Rational Function

$$f(x) = \frac{N(x)}{D(x)} = \frac{a_n x^n + \cdots + a_1 x + a_0}{b_m x^m + \cdots + b_1 x + b_0}$$

$N(x)$ and $D(x)$ are polynomials.

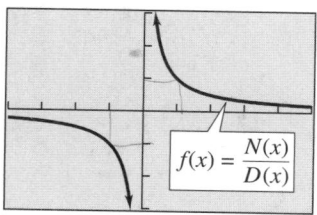

$$f(x) = \frac{N(x)}{D(x)}$$

Domain: all real numbers, $D \neq 0$

Range: $(-\infty, 0)$, $(0, \infty)$

y-intercept: $(0, f(x))$, if $f(0)$ exists

x-intercept(s): zeros of N

Vertical asymptotes: zeros of D

Horizontal asymptote:

$\quad y = 0$ if $n < m$

$\quad y = a_n/b_m$ if $n = m$

Exponential Function

$$f(x) = a^x, \ a > 0$$

$$f(x) = a^{-x}, \ a > 0$$

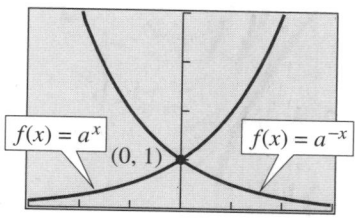

$f(x) = a^x$

$f(x) = a^{-x}$

$(0, 1)$

Domain: $(-\infty, \infty)$

Range: $(0, \infty)$

y-intercept: $(0, 1)$

Asymptote: $y = 0$

Logarithmic Function

$$f(x) = \log_a x, \ a > 1$$

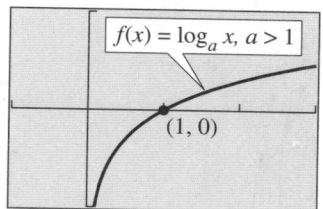

$f(x) = \log_a x, \ a > 1$

$(1, 0)$

Domain: $(0, \infty)$

Range: $(-\infty, \infty)$

x-intercept: $(1, 0)$

Asymptote: $x = 0$

College Algebra

College Algebra
A Graphing Approach

Third Edition

Ron Larson
Robert P. Hostetler
The Pennsylvania State University
The Behrend College

Bruce H. Edwards
University of Florida

With the assistance of David C. Falvo
The Pennsylvania State University
The Behrend College

Houghton Mifflin Company   Boston   New York

Editor-in-Chief: Jack Shira
Managing Editor: Cathy Cantin
Senior Associate Editor: Maureen Ross
Associate Editor: Laura Wheel
Assistant Editor: Carolyn Johnson
Supervising Editor: Karen Carter
Project Editor: Patty Bergin
Editorial Assistant: Kate Hartke
Art Supervisor: Gary Crespo
Senior Manufacturing Coordinator: Sally Culler
Marketing Manager: Michael Busnach
Freelance Development Editor: Michael Richards
Freelance Project Editor: Kathleen Deselle
Composition and Art: Meridian Creative Group
Cover Images: Meridian Creative Group
Cover Design: Gary Crespo

We have included examples and exercises that use real-life data as well as technology output from a variety of software. This would not have been possible without the help of many people and organizations. Our wholehearted thanks go to all for their time and effort.

Printed in the U.S.A.

Library of Congress Catalog Card Number: 00-104769

ISBN: 0-618-06655-1

123456789–DOW–04 03 02 01 00

Contents

A Word from the Authors

Welcome to *College Algebra: A Graphing Approach*, Third Edition. In this revision we have focused on student success, accessibility, and flexibility.

Accessibility: Over the years we have taken care to write a text for the student. We have paid careful attention to the presentation, using precise mathematical language and clear writing to create an effective learning tool. We believe that every student can learn mathematics and we are committed to providing a text that makes the mathematics within it accessible to all students.

In the Third Edition, we have revised and improved upon many text features designed for this purpose. Our pedagogical approach includes presenting solutions to examples from multiple perspectives—algebraic, graphic, and numeric. The side-by-side format allows students to see that a problem can be solved in more than one way, and to compare the accuracy of the solution methods.

Technology has been fully integrated into the text presentation. Also, the *Exploration* and *Study Tip* features have been expanded. *Chapter Tests*, which give students an opportunity for self-assessment, now follow every chapter in the Third Edition. The exercise sets now contain both *Synthesis* exercises, which check students' conceptual understanding, and *Review* exercises, which reinforce skills learned in previous sections and chapters. Students also have access to several media resources—videotapes, *Interactive College Algebra: A Graphing Approach* CD-ROM, and a *College Algebra: A Graphing Approach* website— that provide additional text-specific support.

Student Success: During our past 30 years of teaching and writing, we have learned many things about the teaching and learning of mathematics. We have found that students are most successful when they know what they are expected to learn and why it is important to learn it. With that in mind, we have restructured the Third Edition to include a thematic study thread in every chapter.

Each chapter begins with a study guide called *How to Study This Chapter*, which includes a comprehensive overview of the chapter concepts (*The Big Picture*), a list of *Important Vocabulary* that is integral to learning *The Big Picture* concepts, a list of study resources, and a general study tip. The study guide allows students to get organized and prepare for the chapter.

An old pedagogical recipe goes something like this, "First I'm going to tell you what I'm going to teach you, then I will teach it to you, and finally I will go over what I taught you." Following this recipe, we have included a set of learning objectives in every section that outlines what students are expected to learn, followed by an interesting real-life application that illustrates why it is important to learn the concepts in that section. Finally, the chapter summary (*What did you learn?*), which reinforces the section objectives, and the chapter *Review Exercises*, which are correlated to the chapter summary, provide additional study support at the conclusion of each chapter.

Our new *Student Success Organizer* supplement takes this study thread one step further, providing a content-based study aid.

Flexibility: From the time we first began writing in the early 1970s, we have always viewed part of our authoring role as that of providing instructors with flexible teaching programs. The optional features within the text allow instructors with different pedagogical approaches to design their courses to meet both their instructional needs and the needs of their students. In addition, we provide several print and media resources to support instructors, including a new *Instructor Success Organizer*.

We hope you enjoy the Third Edition.

Ron Larson

Robert P. Hostetler

Bruce H. Edwards

Acknowledgments

We would like to thank the many people who have helped us prepare the text and the supplements package. Their encouragement, criticisms, and suggestions have been invaluable to us.

Third Edition Reviewers

Jamie Whitehead Ashby, Texarkana College; Teresa Barton, Western New England College; Diane Burleson, Central Piedmont Community College; Alexander Burstein, University of Rhode Island; Victor M. Cornell, Mesa Community College; Marcia Drost, Texas A & M University; Kenny Fister, Murray State University; Susan C. Fleming, Virginia Highlands Community College; Nicholas E. Geller, Collin County Community College; Betty Givan, Eastern Kentucky University; John Kendall, Shelby State Community College; Donna M. Krawczyk, University of Arizona; JoAnn Lewin, Edison Community College; David E. Meel, Bowling Green University; Beverly Michael, University of Pittsburgh; Jon Odell, Richland Community College; Laura Reger, Milwaukee Area Technical College; Craig M. Steenberg, Lewis-Clark State College; Mary Jane Sterling, Bradley University; Ellen Vilas, York Technical College. In addition, we would like to thank all the college algebra instructors who took the time to respond to our survey.

We would like to extend a special thanks to Ellen Vilas for her contributions to this revision.

We would like to thank the staff of Larson Texts, Inc. and the staff of Meridian Creative Group, who assisted in proofreading the manuscript, preparing and proofreading the art package, and typesetting the supplements.

On a personal level, we are grateful to our wives, Deanna Gilbert Larson, Eloise Hostetler, and Consuelo Edwards for their love, patience, and support. Also, a special thanks goes to R. Scott O'Neil.

If you have suggestions for improving this text, please feel free to write to us. Over the past two decades we have received many useful comments from both instructors and students, and we value these very much.

Ron Larson
Robert P. Hostetler
Bruce H. Edwards

Features Highlights

Student Success Tools

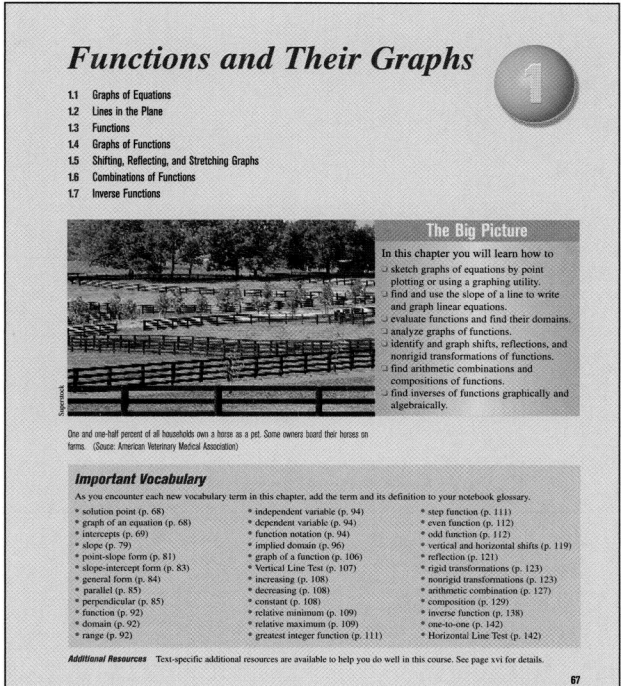

New Chapter Openers include:

▶ **The Big Picture**

An objective-based overview of the main concepts of the chapter.

▶ **Important Vocabulary**

Mathematical terms integral to learning *The Big Picture* concepts.

New Section Openers include:

▶ **"What you should learn"**

Objectives outline the main concepts and help keep students focused on *The Big Picture*.

▶ **"Why you should learn it"**

A real-life application or a reference to other branches of mathematics illustrates the relevance of the section's content.

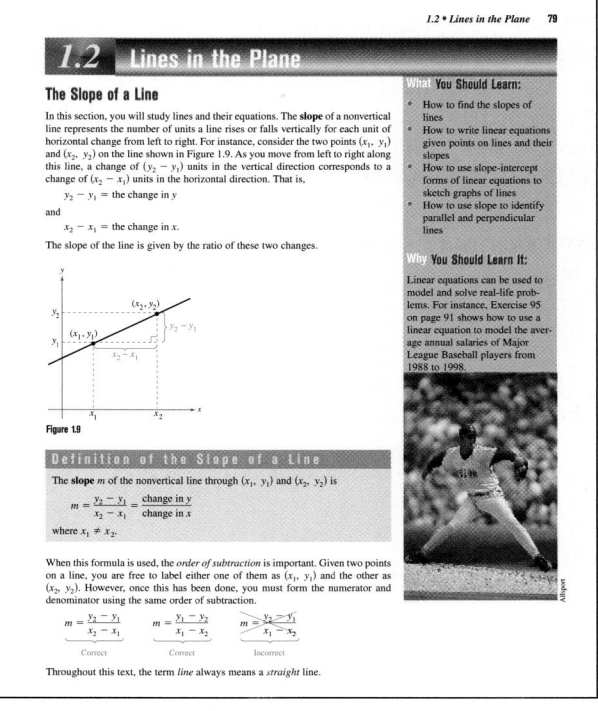

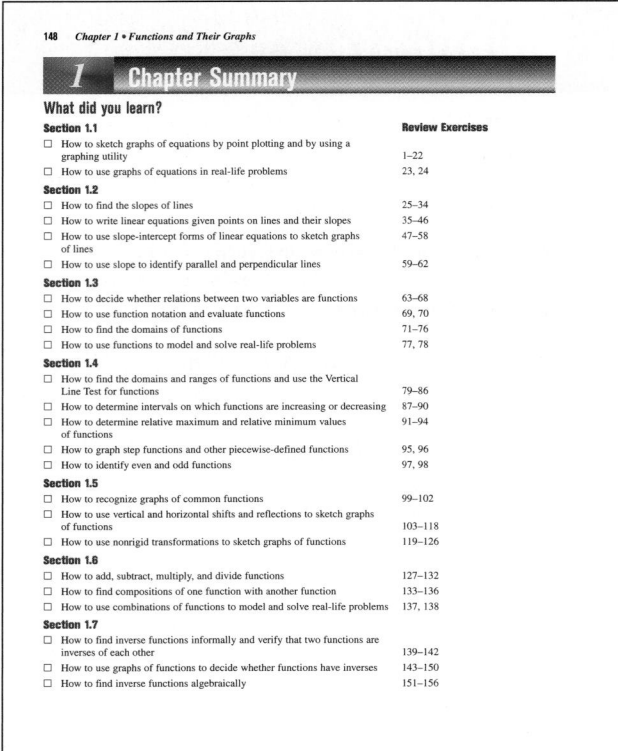

▶ **"What did you learn?" Chapter Summary**

This chapter summary provides a concise, section-by-section review of the section objectives. These objectives are correlated to the chapter Review Exercises.

Flexibility and Accessibility

▶ **Algebraic, Graphical, and Numerical Approach**

- Many examples present solutions from multiple approaches—algebraic, graphical, and numerical.
- Solutions are displayed side-by-side.
- The multiple-approach format shows students different solution methods that can be used to reach the same answer.
- The solution format helps students expand their problem-solving abilities.

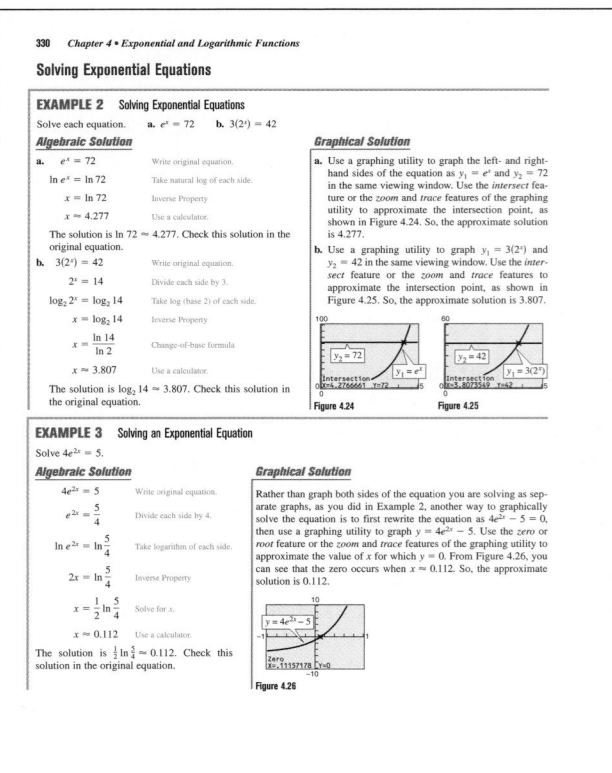

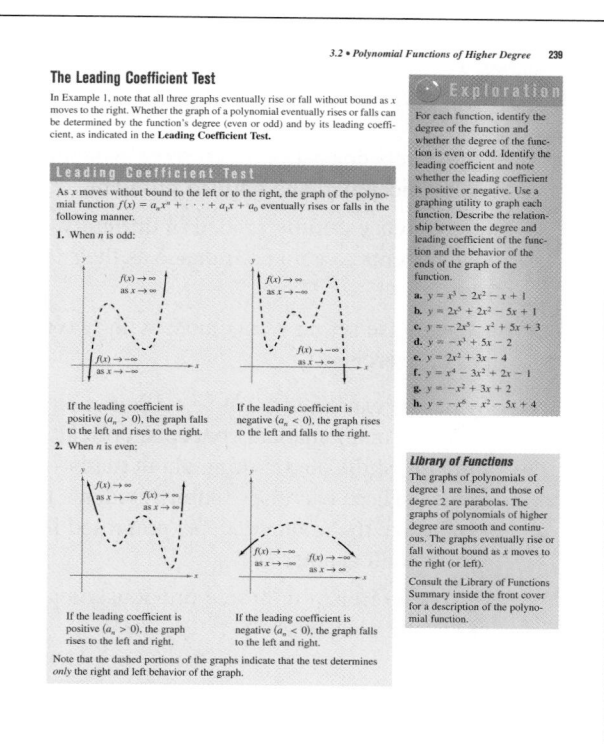

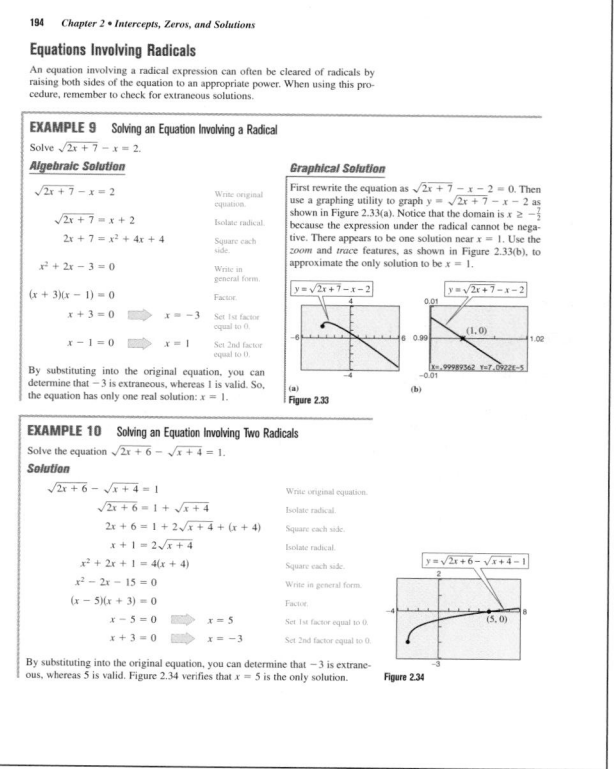

Exploration

- Before introducing selected topics, *Exploration* engages students in active discovery of mathematical concepts and relationships, often through the power of technology.

- *Exploration* strengthens students' critical thinking skills and helps them develop an intuitive understanding of theoretical concepts.

- *Exploration* is an optional feature and can be omitted without loss of continuity in coverage.

▶ **Examples**

- Each example was carefully chosen to illustrate a particular mathematical concept or problem-solving skill.

- Every example contains step-by-step solutions, most with side-by-side explanations that lead students through the solution process.

- Many examples provide side-by-side solutions utilizing two separate approaches.

Revised Exercises and Applications

2.5  EXERCISES

In Exercises 1–4, match the inequality with its graph.
[The graphs are labeled (a), (b), (c), and (d).]

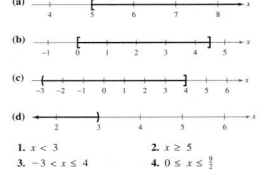

(a)

(b)

(c)

(d)

1. $x < 3$ 2. $x \geq 5$
3. $-3 < x \leq 4$ 4. $0 \leq x \leq \frac{9}{2}$

In Exercises 5–8, determine whether each given value of x is a solution of the inequality.

Inequality	Values
5. $5x - 12 > 0$	(a) $x = 3$ (b) $x = -3$
	(c) $x = \frac{5}{2}$ (d) $x = \frac{3}{2}$
6. $-5 < 2x - 1 \leq 1$	(a) $x = -\frac{1}{2}$ (b) $x = -\frac{5}{2}$
	(c) $x = \frac{4}{3}$ (d) $x = 0$
7. $-1 < \frac{3-x}{2} \leq 1$	(a) $x = 0$ (b) $x = \sqrt{5}$
	(c) $x = 1$ (d) $x = 5$
8. $|x - 10| \geq 3$	(a) $x = 13$ (b) $x = -1$
	(c) $x = 14$ (d) $x = 9$

In Exercises 9–18, solve the inequality and sketch the solution on the real number line. Use a graphing utility to verify your solution graphically.

9. $-10x < 40$ 10. $2x > 3$
11. $4(x + 1) < 2x + 3$ 12. $2x + 7 < 3$
13. $1 < 2x + 3 < 9$ 14. $-2 < 3x + 1 < 10$
15. $-8 \leq 1 - 3(x - 2) < 13$
16. $0 \leq 2(x + 4) < 20$
17. $-4 < \frac{2x - 3}{3} < 4$ 18. $0 \leq \frac{x + 3}{2} < 5$

Graphical Analysis **In Exercises 19–24, use a graphing utility to approximate the solution.**

19. $6x > 12$ 20. $3x - 1 \leq 5$
21. $5 - 2x \geq 1$ 22. $3(x + 1) < x + 7$
23. $-9 < 6x - 1 < 1$ 24. $-10 < 4(x - 3) \leq 8$

In Exercises 25–28, use a graphing utility to graph the equation and graphically approximate the values of x that satisfy the specified inequalities. Then solve each inequality algebraically.

Equation	Inequalities
25. $y = 2x - 3$	(a) $y \geq 1$ (b) $y \leq 0$
26. $y = \frac{2}{3}x + 1$	(a) $y \leq 5$ (b) $y \geq 0$
27. $y = -\frac{1}{2}x + 2$	(a) $0 \leq y \leq 3$ (b) $y \geq 0$
28. $y = -3x + 8$	(a) $-1 \leq y \leq 3$ (b) $y \leq 0$

In Exercises 29–36, solve the inequality and sketch the solution on the real number line.

29. $|5x| > 10$ 30. $|x - 20| \leq 4$
31. $|x - 7| < 6$ 32. $|x - 20| \geq 4$
33. $|x + 14| + 3 > 17$ 34. $\left|\frac{x - 3}{2}\right| \geq 5$
35. $|1 - 2x| < 5$ 36. $3|4 - 5x| \leq 9$

In Exercises 37 and 38, use a graphing utility to graph the equation and graphically approximate the values of x that satisfy the specified inequalities. Then solve each inequality algebraically.

Equation	Inequalities
37. $y = |x - 3|$	(a) $y \leq 2$ (b) $y \geq 4$
38. $y = \left|\frac{1}{2}x + 1\right|$	(a) $y \leq 4$ (b) $y \geq 1$

In Exercises 39–44, use absolute value notation to define each interval (or pair of intervals) on the real number line.

39.

40.

---

75. *Forestry* The number of board feet V in a 16-foot log is approximated by the model

$$V = 0.77x^2 - 1.32x - 9.31, \quad 5 \leq x \leq 40$$

where x is the diameter (in inches) of the log at the small end. (One board foot is a measure of volume equivalent to a board that is 12 inches wide, 12 inches long, and 1 inch thick.)

(a) Use a graphing utility to graph the function.
(b) Estimate the number of board feet in a 16-foot log with a diameter of 16 inches. Use a graphing utility to verify your answer.
(c) Estimate the diameter of a 16-foot log that scaled 500 board feet when the lumber was sold. Use a graphing utility to verify your answer.

76. *Automobile Aerodynamics* The number of horsepower y required to overcome wind drag on a certain automobile is approximated by

$$y = 0.002s^2 + 0.005s - 0.029, \quad 0 \leq s \leq 100$$

where s is the speed of the car in miles per hour.

(a) Use a graphing utility to graph the function.
(b) Graphically estimate the maximum speed of the car if the power required to overcome wind drag is not to exceed 10 horsepower. Verify your result algebraically.

77. *Graphical Analysis* For certain years from 1950 to 1990, the average annual per capita consumption C of cigarettes by Americans (18 and older) can be modeled by $C = 3248.89 + 108.64t - 2.97t^2$ for $0 \leq t \leq 40$, where t is the year, with $t = 0$ corresponding to 1950. (Source: U.S. Department of Agriculture)

(a) Use a graphing utility to graph the model.
(b) Use the graph of the model to approximate the maximum average annual consumption. Beginning in 1966, all cigarette packages were required by law to carry a health warning. Do you think the warning had any effect? Explain.
(c) In 1960, the U.S. population (18 and over) was 116,530,000. Of those, about 48,500,000 were smokers. What was the average annual cigarette consumption *per smoker* in 1960? What was the average daily cigarette consumption *per smoker?*

78. *Data Analysis* The number y (in millions) of VCRs in use in the United States for the years 1987 through 1996 are shown in the table. The variable t represents time (in years), with $t = 7$ corresponding to 1987.

t	7	8	9	10	11	12	13	14	15	16
y	43	51	58	63	67	69	72	74	77	79

(Source: Television Bureau of Advertising, Inc.)

(a) Use a graphing utility to sketch a scatter plot of the data.
(b) Use the regression capabilities of a graphing utility to fit a quadratic model to the data.
(c) Use a graphing utility to graph the model in the same viewing window as the scatter plot.
(d) Do you think the model can be used to estimate VCR utilization in the year 2005? Explain.

Synthesis

True or False? **In Exercises 79 and 80, determine whether the statement is true or false. Justify your answer.**

79. The function $f(x) = -12x^2 - 1$ has no x-intercepts.
80. The graphs of $f(x) = -4x^2 - 10x + 7$ and $g(x) = 12x^2 + 30x + 1$ have the same axis of symmetry.

81. *Think About It* The profits P (in millions of dollars) for a company are modeled by a quadratic function of the form $P = at^2 + bt + c$, where t represents the year. If you were president of the company, which of the models would you prefer? Explain your reasoning.

(a) a is positive and $t \geq -b/(2a)$.
(b) a is positive and $t \leq -b/(2a)$.
(c) a is negative and $t \geq -b/(2a)$.
(d) a is negative and $t \leq -b/(2a)$.

Review

In Exercises 82–85, determine algebraically any points of intersection of the graphs of the equations. Verify your results using the *intersect* feature of a graphing utility.

82. $x + y = 8$ 83. $y = 3x - 10$
   $-\frac{2}{3}x + y = 6$ $y = \frac{1}{4}x + 1$
84. $y = 9 - x^2$ 85. $y = x^3 + 2x - 1$
   $y = x + 3$ $y = -2x + 15$

In Exercises 86–89, perform the operation and write the result in standard form.

86. $(6 - i) - (2i + 11)$ 87. $(2i + 5)^2 - 21$
88. $(3i + 7)(-4i + 1)$ 89. $(4 - i)^3$

▶ **Exercises**

- Exercise sets consist of a variety of computational, conceptual, and applied problems.
- Exercise sets carefully graded in difficulty allow students to gain confidence as they progress.
- Each exercise set now concludes with two new types of exercises:

  - *Synthesis* exercises promote further exploration of mathematical concepts, critical thinking skills, and writing about mathematics. These exercises require students to synthesize the main concepts presented in the section and chapter.
  - *Review* exercises reinforce previously learned skills and concepts.

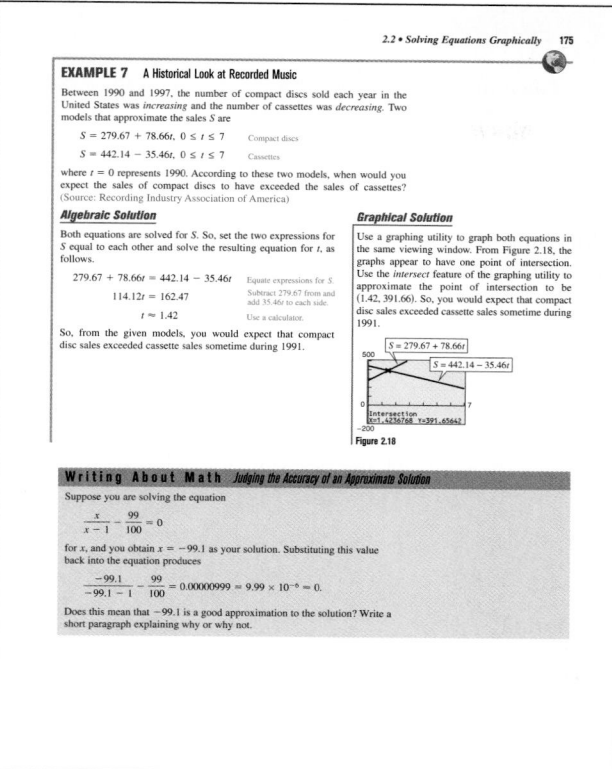

EXAMPLE 7 A Historical Look at Recorded Music

Between 1990 and 1997, the number of compact discs sold each year in the United States was *increasing* and the number of cassettes was *decreasing*. Two models that approximate the sales S are

$$S = 279.67 + 78.66t, \quad 0 \le t \le 7 \qquad \text{Compact discs}$$
$$S = 442.14 - 35.46t, \quad 0 \le t \le 7 \qquad \text{Cassettes}$$

where $t = 0$ represents 1990. According to these two models, when would you expect the sales of compact discs to have exceeded the sales of cassettes? (Source: Recording Industry Association of America)

Algebraic Solution

Both equations are solved for S. So, set the two expressions for S equal to each other and solve the resulting equation for t, as follows.

$$279.67 + 78.66t = 442.14 - 35.46t \qquad \text{Equate expressions for } S.$$
$$114.12t = 162.47 \qquad \text{Subtract 279.67 from and add 35.46t to each side.}$$
$$t \approx 1.42 \qquad \text{Use a calculator.}$$

So, from the given models, you would expect that compact disc sales exceeded cassette sales sometime during 1991.

Graphical Solution

Use a graphing utility to graph both equations in the same viewing window. From Figure 2.18, the graphs appear to have one point of intersection. Use the *intersect* feature of the graphing utility to approximate the point of intersection to be (1.42, 391.66). So, you would expect that compact disc sales exceeded cassette sales sometime during 1991.

Figure 2.18

Writing About Math *Judging the Accuracy of an Approximate Solution*

Suppose you are solving the equation

$$\frac{x}{x - 1} - \frac{99}{100} = 0$$

for x, and you obtain $x = -99.1$ as your solution. Substituting this value back into the equation produces

$$\frac{-99.1}{-99.1 - 1} - \frac{99}{100} = 0.00000999 = 9.99 \times 10^{-6} = 0.$$

Does this mean that -99.1 is a good approximation to the solution? Write a short paragraph explaining why or why not.

▶ **Real-Life Applications**

• A wide variety of real-life applications, many using current, real data, are integrated throughout the examples and exercises.

• The icon 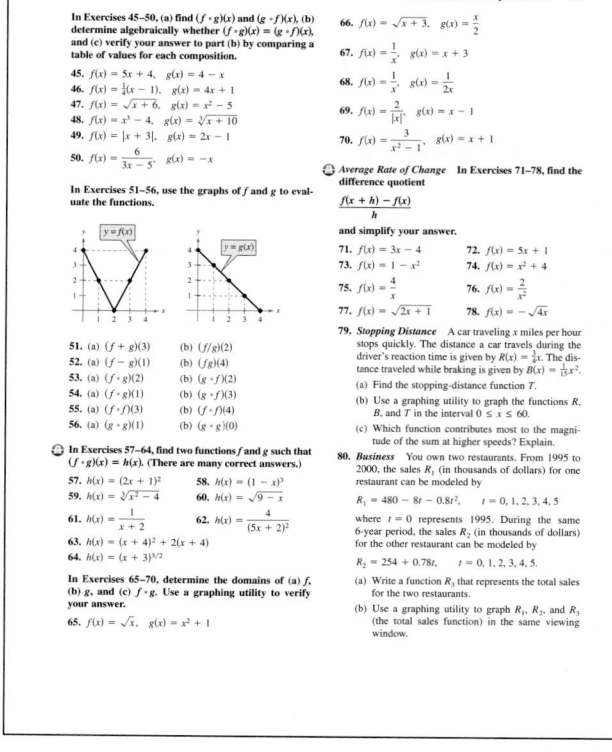 indicates an example that involves a real-life application.

▶ **Algebra of Calculus**

• Special emphasis is given to the algebraic techniques used in calculus.

• Algebra of Calculus examples and exercises are integrated throughout the text.

• The symbol indicates an example or exercise in which the Algebra of Calculus is featured.

▶ **Additional Features**

Carefully crafted learning tools designed to create a rich learning environment can be found throughout the text. These learning tools include a Library of Functions, Study Tips, Historical Notes, Writing About Math, Chapter Projects, Chapter Review Exercises, Chapter Tests, Cumulative Tests, and an extensive art program.

In Exercises 45–50, (a) find $(f \circ g)(x)$ and $(g \circ f)(x)$, (b) determine algebraically whether $(f \circ g)(x) = (g \circ f)(x)$, and (c) verify your answer to part (b) by comparing a table of values for each composition.

45. $f(x) = 5x + 4$, $g(x) = 4 - x$
46. $f(x) = \frac{1}{4}(x - 1)$, $g(x) = 4x + 1$
47. $f(x) = \sqrt{x + 6}$, $g(x) = x^2 - 5$
48. $f(x) = x^3 - 4$, $g(x) = \sqrt[3]{x + 10}$
49. $f(x) = |x + 3|$, $g(x) = 2x - 1$
50. $f(x) = \frac{6}{3x - 5}$, $g(x) = -x$

In Exercises 51–56, use the graphs of f and g to evaluate the functions.

51. (a) $(f + g)(3)$ (b) $(f/g)(2)$
52. (a) $(f - g)(1)$ (b) $(fg)(4)$
53. (a) $(f \circ g)(2)$ (b) $(g \circ f)(2)$
54. (a) $(f \circ g)(1)$ (b) $(g \circ f)(3)$
55. (a) $(f \circ f)(3)$ (b) $(f \circ f)(4)$
56. (a) $(g \circ g)(1)$ (b) $(g \circ g)(0)$

In Exercises 57–64, find two functions f and g such that $(f \circ g)(x) = h(x)$. (There are many correct answers.)

57. $h(x) = (2x + 1)^2$
58. $h(x) = (1 - x)^3$
59. $h(x) = \sqrt[3]{x^2 - 4}$
60. $h(x) = \sqrt{9 - x}$
61. $h(x) = \frac{1}{x + 2}$
62. $h(x) = \frac{4}{(5x + 2)^2}$
63. $h(x) = (x + 4)^2 + 2(x + 4)$
64. $h(x) = (x + 3)^{3/2}$

In Exercises 65–70, determine the domains of (a) f, (b) g, and (c) $f \circ g$. Use a graphing utility to verify your answer.

65. $f(x) = \sqrt{x}$, $g(x) = x^2 + 1$

66. $f(x) = \sqrt{x + 3}$, $g(x) = \frac{x}{2}$
67. $f(x) = \frac{1}{x}$, $g(x) = x + 3$
68. $f(x) = \frac{1}{x}$, $g(x) = \frac{1}{2x}$
69. $f(x) = \frac{2}{|x|}$, $g(x) = x - 1$
70. $f(x) = \frac{3}{x^2 - 1}$, $g(x) = x + 1$

Average Rate of Change In Exercises 71–78, find the difference quotient

$$\frac{f(x + h) - f(x)}{h}$$

and simplify your answer.

71. $f(x) = 3x - 4$ **72.** $f(x) = 5x + 1$
73. $f(x) = 1 - x^2$ **74.** $f(x) = x^2 + 4$
75. $f(x) = \frac{4}{x}$ **76.** $f(x) = \frac{2}{x^2}$
77. $f(x) = \sqrt{2x + 1}$ **78.** $f(x) = -\sqrt{4x}$

79. *Stopping Distance* A car traveling x miles per hour stops quickly. The distance a car travels during the driver's reaction time is given by $R(x) = \frac{3}{4}x$. The distance traveled while braking is given by $B(x) = \frac{1}{15}x^2$.

(a) Find the stopping-distance function T.

(b) Use a graphing utility to graph the functions R, B, and T in the interval $0 \le x \le 60$.

(c) Which function contributes most to the magnitude of the sum at higher speeds? Explain.

80. *Business* You own two restaurants. From 1995 to 2000, the sales R_1 (in thousands of dollars) for one restaurant can be modeled by

$$R_1 = 480 - 8t - 0.8t^2, \quad t = 0, 1, 2, 3, 4, 5$$

where $t = 0$ represents 1995. During the same 6-year period, the sales R_2 (in thousands of dollars) for the other restaurant can be modeled by

$$R_2 = 254 + 0.78t, \quad t = 0, 1, 2, 3, 4, 5.$$

(a) Write a function R_3 that represents the total sales for the two restaurants.

(b) Use a graphing utility to graph R_1, R_2, and R_3 (the total sales function) in the same viewing window.

Supplements

Resources

Website (*college.hmco.com*)
Many additional text-specific study and interactive features for students and instructors can be found at the Houghton Mifflin website. These features include, but are not limited to, the following.

- Glossary
- Video clips
- Graphing calculator emulator
- Sample chapters
- Presentation slides

For the Student

Student Success Organizer

Study and Solutions Guide by Bruce H. Edwards (University of Florida)

Graphing Technology Guide by Benjamin N. Levy and Laurel Technical Services

Instructional Videotapes by Dana Mosely

Instructional Videotapes for Graphing Calculators by Dana Mosely

For the Instructor

Instructor's Annotated Edition

Instructor Success Organizer

Complete Solutions Guide by Bruce H. Edwards (University of Florida)

Test Item File

Problem Solving, Modeling, and Data Analysis Labs by Wendy Metzger (Palomar College)

Computerized Testing (Windows, Macintosh)

Instructor's CD-ROM

An Introduction to Graphing Utilities

Graphing utilities such as graphing calculators and computers with graphing software are very valuable tools for visualizing mathematical principles, verifying solutions to equations, exploring mathematical ideas, and developing mathematical models. Although graphing utilities are extremely helpful in learning mathematics, their use does not mean that learning algebra is any less important. In fact, the combination of knowledge of mathematics and the use of graphing utilities allows you to explore mathematics more easily and to a greater depth. If you are using a graphing utility in this course, it is up to you to learn its capabilities and to practice using this tool to enhance your mathematical learning.

In this text there are many opportunities to use a graphing utility, some of which are described below.

Some Uses of a Graphing Utility

A graphing utility can be used to

- check or validate answers to problems obtained using algebraic methods.
- discover and explore algebraic properties, rules, and concepts.
- graph functions, and approximate solutions to equations involving functions.
- efficiently perform complicated mathematical procedures such as those found in many real-life applications.
- find mathematical models for sets of data.

In this introduction, the features of graphing utilities are discussed from a generic perspective. To learn how to use the features of a specific graphing utility, consult your user's manual or the website for this text found at *college.hmco.com*. Additionally, keystroke guides are available for most graphing utilities, and your college library may have a videotape on how to use your graphing utility.

The Equation Editor

Many graphing utilities are designed to act as "function graphers." In this course, you will study functions and their graphs in detail. You may recall from previous courses that a function can be thought of as a rule that describes the relationship between two variables. These rules are frequently written in terms of x and y. For example, the equation $y = 3x + 5$ represents y as a function of x.

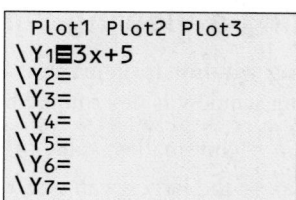

Figure 1

Many graphing utilities have an equation editor that requires an equation to be written in "$y =$" form in order to be entered, as shown in Figure 1. (You should note that your equation editor screen may not look like the screen shown in Figure 1.) To determine exactly how to enter an equation into your graphing utility, consult your user's manual.

The Table Feature

Most graphing utilities are capable of displaying a table of values with x-values and one or more corresponding y-values. These tables can be used to check solutions of an equation and to generate ordered pairs to assist in graphing an equation.

To use the *table* feature, enter an equation into the equation editor in "$y =$" form. The table may have a setup screen, which allows you to select the starting x-value and the table step or x-increment. You may then have the option of automatically generating values for x and y or building your own table using the *ask* mode. In the *ask* mode, you enter a value for x and the graphing utility displays the y-value.

For example, enter the equation

$$y = \frac{3x}{x + 2}$$

into the equation editor, as shown in Figure 2. In the table setup screen, set the table to start at $x = -4$ and set the table step to 1. When you view the table, notice that the first x-value is -4 and each value after it increases by 1. Also notice that the Y_1 column gives the resulting y-value for each x-value, as shown in Figure 3. The table shows that the y-value when $x = -2$ is ERROR. This means that the variable x may not take on the value -2 in this equation.

With the same equation in the equation editor, set the table to *ask* mode. In this mode you do not need to set the starting x-value or the table step, because you are entering any value you choose for x. You may enter any real value for x—integers, fractions, decimals, irrational numbers, and so forth. If you enter $x = 1 + \sqrt{3}$, the graphing utility may rewrite the number as a decimal approximation, as shown in Figure 4. You can continue to build your own table by entering additional x-values in order to generate y-values.

If you have several equations in the equation editor, the table may generate y-values for each equation.

```
 Plot1 Plot2 Plot3
\Y1⊟3x/(X+2)■
\Y2=
\Y3=
\Y4=
\Y5=
\Y6=
\Y7=
```

Figure 2

X	Y1	
-4	6	
-3	9	
-2	ERROR	
-1	-3	
0	0	
1	1	
2	1.5	

X=-4

Figure 3

X	Y1	
2.7321	1.7321	

X=

Figure 4

Creating a Viewing Window

A **viewing window** for a graph is a rectangular portion of the coordinate plane. A viewing window is determined by the following six values.

> Xmin = the smallest value of x
>
> Xmax = the largest value of x
>
> Xscl = the number of units per tick mark on the x-axis
>
> Ymin = the smallest value of y
>
> Ymax = the largest value of y
>
> Yscl = the number of units per tick mark on the y-axis

When you enter these six values into a graphing utility, you are setting the viewing window. Some graphing utilities have a standard viewing window, as shown in Figure 5.

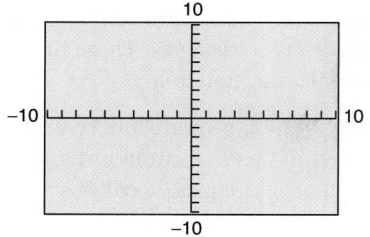

Figure 5

By choosing different viewing windows for a graph, it is possible to obtain very different impressions of the graph's shape. For instance, Figure 6 shows four different viewing windows for the graph of

$$y = 0.1x^4 - x^3 + 2x^2.$$

Of these, the view shown in part (a) is the most complete.

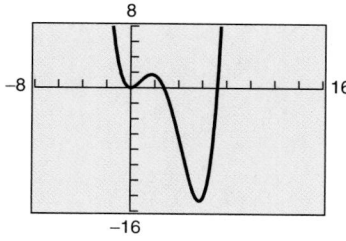

(a)

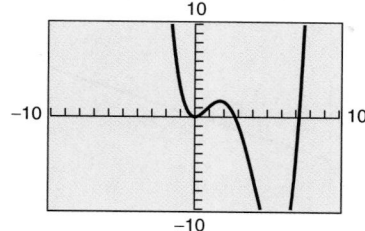

(b)

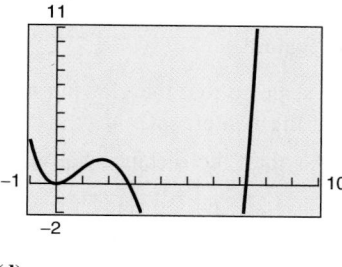

(c)   **(d)**

Figure 6

On most graphing utilities, the display screen is two-thirds as high as it is wide. On such screens, you can obtain a graph with a true geometric perspective by using **a square setting**—one in which

$$\frac{\text{Ymax} - \text{Ymin}}{\text{Xmax} - \text{Xmin}} = \frac{2}{3}.$$

One such setting is shown in Figure 7. Notice that the x and y tick marks are equally spaced on a square setting, but not on a standard setting.

To see how the viewing window affects the geometric perspective, graph the semicircles $y_1 = \sqrt{9 - x^2}$ and $y_2 = -\sqrt{9 - x^2}$ in a standard viewing window. Then graph y_1 and y_2 in a square window. Note the difference in the shapes of the circles.

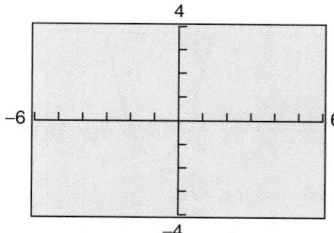

Figure 7

Zoom and Trace Features

When you graph an equation, you can move from point to point along its graph using the *trace* feature. As you trace the graph, the coordinates of each point are displayed, as shown in Figure 8. The *trace* feature combined with the *zoom* feature allows you to obtain better and better approximations of desired points on a graph. For instance, you can use the *zoom* feature of a graphing utility to approximate the x-intercept(s) of a graph [the point(s) where the graph crosses the x-axis]. Suppose you want to approximate the x-intercept(s) of the graph of $y = 2x^3 - 3x + 2$.

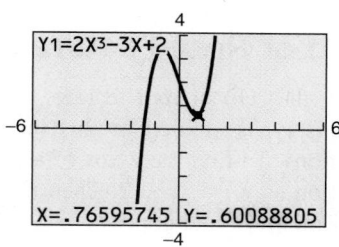

Figure 8

Begin by graphing the equation, as shown in Figure 9(a). From the viewing window shown, the graph appears to have only one *x*-intercept. This intercept lies between -2 and -1. By zooming in on the intercept, you can improve the approximation, as shown in Figure 9(b). To three decimal places, the solution is $x \approx -1.476$.

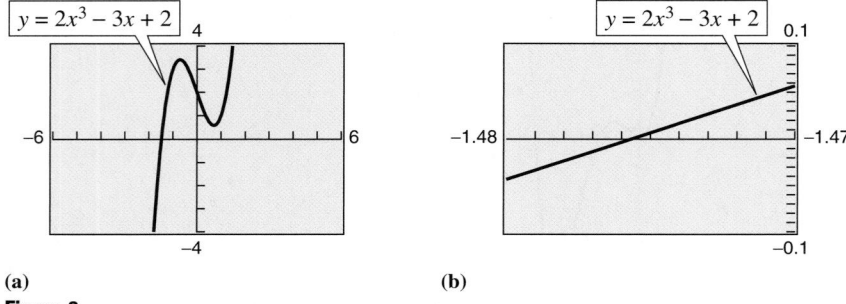

(a)   **(b)**

Figure 9

Here are some suggestions for using the *zoom* feature.

1. With each successive zoom-in, adjust the *x*-scale so that the viewing window shows at least one tick mark on each side of the *x*-intercept.

2. The error in your approximation will be less than the distance between two scale marks.

3. The *trace* feature can usually be used to add one more decimal place of accuracy without changing the viewing window.

Figure 10(a) shows the graph of $y = x^2 - 5x + 3$. Figures 10(b) and 10(c) show "zoom-in views" of the two *x*-intercepts. From these views, you can approximate the *x*-intercepts to be $x \approx 0.697$ and $x \approx 4.303$.

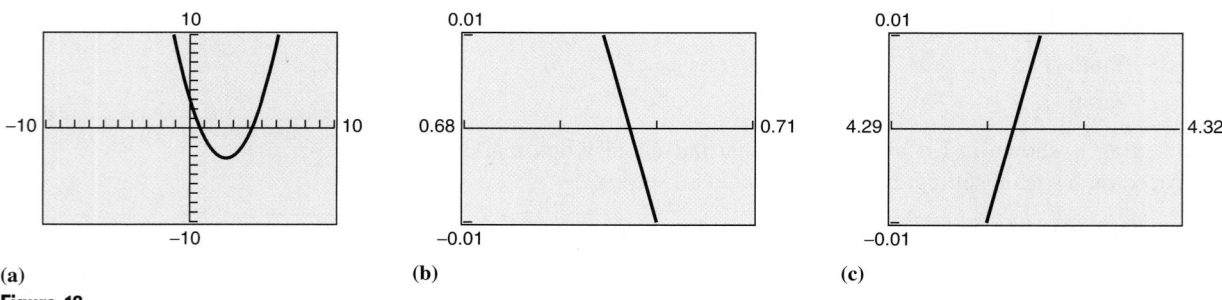

(a)   **(b)**   **(c)**

Figure 10

Zero or Root Feature

Using the *zero* or *root* feature, you can find the real zeros of functions of the various types studied in this text—polynomial, exponential, and logarithmic functions. To find the zeros of a function such as $f(x) = \frac{3}{4}x - 2$, first enter the function as $y_1 = \frac{3}{4}x - 2$. Then use the *zero* or *root* feature, which may require entering lower and upper bound estimates of the root, as shown in Figure 11.

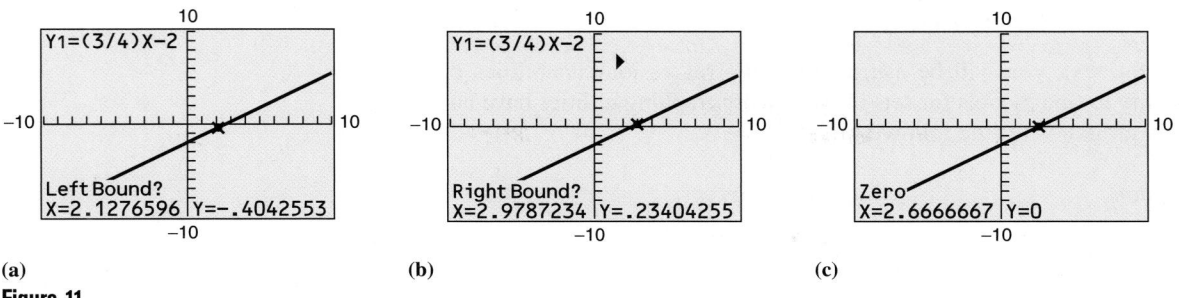

(a)   **(b)**   **(c)**

Figure 11

In Figure 11(c), you can see that the zero is $x = 2.6666667 \approx 2\frac{2}{3}$.

Intersect Feature

To find the points of intersection of two graphs, you can use the *intersect* feature. For instance, to find the points of intersection of the graphs of $y_1 = -x + 2$ and $y_2 = x + 4$, enter these two functions and use the *intersect* feature, as shown in Figure 12.

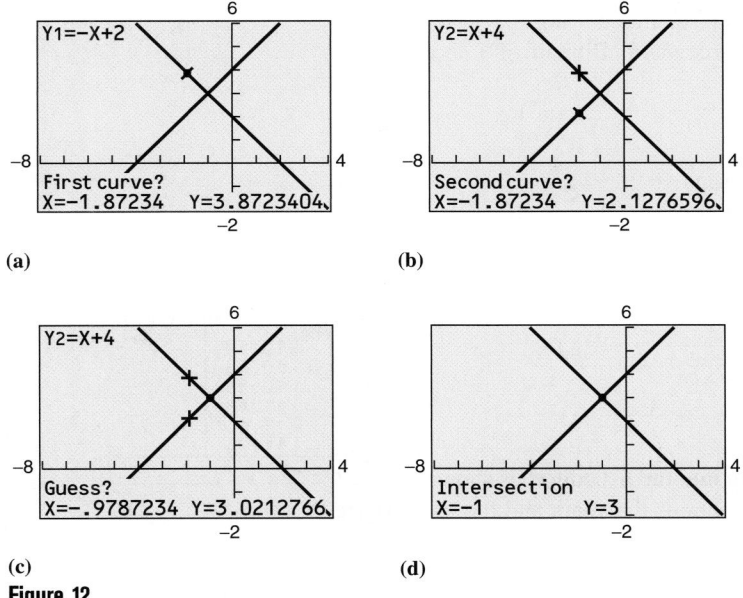

(a)   **(b)**

(c)   **(d)**

Figure 12

From Figure 12(d), you can see that the point of intersection is $(-1, 3)$.

Regression Capabilities

Throughout the text, you will be asked to use the regression capabilities of a graphing utility to find models for sets of data. Most graphing utilities have built-in regression programs for the following.

Regression	*Form of Model*
Linear	$y = ax + b$
Quadratic	$y = ax^2 + bx + c$
Cubic	$y = ax^3 + bx^2 + cx + d$
Quartic	$y = ax^4 + bx^3 + cx^2 + dx + e$
Logarithmic	$y = a + b \ln(x)$
Exponential	$y = ab^x$
Power	$y = ax^b$
Logistic	$y = \dfrac{c}{1 + ae^{-bx}}$
Sine	$y = a \sin(bx + c) + d$

For instance, you can find the linear regression model for the average hourly wages y (in dollars per hour) of production workers in manufacturing industries from 1987 through 1997 shown in the table. (Source: U.S. Bureau of Labor Statistics)

Year	1987	1988	1989	1990	1991	1992
y	9.91	10.19	10.48	10.83	11.18	11.46

Year	1993	1994	1995	1996	1997
y	11.74	12.06	12.37	12.78	13.17

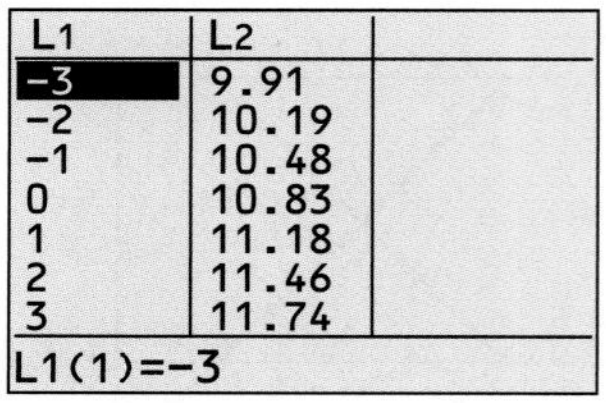

Figure 13

First, let $x = 0$ correspond to 1990 and enter the data into the list editor, as shown in Figure 13. Note that the list in the first column contains the years and the list in the second column contains the hourly wages that correspond to the years. Run your graphing utility's built-in linear regression program to obtain the coefficients a and b for the model $y = ax + b$, as shown in Figure 14. So, a linear model for the data is

$$y \approx 0.321x + 10.83.$$

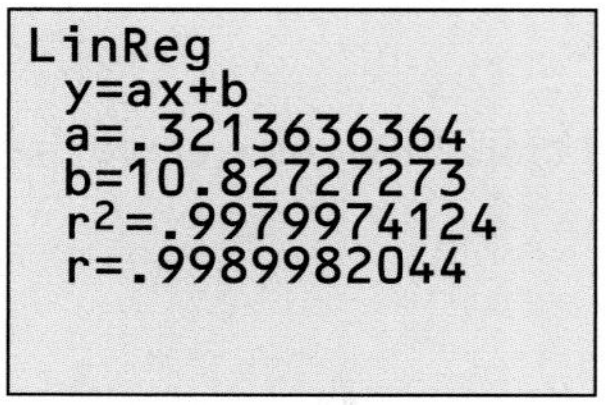

When you run some regression programs, you may obtain an "r-value," which gives a measure of how well the model fits the data. The closer the value of $|r|$ is to 1, the better the fit. For the data in the table above, $r \approx 0.999$, which implies that the model is a very good fit.

Figure 14

Prerequisites

P.1 Real Numbers
P.2 Exponents and Radicals
P.3 Polynomials and Factoring

P.4 Rational Expressions
P.5 Graphical Representation of Data

The Big Picture

In this chapter you will learn how to

❏ represent, classify, and order real numbers and use inequalities.
❏ evaluate algebraic expressions using the basic rules of algebra.
❏ use properties of exponents and radicals to simplify and evaluate expressions.
❏ add, subtract, and multiply polynomials.
❏ factor expressions completely.
❏ determine the domains of algebraic expressions and simplify rational expressions.
❏ avoid common algebraic errors and use algebraic techniques common in calculus.
❏ plot points in the coordinate plane and use the Distance and Midpoint Formulas.

In 1997, over $24 billion worth of corrugated and solid fiber boxes were produced to create shipping containers. (Source: U.S. Bureau of the Census)

Important Vocabulary

As you encounter each new vocabulary term in this chapter, add the term and its definition to your notebook glossary.

- real numbers (p. 2)
- rational numbers (p. 2)
- irrational numbers (p. 2)
- real number line (p. 2)
- origin (p. 2)
- coordinate (p. 2)
- inequality (p. 3)
- positive infinity (p. 4)
- negative infinity (p. 4)
- absolute value (p. 5)
- distance between two points (p. 5)
- variable (p. 6)
- constant (p. 6)
- algebraic expressions (p. 6)

- evaluate an expression (p. 6)
- additive inverse (p. 6)
- multiplicative inverse (p. 6)
- factors (p. 8)
- prime number (p. 8)
- composite number (p. 8)
- exponential form (p. 12)
- exponent (p. 12)
- base (p. 12)
- scientific notation (p. 14)
- square root (p. 15)
- cube root (p. 15)
- principal nth root (p. 15)
- simplest form (p. 17)

- conjugate (p. 18)
- rational exponent (p. 19)
- polynomial (p. 24)
- FOIL Method (p. 25)
- factoring (p. 27)
- factoring by grouping (p. 31)
- domain (p. 37)
- equivalent (p. 37)
- rational expression (p. 37)
- complex fractions (p. 41)
- Cartesian plane (p. 47)
- rectangular coordinate system (p. 47)
- Distance Formula (p. 50)
- Midpoint Formula (p. 52)

Additional Resources   Text-specific additional resources are available to help you do well in this course. See page xvi for details.

Superstock

P.1 Real Numbers

Real Numbers

Real numbers are used in everyday life to describe quantities such as age, miles per gallon, container size, and population. Real numbers are represented by symbols such as

$$-5, 9, 0, \tfrac{4}{3}, 0.666 \ldots, 28.21, \sqrt{2}, \pi, \text{ and } \sqrt[3]{-32}.$$

Here are some important subsets of the set of real numbers.

$$\{1, 2, 3, 4, \ldots\} \qquad \text{Set of natural numbers}$$

$$\{0, 1, 2, 3, 4, \ldots\} \qquad \text{Set of whole numbers}$$

$$\{\ldots -3, -2, -1, 0, 1, 2, 3, \ldots\} \qquad \text{Set of integers}$$

A real number is **rational** if it can be written as the ratio p/q of two integers, where $q \neq 0$. For instance, the numbers

$$\frac{1}{3} = 0.3333 \ldots, \quad \frac{1}{8} = 0.125, \quad \text{and} \quad \frac{125}{111} = 1.126126 \ldots = 1.\overline{126}$$

are rational. The decimal representation of a rational number either *repeats* (as in $\frac{173}{55} = 3.1\overline{45}$) or *terminates* (as in $\frac{1}{2} = 0.5$). A real number that cannot be written as the ratio of two integers is called **irrational.** Irrational numbers have infinite nonrepeating decimal representations. For instance, the numbers

$$\sqrt{2} \approx 1.4142136 \quad \text{and} \quad \pi \approx 3.1415927$$

are irrational. (The symbol $\approx$ means "is approximately equal to.")

Real numbers are represented graphically by a **real number line.** The point 0 on the real number line is the **origin.** Numbers to the right of 0 are positive, and numbers to the left of 0 are negative, as shown in Figure P.1. The term **nonnegative** describes a number that is either positive or zero.

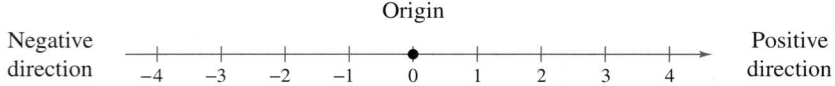

Figure P.1 *The Real Number Line*

There is a *one-to-one correspondence* between real numbers and points on the real number line. That is, every point on the real number line corresponds to exactly one real number called its **coordinate,** and every real number corresponds to exactly one point on the real number line, as shown in Figure P.2.

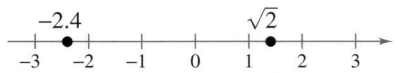

Every point on the real number line corresponds to exactly one real number.

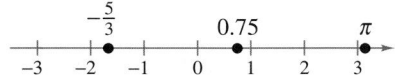

Every real number corresponds to exactly one point on the real number line.

Figure P.2 *One-to-One Correspondence*

Superstock

What You Should Learn:

- How to represent and classify real numbers
- How to order real numbers and use inequalities
- How to find the absolute values of real numbers and the distance between two real numbers
- How to evaluate algebraic expressions
- How to use the basic rules and properties of algebra

Why You Should Learn It:

Real numbers are used in every aspect of our daily lives, such as the variance of a budget in Exercises 81–84 on page 10.

Ordering Real Numbers

One important property of real numbers is that they are **ordered.**

Definition of Order on the Real Number Line

If a and b are real numbers, a is **less than** b if $b - a$ is positive. This order is denoted by the **inequality**

$$a < b.$$

This relationship can also be described by saying that b is **greater than** a and writing $b > a$. The inequality $a \leq b$ means that a is **less than or equal to** b, and the inequality $b \geq a$ means that b is **greater than or equal to** a. The symbols $<$, $>$, $\leq$, and $\geq$ are **inequality symbols.**

Geometrically, this definition implies that $a < b$ if and only if a lies to the *left* of b on the real number line, as shown in Figure P.3.

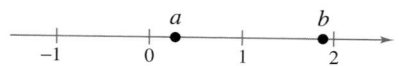

Figure P.3 $a < b$ if and only if a lies to the left of b.

EXAMPLE 1 Interpreting Inequalities

Describe the subset of real numbers represented by each inequality.

a. $x \leq 2$ **b.** $x > -1$ **c.** $-2 \leq x \leq 3$

Solution

a. The inequality $x \leq 2$ denotes all real numbers less than or equal to 2, as shown in Figure P.4(a).

b. The inequality $x > -1$ denotes all real numbers greater than -1, as shown in Figure P.4(b).

c. The inequality $-2 \leq x < 3$ means that $x \geq -2$ *and* $x < 3$. The "double inequality" denotes all real numbers between -2 and 3, including -2 but not including 3, as shown in Figure P.4(c).

Inequalities can be used to describe subsets of real numbers called **intervals.** In the bounded intervals below, the real numbers a and b are the **endpoints** of each interval.

A computer animation of this example appears in the *Interactive* CD-ROM and *Internet* versions of this text.

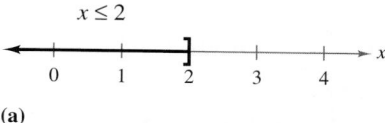

(a)

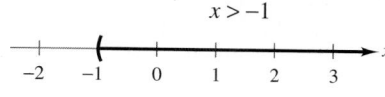

(b)

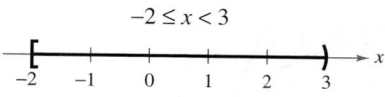

(c)

Figure P.4

Bounded Intervals on the Real Number Line

Notation	Interval Type	Inequality	Graph
$[a, b]$	Closed	$a \leq x \leq b$	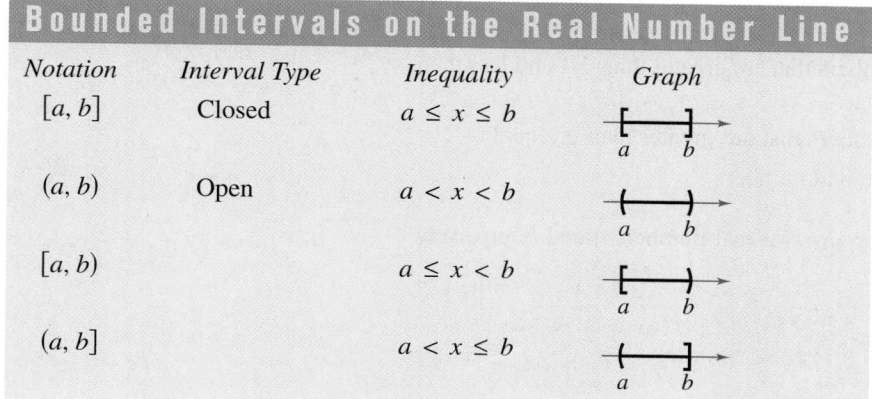
(a, b)	Open	$a < x < b$	
$[a, b)$		$a \leq x < b$	
$(a, b]$		$a < x \leq b$	

The symbols ∞, **positive infinity,** and −∞, **negative infinity,** do not represent real numbers. They are simply convenient symbols used to describe the unboundedness of an interval such as $(1, \infty)$ or $(-\infty, 3]$.

Unbounded Intervals on the Real Number Line

Notation	Interval Type	Inequality	Graph
$[a, \infty)$		$x \geq a$	
(a, ∞)	Open	$x > a$	
$(-\infty, b]$		$x \leq b$	
$(-\infty, b)$	Open	$x < b$	
$(-\infty, \infty)$	Entire real line		

Additional Examples
Use inequality notation to describe each of the following.
a. m is at least -3.
b. All x in the interval $[-2, 2]$
c. w is at least 1 and at most 5.
d. All q in the interval $(-12, 0)$
Solution
a. $m \geq -3$
b. $-2 \leq x \leq 2$
c. $1 \leq w \leq 5$
d. $-12 < q < 0$

EXAMPLE 2   Using Inequalities to Represent Intervals

Use inequality notation to describe each of the following.

a. c is at most 2.

b. All x in the interval $(-3, 5]$

Solution

a. The statement "c is at most 2" can be represented by $c \leq 2$.

b. "All x in the interval $(-3, 5]$" can be represented by $-3 < x \leq 5$.

The *Interactive* CD-ROM and *Internet* versions of this text show every example with its solution; clicking on the *Try It!* button brings up similar problems. Guided Examples and Integrated Examples show step-by-step solutions to additional examples. Integrated Examples are related to several concepts in the section.

EXAMPLE 3   Interpreting Intervals

Give a verbal description of each interval.

a. $(-1, 0)$ **b.** $[2, \infty)$ **c.** $(-\infty, 0)$

Solution

a. This interval consists of all real numbers that are greater than -1 and less than 0.

b. This interval consists of all real numbers that are greater than or equal to 2.

c. This interval consists of all negative real numbers.

The **Law of Trichotomy** states that for any two real numbers a and b, precisely one of three relationships is possible:

   $a = b, \quad a < b, \quad \text{or} \quad a > b.$ Law of Trichotomy

Absolute Value and Distance

The **absolute value** of a real number is its distance from the origin on the real number line.

Definition of Absolute Value

If a is a real number, the **absolute value** of a is

$$|a| = \begin{cases} a, & \text{if } a \geq 0 \\ -a, & \text{if } a < 0 \end{cases}$$

Notice from this definition that the absolute value of a real number is never negative. For instance, if $a = -5$, then $|-5| = -(-5) = 5$. The absolute value of a real number is either positive or zero. Moreover, 0 is the only real number whose absolute value is 0. So, $|0| = 0$.

EXAMPLE 4   Evaluating the Absolute Value of a Number

Evaluate $\dfrac{|x|}{x}$ for (a) $x > 0$ and (b) $x < 0$.

Solution

a. If $x > 0$, then $|x| = x$ and $\dfrac{|x|}{x} = \dfrac{x}{x} = 1$.

b. If $x < 0$, then $|x| = -x$ and $\dfrac{|x|}{x} = \dfrac{-x}{x} = -1$.

Properties of Absolute Value

1. $|a| \geq 0$ **2.** $|-a| = |a|$

3. $|ab| = |a||b|$ **4.** $\left|\dfrac{a}{b}\right| = \dfrac{|a|}{|b|}, \quad b \neq 0$

Absolute value can be used to define the distance between two points on the real number line. For instance, the distance between -3 and 4 is

$$|-3 - 4| = |-7| = 7$$

as shown in Figure P.5.

Distance Between Two Points on the Real Line

Let a and b be real numbers. The **distance between a and b** is

$$d(a, b) = |b - a| = |a - b|.$$

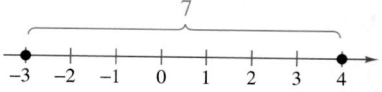

Figure P.5   *The distance between -3 and 4 is 7.*

Algebraic Expressions

One characteristic of algebra is the use of letters to represent numbers. The letters are **variables,** and combinations of letters and numbers are **algebraic expressions.** Here are a few examples of algebraic expressions.

$$5x, \quad 2x - 3, \quad \frac{4}{x^2 + 2}, \quad 7x + y$$

Definition of Algebraic Expression

A collection of letters (**variables**) and real numbers (**constants**) combined using the operations of addition, subtraction, multiplication, division, and exponentiation is an **algebraic expression.**

The **terms** of an algebraic expression are those parts that are separated by *addition*. For example,

$$x^2 - 5x + 8 = x^2 + (-5x) + 8$$

has three terms: x^2 and $-5x$ are the **variable terms** and 8 is the **constant term.** The numerical factor of a variable term is the **coefficient** of the variable term. For instance, the coefficient of $-5x$ is -5, and the coefficient of x^2 is 1.

To **evaluate** an algebraic expression, substitute numerical values for each of the variables in the expression. Here are two examples.

A computer animation of this concept appears in the *Interactive* CD-ROM and *Internet* versions of this text.

Expression	Value of Variable	Substitute	Value of Expression
$-3x + 5$	$x = 3$	$-3(3) + 5$	$-9 + 5 = -4$
$3x^2 + 2x - 1$	$x = -1$	$3(-1)^2 + 2(-1) - 1$	$3 - 2 - 1 = 0$

When an algebraic expression is evaluated, the **Substitution Principle** is used. It states, "If $a = b$, then a can be replaced by b in any expression involving a." In the first evaluation shown above, for instance, 3 is *substituted* for x in the expression $-3x + 5$.

Basic Rules of Algebra

There are four arithmetic operations with real numbers: *addition, multiplication, subtraction,* and *division,* denoted by the symbols $+$, $\times$ or $\cdot$, $-$, and $\div$ or $/$. Of these, addition and multiplication are the two primary operations. Subtraction and division are the inverse operations of addition and multiplication, respectively.

Subtraction: Add the opposite. $\qquad$ *Division: Multiply by the reciprocal.*

$$a - b = a + (-b) \qquad \text{If } b \neq 0, \text{ then } a/b = a\left(\frac{1}{b}\right) = \frac{a}{b}.$$

In these definitions, $-b$ is the **additive inverse** (or opposite) of b, and $1/b$ is the **multiplicative inverse** (or reciprocal) of b. In the fractional form a/b, a is the **numerator** of the fraction and b is the **denominator.**

Because the properties of real numbers below are true for variables and algebraic expressions, as well as for real numbers, they are often called the **Basic Rules of Algebra.** Try to formulate a verbal description of each property. For instance, the first property states that *the order in which two real numbers are added does not affect their sum.*

Basic Rules of Algebra

Let a, b, and c be real numbers, variables, or algebraic expressions.

Property		*Example*
Commutative Property of Addition:	$a + b = b + a$	$4x + x^2 = x^2 + 4x$
Commutative Property of Multiplication:	$ab = ba$	$(4 - x)x^2 = x^2(4 - x)$
Associative Property of Addition:	$(a + b) + c = a + (b + c)$	$(x + 5) + x^2 = x + (5 + x^2)$
Associative Property of Multiplication:	$(ab)c = a(bc)$	$(2x \cdot 3y)(8) = (2x)(3y \cdot 8)$
Distributive Properties:	$a(b + c) = ab + ac$ $(a + b)c = ac + bc$	$3x(5 + 2x) = 3x \cdot 5 + 3x \cdot 2x$ $(y + 8)y = y \cdot y + 8 \cdot y$
Additive Identity Property:	$a + 0 = a$	$5y^2 + 0 = 5y^2$
Multiplicative Identity Property:	$a \cdot 1 = a$	$(4x^2)(1) = 4x^2$
Additive Inverse Property:	$a + (-a) = 0$	$5x^3 + (-5x^3) = 0$
Multiplicative Inverse Property:	$a \cdot \dfrac{1}{a} = 1, \quad a \neq 0$	$(x^2 + 4)\left(\dfrac{1}{x^2 + 4}\right) = 1$

Because subtraction is defined as "adding the opposite," the Distributive Properties are also true for subtraction. For instance, the "subtraction form" of $a(b + c) = ab + ac$ is

$$a(b - c) = ab - ac.$$

Properties of Negation and Equality

Let a, b, and c be real numbers, variables, or algebraic expressions.

Property	*Example*
1. $(-1)a = -a$	$(-1)7 = -7$
2. $-(-a) = a$	$-(-6) = 6$
3. $(-a)b = -(ab) = a(-b)$	$(-5)3 = -(5 \cdot 3) = 5(-3)$
4. $(-a)(-b) = ab$	$(-2)(-x) = 2x$
5. $-(a + b) = (-a) + (-b)$	$-(x + 8) = (-x) + (-8) = -x - 8$
6. If $a = b$, then $a + c = b + c$.	$\frac{1}{2} + 3 = 0.5 + 3$
7. If $a = b$, then $ac = bc$.	$4^2(2) = 16(2)$
8. If $a + c = b + c$, then $a = b$.	$1.4 - 1 = \frac{7}{5} - 1$
9. If $ac = bc$ and $c \neq 0$, then $a = b$.	$\dfrac{3}{4} = \dfrac{\sqrt{9}}{4}$

STUDY TIP

Be sure you see the difference between the opposite of a number and a negative number. If a is already negative, then its opposite, $-a$, is positive. For instance, if $a = -5$, then $-a = -(-5) = 5$.

Properties of Zero

Let a and b be real numbers, variables, or algebraic expressions.

1. $a + 0 = a$ and $a - 0 = a$ **2.** $a \cdot 0 = 0$

3. $\dfrac{0}{a} = 0$, $a \neq 0$ **4.** $\dfrac{a}{0}$ is undefined.

5. Zero-Factor Property: If $ab = 0$, then $a = 0$ or $b = 0$.

Properties and Operations of Fractions

Let a, b, c, and d be real numbers, variables, or algebraic expressions such that $b \neq 0$ and $d \neq 0$.

1. Equivalent Fractions: $\dfrac{a}{b} = \dfrac{c}{d}$ if and only if $ad = bc$.

2. Rules of Signs: $-\dfrac{a}{b} = \dfrac{-a}{b} = \dfrac{a}{-b}$ and $\dfrac{-a}{-b} = \dfrac{a}{b}$

3. Generate Equivalent Fractions: $\dfrac{a}{b} = \dfrac{ac}{bc}$, $c \neq 0$

4. Add or Subtract with Like Denominators: $\dfrac{a}{b} \pm \dfrac{c}{b} = \dfrac{a \pm c}{b}$

5. Add or Subtract with Unlike Denominators: $\dfrac{a}{b} \pm \dfrac{c}{d} = \dfrac{ad \pm bc}{bd}$

6. Multiply Fractions: $\dfrac{a}{b} \cdot \dfrac{c}{d} = \dfrac{ac}{bd}$

7. Divide Fractions: $\dfrac{a}{b} \div \dfrac{c}{d} = \dfrac{a}{b} \cdot \dfrac{d}{c} = \dfrac{ad}{bc}$, $c \neq 0$

Activities
1. Evaluate: $4 - |-3|$.
   Answer: 1
2. Find the distance between -41 and 16.
   Answer: 57
3. Use inequality notation to describe the set of nonnegative numbers.
   Answer: $x \geq 0$
4. Use interval notation to describe the inequality $-6 < x \leq 13$.
   Answer: $(-6, 13]$

EXAMPLE 5   Properties and Operations of Fractions

a. $\dfrac{x}{5} = \dfrac{3 \cdot x}{3 \cdot 5} = \dfrac{3x}{15}$ Write equivalent fractions.

b. $\dfrac{x}{3} + \dfrac{2x}{5} = \dfrac{5 \cdot x + 3 \cdot 2x}{15} = \dfrac{11x}{15}$ Add fractions with unlike denominators.

c. $\dfrac{7}{x} \div \dfrac{3}{2} = \dfrac{7}{x} \cdot \dfrac{2}{3} = \dfrac{14}{3x}$ Divide fractions.

Point out to students that to add or subtract fractions with unlike denominators, they can either use Property 5 of fractions as in Example 5(b), or they can rewrite the fractions with like denominators using the least common denominator (LCD) of the fractions.

If a, b, and c are integers such that $ab = c$, then a and b are **factors** or **divisors** of c. A **prime number** is an integer that has exactly two positive factors: itself and 1. For example, 2, 3, 5, 7, and 11 are prime numbers. The numbers 4, 6, 8, 9, and 10 are **composite** because they can be written as the product of two or more prime numbers. The number 1 is neither prime nor composite. The **Fundamental Theorem of Arithmetic** states that every positive integer greater than 1 can be written as the product of prime numbers in precisely one way (disregarding order). For instance, the *prime factorization* of 24 is $24 = 2 \cdot 2 \cdot 2 \cdot 3$.

P.1 Exercises

In Exercises 1–6, determine which numbers are (a) natural numbers, (b) integers, (c) rational numbers, and (d) irrational numbers.

1. $-9, -\frac{7}{2}, 5, \frac{2}{3}, \sqrt{2}, 0, 1, -4, -1$

2. $\sqrt{5}, -7, -\frac{7}{3}, 0, 3.12, \frac{5}{4}, -2, -8, 3$

3. $2.01, 0.666\ldots, -13, 0.010110111\ldots,$
$1, -10, 20$

4. $2.3030030003\ldots, 0.7575, -4.63, \sqrt{10}, -2,$
$0.03, -10$

5. $-\pi, -\frac{1}{3}, \frac{6}{3}, \frac{1}{2}\sqrt{2}, -7.5, -2, 3, -3$

6. $25, -17, -\frac{12}{5}, \sqrt{9}, 3.12, \frac{1}{2}\pi, 6, -4, 18$

In Exercises 7–10, use a calculator to find the decimal form of the rational number. If it is a nonterminating decimal, write the repeating pattern.

7. $\frac{5}{8}$ 0.625

8. $\frac{1}{3}$ 0.333

9. $\frac{41}{333}$ 0.123123

10. $\frac{6}{11}$ 0.5454..

In Exercises 11–16, use a graphing utility to rewrite the rational number as the ratio of two integers.

11. 4.6 $\frac{46}{10} = \frac{23}{5}$

12. 12.3 $\frac{123}{10}$ 249

13. 6.5 $\frac{65}{10}$

14. 3.81 $\frac{381}{10}$

15. -1.83 $\frac{183}{100}$

16. -2.490 $\frac{2.490}{1000}$ $\frac{1245}{500}$

In Exercises 17 and 18, approximate the numbers and place the correct inequality symbol (< or >) between them.

17.

$-1 < a < 3$

18.

$-6 < a < -2$

In Exercises 19–24, plot the two real numbers on the real number line. Then place the correct inequality symbol (< or >) between them.

19. $-4, -8$ $-8 < a < -4$

20. $-3.5, 1$ $-3.5 < a < 1$

21. $\frac{3}{2}, 7$ $\frac{3}{2} < a < 7$

22. $1, \frac{16}{3}$ $1 < a < \frac{16}{3}$

23. $\frac{5}{6}, \frac{2}{3}$ $\frac{2}{3} < a < \frac{5}{6}$ 0.83

24. $-\frac{8}{7}, -\frac{3}{7}$ $-\frac{8}{7} < a < -\frac{3}{7}$

In Exercises 25–34, (a) verbally describe the subset of real numbers represented by the inequality, (b) sketch the subset on the real number line, and (c) state whether the interval is bounded or unbounded.

25. $x \le 5$

26. $x \ge -2$

27. $x < 0$

28. $x > 3$

29. $x \ge 4$

30. $x < 2$

31. $-2 < x < 2$

32. $0 \le x \le 5$

33. $-1 \le x < 0$

34. $0 < x \le 6$

In Exercises 35 and 36, use a calculator to order the numbers from least to greatest.

35. $\frac{7071}{5000}, \frac{584}{413}, \sqrt{2}, \frac{47}{33}, \frac{127}{90}$

36. $\frac{26}{15}, \sqrt{3}, 1.732, \frac{381}{220}, \frac{2103}{1214}$

In Exercises 37–46, use inequality and interval notation to describe the set.

37. x is negative.

38. z is at least 10.

39. y is nonnegative.

40. y is no more than 25.

41. c is at least 12 and at most 32.

42. p is less than 8 but no less than -1.

43. The dog's weight W is more than 45 pounds.

44. The annual rate of inflation r is expected to be at least 2.5%, but no more than 5%.

In Exercises 45 and 46, give a verbal description of the interval.

45. $(-6, \infty)$

46. $(-\infty, 4]$

In Exercises 47–56, evaluate the expression.

47. $|-10|$

48. $|0|$

49. $|3 - \pi|$

50. $|4 - \pi|$

51. $\dfrac{-5}{|-5|}$

52. $-3 - |-3|$

53. $-3|-3|$

54. $|-1| - |-2|$

55. $\dfrac{|x + 2|}{x + 2}$

56. $\dfrac{|x - 1|}{x - 1}$

The *Interactive* CD-ROM and *Internet* versions of this text contain step-by-step solutions to all odd-numbered Section and Review Exercises. They also provide Tutorial Exercises, which link to Guided Examples for additional help.

In Exercises 57–62, place the correct symbol ($<$, $>$, or $=$) between the pair of real numbers.

57. $|-3|$ ___ $-|-3|$ **58.** $|-4|$ ___ $|4|$

59. -5 ___ $-|5|$ **60.** $-|-6|$ ___ $|-6|$

61. $-|-2|$ ___ $-|2|$ **62.** $-(-2)$ ___ -2

In Exercises 63–70, find the distance between a and b.

63.

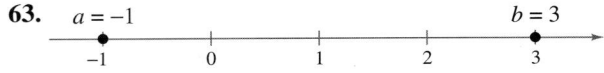

64.

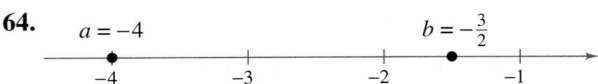

65. $a = 126, b = 75$ **66.** $a = -126, b = -75$

67. $a = -\frac{5}{2}, b = 0$ **68.** $a = \frac{1}{4}, b = \frac{11}{4}$

69. $a = \frac{16}{5}, b = \frac{112}{75}$ **70.** $a = 9.34, b = -5.65$

In Exercises 71 and 72, use the real numbers A, B, and C shown on the number line. Determine the sign of each expression.

71. (a) $-A$ **72.** (a) $-C$

(b) $B - A$ (b) $A - C$

In Exercises 73–80, use absolute value notation to describe the situation.

73. The distance between x and 5 is no more than 3.

74. The distance between x and -10 is at least 6.

75. y is at least six units from 0.

76. y is at most two units from a.

77. *Distance* While traveling, you pass milepost 7, then milepost 18. How far do you travel during that time period?

78. *Distance* While traveling, you pass milepost 103, then milepost 86. How far do you travel during that time period?

79. *Temperature* The temperature was $50°$ at noon, then $27°$ at midnight. What was the change in temperature over the twelve-hour period?

80. *Temperature* The temperature was $38°$ last night at midnight, then $78°$ at noon today. What was the change in temperature over the twelve-hour period?

Budget Variance **In Exercises 81–84, the accounting department of a company is checking to see whether the actual expenses of a department differ from the budgeted expenses by more than \$500 or by more than 5%. Fill in the missing parts of the table, and determine whether the actual expense passes the "budget variance test."**

		Budgeted Expense, b	Actual Expense, a	$|a - b|$	0.05b
81.	Wages	\$112,700	\$113,356		
82.	Utilities	\$9400	\$9772		
83.	Taxes	\$37,640	\$37,335		
84.	Insurance	\$2575	\$2613		

Federal Deficit **In Exercises 85–90, use the bar graph, which shows the receipts of the federal government (in billions of dollars) for selected years from 1960 through 1998. In each exercise you are given the outlay of the federal government. Find the magnitude of the surplus or deficit for the year.** (Source: U.S. Office of Management and Budget)

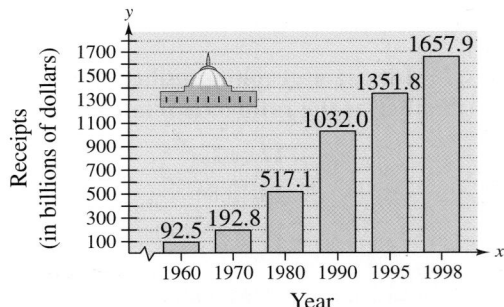

	Receipts, y	Outlay, x	$|y - x|$
85.	1960	\$92.2 billion	
86.	1970	\$195.6 billion	
87.	1980	\$590.9 billion	
88.	1990	\$1253.2 billion	
89.	1995	\$1515.7 billion	
90.	1998	\$1667.8 billion	

In Exercises 91–96, identify the terms. Then identify the coefficients of the variable terms of the expression.

91. $7x + 4$ **92.** $2x - 9$

93. $3x^2 - 8x - 11$ **94.** $7\sqrt{5}x^2 + 3$

95. $4x^3 + \frac{x}{2} - 5$ **96.** $3x^4 + 3x^3$

In Exercises 97–102, evaluate the expression for each value of x. (If not possible, state the reason.)

Expression	Values
97. $4x - 6$	(a) $x = -1$ (b) $x = 0$
98. $9 - 7x$	(a) $x = -3$ (b) $x = 3$
99. $x^2 - 3x + 4$	(a) $x = -2$ (b) $x = 2$
100. $-x^2 + 5x - 4$	(a) $x = -1$ (b) $x = 1$
101. $\dfrac{x + 1}{x - 1}$	(a) $x = 1$ (b) $x = -1$
102. $\dfrac{x}{x + 2}$	(a) $x = 2$ (b) $x = -2$

In Exercises 103–112, identify the rule(s) of algebra illustrated by the equation.

103. $x + 9 = 9 + x$

104. $2\left(\frac{1}{2}\right) = 1$

105. $\dfrac{1}{h + 6}(h + 6) = 1, \quad h \neq -6$

106. $(x + 3) - (x + 3) = 0$

107. $2(x + 3) = 2x + 6$

108. $(z - 2) + 0 = z - 2$

109. $1 \cdot (1 + x) = 1 + x$

110. $x + (y + 10) = (x + y) + 10$

111. $x(3y) = (x \cdot 3)y = (3x)y$

112. $\frac{1}{7}(7 \cdot 12) = \left(\frac{1}{7} \cdot 7\right)12 = 1 \cdot 12 = 12$

In Exercises 113–116, evaluate the expression. (If not possible, state the reason.)

113. $\dfrac{81 - (90 - 9)}{5}$

114. $10(23 - 30 + 7)$

115. $\dfrac{8 - 8}{-9 + (6 + 3)}$

116. $15 - \dfrac{3 - 3}{5}$

In Exercises 117–124, perform the operations. (Write fractional answers in simplest form.)

117. $\frac{3}{16} + \frac{5}{16}$

118. $\frac{6}{7} - \frac{4}{7}$

119. $\frac{5}{8} - \frac{5}{12} + \frac{1}{6}$

120. $\frac{10}{11} + \frac{6}{33} - \frac{13}{66}$

121. $\dfrac{x}{6} + \dfrac{3x}{4}$

122. $\dfrac{11}{x} \div \dfrac{3}{4}$

123. $12 \div \frac{1}{4}$

124. $\left(\frac{3}{5} \div 3\right) - \left(6 \cdot \frac{4}{8}\right)$

In Exercises 125–128, use a calculator to evaluate the expression. (Round your answer to two decimal places.)

125. $-3 + \frac{3}{7}$

126. $3\left(-\frac{5}{12} + \frac{3}{8}\right)$

127. $\dfrac{11.46 - 5.37}{3.91}$

128. $\dfrac{\frac{1}{5}(-8 - 9)}{-\frac{1}{3}}$

129. (a) Use a calculator to complete the table.

n	1	0.5	0.01	0.0001	0.000001
$5/n$					

    (b) Use the result from part (a) to make a conjecture about the value of $\dfrac{5}{n}$ as n approaches 0.

130. (a) Use a calculator to complete the table.

n	1	10	100	10,000	100,000
$5/n$					

    (b) Use the result from part (a) to make a conjecture about the value of $\dfrac{5}{n}$ as n increases without bound.

Synthesis

131. **Exploration**   Consider $|u + v|$ and $|u| + |v|$.

    (a) Are the values of the expressions always equal? If not, under what conditions are they unequal?

    (b) If the two expressions are not equal for certain values of u and v, is one of the expressions always greater than the other? Explain.

132. **Think About It**   Is there a difference between saying that a real number is positive and saying that a real number is nonnegative? Explain.

133. **Writing**   Describe the differences among the sets of natural numbers, integers, rational numbers, and irrational numbers.

True or False?   **In Exercises 134 and 135, determine whether the statement is true or false. Justify your answer.**

134. Let $a > b$, then $\dfrac{1}{a} > \dfrac{1}{b}$, where $a \neq 0$ and $b \neq 0$.

135. Because $\dfrac{a + b}{c} = \dfrac{a}{c} + \dfrac{b}{c}$, then $\dfrac{c}{a + b} = \dfrac{c}{a} + \dfrac{c}{b}$.

P.2 Exponents and Radicals

Exponents

Repeated *multiplication* can be written in **exponential form.** Here are some examples.

Repeated Multiplication	Exponential Form
$a \cdot a \cdot a \cdot a \cdot a$	a^5
$(-4)(-4)(-4)$	$(-4)^3$
$(2x)(2x)(2x)(2x)$	$(2x)^4$

In general, if a is a real number, variable, or algebraic expression and n is a positive integer, then

$$a^n = \underbrace{a \cdot a \cdot a \cdots a}_{n \text{ factors}}$$

where n is the **exponent** and a is the **base.** The expression a^n is read "a to the nth **power.**" An exponent can be negative. Property 3 below shows how to use a negative exponent.

Properties of Exponents

Let a and b be real numbers, variables, or algebraic expressions, and let m and n be integers. (All denominators and bases are nonzero.)

Property	Example
1. $a^m a^n = a^{m+n}$	$3^2 \cdot 3^4 = 3^{2+4} = 3^6 = 729$
2. $\dfrac{a^m}{a^n} = a^{m-n}$	$\dfrac{x^7}{x^4} = x^{7-4} = x^3$
3. $a^{-n} = \dfrac{1}{a^n} = \left(\dfrac{1}{a}\right)^n$	$y^{-4} = \dfrac{1}{y^4} = \left(\dfrac{1}{y}\right)^4$
4. $a^0 = 1, \quad a \neq 0$	$(x^2 + 1)^0 = 1$
5. $(ab)^m = a^m b^m$	$(5x)^3 = 5^3 x^3 = 125x^3$
6. $(a^m)^n = a^{mn}$	$(y^3)^{-4} = y^{3(-4)} = y^{-12} = \dfrac{1}{y^{12}}$
7. $\left(\dfrac{a}{b}\right)^m = \dfrac{a^m}{b^m}$	$\left(\dfrac{2}{x}\right)^3 = \dfrac{2^3}{x^3} = \dfrac{8}{x^3}$
8. $|a^2| = |a|^2 = a^2$	$|(-2)^2| = |-2|^2 = (-2)^2 = 4$

It is important to recognize the difference between expressions such as $(-2)^4$ and -2^4. In $(-2)^4$, the parentheses indicate that the exponent applies to the negative sign as well as to the 2, but in $-2^4 = -(2^4)$, the exponent applies only to the 2. So, $(-2)^4 = 16$, whereas $-2^4 = -16$.

What You Should Learn:

- How to use properties of exponents
- How to use scientific notation to represent real numbers
- How to use properties of radicals
- How to simplify and combine radicals
- How to rationalize denominators and numerators
- How to use properties of rational exponents

Why You Should Learn It:

Real numbers and algebraic expressions are often written with exponents and radicals. For instance, in Exercise 100 on page 23, you will use an expression involving a radical to find the size of a particle that can be carried by a stream moving at a certain velocity.

Superstock

The properties of exponents listed on the previous page apply to *all* integers m and n, not just positive integers. For instance, by Property 2, you can write

$$\frac{3^4}{3^{-5}} = 3^{4-(-5)} = 3^{4+5} = 3^9.$$

EXAMPLE 1   Using Properties of Exponents

a. $(-3ab^4)(4ab^{-3}) = -12(a)(a)(b^4)(b^{-3}) = -12a^2b$

b. $(2xy^2)^3 = 2^3(x)^3(y^2)^3 = 8x^3y^6$

c. $3a(-4a^2)^0 = 3a(1) = 3a, \qquad a \neq 0$

d. $\left(\dfrac{5x^3}{y}\right)^2 = \dfrac{5^2(x^3)^2}{y^2} = \dfrac{25x^6}{y^2}$

EXAMPLE 2   Rewriting with Positive Exponents

a. $x^{-1} = \dfrac{1}{x}$ Property 3

b. $\dfrac{1}{3x^{-2}} = \dfrac{1(x^2)}{3} = \dfrac{x^2}{3}$ The exponent -2 does not apply to 3.

c. $\dfrac{1}{(3x)^{-2}} = (3x)^2 = 9x^2$ The exponent -2 does apply to 3.

d. $\dfrac{12a^3b^{-4}}{4a^{-2}b} = \dfrac{12a^3 \cdot a^2}{4b \cdot b^4} = \dfrac{3a^5}{b^5}$

e. $\left(\dfrac{3x^2}{y}\right)^{-2} = \dfrac{3^{-2}(x^2)^{-2}}{y^{-2}}$ Properties 5 and 7

$\qquad = \dfrac{3^{-2}x^{-4}}{y^{-2}}$ Property 6

$\qquad = \dfrac{y^2}{3^2x^4}$ Property 3

$\qquad = \dfrac{y^2}{9x^4}$ Simplify.

EXAMPLE 3   Calculators and Exponents

Expression	Graphing Calculator Keystrokes	Display
a. $13^4 + 5$	13 ⌃ 4 ⊕ 5 ENTER	28566
b. $3^{-2} + 4^{-1}$	3 ⌃ (−) 2 ⊕ 4 ⌃ (−) 1 ENTER	.3611111111
c. $\dfrac{3^5 + 1}{3^5 - 1}$	(3 ⌃ 5 ⊕ 1) ÷ (3 ⌃ 5 ⊖ 1) ENTER	1.008264463

The graphing calculator keystrokes given in this text may not be the same as the keystrokes for your graphing calculator. Be sure you are familiar with the use of the keys on your own calculator.

The French mathematician Nicolas Chuquet (ca. 1500) wrote *Triparty en la science des nombres*, in which a form of exponent notation was used. Our expressions $6x^3$ and $10x^2$ were written as .6.³ and .10.². Zero and negative exponents were also represented, so x^0 would be written as .1.⁰ and $3x^{-2}$ as .3.²ᵐ. Chuquet wrote that .72.¹ divided by .8.³ is .9.²ᵐ. That is, $72x \div 8x^3 = 9x^{-2}$.

STUDY T!P

Rarely in algebra is there only one way to solve a problem. Don't be concerned if the steps you use to solve a problem are not exactly the same as the steps presented in this text. The important thing is to use steps that you understand *and*, of course, that are justified by the rules of algebra. For instance, you might prefer the following steps for Example 2(e).

$$\left(\frac{3x^2}{y}\right)^{-2} = \left(\frac{y}{3x^2}\right)^2 = \frac{y^2}{9x^4}$$

Additional Examples

a. $4x^{-1} = \dfrac{4}{x}$

b. $\dfrac{3}{2x^{-2}} = \dfrac{3x^2}{2}$

c. $\left(\dfrac{2}{5}\right)^{-1} = \dfrac{5}{2}$

Scientific Notation

Exponents provide an efficient way of writing and computing with very large (or very small) numbers. For instance, there are about 326 billion billion gallons of water on Earth—that is, 326 followed by 18 zeros.

326,000,000,000,000,000,000

It is convenient to write such numbers in **scientific notation.** This notation has the form $\pm c \times 10^n$, where $1 \leq c < 10$ and n is an integer. So, the number of gallons of water on Earth can be written in scientific notation as

$$3.26 \times 100,000,000,000,000,000,000 = 3.26 \times 10^{20}.$$

The *positive* exponent 20 indicates that the number is *large* (10 or more) and that the decimal point has been moved 20 places. A *negative* exponent indicates that the number is *small* (less than 1). For instance, the mass (in grams) of one electron is approximately

$$9.0 \times 10^{-28} = \underbrace{0.0000000000000000000000000009.}_{28 \text{ decimal places}}$$

Activities

1. Rewrite using the Distributive Property: $3(x - y)$.
   Answer: $3x - 3y$

2. Simplify: $\left(\dfrac{6x^{-1}y}{y^3}\right)^{-2}$.
   Answer: $\dfrac{x^2y^4}{36}$

3. Write in scientific notation: 39,000,000.
   Answer: 3.9×10^7

EXAMPLE 4   Scientific Notation

a. $1.345 \times 10^2 = 134.5$

b. $0.0000782 = 7.82 \times 10^{-5}$

c. $-9.36 \times 10^{-6} = -0.00000936$

d. $836,100,000 = 8.361 \times 10^8$

Most calculators switch to scientific notation when they are showing large or small numbers that exceed the display range. Try evaluating $86,500,000 \times 6000$. If your calculator follows standard conventions, its display should be

$\boxed{5.19 \ 11}$ or $\boxed{5.19 \ \text{E} \ 11}$

which is 5.19×10^{11}.

EXAMPLE 5   Using Scientific Notation with a Calculator

Use a calculator to evaluate $65,000 \times 3,400,000,000$.

Solution

Because $65,000 = 6.5 \times 10^4$ and $3,400,000,000 = 3.4 \times 10^9$, you can multiply the two numbers using the following graphing calculator steps.

6.5 $\boxed{\text{EE}}$ 4 $\boxed{\times}$ 3.4 $\boxed{\text{EE}}$ 9 $\boxed{\text{ENTER}}$

After entering these keystrokes, the calculator display should read $\boxed{2.21 \ \text{E} \ 14}$. Therefore, the product of the two numbers is

$$(6.5 \times 10^4)(3.4 \times 10^9) = 2.21 \times 10^{14}$$

$$= 221,000,000,000,000.$$

Radicals and Their Properties

A **square root** of a number is one of its two equal factors. For example, 5 is a square root of 25 because 5 is one of the two equal factors of $25 = 5 \cdot 5$. In a similar way, a **cube root** of a number is one of its three equal factors, as in $125 = 5^3$.

Use pattern recognition to help students identify perfect squares, cubes, etc., of both positive and negative integers when simplifying radicals. Have students construct a table of powers for several integers. For example:

n	n^2	n^3	n^4
-3	9	-27	81
-2	4	-8	16
-1	1	-1	1
0	0	0	0
1	1	1	1
2	4	8	16
3	9	27	81

> ## Definition of the nth Root of a Number
>
> Let a and b be real numbers and let $n \geq 2$ be a positive integer. If
>
> $$a = b^n$$
>
> then b is an n**th root of** a. If $n = 2$, the root is a **square root.** If $n = 3$, the root is a **cube root.**

Some numbers have more than one nth root. For example, both 5 and -5 are square roots of 25. The *principal square root* of 25, written as $\sqrt{25}$, is the positive root, 5. The **principal nth root** of a number is defined as follows.

> ## Principal nth Root of a Number
>
> Let a be a real number that has at least one nth root. The **principal nth root of** a is the nth root that has the same sign as a. It is denoted by a **radical symbol**
>
> $$\sqrt[n]{a}.$$ Principal nth root
>
> The positive integer n is the **index** of the radical, and the number a is the **radicand.** If $n = 2$, omit the index and write $\sqrt{a}$ rather than $\sqrt[2]{a}$. (The plural of index is *indices*.)

A common misunderstanding is that the square root sign implies both negative and positive roots. This is not correct. The square root sign implies only a positive root. When a negative root is needed, you must use the negative sign with the square root sign.

Incorrect: $\sqrt{4} = \pm 2$ Correct: $-\sqrt{4} = -2$ and $\sqrt{4} = 2$

EXAMPLE 6   Evaluating Expressions Involving Radicals

a. $\sqrt{36} = 6$ because $6^2 = 36$.

b. $-\sqrt{36} = -6$ because $-\left(\sqrt{36}\right) = -(6) = -6$.

c. $\sqrt[3]{\dfrac{125}{64}} = \dfrac{5}{4}$ because $\left(\dfrac{5}{4}\right)^3 = \dfrac{5^3}{4^3} = \dfrac{125}{64}$.

d. $\sqrt[5]{-32} = -2$ because $(-2)^5 = -32$.

e. $\sqrt[4]{-81}$ is not a real number because there is no real number that can be raised to the fourth power to produce -81.

Here are some generalizations about the *n*th roots of a real number.

Generalizations About *n*th Roots of Real Numbers

Real Number a	Integer n	Root(s) of a	Example
$a > 0$	$n > 0, n$ is even	$\sqrt[n]{a},\ -\sqrt[n]{a}$	$\sqrt[4]{81} = 3,\ -\sqrt[4]{81} = -3$
$a > 0$ or $a < 0$	n is odd	$\sqrt[n]{a}$	$\sqrt[3]{-8} = -2$
$a < 0$	n is even	No real roots	$\sqrt{-4}$ is not real
$a = 0$	n is even or odd	$\sqrt[n]{0} = 0$	$\sqrt[5]{0} = 0$

Integers such as 1, 4, 9, 16, 25, and 36 are called **perfect squares** because they have integer square roots. Similarly, integers such as 1, 8, 27, 64, and 125 are called **perfect cubes** because they have integer cube roots.

Properties of Radicals

Let a and b be real numbers, variables, or algebraic expressions such that the indicated roots are real numbers, and let m and n be positive integers.

Property

1. $\sqrt[n]{a^m} = \left(\sqrt[n]{a}\right)^m$
2. $\sqrt[n]{a} \cdot \sqrt[n]{b} = \sqrt[n]{ab}$
3. $\dfrac{\sqrt[n]{a}}{\sqrt[n]{b}} = \sqrt[n]{\dfrac{a}{b}},\qquad b \neq 0$
4. $\sqrt[m]{\sqrt[n]{a}} = \sqrt[mn]{a}$
5. $\left(\sqrt[n]{a}\right)^n = a$
6. For n even, $\sqrt[n]{a^n} = |a|$.
   For n odd, $\sqrt[n]{a^n} = a$.

Example

$\sqrt[3]{8^2} = \left(\sqrt[3]{8}\right)^2 = (2)^2 = 4$

$\sqrt{5} \cdot \sqrt{7} = \sqrt{5 \cdot 7} = \sqrt{35}$

$\dfrac{\sqrt[4]{27}}{\sqrt[4]{9}} = \sqrt[4]{\dfrac{27}{9}} = \sqrt[4]{3}$

$\sqrt[3]{\sqrt{10}} = \sqrt[6]{10}$

$\left(\sqrt{3}\right)^2 = 3$

$\sqrt{(-12)^2} = |-12| = 12$

$\sqrt[3]{(-12)^3} = -12$

A common special case of Property 6 is $\sqrt{a^2} = |a|$.

EXAMPLE 7   Using Properties of Radicals

Use the properties of radicals to simplify each expression.

a. $\sqrt{8} \cdot \sqrt{2}$ **b.** $\left(\sqrt[3]{5}\right)^3$

c. $\sqrt[3]{x^3}$ **d.** $\sqrt[6]{y^6}$

Solution
a. $\sqrt{8} \cdot \sqrt{2} = \sqrt{8 \cdot 2} = \sqrt{16} = 4$
b. $\left(\sqrt[3]{5}\right)^3 = 5$
c. $\sqrt[3]{x^3} = x$
d. $\sqrt[6]{y^6} = |y|$

Additional Examples

a. $\sqrt{50} = \sqrt{25 \cdot 2} = 5\sqrt{2}$

b. $\sqrt{\dfrac{3}{4}} = \dfrac{\sqrt{3}}{\sqrt{4}} = \dfrac{\sqrt{3}}{2}$

c. $\left(\sqrt{10}\right)^2 = 10$

STUDY T!P

There are four methods of evaluating radicals on most graphing calculators. For square roots, you can use the *square root key* ☑. For cube roots, you can use the *cube root key* ☑ (or menu choice). For other roots, you can first convert the radical to exponential form and then use the *exponential key* ☐ or you can use the *nth root key* ☑.

Simplifying Radicals

An expression involving radicals is in **simplest form** when the following conditions are satisfied.

1. All possible factors have been removed from the radical.

2. All fractions have radical-free denominators (accomplished by a process called *rationalizing the denominator*).

3. The index of the radical is reduced.

To simplify a radical, factor the radicand into factors whose exponents are multiples of the index. The roots of these factors are written outside the radical, and the "leftover" factors make up the new radicand.

EXAMPLE 8   Simplifying Even Roots

Perfect 4th power — Leftover factor

a. $\sqrt[4]{48} = \sqrt[4]{16 \cdot 3} = \sqrt[4]{2^4 \cdot 3} = 2\sqrt[4]{3}$

Perfect square — Leftover factor

b. $\sqrt{75x^3} = \sqrt{25x^2 \cdot 3x}$ Find largest square factor.

$\qquad = \sqrt{(5x)^2 \cdot 3x}$

$\qquad = 5x\sqrt{3x}$ Find root of perfect square.

c. $\sqrt[4]{(5x)^4} = |5x| = 5|x|$

In Example 8(b), the expression $\sqrt{75x^3}$ makes sense only for nonnegative values of x.

STUDY T!P

When you simplify a radical, it is important that both expressions are defined for the same values of the variable. For instance, in Example 8(b), $\sqrt{75x^3}$ and $5x\sqrt{3x}$ are both defined only for nonnegative values of x. Similarly, in Example 8(c), $\sqrt[4]{(5x)^4}$ and $5|x|$ are both defined for all real values of x.

EXAMPLE 9   Simplifying Odd Roots

Perfect cube — Leftover factor

a. $\sqrt[3]{24} = \sqrt[3]{8 \cdot 3} = \sqrt[3]{2^3 \cdot 3} = 2\sqrt[3]{3}$

Perfect cube — Leftover factor

b. $\sqrt[3]{24a^4} = \sqrt[3]{8a^3 \cdot 3a}$ Find largest cube factor.

$\qquad = \sqrt[3]{(2a)^3 \cdot 3a}$

$\qquad = 2a\sqrt[3]{3a}$ Find root of perfect cube.

c. $\sqrt[3]{-40x^6} = \sqrt[3]{(-8x^6) \cdot 5}$ Find largest cube factor.

$\qquad = \sqrt[3]{(-2x^2)^3 \cdot 5}$

$\qquad = -2x^2\sqrt[3]{5}$ Find root of perfect cube.

Radical expressions can be combined (added or subtracted) if they are **like radicals**—that is, if they have the same index and radicand. For instance, $\sqrt{2}$, $3\sqrt{2}$, and $\frac{1}{2}\sqrt{2}$ are like radicals, but $\sqrt{3}$ and $\sqrt{2}$ are unlike radicals. To determine whether two radicals can be combined, you should first simplify each radical.

EXAMPLE 10   Combining Radicals

a. $2\sqrt{48} - 3\sqrt{27} = 2\sqrt{16 \cdot 3} - 3\sqrt{9 \cdot 3}$ Find square factors.

$\qquad\qquad\qquad = 8\sqrt{3} - 9\sqrt{3}$ Find square roots.

$\qquad\qquad\qquad = (8 - 9)\sqrt{3}$ Combine like terms.

$\qquad\qquad\qquad = -\sqrt{3}$

b. $\sqrt[3]{16x} - \sqrt[3]{54x^4} = \sqrt[3]{8 \cdot 2x} - \sqrt[3]{27 \cdot x^3 \cdot 2x}$ Find cube factors.

$\qquad\qquad\qquad = 2\sqrt[3]{2x} - 3x\sqrt[3]{2x}$ Find cube roots.

$\qquad\qquad\qquad = (2 - 3x)\sqrt[3]{2x}$ Combine like terms.

Try using your calculator to check the result of Example 10(a). You should obtain -1.732050808, which is the same as the calculator's approximation for $-\sqrt{3}$.

Rationalizing Denominators and Numerators

To rationalize a denominator or numerator of the form $a - b\sqrt{m}$ or $a + b\sqrt{m}$, multiply both numerator and denominator by a **conjugate:** $a + b\sqrt{m}$ and $a - b\sqrt{m}$ are conjugates of each other. If $a = 0$, the rationalizing factor for $\sqrt{m}$ is itself, $\sqrt{m}$.

EXAMPLE 11   Rationalizing Denominators

Rationalize the denominator of

a. $\dfrac{5}{2\sqrt{3}}$ **b.** $\dfrac{2}{\sqrt[3]{5}}$.

Solution

a. $\dfrac{5}{2\sqrt{3}} = \dfrac{5}{2\sqrt{3}} \cdot \dfrac{\sqrt{3}}{\sqrt{3}}$ $\sqrt{3}$ is rationalizing factor.

$\qquad = \dfrac{5\sqrt{3}}{2(3)}$

$\qquad = \dfrac{5\sqrt{3}}{6}$

b. $\dfrac{2}{\sqrt[3]{5}} = \dfrac{2}{\sqrt[3]{5}} \cdot \dfrac{\sqrt[3]{5^2}}{\sqrt[3]{5^2}}$ $\sqrt[3]{5^2}$ is rationalizing factor.

$\qquad = \dfrac{2\sqrt[3]{5^2}}{\sqrt[3]{5^3}}$

$\qquad = \dfrac{2\sqrt[3]{25}}{5}$

> **STUDY TIP**
>
> Notice in Example 11(b) that the numerator and denominator are multiplied by $\sqrt[3]{5^2}$ to produce a perfect cube radicand.

EXAMPLE 12   Rationalizing a Denominator with Two Terms

Rationalize the denominator of $\dfrac{2}{3 + \sqrt{7}}$.

Solution

$$\frac{2}{3 + \sqrt{7}} = \frac{2}{3 + \sqrt{7}} \cdot \frac{3 - \sqrt{7}}{3 - \sqrt{7}}$$

Multiply numerator and denominator by conjugate of denominator.

$$= \frac{2(3 - \sqrt{7})}{(3)^2 - (\sqrt{7})^2}$$

Find products. In denominator, $(a + b)(a - b) = a^2 - b^2$.

$$= \frac{2(3 - \sqrt{7})}{2} = 3 - \sqrt{7}$$

Simplify and divide out like factors.

Additional Examples

a. $\dfrac{3}{\sqrt{7}} = \dfrac{3}{\sqrt{7}} \cdot \dfrac{\sqrt{7}}{\sqrt{7}} = \dfrac{3\sqrt{7}}{7}$

b. $\dfrac{2}{\sqrt[3]{4}} = \dfrac{2}{\sqrt[3]{4}} \cdot \dfrac{\sqrt[3]{2}}{\sqrt[3]{2}}$

$\qquad = \dfrac{2\sqrt[3]{2}}{2} = \sqrt[3]{2}$

c. $\dfrac{6}{\sqrt{2} + \sqrt{3}}$

$\qquad = \dfrac{6}{\sqrt{2} + \sqrt{3}} \cdot \dfrac{\sqrt{2} - \sqrt{3}}{\sqrt{2} - \sqrt{3}}$

$\qquad = \dfrac{6(\sqrt{2} - \sqrt{3})}{-1}$

$\qquad = -6\sqrt{2} + 6\sqrt{3}$

Sometimes it is necessary to rationalize the numerator of an expression. For instance, in Section P.4 you will use the technique shown in the next example to rationalize the numerator of an expression from calculus.

EXAMPLE 13   Rationalizing a Numerator

Rationalize the numerator of $\dfrac{\sqrt{5} - \sqrt{7}}{2}$.

Solution

$$\frac{\sqrt{5} - \sqrt{7}}{2} = \frac{\sqrt{5} - \sqrt{7}}{2} \cdot \frac{\sqrt{5} + \sqrt{7}}{\sqrt{5} + \sqrt{7}}$$

Multiply numerator and denominator by conjugate of numerator.

$$= \frac{(\sqrt{5})^2 - (\sqrt{7})^2}{2(\sqrt{5} + \sqrt{7})}$$

Find products. In numerator, $(a + b)(a - b) = a^2 - b^2$.

$$= \frac{-2}{2(\sqrt{5} + \sqrt{7})} = \frac{-1}{\sqrt{5} + \sqrt{7}}$$

Simplify and divide out like terms.

> **STUDY T!P**
>
> Do not confuse the expression $\sqrt{5} + \sqrt{7}$ with the expression $\sqrt{5 + 7}$. In general, $\sqrt{x + y}$ does not equal $\sqrt{x} + \sqrt{y}$. Similarly, $\sqrt{x^2 + y^2}$ does not equal $x + y$.

Rational Exponents

Rationalizing the numerator is especially useful when finding limits in calculus.

> ### Definition of Rational Exponents
>
> If a is a real number and n is a positive integer such that the principal nth root of a exists, then $a^{1/n}$ is defined as
>
> $$a^{1/n} = \sqrt[n]{a} \quad \text{where } 1/n \text{ is the } \textbf{rational exponent} \text{ of } a.$$
>
> Moreover, if m is a positive integer that has no common factor with n, then
>
> $$a^{m/n} = (a^{1/n})^m = (\sqrt[n]{a})^m \quad \text{and} \quad a^{m/n} = (a^m)^{1/n} = \sqrt[n]{a^m}.$$

The symbol ⬤ indicates an example or exercise that highlights algebraic techniques specifically used in calculus.

The numerator of a rational exponent denotes the *power* to which the base is raised, and the denominator denotes the *index* or the *root* to be taken.

$$b^{m/n} = \left(\sqrt[n]{b}\right)^m = \sqrt[n]{b^m}$$

with "Power", "Index" labels pointing to the exponent positions.

When you are working with rational exponents, the properties of integer exponents still apply. For instance,

$$2^{1/2}2^{1/3} = 2^{(1/2)+(1/3)} = 2^{5/6}.$$

EXAMPLE 14 Changing from Radical to Exponential Form

a. $\sqrt{3} = 3^{1/2}$

b. $\sqrt{(3xy)^5} = \sqrt[2]{(3xy)^5} = (3xy)^{(5/2)}$

c. $2x\sqrt[4]{x^3} = (2x)(x^{3/4}) = 2x^{1+(3/4)} = 2x^{7/4}$

EXAMPLE 15 Changing from Exponential to Radical Form

a. $(x^2 + y^2)^{3/2} = \left(\sqrt{x^2 + y^2}\right)^3 = \sqrt{(x^2 + y^2)^3}$

b. $2y^{3/4}z^{1/4} = 2(y^3z)^{1/4} = 2\sqrt[4]{y^3z}$

c. $a^{-3/2} = \dfrac{1}{a^{3/2}} = \dfrac{1}{\sqrt{a^3}}$

d. $x^{0.2} = x^{1/5} = \sqrt[5]{x}$

Rational exponents are useful for evaluating roots of numbers on a calculator, reducing the index of a radical, and simplifying calculus expressions.

EXAMPLE 16 Simplifying with Rational Exponents

a. $(-32)^{-4/5} = \left(\sqrt[5]{-32}\right)^{-4} = (-2)^{-4} = \dfrac{1}{(-2)^4} = \dfrac{1}{16}$

b. $(-5x^{5/3})(3x^{-3/4}) = -15x^{(5/3)-(3/4)} = -15x^{11/12}, \qquad x \neq 0$

c. $\sqrt[9]{a^3} = a^{3/9} = a^{1/3} = \sqrt[3]{a}$ Reduce index.

d. $\sqrt[3]{\sqrt{125}} = \sqrt[6]{125} = \sqrt[6]{(5)^3} = 5^{3/6} = 5^{1/2} = \sqrt{5}$

e. $(2x - 1)^{4/3}(2x - 1)^{-1/3} = (2x - 1)^{(4/3)-(1/3)} = 2x - 1, \qquad x \neq \dfrac{1}{2}$

f. $\dfrac{x - 1}{(x - 1)^{-1/2}} = \dfrac{x - 1}{(x - 1)^{-1/2}} \cdot \dfrac{(x - 1)^{1/2}}{(x - 1)^{1/2}}$

$$= \dfrac{(x - 1)^{3/2}}{(x - 1)^0}$$

$$= (x - 1)^{3/2}, \qquad x \neq 1$$

Additional Examples

a. $\dfrac{9^{2/3}}{9^{1/6}} = 9^{(2/3)-(1/6)}$

$\qquad = 9^{1/2}$

$\qquad = 3$

b. $\sqrt[3]{6} + \sqrt[3]{48} = \sqrt[3]{6} + \sqrt[3]{8 \cdot 6}$

$\qquad = \sqrt[3]{6} + 2\sqrt[3]{6}$

$\qquad = 3\sqrt[3]{6}$

Activities

1. Simplify: $\sqrt[3]{250x^6y^4}$.

   Answer: $5x^2y\sqrt[3]{2y}$

2. Evaluate: $\sqrt[3]{64^2}$.

   Answer: 16

3. Are the two expressions equivalent?

   $\dfrac{2}{\sqrt{3} - 1} \qquad \sqrt{3} + 1$

   Answer: yes

P.2 Exercises

In Exercises 1–8, evaluate each expression.

1. (a) $4^2 \cdot 3$ (b) $3 \cdot 3^3$

2. (a) $\dfrac{5^5}{5^2}$ (b) $\dfrac{3^2}{3^4}$

3. (a) $(3^3)^2$ (b) -3^2

4. (a) $(2^3 \cdot 3^2)^2$ (b) $\left(-\dfrac{3}{5}\right)^3 \left(\dfrac{5}{3}\right)^2$

5. (a) $\dfrac{3}{3^{-4}}$ (b) $24(-2)^{-5}$

6. (a) $\dfrac{4 \cdot 3^{-2}}{2^{-2} \cdot 3^{-1}}$ (b) $(-2)^0$

7. (a) $2^{-1} + 3^{-1}$ (b) $(2^{-1})^{-2}$

8. (a) $3^{-1} + 2^{-2}$ (b) $(3^{-2})^2$

In Exercises 9–12, use a calculator to evaluate the expression. (Round your answer to three decimal places.)

9. $(-4)^3(5^2)$ **10.** $(8^{-4})(10^3)$

11. $\dfrac{3^6}{7^3}$ **12.** $\dfrac{4^3}{3^{-4}}$

In Exercises 13–18, evaluate the expression for the value of x.

Expression	Value
13. $7x^{-2}$	4
14. $6x^0 - (6x)^0$	10
15. $4x^3$	-3
16. $-5x^4$	-2
17. $6x^2$	$-\frac{1}{2}$
18. $4(-x)^3$	$\frac{1}{3}$

In Exercises 19–26, simplify each expression.

19. (a) $(-5z)^3$ (b) $5x^4(x^2)$

20. (a) $(3x)^2$ (b) $(4x^3)^2$

21. (a) $\dfrac{7x^2}{x^3}$ (b) $\dfrac{12(x + y)^3}{9(x + y)}$

22. (a) $\dfrac{r^4}{r^6}$ (b) $\left(\dfrac{4}{y}\right)^3 \left(\dfrac{3}{y}\right)^4$

23. (a) $(x + 5)^0, \quad x \neq -5$ (b) $(2x^2)^{-2}$

24. (a) $(2x^5)^0, \quad x \neq 0$ (b) $(z + 2)^{-3}(z + 2)^{-1}$

25. (a) $[(x^2y^{-2})^{-1}]^{-1}$ (b) $(5x^2z^6)^3(5x^2z^6)^{-3}$

26. (a) $3^n \cdot 3^{2n}$ (b) $\left(\dfrac{a^{-2}}{b^{-2}}\right)\left(\dfrac{b}{a}\right)^3$

In Exercises 27–34, fill in the missing description.

Radical Form	Rational Exponent Form
27. $\sqrt[3]{64} = 4$	$64^{1/3}$
28.	$-(144^{1/2}) = -12$
29.	$196^{1/2} = 14$
30. $\sqrt[3]{614.125} = 8.5$	
31. $\sqrt[3]{-216} = -6$	
32.	$(-243)^{1/5} = -3$
33. $\sqrt[4]{81^3} = 27$	
34.	$16^{5/4} = 32$

In Exercises 35–44, evaluate each expression without using a calculator.

35. $\sqrt{9}$ **36.** $\sqrt{49}$

37. $-\sqrt[3]{-27}$ **38.** $\dfrac{\sqrt[4]{81}}{3}$

39. $\left(\sqrt[3]{-125}\right)^3$ **40.** $\sqrt[4]{562^4}$

41. $32^{-3/5}$ **42.** $\left(\dfrac{9}{4}\right)^{-1/2}$

43. $\left(-\dfrac{1}{64}\right)^{-1/3}$ **44.** $-\left(\dfrac{1}{125}\right)^{-4/3}$

In Exercises 45–50, use a calculator to approximate the number. (Round your answer to three decimal places.)

45. $\sqrt[5]{-27^3}$ **46.** $\sqrt[3]{45^2}$

47. $(3.4)^{2.5}$ **48.** $(6.1)^{-2.9}$

49. $(1.2^{-2})\sqrt{75} + 3\sqrt{8}$ **50.** $\dfrac{-5 + \sqrt{33}}{5}$

In Exercises 51–54, simplify by removing all possible factors from the radical.

51. (a) $\sqrt{8}$ (b) $\sqrt[3]{24}$

52. (a) $\sqrt[3]{\frac{16}{27}}$ (b) $\sqrt{\frac{75}{4}}$

53. (a) $\sqrt{54xy^4}$ (b) $\sqrt{\frac{32a^4}{b^2}}$

54. (a) $\sqrt[4]{(3x^2)^4}$ (b) $\sqrt[5]{96x^5}$

In Exercises 55–60, perform the operations and simplify.

55. $5^{4/3} \cdot 5^{8/3}$ **56.** $\dfrac{8^{12/5}}{8^{2/5}}$

57. $\dfrac{(2x^2)^{3/2}}{2^{1/2}x^4}$ **58.** $\dfrac{x^{4/3}y^{2/3}}{(xy)^{1/3}}$

59. $\dfrac{x^{-3} \cdot x^{1/2}}{x^{3/2} \cdot x^{-1}}$ **60.** $\dfrac{5^{-1/2} \cdot 5x^{5/2}}{(5x)^{3/2}}$

In Exercises 61–64, rationalize the denominator of each expression. Then simplify your answer.

61. (a) $\dfrac{1}{\sqrt{3}}$ (b) $\dfrac{8}{\sqrt[3]{2}}$

62. (a) $\dfrac{5}{\sqrt{10}}$ (b) $\dfrac{5}{\sqrt[3]{(5x)^2}}$

63. (a) $\dfrac{2x}{5 - \sqrt{3}}$ (b) $\dfrac{3}{\sqrt{5} + \sqrt{6}}$

64. (a) $\dfrac{5}{\sqrt{14} - 2}$ (b) $\dfrac{5}{2\sqrt{10} - 5}$

In Exercises 65–68, rationalize the numerator of each expression. Then simplify your answer.

65. $\dfrac{\sqrt{8}}{2}$ **66.** $\dfrac{\sqrt{2}}{3}$

67. $\dfrac{\sqrt{5} + \sqrt{3}}{3}$ **68.** $\dfrac{\sqrt{3} - \sqrt{2}}{2}$

In Exercises 69 and 70, reduce the index of each radical.

69. (a) $\sqrt[4]{3^2}$ (b) $\sqrt[6]{(x + 1)^4}$

70. (a) $\sqrt[6]{x^3}$ (b) $\sqrt[4]{(3x^2)^4}$

In Exercises 71 and 72, write each expression as a single radical. Then simplify your answer.

71. (a) $\sqrt{\sqrt{32}}$ (b) $\sqrt{\sqrt[4]{2x}}$

72. (a) $\sqrt{\sqrt{243(x + 1)}}$ (b) $\sqrt{\sqrt[3]{10a^7b}}$

In Exercises 73–76, simplify each expression.

73. (a) $2\sqrt{50} + 12\sqrt{8}$ (b) $10\sqrt{32} - 6\sqrt{18}$

74. (a) $5\sqrt{x} - 3\sqrt{x}$ (b) $-2\sqrt{9y} + 10\sqrt{y}$

75. (a) $3\sqrt{x + 1} + 10\sqrt{x + 1}$
     (b) $7\sqrt{80x} - 2\sqrt{125x}$

76. (a) $5\sqrt{10x^2} - \sqrt{90x^2}$
     (b) $8\sqrt[3]{27x} - \frac{1}{2}\sqrt[3]{64x}$

In Exercises 77–80, fill in the blank with <, =, or >.

77. $\sqrt{5} + \sqrt{3}$ ▢ $\sqrt{5 + 3}$

78. $\sqrt{\dfrac{3}{11}}$ ▢ $\dfrac{\sqrt{3}}{\sqrt{11}}$

79. 5 ▢ $\sqrt{3^2 + 2^2}$ **80.** 5 ▢ $\sqrt{3^2 + 4^2}$

In Exercises 81–84, write the number in scientific notation.

81. Land Area of Earth: 57,300,000 square miles

82. Light Year: 9,460,000,000,000,000 kilometers

83. Relative Density of Hydrogen: 0.0000899 gram per cm^3

84. One Micron (Millionth of a Meter): 0.00003937 inch

In Exercises 85–88, write the number in decimal form.

85. U.S. Daily Coca-Cola Consumption: 6.048×10^8 servings   (Source: The World of Coca-Cola Pavilion)

86. Interior Temperature of Sun: 1.5×10^7 degrees Celsius

87. Charge of Electron: 1.602×10^{-19} coulomb

88. Width of Human Hair: 9.0×10^{-5} meter

In Exercises 89–92, use a calculator to evaluate each expression. (Round your answer to three decimal places.)

89. (a) $750\left(1 + \dfrac{0.11}{365}\right)^{800}$ (b) $\dfrac{67,000,000 + 93,000,000}{0.0052}$

The symbol ⬒ indicates an example or exercise that highlights algebraic techniques specifically used in calculus.

90. (a) $(9.3 \times 10^6)^3(6.1 \times 10^{-4})$

(b) $\dfrac{(2.414 \times 10^4)^6}{(1.68 \times 10^5)^5}$

91. (a) $\sqrt{4.5 \times 10^9}$ (b) $\sqrt[3]{6.3 \times 10^4}$

92. (a) $(2.65 \times 10^{-4})^{1/3}$ (b) $\sqrt{9 \times 10^{-4}}$

In Exercises 93 and 94, evaluate each expression without using a calculator.

93. (a) $\sqrt{25 \times 10^8}$ (b) $\sqrt[3]{8 \times 10^{15}}$

94. (a) $(1.2 \times 10^7)(5 \times 10^{-3})$

(b) $\dfrac{(6.0 \times 10^8)}{(3.0 \times 10^{-3})}$

95. *Exploration*   List all possible digits that occur in the units place of the square of a positive integer. Use that list to determine whether $\sqrt{5233}$ is an integer.

96. *Think About It*   Square the real number $2/\sqrt{5}$ and note that the radical is eliminated from the denominator. Is this equivalent to rationalizing the denominator? Why or why not?

97. *Declining Balances Depreciation*   For the data in the graph, find the annual depreciation rate r by the declining balances method, which uses the formula

$$r = 1 - \left(\frac{S}{C}\right)^{1/n}$$

where n is the useful life of the item (in years), S is the salvage value (in dollars), and C is the original cost (in dollars).

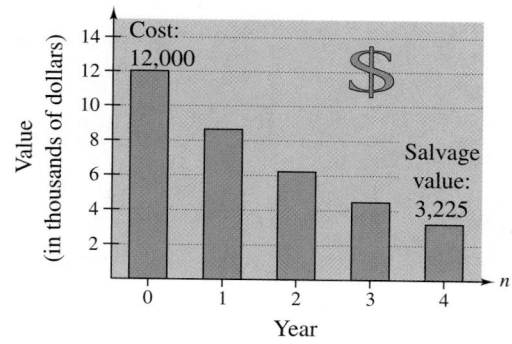

98. *Period of a Pendulum*   The period T (in seconds) of a pendulum is

$$T = 2\pi\sqrt{\frac{L}{32}}$$

where L is the length of the pendulum (in feet). Find the period of a pendulum of length 2 feet.

99. *Mathematical Modeling*   A funnel is filled with water to a height of h centimeters. The time t (in seconds) for the funnel to empty is

$$t = 0.03[12^{5/2} - (12 - h)^{5/2}], \quad 0 \le h \le 12.$$

Find t for $h = 7$ centimeters.

100. *Erosion*   A stream of water moving at the rate of v feet per second can carry particles of size $0.03\sqrt{v}$ inches. Find the size of the particle that can be carried by a stream flowing at the rate of $\frac{3}{4}$ foot per second.

101. *Speed of Light*   The speed of light is 11,160,000 miles per minute. The distance from the sun to the earth is 93,000,000 miles. Find the time for light to travel from the sun to the earth.

102. *Environment*   There were 2.097×10^8 million tons of municipal waste generated in 1996. Find the number of tons for each of the categories in the graph.   (Source: Franklin Associates)

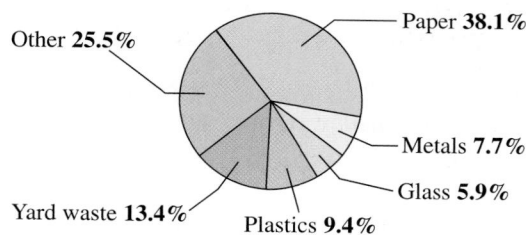

Synthesis

True or False?   **In Exercises 103 and 104, determine whether the statement is true or false. Justify your answer.**

103. $\dfrac{x^{k+1}}{x} = x^k$ **104.** $(a^n)^k = a^{(n^k)}$

105. *Think About It*   Verify that $a^0 = 1$, $a \ne 0$. (*Hint:* Use the property of exponents $\dfrac{a^m}{a^n} = a^{m-n}$.)

106. *Think About It*   Is the real number 52.7×10^5 written in scientific notation? Explain.

P.3 Polynomials and Factoring

Polynomials

An algebraic expression is a collection of variables and real numbers. The most common type of algebraic expression is the **polynomial.** Some examples are

$$2x + 5, \quad 3x^4 - 7x^2 + 2x + 4, \quad \text{and} \quad 5x^2y^2 - xy + 3.$$

The first two are *polynomials in x and the third is a *polynomial in x and y*. The terms of a polynomial in *x* have the form ax^k, where *a* is the **coefficient** and *k* is the **degree** of the term. For instance, the third-degree polynomial

$$2x^3 - 5x^2 + 1 = 2x^3 + (-5)x^2 + (0)x + 1$$

has coefficients 2, −5, 0, and 1.

> ### Definition of a Polynomial in x
>
> Let $a_0, a_1, a_2, \ldots, a_n$ be *real numbers* and let *n* be a *nonnegative integer*. A **polynomial in x** is an expression of the form
> $$a_n x^n + a_{n-1}x^{n-1} + \cdots + a_1 x + a_0$$
> where $a_n \neq 0$. The polynomial is of **degree** *n*, a_n is the **leading coefficient,** and a_0 is the **constant term.**

In **standard form,** a polynomial in *x* is written with descending powers of *x*. Polynomials with one, two, and three terms are called **monomials, binomials,** and **trinomials,** respectively.

A polynomial that has all zero coefficients is called the **zero polynomial,** denoted by 0. No degree is assigned to this particular polynomial. For polynomials in more than one variable, the degree of a *term* is the sum of the exponents of the variables in the term. The degree of the *polynomial* is the highest degree of its terms. Expressions such as the following are not polynomials.

$$x^3 - \sqrt{3}x = x^3 - (3x)^{1/2} \qquad \text{Exponent in } \sqrt{3}x \text{ is not an integer.}$$

$$x^2 + 5x^{-1} \qquad \text{Exponent in } 5x^{-1} \text{ is not a nonnegative integer.}$$

What You Should Learn:

- How to write polynomials in standard form
- How to add, subtract, and multiply polynomials
- How to use special products to multiply polynomials
- How to remove common factors from polynomials
- How to factor special polynomial forms
- How to factor trinomials as the product of two binomials
- How to factor by grouping

Why You Should Learn It:

Polynomials can be used to model and solve real-life problems. For instance, in Exercise 159 on page 34, a polynomial is used to model the stopping distance of an automobile.

Allen Russell/Index Stock

EXAMPLE 1 Writing Polynomials in Standard Form

Polynomial	*Standard Form*	*Degree*
a. $4x^2 - 5x^7 - 2 + 3x$	$-5x^7 + 4x^2 + 3x - 2$	7
b. $4 - 9x^2$	$-9x^2 + 4$	2
c. 8	$8 \ (8 = 8x^0)$	0

Operations with Polynomials

You can add and subtract polynomials in much the same way you add and subtract real numbers. Simply add or subtract the *like terms* (terms having the same variables to the same powers) by adding their coefficients. For instance, $-3xy^2$ and $5xy^2$ are like terms and their sum is

$$-3xy^2 + 5xy^2 = (-3 + 5)xy^2 = 2xy^2.$$

EXAMPLE 2 Sums and Differences of Polynomials

Perform the indicated operation.

a. $(5x^3 - 7x^2 - 3) + (x^3 + 2x^2 - x + 8)$
b. $(7x^4 - x^2 - 4x + 2) - (3x^4 - 4x^2 + 3x)$

Solution

a. $(5x^3 - 7x^2 - 3) + (x^3 + 2x^2 - x + 8)$

$\qquad = (5x^3 + x^3) + (2x^2 - 7x^2) - x + (8 - 3)$ Group like terms.

$\qquad = 6x^3 - 5x^2 - x + 5$ Combine like terms.

b. $(7x^4 - x^2 - 4x + 2) - (3x^4 - 4x^2 + 3x)$

$\qquad = 7x^4 - x^2 - 4x + 2 - 3x^4 + 4x^2 - 3x$ Distributive Property

$\qquad = (7x^4 - 3x^4) + (4x^2 - x^2) + (-3x - 4x) + 2$ Group like terms.

$\qquad = 4x^4 + 3x^2 - 7x + 2$ Combine like terms.

To find the product of two polynomials, use the left and right Distributive Properties.

EXAMPLE 3 Multiplying Polynomials: The FOIL Method

Multiply $(3x - 2)$ by $(5x + 7)$.

Solution

$$(3x - 2)(5x + 7) = 3x(5x + 7) - 2(5x + 7)$$

$$= (3x)(5x) + (3x)(7) - (2)(5x) - (2)(7)$$

$$= 15x^2 + 21x - 10x - 14$$

Product of	Product of	Product of	Product of
First terms	**Outer** terms	**Inner** terms	**Last** terms

$$= 15x^2 + 11x - 14$$

Note in this **FOIL Method** that for binomials the outer (O) and inner (I) terms are alike and can be combined into one term.

When using the FOIL method, the following scheme may be helpful.

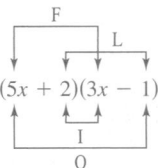

A computer simulation to accompany this example appears in the *Interactive CD-ROM* and *Internet* versions of this text.

EXAMPLE 4   The Product of Two Trinomials

Find the product of $(4x^2 + x - 2)$ and $(-x^2 + 3x + 5)$.

Solution

When multiplying two polynomials, be sure to multiply *each* term of one polynomial by *each* term of the other. A vertical format is helpful.

$$
\begin{array}{r}
4x^2 + x - 2 \quad\text{Standard form}\\
\times \qquad\quad -x^2 + 3x + 5 \quad\text{Standard form}\\
\hline
20x^2 + 5x - 10 \qquad 5(4x^2 + x - 2)\\
12x^3 + 3x^2 - 6x \qquad 3x(4x^2 + x - 2)\\
-4x^4 - x^3 + 2x^2 \qquad -x^2(4x^2 + x - 2)\\
\hline
-4x^4 + 11x^3 + 25x^2 - x - 10
\end{array}
$$

To understand the individual patterns of special products, have students "derive" each product. Then explain how they save time and that the pattern of the product must be recognized to factor expressions.

The *Interactive* CD-ROM and *Internet* versions of this text offer a built-in calculator, which can be used with the Examples, Explorations, and Exercises.

Special Products

Some binomial products have special forms that occur frequently in algebra.

Special Products

Let u and v be real numbers, variables, or algebraic expressions.

Special Product	*Example*
Sum and Difference of Same Terms	
$(u + v)(u - v) = u^2 - v^2$	$(x + 4)(x - 4) = x^2 - 4^2 = x^2 - 16$
Square of a Binomial	
$(u + v)^2 = u^2 + 2uv + v^2$	$(x + 3)^2 = x^2 + 2(x)(3) + 3^2 = x^2 + 6x + 9$
$(u - v)^2 = u^2 - 2uv + v^2$	$(3x - 2)^2 = (3x)^2 - 2(3x)(2) + 2^2 = 9x^2 - 12x + 4$
Cube of a Binomial	
$(u + v)^3 = u^3 + 3u^2v + 3uv^2 + v^3$	$(x + 2)^3 = x^3 + 3x^2(2) + 3x(2^2) + 2^3 = x^3 + 6x^2 + 12x + 8$
$(u - v)^3 = u^3 - 3u^2v + 3uv^2 - v^3$	$(x - 1)^3 = x^3 - 3x^2(1) + 3x(1^2) - 1^3 = x^3 - 3x^2 + 3x - 1$

EXAMPLE 5   The Product of Two Trinomials

Find the product of $(x + y - 2)$ and $(x + y + 2)$.

Solution

By grouping $x + y$ in parentheses, you can write the product of the trinomials as a special product.

$$
\begin{aligned}
(x + y - 2)(x + y + 2) &= [(x + y) - 2][(x + y) + 2]\\
&= (x + y)^2 - 2^2\\
&= x^2 + 2xy + y^2 - 4
\end{aligned}
$$

Factoring

The process of writing a polynomial as a product is called **factoring.** It is an important tool for solving equations and for simplifying fractional expressions.

Unless noted otherwise, when you are asked to factor a polynomial, you can assume that you are looking for factors with integer coefficients. If a polynomial cannot be factored using integer coefficients, it is **prime** or **irreducible over the integers.** For instance, the polynomial $x^2 - 3$ is irreducible over the integers. Over the real numbers, this polynomial can be factored as

$$x^2 - 3 = \left(x + \sqrt{3}\right)\left(x - \sqrt{3}\right).$$

A polynomial is **completely factored** when each of its factors is prime.

EXAMPLE 6   Recognizing Completely Factored Polynomials

a. $x^3 - x^2 + 4x - 4 = (x - 1)(x^2 + 4)$

is completely factored.

b. $x^3 - x^2 - 4x + 4 = (x - 1)(x^2 - 4)$

is not completely factored. Its complete factorization would be

$$x^3 - x^2 - 4x + 4 = (x - 1)(x + 2)(x - 2).$$

The simplest type of factoring involves a polynomial that can be written as the product of a monomial and another polynomial. The technique used here is the Distributive Property, $a(b + c) = ab + ac$, in the *reverse* direction.

$$ab + ac = a(b + c) \qquad \text{\textit{a} is a common factor.}$$

For instance, the polynomial $5x^2 + 15x$ can be factored as follows.

$$5x^2 + 15x = 5x(x) + 5x(3)$$
$$= 5x(x + 3)$$

The first step in completely factoring a polynomial is to remove (factor out) any common factors, as shown in the next example.

EXAMPLE 7   Removing Common Factors

Factor each polynomial.

a. $6x^3 - 4x$ **b.** $3x^4 + 9x^3 + 6x^2$ **c.** $(x - 2)(2x) + (x - 2)(3)$

Solution

a. $6x^3 - 4x = 2x(3x^2) - 2x(2)$ $\qquad 2x$ is a common factor.

$\qquad\qquad = 2x(3x^2 - 2)$

b. $3x^4 + 9x^3 + 6x^2 = 3x^2(x^2) + 3x^2(3x) + 3x^2(2)$ $\qquad 3x^2$ is a common factor.

$\qquad\qquad\qquad = 3x^2(x^2 + 3x + 2)$

c. $(x - 2)(2x) + (x - 2)(3) = (x - 2)(2x + 3)$ $\qquad x - 2$ is a common factor.

Activities

1. Explain what happens when the parentheses are removed from the algebraic statement: $-(3x^2 - 4x + 2)$.

2. Multiply using special products: $\left(\sqrt{2} + \sqrt{3}\right)^2$.
   Answer: $5 + 2\sqrt{6}$

3. Multiply: $(2x + 1)(x - 5)$.
   Answer: $2x^2 - 9x - 5$

Factoring Special Polynomial Forms

Some polynomials have special forms you should learn to recognize so that they can be factored easily.

Factoring Special Polynomial Forms

Factored Form	*Example*
Difference of Two Squares	
$u^2 - v^2 = (u + v)(u - v)$	$9x^2 - 4 = (3x)^2 - 2^2 = (3x + 2)(3x - 2)$
Perfect Square Trinomial	
$u^2 + 2uv + v^2 = (u + v)^2$	$x^2 + 6x + 9 = x^2 + 2(x)(3) + 3^2 = (x + 3)^2$
$u^2 - 2uv + v^2 = (u - v)^2$	$x^2 - 6x + 9 = x^2 - 2(x)(3) + 3^2 = (x - 3)^2$
Sum or Difference of Two Cubes	
$u^3 + v^3 = (u + v)(u^2 - uv + v^2)$	$x^3 + 8 = x^3 + 2^3 = (x + 2)(x^2 - 2x + 4)$
$u^3 - v^3 = (u - v)(u^2 + uv + v^2)$	$27x^3 - 1 = (3x)^3 - 1^3 = (3x - 1)(9x^2 + 3x + 1)$

One of the easiest special polynomial forms to factor is the difference of two squares. Think of this form as follows.

$$u^2 - v^2 = (u + v)(u - v)$$

Difference   Opposite signs

To recognize perfect square terms, look for coefficients that are squares of integers and variables raised to *even powers.*

EXAMPLE 8   Removing a Common Factor First

$$3 - 12x^2 = 3(1 - 4x^2) \qquad \text{3 is a common factor.}$$

$$= 3[1^2 - (2x)^2]$$

$$= 3(1 + 2x)(1 - 2x) \qquad \text{Difference of two squares}$$

EXAMPLE 9   Factoring the Difference of Two Squares

a. $(x + 2)^2 - y^2 = [(x + 2) + y][(x + 2) - y]$

$$= (x + 2 + y)(x + 2 - y)$$

b. $16x^4 - 81 = (4x^2)^2 - 9^2$

$$= (4x^2 + 9)(4x^2 - 9) \qquad \text{Difference of two squares}$$

$$= (4x^2 + 9)[(2x)^2 - 3^2]$$

$$= (4x^2 + 9)(2x + 3)(2x - 3) \qquad \text{Difference of two squares}$$

A perfect square trinomial is the square of a binomial, and it has the following form.

$$u^2 + 2uv + v^2 = (u + v)^2 \qquad \text{or} \qquad u^2 - 2uv + v^2 = (u - v)^2$$

Like signs   Like signs

Note that the first and last terms are squares and the middle term is twice the product of u and v.

EXAMPLE 10   Factoring Perfect Square Trinomials

Factor each trinomial.

a. $x^2 - 10x + 25$ **b.** $16x^2 + 8x + 1$

Solution

a. $x^2 - 10x + 25 = x^2 - 2(x)(5) + 5^2$ Rewrite in $u^2 - 2uv + v^2$ form.

$\qquad\qquad\qquad\; = (x - 5)^2$

b. $16x^2 + 8x + 1 = (4x)^2 + 2(4x)(1) + 1^2$ Rewrite in $u^2 + 2uv + v^2$ form.

$\qquad\qquad\qquad\; = (4x + 1)^2$

The next two formulas show the sums and differences of cubes. Pay special attention to the signs of the terms.

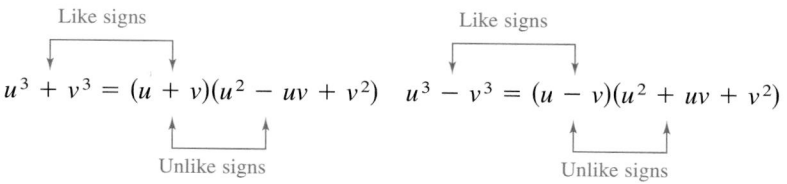

Like signs   Like signs

$$u^3 + v^3 = (u + v)(u^2 - uv + v^2) \quad u^3 - v^3 = (u - v)(u^2 + uv + v^2)$$

Unlike signs   Unlike signs

Exploration

Rewrite $u^6 - v^6$ as the difference of two squares. Then find a formula for completely factoring $u^6 - v^6$. Use your formula to completely factor $x^6 - 1$ and $x^6 - 64$.

EXAMPLE 11   Factoring the Difference of Cubes

Factor $x^3 - 27$.

Solution

$$x^3 - 27 = x^3 - 3^3 \qquad\qquad \text{Rewrite 27 as } 3^3.$$

$$\qquad = (x - 3)(x^2 + 3x + 9) \qquad \text{Factor.}$$

EXAMPLE 12   Factoring the Sum of Cubes

a. $y^3 + 8 = y^3 + 2^3$ Rewrite 8 as 2^3.

$\qquad\; = (y + 2)(y^2 - 2y + 4)$ Factor.

b. $3(x^3 + 64) = 3(x^3 + 4^3)$ Rewrite 64 as 4^3.

$\qquad\qquad = 3(x + 4)(x^2 - 4x + 16)$ Factor.

Trinomials with Binomial Factors

To factor a trinomial of the form $ax^2 + bx + c$, use the following pattern.

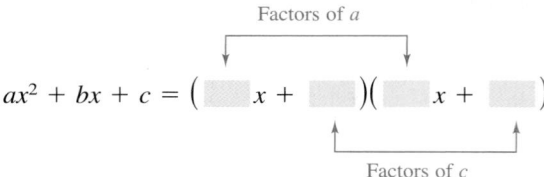

Factors of a

$$ax^2 + bx + c = (\quad x + \quad)(\quad x + \quad)$$

Factors of c

The goal is to find a combination of factors of a and c so that the outer and inner products add up to the middle term bx. For instance, in the trinomial $6x^2 + 17x + 5$, you can write all possible factorizations and determine which one has outer and inner products that add up to $17x$.

$(6x + 5)(x + 1)$ $\qquad$ $(2x + 1)(3x + 5)$

$(6x + 1)(x + 5)$ $\qquad$ $(2x + 5)(3x + 1)$

You can see that $(2x + 5)(3x + 1)$ is the correct factorization because the outer (O) and inner (I) products add up to $17x$.

F $\quad$ O $\quad$ I $\quad$ L $\qquad$ O + I

$$(2x + 5)(3x + 1) = 6x^2 + 2x + 15x + 5 = 6x^2 + 17x + 5.$$

EXAMPLE 13 Factoring a Trinomial: Leading Coefficient Is 1

Factor $x^2 - 7x + 12$.

Solution
The possible factorizations are

$$(x - 2)(x - 6), \quad (x - 1)(x - 12), \quad \text{and} \quad (x - 3)(x - 4).$$

Testing the middle term, you will find the correct factorization to be

$$x^2 - 7x + 12 = (x - 3)(x - 4). \qquad \text{O + I} = -4x + (-3x) = -7x$$

EXAMPLE 14 Factoring a Trinomial: Leading Coefficient Is Not 1

Factor $2x^2 + x - 15$.

Solution
The eight possible factorizations are as follows.

$(2x - 1)(x + 15)$ $\qquad$ $(2x + 1)(x - 15)$

$(2x - 3)(x + 5)$ $\qquad$ $(2x + 3)(x - 5)$

$(2x - 5)(x + 3)$ $\qquad$ $(2x + 5)(x - 3)$

$(2x - 15)(x + 1)$ $\qquad$ $(2x + 15)(x - 1)$

Testing the middle term, you will find the correct factorization to be

$$2x^2 + x - 15 = (2x - 5)(x + 3). \qquad \text{O + I} = 6x - 5x = x$$

You can draw arrows to find the correct middle term. (Encourage students to find the middle term mentally.)

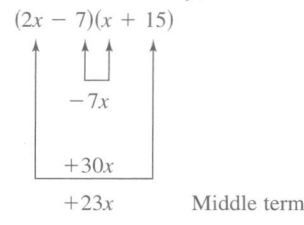

$(2x - 7)(x + 15)$

$-7x$

$+30x$

$+23x$ $\qquad$ Middle term

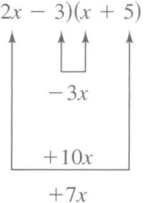

$(2x - 3)(x + 5)$

$-3x$

$+10x$

$+7x$ $\qquad$ Middle term

Point out to students that "testing the middle term" means using the FOIL method to find the sum of the outer and inner terms.

STUDY T!P

Factoring a trinomial can involve trial and error. However, once you have produced the factored form, it is an easy matter to check your answer. For instance, you can verify the factorization in Example 13 by multiplying out the expression $(x - 3)(x - 4)$ to see that you obtain the original trinomial, $x^2 - 7x + 12$.

A computer animation of this example appears in the *Interactive* CD-ROM and *Internet* versions of this text.

Factoring by Grouping

Sometimes polynomials with more than three terms can be factored by a method called **factoring by grouping.** It is not always obvious which terms to group, and sometimes several different groupings will work.

EXAMPLE 15   Factoring by Grouping

Use factoring by grouping to factor

$$x^3 - 2x^2 - 3x + 6.$$

Solution

$$
\begin{aligned}
x^3 - 2x^2 - 3x + 6 &= (x^3 - 2x^2) - (3x - 6) && \text{Group terms.}\\
&= x^2(x - 2) - 3(x - 2) && \text{Factor groups.}\\
&= (x - 2)(x^2 - 3) && \text{Distributive Property}
\end{aligned}
$$

Factoring a trinomial can involve quite a bit of trial and error. Some of this trial and error can be lessened by using factoring by grouping.

Activities

1. Completely factor $4x^2 - 4x + 1$.
   Answer: $(2x - 1)^2$
2. Completely factor $9x^4 - 144$.
   Answer: $9(x^2 + 4)(x - 2)(x + 2)$

EXAMPLE 16   Factoring a Trinomial by Grouping

Use factoring by grouping to factor

$$2x^2 + 5x - 3.$$

Solution

In the trinomial $2x^2 + 5x - 3$, $a = 2$ and $c = -3$, which implies that the product ac is -6. Now, because -6 factors as $(6)(-1)$ and $6 - 1 = 5 = b$, rewrite the middle term as $5x = 6x - x$. This produces the following.

$$
\begin{aligned}
2x^2 + 5x - 3 &= 2x^2 + 6x - x - 3 && \text{Rewrite middle term.}\\
&= (2x^2 + 6x) - (x + 3) && \text{Group terms.}\\
&= 2x(x + 3) - (x + 3) && \text{Factor groups.}\\
&= (x + 3)(2x - 1) && \text{Distributive Property}
\end{aligned}
$$

So, the trinomial factors as

$$2x^2 + 5x - 3 = (x + 3)(2x - 1).$$

G u i d e l i n e s   f o r   F a c t o r i n g   P o l y n o m i a l s

1. Factor out any common factors using the Distributive Property.
2. Factor according to one of the special polynomial forms.
3. Factor as $ax^2 + bx + c = (mx + r)(nx + s)$.
4. Factor by grouping.

P.3   E x e r c i s e s

In Exercises 1–6, match the polynomial with its description. [The polynomials are labeled (a), (b), (c), (d), (e), and (f).]

(a) $5x^2$

(b) $1 - 4x^3$

(c) $x^3 + 2x^2 - 4x + 1$

(d) 18

(e) $-3x^5 + 2x^3 + x$

(f) $\frac{3}{4}x^4 + x^2 + 14$

1. A polynomial of degree zero

2. A trinomial of degree five

3. A binomial with leading coefficient -4

4. A monomial of positive degree

5. A trinomial with leading coefficient $\frac{3}{4}$

6. A third-degree polynomial with leading coefficient 1

In Exercises 7–10, write a polynomial for the description. (There are many correct answers.)

7. A third-degree polynomial with leading coefficient -2

8. A fifth-degree polynomial with leading coefficient 8

9. A fourth-degree polynomial with a negative leading coefficient

10. A third-degree trinomial with an even leading coefficient

In Exercises 11–16, find the degree and leading coefficient of the polynomial.

11. $5x^2 - x + 1$

12. $-3x^4 + x^2 - 4$

13. $x^7 - 1$

14. $9x$

15. $1 - x + 6x^4 - 2x^5$

16. $7 + 3x$

In Exercises 17–22, determine whether the expression is a polynomial. If so, write the polynomial in standard form.

17. $7x - 2x^3 + 10$

18. $4x^3 + x - x^{-1}$

19. $\dfrac{9x + 4}{x}$

20. $\dfrac{x^2 + 2x - 3}{6}$

21. $x^2 - x^4 + x^3 - x$

22. $\sqrt{x^2 - x^4}$

In Exercises 23–38, perform the operations and write the result in standard form.

23. $(6x + 5) - (8x + 15)$

24. $(2x^2 + 1) - (x^2 - 2x + 1)$

25. $-(x^3 - 2) + (4x^3 - 2x)$

26. $-(5x^2 - 1) - (-3x^2 + 5)$

27. $(15x^2 - 6) - (-8.1x^3 - 14.7x^2 - 17)$

28. $(15.6x^4 - 18x - 19.4) - (13.9x^4 - 9.2x + 15)$

29. $3x(x^2 - 2x + 1)$ **30.** $y^2(4y^2 + 2y - 3)$

31. $-5z(3z - 1)$ **32.** $(-3x)(5x + 2)$

33. $(1 - x^3)(4x)$ **34.** $-4x(3 - x^3)$

35. $(2.5x^2 + 5)(3x)$ **36.** $(2 - 3.5y)(4y^3)$

37. $-2x(\frac{1}{8}x + 3)$ **38.** $6y(4 - \frac{3}{8}y)$

In Exercises 39–70, multiply or find the special product.

39. $(x + 3)(x + 4)$ **40.** $(x - 5)(x + 10)$

41. $(3x - 5)(2x + 1)$ **42.** $(7x - 2)(4x - 3)$

43. $(2x - 5y)^2$ **44.** $(5 - 8x)^2$

45. $(x + 10)(x - 10)$ **46.** $(2x + 3)(2x - 3)$

47. $(x + 2y)(x - 2y)$ **48.** $(2x + 3y)(2x - 3y)$

49. $[(m - 3) + n][(m - 3) - n]$

50. $[(x + y) + 1][(x + y) - 1]$

51. $[(x - 3) + y]^2$ **52.** $[(x + 1) - y]^2$

53. $(2r^2 - 5)(2r^2 + 5)$

54. $(3a^3 - 4b^2)(3a^3 + 4b^2)$

55. $(x + 1)^3$ **56.** $(x - 2)^3$

57. $(2x - y)^3$ **58.** $(3x + 2y)^3$

59. $(\frac{1}{2}x - 5)^2$ **60.** $(\frac{3}{5}t + 4)^2$

61. $(\frac{1}{4}x - 3)(\frac{1}{4}x + 3)$ **62.** $(2x + \frac{1}{6})(2x - \frac{1}{6})$

63. $(2.4x + 3)^2$ **64.** $(1.8y - 5)^2$

65. $(1.5x - 4)(1.5x + 4)$ **66.** $(3.3y + 1)(3.3y - 1)$

67. $5x(x + 1) - 3x(x + 1)$

68. $(2x - 1)(x + 3) + 3(x + 3)$

69. $(u + 2)(u - 2)(u^2 + 4)$

70. $(x + y)(x - y)(x^2 + y^2)$

In Exercises 71–76, factor out the common factor.

71. $3x + 6$ **72.** $5y - 30$

73. $2x^3 - 6x$ **74.** $4x^3 - 6x^2 + 12x$

75. $3x(x - 5) + 8(x - 5)$ **76.** $(3x - 1)^2 + (3x - 1)$

In Exercises 77–84, factor the difference of two squares.

77. $x^2 - 36$

78. $x^2 - \frac{1}{4}$

79. $16y^2 - 9$

80. $49 - 9y^2$

81. $4x^2 - \frac{1}{9}$

82. $\frac{25}{36}y^2 - 49$

83. $(x - 1)^2 - 4$

84. $25 - (z + 5)^2$

In Exercises 85–92, factor the perfect square trinomial.

85. $x^2 - 4x + 4$

86. $x^2 + 10x + 25$

87. $x^2 + x + \frac{1}{4}$

88. $x^2 - \frac{4}{3}x + \frac{4}{9}$

89. $4t^2 + 4t + 1$

90. $9x^2 - 12x + 4$

91. $9t^2 + \frac{3}{2}t + \frac{1}{16}$

92. $4t^2 + \frac{8}{5}t + \frac{4}{25}$

In Exercises 93–106, factor the trinomial.

93. $x^2 + x - 2$

94. $x^2 + 5x + 6$

95. $s^2 - 5s + 6$

96. $t^2 - t - 6$

97. $20 - y - y^2$

98. $24 + 5z - z^2$

99. $3x^2 - 5x + 2$

100. $3x^2 + 13x - 10$

101. $2x^2 - x - 1$

102. $2x^2 - x - 21$

103. $5x^2 + 26x + 5$

104. $8x^2 - 45x - 18$

105. $-5u^2 - 13u + 6$

106. $-6x^2 + 23x + 4$

In Exercises 107–116, factor the sum or difference of cubes.

107. $x^3 - 8$

108. $x^3 - 27$

109. $y^3 + 64$

110. $z^3 + 125$

111. $x^3 - \frac{8}{27}$

112. $x^3 + \frac{8}{125}$

113. $8x^3 - 1$

114. $27x^3 + 8$

115. $\frac{1}{8}x^3 + 1$

116. $\frac{27}{64}x^3 - 1$

In Exercises 117–120, factor by grouping.

117. $x^3 - x^2 + 2x - 2$

118. $x^3 + 5x^2 - 5x - 25$

119. $2x^3 - x^2 - 6x + 3$

120. $5x^3 - 10x^2 + 3x - 6$

In Exercises 121–154, completely factor the expression.

121. $x^3 - 9x$

122. $12x^2 - 48$

123. $x^3 - 4x^2$

124. $6x^2 - 54$

125. $x^2 - 2x + 1$

126. $16 + 6x - x^2$

127. $1 - 4x + 4x^2$

128. $-9x^2 + 6x - 1$

129. $2x^2 + 4x - 2x^3$

130. $2y^3 - 7y^2 - 15y$

131. $9x^2 + 10x + 1$

132. $13x + 6 + 5x^2$

133. $\frac{1}{8}x^2 - \frac{1}{96}x - \frac{1}{16}$

134. $\frac{1}{81}x^2 + \frac{2}{9}x - 8$

135. $3x^3 + x^2 + 15x + 5$

136. $5 - x + 5x^2 - x^3$

137. $x^4 - 4x^3 + x^2 - 4x$

138. $3u - 2u^2 + 6 - u^3$

139. $25 - (z + 5)^2$

140. $(t - 1)^2 - 49$

141. $(x^2 + 1)^2 - 4x^2$

142. $(x^2 + 8)^2 - 36x^2$

143. $2t^3 - 16$

144. $5x^3 + 40$

145. $4x(2x - 1) + (2x - 1)^2$

146. $5(3 - 4x)^2 - 8(3 - 4x)(5x - 1)$

147. $2(x + 1)(x - 3)^2 - 3(x + 1)^2(x - 3)$

148. $7(3x + 2)^2(1 - x)^2 + (3x + 2)(1 - x)^3$

149. $7x(2)(x^2 + 1)(2x) - (x^2 + 1)^2(7)$

150. $3(x - 2)^2(x + 1)^4 + (x - 2)^3(4)(x + 1)^3$

151. $2x(x - 5)^4 - x^2(4)(x - 5)^3$

152. $5(x^6 + 1)^4(6x^5)(3x + 2)^3 + 3(3x + 2)^2(3)(x^6 + 1)^5$

153. $\dfrac{x^2}{2}(x^2 + 1)^4 - (x^2 + 1)^5$

154. $5w^3(9w + 1)^4(9) + (2w + 1)^5(3w^2)$

155. *Finance* After 2 years, an investment of $500 compounded annually at an interest rate r will yield an amount of

$$500(1 + r)^2.$$

(a) Write this polynomial in standard form.

(b) Use a calculator to evaluate the polynomial for the values of r in the table.

r	$2\frac{1}{2}\%$	3%	4%	$4\frac{1}{2}\%$	5%
$500(1 + r)^2$					

(c) What conclusion can you make from the table?

156. Finance   After 3 years, an investment of $1200 compounded annually at an interest rate r will yield an amount of

$$1200(1 + r)^3.$$

(a) Write this polynomial in standard form.

(b) Use a calculator to evaluate the polynomial for the values of r in the table.

r	2%	3%	$3\frac{1}{2}$%	4%	$4\frac{1}{2}$%
$1200(1 + r)^3$					

(c) What conclusion can you make from the table?

157. Volume of a Box   A closed box is constructed by cutting along the solid lines and folding along the broken lines on the rectangular piece of metal shown in the figure. The length and width of the rectangle are 45 centimeters and 15 centimeters, respectively. Find the volume of the box in terms of x. Find the volume when $x = 3$, $x = 5$, and $x = 7$.

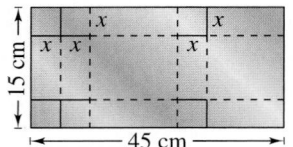
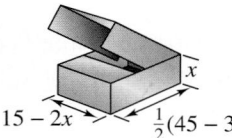

158. Volume of a Box   An open box is made by cutting squares out of the corners of a piece of metal that is 18 centimeters by 26 centimeters. If the edge of each cut-out square is x inches, find the volume when $x = 1$, $x = 2$, and $x = 3$.

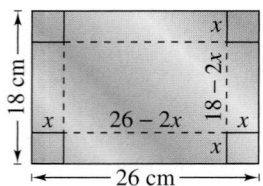
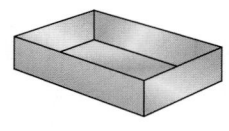

159. Stopping Distance   The stopping distance of an automobile is the distance traveled during the driver's reaction time plus the distance traveled after the brakes are applied. In an experiment, these distances were measured (in feet) when the automobile was traveling at a speed of x miles per hour. The distance traveled during the reaction time was $R = 1.1x$, and the braking distance was

$$B = 0.14x^2 - 4.43x + 58.40.$$

(a) Determine the polynomial that represents the total stopping distance.

(b) Use the result of part (a) to estimate the total stopping distance when $x = 30$, $x = 40$, and $x = 55$.

(c) Use the bar graph below to make a statement about the total stopping distance required for increasing speeds.

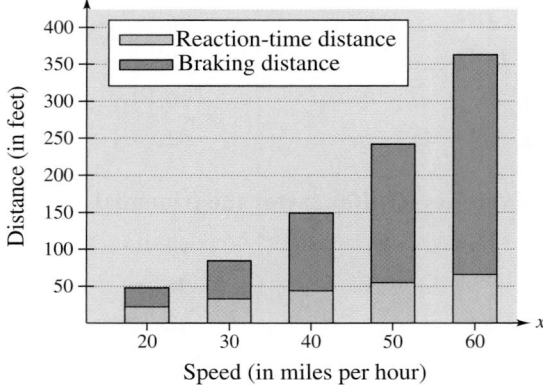

160. Engineering   A uniformly distributed load is placed on a 1-inch-wide steel beam. When the span of the beam is x feet and its depth is 6 inches, the safe load S is approximated by

$$S_6 = (0.06x^2 - 2.42x + 38.71)^2.$$

When the depth is 8 inches, the safe load is approximated by

$$S_8 = (0.08x^2 - 3.30x + 51.93)^2.$$

(a) Use the bar graph below to estimate the difference in the safe loads of these two beams when the span is 12 feet.

(b) How does the difference in safe load change as the span increases?

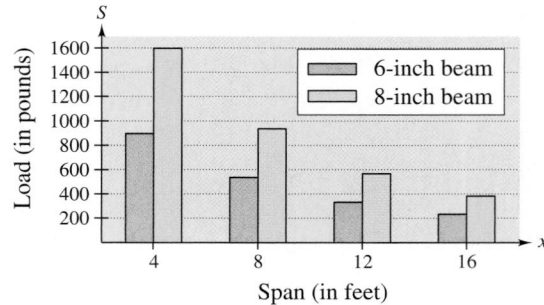

Geometry In Exercises 161 and 162, use the area model to write two different expressions for the area. Then equate the two expressions and name the algebraic property that is illustrated.

161.

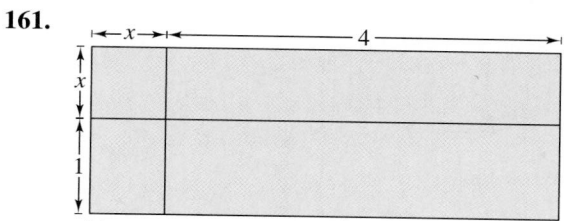

162.

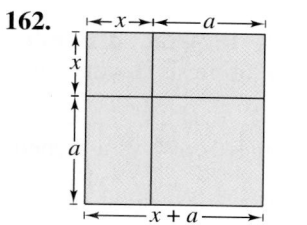

Geometry In Exercises 163–166, match the factoring formula with the correct geometric factoring model. [The models are labeled (a), (b), (c), and (d).] For instance, a factoring model for

$$2x^2 + 3x + 1 = (2x + 1)(x + 1)$$

is shown in the figure.

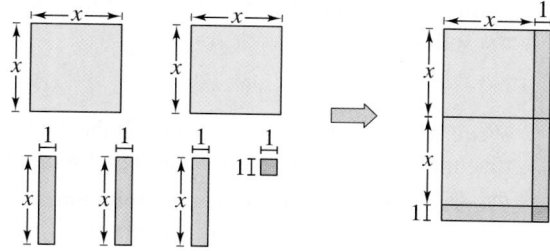

(a)

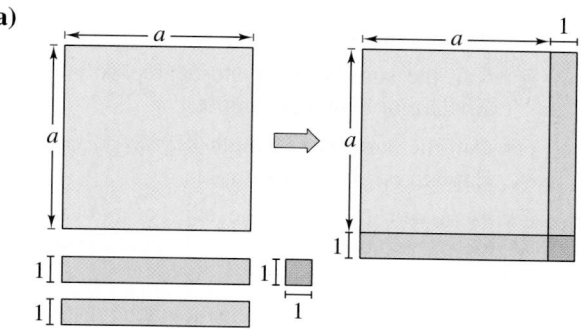

(b)

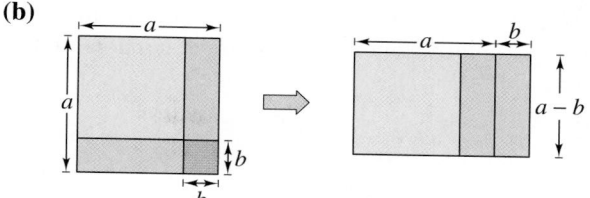

(c)

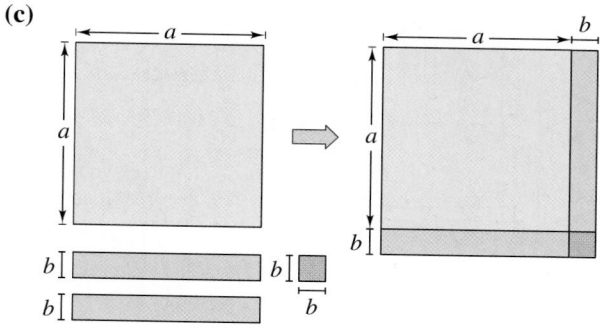

(d)

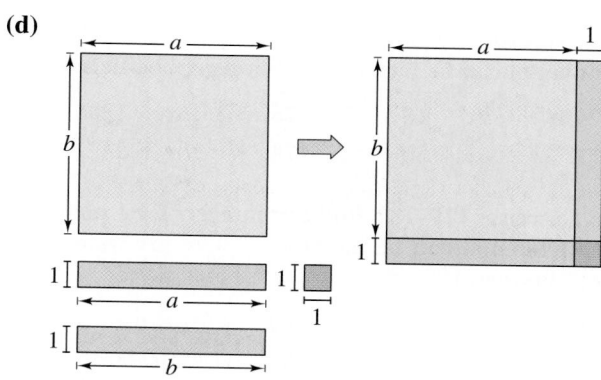

163. $a^2 - b^2 = (a + b)(a - b)$

164. $a^2 + 2ab + b^2 = (a + b)^2$

165. $a^2 + 2a + 1 = (a + 1)^2$

166. $ab + a + b + 1 = (a + 1)(b + 1)$

Geometry In Exercises 167–170, draw a geometric factoring model to represent the factorization.

167. $3x^2 + 7x + 2 = (3x + 1)(x + 2)$

168. $x^2 + 4x + 3 = (x + 3)(x + 1)$

169. $2x^2 + 7x + 3 = (2x + 1)(x + 3)$

170. $x^2 + 3x + 2 = (x + 2)(x + 1)$

Geometry   In Exercises 171–174, write, in factored form, an expression for the shaded portion of the figure.

171.

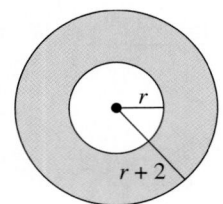

172.

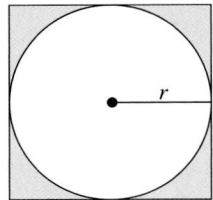

173.

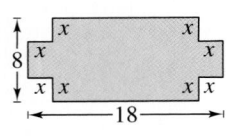

174.

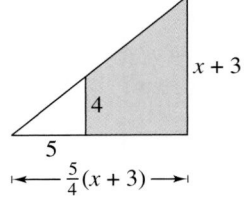

In Exercises 175–178, find all values of b for which the trinomial can be factored with integer coefficients.

175. $x^2 + bx - 15$ **176.** $x^2 + bx - 12$

177. $x^2 + bx + 50$ **178.** $x^2 + bx + 24$

In Exercises 179–182, find two integers for c such that the trinomial can be factored. (There are many correct answers.)

179. $2x^2 + 5x + c$ **180.** $3x^2 - x + c$

181. $3x^2 - 10x + c$ **182.** $2x^2 + 9x + c$

183. *Error Analysis*   Describe the error.

$$9x^2 - 9x - 54 = (3x + 6)(3x - 9)$$
$$= 3(x + 2)(x - 3)$$

184. *Think About It*   Is $(3x - 6)(x + 1)$ completely factored? Explain.

185. *Chemistry*   The rate of change of an autocatalytic chemical reaction is $kQx - kx^2$, where Q is the amount of the original substance, x is the amount of substance formed, and k is a constant of proportionality. Factor the expression.

186. *Geometry*   The cylindrical shell shown in the figure has a volume of

$$V = \pi R^2 h - \pi r^2 h.$$

(a) Factor the expression for the volume.

(b) From the result of part (a), show that the volume is 2π (average radius)(thickness of the shell)h.

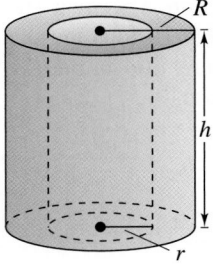

FIGURE FOR 186

Synthesis

True or False?   In Exercises 187–189, determine whether the statement is true or false. Justify your answer.

187. The product of two binomials is always a second-degree polynomial.

188. The difference of two perfect squares can be factored as the product of conjugate pairs.

189. The sum of two perfect squares can be factored as the binomial sum squared.

190. *Exploration*   Find the degree of the product of two polynomials of degrees m and n.

191. *Exploration*   Find the degree of the sum of two polynomials of degrees m and n if $m < n$.

192. *Writing*   A student's homework paper included the following.

$$(x - 3)^2 = x^2 + 9$$

Write a paragraph fully explaining the error and give the correct method for squaring a binomial.

193. *Think About It*   A third-degree polynomial and a fourth-degree polynomial are added.

(a) Can the sum be a fourth-degree polynomial? Explain or give an example.

(b) Can the sum be a second-degree polynomial? Explain or give an example.

(c) Can the sum be a seventh-degree polynomial? Explain or give an example.

194. *Think About It*   Must the sum of two second-degree polynomials be a second-degree polynomial? If not, give an example.

195. *Writing*   Explain what is meant when it is said that a polynomial is in factored form.

P.4 Rational Expressions

Domain of an Algebraic Expression

The set of real numbers for which an algebraic expression is defined is the **domain** of the expression. Two algebraic expressions are **equivalent** if they have the same domain and yield the same values for all numbers in their domain. For instance, the expressions $(x + 1) + (x + 2)$ and $2x + 3$ are equivalent because

$$(x + 1) + (x + 2) = x + 1 + x + 2$$
$$= x + x + 1 + 2$$
$$= 2x + 3.$$

EXAMPLE 1 Finding the Domain of an Algebraic Expression

a. The domain of the polynomial

$$2x^3 + 3x + 4$$

is the set of all real numbers. In fact, the domain of any polynomial is the set of all real numbers, unless the domain is specifically restricted.

b. The domain of the radical expression

$$\sqrt{x - 2}$$

is the set of real numbers greater than or equal to 2, because the square root of a negative number is not a real number.

c. The domain of the expression

$$\frac{x + 2}{x - 3}$$

is the set of all real numbers except $x = 3$, which would produce an undefined division by zero.

The quotient of two algebraic expressions is a **fractional expression.** Moreover, the quotient of two *polynomials* such as

$$\frac{1}{x}, \qquad \frac{2x - 1}{x + 1}, \qquad \text{or} \qquad \frac{x^2 - 1}{x^2 + 1}$$

is a **rational expression.**

Simplifying Rational Expressions

Recall that a fraction is in simplest form if its numerator and denominator have no factors in common aside from ± 1. To write a fraction in simplest form, divide out common factors.

$$\frac{a \cdot \cancel{c}}{b \cdot \cancel{c}} = \frac{a}{b}, \qquad c \neq 0.$$

What You Should Learn:

- How to find domains of algebraic expressions
- How to simplify rational expressions
- How to add, subtract, multiply, and divide rational expressions
- How to simplify complex fractions

Why You Should Learn It:

Rational expressions are useful in estimating prices and determining behavioral trends over time. For instance, a rational expression is used in Exercise 82 on page 46 to model costs of precious metals from 1992 to 1997.

Alert students to the importance of the domain of an expression in graphing functions later in this course and in calculus.

The key to success in simplifying rational expressions lies in your ability to *factor* polynomials.

EXAMPLE 2   Simplifying a Rational Expression

Write $\dfrac{x^2 + 4x - 12}{3x - 6}$ in simplest form.

Solution

$$\frac{x^2 + 4x - 12}{3x - 6} = \frac{(x + 6)(x - 2)}{3(x - 2)} \qquad \text{Factor completely.}$$

$$= \frac{x + 6}{3}, \qquad x \neq 2 \qquad \text{Divide out common factors.}$$

Note that the original expression is undefined when $x = 2$ (because division by zero is undefined). To make sure that the simplified expression is *equivalent* to the original expression, you must restrict the domain of the simplified expression by excluding the value $x = 2$.

When simplifying rational expressions, be sure to factor each polynomial completely before concluding that the numerator and denominator have no factors in common. Moreover, changing the sign of a factor may allow further simplification, as shown in part (b) of the next example.

EXAMPLE 3   Simplifying Rational Expressions

Write each expression in simplest form.

a. $\dfrac{x^3 - 4x}{x^2 + x - 2}$ **b.** $\dfrac{12 + x - x^2}{2x^2 - 9x + 4}$

Solution

a. $\dfrac{x^3 - 4x}{x^2 + x - 2} = \dfrac{x(x^2 - 4)}{(x + 2)(x - 1)}$

$$= \frac{x(x + 2)(x - 2)}{(x + 2)(x - 1)} \qquad \text{Factor completely.}$$

$$= \frac{x(x - 2)}{x - 1}, \qquad x \neq -2 \qquad \text{Divide out common factors.}$$

b. $\dfrac{12 + x - x^2}{2x^2 - 9x + 4} = \dfrac{(4 - x)(3 + x)}{(2x - 1)(x - 4)} \qquad \text{Factor completely.}$

$$= \frac{-(x - 4)(3 + x)}{(2x - 1)(x - 4)} \qquad (4 - x) = -(x - 4)$$

$$= -\frac{3 + x}{2x - 1}, \qquad x \neq 4 \qquad \text{Divide out common factors.}$$

STUDY T!P

In Example 2, do not make the mistake of trying to simplify further by dividing *terms*.

$$\frac{x + 6}{3} \neq \frac{x + 6}{3}^{2} \neq x + 2$$

Remember that to simplify fractions, divide out common *factors*, not terms.

The factoring technique used in equating $(4 - x)$ and $-(x - 4)$ is not always obvious to students. Identify the technique in one or two examples.

Operations with Rational Expressions

To multiply or divide rational expressions, you can use the properties of fractions discussed in Section P.1. Recall that to divide fractions you invert the divisor and multiply.

EXAMPLE 4 Multiplying Rational Expressions

$$\frac{2x^2 + x - 6}{x^2 + 4x - 5} \cdot \frac{x^3 - 3x^2 + 2x}{4x^2 - 6x} = \frac{(2x - 3)(x + 2)}{(x + 5)(x - 1)} \cdot \frac{x(x - 2)(x - 1)}{2x(2x - 3)}$$

$$= \frac{(x + 2)(x - 2)}{2(x + 5)}, \quad x \neq 0, x \neq 1, x \neq \frac{3}{2}$$

EXAMPLE 5 Dividing Rational Expressions

Divide $\dfrac{x^3 - 8}{x^2 - 4}$ by $\dfrac{x^2 + 2x + 4}{x^3 + 8}$.

Solution

$$\frac{x^3 - 8}{x^2 - 4} \div \frac{x^2 + 2x + 4}{x^3 + 8} = \frac{x^3 - 8}{x^2 - 4} \cdot \frac{x^3 + 8}{x^2 + 2x + 4} \qquad \text{Invert and multiply.}$$

$$= \frac{(x - 2)(x^2 + 2x + 4)}{(x + 2)(x - 2)} \cdot \frac{(x + 2)(x^2 - 2x + 4)}{x^2 + 2x + 4}$$

$$= x^2 - 2x + 4, \quad x \neq \pm 2$$

To add or subtract rational expressions, you can use the LCD (least common denominator) method or the basic definition

$$\frac{a}{b} \pm \frac{c}{d} = \frac{ad \pm bc}{bd}, \qquad b \neq 0 \text{ and } d \neq 0. \qquad \text{Basic definition}$$

This definition provides an efficient way of adding or subtracting *two* fractions that have no common factors in their denominators.

EXAMPLE 6 Subtracting Rational Expressions

Subtract $\dfrac{2}{3x + 4}$ from $\dfrac{x}{x - 3}$.

Solution

$$\frac{x}{x - 3} - \frac{2}{3x + 4} = \frac{x(3x + 4) - 2(x - 3)}{(x - 3)(3x + 4)} \qquad \text{Basic definition}$$

$$= \frac{3x^2 + 4x - 2x + 6}{(x - 3)(3x + 4)} \qquad \text{Distributive Property}$$

$$= \frac{3x^2 + 2x + 6}{(x - 3)(3x + 4)} \qquad \text{Combine like terms.}$$

For three or more fractions, or for fractions with a repeated factor in the denominators, the LCD method works well. Recall that the least common denominator of several fractions consists of the product of all prime factors in the denominators, with each factor given the highest power of its occurrence in any denominator. Here is a numerical example.

$$\frac{1}{6} + \frac{3}{4} - \frac{2}{3} = \frac{1 \cdot 2}{6 \cdot 2} + \frac{3 \cdot 3}{4 \cdot 3} - \frac{2 \cdot 4}{3 \cdot 4} \qquad \text{The LCD is 12.}$$

$$= \frac{2}{12} + \frac{9}{12} - \frac{8}{12}$$

$$= \frac{3}{12}$$

$$= \frac{1}{4}$$

Sometimes the numerator of the answer has a factor in common with the denominator. In such cases the answer should be simplified. For instance, in the example above, $\frac{3}{12}$ was simplified to $\frac{1}{4}$.

EXAMPLE 7 • Combining Rational Expressions: The LCD Method

Perform the operations and simplify.

$$\frac{3}{x - 1} - \frac{2}{x} + \frac{x + 3}{x^2 - 1}$$

Solution

Using the factored denominators $(x - 1)$, x, and $(x + 1)(x - 1)$, you can see that the LCD is $x(x + 1)(x - 1)$.

$$\frac{3}{x - 1} - \frac{2}{x} + \frac{x + 3}{(x + 1)(x - 1)}$$

$$= \frac{3(x)(x + 1)}{x(x + 1)(x - 1)} - \frac{2(x + 1)(x - 1)}{x(x + 1)(x - 1)} + \frac{(x + 3)(x)}{x(x + 1)(x - 1)}$$

$$= \frac{3(x)(x + 1) - 2(x + 1)(x - 1) + (x + 3)(x)}{x(x + 1)(x - 1)}$$

$$= \frac{3x^2 + 3x - 2x^2 + 2 + x^2 + 3x}{x(x + 1)(x - 1)} \qquad \text{Distributive Property}$$

$$= \frac{3x^2 - 2x^2 + x^2 + 3x + 3x + 2}{x(x + 1)(x - 1)} \qquad \text{Group like terms.}$$

$$= \frac{2x^2 + 6x + 2}{x(x + 1)(x - 1)} \qquad \text{Combine like terms.}$$

$$= \frac{2(x^2 + 3x + 1)}{x(x + 1)(x - 1)} \qquad \text{Factor.}$$

Complex Fractions

Fractional expressions with separate fractions in the numerator, denominator, or both, are called **complex fractions.** Here are two examples.

$$\frac{\left(\dfrac{1}{x}\right)}{x^2 + 1} \quad \text{and} \quad \frac{\left(\dfrac{1}{x}\right)}{\left(\dfrac{1}{x^2 + 1}\right)}$$

A complex fraction can be simplified by first combining both its numerator and its denominator into single fractions, then inverting the denominator and multiplying.

EXAMPLE 8   Simplifying a Complex Fraction

$$\frac{\left(\dfrac{2}{x} - 3\right)}{\left(1 - \dfrac{1}{x - 1}\right)} = \frac{\left[\dfrac{2 - 3(x)}{x}\right]}{\left[\dfrac{1(x - 1) - 1}{x - 1}\right]} \qquad \text{Combine fractions.}$$

$$= \frac{\left(\dfrac{2 - 3x}{x}\right)}{\left(\dfrac{x - 2}{x - 1}\right)} \qquad \text{Simplify.}$$

$$= \frac{2 - 3x}{x} \cdot \frac{x - 1}{x - 2} \qquad \text{Invert and multiply.}$$

$$= \frac{(2 - 3x)(x - 1)}{x(x - 2)}, \qquad x \neq 1$$

In Example 8, the disclaimer $x \neq 1$ is added to the final expression to make its domain agree with the domain of the original expression.

Another way to simplify a complex fraction is to multiply each term in its numerator and denominator by the LCD of all fractions in its numerator and denominator. This method is applied to the fraction in Example 8 as follows.

$$\frac{\left(\dfrac{2}{x} - 3\right)}{\left(1 - \dfrac{1}{x - 1}\right)} = \frac{\left(\dfrac{2}{x} - 3\right)}{\left(1 - \dfrac{1}{x - 1}\right)} \cdot \frac{x(x - 1)}{x(x - 1)} \qquad \text{LCD is } x(x - 1).$$

$$= \frac{\left(\dfrac{2 - 3x}{x}\right) \cdot x(x - 1)}{\left(\dfrac{x - 2}{x - 1}\right) \cdot x(x - 1)} \qquad \text{Combine fractions.}$$

$$= \frac{(2 - 3x)(x - 1)}{x(x - 2)}, \qquad x \neq 1 \qquad \text{Simplify.}$$

Additional Example

$$\frac{\left(\dfrac{x}{4} + \dfrac{3}{2}\right)}{\left(2 - \dfrac{3}{x}\right)} = \frac{\left(\dfrac{x + 6}{4}\right)}{\left(\dfrac{2x - 3}{x}\right)}$$

$$= \left(\frac{x + 6}{4}\right) \cdot \left(\frac{x}{2x - 3}\right)$$

$$= \frac{x(x + 6)}{4(2x - 3)}, x \neq 0$$

Point out to your students that two different methods are shown here for simplifying the same compound fraction. Emphasize that both yield the same result.

The next three examples illustrate some methods for simplifying rational expressions involving radicals and negative exponents. These types of expressions occur frequently in calculus.

To simplify an expression with negative exponents, begin by factoring out the common factor with the smaller exponent. Remember that when factoring, you subtract exponents. For instance, in $3x^{-5/2} + 2x^{-3/2}$ the smaller exponent is $-\frac{5}{2}$ and the common factor is $x^{-5/2}$.

$$3x^{-5/2} + 2x^{-3/2} = x^{-5/2}\left(3(1) + 2x^{-3/2-(-5/2)}\right)$$

$$= x^{-5/2}(3 + 2x^1)$$

$$= \frac{3 + 2x}{x^{5/2}}$$

EXAMPLE 9   Simplifying an Expression with Negative Exponents

Simplify

$$x(1 - 2x)^{-3/2} + (1 - 2x)^{-1/2}.$$

Solution

Begin by factoring out the common factor with the *smaller exponent.*

$$x(1 - 2x)^{-3/2} + (1 - 2x)^{-1/2} = (1 - 2x)^{-3/2}[x + (1 - 2x)^{(-1/2)-(-3/2)}]$$

$$= (1 - 2x)^{-3/2}[x + (1 - 2x)^1]$$

$$= \frac{1 - x}{(1 - 2x)^{3/2}}$$

A second method for simplifying an expression with negative exponents is shown in the next example. This method involves multiplying the numerator and denominator by a term to eliminate the negative exponent.

EXAMPLE 10   Simplifying a Complex Fraction

Simplify

$$\frac{(4 - x^2)^{1/2} + x^2(4 - x^2)^{-1/2}}{4 - x^2}.$$

Solution

$$\frac{(4 - x^2)^{1/2} + x^2(4 - x^2)^{-1/2}}{4 - x^2}$$

$$= \frac{(4 - x^2)^{1/2} + x^2(4 - x^2)^{-1/2}}{4 - x^2} \cdot \frac{(4 - x^2)^{1/2}}{(4 - x^2)^{1/2}}$$

$$= \frac{(4 - x^2)^1 + x^2(4 - x^2)^0}{(4 - x^2)^{3/2}}$$

$$= \frac{4 - x^2 + x^2}{(4 - x^2)^{3/2}} = \frac{4}{(4 - x^2)^{3/2}}$$

Activities

1. What is the domain of $\sqrt{3 - x}$?

   Answer: The set of all real numbers less than or equal to 3.

2. The implied domain excludes what values of x from the domain of
   $$\frac{x^2 + 6x + 9}{x^2 - 9}?$$
   Answer: $x = 3, x = -3$

3. Simplify: $\dfrac{\dfrac{1}{x} - \dfrac{1}{x + 1}}{x + 1}$.

   Answer: $\dfrac{1}{x(x + 1)^2}$

EXAMPLE 11   Rewriting a Difference Quotient

The expression from calculus

$$\frac{\sqrt{x + h} - \sqrt{x}}{h}$$

is an example of a *difference quotient*. Rewrite this expression by rationalizing its numerator.

Solution

$$\frac{\sqrt{x + h} - \sqrt{x}}{h} = \frac{\sqrt{x + h} - \sqrt{x}}{h} \cdot \frac{\sqrt{x + h} + \sqrt{x}}{\sqrt{x + h} + \sqrt{x}}$$

$$= \frac{\left(\sqrt{x + h}\right)^2 - \left(\sqrt{x}\right)^2}{h\left(\sqrt{x + h} + \sqrt{x}\right)}$$

$$= \frac{h}{h\left(\sqrt{x + h} + \sqrt{x}\right)}$$

$$= \frac{1}{\sqrt{x + h} + \sqrt{x}}, \qquad h \neq 0$$

Notice that the original expression is undefined when $h = 0$. So, you must exclude $h = 0$ from the domain of the simplified expressions so that the expressions are equivalent.

Difference quotients, like that in Example 11, occur frequently in calculus. Often, they need to be rewritten in an equivalent form that can be evaluated when $h = 0$. Note that the equivalent form is not simpler than the original form, but it has the advantage in that it is defined when $h = 0$.

Writing About Math   *Comparing the Domains of Two Expressions*

Complete the table by evaluating the expressions

$$\frac{x^2 - 3x + 2}{x - 2} \quad \text{and} \quad x - 1$$

for the values of x. If your graphing utility has a *table* feature, use it to help create the table. Write a short paragraph describing the equivalence or non-equivalence of the two expressions.

x	-3	-2	-1	0	1	2	3
$\dfrac{x^2 - 3x + 2}{x - 2}$							
$x - 1$							

P.4 E X E R C I S E S

In Exercises 1–8, find the domain of the expression.

1. $3x^2 - 4x + 7$

2. $2x^2 + 5x - 2$

3. $4x^3 + 3, \quad x \geq 0$

4. $6x^2 - 9, \quad x > 0$

5. $\dfrac{1}{x - 2}$

6. $\dfrac{x + 1}{2x + 1}$

7. $\sqrt{x + 1}$

8. $\sqrt{6 - x}$

In Exercises 9 and 10, find the missing factor in the numerator so that the two fractions are equivalent.

9. $\dfrac{5}{2x} = \dfrac{5(\quad)}{6x^2}$

10. $\dfrac{3}{4} = \dfrac{3(\quad)}{4(x + 1)}$

In Exercises 11–28, write the rational expression in simplest form.

11. $\dfrac{15x^2}{10x}$

12. $\dfrac{18y^2}{60y^5}$

13. $\dfrac{3xy}{xy + x}$

14. $\dfrac{2x^2y}{xy - y}$

15. $\dfrac{4y - 8y^2}{10y - 5}$

16. $\dfrac{9x^2 + 9x}{2x + 2}$

17. $\dfrac{x - 5}{10 - 2x}$

18. $\dfrac{12 - 4x}{x - 3}$

19. $\dfrac{y^2 - 16}{y + 4}$

20. $\dfrac{x^2 - 25}{5 - x}$

21. $\dfrac{x^3 + 5x^2 + 6x}{x^2 - 4}$

22. $\dfrac{x^2 + 8x - 20}{x^2 + 11x + 10}$

23. $\dfrac{y^2 - 7y + 12}{y^2 + 3y - 18}$

24. $\dfrac{3 - x}{x^2 + 11x + 10}$

25. $\dfrac{2 - x + 2x^2 - x^3}{x - 2}$

26. $\dfrac{x^2 - 9}{x^3 + x^2 - 9x - 9}$

27. $\dfrac{z^3 - 8}{z^2 + 2z + 4}$

28. $\dfrac{y^3 - 2y^2 - 3y}{y^3 + 1}$

In Exercises 29 and 30, complete the table. What can you conclude?

29.

x	0	1	2	3	4	5	6
$\dfrac{x^2 - 2x - 3}{x - 3}$							
$x + 1$							

30.

x	0	1	2	3	4	5	6
$\dfrac{x - 3}{x^2 - x - 6}$							
$\dfrac{1}{x + 2}$							

31. *Error Analysis*   Describe the error.

$$\frac{5x^3}{2x^3 + 4} = \frac{5\cancel{x^3}}{2\cancel{x^3} + 4} = \frac{5}{2 + 4} = \frac{5}{6}$$ ✗

32. *Error Analysis*   Describe the error.

$$\frac{x^3 + 25x}{x^2 - 2x - 15} = \frac{x(x^2 + 25)}{(x - 5)(x + 3)}$$

$$= \frac{x(x - 5)(x + 5)}{(x - 5)(x + 3)}$$

$$= \frac{x(x + 5)}{x + 3}$$ ✗

In Exercises 33 and 34, find the ratio of the area of the shaded portion of the figure to the total area of the figure.

33.

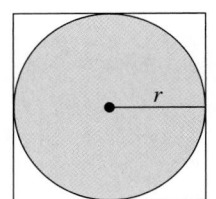

34.

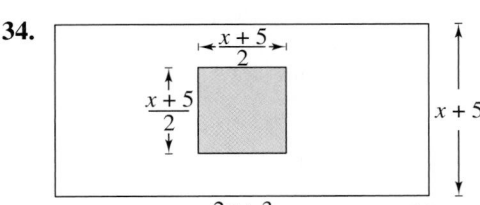

In Exercises 35–42, perform the multiplication or division and simplify.

35. $\dfrac{5}{x-1} \cdot \dfrac{x-1}{25(x-2)}$

36. $\dfrac{x+13}{x^3(3-x)} \cdot \dfrac{x(x-3)}{5}$

37. $\dfrac{r}{r-1} \cdot \dfrac{r^2-1}{r^2}$

38. $\dfrac{4y-16}{5y+15} \cdot \dfrac{2y+6}{4-y}$

39. $\dfrac{t^2-t-6}{t^2+6t+9} \cdot \dfrac{t+3}{t^2-4}$

40. $\dfrac{y^3-8}{2y^3} \cdot \dfrac{4y}{y^2-5y+6}$

41. $\dfrac{3(x+y)}{4} \div \dfrac{x+y}{2}$

42. $\dfrac{x+2}{5(x-3)} \div \dfrac{x-2}{5(x-3)}$

In Exercises 43–52, perform the addition or subtraction and simplify.

43. $\dfrac{5}{x-1} + \dfrac{x}{x-1}$

44. $\dfrac{2x-1}{x+3} + \dfrac{1-x}{x+3}$

45. $6 - \dfrac{5}{x+3}$

46. $\dfrac{3}{x-1} - 5$

47. $\dfrac{3}{x-2} + \dfrac{5}{2-x}$

48. $\dfrac{2x}{x-5} - \dfrac{5}{5-x}$

49. $\dfrac{1}{x^2-x-2} - \dfrac{x}{x^2-5x+6}$

50. $\dfrac{2}{x^2-x-2} + \dfrac{10}{x^2+2x-8}$

51. $-\dfrac{1}{x} + \dfrac{2}{x^2+1} + \dfrac{1}{x^3+x}$

52. $\dfrac{2}{x+1} + \dfrac{2}{x-1} + \dfrac{1}{x^2-1}$

In Exercises 53–60, simplify the expression by removing the common factor with the smaller exponent.

53. $x^5 - 2x^{-2}$

54. $x^5 - 5x^{-3}$

55. $3x^{3/2} - 2x^{-1/2}$

56. $5x^5 - 3x^{-3/2}$

57. $x^2(x^2+1)^{-5} - (x^2+1)^{-4}$

58. $2x(x-5)^{-3} - 4x^2(x-5)^{-4}$

59. $2x^2(x-1)^{1/2} - 5(x-1)^{-1/2}$

60. $4x^3(2x-1)^{3/2} - 2x(2x-1)^{-1/2}$

In Exercises 61–70, simplify the complex fraction.

61. $\dfrac{\left(\dfrac{x}{2}-1\right)}{(x-2)}$

62. $\dfrac{(x-4)}{\left(\dfrac{x}{4}-\dfrac{4}{x}\right)}$

63. $\dfrac{\left[\dfrac{x^2}{(x+1)^2}\right]}{\left[\dfrac{x}{(x+1)^3}\right]}$

64. $\dfrac{\left(\dfrac{x^2-1}{x}\right)}{\left[\dfrac{(x-1)^2}{x}\right]}$

65. $\dfrac{\left[\dfrac{1}{(x+h)^2} - \dfrac{1}{x^2}\right]}{h}$

66. $\dfrac{\left(\dfrac{x+h}{x+h+1} - \dfrac{x}{x+1}\right)}{h}$

67. $\dfrac{\left(\sqrt{x} - \dfrac{1}{2\sqrt{x}}\right)}{\sqrt{x}}$

68. $\dfrac{\left(\dfrac{t^2}{\sqrt{t^2+1}} - \sqrt{t^2+1}\right)}{t^2}$

69. $\dfrac{3x^{1/3} - x^{-2/3}}{3x^{-2/3}}$

70. $\dfrac{-x^3(1-x^2)^{-1/2} - 2x(1-x^2)^{1/2}}{x^4}$

In Exercises 71 and 72, rationalize the numerator of the expression.

71. $\dfrac{\sqrt{x+2} - \sqrt{x}}{2}$

72. $\dfrac{\sqrt{z-3} - \sqrt{z}}{3}$

73. *Rate* A photocopier copies at a rate of 16 pages per minute.

(a) Find the time required to copy one page.

(b) Find the time required to copy x pages.

(c) Find the time required to copy 60 pages.

74. *Rate* After working together for t hours on a common task, two workers have done fractional parts of the job equal to $t/3$ and $t/5$, respectively. What fractional part of the task has been completed?

75. *Average* Determine the average of the two real numbers $x/3$ and $2x/5$.

76. *Partition into Equal Parts* Find three real numbers that divide the real number line between $x/3$ and $3x/4$ into four equal parts.

Probability In Exercises 77 and 78, consider an experiment in which a marble is tossed into a box whose base is shown in the figure. The probability that the marble will come to rest in the shaded portion of the box is equal to the ratio of the shaded area to the total area of the figure. Find the probability.

77.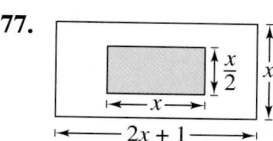

78.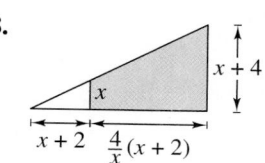

Monthly Payment In Exercises 79 and 80, use the formula that gives the approximate annual interest rate r of a monthly installment loan

$$r = \frac{\left[\dfrac{24(NM - P)}{N}\right]}{\left(P + \dfrac{NM}{12}\right)}$$

where N is the total number of payments, M is the monthly payment, and P is the amount financed.

79. (a) Approximate the annual interest rate for a 4-year car loan of $16,000 that has monthly payments of $400.

    (b) Simplify the expression for the annual interest rate r, and then rework part (a).

80. (a) Approximate the annual interest rate for a 5-year car loan of $20,000 that has monthly payments of $400.

    (b) Simplify the expression for the annual interest rate r, and then rework part (a).

81. *Refrigeration* When food (at room temperature) is placed in the refrigerator, the time required for the food to cool depends on the amount of food, the air circulation in the refrigerator, the original temperature of the food, and the temperature of the refrigerator. Consider the model that gives the temperature of the food that is at 75°F and is placed in a 40°F refrigerator as

$$T = 10\left(\frac{4t^2 + 16t + 75}{t^2 + 4t + 10}\right)$$

where T is the temperature (in degrees Fahrenheit) and t is the time (in hours).

(a) Complete the table.

t	0	2	4	6	8	10
T						

t	12	14	16	18	20	22
T						

(b) What value of T does the mathematical model appear to be approaching?

82. *Precious Metals* The costs per fine ounce of gold and silver for the years 1992 through 1997 are given in the table. (Source: U.S. Bureau of Mines, U.S. Geological Survey)

Year	1992	1993	1994	1995	1996	1997
Gold	$345	$361	$385	$386	$389	$333
Silver	$3.94	$4.30	$5.29	$5.15	$5.19	$4.90

Mathematical models for this data are

$$\text{Cost of gold} = \frac{-38.5t + 310.1}{0.007t^2 - 0.176t + 1}$$

and

$$\text{Cost of silver} = \frac{0.42t^2 - 2.56t + 4.26}{0.09t^2 - 0.58t + 1}$$

where $t = 2$ corresponds to the year 1992.

(a) Create a table using the models to estimate the prices of each metal for the given years. Compare the estimates given by the models with the actual prices.

(b) Determine a model for the ratio of the price of gold to the price of silver. Use the model to find this ratio over the given years. Over this period of time, did the price of gold become more expensive or less expensive relative to the price of silver?

Synthesis

True or False? In Exercises 83–85, determine whether the statement is true or false. Justify your answer.

83. $\dfrac{x^{2n} - 1^{2n}}{x^n - 1^n} = x^n + 1^n$

84. $\dfrac{x^2 - 3x + 2}{x - 1} = x - 2$ for all values of x.

85. The least common denominator of two or more fractions is always the product of all the denominators of the fractions.

86. *Think About It* How do you determine whether a rational expression is in simplest form?

87. *Think About It* Is the following statement true for all nonzero real numbers a and b? Explain.

$$\frac{ax - b}{b - ax} = -1$$

P.5   Graphical Representation of Data

The Cartesian Plane

Just as you can represent real numbers by points on a real number line, you can represent ordered pairs of real numbers by points in a plane called the **rectangular coordinate system,** or the **Cartesian plane,** after the French mathematician René Descartes (1596–1650).

The Cartesian plane is formed by using two real number lines intersecting at right angles, as shown in Figure P.6. The horizontal real number line is usually called the **x-axis,** and the vertical real number line is usually called the **y-axis.** The point of intersection of these two axes is the **origin,** and the two axes divide the plane into four parts called **quadrants.**

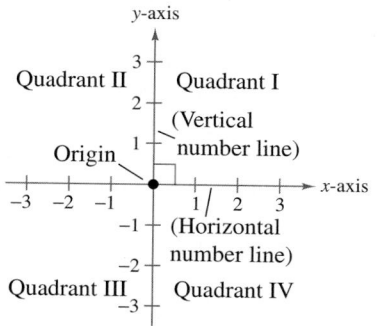

Figure P.6   *The Cartesian Plane*

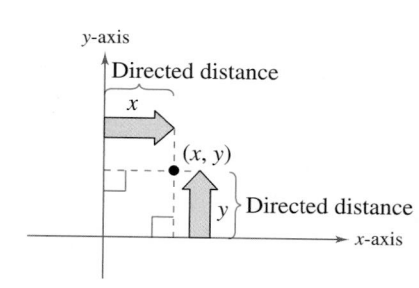

Figure P.7   *Ordered Pair (x, y)*

Each point in the plane corresponds to an **ordered pair** (x, y) of real numbers x and y, called **coordinates** of the point. The **x-coordinate** represents the directed distance from the y-axis to the point, and the **y-coordinate** represents the directed distance from the x-axis to the point, as shown in Figure P.7.

$$\text{Directed distance} \quad (x, y) \quad \text{Directed distance}$$
$$\text{from } y\text{-axis} \qquad\qquad \text{from } x\text{-axis}$$

The notation (x, y) denotes both a point in the plane and an open interval on the real number line. The context will tell you which meaning is intended.

EXAMPLE 1   Plotting Points in the Cartesian Plane

Plot the points $(-1, 2)$, $(3, 4)$, $(0, 0)$, $(3, 0)$, and $(-2, -3)$.

Solution

To plot the point $(-1, 2)$, imagine a vertical line through -1 on the x-axis and a horizontal line through 2 on the y-axis. The intersection of these two lines is the point $(-1, 2)$. This point is 1 unit to the left of the y-axis and 2 units up from the x-axis. The other four points can be plotted in a similar way (see Figure P.8).

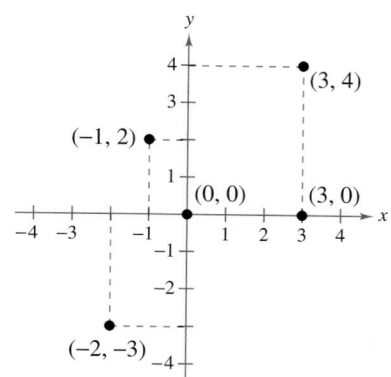

Figure P.8

EXAMPLE 2   Translating Points in the Plane

The triangle in Figure P.9(a) has vertices at the points $(-1, 2)$, $(1, -4)$, and $(2, 3)$. Shift the triangle three units to the right and two units up and find the vertices of the shifted triangle, as shown in Figure P.9(b).

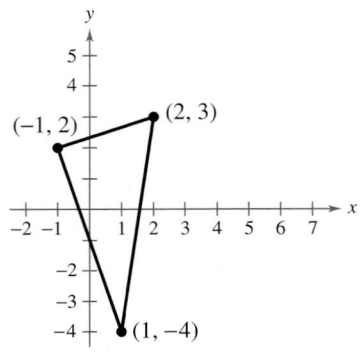

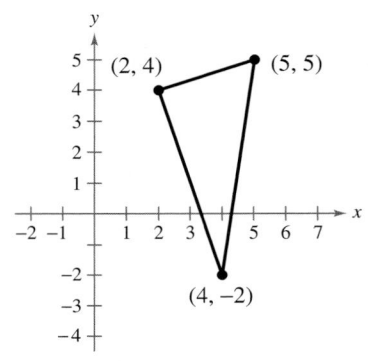

(a)   **(b)**

Figure P.9

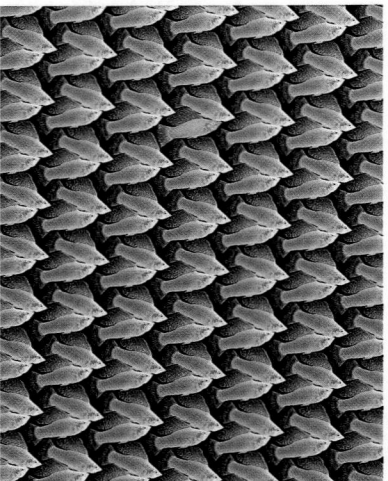

Paul Morrell

Much of computer graphics, including this computer-generated goldfish tessellation, consists of transformations of points in a coordinate plane. One type of transformation, a translation, is illustrated in Example 2. Other types include reflections, rotations, and stretches.

Solution

To shift the vertices three units to the right, add 3 to each of the x-coordinates. To shift the vertices two units up, add 2 to each of the y-coordinates.

Original Point	*Translated Point*
$(-1, 2)$	$(-1 + 3, 2 + 2) = (2, 4)$
$(1, -4)$	$(1 + 3, -4 + 2) = (4, -2)$
$(2, 3)$	$(2 + 3, 3 + 2) = (5, 5)$

Plotting the translated points and sketching the line segments between them produces the shifted triangle shown in Figure P.9(b).

A computer animation of this example appears in the *Interactive* CD-ROM and *Internet* versions of this text.

Example 2 shows how to translate points in a coordinate plane. The following transformed points are related to the original points as follows.

Original Point	*Transformed Point*	
(x, y)	$(-x, y)$	$(-x, y)$ is a reflection of the original point in the y-axis.
(x, y)	$(x, -y)$	$(x, -y)$ is a reflection of the original point in the x-axis.
(x, y)	$(-x, -y)$	$(-x, -y)$ is a reflection of the original point through the origin.

Representing Data Graphically

The beauty of a rectangular coordinate system is that it allows you to see relationships between two variables. It would be difficult to overestimate the importance of Descartes's introduction of coordinates to the plane. Today, his ideas are in common use in virtually every scientific and business-related field.

EXAMPLE 3   Sketching a Scatter Plot, Bar Graph, and Line Graph

From 1988 through 1997, the amount A (in millions of dollars) spent on archery equipment in the United States is given in the table, where t represents the year. (a) Sketch a scatter plot of the data. (b) Sketch a bar graph of the data. (c) Sketch a line graph of the data.   (Source: National Sporting Goods Association)

A computer animation of this example appears in the *Interactive* CD-ROM and *Internet* versions of this text.

t	1988	1989	1990	1991	1992	1993	1994	1995	1996	1997
A	235	261	265	270	334	285	306	287	272	273

Solution

a. To sketch a *scatter plot* of the data given in the table, you simply represent each pair of values by an ordered pair (t, A) and plot the resulting points, as shown in Figure P.10. For instance, the first pair of values is represented by the ordered pair $(1988, 235)$. Note that the break in the t-axis indicates that the numbers between 0 and 1988 have been omitted.

b. To create a *bar graph*, begin by drawing a vertical axis to represent the amount (in millions of dollars) and a horizontal axis to represent the year. Then for each value of t in the table, draw a vertical bar whose height is the corresponding value A. The bar graph is shown in Figure P.11.

c. To draw a *line graph*, begin by drawing a vertical axis to represent the amount (in millions of dollars). Then label the horizontal axis with years and plot the points given in the table. Finally, connect the points with line segments, as shown in Figure P.12.

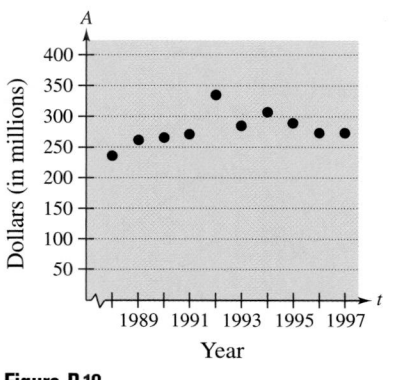

Figure P.10

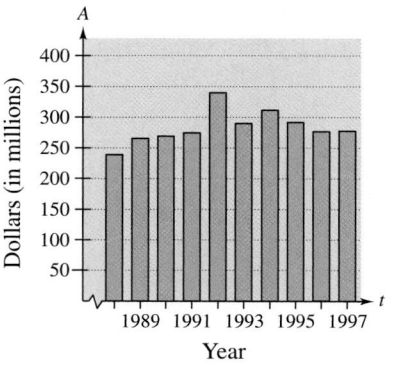

Figure P.11

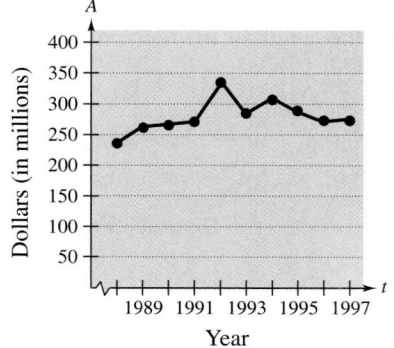

Figure P.12

In Example 3, you could have let $t = 1$ represent the year 1988. In that case, the horizontal axis of each graph would not have been broken, and the tick marks would have been labeled 1 through 10 (instead of 1988 through 1997).

EXAMPLE 4   Interpreting a Population Model

The population (in millions) of North Carolina from 1990 to 1997 can be modeled by $y = 0.11x + 6.63$, where x is the time in years, with $x = 0$ corresponding to 1990. During which year did the population exceed 7 million?

Graphical Solution

You can use the *statistical plotting* feature of a graphing utility to create a bar graph of the data. On the same viewing window, graph the line $y = 7$.

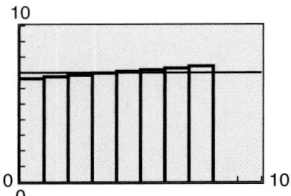

Figure P.13

From the graph in Figure P.13 you can see that the bars that correspond to $x = 0, 1, 2,$ and 3 are less than 7. The bar that corresponds to $x = 4$ is the first bar greater than 7, so the population exceeded 7 million sometime during 1993.

Numerical Solution

You can use the *table* feature of a graphing utility to evaluate the model $y = 0.11x + 6.63$ for different years. Enter the model into the equation editor. Then create a table such as the one below.

X	Y1
0	6.63
1	6.74
2	6.85
3	6.96
4	7.07
5	7.18
6	7.29

X=3

Figure P.14

From the table in Figure P.14, you can see that the value of y when $x = 3$ is 6.96, and the value of y when $x = 4$ is 7.07. So, the population exceeded 7 million when x is greater than 3 and less than 4, or sometime during 1993.

The Distance Formula

Recall from the Pythagorean Theorem that for a right triangle with hypotenuse of length c and sides of lengths a and b, you have $a^2 + b^2 = c^2$ as shown in Figure P.15. (The converse is also true. That is, if $a^2 + b^2 = c^2$, the triangle is a right triangle.)

    Suppose you want to determine the distance d between two points (x_1, y_1) and (x_2, y_2) in the plane. With these two points, a right triangle can be formed, as shown in Figure P.16. The length of the vertical side of the triangle is $|y_2 - y_1|$, and the length of the horizontal side is $|x_2 - x_1|$. By the Pythagorean Theorem,

$$d^2 = |x_2 - x_1|^2 + |y_2 - y_1|^2$$

$$d = \sqrt{|x_2 - x_1|^2 + |y_2 - y_1|^2}$$

$$d = \sqrt{(x_2 - x_1)^2 + (y_2 - y_1)^2}.$$

This result is the **Distance Formula.**

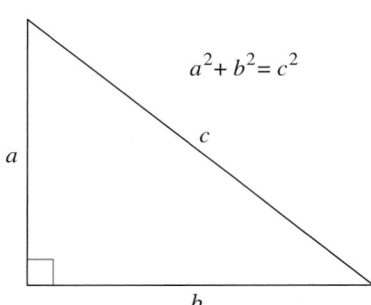

Figure P.15

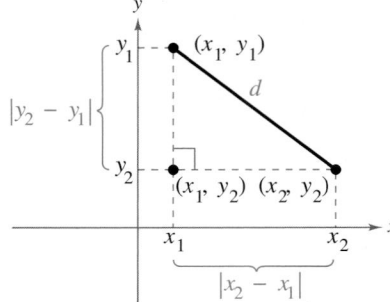

Figure P.16

The Distance Formula

The distance d between the points (x_1, y_1) and (x_2, y_2) in the plane is

$$d = \sqrt{(x_2 - x_1)^2 + (y_2 - y_1)^2}.$$

EXAMPLE 5 Finding a Distance

Find the distance between the points $(-2, 1)$ and $(3, 4)$.

Algebraic Solution

Let $(x_1, y_1) = (-2, 1)$ and $(x_2, y_2) = (3, 4)$. Then apply the Distance Formula as follows.

$$d = \sqrt{(x_2 - x_1)^2 + (y_2 - y_1)^2} \qquad \text{Distance Formula}$$

$$= \sqrt{[3 - (-2)]^2 + (4 - 1)^2} \qquad \begin{array}{l}\text{Substitute for}\\ x_1, y_1, x_2, \text{ and } y_2.\end{array}$$

$$= \sqrt{(5)^2 + (3)^2} \qquad \text{Simplify.}$$

$$= \sqrt{34}$$

$$\approx 5.83 \qquad \text{Use a calculator.}$$

So, the distance between the points is about 5.83 units.

    You can use the Pythagorean Theorem to check that the distance is correct.

$$d^2 \overset{?}{=} 3^2 + 5^2 \qquad \text{Pythagorean Theorem}$$

$$\left(\sqrt{34}\right)^2 \overset{?}{=} 3^2 + 5^2 \qquad \text{Substitute for } d.$$

$$34 = 34 \qquad \text{Distance checks. } \checkmark$$

Graphical Solution

Use centimeter graph paper to plot the points A and B. Carefully sketch the line segment from A to B. Then use a centimeter ruler to measure the length of the segment.

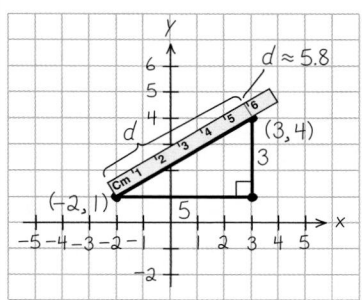

Figure P.17

The line segment measures about 5.8 centimeters as shown in Figure P.17. So, the distance between the points is about 5.8 units.

EXAMPLE 6 Verifying a Right Triangle

Show that the points $(2, 1)$, $(4, 0)$, and $(5, 7)$ are vertices of a right triangle.

Solution

The three points are plotted in Figure P.18. Using the Distance Formula, you can find the lengths of the three sides as follows.

$$d_1 = \sqrt{(5 - 2)^2 + (7 - 1)^2} = \sqrt{9 + 36} = \sqrt{45}$$

$$d_2 = \sqrt{(4 - 2)^2 + (0 - 1)^2} = \sqrt{4 + 1} = \sqrt{5}$$

$$d_3 = \sqrt{(5 - 4)^2 + (7 - 0)^2} = \sqrt{1 + 49} = \sqrt{50}$$

Because

$$d_1{}^2 + d_2{}^2 = 45 + 5 = 50 = d_3{}^2$$

you can conclude that the triangle must be a right triangle.

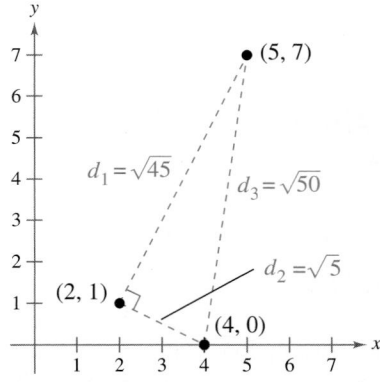

Figure P.18

An overhead projector is useful for showing how to plot points and equations. Try projecting a grid onto the chalkboard, or try using overhead markers and graph directly on the transparency. A viewscreen, a device used with an overhead projector to project a graphing calculator's screen image, is also useful.

The figure provided with Example 6 was not really essential to the solution. Nevertheless, it is strongly recommended that you develop the habit of including sketches with your solutions—even if they are not required.

The Midpoint Formula

To find the **midpoint** of the line segment that joins two points in a coordinate plane, you can simply find the average values of the respective coordinates of the two endpoints using the **Midpoint Formula.** (See Appendix A for a proof of the Midpoint Formula.)

Exercises 53 and 54 on page 55 help develop a general understanding of the Midpoint Formula.

> ## The Midpoint Formula
>
> The midpoint of the segment joining the points (x_1, y_1) and (x_2, y_2) is given by the Midpoint Formula
>
> $$\text{Midpoint} = \left(\frac{x_1 + x_2}{2}, \frac{y_1 + y_2}{2}\right).$$

EXAMPLE 7   Finding a Line Segment's Midpoint

Find the midpoint of the line segment joining the points $(-5, -3)$ and $(9, 3)$, as shown in Figure P.19.

Solution
Let $(x_1, y_1) = (-5, -3)$ and $(x_2, y_2) = (9, 3)$.

$$\text{Midpoint} = \left(\frac{x_1 + x_2}{2}, \frac{y_1 + y_2}{2}\right) \qquad \text{Midpoint Formula}$$

$$= \left(\frac{-5 + 9}{2}, \frac{-3 + 3}{2}\right) \qquad \text{Substitute for } x_1, y_1, x_2, \text{ and } y_2.$$

$$= (2, 0) \qquad \text{Simplify.}$$

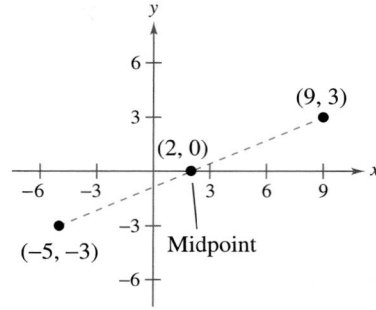

Figure P.19

EXAMPLE 8   Estimating Annual Sales

Winn-Dixie Stores had annual sales of $1.30 billion in 1996 and $1.36 billion in 1998. Without knowing any additional information, what would you estimate the 1997 sales to have been?   (Source: Winn-Dixie Stores, Inc.)

Solution
One solution to the problem is to assume that sales followed a linear pattern. With this assumption, you can estimate the 1997 sales by finding the midpoint of the segment connecting the points (1996, 1.30) and (1998, 1.36).

$$\text{Midpoint} = \left(\frac{1996 + 1998}{2}, \frac{1.30 + 1.36}{2}\right)$$

$$= (1997, 1.33)$$

So, you would estimate the 1997 sales to have been about $1.33 billion, as shown in Figure P.20. (The actual 1997 sales were $1.32 billion.)

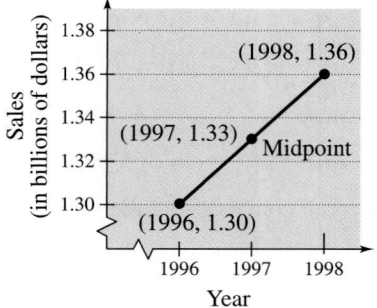

Winn-Dixie Stores Annual Sales

Figure P.20

The Equation of a Circle

The Distance Formula provides a convenient way to define circles. A **circle of radius r** with center at the point (h, k) is shown in Figure P.21. The point (x, y) is on this circle if and only if its distance from the center (h, k) is r. This means that a **circle** in the plane consists of all points (x, y) that are a given positive distance r from a fixed point (h, k). Using the Distance Formula, you can express this relationship by saying that the point (x, y) lies on the circle if and only if

$$\sqrt{(x - h)^2 + (y - k)^2} = r.$$

By squaring both sides of this equation, you can obtain the **standard form of the equation of a circle.**

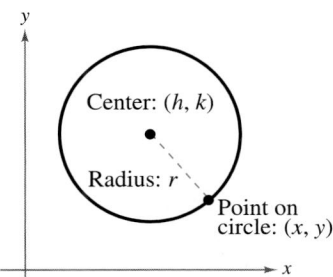

y

Center: (h, k)

Radius: r

Point on circle: (x, y)

x

Figure P.21

Standard Form of the Equation of a Circle

The **standard form of the equation of a circle** is

$$(x - h)^2 + (y - k)^2 = r^2.$$

The point (h, k) is the **center** of the circle, and the positive number r is the **radius** of the circle. The standard form of the equation of a circle whose center is the origin is $x^2 + y^2 = r^2$.

EXAMPLE 9   Finding an Equation of a Circle

The point $(3, 4)$ lies on a circle whose center is at $(-1, 2)$, as shown in Figure P.22. Find an equation for the circle.

Solution

The radius r of the circle is the distance between $(-1, 2)$ and $(3, 4)$.

$$r = \sqrt{[3 - (-1)]^2 + (4 - 2)^2}$$
$$= \sqrt{16 + 4} = \sqrt{20}$$

So, the center of the circle is $(h, k) = (-1, 2)$ and the radius is $r = \sqrt{20}$, and you can write the standard form of the equation of the circle as follows.

$$(x - h)^2 + (y - k)^2 = r^2 \qquad \text{Standard form}$$
$$[x - (-1)]^2 + (y - 2)^2 = \left(\sqrt{20}\right)^2 \qquad \text{Substitute for } h, k, \text{ and } r.$$
$$(x + 1)^2 + (y - 2)^2 = 20 \qquad \text{Equation of circle}$$

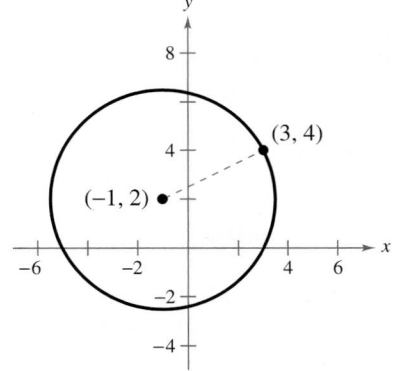

y

$(3, 4)$

$(-1, 2)$

Figure P.22

P.5 Exercises

In Exercises 1–4, sketch the polygon with the indicated vertices.

1. Triangle: $(-1, 1), (2, -1), (3, 4)$
2. Triangle: $(0, 3), (-1, -2), (4, 8)$
3. Square: $(2, 4), (5, 1), (2, -2), (-1, 1)$
4. Parallelogram: $(5, 2), (7, 0), (1, -2), (-1, 0)$

In Exercises 5–8, approximate the coordinates of the points.

5.
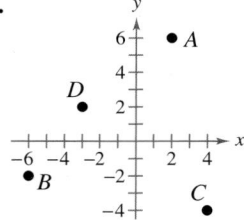

6.
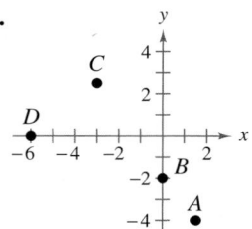

7.
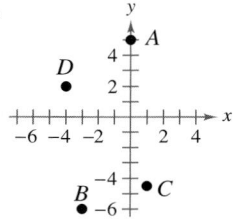

8.
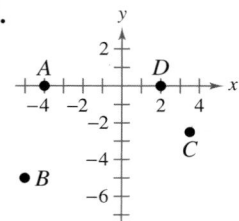

In Exercises 9–12, find the coordinates of the point.

9. The point is located three units to the left of the y-axis and four units above the x-axis.
10. The point is located eight units below the x-axis and four units to the right of the y-axis.
11. The point is located five units below the x-axis and the coordinates of the point are equal.
12. The point is on the x-axis and twelve units to the left of the y-axis.

In Exercises 13–22, determine the quadrant(s) in which (x, y) is located so that the condition(s) is (are) satisfied.

13. $x > 0$ and $y < 0$
14. $x < 0$ and $y < 0$
15. $x = -4$ and $y > 0$
16. $x > 2$ and $y = 3$
17. $y < -5$
18. $x > 4$
19. $(x, -y)$ is in the second quadrant.
20. $(-x, y)$ is in the fourth quadrant.
21. $xy > 0$
22. $xy < 0$

In Exercises 23 and 24, the polygon is shifted to a new position in the plane. Find the coordinates of the vertices of the polygon in its new position.

23. Shift: 5 units up, 2 units to the right

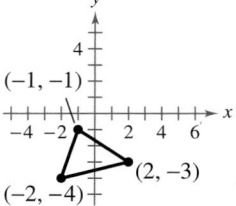

24. Shift: 3 units down, 6 units to the right

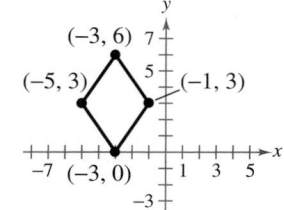

In Exercises 25–30, find the distance between the points algebraically and verify graphically by using centimeter graph paper and a centimeter ruler.

25. $(6, -3), (6, 5)$
26. $(1, 4), (8, 4)$
27. $(-3, -1), (2, -1)$
28. $(-3, -4), (-3, 6)$
29. $(-2, 6), (3, -6)$
30. $(8, 5), (0, 20)$

In Exercises 31–42, (a) plot the points, (b) find the distance between the points, and (c) find the midpoint of the line segment joining the points.

31. $(1, 1), (9, 7)$
32. $(1, 12), (6, 0)$
33. $(-4, 10), (4, -5)$
34. $(-7, -4), (2, 8)$
35. $(-1, 2), (5, 4)$
36. $(2, 10), (10, 2)$
37. $\left(\frac{1}{2}, 1\right), \left(-\frac{5}{2}, \frac{4}{3}\right)$
38. $\left(-\frac{1}{3}, -\frac{1}{3}\right), \left(-\frac{1}{6}, -\frac{1}{2}\right)$
39. $(6.2, 5.4), (-3.7, 1.8)$
40. $(-16.8, 12.3), (5.6, 4.9)$
41. $(-36, -18), (48, -72)$
42. $(1.451, 3.051), (5.906, 11.360)$

In Exercises 43–46, (a) find the length of each side of a right triangle and (b) show that these lengths satisfy the Pythagorean Theorem.

43.

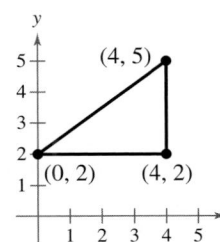

44.

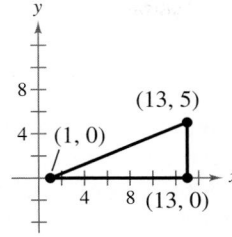

45.

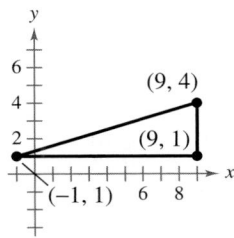

46.

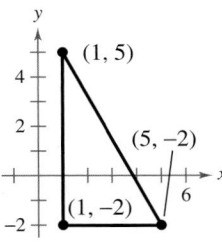

Business **In Exercises 47 and 48, estimate the sales of a company in 1998, given the sales in 1996 and 2000. Assume the sales followed a linear pattern.**

47.

Year	1996	2000
Sales	$520,000	$740,000

48.

Year	1996	2000
Sales	$4,200,000	$5,650,000

In Exercises 49–52, show that the points form the vertices of the polygon.

49. Right triangle: $(4, 0), (2, 1), (-1, -5)$

50. Isosceles triangle: $(1, -3), (3, 2), (-2, 4)$

51. Parallelogram: $(2, 5), (0, 9), (-2, 0), (0, -4)$

52. Parallelogram: $(0, 1), (3, 7), (4, 4), (1, -2)$

53. *Exploration* A line segment has (x_1, y_1) as one endpoint and (x_m, y_m) as its midpoint. Find the other endpoint (x_2, y_2) of the line segment in terms of $x_1, y_1, x_m,$ and y_m. Use the result to find the coordinates of the endpoint of a line segment if the coordinates of the other endpoint and midpoint are, respectively,

(a) $(1, -2), (4, -1)$ (b) $(-5, 11), (2, 4)$.

54. *Exploration* Use the Midpoint Formula three times to find the three points that divide the line segment joining (x_1, y_1) and (x_2, y_2) into four parts. Use the result to find the points that divide the line segment joining the given points into four equal parts.

(a) $(1, -2), (4, -1)$ (b) $(-2, -3), (0, 0)$

In Exercises 55–62, find the standard form of the equation of the specified circle.

55. Center: $(0, 0)$; radius: 3

56. Center: $(0, 0)$; radius: 5

57. Center: $(2, -1)$; radius: 4

58. Center: $\left(0, \frac{1}{3}\right)$; radius: $\frac{1}{3}$

59. Center: $(-1, 2)$; solution point: $(0, 0)$

60. Center: $(3, -2)$; solution point: $(-1, 1)$

61. Endpoints of a diameter: $(0, 0), (6, 8)$

62. Endpoints of a diameter: $(-4, -1), (4, 1)$

In Exercises 63–68, find the center and radius, and sketch the circle.

63. $x^2 + y^2 = 4$

64. $x^2 + y^2 = 16$

65. $(x - 1)^2 + (y + 3)^2 = 4$

66. $x^2 + (y - 1)^2 = 4$

67. $\left(x - \frac{1}{2}\right)^2 + \left(y - \frac{1}{2}\right)^2 = \frac{9}{4}$

68. $\left(x - \frac{2}{3}\right)^2 + \left(y + \frac{1}{4}\right)^2 = \frac{25}{9}$

In Exercises 69 and 70, sketch a scatter plot of the data given in the table.

69. *Meteorology* The table shows the lowest temperature of record y (in degrees Fahrenheit) in Duluth, Minnesota, for each month x, where $x = 1$ represents January.   (Source: NOAA)

x	1	2	3	4	5	6
y	-39	-33	-29	-5	17	27

x	7	8	9	10	11	12
y	35	32	22	8	-23	-34

70. *Business* The table shows the number y of Wal-Mart stores for each year x from 1992 through 1999. (Source: Wal-Mart Stores, Inc.)

x	1992	1993	1994	1995
y	2136	2440	2759	2943

x	1996	1997	1998	1999
y	3054	3406	3630	3815

Milk Prices In Exercises 71 and 72, use the graph below, which shows the average retail price of one-half gallon of milk from 1992 to 1997. (Source: U.S. Bureau of Labor Statistics)

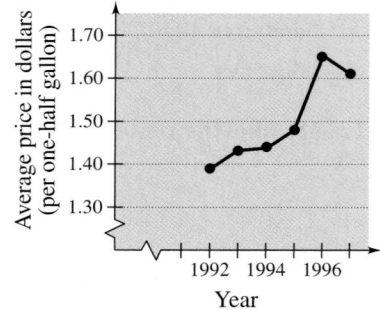

71. Approximate the highest price of one-half gallon of milk shown in the graph. When did this occur?

72. Approximate the difference in the price of milk from the highest price shown in the graph to the price in 1992.

Advertising In Exercises 73 and 74, use the graph below, which shows the cost of a 30-second television spot (in thousands of dollars) during the Super Bowl from 1987 to 1999. (Source: USA Today Research)

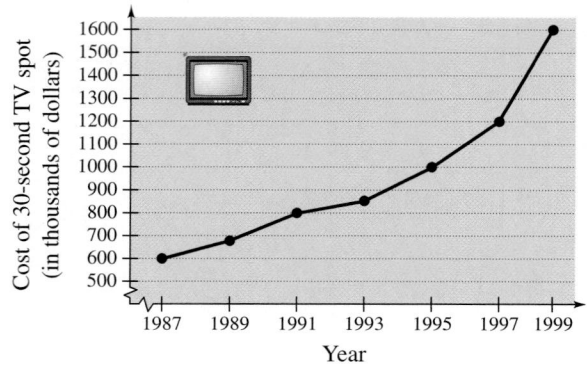

73. Approximate the percent increase in cost of a 30-second spot from Super Bowl XXI in 1987 to Super Bowl XXXIII in 1999.

74. Estimate the increase in cost of a 30-second spot (a) from Super Bowl XXI to Super Bowl XXVII, and (b) from Super Bowl XXVII to Super Bowl XXXIII.

Analyzing Data In Exercises 75 and 76, refer to the scatter plot, which shows the mathematics entrance test scores x and the final examination scores y in an algebra course for a sample of 10 students.

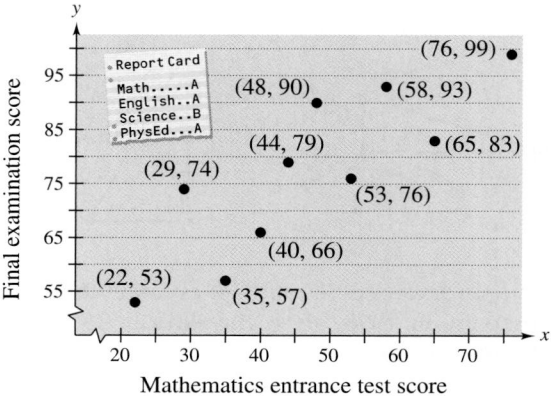

75. Find the entrance exam score of any student with a final exam score in the 80s.

76. Does a higher entrance exam score necessarily imply a higher final exam score? Explain.

77. *Food Production* The double bar graph shows the production and exports (in millions of metric tons) of corn, soybeans, and wheat for the year 1997. Approximate the percent of each product that is exported. (Source: U.S. Department of Agriculture)

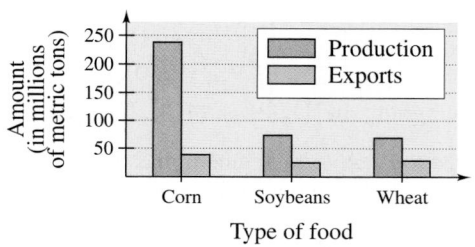

78. *Fruit Crops* The table shows farmers' cash receipts (in millions of dollars) from fruit crops in 1996. Construct a bar graph for the data. (Source: U.S. Department of Agriculture)

Fruit	Receipts	Fruit	Receipts
Apples	1846	Oranges	1798
Cherries	264	Peaches	380
Cranberries	246	Pears	292
Grapes	2334	Plums and Prunes	295
Lemons	228	Strawberries	770

79. *Sports Participants* The table shows the number of males and females (in millions) over the age of seven that participated in popular sports activities in 1996 in the United States. Construct a double bar graph for the data. (Source: National Sporting Goods Association)

Activity	Male	Female
Aerobic exercising	5.3	18.8
Basketball	22.4	10.9
Bicycling	28.6	24.7
Bowling	22.6	20.3
Camping	24.1	20.6
Exercise walking	26.7	46.6
Running	12.3	9.9
Swimming	29.1	31.1

80. *Oil Imports* The table shows the amount of crude oil imported into the United States (in millions of barrels) for the years 1988 through 1997. Construct a line graph for the data and state what information the graph reveals. (Source: Energy Information Administration)

Year	1988	1989	1990	1991	1992
Imports	1864	2133	2151	2110	2220

Year	1993	1994	1995	1996	1997
Imports	2477	2578	2643	2748	2918

81. *Personal Savings* The line graph shows the percent of disposable income saved in the United States in selected years from 1980 to 1997. (Source: U.S. Bureau of Economic Analysis)

(a) Determine the percent decrease in the rate of saving from 1980 to 1997.

(b) Is the trend shown in the line graph good for the country? Explain your reasoning.

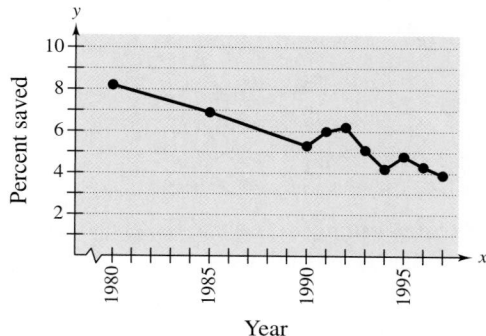

82. *Population* The population P (in millions) of Texas from 1990 to 1997 can be modeled by

$$P = 0.35x + 16.99$$

where x is the time in years, with $x = 0$ corresponding to 1990. (Source: U.S. Bureau of the Census)

(a) Use your graphing utility to create a bar graph of the model for the years 1990 to 1997. Use the graph to determine when the population of Texas exceeded 19 million.

(b) Determine algebraically when the population of Texas exceeded 19 million. Use your graph from part (a) to check your answer.

83. *Health* The average patient cost C to a community hospital per day in the United States from 1989 to 1996 can be modeled by

$$C = -2.37t^2 + 66.44t + 696.39$$

where t is the time in years, with $t = 0$ corresponding to 1990. (Source: American Hospital Association)

(a) Determine algebraically when the average cost exceeded $900 per day.

(b) Check your answer in part (a) by constructing a line graph of the model for the years 1989 to 1996. Use your graph to approximate when the average cost exceeded $900 per day.

84. *Sports*   In a football game, a quarterback throws a pass from the 15-yard line, 10 yards from the sideline as shown in the figure. The pass is caught on the 40-yard line, 45 yards from the same sideline. How long is the pass?

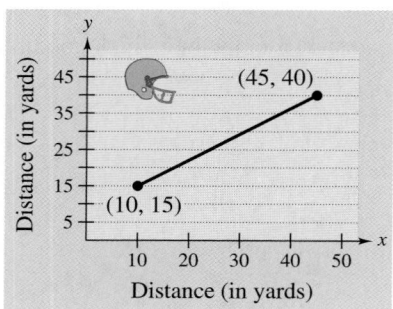

85. *Flying Distance*   A plane flies in a straight line to a city that is 100 kilometers east and 150 kilometers north of the point of departure. How far does it fly?

86. *Make a Conjecture*   Plot the points $(2, 1)$, $(-3, 5)$, and $(7, -3)$ on a rectangular coordinate system. Then change the sign of the indicated coordinate(s) of each point and plot the three new points on the same rectangular coordinate system. Make a conjecture about the location of a point when

(a) the sign of the *x*-coordinate is changed;

(b) the sign of the *y*-coordinate is changed;

(c) the sign of both the *x*- and *y*-coordinates are changed.

87. *Rock and Roll Hall of Fame*   The graph below shows the number of recording artists who were elected to the Rock and Roll Hall of Fame from 1986 to 1999.

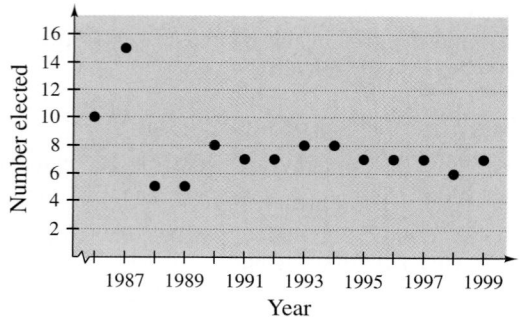

(a) Describe any trends in the data. From these trends, estimate the number of artists that will be elected in 2001.

(b) Why do you think the numbers elected in 1986 and 1987 were greater than in other years?

88. *Business*   Starbucks Corporation had annual sales of $696.5 million in 1996 and $1308.7 million in 1998. Use the Midpoint Formula to estimate the 1997 sales.   (Source: Starbucks Corporation)

89. *Business*   Lands' End, Inc., had annual sales of $1118.7 million in 1996 and $1371.4 million in 1998. Use the Midpoint Formula to estimate the 1997 sales.   (Source: Lands' End, Inc.)

Synthesis

True or False?   **In Exercises 90–92, determine whether the statement is true or false. Justify your answer.**

90. In order to divide a line segment into 16 equal parts, you would have to use the Midpoint Formula 16 times.

91. The points $(-8, 4)$, $(2, 11)$, and $(-5, 1)$ represent the vertices of an isosceles triangle.

92. If four points represent the vertices of a polygon, and the four sides are equal, then the polygon must be a square.

93. *Think About It*   What is the *y*-coordinate of any point on the *x*-axis? What is the *x*-coordinate of any point on the *y*-axis?

94. *Think About It*   When plotting points on the rectangular coordinate system, is it true that the scales on the *x*- and *y*-axes must be the same? Explain.

P   Chapter Summary

What did you learn?

Section P.1	Review Exercises
☐ How to represent and classify real numbers	1, 2
☐ How to order real numbers and use inequalities	3–6
☐ How to find the absolute values of real numbers and the distance between two real numbers	7–12
☐ How to evaluate algebraic expressions	13–16
☐ How to use the basic rules and properties of algebra	17–26

Section P.2
☐ How to use properties of exponents	27–30
☐ How to use scientific notation to represent real numbers	31–34
☐ How to use properties of radicals	35, 36
☐ How to simplify and combine radicals	37–49
☐ How to rationalize denominators and numerators	50–53
☐ How to use properties of rational exponents	54–59

Section P.3
☐ How to write polynomials in standard form	60, 61
☐ How to add, subtract, and multiply polynomials	62–69
☐ How to use special products to multiply polynomials	70–77
☐ How to remove common factors from polynomials	78–85
☐ How to factor special polynomial forms	86–89
☐ How to factor trinomials as the product of two binomials	90–93
☐ How to factor by grouping	94–97

Section P.4
☐ How to find domains of algebraic expressions	98–101
☐ How to simplify rational expressions	102–105
☐ How to add, subtract, multiply, and divide rational expressions	106–113
☐ How to simplify complex fractions	114, 115

Section P.5
☐ How to plot points in the Cartesian plane	116–121
☐ How to represent data graphically using scatter plots, bar graphs, and line graphs	122–124
☐ How to use the Distance Formula to find the distance between two points	125–128
☐ How to use the Midpoint Formula to find the midpoint of a line segment	129–131
☐ How to find the equation of a circle	132, 133

P Review Exercises

P.1 In Exercises 1 and 2, determine which numbers are (a) natural numbers, (b) integers, (c) rational numbers, and (d) irrational numbers.

1. $11, -14, -\frac{8}{9}, \frac{5}{2}, \sqrt{6}, 0.4$

2. $\sqrt{15}, -22, -\frac{10}{3}, 0, 5.2, \frac{3}{7}$

In Exercises 3 and 4, use a calculator to find the decimal form of the rational number. If it is a nonterminating decimal, write the repeating pattern. Then place the correct inequality symbol ($<$ or $>$) between the numbers.

3. $\frac{5}{6}, \frac{7}{8}$

4. $\frac{9}{25}, \frac{5}{7}$

In Exercises 5 and 6, give a verbal description of the real numbers that are represented by the inequality. Then sketch the inequality on the real number line.

5. $x \le 7$

6. $x > 1$

In Exercises 7 and 8, find the distance between a and b.

7. $a = -74, \quad b = 48$

8. $a = -123, \quad b = -9$

In Exercises 9–12, use absolute value notation to describe the expression.

9. The distance between x and 7 is at least 4.

10. The distance between x and 25 is no more than 10.

11. The distance between y and -30 is less than 5.

12. The distance between y and $\frac{1}{2}$ is more than 2.

In Exercises 13–16, evaluate the expression for each value of x. (If not possible, state the reason.)

Expression	Values	
13. $10x - 3$	(a) $x = -1$	(b) $x = 3$
14. $x^2 - 11x + 24$	(a) $x = -2$	(b) $x = 2$
15. $-2x^2 - x + 3$	(a) $x = 3$	(b) $x = -3$
16. $\dfrac{4x}{x - 1}$	(a) $x = -1$	(b) $x = 1$

In Exercises 17–20, identify the rule of algebra illustrated by the equation.

17. $2x + (3x - 10) = (2x + 3x) - 10$

18. $\dfrac{2}{y + 4} \cdot \dfrac{y + 4}{2} = 1, \quad y \ne -4$

19. $(t + 4)(2t) = (2t)(t + 4)$

20. $0 + (a - 5) = a - 5$

In Exercises 21–26, perform the operations. (Write fractional answers in simplest form.)

21. $\frac{2}{3} + \frac{8}{9}$

22. $\frac{3}{4} - \frac{1}{6} + \frac{1}{8}$

23. $\frac{3}{16} \div \frac{9}{2}$

24. $\frac{5}{8} \cdot \frac{2}{3}$

25. $\frac{x}{5} + \frac{7x}{12}$

26. $\frac{9}{x} \div \frac{1}{6}$

P.2 In Exercises 27–30, simplify each expression.

27. (a) $(-2z)^3$ (b) $(a^2 b^4)(3ab^{-2})$

28. (a) $\dfrac{(8y)^0}{y^2}$ (b) $\dfrac{40(b - 3)^5}{75(b - 3)^2}$

29. (a) $\dfrac{6^2 u^3 v^{-3}}{12u^{-2}v}$ (b) $\dfrac{3^{-4}m^{-1}n^{-3}}{9^{-2}mn^{-3}}$

30. (a) $(x + y^{-1})^{-1}$ (b) $\left(\dfrac{x^{-3}}{y}\right)\left(\dfrac{x}{y}\right)^{-1}$

In Exercises 31 and 32, write the number in scientific notation.

31. *Sales of K-Mart Corporation in 1998:* $33,674,000,000 (Source: K-Mart Corporation)

32. *Number of Meters in One Foot:* 0.3048

In Exercises 33 and 34, write the number in decimal form.

33. *Distance between Sun and Jupiter:* 4.833×10^8 miles

34. *Ratio of Day to Year:* 2.74×10^{-3}

In Exercises 35 and 36, use the properties of radicals to simplify the expression.

35. $\left(\sqrt[4]{78}\right)^4$

36. $\sqrt[3]{9} \cdot \sqrt[3]{3}$

In Exercises 37–42, simplify by removing all possible factors from the radical.

37. $\sqrt{4x^4}$

38. $\sqrt[5]{64x^6}$

39. $\sqrt{\frac{81}{144}}$

40. $\sqrt[3]{\frac{125}{216}}$

41. $\sqrt[3]{\dfrac{2x^3}{27}}$

42. $\sqrt{\dfrac{75x^2}{y^4}}$

In Exercises 43–48, simplify the expression.

43. $\sqrt{50} - \sqrt{18}$

44. $3\sqrt{32} + 4\sqrt{98}$

45. $8\sqrt{3x} - 5\sqrt{3x}$

46. $-11\sqrt{36y} - 6\sqrt{y}$

47. $\sqrt{8x^3} + \sqrt{2x}$

48. $3\sqrt{14x^2} - \sqrt{56x^2}$

49. *Strength of a Wooden Beam*   The rectangular cross section of a wooden beam cut from a log of diameter 24 inches will have a maximum strength if its width w and height h are

$$w = 8\sqrt{3} \quad \text{and} \quad h = \sqrt{24^2 - \left(8\sqrt{3}\right)^2}.$$

Find the area of the rectangular cross section and express the answer in simplest form.

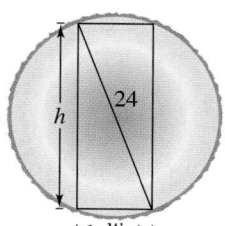

In Exercises 50 and 51, rewrite the expression by rationalizing the denominator. Simplify your answer.

50. $\dfrac{1}{2 - \sqrt{3}}$

51. $\dfrac{1}{\sqrt{x} - 1}$

In Exercises 52 and 53, rewrite the expression by rationalizing the numerator. Simplify your answer.

52. $\dfrac{\sqrt{20}}{4}$

53. $\dfrac{\sqrt{2} - \sqrt{11}}{3}$

In Exercises 54 and 55, fill in the missing description.

Radical Form	*Rational Exponent Form*
54. $\sqrt{16} = 4$	⬜ $= 4$
55. ⬜ $= 2$	$16^{1/4} = 2$

In Exercises 56–59, simplify the expression.

56. $81^{3/2}$

57. $64^{-2/3}$

58. $\left(-3x^{2/5}\right)\left(-2x^{1/2}\right)$

59. $(x - 1)^{1/3}(x - 1)^{-1/4}$

P.3   **In Exercises 60 and 61, write the polynomial in standard form.**

60. $15x^2 - 2x^5 + 3x^3 + 5 - x^4$

61. $-2x^4 + x^2 - 10 - x + x^3$

In Exercises 62–69, perform the operations and write the result in standard form.

62. $-(3x^2 + 2x) + (1 - 5x)$

63. $8y - [2y^2 - (3y - 8)]$

64. $(2x^3 - 5x^2 + 10x - 7) + (4x^2 - 7x - 2)$

65. $(6x^4 - 4x^3 - x + 3 - 20x^2) - (16 + 9x^4 - 11x^2)$

66. $(x^2 - 2x + 1)(x^3 - 1)$

67. $(x^3 - 3x)(2x^2 + 3x + 5)$

68. $(y^2 - y)(y^2 + 1)(y^2 + y + 1)$

69. $\left(x - \dfrac{1}{x}\right)(x + 2)$

In Exercises 70–75, find the product.

70. $(3x - 8)^2$

71. $(7x + 4)(7x - 4)$

72. $(x - 4)^3$

73. $(2x - 1)^3$

74. $\left(3\sqrt{5} + 2\right)\left(3\sqrt{5} - 2\right)$

75. $(x - y - 6)(x - y + 6)$

76. *Geometry*   Use the area model to write two different expressions for the total area. Then equate the two expressions and name the algebraic property illustrated.

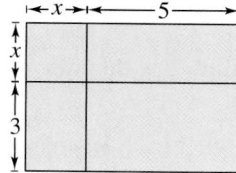

77. *Geometry*   Write an expression for the area of the region and simplify the result.

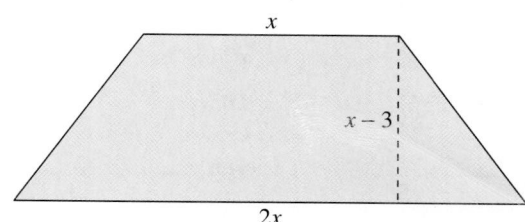

In Exercises 78–83, factor out the common factor.

78. $7x + 35$

79. $10x - 2$

80. $x^3 - x$

81. $x(x - 3) + 4(x - 3)$

82. $2x^3 + 18x^2 - 4x$

83. $-6x^4 - 3x^3 + 12x$

84. *Geometry* The surface area of a right circular cylinder is $S = 2\pi r^2 + 2\pi rh$.

    (a) Draw a right circular cylinder of radius r and height h. Use the figure to explain how the surface area formula was obtained.

    (b) Factor the expression for surface area.

85. *Business* The revenue for selling x units of a product at a price of p dollars per unit is $R = xp$. For a particular product the revenue is

$$R = 1600x - 0.50x^2.$$

Factor the expression and determine an expression that gives the price in terms of x.

In Exercises 86–93, factor the expression.

86. $x^2 - 169$

87. $9x^2 - \frac{1}{25}$

88. $x^3 + 216$

89. $64x^3 - 27$

90. $x^2 - 6x - 27$

91. $x^2 - 9x + 14$

92. $2x^2 + 21x + 10$

93. $3x^2 + 14x + 8$

In Exercises 94–97, factor by grouping.

94. $x^3 - 4x^2 - 3x + 12$

95. $x^3 - 6x^2 - x + 6$

96. $4x^3 - 3x^2 + 20x - 15$

97. $2x^3 + 5x^2 - 14x - 35$

P.4 **In Exercises 98–101, find the domain of the expression.**

98. $-5x^2 - x - 1$

99. $9x^4 + 7, \quad x > 0$

100. $\dfrac{4}{2x - 3}$

101. $\dfrac{\sqrt{x + 12}}{4x}$

In Exercises 102–105, write the rational expression in simplest form.

102. $\dfrac{4x^2}{4x^3 + 28x}$

103. $\dfrac{6xy}{xy + 2x}$

104. $\dfrac{x^2 - x - 30}{x^2 - 25}$

105. $\dfrac{x^2 - 9x + 18}{8x - 48}$

In Exercises 106–113, perform the operation and simplify your answer.

106. $\dfrac{x^2 - 4}{x^4 - 2x^2 - 8} \cdot \dfrac{x^2 + 2}{x^2}$

107. $\dfrac{2x - 1}{x + 1} \cdot \dfrac{x^2 - 1}{2x^2 - 7x + 3}$

108. $\dfrac{x^2(5x - 6)}{2x + 3} \div \dfrac{5x}{2x + 3}$

109. $\dfrac{4x - 6}{(x - 1)^2} \div \dfrac{2x^2 - 3x}{x^2 + 2x - 3}$

110. $x - 1 + \dfrac{1}{x + 2} + \dfrac{1}{x - 1}$

111. $2x + \dfrac{3}{2(x - 4)} - \dfrac{1}{2(x + 2)}$

112. $\dfrac{1}{x} - \dfrac{x - 1}{x^2 + 1}$

113. $\dfrac{1}{x - 1} + \dfrac{1 - x}{x^2 + x + 1}$

In Exercises 114 and 115, simplify the complex fraction.

114. $\dfrac{\left(\dfrac{1}{x} - \dfrac{1}{y}\right)}{(x^2 - y^2)}$

115. $\dfrac{\left(\dfrac{1}{x} - \dfrac{1}{y}\right)}{\left(\dfrac{1}{x} + \dfrac{1}{y}\right)}$

P.5 **In Exercises 116–119, plot the point and determine the quadrant in which it is located.**

116. $(8, -3)$

117. $(-4, -9)$

118. $\left(-\frac{5}{2}, 10\right)$

119. $(-6.5, -0.5)$

In Exercises 120 and 121, determine the quadrant(s) in which (x, y) is located so that the conditions are satisfied.

120. $x > 0$ and $y = -2$

121. $(x, y), \quad xy = 4$

122. *Patents*   The number of patents P (in thousands) issued in the United States from 1988 through 1996 is shown in the table.   (Source: U.S. Patent and Trademark Office)

Year	1988	1989	1990	1991	1992
P	84.4	102.7	99.2	106.8	107.4

Year	1993	1994	1995	1996
P	109.7	113.6	113.8	121.7

(a) Sketch a scatter plot of the data.

(b) What statement can be made about the number of patents issued in the United States?

123. *Weather*   The normal daily maximum and minimum temperatures for each month for the city of Chicago are shown in the table. Make a double line graph for the data.   (Source: NOAA)

Month	Jan.	Feb.	Mar.	Apr.	May	Jun.
Max.	29.0	33.5	45.8	58.6	70.1	79.6
Min.	12.9	17.2	28.5	38.6	47.7	57.5

Month	Jul.	Aug.	Sep.	Oct.	Nov.	Dec.
Max.	83.7	81.8	74.8	63.3	48.4	34.0
Min.	62.6	61.6	53.9	42.2	31.6	19.1

124. *Business*   The net profits (in millions of dollars) for the Progressive Corporation for the years 1994 through 1998 are shown in the table. Create a bar graph for the data.   (Source: Progressive Corporation)

Year	1994	1995	1996	1997	1998
Profits	228.1	250.5	316.6	400.0	456.7

In Exercises 125 and 126, plot the points and find the distance between the points.

125. $(-3, 8), (1, 5)$ **126.** $(5.6, 0), (0, 8.2)$

Geometry   **In Exercises 127 and 128, plot the points and verify that the points form the polygon.**

127. *Right Triangle:* $(2, 3), (13, 11), (5, 22)$

128. *Parallelogram:* $(1, 2), (8, 3), (9, 6), (2, 5)$

In Exercises 129 and 130, plot the points and find the midpoint of the line segment joining the points.

129. $(-12, 5), (4, -7)$

130. $(1.8, 7.4), (-0.6, -14.5)$

131. *Business*   The Sbarro, Inc., restaurant chain had revenues of \$329.5 million in 1996 and \$375.2 million in 1998.   (Source: Sbarro, Inc.)

(a) Without any additional information, what would you estimate the 1997 revenues to have been?

(b) The actual revenue for 1997 was \$349.4 million. How accurate is your estimate?

In Exercises 132 and 133, find the standard form of the equation of the specified circle.

132. Center: $(3, -1)$; solution point: $(-5, 1)$

133. End points of a diameter: $(-4, 6), (10, -2)$

Synthesis

True or False?   **In Exercises 134–136, determine whether the statement is true or false. Justify your answer.**

134. $\dfrac{x^3 - 1}{x - 1} = x^2 + x + 1$ for all values of x.

135. A binomial sum squared is equal to the sum of the terms squared.

136. $x^n - y^n$ factors as conjugates for all values of n.

In Exercises 137–142, describe the error and then make the necessary correction.

137. $\dfrac{x - 1}{1 - x} = 1$

138. $-x^2(-x^2 + 3) = x^4 + 3x^2$

139. $(2x)^4 = 2x^4$

140. $(-x)^6 = -x^6$

141. $\sqrt{3^2 + 4^2} = 3 + 4$

142. $\sqrt{10x} = 10\sqrt{x}$

143. *Writing*   Explain why $\sqrt{5u} + \sqrt{3u} \neq 2\sqrt{2u}$.

Chapter Project *Modeling the Volume of a Box*

Many mathematical results are discovered experimentally by calculating examples and looking for patterns. Prior to the 1950s, this mode of discovery was very time-consuming because the calculations had to be done by hand. The introduction of computer and calculator technology has removed much of this drudgery. In the following project, you are asked to model a real-life situation and solve a problem by looking for patterns in the corresponding data.

Consider a rectangular box with a square base and a surface area of 216 square inches. Let x represent the length (in inches) of each side of the base and let h represent the height (in inches) of the box, as shown at the right. Your goal is to answer this question: "Of all rectangular boxes with square bases and surface area of 216 square inches, which has the greatest volume?"

a. Express the areas of the base, top, and sides in terms of x and h.

b. Find an expression in terms of x and h for the surface area of the box.

c. Use the fact that the surface area is 216 square inches to express the variable h in terms of x.

d. Find an expression for the volume of the box in terms of x alone.

e. Use the expression in part (d) and a graphing utility to complete the table. Then use the results to decide which box has the greatest volume.

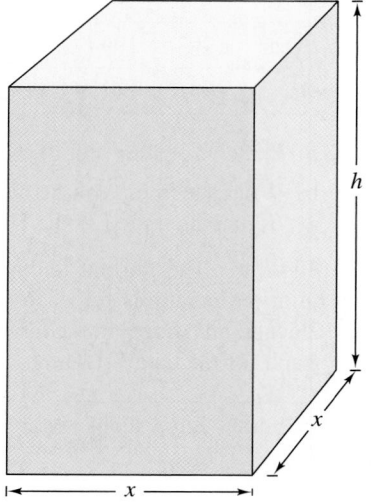

Base, x	Height, h	Surface Area	Volume
1.0	53.5	216.0	53.5
1.5	35.3	216.0	79.3
2.0	26.0	216.0	104.0
⋮	⋮	⋮	⋮
10.0	0.4	216.0	40.0

A computer simulation to accompany this project appears in the *Interactive* CD-ROM and *Internet* versions of this text.

Questions for Further Exploration

1. What happens to the height of the box as x gets closer and closer to 0? Of all boxes with square bases and a surface area of 216 square inches, is there a tallest? Explain your reasoning.

2. What is the maximum value of x? What happens to the height of the box as x gets closer and closer to this maximum value? Is there a shortest box that has a square base and a surface area of 216 square inches? Explain your reasoning.

3. Complete the table. Does it lend further support to your answer to part (e)? Explain.

x	5.9	5.99	5.999	6.001	6.01	6.1
V						

4. Of all rectangular boxes with surface area of 216 square inches and a base that is x inches by $2x$ inches, which has the maximum volume? Explain your reasoning.

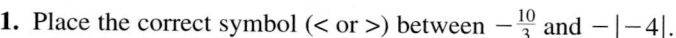

P ## Chapter Test

Take this test as you would take a test in class. After you are done, check your
work against the answers in the back of the book.

1. Place the correct symbol (< or >) between $-\frac{10}{3}$ and $-|-4|$.

2. Find the distance between the real numbers -17 and 39.

In Exercises 3–6, evaluate each quantity without using a calculator.

3. (a) $27\left(-\frac{2}{3}\right)$ (b) $\frac{5}{18} \div \frac{15}{8}$ 4. (a) $\left(-\frac{3}{5}\right)^3$ (b) $\left(\frac{3^2}{2}\right)^{-3}$

5. (a) $\sqrt{5} \cdot \sqrt{125}$ (b) $\frac{\sqrt{72}}{\sqrt{2}}$ 6. (a) $\frac{5.4 \times 10^8}{3 \times 10^3}$ (b) $(3 \times 10^4)^3$

In Exercises 7 and 8, simplify each expression.

7. (a) $3z^2(2z^3)^2$ (b) $(u-2)^{-4}(u-2)^{-3}$ (c) $\left(\frac{x^{-2}y^2}{3}\right)^{-1}$

8. (a) $9z\sqrt{8z} - 3\sqrt{2z^3}$ (b) $-5\sqrt{16y} + 10\sqrt{y}$ (c) $\sqrt[3]{\frac{16}{v^5}}$

In Exercises 9–12, perform the operations and simplify.

9. $(x^2 + 3) - [3x + (8 - x^2)]$ 10. $\left(x + \sqrt{5}\right)\left(x - \sqrt{5}\right)$

11. $\frac{8x}{x-3} + \frac{24}{3-x}$ 12. $\left(\frac{2}{x} - \frac{2}{x+1}\right) \div \left(\frac{4}{x^2-1}\right)$

In Exercises 13–15, factor the expression completely.

13. $2x^4 - 3x^3 - 2x^2$ 14. $x^3 + 2x^2 - 4x - 8$ 15. $8x^3 - 27$

16. Rationalize the denominators of (a) $\frac{16}{\sqrt[3]{16}}$ and (b) $\frac{6}{1 - \sqrt{3}}$.

17. Write an expression for the area of the shaded region in the figure at the
    right and simplify the result.

18. Plot the points $(-2, 5)$ and $(6, 0)$. Find the coordinates of the midpoint of the
    line segment joining the points and the distance between the points.

19. The area of a rectangle of length l is $45l - l^2$. Factor the expression to deter-
    mine the width of the rectangle.

20. The numbers (in millions) of votes cast for the Democratic candidates
    for president in 1980, 1984, 1988, 1992, and 1996 were 35.5, 37.6, 41.8,
    44.9, and 47.4, respectively. Create a bar graph for this data. (Source:
    Congressional Quarterly, Inc.)

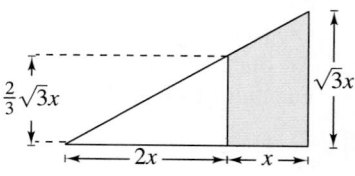

FIGURE FOR 17

LIBRARY OF FUNCTIONS

In Chapter 1, you will be introduced to the concept of a *function*. As you proceed through the text, you will see that functions play a primary role in modeling real-life situations.

Over the past few hundred years, many different types of functions have been introduced and studied. Those that have proven to be most important in modeling real life have come to be known as *elementary functions*. There are three basic types of elementary functions: algebraic functions, exponential and logarithmic functions, and trigonometric and inverse trigonometric functions.

You will also encounter other types of functions in this text, such as functions defined by real-life data and piecewise-defined functions.

Library of Functions

Each time a new type of function is studied in detail in this text, it will be highlighted in a box like this one. For instance, a linear function is highlighted in the Library of Functions box in Section 1.2 because lines are discussed in that section.

In addition, there is a Library of Functions Summary inside the front cover which describes the functions listed below.

Algebraic Functions

Polynomial Functions	
Linear or First-Degree Polynomial Functions	Section 1.2
Quadratic or Second-Degree Polynomial Functions	Section 3.1
Cubic or Third-Degree Polynomial Functions	Section 3.2
Fourth- and Higher-Degree Polynomial Functions	Section 3.2
Rational Functions	Section 3.5
Radical Functions	Section 1.3

Exponential and Logarithmic Functions

Exponential Functions	Section 4.1
Logarithmic Functions	Section 4.2

Trigonometric and Inverse Trigonometric Functions

Trigonometric Functions	Not covered in this text.
Inverse Trigonometric Functions	Not covered in this text.

Nonelementary Functions

Piecewise-Defined Functions	Section 1.3
Greatest Integer Functions	Section 1.4
Absolute Value Functions	Section 1.4
Functions Defined by Real-Life Data	Section 1.3

Functions and Their Graphs

The Big Picture

In this chapter you will learn how to

- ❏ sketch graphs of equations by point plotting or using a graphing utility.
- ❏ find and use the slope of a line to write and graph linear equations.
- ❏ evaluate functions and find their domains.
- ❏ analyze graphs of functions.
- ❏ identify and graph shifts, reflections, and nonrigid transformations of functions.
- ❏ find arithmetic combinations and compositions of functions.
- ❏ find inverses of functions graphically and algebraically.

Superstock

One and one-half percent of all households own a horse as a pet. Some owners board their horses on farms. (Source: American Veterinary Medical Association)

Important Vocabulary

As you encounter each new vocabulary term in this chapter, add the term and its definition to your notebook glossary.

- solution point (p. 68)
- graph of an equation (p. 68)
- intercepts (p. 69)
- slope (p. 79)
- point-slope form (p. 81)
- slope-intercept form (p. 83)
- general form (p. 84)
- parallel (p. 85)
- perpendicular (p. 85)
- function (p. 92)
- domain (p. 92)
- range (p. 92)

- independent variable (p. 94)
- dependent variable (p. 94)
- function notation (p. 94)
- implied domain (p. 96)
- graph of a function (p. 106)
- Vertical Line Test (p. 107)
- increasing (p. 108)
- decreasing (p. 108)
- constant (p. 108)
- relative minimum (p. 109)
- relative maximum (p. 109)
- greatest integer function (p. 111)

- step function (p. 111)
- even function (p. 112)
- odd function (p. 112)
- vertical and horizontal shifts (p. 119)
- reflection (p. 121)
- rigid transformations (p. 123)
- nonrigid transformations (p. 123)
- arithmetic combination (p. 127)
- composition (p. 129)
- inverse function (p. 138)
- one-to-one (p. 142)
- Horizontal Line Test (p. 142)

Additional Resources   Text-specific additional resources are available to help you do well in this course. See page xvi for details.

1.1 Graphs of Equations

The Graph of an Equation

News magazines often show graphs comparing the rate of inflation, the federal deficit, wholesale prices, or the unemployment rate to the time of year. Industrial firms and businesses use graphs to report their monthly production and sales statistics. Such graphs provide geometric pictures of the way one quantity changes with respect to another. Frequently, the relationship between two quantities is expressed as an equation. This section introduces the basic procedure for determining the geometric picture associated with an equation.

For an equation in variables x and y, a point (a, b) is a **solution point** if the substitution of $x = a$ and $y = b$ satisfies the equation. Most equations have *infinitely* many solution points. For example, the equation

$$3x + y = 5$$

has solution points $(0, 5)$, $(1, 2)$, $(2, -1)$, $(3, -4)$, and so on. The set of all solution points of an equation is the **graph of the equation.**

What You Should Learn:

- How to sketch graphs of equations by point plotting
- How to sketch graphs of equations using a graphing utility
- How to use graphs of equations in real-life problems

Why You Should Learn It:

The graph of an equation can help you see relationships between real-life quantities. For example, Exercise 75 on page 78 shows how a graph can be used to understand the relationship between life expectancy and the year a child is born.

Bruce Ayres/Tony Stone Images

EXAMPLE 1   Determining Solution Points

Determine whether each point lies on the graph of $y = 10x - 7$.

a. $(2, 13)$ **b.** $(-1, -3)$

Solution

a. The point $(2, 13)$ lies on the graph of $y = 10x - 7$ because it is a solution point of the equation.

$y = 10x - 7$	Write original equation.
$13 \stackrel{?}{=} 10(2) - 7$	Substitute 2 for x and 13 for y.
$13 = 13$	$(2, 13)$ is a solution. ✓

b. The point $(-1, -3)$ does not lie on the graph of $y = 10x - 7$ because it is not a solution point of the equation.

$y = 10x - 7$	Write original equation.
$-3 \stackrel{?}{=} 10(-1) - 7$	Substitute -1 for x and -3 for y.
$-3 \neq -17$	$(-1, -3)$ is not a solution.

How to Sketch the Graph of an Equation by Point Plotting

1. If possible, rewrite the equation so that one of the variables is isolated on one side of the equation.
2. Make a table of several solution points.
3. Plot these points in the coordinate plane.
4. Connect the points with a smooth curve.

EXAMPLE 2   Sketching a Graph by Point Plotting

Use point plotting and graph paper to sketch the graph of

$$3x + y = 6.$$

Solution

In this case you can isolate the variable y.

$$y = 6 - 3x \qquad \text{Solve equation for } y.$$

Using negative, zero, and positive values for x, you can obtain the following table of values (solution points).

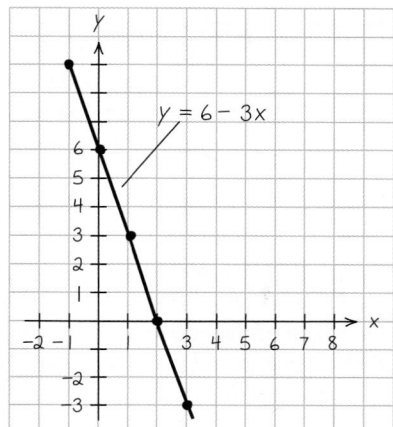

Figure 1.1

x	-1	0	1	2	3
$y = 6 - 3x$	9	6	3	0	-3

Next, plot these points and connect them, as shown in Figure 1.1. It appears that the graph is a straight line. You will study lines extensively in Section 1.2.

The points at which a graph touches or crosses an axis are the **intercepts** of the graph. For instance, in Example 2 the point $(0, 6)$ is the y-intercept of the graph because the graph crosses the y-axis at that point. The point $(2, 0)$ is the x-intercept of the graph because the graph crosses the x-axis at that point.

EXAMPLE 3   Sketching a Graph by Point Plotting

Use point plotting and graph paper to sketch the graph of $y = x^2 - 2$.

Solution

First, make a table of values by choosing several convenient values of x and calculating the corresponding values of y.

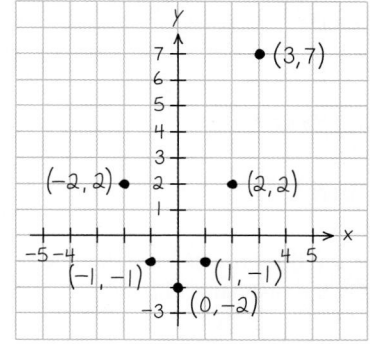

(a)

x	-2	-1	0	1	2	3
$y = x^2 - 2$	2	-1	-2	-1	2	7

Next, plot the corresponding solution points, as shown in Figure 1.2(a). Finally, connect the points with a smooth curve, as shown in Figure 1.2(b). This graph is called a *parabola*. You will study parabolas in Section 3.1.

In this text, you will study two basic ways to create graphs: *by hand* and *using a graphing utility*. For instance, the graphs in Figures 1.1 and 1.2 were sketched by hand and the graph in Figure 1.4 was sketched using a graphing utility.

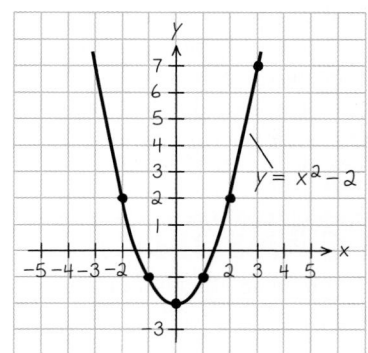

(b)
Figure 1.2

A computer animation of this example appears in the *Interactive* CD-ROM and *Internet* versions of this text.

Using a Graphing Utility

One of the disadvantages of the point-plotting method is that to get a good idea about the shape of a graph you need to plot *many* points. With only a few points, you could badly misrepresent the graph. For instance, consider the equation

$$y = \frac{1}{30}x(x^4 - 10x^2 + 39).$$

Suppose you plotted only five points: $(-3, -3), (-1, -1), (0, 0), (1, 1)$, and $(3, 3)$, as shown in Figure 1.3(a). From these five points, you might assume that the graph of the equation is a straight line. That, however, is not correct. By plotting several more points, you can see that the actual graph is not straight at all, as shown in Figure 1.3(b).

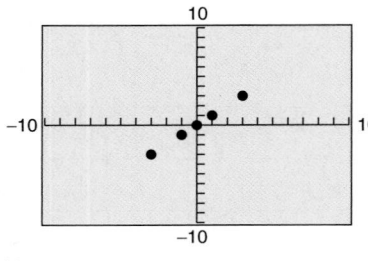

(a)

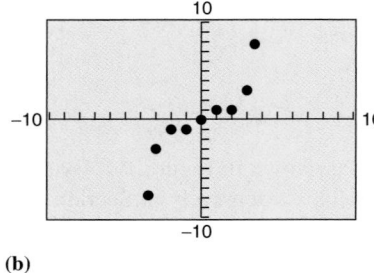

(b)

Figure 1.3

> **STUDY T!P**
>
> This section presents a brief overview of how to use a graphing utility to graph an equation. For more extensive coverage on this topic, see "An Introduction to Graphing Utilities" on pages xvii–xxii, and the *Graphing Technology Guide.*

From this, you can see that the point-plotting method leaves you with a dilemma. On the one hand, the method can be very inaccurate if only a few points are plotted. But on the other hand, it is very time-consuming to plot a dozen (or more) points. Technology can help solve this dilemma. Plotting several (even several hundred) points on a rectangular coordinate system is something that a computer or calculator can do easily.

The point-plotting method is the method used by *all* graphing utilities. Each computer or calculator screen is made up of a grid of hundreds or thousands of small areas called *pixels*. Screens that have many pixels per square inch are said to have a higher *resolution* than screens with fewer pixels.

Using a Graphing Utility to Graph an Equation

To graph an equation involving x and y on a graphing utility, use the following procedure.

1. Rewrite the equation so that y is isolated on the left side.

2. Enter the equation into a graphing utility.

3. Determine a *viewing window* that shows all important features of the graph.

4. Graph the equation.

EXAMPLE 4   Using a Graphing Utility to Graph an Equation

Use a graphing utility to graph $2y + x^3 = 4x$.

Solution

To begin, solve the equation for y in terms of x.

$$2y + x^3 = 4x \qquad \text{Write original equation.}$$

$$2y = -x^3 + 4x \qquad \text{Subtract } x^3 \text{ from each side.}$$

$$y = -\frac{1}{2}x^3 + 2x \qquad \text{Divide each side by 2.}$$

Now, by entering this equation into a graphing utility (using a standard viewing window), you can obtain the graph shown in Figure 1.4.

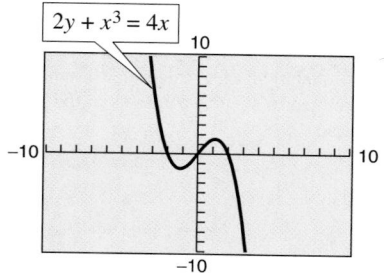

Figure 1.4

By choosing different viewing windows for a graph, it is possible to obtain very different impressions of the graph's shape. For instance, Figure 1.5 shows four different viewing windows for the graph of the equation in Example 4. None of these views shows *all* of the important features of the graph as Figure 1.4 does.

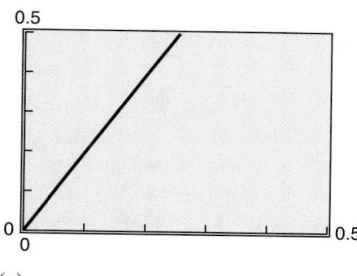

(a)

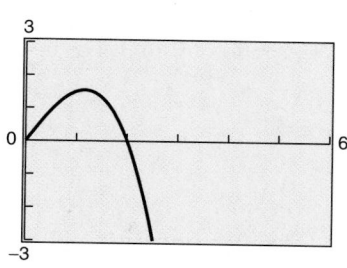

(b)

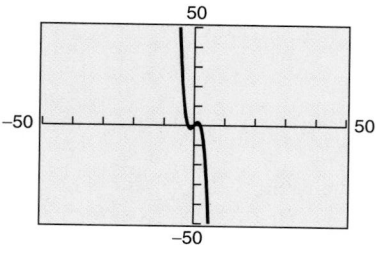

(c)

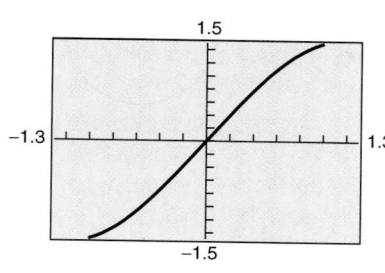

(d)

Figure 1.5

The standard viewing window on many graphing utilities does not give a true geometric perspective. That is, perpendicular lines will not appear to be perpendicular and circles will not appear to be circular. To overcome this, you can use a *square setting*, as demonstrated in Example 5.

EXAMPLE 5   Sketching a Circle with a Graphing Utility

Use a graphing utility to graph

$x^2 + y^2 = 9.$

Solution

The graph of $x^2 + y^2 = 9$ is a circle whose center is the origin and whose radius is 3. (See Section P.5.) To graph the equation, begin by solving the equation for y.

$x^2 + y^2 = 9$	Write original equation.
$y^2 = 9 - x^2$	Subtract x^2 from each side.
$y = \pm\sqrt{9 - x^2}$	Take square root of each side.

The graph of

$y = \sqrt{9 - x^2}$ Upper semicircle

is the upper semicircle. The graph of

$y = -\sqrt{9 - x^2}$ Lower semicircle

is the lower semicircle. Enter *both* equations in your graphing utility and generate the resulting graphs. In Figure 1.6(a), note that if you use a standard viewing window, the two graphs do not appear to form a circle. You can overcome this problem by using a *square setting*, in which the horizontal and vertical tick marks have equal spacing, as shown in Figure 1.6(b). On many graphing utilities, a square setting can be obtained by using a y to x ratio of 2 to 3. For instance, in Figure 1.6(b), the y to x ratio is

$$\frac{Y_{max} - Y_{min}}{X_{max} - X_{min}} = \frac{4 - (-4)}{6 - (-6)} = \frac{8}{12} = \frac{2}{3}.$$

The *Interactive* CD-ROM and *Internet* versions of this text show every example with its solution; clicking on the *Try It!* button brings up similar problems. Guided Examples and Integrated Examples show step-by-step solutions to additional examples. Integrated Examples are related to several concepts in the section.

Notice that when you graph a circle by graphing two separate equations for y, a graphing utility may not show the two semicircles as being connected. You may wish to point out to your students that some graphing utilities have commands that allow the user to draw complete circles by specifying the coordinates of the center and the radius.

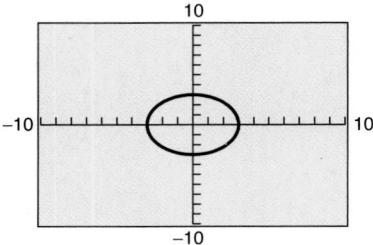

(a)

(b)

Figure 1.6

Throughout this course, you will learn that there are many ways to approach a problem. Two of the three common approaches are illustrated in Example 6.

A Numerical Approach: Construct and use a table.
A Graphical Approach: Draw and use a graph.
An Analytic Approach: Use the rules of algebra.

We recommend that you habitually use at least two approaches with every problem to help build your intuition and check that your answer is reasonable.

Applications

The following two applications show how to develop mathematical models to represent real-world situations. You will see that both a graphing utility and algebra can be used to understand and solve the problems posed.

> **STUDY T!P**
>
> In applications, it is convenient to use variable names that suggest real-life quantities: d for distance, t for time, and so on. Most graphing utilities, however, require the variable names to be x and y.

EXAMPLE 6   Running a Marathon

A runner runs at a constant rate of 4.9 miles per hour. The verbal model and algebraic equation relating distance run and elapsed time are as follows.

Verbal Model: $\boxed{\text{Distance}} = \boxed{\text{Rate}} \cdot \boxed{\text{Time}}$ *Equation:* $d = 4.9t$

a. Determine how far the runner can run in 3.1 hours.

b. Determine how long it will take to run a 26.2-mile marathon.

Graphical Solution

a. To begin, use a graphing utility to graph the equation $d = 4.9t$. (Represent d by y and t by x.) Be sure to use a viewing window that shows the graph when $x = 3.1$. Then use the *value* feature or *zoom* and *trace* features of the graphing utility to estimate that when $x = 3.1$, the distance is $y \approx 15.2$ miles, as shown in Figure 1.7(a).

b. Adjust the viewing window so that it shows the graph when $y = 26.2$. Use the *value* feature or *zoom* and *trace* features to estimate that when $y = 26.2$, the time is $x \approx 5.4$ hours, as shown in Figure 1.7(b).

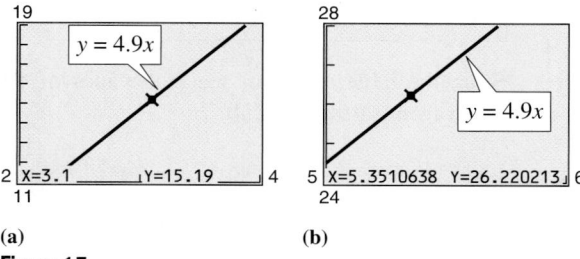

(a)   (b)
Figure 1.7

Note that the viewing window on your graphing utility may differ slightly from those shown in Figure 1.7.

Algebraic Solution

a. To find how far the runner can run in 3.1 hours, substitute 3.1 for t in the equation.

$$d = 4.9t \qquad \text{Write original equation.}$$
$$= 4.9(3.1) \qquad \text{Substitute 3.1 for } t.$$
$$\approx 15.2 \qquad \text{Use a calculator.}$$

So, a runner can run about 15.2 miles in 3.1 hours. Use estimation to check your answer. Because 4.9 is about 5 and 3.1 is about 3, the distance is about $5(3) = 15$. So 15.2 is reasonable.

b. You can find how long it will take to run a 26.2-mile marathon as follows. (For help with solving linear equations see Appendix C.)

$$d = 4.9t \qquad \text{Write original equation.}$$
$$\frac{d}{4.9} = t \qquad \text{Divide each side by 4.9.}$$
$$\frac{26.2}{4.9} = t \qquad \text{Substitute 26.2 for } d.$$
$$5.3 \approx t \qquad \text{Use a calculator.}$$

So, it will take about 5.3 hours to run 26.2 miles.

EXAMPLE 7 Monthly Wages

You receive a monthly salary of $2000 plus a commission of 10% of sales. The verbal model and algebraic equations relating the wages, the salary, and the commission are as follows.

Verbal Model: Wages = Salary + Commission on Sales   *Equation:* $y = 2000 + 0.1x$

a. If sales are $x = 1480$ in August, what are your wages for that month?

b. If you receive $2225 for September, what are your sales for that month?

Graphical Solution

a. You can use a graphing utility to graph $y = 2000 + 0.1x$ and then estimate the wages when $x = 1480$. Because $x \geq 0$ and the monthly wages are at least $2000, a reasonable viewing window is the one shown in Figure 1.8(a). Using the *value* feature or *zoom* and *trace* features near $x = 1480$ shows that the wages are about $2148.

b. Use the graphing utility to find the value along the *x*-axis (sales) that corresponds to a *y*-value of 2225 (wages). Beginning with Figure 1.8(b) and using the *value* feature or *zoom* and *trace* features, you can estimate the sales to be about $2250.

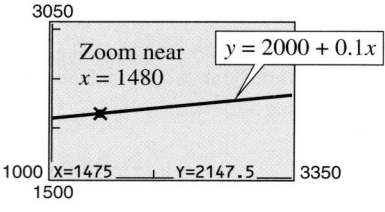

(a)

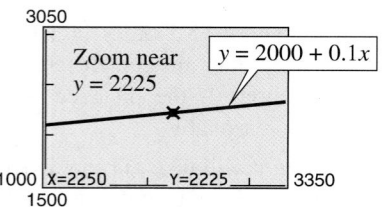

(b)

Figure 1.8

Numerical Solution

a. To find the wages in August, evaluate the equation when $x = 1480$.

$$y = 2000 + 0.1x \qquad \text{Write original equation.}$$
$$= 2000 + 0.1(1480) \qquad \text{Substitute 1480 for } x.$$
$$= 2148 \qquad \text{Simplify.}$$

So, the wages in August are $2148.

b. The table shows the wages for different amounts of sales.

Sales x	2000	2100	2200	2300	2400
Wages y	2200	2210	2220	2230	2240

From the table, you can see that wages of $2225 result from sales between $2200 and $2300. You can improve this estimate by making a table similar to the one below.

Sales x	2210	2220	2230	2240	2250
Wages y	2221	2222	2223	2224	2225

Sales x	2260	2270	2280	2290
Wages y	2226	2227	2228	2229

From the table, you can see that wages of $2225 result from sales of $2250.

Writing About Math *Comparison of Wages*

Your employer offers you a choice of wage scales: a monthly salary of $3000 plus commission of 7% of sales or a salary of $3400 plus a 5% commission. Write a short paragraph discussing how you would choose your option. At what sales level would the options yield the same salary? Be sure to take advantage of your graphing utility to make your decision.

1.1 Exercises

In Exercises 1–8, determine whether the points lie on the graph of the equation.

Equation	Points
1. $y = \sqrt{x} + 4$	(a) $(0, 2)$ (b) $(5, 3)$
2. $y = x^2 - 3x + 2$	(a) $(2, 0)$ (b) $(-2, 8)$
3. $y = 4 - |x - 2|$	(a) $(1, 5)$ (b) $(1.2, 3.2)$
4. $y = \dfrac{1}{x^2 + 1}$	(a) $(0, 0)$ (b) $(3, 0.1)$
5. $2x - y - 3 = 0$	(a) $(1, 2)$ (b) $(1, -1)$
6. $x^2 + y^2 = 20$	(a) $(3, -2)$ (b) $(-4, 2)$
7. $x^2 y - x^2 + 4y = 0$	(a) $\left(1, \frac{1}{5}\right)$ (b) $\left(2, \frac{1}{2}\right)$
8. $y = \frac{1}{3}x^3 - 2x^2$	(a) $\left(2, -\frac{16}{3}\right)$ (b) $(-3, 9)$

In Exercises 9–14, complete the table. Use the resulting solution points to sketch the graph of the equation. Use a graphing utility to verify the graph.

9. $y = -2x + 3$

x	-1	0	1	$\frac{3}{2}$	2
y					

10. $y = \frac{3}{2}x - 1$

x	-2	0	$\frac{2}{3}$	1	2
y					

11. $y = x^2 - 2x$

x	-1	0	1	2	3
y					

12. $y = 4 - x^2$

x	-2	-1	0	1	2
y					

13. $y = 3 - |x - 2|$

x	0	1	2	3	4
y					

14. $y = \sqrt{x - 1}$

x	1	2	5	10	17
y					

15. *Exploration*

(a) Complete the table for the equation $y = \frac{1}{4}x - 3$.

x	-2	-1	0	1	2
y					

(b) Use the resulting solution points to sketch its graph. Then use a graphing utility to verify the graph.

(c) Repeat parts (a) and (b) for the equation $y = -\frac{1}{4}x - 3$. Use the result to describe any differences between the graphs.

16. *Exploration*

(a) Complete the table for the equation $y = \dfrac{6x}{x^{-2} + 1}$.

x	-2	-1	0	1	2
y					

(b) Use the resulting solution points to sketch its graph. Then use a graphing utility to verify the graph.

(c) Continue the table in part (a) for x-values of 5, 10, 20, and 40. What is the value of y approaching? Can y be negative for positive values of x? Explain.

The *Interactive* CD-ROM and *Internet* versions of this text contain step-by-step solutions to all odd-numbered Section and Review Exercises. They also provide Tutorial Exercises, which link to Guided Examples for additional help.

In Exercises 17–22, match the equation with its graph. [The graphs are labeled (a), (b), (c), (d), (e), and (f).]

(a)

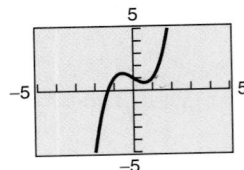

(b)

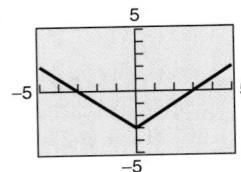

(c)

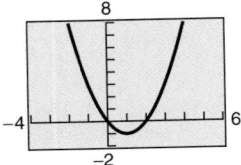

(d)

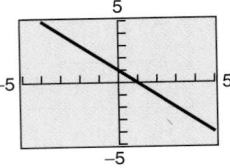

(e)

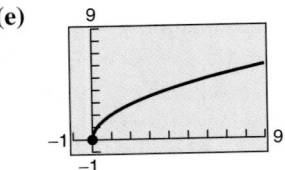

(f)

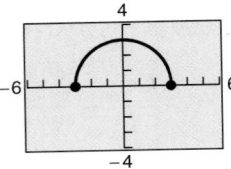

17. $y = 1 - x$

18. $y = x^2 - 2x$

19. $y = \sqrt{9 - x^2}$

20. $y = 2\sqrt{x}$

21. $y = x^3 - x + 1$

22. $y = |x| - 3$

In Exercises 23–36, sketch the graph of the equation.

23. $y = -3x + 2$

24. $y = 2x - 3$

25. $y = 1 - x^2$

26. $y = x^2 - 1$

27. $y = x^2 - 3x$

28. $y = -x^2 - 4x$

29. $y = x^3 + 2$

30. $y = x^3 - 1$

31. $y = \sqrt{x - 3}$

32. $y = \sqrt{1 - x}$

33. $y = |x - 2|$

34. $y = 4 - |x|$

35. $x = y^2 - 1$

36. $x = y^2 - 4$

In Exercises 37–50, use a graphing utility to graph the equation. Use a standard viewing window. Approximate any x- or y-intercepts of the graph.

37. $y = x - 5$

38. $y = (x + 1)(x - 3)$

39. $y = 3 - \frac{1}{2}x$

40. $y = \frac{2}{3}x - 1$

41. $y = x^2 - 4x + 3$

42. $y = \frac{1}{2}(x + 4)(x - 2)$

43. $y = x(x - 2)^2$

44. $y = \dfrac{4}{x^2 + 1}$

45. $y = \dfrac{2x}{x - 1}$

46. $y = \dfrac{4}{x}$

47. $y = x\sqrt{x + 6}$

48. $y = (6 - x)\sqrt{x}$

49. $y = \sqrt[3]{x}$

50. $y = \sqrt[3]{x + 1}$

In Exercises 51–54, use a graphing utility to sketch the graph of the equation. Begin by using a standard viewing window. Then graph the equation a second time using the specified viewing window. Which viewing window is better? Explain.

51. $y = \frac{5}{2}x + 5$

52. $y = -3x + 50$

| Xmin = 0 |
| Xmax = 6 |
| Xscl = 1 |
| Ymin = 0 |
| Ymax = 10 |
| Yscl = 1 |

| Xmin = -1 |
| Xmax = 4 |
| Xscl = 1 |
| Ymin = -5 |
| Ymax = 60 |
| Yscl = 5 |

53. $y = -x^2 + 10x - 5$

54. $y = 4(x + 5)\sqrt{4 - x}$

| Xmin = -1 |
| Xmax = 11 |
| Xscl = 1 |
| Ymin = -5 |
| Ymax = 25 |
| Yscl = 2 |

| Xmin = -6 |
| Xmax = 6 |
| Xscl = 1 |
| Ymin = -5 |
| Ymax = 50 |
| Yscl = 4 |

In Exercises 55–58, describe the viewing window of the graph.

55. $y = 4x^2 - 25$

56. $y = x^3 - 3x^2 + 4$

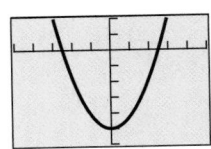

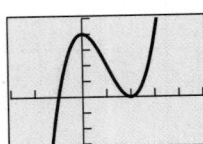

57. $y = |x| + |x - 10|$

58. $y = 8\sqrt[3]{x - 6}$

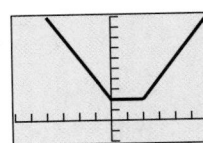

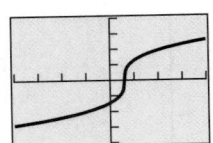

In Exercises 59–62, solve for y and use a graphing utility to graph each of the resulting equations in the same viewing window. Adjust the viewing window so that a circle really does appear circular.

59. $x^2 + y^2 = 64$

60. $(x - 1)^2 + (y - 2)^2 = 16$

61. $x^2 + y^2 = 49$

62. $(x - 3)^2 + (y - 1)^2 = 25$

In Exercises 63–66, explain how to use a graphing utility to verify that $y_1 = y_2$. Identify the rule of algebra that is illustrated.

63. $y_1 = \frac{1}{4}(x^2 - 8)$

   $y_2 = \frac{1}{4}x^2 - 2$

64. $y_1 = \frac{1}{2}x + (x + 1)$

   $y_2 = \frac{3}{2}x + 1$

65. $y_1 = \frac{1}{5}[10(x^2 - 1)]$

   $y_2 = 2(x^2 - 1)$

66. $y_1 = (x - 3) \cdot \dfrac{1}{x - 3}$

   $y_2 = 1$

In Exercises 67–70, use a graphing utility to graph the equation. Move the cursor along the curve to approximate the unknown coordinate of each solution point accurate to two decimal places. (*Hint:* You may need to use the *zoom* feature of the graphing utility to obtain the required accuracy.)

67. $y = \sqrt{5 - x}$

   (a) $(2, y)$

   (b) $(x, 3)$

68. $y = x^3(x - 3)$

   (a) $(2.25, y)$

   (b) $(x, 20)$

69. $y = x^5 - 5x$

   (a) $(-0.5, y)$

   (b) $(x, -4)$

70. $y = |x^2 - 6x + 5|$

   (a) $(2, y)$

   (b) $(x, 1.5)$

71. *Business* A manufacturing plant purchases a new molding machine for $225,000. The depreciated value y after t years is

$$y = 225,000 - 20,000t, \qquad 0 \le t \le 8.$$

(a) Use the constraints of the model to determine an appropriate viewing window.

(b) Use a graphing utility to graph the equation.

(c) Use the *value* feature or *zoom* and *trace* features of your graphing utility to determine the value of y when $t = 5.8$. Verify your answer algebraically.

(d) Use the *value* feature or *zoom* and *trace* features of your graphing utility to determine the value of y when $t = 2.35$. Verify your answer algebraically.

72. *Consumerism* You purchase a personal watercraft for $8100. The depreciated value y after t years is

$$y = 8100 - 929t, \qquad 0 \le t \le 6.$$

(a) Use the constraints of the model to determine an appropriate viewing window.

(b) Use a graphing utility to graph the equation.

(c) Use the *value* feature or *zoom* and *trace* features of your graphing utility to determine the value of t when $y = 5545.25$. Verify your answer algebraically.

(d) Use the *value* feature or *zoom* and *trace* features of your graphing utility to determine the value of y when $t = 5.5$. Verify your answer algebraically.

73. *Geometry* A rectangle of length x and width w has a perimeter of 12 meters.

(a) Draw a diagram to represent the rectangle. Use the specified variables to label its sides.

(b) Show that $w = 6 - x$ is the width of the rectangle and that $A = x(6 - x)$ is its area.

(c) Use a graphing utility to graph the area equation.

(d) Use the *zoom* and *trace* features of your graphing utility to determine the value of A when $w = 4.9$ meters. Verify your answer algebraically.

(e) From the graph in part (c), estimate the dimensions of the rectangle that yield a maximum area.

74. *Federal Debt* The table shows the per capita U.S. federal debt for several years. (Sources: U.S. Treasury Department; U.S. Bureau of the Census)

Year	1950	1960	1970	1980
Per Capita Debt	$1688	$1572	$1807	$3981

Year	1990	1994	1997	1998
Per Capita Debt	$12,848	$15,750	$20,063	$20,513

A model for the per capita debt during this period is

$$y = 0.223t^3 - 0.733t^2 - 78.255t + 1837.433$$

where y represents the per capita debt and t is the time in years, with $t = 0$ corresponding to 1950.

(a) Use the *value* feature or *zoom* and *trace* features of your graphing utility to find the per capita federal debt in 1975 and 1992. Verify your answers algebraically.

(b) Use your graphing utility to determine during which year the per capita federal debt exceeded $10,200.

(c) Use the model to estimate the per capita federal debt in 2002 and 2004.

75. *Population Statistics* The table gives the life expectancy of a child (at birth) in the United States for selected years from 1920 to 2000. (Source: U.S. National Center for Health Statistics)

Year	1920	1930	1940	1950
Life Expectancy	54.1	59.7	62.9	68.2

Year	1960	1970	1980	1990	2000
Life Expectancy	69.7	70.8	73.7	75.4	76.4

A model for the life expectancy during this period is

$$y = \frac{66.93 + t}{1 + 0.01t}$$

where y represents the life expectancy and t is the time in years, with $t = 0$ corresponding to 1950.

(a) What does the y-intercept of the graph of the model represent?

(b) Use your graphing utility to determine the year when the life expectancy was 73.2. Verify your answer algebraically.

(c) Determine the life expectancy in 1948 both graphically and algebraically.

(d) Use the model to estimate the life expectancy of a child born in 2005.

76. *Finance* The dividends declared per share of Procter & Gamble Company from 1992 to 1998 can be approximated by the model

$$y = 0.464 + 0.091t, \qquad 0 \le t \le 6$$

where y is the dividend (in dollars) and t is the time (in years), with $t = 0$ corresponding to 1992. (Source: Procter & Gamble Company)

(a) Create a table showing the dividends y for the years 1992 through 1998. From your table, determine the year during which the dividend was $0.65.

(b) Use your graphing utility to graph the model.

(c) Verify your answer to part (a) by using the *zoom* and *trace* features of your graphing utility to determine the year when $y = 0.65$.

(d) Determine the value of y in 1997 algebraically.

(e) Use the model to estimate the value of y in 2002.

77. *Copper Wire* The resistance y in ohms of 1000 feet of solid copper wire at 77°F can be approximated by the mathematical model

$$y = \frac{10{,}770}{x^2} - 0.37, \qquad 5 \le x \le 100$$

where x is the diameter of the wire in mils (0.001 in.). (Source: American Wire Gage)

(a) Complete the table.

x	10	20	30	40	50	60	70	80	90	100
y										

(b) Use your table to approximate the value of x when the resistance is 4.8 ohms. Then determine the answer algebraically.

(c) Use the *value* feature or *zoom* and *trace* features of your graphing utility to determine the resistance when $x = 85.5$.

(d) What can you conclude in general about the relationship between the diameter of the copper wire and the resistance?

Synthesis

True or False? **In Exercises 78 and 79, determine whether the statement is true or false. Justify your answer.**

78. A parabola can have only one x-intercept.

79. The graph of a linear equation can have either no x-intercepts or only one x-intercept.

80. *Think About It* Find a and b if the x-intercepts of the graph of $y = (x - a)(x - b)$ are $(-2, 0)$ and $(5, 0)$.

81. *Writing* Explain how to find an appropriate viewing window for the graph of an equation.

Review

In Exercises 82–85, perform the operations and simplify.

82. $7\sqrt{72} - 5\sqrt{18}$

83. $-10\sqrt{25y} - \sqrt{y}$

84. $7^{3/2} \cdot 7^{11/2}$

85. $\dfrac{10^{17/4}}{10^{5/4}}$

In Exercises 86–89, perform the operations and write the result in standard form.

86. $(9x - 4) + (2x^2 - x + 15)$

87. $4x(11 - x + 3x^2)$

88. $(2x + 9)(x - 7)$

89. $(3x^2 - 5)(-x^2 + 1)$

1.2 Lines in the Plane

The Slope of a Line

In this section, you will study lines and their equations. The **slope** of a nonvertical line represents the number of units a line rises or falls vertically for each unit of horizontal change from left to right. For instance, consider the two points (x_1, y_1) and (x_2, y_2) on the line shown in Figure 1.9. As you move from left to right along this line, a change of $(y_2 - y_1)$ units in the vertical direction corresponds to a change of $(x_2 - x_1)$ units in the horizontal direction. That is,

$$y_2 - y_1 = \text{the change in } y$$

and

$$x_2 - x_1 = \text{the change in } x.$$

The slope of the line is given by the ratio of these two changes.

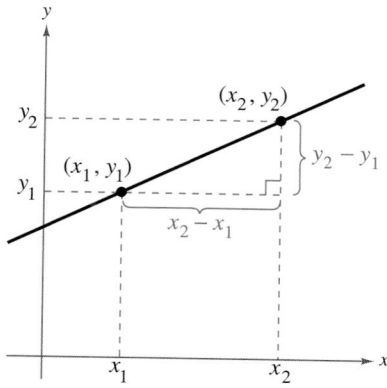

Figure 1.9

What You Should Learn:

- How to find the slopes of lines
- How to write linear equations given points on lines and their slopes
- How to use slope-intercept forms of linear equations to sketch graphs of lines
- How to use slope to identify parallel and perpendicular lines

Why You Should Learn It:

Linear equations can be used to model and solve real-life problems. For instance, Exercise 95 on page 91 shows how to use a linear equation to model the average annual salaries of Major League Baseball players from 1988 to 1998.

Allsport

Definition of the Slope of a Line

The **slope** m of the nonvertical line through (x_1, y_1) and (x_2, y_2) is

$$m = \frac{y_2 - y_1}{x_2 - x_1} = \frac{\text{change in } y}{\text{change in } x}$$

where $x_1 \neq x_2$.

When this formula is used, the *order of subtraction* is important. Given two points on a line, you are free to label either one of them as (x_1, y_1) and the other as (x_2, y_2). However, once this has been done, you must form the numerator and denominator using the same order of subtraction.

$$m = \frac{y_2 - y_1}{x_2 - x_1}$$
Correct

$$m = \frac{y_1 - y_2}{x_1 - x_2}$$
Correct

$$m = \frac{y_2 - y_1}{x_1 - x_2}$$
Incorrect

Throughout this text, the term *line* always means a *straight* line.

EXAMPLE 1   Finding the Slope of a Line

Find the slope of the line passing through each pair of points.

a. $(-2, 0)$ and $(3, 1)$ **b.** $(-1, 2)$ and $(2, 2)$ **c.** $(0, 4)$ and $(1, -1)$

Solution

Difference in *y*-values

a. $m = \dfrac{y_2 - y_1}{x_2 - x_1} = \dfrac{1 - 0}{3 - (-2)} = \dfrac{1}{3 + 2} = \dfrac{1}{5}$

Difference in *x*-values

b. $m = \dfrac{2 - 2}{2 - (-1)} = \dfrac{0}{3} = 0$

c. $m = \dfrac{-1 - 4}{1 - 0} = \dfrac{-5}{1} = -5$

The graphs of the three lines are shown in Figure 1.10. Note that the square setting gives the correct "steepness" of the lines.

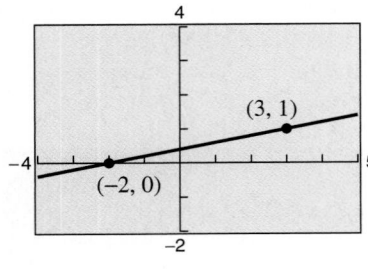
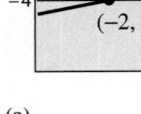
(a)

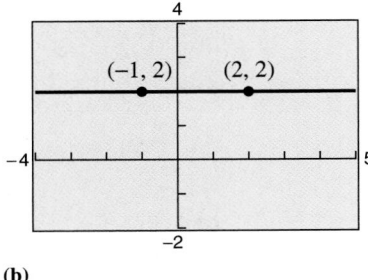
(b)

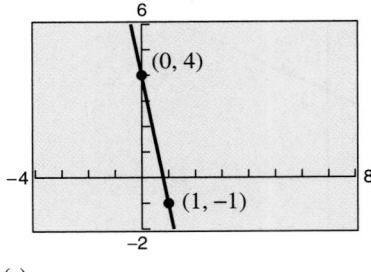
(c)

Figure 1.10

The definition of slope does not apply to vertical lines. For instance, consider the points $(3, 4)$ and $(3, 1)$ on the vertical line shown in Figure 1.11. Applying the formula for slope, you obtain

$$m = \frac{4 - 1}{3 - 3} = \frac{3}{0}. \qquad \text{Undefined}$$

Because division by zero is undefined, the slope of a vertical line is undefined.

From the slopes of the lines shown in Figures 1.10 and 1.11, you can make the following generalizations about the slope of a line.

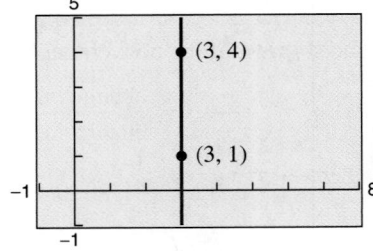
Figure 1.11

The Slope of a Line

1. A line with positive slope $(m > 0)$ *rises* from left to right.
2. A line with negative slope $(m < 0)$ *falls* from left to right.
3. A line with zero slope $(m = 0)$ is *horizontal*.
4. A line with undefined slope is *vertical*.

Exploration

Use a graphing utility to compare the slopes of the lines $y = 0.5x$, $y = x$, $y = 2x$, and $y = 4x$. What do you observe about these lines? Compare the slopes of the lines $y = -0.5x$, $y = -x$, $y = -2x$, and $y = -4x$. What do you observe about these lines? (*Hint:* Use a square setting to guarantee a true geometric perspective.)

Common Error

A common error when finding the slope of a line is combining *x* and *y* coordinates in either the numerator or denominator, as in

$$m = \frac{y_2 - x_1}{x_2 - y_1}.$$

Point out to your students that the vertical line shown in Figure 1.11 must be drawn on a graphing utility with a special command because there is no way to express the line's equation in the $y =$ format.

The Point-Slope Form of the Equation of a Line

If you know the slope of a line *and* you also know the coordinates of one point on the line, you can find an equation for the line. For instance, in Figure 1.12, let (x_1, y_1) be a given point on the line whose slope is m. If (x, y) is any *other* point on the line, it follows that

$$\frac{y - y_1}{x - x_1} = m.$$

This equation in the variables x and y can be rewritten in the **point-slope form** of the equation of a line.

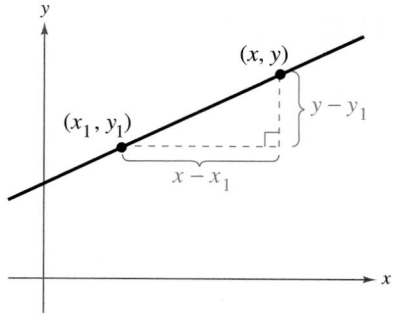

Figure 1.12

Point-Slope Form of the Equation of a Line

The **point-slope form** of the equation of the line that passes through the point (x_1, y_1) and has a slope of m is

$$y - y_1 = m(x - x_1).$$

EXAMPLE 2   The Point-Slope Form of the Equation of a Line

Find an equation of the line that passes through the point $(1, -2)$ and has a slope of 3.

Solution

$$y - y_1 = m(x - x_1) \qquad \text{Point-slope form}$$
$$y - (-2) = 3(x - 1) \qquad \text{Substitute for } y_1, m, \text{ and } x_1.$$
$$y + 2 = 3x - 3$$
$$y = 3x - 5$$

This line is shown in Figure 1.13.

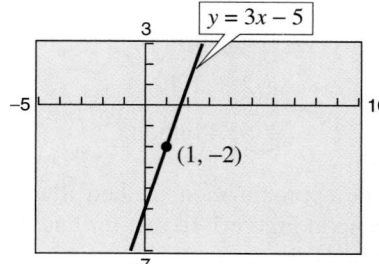

Figure 1.13

The point-slope form can be used to find an equation of a nonvertical line passing through two points (x_1, y_1) and (x_2, y_2). First, use the formula for the slope of the line passing through two points.

$$m = \frac{y_2 - y_1}{x_2 - x_1}$$

Then, once you know the slope, use the point-slope form to obtain the equation

$$y - y_1 = m(x - x_1)$$
$$= \frac{y_2 - y_1}{x_2 - x_1}(x - x_1).$$

This is sometimes called the **two-point form** of the equation of a line.

EXAMPLE 3   A Linear Model for Sales Prediction

During 1997, Barnes & Noble's net sales were $2.8 billion, and in 1998 net sales were $3.0 billion.   (Source: Barnes & Noble, Inc.)

a. Write a linear equation giving the net sales y in terms of the year x.

b. Use the equation to estimate the net sales during 2000.

Solution

a. Let $x = 7$ represent 1997. In Figure 1.14, let $(7, 2.8)$ and $(8, 3.0)$ be two points on the line representing the net sales. The slope of the line passing through these two points is

$$m = \frac{3.0 - 2.8}{8 - 7} = 0.2. \qquad m = \frac{y_2 - y_1}{x_2 - x_1}$$

By the point-slope form, the equation of the line is as follows.

$$y - y_1 = m(x - x_1) \qquad \text{Point-slope form}$$

$$y - 2.8 = 0.2(x - 7) \qquad \text{Substitute for } y_1, m, \text{ and } x_1.$$

$$y = 0.2x - 1.4 + 2.8$$

$$y = 0.2x + 1.4 \qquad \text{Simplify.}$$

b. Using the equation from part (a), estimate the 2000 net sales $(x = 10)$ to be

$$y = 0.2(10) + 1.4$$

$$= 2 + 1.4$$

$$= \$3.4 \text{ billion.}$$

The approximation method illustrated in Example 3 is **linear extrapolation.** Note in Figure 1.15 that for linear extrapolation, the estimated point lies *outside* of the given points. When the estimated point lies *between* two given points, the procedure is called **linear interpolation.**

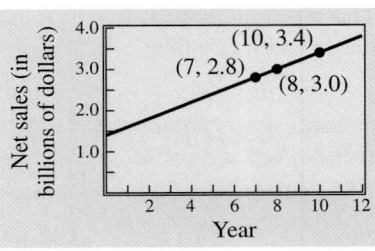

Figure 1.14

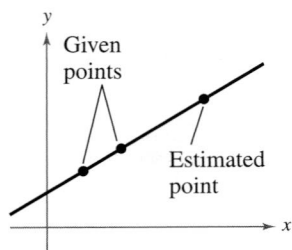

Linear Extrapolation
Figure 1.15

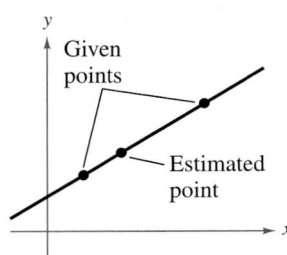

Linear Interpolation

Library of Functions

In the next section, you will be introduced to the precise meaning of the term *function*. The simplest type of function is a linear function and has the form

$$y = mx + b.$$

As its name implies, the graph of a linear function is a line that has a slope of m and a y-intercept at $(0, b)$.

Consult the Library of Functions Summary inside the front cover for a description of the linear function.

Sketching Graphs of Lines

Many problems in coordinate geometry can be classified as follows.

1. Given a graph (or parts of it), find its equation.

2. Given an equation, sketch its graph.

For lines, the first problem is solved easily by using the point-slope form. This formula, however, is not particularly useful for solving the second type of problem. The form that is better suited to graphing linear equations is the **slope-intercept form,** $y = mx + b$, of the equation of a line.

Slope-Intercept Form of the Equation of a Line

The graph of the equation

$$y = mx + b$$

is a line whose slope is m and whose y-intercept is $(0, b)$.

A computer simulation of this concept appears in the *Interactive* CD-ROM and *Internet* versions of this text.

EXAMPLE 4   Using the Slope-Intercept Form

Determine the slope and y-intercept of each linear equation. Then describe its graph.

a. $x + y = 2$ **b.** $y = 2$

Algebraic Solution

a. Begin by writing the equation in slope-intercept form.

$$x + y = 2 \qquad \text{Write original equation.}$$

$$y = 2 - x \qquad \text{Subtract } x \text{ from each side.}$$

$$y = -x + 2 \qquad \text{Slope-intercept form}$$

From the slope-intercept form of the equation, the slope is -1 and the y-intercept is $(0, 2)$. Because the slope is negative, you know that the graph of the equation is a line that falls one unit for every unit it moves to the right.

b. By writing the equation $y = 2$ in slope-intercept form

$$y = (0)x + 2$$

you can see that the slope is 0 and the y-intercept is $(0, 2)$. A zero slope implies that the line is horizontal.

Graphical Solution

a. Solve the equation for y to obtain $y = 2 - x$. Enter this equation in your graphing utility. Use a decimal viewing window to graph the equation as shown in Figure 1.16(a).

To find the y-intercept, use the *value* or *trace* feature. When $x = 0$, $y = 2$. So, the y-intercept is $(0, 2)$. To find the slope, continue to use the *trace* feature. Move the cursor along the line until $x = 1$. At this point, $y = 1$. So the graph falls 1 unit for every unit it moves to the right, and the slope is -1.

b. Enter the equation $y = 2$ in your graphing utility and graph the equation as shown in Figure 1.16(b). Use the *trace* feature to verify the y-intercept $(0, 2)$ and to see that the value of y is the same for all values of x. So, the slope of the horizontal line is 0.

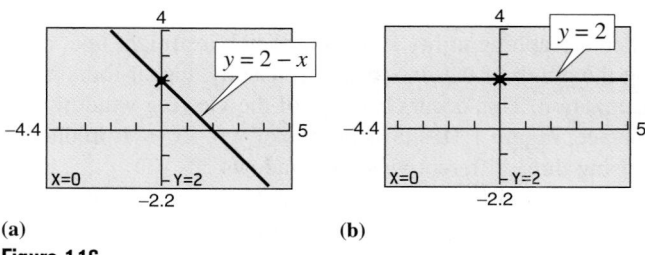

(a)   (b)

Figure 1.16

From the slope-intercept form of the equation of a line, you can see that a horizontal line ($m = 0$) has an equation of the form $y = b$. This is consistent with the fact that each point on a horizontal line through $(0, b)$ has a y-coordinate of b.

Similarly, each point on a vertical line through $(a, 0)$ has an x-coordinate of a. So, a vertical line has an equation of the form $x = a$. This equation cannot be written in the slope-intercept form, because the slope of a vertical line is undefined. However, *every* line has an equation that can be written in the **general form**

$$Ax + By + C = 0 \qquad \text{General form of the equation of a line}$$

where A and B are not *both* zero.

Summary of Equations of Lines

1. General form: $Ax + By + C = 0$
2. Vertical line: $x = a$
3. Horizontal line: $y = b$
4. Slope-intercept form: $y = mx + b$
5. Point-slope form: $y - y_1 = m(x - x_1)$

EXAMPLE 5   Different Viewing Windows

The graphs of the two lines

$$y = -x - 1 \qquad \text{and} \qquad y = -10x - 1$$

are shown in Figure 1.17. Even though the slopes of these lines are quite different (-1 and -10, respectively), the graphs seem misleadingly similar because the viewing windows are different.

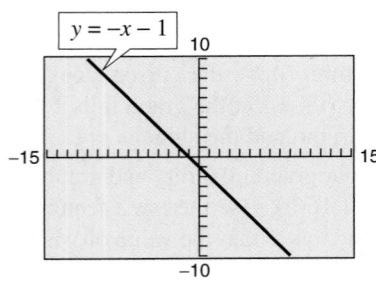
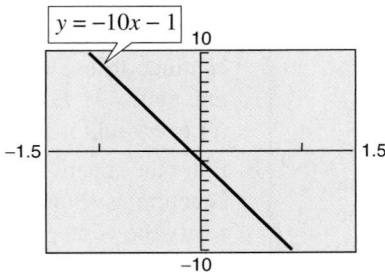

Figure 1.17

When a graphing utility is used to sketch a straight line, it is important to realize that the graph of the line may not visually appear to have the slope indicated by its equation. This occurs because of the viewing window used for the graph. For instance, Figure 1.18 shows graphs of $y = 2x + 1$ produced on a graphing utility using three different viewing windows.

Notice that the slopes in Figure 1.18(a) and (b) do not visually appear to be equal to 2. However, if you use the *square* viewing window, as in Figure 1.18(c), the slope visually appears to be 2. In general, two graphs of the same equation can appear to be quite different depending on the viewing window selected.

Exploration

Graph the lines $y = 2x + 1$, $y = \frac{1}{2}x + 1$, and $y = -2x + 1$ in the same viewing window. What do you observe?

Graph the lines $y = 2x + 1$, $y = 2x$, and $y = 2x - 1$ in the same viewing window. What do

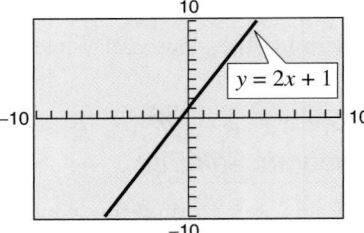

(a)

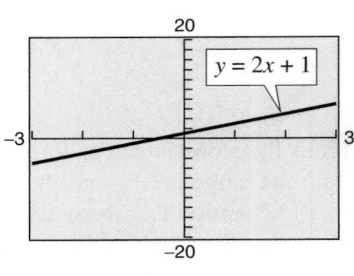

(b)

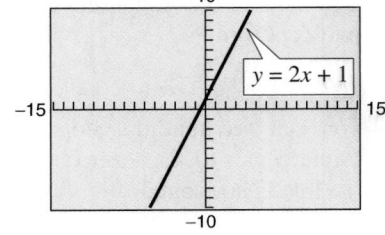

(c)

Figure 1.18

Parallel and Perpendicular Lines

The slope of a line is a convenient tool for determining whether two lines are parallel or perpendicular.

Parallel Lines

Two distinct nonvertical lines are **parallel** if and only if their slopes are equal.

EXAMPLE 6 Equations of Parallel Lines

Find the slope-intercept form of the equation of the line that passes through the point $(2, -1)$ and is parallel to the line $2x - 3y = 5$.

Solution

Begin by finding the slope of the given line.

$2x - 3y = 5$ Write original equation.

$-2x + 3y = -5$ Multiply by -1.

$3y = 2x - 5$ Add $2x$ to each side.

$y = \dfrac{2}{3}x - \dfrac{5}{3}$ Write in slope-intercept form.

Therefore, the given line has a slope of $m = \frac{2}{3}$. Because any line parallel to the given line must also have a slope of $\frac{2}{3}$, the required line through $(2, -1)$ has the following equation.

$y - (-1) = \dfrac{2}{3}(x - 2)$ Substitute for m, x_1, and y_1 in point-slope form.

$y + 1 = \dfrac{2}{3}x - \dfrac{4}{3}$ Simplify.

$y = \dfrac{2}{3}x - \dfrac{4}{3} - 1$ Subtract 1 from each side.

$y = \dfrac{2}{3}x - \dfrac{7}{3}$ Write in slope-intercept form.

Notice the similarity between the slope-intercept form of the original equation and the slope-intercept form of the parallel equation. The graphs of both equations are shown in Figure 1.19.

Perpendicular Lines

Two nonvertical lines are **perpendicular** if and only if their slopes are negative reciprocals of each other. That is,

$$m_1 = -\dfrac{1}{m_2}.$$

Be careful when you graph equations such as $y = \frac{2}{3}x - \frac{7}{3}$ on your graphing utility. A common mistake is to type it in as

Y1 = 2/3X − 7/3,

which may not be interpreted as the original equation by your graphing utility. You should use one of the following formulas.

Y1 = 2X/3 − 7/3

Y1 = (2/3)X − 7/3

Do you see why?

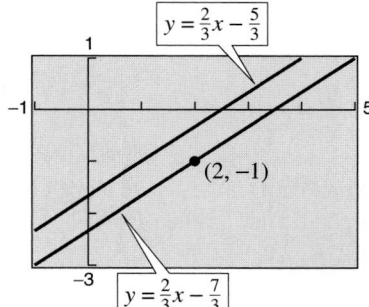

Figure 1.19

Activities

1. Write an equation of the line that passes through the points $(-2, 1)$ and $(3, 2)$.

   Answer: $x - 5y + 7 = 0$

2. Find the slope of the line that is perpendicular to the line $4x - 7y = 12$.

   Answer: $m = -\frac{7}{4}$

3. Write the equation of the vertical line that passes through the point $(3, 2)$.

   Answer: $x = 3$

EXAMPLE 7   Equations of Perpendicular Lines

Find an equation of the line that passes through the point $(2, -1)$ and is perpendicular to the line $2x - 3y = 5$.

Solution

By writing the given line in the form $y = \frac{2}{3}x - \frac{5}{3}$, you can see that the line has a slope of $\frac{2}{3}$. So, any line that is perpendicular to this line must have a slope of $-\frac{3}{2}$ (because $-\frac{3}{2}$ is the negative reciprocal of $\frac{2}{3}$). Therefore, the required line through the point $(2, -1)$ has the following equation.

$$y - (-1) = -\frac{3}{2}(x - 2)$$ Substitute for m, x_1, and y_1 in point-slope form.

$$y + 1 = -\frac{3}{2}x + 3$$ Simplify.

$$y = -\frac{3}{2}x + 3 - 1$$ Subtract 1 from each side.

$$y = -\frac{3}{2}x + 2$$ Slope-intercept form

The graphs of both equations are shown in Figure 1.20.

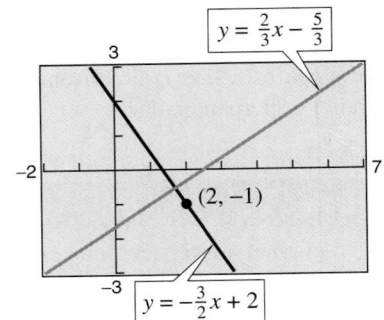

Figure 1.20

EXAMPLE 8   Graphs of Perpendicular Lines

Use a graphing utility to graph the lines

$$y = x + 1$$

and

$$y = -x + 3.$$

Display *both* graphs in the same viewing window. The lines are supposed to be perpendicular (they have slopes of $m_1 = 1$ and $m_2 = -1$). Do they appear to be perpendicular on the display?

Solution

If the viewing window is nonsquare, as in Figure 1.21(a), the two lines will not appear perpendicular. If, however, the viewing window is square, as in Figure 1.21(b), the lines will appear perpendicular.

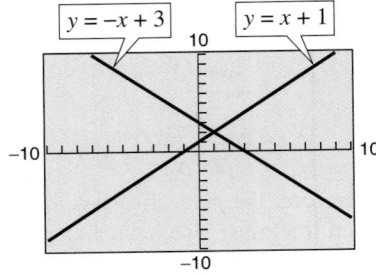

(a)

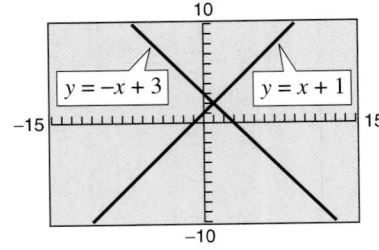

(b)
Figure 1.21

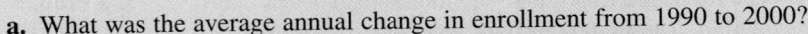

Writing About Math   *An Application of Slope*

In 1990, a college had an enrollment of 5500 students. By 2000, the enrollment had increased to 7000 students.

a. What was the average annual change in enrollment from 1990 to 2000?

b. Use the average annual change in enrollment to estimate the enrollments in 1993, 1997, and 1999.

c. Write the equation of the line that represents the data in part (b). What is its slope? Interpret the slope in the context of the problem.

d. Write a short paragraph discussing the concepts of *slope* and *average rate of change*.

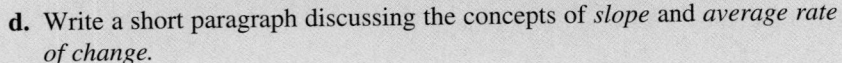

1.2 E x e r c i s e s

In Exercises 1 and 2, identify the line that has the specified slope.

1. (a) $m = \frac{2}{3}$ (b) m is undefined. (c) $m = -2$

2. (a) $m = 0$ (b) $m = -\frac{3}{4}$ (c) $m = 1$

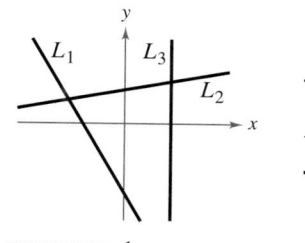

FIGURE FOR 1

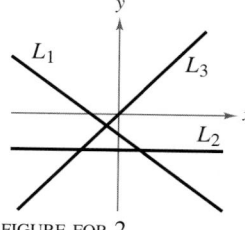

FIGURE FOR 2

In Exercises 3 and 4, sketch the line through the point with each indicated slope on the same set of coordinate axes.

Point			*Slopes*	
3. $(2, 3)$	(a) 0	(b) 1	(c) 2	(d) -3
4. $(-4, 1)$	(a) 3	(b) -3	(c) $\frac{1}{2}$	(d) Undefined

In Exercises 5–10, estimate the slope of the line.

5.

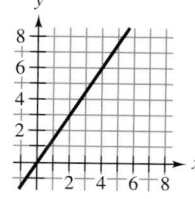

6.

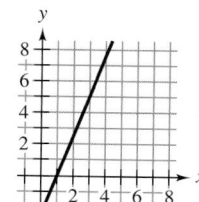

7.

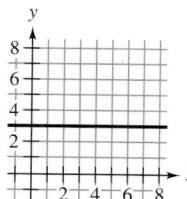

8.

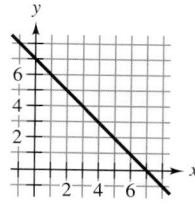

9.

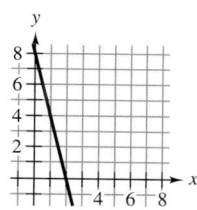

10.

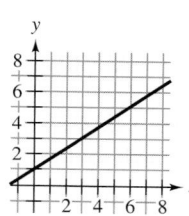

In Exercises 11–14, plot the points and find the slope of the line passing through the points. Verify the slope using the *draw* feature on your graphing utility to graph the line segment connecting the two points. (Use a square setting.)

11. $(0, -10), (-4, 0)$ **12.** $(2, 4), (4, -4)$

13. $(-6, -1), (-6, 4)$ **14.** $(-3, -2), (1, 6)$

In Exercises 15–20, you are given the slope of the line and a point on the line. Find three additional points through which the line passes. (There are many correct answers.)

	Point	*Slope*
15.	$(2, 1)$	$m = 0$
16.	$(-4, 1)$	m is undefined.
17.	$(-5, 4)$	$m = 2$
18.	$(0, -9)$	$m = -2$
19.	$(7, -2)$	$m = \frac{1}{2}$
20.	$(-1, -6)$	$m = -\frac{1}{2}$

In Exercises 21–24, determine whether the lines L_1 and L_2 passing through the pairs of points are parallel, perpendicular, or neither. Use a graphing utility to graph the line segments connecting the pairs of points on the respective lines. (Use a square setting.)

21. $L_1: (0, -1), (5, 9)$ **22.** $L_1: (-2, -1), (1, 5)$
   $L_2: (0, 3), (4, 1)$ $L_2: (1, 3), (5, -5)$

23. $L_1: (3, 6), (-6, 0)$ **24.** $L_1: (4, 8), (-4, 2)$
   $L_2: (0, -1), \left(5, \frac{7}{3}\right)$ $L_2: (3, -5), \left(-1, \frac{1}{3}\right)$

In Exercises 25–32, (a) find the slope and y-intercept (if possible) of the equation of the line algebraically, (b) sketch the line by hand, and (c) use a graphing utility to verify your answers to parts (a) and (b).

25. $5x - y + 3 = 0$ **26.** $2x + 3y - 9 = 0$

27. $5x - 2 = 0$ **28.** $3x + 7 = 0$

29. $3y + 5 = 0$ **30.** $-11 - 8y = 0$

31. $7x + 6y - 30 = 0$ **32.** $x - y - 10 = 0$

In Exercises 33–42, find the general form of the equation of the line that passes through the given point and has the indicated slope. Sketch the line by hand. Use a graphing utility to verify your sketch.

Point	Slope
33. $(0, -2)$	$m = 3$
34. $(0, 10)$	$m = -1$
35. $(-3, 6)$	$m = -2$
36. $(0, 0)$	$m = 4$
37. $(4, 0)$	$m = -\frac{1}{3}$
38. $(-2, -5)$	$m = \frac{3}{4}$
39. $(6, -1)$	m is undefined.
40. $(-10, 4)$	$m = 0$
41. $\left(-\frac{1}{2}, \frac{3}{2}\right)$	$m = -3$
42. $(2.3, -8.5)$	$m = -\frac{5}{2}$

In Exercises 43–52, find the general form of the equation of the line that passes through the points. Use a graphing utility to sketch the line.

43. $(5, -1), (-5, 5)$ **44.** $(4, 3), (-4, -4)$

45. $(-8, 1), (-8, 7)$ **46.** $(-1, 4), (6, 4)$

47. $\left(2, \frac{1}{2}\right), \left(\frac{1}{2}, \frac{5}{4}\right)$ **48.** $\left(1, 1\right), \left(6, -\frac{2}{3}\right)$

49. $\left(-\frac{1}{10}, -\frac{3}{5}\right), \left(\frac{9}{10}, -\frac{9}{5}\right)$ **50.** $\left(\frac{3}{4}, \frac{3}{2}\right), \left(-\frac{4}{3}, \frac{7}{4}\right)$

51. $(1, 0.6), (-2, -0.6)$ **52.** $(-8, 0.6), (2, -2.4)$

Exploration   In Exercises 53 and 54, use the values of a and b and a graphing utility to graph the equation of the line

$$\frac{x}{a} + \frac{y}{b} = 1, \qquad a \neq 0, b \neq 0.$$

Use the graphs to make a conjecture about what a and b represent. Verify your conjecture.

53. $a = 5, \quad b = -3$ **54.** $a = -6, \quad b = 2$

In Exercises 55–58, use the results of Exercises 53 and 54 to write an equation of the line that passes through the points.

55. x-intercept: $(2, 0)$
    y-intercept: $(0, 3)$

56. x-intercept: $(-5, 0)$
    y-intercept: $(0, -4)$

57. x-intercept: $\left(-\frac{1}{6}, 0\right)$
    y-intercept: $\left(0, -\frac{2}{3}\right)$

58. x-intercept: $\left(\frac{3}{4}, 0\right)$
    y-intercept: $\left(0, \frac{4}{5}\right)$

In Exercises 59 and 60, use a graphing utility to graph the equation using each of the suggested viewing windows. Describe the difference between the two graphs.

59. $y = 0.5x - 3$

Xmin = -5	Xmin = -2
Xmax = 10	Xmax = 10
Xscl = 1	Xscl = 1
Ymin = -1	Ymin = -4
Ymax = 10	Ymax = 1
Yscl = 1	Yscl = 1

60. $y = -8x + 5$

Xmin = -5	Xmin = -5
Xmax = 5	Xmax = 10
Xscl = 1	Xscl = 1
Ymin = -10	Ymin = -80
Ymax = 10	Ymax = 80
Yscl = 1	Yscl = 20

Graphical Analysis   In Exercises 61–64, use a graphing utility to graph the three equations in the same viewing window. Adjust the viewing window so that the slope appears visually correct. Identify any relationships that exist among the lines. Use the slope of the lines to verify your results.

61. (a) $y = 2x$ (b) $y = -2x$ (c) $y = \frac{1}{2}x$

62. (a) $y = \frac{2}{3}x$ (b) $y = -\frac{3}{2}x$ (c) $y = \frac{2}{3}x + 2$

63. (a) $y = -\frac{1}{2}x$ (b) $y = -\frac{1}{2}x + 3$ (c) $y = 2x - 4$

64. (a) $y = x - 8$ (b) $y = x + 1$ (c) $y = -x + 3$

In Exercises 65–70, write equations of the lines through the given point (a) parallel to the given line and (b) perpendicular to the given line.

Point	Line
65. $(2, 1)$	$4x - 2y = 3$
66. $(-3, 2)$	$x + y = 7$
67. $\left(-\frac{2}{3}, \frac{7}{8}\right)$	$3x + 4y = 7$
68. $\left(\frac{7}{8}, \frac{3}{4}\right)$	$5x + 3y = 0$
69. $(2.5, 6.8)$	$x - y = 4$
70. $(-3.9, -1.4)$	$6x + 2y = 9$

In Exercises 71 and 72, find a relationship between x and y such that (x, y) is equidistant from the two points.

71. $(4, -1), (-2, 3)$ **72.** $(3, -2), (-7, 1)$

73. *Business* The slopes are the slopes of lines representing annual sales y in terms of time x in years. Use each slope to interpret any change in annual sales for a 1-year increase in time.

(a) The line has a slope of $m = 135$.

(b) The line has a slope of $m = 0$.

(c) The line has a slope of $m = -40$.

74. *Business* The slopes are the slopes of lines representing daily revenues y in terms of time x in days. Use each slope to interpret any change in daily revenues for a 1-day increase in time.

(a) The line has a slope of $m = 400$.

(b) The line has a slope of $m = 100$.

(c) The line has a slope of $m = 0$.

75. *Business* The graph shows the earnings per share of stock for the Kellogg Company for the years 1988 through 1998. (Source: Kellogg Company)

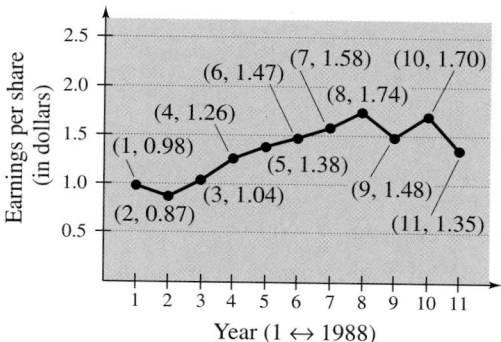

(a) Use the slopes to determine the year(s) when the earnings per share showed the greatest increase and decrease.

(b) Find the equation of the line between the years 1988 and 1998.

(c) Interpret the meaning of the slope in the equation from part (b) in the context of the problem.

(d) Use the equation from part (b) to estimate the earnings per share of stock for the year 2001. Do you think this is an accurate estimation? Explain.

76. *Business* The graph shows the dividends declared per share of stock for the Colgate-Palmolive Company for the years 1988 through 1998. (Source: Colgate-Palmolive Company)

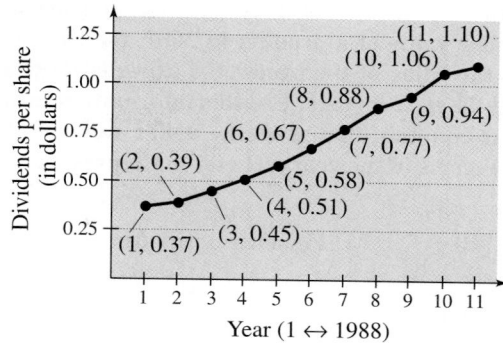

(a) Use the slopes to determine the years when the dividends declared per share showed the greatest increase and the smallest increase.

(b) Find the equation of the line between the years 1988 and 1998.

(c) Interpret the meaning of the slope in the equation from part (b) in the context of the problem.

(d) Use the equation from part (b) to estimate the dividends declared per share for the year 2001. Do you think this is an accurate estimation? Explain.

77. *Driving* When driving down a mountain road, you notice warning signs indicating that it is a "12% grade." This means that the slope of the road is $-\frac{12}{100}$. Approximate the amount of horizontal change in your position if you note from elevation markers that you have descended 2000 feet vertically.

78. *Attic Height* The "rise to run" ratio of the roof of a house determines the steepness of the roof. Suppose the rise to run ratio of a roof is 3 to 4. Determine the maximum height in the attic of the house if the house is 32 feet wide.

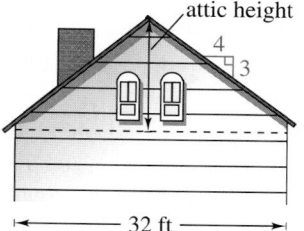

Rate of Change   In Exercises 79–82, you are given the dollar value of a product in 2001 and the rate at which the value of the product is expected to change during the next 5 years. Use this information to write a linear equation that gives the dollar value V of the item in terms of the year t. (Let $t = 1$ represent 2001.)

	2001 Value	Rate
79.	$2540	$125 increase per year
80.	$156	$4.50 increase per year
81.	$20,400	$2000 decrease per year
82.	$245,000	$5600 decrease per year

Graphical Interpretation   In Exercises 83–86, match the description with its graph. Also determine the slope and how it is interpreted in the situation. [The graphs are labeled (a), (b), (c), and (d).]

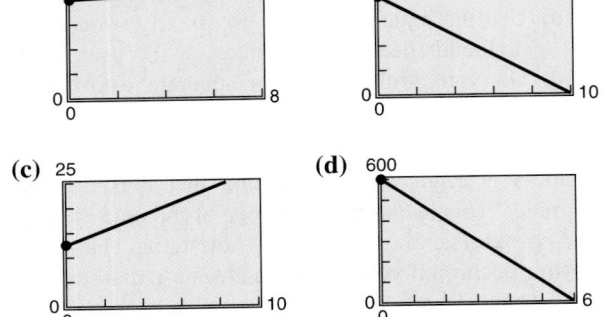

83. A person is paying $10 per week to a friend to repay a $100 loan.

84. An employee is paid $12.50 per hour plus $1.50 for each unit produced per hour.

85. A sales representative receives $20 per day for food plus $0.25 for each mile traveled.

86. A word processor that was purchased for $600 depreciates $100 per year.

87. *Temperature*   Find the equation of the line that shows the relationship between the temperature in degrees Celsius C and degrees Fahrenheit F. Remember that water freezes at 0°C (32°F) and boils at 100°C (212°F).

88. *Temperature*   Use the result of Exercise 87 to complete the table.

C		$-10°$	$10°$			177°
F	0°			68°	90°	

89. *Finance*   Your salary was $28,500 in 1998 and $32,900 in 2000. If your salary follows a linear growth pattern, what will your salary be in 2003?

90. *College Enrollment*   A small college had 2546 students in 1998 and 2702 students in 2000. If the enrollment follows a linear growth pattern, how many students will the college have in 2004?

91. *Business*   A small business purchases a fax machine for $875. After 5 years, the fax machine will be outdated and have no value.

(a) Write a linear equation giving the value V of the fax machine during the 5 years it will be used.

(b) Use a graphing utility to graph the linear equation representing the depreciation of the fax machine, and use the *value* or *trace* feature to complete the table.

t	0	1	2	3	4	5
V						

(c) Verify your answers in part (b) algebraically by using the equation you found in part (a).

92. *Business*   A small business purchases a computer network system for $25,000. After 10 years, the system will have to be replaced. Its value at that time is expected to be $2000.

(a) Write a linear equation giving the value V of the system during the 10 years it will be used.

(b) Use a graphing utility to graph the linear equation representing the depreciation of the system, and use the *value* or *trace* feature to complete the table.

t	0	1	2	3	4	5	6	7	8	9	10
V											

(c) Verify your answers in part (b) algebraically by using the equation you found in part (a).

93. *Business*   A contractor purchases a bulldozer for $36,500. The bulldozer requires an average expenditure of $5.25 per hour for fuel and maintenance, and the operator is paid $11.50 per hour.

(a) Write a linear equation giving the total cost C of operating the bulldozer for t hours. (Include the purchase cost of the bulldozer.)

(b) Assuming that customers are charged $27 per hour of bulldozer use, write an equation for the revenue R derived from t hours of use.

(c) Use the formula for profit ($P = R - C$) to write an equation for the profit derived from t hours of use.

(d) Use the result of part (c) to find the break-even point (the number of hours the bulldozer must be used to yield a profit of 0 dollars).

94. *Real Estate Purchase* A real estate office handles an apartment complex with 50 units. When the rent per unit is $580 per month, all 50 units are occupied. However, when the rent is $625 per month, the average number of occupied units drops to 47. Assume that the relationship between the monthly rent p and the demand x is linear.

(a) Write the equation of the line giving the demand x in terms of the rent p.

(b) Use a graphing utility to graph the demand equation and use the *trace* feature to estimate the number of units occupied if the rent is raised to $655. Verify your answer algebraically.

(c) Use the demand equation to estimate the number of units occupied if the rent is lowered to $595. Verify your answer graphically.

95. *Sports* The average annual salaries of Major League Baseball players (in thousands of dollars) from 1988 to 1998 are shown in the scatter plot. Let y represent the average salary and let t represent the year, with $t = 0$ corresponding to 1988. (Source: Major League Baseball Player Relations Committee)

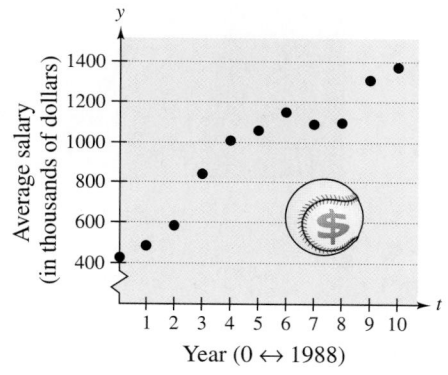

(a) Use the regression capabilities of a graphing utility to find the line that best fits the data.

(b) Use the regression line to estimate the average salary in the year 2000.

(c) Interpret the meaning of the slope of the regression line.

Synthesis

True or False? **In Exercises 96 and 97, determine whether the statement is true or false. Justify your answer.**

96. The line through $(-8, 2)$ and $(-1, 4)$ and the line through $(0, -4)$ and $(-7, 7)$ are parallel.

97. If the points $(10, -3)$ and $(2, -9)$ lie on the same line, then the point $\left(-12, -\frac{37}{2}\right)$ also lies on that line.

98. *Writing* Explain how you could show that the points $A(2, 3)$, $B(2, 9)$, and $C(7, 3)$ are the vertices of a right triangle.

99. *Think About It* The slopes of two lines are -4 and $\frac{5}{2}$. Which is steeper?

100. *Writing* Write a brief paragraph explaining whether or not any pair of points on a line can be used to calculate the slope of the line.

101. *Think About It* Is it possible for two lines with positive slopes to be perpendicular? Explain.

Review

In Exercises 102–107, determine whether the expression is a polynomial. If it is, write the polynomial in standard form.

102. $x + 20$

103. $3x - 10x^2 + 1$

104. $4x^2 + x^{-1} - 3$

105. $2x^2 - 2x^4 - x^3 + 2$

106. $\dfrac{x^2 + 3x + 4}{x^2 - 9}$

107. $\sqrt{x^2 + 7x + 6}$

In Exercises 108–111, factor the trinomial.

108. $x^2 - 6x - 27$

109. $x^2 - 11x + 28$

110. $2x^2 + 11x - 40$

111. $3x^2 - 16x + 5$

In Exercises 112–115, find the standard form of the equation of the specified circle.

112. Center: $(0, 0)$; radius: 9

113. Center: $(-8, -5)$; radius: $\frac{3}{4}$

114. Center: $(10, 1)$; solution point: $(-2, -4)$

115. Endpoints of a diameter: $(6, -5)$, $(-2, 7)$

1.3 Functions

Introduction to Functions

Many everyday phenomena involve pairs of quantities that are related to each other by some rule of correspondence. The mathematical term for such a rule of correspondence is a **relation.** Here are two examples.

1. The simple interest I earned on an investment of $1000 for 1 year is related to the annual interest rate r by the formula $I = 1000r$.

2. The area A of a circle is related to its radius r by the formula $A = \pi r^2$.

Not all relations have simple mathematical formulas. For instance, people commonly match up NFL starting quarterbacks with touchdown passes, and hours of the day with temperature. In each of these cases, however, there is some relation that matches each item from one set with exactly one item from a different set. Such a relation is called a **function.**

Definition of a Function

A **function** f from a set A to a set B is a relation that assigns to each element x in the set A exactly one element y in the set B. The set A is the **domain** (or set of inputs) of the function f, and the set B contains the **range** (or set of outputs).

To help understand this definition, look at the function in Figure 1.22.

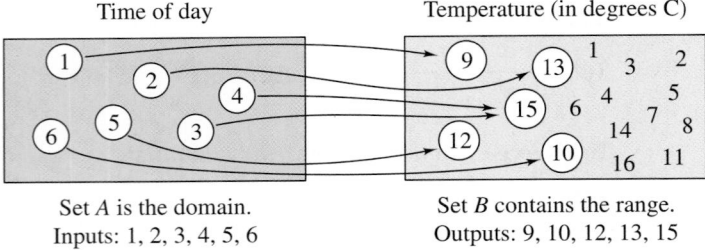

Time of day   Temperature (in degrees C)

Set A is the domain.   Set B contains the range.
Inputs: 1, 2, 3, 4, 5, 6   Outputs: 9, 10, 12, 13, 15

Figure 1.22

This function can be represented by the ordered pairs $\{(1, 9°), (2, 13°), (3, 15°), (4, 15°), (5, 12°), (6, 10°)\}$. In each ordered pair, the first coordinate is the **input** and the second coordinate is the **output.** In this example, note the following characteristics of a function.

1. Each element in A must be matched with an element of B.

2. Some elements in B may not be matched with any element in A.

3. Two or more elements of A may be matched with the same element of B.

The converse of the third statement is not true. That is, an element of A (the domain) cannot be matched with two different elements of B. In other words, each element of A must be matched with only one element of B.

What You Should Learn:

- How to decide whether relations between two variables are functions
- How to use function notation and evaluate functions
- How to find the domains of functions
- How to use functions to model and solve real-life problems

Why You Should Learn It:

Many natural phenomena can be modeled by functions, such as the force of water against the face of a dam, in Exercise 100 on page 104.

Kunio Owaki/The Stock Market

Functions are commonly represented in four ways.

1. *Verbally* by a sentence that describes how the input variable is related to the output variable
2. *Numerically* by a table or a list of ordered pairs that matches input values with output values
3. *Graphically* by points on a graph in a coordinate plane in which the input values are represented by the horizontal axis and the output values are represented by the vertical axis
4. *Algebraically* by an equation in two variables

In the following example, you are asked to decide whether the given relation is a function. To do this, you must decide whether each input value is matched with exactly one output value. If any input value is matched with two or more output values, the relation is not a function.

Library of Functions

Many functions do not have simple mathematical formulas but are defined by real-life data. Such functions arise when you are using collections of data to model real-life applications. You will see that it is often convenient to approximate the data using a mathematical model or formula.

Consult the Library of Functions Summary inside the front cover for a description of functions used to model data.

EXAMPLE 1   Testing for Functions

Decide whether the description represents y as a function of x.

a. The input value x is the number of representatives from a state and the output value y is the number of senators.

Have your students pay special attention to the concepts of *function*, *domain*, and *range*, because they will be used throughout the text and in calculus.

b.

Input x	2	2	3	4	5
Output y	11	10	8	5	1

c.

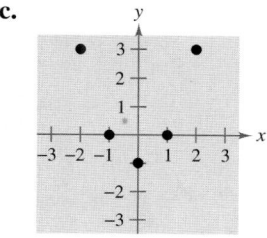

Figure 1.23

STUDY T!P

Be sure you see that the *range* of a function is not the same as the use of *range* relating to the viewing window.

Solution

a. This verbal description does describe y as a function of x. Regardless of the value of x, the value of y is always 2. Such functions are called *constant functions*.

b. This table does not describe y as a function of x. The input value 2 is mapped to two different y-values.

c. The graph in Figure 1.23 does describe y as a function of x. No input value is mapped to two output values.

Representing functions by sets of ordered pairs is common in *discrete mathematics*. For instance, a function that relates the number of units produced or sold in business to the profit could be represented by sets of ordered pairs. In algebra, however, it is more common to assume that the variables can be any real value and represent functions by equations or formulas involving two variables.

For instance, the equation

$$y = x^2 \qquad \text{y is a function of x.}$$

represents the variable y as a function of the variable x. In this equation, x is the **independent variable** and y is the **dependent variable.** The domain of the function is the set of all values taken on by the independent variable x, and the range of the function is the set of all values taken on by the dependent variable y.

EXAMPLE 2   Testing for Functions Represented Algebraically

Which of the equations represents y as a function of x?

a. $x^2 + y = 1$ **b.** $-x + y^2 = 1$

Solution
To determine whether y is a function of x, try to solve for y in terms of x.
a. Solving for y yields

$x^2 + y = 1$	Write original equation.
$y = 1 - x^2.$	Solve for y.

To each value of x there corresponds exactly one value of y. So, y *is* a function of x.

b. Solving for y yields

$-x + y^2 = 1$	Write original equation.
$y^2 = 1 + x$	Add x to each side.
$y = \pm\sqrt{1 + x}.$	Solve for y.

The $\pm$ indicates that for a given value of x there correspond two values of y. So, y *is not* a function of x.

Function Notation

When an equation is used to represent a function, it is convenient to name the function so that it can be referenced easily. For example, you know that the equation $y = 1 - x^2$ describes y as a function of x. Suppose you give this function the name "f." Then you can use the following **function notation.**

Input	Output	Equation
x	$f(x)$	$f(x) = 1 - x^2$

The symbol $f(x)$ is read as the *value of f at x* or simply *f of x.* The symbol $f(x)$ corresponds to the y-value for a given x. So, you can write $y = f(x)$. Keep in mind that f is the *name* of the function, whereas $f(x)$ is the *output value* of the function at the *input value* x. In function notation, the *input* is the independent variable and the *output* is the dependent variable. For instance, the function $f(x) = 3 - 2x$ has *function values* denoted by $f(-1), f(0), f(2)$, and so on. To find these values, substitute the specified input values into the given equation.

For $x = -1$,	$f(-1) = 3 - 2(-1) = 3 + 2 = 5.$
For $x = 0$,	$f(0) = 3 - 2(0) = 3 - 0 = 3.$
For $x = 2$,	$f(2) = 3 - 2(2) = 3 - 4 = -1.$

Exploration

Use a graphing utility to graph $x^2 + y = 1$. Then use the graph to write a convincing argument that each x-value has at most one y-value.

Use a graphing utility to graph $-x + y^2 = 1$. (*Hint:* You will need to use two equations.) Then use the graph to find an x-value that corresponds to two y-values. Does the graph represent y as a function of x? Explain.

The *Interactive* CD-ROM and *Internet* versions of this text offer a built-in graphing calculator, which can be used with the Examples, Explorations, and Exercises.

Understanding the concept of functions is essential. Be sure students understand functional notation. Frequently $f(x)$ is misinterpreted as "f times x" rather than "f of x."

STUDY T!P

You can use a graphing utility to evaluate a function. On the website *college.hmco.com*, you will find the graphing utility program EVALUATE. The program will prompt you for a value of x, and then evaluate the expression in the equation editor for that value of x. Try using the program to evaluate several different functions of x.

Although f is often used as a convenient function name and x is often used as the independent variable, you can use other letters. For instance,

$$f(x) = x^2 - 4x + 7, \quad f(t) = t^2 - 4t + 7, \quad \text{and} \quad g(s) = s^2 - 4s + 7$$

all define the same function. In fact, the role of the independent variable is that of a "placeholder." Consequently, the function could be described by

$$f(\ \ ) = (\ \ )^2 - 4(\ \ ) + 7.$$

Library of Functions

The function in Example 4 is a *piecewise-defined* function. This means that the function is defined by two or more equations over a specified domain. In Example 4, you use the top equation for all x-values less than 0, and the bottom equation for all x-values greater than or equal to 0.

Consult the Library of Functions Summary inside the front cover for a description of the piecewise-defined function.

EXAMPLE 3 Evaluating a Function

Let $g(x) = -x^2 + 4x + 1$ and find

a. $g(2)$ **b.** $g(t)$ **c.** $g(x + 2)$.

Solution

a. Replacing x with 2 in $g(x) = -x^2 + 4x + 1$ yields the following.

$$g(2) = -(2)^2 + 4(2) + 1 = -4 + 8 + 1 = 5$$

b. Replacing x with t yields the following.

$$g(t) = -(t)^2 + 4(t) + 1 = -t^2 + 4t + 1$$

c. Replacing x with $x + 2$ yields the following.

$$
\begin{array}{ll}
g(x + 2) = -(x + 2)^2 + 4(x + 2) + 1 & \text{Substitute } x + 2 \text{ for } x. \\
\quad = -(x^2 + 4x + 4) + 4x + 8 + 1 & \text{Multiply.} \\
\quad = -x^2 - 4x - 4 + 4x + 8 + 1 & \text{Distributive Property} \\
\quad = -x^2 + 5 & \text{Simplify.}
\end{array}
$$

In Example 3, note that $g(x + 2)$ is not equal to $g(x) + g(2)$. In general, $g(u + v) \neq g(u) + g(v)$.

Sometimes a function is defined by more than one equation. An illustration of this is given in Example 4.

Additional Example

Evaluate at $x = 0, 1, 3$.

$$f(x) = \begin{cases} \dfrac{x}{2} + 1, & x \leq 1 \\ 3x + 2, & x > 1 \end{cases}$$

Solution

Because $x = 0$ is less than or equal to 1, use $f(x) = (x/2) + 1$ to obtain

$$f(0) = \frac{0}{2} + 1 = 1.$$

For $x = 1$, use $f(x) = (x/2) + 1$ to obtain

$$f(1) = \frac{1}{2} + 1 = 1\frac{1}{2}.$$

For $x = 3$, use $f(x) = 3x + 2$ to obtain

$$f(3) = 3(3) + 2 = 11.$$

EXAMPLE 4 A Piecewise–Defined Function

Evaluate the function when $x = -1, 0,$ and 1.

$$f(x) = \begin{cases} x^2 + 1, & x < 0 \\ x - 1, & x \geq 0 \end{cases}$$

Solution

Because $x = -1$ is less than 0, use $f(x) = x^2 + 1$ to obtain

$$f(-1) = (-1)^2 + 1 = 2.$$

For $x = 0$, use $f(x) = x - 1$ to obtain

$$f(0) = (0) - 1 = -1.$$

For $x = 1$, use $f(x) = x - 1$ to obtain

$$f(1) = (1) - 1 = 0.$$

STUDY TIP

Most graphing utilities can graph functions that are defined piecewise. For instructions on how to enter a piecewise-defined function into your graphing utility, consult your user's manual. You may find it helpful to set your graphing utility to *dot mode* before graphing.

The Domain of a Function

The domain of a function is the set of all values of the independent variable for which the function is defined. If x is in the domain of f, f is said to be *defined* at x. If x is not in the domain of f, f is said to be *undefined* at x.

The domain of a function can be described explicitly or it can be *implied* by the expression used to define the function. The **implied domain** is the set of all real numbers for which the expression is defined. For instance, the function

$$f(x) = \frac{1}{x^2 - 4}$$ Domain excludes x-values that result in division by zero.

has an implied domain that consists of all real x other than $x = \pm 2$. These two values are excluded from the domain because division by zero is undefined. Another common type of implied domain is that used to avoid even roots of negative numbers. For example, the function

$$f(x) = \sqrt{x}$$ Domain excludes x-values that result in even roots of negative numbers.

is defined only for $x \geq 0$. So, its implied domain is the interval $[0, \infty)$. In general, the domain of a function *excludes* values that would cause division by zero *or* result in the even root of a negative number.

EXAMPLE 5   Finding the Domain of a Function

Find the domain of each function.

a. $f: \{(-3, 0), (-1, 4), (0, 2), (2, 2), (4, -1)\}$

b. $g(x) = -3x^2 + 4x + 5$ **c.** $h(x) = \dfrac{1}{x + 5}$

d. Volume of a sphere: $V = \frac{4}{3}\pi r^3$ **e.** $k(x) = \sqrt{4 - 3x}$

Solution

a. The domain of f consists of all first coordinates in the set of ordered pairs.

   Domain $= \{-3, -1, 0, 2, 4\}$.

b. The domain of g is the set of all real numbers.

c. Excluding x-values that yield zero in the denominator, the domain of h is the set of all real numbers $x \neq -5$.

d. Because this function represents the volume of a sphere, the values of the radius r must be positive. So, the domain is the set of all real numbers r such that $r > 0$.

e. This function is defined only for x-values for which

   $4 - 3x \geq 0$.

The domain of k is all real numbers that are less than or equal to $\frac{4}{3}$.

In Example 5(d), note that the *domain of a function may be implied by the physical context*. For instance, from the equation $V = \frac{4}{3}\pi r^3$, you would have no reason to restrict r to positive values, but the physical context implies that a sphere cannot have a negative or zero radius.

Exploration

Use a graphing utility to graph $y = \sqrt{4 - x^2}$. What is the domain of this function? Then graph $y = \sqrt{x^2 - 4}$. What is the domain of this function? Do the domains of these two functions overlap? If so, for what values?

Library of Functions

The *square root* function $f(x) = \sqrt{x}$ is not defined for $x < 0$. This means that you must be careful when analyzing the domain of complicated functions involving the square root symbol.

Consult the Library of Functions Summary inside the front cover for a description of the square root or radical function.

STUDY TIP

In Example 5(e), $4 - 3x \geq 0$ is a *linear inequality*. For help with solving linear inequalities see Appendix C. You will study more about inequalities in Section 2.5.

Applications

$$\boxed{\frac{h}{r} = 4}$$

$\vert\!\!\leftarrow r \rightarrow\!\!\vert$

EXAMPLE 6 The Dimensions of a Container

You work in the marketing department of a soft-drink company and are experimenting with a new soft-drink can that is slightly narrower and taller than a standard can. For your experimental can, the ratio of the height to the radius is 4, as shown in Figure 1.24.

a. Express the volume of the can as a function of the radius r.

b. Express the volume of the can as a function of the height h.

Solution

The volume of a right circular cylinder is $V = \pi r^2 h$.

a. To write the volume as a function of the radius, use the fact that $h = 4r$.

$$V(r) = \pi r^2 h = \pi r^2 (4r) = 4\pi r^3 \qquad \text{Write } V \text{ as a function of } r.$$

b. To write the volume as a function of the height, use the fact that $r = h/4$.

$$V(h) = \pi r^2 h = \pi \left(\frac{h}{4}\right)^2 h = \frac{\pi h^3}{16} \qquad \text{Write } V \text{ as a function of } h.$$

Figure 1.24

EXAMPLE 7 The Path of a Baseball

A baseball is hit at a point 3 feet above ground at a velocity of 100 feet per second and an angle of 45°. The path of the baseball is given by the function

$$f(x) = -0.0032x^2 + x + 3$$

where y and x are measured in feet. Will the baseball clear a 10-foot fence located 300 feet from home plate?

Algebraic Solution

The height of the baseball is a function of the horizontal distance from home plate. When $x = 300$, you can find the height of the baseball as follows.

$$f(x) = -0.0032x^2 + x + 3 \qquad \begin{array}{l}\text{Write original}\\\text{equation.}\end{array}$$

$$f(300) = -0.0032(300)^2 + 300 + 3 \qquad \begin{array}{l}\text{Substitute 300}\\\text{for } x.\end{array}$$

$$= 15 \qquad \text{Simplify.}$$

When $x = 300$, the height of the baseball is 15 feet, so the baseball will clear a 10-foot fence.

Graphical Solution

Use a graphing utility to graph the function $y = -0.0032x^2 + x + 3$, as shown in Figure 1.25.

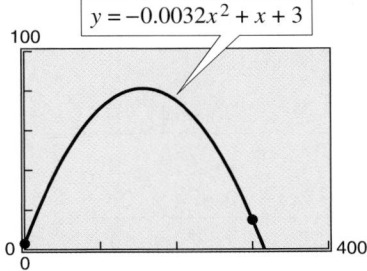

Figure 1.25

Use the *value* feature or *zoom* and *trace* features of the graphing utility to estimate that $y = 15$ when $x = 300$. So, the ball will clear a 10-foot fence.

EXAMPLE 8   Direct Mail Advertising

The money C (in billions of dollars) spent for direct mail advertising in the United States increased in a linear pattern from 1990 to 1992, as shown in Figure 1.26. Then, in 1993, the money spent took a jump and, until 1996, increased in a *different* linear pattern. These two patterns can be approximated by the function

$$C(t) = \begin{cases} 23.40 + 1.01t & 0 \le t \le 2 \\ 19.85 + 2.50t & 3 \le t \le 6 \end{cases}$$

where $t = 0$ represents 1990. Use this function to approximate the total amount spent for direct mail advertising between 1990 and 1996.   (Source: McCann-Erickson)

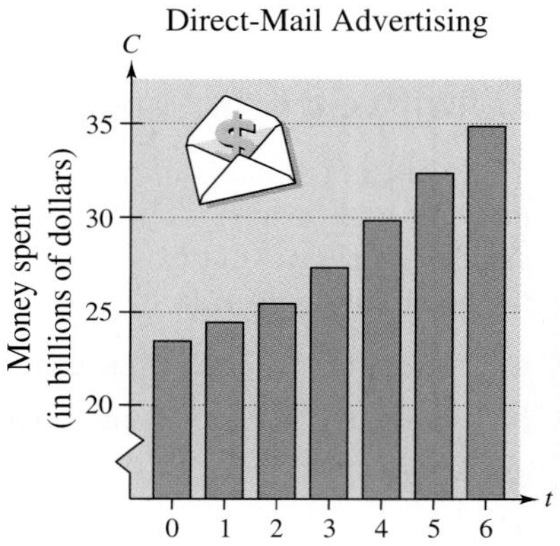

Solution

From 1990 to 1992, use the formula $C(t) = 23.40 + 1.01t$.

$$\$23.40, \quad \$24.41, \quad \$25.42$$

$$\underbrace{\quad}_{1990} \quad \underbrace{\quad}_{1991} \quad \underbrace{\quad}_{1992}$$

From 1993 to 1996, use the formula $C(t) = 19.85 + 2.50t$.

$$\$27.35, \quad \$29.85, \quad \$32.35, \quad \$34.85$$

$$\underbrace{\quad}_{1993} \quad \underbrace{\quad}_{1994} \quad \underbrace{\quad}_{1995} \quad \underbrace{\quad}_{1996}$$

The total of these seven amounts is $197.63, which implies that the total amount spent was approximately $197,630,000,000.

One of the basic definitions in calculus employs the ratio

$$\frac{f(x + h) - f(x)}{h}, \qquad h \ne 0.$$

This ratio is called a **difference quotient,** as illustrated in Examples 9 and 10.

Direct-Mail Advertising

Figure 1.26

EXAMPLE 9   Evaluating a Difference Quotient

For $f(x) = -2x + 4$, find $\dfrac{f(x + h) - f(x)}{h}$.

Solution

$$\frac{f(x + h) - f(x)}{h} = \frac{[-2(x + h) + 4] - (-2x + 4)}{h} \qquad \text{Substitute } x + h \text{ for } x.$$

$$= \frac{-2x - 2h + 4 + 2x - 4}{h} \qquad \text{Distributive Property}$$

$$= \frac{-2h}{h} = -2, \quad h \ne 0 \qquad \text{Simplify and divide out common factor.}$$

> ### STUDY T!P
>
> Notice in Example 9 that h cannot be zero in the original expression. So, you must restrict the domain of the simplified expression by adding $h \ne 0$ so that the simplified expression is equivalent to the original expression.

The symbol 🔵 indicates an example or exercise that highlights algebraic techniques specifically used in calculus.

EXAMPLE 10 Evaluating a Difference Quotient

For $f(x) = x^2 - 4x + 7$, find $\dfrac{f(x + h) - f(x)}{h}$.

Solution

$$\frac{f(x + h) - f(x)}{h} = \frac{[(x + h)^2 - 4(x + h) + 7] - (x^2 - 4x + 7)}{h}$$

$$= \frac{x^2 + 2xh + h^2 - 4x - 4h + 7 - x^2 + 4x - 7}{h}$$

$$= \frac{2xh + h^2 - 4h}{h}$$

$$= \frac{h(2x + h - 4)}{h} = 2x + h - 4, \quad h \neq 0$$

Activities

1. Evaluate $f(x) = 2 + 3x - x^2$ for
   a. $f(-3)$
   b. $f(x + 1)$
   c. $f(x + h) - f(x)$
   Answers:
   a. -16
   b. $-x^2 + x + 4$
   c. $3h - 2xh - h^2$

2. Determine if y is a function of x:
   $2x^3 + 3x^2y^2 + 1 = 0$.
   Answer: No

3. Find the domain: $f(x) = \dfrac{3}{x + 1}$.
   Answer: $(-\infty, -1), (-1, \infty)$

The Granger Collection

Leonhard Euler (1707–1783), a Swiss mathematician, is considered to have been the most prolific and productive mathematician in history. One of his greatest influences on mathematics was his use of symbols, or notation. The function notation $y = f(x)$ was introduced by Euler.

Summary of Function Terminology

Function: A **function** is a relationship between two variables such that to each value of the independent variable there corresponds exactly one value of the dependent variable.

Function Notation: $y = f(x)$
   f is the *name* of the function.
   y is the **dependent variable,** or output value.
   x is the **independent variable,** or input value.
   $f(x)$ is the *value of the function at x.*

Domain: The **domain** of a function is the set of all values (inputs) of the independent variable for which the function is defined.

Range: The **range** of a function is the set of all values (outputs) assumed by the dependent variable (that is, the set of all function values).

Implied Domain: If f is defined by an algebraic expression and the domain is not specified, the **implied domain** consists of all real numbers for which the expression is defined.

Writing About Math   *Modeling with Piecewise-Defined Functions*

x	y
1	5.2
2	5.6
3	6.6
4	8.3
5	11.5
6	15.8

x	y
7	12.8
8	10.1
9	8.6
10	6.9
11	4.5
12	2.7

The table at the left shows the monthly revenue y (in thousands of dollars) for one year of a landscaping business, with $x = 1$ representing January.

A mathematical model that represents this data is

$$f(x) = \begin{cases} -1.97x + 26.33 \\ 0.51x^2 - 1.47x + 6.31. \end{cases}$$

What is the domain of each part of the piecewise-defined function? How can you tell? Explain your reasoning.

Find $f(5)$ and $f(11)$, and interpret your results in the context of the problem. How do these model values compare with the actual data values?

1.3 E x e r c i s e s

In Exercises 1–4, is the relationship a function?

1. *Domain   Range*

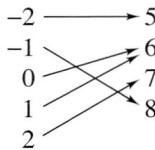

2. *Domain   Range*

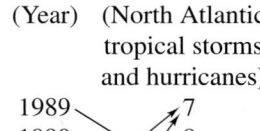

3. *Domain   Range*

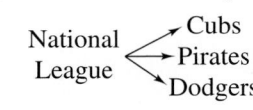

4. *Domain   Range*

(Year)   (North Atlantic tropical storms and hurricanes)

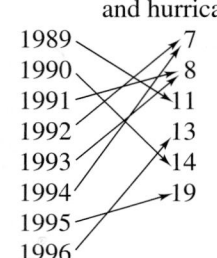

In Exercises 5–8, does the table describe a function? Explain your reasoning.

5.

Input Value	-2	-1	0	1	2
Output Value	-8	-1	0	1	8

6.

Input Value	0	1	2	1	0
Output Value	-4	-2	0	2	4

7.

Input Value	10	7	4	7	10
Output Value	3	6	9	12	15

8.

Input Value	0	3	9	12	15
Output Value	3	3	3	3	3

In Exercises 9 and 10, which sets of ordered pairs represent function(s) from *A* to *B*? Explain.

9. $A = \{0, 1, 2, 3\}$ and $B = \{-2, -1, 0, 1, 2\}$

(a) $\{(0, 1), (1, -2), (2, 0), (3, 2)\}$

(b) $\{(0, -1), (2, 2), (1, -2), (3, 0), (1, 1)\}$

(c) $\{(0, 0), (1, 0), (2, 0), (3, 0)\}$

(d) $\{(0, 2), (3, 0) \ (1, 1)\}$

10. $A = \{a, b, c\}$ and $B = \{0, 1, 2, 3\}$

(a) $\{(a, 1), (c, 2), (c, 3), (b, 3)\}$

(b) $\{(a, 1), (b, 2), (c, 3)\}$

(c) $\{(1, a), (0, a), (2, c), (3, b)\}$

(d) $\{(c, 0), (b, 0 \ ), (a, 3)\}$

Circulation of Newspapers **In Exercises 11 and 12, use the graph, which shows the circulation (in millions) of daily newspapers in the United States.** (Source: Editor & Publisher Company)

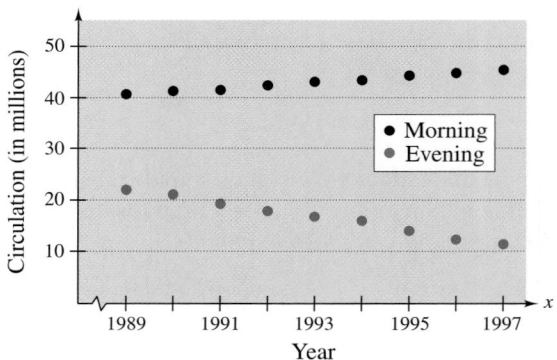

11. Is the circulation of morning newspapers a function of the year? Is the circulation of evening newspapers a function of the year? Explain.

12. Let $f(x)$ represent the circulation of evening newspapers in year x. Find $f(1994)$.

In Exercises 13–24, determine if the equation represents *y* as a function of *x*.

13. $x^2 + y^2 = 4$ **14.** $x = y^2$

15. $x^2 + y = 4$ **16.** $x + y^2 = 4$

17. $2x + 3y = 4$ **18.** $x = -y + 5$

19. $y^2 = x^2 - 1$ **20.** $y = \sqrt{x + 5}$

21. $y = |4 - x|$ **22.** $|y| = 4 - x$

23. $x = 4$ **24.** $y = -2$

In Exercises 25 and 26, fill in the blanks using the specified function and the given values of the independent variable. Simplify the result.

25. $f(x) = \dfrac{1}{x + 1}$

   (a) $f(4) = \dfrac{1}{(\quad) + 1}$

   (b) $f(0) = \dfrac{1}{(\quad) + 1}$

   (c) $f(4t) = \dfrac{1}{(\quad) + 1}$

   (d) $f(x + c) = \dfrac{1}{(\quad) + 1}$

26. $g(x) = x^2 - 2x$

   (a) $g(2) = (\quad)^2 - 2(\quad)$

   (b) $g(-3) = (\quad)^2 - 2(\quad)$

   (c) $g(t + 1) = (\quad)^2 - 2(\quad)$

   (d) $g(x + c) = (\quad)^2 - 2(\quad)$

In Exercises 27–38, evaluate the function at each specified value of the independent variable and simplify.

27. $f(x) = 2x - 3$

   (a) $f(1)$ (b) $f(-3)$ (c) $f(x - 1)$

28. $g(y) = 7 - 3y$

   (a) $g(0)$ (b) $g\left(\frac{7}{3}\right)$ (c) $g(s + 2)$

29. $h(t) = t^2 - 2t$

   (a) $h(2)$ (b) $h(1.5)$ (c) $h(x + 2)$

30. $V(r) = \frac{4}{3}\pi r^3$

   (a) $V(3)$ (b) $V\left(\frac{3}{2}\right)$ (c) $V(2r)$

31. $f(y) = 3 - \sqrt{y}$

   (a) $f(4)$ (b) $f(0.25)$ (c) $f(4x^2)$

32. $f(x) = \sqrt{x + 8} + 2$

   (a) $f(-8)$ (b) $f(1)$ (c) $f(x - 8)$

33. $q(x) = \dfrac{1}{x^2 - 9}$

   (a) $q(0)$ (b) $q(3)$ (c) $q(y + 3)$

34. $q(t) = \dfrac{2t^2 + 3}{t^2}$

   (a) $q(2)$ (b) $q(0)$ (c) $q(-x)$

35. $f(x) = \dfrac{|x|}{x}$

   (a) $f(2)$ (b) $f(-2)$ (c) $f(x^2)$

36. $f(x) = |x| + 4$

   (a) $f(2)$ (b) $f(-2)$ (c) $f(x^2)$

37. $f(x) = \begin{cases} 2x + 1, & x < 0 \\ 2x + 2, & x \geq 0 \end{cases}$

   (a) $f(-1)$ (b) $f(0)$ (c) $f(2)$

38. $f(x) = \begin{cases} x^2 + 2, & x \leq 1 \\ 2x^2 + 2, & x > 1 \end{cases}$

   (a) $f(-2)$ (b) $f(1)$ (c) $f(2)$

In Exercises 39–44, complete the table.

39. $f(x) = x^2 - 3$

x	-2	-1	0	1	2
$f(x)$					

40. $g(x) = \sqrt{x - 3}$

x	3	4	5	6	7
$g(x)$					

41. $h(t) = \frac{1}{2}|t + 3|$

t	-5	-4	-3	-2	-1
$h(t)$					

42. $f(s) = \dfrac{|s - 2|}{s - 2}$

s	0	1	$\frac{3}{2}$	$\frac{5}{2}$	4
$f(s)$					

43. $f(x) = \begin{cases} -\frac{1}{2}x + 4, & x \leq 0 \\ (x - 2)^2, & x > 0 \end{cases}$

x	-2	-1	0	1	2
$f(x)$					

44. $h(x) = \begin{cases} 9 - x^2, & x < 3 \\ x - 3, & x \geq 3 \end{cases}$

x	1	2	3	4	5
$h(x)$					

In Exercises 45–52, find all real values of x such that $f(x) = 0$.

45. $f(x) = 15 - 3x$

46. $f(x) = 5x + 1$

47. $f(x) = \dfrac{3x - 4}{5}$

48. $f(x) = \dfrac{12 - x^2}{5}$

49. $f(x) = x^2 - 9$

50. $f(x) = x^3 - x$

51. $f(x) = \sqrt{x^2 - 16}$

52. $f(x) = \sqrt{4x^2 - x}$

In Exercises 53–56, find the value(s) of x for which $f(x) = g(x)$.

53. $f(x) = x^2$, $g(x) = x + 2$

54. $f(x) = x^2 + 2x + 1$, $g(x) = 3x + 3$

55. $f(x) = \sqrt{3x} + 1$, $g(x) = x + 1$

56. $f(x) = x^4 - 2x^2$, $g(x) = 2x^2$

In Exercises 57–70, determine the domain of the function.

57. $f(x) = 5x^2 + 2x - 1$

58. $g(x) = 1 - 2x^2$

59. $h(t) = \dfrac{4}{t}$

60. $s(y) = \dfrac{3y}{y + 5}$

61. $g(y) = \sqrt{y - 10}$

62. $f(t) = \sqrt[3]{t + 4}$

63. $f(x) = \sqrt[4]{1 - x^2}$

64. $f(x) = \sqrt[4]{x^2 + 3x}$

65. $g(x) = \dfrac{1}{x} - \dfrac{3}{x + 2}$

66. $h(x) = \dfrac{10}{x^2 - 2x}$

67. $f(s) = \dfrac{\sqrt{s - 1}}{s - 4}$

68. $f(x) = \dfrac{\sqrt{x + 6}}{6 + x}$

69. $f(x) = \dfrac{\sqrt[3]{x - 4}}{x}$

70. $f(x) = \dfrac{x - 5}{\sqrt[4]{x^2 - 9}}$

In Exercises 71–74, assume that the domain of f is the set $A = \{-2, -1, 0, 1, 2\}$. Determine the set of ordered pairs representing the function f.

71. $f(x) = x^2$

72. $f(x) = \dfrac{2x}{x^2 + 1}$

73. $f(x) = \sqrt{x + 2}$

74. $f(x) = |x + 1|$

Exploration   In Exercises 75–78, select a function from $f(x) = cx$, $g(x) = cx^2$, $h(x) = c\sqrt{|x|}$, or $r(x) = c/x$ and determine the value of the constant c such that the function fits the data given in the table.

75.

x	-4	-1	0	1	4
y	-32	-2	0	-2	-32

76.

x	-4	-1	0	1	4
y	-1	$-\frac{1}{4}$	0	$\frac{1}{4}$	1

77.

x	-4	-1	0	1	4
y	-8	-32	Undef.	32	8

78.

x	-4	-1	0	1	4
y	6	3	0	3	6

🔵 **In Exercises 79–86, find the difference quotient and simplify your answer.**

79. $f(x) = 2x$, $\dfrac{f(x + c) - f(x)}{c}, \; c \neq 0$

80. $g(x) = 3x - 1$, $\dfrac{g(x + h) - g(x)}{h}, \; h \neq 0$

81. $f(x) = x^2 - x + 1$, $\dfrac{f(2 + h) - f(2)}{h}, \; h \neq 0$

82. $f(x) = 5x - x^2$, $\dfrac{f(5 + h) - f(5)}{h}, \; h \neq 0$

83. $f(x) = x^3$, $\dfrac{f(x + c) - f(x)}{c}, \; c \neq 0$

84. $f(x) = x^3 + x$, $\dfrac{f(x + h) - f(x)}{h}, \; h \neq 0$

85. $f(t) = \dfrac{1}{t}$, $\dfrac{f(t) - f(1)}{t - 1}, \; t \neq 1$

86. $f(x) = \dfrac{4}{x + 1}$, $\dfrac{f(x) - f(7)}{x - 7}, \; x \neq 7$

87. Geometry   Express the area A of a circle as a function of its circumference C.

88. Geometry   Express the area A of an equilateral triangle as a function of the length s of its sides.

89. Geometry   Express the area A of an isosceles right triangle as a function of the length s of one of its two equal sides.

90. Geometry   Express the area A of an equilateral triangle as a function of the height of the triangle.

The symbol 🔵 indicates an example or exercise that highlights algebraic techniques specifically used in calculus.

91. *Exploration* An open box of maximum volume is to be made from a square piece of material, 24 centimeters on a side, by cutting equal squares from the corners and turning up the sides.

(a) Use the *table* feature of a graphing utility to complete six rows of the table. Use the result to guess the maximum volume.

Height, x	Width	Volume, V
1	$24 - 2(1)$	$1[24 - 2(1)]^2 = 484$
2	$24 - 2(2)$	$2[24 - 2(2)]^2 = 800$

(b) Write the volume V as a function of x, and determine its domain. Use a graphing utility to graph the function.

(c) Use the *value* feature or *zoom* and *trace* features of the graphing utility to approximate V when $x = 9$ and when $x = 10$.

(d) Verify your answers to part (c) algebraically.

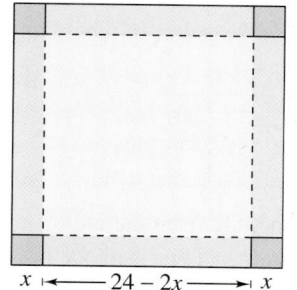

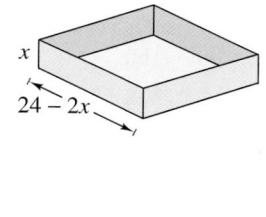

92. *Exploration* The cost per unit of a certain radio model is $60. The manufacturer charges $90 per unit for orders of 100 or less. To encourage large orders, the manufacturer reduces the charge by $0.15 per radio for each unit ordered in excess of 100 (i.e., there would be a charge of $87 per radio for an order size of 120).

(a) Use the *table* feature of a graphing utility to complete six rows of the table. Use the result to estimate the maximum profit.

Units, x	Price, p	Profit, P
110	$90 - 10(0.15)$	$xp - 110(60)$
120	$90 - 20(0.15)$	$xp - 120(60)$

(b) Write the profit P as a function of x, and determine its domain. Use a graphing utility to graph the function.

(c) Use the *value* feature or *zoom* and *trace* features of the graphing utility to approximate P when $x = 120, 130,$ and 140.

(d) Verify your answers to part (c) algebraically.

93. *Geometry* A right triangle is formed in the first quadrant by the x- and y-axes and a line through the point $(2, 1)$. Write the area of the triangle as a function of x, and determine the domain of the function.

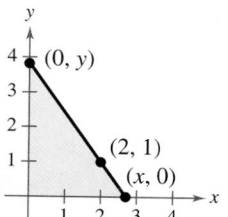

94. *Geometry* A rectangle is bounded by the x-axis and the semicircle $y = \sqrt{36 - x^2}$. Write the area of the rectangle as a function of x, and determine the domain of the function.

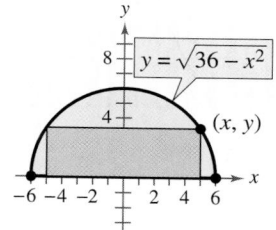

95. *Geometry* A rectangular package to be sent by the U.S. Postal Service can have a maximum combined length and girth (perimeter of a cross section) of 108 inches.

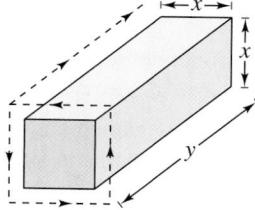

(a) Write the volume of the package as a function of x.

(b) What is the domain of the function?

(c) Use a graphing utility to graph the function. Be sure to use the appropriate viewing window.

(d) What dimensions will maximize the volume of the package? Explain your answer.

96. *Mobile Home Prices* The average price p (in thousands of dollars) of a new mobile home in the United States from 1974 to 1997 can be approximated by the model

$$p(t) = \begin{cases} 17.27 + 1.036t, & -6 \leq t \leq 11 \\ -4.807 + 2.882t + 0.011t^2, & 12 \leq t \leq 17 \end{cases}$$

where $t = 0$ represents 1980. Use a graphing utility to graph this model. Then use the *value* feature or *zoom* and *trace* features to find the average price of a mobile home in 1978, 1988, 1993, and 1997. (Source: U.S. Bureau of the Census, *Construction Reports*)

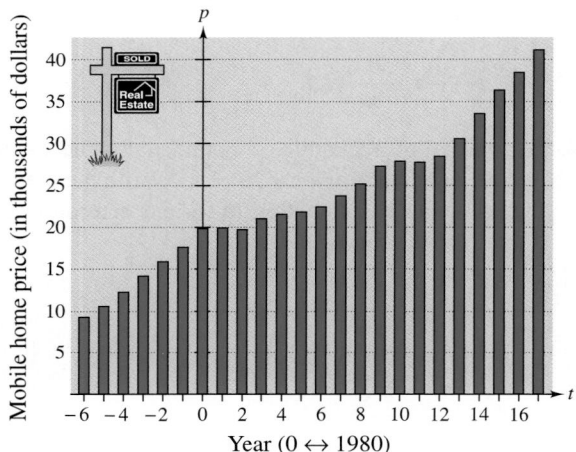

Year (0 ↔ 1980)

97. *Business* A company produces a toy for which the variable cost is $12.30 per unit and the fixed costs are $98,000. The toy sells for $17.98. Let x be the number of units produced and sold.

    (a) Write the total cost C as a function of the number of units produced.

    (b) Write the revenue R as a function of the number of units sold.

    (c) Write the profit P as a function of the number of units sold. (*Note:* $P = R - C$.)

98. *Business* The inventor of a new game believes that the variable cost for producing the game is $0.95 per unit and the fixed costs are $6000. The inventor sells each game for $1.69. Let x be the number of games sold.

    (a) Write the total cost C as a function of the number of games sold.

    (b) Write the average cost per unit $\overline{C} = C/x$ as a function of x.

99. *Charter Bus Fares* For groups of 80 or more people, a charter bus company determines the rate per person according to the formula

$$\text{Rate} = 8 - 0.05(n - 80), \quad n \geq 80$$

where the rate is given in dollars and n is the number of people.

    (a) Express the revenue R for the bus company as a function of n.

    (b) Use the function from part (a) to complete the table. What can you conclude?

n	90	100	110	120	130	140	150
$R(n)$							

    (c) Use a graphing utility to graph R and determine the number of people that will produce a maximum revenue. Compare the result with your conclusion from part (b).

100. *Physics* The force F (in tons) of water against the face of a dam is a function $F(y) = 149.76\sqrt{10}y^{5/2}$, where y is the depth of the water in feet. Complete the table.

y	5	10	20	30	40
$F(y)$					

    (a) What can you conclude from the table?

    (b) Use a graphing utility to graph the function. Describe your viewing window.

    (c) Use the table to approximate the depth at which the force against the dam is 1,000,000 tons. How could you find a better estimate?

    (d) Verify your answer in part (c) graphically.

101. *Height of a Balloon* A balloon carrying a transmitter ascends vertically from a point 3000 feet from the receiving station.

    (a) Draw a diagram to represent the problem. Let h represent the height of the balloon and let d represent the distance between the balloon and the receiving station.

    (b) Express the height of the balloon as a function of d. What is the domain of the function?

    (c) Use a graphing utility to graph the function in part (b). Describe your viewing window.

    (d) Graphically find the height of the balloon when $d = 10,000$ feet. Verify your answer algebraically.

102. ***Biology***   The graph below shows the lynx population from 1988 through 1995 in a 350-square-kilometer region of the Yukon territory in Canada. Let $f(t)$ represent the number of lynx in year t. (Source: Kluane Boreal Forest Ecosystem Project)

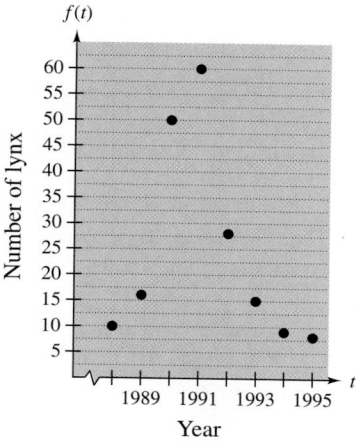

Year

(a) Find $f(1992)$.

(b) Find $\dfrac{f(1994) - f(1991)}{1994 - 1991}$

and interpret the result in the context of the problem.

(c) An approximate model for the function is

$$N(t) = \frac{434t + 4387}{45t^2 - 55t + 100}$$

where N is the number of lynx and t is the time in years, with $t = 0$ corresponding to 1990. Complete the table and compare the result with the data. Use a graphing utility to graph the model and data in the same viewing window. Comment on the validity of the model.

t	1988	1989	1990	1991
N				

t	1992	1993	1994	1995
N				

Synthesis

True or False?   **In Exercises 103 and 104, determine whether the statement is true or false. Justify your answer.**

103. The domain of the function $f(x) = x^4 - 1$ is $(-\infty, \infty)$, and the range of $f(x)$ is $(0, \infty)$.

104. The set of ordered pairs $\{(-8, -2),\ (-6, 0),\ (-4, 0),\ (-2, 2),\ (0, 4), (2, -2)\}$ represents a function.

105. ***Think About It***   Does the relationship shown in the figure represent a function from set A to set B? Explain.

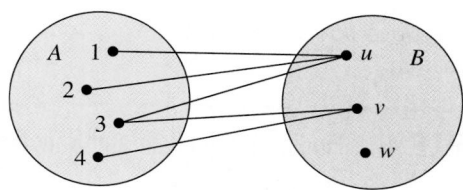

106. ***Writing***   In your own words, explain the meaning of domain and range.

107. ***Think About It***   Describe an advantage of function notation.

Review

In Exercises 108–111, perform the operations and simplify.

108. $12 - \dfrac{4}{x + 2}$

109. $\dfrac{3}{x^2 + x - 20} + \dfrac{x}{x^2 + 4x - 5}$

110. $\dfrac{2x^3 + 11x^2 - 6x}{5x} \cdot \dfrac{x + 10}{2x^2 + 5x - 3}$

111. $\dfrac{x + 7}{2(x - 9)} \div \dfrac{x - 7}{2(x - 9)}$

In Exercises 112–115, sketch the graph of the equation using the point-plotting method.

112. $y = -2x - 5$ **113.** $y = -x^2 - 3x$

114. $y = \sqrt{x - 6}$ **115.** $y = x^3 - 2$

1.4   Graphs of Functions

The Graph of a Function

In Section 1.3 functions were represented graphically by points on a graph in a coordinate plane in which the input values are represented by the horizontal axis and the output values are represented by the vertical axis. The **graph of a function** f is the collection of ordered pairs $(x, f(x))$ such that x is in the domain of f. As you study this section, remember the following geometrical interpretation of x and $f(x)$.

$$x = \text{the directed distance from the } y\text{-axis}$$

$$f(x) = \text{the directed distance from the } x\text{-axis}$$

Example 1 shows how to use the graph of a function to find the domain and range of the function.

EXAMPLE 1   Finding the Domain and Range of a Function

Use the graph of the function f shown in Figure 1.27 to find (a) the domain of f, (b) the function values $f(-1)$ and $f(2)$, and (c) the range of f.

Solution

a. The closed dot (on the left) indicates that $x = -1$ is in the domain of f, whereas the open dot (on the right) indicates that $x = 4$ is not in the domain. So, the domain of f is all x in the interval $[-1, 4)$.

b. Because $(-1, -5)$ is a point on the graph of f, it follows that

$$f(-1) = -5.$$

Similarly, because $(2, 4)$ is a point on the graph of f, it follows that

$$f(2) = 4.$$

c. Because the graph does not extend below $f(-1) = -5$ or above $f(2) = 4$, the range of f is the interval $[-5, 4]$.

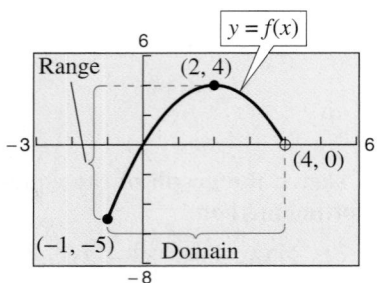

Figure 1.27

What You Should Learn:

- How to find the domains and ranges of functions
- How to use the Vertical Line Test for functions
- How to determine intervals on which functions are increasing or decreasing
- How to determine relative maximum and relative minimum values of functions
- How to identify and graph step functions and other piecewise-defined functions
- How to identify even and odd functions

Why You Should Learn It:

Graphs of functions provide a visual relationship between two variables. Exercise 87 on page 116 shows how the graph of a step function can represent the cost of a telephone call.

Jeff Greenberg/Peter Arnold, Inc.

The use of dots (open or closed) at the extreme left and right points of a graph indicates that the graph does not extend beyond these points. If no such dots are shown, assume that the graph extends beyond these points.

EXAMPLE 2 Finding the Domain and Range of a Function

Find the domain and range of $f(x) = \sqrt{x - 4}$.

Algebraic Solution

Because the expression under a radical cannot be negative, the domain of $f(x) = \sqrt{x - 4}$ is the set of all real numbers such that $x - 4 \geq 0$. Solve this linear inequality for x as follows. (For help with solving linear inequalities, see Appendix C.)

$x - 4 \geq 0$ Write original inequality.

$x \geq 4$ Add 4 to each side.

So, the domain is the set of all real numbers greater than or equal to 4. Because the value of a radical expression is never negative, the range of $f(x) = \sqrt{x - 4}$ is the set of all nonnegative real numbers.

Graphical Solution

Use a graphing utility to graph the equation $y = \sqrt{x - 4}$, as shown in Figure 1.28. Use the *trace* feature to determine that the x-coordinates of points on the graph extend from 4 to the right. When x is greater than or equal to 4, the expression under the radical is nonnegative. So, you can conclude that the domain is the set of all real numbers greater than or equal to 4. From the graph, you can see that the y-coordinates of points on the graph extend from 0 upwards. So you can estimate the range to be the set of all nonnegative real numbers.

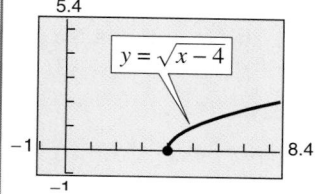

Figure 1.28

By the definition of a function, at most one y-value corresponds to a given x-value. It follows, then, that a vertical line can intersect the graph of a function at most once. This leads to the **Vertical Line Test** for functions.

Vertical Line Test for Functions

A set of points in a coordinate plane is the graph of y as a function of x if and only if no vertical line intersects the graph at more than one point.

EXAMPLE 3 Vertical Line Test for Functions

Which of the graphs in Figure 1.29 represent y as a function of x?

Solution

a. This *is not* a graph of y as a function of x because you can find a vertical line that intersects the graph twice.

b. This *is* a graph of y as a function of x because every vertical line intersects the graph at most once.

c. This *is* a graph of y as a function of x. (Note that if a vertical line does not intersect the graph, it simply means that the function is undefined for that particular value of x.)

Most graphing utilities are designed to graph functions of x more easily than other types of equations. For instance, the graph shown in Figure 1.29(a) represents the equation $x - (y - 1)^2 = 0$. To use a graphing utility to duplicate this graph you must first solve the equation for y to obtain $y = 1 \pm \sqrt{x}$, and then graph the two equations $y_1 = 1 + \sqrt{x}$ and $y_2 = 1 - \sqrt{x}$ in the same viewing window.

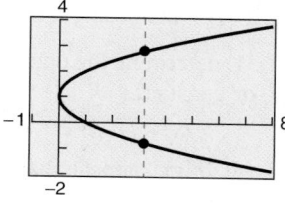

(a)

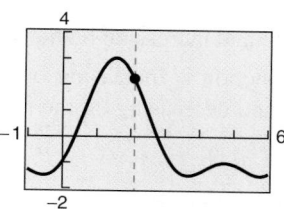

(b)

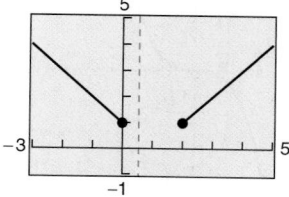

(c)
Figure 1.29

Increasing and Decreasing Functions

The more you know about the graph of a function, the more you know about the function itself. Consider the graph shown in Figure 1.30. Moving from *left to right,* this graph falls from $x = -2$ to $x = 0$, is constant from $x = 0$ to $x = 2$, and rises from $x = 2$ to $x = 4$.

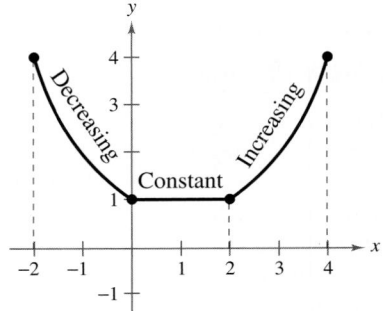

Figure 1.30

> ## Increasing, Decreasing, and Constant Functions
>
> A function f is **increasing** on an interval if, for any x_1 and x_2 in the interval,
>
> $$x_1 < x_2 \text{ implies } f(x_1) < f(x_2).$$
>
> A function f is **decreasing** on an interval if, for any x_1 and x_2 in the interval,
>
> $$x_1 < x_2 \text{ implies } f(x_1) > f(x_2).$$
>
> A function f is **constant** on an interval if, for any x_1 and x_2 in the interval,
>
> $$f(x_1) = f(x_2).$$

EXAMPLE 4   Increasing and Decreasing Functions

In Figure 1.31, determine the open intervals on which each function is increasing, decreasing, or constant.

Solution

a. Although it might appear that there is an interval in which this function is constant, you can see that if $x_1 < x_2$, then $(x_1)^3 < (x_2)^3$, which implies that $f(x_1) < f(x_2)$. So, the function is increasing over the entire real line.

b. This function is increasing on the interval $(-\infty, -1)$, decreasing on the interval $(-1, 1)$, and increasing on the interval $(1, \infty)$.

c. This function is increasing on the interval $(-\infty, 0)$, constant on the interval $(0, 2)$, and decreasing on the interval $(2, \infty)$.

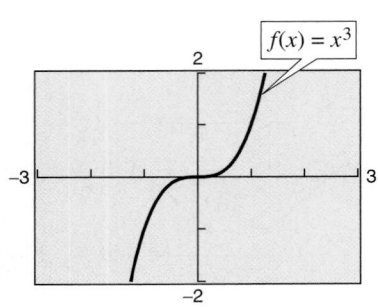

(a)

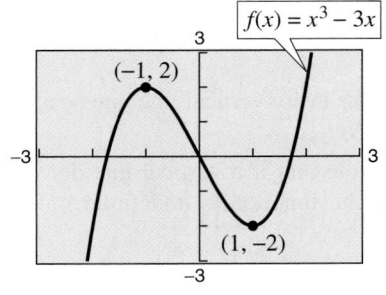

(b)

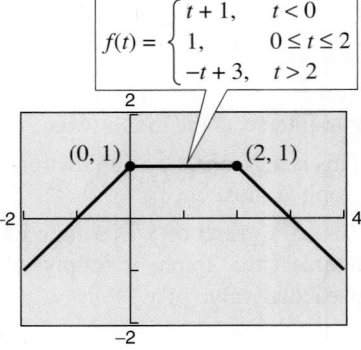

(c)

Figure 1.31

Relative Minimum and Maximum Values

The points at which a function changes its increasing, decreasing, or constant behavior are helpful in determining the relative maximum or relative minimum values of the function.

> ### Definition of Relative Minimum and Relative Maximum
>
> A function value $f(a)$ is called a **relative minimum** of f if there exists an interval (x_1, x_2) that contains a such that
>
> $$x_1 < x < x_2 \quad \text{implies} \quad f(a) \leq f(x).$$
>
> A function value $f(a)$ is called a **relative maximum** of f if there exists an interval (x_1, x_2) that contains a such that
>
> $$x_1 < x < x_2 \quad \text{implies} \quad f(a) \geq f(x).$$

Figure 1.32 shows several different examples of relative minimums and relative maximums. In Section 3.1, you will study a technique for finding the *exact points* at which a second-degree polynomial function has a relative minimum or relative maximum. For the time being, however, you can use a graphing utility to find reasonable approximations of these points.

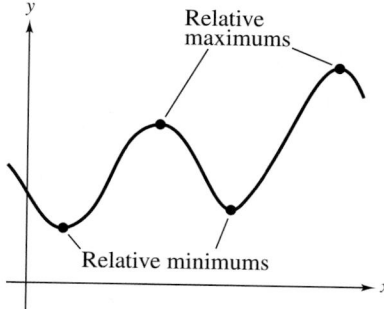

Figure 1.32

EXAMPLE 5   Approximating a Relative Minimum

Use a graphing utility to approximate the relative minimum of the function $f(x) = 3x^2 - 4x - 2$.

Solution

The graph of f is shown in Figure 1.33. By using the *zoom* and *trace* features of a graphing utility, you can estimate that the function has a relative minimum at the point

$(0.67, -3.33).$ Approximate relative minimum

Later, in Section 3.1, you will be able to determine that the exact point at which the relative minimum occurs is $\left(\frac{2}{3}, -\frac{10}{3}\right)$.

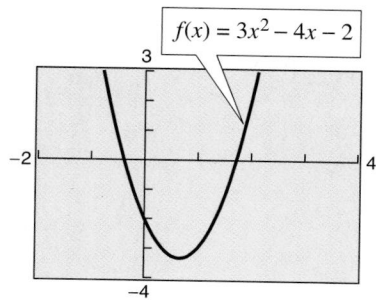

Figure 1.33

STUDY T!P

When you use a graphing utility to estimate *x*- and *y*-values of a relative minimum or relative maximum, the automatic *zoom* feature will often produce graphs that are nearly flat. To overcome this problem, you can manually change the vertical setting of the viewing window. The graph will vertically stretch if the values of Ymin and Ymax are closer together.

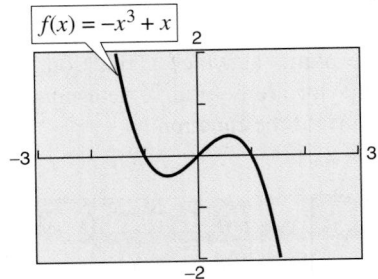

Figure 1.34

EXAMPLE 6 Approximating Relative Minimums and Maximums

Use a graphing utility to approximate the relative minimum and relative maximum of the function $f(x) = -x^3 + x$.

Solution
A sketch of the graph of f is shown in Figure 1.34. By using the *zoom* and *trace* features of the graphing utility, you can estimate that the function has a relative minimum at the point

$(-0.58, -0.38)$ Approximate relative minimum

and a relative maximum at the point

$(0.58, 0.38)$.   Approximate relative maximum

If you go on to take a course in calculus, you will learn a technique for finding the exact points at which this function has a relative minimum and a relative maximum.

> ## STUDY T!P
>
> Some graphing utilities have built-in programs that will find minimum or maximum values. If your graphing utility has such features, try using them to rework Example 6.

EXAMPLE 7 Bowling Equipment Sales

During the 1990s, the sales of bowling equipment in the United States increased and then decreased according to the model

$$C = 0.165t^3 - 7.16t^2 + 100.6t - 303.1, \qquad 8 \le t \le 16$$

where C is the sales of bowling equipment (in millions of dollars) and t represents the year, with $t = 8$ corresponding to 1988. According to this model, during which years were bowling equipment sales increasing? During which years were bowling equipment sales decreasing? Approximate the maximum amount of bowling equipment sales between 1988 and 1996. (Source: National Sporting Goods Association)

Solution
To solve this problem graph the function, as shown in Figure 1.35. From the graph, you can see that the bowling equipment sales increased from 1988 until 1992. Then, from 1992 to 1996, the sales decreased. The maximum amount of bowling equipment sales during the 8-year period was approximately $158 million.

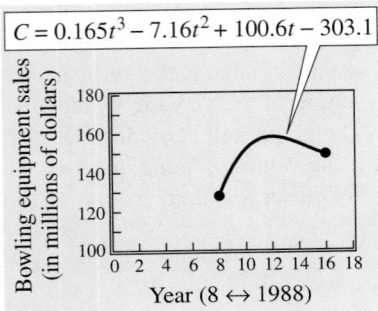

Figure 1.35

Graphing Step Functions and Piecewise-Defined Functions

The **greatest integer function** is denoted by $[\![x]\!]$ and is defined by

$$f(x) = [\![x]\!] = \text{the greatest integer less than or equal to } x.$$

The graph of this function is shown in Figure 1.36.

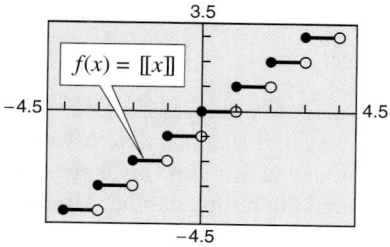

Figure 1.36

The graph of the greatest integer function jumps vertically one unit at each integer and is constant (a horizontal line segment) between each pair of consecutive integers. Because of these jumps, the greatest integer function is an example of a **step function** whose graph resembles a set of stair steps. Some values of the greatest integer function are as follows.

$$[\![-2]\!] = -2 \qquad [\![-1.5]\!] = -2 \qquad [\![-1]\!] = -1$$
$$[\![-0.5]\!] = -1 \qquad [\![0]\!] = 0 \qquad [\![0.5]\!] = 0$$
$$[\![1]\!] = 1 \qquad [\![1.5]\!] = 1 \qquad [\![2]\!] = 2$$

The range of the greatest integer function is the set of all integers.

In Section 1.3, you learned that a piecewise-defined function is a function that is defined by two or more equations over a specified domain. To sketch the graph of a piecewise-defined function, you need to sketch the graph of each equation on the appropriate portion of the domain.

EXAMPLE 8   Graphing a Piecewise-Defined Function

Sketch the graph of $f(x) = \begin{cases} 2x + 3, & x \le 1 \\ -x + 4, & x > 1 \end{cases}$.

Solution

This piecewise-defined function is composed of two linear functions. To the left of $x = 1$, the graph is the line given by $y = 2x + 3$. To the right of $x = 1$, the graph is the line given by $y = -x + 4$ (see Figure 1.37). Notice that the point $(1, 5)$ is a solid dot and the point $(1, 3)$ is an open dot. This is because $f(1) = 5$.

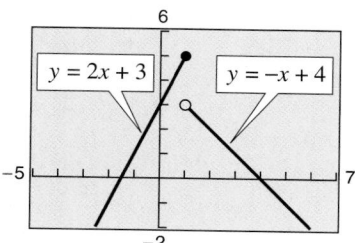

Figure 1.37

Library of Functions

The *greatest integer* function has an infinite number of breaks or steps—one at each integer value in its domain. Could you describe the greatest integer function using a piecewise-defined function? How does the graph of the greatest integer function differ from the graph of a line with zero slope?

Consult the Library of Functions Summary inside the front cover for a description of the greatest integer function.

STUDY TIP

Most graphing utilities display graphs in *connected mode*, which means that the graph has no breaks. When you are sketching graphs that do have breaks, it is better to use *dot mode*. Graph the greatest integer function [often called Int (x)] in connected and dot modes, and compare the two results.

Demonstrate the real-life nature of step functions by discussing Exercises 87 and 88 in this section. If writing is a part of your course, this section provides a good opportunity for students to find other examples of step functions and write brief essays on the application of these functions.

Even and Odd Functions

A graph has *symmetry with respect to the y-axis* if whenever (x, y) is on the graph, so is the point $(-x, y)$. A graph has *symmetry with respect to the origin* if whenever (x, y) is on the graph, so is the point $(-x, -y)$. A graph has *symmetry with respect to the x-axis* if whenever (x, y) is on the graph, so is the point $(x, -y)$. A function whose graph is symmetric with respect to the y-axis is an **even** function. A function whose graph is symmetric with respect to the origin is an **odd** function. The graph of a (nonzero) function cannot be symmetric with respect to the x-axis. These three types of symmetry are illustrated in Figure 1.38.

A computer animation of this concept appears in the *Interactive* CD-ROM and *Internet* versions of this text.

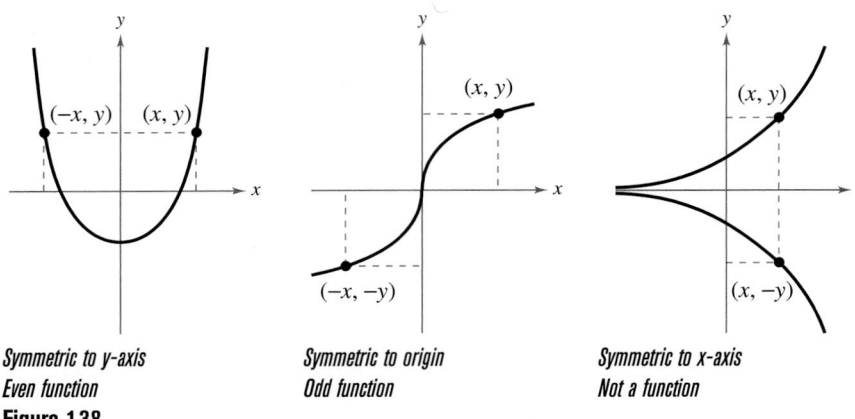

Symmetric to y-axis
Even function
Figure 1.38

Symmetric to origin
Odd function

Symmetric to x-axis
Not a function

Library of Functions

The *absolute value* function can be expressed as a piecewise-defined function.

$$|x| = \begin{cases} -x, & x < 0 \\ x, & x \geq 0 \end{cases}$$

Use this definition to show that $|-5| = 5$ and $|0| = 0$.

Consult the Library of Functions Summary inside the front cover for a description of the absolute value function.

Test for Even and Odd Functions

A function f is **even** if, for each x in the domain of f, $f(-x) = f(x)$.

A function f is **odd** if, for each x in the domain of f, $f(-x) = -f(x)$.

EXAMPLE 9   Testing for Evenness and Oddness

Is the function $f(x) = |x|$ even, odd, or neither?

Algebraic Solution

This function is even because

$$f(-x) = |-x|$$
$$= |x|$$
$$= f(x).$$

Graphical Solution

Use a graphing utility to graph $y = |x|$, as shown in Figure 1.39. You can see that the graph appears to be symmetric about the y-axis. So, the function is even.

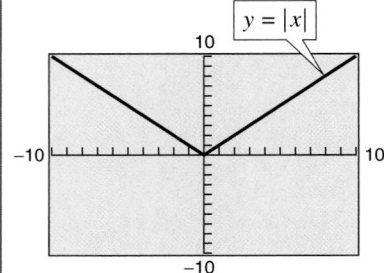

Figure 1.39

EXAMPLE 10 Even and Odd Functions

Determine whether each function is even, odd, or neither.

a. $g(x) = x^3 - x$ **b.** $h(x) = x^2 + 1$ **c.** $f(x) = x^3 - 1$

A computer animation of this concept appears in the *Interactive* CD-ROM and *Internet* versions of this text.

Algebraic Solution

a. This function is odd because

$$g(-x) = (-x)^3 - (-x)$$

$$= -x^3 + x$$

$$= -(x^3 - x)$$

$$= -g(x).$$

b. This function is even because

$$h(-x) = (-x)^2 + 1$$

$$= x^2 + 1$$

$$= h(x).$$

c. Substituting $-x$ for x produces

$$f(-x) = (-x)^3 - 1$$

$$= -x^3 - 1.$$

Because $f(x) = x^3 - 1$ and $-f(x) = -x^3 + 1$, you can conclude that $f(-x) \neq f(x)$ and $f(-x) \neq -f(x)$. So, the function is neither even nor odd.

Graphical Solution

a. In Figure 1.40(a), the graph is symmetric with respect to the origin. So, this function is odd.

b. In Figure 1.40(b), the graph is symmetric with respect to the y-axis. So, this function is even.

c. In Figure 1.40(c), the graph is neither symmetric to the origin nor to the y-axis. So, this function is neither even nor odd.

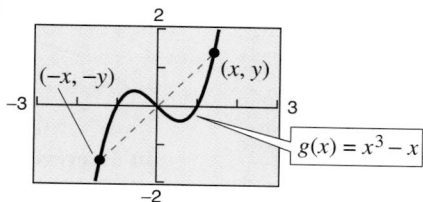

(a)

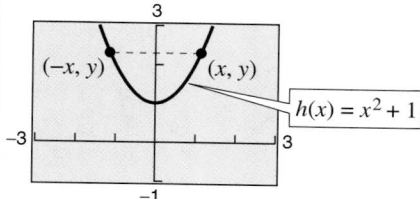

(b)

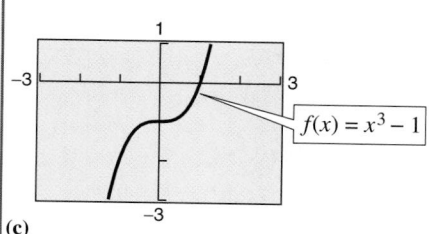

(c)

Figure 1.40

Writing About Math *Increasing and Decreasing Functions*

Write a short paragraph describing three different functions that represent quantities between 1985 and 2000. Describe one that decreased during this time, one that increased, and one that was constant. For instance, the value of the dollar decreased, the cost of first-class postage increased, and the land size of the United States remained constant. Present your results graphically.

1.4 Exercises

In Exercises 1–6, find the domain and range of the function.

1. $f(x) = 1 - x^2$

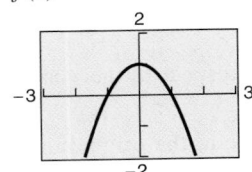

2. $f(x) = x^3 - 3x + 2$

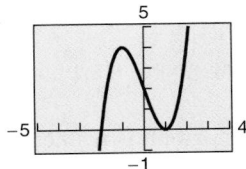

3. $f(x) = \sqrt{x^2 - 1}$

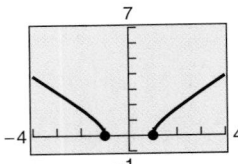

4. $h(x) = \sqrt{16 - x^2}$

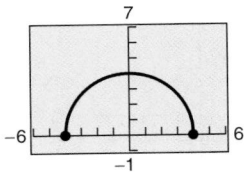

5. $f(x) = \frac{1}{2}|x - 2|$

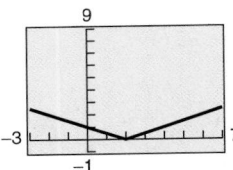

6. $g(x) = -|x - 1|$

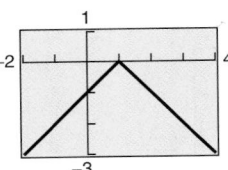

In Exercises 7–12, use a graphing utility to graph the function and estimate its domain and range. Then find the domain and range algebraically.

7. $f(x) = 2x^2 + 3$

8. $f(x) = -x^2 - 1$

9. $f(x) = \sqrt{x - 1}$

10. $h(t) = \sqrt{4 - t^2}$

11. $f(x) = |x + 3|$

12. $f(x) = -\frac{1}{4}|x - 5|$

In Exercises 13–18, use the Vertical Line Test to determine whether y is a function of x. Describe how you can use a graphing utility to produce the given graph.

13. $y = \frac{1}{2}x^2$

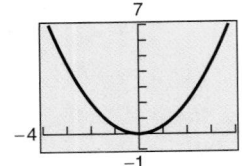

14. $y = \frac{1}{4}x^3$

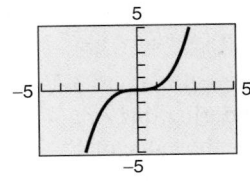

15. $x - y^2 = 1$

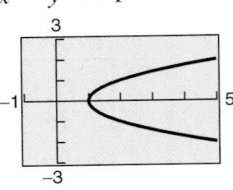

16. $x^2 + y^2 = 25$

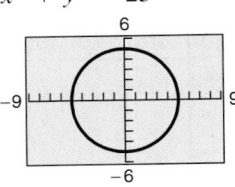

17. $x^2 = 2xy - 1$

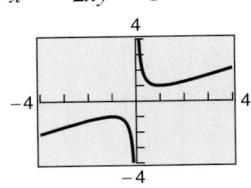

18. $x = |y + 2|$

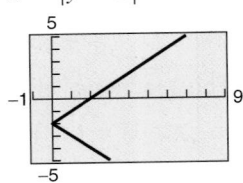

In Exercises 19–22, (a) determine the intervals over which the function is increasing, decreasing, or constant and (b) determine whether the function is even, odd, or neither.

19. $f(x) = \frac{3}{2}x$

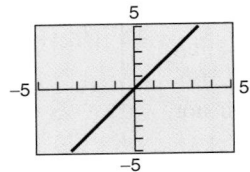

20. $f(x) = x^2 - 4x$

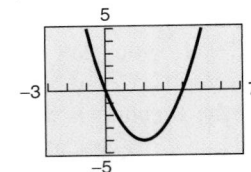

21. $f(x) = x^3 - 3x^2 + 2$

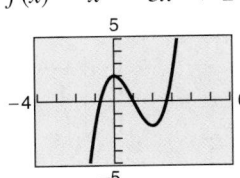

22. $f(x) = \sqrt{x^2 - 1}$

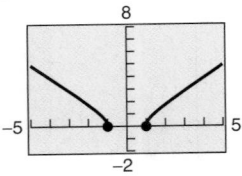

In Exercises 23–30, (a) use a graphing utility to graph the function; (b) determine the intervals over which the function is increasing, decreasing, or constant; and (c) determine whether the function is even, odd, or neither.

23. $f(x) = 3x^4 - 6x^2$

24. $f(x) = -x^6 - 2x^4$

25. $f(x) = x^{2/3}$

26. $f(x) = -x^{3/4}$

27. $f(x) = x\sqrt{x + 3}$ **28.** $f(x) = x(x^2 + 1)^{1/2}$

29. $f(x) = |x + 1| + |x - 1|$

30. $f(x) = -|x + 4| - |x + 1|$

In Exercises 31–36, use a graphing utility to approximate (to two decimal places) any relative minimum or maximum values of the function.

31. $f(x) = x^2 - 6x$ **32.** $f(x) = 3x^2 - 2x - 5$

33. $y = 2x^3 + 3x^2 - 12x$ **34.** $y = x^3 - 6x^2 + 15$

35. $h(x) = (x - 1)\sqrt{x}$ **36.** $g(x) = x\sqrt{4 - x}$

In Exercises 37–42, (a) approximate the relative minimum or maximum values of the function by sketching its graph using the point-plotting method, (b) use a graphing utility to approximate (to two decimal places) any relative minimum or maximum values, and (c) compare your answers from parts (a) and (b).

37. $f(x) = x^2 - 4x - 5$ **38.** $f(x) = 3x^2 - 12$

39. $f(x) = x^3 - 8x$ **40.** $f(x) = -x^3 + 7x$

41. $f(x) = (x - 4)^{2/3}$ **42.** $f(x) = \sqrt{4x^2 + 1}$

In Exercises 43–46, use a graphing utility to graph the piecewise-defined function.

43. $f(x) = \begin{cases} 2x + 3, & x < 0 \\ 3 - x, & x \geq 0 \end{cases}$

44. $f(x) = \begin{cases} x^2 + 5, & x \leq 1 \\ -x^2 + 4x + 3, & x > 1 \end{cases}$

45. $f(x) = \begin{cases} \sqrt{4 + x}, & x < 0 \\ \sqrt{4 - x}, & x \geq 0 \end{cases}$

46. $f(x) = \begin{cases} 1 - (x - 1)^2, & x \leq 2 \\ \sqrt{x - 2}, & x > 2 \end{cases}$

In Exercises 47–54, algebraically determine whether the function is even, odd, or neither. Verify your answer using a graphing utility.

47. $f(t) = t^2 + 2t - 3$ **48.** $f(x) = x^6 - 2x^2 + 3$

49. $g(x) = x^3 - 5x$ **50.** $h(x) = x^3 - 5$

51. $f(x) = x\sqrt{1 - x^2}$ **52.** $f(x) = x\sqrt{x + 5}$

53. $g(s) = 4s^{2/3}$ **54.** $f(s) = 4s^{3/2}$

Think About It In Exercises 55–60, find the coordinates of a second point on the graph of a function f if the given point is on the graph and the function is (a) even and (b) odd.

55. $\left(-\frac{3}{2}, 4\right)$ **56.** $\left(-\frac{5}{3}, -7\right)$

57. $(4, 9)$ **58.** $(5, -1)$

59. $(x, -y)$ **60.** $(2a, 2c)$

In Exercises 61–72, use a graphing utility to graph the function and determine whether it is even, odd, or neither. Verify your answer algebraically.

61. $f(x) = 5$ **62.** $f(x) = -9$

63. $f(x) = 3x - 2$ **64.** $f(x) = 5 - 3x$

65. $h(x) = x^2 - 4$ **66.** $f(x) = -x^2 - 8$

67. $f(x) = \sqrt{1 - x}$ **68.** $g(t) = \sqrt[3]{t - 1}$

69. $f(x) = |x + 2|$ **70.** $f(x) = -|x - 5|$

71. $f(x) = \begin{cases} x + 3, & x \leq 0 \\ 3, & 0 < x \leq 2 \\ 2x - 1, & x > 2 \end{cases}$

72. $f(x) = \begin{cases} 2x + 1, & x \leq -1 \\ x^2 - 2, & x > -1 \end{cases}$

In Exercises 73–82, graph the function and determine the interval(s) (if any) on the real axis for which $f(x) \geq 0$. Use a graphing utility to verify your results.

73. $f(x) = 4 - x$ **74.** $f(x) = 4x + 2$

75. $f(x) = x^2 - 9$ **76.** $f(x) = x^2 - 4x$

77. $f(x) = 1 - x^4$ **78.** $f(x) = x^2 + 1$

79. $f(x) = \sqrt{x + 2}$ **80.** $f(x) = -2\sqrt{x - 3}$

81. $f(x) = -(1 + |x|)$ **82.** $f(x) = \frac{1}{2}(2 + |x|)$

In Exercises 83 and 84, use a graphing utility to graph the function. State the domain and range of the function. Describe the pattern of the graph.

83. $s(x) = 2\left(\frac{1}{4}x - \left[\!\left[\frac{1}{4}x\right]\!\right]\right)$ **84.** $g(x) = 2\left(\frac{1}{4}x - \left[\!\left[\frac{1}{4}x\right]\!\right]\right)^2$

85. *Geometry* The perimeter of a rectangle is 100 meters.

     (a) Show that the area of the rectangle is $A = x(50 - x)$, where x is its length.

     (b) Use a graphing utility to graph the area function.

     (c) Use a graphing utility to approximate the maximum area of the rectangle and the dimensions that yield the maximum area.

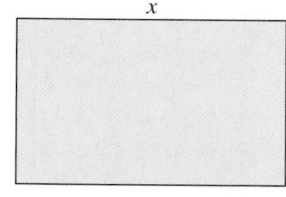

86. Business The marketing department of a company estimates that the demand for a product is

$$p = 100 - 0.0001x$$

where p is the price per unit and x is the number of units. The cost of producing x units is

$$C = 350,000 + 30x$$

and the profit for producing and selling x units is

$$P = R - C = xp - C.$$

Use a graphing utility to graph the profit function and estimate the number of units that would produce a maximum profit.

87. Communications The cost of using a telephone calling card is $1.05 for the first minute and $0.38 for each additional minute.

(a) Which of the following is the appropriate model for the cost C of a telephone call lasting t minutes? Explain.

$$C_1(t) = 1.05 + 0.38[\![t - 1]\!]$$

$$C_2(t) = 1.05 - 0.38[\![-(t - 1)]\!]$$

(b) Use a graphing utility to graph the appropriate model. Use the *value* feature or *zoom* and *trace* features to estimate the cost of a call lasting 18 minutes and 45 seconds.

88. Delivery Service Suppose that the cost of sending an overnight package from New York to Atlanta is $9.80 for under one pound and $2.50 for each additional pound. Use the greatest integer function to create a model for the cost C of overnight delivery of a package weighing x pounds where $x > 0$. Sketch the graph of the function.

 In Exercises 89–92, write the height h of the rectangle as a function of x.

89.

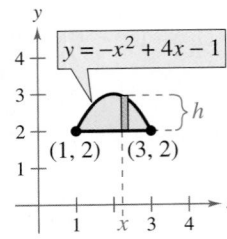

90.

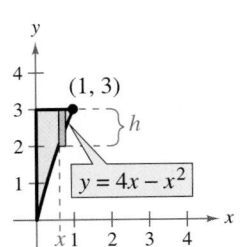

91.

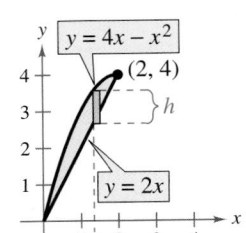

92.

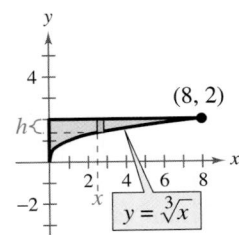

In Exercises 93 and 94, write the length L of the rectangle as a function of y.

93.

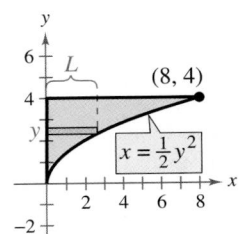

94.

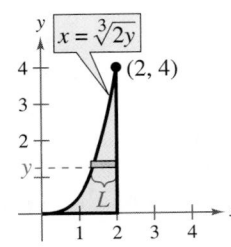

95. Data Analysis The table shows the amount y (in billions of dollars) of the merchandise trade balance of the United States for the years 1990 through 1997. (Source: U.S. International Trade Administration)

Year	1990	1991	1992	1993
y	-101.7	-66.7	-84.5	-115.6

Year	1994	1995	1996	1997
y	-150.6	-158.7	-170.2	-181.5

(a) Use the regression capabilities of a graphing utility to find a cubic model for the data. Let x be the time (in years), with $x = 0$ corresponding to 1990.

(b) What is the domain of the model?

(c) Use a graphing utility to graph the data and the model on the same viewing window.

(d) For which year does the model most accurately estimate the actual data? During which year is it least accurate?

(e) If this model remained valid in the future, would the economy show improvement? Explain your answer.

96. *Fluid Flow*   The intake pipe of a 100-gallon tank has a flow rate of 10 gallons per minute, and two drain pipes have a flow rate of 5 gallons per minute each. The graph shows the volume V of fluid in the tank as a function of time t. Determine the pipes in which the fluid is flowing in specific subintervals of the 1 hour of time shown on the graph. (There are many correct answers.)

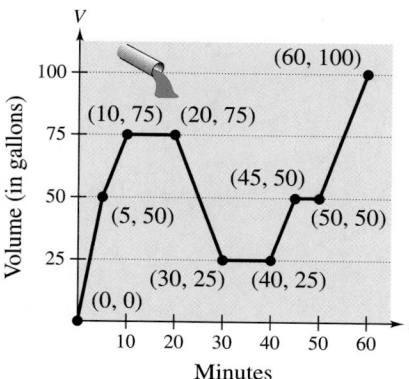

Synthesis

True or False?   **In Exercises 97 and 98, determine whether the statement is true or false. Justify your answer.**

97. A function with a square root cannot have a domain that is the set of all real numbers.

98. It is possible for an odd function to have the interval $[0, \infty)$ as its domain.

99. Prove that a function of the following form is odd.

$$y = a_{2n+1}x^{2n+1} + a_{2n-1}x^{2n-1} + \cdots + a_3x^3 + a_1x$$

100. Prove that a function of the following form is even.

$$y = a_{2n}x^{2n} + a_{2n-2}x^{2n-2} + \cdots + a_2x^2 + a_0$$

101. If f is an even function, determine if g is even, odd, or neither. Explain.

  (a) $g(x) = -f(x)$ (b) $g(x) = f(-x)$

  (c) $g(x) = f(x) - 2$ (d) $g(x) = -f(x - 2)$

102. *Think About It*   Does the graph of $x - y^2 = 1$ represent x as a function of y? Explain.

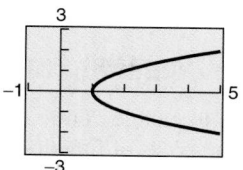

103. *Think About It*   Does the graph of $x^2 + y^2 = 25$ represent x as a function of y? Explain.

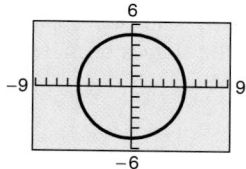

Review

In Exercises 104–107, find (a) the distance between the two points and (b) the midpoint of the segment joining the points.

104. $(-2, 7), (6, 3)$ **105.** $(-5, 0), (3, 6)$

106. $\left(\frac{5}{2}, -1\right), \left(-\frac{3}{2}, 4\right)$ **107.** $\left(-6, \frac{2}{3}\right), \left(\frac{3}{4}, \frac{1}{6}\right)$

In Exercises 108–111, evaluate the function at each specified value of the independent variable and simplify.

108. $f(x) = 5x - 1$

  (a) $f(6)$ (b) $f(-1)$ (c) $f(x - 3)$

109. $f(x) = -x^2 - x + 3$

  (a) $f(4)$ (b) $f(-2)$ (c) $f(x - 2)$

110. $f(x) = x\sqrt{x - 3}$

  (a) $f(3)$ (b) $f(12)$ (c) $f(6)$

111. $f(x) = -\frac{1}{2}x|x + 1|$

  (a) $f(-4)$ (b) $f(10)$ (c) $f\left(-\frac{2}{3}\right)$

In Exercises 112 and 113, find the difference quotient.

112. $f(x) = x^2 - 2x + 9, \dfrac{f(3 + h) - f(3)}{h}, h \neq 0$

113. $f(x) = 5 + 6x - x^2, \dfrac{f(6 + h) - f(6)}{h}, h \neq 0$

1.5 Shifting, Reflecting, and Stretching Graphs

Summary of Graphs of Common Functions

One of the goals of this text is to enable you to build your intuition for the basic shapes of the graphs of different types of functions. For instance, from your study of lines in Section 1.2, you can determine the basic shape of the graph of the linear function $f(x) = mx + b$. Specifically, you know that the graph of this function is a line whose slope is m and whose y-intercept is b.

The six graphs shown in Figure 1.41 represent the most commonly used functions in algebra. Familiarity with the basic characteristics of these simple graphs will help you analyze the shapes of more complicated graphs.

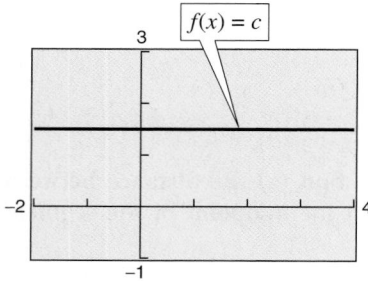

(a) Constant Function

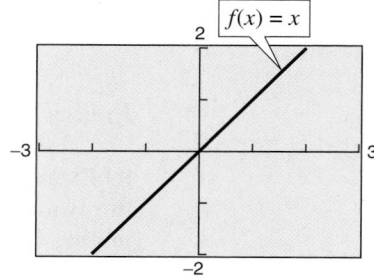

(b) Identity Function

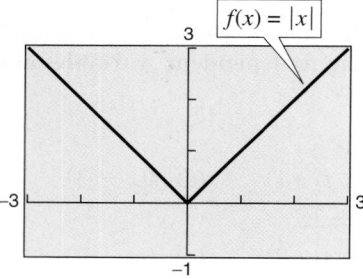

(c) Absolute Value Function

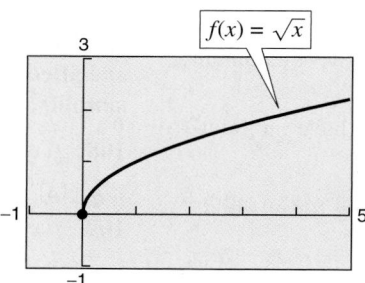

(d) Square Root Function

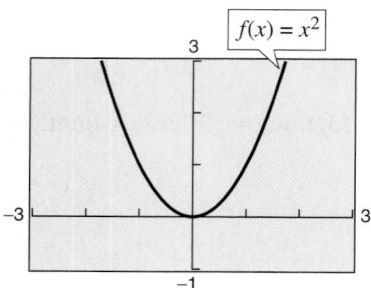

(e) Quadratic Function

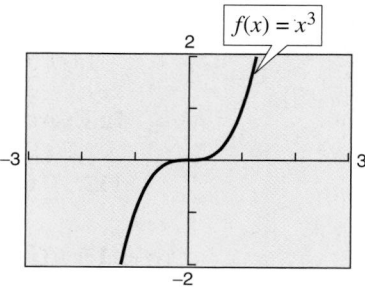

(f) Cubic Function

Figure 1.41

What You Should Learn:

- How to recognize graphs of common functions
- How to use vertical and horizontal shifts and reflections to sketch graphs of functions
- How to use nonrigid transformations to sketch graphs of functions

Why You Should Learn It:

Knowing the graphs of common functions and knowing how to shift, reflect, and stretch graphs of functions can help you sketch a wide variety of simple functions by hand. This skill is useful in sketching graphs of functions that model real-life data, such as in Exercise 77 on page 126, where you are asked to sketch a function that models the amount of fuel used by trucks from 1980 through 1996.

Index Stock

Emphasize that the graph of a function is related to a "family" of graphs, and if students learn these "families" of common graphs, graphing will be much easier. You can reinforce this concept with discovery methods such as graphing $f(x) = x^2$, $f(x) = x^2 + 2$, $f(x) = (x - 1)^2$, and $f(x) = (x - 1)^2 + 2$ and noting similarities and differences.

Vertical and Horizontal Shifts

Many functions have graphs that are simple transformations of the common graphs summarized in Figure 1.41. For example, you can obtain the graph of

$$h(x) = x^2 + 2$$

by shifting the graph of $f(x) = x^2$ *up* two units, as shown in Figure 1.42. In function notation, h and f are related as follows.

$$h(x) = x^2 + 2$$
$$= f(x) + 2 \qquad \text{Upward shift of 2}$$

Similarly, you can obtain the graph of

$$g(x) = (x - 2)^2$$

by shifting the graph of $f(x) = x^2$ to the *right* two units, as shown in Figure 1.43. In this case, the functions g and f have the following relationship.

$$g(x) = (x - 2)^2$$
$$= f(x - 2) \qquad \text{Right shift of 2}$$

A computer animation of this concept appears in the *Interactive* CD-ROM and *Internet* versions of this text.

Exploration

Use a graphing utility to display the graphs of $y = x^2 + c$, where $c = -4, -2, 0, 2$, and 4. Use the result to describe the effect that c has on the graph. Use a graphing utility to display the graphs of $y = (x + c)^2$, where $c = -2, 0, 2$, and 4. Use the result to describe the effect that c has on the graph.

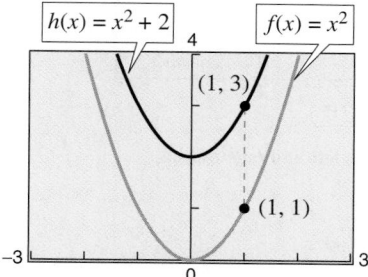

Figure 1.42 *Vertical shift upward: two units*

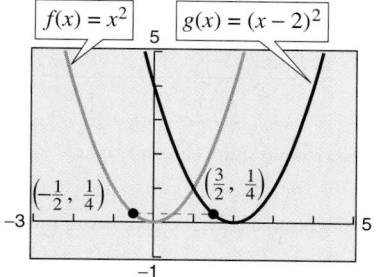

Figure 1.43 *Horizontal shift to the right: two units*

The following list summarizes this discussion about horizontal and vertical shifts.

Vertical and Horizontal Shifts

Let c be a positive real number. **Vertical and horizontal shifts** in the graph of $y = f(x)$ are represented as follows.

1. Vertical shift c units *upward:* $\qquad h(x) = f(x) + c$
2. Vertical shift c units *downward:* $\qquad h(x) = f(x) - c$
3. Horizontal shift c units to the *right:* $\qquad h(x) = f(x - c)$
4. Horizontal shift c units to the *left:* $\qquad h(x) = f(x + c)$

In items 3 and 4, be sure you see that $h(x) = f(x - c)$ corresponds to a *right* shift and $h(x) = f(x + c)$ corresponds to a *left* shift for $c > 0$.

You might also wish to illustrate simple transformations of functions numerically using tables to emphasize what happens to individual ordered pairs. For instance, suppose you have

$$f(x) = x^2, \quad h(x) = x^2 + 2 = f(x) + 2$$

and

$$g(x) = (x - 2)^2 = f(x - 2)$$

then you can illustrate these transformations with the following tables.

x	$f(x)$	$h(x) = f(x) + 2$
-2	4	$4 + 2 = 6$
-1	1	$1 + 2 = 3$
0	0	$0 + 2 = 2$
1	1	$1 + 2 = 3$
2	4	$4 + 2 = 6$

x	$x - 2$	$g(x) = f(x - 2)$
0	$0 - 2 = -2$	4
1	$1 - 2 = -1$	1
2	$2 - 2 = 0$	0
3	$3 - 2 = 1$	1
4	$4 - 2 = 2$	4

EXAMPLE 1 Shifts in the Graph of a Function

Compare the graph of each function with the graph of $f(x) = x^3$.

a. $g(x) = x^3 - 1$ **b.** $h(x) = (x - 1)^3$ **c.** $k(x) = (x + 2)^3 + 1$

Solution

a. Graph $f(x) = x^3$ and $g(x) = x^3 - 1$ [see Figure 1.44(a)]. You can see that you can obtain the graph of g by shifting the graph of f one unit down.

b. Graph $f(x) = x^3$ and $h(x) = (x - 1)^3$ [see Figure 1.44(b)]. You can obtain the graph of h by shifting the graph of f one unit to the right.

c. Graph $f(x) = x^3$ and $k(x) = (x + 2)^3 + 1$ [see Figure 1.44(c)]. You can see that you can obtain the graph of k by shifting the graph of f two units to the left and then one unit up.

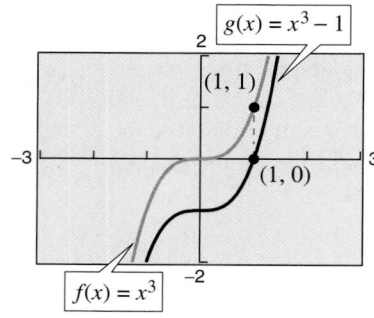
(a) Vertical shift: one unit down

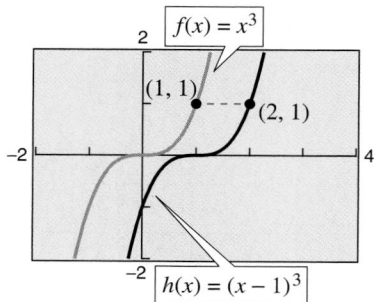
(b) Horizontal shift: one unit right

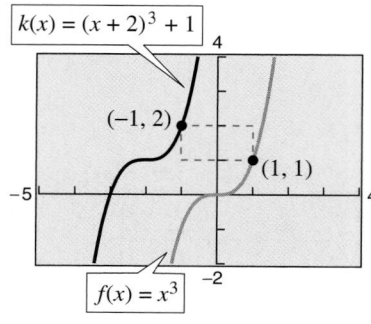
(c) Two units left and one unit up

Figure 1.44

EXAMPLE 2 Finding Equations from Graphs

The graphs shown in Figures 1.45 (b) and (c) are shifts of the graph of $f(x) = x^2$ shown in Figure 1.45 (a). Find equations for g and h.

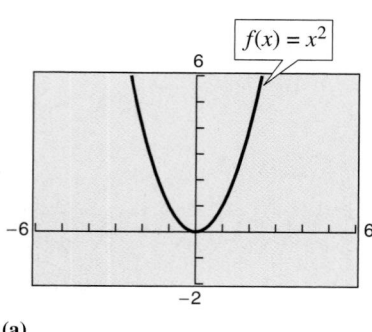
(a)

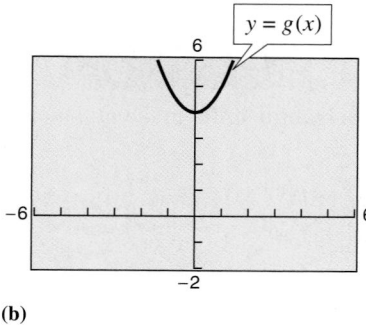
(b)

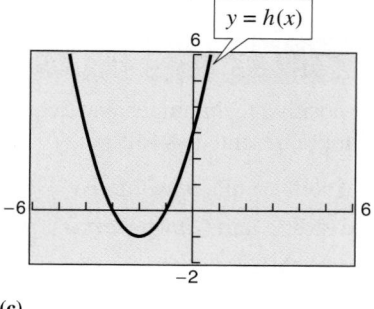
(c)

Figure 1.45

Solution

a. The graph of g is a vertical shift of four units upward of the graph of $f(x) = x^2$. So, the equation for g is $g(x) = x^2 + 4$.

b. The graph of h is a horizontal shift of two units to the left of the graph of $f(x) = x^2$ and one unit downward. So, the equation for h is $h(x) = (x + 2)^2 - 1$.

Reflecting Graphs

The second common type of transformation is called a **reflection.** For instance, if you consider the x-axis to be a mirror, the graph of $h(x) = -x^2$ is the mirror image (or reflection) of the graph of $f(x) = x^2$ (see Figure 1.46).

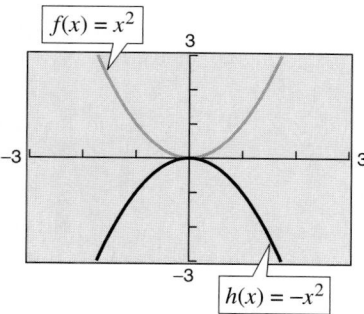

Figure 1.46

Exploration

Compare the graph of each function with the graph of $f(x) = x^2$ by using a graphing utility to graph the function and f in the same viewing window. Describe the transformation.

a. $g(x) = -x^2$

b. $h(x) = (-x)^2$

Reflections in the Coordinate Axes

Reflections in the coordinate axes of the graph of $y = f(x)$ are represented as follows.

1. Reflection in the x-axis: $h(x) = -f(x)$
2. Reflection in the y-axis: $h(x) = f(-x)$

A computer animation of this concept appears in the *Interactive* CD-ROM and *Internet* versions of this text.

EXAMPLE 3   Finding Equations from Graphs

Each of the graphs shown in Figure 1.48 is a transformation of the graph of $f(x) = x^4$ (see Figure 1.47). Find an equation of each function.

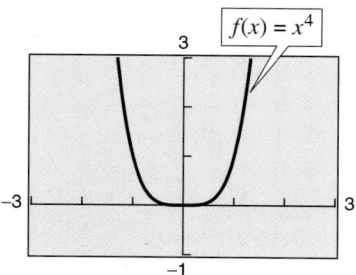

Figure 1.47

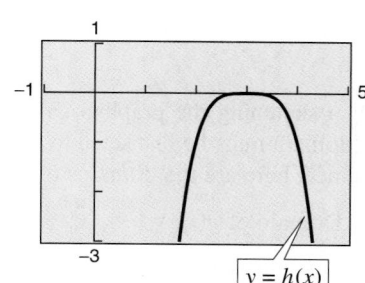

(a)

(b)
Figure 1.48

Solution

a. The graph of g is a reflection in the x-axis followed by an upward shift of two units of the graph of $f(x) = x^4$. So, the equation for g is $g(x) = -x^4 + 2$.

b. The graph of h is a horizontal shift of three units to the right followed by a reflection in the x-axis of the graph of $f(x) = x^4$. So, the equation for h is $h(x) = -(x - 3)^4$.

EXAMPLE 4   Reflections and Shifts

Compare the graph of each function with the graph of $f(x) = \sqrt{x}$.

a. $g(x) = -\sqrt{x}$ **b.** $h(x) = \sqrt{-x}$ **c.** $k(x) = -\sqrt{x+2}$

Algebraic Solution

a. Relative to the graph of $f(x) = \sqrt{x}$, the graph of g is a reflection in the x-axis because

$$g(x) = -\sqrt{x}$$

$$= -f(x).$$

b. The graph of h is a reflection of the graph of $f(x) = \sqrt{x}$ in the y-axis because

$$h(x) = \sqrt{-x}$$

$$= f(-x).$$

c. From the equation

$$k(x) = -\sqrt{x+2}$$

$$= -f(x+2)$$

you can conclude that the graph of k is a left shift of two units, followed by a reflection in the x-axis.

Graphical Solution

a. Use a graphing utility to graph f and g in the same viewing window. From the graph in Figure 1.49(a), you can see that the graph of g is a reflection of the graph of f in the x-axis.

b. Use a graphing utility to graph f and h in the same viewing window. From the graph in Figure 1.49(b), you can see that the graph of h is a reflection of the graph of f in the y-axis.

c. Use a graphing utility to graph f and k in the same viewing window. From the graph in Figure 1.49(c), you can see that the graph of k is a left shift of the graph of f of two units, followed by a reflection in the x-axis.

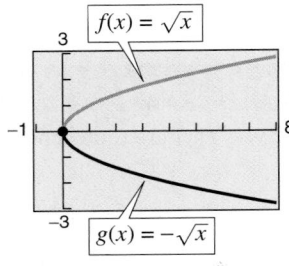

(a)

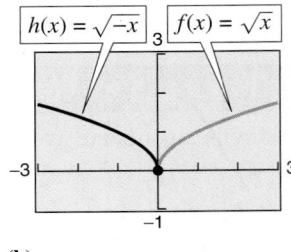

(b)

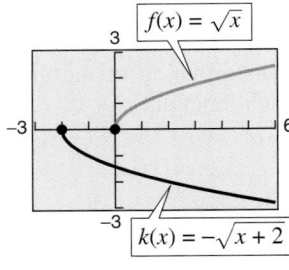

(c)

Figure 1.49

When sketching the graphs of functions involving square roots, remember that the domain must be restricted to exclude negative numbers inside the radical. For instance, here are the domains of the functions in Example 4.

Domain of $g(x) = -\sqrt{x}$: $x \geq 0$

Domain of $h(x) = \sqrt{-x}$: $x \leq 0$

Domain of $k(x) = -\sqrt{x+2}$: $x \geq -2$

Activities

1. Compare the graph of $f(x) = |x|$ to the graph of $g(x) = |x - 9|$.

   Answer: $g(x)$ is $f(x)$ shifted to the right nine units.

2. Does the graph of

   $$f(x) = -(x+1)^3 + 4$$

   represent a horizontal shift of one unit to the left, followed by a vertical shift of four units up, followed by a reflection in the x-axis?

   Answer: No, it represents a horizontal shift of one unit to the left, followed by a reflection in the x-axis, followed by a vertical shift of four units.

Nonrigid Transformations

Horizontal shifts, vertical shifts, and reflections are called **rigid transformations** because the basic shape of the graph is unchanged. These transformations change only the *position* of the graph in the *xy*-plane. **Nonrigid transformations** are those that cause a *distortion*—a change in the shape of the original graph. For instance, a nonrigid transformation of the graph of $y = f(x)$ is represented by $y = cf(x)$, where the transformation is a **vertical stretch** if $c > 1$ and a **vertical shrink** if $0 < c < 1$.

A computer animation of this concept appears in the *Interactive* CD-ROM and *Internet* versions of this text.

EXAMPLE 5 Nonrigid Transformations

Compare the graph of each function with the graph of $f(x) = |x|$.

a. $h(x) = 3|x|$ **b.** $g(x) = \dfrac{1}{3}|x|$

Solution

a. Relative to the graph of $f(x) = |x|$, the graph of

$$h(x) = 3|x|$$
$$= 3f(x)$$

is a vertical stretch (multiply each *y*-value by 3) of the graph of *f*.

b. Similarly, the equation

$$g(x) = \frac{1}{3}|x|$$
$$= \frac{1}{3}f(x)$$

indicates that the graph of *g* is a vertical shrink $\left(\text{multiply each } y\text{-value by } \frac{1}{3}\right)$ of the graph of *f*.

The graphs of all three functions are shown in Figure 1.50.

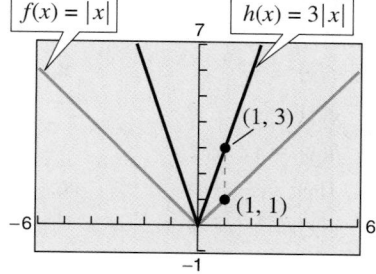

(a)

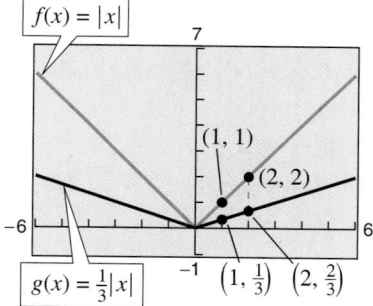

(b)

Figure 1.50

EXAMPLE 6 Sequences of Nonrigid Transformations

Use a graphing utility to graph the two functions

$$g(x) = 5(x^2 - 2) \quad \text{and} \quad h(x) = 5x^2 - 2$$

in the same viewing window. Describe how each function was obtained from $f(x) = x^2$ as a sequence of shifts and stretches.

Solution

Notice that $g(x)$ and $h(x)$ in Figure 1.51 are different. The graph of *g* is a downward shift of *f* of two units followed by a vertical stretch, whereas *h* is a vertical stretch of *f* followed by a downward shift of two units. So, the order of applying the transformations that include nonrigid transformations is important.

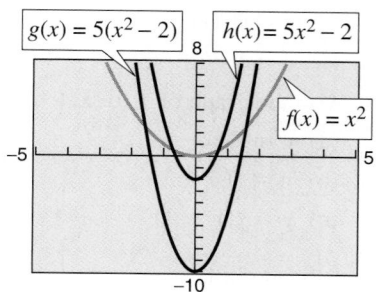

Figure 1.51

1.5 Exercises

In Exercises 1–12, sketch the graphs of the three functions by hand on the same rectangular coordinate system. Verify your result with a graphing utility.

1. $f(x) = x$
  $g(x) = x - 4$
  $h(x) = 3x$

2. $f(x) = \frac{1}{2}x$
  $g(x) = \frac{1}{2}x + 2$
  $h(x) = \frac{1}{2}(x - 2)$

3. $f(x) = x^2$
  $g(x) = x^2 + 2$
  $h(x) = (x - 2)^2$

4. $f(x) = x^2$
  $g(x) = x^2 - 4$
  $h(x) = (x + 2)^2 + 1$

5. $f(x) = -x^2$
  $g(x) = -x^2 + 1$
  $h(x) = -(x - 2)^2$

6. $f(x) = (x - 2)^2$
  $g(x) = (x - 2)^2 + 2$
  $h(x) = -(x - 2)^2 + 4$

7. $f(x) = x^2$
  $g(x) = \frac{1}{2}x^2$
  $h(x) = 2x^2$

8. $f(x) = x^2$
  $g(x) = \frac{1}{4}x^2 + 2$
  $h(x) = -\frac{1}{4}x^2$

9. $f(x) = |x|$
  $g(x) = |x| - 1$
  $h(x) = |x - 3|$

10. $f(x) = |x|$
  $g(x) = 2|x|$
  $h(x) = -2|x + 2| - 1$

11. $f(x) = \sqrt{x}$
  $g(x) = \sqrt{x + 1}$
  $h(x) = \sqrt{x - 2} + 1$

12. $f(x) = \sqrt{x}$
  $g(x) = \frac{1}{2}\sqrt{x}$
  $h(x) = -\frac{1}{2}\sqrt{x + 4}$

13. Use the graph of f to sketch each graph.
  (a) $y = f(x) + 2$
  (b) $y = -f(x)$
  (c) $y = f(x - 2)$
  (d) $y = f(x + 3)$
  (e) $y = 2f(x)$
  (f) $y = f(-x)$

14. Use the graph of f to sketch each graph.
  (a) $y = f(x) - 1$
  (b) $y = f(x + 1)$
  (c) $y = f(x - 1)$
  (d) $y = -f(x - 2)$
  (e) $y = f(-x)$
  (f) $y = \frac{1}{2}f(x)$

In Exercises 15–26, identify the common function and the transformation shown in the graph. Write the formula for the graphed function.

15.
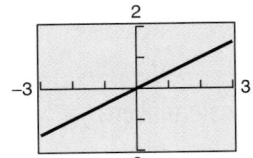

16.
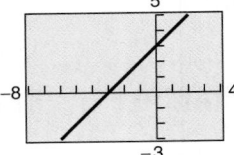

17.
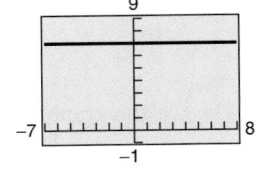

18.
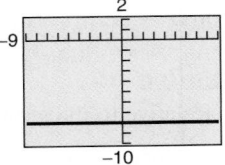

19.
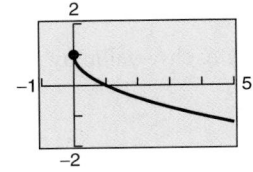

20.
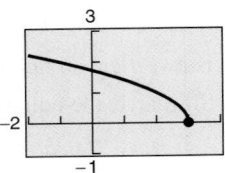

21.
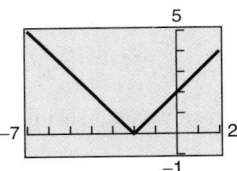

22.
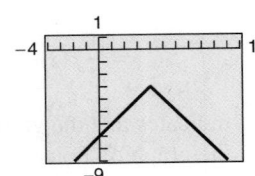

23.
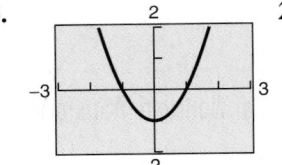

24.
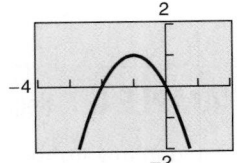

25.
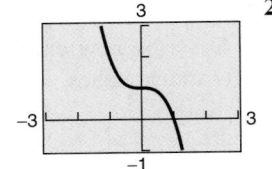

26.
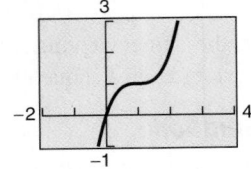

In Exercises 27–32, compare the graph of the function with the graph of $f(x) = \sqrt{x}$.

27. $y = \sqrt{x} + 2$ **28.** $y = -\sqrt{x} - 1$

29. $y = \sqrt{x} - 2$ **30.** $y = \sqrt{x} + 3$

31. $y = 2\sqrt{x}$ **32.** $y = \sqrt{-x} + 3$

In Exercises 33–38, compare the graph of the function with the graph of $f(x) = |x|$.

33. $y = |x + 2|$ **34.** $y = |x| - 3$

35. $y = -|x|$ **36.** $y = |-x|$

37. $y = \frac{1}{3}|x|$ **38.** $y = \frac{1}{2}|x|$

In Exercises 39–44, specify the sequence of transformations that will yield the graph of the given function from the graph of the function $f(x) = x^3$.

39. $g(x) = 4 - x^3$ **40.** $g(x) = -(x - 4)^3$

41. $h(x) = \frac{1}{4}(x + 2)^3$ **42.** $h(x) = -2(x - 1)^3 + 3$

43. $p(x) = \frac{1}{3}x^3 + 2$ **44.** $p(x) = [3(x - 2)]^3$

In Exercises 45–48, use a graphing utility to graph the three functions in the same viewing window. Describe the graphs of g and h relative to the graph of f.

45. $f(x) = x^3 - 3x^2$
     $g(x) = f(x + 2)$
     $h(x) = \frac{1}{2}f(x)$

46. $f(x) = x^3 - 3x^2 + 2$
     $g(x) = f(x - 1)$
     $h(x) = 2f(x)$

47. $f(x) = x^3 - 3x^2$
     $g(x) = -\frac{1}{3}f(x)$
     $h(x) = f(-x)$

48. $f(x) = x^3 - 3x^2 + 2$
     $g(x) = -f(x)$
     $h(x) = f(-x)$

In Exercises 49 and 50, use the graph of $f(x) = x^3 - 3x^2$ (see Exercise 45) to write a formula for the function g shown in the graph.

49.

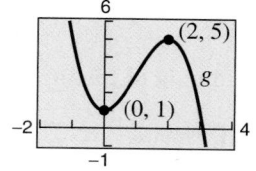

50.

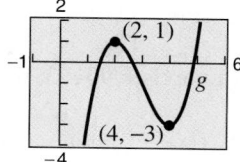

In Exercises 51–74, g is related to one of the six common functions on page 118. (a) Identify the common function f. (b) Describe the sequence of transformations from f to g. (c) Sketch the graph of g. (d) Use function notation to write g in terms of the common function f.

51. $g(x) = 12 - x^2$ **52.** $g(x) = (x - 8)^2$

53. $g(x) = 2 - (x + 5)^2$ **54.** $g(x) = -(x + 10)^2 + 5$

55. $g(x) = 3 + 2(x - 4)^2$

56. $g(x) = -\frac{1}{4}(x + 2)^2 - 2$

57. $g(x) = x^3 + 7$ **58.** $g(x) = -x^3 - 1$

59. $g(x) = (x - 1)^3 + 2$ **60.** $g(x) = -(x + 3)^3 - 10$

61. $g(x) = 3(x - 2)^3$ **62.** $g(x) = -\frac{1}{2}(x + 1)^3 - 5$

63. $g(x) = -|x| - 2$ **64.** $g(x) = 6 - |x + 5|$

65. $g(x) = -|x + 4| + 8$ **66.** $g(x) = |-x + 3| + 9$

67. $g(x) = -2|x - 1|$ **68.** $g(x) = \frac{1}{2}|x - 2| - 3$

69. $g(x) = \sqrt{x - 9}$ **70.** $g(x) = \sqrt{x + 4} + 8$

71. $g(x) = \sqrt{7 - x} - 2$ **72.** $g(x) = -\sqrt{x + 1} - 6$

73. $g(x) = 4\sqrt{x - 1}$

74. $g(x) = -\frac{1}{2}\sqrt{x + 3} - 1$

75. *Profit*   The profit P per week on a certain product is given by the model

$$P(x) = 80 + 20x - 0.5x^2, \qquad 0 \le x \le 20$$

where x is the amount spent on advertising. In this model, x and P are both measured in hundreds of dollars.

(a) Use a graphing utility to graph the profit function.

(b) The business estimates that taxes and operating costs will increase by an average of \$2500 per week during the next year. Rewrite the profit equation to reflect this expected decrease in profits. Identify the type of transformation applied to the graph of the equation.

(c) Rewrite the profit equation so that x measures advertising expenditures in dollars. [Find $P\left(\frac{x}{100}\right)$.] Identify the type of transformation applied to the graph of the profit function.

76. *Automobile Aerodynamics*   The number of horsepower H required to overcome wind drag on a certain automobile is approximated by

$$H(x) = 0.002x^2 + 0.005x - 0.029, \quad 10 \le x \le 100$$

where x is the speed of the car in miles per hour.

(a) Use a graphing utility to graph the power function.

(b) Rewrite the power function so that x represents the speed in kilometers per hour. [Find $H(x/1.6)$.] Identify the type of transformation applied to the graph of the power function.

77. *Energy* The amount of fuel F (in billions of gallons) used by trucks from 1980 through 1996 can be approximated by the function

$$F(t) = 20.46 + 0.04t^2$$

where $t = 0$ represents 1980. (Source: U.S. Federal Highway Administration)

(a) Describe how F can be obtained from the common function $f(x) = x^2$. Then sketch the graph over the interval $0 \leq t \leq 16$.

(b) Rewrite the function so that $t = 0$ represents 1990. Explain how you got your answer.

78. *Finance* The amount of mortgage debt outstanding M (in billions of dollars) in the United States from 1985 through 1997 can be approximated by the function

$$M(t) = 1.5\sqrt{t} - 1.25$$

where $t = 5$ represents 1985. (Source: Board of Governors of the Federal Reserve System)

(a) Describe how M can be obtained from the common function $f(x) = \sqrt{x}$. Then sketch the graph over the interval $5 \leq t \leq 17$.

(b) Rewrite the function so that $t = 5$ represents 1995. Explain how you got your answer.

79. *Graphical Reasoning* An electronically controlled thermostat in a home is programmed to automatically lower the temperature at night (see figure). The temperature in the house T, in degrees Fahrenheit, is given in terms of t, the time (in hours) on a 24-hour clock.

(a) Explain why T is a function of t.

(b) Approximate $T(4)$ and $T(15)$.

(c) Suppose the thermostat were reprogrammed to produce a temperature H where $H(t) = T(t - 1)$. How would this change the temperature in the house? Explain.

(d) Suppose the thermostat were reprogrammed to produce a temperature H where $H(t) = T(t) - 1$. How would this change the temperature in the house? Explain.

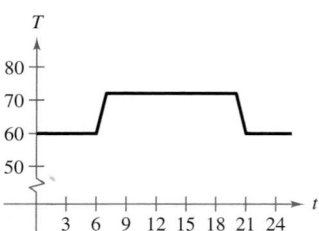

Synthesis

True or False?   In Exercises 80 and 81, determine whether the statement is true or false. Justify your answer.

80. The graphs of $f(x) = |x| - 5$ and $g(x) = |-x| - 5$ are identical.

81. If the graph of the common function $f(x) = x^2$ is moved 6 units to the right, 3 units up, and reflected in the x-axis, then the point $(-1, 28)$ will lie on the graph of the transformation.

82. *Exploration* Use a graphing utility to graph each function. Describe any similarities and differences you observe among the graphs.

(a) $y = x$ (b) $y = x^2$ (c) $y = x^3$
(d) $y = x^4$ (e) $y = x^5$ (f) $y = x^6$

83. *Conjecture* Use the results of Exercise 82 to make a conjecture about the shapes of the graphs of $y = x^7$ and $y = x^8$. Use a graphing utility to verify your conjecture.

84. Use the results of Exercise 82 to sketch the graph of $y = (x - 3)^3$ by hand. Use a graphing utility to verify your graph.

85. Use the results of Exercise 82 to sketch the graph of $y = (x + 1)^2$ by hand. Use a graphing utility to verify your graph.

Conjecture   In Exercises 86–89, use the results of Exercise 82 to make a conjecture about the shape of the graph of the function. Use a graphing utility to verify your conjecture.

86. $f(x) = x^2(x - 6)^2$ **87.** $f(x) = x^3(x - 6)^2$
88. $f(x) = x^2(x - 6)^3$ **89.** $f(x) = x^3(x - 6)^3$

Review

In Exercises 90–93, find the domain of the function.

90. $f(x) = \dfrac{4}{9 - x}$ **91.** $f(x) = \dfrac{\sqrt{x - 5}}{x - 7}$

92. $f(x) = \sqrt{100 - x^2}$ **93.** $f(x) = \sqrt[3]{16 - x^2}$

In Exercises 94–99, sketch a graph of the equation. Use a graphing utility to verify your graph.

94. $y = -x - 7$ **95.** $y = 9 - 4x$
96. $y = x^2 - 4x$ **97.** $y = -x^3 - 3$
98. $y = \sqrt{9 - x}$ **99.** $y = 5 - 2|3x|$

1.6 Combinations of Functions

Arithmetic Combinations of Functions

Just as two real numbers can be combined by the operations of addition, subtraction, multiplication, and division to form other real numbers, two *functions* can be combined to create new functions. If $f(x) = 2x - 3$ and $g(x) = x^2 - 1$ you can form the sum, difference, product, and quotient of f and g as follows.

$$f(x) + g(x) = (2x - 3) + (x^2 - 1)$$
$$= x^2 + 2x - 4 \qquad \text{Sum}$$

$$f(x) - g(x) = (2x - 3) - (x^2 - 1)$$
$$= -x^2 + 2x - 2 \qquad \text{Difference}$$

$$f(x) \cdot g(x) = (2x - 3)(x^2 - 1)$$
$$= 2x^3 - 3x^2 - 2x + 3 \qquad \text{Product}$$

$$\frac{f(x)}{g(x)} = \frac{2x - 3}{x^2 - 1}, \qquad x \neq \pm 1 \qquad \text{Quotient}$$

The domain of an **arithmetic combination** of functions f and g consists of all real numbers that are common to the domains of f and g. In the case of the quotient $f(x)/g(x)$, there is the further restriction that $g(x) \neq 0$.

Sum, Difference, Product, and Quotient of Functions

Let f and g be two functions with overlapping domains. Then, for all x common to both domains, the sum, difference, product, and quotient of f and g are defined as follows.

1. **Sum:** $\quad (f + g)(x) = f(x) + g(x)$
2. **Difference:** $\quad (f - g)(x) = f(x) - g(x)$
3. **Product:** $\quad (fg)(x) = f(x) \cdot g(x)$
4. **Quotient:** $\quad \left(\dfrac{f}{g}\right)(x) = \dfrac{f(x)}{g(x)}, \quad g(x) \neq 0$

What You Should Learn:

- How to add, subtract, multiply, and divide functions
- How to find compositions of one function with another function
- How to use combinations of functions to model and solve real-life problems

Why You Should Learn It:

Combining functions can sometimes help you better understand the bigger picture. For instance, Exercises 81 and 82 on page 136 show how to use combinations of functions to analyze U.S. health expenditures.

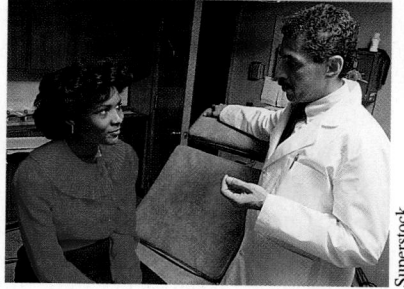

A computer animation of this concept appears in the *Interactive* CD-ROM and *Internet* versions of this text.

EXAMPLE 1   Finding the Sum of Two Functions

Find $(f + g)(x)$ for the functions $f(x) = 2x + 1$ and $g(x) = x^2 + 2x - 1$. Then evaluate the sum when $x = 2$.

Solution

$$(f + g)(x) = f(x) + g(x)$$
$$= (2x + 1) + (x^2 + 2x - 1)$$
$$= x^2 + 4x$$

When $x = 2$, the value of this sum is $(f + g)(2) = 2^2 + 4(2) = 12$.

EXAMPLE 2 Finding the Difference of Two Functions

Evaluate $(f - g)(x)$ for the functions

$$f(x) = 2x + 1 \quad \text{and} \quad g(x) = x^2 + 2x - 1$$

when $x = 2$.

Algebraic Solution

The difference of the functions f and g is

$$
\begin{aligned}
(f - g)(x) &= f(x) - g(x) \\
&= (2x + 1) - (x^2 + 2x - 1) \\
&= -x^2 + 2.
\end{aligned}
$$

When $x = 2$, the value of this difference is

$$
\begin{aligned}
(f - g)(2) &= -(2)^2 + 2 \\
&= -2.
\end{aligned}
$$

Note that $(f - g)(2)$ can also be evaluated as follows.

$$
\begin{aligned}
(f - g)(2) &= f(2) - g(2) \\
&= [2(2) + 1] - [2^2 + 2(2) - 1] \\
&= 5 - 7 \\
&= -2
\end{aligned}
$$

Graphical Solution

You can use a graphing utility to graph the difference of two functions. Enter the functions as follows.

$$y_1 = 2x + 1$$

$$y_2 = x^2 + 2x - 1$$

$$y_3 = y_1 - y_2$$

Graph y_3 as shown in Figure 1.52. Then use the *value* feature or *zoom* and *trace* features to estimate that the value of the difference when $x = 2$ is -2.

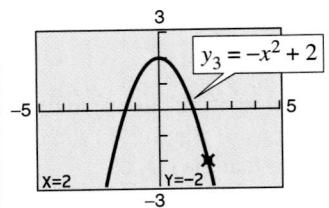

Figure 1.52

In Examples 1 and 2, both f and g have domains that consist of all real numbers. So, the domain of both $(f + g)$ and $(f - g)$ is also the set of all real numbers. Remember that any restrictions on the domains of f or g must be taken into account when forming the sum, difference, product, or quotient of f and g. For instance, the domain of $f(x) = 1/x$ is all $x \neq 0$, and the domain of $g(x) = \sqrt{x}$ is $[0, \infty)$. This implies that the domain of $f + g$ is $(0, \infty)$.

EXAMPLE 3 Finding the Product of Two Functions

Given the functions $f(x) = x^2$ and $g(x) = x - 3$, find the product of f and g. Then evaluate the product when $x = 4$.

Solution

$$
\begin{aligned}
(fg)(x) &= f(x)g(x) \\
&= (x^2)(x - 3) \\
&= x^3 - 3x^2
\end{aligned}
$$

When $x = 4$, the value of this product is

$$
\begin{aligned}
(fg)(4) &= 4^3 - 3(4)^2 \\
&= 16.
\end{aligned}
$$

Additional Examples

a. Find $(fg)(x)$ given that $f(x) = x + 5$ and $g(x) = 3x$.

Solution

$$
\begin{aligned}
(fg)(x) &= f(x) \cdot g(x) \\
&= (x + 5)(3x) \\
&= 3x^2 + 15x
\end{aligned}
$$

b. Find $(gf)(x)$ given that $f(x) = \dfrac{1}{x}$ and $g(x) = \dfrac{x}{x + 1}$.

Solution

$$
\begin{aligned}
(gf)(x) &= g(x) \cdot f(x) \\
&= \left(\frac{x}{x + 1}\right)\left(\frac{1}{x}\right) \\
&= \frac{1}{x + 1}, \quad x \neq 0
\end{aligned}
$$

EXAMPLE 4   Finding the Quotient of Two Functions

Find $\left(\dfrac{f}{g}\right)(x)$ and $\left(\dfrac{g}{f}\right)(x)$ for the functions $f(x) = \sqrt{x}$ and $g(x) = \sqrt{4 - x^2}$. Then find the domains of f/g and g/f.

Solution

The quotient of f and g is

$$\left(\frac{f}{g}\right)(x) = \frac{f(x)}{g(x)} = \frac{\sqrt{x}}{\sqrt{4 - x^2}},$$

and the quotient of g and f is

$$\left(\frac{g}{f}\right)(x) = \frac{g(x)}{f(x)} = \frac{\sqrt{4 - x^2}}{\sqrt{x}}.$$

The domain of f is $[0, \infty)$ and the domain of g is $[-2, 2]$. The intersection of these domains is $[0, 2]$. So, the domains for f/g and g/f are as follows.

$$\text{Domain of } \frac{f}{g}: [0, 2) \qquad \text{Domain of } \frac{g}{f}: (0, 2]$$

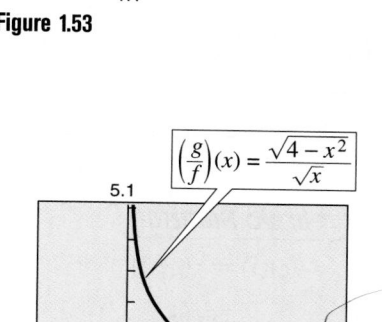

Figure 1.53

Can you see why these two domains differ slightly? You can confirm the domain of f/g in Example 4 with your graphing utility by entering the three functions

$$y_1 = \sqrt{x} \qquad y_2 = \sqrt{(4 - x^2)} \qquad y_3 = \frac{y_1}{y_2}$$

and graphing y_3 as shown in Figure 1.53.

Use the *trace* feature to determine that the x-coordinates of points on the graph extend from 0 to 2 but do not include 2. So, you can estimate the domain of f/g to be $[0, 2)$. You can confirm the domain of g/f in Example 4 by entering $y_4 = y_2/y_1$ and graphing y_4 as shown in Figure 1.54. Use the *trace* feature to determine that the x-coordinates of points on the graph extend from 0 to 2 but do not include 0. So, you can estimate the domain of g/f to be $(0, 2]$.

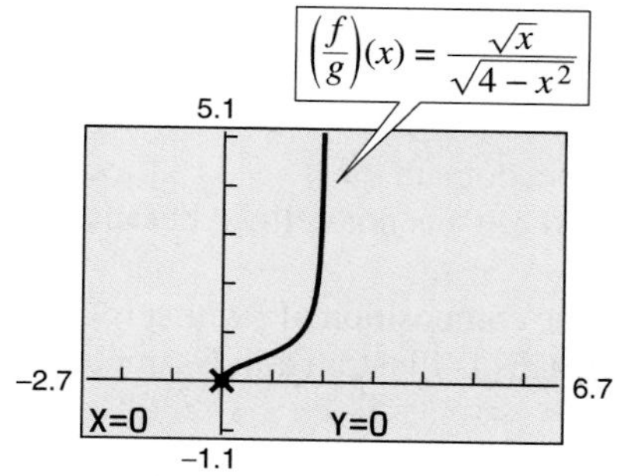

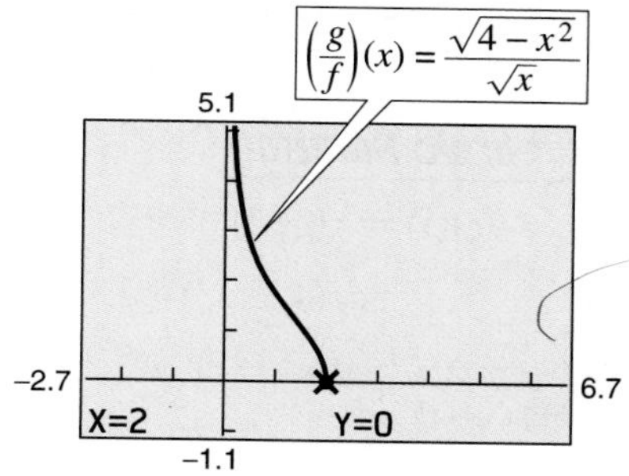

Figure 1.54

Compositions of Functions

Another way of combining two functions is to form the **composition** of one with the other. For instance, if $f(x) = x^2$ and $g(x) = x + 1$, the composition of f with g is

$$f(g(x)) = f(x + 1) = (x + 1)^2.$$

This composition is denoted as $f \circ g$.

A computer animation of this concept appears in the *Interactive* CD-ROM and *Internet* versions of this text.

Definition of Composition of Two Functions

The **composition** of the function f with g is

$$(f \circ g)(x) = f(g(x)).$$

The domain of $f \circ g$ is the set of all x in the domain of g such that $g(x)$ is in the domain of f. (See Figure 1.55.)

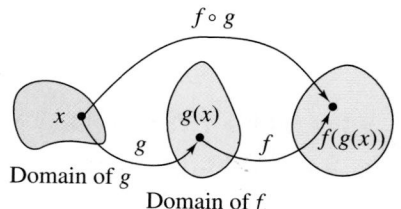

Figure 1.55

EXAMPLE 5   Forming the Composition of *f* with *g*

Find $(f \circ g)(x)$ for $f(x) = \sqrt{x}$, $x \geq 0$, and $g(x) = x - 1$, $x \geq 1$. If possible, find $(f \circ g)(2)$ and $(f \circ g)(0)$.

Solution

$$(f \circ g)(x) = f(g(x)) \qquad \text{Definition of } f \circ g$$

$$= f(x - 1) \qquad \text{Definition of } g(x)$$

$$= \sqrt{x - 1}, \quad x \geq 1 \qquad \text{Definition of } f(x)$$

The domain of $f \circ g$ is $[1, \infty)$. So, $(f \circ g)(2) = \sqrt{2 - 1} = 1$ is defined, but $(f \circ g)(0)$ is not defined because 0 is not in the domain of $f \circ g$.

The composition of *f* with *g* is generally not the same as the composition of *g* with *f*. This is illustrated in Example 6.

Exploration

Let $f(x) = x + 2$ and $g(x) = 4 - x^2$. Are the compositions $f \circ g$ and $g \circ f$ equal? You can use your graphing utility to answer this question by entering and graphing the following functions.

$$Y_1 = (4 - x^2) + 2$$

$$Y_2 = 4 - (x + 2)^2$$

What do you observe? Which function represents $f \circ g$ and which represents $g \circ f$?

EXAMPLE 6   Compositions of Functions

Given $f(x) = x + 2$ and $g(x) = 4 - x^2$, evaluate the following when $x = 0, 1, 2$, and 3.

a. $(f \circ g)(x)$ **b.** $(g \circ f)(x)$

Algebraic Solution

a. $(f \circ g)(x) = f(g(x))$ Definition of $f \circ g$

$$= f(4 - x^2) \qquad \text{Definition of } g(x)$$

$$= (4 - x^2) + 2 \qquad \text{Definition of } f(x)$$

$$= -x^2 + 6$$

$$(f \circ g)(0) = -0^2 + 6 = 6$$

$$(f \circ g)(1) = -1^2 + 6 = 5$$

$$(f \circ g)(2) = -2^2 + 6 = 2$$

$$(f \circ g)(3) = -3^2 + 6 = -3$$

b. $(g \circ f)(x) = g(f(x))$ Definition of $g \circ f$

$$= g(x + 2) \qquad \text{Definition of } f(x)$$

$$= 4 - (x + 2)^2 \qquad \text{Definition of } g(x)$$

$$= 4 - (x^2 + 4x + 4)$$

$$= -x^2 - 4x$$

$$(g \circ f)(0) = -0^2 - 4(0) = 0$$

$$(g \circ f)(1) = -1^2 - 4(1) = -5$$

$$(g \circ f)(2) = -2^2 - 4(2) = -12$$

$$(g \circ f)(3) = -3^2 - 4(3) = -21$$

Note that $(f \circ g)(x) \neq (g \circ f)(x)$.

Numerical Solution

a. You can use a table to evaluate $f \circ g$ when $x = 0, 1, 2$, and 3. First evaluate $g(x)$ for the values of x in the table. Then evaluate $f(g(x))$ for the values of $g(x)$ in the table.

x	0	1	2	3
$g(x)$	4	3	0	-5
$f(g(x))$	6	5	2	-3

b. To evaluate $g \circ f$ when $x = 0, 1, 2$, and 3, first evaluate $f(x)$ for the values of x in the table. Then evaluate $g(f(x))$ for the values of $f(x)$ in the table.

x	0	1	2	3
$f(x)$	2	3	4	5
$g(f(x))$	0	-5	-12	-21

From the tables you can see that

$$(f \circ g)(x) \neq (g \circ f)(x).$$

To determine the domain of a composite function $f \circ g$, you need to restrict the outputs of g so that they are in the domain of f. For instance, to find the domain of $f \circ g$ given that $f(x) = 1/x$, and $g(x) = x + 1$, consider the outputs of g. These can be any real number. However, the domain of f is restricted to all real numbers except 0. So, the outputs of g must be restricted to all real numbers except 0. This means that $g(x) = x + 1 \neq 0$, or $x \neq -1$. So, the domain of $f \circ g$ is all real numbers except $x = -1$.

EXAMPLE 7   Finding the Domain of a Composite Function

Find the domain of the composition $(f \circ g)(x)$ for the functions

$$f(x) = x^2 - 9 \quad \text{and} \quad g(x) = \sqrt{9 - x^2}.$$

Algebraic Solution

The composition of the functions is as follows.

$$(f \circ g)(x) = f(g(x))$$

$$= f\left(\sqrt{9 - x^2}\right)$$

$$= \left(\sqrt{9 - x^2}\right)^2 - 9$$

$$= 9 - x^2 - 9$$

$$= -x^2$$

From this, it might appear that the domain of the composition is the set of all real numbers. This, however, is not true because the domain of g is $-3 \leq x \leq 3$. So, the domain of $f \circ g$ is $-3 \leq x \leq 3$.

Graphical Solution

You can use a graphing utility to graph the composition of the functions $(f \circ g)(x)$ as $y = \left(\sqrt{9 - x^2}\right)^2 - 9$. Enter the functions as follows.

$$y_1 = \sqrt{(9 - x^2)}$$

$$y_2 = y_1{}^2 - 9$$

Graph y_2 as shown in Figure 1.56. Use the *trace* feature to determine that the x-coordinates of points on the graph extend from -3 to 3. So, you can graphically estimate the domain of $(f \circ g)(x)$ to be $-3 \leq x \leq 3$.

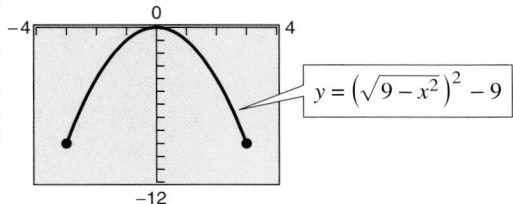

$$y = \left(\sqrt{9 - x^2}\right)^2 - 9$$

Figure 1.56

EXAMPLE 8   A Case in Which $f \circ g = g \circ f$

Given $f(x) = 2x + 3$ and $g(x) = \frac{1}{2}(x - 3)$, find the following.

a. $(f \circ g)(x)$ **b.** $(g \circ f)(x)$

Solution

a. $(f \circ g)(x) = f(g(x))$

$$= f\left(\frac{1}{2}(x - 3)\right)$$

$$= 2\left(\frac{1}{2}(x - 3)\right) + 3$$

$$= x - 3 + 3$$

$$= x$$

b. $(g \circ f)(x) = g(f(x))$

$$= g(2x + 3)$$

$$= \frac{1}{2}((2x + 3) - 3)$$

$$= \frac{1}{2}(2x)$$

$$= x$$

> ### STUDY T!P
>
> In Example 8, note that the two composite functions $f \circ g$ and $g \circ f$ are equal, and both represent the identity function. That is,
>
> $$(f \circ g)(x) = x$$
> $$(g \circ f)(x) = x.$$
>
> You will study this special case in the next section.

In Examples 5, 6, 7, and 8 you formed the composition of two given functions. In calculus, it is also important to be able to identify two functions that make up a given composite function. For instance, the function h

$$h(x) = (3x - 5)^3$$

is the composition of f with g, where $f(x) = x^3$ and $g(x) = 3x - 5$. That is,

$$h(x) = (3x - 5)^3 = [g(x)]^3 = f(g(x)).$$

Basically, to "decompose" a composite function, look for an "inner" and an "outer" function. In the function h above, $g(x) = 3x - 5$ is the inner function and $f(x) = x^3$ is the outer function.

EXAMPLE 9   Identifying a Composite Function

Express the function

$$h(x) = \frac{1}{(x - 2)^2}$$

as a composition of two functions.

Solution

One way to write h as a composition of two functions is to take the inner function to be $g(x) = x - 2$ and the outer function to be

$$f(x) = \frac{1}{x^2} = x^{-2}.$$

Then you can write

$$h(x) = \frac{1}{(x - 2)^2} = (x - 2)^{-2} = f(x - 2) = f(g(x)).$$

Exploration

The function in Example 9 can be decomposed in other ways. For which of the following pairs of functions is $h(x)$ equal to $f(g(x))$?

a. $g(x) = \dfrac{1}{x - 2}$ and $f(x) = x^2$

b. $g(x) = x^2$ and $f(x) = \dfrac{1}{x - 2}$

c. $g(x) = \dfrac{1}{x}$ and $f(x) = (x - 2)^2$

Activities

1. Find $(f + g)(-1)$ and $\left(\dfrac{f}{g}\right)(2)$ for
   $f(x) = 3x^2 + 2$, $g(x) = 2x$.

   Answer: $3; \dfrac{7}{2}$

2. Given $f(x) = 3x^2 + 2$ and $g(x) = 2x$, find $f \circ g$.

   Answer: $(f \circ g)(x) = 12x^2 + 2$

3. Find two functions f and g such that $(f \circ g)(x) = h(x)$.

   a. $h(x) = \dfrac{1}{\sqrt{3x + 1}}$.

   b. $h(x) = (3x - 5)^3$

   Answers are not unique:

   a. $f(x) = \dfrac{1}{\sqrt{x}}$ and $g(x) = 3x + 1$

   b. $f(x) = x^3$ and $g(x) = 3x - 5$

Application

EXAMPLE 10   Bacteria Count

The number of bacteria in a refrigerated food is

$$N(T) = 20T^2 - 80T + 500, \qquad 2 \leq T \leq 14$$

where T is the temperature of the food in degrees Celsius. When the food is removed from refrigeration, the temperature is

$$T(t) = 4t + 2, \qquad 0 \leq t \leq 3$$

where t is the time (in hours). Find the following.

a. The composite $N(T(t))$. What does this function represent?

b. The number of bacteria in the food when $t = 2$ hours

c. The time when the bacterial count reaches 2000

Solution

a. $N(T(t)) = 20(4t + 2)^2 - 80(4t + 2) + 500$

$$= 20(16t^2 + 16t + 4) - 320t - 160 + 500$$

$$= 320t^2 + 320t + 80 - 320t - 160 + 500$$

$$= 320t^2 + 420$$

This composite function $N(T(t))$ represents the number of bacteria as a function of the amount of time the food has been out of refrigeration.

b. When $t = 2$, the number of bacteria is

$$N = 320(2)^2 + 420 = 1280 + 420 = 1700.$$

c. The bacterial count will reach $N = 2000$ when $320t^2 + 420 = 2000$. You can solve this equation for t algebraically as follows.

$$320t^2 + 420 = 2000$$

$$320t^2 = 1580$$

$$t^2 = \frac{1580}{320} = \frac{79}{16}$$

$$t = \frac{\sqrt{79}}{4} \approx 2.2 \text{ hours}$$

So, the count will reach 2000 when $t \approx 2.2$ hours. When you solve this equation, note that the negative value is rejected because it is not in the domain of the composite function. You can use a graphing utility to approximate the solution, as shown in Figure 1.57.

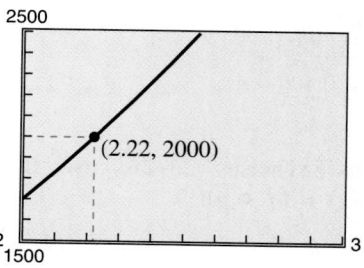

Figure 1.57

1.6 Exercises

In Exercises 1–8, find the following.

(a) $(f + g)(x)$ **(b)** $(f - g)(x)$

(c) $(fg)(x)$ **(d)** $(f/g)(x)$

(e) the domain of f/g

1. $f(x) = x + 1$, $g(x) = x - 1$

2. $f(x) = 2x - 5$, $g(x) = 1 - x$

3. $f(x) = x^2$, $g(x) = 1 - x$

4. $f(x) = 2x - 5$, $g(x) = 5$

5. $f(x) = x^2 + 5$, $g(x) = \sqrt{1 - x}$

6. $f(x) = \sqrt{x^2 - 4}$, $g(x) = \dfrac{x^2}{x^2 + 1}$

7. $f(x) = \dfrac{1}{x}$, $g(x) = \dfrac{1}{x^2}$

8. $f(x) = \dfrac{x}{x + 1}$, $g(x) = x^3$

In Exercises 9–22, evaluate the indicated function for $f(x) = x^2 + 1$ **and** $g(x) = x - 4$ **algebraically. If possible, use a graphing utility to verify your answer.**

9. $(f + g)(3)$ **10.** $(f - g)(-2)$

11. $(f - g)(0)$ **12.** $(f + g)(1)$

13. $(fg)(4)$ **14.** $(fg)(-6)$

15. $\left(\dfrac{f}{g}\right)(5)$ **16.** $\left(\dfrac{f}{g}\right)(0)$

17. $(f - g)(2t)$ **18.** $(f + g)(t - 4)$

19. $(fg)(-5t)$ **20.** $(fg)(3t^2)$

21. $\left(\dfrac{f}{g}\right)(-t)$ **22.** $\left(\dfrac{f}{g}\right)(t + 2)$

In Exercises 23–26, use the graphs to graph $h(x) = (f + g)(x)$.

23. 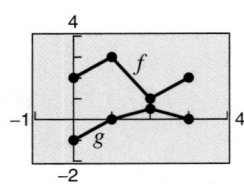   **24.**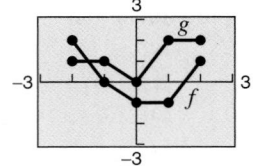

25. 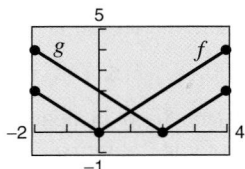   **26.**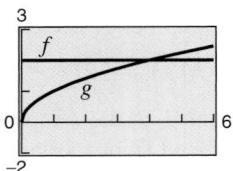

In Exercises 27–30, graph the functions f, g, **and** $f + g$ **in the same viewing window.**

27. $f(x) = \frac{1}{2}x$, $g(x) = x - 1$

28. $f(x) = \frac{1}{3}x$, $g(x) = -x + 4$

29. $f(x) = x^2$, $g(x) = -2x$

30. $f(x) = 4 - x^2$, $g(x) = x$

In Exercises 31–34, use a graphing utility to sketch the graphs of f, g, **and** $f + g$ **in the same viewing window. Which function contributes more to the magnitude of the sum when** $0 \le x \le 2$? **Which function contributes more to the magnitude of the sum when** $x > 6$?

31. $f(x) = 3x$, $g(x) = -\dfrac{x^3}{10}$

32. $f(x) = \dfrac{x}{2}$, $g(x) = \sqrt{x}$

33. $f(x) = 3x + 2$, $g(x) = -\sqrt{x + 5}$

34. $f(x) = x^2 - \frac{1}{2}$, $g(x) = -3x^2 - 1$

In Exercises 35–38, find (a) $f \circ g$ **and (b)** $g \circ f$.

35. $f(x) = x^2$, $g(x) = x - 1$

36. $f(x) = \sqrt[3]{x - 1}$, $g(x) = x^3 + 1$

37. $f(x) = 3x + 5$, $g(x) = 5 - x$

38. $f(x) = x^3$, $g(x) = \dfrac{1}{x}$

In Exercises 39–44, (a) find $f \circ g$ **and** $g \circ f$. **(b) Use a graphing utility to graph** $f \circ g$ **and** $g \circ f$. **Determine whether** $f \circ g = g \circ f$.

39. $f(x) = \sqrt{x + 4}$, $g(x) = x^2$

40. $f(x) = \sqrt[3]{x + 1}$, $g(x) = x^3 - 1$

41. $f(x) = \frac{1}{3}x - 3$, $g(x) = 3x + 1$

42. $f(x) = \sqrt{x}$, $g(x) = \sqrt{x}$

43. $f(x) = x^{2/3}$, $g(x) = x^6$

44. $f(x) = |x|$, $g(x) = x + 6$

In Exercises 45–50, (a) find $(f \circ g)(x)$ and $(g \circ f)(x)$, (b) determine algebraically whether $(f \circ g)(x) = (g \circ f)(x)$, and (c) verify your answer to part (b) by comparing a table of values for each composition.

45. $f(x) = 5x + 4$, $g(x) = 4 - x$

46. $f(x) = \frac{1}{4}(x - 1)$, $g(x) = 4x + 1$

47. $f(x) = \sqrt{x + 6}$, $g(x) = x^2 - 5$

48. $f(x) = x^3 - 4$, $g(x) = \sqrt[3]{x + 10}$

49. $f(x) = |x + 3|$, $g(x) = 2x - 1$

50. $f(x) = \frac{6}{3x - 5}$, $g(x) = -x$

In Exercises 51–56, use the graphs of f and g to evaluate the functions.

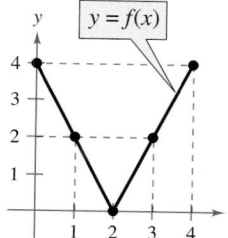
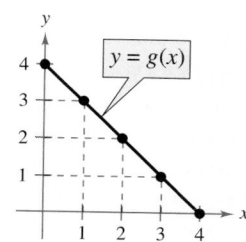

51. (a) $(f + g)(3)$ (b) $(f/g)(2)$

52. (a) $(f - g)(1)$ (b) $(fg)(4)$

53. (a) $(f \circ g)(2)$ (b) $(g \circ f)(2)$

54. (a) $(f \circ g)(1)$ (b) $(g \circ f)(3)$

55. (a) $(f \circ f)(3)$ (b) $(f \circ f)(4)$

56. (a) $(g \circ g)(1)$ (b) $(g \circ g)(0)$

In Exercises 57–64, find two functions f and g such that $(f \circ g)(x) = h(x)$. (There are many correct answers.)

57. $h(x) = (2x + 1)^2$ **58.** $h(x) = (1 - x)^3$

59. $h(x) = \sqrt[3]{x^2 - 4}$ **60.** $h(x) = \sqrt{9 - x}$

61. $h(x) = \dfrac{1}{x + 2}$ **62.** $h(x) = \dfrac{4}{(5x + 2)^2}$

63. $h(x) = (x + 4)^2 + 2(x + 4)$

64. $h(x) = (x + 3)^{3/2}$

In Exercises 65–70, determine the domains of (a) f, (b) g, and (c) $f \circ g$. Use a graphing utility to verify your answer.

65. $f(x) = \sqrt{x}$, $g(x) = x^2 + 1$

66. $f(x) = \sqrt{x + 3}$, $g(x) = \dfrac{x}{2}$

67. $f(x) = \dfrac{1}{x}$, $g(x) = x + 3$

68. $f(x) = \dfrac{1}{x}$, $g(x) = \dfrac{1}{2x}$

69. $f(x) = \dfrac{2}{|x|}$, $g(x) = x - 1$

70. $f(x) = \dfrac{3}{x^2 - 1}$, $g(x) = x + 1$

Average Rate of Change   In Exercises 71–78, find the difference quotient

$$\frac{f(x + h) - f(x)}{h}$$

and simplify your answer.

71. $f(x) = 3x - 4$ **72.** $f(x) = 5x + 1$

73. $f(x) = 1 - x^2$ **74.** $f(x) = x^2 + 4$

75. $f(x) = \dfrac{4}{x}$ **76.** $f(x) = \dfrac{2}{x^2}$

77. $f(x) = \sqrt{2x + 1}$ **78.** $f(x) = -\sqrt{4x}$

79. *Stopping Distance*   A car traveling x miles per hour stops quickly. The distance a car travels during the driver's reaction time is given by $R(x) = \frac{3}{4}x$. The distance traveled while braking is given by $B(x) = \frac{1}{15}x^2$.

(a) Find the stopping-distance function T.

(b) Use a graphing utility to graph the functions R, B, and T in the interval $0 \le x \le 60$.

(c) Which function contributes most to the magnitude of the sum at higher speeds? Explain.

80. *Business*   You own two restaurants. From 1995 to 2000, the sales R_1 (in thousands of dollars) for one restaurant can be modeled by

$$R_1 = 480 - 8t - 0.8t^2, \qquad t = 0, 1, 2, 3, 4, 5$$

where $t = 0$ represents 1995. During the same 6-year period, the sales R_2 (in thousands of dollars) for the other restaurant can be modeled by

$$R_2 = 254 + 0.78t, \qquad t = 0, 1, 2, 3, 4, 5.$$

(a) Write a function R_3 that represents the total sales for the two restaurants.

(b) Use a graphing utility to graph R_1, R_2, and R_3 (the total sales function) in the same viewing window.

Data Analysis In Exercises 81 and 82, use the table, which gives the total amount spent (in billions of dollars) on health services and supplies in the United States and Puerto Rico for the years 1990 through 1996. The variables $y_1, y_2,$ and y_3 represent out-of-pocket payments, insurance premiums, and other types of payments, respectively. (Source: U.S. Health Care Financing Administration)

Year	1990	1991	1992	1993	1994	1995	1996
y_1	144.4	151.6	159.5	163.6	164.8	166.7	171.2
y_2	238.6	259.4	282.5	303.3	315.6	326.9	337.3
y_3	21.9	24.0	25.1	27.3	29.6	31.7	32.4

81. Use a graphing utility to find a mathematical model for each of the variables. Let $t = 0$ represent 1990. Find a quadratic model $(y = ax^2 + bx + c)$ for y_1 and linear models $(y = ax + b)$ for y_2 and y_3.

82. Use a graphing utility to graph y_1, y_2, y_3, and $y_1 + y_2 + y_3$ in the same viewing window. Use the model to estimate the total amount spent on health services and supplies in 2000.

83. *Ripples* A pebble is dropped into a calm pond, causing ripples in the form of concentric circles. The radius (in feet) of the outer ripple is $r(t) = 0.6t$, where t is the time (in seconds) after the pebble strikes the water. The area of the circle is $A(r) = \pi r^2$. Find and interpret $(A \circ r)(t)$.

84. *Geometry* A square concrete foundation was prepared as a base for a large cylindrical gasoline tank.

   (a) Express the radius r of the tank as a function of the length x of the sides of the square.

   (b) Express the area A of the circular base of the tank as a function of the radius r.

   (c) Find and interpret $(A \circ r)(x)$.

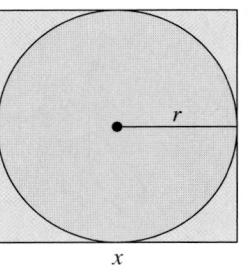

FIGURE FOR 84

85. *Business* The weekly cost of producing x units in a manufacturing process is $C(x) = 60x + 750$. The number of units produced in t hours is $x(t) = 50t$.

   (a) Find and interpret $(C \circ x)(t)$.

   (b) Use a graphing utility to graph the cost as a function of time. Use the *trace* feature to estimate (to two-decimal-place accuracy) the time that must elapse until the cost increases to $15,000.

86. *Air Traffic Control* An air traffic controller spots two planes at the same altitude flying toward each other. Their flight paths form a right angle at point P. One plane is 150 miles from point P and is moving at 450 miles per hour. The other plane is 200 miles from point P and is moving at 450 miles per hour. Write the distance s between the planes as a function of time t.

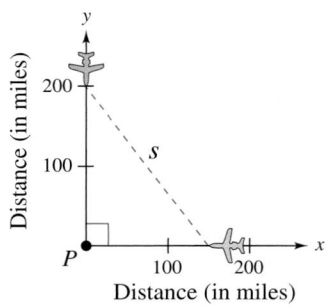

87. *Business* You are a sales representative for an automobile manufacturer. You are paid an annual salary plus a bonus of 3% of your sales over $500,000. Consider the two functions $f(x) = x - 500,000$ and $g(x) = 0.03x$. If x is greater than $500,000, which of the following represents your bonus? Explain.

   (a) $f(g(x))$ (b) $g(f(x))$

88. *Exploration*   The suggested retail price of a new car is p dollars. The dealership advertised a factory rebate of $1200 and an 8% discount.

(a) Write a function R in terms of p, giving the cost of the car after receiving the rebate from the factory.

(b) Write a function S in terms of p, giving the cost of the car after receiving the dealership discount.

(c) Form the composite functions $(R \circ S)(p)$ and $(S \circ R)(p)$, and interpret each.

(d) Find $(R \circ S)(18,400)$ and $(S \circ R)(18,400)$. Which yields the lower cost for the car? Explain.

89. *Data Analysis*   The data in the table shows the circulations of morning and evening newspapers in the United States for the years 1988 through 1997. The variables y_1 and y_2 represent the circulations in millions of the morning and evening papers, respectively.   (Source: Editor & Publisher Co.)

Year	1988	1989	1990	1991	1992
y_1	40.5	40.7	41.3	41.5	42.4
y_2	22.2	21.9	21.0	19.2	17.8

Year	1993	1994	1995	1996	1997
y_1	43.1	43.4	44.3	44.8	45.4
y_2	16.7	15.9	13.9	12.2	11.3

Use a graphing utility to create a scatter plot of each data set. What type of model would best fit the data? Use the regression capabilities of a graphing utility to find models for y_1 and y_2 (use $t = 8$ to represent 1988). Graph the models for y_1, y_2, and $y_1 - y_2$ in the same viewing window. What does the graph of the difference of the functions indicate about newspaper circulation in general?

Synthesis

True or False?   **In Exercises 90 and 91, determine whether the statement is true or false. Justify your answer.**

90. If $f(x) = x + 1$ and $g(x) = 6x$, then

$$(f \circ g)(x) = (g \circ f)(x).$$

91. If you are given two functions $f(x)$ and $g(x)$, you can calculate $(f \circ g)(x)$ if and only if the range of g is a subset of the domain of f.

92. *Think About It*   Prove that the product of two odd functions is an even function and the product of two even functions is an even function.

93. *Conjecture*   Use examples to hypothesize whether the product of an odd function and an even function is even or odd. Then prove your hypothesis.

94. Given a function f, prove that $g(x)$ is even and $h(x)$ is odd where

$$g(x) = \tfrac{1}{2}[f(x) + f(-x)] \quad \text{and}$$
$$h(x) = \tfrac{1}{2}[f(x) - f(-x)].$$

95. Use the result of Exercise 94 to prove that any function can be written as a sum of even and odd functions. (*Hint:* Add the two equations in Exercise 94.)

96. Use the result of Exercise 95 to write each function as a sum of even and odd functions.

(a) $f(x) = x^2 - 2x + 1$ (b) $f(x) = \dfrac{1}{x + 1}$

Review

In Exercises 97–100, find three points that lie on the graph of the equation.

97. $y = -x^2 + x - 5$ **98.** $y = \tfrac{1}{5}x^3 - 4x^2 + 1$

99. $x^2 + y^2 = 24$ **100.** $y = \dfrac{x}{x^2 - 5}$

In Exercises 101–104, find an equation of the line that passes through the two points.

101. $(-4, -2), (-3, 8)$ **102.** $(1, 5), (-8, 2)$

103. $\left(\tfrac{3}{2}, -1\right), \left(-\tfrac{1}{3}, 4\right)$ **104.** $(0, 1.1), (-4, 3.1)$

In Exercises 105–110, use the graph of f to sketch the graph of the specified function.

105. $f(x - 4)$
106. $f(x + 2)$
107. $f(x) + 4$
108. $f(x) - 1$
109. $2f(x)$
110. $\tfrac{1}{2}f(x)$

1.7 Inverse Functions

The Inverse of a Function

Recall from Section 1.3 that a function can be represented by a set of ordered pairs. For instance, the function $f(x) = x + 4$ from the set $A = \{1, 2, 3, 4\}$ to the set $B = \{5, 6, 7, 8\}$ can be written as follows.

$$f(x) = x + 4: \{(1, 5), (2, 6), (3, 7), (4, 8)\}$$

In this case, by interchanging the first and second coordinates of each of these ordered pairs, you can form the **inverse function** of f, which is denoted by f^{-1}. It is a function from the set B to the set A, and can be written as follows.

$$f^{-1}(x) = x - 4: \{(5, 1), (6, 2), (7, 3), (8, 4)\}$$

Note that the domain of f is equal to the range of f^{-1}, and vice versa, as shown in Figure 1.58. Also note that the functions f and f^{-1} have the effect of "undoing" each other. In other words, when you form the composition of f with f^{-1} or the composition of f^{-1} with f, you obtain the identity function.

$$f(f^{-1}(x)) = f(x - 4) = (x - 4) + 4 = x$$

$$f^{-1}(f(x)) = f^{-1}(x + 4) = (x + 4) - 4 = x$$

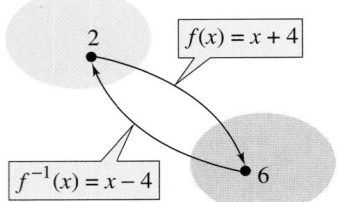

Figure 1.58

What You Should Learn:

- How to find inverse functions informally and verify that two functions are inverses of each other
- How to use graphs of functions to decide whether functions have inverses
- How to find inverse functions algebraically

Why You Should Learn It:

Inverse functions can be helpful in further exploring how two variables relate to each other. Exercise 90 on page 147 investigates the relationship between the exhaust temperature and the percent load on a diesel engine.

David J. Sams/Stock Boston

EXAMPLE 1 Finding Inverse Functions Informally

Find the inverse of $f(x) = 4x$. Then verify that both $f(f^{-1}(x))$ and $f^{-1}(f(x))$ are equal to the identity function.

Solution

The given function *multiplies* each input by 4. To "undo" this function, you need to *divide* each input by 4. So, the inverse function of $f(x) = 4x$ is

$$f^{-1}(x) = \frac{x}{4}.$$

You can verify that both $f(f^{-1}(x))$ and $f^{-1}(f(x))$ are equal to the identity function as follows.

$$f(f^{-1}(x)) = f\left(\frac{x}{4}\right) = 4\left(\frac{x}{4}\right) = x$$

$$f^{-1}(f(x)) = f^{-1}(4x) = \frac{4x}{4} = x$$

EXAMPLE 2 Finding Inverse Functions Informally

Find the inverse of $f(x) = x - 6$. Then verify that both $f(f^{-1}(x))$ and $f^{-1}(f(x))$ are equal to the identity function.

Solution

The given function *subtracts* 6 from each input. To "undo" this function, you need to *add* 6 to each input. So, the inverse function of $f(x) = x - 6$ is

$$f^{-1}(x) = x + 6.$$

You can verify that both $f(f^{-1}(x))$ and $f^{-1}(f(x))$ are equal to the identity function as follows.

$$f(f^{-1}(x)) = f(x + 6) = (x + 6) - 6 = x$$
$$f^{-1}(f(x)) = f^{-1}(x - 6) = (x - 6) + 6 = x$$

A table of values can help you understand inverse functions. For instance, the following table shows several values of the function in Example 2. Interchange the rows of this table to obtain values of the inverse function.

x	-2	-1	0	1	2
$f(x)$	-8	-7	-6	-5	-4

x		-8	-7	-6	-5	-4
$f^{-1}(x)$		-2	-1	0	1	2

In the table at the left, each output is 6 less than the input, and in the table at the right, each output is 6 more than the input.

The formal definition of the inverse of a function is as follows.

Definition of the Inverse of a Function

Let f and g be two functions such that

$$f(g(x)) = x \qquad \text{for every } x \text{ in the domain of } g$$

and

$$g(f(x)) = x \qquad \text{for every } x \text{ in the domain of } f.$$

Under these conditions, the function g is the **inverse** of the function f. The function g is denoted by f^{-1} (read "f-inverse"). So,

$$f(f^{-1}(x)) = x \qquad \text{and} \qquad f^{-1}(f(x)) = x.$$

The domain of f must be equal to the range of f^{-1}, and the range of f must be equal to the domain of f^{-1}.

STUDY T!P

Don't be confused by the use of -1 to denote the inverse function f^{-1}. In this text, whenever f^{-1} is written, it *always* refers to the inverse of the function f and *not* to the reciprocal of $f(x)$, which is

$$\frac{1}{f(x)}.$$

If the function g is the inverse of the function f, it must also be true that the function f is the inverse of the function g. For this reason, you can say that the functions f and g are *inverses of each other*.

EXAMPLE 3 Verifying Inverse Functions Algebraically

Show that the functions are inverses of each other.

$$f(x) = 2x^3 - 1 \quad \text{and} \quad g(x) = \sqrt[3]{\frac{x+1}{2}}$$

Solution

$$f(g(x)) = f\left(\sqrt[3]{\frac{x+1}{2}}\right) = 2\left(\sqrt[3]{\frac{x+1}{2}}\right)^3 - 1$$

$$= 2\left(\frac{x+1}{2}\right) - 1$$

$$= x + 1 - 1$$

$$= x$$

$$g(f(x)) = g(2x^3 - 1) = \sqrt[3]{\frac{(2x^3 - 1) + 1}{2}}$$

$$= \sqrt[3]{\frac{2x^3}{2}}$$

$$= \sqrt[3]{x^3}$$

$$= x$$

EXAMPLE 4 Verifying Inverse Functions Algebraically

Which of the functions is the inverse of $f(x) = \dfrac{5}{x-2}$?

$$g(x) = \frac{x-2}{5} \quad \text{or} \quad h(x) = \frac{5}{x} + 2$$

Solution

By forming the composition of f with g, you have

$$f(g(x)) = f\left(\frac{x-2}{5}\right) = \frac{5}{\dfrac{x-2}{5} - 2} = \frac{25}{x - 12} \neq x.$$

Because this composition is not equal to the identity function x, it follows that g is *not* the inverse of f. By forming the composition of f with h, you have

$$f(h(x)) = f\left(\frac{5}{x} + 2\right) = \frac{5}{\dfrac{5}{x} + 2 - 2} = \frac{5}{5/x} = x.$$

So, it appears that h is the inverse of f. You can confirm this by showing that the composition of h with f is also equal to the identity function.

Point out to students that when using a graphing utility it is important to know a function's behavior because the graphing utility may show an incomplete function. For instance, it is important to know that the domain of $x^{2/3}$ is all real numbers, because a graphing utility may show an incomplete graph of the function, depending on how the function was entered.

STUDY T!P

Most graphing utilities can graph $y = x^{1/3}$ in two ways:

$$y_1 = x \wedge (1/3) \quad \text{or}$$

$$y_1 = \sqrt[3]{x}.$$

However, you may not be able to obtain the complete graph of $y = x^{2/3}$ by entering $y_1 = x \wedge (2/3)$. If not, you should use

$$y_1 = (x \wedge (1/3))^2 \quad \text{or}$$

$$y_1 = \sqrt[3]{x^2}.$$

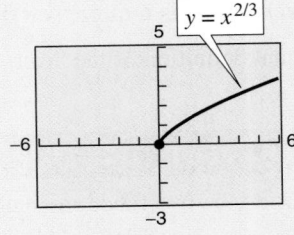

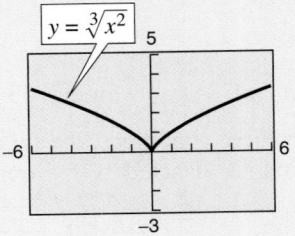

The Graph of an Inverse Function

The graphs of f and f^{-1} are related to each other in the following way. If the point (a, b) lies on the graph of f, then the point (b, a) lies on the graph of f^{-1} and vice versa. This means that the graph of f^{-1} is a reflection of the graph of f in the line $y = x$, as shown in Figure 1.59.

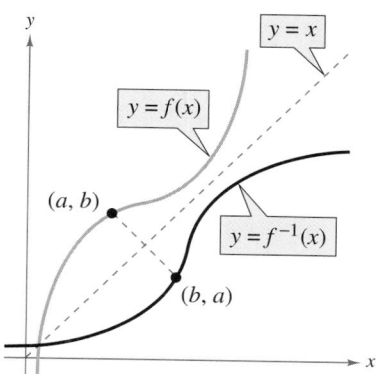

Figure 1.59

A computer animation of this concept appears in the *Interactive* CD-ROM and *Internet* versions of this text.

EXAMPLE 5   Verifying Inverse Functions Graphically and Numerically

Example 3 shows how to verify *algebraically* that the functions

$$f(x) = 2x^3 - 1 \quad \text{and} \quad g(x) = \sqrt[3]{\frac{x + 1}{2}}$$

are inverses of each other. Verify that f and g are inverses of each other graphically and numerically.

Graphical Solution

You can *graphically* verify that f and g are inverses of each other by using a graphing utility to graph f and g in the same viewing window. (Be sure to use a square setting.) From the graph in Figure 1.60, you can verify that the graph of g is the reflection of the graph of f in the line $y = x$.

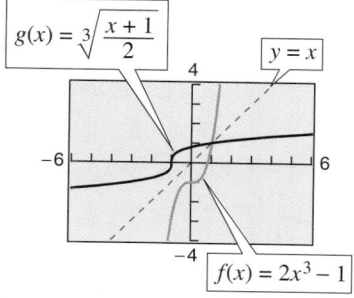

Figure 1.60

Numerical Solution

You can *numerically* verify that f and g are inverses of each other by creating two tables as shown below.

x	-2	-1	0	1	2
$f(x)$	-17	-3	-1	1	15

x	-17	-3	-1	1	15
$g(x)$	-2	-1	0	1	2

Note that the entries in the tables are the same except that their rows are interchanged. From the tables, you can verify that f and g are inverses of each other.

The Existence of an Inverse Function

A function need not have an inverse function. For instance, the function $f(x) = x^2$ has no inverse [assuming a domain of $(-\infty, \infty)$]. You can observe this numerically in the table at the right.

x	-2	-1	0	1	2
$f(x)$	4	1	0	1	4

When you interchange the rows of the tables, you can find two different outputs correspond to the same input. For example, the input 4 corresponds to two different outputs, -2 and 2. So, the bottom table does not represent a function, and therefore $f(x) = x^2$ does not have an inverse.

To have an inverse, a function must be **one-to-one,** which means that no two elements in the domain of f correspond to the same element in the range of f.

x	4	1	0	1	4
$g(x)$	-2	-1	0	1	2

Definition of a One-to-One Function

A function f is **one-to-one** if, for a and b in its domain,

$f(a) = f(b)$ implies that $a = b$.

Existence of an Inverse Function

A function f has an inverse function f^{-1} if and only if f is one-to-one.

From its graph, it is easy to tell whether a function of x is one-to-one. Simply check to see that every horizontal line intersects the graph of the function at most once. For instance, Figure 1.61 shows the graph of $y = x^4$. On the graph, you can find a horizontal line that intersects the graph twice.

Two special types of functions that pass the **Horizontal Line Test** are those that are increasing or decreasing on their entire domains.

1. If f is *increasing* on its entire domain, f is one-to-one.

2. If f is *decreasing* on its entire domain, f is one-to-one.

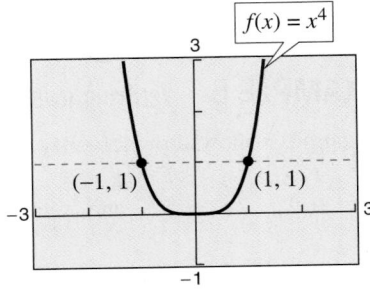

Figure 1.61 $f(x) = x^4$ is not one-to-one.

EXAMPLE 6   Testing for One-to-One Functions

Is the function $f(x) = \sqrt{x} + 1$ one-to-one?

Algebraic Solution

Let a and b be nonnegative real numbers with $f(a) = f(b)$.

$\sqrt{a} + 1 = \sqrt{b} + 1$ Set $f(a) = f(b)$.

$\sqrt{a} = \sqrt{b}$

$a = b$

Therefore,

$f(a) = f(b)$

implies that

$a = b$.

So, f *is* one-to-one.

Graphical Solution

Use a graphing utility to graph the function $y = \sqrt{x} + 1$. From Figure 1.62, you can see that a horizontal line will intersect the graph at most once. So, f is one-to-one.

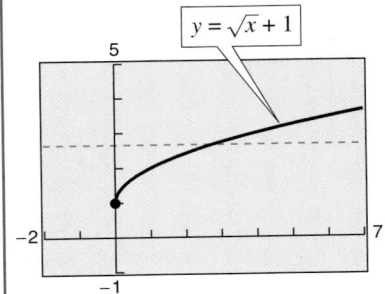

Figure 1.62

Finding Inverse Functions Algebraically

For simple functions (such as the ones in Examples 1 and 2) you can find inverse functions by inspection. For instance, the inverse of $f(x) = 8x$ is $f^{-1}(x) = x/8$. For more complicated functions, however, it is best to use the following procedure for finding the inverse of a function.

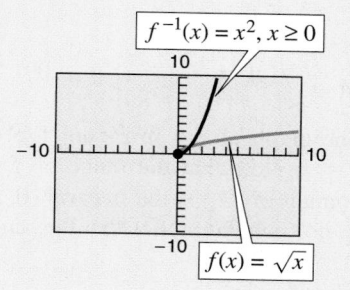
Finding the Inverse of a Function

To find the inverse of f, use the following steps.

1. Use the Horizontal Line Test to decide whether f has an inverse.
2. In the equation for $f(x)$, replace $f(x)$ by y.
3. Interchange the roles of x and y, and solve for y.
4. Replace y by $f^{-1}(x)$ in the new equation.
5. Verify that f and f^{-1} are inverses of each other by showing that $f(f^{-1}(x)) = x$ and $f^{-1}(f(x)) = x$.

It is important to note that in Step 1 above, the domain of f is assumed to be the entire real line. The domain of f may be restricted so that f does have an inverse. For instance, if the domain of $f(x) = x^2$ is restricted to the nonnegative real numbers, then f does have an inverse.

EXAMPLE 7   Finding the Inverse of a Function

Find the inverse (if it exists) of $f(x) = \dfrac{5 - 3x}{2}$.

Solution

The graph of f in Figure 1.63 passes the Horizontal Line Test, so you can see that f is one-to-one, and therefore has an inverse.

$$f(x) = \frac{5 - 3x}{2} \qquad \text{Write original equation.}$$

$$y = \frac{5 - 3x}{2} \qquad \text{Replace } f(x) \text{ by } y.$$

$$x = \frac{5 - 3y}{2} \qquad \text{Interchange } x \text{ and } y.$$

$$2x = 5 - 3y \qquad \text{Multiply each side by 2.}$$

$$3y = 5 - 2x \qquad \text{Isolate the } y\text{-term.}$$

$$y = \frac{5 - 2x}{3} \qquad \text{Solve for } y.$$

$$f^{-1}(x) = \frac{5 - 2x}{3} \qquad \text{Replace } y \text{ by } f^{-1}(x).$$

The domain and range of both f and f^{-1} consist of all real numbers. Verify that $f(f^{-1}(x)) = x$ and $f^{-1}(f(x)) = x$.

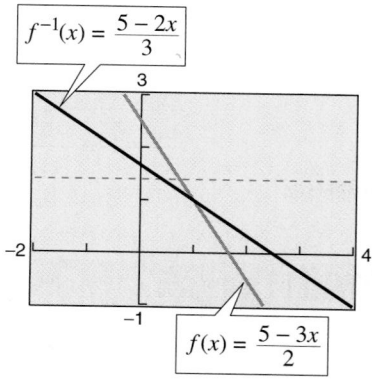

Figure 1.63

The *draw inverse* feature is particularly useful if you cannot find an expression for the inverse of a given function. For example, it would be very difficult to determine the equation for the inverse of the one-to-one function

$$f(x) = \tfrac{1}{4}x^5 + \tfrac{1}{4}x^3 + \tfrac{1}{2}x - 1.$$

However, it is easy to use the technique outlined above to obtain the *graph* of the inverse of this function.

EXAMPLE 8   Finding the Inverse of a Function

Find the inverse of $f(x) = \sqrt{2x - 3}$ and sketch the graphs of f and f^{-1}.

Solution

The graph of f in Figure 1.64 passes the Horizontal Line Test, so you can see that f is one-to-one and therefore has an inverse.

$f(x) = \sqrt{2x - 3}$	Write original equation.
$y = \sqrt{2x - 3}$	Replace $f(x)$ by y.
$x = \sqrt{2y - 3}$	Interchange x and y.
$x^2 = 2y - 3$	
$2y = x^2 + 3$	
$y = \dfrac{x^2 + 3}{2}$	Solve for y.
$f^{-1}(x) = \dfrac{x^2 + 3}{2}, \quad x \geq 0$	Replace y by $f^{-1}(x)$.

The graph of f^{-1} in Figure 1.64 is the reflection of the graph of f in the line $y = x$. Note that the range of f is the interval $[0, \infty)$, which implies that the domain of f^{-1} is the interval $[0, \infty)$. Moreover, the domain of f is the interval $\left[\frac{3}{2}, \infty\right)$, which implies that the range of f^{-1} is the interval $\left[\frac{3}{2}, \infty\right)$.

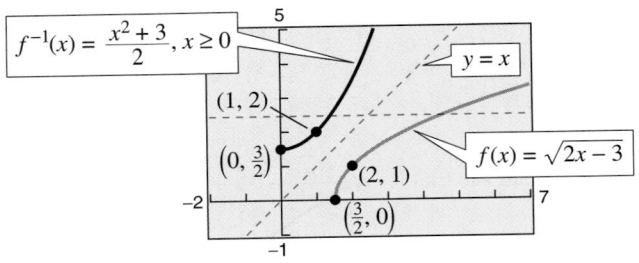

Figure 1.64

Activities

1. Given $f(x) = 5x - 7$, find $f^{-1}(x)$.

   Answer: $f^{-1}(x) = \dfrac{x + 7}{5}$

2. Show that f and g are inverse functions by showing $f(g(x)) = x$ and $g(f(x)) = x$.

   $f(x) = 3x^3 + 1$

   $g(x) = \sqrt[3]{\dfrac{x - 1}{3}}$

3. Describe the graphs of functions that have inverses and show how the graph of a function and its inverse are related.

Writing About Math   *The Existence of an Inverse Function*

Write a short paragraph describing why the following functions do or do not have inverse functions. Give a numerical example for each.

a. Your hourly wage is $7.50 plus $0.90 for each unit x produced per hour. Let $f(x)$ represent your weekly wage for 40 hours of work. Does this function have an inverse?

b. Let x represent the retail price of an item (in dollars), and let $f(x)$ represent the sales tax on the item. Assume that the sales tax is 7% of the retail price *and* that the sales tax is rounded to the nearest cent. Does this function have an inverse? (*Hint:* Can you undo this function? For instance, if you know that the sales tax is $0.14, can you determine *exactly* what the retail price is?)

1.7 E x e r c i s e s

In Exercises 1–4, match the graph of the function with the graph of its inverse. [The graphs of the inverse functions are labeled (a), (b), (c), and (d).]

(a) 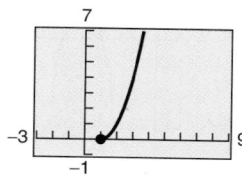   (b)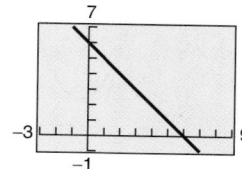

(c) 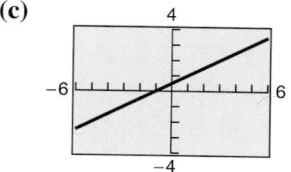   (d)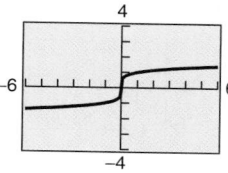

1. 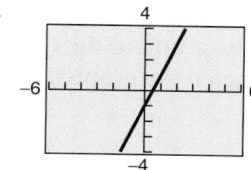   **2.**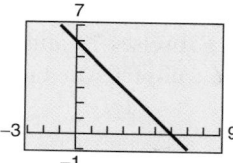

3. 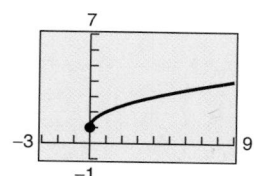   **4.**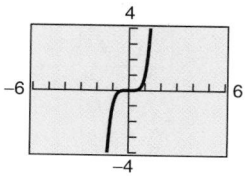

In Exercises 5–12, find the inverse of f informally. Verify that $f(f^{-1}(x)) = x$ and $f^{-1}(f(x)) = x$.

5. $f(x) = 8x$

6. $f(x) = \dfrac{1}{5}x$

7. $f(x) = x + 10$

8. $f(x) = x - 5$

9. $f(x) = 2x + 1$

10. $f(x) = \dfrac{x - 1}{4}$

11. $f(x) = \sqrt[3]{x}$

12. $f(x) = x^5$

In Exercises 13–16, show that f and g are inverse functions (a) algebraically and (b) graphically.

13. $f(x) = 2x, \quad g(x) = \dfrac{x}{2}$

14. $f(x) = x - 5, \quad g(x) = x + 5$

15. $f(x) = 5x + 1, \quad g(x) = \dfrac{x - 1}{5}$

16. $f(x) = 3 - 4x, \quad g(x) = \dfrac{3 - x}{4}$

In Exercises 17–22, show that f and g are inverse functions algebraically. Use a graphing utility to graph f and g in the same viewing window. Describe the relationship between the graphs.

17. $f(x) = x^3, \quad g(x) = \sqrt[3]{x}$

18. $f(x) = \dfrac{1}{x}, \quad g(x) = \dfrac{1}{x}$

19. $f(x) = \sqrt{x - 4}; \quad g(x) = x^2 + 4, \ x \ge 0$

20. $f(x) = 9 - x^2, \quad x \ge 0; \quad g(x) = \sqrt{9 - x}$

21. $f(x) = 1 - x^3, \quad g(x) = \sqrt[3]{1 - x}$

22. $f(x) = \dfrac{1}{1 + x}, \ x \ge 0; \quad g(x) = \dfrac{1 - x}{x}, \ 0 < x \le 1$

In Exercises 23–28, (a) show that f and g are inverse functions algebraically and (b) verify that f and g are inverses numerically by creating a table of values for each function.

23. $f(x) = -\dfrac{7}{2}x - 3, \quad g(x) = -\dfrac{2x + 6}{7}$

24. $f(x) = \dfrac{x + 8}{3}, \quad g(x) = 3x - 8$

25. $f(x) = x^3 + 5, \quad g(x) = \sqrt[3]{x - 5}$

26. $f(x) = \dfrac{x^3}{5}, \quad g(x) = \sqrt[3]{5x}$

27. $f(x) = -\sqrt{x - 8}; \quad g(x) = 8 + x^2, \ x \le 0$

28. $f(x) = \sqrt[3]{3x - 10}, \quad g(x) = \dfrac{x^3 + 10}{3}$

In Exercises 29–42, use a graphing utility to graph the function and use the Horizontal Line Test to determine whether the function is one-to-one.

29. $f(x) = 3 - \tfrac{1}{2}x$

30. $g(x) = \dfrac{4 - x}{6}$

31. $h(x) = \dfrac{x^2}{x^2 + 1}$

32. $f(x) = \tfrac{1}{8}(x + 2)^2 - 1$

33. $h(x) = \sqrt{16 - x^2}$

34. $f(x) = -2x\sqrt{16 - x^2}$

35. $f(x) = \sqrt{x - 2}$

36. $f(x) = 4 - 3x^{2/3}$

37. $f(x) = 10$

38. $f(x) = -0.65$

39. $g(x) = (x + 5)^3$

40. $f(x) = x^5 - 7$

41. $h(x) = |x + 4| - |x - 4|$

42. $f(x) = -\dfrac{|x - 6|}{|x + 6|}$

In Exercises 43–54, find the inverse of the function f. Use a graphing utility to graph both f and f^{-1} in the same viewing window. Describe the relationship between the graphs.

43. $f(x) = 2x - 3$

44. $f(x) = 3x$

45. $f(x) = x^5$

46. $f(x) = x^3 + 1$

47. $f(x) = \sqrt{x}$

48. $f(x) = x^2, \quad x \geq 0$

49. $f(x) = \sqrt{4 - x^2}, \quad 0 \leq x \leq 2$

50. $f(x) = \sqrt{16 - x^2}, \quad -4 \leq x \leq 0$

51. $f(x) = \sqrt[3]{x - 1}$

52. $f(x) = x^{3/5}$

53. $f(x) = \dfrac{4}{x}$

54. $f(x) = \dfrac{6}{\sqrt{x}}$

In Exercises 55–68, determine algebraically whether the function is one-to-one. If it is, find its inverse. Verify your answer graphically.

55. $f(x) = x^4$

56. $f(x) = \dfrac{1}{x^2}$

57. $f(x) = \dfrac{3x + 4}{5}$

58. $f(x) = 3x + 5$

59. $f(x) = (x + 3)^2, \quad x \geq -3$

60. $q(x) = (x - 5)^2, \quad x \leq 5$

61. $h(x) = \dfrac{4}{x^2}$

62. $f(x) = |x - 2|, \quad x \leq 2$

63. $f(x) = \sqrt{2x + 3}$

64. $f(x) = \sqrt{x - 2}$

65. $g(x) = x^2 - x^4$

66. $f(x) = \dfrac{x^2}{x^2 + 1}$

67. $f(x) = ax + b, \quad a \neq 0$

68. $f(x) = c$

Think About It **In Exercises 69–72, delete part of the graph of the function so that the part that remains is one-to-one. Find the inverse of the remaining part and give the domain of the inverse. (There are many correct answers.)**

69. $f(x) = (x - 2)^2$

70. $f(x) = 1 - x^4$

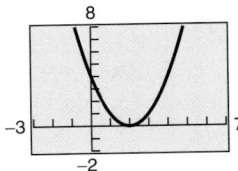

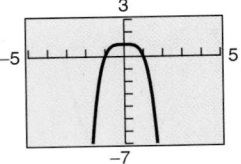

71. $f(x) = |x + 2|$

72. $f(x) = |x - 2|$

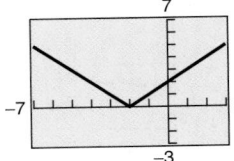

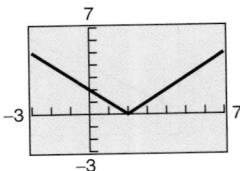

In Exercises 73 and 74, use the graph of the function f to complete the table and sketch the graph of f^{-1}.

73.

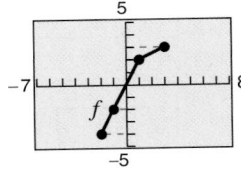

x	$f^{-1}(x)$
-4	
-2	
2	
3	

74.

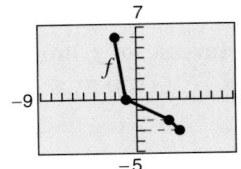

x	$f^{-1}(x)$
-3	
-2	
0	
6	

Graphical Reasoning **In Exercises 75–78, (a) use a graphing utility to graph the function, (b) use the *draw inverse* feature of the graphing utility to draw the inverse of the function, and (c) determine whether the graph of the inverse relation is an inverse function, explaining your reasoning.**

75. $f(x) = x^3 + x + 1$

76. $h(x) = x\sqrt{4 - x^2}$

77. $g(x) = \dfrac{3x^2}{x^2 + 1}$

78. $f(x) = \dfrac{4x}{\sqrt{x^2 + 15}}$

In Exercises 79–84, use the functions $f(x) = \frac{1}{8}x - 3$ and $g(x) = x^3$ to find the indicated value or function.

79. $(f^{-1} \circ g^{-1})(1)$

80. $(g^{-1} \circ f^{-1})(-3)$

81. $(f^{-1} \circ f^{-1})(6)$

82. $(g^{-1} \circ g^{-1})(-4)$

83. $(f \circ g)^{-1}$

84. $g^{-1} \circ f^{-1}$

In Exercises 85–88, use the functions $f(x) = x + 4$ and $g(x) = 2x - 5$ to find the specified functions.

85. $g^{-1} \circ f^{-1}$

86. $f^{-1} \circ g^{-1}$

87. $(f \circ g)^{-1}$

88. $(g \circ f)^{-1}$

89. *Hourly Wage* Your wage is $8.00 per hour plus $0.75 for each unit produced per hour. So, your hourly wage y in terms of the number of units produced is $y = 8 + 0.75x$.

(a) Determine the inverse of the function. What does each variable in the inverse function represent?

(b) Use a graphing utility to graph the function and its inverse.

(c) Use the *trace* feature of your graphing utility to find the hourly wage if 10 units are produced per hour.

(d) Use the *trace* feature of your graphing utility to find the number of units produced when your hourly wage is $22.25.

90. *Diesel Engine* The function

$$y = 0.03x^2 + 254.50, \qquad 0 < x < 100$$

approximates the exhaust temperature y of a diesel engine in degrees Fahrenheit, where x is the percent load on the engine.

(a) Determine the inverse of the function. What does each variable in the inverse function represent?

(b) Use a graphing utility to graph the inverse function.

(c) Determine the percent load interval if the exhaust temperature of the engine must not exceed 500°F.

91. *Transportation* The total value of new car sales f (in billions of dollars) in the United States from 1992 through 1997 is shown in the table. The time (in years) is given by t, with $t = 2$ corresponding to 1992. (Source: National Automobile Dealers Association)

t	2	3	4	5	6	7
$f(t)$	333.8	377.3	430.6	456.2	490.0	507.5

(a) Does f^{-1} exist?

(b) If f^{-1} exists, what does it mean in the context of the problem?

(c) If f^{-1} exists, find $f^{-1}(456.2)$.

(d) If the table above was extended to 1998 and if the total value of new car sales for that year was $430.6 billion, would f^{-1} exist? Explain.

Synthesis

True or False? **In Exercises 92 and 93, determine whether the statement is true or false. Justify your answer.**

92. If f is an even function, f^{-1} exists.

93. If the inverse of f exists, the y-intercept of f is an x-intercept of f^{-1}.

94. Prove that if f and g are one-to-one functions, $(f \circ g)^{-1}(x) = (g^{-1} \circ f^{-1})(x)$.

95. Prove that if f is a one-to-one odd function, f^{-1} is an odd function.

96. *Think About It* The function

$$f(x) = k(2 - x - x^3)$$

is one-to-one and $f^{-1}(3) = -2$. Find k.

Review

In Exercises 97–100, write the rational expression in simplest form.

97. $\dfrac{27x^3}{3x^2}$

98. $\dfrac{5x^2y}{xy + 5x}$

99. $\dfrac{x^2 - 36}{6 - x}$

100. $\dfrac{x^2 + 3x - 40}{x^2 - 3x - 10}$

In Exercises 101–104, evaluate the combination of functions when $f(x) = 2x^2 - 5$ and $g(x) = x - 3$ at the indicated value of x.

101. $(f + g)(-x)$ when $x = -2$

102. $(f - g)(x)$ when $x = 4$

103. $(fg)(-x)$ when $x = -3$

104. $\left(\dfrac{f}{g}\right)(x)$ when $x = \dfrac{3}{2}$

1 Chapter Summary

What did you learn?

	Review Exercises
Section 1.1	
☐ How to sketch graphs of equations by point plotting and by using a graphing utility	1–22
☐ How to use graphs of equations in real-life problems	23, 24
Section 1.2	
☐ How to find the slopes of lines	25–34
☐ How to write linear equations given points on lines and their slopes	35–46
☐ How to use slope-intercept forms of linear equations to sketch graphs of lines	47–58
☐ How to use slope to identify parallel and perpendicular lines	59–62
Section 1.3	
☐ How to decide whether relations between two variables are functions	63–68
☐ How to use function notation and evaluate functions	69, 70
☐ How to find the domains of functions	71–76
☐ How to use functions to model and solve real-life problems	77, 78
Section 1.4	
☐ How to find the domains and ranges of functions and use the Vertical Line Test for functions	79–86
☐ How to determine intervals on which functions are increasing or decreasing	87–90
☐ How to determine relative maximum and relative minimum values of functions	91–94
☐ How to graph step functions and other piecewise-defined functions	95, 96
☐ How to identify even and odd functions	97, 98
Section 1.5	
☐ How to recognize graphs of common functions	99–102
☐ How to use vertical and horizontal shifts and reflections to sketch graphs of functions	103–118
☐ How to use nonrigid transformations to sketch graphs of functions	119–126
Section 1.6	
☐ How to add, subtract, multiply, and divide functions	127–132
☐ How to find compositions of one function with another function	133–136
☐ How to use combinations of functions to model and solve real-life problems	137, 138
Section 1.7	
☐ How to find inverse functions informally and verify that two functions are inverses of each other	139–142
☐ How to use graphs of functions to decide whether functions have inverses	143–150
☐ How to find inverse functions algebraically	151–156

1 Review Exercises

1.1 **In Exercises 1 and 2, complete the table. Use the resulting solution points to sketch the graph of the equation. Use a graphing utility to verify the graph.**

1. $y = -\frac{1}{2}x + 2$

x	-2	0	2	3	4
y					

2. $y = x^2 - 3x$

x	-1	0	1	2	3
y					

In Exercises 3–12, sketch the graph of the equation *by hand*. Use a graphing utility to verify the graph.

3. $y - 2x - 3 = 0$

4. $3x + 2y + 6 = 0$

5. $x - 5 = 0$

6. $y = 8 - |x|$

7. $y = \sqrt{5 - x}$

8. $y = \sqrt{x + 2}$

9. $y + 2x^2 = 0$

10. $y = x^2 - 4x$

11. $x + y^2 = 9$

12. $x^2 + y^2 = 10$

In Exercises 13–20, use a graphing utility to graph the equation. Approximate any intercepts.

13. $y = \frac{1}{4}(x + 1)^3$

14. $y = 4 - (x - 4)^2$

15. $y = \frac{1}{4}x^4 - 2x^2$

16. $y = \frac{1}{4}x^3 - 3x$

17. $y = x\sqrt{9 - x^2}$

18. $y = x\sqrt{x + 3}$

19. $y = |x - 4| - 4$

20. $y = |x + 2| + |3 - x|$

In Exercises 21 and 22, find a viewing window on a graphing utility such that the graph of the equation agrees with the graph shown.

21. $y = 0.002x^2 - 0.06x - 1$

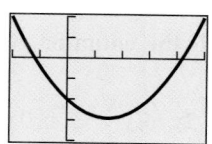

22. $y = 10x^3 - 21x^2$

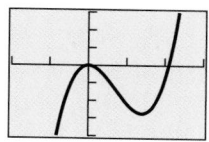

Data Analysis **In Exercises 23 and 24, (a) use a graphing utility to plot the data; (b) use the regression capabilities of a graphing utility to find the best-fitting linear model (let $t = 2$ correspond to 1992); (c) graph the model in the same viewing window with the data; and (d) use the model to estimate the values of y for the years 2000 and 2002.**

23. The average expenditures y for automobile insurance per insured vehicle from 1992 through 1996 are shown in the table. (Source: National Association of Insurance Commissioners)

x	1992	1993	1994	1995	1996
y	616	638	651	667	685

24. The total number y of Coast Guard personnel on active duty (in thousands) from 1992 through 1997 are shown in the table. (Source: U.S. Department of Transportation)

x	1992	1993	1994	1995	1996	1997
y	39.4	39.2	37.8	36.7	35.2	34.9

1.2 **In Exercises 25–30, plot the two points and find the slope of the line that passes through the points.**

25. $(-3, 2), (8, 2)$

26. $(7, -1), (7, 12)$

27. $\left(\frac{3}{2}, 1\right), \left(5, \frac{5}{2}\right)$

28. $\left(-\frac{3}{4}, \frac{5}{6}\right), \left(\frac{1}{2}, -\frac{5}{2}\right)$

29. $(-4.5, 6), (2.1, 3)$

30. $(-2.7, -6.3), (-1, -1.2)$

In Exercises 31–34, use the concept of slope to find t such that the three points are collinear.

31. $(-2, 5), (0, t), (1, 1)$

32. $(-6, 1), (1, t), (10, 5)$

33. $(1, -4), (t, 3), (5, 10)$

34. $(-3, 3), (t, -1), (8, 6)$

In Exercises 35–46, (a) find an equation of the line that passes through the given point and has the specified slope, and (b) find three additional points through which the line passes.

	Point	Slope
35.	$(2, -1)$	$m = \frac{1}{4}$
36.	$(-3, 5)$	$m = -\frac{3}{2}$
37.	$(0, -5)$	$m = \frac{3}{2}$
38.	$(3, 0)$	$m = -\frac{2}{3}$
39.	$(-6, -5)$	$m = -2$
40.	$(-7, 2)$	$m = 4$
41.	$\left(\frac{1}{5}, -5\right)$	$m = -1$
42.	$\left(0, \frac{7}{8}\right)$	$m = -\frac{4}{5}$
43.	$(-2, 6)$	$m = 0$
44.	$(-8, 8)$	$m = 0$
45.	$(10, -6)$	m is undefined.
46.	$(5, 4)$	m is undefined.

In Exercises 47–52, (a) find an equation of the line (in slope-intercept form) that passes through the points and (b) sketch the graph of the equation.

47. $(2, -1), (4, -1)$ **48.** $(0, 0), (0, 10)$

49. $(2, 1), (14, 6)$ **50.** $(-2, 2), (3, -10)$

51. $(-1, 0), (6, 2)$ **52.** $(1, 6), (4, 2)$

Rate of Change **In Exercises 53 and 54, you are given the dollar value of a product in 2000 *and* the rate at which the value of the item is expected to change during the 5 years following. Use this information to write a linear equation that gives the dollar value V of the product in terms of the year t. (Let $t = 0$ represent 2000.)**

	2000 Value	Rate
53.	$12,500	$850 increase per year
54.	$72.95	$5.15 increase per year

Exploration **In Exercises 55 and 56, find a relationship between x and y such that (x, y) is equidistant from the two points.**

55. $(-2, -5), (6, 3)$ **56.** $\left(1, \frac{7}{2}\right), (5, 0)$

57. *Business* During the second and third quarters of the year, a business had sales of $160,000 and $185,000, respectively. If the growth of sales follows a linear pattern, estimate sales during the fourth quarter.

58. *Dollar Value* The dollar value of a product in 2000 is $85, and the product will increase in value at an expected rate of $3.75 per year.

(a) Write a linear equation that gives the dollar value V of the product in terms of the year t. (Let $t = 0$ represent 2000.)

(b) Use a graphing utility to graph the sales equation.

(c) Use the *value* or *trace* feature of your graphing utility to estimate the dollar value of the product in 2005.

In Exercises 59–62, write equations of the lines through the point (a) parallel to the given line and (b) perpendicular to the given line. Verify your result with a graphing utility (use a square setting).

	Point	Line
59.	$(3, -2)$	$5x - 4y = 8$
60.	$(-8, 3)$	$2x + 3y = 5$
61.	$(-6, 2)$	$x = 4$
62.	$(3, -4)$	$y = 2$

1.3 **In Exercises 63 and 64, determine which of the sets of ordered pairs represents a function from A to B. Give reasons for your answers.**

63. $A = \{10, 20, 30, 40\}$ and $B = \{0, 2, 4, 6\}$
(a) $\{(20, 4), (40, 0), (20, 6), (30, 2)\}$
(b) $\{(10, 4), (20, 4), (30, 4), (40, 4)\}$
(c) $\{(40, 0), (30, 2), (20, 4), (10, 6)\}$
(d) $\{(20, 2), (10, 0), (40, 4)\}$

64. $A = \{u, v, w\}$ and $B = \{-2, -1, 0, 1, 2\}$
(a) $\{(v, -1), (u, 2), (w, 0), (u, -2)\}$
(b) $\{(u, -2), (v, 2), (w, 1)\}$
(c) $\{(u, 2), (v, 2), (w, 1), (w, 1)\}$
(d) $\{(w, -2), (v, 0), (w, 2)\}$

In Exercises 65–68, determine if the equation represents y as a function of x.

65. $16x - y^4 = 0$ **66.** $2x - y - 3 = 0$

67. $y = \sqrt{1 - x}$ **68.** $|y| = x + 2$

In Exercises 69 and 70, evaluate the function at each value of the specified variable. Simplify your answers.

69. $f(x) = x^2 + 1$

    (a) $f(2)$ (b) $f(-4)$

    (c) $f(t^2)$ (d) $-f(x)$

70. $g(x) = x^{4/3}$

    (a) $g(8)$ (b) $g(t + 1)$

    (c) $\dfrac{g(8) - g(1)}{8 - 1}$ (d) $g(-x)$

In Exercises 71–76, determine the domain of the function. Verify your result with a graphing utility.

71. $f(x) = (x - 1)(x + 2)$ **72.** $f(x) = x^2 - 4x - 32$

73. $f(x) = \sqrt{25 - x^2}$ **74.** $f(x) = \sqrt{x^2 + 8x}$

75. $g(s) = \dfrac{5}{3s - 9}$ **76.** $f(x) = \dfrac{2}{3x + 4}$

77. *Business* A company produces a product for which the variable cost is \$5.35 per unit and the fixed costs are \$16,000. The company sells the product for \$8.20 and can sell all that it produces.

    (a) Find the total cost as a function of x, the number of units produced.

    (b) Find the profit as a function of x.

78. *Boating* The retail expenditures B (in billions of dollars) on boating in the United States from 1985 to 1996 can be represented by the piecewise-defined function

$$B(t) = \begin{cases} -0.631t^2 - 2.845t + 14.160, & -5 \le t < 2 \\ 2.088t + 5.768, & 2 \le t \le 6 \end{cases}$$

where $t = 0$ represents 1990. Use a graphing utility to graph the model and find the amount spent on boating in 1985, 1990, and 1995. (Source: National Marine Manufacturers Association)

1.4 In Exercises 79–82, find the domain and range of the function.

79. $f(x) = 3 - 2x^2$ **80.** $f(x) = \sqrt{2x^2 - 1}$

81. $h(x) = \sqrt{36 - x^2}$ **82.** $g(x) = |x + 5|$

In Exercises 83–86, (a) use a graphing utility to graph the equation and (b) use the Vertical Line Test to determine whether y is a function of x.

83. $y = \dfrac{x^2 + 3x}{6}$ **84.** $y = -\frac{2}{3}|x + 5|$

85. $3x + y^2 = 2$ **86.** $x^2 + y^2 = 49$

In Exercises 87–90, determine the open intervals over which the function is increasing, decreasing, or constant.

87. $f(x) = x^3 - 3x$ **88.** $f(x) = \sqrt{x^2 - 9}$

89. $f(x) = x\sqrt{x - 6}$ **90.** $f(x) = \dfrac{|x + 8|}{2}$

Graphical Analysis In Exercises 91–94, use a graphing utility to approximate (to two-decimal-place accuracy) any relative maximum or minimum values of the function.

91. $f(x) = (x^2 - 4)^2$ **92.** $f(x) = x^2 - x - 1$

93. $h(x) = 4x^3 - x^4$ **94.** $f(x) = x^3 - 4x^2 - 1$

In Exercises 95 and 96, sketch the graph of the piecewise-defined function by hand. Verify using a graphing utility.

95. $f(x) = \begin{cases} 3x + 5, & x < 0 \\ x - 4, & x \ge 0 \end{cases}$

96. $f(x) = \begin{cases} x^2 + 7, & x < 1 \\ x^2 - 5x + 6, & x \ge 1 \end{cases}$

In Exercises 97 and 98, determine whether the function is even, odd, or neither.

97. $f(x) = (x^2 - 8)^2$ **98.** $f(x) = 2x^3 - x^2$

1.5 In Exercises 99–102, the graph is related to one of the common functions on page 118. Identify the common function and describe the transformation shown in the graph. Write the equation for the graphed function.

99.

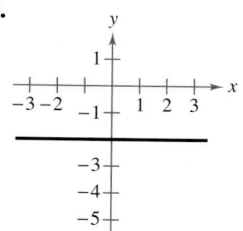

100.

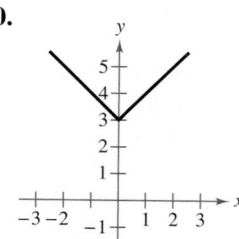

101.

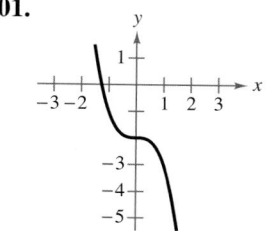

102.

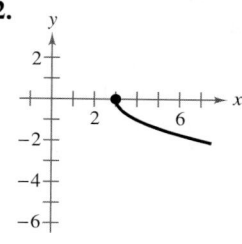

In Exercises 103–126, sketch the graph of the function by hand.

103. $f(x) = x^2 - 6$ **104.** $f(x) = (x - 3)^2 - 2$

105. $f(x) = (x - 1)^3 + 7$ **106.** $f(x) = (x + 2)^3 + 5$

107. $f(x) = \sqrt{x} - 5$ **108.** $f(x) = \sqrt{x + 5} + 4$

109. $f(x) = 7 + |x|$ **110.** $f(x) = |x + 8| - 1$

111. $f(x) = -x^2 - 3$

112. $f(x) = -(x - 2)^2 - 8$

113. $f(x) = -(x + 5)^3 - 6$

114. $f(x) = 3 - x^3$ **115.** $f(x) = -\sqrt{x + 4} - 3$

116. $f(x) = \sqrt{-x - 1} + 7$

117. $f(x) = -|x + 2| - 1$

118. $f(x) = 1 - |-x|$

119. $f(x) = -2x^2 + 3$ **120.** $f(x) = \frac{1}{2}(x - 3)^2 + 6$

121. $f(x) = -\frac{1}{4}(1 - x)^3 - 2$

122. $f(x) = 5(x - 1)^3 - 5$

123. $f(x) = -\frac{1}{2}|x| + 9$ **124.** $f(x) = -2|-x - 4|$

125. $f(x) = -3\sqrt{6 - x} + 4$

126. $f(x) = 4\sqrt{x + 1} - 8$

1.6 **In Exercises 127–136, let $f(x) = 3 - 2x$, $g(x) = \sqrt{x}$, and $h(x) = 3x^2 + 2$, and find the indicated values.**

127. $(f - g)(4)$

128. $(f + h)(5)$

129. $(f + g)(25)$

130. $(g - h)(1)$

131. $(fh)(1)$

132. $\left(\dfrac{g}{h}\right)(1)$

133. $(h \circ g)(7)$

134. $(g \circ f)(-2)$

135. $(f \circ h)(-4)$

136. $(g \circ h)(6)$

Data Analysis **In Exercises 137 and 138, use the table, which shows the total value (in billions of dollars) of U.S. imports from China and Taiwan for the years 1992 through 1997. The variables y_1 and y_2 represent the total value of imports from China and Taiwan, respectively.** (Source: U.S. Bureau of the Census)

Year	1992	1993	1994	1995	1996	1997
y_1	25.7	31.5	38.8	45.5	51.5	62.6
y_2	24.6	25.1	26.7	29.0	29.9	32.6

137. Use the regression capabilities of a graphing utility to find quadratic models for each of the variables. Let $t = 2$ represent 1992.

138. Use a graphing utility to graph y_1, y_2, and $y_1 + y_2$ in the same viewing window. Use the model to estimate the total value of U.S. imports from China and Taiwan in 2002.

1.7 **In Exercises 139–142, find the inverse of f informally. Verify that $f(f^{-1}(x)) = f^{-1}(f(x)) = x$.**

139. $f(x) = 6x$ **140.** $f(x) = \frac{1}{12}x$

141. $f(x) = x - 7$ **142.** $f(x) = x + 5$

In Exercises 143–146, (a) find f^{-1}, (b) graph f and f^{-1} in the same viewing window, and (c) verify that $f^{-1}(f(x)) = x$ and $f(f^{-1}(x)) = x$.

143. $f(x) = \frac{1}{2}x - 3$ **144.** $f(x) = 5x - 7$

145. $f(x) = \sqrt{x + 1}$ **146.** $f(x) = x^3 + 2$

In Exercises 147–150, restrict the domain of the function f to an interval over which the function is increasing, and determine f^{-1} over that interval. Use a graphing utility to graph f and f^{-1} in the same viewing window.

147. $f(x) = 2(x - 4)^2$ **148.** $f(x) = -x^2 + 4$

149. $f(x) = |x - 2|$ **150.** $f(x) = \frac{1}{2}|x + 4|$

In Exercises 151–156, find the inverse of f algebraically.

151. $f(x) = \dfrac{x}{12}$ **152.** $f(x) = \dfrac{7x + 3}{8}$

153. $f(x) = 4x^3 - 3$ **154.** $f(x) = x^3 - 2$

155. $f(x) = \sqrt{x + 10}$ **156.** $f(x) = 4\sqrt{6 - x}$

Synthesis

True or False? **In Exercises 157–159, determine whether the statement is true or false. Justify your answer.**

157. Relative to the graph of $f(x) = \sqrt{x}$, the function $h(x) = -\sqrt{x + 9} - 13$ is shifted 9 units to the left and 13 units down, then reflected in the x-axis.

158. If $f(x) = x^n$ where n is odd, f^{-1} exists.

159. There exists no function f such that $f = f^{-1}$.

160. Explain why not all equations of lines are functions.

Chapter Project   *Modeling the Area of a Plot*

Many real-life problems can be analyzed from a *graphical,* a *numerical,* and an *algebraic* perspective. In this project, you will use all three strategies to determine the maximum size of a rectangular plot that can be enclosed by a fixed amount of fencing.

You have 100 meters of fencing material to enclose a rectangular plot. Your goal is to determine the dimensions of the plot such that you enclose the maximum area possible.

a. Express the area $A(x)$ of the rectangular plot as a function of the length x of one side, as shown in the figure below.

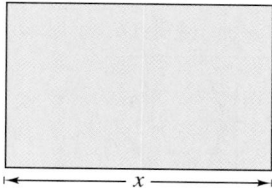

b. Analyze the problem *numerically* by completing the table.

x	0	5	10	15	20	25	30	35	40	45	50
$A(x)$											

According to this table, what do you think the dimensions of the plot should be to enclose the maximum area? Explain.

c. Use a graphing utility to graph the area function. What is the domain of the function? Solve the problem *graphically* by using the *trace* feature of your graphing utility to find the value of x that yields the maximum area.

d. Solve the problem *algebraically* by showing that the area function can be written as $A(x) = 625 - (x - 25)^2$. How does this form of the function allow you to find the dimensions that produce a maximum area?

e. Discuss the strengths and weaknesses of the three strategies used in parts (b), (c), and (d).

Questions for Further Exploration

1. Suppose you were not restricted to a rectangular plot. Would you be able to use 100 meters of fencing to enclose a greater area? Explain.

2. In the project above, you found the maximum area that can be enclosed in a rectangular plot using 100 meters of fencing. If you doubled the amount of fencing, could you enclose twice as much area? Use numerical, graphical, and algebraic approaches and explain your reasoning.

3. Suppose the rectangular plot runs along a building, so that you need to fence only three sides. What dimensions will now yield a maximum area with 100 meters of fencing?

1 Chapter Test

Take this test as you would take a test in class. After you are done, check your work against the answers in the back of the book.

The *Interactive* CD-ROM and *Internet* versions of this text provide answers to the Chapter Tests and Cumulative Tests. They also offer Chapter Pre-Tests (that test key skills and concepts covered in previous chapters) and Chapter Post-Tests, both of which have randomly generated exercises with diagnostic capabilities.

In Exercises 1–6, use the point-plotting method to graph the equation and identify any intercepts. Verify your results using a graphing utility.

1. $y = 4 - \frac{3}{4}|x|$ **2.** $y = 4 - (x - 2)^2$ **3.** $y = x - x^3$

4. $y = -x^3 + 2x - 4$ **5.** $y = \sqrt{3 - x}$ **6.** $y = \frac{1}{2}x\sqrt{x + 3}$

7. A line passes through the point $(3, -1)$ with slope $m = \frac{3}{2}$. List three additional points on the line. Then sketch the line.

8. Find the x- and y-intercepts of the graph of $3x - 2y - 9 = 0$.

9. Find an equation of the line that passes through the point $(0, 4)$ and is perpendicular to the line $5x + 2y = 3$.

10. Does the graph at the right represent y as a function of x? Explain.

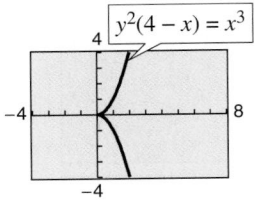

FIGURE FOR 10

In Exercises 11–14, use the function $f(x) = 10 - \sqrt{3 - x}$.

11. Evaluate: $f(-6)$ **12.** Simplify: $f(t - 3)$

13. Simplify: $\dfrac{f(x) - f(2)}{x - 2}$ **14.** Determine the domain of f.

15. A company produces a product for which the variable cost is $5.60 and the fixed costs are $24,000. The product sells for $9.20. Write the total cost C as a function of x. Write the profit P as a function of x.

In Exercises 16 and 17, find the open intervals for which the function is increasing, decreasing, or constant.

16. $h(x) = \frac{1}{4}x^4 - 2x^2$ **17.** $g(t) = |t + 2| - |t - 2|$

In Exercises 18 and 19, use a graphing utility to approximate (to two decimal places) any relative minimum or maximum function values.

18. $f(x) = -x^3 - 5x^2 + 12$ **19.** $f(x) = x^5 - x^3 + 2$

In Exercises 20–22, (a) identify the common function, (b) describe the transformation, and (c) sketch the graph of the function.

20. $f(x) = -2(x - 5)^3 + 3$ **21.** $f(x) = \sqrt{-x} - 7$ **22.** $f(x) = 4|-x| - 7$

23. Use the functions $f(x) = x^2$ and $g(x) = \sqrt{2 - x}$ to find the specified function and its domain.

(a) $(f - g)(x)$ (b) $\left(\dfrac{f}{g}\right)(x)$ (c) $(f \circ g)(x)$ (d) $g^{-1}(x)$

24. A wire 100 inches long is to be cut into four pieces to form a rectangle whose shortest side has a length of x. Express the area A of the rectangle as a function of x. Determine the domain of the function and graph the function over that domain. Approximate the maximum area of the rectangle.

Intercepts, Zeros, and Solutions

2

Bob Krist/Tony Stone Images

The key and action combination of a piano contains more than 9000 parts. The combined tension of the more than 200 strings is greater than 18 tons.

The Big Picture

In this chapter you will learn how to

❏ solve and use linear equations, including those involving fractions.
❏ write and use mathematical models to solve real-life problems.
❏ find intercepts, zeros, and solutions of equations graphically.
❏ perform operations with complex numbers and plot complex numbers in the complex plane.
❏ solve quadratic equations, polynomial equations, equations involving radicals, equations involving fractions, and equations involving absolute values.
❏ solve linear inequalities, inequalities involving absolute values, polynomial inequalities, and rational inequalities.

Important Vocabulary

As you encounter each new vocabulary term in this chapter, add the term and its definition to your notebook glossary.

- equation (p. 156)
- solutions (p. 156)
- linear equation in one variable x (p. 156)
- extraneous (p. 157)
- mathematical modeling (p. 157)
- formulas (p. 160)
- fitting a line to data (p. 162)
- x-intercept (p. 169)
- y-intercept (p. 169)
- zero (p. 170)
- point of intersection (p. 173)

- imaginary unit i (p. 180)
- complex number (p. 180)
- complex conjugates (p. 183)
- fractal geometry (p. 184)
- complex plane (p. 184)
- imaginary axis (p. 184)
- real axis (p. 184)
- fractals (p. 184)
- Mandelbrot Set (p. 184)
- bounded (p. 184)
- unbounded (p. 184)
- quadratic equation in x (p. 188)

- second-degree polynomial equation in x (p. 188)
- position equation (p. 197)
- solutions of an inequality (p. 205)
- graph of an inequality (p. 205)
- properties of inequalities (p. 205)
- equivalent inequalities (p. 205)
- linear inequality (p. 206)
- double inequality (p. 207)
- critical numbers (p. 209)
- test intervals (p. 209)

Additional Resources Text-specific additional resources are available to help you do well in this course. See page xvi for details.

2.1 Modeling with Linear Equations

Equations and Solutions of Equations

An **equation** is a statement that two algebraic expressions are equal. For example, $3x - 5 = 7$, $x^2 - x - 6 = 0$, and $\sqrt{2x} = 4$ are equations. To **solve** an equation in x means to find all values of x for which the equation is true. Such values are **solutions.** For instance, $x = 4$ is a solution of the equation $3x - 5 = 7$, because $3(4) - 5 = 7$ is a true statement.

The solutions of an equation depend on the kinds of numbers being considered. For instance, in the set of rational numbers, $x^2 = 10$ has no solution because there is no rational number whose square is 10. However, in the set of real numbers the equation has the two solutions $\sqrt{10}$ and $-\sqrt{10}$.

An equation that is true for *every* real number in the domain of the variable is called an **identity.** For example, $x^2 - 9 = (x + 3)(x - 3)$ is an identity because it is a true statement for any real value of x, and $x/(3x^2) = 1/(3x)$, where $x \neq 0$, is an identity because it is true for any nonzero real value of x.

An equation that is true for just *some* (or even none) of the real numbers in the domain of the variable is called a **conditional equation.** For example, the equation $x^2 - 9 = 0$ is conditional because $x = 3$ and $x = -3$ are the only values in the domain that satisfy the equation. The equation $2x + 1 = 2x - 3$ is also conditional because it is not true for any value of x. Learning to solve conditional equations is the primary focus of this chapter.

A **linear equation in one variable x** is an equation that can be written in the standard form $ax + b = 0$, where a and b are real numbers, with $a \neq 0$. For a review of solving one- and two-step linear equations, see Appendix C.

To solve an equation involving fractional expressions, find the least common denominator of all terms in the equation and multiply every term by this LCD. This procedure clears the equation of fractions.

What You Should Learn:

- How to solve equations involving fractional expressions
- How to write and use mathematical models to solve real-life problems
- How to use common formulas to solve real-life problems
- How to use scatter plots and a graphing utility to find linear models for data

Why You Should Learn It:

Linear equations are useful in modeling situations in which you need to find missing information. For instance, Exercise 40 on page 165 shows how to use a linear equation to determine the score you must get on a test in order to get an A for the course you are taking.

EXAMPLE 1   Solving an Equation Involving Fractions

$$\frac{x}{3} + \frac{3x}{4} = 2 \qquad \text{Original equation}$$

$$(12)\frac{x}{3} + (12)\frac{3x}{4} = (12)2 \qquad \text{Multiply by the LCD.}$$

$$4x + 9x = 24 \qquad \text{Simplify and multiply.}$$

$$13x = 24 \qquad \text{Combine like terms.}$$

$$x = \frac{24}{13} \qquad \text{Divide each side by 13.}$$

Check

After solving an equation, check the solution in the original equation.

$$\frac{\frac{24}{13}}{3} + \frac{3\left(\frac{24}{13}\right)}{4} \overset{?}{=} 2 \qquad \text{Substitute } \tfrac{24}{13} \text{ for } x.$$

$$2 = 2 \qquad \text{Solution checks. } \checkmark$$

PhotoEdit

When multiplying or dividing an equation by a *variable* expression, it is possible to introduce an **extraneous** solution—one that does not satisfy the original equation. The next example demonstrates the importance of checking your solution when you have multiplied or divided by a variable expression.

As you cover this chapter, you should point out to your students that some equations are best solved algebraically, whereas others are best solved with a graphing utility.

EXAMPLE 2   An Equation with an Extraneous Solution

Solve the equation for x.

$$\frac{1}{x-2} = \frac{3}{x+2} - \frac{6x}{x^2-4}$$

Algebraic Solution

In this case, the LCD is

$$x^2 - 4 = (x+2)(x-2).$$

Multiplying each term by the LCD and simplifying produces the following.

$$\frac{1}{x-2}(x+2)(x-2)$$

$$= \frac{3}{x+2}(x+2)(x-2) - \frac{6x}{x^2-4}(x+2)(x-2)$$

$$x + 2 = 3(x-2) - 6x, \quad x \neq \pm 2$$

$$x + 2 = 3x - 6 - 6x$$

$$4x = -8$$

$$x = -2$$

A check of $x = -2$ in the original equation shows that it yields a denominator of zero. So, $x = -2$ is extraneous, and the equation has *no solution*.

Graphical Solution

Use a graphing utility to graph the left and right sides of the equation in the same viewing window as the functions

$$y_1 = \frac{1}{x-2} \quad \text{and} \quad y_2 = \frac{3}{x+2} - \frac{6x}{x^2-4}$$

as shown in Figure 2.1. The graphs of the functions do not appear to intersect. This means that there is no point for which the left side of the equation $1/(x-2)$ is equal to the right side of the equation

$$\frac{3}{x+2} - \frac{6x}{x^2-4}.$$

So, the equation appears to have *no solution*.

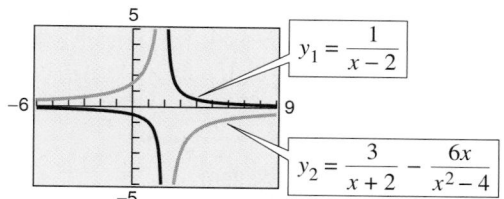

Figure 2.1

Using Mathematical Models to Solve Problems

One of the primary goals of this text is to learn how algebra can be used to solve problems that occur in real-life situations. This procedure is called **mathematical modeling.**

A good approach to mathematical modeling is to use two stages. Begin by using the verbal description of the problem to form a *verbal model*. Then, after assigning labels to the quantities in the verbal model, form a *mathematical model* or *algebraic equation*.

An ancient Egyptian papyrus, discovered in 1858, contains one of the earliest examples of mathematical writing in existence. The papyrus itself dates back to around 1650 B.C., but it is actually a copy of writings from two centuries earlier. The algebraic equations on the papyrus were written in words. Diophantus, a Greek who lived around A.D. 250, is often called the Father of Algebra. He was the first to use abbreviated word forms in equations.

| Verbal description | ⇒ | Verbal model | ⇒ | Algebraic equation |

When you are trying to construct a verbal model, it is helpful to look for a *hidden equality*—a statement that two algebraic expressions are equal. These two expressions might be explicitly stated as being equal, or they might be known to be equal (based on prior knowledge or experience).

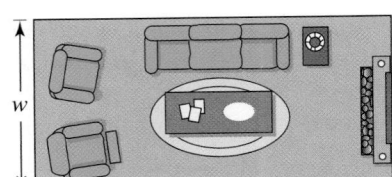

Figure 2.2

EXAMPLE 3   Finding the Dimensions of a Room

A rectangular family room is twice as long as it is wide, and its perimeter is 84 feet. Find the dimensions of the family room.

Solution

For this problem, it helps to draw a diagram, as shown in Figure 2.2.

Verbal Model: $2 \cdot$ Length $+ \, 2 \cdot$ Width $=$ Perimeter

Labels: Perimeter $= 84$ (feet)
Width $= w$ (feet)
Length $= l = 2w$ (feet)

Equation: $2(2w) + 2w = 84$ Write original equation.

$6w = 84$ Group like terms.

$w = 14$ Divide each side by 6.

Because the length is twice the width, you have

$l = 2w$ Length is twice width.

$= 2(14) = 28.$ Substitute 14 for w and simplify.

So, the dimensions of the room are 14 feet by 28 feet.
You can check that the dimensions are correct as follows.

$2 \cdot$ Length $+ \, 2 \cdot$ Width $=$ Perimeter

$2 \cdot 28 + 2 \cdot 14 \overset{?}{=} 84$ Substitute.

$84 = 84$ Solution checks. ✓

The figure provided with Example 3 was not really essential to the solution. Nevertheless, strongly encourage your students to develop the habit of including sketches with their solutions even if they are not required.

STUDY T!P

Students sometimes say that although a solution looks easy when it is worked out in class, they don't see where to begin when solving a problem alone. Keep in mind that no one—not even great mathematicians—can expect to look at every mathematical problem and know immediately where to begin. Many problems involve some trial and error before a solution is found. To make algebra work for you, put in a lot of time, expect to try solution methods that end up not working, and learn from both your successes and your failures.

EXAMPLE 4   A Distance Problem

A plane is flying nonstop from New York to San Francisco, a distance of about 2700 miles, as shown in Figure 2.3. After $1\frac{1}{2}$ hours in the air, the plane flies over Chicago (a distance of 800 miles from New York). Estimate the time it will take the plane to fly from New York to San Francisco.

Solution

Verbal Model: Distance $=$ Rate $\cdot$ Time

Labels: Distance $= 2700$ (miles)
Time $= t$ (hours)
Rate $= \dfrac{\text{Distance to Chicago}}{\text{Time to Chicago}} = \dfrac{800}{1.5}$ (miles per hour)

Equation: $2700 = \dfrac{800}{1.5}t$

$5.06 \approx t$

The trip will take about 5.06 hours or about 5 hours and 4 minutes.

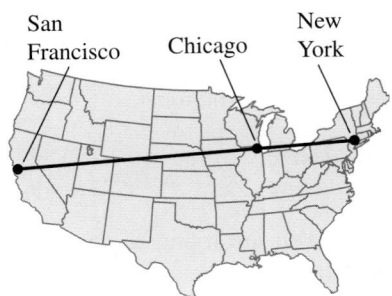

Figure 2.3

EXAMPLE 5   Height of a Building

To measure the height of the twin towers of the World Trade Center, you measure the shadow cast by one of the buildings and find it to be 170.25 feet long, as shown in Figure 2.4. Then you measure the shadow cast by a 4-foot post and find it to be 6 inches long. Estimate the building's height.

Solution

To solve this problem, you use a result from geometry that states that the ratios of corresponding sides of similar triangles are equal.

Verbal Model: $\dfrac{\text{Height of building}}{\text{Length of building's shadow}} = \dfrac{\text{Height of post}}{\text{Length of post's shadow}}$

Labels:
Height of building $= x$ (feet)
Length of building's shadow $= 170.25$ (feet)
Height of post $= 4$ feet $= 48$ inches   (inches)
Length of post's shadow $= 6$ (inches)

Equation: $\dfrac{x}{170.25} = \dfrac{48}{6}$

$$x = 1362$$

So, the World Trade Center is about 1362 feet high.

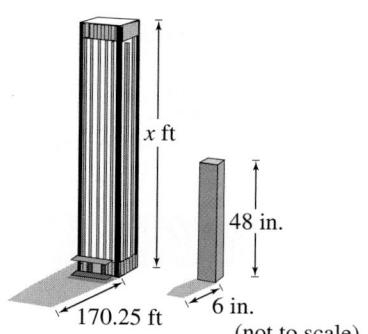

Figure 2.4

x ft

48 in.

170.25 ft   6 in.
(not to scale)

The *Interactive* CD-ROM and *Internet* versions of this text show every example with its solution; clicking on the *Try It!* button brings up similar problems. Guided Examples and Integrated Examples show step-by-step solutions to additional examples. Integrated Examples are related to several concepts in the section.

EXAMPLE 6   An Inventory Problem

A store has $30,000 of inventory in 12-inch and 19-inch color televisions. The profit on a 12-inch set is 22% and the profit on a 19-inch set is 40%. The profit for the entire stock is 35%. How much was invested in each type of television?

Solution

Verbal Model: $\boxed{\begin{array}{c}\text{Profit from}\\ \text{12-inch sets}\end{array}} + \boxed{\begin{array}{c}\text{Profit from}\\ \text{19-inch sets}\end{array}} = \boxed{\begin{array}{c}\text{Total}\\ \text{profit}\end{array}}$

Labels:
Inventory of 12-inch sets $= x$ (dollars)
Inventory of 19-inch sets $= 30,000 - x$ (dollars)
Profit from 12-inch sets $= 0.22x$ (dollars)
Profit from 19-inch sets $= 0.40(30,000 - x)$ (dollars)
Total profit $= 0.35(30,000) = 10,500$ (dollars)

Equation: $0.22x + 0.40(30,000 - x) = 10,500$

$$-0.18x = -1500$$

$$x \approx 8333.33$$

$$30,000 - x \approx 21,666.67$$

So, about $8333.33 is invested in 12-inch sets and about $21,666.67 is invested in 19-inch sets.

STUDY T!P

Notice in Example 6 that percents are expressed as decimals. For instance, 22% is written as 0.22.

You might want to remind your students that words and phrases such as *is, are, will be,* and *represents* indicate equality; *sum, plus, greater, increased by, more than, exceeds,* and *total of* indicate addition; *difference, minus, less than, decreased by, subtracted from, reduced by,* and *the remainder* indicate subtraction; *product, multiplied by, twice, times,* and *percent of* indicate multiplication; and *quotient, divided by, ratio,* and *per* indicate division.

Common Formulas

Many common types of geometric, scientific, and investment problems use ready-made equations, called **formulas.** Knowing these formulas will help you translate and solve a wide variety of real-life applications.

Common Formulas for Area *A*, Perimeter *P*, Circumference *C*, and Volume *V*

Square	*Rectangle*	*Circle*	*Triangle*
$A = s^2$	$A = lw$	$A = \pi r^2$	$A = \dfrac{1}{2}bh$
$P = 4s$	$P = 2l + 2w$	$C = 2\pi r$	$P = a + b + c$

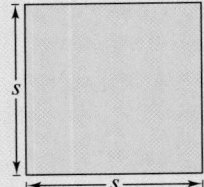 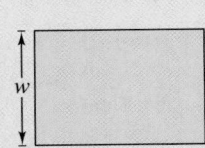 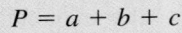 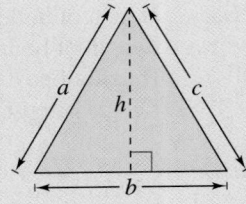

Cube	*Rectangular Solid*	*Circular Cylinder*	*Sphere*
$V = s^3$	$V = lwh$	$V = \pi r^2 h$	$V = \dfrac{4}{3}\pi r^3$

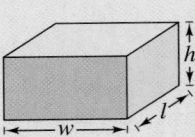 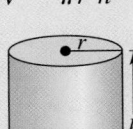 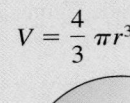 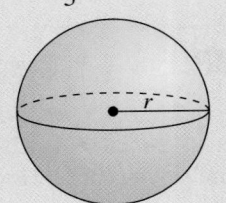

Miscellaneous Common Formulas

Temperature: $F = \dfrac{9}{5}C + 32$ F = degrees Fahrenheit, C = degrees Celsius

Simple Interest: $I = Prt$ I = interest, P = principal, r = annual interest rate, t = time in years

Compound Interest: $A = P\left(1 + \dfrac{r}{n}\right)^{nt}$ A = balance, P = principal, r = annual interest rate,

n = compoundings per year, t = time in years

Distance: $d = rt$ d = distance traveled, r = rate, t = time

When working with applied problems you often need to rewrite one of the common formulas. For instance, the formula for the perimeter of a rectangle, $P = 2l + 2w$, can be solved for w as $w = \frac{1}{2}(P - 2l)$.

EXAMPLE 7   Height of a Can

A cylindrical can has a volume of 300 cubic centimeters (cm^3) and a radius of 3 centimeters (cm), as shown in Figure 2.5. Find the height of the can.

Solution

The formula for the volume of a cylinder is $V = \pi r^2 h$. To find the height of the can, solve for h as $h = V/\pi r^2$.

Then, using $V = 300$ cm^3 and $r = 3$ cm, find the height.

$$h = \frac{300}{\pi(3)^2} = \frac{300}{9\pi} \approx 10.61$$

You can use unit analysis to check your answer: $\dfrac{300 \text{ cm}^3}{9\pi \text{ cm}^2} \approx 10.61$ cm.

3 cm

green valley

carrots

h

Figure 2.5

Fitting a Line to Data

Many real-life situations involve finding relationships between two variables, such as the year and the number of people in the labor force. In a typical situation, data is collected and written as a set of ordered pairs. The graph of such a set, a *scatter plot*, was discussed briefly in Section P.5.

EXAMPLE 8   Constructing a Scatter Plot

The data in the table shows the number of people P (in millions) in the United States who were part of the labor force from 1987 through 1997. In the table, t represents the year, with $t = 7$ corresponding to 1987. Sketch a scatter plot of the data.   (Source: U.S. Bureau of Labor Statistics)

t	7	8	9	10	11	12	13	14	15	16	17
P	120	122	124	126	126	128	129	131	132	134	136

Solution

Begin by representing the data with a set of ordered pairs.

(7, 120), (8, 122), (9, 124), (10, 126), (11, 126), (12, 128),

(13, 129), (14, 131), (15, 132), (16, 134), (17, 136)

Then plot each point in a coordinate plane, as shown in Figure 2.6.

From the scatter plot in Figure 2.6, it appears that the points describe a relationship that is nearly linear. The relationship is not *exactly* linear because the labor force did not increase by precisely the same amount each year.

A mathematical equation that approximates the relationship between t and P is a *mathematical model*. When developing a mathematical model to describe a set of data, you strive for two (often conflicting) goals—accuracy and simplicity. For the data above, a linear model of the form $P = at + b$ appears to be best. It is simple and relatively accurate.

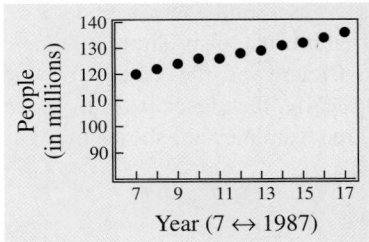

Figure 2.6

Finding a linear model to represent the relationship described by a scatter plot is called **fitting a line to data.** You can do this graphically by simply sketching the line that appears to fit the points, finding two points on the line, and then finding the equation of the line that passes through the two points.

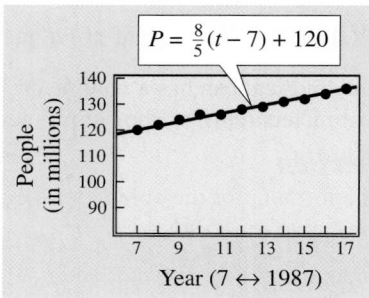

EXAMPLE 9 Fitting a Line to Data

Find a linear model that relates the year with the number of people in the United States labor force. (See Example 8.)

Figure 2.7

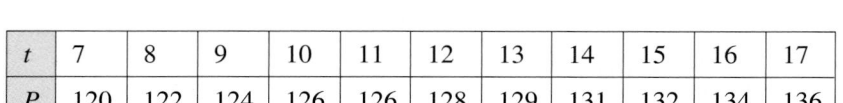

t	7	8	9	10	11	12	13	14	15	16	17
P	120	122	124	126	126	128	129	131	132	134	136

Solution

After plotting the data in the table, draw the line that you think best represents the data, as shown in Figure 2.7. Two points that lie on this line are (7, 120) and (17, 136). Using the point-slope form, you can find the equation of the line to be

$$P = \frac{8}{5}(t - 7) + 120. \qquad \text{Linear model}$$

Once you have found a model, you can measure how well the model fits the data by comparing the actual values with the values given by the model, as shown in the following table.

> ## STUDY T!P
>
> The model in Example 9 is based on the two data points chosen. If different points were chosen, the model may change somewhat. For instance, if you choose (10, 126) and (15, 132), the new model is
> $$P = \frac{6}{5}(t - 10) + 126.$$

	t	7	8	9	10	11	12	13	14	15	16	17
Actual ⇨	P	120	122	124	126	126	128	129	131	132	134	136
Model ⇨	P	120	121.6	123.2	124.8	126.4	128	129.6	131.2	132.8	134.4	136

If you use the regression capabilities of a graphing calculator or computer program to find a linear model for the data in Example 9, you will notice that the program may also output a value of $r \approx 0.995$. This number is the **correlation coefficient** of the data. Correlation coefficients vary between -1 and 1. Basically, the closer $|r|$ is to 1, the better the points can be described by a line. Three examples are shown in Figure 2.8.

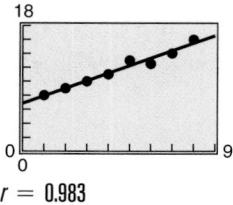
$r = 0.983$

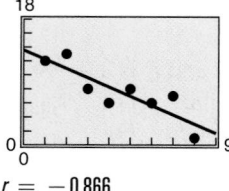
$r = -0.866$

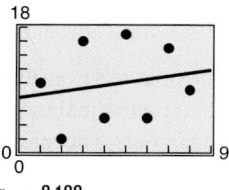
$r = 0.190$

Figure 2.8

EXAMPLE 10   A Mathematical Model

The average number of students s out of one thousand 11th- and 12th-grade students who took advanced placement exams for the years 1984 through 1995 are shown in the table.   (Source: U.S. National Center for Education Statistics)

Year	1984	1985	1986	1987	1988	1989
s	24	29	33	36	39	44

Year	1990	1991	1992	1993	1994	1995
s	48	53	57	62	60	66

a. Use the regression capabilities of a graphing utility to find a linear model for the data. Let t represent the year with $t = 4$ corresponding to 1984.

b. How closely does the model represent the data?

Graphical Solution

a. Using the regression capabilities of a graphing utility, you can find that a linear model for the data is $s = 3.8t + 9.5$.

b. You can use a graphing utility to graph the actual data and the model in the same viewing window. From Figure 2.9, it appears that the model is a "good fit" for the actual data. This is verified by the fact that the graphing utility outputs a value of $r \approx 0.994$.

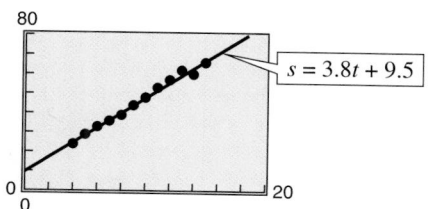

Figure 2.9

Numerical Solution

a. Using the regression capabilities of a graphing utility, you can find that a linear model for the data is $s = 3.8t + 9.5$.

b. You can see how well the model fits the data by comparing the actual values of s with the values of s given by the model, which are labeled $s*$ in the table below.

Year	1984	1985	1986	1987	1988	1989
s	24	29	33	36	39	44
$s*$	24.7	28.5	32.3	36.1	39.9	43.7

Year	1990	1991	1992	1993	1994	1995
s	48	53	57	62	60	66
$s*$	47.5	51.3	55.1	58.9	62.7	66.5

From the table, you can see that the model appears to be a good fit for the actual data.

Writing About Math   *Research Project*

Use your school's library or some other reference source to locate data that you think describes a linear relationship. Create a scatter plot of the data, and use the regression capabilities of a graphing utility to find a linear model for the data. Interpret the slope and y-intercept in the context of the data. Write a summary of your findings.

2.1 Exercises

In Exercises 1–6, determine whether the given values of x are solutions of the equation.

Equation   *Values*

1. $\dfrac{5}{2x} - \dfrac{4}{x} = 3$
(a) $x = -\frac{1}{2}$ (b) $x = 4$
(c) $x = 0$ (d) $x = \frac{1}{4}$

2. $\dfrac{x}{2} + \dfrac{6x}{7} = \dfrac{19}{14}$
(a) $x = -2$ (b) $x = 1$
(c) $x = \frac{1}{2}$ (d) $x = 7$

3. $3 + \dfrac{1}{x + 2} = 4$
(a) $x = -1$ (b) $x = -2$
(c) $x = 0$ (d) $x = 5$

4. $\dfrac{(x + 5)(x - 3)}{2} = 24$
(a) $x = -3$ (b) $x = -2$
(c) $x = 7$ (d) $x = 9$

5. $\dfrac{\sqrt{x + 4}}{6} + 3 = 4$
(a) $x = -3$ (b) $x = 0$
(c) $x = 21$ (d) $x = 32$

6. $\dfrac{\sqrt[3]{x - 8}}{3} = -\dfrac{2}{3}$
(a) $x = -16$ (b) $x = 0$
(c) $x = 9$ (d) $x = 16$

In Exercises 7–12, determine whether the equation is an identity or a conditional equation.

7. $2(x - 1) = 2x - 2$

8. $-7(x - 3) + 4x = 3(7 - x)$

9. $x^2 - 8x + 5 = (x - 4)^2 - 11$

10. $x^2 + 2(3x - 2) = x^2 + 6x - 4$

11. $3 + \dfrac{1}{x + 1} = \dfrac{4x}{x + 1}$ **12.** $\dfrac{5}{x} + \dfrac{3}{x} = 24$

In Exercises 13 and 14, solve the equation in two ways. Then explain which way was easier for you.

13. $\dfrac{3x}{8} - \dfrac{4x}{3} = 4$ **14.** $\dfrac{3z}{8} - \dfrac{z}{10} = 6$

The *Interactive* CD-ROM and *Internet* versions of this text contain step-by-step solutions to all odd-numbered Section and Review Exercises. They also provide Tutorial Exercises, which link to Guided Examples for additional help.

In Exercises 15–30, solve the equation (if possible). Then use a graphing utility to verify your solution.

15. $\dfrac{5x}{4} + \dfrac{1}{2} = x - \dfrac{1}{2}$ **16.** $\dfrac{x}{5} - \dfrac{x}{2} = 3$

17. $\dfrac{3}{2}(z + 5) - \dfrac{1}{4}(z + 24) = 0$

18. $\dfrac{3x}{2} + \dfrac{1}{4}(x - 2) = 10$

19. $\dfrac{100 - 4u}{3} = \dfrac{5u + 6}{4} + 6$

20. $\dfrac{17 + y}{y} + \dfrac{32 + y}{y} = 100$

21. $\dfrac{5x - 4}{5x + 4} = \dfrac{2}{3}$ **22.** $\dfrac{15}{x} - 4 = \dfrac{6}{x} + 3$

23. $\dfrac{1}{x - 3} + \dfrac{1}{x + 3} = \dfrac{10}{x^2 - 9}$

24. $\dfrac{1}{x - 2} + \dfrac{3}{x + 3} = \dfrac{4}{x^2 + x - 6}$

25. $\dfrac{7}{2x + 1} - \dfrac{8x}{2x - 1} = -4$

26. $\dfrac{4}{u - 1} + \dfrac{6}{3u + 1} = \dfrac{15}{3u + 1}$

27. $\dfrac{1}{x} + \dfrac{2}{x - 5} = 0$ **28.** $\dfrac{6}{x} - \dfrac{2}{x + 3} = \dfrac{3(x + 5)}{x(x + 3)}$

29. $\dfrac{3}{x(x - 3)} + \dfrac{4}{x} = \dfrac{1}{x - 3}$

30. $3 = 2 + \dfrac{2}{z + 2}$

In Exercises 31–34, solve for the indicated variable.

31. *Area of a Triangle*
Solve for h: $A = \frac{1}{2}bh$

32. *Investment at Compound Interest*
Solve for P: $A = P\left(1 + \dfrac{r}{n}\right)^{nt}$

33. *Area of a Trapezoid*
Solve for b: $A = \frac{1}{2}(a + b)h$

34. *Geometric Progression*
Solve for r: $S = \dfrac{rL - a}{r - 1}$

Human Height In Exercises 35 and 36, use the following information. The relationship between the length of an adult's thigh bone and the height of the adult can be approximated by the linear equations

$$y = 0.432x - 10.44 \qquad \textbf{Female}$$

$$y = 0.449x - 12.15 \qquad \textbf{Male}$$

where *y* is the length of the femur (thigh bone) in inches and *x* is the height in inches (see figure).

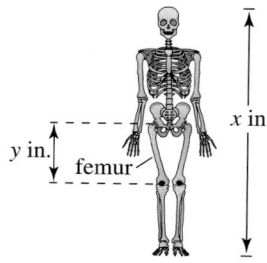

35. An anthropologist discovers a thigh bone belonging to an adult human female. The bone is 16 inches long. Estimate the height of the female.

36. From the foot bones of an adult human male, an anthropologist estimates that the height of the male was 69 inches. A few feet away from the site where the foot bones were discovered, the anthropologist discovered a male adult thigh bone that was 19 inches long. Is it possible that both the foot bones and the thigh bone came from the same person?

37. *Operating Cost* A delivery company has a fleet of vans. The annual operating cost per van is

$$C = 0.32m + 2500$$

where *m* is the number of miles traveled by a van in a year. What number of miles will yield an annual operating cost of $10,000?

38. *Dimensions of a Room* A room is 1.5 times as long as it is wide, and its perimeter is 25 meters.

  (a) Draw a diagram that gives a visual representation of the problem. Identify the length as *l* and the width as *w*.

  (b) Write *l* in terms of *w* and write an equation for the perimeter in terms of *w*.

  (c) Find the dimensions of the room.

39. *Dimensions of a Picture Frame* A picture frame has a total perimeter of 3 meters. The height of the frame is $\frac{2}{3}$ times its width.

  (a) Draw a diagram that gives a visual representation of the problem. Identify the width as *w* and the height as *h*.

  (b) Write *h* in terms of *w* and write an equation for the perimeter in terms of *w*.

  (c) Find the dimensions of the picture frame.

40. *Course Grade* To get an A in a course, you must have an average of at least 90 on four tests of 100 points each. The scores on your first three tests were 87, 92, and 84.

  (a) Write a verbal model for the test average for the course.

  (b) What must you score on the fourth test to get an A for the course?

41. *Course Grade* Suppose you are taking a course that has four tests. The first three tests are 100 points each and the fourth test is 200 points. To get an A in the course, you must have an average of at least 90% on the four tests. Your scores on the first three tests were 87, 92, and 84. What must you score on the fourth test to get an A for the course?

42. *Travel Time* Suppose you are driving on a Canadian freeway to a town that is 300 kilometers from your home. After 30 minutes you pass a freeway exit that you know is 50 kilometers from your home. Assuming that you continue at the same constant speed, how long will it take for the entire trip?

43. *Travel Time* On the first part of a 317-mile trip, a salesman averaged 58 miles per hour. He averaged only 52 miles per hour on the last part of the trip because of an increased volume of traffic. Find the amount of time at each of the speeds if the total time was 5 hours and 45 minutes.

44. *Travel Time* Two families meet at a park for a picnic. At the end of the day one family travels east at an average speed of 42 miles per hour and the other travels west at an average speed of 50 miles per hour. Both families have approximately 160 miles to travel.

  (a) Find the time it takes each family to get home.

  (b) Find the time that will have elapsed when they are 100 miles apart.

  (c) Find the distance the eastbound family has to travel after the westbound family has arrived home.

45. *Average Speed* A truck driver traveled at an average speed of 55 miles per hour on a 200-mile trip to pick up a load of freight. On the return trip (with the truck fully loaded), the average speed was 40 miles per hour. Find the average speed for the round trip.

46. *Wind Speed* An executive flew in the corporate jet to a meeting in a city 1500 kilometers away. After traveling the same amount of time on the return flight, the pilot mentioned that they still had 300 kilometers to go. If the air speed of the plane was 600 kilometers per hour, how fast was the wind blowing? (Assume that the wind direction was parallel to the flight path and constant all day.)

47. *Speed of Light* Light travels at the speed of 3.0×10^8 meters per second. Find the time in minutes required for light to travel from the sun to the earth (a distance of 1.5×10^{11} meters).

48. *Radio Waves* Radio waves travel at the same speed as light, 3.0×10^8 meters per second. Find the time required for a radio wave to travel from mission control in Houston to NASA astronauts on the surface of the moon 3.86×10^8 meters away.

49. *Height of a Tree* To obtain the height of a tree, you measure the tree's shadow and find that it is 8 meters long. You also measure the shadow of a 2-meter lamppost and find that it is 75 centimeters long. How tall is the tree?

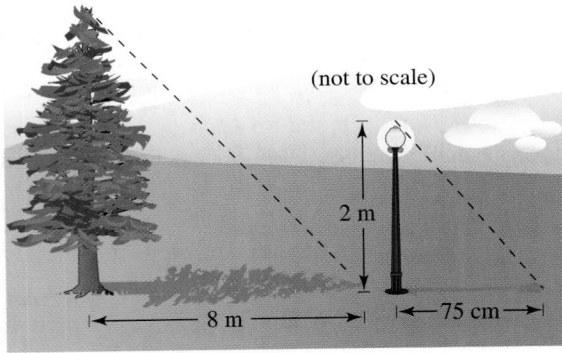

(not to scale)

2 m

8 m

75 cm

50. *Height of a Building* To obtain the height of a building, you measure the building's shadow and find that it is 80 feet long. You also measure the shadow of a 4-foot stake and find that it is $3\frac{1}{2}$ feet long.

(a) Draw a diagram to represent the problem. Let h represent the height of the building.

(b) Find the height of the building.

51. *Height of a Flagpole* A person who is 6 feet tall walks away from a flagpole toward the tip of the shadow of the pole. When the person is 30 feet from the pole, the tips of the person's shadow and the shadow cast by the pole coincide at a point 5 feet in front of the person.

(a) Draw a diagram to represent the problem. Let h represent the height of the pole.

(b) Find the height of the pole.

52. *Investment* You plan to invest $12,000 in two funds paying $4\frac{1}{2}\%$ and 5% simple interest. (There is more risk in the 5% fund.) Your goal is to obtain a total annual interest income of $560 from the investments. What is the smallest amount you can invest in the 5% fund in order to meet your objective?

53. *Investment* You plan to invest $25,000 in two funds paying 3% and $4\frac{1}{2}\%$ simple interest. (There is more risk in the $4\frac{1}{2}\%$ fund.) Your goal is to obtain a total annual interest income of $1000 from the investments. What is the smallest amount you can invest in the $4\frac{1}{2}\%$ fund in order to meet your objective?

54. *Investment* Suppose you invested $12,000 in a fund paying $3\frac{1}{2}\%$ simple interest and $10,000 in a fund with a variable interest rate. At the end of the year you were notified that the total interest for both funds was $870. Find the equivalent simple interest rate on the variable-rate fund.

55. *Investment* Suppose you have $10,000 on deposit earning simple interest with the interest rate linked to the prime rate. Because of a drop in the prime rate, the rate on your investment dropped by $1\frac{1}{2}\%$ for the last quarter of the year. Your annual earnings on the fund were $387.50. Find the interest rate for the first three quarters of the year and the interest rate for the last quarter.

56. *Mixture Problem* A grocer mixes two kinds of nuts that cost $2.49 per pound and $3.89 per pound, respectively, to make 100 pounds of a mixture that costs $3.19 per pound. How much of each kind of nut is put into the mixture?

57. *Production Limit* A company has fixed costs of $10,000 per month and variable costs of $8.50 per unit manufactured. The company has $85,000 available to cover the monthly costs. How many units can the company manufacture? (Fixed costs are those that occur regardless of the level of production. Variable costs depend on the level of production.)

Statics Problems   In Exercises **58** and **59**, suppose you have a uniform beam of length L with a fulcrum x feet from one end. If objects with weights W_1 and W_2 are placed at opposite ends of the beam, the beam will balance if

$$W_1 x = W_2(L - x).$$

Find x such that the beam will balance.

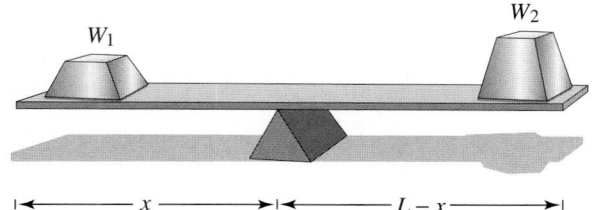

58. Two children weighing 50 pounds and 75 pounds are going to play on a seesaw that is 10 feet long.

59. A person weighing 200 pounds is attempting to move a 550-pound rock with a bar that is 5 feet long.

In Exercises 60–63, use the formulas on page 160.

60. ***Dimensions of a Sail***   A triangular sail has an area of 182.25 square feet. The sail has a base of 13.5 feet. Find the height of the sail.

61. ***Dimensions of a Package***   The volume of a rectangular package is 2304 cubic inches. The length of the package is 3 times its width, and the height is one and a half times its width.

(a) Draw a diagram to represent the problem. Label the height, width, and length accordingly.

(b) Find the dimensions of the package.

62. ***Geometry***   The volume of a globe is about 47,712.94 cubic centimeters. Use a graphing utility to find the radius of the globe. Round your result to two decimal places.

63. ***Temperature***   The line graph shows the temperatures (in degrees Fahrenheit) on a particular day from 10:00 A.M. to 6:00 P.M. Create a new line graph showing the temperatures throughout the day in degrees Celsius.

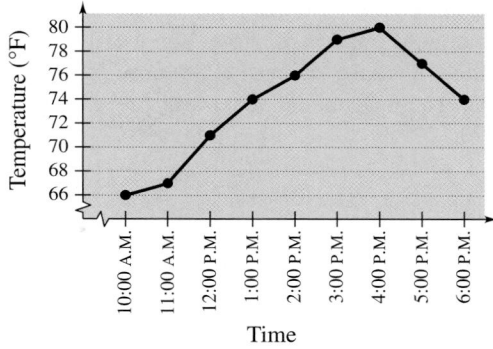

FIGURE FOR 63

64. ***Quiz Scores***   The following ordered pairs give the scores of two consecutive 15-point quizzes for a class of 18 students.

(7, 13), (9, 7), (14, 14), (15, 15), (10, 15),

(9, 7), (14, 11), (14, 15), (8, 10), (9, 10),

(15, 9), (10, 11), (11, 14), (7, 14),

(11, 10), (14, 11), (10, 15), (9, 6)

(a) Create a scatter plot for the data.

(b) Does the relationship between consecutive quiz scores appear to be approximately linear? If not, give some possible explanations.

65. ***Dentists***   The data in the table shows the number of dentists D (in thousands) in the United States from 1985 through 1996. In the table, t represents the year, with $t = 5$ representing 1985.

t	5	6	7	8	9	10
D	156	158	161	164	168	173

t	11	12	13	14	15	16
D	179	183	187	191	194	196

(a) Sketch a scatter plot of the data.

(b) Find the equation of the line that seems to best fit the data.

(c) Use the regression capabilities of a graphing utility to find a linear model for the data. Compare with your answer to part (b).

(d) Use the model from part (c) to estimate the number of dentists in the United States in 2000, 2002, and 2005.

66. *Consumerism* The data in the table shows the per capita consumption W (in gallons) of bottled water in the United States from 1988 through 1996. In the table, t represents the year, with $t = 0$ representing 1990. (Source: U.S. Department of Agriculture)

t	-2	-1	0	1	2
W	6.5	7.4	8	8	8.2

t	3	4	5	6
W	9.4	10.7	11.6	12.4

(a) Sketch a scatter plot of the data.

(b) Find the equation of a line that best fits the data.

(c) Use the regression capabilities of a graphing utility to find a linear model for the data. Compare with your answer to part (b).

(d) Use the model from part (c) to estimate the per capita consumption in 2000, 2004, and 2007.

67. *Advertising and Sales* The table shows the advertising expenditures x and sales volume y for a company for seven randomly selected months. Both are measured in thousands of dollars.

Month	1	2	3	4	5	6	7
x	2.4	1.6	2.0	2.6	1.4	1.6	2.0
y	202	184	220	240	180	164	186

(a) Use the regression capabilities of a graphing utility to find a linear model for y as a function of x.

(b) Use a graphing utility to plot the data and graph the model.

(c) Interpret the slope in the context of the problem.

(d) Use the model to estimate sales for advertising expenditures of $1500.

68. *World Food Production* The data in the table shows the world production P (in millions of metric tons) of vegetables (including melons) for 1990 through 1997. (Source: U.S. Department of Agriculture)

Year	1990	1991	1992	1993
P	461.4	462.4	478.6	509.5

Year	1994	1995	1996	1997
P	532.9	559.9	589.1	595.6

(a) Use the regression capabilities of a graphing utility to find a linear model for the data.

(b) Use a graphing utility to graph the actual data and the model in the same viewing window. How closely does the model represent the data?

(c) Create a table showing the actual values of P and the values of P given by the model.

Synthesis

True or False? In Exercises 69 and 70, determine whether the statement is true or false. Justify your answer.

69. The volume of a cube with a side length of 9.5 inches is greater than the volume of a sphere with a radius of 5.9 inches.

70. If the correlation coefficient for a set of data with respect to a linear least squares regression model is -0.9824, you can conclude that the data points cannot be described by a linear model.

In Exercises 71 and 72, write a linear equation that has the given solution. (There are many correct answers.)

71. $x = -3$ **72.** $x = \frac{1}{4}$

73. *Think About It* What is meant by equivalent equations? Give an example of two equivalent equations.

74. *Writing* In your own words, describe how to clear an equation of fractions.

Review

In Exercises 75–80, sketch the graph of the equation by hand. Verify using a graphing utility.

75. $y = \frac{5}{8}x - 2$ **76.** $y = \dfrac{3x - 5}{2} + 2$

77. $y = (x - 3)^2 + 7$ **78.** $y = \frac{1}{3}x^2 - 4$

79. $y = -\frac{1}{2}|x + 4| - 1$ **80.** $y = |x - 2| + 10$

In Exercises 81–84, evaluate the combination of functions for $f(x) = -x^2 + 4$ and $g(x) = 6x - 5$.

81. $(f + g)(-3)$ **82.** $(g - f)(-1)$

83. $(f \circ g)(4)$ **84.** $(g \circ f)(2)$

2.2 Solving Equations Graphically

Intercepts, Zeros, and Solutions

In Section 1.1, you learned that the intercepts of a graph are the points at which the graph intersects the x- or y-axis.

Definition of Intercepts

1. The point $(a, 0)$ is called an **x-intercept** of the graph of an equation if it is a solution point of the equation. To find the x-intercept(s), let $y = 0$ and solve the equation for x.

2. The point $(0, b)$ is called a **y-intercept** of the graph of an equation if it is a solution point of the equation. To find the y-intercept(s), let $x = 0$ and solve the equation for y.

Sometimes it is convenient to denote the x-intercept as simply the x-coordinate of the point $(a, 0)$ rather than the point itself. Unless it is necessary to make a distinction, "intercept" will be used to mean either the point or the coordinate.

It is possible that a particular graph will have no intercepts or several intercepts. For instance, consider the four graphs in Figure 2.10.

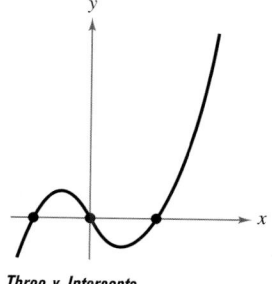

Three x-Intercepts
One y-Intercept

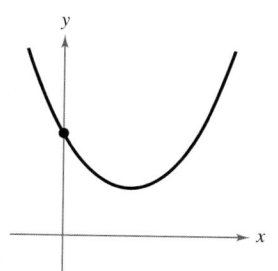

No x-Intercepts
One y-Intercept

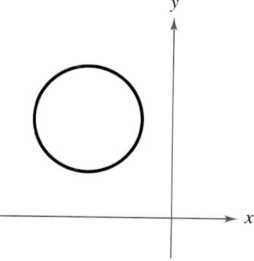

No Intercepts

Figure 2.10

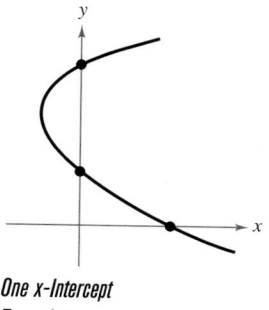

One x-Intercept
Two y-Intercepts

EXAMPLE 1   Finding *x*- and *y*-Intercepts

Find the *x*- and *y*-intercepts of the graph of $2x + 3y = 5$.

Solution

To find the *x*-intercept, let $y = 0$. This produces

$$2x = 5 \quad \Longrightarrow \quad x = \frac{5}{2}$$

which implies that the graph has one *x*-intercept: $\left(\frac{5}{2}, 0\right)$. To find the *y*-intercept, let $x = 0$. This produces

$$3y = 5 \quad \Longrightarrow \quad y = \frac{5}{3}$$

which implies that the graph has one *y*-intercept: $\left(0, \frac{5}{3}\right)$. See Figure 2.11.

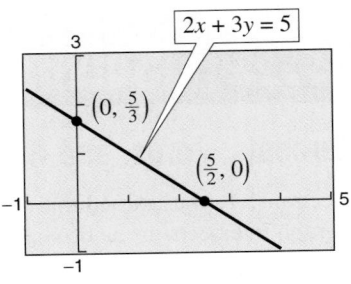

Figure 2.11

A **zero** of a function $y = f(x)$ is a number a such that $f(a) = 0$. So, to find the zeros of a function, you must solve the equation $f(x) = 0$.

The concepts of *x*-intercepts, zeros of functions, and solutions of equations are closely related. In fact, the following statements are equivalent.

The *Interactive* CD-ROM and *Internet* versions of this text offer a built-in graphing calculator, which can be used with the Examples, Explorations, and Exercises.

1. The point $(a, 0)$ is an *x-intercept* of the graph of $y = f(x)$.

2. The number a is a *zero* of the function f.

3. The number a is a *solution* of the equation $f(x) = 0$.

EXAMPLE 2   Verifying Zeros of Functions

Verify that the real numbers -2 and 3 are zeros of the function $f(x) = x^2 - x - 6$.

Algebraic Solution

To verify that -2 is a zero of f, check that $f(-2) = 0$.

$f(x) = x^2 - x - 6$ Write original equation.

$f(-2) = (-2)^2 - (-2) - 6$ Substitute -2 for x.

$\quad\quad = 4 + 2 - 6$ Simplify.

$\quad\quad = 0$ -2 is a solution. ✓

To verify that 3 is a zero of $f(x) = x^2 - x - 6$, check that $f(3) = 0$.

$f(x) = x^2 - x - 6$ Write original equation.

$f(3) = (3)^2 - (3) - 6$ Substitute 3 for x.

$\quad\quad = 9 - 3 - 6$ Simplify.

$\quad\quad = 0$ 3 is a solution. ✓

Graphical Solution

Use a graphing utility to graph $y = x^2 - x - 6$. From the graph in Figure 2.12, it appears that the function has *x*-intercepts (where *y* is zero) when $x = -2$ and when $x = 3$. So, you can approximate the zeros of the function to be -2 and 3.

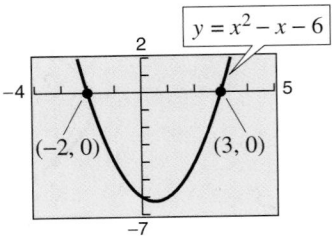

Figure 2.12

Note that the graph of $y = x^2 - x - 6$ in Figure 2.12 has *x-intercepts* of $(3, 0)$ and $(-2, 0)$ because the equation $0 = x^2 - x - 6$ has the *solutions* $x = 3$ and $x = -2$.

This close connection among *x*-intercepts, zeros, and solutions described on page 170 is crucial to our study of algebra, and you can take advantage of this connection in two basic ways. You can use your algebraic "equation-solving skills" to find the *x*-intercepts of a graph and your "graphing skills" to approximate the solutions of an equation.

Finding Solutions Graphically

Polynomial equations of degree 1 or 2 can be solved in relatively straightforward ways. Polynomial equations of higher degrees can, however, be quite difficult, especially if you rely only on algebraic techniques. For such equations, a graphing utility can be very helpful.

Graphical Approximations of Solutions of an Equation

1. Write the equation in *general form*, $f(x) = 0$, with the nonzero terms on one side of the equation and zero on the other side.
2. Use a graphing utility to graph the function $y = f(x)$. Be sure the viewing window shows all the relevant features of the graph.
3. Use the *zero* or *root* feature or the *zoom* and *trace* features of the graphing utility to approximate each of the *x*-intercepts of the graph of *f*. Remember that a graph can have more than one *x*-intercept, so you may need to change the viewing window a few times.

In Chapter 3 you will learn techniques for determining the number of solutions of a polynomial equation. For now, you should know that a polynomial equation of degree *n* cannot have more than *n* different solutions.

EXAMPLE 3   Finding Solutions of an Equation Graphically

Use a graphing utility to approximate the solutions of $2x^3 - 3x + 2 = 0$.

Solution
Begin by graphing the function $y = 2x^3 - 3x + 2$, as shown in Figure 2.13. You can see from the graph that there is only one *x*-intercept. It lies between -1 and -2 and is approximately -1.5. By using the *zero* or *root* feature of a graphing utility you can improve the approximation. To three-decimal-place accuracy, the solution is $x \approx -1.476$. Check this approximation on your calculator. You will find that the value of *y* is $y = 2(-1.476)^3 - 3(-1.476) + 2 \approx -0.003$.

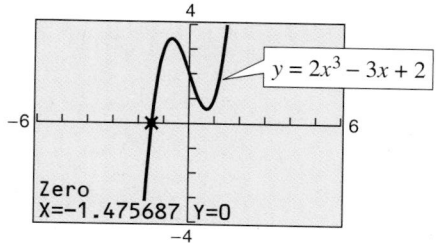

$y = 2x^3 - 3x + 2$

Zero
X=-1.475687 Y=0

Figure 2.13

You can also use a graphing calculator's *zoom* and *trace* features to approximate the solution of an equation. Here are some suggestions for using the *zoom-in* feature of a graphing utility.

1. With each successive zoom-in, adjust the *x*-scale (if necessary) so that the resulting viewing window shows at least the two scale marks between which the solution lies.

2. The accuracy of the approximation will always be such that the error is less than the distance between two scale marks.

3. If you have a *trace* feature on your graphing utility, you can generally add one more decimal place of accuracy without changing the viewing window.

Unless stated otherwise, this book will approximate all real solutions with an error of *at most* 0.01.

EXAMPLE 4   Approximating Solutions of an Equation Graphically

Use a graphing utility to approximate the solutions of $x^2 + 3 = 5x$.

Solution

In general form, this equation is

$$x^2 - 5x + 3 = 0. \qquad \text{Equation in general form}$$

So, you can begin by graphing

$$y = x^2 - 5x + 3 \qquad \text{Function to be graphed}$$

as shown in Figure 2.14(a). This graph has two *x*-intercepts, and by using the *zoom* and *trace* features you can approximate the corresponding solutions to be $x \approx 0.70$ and $x \approx 4.30$, as shown in Figures 2.14(b) and 2.14(c).

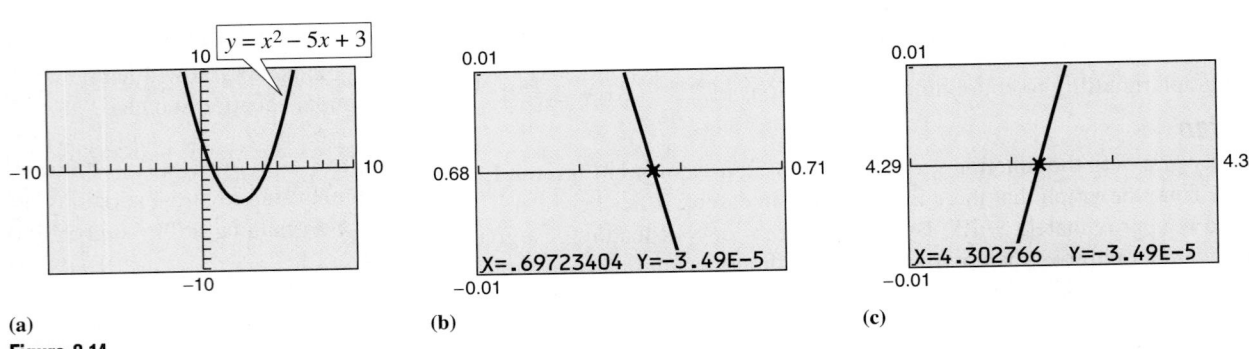

(a)   **(b)**   **(c)**

Figure 2.14

The built-in *zero* or *root* programs of a graphing utility will approximate solutions of equations or approximate *x*-intercepts of graphs. If your graphing utility has such features, try using them to approximate the solutions in Example 4.

Points of Intersection of Two Graphs

An ordered pair that is a solution of two different equations is called a **point of intersection** of the graphs of the two equations. For instance, in Figure 2.15 you can see that the graphs of the following equations have two points of intersection.

$y = x + 2$ Equation 1

$y = x^2 - 2x - 2$ Equation 2

The point $(-1, 1)$ is a solution of both equations, and the point $(4, 6)$ is a solution of both equations. To check this algebraically, substitute -1 and 4 into each equation.

Check that $(-1, 1)$ is a solution.

Equation 1: $y = -1 + 2 = 1$ Solution checks. ✓

Equation 2: $y = (-1)^2 - 2(-1) - 2$

$\qquad = 1$ Solution checks. ✓

Check that $(4, 6)$ is a solution.

Equation 1: $y = 4 + 2$

$\qquad = 6$ Solution checks. ✓

Equation 2: $y = (4)^2 - 2(4) - 2$

$\qquad = 6$ Solution checks. ✓

To find the points of intersection of the graphs of two equations, solve each equation for y (or x) and set the two results equal to each other. The resulting equation will be an equation in one variable, which can be solved using standard procedures, as shown in Example 5.

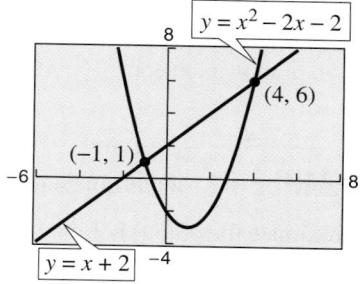

Figure 2.15

STUDY T!P

The table shows some points of the graphs of the equations at the left. Find the points of intersection of the graphs by finding the values of x for which y_1 and y_2 are equal.

X	Y1	Y2
-2	0	6
-1	1	1
0	2	-2
1	3	-2
2	4	-2
3	5	1
4	6	6
X=-2		

EXAMPLE 5 Finding Points of Intersection

Find the points of intersection of the graphs of $2x - 3y = -2$ and $4x - y = 6$.

Algebraic Solution

To begin, solve each equation for y to obtain

$$y = \frac{2}{3}x + \frac{2}{3} \quad \text{and} \quad y = 4x - 6.$$

Next, set the two expressions for y equal to each other and solve the resulting equation for x, as follows.

$\dfrac{2}{3}x + \dfrac{2}{3} = 4x - 6$ Equate expressions for y.

$2x + 2 = 12x - 18$ Multiply each side by 3.

$-10x = -20$ Subtract $12x$ and 2 from each side.

$x = 2$ Divide each side by -10.

When $x = 2$, the y-value of each of the given equations is 2. So, the point of intersection is $(2, 2)$.

Graphical Solution

To begin, solve each equation for y to obtain $y_1 = \frac{2}{3}x + \frac{2}{3}$ and $y_2 = 4x - 6$. Then use a graphing utility to graph both equations in the same viewing window. In Figure 2.16, the graphs appear to have one point of intersection. Use the *intersect* feature of the graphing utility to approximate the point of intersection to be $(2, 2)$.

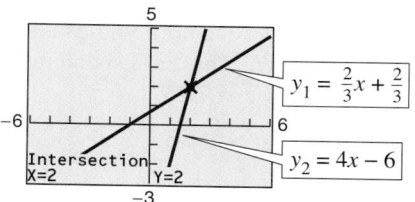

Figure 2.16

Another way to approximate points of intersection of two graphs is to graph both equations and use the *zoom* and *trace* features to find the point or points at which the two graphs intersect.

Additional Example

Approximate the point(s) of intersection of the graphs of $y = x^3 - 6x^2 + 6x + 3$ and $y = -x^2 + 7x - 2$.

Solution

Use a graphing utility to graph both functions. Use the *zoom* and *trace* features or the *intersect* feature to approximate the points of intersection to be $(1, 4)$, $(5, 8)$, and $(-1, -10)$.

EXAMPLE 6   Approximating Points of Intersection Graphically

Approximate the point(s) of intersection of the graphs of the following equations.

$$y = x^2 - 3x - 4 \qquad \text{Equation 1 (quadratic function)}$$

$$y = x^3 + 3x^2 - 2x - 1 \qquad \text{Equation 2 (cubic function)}$$

Solution

Begin by using a graphing utility to graph both functions, as shown in Figure 2.17. From this display, you can see that the two graphs have only one point of intersection. Then, using the *zoom* and *trace* features, approximate the point of intersection to be $(-2.17, 7.25)$. To test the reasonableness of this approximation, you can evaluate both functions when $x = -2.17$.

Quadratic Function:

$$y = (-2.17)^2 - 3(-2.17) - 4$$

$$\approx 7.22$$

Cubic Function:

$$y = (-2.17)^3 + 3(-2.17)^2 - 2(-2.17) - 1$$

$$\approx 7.25$$

Because both functions yield approximately the same y-value, you can conclude that the approximate coordinates of the point of intersection are $x \approx -2.17$ and $y \approx 7.25$.

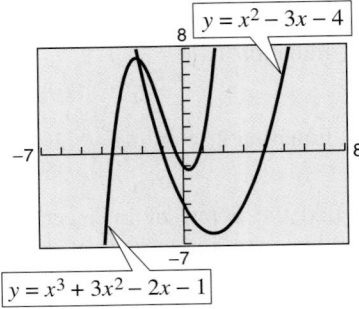

Figure 2.17

The method shown in Example 6 gives a nice graphical picture of the points of intersection of two graphs. However, for actual approximation purposes, it is better to use the algebraic procedure described in Example 5. That is, the point of intersection of $y = x^2 - 3x - 4$ and $y = x^3 + 3x^2 - 2x - 1$ coincides with the solution of the equation

$$x^3 + 3x^2 - 2x - 1 = x^2 - 3x - 4 \qquad \text{Equate } y\text{-values.}$$

$$x^3 + 2x^2 + x + 3 = 0. \qquad \text{Write in general form.}$$

By graphing $y = x^3 + 2x^2 + x + 3$ on a graphing utility and using the *zoom* and *trace* features (or the *zero* or *root* feature), you can approximate the solution of this equation to be $x \approx -2.17$. The corresponding y-value for *both* of the functions given in Example 6 is $y \approx 7.25$.

EXAMPLE 7   A Historical Look at Recorded Music

Between 1990 and 1997, the number of compact discs sold each year in the United States was *increasing* and the number of cassettes was *decreasing*. Two models that approximate the sales S are

$$S = 279.67 + 78.66t, \ 0 \le t \le 7 \qquad \text{Compact discs}$$

$$S = 442.14 - 35.46t, \ 0 \le t \le 7 \qquad \text{Cassettes}$$

where $t = 0$ represents 1990. According to these two models, when would you expect the sales of compact discs to have exceeded the sales of cassettes? (Source: Recording Industry Association of America)

Algebraic Solution

Both equations are solved for S. So, set the two expressions for S equal to each other and solve the resulting equation for t, as follows.

$$279.67 + 78.66t = 442.14 - 35.46t \qquad \text{Equate expressions for } S.$$

$$114.12t = 162.47 \qquad \begin{array}{l}\text{Subtract 279.67 from and} \\ \text{add 35.46}t \text{ to each side.}\end{array}$$

$$t \approx 1.42 \qquad \text{Use a calculator.}$$

So, from the given models, you would expect that compact disc sales exceeded cassette sales sometime during 1991.

Graphical Solution

Use a graphing utility to graph both equations in the same viewing window. From Figure 2.18, the graphs appear to have one point of intersection. Use the *intersect* feature of the graphing utility to approximate the point of intersection to be (1.42, 391.66). So, you would expect that compact disc sales exceeded cassette sales sometime during 1991.

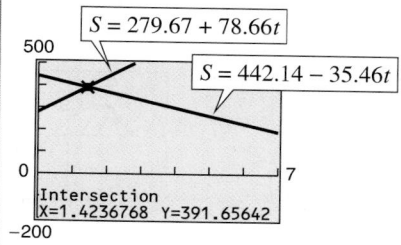

Figure 2.18

W r i t i n g   A b o u t   M a t h   *Judging the Accuracy of an Approximate Solution*

Suppose you are solving the equation

$$\frac{x}{x-1} - \frac{99}{100} = 0$$

for x, and you obtain $x = -99.1$ as your solution. Substituting this value back into the equation produces

$$\frac{-99.1}{-99.1 - 1} - \frac{99}{100} = 0.00000999 = 9.99 \times 10^{-6} \approx 0.$$

Does this mean that -99.1 is a good approximation to the solution? Write a short paragraph explaining why or why not.

2.2 Exercises

In Exercises 1–12, find the x- and y-intercepts of the graph of the equation.

1. $y = x - 5$

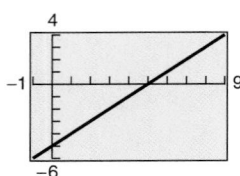

2. $y = -\frac{3}{4}x - 3$

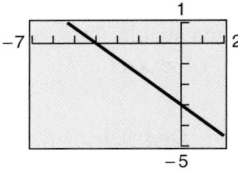

3. $y = x^2 + x - 2$

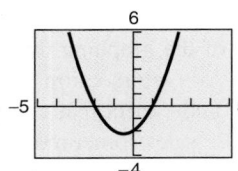

4. $y = 4 - x^2$

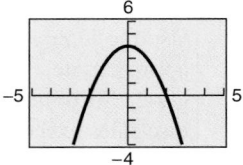

5. $y = x\sqrt{x + 2}$

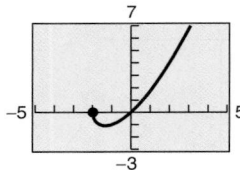

6. $y = -\frac{1}{2}x\sqrt{x + 3} + 1$

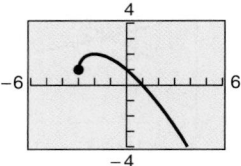

7. $xy = 4$

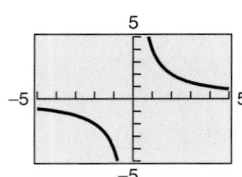

8. $4xy = 3x - 1$

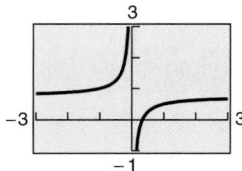

9. $y = |x - 2| - 4$

10. $y = 3 - \frac{1}{2}|x + 1|$

11. $xy - 2y - x + 1 = 0$

12. $x^2y - x^2 + 4y = 0$

In Exercises 13–18, the zero(s) of the function are given. Verify the zero(s) both algebraically and graphically.

Function	*Zero(s)*
13. $f(x) = 12 - 4x$	$x = 3$
14. $f(x) = 3(x - 5) + 9$	$x = 2$
15. $f(x) = x^2 - 2.5x - 6$	$x = -1.5, 4$
16. $f(x) = x^3 - 9x^2 + 18x$	$x = 0, 3, 6$
17. $f(x) = \dfrac{x + 2}{3} - \dfrac{x - 1}{5} - 1$	$x = 1$
18. $f(x) = x - 3 - \dfrac{10}{x}$	$x = -2, 5$

Graphical Analysis **In Exercises 19–22, use a graphing utility to graph the equation and approximate any x-intercepts. Set $y = 0$ and solve the resulting equation. Compare the results with the x-intercepts of the graph.**

19. $y = 2(x - 1) - 4$ **20.** $y = \frac{4}{3}x + 2$

21. $y = 20 - (3x - 10)$ **22.** $y = 10 + 2(x - 2)$

In Exercises 23–34, solve the equation algebraically. Then write the equation in the form $f(x) = 0$ and use a graphing utility to verify the algebraic solution.

23. $27 - 4x = 12$ **24.** $3.5x - 8 = 0.5x$

25. $25(x - 3) = 12(x + 2) - 10$

26. $1200 = 300 + 2(x - 500)$

27. $\dfrac{3x}{2} + \dfrac{1}{4}(x - 2) = 10$

28. $0.60x + 0.40(100 - x) = 50$

29. $\dfrac{2x}{3} = 10 - \dfrac{24}{x}$ **30.** $\dfrac{x - 3}{25} = \dfrac{x - 5}{12}$

31. $\dfrac{3}{x + 2} - \dfrac{4}{x - 2} = 5$ **32.** $\dfrac{6}{x} + \dfrac{8}{x + 5} = 3$

33. $3(x + 3) = 5(1 - x) - 1$

34. $(x + 1)^2 + 2(x - 2) = (x + 1)(x - 2)$

In Exercises 35–46, use a graphing utility to approximate any solutions (accurate to three decimal places) of the equation. [Remember to write the equation in the form $f(x) = 0$.]

35. $\frac{1}{4}(x^2 - 10x + 17) = 0$ **36.** $-2(x^2 - 6x + 6) = 0$

37. $x^3 + x + 4 = 0$ **38.** $\frac{1}{9}x^3 + x + 4 = 0$

39. $2x^3 - x^2 - 18x + 9 = 0$

40. $4x^3 + 12x^2 - 26x - 24 = 0$

41. $x^4 = 2x^3 + 1$ **42.** $x^5 = 3 + 2x^3$

43. $\dfrac{2}{x + 2} = 3$ **44.** $\dfrac{5}{x} = 1 + \dfrac{3}{x + 2}$

45. $|x - 3| = 4$ **46.** $\sqrt{x - 2} = 3$

47. *Exploration*

(a) Use a graphing utility to complete the table.

x	-1	0	1	2	3	4
$3.2x - 5.8$						

(b) Use the table in part (a) to determine the interval in which the solution to the equation $3.2x - 5.8 = 0$ is located. Explain your reasoning.

(c) Use a graphing utility to complete the table.

x	1.5	1.6	1.7	1.8	1.9	2
$3.2x - 5.8$						

(d) Use the table in part (c) to determine the interval in which the solution to the equation $3.2x - 5.8 = 0$ is located. Explain how this process can be used to approximate the solution to any desired degree of accuracy.

(e) Use a graphing utility to verify graphically the solution to $3.2x - 5.8 = 0$ found in part (d).

48. *Exploration* Use the procedure of Exercise 47 to approximate the solution of the equation

$$0.3(x - 1.5) - 2 = 0$$

accurate to two decimal places.

In Exercises 49–54, determine any point(s) of intersection algebraically. Then verify your result numerically by creating a table of values for each function.

49. $y = 2 - x$
  $y = 2x - 1$

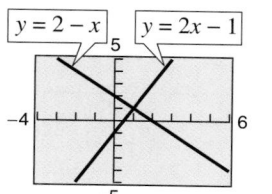

50. $y = 7 - x$
  $y = \frac{3}{2} - \frac{11}{2}x$

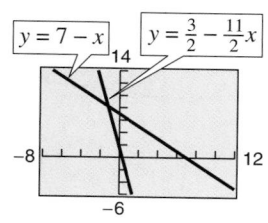

51. $2x + y = 6$
  $-x + y = 0$

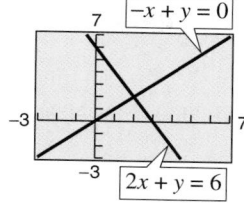

52. $x - y = -4$
  $x + 2y = 5$

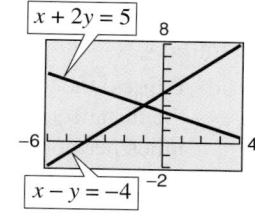

53. $x - y = -4$
  $x^2 - y = -2$

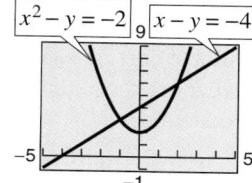

54. $3x + y = 2$
  $x^3 + y = 0$

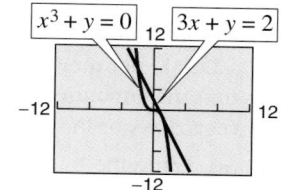

In Exercises 55–62, use a graphing utility to approximate any points of intersection (accurate to three decimal places) of the graphs of equations. Verify your results algebraically.

55. $y = 9 - 2x$
  $y = x - 3$

56. $y = \frac{1}{3}x + 2$
  $y = \frac{5}{2}x - 11$

57. $y = 4 - x^2$
  $y = 2x - 1$

58. $y = x^3 - 3$
  $y = 5 - 2x$

59. $y = 8$
  $y = 3x^2 + 2x$

60. $y = 32$
  $y = x^5 - x^2$

61. $y = 2x^2$
  $y = x^4 - 2x^2$

62. $y = -x$
  $y = 2x - x^2$

In Exercises 63 and 64, evaluate the expression in two ways. (a) Calculate entirely on your calculator by storing intermediate results and then rounding the final answer to two decimal places. (b) Round both the numerator and denominator to two decimal places before dividing, and then round the final answer to two decimal places. Does the method in part (b) decrease the accuracy? Explain.

63. $\dfrac{1 + 0.73205}{1 - 0.73205}$ **64.** $\dfrac{1 + 0.86603}{1 - 0.86603}$

65. *Travel Time* On the first part of a 280-mile trip, a sales person averaged 63 miles per hour. The sales person averaged only 54 miles per hour on the last part of the trip because of an increased volume of traffic.

(a) Express the total time for the trip as a function of the distance x traveled at an average speed of 63 miles per hour.

(b) Use a graphing utility to graph the time function. What is the domain of the function?

(c) Approximate the number of miles traveled at 63 miles per hour if the total time was 4 hours and 45 minutes.

66. *Production Limit* A company has fixed costs of $25,000 per month and a variable cost of $18.65 per unit manufactured. (*Fixed costs* are those that occur regardless of the level of production.)

(a) Write the total monthly costs C as a function of the number of units x produced.

(b) Use a graphing utility to graph the cost function. Approximate the number of units that can be produced per month if total costs cannot exceed $200,000. Verify algebraically. Is this better solved algebraically or graphically? Explain.

67. *Mixture Problem* A 55-gallon barrel contains a mixture with a concentration of 33%. You remove x gallons of this mixture and replace it with 100% concentrate.

(a) Write the amount of concentrate in the final mixture as a function of x.

(b) Use a graphing utility to graph the concentration function. What is the domain of the function?

(c) Approximate (accurate to one decimal place) the value of x if the final mixture is 60% concentrate.

68. *Geometry* A rectangular region with a perimeter of 230 meters has a length of x.

(a) Draw a diagram to represent the problem.

(b) Express the rectangle's area as a function of x.

(c) Use a graphing utility to graph the area function. Because area is nonnegative, what is the domain of the function?

(d) Approximate (accurate to one decimal place) the dimensions of the region if its area is 2000 square feet.

Geometry In Exercises 69 and 70, (a) write a function for the area of the region, (b) use a graphing utility to graph the function, and (c) approximate the value of x if the area of the region is 200 square units.

69. **70.**

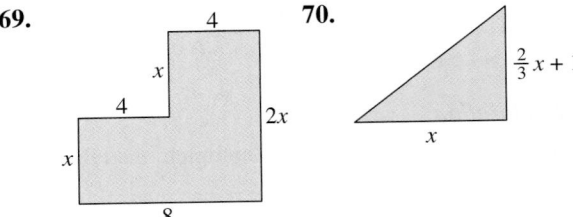

71. *Volume* Consider the swimming pool in the figure below. (When finding its volume, use the fact that the volume is the area of the region on the vertical side-wall times the width of the pool.)

(a) Find the volume of the pool.

(b) Find an equation of the line representing the base of the pool.

(c) If the depth of the water at the deep end of the pool is d, show that the volume of water is

$$V(d) = \begin{cases} 80d^2, & 0 \le d \le 5 \\ 800d - 2000, & 5 < d \le 9 \end{cases}.$$

(d) Graph the volume function.

(e) Use a graphing utility to complete the table.

d	3	5	7	9
V				

(f) Approximate the depth of the water at the deep end if the volume is 4800 cubic feet.

(g) How many gallons of water are in the pool? (There are 7.48 gallons of water in 1 cubic foot.)

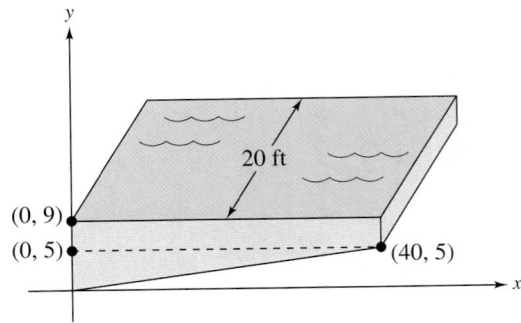

72. *Negative Income Tax* The following information describes a possible negative income tax for a family consisting of two adults and two children. The plan would guarantee the poor a minimum income while encouraging a family to increase its private income ($0 \leq x \leq 20,000$).

Family's earned income: $I = x$

Subsidy: $S = 10,000 - \frac{1}{2}x$

Total income: $T = I + S$

(a) Express the total income T in terms of x.

(b) Use a graphing utility to find the earned income x if the subsidy is $6600. Verify your answer algebraically.

(c) Use a graphing utility to find the earned income x if the total income is $13,800. Verify your answer algebraically.

(d) Find the subsidy S graphically if the total income is $12,500.

73. *Labor Force* The number of married women y in the civilian work force (in millions) in the United States from 1990 to 1997 can be approximated by the model

$y = 0.46x + 30.81$

where $t = 0$ represents 1990. According to this model, during which year did this number reach 33 million? Explain how to answer the question graphically and algebraically. (Source: U.S. Bureau of Labor Statistics)

74. *Recommended Weight* The median recommended weight of women of small frame who are 25 to 59 years old can be approximated by the mathematical model

$y = 0.041x^2 - 2.525x + 113.639, \quad 58 \leq x \leq 72$

where y is the median recommended weight in pounds and x is the height in inches. Suppose you are an insurance agent. After taking information from a female client, you compute her recommended weight to be 123 pounds. Later, when you are filling out her paperwork, you are unable to remember her height. Use the model and a graphing utility to estimate your client's height based on her recommended weight. (Source: Metropolitan Life Insurance Company)

75. *Per Capita Utilization* The per capita utilization (in pounds) of nectarines and peaches N, and cucumbers C, from 1991 through 1996 can be modeled by

$N = -0.37t + 6.88$

$C = 0.27t + 4.42$

where $t = 1$ represents 1991. (Source: U.S. Department of Agriculture)

(a) What does the intersection of the graphs of these equations represent?

(b) Find the point of intersection of the graphs algebraically.

(c) Verify your answer to part (b) using the *zoom* and *trace* features of a graphing utility.

Synthesis

True or False? **In Exercises 76–78, determine whether the statement is true or false. Justify your answer.**

76. To find the y-intercept of a graph, let $x = 0$ and solve the equation for y.

77. Every linear equation has at least one y-intercept or x-intercept.

78. Two linear equations can have either one point of intersection or no points of intersection.

Review

In Exercises 79–82, rationalize the denominator.

79. $\dfrac{12}{5\sqrt{3}}$

80. $\dfrac{4}{\sqrt{10} - 2}$

81. $\dfrac{3}{8 + \sqrt{11}}$

82. $\dfrac{14}{3\sqrt{10} - 1}$

In Exercises 83–88, find the product.

83. $(x + 6)(3x - 5)$

84. $(3x + 13)(4x - 7)$

85. $(2x - 9)(2x + 9)$

86. $(4x + 1)^2$

87. $(2x^2 - y)(3x^2 + 4y)$

88. $(4x^3 + 7y^2)(3x^3 - y^2)$

In Exercises 89 and 90, determine the open intervals over which the function is increasing, decreasing, or constant.

89. $f(x) = -x^2 - 8$

90. $f(x) = 2x^4 - 3x^2$

2.3   Complex Numbers

The Imaginary Unit i

Some quadratic equations have no real solutions. For instance, the quadratic equation $x^2 + 1 = 0$ has no real solution because there is no real number x that can be squared to produce -1. To overcome this deficiency, mathematicians created an expanded system of numbers using the **imaginary unit i,** defined as

$$i = \sqrt{-1} \qquad \text{Imaginary unit}$$

where $i^2 = -1$. By adding real numbers to real multiples of this imaginary unit, you obtain the set of **complex numbers.** Each complex number can be written in the **standard form** $a + bi$. For instance, the standard form of the complex number $\sqrt{-9} - 5$ is $-5 + 3i$ because

$$\sqrt{-9} - 5 = \sqrt{3^2(-1)} - 5 = 3\sqrt{-1} - 5 = -5 + 3i.$$

In the standard form $a + bi$, the real number a is called the **real part** of the complex number and the number bi (where b is a real number) is called the **imaginary part** of the complex number.

Definition of a Complex Number

If a and b are real numbers, the number $a + bi$ is a **complex number,** and it is said to be written in **standard form.** If $b = 0$, the number $a + bi = a$ is a real number. If $b \neq 0$, the number $a + bi$ is called an **imaginary number.** A number of the form bi, where $b \neq 0$, is called a **pure imaginary number.**

The set of real numbers is a subset of the set of complex numbers, as shown in Figure 2.19. This is true because every real number a can be written as a complex number using $b = 0$. That is, for every real number a, you can write $a = a + 0i$.

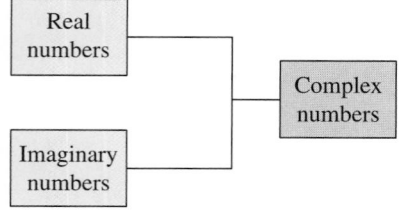

Figure 2.19

Equality of Complex Numbers

Two complex numbers $a + bi$ and $c + di$, written in standard form, are equal to each other

$$a + bi = c + di \qquad \text{Equality of two complex numbers}$$

if and only if $a = c$ and $b = d$.

What You Should Learn:

- How to use the imaginary unit i to write complex numbers
- How to add, subtract, and multiply complex numbers
- How to use complex conjugates to divide complex numbers
- How to plot complex numbers in the complex plane

Why You Should Learn It:

Complex numbers are used to model numerous aspects of the natural world, such as the impedance of an electrical circuit, as shown in Exercise 83 on page 187.

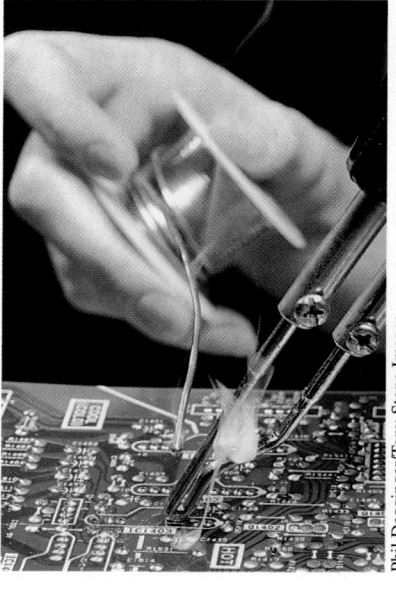

Phil Degginger/Tony Stone Images

Operations with Complex Numbers

To add (or subtract) two complex numbers, you add (or subtract) the real and imaginary parts of the numbers separately.

> ### Addition and Subtraction of Complex Numbers
>
> If $a + bi$ and $c + di$ are two complex numbers written in standard form, their sum and difference are defined as follows.
>
> *Sum:* $(a + bi) + (c + di) = (a + c) + (b + d)i$
>
> *Difference:* $(a + bi) - (c + di) = (a - c) + (b - d)i$

The **additive identity** in the complex number system is zero (the same as in the real number system). Furthermore, the **additive inverse** of the complex number $a + bi$ is

$$-(a + bi) = -a - bi. \qquad \text{Additive inverse}$$

So, you have

$$(a + bi) + (-a - bi) = 0 + 0i = 0.$$

Corbis-Bettmann

Carl Friedrich Gauss (1777–1855) proved that all the roots of any algebraic equation are "numbers" of the form $a + bi$, where a and b are real numbers and i is the square root of -1. These "numbers" are called complex.

EXAMPLE 1 Adding and Subtracting Complex Numbers

a. $(3 - i) + (2 + 3i) = 3 - i + 2 + 3i$ Remove parentheses.

$\qquad\qquad\qquad = 3 + 2 - i + 3i$ Group like terms.

$\qquad\qquad\qquad = (3 + 2) + (-1 + 3)i$

$\qquad\qquad\qquad = 5 + 2i$ Write in standard form.

b. $2i + (-4 - 2i) = 2i - 4 - 2i$ Remove parentheses.

$\qquad\qquad\qquad = -4 + 2i - 2i$ Group like terms.

$\qquad\qquad\qquad = -4$ Write in standard form.

c. $3 - (-2 + 3i) + (-5 + i) = 3 + 2 - 3i - 5 + i$

$\qquad\qquad\qquad\qquad = 3 + 2 - 5 - 3i + i$

$\qquad\qquad\qquad\qquad = 0 - 2i$

$\qquad\qquad\qquad\qquad = -2i$

d. $(3 + 2i) + (4 - i) - (7 + i) = 3 + 2i + 4 - i - 7 - i$

$\qquad\qquad\qquad\qquad = 3 + 4 - 7 + 2i - i - i$

$\qquad\qquad\qquad\qquad = 0 + 0i$

$\qquad\qquad\qquad\qquad = 0$

For each operation on complex numbers, you can show the parallel operations on polynomials.

In Examples 1(b) and 1(d) note that the sum of complex numbers can be a real number.

Many of the properties of real numbers are valid for complex numbers as well. Here are some examples.

Associative Property of Addition and Multiplication
Commutative Property of Addition and Multiplication
Distributive Property of Multiplication over Addition

Notice how these properties are used when two complex numbers are multiplied.

$$(a + bi)(c + di) = a(c + di) + bi(c + di) \qquad \text{Distributive Property}$$

$$= ac + (ad)i + (bc)i + (bd)i^2 \qquad \text{Distributive Property}$$

$$= ac + (ad)i + (bc)i + (bd)(-1) \qquad i^2 = -1$$

$$= ac - bd + (ad)i + (bc)i \qquad \text{Commutative Property}$$

$$= (ac - bd) + (ad + bc)i \qquad \text{Distributive Property}$$

Rather than trying to memorize this multiplication rule, you should simply remember how the distributive property is used to multiply two complex numbers. The procedure is similar to multiplying two polynomials and combining like terms (as in the FOIL Method) shown in Section P.3.

> ### Exploration
>
> Complete the table:
>
> | | |
> |---|---|
> | $i^1 = i$ | $i^7 = \boxed{}$ |
> | $i^2 = -1$ | $i^8 = \boxed{}$ |
> | $i^3 = -i$ | $i^9 = \boxed{}$ |
> | $i^4 = 1$ | $i^{10} = \boxed{}$ |
> | $i^5 = \boxed{}$ | $i^{11} = \boxed{}$ |
> | $i^6 = \boxed{}$ | $i^{12} = \boxed{}$ |
>
> What pattern do you see? Write a brief description of how you would find i raised to any positive integer power.

EXAMPLE 2 Multiplying Complex Numbers

a. $(i)(-3i) = -3i^2$ Multiply.

$$= -3(-1) \qquad i^2 = -1$$

$$= 3 \qquad \text{Simplify.}$$

b. $\sqrt{-4} \cdot \sqrt{-16} = (2i)(4i)$ Write each factor in standard form.

$$= 8i^2 \qquad \text{Multiply.}$$

$$= 8(-1) \qquad i^2 = -1$$

$$= -8 \qquad \text{Simplify.}$$

c. $(2 - i)(4 + 3i) = 8 + 6i - 4i - 3i^2$ Product of binomials

$$= 8 + 6i - 4i - 3(-1) \qquad i^2 = -1$$

$$= 8 + 3 + 6i - 4i \qquad \text{Group like terms.}$$

$$= 11 + 2i \qquad \text{Write in standard form.}$$

d. $(3 + 2i)(3 - 2i) = 9 - 6i + 6i - 4i^2$ Product of binomials

$$= 9 - 4(-1) \qquad i^2 = -1$$

$$= 9 + 4 \qquad \text{Simplify.}$$

$$= 13 \qquad \text{Write in standard form.}$$

e. $(3 + 2i)^2 = 9 + 6i + 6i + 4i^2$ Product of binomials

$$= 9 + 4(-1) + 12i \qquad i^2 = -1$$

$$= 9 - 4 + 12i \qquad \text{Simplify.}$$

$$= 5 + 12i \qquad \text{Write in standard form.}$$

> ### STUDY T!P
>
> Note in Example 2(b) that
> $$\sqrt{-4} \cdot \sqrt{-16} \neq \sqrt{(-4)(-16)}$$
> $$= \sqrt{64}$$
> $$= 8.$$

Complex Conjugates and Division

Notice in Example 2(d) that the product of two complex numbers can be a real number. This occurs with pairs of complex numbers of the form $a + bi$ and $a - bi$, called **complex conjugates.**

$$(a + bi)(a - bi) = a^2 - abi + abi - b^2i^2$$
$$= a^2 - b^2(-1)$$
$$= a^2 + b^2$$

To find the quotient of $a + bi$ and $c + di$ where c and d are not both zero, multiply the numerator and denominator by the conjugate of the *denominator* to obtain

$$\frac{a + bi}{c + di} = \frac{a + bi}{c + di}\left(\frac{c - di}{c - di}\right)$$

$$= \frac{(ac + bd) + (bc - ad)i}{c^2 + d^2}.$$

A comparison with the method of rationalizing denominators (Section P.2) may be helpful.

EXAMPLE 3 Dividing Complex Numbers

$$\frac{1}{1 + i} = \frac{1}{1 + i}\left(\frac{1 - i}{1 - i}\right) \qquad \text{Multiply numerator and denominator by conjugate of denominator.}$$

$$= \frac{1 - i}{1^2 - i^2} \qquad \text{Expand.}$$

$$= \frac{1 - i}{1 - (-1)} \qquad i^2 = -1$$

$$= \frac{1 - i}{2} \qquad \text{Simplify.}$$

$$= \frac{1}{2} - \frac{1}{2}i \qquad \text{Write in standard form.}$$

EXAMPLE 4 Dividing Complex Numbers

$$\frac{2 + 3i}{4 - 2i} = \frac{2 + 3i}{4 - 2i}\left(\frac{4 + 2i}{4 + 2i}\right) \qquad \text{Multiply numerator and denominator by conjugate of denominator.}$$

$$= \frac{8 + 4i + 12i + 6i^2}{16 - 4i^2} \qquad \text{Expand.}$$

$$= \frac{8 - 6 + 16i}{16 + 4} \qquad i^2 = -1$$

$$= \frac{(2 + 16i)}{20} \qquad \text{Simplify.}$$

$$= \frac{1}{10} + \frac{4}{5}i \qquad \text{Write in standard form.}$$

STUDY T!P

Some graphing utilities can perform operations with complex numbers. For instance, on some graphing utilities, to divide $2 + 3i$ by $4 - 2i$, enter

$$\boxed{(}\ 2\ \boxed{+}\ 3\ \boxed{i}\ \boxed{)}\ \boxed{\div}$$
$$\boxed{(}\ 4\ \boxed{-}\ 2\ \boxed{i}\ \boxed{)}\ \boxed{\text{ENTER}}.$$

The display will be as follows.

$$.1 + .8i \quad \text{or} \quad \frac{1}{10} + \frac{4}{5}i$$

Consult your user's manual for specific instructions on performing operations with complex numbers.

Applications

Most applications involving complex numbers are either theoretical or very technical, and are therefore not appropriate for inclusion in this text. However, to give you some idea of how complex numbers can be used in applications, we give a general description of their use in **fractal geometry.**

To begin, consider a coordinate system called the **complex plane.** Just as every real number corresponds to a point on the real number line, every complex number corresponds to a point in the complex plane, as shown in Figure 2.20. In this figure, note that the vertical axis is the **imaginary axis** and the horizontal axis is the **real axis.** The point that corresponds to the complex number $a + bi$ is (a, b).

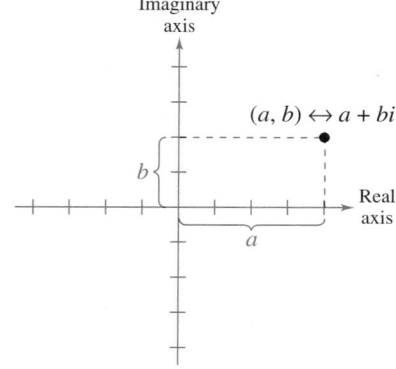

Figure 2.20

EXAMPLE 5   Plotting Complex Numbers

Plot each complex number in the complex plane.

a. $2 + 3i$ **b.** $-1 + 2i$

c. 4 **d.** $-3i$

Solution

a. To plot the complex number $2 + 3i$, move (from the origin) two units to the right on the real axis and then three units up, as shown in Figure 2.21. In other words, plotting the complex number $2 + 3i$ in the complex plane is comparable to plotting the point $(2, 3)$ in the Cartesian plane.

b. The complex number $-1 + 2i$ corresponds to the point $(-1, 2)$, as shown in Figure 2.21.

c. The complex number 4 corresponds to the point $(4, 0)$, as shown in Figure 2.21.

d. The complex number $-3i$ corresponds to the point $(0, 3)$, as shown in Figure 2.21.

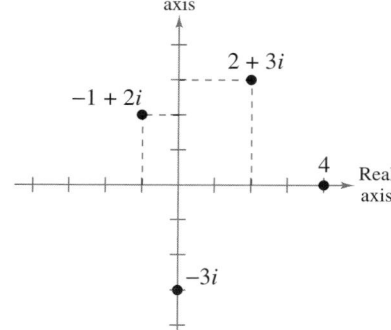

Figure 2.21

In the hands of a person who understands fractal geometry, the complex plane can become an easel on which stunning pictures, called **fractals,** can be drawn. The most famous such picture is called the **Mandelbrot Set,** named after the Polish-born mathematician Benoit Mandelbrot. To draw the Mandelbrot Set, consider the following sequence of numbers.

$$c, \; c^2 + c, \; (c^2 + c)^2 + c, \; [(c^2 + c)^2 + c]^2 + c, \ldots$$

The behavior of this sequence depends on the value of the complex number c. For some values of c this sequence is **bounded,** which means that all elements in the sequence are less than some fixed number N. For other values it is **unbounded,** which means that the elements in the sequence become infinitely large. If the sequence is bounded, the complex number c is in the Mandelbrot Set; if the sequence is unbounded, the complex number c is not in the Mandelbrot Set.

Activities

1. Perform the indicated operations and write the result in standard form.

    $\left(4 - \sqrt{-9}\right)\left(2 + \sqrt{-9}\right)$

    Answer: $17 + 6i$

2. Write $\dfrac{3 + i}{i}$ in standard form.

    Answer: $1 - 3i$

3. Plot $6 - 5i$ and $-3 + 2i$ in the complex plane.

EXAMPLE 6 Members of the Mandelbrot Set

a. The complex number -2 is in the Mandelbrot Set because for $c = -2$, the corresponding Mandelbrot sequence is $-2, 2, 2, 2, 2, 2, \ldots$, which is bounded.

b. The complex number i is also in the Mandelbrot Set because for $c = i$, the corresponding Mandelbrot sequence is

$$i, \quad -1 + i, \quad -i, \quad -1 + i, \quad -i, \quad -1 + i, \quad \ldots$$

which is bounded.

c. The complex number $1 + i$ is not in the Mandelbrot Set because for $c = 1 + i$, the corresponding Mandelbrot sequence is

$$1 + i, \quad 1 + 3i, \quad -7 + 7i, \quad 1 - 97i, \quad -9407 - 193i,$$

$$88454401 + 3631103i, \quad \ldots$$

which is unbounded.

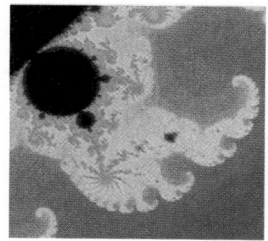

With this definition, a picture of the Mandelbrot Set would have only two colors: one color for points that are in the set (the sequence is bounded), and one for points that are outside the set (the sequence is unbounded). Figure 2.22 shows a black and yellow picture of the Mandelbrot Set. The points that are black are in the Mandelbrot Set and the points that are yellow are not.

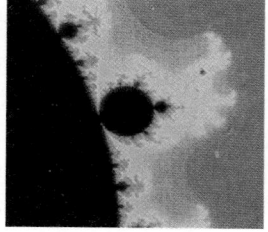

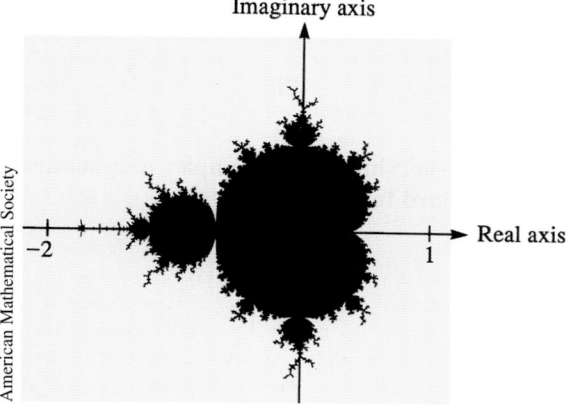

Figure 2.22

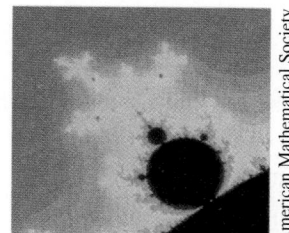

Figure 2.23

To add more interest to the picture, computer scientists discovered that the points that are not in the Mandelbrot Set can be assigned a variety of colors, depending on "how quickly" their sequences diverge. Figure 2.23 shows three different appendages of the Mandelbrot Set. (The black portions of the picture represent points that are in the Mandelbrot Set.)

Figures 2.24 shows another type of fractal. From this picture, you can see why fractals have fascinated people since their discovery (around 1980). The fractal shown was produced on a graphing calculator.

Figure 2.24 *A Fractal Fern*

2.3   E X E R C I S E S

In Exercises 1–4, solve for a and b.

1. $a + bi = -9 + 4i$ **2.** $a + bi = 12 + 5i$

3. $(a - 1) + (b + 3)i = 5 + 8i$

4. $(a + 6) + 2bi = 6 - 5i$

In Exercises 5–14, write in standard form.

5. $4 + \sqrt{-25}$ **6.** $3 + \sqrt{-9}$

7. 12 **8.** 42

9. $-5i + i^2$ **10.** $-3i^2 + i$

11. $\left(\sqrt{-75}\right)^2$ **12.** $\left(\sqrt{-4}\right)^2 - 7$

13. $\sqrt{-0.09}$ **14.** $\sqrt{-0.0004}$

In Exercises 15–24, perform the addition or subtraction and write the result in standard form.

15. $(4 + i) + (7 - 2i)$ **16.** $(11 - 2i) + (-3 + 6i)$

17. $\left(-1 + \sqrt{-8}\right) + \left(8 - \sqrt{-50}\right)$

18. $\left(7 + \sqrt{-18}\right) - \left(3 + 3\sqrt{2}i\right)$

19. $13i - (14 - 7i)$ **20.** $22 + (-5 + 8i) + 10i$

21. $-\left(\frac{3}{2} + \frac{5}{2}i\right) + \left(\frac{5}{3} + \frac{11}{3}i\right)$ **22.** $-\left(\frac{3}{4} + \frac{7}{5}i\right) - \left(\frac{5}{6} - \frac{1}{6}i\right)$

23. $(1.6 + 3.2i) + (-5.8 + 4.3i)$

24. $-(-3.7 - 12.8i) - \left(6.1 - \sqrt{-24.5}\right)$

In Exercises 25–36, perform the operation and write the result in standard form.

25. $\sqrt{-6} \cdot \sqrt{-2}$ **26.** $\sqrt{-5} \cdot \sqrt{-10}$

27. $\left(\sqrt{-10}\right)^2$ **28.** $\left(\sqrt{-75}\right)^2$

29. $(1 + i)(3 - 2i)$ **30.** $(6 - 2i)(2 - 3i)$

31. $6i(5 - 2i)$ **32.** $-8i(9 + 4i)$

33. $\left(\sqrt{14} + \sqrt{10}i\right)\left(\sqrt{14} - \sqrt{10}i\right)$

34. $\left(3 + \sqrt{-5}\right)\left(7 - \sqrt{-10}\right)$

35. $(4 + 5i)^2$ **36.** $(1 - 2i)^2 - (1 + 2i)^2$

37. *Error Analysis* Describe the error.

$$\sqrt{-6}\sqrt{-6} = \sqrt{(-6)(-6)} = \sqrt{36} = 6 \quad \times$$

38. *Error Analysis* Describe the error.

$$-i\left(\sqrt{-4} - 1\right) = -i(4i - 1) \quad \times$$

$$= -4i^2 - i$$

$$= 4 - i$$

In Exercises 39–46, find the product of the number and its conjugate.

39. $4 + 3i$ **40.** $8 - 12i$

41. $-6 - \sqrt{5}i$ **42.** $-3 + \sqrt{2}i$

43. $22i$ **44.** $\sqrt{-13}$

45. $3 - \sqrt{-2}$ **46.** $1 + \sqrt{-8}$

In Exercises 47–58, perform the operation and write the result in standard form.

47. $\dfrac{6}{i}$ **48.** $-\dfrac{5}{i}$

49. $\dfrac{4}{4 - 5i}$ **50.** $\dfrac{3}{1 - i}$

51. $\dfrac{2 + i}{2 - i}$ **52.** $\dfrac{8 - 7i}{1 - 2i}$

53. $\dfrac{6 - 7i}{i}$ **54.** $\dfrac{8 + 20i}{2i}$

55. $\dfrac{1}{(4 - 5i)^2}$ **56.** $\dfrac{(2 - 3i)(5i)}{2 + 3i}$

57. $\dfrac{2}{1 + i} - \dfrac{3}{1 - i}$ **58.** $\dfrac{2i}{2 + i} + \dfrac{5}{2 - i}$

In Exercises 59–66, simplify the complex number and write it in standard form.

59. $-6i^3 + i^2$ **60.** $4i^2 - 2i^3$

61. $-5i^5$ **62.** $(-i)^3$

63. $\left(\sqrt{-75}\right)^3$ **64.** $\left(\sqrt{-2}\right)^6$

65. $\dfrac{1}{i^3}$ **66.** $\dfrac{1}{(2i)^3}$

In Exercises 67–70, determine the complex number shown in the complex plane.

67.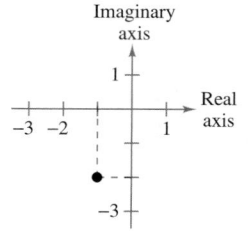

68.

69.

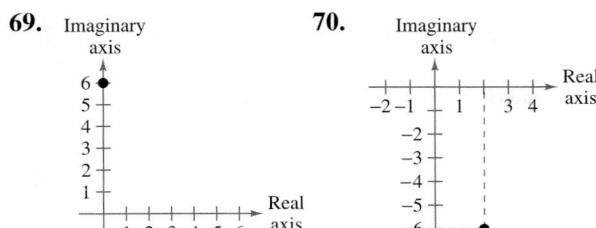

Imaginary axis

6, 5, 4, 3, 2, 1

1 2 3 4 5 6 Real axis

70.

Imaginary axis

Real axis

-2 -1   1   3 4

-2, -3, -4, -5, -6

In Exercises 71–74, plot the complex number in the complex plane.

71. $4 - 5i$ **72.** $3i$

73. -6 **74.** $-7 + 2i$

Fractals   In Exercises 75–80, find the first six terms in the following sequence.

$$c, \ c^2 + c, \ (c^2 + c)^2 + c, \ [(c^2 + c)^2 + c]^2 + c, \ \dots$$

From these terms, do you think the given complex number is in the Mandelbrot Set? Explain your reasoning.

75. $c = 0$ **76.** $c = 2$

77. $c = \frac{1}{2}i$ **78.** $c = -i$

79. $c = 1$ **80.** $c = -1$

81. Cube each complex number. What do you notice?

(a) 2 (b) $-1 + \sqrt{3}i$ (c) $-1 - \sqrt{3}i$

82. Raise each number to the fourth power.

(a) 2 (b) -2 (c) $2i$ (d) $-2i$

83. *Impedance*   The opposition to current in an electrical circuit is called its impedance. The impedance in a parallel circuit with two pathways satisfies the equation

$$\frac{1}{z} = \frac{1}{z_1} + \frac{1}{z_2}$$

when z_1 is the impedance (in ohms) of pathway 1 and z_2 is the impedance (in ohms) of pathway 2. Use the table to determine the impedance of each parallel circuit. (*Hint:* You can find the impedance of each pathway by adding the impedance of each component in the pathway.)

	Resistor	Inductor	Capacitor
	─w─	─◠◠◠─	─┤├─
Symbol	$a \ \Omega$	$b \ \Omega$	$c \ \Omega$
Impedance	a	bi	$-ci$

(a)

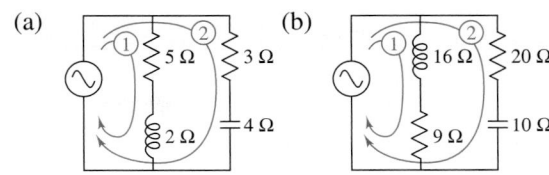

1   5 Ω   2   3 Ω

2 Ω   4 Ω

(b)

1   16 Ω   2   20 Ω

9 Ω   10 Ω

Synthesis

True or False?   In Exercises 84–86, determine whether the statement is true or false. Justify your answer.

84. There is no complex number that is equal to its conjugate.

85. $-i\sqrt{6}$ is a solution of $x^4 - x^2 + 14 = 56$.

86. $i^{44} + i^{150} - i^{74} - i^{109} + i^{61} = -1$

87. Express each of the following powers of i as i, $-i$, 1, or -1.

(a) i^{40} (b) i^{25} (c) i^{50} (d) i^{67}

88. Prove that the sum of a complex number $a + bi$ and its conjugate is a real number, and that the difference of a complex number $a + bi$ and its conjugate is an imaginary number.

89. Prove that the product of a complex number $a + bi$ and its conjugate is a real number.

Review

In Exercises 90–93 perform the operations and write the result in standard form.

90. $(4 + 3x) + (8 - 6x - x^2)$

91. $(x^3 - 3x^2) - (6 - 2x - 4x^2)$

92. $\left(3x - \frac{1}{2}\right)(x + 4)$

93. $(2x - 5)^2$

In Exercises 94–97, find the *x*- and *y*-intercepts of the graph of the equation.

94. $y = -x^2 + 6$ **95.** $y = x^2 + 2x - 8$

96. $y = |x - 4| + 1$ **97.** $y = |x| - 1$

98. *Mixture Problem*   A 5-liter container contains a mixture with a concentration of 50%. How much of this mixture must be withdrawn and replaced by 100% concentrate to bring the mixture up to 60% concentration?

2.4   Solving Equations Algebraically

Quadratic Equations

A **quadratic equation in** x is an equation that can be written in the general form

$$ax^2 + bx + c = 0$$

where a, b, and c are real numbers with $a \neq 0$. Another name for a quadratic equation in x is a **second-degree polynomial equation in** x. You should be familiar with the following four methods for solving quadratic equations.

Solving a Quadratic Equation

Factoring: If $ab = 0$, then $a = 0$ or $b = 0$.

Example: $x^2 - x - 6 = 0$

$$(x - 3)(x + 2) = 0$$

$$x - 3 = 0 \implies x = 3$$

$$x + 2 = 0 \implies x = -2$$

Extracting Square Roots: If $u^2 = c$, where $c > 0$, then $u = \pm\sqrt{c}$.

Example: $(x + 3)^2 = 16$

$$x + 3 = \pm 4$$

$$x = -3 \pm 4$$

$$x = 1 \quad \text{or} \quad x = -7$$

Completing the Square: If $x^2 + bx = c$, then

$$x^2 + bx + \left(\frac{b}{2}\right)^2 = c + \left(\frac{b}{2}\right)^2$$

$$\left(x + \frac{b}{2}\right)^2 = c + \frac{b^2}{4}.$$

Example: $x^2 + 6x = 5$

$$x^2 + 6x + 3^2 = 5 + 3^2$$

$$(x + 3)^2 = 14$$

$$x + 3 = \pm\sqrt{14}$$

$$x = -3 \pm \sqrt{14}$$

Quadratic Formula: If $ax^2 + bx + c = 0$, then $x = \dfrac{-b \pm \sqrt{b^2 - 4ac}}{2a}$.

Example: $2x^2 + 3x - 1 = 0$

$$x = \frac{-3 \pm \sqrt{3^2 - 4(2)(-1)}}{2(2)} = \frac{-3 \pm \sqrt{17}}{4}$$

What You Should Learn:

- How to solve quadratic equations by factoring, extracting square roots, completing the square, and using the Quadratic Formula
- How to solve polynomial equations of degree three or greater
- How to solve equations involving radicals
- How to solve equations involving fractions or absolute values
- How to use quadratic equations to model and solve real-life problems

Why You Should Learn It:

Knowing how to solve quadratic and other types of equations algebraically can help you solve real-life problems, such as Exercise 132 on page 203, where you determine the greatest distance a car can travel on a tank of fuel.

Paul Souders/Tony Stone Images

EXAMPLE 1   Solving a Quadratic Equation by Factoring

Solve each quadratic equation by factoring.

a. $6x^2 = 3x$ **b.** $9x^2 - 6x + 1 = 0$

Solution

a.

$6x^2 = 3x$	Write original equation.
$6x^2 - 3x = 0$	Write in general form.
$3x(2x - 1) = 0$	Factor.
$3x = 0 \implies x = 0$	Set 1st factor equal to 0.
$2x - 1 = 0 \implies x = \frac{1}{2}$	Set 2nd factor equal to 0.

b.

$9x^2 - 6x + 1 = 0$	Write original equation.
$(3x - 1)^2 = 0$	Factor.
$3x - 1 = 0 \implies x = \frac{1}{3}$	Set repeated factor equal to 0.

Throughout the text, when solving equations, be sure to check your solutions either *algebraically* by substituting in the original equation or *graphically*.

Check

a.

$6x^2 = 3x$	Write original equation.
$6(0)^2 \stackrel{?}{=} 3(0)$	Substitute 0 for x.
$0 = 0$	Solution checks. ✓
$6\left(\frac{1}{2}\right)^2 \stackrel{?}{=} 3\left(\frac{1}{2}\right)$	Substitute $\frac{1}{2}$ for x.
$\frac{6}{4} = \frac{3}{2}$	Solution checks. ✓

b.

$9x^2 - 6x + 1 = 0$	Write original equation.
$9\left(\frac{1}{3}\right)^2 - 6\left(\frac{1}{3}\right) + 1 \stackrel{?}{=} 0$	Substitute $\frac{1}{3}$ for x.
$1 - 2 + 1 \stackrel{?}{=} 0$	Simplify.
$0 = 0$	Solution checks. ✓

Similarly, you can approximate the solutions using the graphs in Figure 2.25 to graphically check your solutions.

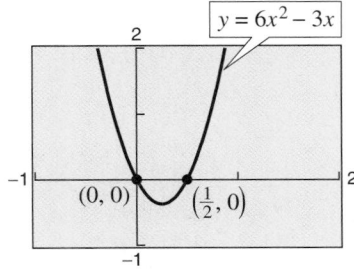

(a)   (b)

Figure 2.25

Encourage your students to use the Quadratic Formula program on the website *college.hmco.com* as a quick and easy check of their work when solving quadratic equations.

Exploration

Try programming the Quadratic Formula into a computer or graphing calculator. Programs for several graphing calculator models may be found on the website *college.hmco.com*.

To use one of the programs, you must first write the equation in general form. Then enter the values of *a*, *b*, and *c*. After the final value has been entered, the program will display either two real solutions *or* the words "NO REAL SOLUTION," *or* the program will give both real and complex solutions.

Solving a quadratic equation by extracting square roots is an efficient method to use when the quadratic equation can be written in the form $ax^2 + c = 0$, as shown in Example 2.

EXAMPLE 2   Extracting Square Roots

Solve each quadratic equation.

a. $4x^2 = 12$ **b.** $(x - 3)^2 = 7$

Solution

a. $4x^2 = 12$ Write original equation.

   $x^2 = 3$ Divide each side by 4.

   $x = \pm\sqrt{3}$ Take square root of each side.

b. $(x - 3)^2 = 7$ Write original equation.

   $x - 3 = \pm\sqrt{7}$ Take square root of each side.

   $x = 3 \pm \sqrt{7}$ Add 3 to each side.

The graphs of $y = 4x^2 - 12$ and $y = (x - 3)^2 - 7$, as shown in Figure 2.26, verify the solutions graphically.

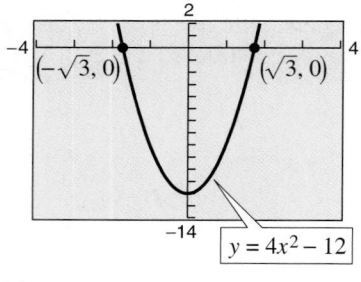

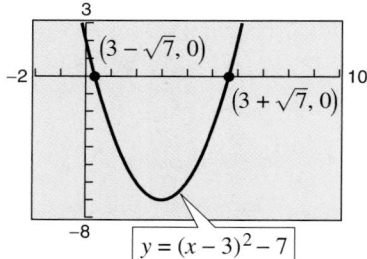

(a)   **(b)**

Figure 2.26

Note that the solutions shown in Example 2 are listed in *exact* form. Most graphing utilities produce decimal approximations of solutions rather than exact forms. For instance, if you solve the equations in Example 2 using a graphing utility, you will obtain $x \approx \pm 1.732$ in part (a) and $x \approx 5.646$ and $x \approx 0.354$ in part (b).

Some graphing utilities have symbolic algebra programs that *can* list the exact form of a solution.

Completing the square can be used to solve any quadratic equation, but it is best suited for quadratic equations in general form $ax^2 + bx + c = 0$ with $a = 1$ and b an even number. If the leading coefficient of the quadratic is not 1, divide each side of the equation by this coefficient *before* completing the square, as shown in Example 3.

A computer animation of this example appears in the *Interactive* CD-ROM and *Internet* versions of this text.

2.4 • Solving Equations Algebraically   **191**

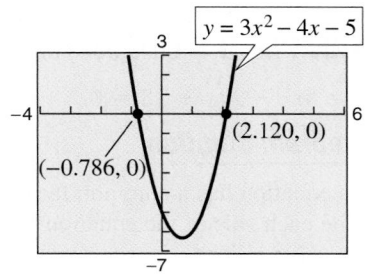

EXAMPLE 3   Completing the Square: Leading Coefficient Is Not 1

Solve $3x^2 - 4x - 5 = 0$ by completing the square.

Solution

$$3x^2 - 4x - 5 = 0 \qquad \text{Write original equation.}$$

$$3x^2 - 4x = 5 \qquad \text{Add 5 to each side.}$$

$$x^2 - \frac{4}{3}x = \frac{5}{3} \qquad \text{Divide each side by 3.}$$

$$x^2 - \frac{4}{3}x + \left(\frac{2}{3}\right)^2 = \frac{5}{3} + \left(\frac{2}{3}\right)^2 \qquad \text{Add } \left(\tfrac{2}{3}\right)^2 \text{ to each side.}$$

$$\left(\text{Half of } \tfrac{4}{3}\right)^2$$

$$\left(x - \frac{2}{3}\right)^2 = \frac{19}{9}$$

$$x - \frac{2}{3} = \pm\frac{\sqrt{19}}{3} \qquad \text{Take square root of each side.}$$

$$x = \frac{2}{3} \pm \frac{\sqrt{19}}{3} \qquad \text{Solutions}$$

Using a calculator, the two solutions are approximately 2.11963 and -0.78630, which agree with the graphical solution shown in Figure 2.27.

Figure 2.27

$y = 3x^2 - 4x - 5$

$(2.120, 0)$

$(-0.786, 0)$

Exploration

Use a graphing utility to graph the three quadratic equations

$$y_1 = x^2 - 2x$$

$$y_2 = x^2 - 2x + 1$$

$$y_3 = x^2 - 2x + 2$$

in the same viewing window. Compute the *discriminant* $\sqrt{b^2 - 4ac}$ for each and discuss the relationship between the discriminant and the number of zeros of the quadratic function.

EXAMPLE 4   Quadratic Formula: Two Distinct Solutions

Solve $x^3 + 3x = 9$ using the Quadratic Formula.

 A computer animation of this example appears in the *Interactive* CD-ROM and *Internet* versions of this text.

Algebraic Solution

$$x^2 + 3x = 9 \qquad \text{Write original equation.}$$

$$x^2 + 3x - 9 = 0 \qquad \text{Write in general form.}$$

$$x = \frac{-b \pm \sqrt{b^2 - 4ac}}{2a} \qquad \text{Quadratic Formula}$$

$$x = \frac{-3 \pm \sqrt{3^2 - 4(1)(-9)}}{2(1)} \qquad \text{Substitute 3 for } b, 1 \text{ for } a, \text{ and } -9 \text{ for } c.$$

$$x = \frac{-3 \pm \sqrt{45}}{2} \qquad \text{Simplify.}$$

$$x = \frac{-3 \pm 3\sqrt{5}}{2} \qquad \text{Simplify radical.}$$

$$x \approx 1.85 \text{ or } -4.85 \qquad \text{Solutions}$$

The equation has two solutions: $x \approx 1.85$ and $x \approx -4.85$. Check these solutions in the original equation.

Graphical Solution

Use a graphing utility to graph $y_1 = x^2 + 3x$ and $y_2 = 9$ in the same viewing window. Use the *intersect* feature of the graphing utility to approximate the points where the graphs intersect. From Figure 2.28, it appears that the graphs intersect when $x \approx 1.85$ and $x \approx -4.85$. These x-coordinates of the intersection points are solutions of the equation $x^2 + 3x = 9$.

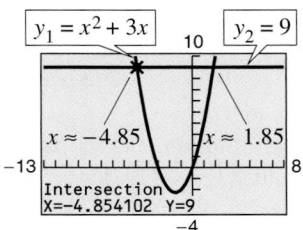

$y_1 = x^2 + 3x$ $y_2 = 9$

$x \approx -4.85$ $x \approx 1.85$

Intersection
X=-4.854102 Y=9

Figure 2.28

EXAMPLE 5   Quadratic Formula: One Repeated Solution

Solve $8x^2 - 24x + 18 = 0$.

Algebraic Solution

This equation has a common factor of 2. To simplify things, first divide each side of the equation by 2.

$$8x^2 - 24x + 18 = 0 \qquad \text{Write original equation.}$$

$$4x^2 - 12x + 9 = 0 \qquad \text{Divide each side by 2.}$$

$$x = \frac{-b \pm \sqrt{b^2 - 4ac}}{2a} \qquad \text{Quadratic Formula}$$

$$x = \frac{-(-12) \pm \sqrt{(-12)^2 - 4(4)(9)}}{2(4)}$$

$$x = \frac{12 \pm \sqrt{0}}{8} = \frac{3}{2} \qquad \text{Repeated solution}$$

This quadratic equation has only one solution: $\frac{3}{2}$. Check this solution in the original equation.

Graphical Solution

Use a graphing utility to graph

$$y = 8x^2 - 24x + 18.$$

Use the *zoom* and *trace* features of the graphing utility to approximate the values of x for which the function is equal to zero. From the graph in Figure 2.29, it appears that the function is equal to when $x = \frac{3}{2}$. This is the only solution of the equation $8x^2 - 24x + 18 = 0$.

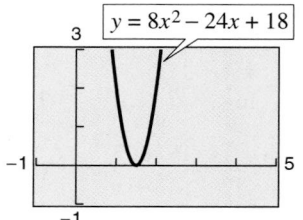

Figure 2.29

EXAMPLE 6   Complex Solutions of a Quadratic Equation

Solve $3x^2 - 2x + 5 = 0$.

Algebraic Solution

By the Quadratic Formula, you can write the solutions as follows.

$$3x^2 - 2x + 5 = 0 \qquad \text{Write original equation.}$$

$$x = \frac{-b \pm \sqrt{b^2 - 4ac}}{2a} \qquad \text{Quadratic Formula}$$

$$= \frac{-(-2) \pm \sqrt{(-2)^2 - 4(3)(5)}}{2(3)} \qquad \begin{array}{l}\text{Substitute } -2 \text{ for } b, \\ 3 \text{ for } a, \text{ and } 5 \text{ for } c.\end{array}$$

$$= \frac{2 \pm \sqrt{-56}}{6} \qquad \text{Simplify.}$$

$$= \frac{2 \pm 2\sqrt{14}\,i}{6} \qquad \text{Simplify radical.}$$

$$= \frac{1}{3} \pm \frac{\sqrt{14}}{3}\,i \qquad \text{Solutions}$$

The equation has no real solution, but it has two complex solutions: $\frac{1}{3}\left(1 + \sqrt{14}\,i\right)$ and $\frac{1}{3}\left(1 - \sqrt{14}\,i\right)$.

Graphical Solution

Use a graphing utility to graph

$$y = 3x^2 - 2x + 5.$$

Note in Figure 2.30 that the graph of the function appears to have no x-intercepts. From this you can conclude that the equation $3x^2 - 2x + 5 = 0$ has no real solution. You can solve the equation algebraically to find the complex solutions.

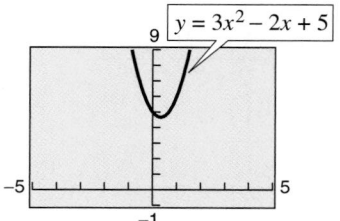

Figure 2.30

Polynomial Equations of Higher Degree

The methods used to solve quadratic equations can sometimes be extended to polynomial equations of higher degree, as shown in the next two examples.

A common mistake that students make when solving polynomial equations of higher degree such as $3x^4 = 48x^2$ is dividing both sides of the equation by the common variable factor x^2. This loses the solution $x = 0$. When your students are factoring to solve an equation, remind them to be sure to set *each* factor equal to zero.

EXAMPLE 7   Solving an Equation of Quadratic Type

Solve the equation $x^4 - 3x^2 + 2 = 0$.

Solution

The expression $x^4 - 3x^2 + 2$ is said to be in *quadratic form* because it is written in the form $au^2 + bu + c$, where u is any expression in x, namely x^2. You can use factoring to solve the equation as follows.

$$x^4 - 3x^2 + 2 = 0 \qquad \text{Write original equation.}$$
$$(x^2)^2 - 3(x^2) + 2 = 0 \qquad \text{Write in quadratic form in } x^2.$$
$$(x^2 - 1)(x^2 - 2) = 0 \qquad \text{Partially factor.}$$
$$(x + 1)(x - 1)(x^2 - 2) = 0 \qquad \text{Factor.}$$
$$x + 1 = 0 \implies x = -1$$
$$x - 1 = 0 \implies x = 1$$
$$x^2 - 2 = 0 \implies x = \pm\sqrt{2}$$

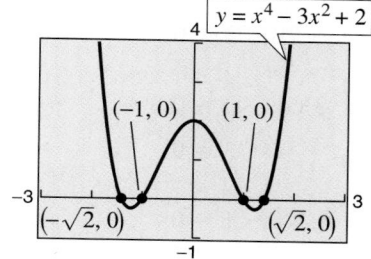

Figure 2.31

The equation has four solutions: -1, 1, $\sqrt{2}$, and $-\sqrt{2}$. Check these solutions in the original equation. The graph of $y = x^4 - 3x^2 + 2$, as shown in Figure 2.31, verifies the solutions graphically.

EXAMPLE 8   Solving a Polynomial Equation by Factoring

Solve the equation $2x^3 - 6x^2 - 6x + 18 = 0$.

Solution

This equation has a common factor of 2. To simplify things, first divide each side of the equation by 2.

$$2x^3 - 6x^2 - 6x + 18 = 0 \qquad \text{Write original equation.}$$
$$x^3 - 3x^2 - 3x + 9 = 0 \qquad \text{Divide each side by 2.}$$
$$x^2(x - 3) - 3(x - 3) = 0 \qquad \text{Group terms.}$$
$$(x - 3)(x^2 - 3) = 0 \qquad \text{Factor by grouping.}$$
$$x - 3 = 0 \implies x = 3$$
$$x^2 - 3 = 0 \implies x = \pm\sqrt{3}$$

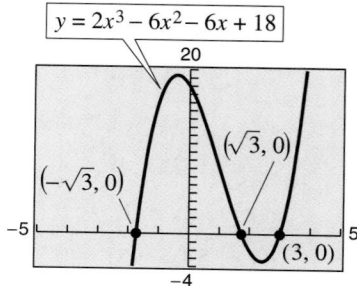

Figure 2.32

The equation has three solutions: 3, $\sqrt{3}$, and $-\sqrt{3}$. Check these solutions in the original equation. The graph of $y = 2x^3 - 6x^2 - 6x + 18$, as shown in Figure 2.32, verifies the solutions graphically.

Equations Involving Radicals

An equation involving a radical expression can often be cleared of radicals by raising both sides of the equation to an appropriate power. When using this procedure, remember to check for extraneous solutions.

To show why the radical should be isolated, have students square both sides of the equation before isolating the radical. Compare problem-solving strategies to help convince students of the need to isolate the radical.

EXAMPLE 9   Solving an Equation Involving a Radical

Solve $\sqrt{2x + 7} - x = 2$.

Algebraic Solution

$\sqrt{2x + 7} - x = 2$	Write original equation.
$\sqrt{2x + 7} = x + 2$	Isolate radical.
$2x + 7 = x^2 + 4x + 4$	Square each side.
$x^2 + 2x - 3 = 0$	Write in general form.
$(x + 3)(x - 1) = 0$	Factor.
$x + 3 = 0 \implies x = -3$	Set 1st factor equal to 0.
$x - 1 = 0 \implies x = 1$	Set 2nd factor equal to 0.

By substituting into the original equation, you can determine that -3 is extraneous, whereas 1 is valid. So, the equation has only one real solution: $x = 1$.

Graphical Solution

First rewrite the equation as $\sqrt{2x + 7} - x - 2 = 0$. Then use a graphing utility to graph $y = \sqrt{2x + 7} - x - 2$ as shown in Figure 2.33(a). Notice that the domain is $x \geq -\frac{7}{2}$ because the expression under the radical cannot be negative. There appears to be one solution near $x = 1$. Use the *zoom* and *trace* features, as shown in Figure 2.33(b), to approximate the only solution to be $x = 1$.

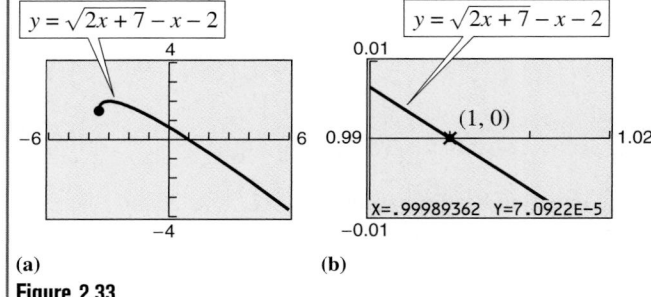

(a)   (b)

Figure 2.33

EXAMPLE 10   Solving an Equation Involving Two Radicals

Solve the equation $\sqrt{2x + 6} - \sqrt{x + 4} = 1$.

Solution

$\sqrt{2x + 6} - \sqrt{x + 4} = 1$	Write original equation.
$\sqrt{2x + 6} = 1 + \sqrt{x + 4}$	Isolate radical.
$2x + 6 = 1 + 2\sqrt{x + 4} + (x + 4)$	Square each side.
$x + 1 = 2\sqrt{x + 4}$	Isolate radical.
$x^2 + 2x + 1 = 4(x + 4)$	Square each side.
$x^2 - 2x - 15 = 0$	Write in general form.
$(x - 5)(x + 3) = 0$	Factor.
$x - 5 = 0 \implies x = 5$	Set 1st factor equal to 0.
$x + 3 = 0 \implies x = -3$	Set 2nd factor equal to 0.

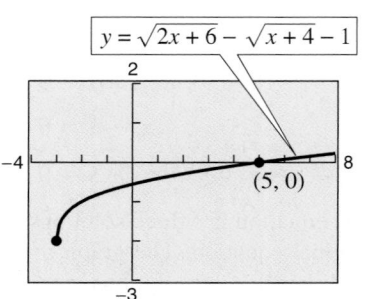

By substituting into the original equation, you can determine that -3 is extraneous, whereas 5 is valid. Figure 2.34 verifies that $x = 5$ is the only solution.

Figure 2.34

EXAMPLE 11 Solving an Equation with Rational Exponents

Solve $(x + 1)^{2/3} = 4$.

Algebraic Solution

$$(x + 1)^{2/3} = 4$$ Write original equation.

$$\sqrt[3]{(x + 1)^2} = 4$$ Rewrite with radical sign.

$$(x + 1)^2 = 64$$ Cube each side.

$$x + 1 = \pm 8$$ Take square root of each side.

$$x = -9, x = 7$$ Subtract 1 from each side.

Substitute $x = -9$ and $x = 7$ into the original equation to determine that both are valid solutions.

Graphical Solution

Use a graphing utility to graph $y_1 = \sqrt[3]{(x + 1)^2}$ and $y_2 = 4$ in the same viewing window, as shown in Figure 2.35. Use the *intersect* feature of the graphing utility to approximate the solutions to be $x = -9$ and $x = 7$.

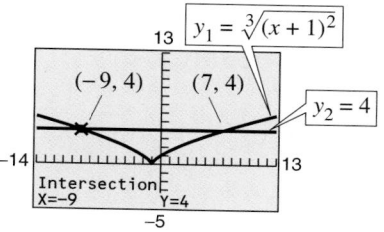

Figure 2.35

Equations Involving Fractions or Absolute Values

As demonstrated in Section 2.1, you can algebraically solve an equation involving fractions by multiplying both sides of the equation by the least common denominator of each term in the equation to "clear an equation of fractions."

EXAMPLE 12 Solving an Equation Involving Fractions

Solve $\dfrac{2}{x} = \dfrac{3}{x - 2} - 1$.

Solution

For this equation, the least common denominator of the three terms is $x(x - 2)$, so you can begin by multiplying each term in the equation by this expression.

$$\frac{2}{x} = \frac{3}{x - 2} - 1$$

$$x(x - 2)\frac{2}{x} = x(x - 2)\frac{3}{x - 2} - x(x - 2)(1)$$

$$2(x - 2) = 3x - x(x - 2), \qquad x \neq 0, 2$$

$$x^2 - 3x - 4 = 0$$

$$(x - 4)(x + 1) = 0$$

$$x - 4 = 0 \quad \Longrightarrow \quad x = 4$$

$$x + 1 = 0 \quad \Longrightarrow \quad x = -1$$

The equation has two solutions: 4 and -1. Check these solutions in the original equation. Use a graphing utility to verify these solutions graphically.

Exploration

Using dot mode, graph the two functions

$$y_1 = \frac{2}{x}$$

$$y_2 = \frac{3}{x - 2} - 1$$

in the same viewing window. How many times do the graphs of the functions intersect? What does this tell you about the solution to Example 12?

STUDY T!P

Graphs of functions involving variable denominators can be tricky because of the way graphing utilities skip over points where the denominator is zero. You will study graphs of such functions in Sections 3.5 and 3.6.

EXAMPLE 13   Solving an Equation Involving Absolute Value

Solve $|x^2 - 3x| = -4x + 6$.

Solution

Begin by writing the equation as $|x^2 - 3x| + 4x - 6 = 0$. From the graph of $y = |x^2 - 3x| + 4x - 6$ in Figure 2.36, you can estimate the solutions to be -3 and 1. These can be verified by substitution into the equation. To solve *algebraically* an equation involving an absolute value, you must consider the fact that the expression inside the absolute value symbols can be positive or negative. This consideration results in *two* separate equations, each of which must be solved.

First Equation:

$x^2 - 3x = -4x + 6$	Use positive expression.
$x^2 + x - 6 = 0$	Write in general form.
$(x + 3)(x - 2) = 0$	Factor.
$x + 3 = 0 \quad \Longrightarrow \quad x = -3$	Set 1st factor equal to 0.
$x - 2 = 0 \quad \Longrightarrow \quad x = 2$	Set 2nd factor equal to 0.

Second Equation:

$$-x^3 + 32 + 4x - 6 = 0$$

$-(x^2 - 3x) = -4x + 6$	Use negative expression.
$-x^2 + 7x - 6 = 0$	
$x^2 - 7x + 6 = 0$	Write in general form.
$(x - 1)(x - 6) = 0$	Factor.
$x - 1 = 0 \quad \Longrightarrow \quad x = 1$	Set 1st factor equal to 0.
$x - 6 = 0 \quad \Longrightarrow \quad x = 6$	Set 2nd factor equal to 0.

Check

$\|(-3)^2 - 3(-3)\| \stackrel{?}{=} -4(-3) + 6$	Substitute -3 for x.
$18 = 18$	-3 checks. ✔
$\|2^2 - 3(2)\| \stackrel{?}{=} -4(2) + 6$	Substitute 2 for x.
$2 \neq -2$	2 does not check.
$\|1^2 - 3(1)\| \stackrel{?}{=} -4(1) + 6$	Substitute 1 for x.
$2 = 2$	1 checks. ✔
$\|6^2 - 3(6)\| \stackrel{?}{=} -4(6) + 6$	Substitute 6 for x.
$18 \neq -18$	6 does not check.

The equation has only two solutions: -3 and 1, just as you obtained by graphing.

In Figure 2.36, the graph of $y = |x^2 - 3x| + 4x - 6$ appears to be a straight line to the right of the y-axis. Is it? Explain how you decided.

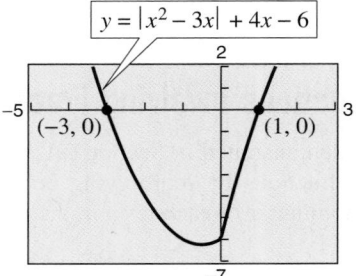

Figure 2.36

Applications

A common application of quadratic equations involves an object that is falling (or projected into the air). The general equation that gives the height of such an object is called a **position equation,** and on *earth's* surface it has the form

$$s = -16t^2 + v_0t + s_0.$$

In this equation, s represents the height of the object (in feet), v_0 represents the original velocity of the object (in feet per second), s_0 represents the original height of the object (in feet), and t represents the time (in seconds). Note that this position equation ignores air resistance.

EXAMPLE 14   Falling Time

A construction worker on the 24th floor of a building project (see Figure 2.37) accidentally drops a wrench and yells, "Look out below!" Could a person at ground level hear this warning in time to get out of the way?

Solution

Assume that each floor of the building is 10 feet high, so that the wrench is dropped from a height of 240 feet. Because sound travels at about 1100 feet per second, it follows that a person at ground level hears the warning within 1 second of the time the wrench is dropped. To set up a mathematical model for the height of the wrench, use the position equation

$$s = -16t^2 + v_0t + s_0. \qquad \text{Position equation}$$

Because the object is dropped rather than thrown, the initial velocity is $v_0 = 0$. So, with an initial height of $s_0 = 240$ feet, you have the following model.

$$s = -16t^2 + 240$$

After falling for 1 second, the height of the wrench is

$$-16(1)^2 + 240 = 224.$$

After falling for 2 seconds, the height of the wrench is

$$-16(2)^2 + 240 = 176.$$

To find the number of seconds it takes the wrench to hit the ground, let the height s be zero and solve the equation for t.

$$s = -16t^2 + 240 \qquad \text{Position equation}$$
$$0 = -16t^2 + 240 \qquad \text{Substitute 0 for } s.$$
$$16t^2 = 240 \qquad \text{Add } 16t^2 \text{ to each side.}$$
$$t^2 = 15 \qquad \text{Divide each side by 16.}$$
$$t = \sqrt{15} \approx 3.87 \qquad \text{Extract positive square root.}$$

The wrench will take about 3.87 seconds to hit the ground. If the person hears the warning 1 second after the wrench is dropped, the person still has almost 3 more seconds to get out of the way.

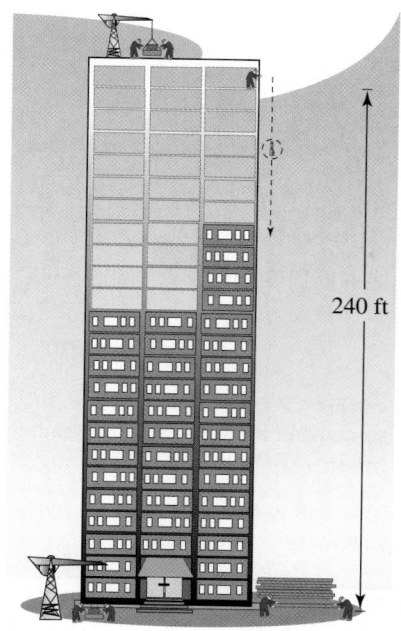

240 ft

Figure 2.37

EXAMPLE 15   Quadratic Modeling: Internet Use

From 1992 to 2000, the number of hours spent annually per person using the Internet in the United States closely followed the quadratic model

$$\text{Hours} = 0.39t^2 + 0.26t - 1.12$$

where $t = 2$ represents 1992. The number of hours per year is shown graphically in Figure 2.38. According to this model, in which year will the number of hours spent per person reach or surpass 100?   (Source: Veronis, Suhler, & Associates)

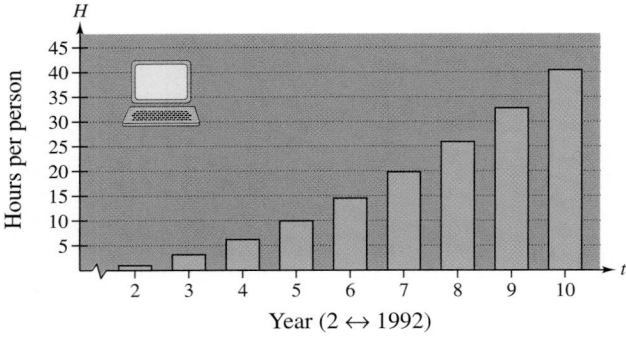

Figure 2.38

Solution

To find when the number of hours spent per person will reach 100, you need to solve the equation

$$0.39t^2 + 0.26t - 1.12 = 100$$

To begin, write the equation in general form.

$$0.39t^2 + 0.26t - 101.12 = 0$$

Then apply the Quadratic Formula.

$$t = \frac{-0.26 \pm \sqrt{(0.26)^2 - 4(0.39)(-101.12)}}{2(0.39)}$$

Because time is nonnegative, choose the positive solution

$$t = \frac{-0.26 + \sqrt{(0.26)^2 - 4(0.39)(-101.12)}}{2(0.39)} \approx 15.8.$$

Because $t = 2$ corresponds to 1992, it follows that $t = 15.8$ must correspond to some time in 2005. So, the number of hours spent annually per person using the Internet should reach 100 during 2005.

You can solve Example 15 with your graphing utility by graphing the two functions

$$y_1 = 0.39t^2 + 0.26t - 1.12$$

$$y_2 = 100$$

in the same viewing window and finding their point of intersection. You should obtain $x \approx 15.8$, which verifies the answer obtained analytically.

Another type of application that often involves a quadratic equation is one dealing with the hypotenuse of a right triangle. These types of applications often use the Pythagorean Theorem, which states that

$$a^2 + b^2 = c^2 \qquad \text{Pythagorean Theorem}$$

where a and b are the legs of a right triangle and c is the hypotenuse, as indicated in Figure 2.39.

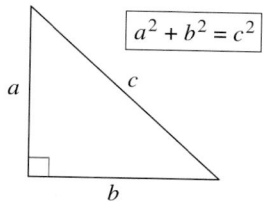

Figure 2.39

EXAMPLE 16   Cutting Across the Lawn

Your house is on a large corner lot. Several of the children in the neighborhood cut across your lawn, as shown in Figure 2.40. The distance across the lawn is 32 feet. How many feet does a person save by walking across the lawn instead of walking on the sidewalk?

Solution

In Figure 2.40, let x represent the length of the shorter part of the sidewalk. Using a ruler, you can find that the length of the longer part of the sidewalk is twice the shorter, so you can represent its length by $2x$. Now, using the Pythagorean Theorem, you have

$$a^2 + b^2 = c^2 \qquad \text{Pythagorean Theorem}$$

$$x^2 + (2x)^2 = 32^2 \qquad \text{Substitute for } a, b, \text{ and } c.$$

$$5x^2 = 1024 \qquad \text{Combine like terms.}$$

$$x^2 = 204.8 \qquad \text{Divide each side by 5.}$$

$$x = \pm\sqrt{204.8} \qquad \text{Take square root of each side.}$$

Choose the positive square root. The total distance on the sidewalk is

$$x + 2x = 3x = 3\sqrt{204.8} \approx 42.9 \text{ feet.}$$

Cutting across the lawn saves a person about $42.9 - 32$ or 10.9 feet.

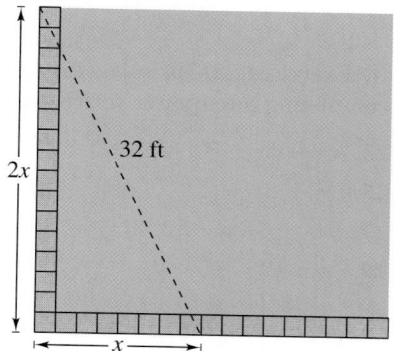

Figure 2.40

Writing About Math   *Investigating Intercepts*

On a graphing utility, store the value 5 in A, -2 in B, and 1 in C. Use a graphing utility to sketch the graph of $y = C(x - A)(x - B)$. Explain how the values of A and B can be determined from the graph. Now store any other nonzero value in C. Does the value of C affect the x-intercepts of the graph? Explain. Find values of A, B, and C such that the graph opens downward and has x-intercepts at $(-5, 0)$ and $(0, 0)$. Summarize your findings.

2.4   Exercises

In Exercises 1–4, write the quadratic equation in general form.

1. $2x^2 = 3 - 5x$

2. $x^2 = 25x$

3. $\frac{1}{5}(3x^2 - 10) = 12x$

4. $x(x + 2) = 3x^2 + 1$

In Exercises 5–14, solve the quadratic equation by factoring. Check your solutions in the original equation.

5. $6x^2 + 3x = 0$

6. $9x^2 - 1 = 0$

7. $x^2 - 2x - 8 = 0$

8. $x^2 - 10x + 9 = 0$

9. $3 + 5x - 2x^2 = 0$

10. $2x^2 = 19x + 33$

11. $x^2 + 4x = 12$

12. $-x^2 + 8x = 12$

13. $(x + a)^2 - b^2 = 0$

14. $x^2 + 2ax + a^2 = 0$

In Exercises 15–22, solve the equation by extracting square roots. List both the exact solution and the decimal solution rounded to two decimal places.

15. $x^2 = 7$

16. $9x^2 = 25$

17. $(x - 12)^2 = 18$

18. $(x - 5)^2 = 20$

19. $(2x - 1)^2 = 18$

20. $(4x + 7)^2 = 44$

21. $(x - 7)^2 = (x + 3)^2$

22. $(x + 5)^2 = (x + 4)^2$

In Exercises 23–30, solve the quadratic equation by completing the square. Verify your answer graphically.

23. $x^2 + 4x - 32 = 0$

24. $x^2 - 2x - 3 = 0$

25. $x^2 + 6x + 2 = 0$

26. $x^2 + 8x + 14 = 0$

27. $9x^2 - 18x + 3 = 0$

28. $9x^2 - 12x - 14 = 0$

29. $8 + 4x - x^2 = 0$

30. $4x^2 - 4x - 99 = 0$

Graphical Reasoning   In Exercises 31–38, (a) use a graphing utility to graph the equation, (b) use the graph to approximate any x-intercepts, (c) set $y = 0$ and solve the resulting equation, and (d) compare the result with the x-intercepts of the graph.

31. $y = (x + 3)^2 - 4$

32. $y = 1 - (x - 2)^2$

33. $y = -4x^2 + 4x + 3$

34. $y = x^2 + 3x - 4$

35. $y = \frac{1}{4}(4x^2 - 20x + 25)$

36. $y = -(x^2 - 4x + 3)$

37. $y = -(x^2 - 4x + 5)$

38. $y = \frac{1}{4}(x^2 - 2x + 9)$

In Exercises 39–44, use a graphing utility to determine the number of real solutions of the quadratic equation.

39. $2x^2 - 5x + 5 = 0$

40. $2x^2 - x - 1 = 0$

41. $\frac{1}{5}x^2 + \frac{6}{5}x - 8 = 0$

42. $\frac{1}{3}x^2 - 5x + 25 = 0$

43. $-4.1x^2 + 2.9x - 1.5 = 0$

44. $9 + 2.4x - 8.3x^2$

In Exercises 45–52, use the Quadratic Formula to solve the equation. Use a graphing utility to verify your solutions graphically.

45. $2 + 2x - x^2 = 0$

46. $x^2 - 10x + 22 = 0$

47. $x^2 + 8x - 4 = 0$

48. $4x^2 - 4x - 4 = 0$

49. $28x - 49x^2 = 4$

50. $9x^2 + 24x + 16 = 0$

51. $4x^2 + 16x + 15 = 0$

52. $9x^2 - 6x - 35 = 0$

In Exercises 53–60, solve the equation by any convenient method.

53. $x^2 - 2x - 1 = 0$

54. $11x^2 + 33x = 0$

55 $(x + 3)^2 = 81$

56. $x^2 - 14x + 49 = 0$

57. $x^2 - x - \frac{11}{4} = 0$

58. $x^2 + 3x - \frac{3}{4} = 0$

59. $(x + 1)^2 = x^2$

60. $a^2x^2 - b^2 = 0,\ a \neq 0$

In Exercises 61–76, find all solutions of the equation. Use a graphing utility to verify the solutions graphically.

61. $4x^4 - 18x^2 = 0$

62. $20x^3 - 125x = 0$

63. $x^4 - 81 = 0$

64. $x^6 - 64 = 0$

65. $5x^3 + 30x^2 + 45x = 0$

66. $9x^4 - 24x^3 + 16x^2 = 0$

67. $x^3 - 3x^2 - x + 3 = 0$

68. $x^4 + 2x^3 - 8x - 16 = 0$

69. $x^4 - 4x^2 + 3 = 0$

70. $x^4 + 5x^2 - 36 = 0$

71. $4x^4 - 65x^2 + 16 = 0$

72. $36t^4 + 29t^2 - 7 = 0$

73. $\dfrac{1}{t^2} + \dfrac{8}{t} + 15 = 0$

74. $6\left(\dfrac{s}{s + 1}\right)^2 + 5\left(\dfrac{s}{s + 1}\right) - 6 = 0$

75. $2x + 9\sqrt{x} - 5 = 0$

76. $3x^{1/3} + 2x^{2/3} = 5$

Graphical Analysis In Exercises 77–80, (a) use a graphing utility to graph the equation, (b) use the graph to approximate any x-intercepts of the graph, (c) set $y = 0$ and solve the resulting equation, and (d) compare the result with the x-intercepts of the graph.

77. $y = x^3 - 2x^2 - 3x$

78. $y = 2x^4 - 15x^3 + 18x^2$

79. $y = x^4 - 10x^2 + 9$

80. $y = x^4 - 29x^2 + 100$

In Exercises 81–90, find all solutions of the equation algebraically. Check your solutions both algebraically and graphically.

81. $\sqrt{x - 10} - 4 = 0$ **82.** $\sqrt[3]{2x + 5} + 3 = 0$

83. $\sqrt{x + 1} - 3x = 1$ **84.** $\sqrt{x + 5} = \sqrt{x - 5}$

85. $\sqrt{x} - \sqrt{x - 5} = 1$ **86.** $\sqrt{x} + \sqrt{x - 20} = 10$

87. $(x - 5)^{2/3} = 16$

88. $(x^2 - x - 22)^{4/3} = 16$

89. $3x(x - 1)^{1/2} + 2(x - 1)^{3/2} = 0$

90. $4x^2(x - 1)^{1/3} + 6x(x - 1)^{4/3} = 0$

Graphical Analysis In Exercises 91–94, (a) use a graphing utility to graph the equation, (b) use the graph to approximate any x-intercepts of the graph, (c) set $y = 0$ and solve the resulting equation, and (d) compare the result with the x-intercepts of the graph.

91. $y = \sqrt{11x - 30} - x$ **92.** $y = 2x - \sqrt{15 - 4x}$

93. $y = \sqrt{7x + 36} - \sqrt{5x + 16} - 2$

94. $y = 3\sqrt{x} - \dfrac{4}{\sqrt{x}} - 4$

In Exercises 95–104, find all solutions of the equation. Use a graphing utility to verify your solutions graphically.

95. $\dfrac{20 - x}{x} = x$ **96.** $\dfrac{4}{x} - \dfrac{5}{3} = \dfrac{x}{6}$

97. $\dfrac{1}{x} - \dfrac{1}{x + 1} = 3$ **98.** $\dfrac{x}{x^2 - 4} + \dfrac{1}{x + 2} = 3$

99. $x = \dfrac{3}{x} + \dfrac{1}{2}$ **100.** $4x + 1 = \dfrac{3}{x}$

101. $|2x - 1| = 5$ **102.** $|3x + 2| = 7$

103. $|x| = x^2 + x - 3$ **104.** $|x - 10| = x^2 - 10x$

Graphical Analysis In Exercises 105–108, (a) use a graphing utility to graph the equation, (b) use the graph to approximate any x-intercepts of the graph, (c) set $y = 0$ and solve the resulting equation, and (d) compare the result with the x-intercepts of the graph.

105. $y = \dfrac{1}{x} - \dfrac{4}{x - 1} - 1$ **106.** $y = x + \dfrac{9}{x + 1} - 5$

107. $y = |x + 1| - 2$ **108.** $y = |x - 2| - 3$

In Exercises 109–116, find an equation having the given solutions. (There are many correct answers.)

109. $-6, 5$ **110.** $0, 4, 7$

111. $-\dfrac{7}{3}, \dfrac{6}{7}$ **112.** $-\dfrac{1}{8}, -\dfrac{4}{5}$

113. $\sqrt{2}, -\sqrt{2}, 4$ **114.** $2, \sqrt{5}, -\sqrt{5}$

115. $-2, 2, i, -i$ **116.** $4i, -4i, 6, -6$

Think About It In Exercises 117 and 118, find x such that the distance between the points is 13.

117. $(1, 2), (x, -10)$ **118.** $(-8, 0), (x, 5)$

In Exercises 119 and 120, solve for the variable.

119. *Surface Area of a Cone*
Solve for h: $S = \pi r\sqrt{r^2 + h^2}$

120. *Inductance*
Solve for Q: $i = \pm\sqrt{\dfrac{1}{LC}}\sqrt{Q^2 - q}$

121. *Floor Space* The floor of a one-story building is 14 feet longer than it is wide. The building has 1632 square feet of floor space.

(a) Draw a diagram to represent the floor space. Represent the width as w and show the length in terms of w.

(b) Write a quadratic equation in terms of w.

(c) Find the length and width of the building floor.

122. *Packaging* An open box with a square base is to be constructed from 84 square inches of material. What should the dimensions of the base be if the height of the box is to be 2 inches? (*Hint:* The surface area is $S = x^2 + 4xh$.)

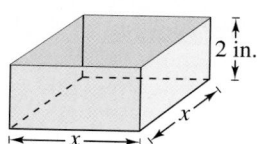

123. *Packaging* An open box is to be made from a square piece of material by cutting 2-centimeter squares from each corner and turning up the sides. The volume of the finished box is to be 200 cubic centimeters. Find the size of the original piece of material.

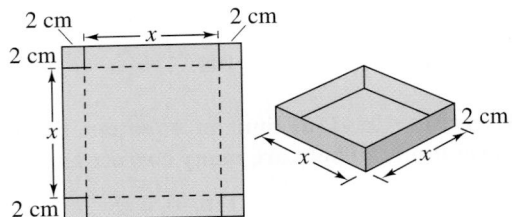

124. *Exploration* A rancher has 100 meters of fencing to enclose two adjacent rectangular corrals as shown in the figure.

(a) Write the area of the enclosed region as a function of x.

(b) Use a graphing utility to generate additional rows of the table. Use the table to estimate the dimensions that will produce a maximum area.

x	y	Area
2	$\frac{92}{3}$	$\frac{368}{3} \approx 123$
4	28	224

(c) Use a graphing utility to graph the area function, and use the graph to estimate the dimensions that will produce a maximum area.

(d) Use the graph to approximate the dimensions such that the enclosed area will be 350 square meters.

(e) Find the required dimensions of part (d) algebraically.

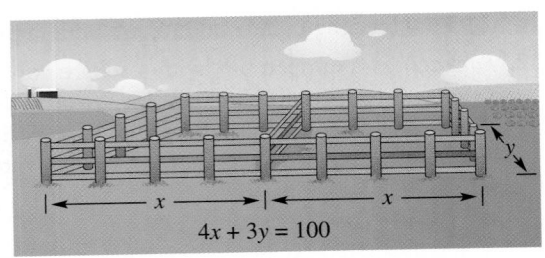

$4x + 3y = 100$

In Exercises 125–128, use the position equation on page 197 as the model for the problem.

125. *CN Tower* At 1821 feet tall, the CN Tower in Toronto, Ontario, is the world's tallest self-supporting structure. Suppose an object were dropped from the top of the tower.

(a) Find the position equation

$$s = -16t^2 + v_0t + s_0.$$

(b) Complete the table.

t	0	2	4	6	8	10
s						

(c) From the table of part (b) you know the time until the object reaches ground level is greater than how many seconds? Find the time algebraically.

126. *Warfare* A cargo plane flying at 8000 feet over level terrain drops a 500-pound supply package.

(a) How long will it take until the package strikes the ground?

(b) If the plane is flying at 600 miles per hour, how far will the package travel horizontally during its descent?

127. *World Trade Center* Suppose you drop a penny from the top of One World Trade Center in New York City. The building has a height of 1368 feet.

(a) Use the position equation to write a mathematical model for the height of the penny.

(b) Find the height of the penny after 4 seconds.

(c) How long will it take before the penny strikes the ground?

(d) Use a graphing utility with the appropriate viewing window to verify your answer in part (c).

128. *Baseball* You throw a baseball straight up into the air at a velocity of 45 feet per second. You release the baseball at a height of 5.5 feet and are going to catch it when it falls back to a height of 6 feet.

(a) Use the position equation to write a mathematical model for the height of the baseball.

(b) Find the height of the baseball after 0.5 seconds.

(c) How many seconds will the baseball be in the air?

(d) Use a graphing utility to verify your answer in part (c).

129. *Airline Traffic* The total number y of annual aircraft departures in the United States from 1990 through 1996 can be approximated by the mathematical model

$$y = 0.036t^2 + 0.032t + 6.839, \quad 0 \le t \le 6$$

where y is in millions and t is the year, with $t = 0$ corresponding to 1990. (Source: Air Transport Association of America)

(a) Determine algebraically when the number of departures reached 8 million.

(b) Verify your answer to part (a) by creating a table of values for the model.

(c) Use a graphing utility to graph the model.

(d) Use the *zoom* and *trace* features of a graphing utility to find the year in which the total number of departures reached 7.0 million.

(e) Verify your answer to part (d) algebraically.

130. *Boating* The total number of dollars spent on boating in the United States from 1991 through 1996 can be approximated by the model

$$S = 0.23t^2 + 0.088t + 9.75, \quad 1 \le t \le 6$$

where S is the spending (in billions of dollars) and t is the time, with $t = 0$ corresponding to 1990. (Source: National Marine Manufacturers Association)

(a) Use a graphing utility to graph the model.

(b) Extend the model past 1996. Does the model predict that sales ever exceed 25 billion dollars? If so, estimate the year.

131. *Biology* The metabolic rate of ectothermic organisms increases with increasing temperature within a certain range. Experimental data for oxygen consumption (microliters per gram per hour) of a beetle for certain temperatures yielded the model

$$C = 0.45x^2 - 1.65x + 50.75, \quad 10 \le x \le 25$$

where x is the air temperature in degrees Celsius.

(a) Use a graphing utility to graph the consumption function over the specified domain.

(b) Use the graph to approximate the air temperature resulting in oxygen consumption of 150 microliters per gram per hour.

(c) If the temperature is increased from 10 to 20 degrees, the oxygen consumption is increased by approximately what factor?

132. *Fuel Efficiency* The distance d (in miles) a car can travel on one tank of fuel is approximated by $d = -0.024s^2 + 1.455s + 431.5$ for $0 < s \le 75$, where s is the average speed of the car in mph.

(a) Use a graphing utility to graph the distance function over the specified domain.

(b) Use the graph to determine the greatest distance that can be traveled on a tank of fuel. How long will the trip take?

(c) Determine the greatest distance that can be traveled in this car in 8 hours with no refueling. How fast should the car be driven? [*Hint:* The distance traveled in 8 hours is $8s$. Graph this expression in the same viewing window as the graph in part (a) and approximate the point of intersection.]

133. *Saturated Steam* The temperature T (in degrees Fahrenheit) of saturated steam increases as pressure increases. This relationship is approximated by

$$T = 75.82 - 2.11x + 43.51\sqrt{x}, \quad 5 \le x \le 40$$

where x is the absolute pressure in pounds per square inch.

(a) Use a graphing utility to graph the temperature function over the specified domain.

(b) The temperature of steam at sea level ($x = 14.696$) is 212°F. Evaluate the model at this pressure and verify the result graphically.

(c) Use the model to approximate the pressure for a steam temperature of 240°F.

134. *Exploration* A meteorologist is positioned 100 feet from the point where a weather balloon is launched. When the balloon is at height h, the distance d between the meteorologist and the balloon is $d = \sqrt{100^2 + h^2}$.

(a) Use a graphing utility to graph the equation. Use the trace feature to approximate the value of h when $d = 200$.

(b) Complete the table. Use the table to approximate the value of h when $d = 200$.

h	160	165	170	175	180	185
d						

(c) Find h algebraically when $d = 200$.

(d) Compare the results of each method. In each case, what information did you gain that wasn't revealed by another solution method?

135. *Economics*   The demand equation for a certain product is $p = 20 - 0.0002x$, where p is the price per unit and x is the number of units sold. The total revenue for selling x units is

Revenue $= xp = x(20 - 0.0002x)$.

How many units must be sold to produce a revenue of $500,000?

136. *Economics*   The demand equation for a certain product is $p = 60 - 0.0004x$, where p is the price per unit and x is the number of units sold. The total revenue for selling x units is

Revenue $= xp = x(60 - 0.0004x)$.

How many units must be sold to produce a revenue of $220,000?

137. *Geometry*   The hypotenuse of an isosceles right triangle is 5 centimeters long. How long are its right sides?

138. *Geometry*   An equilateral triangle has a height of 10 inches. How long are each of its sides? (*Hint:* Use the height of the triangle to partition the triangle into two congruent right triangles.)

139. *Flying Speed*   Two planes leave simultaneously from the same airport, one flying due north and the other due east. The northbound plane is flying 50 miles per hour faster than the eastbound plane. After 3 hours the planes are 2440 miles apart. Find the speed of each plane.

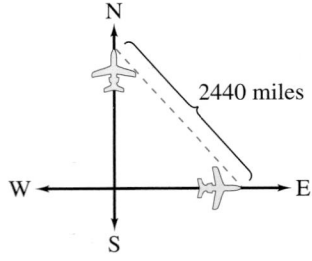

140. *Flying Distance*   A small commuter airline flies to three cities whose locations form the vertices of a right triangle. The total flight distance (from City A to City B to City C and back to City A) is 1400 kilometers. It is 600 kilometers between the two cities that are farthest apart. Approximate the other two distances between cities.

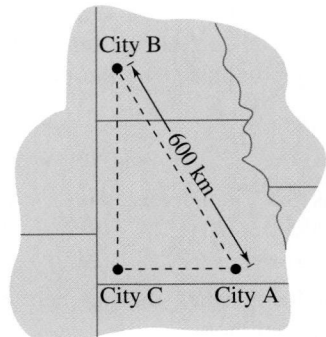

FIGURE FOR 140

Synthesis

True or False?   **In Exercises 141–143, determine whether the statement is true or false. Justify your answer.**

141. The quadratic equation $-3x^2 - x = 10$ has two real solutions.

142. If $(2x - 3)(x + 5) = 8$, then $2x - 3 = 8$ or $x + 5 = 8$.

143. An equation can never have more than one extraneous solution.

144. *Exploration*   Solve the equation $3(x + 4)^2 + (x + 4) - 2 = 0$ in two ways.

(a) Let $u = x + 4$, and solve the resulting equation for u. Then find the corresponding values of x that are solutions of the original equation.

(b) Expand and collect like terms in the original equation, and solve the resulting equation for x.

(c) Which method is easier? Explain.

145. *Exploration*   Given that a and b are nonzero real numbers, determine the solutions of the equations.

(a) $ax^2 + bx = 0$ (b) $ax^2 - ax = 0$

Review

In Exercises 146–149, completely factor the expression over the real numbers.

146. $x^5 - 27x^2$

147. $x^3 - 5x^2 - 14x$

148. $x^3 + 5x^2 - 2x - 10$

149. $5(x + 5)x^{1/3} + 4x^{4/3}$

In Exercises 150–155, determine whether y is a function of x.

150. $5x + 8y = -1$

151. $-x^2 + y^2 = 2$

152. $x + y^2 = 10$

153. $-2y = \sqrt{x + 6}$

154. $y = |x - 3|$

155. $|y| = 1 - x$

2.5 Solving Inequalities Algebraically and Graphically

Properties of Inequalities

Simple inequalities were reviewed in Section P.1. There, the inequality symbols $<$, $\leq$, $>$, and $\geq$ were used to compare two numbers and to denote subsets of real numbers. For instance, the simple inequality $x \geq 3$ denotes all real numbers x that are greater than or equal to 3. In this section you will study inequalities that contain more involved statements such as

$$5x - 7 > 3x + 9 \qquad \text{and} \qquad -3 \leq 6x - 1 < 3.$$

As with an equation, you **solve an inequality** in the variable x by finding all values of x for which the inequality is true. These values are **solutions** of the inequality and are said to **satisfy** the inequality. For instance, the number 9 is a solution of the first inequality listed above because

$$5(9) - 7 > 3(9) + 9$$

$$38 > 36.$$

On the other hand, the number 7 is not a solution because

$$5(7) - 7 \not> 3(7) + 9$$

$$28 \not> 30.$$

The set of all real numbers that are solutions of an inequality is the **solution set** of the inequality.

The set of all points on the real number line that represent the solution set is the **graph of the inequality.** Graphs of many types of inequalities consist of intervals on the real number line.

The procedures for solving linear inequalities in one variable are much like those for solving linear equations. To isolate the variable you can make use of the **properties of inequalities.** These properties are similar to the properties of equality, but there are two important exceptions. When both sides of an inequality are multiplied or divided by a negative number, *the direction of the inequality symbol must be reversed.* Here is an example.

$$-2 < 5 \qquad \text{Write original inequality.}$$

$$(-3)(-2) > (-3)(5) \qquad \text{Multiply each side by } -3 \text{ and reverse inequality.}$$

$$6 > -15 \qquad \text{New inequality}$$

Two inequalities that have the same solution set are **equivalent inequalities.** The properties listed at the top of the next page describe operations that can be used to create equivalent inequalities.

What You Should Learn:

- How to use properties of inequalities to solve linear inequalities
- How to solve inequalities involving absolute values
- How to solve polynomial inequalities
- How to solve rational inequalities
- How to use inequalities to model and solve real-life problems

Why You Should Learn It:

An inequality can be used to describe the time when a level of real-life quantity is exceeded. For instance, Exercise 70 on page 215 shows how to use a quadratic inequality to determine when the total number of education degrees conferred in the United States exceeds 2.5 million.

Cliff Hollis/Liaison International

Properties of Inequalities

Let a, b, c, and d be real numbers.

1. *Transitive Property*

$a < b$ and $b < c$ ⟹ $a < c$

2. *Addition of Inequalities*

$a < b$ and $c < d$ ⟹ $a + c < b + d$

3. *Addition of a Constant*

$a < b$ ⟹ $a + c < b + c$

4. *Multiplying by a Constant*

For $c > 0$, $a < b$ ⟹ $ac < bc$

For $c < 0$, $a < b$ ⟹ $ac > bc$

Each of the properties above is true if the symbol $<$ is replaced by $\leq$ and $>$ is replaced by $\geq$. For instance, another form of Property 3 would be as follows.

$a \leq b$ ⟹ $a + c \leq b + c$

Solving a Linear Inequality

The simplest type of inequality to solve is a **linear inequality** in a single variable, such as $2x + 3 > 4$. (See Appendix C for help with solving one-step linear inequalities.)

EXAMPLE 1 Solving a Linear Inequality

Solve the inequality

$5x - 7 > 3x + 9.$

Solution

$5x - 7 > 3x + 9$	Write original inequality.
$5x > 3x + 16$	Add 7 to each side.
$5x - 3x > 16$	Subtract $3x$ from each side.
$2x > 16$	Combine like terms.
$x > 8$	Divide each side by 2.

So, the solution set consists of all real numbers that are greater than 8. The interval notation for this solution set is $(8, \infty)$. The number line graph of this solution set is shown in Figure 2.41.

Note that the five inequalities forming the solution steps of Example 1 are all *equivalent* in the sense that each has the same solution set.

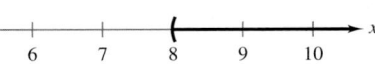

EXAMPLE 2   Solving an Inequality

Solve $1 - \dfrac{3x}{2} \geq x - 4$.

Algebraic Solution

$$1 - \frac{3x}{2} \geq x - 4 \qquad \text{Write original inequality.}$$

$$2 - 3x \geq 2x - 8 \qquad \text{Multiply each side by the LCD.}$$

$$-3x \geq 2x - 10 \qquad \text{Subtract 2 from each side.}$$

$$-5x \geq -10 \qquad \text{Subtract } 2x \text{ from each side.}$$

$$x \leq 2 \qquad \begin{array}{l}\text{Divide each side by } -5 \\ \text{and reverse inequality.}\end{array}$$

The solution set consists of all real numbers that are less than or equal to 2. The interval notation for this solution set is $(-\infty, 2]$. The number line graph of this solution set is shown in Figure 2.42.

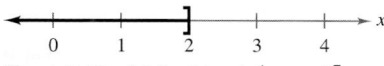

Figure 2.42 *Solution interval:* $(-\infty, 2]$

Graphical Solution

Use a graphing utility to graph $y_1 = 1 - (3x)/2$ and $y_2 = x - 4$ in the same viewing window. In Figure 2.43, you can see that the graphs appear to intersect at the point $(2, -2)$. Use the *intersect* feature of the graphing utility to confirm this. The graph of y_1 lies above the graph of y_2 to the left of their point of intersection, which implies that $y_1 \geq y_2$ for all $x \leq 2$.

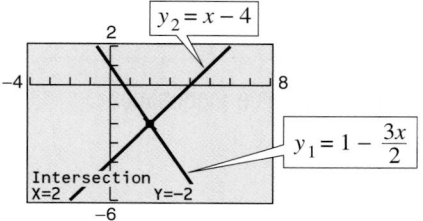

Figure 2.43

Sometimes it is possible to write two inequalities as a **double inequality.** For instance, you can write the two inequalities $-4 \leq 5x - 2$ and $5x - 2 < 7$ more simply as $-4 \leq 5x - 2 < 7$, so you can solve the two inequalities together.

EXAMPLE 3   Solving a Double Inequality

Solve $-3 \leq 6x - 1 < 3$.

Algebraic Solution

$$-3 \leq 6x - 1 < 3 \qquad \text{Write original inequality.}$$

$$-2 \leq 6x < 4 \qquad \text{Add 1 to all three parts.}$$

$$-\frac{1}{3} \leq x < \frac{2}{3} \qquad \text{Divide by 6 and simplify.}$$

The solution set consists of all real numbers that are greater than or equal to $-\frac{1}{3}$ *and* less than $\frac{2}{3}$. The interval notation for this solution set is $\left[-\frac{1}{3}, \frac{2}{3}\right)$. The number line graph of this solution set is shown in Figure 2.44.

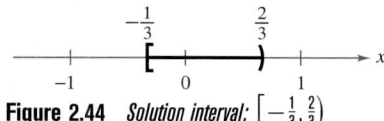

Figure 2.44 *Solution interval:* $\left[-\frac{1}{3}, \frac{2}{3}\right)$

Graphical Solution

Use a graphing utility to graph $y_1 = 6x - 1$, $y_2 = -3$, and $y_3 = 3$ in the same viewing window. In Figure 2.45, you can see that the graphs appear to intersect at the points $\left(-\frac{1}{3}, -3\right)$ and $\left(\frac{2}{3}, 3\right)$. Use the *intersect* feature of the graphing utility to confirm this. The graph of y_1 lies above the graph of y_2 to the right of $\left(-\frac{1}{3}, -3\right)$ *and* the graph of y_1 lies below the graph of y_3 to the left of $\left(\frac{2}{3}, 3\right)$. This implies that $y_2 \leq y_1 < y_3$ when $-\frac{1}{3} \leq x < \frac{2}{3}$.

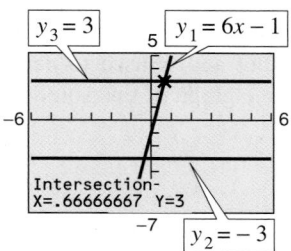

Figure 2.45

Inequalities Involving Absolute Value

You may need to remind your students that $|x| = a$ corresponds to $x = a$ and $x = -a$.

Solving an Absolute Value Inequality

Let x be a variable or an algebraic expression and let a be a real number such that $a \geq 0$.

1. The solutions of $|x| < a$ are all values of x that lie between $-a$ and a.

$$|x| < a \quad \text{if and only if} \quad -a < x < a.$$

2. The solutions of $|x| > a$ are all values of x that are less than $-a$ or greater than a.

$$|x| > a \quad \text{if and only if} \quad x < -a \quad \text{or} \quad x > a.$$

These rules are also valid if $<$ is replaced by $\leq$ and $>$ is replaced by $\geq$.

EXAMPLE 4   Solving Absolute Value Inequalities

Solve each inequality.

a. $|x - 5| < 2$ **b.** $|x - 5| > 2$

Algebraic Solution

a.

$|x - 5| < 2$	Write original inequality.
$-2 < x - 5 < 2$	Equivalent inequalities
$-2 + 5 < x - 5 + 5 < 2 + 5$	Add 5 to all three parts.
$3 < x < 7$	Simplify.

The solution set is all real numbers that are greater than 3 *and* less than 7. The interval notation for this solution set is $(3, 7)$. The number line graph of this solution set is shown in Figure 2.46.

b. The absolute value inequality $|x - 5| > 2$ is equivalent to the following compound inequality.

$$x - 5 < -2 \quad \text{or} \quad x - 5 > 2$$

Solve first inequality: $x - 5 < -2$	Write first inequality.
$x < 3$	Add 5 to each side.
Solve second inequality: $x - 5 > 2$	Write second inequality.
$x > 7$	Add 5 to each side.

The solution is all real numbers that are less than -3 *or* greater than 7. The interval notation for this solution set is $(-\infty, 3) \cup (7, \infty)$. The symbol $\cup$ is called a *union* symbol and is used to denote the combining of two sets. The number line graph of this solution set is shown in Figure 2.47.

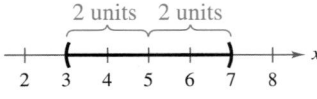

Figure 2.46 $|x - 5| < 2$ **Figure 2.47** $|x - 5| > 2$

Graphical Solution

a. Use a graphing utility to graph $y_1 = |x - 5|$ and $y_2 = 2$ in the same viewing window. In Figure 2.48, you can see that the graphs appear to intersect at the points $(3, 2)$ and $(7, 2)$. Use the *intersect* feature of the graphing utility to confirm this. The graph of y_1 lies below the graph of y_2 when $3 < x < 7$. So, you can approximate the solution set to be all real numbers greater than 3 *and* less than 7.

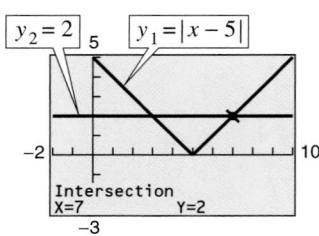

Figure 2.48

b. In Figure 2.48, you can see that the graph of y_1 lies above the graph of y_2 when $x < 3$ *or* when $x > 7$. So, you can approximate the solution set to be all real numbers that are less than 3 *or* greater than 7.

Polynomial Inequalities

To solve a polynomial inequality such as $x^2 - 2x - 3 < 0$, use the fact that a polynomial can change signs only at its zeros (the x-values that make the polynomial equal to zero). Between two consecutive zeros a polynomial must be entirely positive or entirely negative. This means that when the real zeros of a polynomial are put in order, they divide the real number line into intervals in which the polynomial has no sign changes. These zeros are the **critical numbers** of the inequality, and the resulting open intervals are the **test intervals** for the inequality. For instance, the polynomial

$$x^2 - 2x - 3 = (x + 1)(x - 3)$$

has two zeros, $x = -1$ and $x = 3$, which divide the real number line into three test intervals: $(-\infty, -1)$, $(-1, 3)$, and $(3, \infty)$. To solve the inequality $x^2 - 2x - 3 < 0$, you only need to test one value from each test interval.

Finding Test Intervals for a Polynomial

To determine the intervals on which the values of a polynomial are entirely negative or entirely positive, use the following steps.

1. Find all real zeros of the polynomial, and arrange the zeros in increasing order. The zeros of a polynomial are its **critical numbers.**

2. Use the critical numbers of the polynomial to determine its **test intervals.**

3. Choose one representative x-value in each test interval and evaluate the polynomial at that value. If the value of the polynomial is negative, the polynomial will have negative values for *every* x-value in the interval. If the value of the polynomial is positive, the polynomial will have positive values for *every* x-value in the interval.

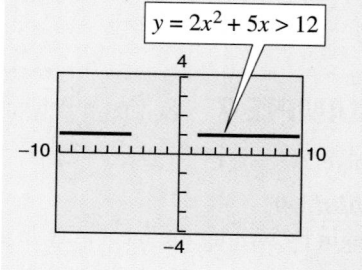
EXAMPLE 5   Investigating Polynomial Behavior

To determine the intervals on which $x^2 - x - 6$ is entirely negative and those on which it is entirely positive, factor the quadratic as

$$x^2 - x - 6 = (x + 2)(x - 3).$$

The critical numbers occur at $x = -2$ and $x = 3$. So, the test intervals for the quadratic are $(-\infty, -2)$, $(-2, 3)$, and $(3, \infty)$. In each test interval, choose a representative x-value and evaluate the polynomial, as shown in the table.

Interval	x-Value	Value of Polynomial	Sign of Polynomial
$(-\infty, -2)$	$x = -3$	$(-3)^2 - (-3) - 6 = 6$	Positive
$(-2, 3)$	$x = 0$	$(0)^2 - (0) - 6 = -6$	Negative
$(3, \infty)$	$x = 5$	$(5)^2 - (5) - 6 = 14$	Positive

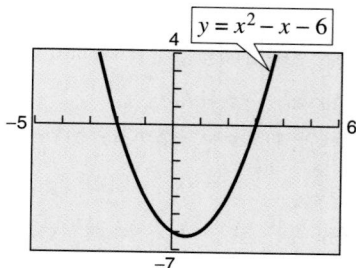

Figure 2.49

The polynomial has negative values for every x in the interval $(-2, 3)$ and positive values for every x in the intervals $(-\infty, -2)$ and $(3, \infty)$. This result is shown graphically in Figure 2.49.

To determine the test intervals for a polynomial inequality, the inequality must first be written in general form with the polynomial on one side.

EXAMPLE 6   Solving a Polynomial Inequality

Solve $2x^2 + 5x > 12$.

Algebraic Solution

$$2x^2 + 5x > 12 \qquad \text{Write original inequality.}$$
$$2x^2 + 5x - 12 > 0 \qquad \text{Write in general form.}$$
$$(x + 4)(2x - 3) > 0 \qquad \text{Factor.}$$

Critical Numbers: $x = -4, x = \frac{3}{2}$

Test Intervals: $(-\infty, -4), \left(-4, \frac{3}{2}\right), \left(\frac{3}{2}, \infty\right)$

Test: Is $(x + 4)(2x - 3) > 0$?

After testing these intervals, you can see that the polynomial $2x^2 + 5x - 12$ is positive in the open intervals $(-\infty, -4)$ and $\left(\frac{3}{2}, \infty\right)$. Therefore, the solution set of the inequality is

$$(-\infty, -4) \cup \left(\tfrac{3}{2}, \infty\right).$$

Graphical Solution

First write the polynomial inequality $2x^2 + 5x > 12$ as $2x^2 + 5x - 12 > 0$. Then use a graphing utility to graph $y = 2x^2 + 5x - 12$. In Figure 2.50, you can see that the graph is *above* the *x*-axis when *x* is less than -4 *or* when *x* is greater than $\frac{3}{2}$. So, you can graphically approximate the solution set to be $(-\infty, -4) \cup \left(\frac{3}{2}, \infty\right)$.

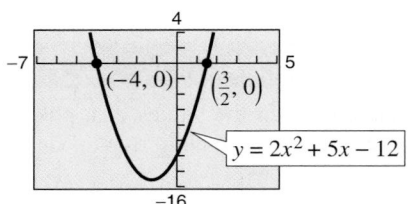

Figure 2.50

EXAMPLE 7   Solving a Polynomial Inequality

Solve $2x^3 - 3x^2 - 32x > -48$

Solution

Begin by writing the inequality in general form.

$$2x^3 - 3x^2 - 32x > -48 \qquad \text{Write original inequality.}$$
$$2x^3 - 3x^2 - 32x + 48 > 0 \qquad \text{Write in general form.}$$
$$x^2(2x - 3) - 16(2x - 3) > 0 \qquad \text{Factor by grouping.}$$
$$(x^2 - 16)(2x - 3) > 0 \qquad \text{Distributive Property}$$
$$(x - 4)(x + 4)(2x - 3) > 0 \qquad \text{Factor difference of two squares.}$$

The critical numbers are $x = -4, x = \frac{3}{2}$, and $x = 4$; and the test intervals are $(-\infty, -4), \left(-4, \frac{3}{2}\right), \left(\frac{3}{2}, 4\right)$, and $(4, \infty)$.

Interval	x-Value	Polynomial Value	Conclusion
$(-\infty, -4)$	$x = -5$	$2(-5)^3 - 3(-5)^2 - 32(-5) + 48 = -117$	Negative
$\left(-4, \frac{3}{2}\right)$	$x = 0$	$2(0)^3 - 3(0)^2 - 32(0) + 48 = 48$	Positive
$\left(\frac{3}{2}, 4\right)$	$x = 2$	$2(2)^3 - 3(2)^2 - 32(2) + 48 = -12$	Negative
$(4, \infty)$	$x = 5$	$2(5)^3 - 3(5)^2 - 32(5) + 48 = 63$	Positive

From this you can conclude that the polynomial $2x^3 - 3x^2 - 32x + 48$ is positive on the open intervals $\left(-4, \frac{3}{2}\right)$ and $(4, \infty)$. Therefore, the solution set consists of all real numbers in the intervals $\left(-4, \frac{3}{2}\right)$ and $(4, \infty)$.

STUDY T!P

When solving a quadratic inequality, be sure you have accounted for the particular type of inequality symbol given in the inequality. For instance, in Example 7, note that the original inequality contained a "greater than" symbol and the solution consisted of two open intervals. If the original inequality had been

$$2x^3 - 3x^2 + 32x \geq -48,$$

the solution would have consisted of the closed interval $\left[-4, \frac{3}{2}\right]$ and the interval $[4, \infty)$.

EXAMPLE 8   Unusual Solution Sets

a. The solution set of

$$x^2 + 2x + 4 > 0$$

consists of the entire set of real numbers, $(-\infty, \infty)$. In other words, the quadratic $x^2 + 2x + 4$ is positive for every real value of x, as indicated in Figure 2.51(a). (Note that this quadratic inequality has *no* critical numbers. In such a case, there is only one test interval—the entire real number line.)

b. The solution set of

$$x^2 + 2x + 1 \le 0$$

consists of the single real number -1, because the graph touches the x-axis only at -1, as shown in Figure 2.51(b).

c. The solution set of

$$x^2 + 3x + 5 < 0$$

is empty. In other words, the quadratic $x^2 + 3x + 5$ is not less than zero for any value of x, as indicated in Figure 2.51(c).

d. The solution set of

$$x^2 - 4x + 4 > 0$$

consists of all real numbers *except* the number 2. In interval notation, this solution set can be written as $(-\infty, 2) \cup (2, \infty)$. The graph of $x^2 - 4x + 4$ lies above the x-axis except at $x = 2$, where it touches it, as indicated in Figure 2.51(d).

STUDY T!P

One of the advantages of technology is that you can solve complicated polynomial inequalities that might be difficult, or even impossible, to factor. For instance, you could use a graphing utility to approximate the solution to the inequality

$$x^3 - 0.26x^2 - 3.1416x + 1.414 < 0.$$

Remind students that they can check the answers to inequality problems in two ways.

Algebraically: Substitute x-values into the original inequality.

Graphically: Sketch the graph of the polynomial written in standard form and note where the graph is relative to the x-axis.

Students can also use a graphing utility to check their answers as indicated in the Study Tip on page 209.

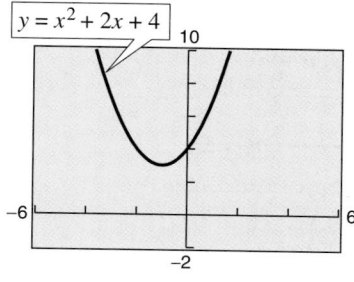

(a)

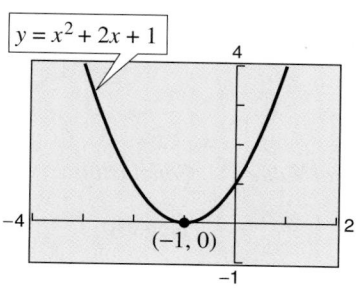

(b)

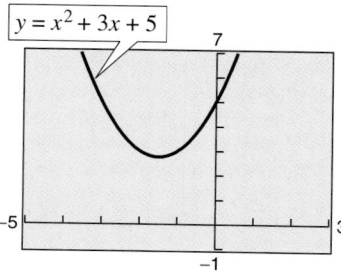

(c)

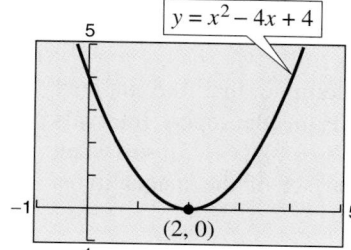

(d)

Figure 2.51

Rational Inequalities

The concepts of critical numbers and test intervals can be extended to inequalities involving rational expressions. To do this, use the fact that the value of a rational expression can change sign only at its *zeros* (the *x*-values for which its numerator is zero) and its *undefined values* (the *x*-values for which its denominator is zero). These two types of numbers make up the *critical numbers* of a rational inequality.

EXAMPLE 9   Solving a Rational Inequality

Solve $\dfrac{2x - 7}{x - 5} \le 3$.

Algebraic Solution

$$\frac{2x - 7}{x - 5} \le 3 \qquad \text{Write original inequality.}$$

$$\frac{2x - 7}{x - 5} - 3 \le 0 \qquad \text{Write in standard form.}$$

$$\frac{2x - 7 - 3x + 15}{x - 5} \le 0 \qquad \text{Write as single fraction.}$$

$$\frac{-x + 8}{x - 5} \le 0 \qquad \text{Simplify.}$$

Now, in standard form you can see that the critical numbers are 5 and 8, and you can proceed as follows.

Critical Numbers: $x = 5, x = 8$

Test Intervals: $(-\infty, 5), (5, 8), (8, \infty)$

Test: Is $\dfrac{-x + 8}{x - 5} \le 0$?

Interval	x-Value	Polynomial Value	Conclusion
$(-\infty, 5)$	$x = 0$	$\dfrac{-0 + 8}{0 - 5} = -\dfrac{8}{5}$	Negative
$(5, 8)$	$x = 6$	$\dfrac{-6 + 8}{6 - 5} = 2$	Positive
$(8, \infty)$	$x = 9$	$\dfrac{-9 + 8}{9 - 5} = -\dfrac{1}{4}$	Negative

By testing these intervals, you can determine that the rational expression $(-x + 8)/(x - 5)$ is negative in the open intervals $(-\infty, 5)$ and $(8, \infty)$. Moreover, because $(-x + 8)/(x - 5) = 0$ when $x = 8$, you can conclude that the solution set of the inequality is $(-\infty, 5) \cup [8, \infty)$.

Graphical Solution

Use a graphing utility to graph

$$y_1 = \frac{2x - 7}{x - 5} \quad \text{and} \quad y_2 = 3$$

in the same viewing window. In Figure 2.52, you can see that the graphs appear to intersect at the point (8, 3). Use the *intersect* feature of the graphing utility to confirm this. The graph of y_1 lies below the graph of y_2 in the intervals $(-\infty, 5)$ and $[8, \infty)$. So, you can graphically approximate the solution set to be all real numbers less than 5 *or* all real numbers greater than or equal to 8.

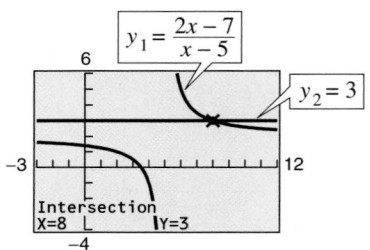

Figure 2.52

Note in Example 9 that $x = 5$ is not included in the solution set because the inequality is undefined when $x = 5$.

Applications

In Section 1.3 you studied the *implied domain* of a function, the set of all x-values for which a function is defined. A common type of implied domain is that used to avoid even roots of negative numbers, as shown in Example 10.

EXAMPLE 10   Finding the Domain of an Expression

Find the domain of

$$\sqrt{64 - 4x^2}.$$

Solution

Because $\sqrt{64 - 4x^2}$ is defined only if $64 - 4x^2$ is nonnegative, the domain is given by $64 - 4x^2 \geq 0$.

$64 - 4x^2 \geq 0$	Write in general form.
$16 - x^2 \geq 0$	Divide each side by 4.
$(4 - x)(4 + x) \geq 0$	Factor.

The inequality has two critical numbers: -4 and 4. A test shows that $64 - 4x^2 \geq 0$ in the *closed interval* $[-4, 4]$. The graph of $y = \sqrt{64 - 4x^2}$, shown in Figure 2.53, confirms that the domain is $[-4, 4]$.

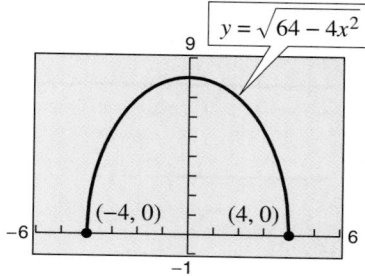

Figure 2.53

EXAMPLE 11   The Height of a Projectile

A projectile is fired straight upward from ground level with an initial velocity of 384 feet per second. During what time period will its height exceed 2000 feet?

Solution

In Section 2.4 you saw that the position of an object moving vertically can be modeled by the *position equation*

$$s = -16t^2 + v_0 t + s_0,$$

where s is the height in feet and t is the time in seconds. In this case, $s_0 = 0$ and $v_0 = 384$. So, you need to solve the inequality $-16t^2 + 384t > 2000$. Using a graphing utility, graph $s = -16t^2 + 384t$ and $s = 2000$, as shown in Figure 2.54. From the graph, you can determine that $-16t^2 + 384t > 2000$ for t between approximately 7.6 and 16.4. You can verify this result algebraically as follows.

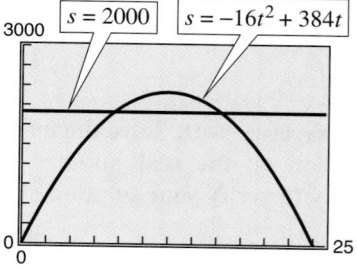

Figure 2.54

$-16t^2 + 384t > 2000$	Write original inequality.
$t^2 - 24t < -125$	Divide by -16 and reverse inequality.
$t^2 - 24t + 125 < 0$	Write in general form.

By the Quadratic Formula the critical numbers are $12 - \sqrt{19}$ and $12 + \sqrt{19}$, or approximately 7.64 and 16.36. A test will verify that the height of the projectile will exceed 2000 feet when $7.64 < t < 16.36$, that is, during the time interval $(7.64, 16.36)$ seconds.

2.5 Exercises

In Exercises 1–4, match the inequality with its graph. [The graphs are labeled (a), (b), (c), and (d).]

(a)
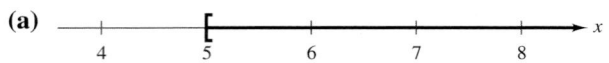

(b)

(c)

(d)

1. $x < 3$

2. $x \geq 5$

3. $-3 < x \leq 4$

4. $0 \leq x \leq \frac{9}{2}$

In Exercises 5–8, determine whether each given value of x is a solution of the inequality.

Inequality   *Values*

5. $5x - 12 > 0$ (a) $x = 3$ (b) $x = -3$
               (c) $x = \frac{5}{2}$ (d) $x = \frac{3}{2}$

6. $-5 < 2x - 1 \leq 1$ (a) $x = -\frac{1}{2}$ (b) $x = -\frac{5}{2}$
               (c) $x = \frac{4}{3}$ (d) $x = 0$

7. $-1 < \dfrac{3 - x}{2} \leq 1$ (a) $x = 0$ (b) $x = \sqrt{5}$
               (c) $x = 1$ (d) $x = 5$

8. $|x - 10| \geq 3$ (a) $x = 13$ (b) $x = -1$
               (c) $x = 14$ (d) $x = 9$

In Exercises 9–18, solve the inequality and sketch the solution on the real number line. Use a graphing utility to verify your solution graphically.

9. $-10x < 40$

10. $2x > 3$

11. $4(x + 1) < 2x + 3$

12. $2x + 7 < 3$

13. $1 < 2x + 3 < 9$

14. $-2 < 3x + 1 < 10$

15. $-8 \leq 1 - 3(x - 2) < 13$

16. $0 \leq 2(x + 4) < 20$

17. $-4 < \dfrac{2x - 3}{3} < 4$

18. $0 \leq \dfrac{x + 3}{2} < 5$

Graphical Analysis **In Exercises 19–24, use a graphing utility to approximate the solution.**

19. $6x > 12$

20. $3x - 1 \leq 5$

21. $5 - 2x \geq 1$

22. $3(x + 1) < x + 7$

23. $-9 < 6x - 1 < 1$

24. $-10 < 4(x - 3) \leq 8$

In Exercises 25–28, use a graphing utility to graph the equation and graphically approximate the values of x that satisfy the specified inequalities. Then solve each inequality algebraically.

Equation   *Inequalities*

25. $y = 2x - 3$ (a) $y \geq 1$ (b) $y \leq 0$

26. $y = \frac{2}{3}x + 1$ (a) $y \leq 5$ (b) $y \geq 0$

27. $y = -\frac{1}{2}x + 2$ (a) $0 \leq y \leq 3$ (b) $y \geq 0$

28. $y = -3x + 8$ (a) $-1 \leq y \leq 3$ (b) $y \leq 0$

In Exercises 29–36, solve the inequality and sketch the solution on the real number line.

29. $|5x| > 10$

30. $|x - 20| \leq 4$

31. $|x - 7| < 6$

32. $|x - 20| \geq 4$

33. $|x + 14| + 3 > 17$

34. $\left| \dfrac{x - 3}{2} \right| \geq 5$

35. $|1 - 2x| < 5$

36. $3|4 - 5x| \leq 9$

In Exercises 37 and 38, use a graphing utility to graph the equation and graphically approximate the values of x that satisfy the specified inequalities. Then solve each inequality algebraically.

Equation   *Inequalities*

37. $y = |x - 3|$ (a) $y \leq 2$ (b) $y \geq 4$

38. $y = \left| \frac{1}{2}x + 1 \right|$ (a) $y \leq 4$ (b) $y \geq 1$

In Exercises 39–44, use absolute value notation to define each interval (or pair of intervals) on the real number line.

39.

40.
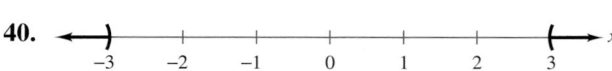

41.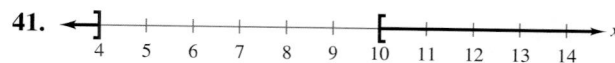

42.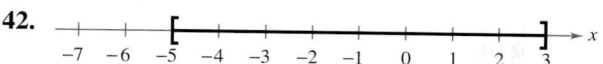

43. All real numbers within 10 units of 12

44. All real numbers whose distances from -3 are more than 5

In Exercises 45–50, solve the inequality and graph the solution on the real number line. Use a graphing utility to verify your solution graphically.

45. $(x + 2)^2 < 25$

46. $(x + 6)^2 \leq 8$

47. $x^2 + 4x + 4 \geq 9$

48. $x^2 - 6x + 9 < 16$

49. $x^3 - 4x \geq 0$

50. $x^4(x - 3) \leq 0$

In Exercises 51–54, use a graphing utility to graph the equation and graphically approximate the values of x that satisfy the specified inequalities. Then solve each inequality algebraically.

Equation	Inequalities
51. $y = -x^2 + 2x + 3$	(a) $y \leq 0$ (b) $y \geq 3$
52. $y = \frac{1}{2}x^2 - 2x + 1$	(a) $y \leq 1$ (b) $y \geq 7$
53. $y = \frac{1}{8}x^3 - \frac{1}{2}x$	(a) $y \geq 0$ (b) $y \leq 6$
54. $y = x^3 - x^2 - 16x + 16$	(a) $y \leq 0$ (b) $y \geq 36$

In Exercises 55–58, solve the inequality and graph the solution on the real number line. Use a graphing utility to verify your solution graphically.

55. $\dfrac{1}{x} - x > 0$

56. $\dfrac{1}{x} - 4 < 0$

57. $\dfrac{x + 6}{x + 1} - 2 < 0$

58. $\dfrac{x + 12}{x + 2} - 3 \geq 0$

In Exercises 59–62, use a graphing utility to graph the equation and graphically approximate the values of x that satisfy the specified inequalities. Then solve each inequality algebraically.

Equation	Inequalities
59. $y = \dfrac{3x}{x - 2}$	(a) $y \leq 0$ (b) $y \geq 6$
60. $y = \dfrac{2(x - 2)}{x + 1}$	(a) $y \leq 0$ (b) $y \geq 8$
61. $y = \dfrac{2x^2}{x^2 + 4}$	(a) $y \geq 1$ (b) $y \leq 2$
62. $y = \dfrac{5x}{x^2 + 4}$	(a) $y \geq 1$ (b) $y \leq 0$

In Exercises 63–68, find the domain of x in the expression.

63. $\sqrt{x - 5}$

64. $\sqrt{x^2 - 4}$

65. $\sqrt[3]{6 - x}$

66. $\sqrt[3]{2x^2 - 8}$

67. $\sqrt[4]{6x + 15}$

68. $\sqrt[4]{4 - x^2}$

69. *Data Analysis* You want to determine whether there is a relationship between an athlete's weight x (in pounds) and the athlete's maximum bench-press weight y (in pounds). The table shows a sample of 12 athletes.

x	165	184	150	210	196	240
y	170	185	200	255	205	295

x	202	170	185	190	230	160
y	190	175	195	185	250	155

(a) Use a graphing utility to plot the data.

(b) A model for this data is $y = 1.266x - 35.766$. Use a graphing utility to graph the equation on the same display used in part (a).

(c) Use the graph to estimate the values of x that estimate a maximum bench-press weight of at least 200 pounds.

(d) Use the graph to write a statement about the accuracy of the model. If you think the graph indicates that an athlete's weight is not a particularly good indicator of the athlete's maximum bench-press weight, list other factors that may influence an individual's maximum bench-press weight.

70. *Educational Degrees* The number D (in thousands) of earned degrees conferred annually in the United States from 1950 to 1995 is approximated by the model

$$D = -0.0977t^2 + 47.1174t + 291.5651$$

where $t = 0$ represents 1950. (Source: U.S. National Center for Education Statistics)

(a) Use a graphing utility to graph the model.

(b) According to this model, estimate when the number of degrees will exceed 2,500,000.

71. Height The height h of two-thirds of the members of a certain population satisfies the inequality

$$\left|\frac{h - 68.5}{2.7}\right| \leq 1$$

where h is measured in inches. Determine the interval on the real number line in which these heights lie.

72. Meteorology A certain electronic device is to be operated in an environment with relative humidity h in the interval defined by

$$|h - 50| \leq 30.$$

What are the minimum and maximum relative humidities for the operation of this device?

73. Music Michael Kasha of Florida State University used physics and mathematics to design a new classical guitar. He used the model for the frequency of the vibrations on a circular plate

$$v = \frac{2.6t}{d^2}\sqrt{\frac{E}{\rho}}$$

where v is the frequency, t is the plate thickness, d is the diameter, E is the elasticity of the plate material, and ρ is the density of the plate material. For fixed values of d, E, and ρ, the graph of the equation is a line, as shown below.

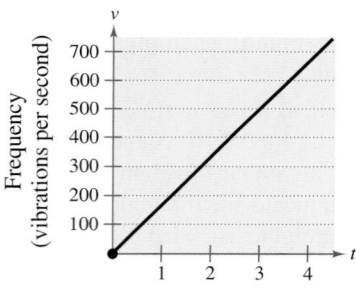

Plate thickness (millimeters)

(a) Estimate the frequency if the plate thickness is 2 millimeters.

(b) Estimate the plate thickness if the frequency is 600 vibrations per second.

(c) Approximate the interval for the plate thickness if the frequency is between 200 and 400 vibrations per second.

(d) Approximate the interval for the frequency if the plate thickness is less than 3 millimeters.

Synthesis

True or False? In Exercises 74 and 75, determine whether the statement is true or false. Justify your answer.

74. If a, b, and c are real numbers, and $a \leq b$, then $ac \leq bc$.

75. If $-10 \leq x \leq 8$, then $-10 \geq -x$ and $-x \geq -8$.

76. Identify the solution of the inequality $|x - a| \geq 2$.

(a)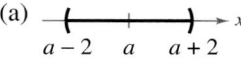

(b)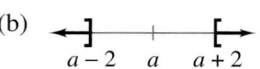

(c)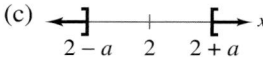

(d)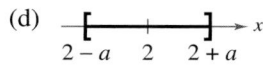

77. Consider the polynomial $(x - a)(x - b)$ and the real number line (see figure).

(a) Identify the points on the line where the polynomial is zero.

(b) In each of the three subintervals of the line, write the sign of each factor and the sign of the product.

(c) For which x-values does a polynomial possibly change signs?

Review

In Exercises 78–81, find the distance between each pair of points. Then find the midpoint of the line segment joining the points.

78. $(-4, 2)$, $(1, 12)$ **79.** $(1, -2)$, $(10, 3)$

80. $(3, 6)$, $(-5, -8)$ **81.** $(0, -3)$, $(-6, 9)$

In Exercises 82–87, sketch a graph of the function.

82. $f(x) = -x^2 + 6$ **83.** $f(x) = \frac{1}{3}(x - 5)^2$

84. $f(x) = -|x + 5| - 6$ **85.** $f(x) = \frac{1}{2}|-x| - 4$

86. $f(x) = -2\sqrt{x - 3} + 7$

87. $f(x) = \sqrt{4 - x} - 10$

In Exercises 88–91, find the inverse of the function.

88. $y = 12x$ **89.** $y = 5x + 8$

90. $y = x^3 + 7$ **91.** $y = \sqrt[3]{x} - 7$

2 Chapter Summary

What did you learn?

Section 2.1

Section 2.2

Section 2.3

Section 2.4

Section 2.5

2 Review Exercises

2.1 In Exercises 1 and 2, determine whether each given value of x is a solution of the equation.

Equation	Values

1. $6 + \dfrac{3}{x - 4} = 5$
   (a) $x = 5$ (b) $x = 0$
   (c) $x = -2$ (d) $x = 1$

2. $6 + \dfrac{2}{x + 3} = \dfrac{6x + 1}{3}$
   (a) $x = -3$ (b) $x = 3$
   (c) $x = 0$ (d) $x = -\frac{2}{3}$

In Exercises 3–6, solve the equation (if possible) and use a graphing utility to verify your solution.

3. $14 + \dfrac{2}{x - 1} = 10$ **4.** $6 - \dfrac{11}{x} = 3 + \dfrac{7}{x}$

5. $\dfrac{9x}{3x - 1} - \dfrac{4}{3x + 1} = 3$

6. $\dfrac{5}{x - 5} + \dfrac{1}{x + 5} = \dfrac{2}{x^2 - 25}$

7. *Monthly Profit* In October, a company's total profit was 12% more than it was in September. The total profit for the two months was $689,000. Find the profit for each month.

8. *Discount Rate* The price of a television set has been discounted $85. The sale price is $340. What is the percent discount?

9. *Mixture Problem* A car radiator contains 10 liters of a 30% antifreeze solution. How many liters will have to be replaced with pure antifreeze if the resulting solution is to be 50% antifreeze?

10. *Starting Positions* A fitness center has two running tracks around a rectangular playing floor. The tracks are 1 meter wide and form semicircles at the narrow ends of the rectangular floor. Determine the distance between the starting positions if two runners must run the same distance to the finish line in one lap around the track.

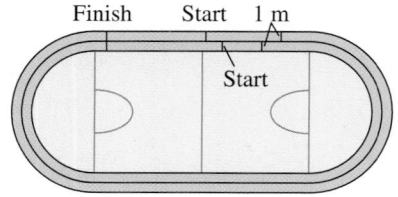

11. *Cost Sharing* A group of farmers agree to share equally in the cost of a $48,000 piece of machinery. If they could find two more farmers to join the group, each person's share of the cost would decrease by $4000. How many farmers are presently in the group?

12. *Venture Capital* An individual is planning on starting a small business that will require $90,000 before any income can be generated. Because it is difficult to borrow for new ventures, the individual wants a group of friends to divide the cost equally for future shares of the profit. Some are willing, but three more are needed so that the price per person will be $2500 less. How many investors are needed?

13. *Average Speed* You drove 56 miles one way on a service call. On the return, your average speed was 8 miles per hour greater and took 10 fewer minutes. What was your average speed on the return trip?

14. *Geometry* A triangle whose area is 80 square inches has a base that is two and a half times its height. Find the base and height of the triangle.

15. *Geometry* A basketball and a baseball have circumferences of 30 inches and $9\frac{1}{4}$ inches, respectively. Find the volume of each.

16. *Sales* The sales manager of a company wants to determine whether there is a relationship between sales and years of experience for sales personnel who have been with the company 4 or fewer years. The table shows the years of experience x for eight of the firm's sales personnel and monthly sales y (in thousands of dollars).

x	1.5	1.0	0.3	3.0
y	46.7	32.9	19.2	48.4

x	4.0	0.5	2.5	1.8
y	51.2	28.5	53.4	35.5

(a) Use the regression capabilities of a graphing utility to find a linear model for the data.

(b) Use a graphing utility to plot the data and graph the model. Interpret the slope of the model in the context of the problem.

(c) Use the model to estimate monthly sales of a salesperson with 5 years of experience.

17. *Stress Test*   A machine part was tested by bending it x centimeters 10 times per minute until it failed (y = time to failure, in hours). The results are recorded in the table.

x	3	6	9	12	15
y	61	56	53	55	48

x	18	21	24	27	30
y	35	36	33	44	23

(a) Use the regression capabilities of a graphing utility to find a linear model for the data.

(b) Use a graphing utility to plot the data and graph the model.

(c) Use the graph to determine if there may have been an error made in conducting one of the tests or in recording the results. If so, eliminate the point and find the model for the remaining data.

2.2 In Exercises 18–21, determine the x- and y-intercepts of the graph of the equation algebraically. Use a graphing utility to verify your answer.

18. $-x + y = 3$

19. $x - 5y = 20$

20. $y = x^2 - 9x + 8$

21. $y = 25 - x^2$

In Exercises 22 and 23, use a graphing utility to graph the equation and approximate the x- and y-intercepts.

22. $y = -|x + 5| - 2$

23. $y = 6 - 2|x - 3|$

In Exercises 24–29, use a graphing utility to approximate any solutions (accurate to three decimal places) of the equation.

24. $5(x - 2) - 1 = 0$

25. $12 - 5(x - 7) = 0$

26. $3x^3 - 2x + 4 = 0$

27. $\frac{1}{3}x^3 - x + 4 = 0$

28. $x^4 - 3x + 1 = 0$

29. $6 - \frac{1}{2}x^2 + \frac{5}{6}x^4 = 0$

In Exercises 30–33, determine algebraically any points of intersection of the graphs of the equations. Use a graphing utility to verify your answer(s).

30. $3x + 5y = -7$
$\quad\ -x - 2y = \ \ 3$

31. $\ x - y = \ \ 3$
$\quad 2x + y = 12$

32. $x^2 + 2y = 14$
$\quad 3x + 4y = 1$

33. $y = -x + 7$
$\quad y = 2x^3 - x + 9$

2.3 In Exercises 34–37, write in standard form.

34. $6 + \sqrt{-25}$

35. $-\sqrt{-12} + 3$

36. $-2i^2 + 7i$

37. $-i^2 - 4i$

In Exercises 38–49, perform the operations and write the result in standard form.

38. $(7 + 5i) + (-4 + 2i)$

39. $\left(\dfrac{\sqrt{2}}{2} - \dfrac{\sqrt{2}}{2}i\right) - \left(\dfrac{\sqrt{2}}{2} + \dfrac{\sqrt{2}}{2}i\right)$

40. $5i(13 - 8i)$

41. $(1 + 6i)(5 - 2i)$

42. $(10 - 8i)(2 - 3i)$

43. $i(6 + i)(3 - 2i)$

44. $(3 + 7i)^2 + (3 - 7i)^2$

45. $(4 - i)^2 - (4 + i)^2$

46. $\dfrac{6 + i}{i}$

47. $\dfrac{3 + 2i}{5 + i}$

48. $\dfrac{4}{-3i}$

49. $\dfrac{1}{(2 + i)^4}$

In Exercises 50–53, plot the complex number in the complex plane.

50. $2 - 5i$

51. $-1 + 4i$

52. $-6i$

53. $7i$

2.4 In Exercises 54–63, use any method to solve the equation. Use a graphing utility to verify your solution(s).

54. $6x = 3x^2$

55. $15 + x - 2x^2 = 0$

56. $(x + 4)^2 = 18$

57. $16x^2 = 25$

58. $x^2 - 12x + 30 = 0$

59. $x^2 + 6x - 3 = 0$

60. $2x^2 + 9x - 5 = 0$

61. $-x^2 - x + 15 = 0$

62. $x^2 - 4x - 10 = 0$

63. $-2x^2 - 13x = 0$

In Exercises 64–85, solve the equation (if possible) and use a graphing utility to verify your solution.

64. $3x^3 - 26x^2 + 16x = 0$

65. $216x^4 - x = 0$

66. $5x^4 - 12x^3 = 0$

67. $4x^3 - 6x^2 = 0$

68. $\sqrt{x + 4} = 3$

69. $\sqrt{x - 2} - 8 = 0$

70. $2\sqrt{x} - 5 = 0$

71. $\sqrt{3x - 2} = 4 - x$

72. $\sqrt{2x + 3} + \sqrt{x - 2} = 2$

73. $5\sqrt{x} - \sqrt{x - 1} = 6$

74. $(x - 1)^{2/3} - 25 = 0$

75. $(x + 2)^{3/4} = 27$

76. $(x + 4)^{1/2} + 5x(x + 4)^{3/2} = 0$

77. $8x^2(x^2 - 4)^{1/3} + (x^2 - 4)^{4/3} = 0$

78. $3\left(1 - \dfrac{1}{5t}\right) = 0$

79. $\dfrac{1}{x - 2} = 3$

80. $\dfrac{4}{(x - 4)^2} = 1$

81. $\dfrac{1}{(t + 1)^2} = 1$

82. $|x - 5| = 10$

83. $|2x + 3| = 7$

84. $|x^2 - 3| = 2x$

85. $|x^2 - 6| = x$

86. *Population*   The population P of Wyoming (in thousands) from 1990 through 1997 can be approximated by the model

$$P = -0.435t^2 + 7.125t + 452.542$$

where $t = 0$ represents 1990.   (Source: U.S. Bureau of the Census)

(a) Use a graphing utility to graph the model.

(b) Use the *zoom* and *trace* features of a graphing utility to determine when the population exceeded 465,000.

(c) According to the model, when will the population reach 490,000?

(d) Verify your answer to part (c) numerically by creating a table of values for the model.

(e) Do you think this is an accurate model for the population? Explain.

87. *Life Insurance*   The number y of life insurance companies in the United States from 1989 through 1996 can be modeled by

$$y = 7.73t^2 - 127.7t + 2164.4$$

where $t = 0$ represents 1990.   (Source: American Council of Life Insurance)

(a) Use a graphing utility to graph the model.

(b) Use the model to determine the year when there were about 2000 life insurance companies.

(c) Is this model accurate for predicting the number of life insurance companies in the future? Explain.

2.5   In Exercises 88–105, solve the inequality and graph the solution on the real number line. Use a graphing utility to verify your solution.

88. $8x - 3 < 6x + 15$

89. $\frac{1}{2}(3 - x) > \frac{1}{3}(2 - 3x)$

90. $-2 < -x + 7 \le 10$

91. $-6 \le 3 - 2(x - 5) < 14$

92. $|x - 2| < 1$

93. $|x| \le 4$

94. $\left|x - \frac{3}{2}\right| \ge \frac{3}{2}$

95. $|x - 3| > 4$

96. $4|3 - 2x| \le 16$

97. $|x + 9| + 7 > 19$

98. $x^2 - 2x \ge 3$

99. $4x^2 - 23x \le 6$

100. $x^3 - 16x \ge 0$

101. $12x^3 - 20x^2 < 0$

102. $\dfrac{x - 5}{3 - x} < 0$

103. $\dfrac{2}{x + 1} \le \dfrac{3}{x - 1}$

104. $\dfrac{3x + 8}{x - 3} \le 4$

105. $\dfrac{x + 8}{x + 5} - 2 < 0$

106. *Accuracy of Measurement*   The side of a square is measured as 20.8 inches with a possible error of $\frac{1}{16}$ inch. Using these measurements, determine the interval containing the area of the square.

107. *Fuel Consumption*   The total fuel consumption F (in billions of gallons) in the United States from 1985 through 1996 can be approximated by the model

$$F = 0.107t^2 - 0.235t + 122.446$$

where t is the time in years, with $t = 5$ corresponding to 1985.   (Source: U.S. Federal Highway Administration)

(a) Use a graphing utility to graph the model over the indicated years.

(b) According to this model, estimate the year of an annual fuel consumption of more than 165 billion gallons. Solve algebraically and graphically.

Synthesis

True or False?   **In Exercises 108–110, determine whether the statement is true or false. Justify your answer.**

108. The graph of a function may have two distinct y-intercepts.

109. The sum of two complex numbers cannot be a real number.

110. The sign of the slope of the regression line is always positive.

111. In your own words, explain the difference between an identity and a conditional equation.

112. Describe the relationship among the x-intercepts of a graph, the zeros of a function, and the solutions of an equation.

113. Consider the linear equation $ax + b = 0$.

(a) What is the sign of the solution if $ab > 0$?

(b) What is the sign of the solution if $ab < 0$?

Chapter Project *Mozart and the Golden Ratio*

Music and mathematics have always been closely related. In this project, you will discover a curious relationship between the structure of Mozart's (1756–1791) piano sonatas and Euclid's (ca. 300 B.C.) famous golden ratio.   (Source: John F. Putz, *Mathematics Magazine,* October 1995)

Sonatas can be naturally divided into two parts: the *exposition,* which introduces the musical theme, and the *development and recapitulation,* which develop and repeat the theme. The data at the right shows all of Mozart's piano sonata movements that have these two parts. The first column identifies the sonata movement. The second column, labeled x, identifies the length of the development and recapitulation in measures. The third column, labeled y, identifies the length of the exposition in measures.

a. Enter the points (x, y) in a graphing utility and sketch a scatter plot of the points. Describe the relationship between x and y.

b. Use the statistical capabilities of a graphing utility to find the least squares regression line for the data. How well does the line fit the data? Explain. Interpret the meaning of the slope and the y-intercept.

c. The **golden section** was defined by Euclid as the point B on a line segment AC such that

$$\frac{AB}{BC} = \frac{BC}{AC}.$$ Assume that $AC = 1$ and $BC = r$.

Then this proportion can be written as $\dfrac{1 - r}{r} = \dfrac{r}{1}$.

Use a graphing utility to graph $y_1 = \dfrac{1 - x}{x}$ and $y_2 = \dfrac{x}{1}$

and approximate their point of intersection in Quadrant I. This value is called the golden ratio. How does it compare to the line in part (b)?

Sonata	x	y	Sonata	x	y
279, I	62	38	310, I	84	49
279, II	46	28	311, I	73	39
279, III	102	56	330, I	92	58
280, I	88	56	330, III	103	68
280, II	36	24	332, I	136	93
280, III	113	77	332, III	155	90
281, I	69	40	333, I	102	63
281, II	60	46	333, III	50	31
282, I	18	15	457, I	93	74
282, III	63	39	533, I	137	102
283, I	67	53	533, II	76	46
283, II	23	14	545, I	45	28
283, III	171	102	547a, I	118	78
284, I	76	51	570, I	130	79
309, I	97	58			

For Question 1, you might also suggest another approach to your students: use a graphing utility to create a scatter plot of x (vertical axis) versus $x + y$ (horizontal axis) and then use the graphing utility's regression capabilities to find the best-fitting line for the data. How does the slope of this line relate to the golden ratio?

Questions for Further Exploration

1. Use the data for Mozart's sonatas to complete a table that calculates ratios of the form $x/(x + y)$. How do these ratios compare with the golden ratio?

2. The Fibonacci Sequence is given by 1, 1, 2, 3, 5, 8, 13, 21, 34, ...

  (a) Explain how to generate succeeding terms in the sequence.

  (b) Complete and expand the table, which shows decimal approximations of ratios of adjacent terms in the sequence.

$\frac{1}{1}$	$\frac{1}{2}$	$\frac{2}{3}$	$\frac{3}{5}$	$\frac{5}{8}$	$\frac{8}{13}$	$\frac{13}{21}$	$\frac{21}{34}$
1.000	0.500	0.667					

What can you conclude about the ratios?

3. *Research Project*   Obtain a copy of the article "The Golden Section and the Piano Sonatas of Mozart," John F. Putz, *Mathematics Magazine*, Vol. 68, No. 4, October 1995, pp. 275–282. Read the article and write a short paper about other aspects of Mozart's sonatas and the golden ratio.

2 Chapter Test

Take this test as you would take a test in class. After you are done, check your work against the answers in the back of the book.

In Exercises 1 and 2, solve the equation and use a graphing utility to verify your solution.

1. $\dfrac{12}{x} - 7 = -\dfrac{27}{x} + 6$

2. $\dfrac{4}{3x - 2} - \dfrac{9x}{3x + 2} = -3$

The *Interactive* CD-ROM and *Internet* versions of this text provide answers to the Chapter Tests and Cumulative Tests. They also offer Chapter Pre-Tests (which test key skills and concepts covered in previous chapters) and Chapter Post-Tests, both of which have randomly generated exercises with diagnostic capabilities.

In Exercises 3–8, perform the operation.

3. $(-8 - 3i) + (-1 - 15i)$

4. $\left(10 + \sqrt{-20}\right) - \left(4 - \sqrt{-14}\right)$

5. $(2 + i)(6 - i)$

6. $(4 + 3i)^2 - (5 + i)^2$

7. $\dfrac{8 + 5i}{6 - i}$

8. $\dfrac{i}{4 - 5i} + \dfrac{5i}{2 + i}$

In Exercises 9–12, use a graphing utility to graph the equation. Determine the number of x-intercepts of the graph and compare these intercepts with the real zeros of the function.

9. $y = 3x^2 + 1$

10. $y = x^3 + x$

11. $y = x^3 - 4x^2 + 5x$

12. $y = 2 + 8x^{-2}$

In Exercises 13–16, use any method to solve the equation. Check your solutions algebraically and graphically.

13. $x^2 - 10x + 9 = 0$

14. $x^2 + 12x - 2 = 0$

15. $4x^2 - 81 = 0$

16. $5x^2 + 14x - 3 = 0$

In Exercises 17–20, find all real solutions of the equation. Check your solution(s) algebraically and graphically.

17. $3x^3 - 4x^2 - 12x + 16 = 0$

18. $x + \sqrt{22 - 3x} = 6$

19. $(x^2 + 6)^{2/3} = 16$

20. $|8x - 1| = 21$

In Exercises 21–23, solve the inequality and sketch the solution on the real number line. Use a graphing utility to verify your solution.

21. $-\dfrac{5}{6} < x - 2 < \dfrac{1}{8}$

22. $2|x - 8| < 10$

23. $\dfrac{3 - 5x}{2 + 3x} < -2$

t	C
-1	389
0	402
1	416
2	434
3	447
4	465
5	484
6	504

24. The table shows the number of local telephone calls C (in billions) in the United States from 1989 through 1996, where $t = 0$ represents 1990. Use the regression capabilities of a graphing utility to find a linear model for the data. Determine algebraically and graphically when the annual number of local calls will be about 600 billion. (Source: U.S. Federal Communications Commission)

25. You buy a bag of tomatoes for $1.62 per pound. The weight that is listed on the bag is 4.55 pounds. The scale is accurate to within 1 ounce. How much might you have been undercharged or overcharged?

P–2 Cumulative Test

Take this test to review the material from earlier chapters. After you are
done, check your work against the answers in the back of the book.

In Exercises 1–3, simplify the expression.

1. $\dfrac{14x^2y^{-3}}{32x^{-1}y^2}$

2. $8\sqrt{60} - 2\sqrt{135} - \sqrt{15}$ **3.** $\sqrt{28x^4y^3}$

In Exercises 4–6, perform the operations and simplify the result.

4. $4x - [2x + 5(2 - x)]$ **5.** $(x - 2)(x^2 + x - 3)$ **6.** $\dfrac{2}{x + 3} - \dfrac{1}{x + 1}$

In Exercises 7–9, factor the expression completely.

7. $25 - (x - 2)^2$ **8.** $x - 5x^2 - 6x^3$ **9.** $54 - 16x^3$

10. Find the midpoint of the line segment connecting the points $\left(-\frac{7}{2}, 4\right)$ and
$(6.5, -8)$. Then find the distance between the points.

11. Find the standard form of the equation of a circle with center at $\left(-\frac{1}{2}, -8\right)$ and
radius of $\frac{5}{4}$.

In Exercises 12–14, use point plotting to sketch a graph of the equation.

12. $x - 3y + 12 = 0$ **13.** $y = x^2 - 9$ **14.** $y = \sqrt{4 - x}$

**In Exercises 15–17, (a) find the equation of the line that satisfies the given
conditions and (b) find three additional points that lie on that line.**

15. The line contains the points $(-5, 8)$ and $\left(\frac{1}{2}, -6\right)$.

16. The line contains the point $\left(-\frac{1}{2}, 1\right)$ and has a slope of -2.

17. The line has an undefined slope and contains the point $\left(-\frac{3}{7}, \frac{1}{8}\right)$.

18. Does the graph at the right represent y as a function of x? Explain.

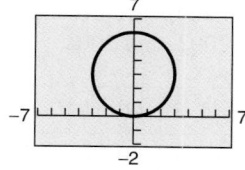

FIGURE FOR 18

**In Exercises 19 and 20, evaluate the function at each specified value of the
independent variable and simplify.**

19. $f(x) = \dfrac{x}{x - 2}$

20. $f(x) = \begin{cases} 3x - 8, & x \le -\frac{5}{3} \\ 3x^2 + 9x - 8, & x > -\frac{5}{3} \end{cases}$

   (a) $f(6)$ (b) $f(2)$ (c) $f(s + 2)$ (a) $f\left(-\frac{5}{3}\right)$ (b) $f(-1)$ (c) $f(0)$

21. Use a graphing utility to graph the function $f(x) = 2|x - 5| - |x + 5|$.
Then determine the open intervals over which the function is increasing,
decreasing, or constant.

22. Compare the graphs of each function with the graph of $y = \sqrt[3]{x}$.

   (a) $r(x) = \dfrac{1}{2}\sqrt[3]{x}$ (b) $h(x) = \sqrt[3]{x} + 2$ (c) $g(x) = \sqrt[3]{x + 2}$

In Exercises 23–26, evaluate the indicated function for

$f(x) = -x^2 + 3x - 10$ and $g(x) = 4x + 1.$

23. $(f + g)(-4)$ **24.** $(g - f)\left(\frac{3}{4}\right)$ **25.** $(g \circ f)(-2)$ **26.** $(fg)(-1)$

27. Plot the complex number $-5 + 4i$ in the complex plane.

28. Write the quadratic equation $9x(x - 1) = -4x^2 - 6$ in general form.

In Exercises 29–32, use a graphing utility to graph the equation and approximate any x-intercepts of the graph. Find any x-intercepts algebraically and compare your results to those you approximated graphically.

29. $y = 4x^3 - 12x^2 + 8x$ **30.** $y = 12x^3 - 84x^2 + 120x$

31. $y = |2x - 3| - 5$ **32.** $y = \sqrt{x^2 + 1} + x - 9$

In Exercises 33 and 34, solve the equation for the indicated variable.

33. Solve for X: $Z = \sqrt{R^2 - X^2}$ **34.** Solve for p: $L = \dfrac{k}{3\pi r^2 p}$

In Exercises 35 and 36, find the constant C such that the ordered pair is a solution point of the equation.

35. $y = C\sqrt{x + 1}$, $(3, 8)$ **36.** $x + C(y + 2) = 0$, $(4, 3)$

In Exercises 37–39, use a graphing utility to approximate the solution to the inequality. Verify your answer algebraically.

37. $\dfrac{x}{5} - 6 \le -\dfrac{x}{2} + 6$ **38.** $2x^2 + x \ge 15$ **39.** $(x - 4)|x| > 0$

40. The total sales S (in millions of dollars) for the Cooper Tire and Rubber Company from 1989 through 1998 is shown in the table, where $t = 0$ represents 1990. Use the regression capabilities of a graphing utility to find a linear model that represents the data. Estimate algebraically the total sales for 2000, 2002, and 2004.   (Source: Cooper Tire and Rubber Company)

t	-1	0	1	2	3	4	5	6	7	8
S	866.8	895.9	1001.1	1174.7	1193.6	1403.2	1493.6	1619.3	1813.0	1876.1

41. A bowling ball has a volume of about 332.38 cubic inches. Find the radius of the bowling ball (accurate to three decimal places).

42. A rectangular plot of land with a perimeter of 546 feet has a width of x.

(a) Express the area of the plot as a function of x.

(b) Use a graphing utility to graph the area function. What is the domain of the function?

(c) Approximate the dimensions of the plot if its area is 15,000 square feet.

Polynomial and Rational Functions

Pictures Colour Library Ltd./Leo de Wys

The Big Picture

In this chapter you will learn how to

❏ sketch and analyze graphs of quadratic and polynomial functions.
❏ use long division and synthetic division to divide polynomials by other polynomials.
❏ determine the number of rational and real zeros of polynomial functions, and find them.
❏ determine the domain, find asymptotes, and sketch the graphs of rational functions.

U.S. wheat production increased from 2183 million bushels in 1995 to 2527 million bushels in 1997, while the price per bushel dropped from $4.55 to $3.45.   (Source: U.S. Department of Agriculture)

Important Vocabulary

As you encounter each new vocabulary term in this chapter, add the term and its definition to your notebook glossary.

- polynomial function of x with degree n (p. 226)
- constant function (p. 226)
- linear function (p. 226)
- quadratic function (p. 226)
- parabola (p. 226)
- axis of symmetry (p. 227)
- vertex (p. 227)
- standard form of a quadratic function (p. 229)
- continuous (p. 237)
- Leading Coefficient Test (p. 239)

- extrema (p. 240)
- relative minimum (p. 240)
- relative maximum (p. 240)
- repeated zero (p. 242)
- multiplicity (p. 242)
- Intermediate Value Theorem (p. 244)
- long division of polynomials (p. 250)
- Division Algorithm (p. 251)
- synthetic division (p. 253)
- Remainder Theorem (p. 254)
- Factor Theorem (p. 254)

- Rational Zero Test (p. 256)
- upper bound (p. 258)
- lower bound (p. 258)
- Fundamental Theorem of Algebra (p. 264)
- Linear Factorization Theorem (p. 264)
- conjugates (p. 266)
- rational function (p. 271)
- vertical asymptote (p. 272)
- horizontal asymptote (p. 272)
- slant (or oblique) asymptote (p. 284)

Additional Resources   Text-specific additional resources are available to help you do well in this course. See page xvi for details.

3.1 Quadratic Functions

The Graph of a Quadratic Function

In this and the next section, you will study the graphs of polynomial functions.

Definition of Polynomial Function

Let n be a nonnegative integer and let $a_n, a_{n-1}, \ldots, a_2, a_1, a_0$ be real numbers with $a_n \neq 0$. The function

$$f(x) = a_n x^n + a_{n-1} x^{n-1} + \cdots + a_2 x^2 + a_1 x + a_0$$

is called a **polynomial function of x with degree n.**

Polynomial functions are classified by degree. For instance, the polynomial function

$$f(x) = a, \quad a \neq 0 \qquad \text{Constant function}$$

has degree 0 and is called a **constant function.** In Chapter 1, you learned that the graph of this type of function is a horizontal line. The polynomial function

$$f(x) = mx + b, \quad m \neq 0 \qquad \text{Linear function}$$

has degree 1 and is called a **linear function.** You also learned in Chapter 1 that the graph of the linear function $f(x) = mx + b$ is a line whose slope is m and whose y-intercept is $(0, b)$. In this section you will study second-degree polynomial functions, which are called **quadratic functions.**

Definition of Quadratic Function

Let a, b, and c be real numbers with $a \neq 0$. The function

$$f(x) = ax^2 + bx + c \qquad \text{Quadratic function}$$

is called a **quadratic function.**

Often real-life data can be modeled by quadratic functions. For instance, the table shows height h (in feet) of a projectile fired from a height of 6 feet with an initial velocity of 256 feet per second at any time t (in seconds). A quadratic model for the data in the table is $h(t) = -16t^2 + 256t + 6$ for $0 \leq t \leq 16$.

t	0	2	4	6	8	10	12	14	16
h	6	454	774	966	1030	966	774	454	6

The graph of a quadratic function is a special type of U-shaped curve called a **parabola.** Parabolas occur in many real-life applications—especially those involving reflective properties, such as satellite dishes or flashlight reflectors. You will study these properties in Section 8.1.

What You Should Learn:

- How to analyze graphs of quadratic functions
- How to write quadratic functions in standard form and use the results to sketch graphs of functions
- How to use quadratic functions to model and solve real-life problems

Why You Should Learn It:

Quadratic functions can be used to model data to analyze consumer behavior. For instance, Exercise 78 on page 236 shows how a quadratic function can model VCR usage in the United States.

Mary K. Kenny/PhotoEdit

All parabolas are symmetric with respect to a line called the **axis of symmetry,** or simply the **axis** of the parabola. The point where the axis intersects the parabola is the **vertex** of the parabola, as shown in Figure 3.1. If the leading coefficient a is positive, the graph of $f(x) = ax^2 + bx + c$ is a parabola that opens upward; and if the leading coefficient a is negative, the graph of $f(x) = ax^2 + bx + c$ is a parabola that opens downward.

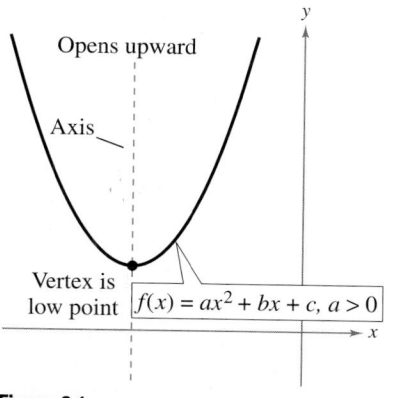
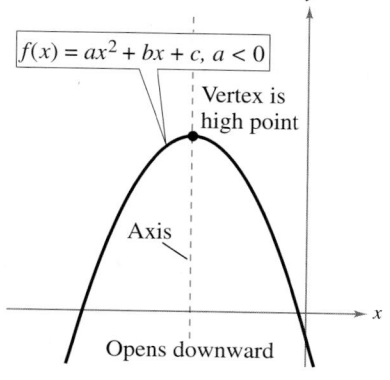

Figure 3.1

The simplest type of quadratic function is

$$f(x) = ax^2.$$

Its graph is a parabola whose vertex is $(0, 0)$. If $a > 0$, the vertex is the *minimum* point on the graph; and if $a < 0$, the vertex is the *maximum* point on the graph, as shown in Figure 3.2.

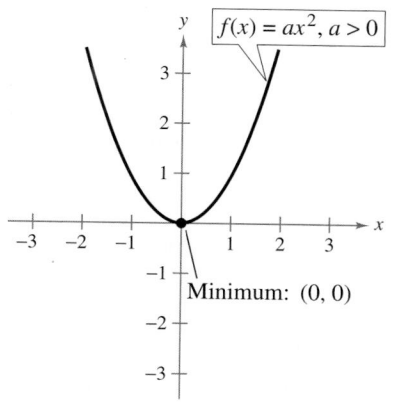
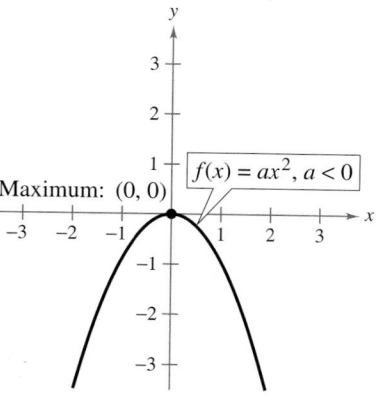

Figure 3.2

When sketching the graph of $f(x) = ax^2$, it is helpful to use the graph of $y = x^2$ as a reference, as discussed in Section 1.5. There you saw that when $a > 1$, the graph of $y = af(x)$ is a vertical stretch of the graph of $y = f(x)$. When $0 < a < 1$, the graph of $y = af(x)$ is a vertical shrink of the graph of $y = f(x)$. This is demonstrated again in Example 1.

Library of Functions

The graph of a quadratic function is called a parabola. Graph $y_1 = x^2$ and $y_2 = |x|$ in the same viewing window. Zoom in near the origin and compare the shape of the two graphs. Which graph grows faster as x gets larger and larger? Why does the definition of a quadratic function require that $a \neq 0$?

Consult the Library of Functions Summary inside the front cover for a description of the quadratic function.

EXAMPLE 1   Graphing Simple Quadratic Functions

Describe how the graph of each function is related to the graph of $y = x^2$.

a. $f(x) = \dfrac{1}{3}x^2$ **b.** $g(x) = 2x^2$

c. $h(x) = -x^2 + 1$ **d.** $k(x) = (x + 2)^2 - 3$

Solution

a. Compared with $y = x^2$, each output of f "shrinks" by a factor of $\frac{1}{3}$. The result is a parabola that opens upward and is broader than the parabola represented by $y = x^2$, as shown in Figure 3.3(a).

b. Compared with $y = x^2$, each output of g "stretches" by a factor of 2, creating a narrower parabola, as shown in Figure 3.3(b).

c. With respect to the graph of $y = x^2$, the negative coefficient in $h(x) = -x^2 + 1$ reflects the graph *downward* and the positive constant term shifts the vertex *up* one unit. The graph of h is shown in Figure 3.3(c).

d. With respect to the graph of $y = x^2$, the graph of $k(x) = (x + 2)^2 - 3$ is obtained by a horizontal shift two units *to the left* and a vertical shift three units *down*, as shown in Figure 3.3(d).

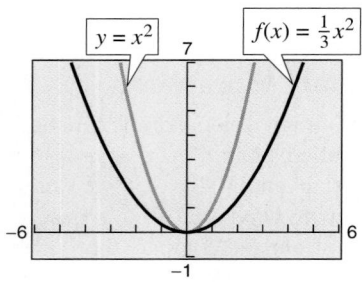

(a)

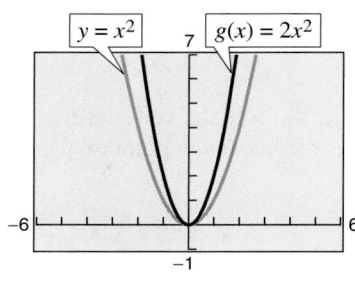

(b)

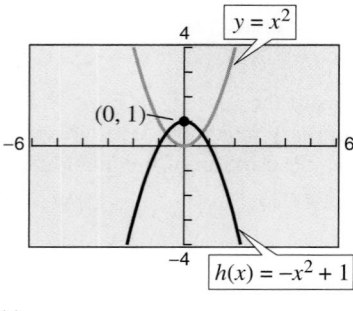

(c)

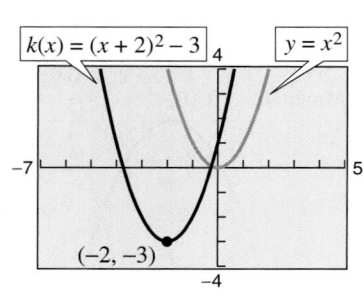

(d)

Figure 3.3

Recall from Section 1.5 that the graphs of $y = f(x \pm c)$, $y = f(x) \pm c$, $y = -f(x)$, and $y = f(-x)$ are rigid transformations of the graph of $y = f(x)$.

$y = f(x \pm c)$	Horizontal shift	$y = -f(x)$	Reflection in x-axis
$y = f(x) \pm c$	Vertical shift	$y = f(-x)$	Reflection in y-axis

Emphasize that the technique illustrated in Example 1 (comparing functions to the "base" function $y = x^2$) is very useful when analyzing functions and preparing to graph them. This kind of exercise (and Exercises 9–12 in the exercise set) also helps build conceptual understanding. You may want to cover extra examples of this technique during class for practice.

STUDY T!P

In Example 1, note that the coefficient a determines how widely the parabola given by $f(x) = ax^2$ opens. If $|a|$ is small, the parabola opens more widely than if $|a|$ is large.

The *Interactive* CD-ROM and *Internet* versions of this text show every example with its solution; clicking on the *Try It!* button brings up similar problems. Guided Examples and Integrated Examples show step-by-step solutions to additional examples. Integrated Examples are related to several concepts in the section.

The Standard Form of a Quadratic Function

The equation in Example 1(d) is written in the **standard form**

$$f(x) = a(x - h)^2 + k.$$

This form is especially convenient for sketching a parabola because it identifies the vertex of the parabola as (h, k).

Standard Form of a Quadratic Function

The quadratic function

$$f(x) = a(x - h)^2 + k, \qquad a \neq 0$$

is said to be in **standard form**. The graph of f is a parabola whose axis is the vertical line $x = h$ and whose vertex is the point (h, k). If $a > 0$, the parabola opens upward, and if $a < 0$, the parabola opens downward.

EXAMPLE 2   Identifying the Vertex of a Quadratic Function

Describe the graph of

$$f(x) = 2x^2 + 8x + 7$$

and identify the vertex.

Solution

Write the quadratic function in standard form by completing the square. Recall that the first step is to factor out any coefficient of x^2 that is different from 1.

To prepare for rewriting a function of $f(x)$ in standard form, review the process of completing the square for an algebraic expression, paying special attention to problems in which $a \neq 1$.

$$
\begin{aligned}
f(x) &= 2x^2 + 8x + 7 && \text{Write original function.}\\
&= 2(x^2 + 4x) + 7 && \text{Factor 2 out of } x\text{-terms.}\\
&= 2(x^2 + 4x + 4 - 4) + 7 && \text{Because } b = 4, \text{ add and subtract}\\
&&& (b/2)^2 = 4 \text{ within parentheses.}
\end{aligned}
$$

$$\left(\frac{b}{2}\right)^2$$

$$
\begin{aligned}
&= 2(x^2 + 4x + 4) - 2(4) + 7 && \text{Regroup terms.}\\
&= 2(x + 2)^2 - 1 && \text{Write in standard form.}
\end{aligned}
$$

From the standard form, you can see that the graph of f is a parabola that opens upward with vertex $(-2, -1)$, as shown in Figure 3.4.

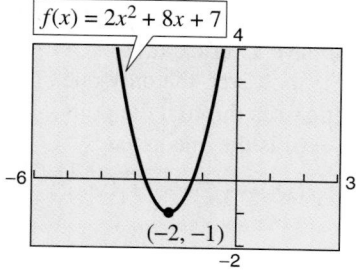

Figure 3.4

To find the x-intercepts of the graph of $f(x) = ax^2 + bx + c$, solve the equation $ax^2 + bx + c = 0$. If $ax^2 + bx + c$ does not factor, you can use the Quadratic Formula to find the x-intercepts, or a graphing utility to approximate the x-intercepts. Remember, however, that a parabola may have no x-intercept.

EXAMPLE 3   Writing a Quadratic Function in Standard Form

Describe the graph of $f(x) = -x^2 + 6x - 8$. Identify any x-intercepts.

Solution

$$f(x) = -x^2 + 6x - 8 \qquad \text{Write original function.}$$

$$= -(x^2 - 6x) - 8 \qquad \text{Factor } -1 \text{ out of } x\text{-terms.}$$

$$= -(x^2 - 6x + 9 - 9) - 8 \qquad \text{Because } b = 6, \text{ add and subtract}$$
$$\left(\frac{b}{2}\right)^2 \qquad (b/2)^2 = 9 \text{ within parentheses.}$$

$$= -(x^2 - 6x + 9) - (-9) - 8 \qquad \text{Regroup terms.}$$

$$= -(x - 3)^2 + 1 \qquad \text{Write in standard form.}$$

The graph of f is a parabola that opens downward with vertex at $(3, 1)$, as shown in Figure 3.5. The x-intercepts are determined as follows.

$$-x^2 + 6x - 8 = 0$$

$$x^2 - 6x + 8 = 0$$

$$(x - 2)(x - 4) = 0$$

$$x = 2, x = 4$$

So, the x-intercepts are $(2, 0)$ and $(4, 0)$, as shown in Figure 3.5.

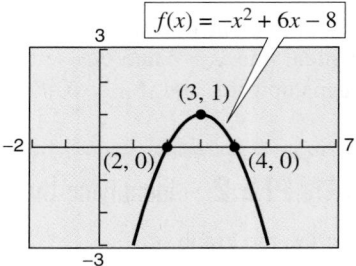

Figure 3.5

EXAMPLE 4   Finding the Equation of a Parabola in Standard Form

Find the standard form of the equation for the parabola that has its vertex at $(1, 2)$ and passes through the point $(3, -6)$, as shown in Figure 3.6.

Solution

Because the parabola has a vertex at $(h, k) = (1, 2)$, the equation has the form

$$f(x) = a(x - 1)^2 + 2. \qquad \text{Standard form}$$

Because the parabola passes through the point $(3, -6)$, it follows that $f(3) = -6$. So, you obtain

$$-6 = a(3 - 1)^2 + 2$$

$$-6 = 4a + 2$$

$$-2 = a.$$

The equation in standard form is $f(x) = -2(x - 1)^2 + 2$. Try graphing $f(x) = -2(x - 1)^2 + 2$ with a graphing utility to confirm that its vertex is $(1, 2)$ and that it passes through the point $(3, -6)$.

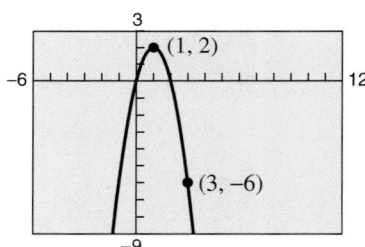

Figure 3.6

STUDY T!P

In Example 4, there are infinitely many different parabolas that have a vertex at $(1, 2)$. Of these, however, the only one that passes through the point $(3, -6)$ is the one given by

$$f(x) = -2(x - 1)^2 + 2.$$

Applications

Many applications involve finding the maximum or minimum value of a quadratic function. By writing the quadratic function $f(x) = ax^2 + bx + c$ in standard form,

$$f(x) = a\left(x + \frac{b}{2a}\right)^2 + \left(c - \frac{b^2}{4a}\right)$$

you can see that the vertex occurs at $x = -b/(2a)$, which implies the following.

1. If $a > 0$, f has a *minimum* that occurs at

$$x = -\frac{b}{2a}.$$

2. If $a < 0$, f has a *maximum* that occurs at

$$x = -\frac{b}{2a}.$$

EXAMPLE 5   The Maximum Height of a Baseball

A baseball is hit 3 feet above ground at a velocity of 100 feet per second and at an angle of 45 degrees with respect to level ground. The path of the baseball is given by the function $f(x) = -0.0032x^2 + x + 3$, where $f(x)$ is the height of the baseball (in feet) and x is the distance from home plate (in feet). What is the maximum height reached by the baseball? (See Example 7 in Section 1.3.)

A computer simulation of this example appears in the *Interactive* CD-ROM and *Internet* versions of this text.

Algebraic Solution

For this quadratic function, you have

$$f(x) = ax^2 + bx + c$$

$$= -0.0032x^2 + x + 3$$

which implies that $a = -0.0032$ and $b = 1$. Because the function has a maximum when $x = -b/(2a)$, you can conclude that the baseball reaches its maximum height when

$$x = -\frac{b}{2a}$$

$$= -\frac{1}{2(-0.0032)}$$

$$= 156.25 \text{ feet}$$

from home plate. At this distance, the maximum height is

$$f(156.25) = -0.0032(156.25)^2 + 156.25 + 3$$

$$= 81.125 \text{ feet}.$$

Graphical Solution

Use a graphing utility to graph $y = -0.0032x^2 + x + 3$ so that you can see the important features of the parabola. In Figure 3.7 the graph appears to have a maximum near $x = 150$. Use the *maximum* feature of the graphing utility or the *zoom* and *trace* features to approximate the maximum height on the graph to be $y \approx 81.125$ feet at $x \approx 156.25$. Note that when using the *zoom* and *trace* features of a graphing utility, you might have to change the y-scale in order to avoid a graph that is "too flat."

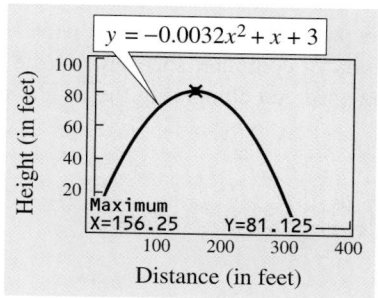

Figure 3.7

EXAMPLE 6 Charitable Contributions

According to a survey conducted by *Independent Sector*, the percent of their income that Americans give to charities is related to their household income. For families with an annual income of $100,000 or less, the percent is approximately

$$P = 0.0014x^2 - 0.1529x + 5.855, \quad 5 \le x \le 100$$

where P is the percent of annual income given and x is the annual income (in thousands of dollars). According to this model, what income level corresponds to the minimum percent of charitable contributions?

Algebraic Solution

Use the fact that the minimum point of the parabola occurs when $x = -b/(2a)$. For this function, you have $a = 0.0014$ and $b = -0.1529$. So,

$$x = -\frac{b}{2a}$$

$$= -\frac{-0.1529}{2(0.0014)}$$

$$\approx 54.6.$$

From this x-value, you can conclude that the minimum percent corresponds to an income level of about $54,600.

Graphical Solution

Use a graphing utility to graph

$$y_1 = 0.0014x^2 - 0.1529x + 5.855$$

for $5 \le x \le 100$, as shown in Figure 3.8. The graph appears to have a minimum near $x = 55$. Use the *minimum* feature of the graphing utility or the *zoom* and *trace* features to approximate the minimum point of the parabola to be $x \approx 54.6$. So, the minimum point corresponds to an income level of about $54,600.

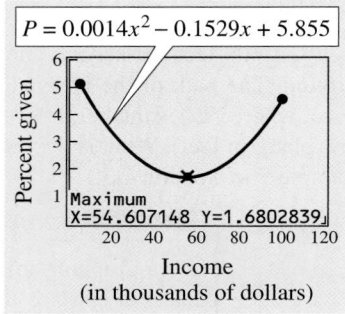

Figure 3.8

Writing About Math *Finding an Equation for a Curve*

The parabola in the figure below has an equation of the form

$$y = ax^2 + bx - 4.$$

Find the equation for this parabola in two different ways, by hand and with technology (graphing utility or computer software). Write a paragraph describing the methods you used and comparing the results of the two methods.

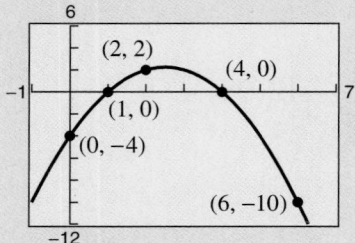

3.1 Exercises

In Exercises 1–8, match the quadratic function with the correct graph. [The graphs are labeled (a), (b), (c), (d), (e), (f), (g), and (h).]

(a)

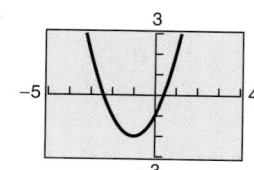

(b)

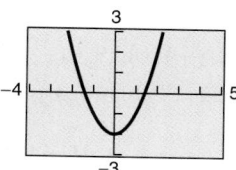

(c)

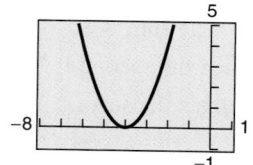

(d)

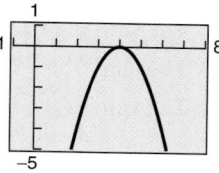

(e)

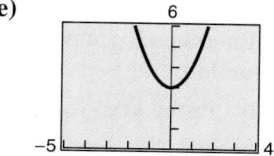

(f)

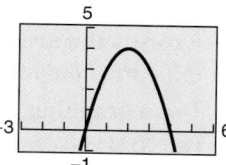

(g)

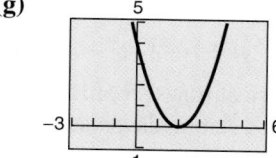

(h)

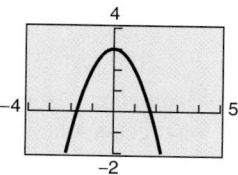

1. $f(x) = (x - 2)^2$

2. $f(x) = (x + 4)^2$

3. $f(x) = x^2 - 2$

4. $f(x) = 3 - x^2$

5. $f(x) = 4 - (x - 2)^2$

6. $f(x) = (x + 1)^2 - 2$

7. $f(x) = x^2 + 3$

8. $f(x) = -(x - 4)^2$

Exploration **In Exercises 9–12, use a graphing utility to graph each equation. Describe how the graph of each equation is related to the graph of $y = x^2$.**

9. (a) $y = \frac{1}{2}x^2$

(b) $y = -\frac{1}{8}x^2$

(c) $y = \frac{3}{2}x^2$

(d) $y = -3x^2$

10. (a) $y = x^2 + 1$

(b) $y = x^2 - 1$

(c) $y = x^2 + 3$

(d) $y = x^2 - 3$

11. (a) $y = (x - 1)^2$

(b) $y = (x + 1)^2$

(c) $y = (x - 3)^2$

(d) $y = (x + 3)^2$

12. (a) $y = -\frac{1}{2}(x - 2)^2 + 1$

(b) $y = \frac{1}{2}(x - 2)^2 + 1$

(c) $y = -\frac{1}{2}(x + 2)^2 - 1$

(d) $y = \frac{1}{2}(x + 2)^2 - 1$

In Exercises 13–26, sketch the graph of the quadratic function. Identify the vertex and intercepts. Use a graphing utility to verify your results.

13. $f(x) = 25 - x^2$

14. $f(x) = x^2 - 7$

15. $f(x) = \frac{1}{2}x^2 - 4$

16. $f(x) = 16 - \frac{1}{4}x^2$

17. $f(x) = (x + 4)^2 - 3$

18. $f(x) = (x - 6)^2 + 3$

19. $h(x) = x^2 - 8x + 16$

20. $g(x) = x^2 + 2x + 1$

21. $f(x) = x^2 - x + \frac{5}{4}$

22. $f(x) = x^2 + 3x + \frac{1}{4}$

23. $f(x) = -x^2 + 2x + 5$

24. $f(x) = -x^2 - 4x + 1$

25. $h(x) = 4x^2 - 4x + 21$

26. $f(x) = 2x^2 - x + 1$

In Exercises 27–34, use a graphing utility to graph the quadratic function. Identify the vertex and intercepts. Then check your results algebraically by completing the square.

27. $f(x) = -(x^2 + 2x - 3)$

28. $f(x) = -(x^2 + x - 30)$

29. $g(x) = x^2 + 8x + 11$

30. $f(x) = x^2 + 10x + 14$

31. $f(x) = 2x^2 - 16x + 31$

32. $f(x) = -4x^2 + 24x - 41$

33. $g(x) = \frac{1}{2}(x^2 + 4x - 2)$

34. $f(x) = \frac{3}{5}(x^2 + 6x - 5)$

In Exercises 35–38, find an equation for the parabola. Use a graphing utility to graph the equation and verify your result.

35.

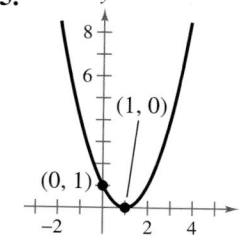

36.

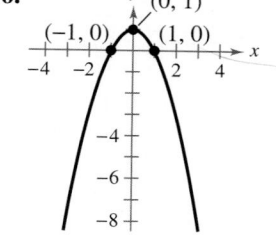

37.

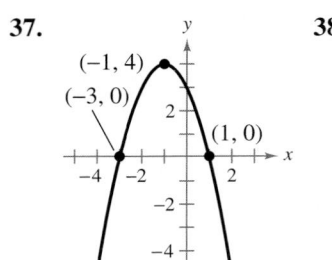

38.

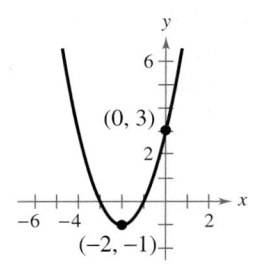

In Exercises 39–46, find the quadratic function that has the indicated vertex and whose graph passes through the given point. Confirm your result with a graphing utility.

39. Vertex: $(-2, 5)$; Point: $(0, 9)$

40. Vertex: $(4, -1)$; Point: $(2, 3)$

41. Vertex: $(3, 4)$; Point: $(1, 2)$

42. Vertex: $(2, 3)$; Point: $(0, 2)$

43. Vertex: $(-2, -2)$; Point: $(-1, 0)$

44. Vertex: $\left(-\frac{1}{4}, \frac{3}{2}\right)$; Point: $(-2, 0)$

45. Vertex: $\left(\frac{5}{2}, -\frac{3}{4}\right)$; Point: $(-2, 4)$

46. Vertex: $\left(-\frac{5}{2}, 0\right)$; Point: $\left(-\frac{7}{2}, -\frac{16}{3}\right)$

Graphical Reasoning **In Exercises 47–50, determine the x-intercepts of the graph visually. How do the x-intercepts correspond to the solutions of the quadratic equation when $y = 0$?**

47.

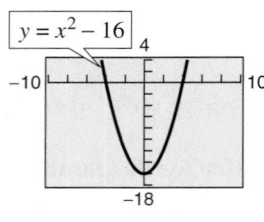

48.

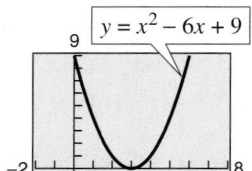

49.

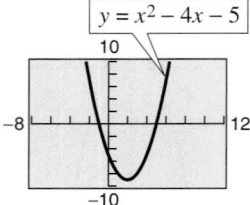

50.

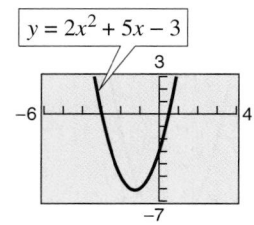

In Exercises 51–56, use a graphing utility to graph the quadratic function. Find the x-intercepts of the graph and compare them with the solutions of the corresponding quadratic equation when $y = 0$.

51. $y = x^2 - 4x$ **52.** $y = -2x^2 + 10x$

53. $y = 2x^2 - 7x - 30$ **54.** $y = 4x^2 + 25x - 21$

55. $y = -\frac{1}{2}(x^2 - 6x - 7)$ **56.** $y = \frac{7}{10}(x^2 + 12x - 45)$

In Exercises 57–60, find two quadratic functions, one that opens upward and one that opens downward, whose graphs have the given x-intercepts. (There are many correct answers.)

57. $(-1, 0), (3, 0)$ **58.** $(0, 0), (10, 0)$

59. $(-3, 0), \left(-\frac{1}{2}, 0\right)$ **60.** $\left(-\frac{5}{2}, 0\right), (2, 0)$

In Exercises 61–64, find two positive real numbers whose product is a maximum.

61. The sum is 110.   **62.** The sum is S.

63. The sum of the first and twice the second is 24.

64. The sum of the first and 3 times the second is 42.

Maximum Area **In Exercises 65 and 66, consider a rectangle of length x and perimeter P.**

(a) Express the area A as a function of x and determine the domain of the function.

(b) Use a graphing utility to graph the area function.

(c) Use the graph to approximate the length and width of the rectangle of maximum area, and verify algebraically.

65. $P = 100$ feet   **66.** $P = 36$ meters

67. *Geometry* An indoor physical fitness room consists of a rectangular region with a semicircle on each end. The perimeter of the room is to be a 200-meter running track.

(a) Draw a diagram to represent the problem. Let x and y represent the length and width of the rectangular region.

(b) Determine the radius of the semicircular ends of the track. Determine the distance, in terms of y, around the two semicircular parts of the track.

(c) Use the result of part (b) to write an equation, in terms of x and y, for the distance traveled in one lap around the track. Solve for y.

(d) Use the result of part (c) to write the area A of the rectangular region as a function of x.

(e) Use a graphing utility to graph the area function of part (d). Use the graph to approximate the dimensions that will produce a maximum area of the rectangle.

68. *Numerical, Graphical, and Analytical Analysis* A rancher has 200 feet of fencing to enclose two adjacent rectangular corrals. Use the following methods to determine the dimensions that will produce a maximum enclosed area.

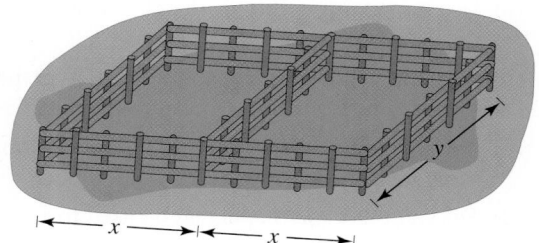

(a) Complete six rows of a table such as the one below. (The first two rows are shown.)

x	y		Area
2	$\frac{1}{3}[200 - 4(2)]$	$2xy = 256$
4	$\frac{1}{3}[200 - 4(4)]$	$2xy \approx 491$

(b) Use a graphing utility to generate additional rows of the table in part (a). Use the table to estimate the dimensions that will produce the maximum enclosed area.

(c) Write the area A as a function of x.

(d) Use a graphing utility to graph the area function. Use the graph to approximate the dimensions that will produce the maximum enclosed area.

(e) Write the area function in standard form to find algebraically the dimensions that will produce the maximum area.

(f) Compare your results from parts (b), (d), and (e).

69. *Business* A manufacturer of lighting fixtures has daily production costs of

$$C = 800 - 10x + 0.25x^2$$

where C is the total cost (in dollars) and x is the number of units produced. How many fixtures should be produced each day to yield a minimum cost?

70. *Business* A textile manufacturer has daily production costs of

$$C = 10,000 - 110x + 0.45x^2$$

where C is the total cost (in dollars) and x is the number of units produced. How many units should be produced each day to yield a minimum cost?

71. *Business* The profit P (in dollars) for a company is

$$P = -0.0002x^2 + 140x - 250,000$$

where x is the number of units sold. What sales level will yield maximum profit?

72. *Business* The profit P (in hundreds of dollars) that a company makes depends on the amount x (in hundreds of dollars) the company spends on advertising according to the model

$$P = 230 + 20x - 0.5x^2.$$

What expenditure for advertising results in the maximum profit?

73. *Trajectory of a Ball* The height y (in feet) of a ball thrown by a child is

$$y = -\frac{1}{12}x^2 + 2x + 4$$

where x is the horizontal distance (in feet) from where the ball is thrown.

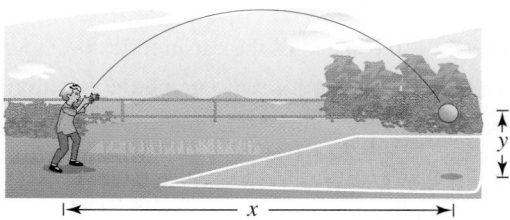

(a) Use a graphing utility to graph the path of the ball.

(b) How high is the ball when it leaves the child's hand? (*Hint:* Find y when $x = 0$.)

(c) How high is the ball when it is at its maximum height?

(d) How far from the child does the ball strike the ground?

74. *Maximum Height of a Dive* The path of a diver is

$$y = -\frac{4}{9}x^2 + \frac{24}{9}x + 12$$

where y is the height (in feet) and x is the horizontal distance (in feet) from the end of the diving board. What is the maximum height of the dive? Verify your answer using a graphing utility.

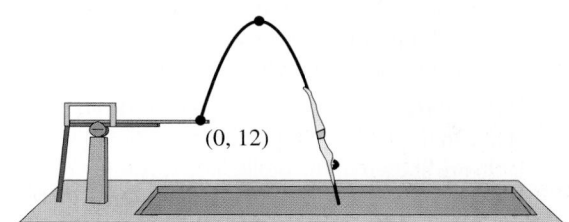

75. Forestry The number of board feet V in a 16-foot log is approximated by the model

$$V = 0.77x^2 - 1.32x - 9.31, \quad 5 \le x \le 40$$

where x is the diameter (in inches) of the log at the small end. (One board foot is a measure of volume equivalent to a board that is 12 inches wide, 12 inches long, and 1 inch thick.)

(a) Use a graphing utility to graph the function.

(b) Estimate the number of board feet in a 16-foot log with a diameter of 16 inches. Use a graphing utility to verify your answer.

(c) Estimate the diameter of a 16-foot log that scaled 500 board feet when the lumber was sold. Use a graphing utility to verify your answer.

76. Automobile Aerodynamics The number of horsepower y required to overcome wind drag on a certain automobile is approximated by

$$y = 0.002s^2 + 0.005s - 0.029, \quad 0 \le s \le 100$$

where s is the speed of the car in miles per hour.

(a) Use a graphing utility to graph the function.

(b) Graphically estimate the maximum speed of the car if the power required to overcome wind drag is not to exceed 10 horsepower. Verify your result algebraically.

77. Graphical Analysis For certain years from 1950 to 1990, the average annual per capita consumption C of cigarettes by Americans (18 and older) can be modeled by $C = 3248.89 + 108.64t - 2.97t^2$ for $0 \le t \le 40$, where t is the year, with $t = 0$ corresponding to 1950. (Source: U.S. Department of Agriculture)

(a) Use a graphing utility to graph the model.

(b) Use the graph of the model to approximate the maximum average annual consumption. Beginning in 1966, all cigarette packages were required by law to carry a health warning. Do you think the warning had any effect? Explain.

(c) In 1960, the U.S. population (18 and over) was 116,530,000. Of those, about 48,500,000 were smokers. What was the average annual cigarette consumption *per smoker* in 1960? What was the average daily cigarette consumption *per smoker*?

78. Data Analysis The number y (in millions) of VCRs in use in the United States for the years 1987 through 1996 are shown in the table. The variable t represents time (in years), with $t = 7$ corresponding to 1987.

t	7	8	9	10	11	12	13	14	15	16
y	43	51	58	63	67	69	72	74	77	79

(Source: Television Bureau of Advertising, Inc.)

(a) Use a graphing utility to sketch a scatter plot of the data.

(b) Use the regression capabilities of a graphing utility to fit a quadratic model to the data.

(c) Use a graphing utility to graph the model in the same viewing window as the scatter plot.

(d) Do you think the model can be used to estimate VCR utilization in the year 2005? Explain.

Synthesis

True or False? In Exercises 79 and 80, determine whether the statement is true or false. Justify your answer.

79. The function $f(x) = -12x^2 - 1$ has no x-intercepts.

80. The graphs of $f(x) = -4x^2 - 10x + 7$ and $g(x) = 12x^2 + 30x + 1$ have the same axis of symmetry.

81. Think About It The profits P (in millions of dollars) for a company are modeled by a quadratic function of the form $P = at^2 + bt + c$, where t represents the year. If you were president of the company, which of the models would you prefer? Explain your reasoning.

(a) a is positive and $t \ge -b/(2a)$.

(b) a is positive and $t \le -b/(2a)$.

(c) a is negative and $t \ge -b/(2a)$.

(d) a is negative and $t \le -b/(2a)$.

Review

In Exercises 82–85, determine algebraically any points of intersection of the graphs of the equations. Verify your results using the *intersect* feature of a graphing utility.

82. $x + y = 8$
$-\frac{2}{3}x + y = 6$

83. $y = 3x - 10$
$y = \frac{1}{4}x + 1$

84. $y = 9 - x^2$
$y = x + 3$

85. $y = x^3 + 2x - 1$
$y = -2x + 15$

In Exercises 86–89, perform the operation and write the result in standard form.

86. $(6 - i) - (2i + 11)$

87. $(2i + 5)^2 - 21$

88. $(3i + 7)(-4i + 1)$

89. $(4 - i)^3$

3.2   Polynomial Functions of Higher Degree

Graphs of Polynomial Functions

You should be able to sketch accurate graphs of polynomial functions of degrees 0, 1, and 2. The graphs of polynomial functions of degree greater than 2 are more difficult to sketch by hand. However, in this section you will learn how to recognize some of the basic features of the graphs of polynomial functions.

The graph of a polynomial function is **continuous**. Essentially, this means that the graph of a polynomial function has no breaks, holes, or gaps, as shown in Figure 3.9. Another feature of the graph of a polynomial function is that it has only smooth, rounded turns, as shown in Figure 3.10(a). It cannot have a sharp, pointed turn such as the one shown in Figure 3.10(b).

What You Should Learn:

- How to use transformations to sketch graphs of polynomial functions
- How to use the Leading Coefficient Test to determine the end behavior of graphs of polynomial functions
- How to find and use zeros of polynomial functions to sketch their graphs
- How to use the Intermediate Value Theorem to help locate zeros of polynomial functions

Why You Should Learn It:

You can use polynomial functions to model various aspects of nature, such as the growth of a red oak tree, as shown in Exercise 98 on page 248.

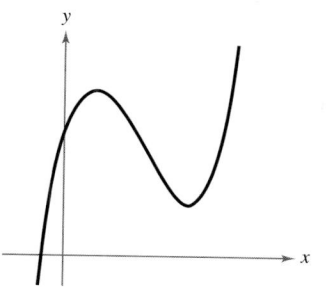

(a) Polynomial functions have continuous graphs.

Figure 3.9

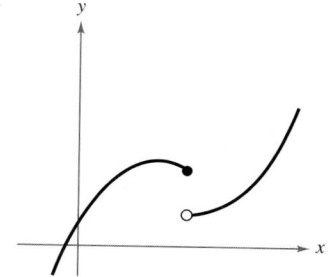

(b) Functions with graphs that are not continuous are not polynomial functions.

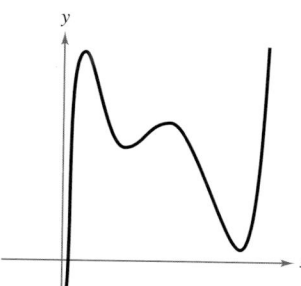

(a) Polynomial functions have smooth, rounded graphs.

Figure 3.10

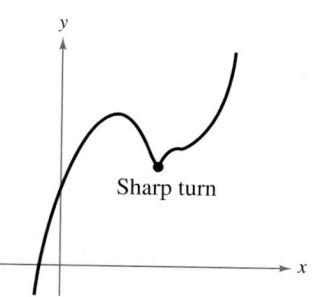

Sharp turn

(b) Graphs of polynomial functions cannot have sharp turns.

The Granger Collection

Informally, you can say that a function is continuous if its graph can be drawn with a pencil without lifting the pencil from the paper.

The polynomial functions that have the simplest graphs are monomials of the form $f(x) = x^n$, where n is an integer greater than zero.

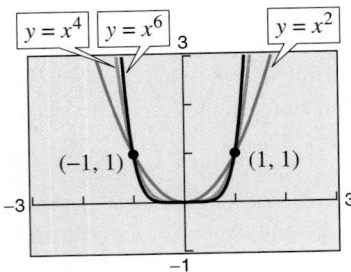

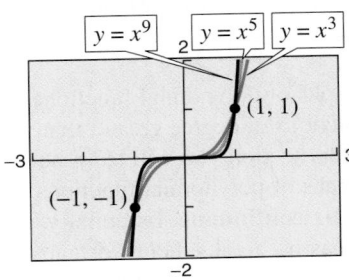

If n is even, the graph of $y = x^n$ touches the axis at the x-intercept.

Figure 3.11

If n is odd, the graph of $y = x^n$ crosses the axis at the x-intercept.

In Figure 3.11, you can see that when n is *even* the graph is similar to the graph of $f(x) = x^2$, and when n is *odd* the graph is similar to the graph of $f(x) = x^3$. Moreover, the greater the value of n, the flatter the graph is on the interval $(-1, 1)$.

Exploration

Use a graphing utility to graph $y = x^n$ with $n = 2$, 4, and 8. (Use the viewing window $-1.5 \leq x \leq 1.5$ and $-1 \leq y \leq 6$.) Compare the graphs. In the interval $(-1, 1)$, which graph is on the bottom? Outside the interval $(-1, 1)$, which graph is on the bottom?

Use a graphing utility to graph $y = x^n$ with $n = 3$, 5, and 7. (Use the viewing window $-1.5 \leq x \leq 1.5$ and $-4 \leq y \leq 4$.) Compare the graphs. In the intervals $(-\infty, -1)$ and $(0, 1)$, which graph is on the bottom? In the intervals $(-1, 0)$ and $(1, \infty)$, which graph is on the bottom?

EXAMPLE 1 Sketching Transformations of Polynomial Functions

Sketch the graph of each polynomial function.

a. $f(x) = -x^5$ **b.** $g(x) = x^4 + 1$ **c.** $h(x) = (x + 1)^4$

Solution

a. Because the degree of $f(x) = -x^5$ is odd, the graph is similar to the graph of $y = x^3$. Moreover, the negative coefficient reflects the graph in the x-axis, as shown in Figure 3.12(a).

b. The graph of $g(x) = x^4 + 1$ is an upward shift, by one unit, of the graph of $y = x^4$, as shown in Figure 3.12(b).

c. The graph of $h(x) = (x + 1)^4$ is a left shift, by one unit, of the graph of $y = x^4$, as shown in Figure 3.12(c).

The *Interactive* CD-ROM and *Internet* versions of this text offer a built-in graphing calculator, which can be used with the Examples, Explorations, and Exercises.

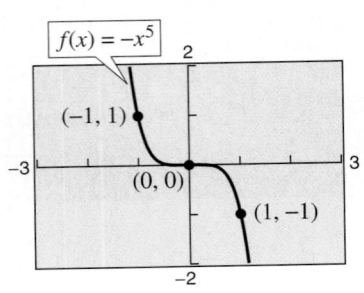

(a)

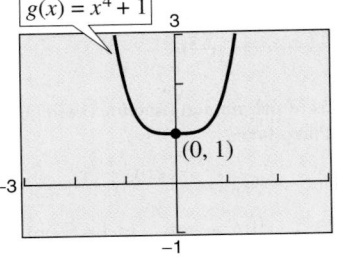

(b)

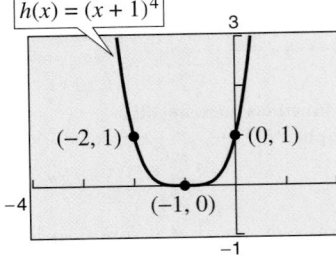

(c)

Figure 3.12

The Leading Coefficient Test

In Example 1, note that all three graphs eventually rise or fall without bound as x moves to the right. Whether the graph of a polynomial eventually rises or falls can be determined by the function's degree (even or odd) and by its leading coefficient, as indicated in the **Leading Coefficient Test.**

Leading Coefficient Test

As x moves without bound to the left or to the right, the graph of the polynomial function $f(x) = a_nx^n + \cdots + a_1x + a_0$ eventually rises or falls in the following manner.

1. When n is odd:

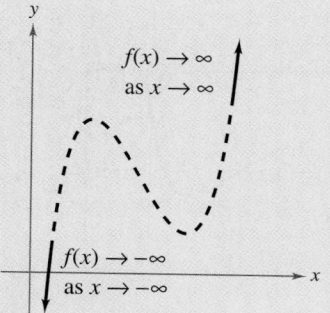 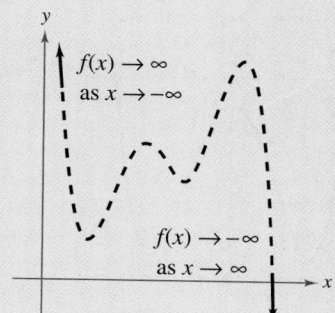

If the leading coefficient is positive $(a_n > 0)$, the graph falls to the left and rises to the right.

If the leading coefficient is negative $(a_n < 0)$, the graph rises to the left and falls to the right.

2. When n is even:

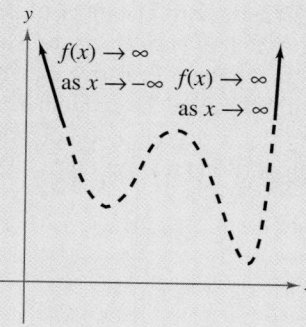 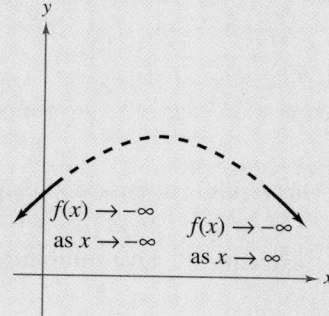

If the leading coefficient is positive $(a_n > 0)$, the graph rises to the left and right.

If the leading coefficient is negative $(a_n < 0)$, the graph falls to the left and right.

Note that the dashed portions of the graphs indicate that the test determines *only* the right and left behavior of the graph.

Exploration

For each function, identify the degree of the function and whether the degree of the function is even or odd. Identify the leading coefficient and note whether the leading coefficient is positive or negative. Use a graphing utility to graph each function. Describe the relationship between the degree and leading coefficient of the function and the behavior of the ends of the graph of the function.

a. $y = x^3 - 2x^2 - x + 1$

b. $y = 2x^5 + 2x^2 - 5x + 1$

c. $y = -2x^5 - x^2 + 5x + 3$

d. $y = -x^3 + 5x - 2$

e. $y = 2x^2 + 3x - 4$

f. $y = x^4 - 3x^2 + 2x - 1$

g. $y = -x^2 + 3x + 2$

h. $y = -x^6 - x^2 - 5x + 4$

Library of Functions

The graphs of polynomials of degree 1 are lines, and those of degree 2 are parabolas. The graphs of polynomials of higher degree are smooth and continuous. The graphs eventually rise or fall without bound as x moves to the right (or left).

Consult the Library of Functions Summary inside the front cover for a description of the polynomial function.

A review of the shapes of the graphs of polynomial functions of degrees 0, 1, and 2 may be used to illustrate the Leading Coefficient Test.

EXAMPLE 2   Applying the Leading Coefficient Test

Use the Leading Coefficient Test to determine the left and right behavior of the graph of each polynomial function.

a. $f(x) = -x^3 + 4x$ **b.** $f(x) = x^4 - 5x^2 + 4$ **c.** $f(x) = x^5 - x$

Solution

a. Because the degree is odd and the leading coefficient is negative, the graph rises to the left and falls to the right, as shown in Figure 3.13(a).

b. Because the degree is even and the leading coefficient is positive, the graph rises to the left and right, as shown in Figure 3.13(b).

c. Because the degree is odd and the leading coefficient is positive, the graph falls to the left and rises to the right, as shown in Figure 3.13(c).

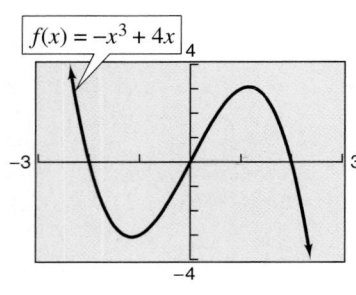
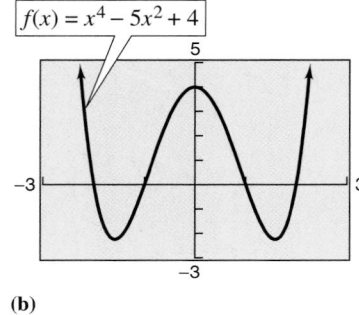
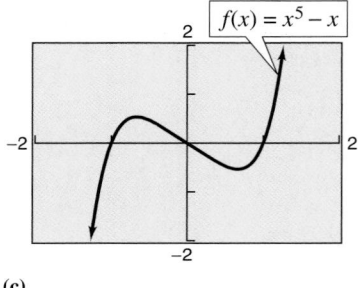

(a) (b) (c)

Figure 3.13

In Example 2, note that the Leading Coefficient Test only tells you whether the graph *eventually* rises or falls to the right or left. Other characteristics of the graph, such as intercepts and minimum and maximum points, must be determined by other tests.

Zeros of Polynomial Functions

It can be shown that for a polynomial function f of degree n, the following statements are true.

1. The graph of f has at most n real zeros. (This result is discussed in detail in Section 3.4.)

2. The function f has at most $n - 1$ relative **extrema** (relative **minimums** or **maximums**).

Recall that a **zero** of a function f is a number x for which $f(x) = 0$. Finding the zeros of polynomial functions is one of the most important problems in algebra. You have already seen that there is a strong interplay between graphical and algebraic approaches to this problem. Sometimes you can use information about the graph of a function to help find its zeros. In other cases you can use information about the zeros of a function to find a good viewing window.

A good test of understanding is to present a graph of a function, without giving its equation, and ask what you can tell about the function's degree and leading coefficient by looking at the graph. You might want to display a few such graphs on an overhead projector during class to practice.

Exploration

For each of the graphs in Figure 3.13, count the number of zeros of the polynomial function and the number of relative extrema, and compare these numbers with the degree of the polynomial. What do you observe?

Additional Examples

Describe the right- and left-hand behavior of the graph of each function.

a. $x^4 + 2x^2 - 3x$

b. $-x^5 + 3x^4 - x$

c. $2x^3 - 3x^2 + 5$

Solution

a. The graph rises to the left and to the right.

b. The graph rises to the left and falls to the right.

c. The graph falls to the left and rises to the right.

Real Zeros of Polynomial Functions

If f is a polynomial function and a is a real number, the following statements are equivalent.

1. $x = a$ is a *zero* of the function f.
2. $x = a$ is a *solution* of the polynomial equation $f(x) = 0$.
3. $(x - a)$ is a *factor* of the polynomial $f(x)$.
4. $(a, 0)$ is an *x-intercept* of the graph of f.

Finding zeros of polynomial functions is closely related to factoring and finding *x*-intercepts, as demonstrated in Examples 3, 4, and 5.

EXAMPLE 3   Finding Zeros of a Polynomial Function

Find all real zeros of $f(x) = x^3 - x^2 - 2x$.

Algebraic Solution

$f(x)$	$= x^3 - x^2 - 2x$	Write original function.
0	$= x^3 - x^2 - 2x$	Substitute 0 for $f(x)$.
	$= x(x^2 - x - 2)$	Remove common monomial factor.
	$= x(x - 2)(x + 1)$	Factor completely.

So, the real zeros are $x = 0$, $x = 2$, and $x = -1$, and the corresponding *x*-intercepts are $(0, 0)$, $(2, 0)$, and $(-1, 0)$.

Check

$(0)^3 - (0)^2 - 2(0) = 0$	$x = 0$ is a zero. ✓
$(2)^3 - (2)^2 - 2(2) = 0$	$x = 2$ is a zero. ✓
$(-1)^3 - (-1)^2 - 2(-1) = 0$	$x = -1$ is a zero. ✓

Graphical Solution

Use a graphing utility to graph $y = x^3 - x^2 - 2x$. In Figure 3.14, the graph appears to have the *x*-intercepts $(0, 0)$, $(2, 0)$, and $(-1, 0)$. Use the *zero* or *root* feature, or the *zoom* and *trace* features, of the graphing utility to verify these intercepts. Note that this third-degree polynomial has two relative extrema.

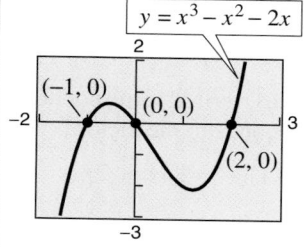

Figure 3.14

EXAMPLE 4   Analyzing a Polynomial Function

Find all real zeros and relative extrema of $f(x) = -2x^4 + 2x^2$.

Solution

$f(x)$	$= -2x^4 + 2x^2$	Write original function.
0	$= -2x^4 + 2x^2$	Substitute 0 for $f(x)$.
	$= -2x^2(x^2 - 1)$	Remove common monomial factor.
	$= -2x^2(x - 1)(x + 1)$	Factor completely.

So, the real zeros are $x = 0$, $x = 1$, and $x = -1$, and the corresponding *x*-intercepts are $(0, 0)$, $(1, 0)$, and $(-1, 0)$, as shown in Figure 3.15. Using the *minimum* and *maximum* features of a graphing utility, you can approximate the three relative extrema to be $(-0.7071, 0.5)$, $(0, 0)$, and $(0.7071, 0.5)$.

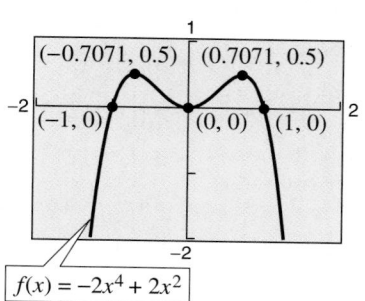

Figure 3.15

In Example 4, the real zero $x = 0$ arising from $-2x^2 = 0$ is a **repeated zero.** In general, a factor of $(x - a)^k$ yields a repeated zero $x = a$ of **multiplicity** k. If k is odd, the graph *crosses* the x-axis at $x = a$. If k is even, the graph *touches* (but does not cross) the x-axis at $x = a$, as shown in Figure 3.15.

EXAMPLE 5 Finding Zeros of a Polynomial Function

Find all real zeros of $f(x) = x^5 - 3x^3 - x^2 - 4x - 1$.

Solution
Use a graphing utility to obtain the graph shown in Figure 3.16. From the graph, you can see that there are three zeros. Using the *zero* or *root* feature, you can determine that the zeros are approximately $x \approx -1.861$, $x \approx -0.254$, and $x \approx 2.115$. It should be noted that this fifth-degree polynomial factors as

$$f(x) = x^5 - 3x^3 - x^2 - 4x - 1$$

$$= (x^2 + 1)(x^3 - 4x - 1).$$

The three zeros obtained above are the zeros of the cubic $x^3 - 4x - 1$ (the quadratic $x^2 + 1$ has two complex zeros and, so, no *real* zeros).

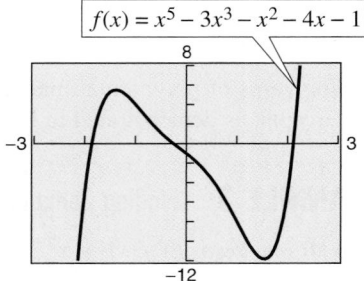

$f(x) = x^5 - 3x^3 - x^2 - 4x - 1$

Figure 3.16

EXAMPLE 6 Finding a Polynomial Function with Given Zeros

Find polynomial functions with the following zeros. (There are many correct solutions.)

a. $-2, -1, 1, 2$ **b.** $-\dfrac{1}{2}, 3, 3$ **c.** $3, 2 + \sqrt{11}, 2 - \sqrt{11}$

Solution
a. For each of the given zeros, form a corresponding factor. For instance, the zero given by $x = -2$ corresponds to the factor $(x + 2)$. So, you can write

$$f(x) = (x + 2)(x + 1)(x - 1)(x - 2)$$

$$= (x^2 - 4)(x^2 - 1) = x^4 - 5x^2 + 4.$$

b. Note that the zero $x = -\frac{1}{2}$ corresponds to either $\left(x + \frac{1}{2}\right)$ or $(2x + 1)$. To avoid fractions, choose the second factor and write

$$f(x) = (2x + 1)(x - 3)^2$$

$$= (2x + 1)(x^2 - 6x + 9) = 2x^3 - 11x^2 + 12x + 9.$$

c. For each of the given zeros, form a corresponding factor and write

$$f(x) = (x - 3)\left[x - \left(2 + \sqrt{11}\right)\right]\left[x - \left(2 - \sqrt{11}\right)\right]$$

$$= (x - 3)\left[(x - 2) - \sqrt{11}\right]\left[(x - 2) + \sqrt{11}\right]$$

$$= (x - 3)\left[(x - 2)^2 - \left(\sqrt{11}\right)^2\right]$$

$$= (x - 3)(x^2 - 4x + 4 - 11)$$

$$= (x - 3)(x^2 - 4x - 7) = x^3 - 7x^2 + 5x + 21.$$

Exploration

Use a graphing utility to graph

$$y_1 = x + 2$$

$$y_2 = (x + 2)(x - 1).$$

Predict the shape of the curve $y = (x + 2)(x - 1)(x - 3)$, and verify your answer with a graphing utility.

EXAMPLE 7   Sketching the Graph of a Polynomial Function

Sketch the graph of $f(x) = 3x^4 - 4x^3$ by hand.

Solution

1. *Apply Leading Coefficient Test.*   Because the leading coefficient is positive and the degree is even, you know that the graph eventually rises to the left and to the right [see Figure 3.17(a)].

2. *Find the Zeros of the Polynomial.*   By factoring

$$f(x) = 3x^4 - 4x^3$$

$$= x^3(3x - 4)$$

you can see that the zeros of f are $x = 0$ (of odd multiplicity 3) and $x = \frac{4}{3}$ (of odd multiplicity 1). So, the x-intercepts occur at $(0, 0)$ and $\left(\frac{4}{3}, 0\right)$. Add these points to your graph, as shown in Figure 3.17(a).

3. *Plot a Few Additional Points.*   To sketch the graph by hand, find a few additional points, as shown in the table. Be sure to choose points between the zeros and to the left and right of the zeros. Then plot the points [see Figure 3.17(b)].

x	-1	0.5	1	1.5
$f(x)$	7	-0.3125	-1	1.6875

4. *Draw the Graph.*   Draw a continuous curve through the points, as shown in Figure 3.17(b). If you are unsure of the shape of the portion of the graph, plot some additional points.

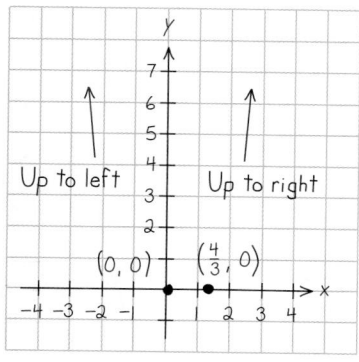

(a)

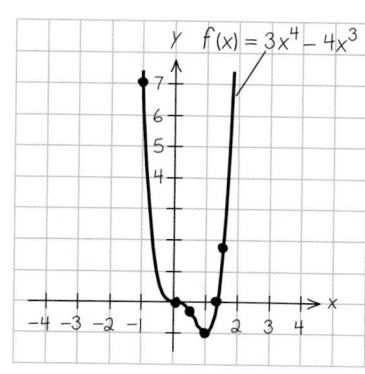

(b)

Figure 3.17

Exploration

Partner Activity   Multiply 3, 4, or 5 distinct linear factors to obtain the equation of a polynomial function that has a degree of 3, 4, or 5. Exchange equations with your partner and sketch, *by hand,* the graph of the equation that your partner wrote. When you are finished, use a graphing utility to check each other's work.

Activities

1. Find all of the zeros of
   $f(x) = 6x^4 - 33x^3 - 18x^2$.
   Answer: $-\frac{1}{2}, 0, 6$

2. Determine the right-hand and left-hand behavior of
   $f(x) = 6x^4 - 33x^3 - 18x^2$.
   Answer: The graph moves up to the left because $f(x) \to \infty$ as $x \to -\infty$, and it moves up to the right because $f(x) \to \infty$ as $x \to \infty$.

3. Find a polynomial function of degree 3 that has zeros of 0, 2, and $-\frac{1}{3}$.
   Answer: $3x^3 - 5x^2 - 2x$

EXAMPLE 8   Sketching the Graph of a Polynomial Function

Sketch the graph of $f(x) = -2x^3 + 6x^2 - \frac{9}{2}x$.

Solution

1. *Apply Leading Coefficient Test.*   Because the leading coefficient is negative and the degree is odd, you know that the graph eventually rises to the left and falls to the right [see Figure 3.18(a)].

2. *Find the Zeros of the Polynomial.*   By factoring

$$f(x) = -2x^3 + 6x^2 - \tfrac{9}{2}x = -\tfrac{1}{2}x(4x^2 - 12x + 9) = -\tfrac{1}{2}x(2x - 3)^2$$

you can see that the zeros of f are

$$x = 0 \text{ (of odd multiplicity 1) and } x = \tfrac{3}{2} \text{ (of even multiplicity 2).}$$

So, the x-intercepts occur at $(0, 0)$ and $\left(\frac{3}{2}, 0\right)$. Add these points to your graph, as shown in Figure 3.18(a).

3. *Plot a Few Additional Points.*   To sketch the graph by hand, find a few additional points, as shown in the table. Then plot the points [see Figure 3.18(b)].

x	-0.5	0.5	1	2
$f(x)$	4	-1	-0.5	-1

4. *Draw the Graph.*   Draw a continuous curve through the points, as shown in Figure 3.18(b). Notice that the graph crosses the x-axis at $(0, 0)$ and touches (but does not cross) the x-axis at $\left(\frac{3}{2}, 0\right)$.

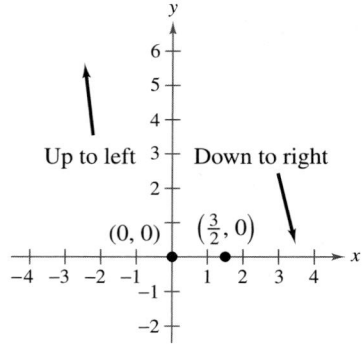

Up to left   Down to right

$(0, 0)$ $\left(\frac{3}{2}, 0\right)$

(a)

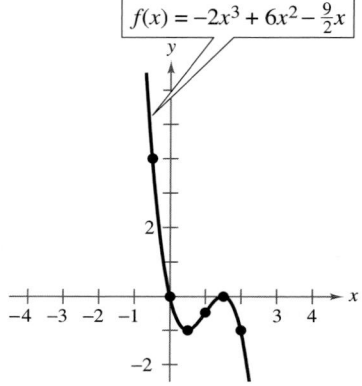

$f(x) = -2x^3 + 6x^2 - \frac{9}{2}x$

(b)
Figure 3.18

The Intermediate Value Theorem

The **Intermediate Value Theorem** concerns the existence of real zeros of polynomial functions. The theorem states that if $(a, f(a))$ and $(b, f(b))$ are two points on the graph of a polynomial function such that $f(a) \neq f(b)$, then for any number d between $f(a)$ and $f(b)$ there must be a number c between a and b such that $f(c) = d$. (See Figure 3.19.)

Intermediate Value Theorem

Let a and b be real numbers such that $a < b$. If f is a polynomial function such that $f(a) \neq f(b)$, then in the interval $[a, b]$, f takes on every value between $f(a)$ and $f(b)$.

This theorem helps locate the real zeros of a polynomial function in the following way. If you can find a value $x = a$ where a polynomial function is positive, and another $x = b$ where it is negative, you can conclude that the function has at least one real zero between these two values. For example, the function $f(x) = x^3 + x^2 + 1$ is negative when $x = -2$ and positive when $x = -1$. Therefore, it follows from the Intermediate Value Theorem that f must have a real zero somewhere between -2 and -1.

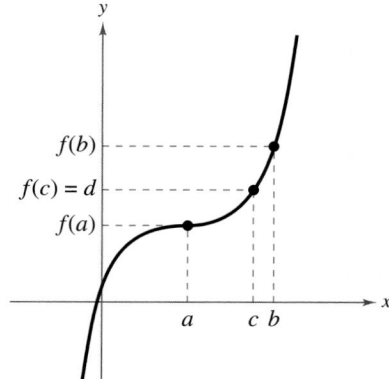

$f(b)$
$f(c) = d$
$f(a)$

a c b

Figure 3.19

EXAMPLE 9   Approximating the Zeros of a Function

Find three intervals of length 1 in which the polynomial

$$f(x) = 12x^3 - 32x^2 + 3x + 5$$

is guaranteed to have a zero.

Graphical Solution

Use a graphing utility to graph

$$y = 12x^3 - 32x^2 + 3x + 5$$

as shown in Figure 3.20.

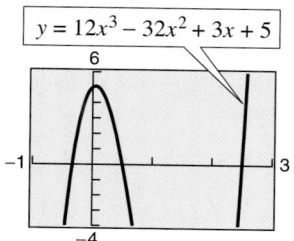

Figure 3.20

From the figure, you can see that the graph crosses the x-axis three times—between -1 and 0, between 0 and 1, and another between 2 and 3. So, you can conclude that the function has zeros in the intervals $(-1, 0)$, $(0, 1)$, and $(2, 3)$.

Numerical Solution

Use the *table* feature of a graphing utility to create a table that shows the function values for $-20 \le x \le 20$ as shown in Figure 3.21.

X	Y1
-2	-225
-1	-42
0	5
1	-12
2	-21
3	50
4	273

X=3

Figure 3.21

Scroll through the table looking for consecutive function values that differ in sign. For instance, from the table you can see that $f(-1)$ and $f(0)$ differ in sign. So, you can conclude from the Intermediate Value Theorem that the function has a zero between -1 and 0. Similarly, $f(0)$ and $f(1)$ differ in sign, so the function has a zero between 0 and 1. Likewise, $f(2)$ and $f(3)$ differ in sign, so the function has a zero between 2 and 3. So, you can conclude that the function has zeros in the intervals $(-1, 0)$, $(0, 1)$, and $(2, 3)$.

Writing About Math   *The Graphs of Cubic Polynomials*

The graphs of cubic polynomials can be categorized according to the four basic shapes below. Match the graph of each function with one of the basic shapes and write a short paragraph describing how you reached your conclusion. Is it possible for a polynomial of odd degree to have no real zeros? Explain.

(a)
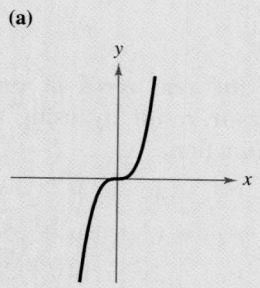

(b)
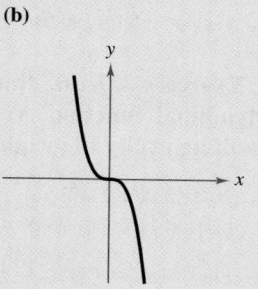

(c)
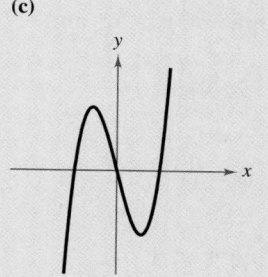

(d)
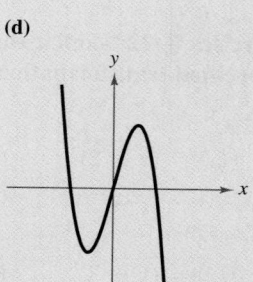

1. $f(x) = -x^3$ **2.** $f(x) = -x^3 + 4x$ **3.** $f(x) = x^3$ **4.** $f(x) = x^3 - 4x$

3.2 Exercises

In Exercises 1–8, match the polynomial function with its graph. [The graphs are labeled (a) through (h).]

(a)
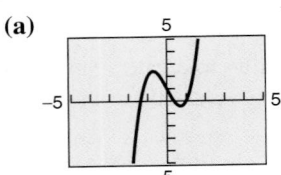

(b)
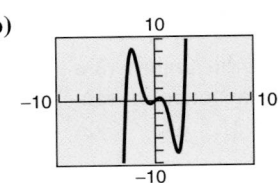

(c)
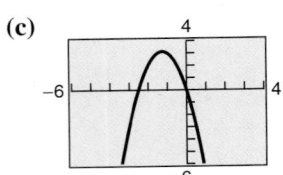

(d)
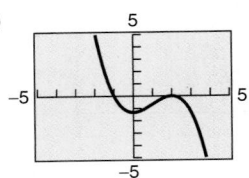

(e)
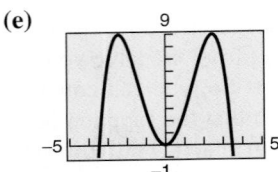

(f)
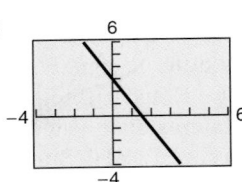

(g)
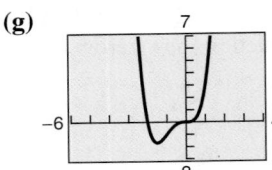

(h)
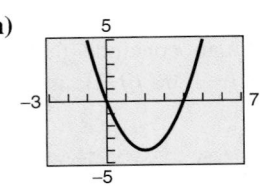

1. $f(x) = -2x + 3$
2. $f(x) = x^2 - 4x$
3. $f(x) = -2x^2 - 5x$
4. $f(x) = 2x^3 - 3x + 1$
5. $f(x) = -\frac{1}{4}x^4 + 3x^2$
6. $f(x) = -\frac{1}{3}x^3 + x^2 - \frac{4}{3}$
7. $f(x) = x^4 + 2x^3$
8. $f(x) = \frac{1}{5}x^5 - 2x^3 + \frac{9}{5}x$

In Exercises 9–12, sketch the graphs of $y = x^n$ and each specified transformation.

9. $y = x^3$
   (a) $f(x) = (x - 2)^3$
   (b) $f(x) = x^3 - 2$
   (c) $f(x) = -\frac{1}{2}x^3$
   (d) $f(x) = (x - 2)^3 - 2$

10. $y = x^5$
    (a) $f(x) = (x + 3)^5$
    (b) $f(x) = x^5 + 3$
    (c) $f(x) = 1 - \frac{1}{2}x^5$
    (d) $f(x) = -\frac{1}{2}(x + 1)^5$

11. $y = x^4$
    (a) $f(x) = (x + 5)^4$
    (b) $f(x) = x^4 - 5$
    (c) $f(x) = 4 - x^4$
    (d) $f(x) = \frac{1}{2}(x - 1)^4$

12. $y = x^6$
    (a) $f(x) = -\frac{1}{8}x^6$
    (b) $f(x) = x^6 - 4$
    (c) $f(x) = -\frac{1}{4}x^6 + 1$
    (d) $f(x) = (x + 2)^6 - 4$

Graphical Analysis In Exercises 13–16, use a graphing utility to graph the functions f and g in the same viewing window. Zoom out sufficiently far to show that the right-hand and left-hand behavior of f and g appear identical. Show the graphs.

13. $f(x) = 3x^3 - 9x + 1,\quad g(x) = 3x^3$
14. $f(x) = -\frac{1}{3}(x^3 - 3x + 2),\quad g(x) = -\frac{1}{3}x^3$
15. $f(x) = -(x^4 - 4x^3 + 16x),\quad g(x) = -x^4$
16. $f(x) = 3x^4 - 6x^2,\quad g(x) = 3x^4$

In Exercises 17–26, use the Leading Coefficient Test to determine the right-hand and left-hand behavior of the graph of the polynomial function. Verify your result by using a graphing utility to graph the function.

17. $f(x) = 2x^2 - 3x + 1$
18. $f(x) = \frac{1}{3}x^3 + 5x$
19. $g(x) = 5 - \frac{7}{2}x - 3x^2$
20. $h(x) = 1 - x^6$
21. $f(x) = -2.1x^5 + 4x^3 - 2$
22. $f(x) = 2x^5 - 5x + 7.5$
23. $f(x) = 6 - 2x + 4x^2 - 5x^3$
24. $f(x) = \dfrac{3x^4 - 2x + 5}{4}$
25. $h(t) = -\frac{2}{3}(t^2 - 5t + 3)$
26. $f(s) = -\frac{7}{8}(s^3 + 5s^2 - 7s + 1)$

In Exercises 27–36, find all the real zeros of the polynomial function. Verify your result by using a graphing utility to graph the function.

27. $f(x) = x^2 - 25$
28. $f(x) = 49 - x^2$
29. $h(t) = t^2 - 6t + 9$
30. $f(x) = x^2 + 10x + 25$
31. $f(x) = x^2 + x - 2$
32. $f(x) = 2x^2 - 14x + 24$
33. $f(t) = t^3 - 4t^2 + 4t$
34. $f(x) = x^4 - x^3 - 20x^2$
35. $f(x) = \frac{1}{2}x^2 + \frac{5}{2}x - \frac{3}{2}$
36. $f(x) = \frac{5}{3}x^2 + \frac{8}{3}x - \frac{4}{3}$

Graphical Analysis In Exercises 37–48, (a) use a graphing utility to graph the function, (b) use the graph to approximate any zeros, and (c) find the zeros algebraically.

37. $f(x) = 3x^2 - 12x + 3$

38. $g(x) = 5(x^2 - 2x - 1)$

39. $g(t) = \frac{1}{2}t^4 - \frac{1}{2}$ **40.** $y = \frac{1}{4}x^3(x^2 - 9)$

41. $f(x) = x^5 + x^3 - 6x$ **42.** $g(t) = t^5 - 6t^3 + 9t$

43. $f(x) = 2x^4 - 2x^2 - 40$

44. $f(x) = 5x^4 + 15x^2 + 10$

45. $f(x) = x^3 - 4x^2 - 25x + 100$

46. $y = 4x^3 + 4x^2 - 7x + 2$

47. $y = 4x^3 - 20x^2 + 25x$ **48.** $y = x^5 - 5x^3 + 4x$

In Exercises 49–52, use a graphing utility to graph the function and approximate (accurate to three decimal places) any relative extrema.

49. $f(x) = 2x^4 - 6x^2 + 1$

50. $f(x) = -3x^3 - 4x^2 + x - 3$

51. $f(x) = x^5 + 3x^3 - x + 6$

52. $f(x) = -\frac{3}{8}x^4 - x^3 + 2x^2 + 5$

In Exercises 53–64, find a polynomial function that has the given zeros. (There are many correct answers.)

53. $0, 12$ **54.** $0, -8$

55. $2, -6$ **56.** $-4, 5$

57. $0, -4, -3$ **58.** $0, 2, 7$

59. $4, -3, 3, 0$ **60.** $-2, -1, 0, 1, 2$

61. $1 + \sqrt{3}, 1 - \sqrt{3}$ **62.** $6 + \sqrt{3}, 6 - \sqrt{3}$

63. $2, 4 + \sqrt{5}, 4 - \sqrt{5}$ **64.** $4, 2 + \sqrt{7}, 2 - \sqrt{7}$

In Exercises 65–78, sketch the graph of the function by (a) applying the Leading Coefficient Test, (b) finding the zeros of the polynomial, (c) plotting sufficient solution points, and (d) drawing a continuous curve through the points.

65. $f(x) = x^3 - 9x$

66. $g(x) = x^4 - 4x^2$

67. $f(t) = \frac{1}{4}(t^2 - 2t + 15)$

68. $g(x) = -x^2 + 10x - 16$

69. $f(x) = x^3 - 3x^2$

70. $f(x) = 1 - x^3$

71. $f(x) = 3x^3 - 15x^2 + 18x$

72. $f(x) = -4x^3 + 4x^2 + 15x$

73. $f(x) = -x^3 - 5x^2$

74. $f(x) = 3x^4 - 48x^2$

75. $f(x) = x^2(x - 4)$

76. $h(x) = \frac{1}{3}x^3(x - 4)^2$

77. $g(t) = -\frac{1}{4}(t - 2)^2(t + 2)^2$

78. $g(x) = \frac{1}{10}(x + 1)^2(x - 3)^2$

In Exercises 79–82, (a) use the Intermediate Value Theorem and a graphing utility to find intervals of length 1 in which the polynomial function is guaranteed to have a zero, (b) use the *root* or *zero* feature of a graphing utility to approximate the zeros of the function, and (c) verify your answers in part (a) by using the *table* feature of a graphing utility.

79. $f(x) = x^3 - 3x^2 + 3$

80. $f(x) = 0.11x^3 - 2.07x^2 + 9.81x - 6.88$

81. $g(x) = 3x^4 + 4x^3 - 3$

82. $h(x) = x^4 - 10x^2 + 2$

In Exercises 83–86, use a graphing utility to graph the function. Describe a viewing window that gives a good view of the basic characteristics of the graph. (There are many correct answers.)

83. $f(x) = -\frac{3}{2}$

84. $h(x) = \frac{1}{3}x - 3$

85. $f(t) = \frac{1}{6}(t^2 - 4t + 21)$

86. $g(x) = -x^2 + 9x - 14$

In Exercises 87–94, use a graphing utility to graph the function. Identify any symmetry with respect to the *x*-axis, *y*-axis, or origin. Determine the number of *x*-intercepts of the graph.

87. $f(x) = x^2(x + 6)$

88. $h(x) = x^3(x - 4)^2$

89. $g(t) = -\frac{1}{2}(t - 4)^2(t + 4)^2$

90. $g(x) = \frac{1}{8}(x + 1)^2(x - 3)^3$

91. $f(x) = x^3 - 4x$

92. $f(x) = x^4 - 2x^2$

93. $g(x) = \frac{1}{5}(x + 1)^2(x - 3)(2x - 9)$

94. $h(x) = \frac{1}{5}(x + 2)^2(3x - 5)^2$

95. *Numerical and Graphical Analysis*   An open box is to be made from a square piece of material 36 centimeters on a side by cutting equal squares from the corners and turning up the sides.

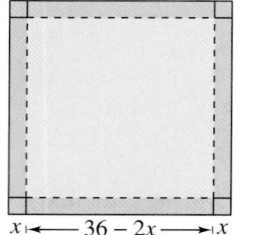
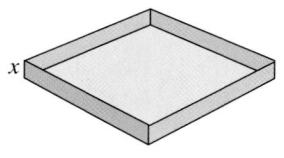

$x \longleftarrow 36 - 2x \longrightarrow x$

(a) Complete four rows of a table like the one below.

Height	Width	Volume
1	$36 - 2(1)$	$1[36 - 2(1)]^2 = 1156$
2	$36 - 2(2)$	$2[36 - 2(2)]^2 = 2048$

(b) Use a graphing utility to generate additional rows of the table. Use the table to estimate a range of dimensions within which the maximum volume is produced.

(c) Verify that the volume of the box is $V(x) = x(36 - 2x)^2$. Determine the domain of the function.

(d) Use a graphing utility to graph V, and use the range of dimensions from part (b) to find the x-value for which $V(x)$ is maximum.

96. *Geometry*   An open box with locking tabs is to be made from a square piece of material 24 inches on a side. This is done by cutting equal squares from the corners and folding along the dashed lines, as shown in the figure.

(a) Show that the volume of the box is

$$V(x) = 8x(6 - x)(12 - x).$$

(b) Determine the domain of the function V.

(c) Sketch the graph of the function and estimate the value of x for which $V(x)$ is maximum.

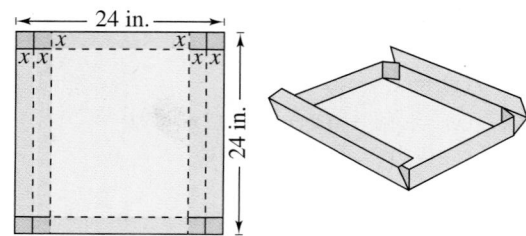

97. *Business*   The total revenue R (in millions of dollars) for a company is related to its advertising expense by the function

$$R = \frac{1}{100,000}(-x^3 + 600x^2), \quad 0 \le x \le 400$$

where x is the amount spent on advertising (in tens of thousands of dollars). Use the graph of the function shown in the figure to estimate the point on the graph at which the function is increasing most rapidly. This point is called the **point of diminishing returns** because any expense above this amount will yield less return per dollar invested in advertising.

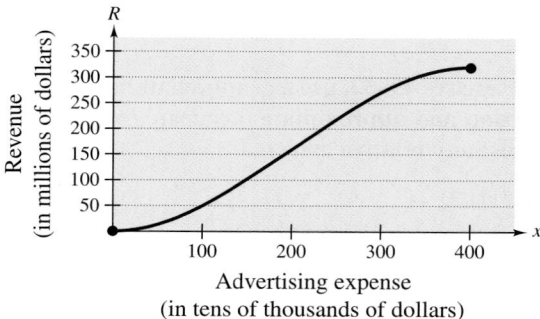

Advertising expense
(in tens of thousands of dollars)

98. *Environment*   The growth of a red oak tree is approximated by the function

$$G = -0.003t^3 + 0.137t^2 + 0.458t - 0.839$$

where G is the height of the tree (in feet) and t ($2 \le t \le 34$) is its age (in years). Use a graphing utility to graph the function and estimate the age of the tree when it is growing most rapidly. This point is called the **point of diminishing returns** because the increase in growth will be less with each additional year. (*Hint:* Use a viewing window in which $-10 \le x \le 45$ and $-5 \le y \le 60$.)

99. *Data Analysis*   The vertical deflection y of a 4-meter beam is measured in $\frac{1}{2}$-meter intervals x. The measurements are given by the following ordered pairs.

(0, 0), (0.5, 0.06), (1, 0.11), (1.5, 0.15), (2, 0.16), (2.5, 0.15), (3, 0.11), (3.5, 0.06), (4, 0)

(a) Use the regression capabilities of a graphing utility to fit a quartic (fourth-degree polynomial) equation to the data.

(b) Use a graphing utility to graph the data and the regression equation in the same viewing window. How do they compare?

(c) Because $y = 0$ when $x = 0$, what should the constant term in the model be? Does your answer agree with the result of part (a)? Explain.

100. *Data Analysis*   The table gives the median values of new privately owned U.S. homes for 1983 through 1997. In the table, t is the time (in years), with $t = 3$ corresponding to 1983, and y_1 and y_2 are the median prices (in thousands of dollars) in the Northeast and the South, respectively. (Sources: U.S. Bureau of the Census; U.S. Department of Housing and Urban Development)

t	3	4	5	6	7	8
y_1	82.2	88.6	103.3	125	140	149
y_2	70.9	72	75	80.2	88	92

t	9	10	11	12	13
y_1	159.6	159	155.9	169	162.6
y_2	96.4	99	100	105.5	115

t	14	15	16	17
y_1	169	180	186	190
y_2	116.9	124.5	126.2	129.6

(a) Use the regression capabilities of a graphing utility to fit a cubic model to the median prices of homes in the Northeast.

(b) Use the regression capabilities of a graphing utility to fit a cubic model to the median prices of homes in the South.

(c) Use the graphs of the models in parts (a) and (b) to write a short paragraph about the relationship between the median prices of homes in the two regions.

Synthesis

True or False?   **In Exercises 101 and 102, determine whether the statement is true or false. Justify your answer.**

101. A fourth-degree polynomial can have four turning points.

102. The graph of the function

$$f(x) = 2 + x - x^2 + x^3 - x^4 + x^5 + x^6 - x^7$$

rises to the left and falls to the right.

103. *Graphical Reasoning*   Use a graphing utility to graph the function $f(x) = x^4$. Explain how the graph of g differs (if it does) from the graph of f and confirm your result with a graphing utility. Determine whether g is odd, even, or neither.

(a) $g(x) = f(x) + 2$ (b) $g(x) = f(x + 2)$

(c) $g(x) = f(-x)$ (d) $g(x) = -f(x)$

(e) $g(x) = f\left(\frac{1}{2}x\right)$ (f) $g(x) = \frac{1}{2}f(x)$

(g) $g(x) = f\left(x^{3/4}\right)$ (h) $g(x) = (f \circ f)(x)$

Review

In Exercises 104–109, let $f(x) = 14x - 3$, and $g(x) = 8x^2$. Find the indicated value.

104. $(f + g)(-4)$ **105.** $(g - f)(3)$

106. $(fg)\left(-\dfrac{4}{7}\right)$ **107.** $\left(\dfrac{f}{g}\right)(-1.5)$

108. $(f \circ g)(-1)$ **109.** $(g \circ f)(0)$

In Exercises 110–113, solve the inequality and sketch the solution on the real number line. Use a graphing utility to verify your solution graphically.

110. $3(x - 5) < 4x - 7$ **111.** $2x^2 - x \geq 1$

112. $\dfrac{5x - 2}{x - 7} \leq 4$ **113.** $|x + 8| - 1 \geq 15$

In Exercises 114–117, find the quadratic function that has the indicated vertex and whose graph passes through the given point.

114. Vertex: $(3, -6)$;   Point: $(-1, 2)$

115. Vertex: $(0, -8)$;   Point: $(5, 9)$

116. Vertex: $(4, -4)$;   Point: $(1, 10)$

117. Vertex: $(-5, -2)$;   Point: $(0, 3)$

3.3   Real Zeros of Polynomial Functions

Long Division of Polynomials

Consider the graph of

$$f(x) = 6x^3 - 19x^2 + 16x - 4.$$

Notice in Figure 3.22 that $x = 2$ appears to be a zero of f. Because $f(2) = 0$, you know that $x = 2$ is a zero of the polynomial function f, and that $(x - 2)$ is a factor of $f(x)$. This means that there exists a second-degree polynomial $q(x)$ such that $f(x) = (x - 2) \cdot q(x)$. To find $q(x)$, you can use **long division of polynomials.**

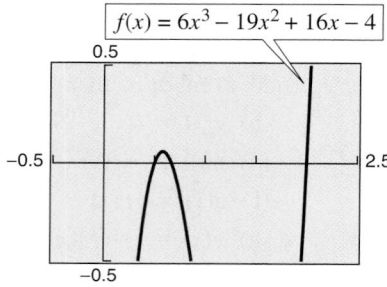

$f(x) = 6x^3 - 19x^2 + 16x - 4$

Figure 3.22

EXAMPLE 1   Long Division of Polynomials

Divide $f(x) = 6x^3 - 19x^2 + 16x - 4$ by $x - 2$, and use the result to factor the function f completely.

Solution

$$
\begin{array}{r}
6x^2 - 7x + 2 \\
x - 2 \overline{\smash{\big)}\ 6x^3 - 19x^2 + 16x - 4} \\
\underline{6x^3 - 12x^2} \\
-7x^2 + 16x \\
\underline{-7x^2 + 14x} \\
2x - 4 \\
\underline{2x - 4} \\
0
\end{array}
$$

Partial quotients

Multiply: $6x^2(x - 2)$.
Subtract.
Multiply: $-7x(x - 2)$.
Subtract.
Multiply: $2(x - 2)$.
Subtract.

You can see that

$$6x^3 - 19x^2 + 16x - 4 = (x - 2)(6x^2 - 7x + 2)$$

$$= (x - 2)(2x - 1)(3x - 2).$$

Note that this factorization agrees with the graph of f (Figure 3.22) in that the three x-intercepts occur at $x = 2$, $x = \frac{1}{2}$, and $x = \frac{2}{3}$.

Stephen Ferry/Liaison International

In Example 1, $x - 2$ is a factor of the polynomial $6x^3 - 19x^2 + 16x - 4$, and the long division process produces a remainder of zero. Often, long division will produce a nonzero remainder. For instance, if you divide $x^2 + 3x + 5$ by $x + 1$, you obtain the following.

Note that one of the many uses of polynomial division is to write a function as a sum of terms to find slant asymptotes (see Section 3.6). This is a skill that is also used frequently in calculus.

$$
\begin{array}{r}
x + 2 \qquad\quad \Leftarrow \text{ Quotient} \\
x + 1 \overline{)\, x^2 + 3x + 5} \quad \Leftarrow \text{ Dividend} \\
\underline{x^2 + x} \qquad\qquad \\
2x + 5 \qquad\quad \\
\underline{2x + 2} \qquad\quad \\
3 \qquad\quad \Leftarrow \text{ Remainder}
\end{array}
$$

Divisor $\Longrightarrow$

In fractional form, you can write this result as follows.

$$
\underbrace{\frac{\overbrace{x^2 + 3x + 5}^{\text{Dividend}}}{\underbrace{x + 1}_{\text{Divisor}}}}_{} = \overbrace{x + 2}^{\text{Quotient}} + \frac{\overset{\text{Remainder}}{\downarrow}{3}}{\underbrace{x + 1}_{\text{Divisor}}}
$$

This implies that

$$x^2 + 3x + 5 = (x + 1)(x + 2) + 3$$

which illustrates the following well-known theorem called the **Division Algorithm.**

The Division Algorithm

If $f(x)$ and $d(x)$ are polynomials such that $d(x) \neq 0$, and the degree of $d(x)$ is less than or equal to the degree of $f(x)$, there exist unique polynomials $q(x)$ and $r(x)$ such that

$$f(x) = d(x)q(x) + r(x)$$

where $r(x) = 0$ *or* the degree of $r(x)$ is less than the degree of $d(x)$. If the remainder $r(x)$ is zero, $d(x)$ *divides evenly* into $f(x)$.

Have students practice identifying the dividend, divisor, quotient, and remainder when dividing polynomials. For instance, in the division problem

$$\frac{x^3 - x + 1}{x - 1} = x^2 + x + \frac{1}{x - 1}$$

the dividend is $x^3 - x + 1$, the divisor is $x - 1$, the quotient is $x^2 + x$, and the remainder is 1.

The Division Algorithm can also be written as

$$\frac{f(x)}{d(x)} = q(x) + \frac{r(x)}{d(x)}.$$

In the Division Algorithm, the rational expression $f(x)/d(x)$ is **improper** because the degree of $f(x)$ is greater than or equal to the degree of $d(x)$. On the other hand, the rational expression $r(x)/d(x)$ is **proper** because the degree of $r(x)$ is less than the degree of $d(x)$.

EXAMPLE 2   Long Division of Polynomials

Divide $x^3 - 1$ by $x - 1$.

Solution

Because there is no x^2-term or x-term in the dividend, you need to line up the subtraction by using zero coefficients (or leaving spaces) for the missing terms.

$$
\begin{array}{r}
x^2 + x + 1 \\
x - 1 \overline{)\,x^3 + 0x^2 + 0x - 1} \\
\underline{x^3 - x^2} \\
x^2 \\
\underline{x^2 - x} \\
x - 1 \\
\underline{x - 1} \\
0
\end{array}
$$

So, $x - 1$ divides evenly into $x^3 - 1$, and you can write

$$\frac{x^3 - 1}{x - 1} = x^2 + x + 1, \qquad x \neq 1.$$

You can check the result of a division problem by multiplying. For instance, in Example 2, try checking that

$$(x - 1)(x^2 + x + 1) = x^3 - 1.$$

EXAMPLE 3   Long Division of Polynomials

Divide $2x^4 + 4x^3 - 5x^2 + 3x - 2$ by $x^2 + 2x - 3$.

Solution

$$
\begin{array}{r}
2x^2 \qquad\quad + 1 \\
x^2 + 2x - 3 \overline{)\,2x^4 + 4x^3 - 5x^2 + 3x - 2} \\
\underline{2x^4 + 4x^3 - 6x^2} \\
x^2 + 3x - 2 \\
\underline{x^2 + 2x - 3} \\
x + 1
\end{array}
$$

A computer animation of this example appears in the *Interactive* CD-ROM and *Internet* versions of this text.

Remind students that when division yields a remainder, it is important that they write the remainder term correctly.

Note that the first subtraction eliminated two terms from the dividend. When this happens, the quotient skips a term. You can write the result as

$$\frac{2x^4 + 4x^3 - 5x^2 + 3x - 2}{x^2 + 2x - 3} = 2x^2 + 1 + \frac{x + 1}{x^2 + 2x - 3}.$$

Synthetic Division

There is a nice shortcut for long division of polynomials by divisors of the form $x - k$. The shortcut is called **synthetic division.** The pattern for synthetic division of a cubic polynomial is summarized as follows. (The pattern for higher-degree polynomials is similar.)

Synthetic Division (of a Cubic Polynomial)

To divide $ax^3 + bx^2 + cx + d$ by $x - k$, use the following pattern.

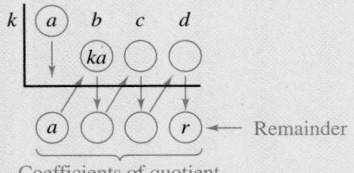

Vertical pattern: Add terms.
Diagonal pattern: Multiply by k.

Note that synthetic division works *only* for divisors of the form $x - k$. [Remember that $x + k = x - (-k)$.] You cannot use synthetic division to divide a polynomial by a quadratic such as $x^2 - 3$.

EXAMPLE 4   Using Synthetic Division

Use synthetic division to divide $x^4 - 10x^2 - 2x + 4$ by $x + 3$.

Solution

You should set up the array as follows. Note that a zero is included for each missing term in the dividend.

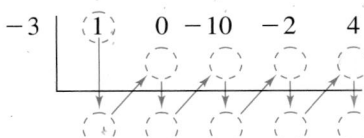

Then, use the synthetic division pattern by adding terms in columns and multiplying the results by -3.

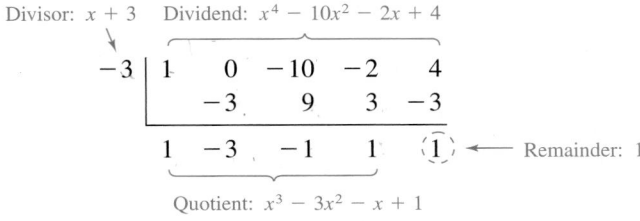

So, you have

$$\frac{x^4 - 10x^2 - 2x + 4}{x + 3} = x^3 - 3x^2 - x + 1 + \frac{1}{x + 3}.$$

Point out to students that they can use a graphing utility to check the answer to a polynomial division problem. When students graph both the original polynomial division problem and the answer on the same viewing window, the graphs should coincide.

A computer animation of this example appears in the *Interactive* CD-ROM and *Internet* versions of this text.

The Remainder and Factor Theorems

The remainder obtained in the synthetic division process has an important interpretation, as described in the **Remainder Theorem.** (A proof of this theorem is given in Appendix A.)

The Remainder Theorem

If a polynomial $f(x)$ is divided by $x - k$, the remainder is

$r = f(k)$.

The Remainder Theorem tells you that synthetic division can be used to evaluate a polynomial function. That is, to evaluate a polynomial function $f(x)$ when $x = k$, divide $f(x)$ by $x - k$. The remainder will be $f(k)$, as illustrated in Example 5.

EXAMPLE 5   Using the Remainder Theorem

Use the Remainder Theorem to evaluate the following function at $x = -2$.

$$f(x) = 3x^3 + 8x^2 + 5x - 7$$

Solution
Using synthetic division, you obtain the following.

$$
\begin{array}{r|rrrr}
-2 & 3 & 8 & 5 & -7 \\
   &   & -6 & -4 & -2 \\
\hline
   & 3 & 2 & 1 & -9
\end{array}
$$

Because the remainder is $r = -9$, you can conclude that

$$f(-2) = -9.$$

This means that $(-2, -9)$ is a point on the graph of f. You can check this by substituting $x = -2$ in the original function.

Check

$$
\begin{aligned}
f(-2) &= 3(-2)^3 + 8(-2)^2 + 5(-2) - 7 \\
&= 3(-8) + 8(4) - 10 - 7 \\
&= -24 + 32 - 10 - 7 \\
&= -9
\end{aligned}
$$

Another important theorem is the **Factor Theorem,** which is stated below. This theorem states that you can test to see whether a polynomial has $(x - k)$ as a factor by evaluating the polynomial at $x = k$. If the result is 0, $(x - k)$ is a factor. For a proof of the Factor Theorem, see Appendix A.

The Factor Theorem

A polynomial $f(x)$ has a factor $(x - k)$ if and only if $f(k) = 0$.

Additional Example

Use the Remainder Theorem to evaluate $f(x) = 4x^2 - 10x - 21$ when $x = 5$.

Solution

Using synthetic division you obtain the following.

$$
\begin{array}{r|rrr}
5 & 4 & -10 & -21 \\
  &   & 20 & 50 \\
\hline
  & 4 & 10 & 29
\end{array}
$$

Because the remainder is 29, you can conclude that $f(5) = 29$.

EXAMPLE 6   Factoring a Polynomial: Repeated Division

Show that $(x - 2)$ and $(x + 3)$ are factors of

$$f(x) = 2x^4 + 7x^3 - 4x^2 - 27x - 18.$$

Then find the remaining factors of $f(x)$.

Algebraic Solution

Using synthetic division with 2 and -3 *repeatedly,* you obtain the following.

```
2 | 2    7    -4   -27   -18
  |      4    22    36    18
  ------------------------------
    2   11    18     9     0
```
0 remainder
$(x - 2)$ is
a factor.

```
-3 | 2   11    18     9
   |     -6   -15    -9
   -----------------------
     2    5     3     0
```
0 remainder
$(x + 3)$ is
a factor.

Because the resulting quadratic factors as

$$2x^2 + 5x + 3 = (2x + 3)(x + 1)$$

the complete factorization of $f(x)$ is

$$f(x) = (x - 2)(x + 3)(2x + 3)(x + 1).$$

Graphical Solution

The graph of a polynomial with factors of $(x - 2)$ and $(x + 3)$ has x-intercepts at $x = 2$ and $x = -3$. Use a graphing utility to graph

$$y = 2x^4 + 7x^3 - 4x^2 - 27x - 18.$$

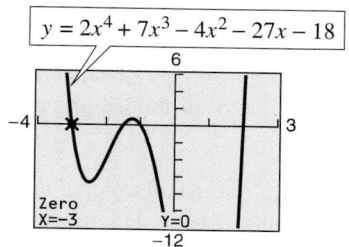

Figure 3.23

From Figure 3.23, you can see that the graph appears to cross the x-axis in two other places, near $x = -1$ and $x = -\frac{3}{2}$. Use the *zero* or *root* feature or the *zoom* and *trace* features to approximate the other two intercepts to be $x = -1$ and $x = -\frac{3}{2}$. So, the factors of f are $(x - 2)$, $(x + 3)$, $\left(x + \frac{3}{2}\right)$, and $(x + 1)$. You can rewrite the factor $\left(x + \frac{3}{2}\right)$ as $(2x + 3)$, so the complete factorization of f is $f(x) = (x - 2)(x + 3)(2x + 3)(x + 1)$.

Using the Remainder in Synthetic Division

In summary, the remainder r, obtained in the synthetic division of $f(x)$ by $x - k$, provides the following information.

1. The remainder r gives the value of f at $x = k$. That is, $r = f(k)$.

2. If $r = 0$, $(x - k)$ is a factor of $f(x)$.

3. If $r = 0$, $(k, 0)$ is an x-intercept of the graph of f.

Throughout this text, the importance of developing several problem-solving strategies has been emphasized. In the exercises for this section, try using more than one strategy to solve several of the exercises. For instance, if you find that $x - k$ divides evenly into $f(x)$, try sketching the graph of f. You should find that $(k, 0)$ is an x-intercept of the graph.

Activities

1. Use synthetic division to determine if $(x + 3)$ is a factor of
$$f(x) = 3x^3 + 4x^2 - 18x - 3.$$
Answer: No, it is not.

2. Divide using long division.
$$\frac{4x^5 - x^3 + 2x^2 - x}{2x + 1}$$
Answer:
$$2x^4 - x^3 + x - 1 + \frac{1}{2x + 1}$$

3. Use the Remainder Theorem to evaluate $f(-3)$ for $f(x) = 2x^3 - 4x^2 + 1$.
Answer: -89

The Rational Zero Test

The **Rational Zero Test** relates the possible rational zeros of a polynomial (having integer coefficients) to the leading coefficient and to the constant term of the polynomial.

The Rational Zero Test

If the polynomial

$$f(x) = a_n x^n + a_{n-1}x^{n-1} + \cdots + a_2 x^2 + a_1 x + a_0$$

has integer coefficients, every rational zero of f has the form

$$\text{Rational zero} = \frac{p}{q}$$

where p and q have no common factors other than 1, p is a factor of the constant term a_0, and q is a factor of the leading coefficient a_n.

To use the Rational Zero Test, first list all rational numbers whose numerators are factors of the constant term and whose denominators are factors of the leading coefficient.

$$\text{Possible rational zeros} = \frac{\text{factors of constant term}}{\text{factors of leading coefficient}}$$

Now that you have formed this list of *possible rational zeros,* use a trial-and-error method to determine which, if any, are actual zeros of the polynomial. Note that when the leading coefficient is 1, the possible rational zeros are simply the factors of the constant term. This case is illustrated in Example 7.

EXAMPLE 7   Rational Zero Test with Leading Coefficient of 1

Find the rational zeros of $f(x) = x^3 + x + 1$.

Solution

Because the leading coefficient is 1, the possible rational zeros are simply the factors of the constant term.

Possible Rational Zeros: ± 1

By testing these possible zeros, you can see that neither works.

$$f(1) = (1)^3 + 1 + 1 = 3$$

$$f(-1) = (-1)^3 + (-1) + 1 = -1$$

So, the polynomial has *no* rational zeros. Note from the graph of f in Figure 3.24 that f does have one real zero (between -1 and 0). However, by the Rational Zero Test, you know that this real zero is *not* a rational number.

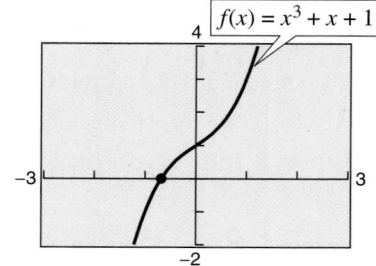

Figure 3.24

If the leading coefficient of a polynomial is not 1, the list of possible rational zeros can increase dramatically. In such cases the search can be shortened in several ways.

1. A programmable calculator can be used to speed up the calculations.
2. A graphing utility can give a good estimate of the locations of the zeros.
3. The Factor Theorem and synthetic division can be used to test the possible rational zeros.

Finding the first zero is often the most difficult part. After that, the search is simplified by working with the lower-degree polynomial obtained in synthetic division.

EXAMPLE 8   Using the Rational Zero Test

Find the rational zeros of

$$f(x) = 2x^3 + 3x^2 - 8x + 3.$$

Solution

The leading coefficient is 2 and the constant term is 3.

Possible Rational Zeros:

$$\frac{\text{Factors of 3}}{\text{Factors of 2}} = \frac{\pm 1, \pm 3}{\pm 1, \pm 2} = \pm 1, \pm 3, \pm \frac{1}{2}, \pm \frac{3}{2}$$

By synthetic division, you can determine that $x = 1$ is a zero.

$$
\begin{array}{r|rrrr}
1 & 2 & 3 & -8 & 3 \\
  &   & 2 & 5 & -3 \\
\hline
  & 2 & 5 & -3 & 0 \\
\end{array}
$$

So, $f(x)$ factors as

$$f(x) = (x - 1)(2x^2 + 5x - 3)$$
$$= (x - 1)(2x - 1)(x + 3)$$

and you can conclude that the rational zeros of f are $x = 1$, $x = \frac{1}{2}$, and $x = -3$, as shown in Figure 3.25.

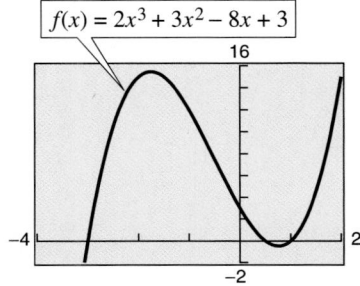

Figure 3.25

A graphing utility can help you determine which possible rational zeros to test, as demonstrated in Example 9.

EXAMPLE 9   Finding Real Zeros of a Polynomial Function

Find all the real zeros of $f(x) = 10x^3 - 15x^2 - 16x + 12$.

Solution

Because the leading coefficient is 10 and the constant term is 12, there is a long list of possible rational zeros.

Possible Rational Zeros:

$$\frac{\text{Factors of 12}}{\text{Factors of 10}} = \frac{\pm 1, \pm 2, \pm 3, \pm 4, \pm 6, \pm 12}{\pm 1, \pm 2, \pm 5, \pm 10}$$

With so many possibilities (32, in fact), it is worth your time to use a graphing utility to focus on just a few. From Figure 3.26, it looks like three reasonable choices would be $x = -\frac{6}{5}$, $x = \frac{1}{2}$, and $x = 2$. Synthetic division shows that only $x = 2$ works. (You could also use the Factor Theorem to test these choices.)

$$
\begin{array}{r|rrrr}
2 & 10 & -15 & -16 & 12 \\
  &   & 20 & 10 & -12 \\
\hline
  & 10 & 5   & -6 & 0
\end{array}
$$

So, $x = 2$ is one zero and you have

$$f(x) = (x - 2)(10x^2 + 5x - 6).$$

Using the Quadratic Formula, you find that the two additional zeros are irrational numbers.

$$x = \frac{-5 + \sqrt{265}}{20} \approx 0.5639 \quad \text{and} \quad x = \frac{-5 - \sqrt{265}}{20} \approx -1.0639$$

Bounds for Real Zeros of Polynomial Functions

The third test for zeros of a polynomial function is related to the sign pattern in the last row of the synthetic division tableau. This test can give you an upper or lower bound of the real zeros of f, which can help you eliminate possible real zeros.

A real number b is an **upper bound** for the real zeros of f if no zeros are greater than b. Similarly, b is a **lower bound** if no real zeros of f are less than b.

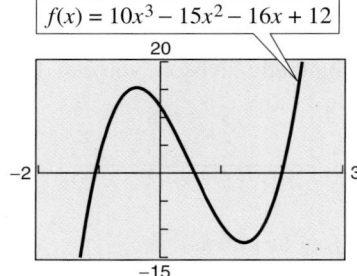

Figure 3.26

Upper and Lower Bound Rule

Let $f(x)$ be a polynomial with real coefficients and a positive leading coefficient. Suppose $f(x)$ is divided by $x - c$, using synthetic division.

1. If $c > 0$ and each number in the last row is either positive or zero, c is an **upper bound** for the real zeros of f.

2. If $c < 0$ and the numbers in the last row are alternately positive and negative (zero entries count as positive or negative), c is a **lower bound** for the real zeros of f.

EXAMPLE 10 Finding the Zeros of a Polynomial Function

Find the real zeros of $f(x) = 6x^3 - 4x^2 + 3x - 2$.

Solution

The possible real zeros are as follows.

$$\frac{\text{Factors of } 2}{\text{Factors of } 6} = \frac{\pm 1, \pm 2}{\pm 1, \pm 2, \pm 3, \pm 6} = \pm 1, \pm \frac{1}{2}, \pm \frac{1}{3}, \pm \frac{1}{6}, \pm \frac{2}{3}, \pm 2$$

Trying $x = 1$ produces the following.

$$
\begin{array}{r|rrrr}
1 & 6 & -4 & 3 & -2 \\
  &   & 6 & 2 & 5 \\
\hline
  & 6 & 2 & 5 & 3
\end{array}
$$

So, $x = 1$ is not a zero, but because the last row has all positive entries, you know that $x = 1$ is an upper bound for the real zeros. Therefore, you can restrict the search to zeros less than 1. By testing the possible rational zeros less than 1, you can determine that $x = \frac{2}{3}$ is a zero. So,

$$f(x) = \left(x - \frac{2}{3}\right)(6x^2 + 3).$$

Because $6x^2 + 3$ has no real zeros, it follows that $x = \frac{2}{3}$ is the only real zero.

Before concluding this section, two additional hints that can help you find the real zeros of a polynomial are listed below.

1. If the terms of $f(x)$ have a common monomial factor, it should be factored out before applying the tests in this section. For instance, by writing

$$f(x) = x^4 - 5x^3 + 3x^2 + x = x(x^3 - 5x^2 + 3x + 1)$$

you can see that $x = 0$ is a zero of f and that the remaining zeros can be obtained by analyzing the cubic factor.

2. If you are able to find all but two zeros of $f(x)$, you can always use the Quadratic Formula on the remaining quadratic factor. For instance, if you succeeded in writing

$$f(x) = x^4 - 5x^3 + 3x^2 + x = x(x - 1)(x^2 - 4x - 1)$$

you can apply the Quadratic Formula to $x^2 - 4x - 1$ to conclude that the two remaining zeros are $x = 2 + \sqrt{5}$ and $x = 2 - \sqrt{5}$.

Writing About Math   *Finding Patterns in Polynomial Division*

Complete the following polynomial divisions.

a. $\dfrac{x^2 - 1}{x - 1} =$ [   ]   **b.** $\dfrac{x^3 - 1}{x - 1} =$ [   ]   **c.** $\dfrac{x^4 - 1}{x - 1} =$ [   ]

Write a brief description of the pattern that you obtain, and use your result to find a formula for the polynomial division $(x^n - 1)/(x - 1)$. Create a numerical example to test your formula.

Exploration

Use a graphing utility to graph

$$y_1 = 6x^3 - 4x^2 + 3x - 2.$$

Notice that the graph intersects the x-axis at the point $\left(\frac{2}{3}, 0\right)$. How does this relate to the real zero found in Example 10? Use a graphing utility to graph

$$y_2 = x^4 - 5x^3 + 3x^2 + x.$$

How many times does the graph intersect the x-axis? How many real zeros does y_2 have?

A computer animation of this example appears in the *Interactive* CD-ROM and *Internet* versions of this text.

Exploration

Use a graphing utility to graph

$$y = x^3 + 4.9x^2 - 126x + 382.5$$

in the standard viewing window. From the graph, what do the real zeros appear to be? Discuss how the mathematical tools of this section might help you realize that the graph does not show all the important features of the polynomial function. Now use the *zoom* feature to find all the zeros of this function.

3.3   E x e r c i s e s

Graphical Analysis   **In Exercises 1–6, use a graphing utility to graph the two equations in the same viewing window. Use the graphs to verify that the expressions are equivalent. Verify the results algebraically.**

1. $y_1 = \dfrac{4x}{x-1}, \quad y_2 = 4 + \dfrac{4}{x-1}$

2. $y_1 = \dfrac{3x-5}{x-3}, \quad y_2 = 3 + \dfrac{4}{x-3}$

3. $y_1 = \dfrac{x^2}{x+2}, \quad y_2 = x - 2 + \dfrac{4}{x+2}$

4. $y_1 = \dfrac{x^4 - 3x^2 - 1}{x^2 + 5}, \quad y_2 = x^2 - 8 + \dfrac{39}{x^2 + 5}$

5. $y_1 = \dfrac{x^5 - 3x^3}{x^2 + 1}, \quad y_2 = x^3 - 4x + \dfrac{4x}{x^2 + 1}$

6. $y_1 = \dfrac{x^3 - 2x^2 + 5}{x^2 + x + 1}, \quad y_2 = x - 3 + \dfrac{2(x+4)}{x^2 + x + 1}$

In Exercises 7–18, divide using long division.

7. Divide $2x^2 + 10x + 12$ by $x + 3$.

8. Divide $5x^2 - 17x - 12$ by $x - 4$.

9. Divide $4x^3 - 7x^2 - 11x + 5$ by $4x + 5$.

10. Divide $x^4 + 5x^3 + 6x^2 - x - 2$ by $x + 2$.

11. Divide $7x + 3$ by $x + 2$.

12. Divide $8x - 5$ by $2x + 1$.

13. $(6x^3 + 10x^2 + x + 8) \div (2x^2 + 1)$

14. $(x^3 - 9) \div (x^2 + 1)$

15. $\dfrac{x^4 + 3x^2 + 1}{x^2 - 2x + 3}$

16. $\dfrac{x^5 + 7}{x^3 - 1}$

17. $\dfrac{2x^3 - 4x^2 - 15x + 5}{(x-1)^2}$

18. $\dfrac{x^4}{(x-1)^3}$

In Exercises 19–28, divide using synthetic division.

19. $(3x^3 - 10x^2 + 12x - 22) \div (x - 4)$

20. $(2x^3 + 6x^2 - 14x + 9) \div (x - 1)$

21. $(6x^3 + 7x^2 - x + 26) \div (x - 3)$

22. $(2x^3 + 14x^2 - 20x + 7) \div (x + 6)$

23. $(9x^3 - 18x^2 - 16x + 32) \div (x - 2)$

24. $(5x^3 + 6x + 8) \div (x + 2)$

25. $\dfrac{x^3 + 512}{x + 8}$

26. $\dfrac{x^3 - 729}{x - 9}$

27. $\dfrac{4x^3 + 16x^2 - 23x - 15}{x + \frac{1}{2}}$

28. $\dfrac{3x^3 - 4x^2 + 5}{x - \frac{3}{2}}$

In Exercises 29–34, express the function in the form $f(x) = (x - k)q(x) + r(x)$ for the given value of k. Use a graphing utility to demonstrate that $f(k) = r$.

Function	*Value of k*
29. $f(x) = x^3 - x^2 - 14x + 11$	$k = 4$
30. $f(x) = 15x^4 + 10x^3 - 6x^2 + 14$	$k = -\frac{2}{3}$
31. $f(x) = x^3 + 3x^2 - 2x - 14$	$k = \sqrt{2}$
32. $f(x) = x^3 + 2x^2 - 5x - 4$	$k = -\sqrt{5}$
33. $f(x) = 4x^3 - 6x^2 - 12x - 4$	$k = 1 - \sqrt{3}$
34. $f(x) = -3x^3 + 8x^2 + 10x - 8$	$k = 2 + \sqrt{2}$

In Exercises 35–38, use synthetic division to find each function value. Use a graphing utility to verify your result.

35. $f(x) = 4x^3 - 13x + 10$

    (a) $f(1)$ (b) $f(-2)$ (c) $f\left(\frac{1}{2}\right)$ (d) $f(8)$

36. $g(x) = x^6 - 4x^4 + 3x^2 + 2$

    (a) $g(2)$ (b) $g(-4)$ (c) $g(3)$ (d) $g(-1)$

37. $h(x) = 3x^3 + 5x^2 - 10x + 1$

    (a) $h(3)$ (b) $h\left(\frac{1}{3}\right)$ (c) $h(-2)$ (d) $h(-5)$

38. $f(x) = 0.4x^4 - 1.6x^3 + 0.7x^2 - 2$

    (a) $f(1)$ (b) $f(-2)$ (c) $f(5)$ (d) $f(-10)$

In Exercises 39–44, use synthetic division to show that x is a solution of the third-degree polynomial equation, and use the result to factor the polynomial completely. List all the real zeros of the function.

Polynomial Equation	*Value of x*
39. $x^3 - 7x + 6 = 0$	$x = 2$
40. $x^3 - 28x - 48 = 0$	$x = -4$
41. $2x^3 - 15x^2 + 27x - 10 = 0$	$x = \frac{1}{2}$
42. $x^3 + 2x^2 - 3x - 6 = 0$	$x = -2$
43. $x^3 + 2x^2 - 2x - 4 = 0$	$x = -2$
44. $x^3 - x^2 - 13x - 3 = 0$	$x = -3$

In Exercises 45–50, (a) verify the given factors of the function f, (b) find the remaining factors of f, (c) use your results to write the complete factorization of f, (d) list all real zeros of f, and (e) confirm your results by using a graphing utility to graph the function.

	Function	Factors
45.	$f(x) = 2x^3 + x^2 - 5x + 2$	$(x + 2), (x - 1)$
46.	$f(x) = 3x^3 + 2x^2 - 19x + 6$	$(x + 3), (x - 2)$
47.	$f(x) = x^4 - 4x^3 - 15x^2 + 58x - 40$	$(x - 5), (x + 4)$
48.	$f(x) = 8x^4 - 14x^3 - 71x^2 - 10x + 24$	$(x + 2), (x - 4)$
49.	$f(x) = 6x^3 + 41x^2 - 9x - 14$	$(2x + 1), (3x - 2)$
50.	$f(x) = 2x^3 - x^2 - 10x + 5$	$(2x - 1), (x + \sqrt{5})$

In Exercises 51–54, use the Rational Zero Test to list all possible rational zeros of f. Verify that the zeros of f shown on the graph are contained in the list.

51. $f(x) = x^3 + 3x^2 - x - 3$

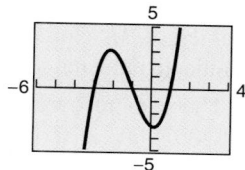

52. $f(x) = x^3 - 4x^2 - 4x + 16$

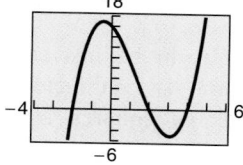

53. $f(x) = 2x^4 - 17x^3 + 35x^2 + 9x - 45$

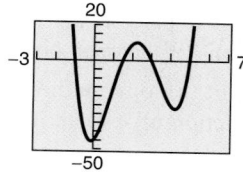

54. $f(x) = 4x^5 - 8x^4 - 5x^3 + 10x^2 + x - 2$

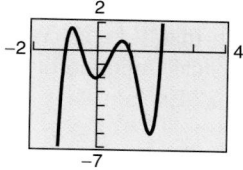

In Exercises 55–62, (a) list the possible rational zeros of f, (b) use a graphing utility to graph f so that some of the possible zeros in part (a) can be disregarded, and (c) determine all the real zeros of f.

55. $f(x) = x^3 + x^2 - 4x - 4$

56. $f(x) = -3x^3 + 20x^2 - 36x + 16$

57. $f(x) = -4x^3 + 15x^2 - 8x - 3$

58. $f(x) = 4x^3 - 12x^2 - x + 15$

59. $f(x) = -2x^4 + 13x^3 - 21x^2 + 2x + 8$

60. $f(x) = 4x^4 - 17x^2 + 4$

61. $f(x) = 6x^3 - x^2 - 13x + 8$

62. $f(x) = 4x^3 + 7x^2 - 11x - 18$

In Exercises 63–68, find all the real solutions of the polynomial equation.

63. $z^4 - z^3 - 2z - 4 = 0$

64. $x^4 - x^3 - 29x^2 - x - 30 = 0$

65. $x^4 - 13x^2 - 12x = 0$

66. $2y^4 + 7y^3 - 26y^2 + 23y - 6 = 0$

67. $2x^4 - 11x^3 - 6x^2 + 64x + 32 = 0$

68. $x^5 - x^4 - 3x^3 + 5x^2 - 2x = 0$

Graphical Analysis In Exercises 69–74, (a) use the *zero* or *root* feature of a graphing utility to approximate (accurate to three decimal places) the zeros of the function, (b) determine one of the exact zeros and use synthetic division to verify your result, and (c) factor the polynomial completely.

69. $f(x) = x^3 - 2x^2 - 5x + 10$

70. $g(x) = x^3 - 4x^2 - 2x + 8$

71. $h(t) = t^3 - 2t^2 - 7t + 2$

72. $f(s) = s^3 - 12s^2 + 40s - 24$

73. $h(x) = x^5 - 7x^4 + 10x^3 + 14x^2 - 24x$

74. $g(x) = 6x^4 - 11x^3 - 51x^2 + 99x - 27$

In Exercises 75–78, use synthetic division to verify the upper bound and lower bound of the zeros of f.

75. $f(x) = x^4 - 4x^3 + 15$

Upper bound: $x = 4$; Lower bound: $x = -1$

76. $f(x) = 2x^3 - 3x^2 - 12x + 8$

Upper bound: $x = 4$; Lower bound: $x = -3$

77. $f(x) = x^4 - 4x^3 + 16x - 16$

Upper bound: $x = 5$; Lower bound: $x = -3$

78. $f(x) = 2x^4 - 8x + 3$

Upper bound: $x = 3$; Lower bound: $x = -4$

In Exercises 79–82, find the rational zeros of the polynomial function.

79. $P(x) = x^4 - \frac{25}{4}x^2 + 9 = \frac{1}{4}(4x^4 - 25x^2 + 36)$

80. $f(x) = x^3 - \frac{3}{2}x^2 - \frac{23}{2}x + 6 = \frac{1}{2}(2x^3 - 3x^2 - 23x + 12)$

81. $f(x) = x^3 - \frac{1}{4}x^2 - x + \frac{1}{4} = \frac{1}{4}(4x^3 - x^2 - 4x + 1)$

82. $f(z) = z^3 + \frac{11}{6}z^2 - \frac{1}{2}z - \frac{1}{3} = \frac{1}{6}(6z^3 + 11z^2 - 3z - 2)$

In Exercises 83–86, match the cubic function with the correct number of rational and irrational zeros.
(a) Rational zeros: 0; Irrational zeros: 1
(b) Rational zeros: 3; Irrational zeros: 0
(c) Rational zeros: 1; Irrational zeros: 2
(d) Rational zeros: 1; Irrational zeros: 0

83. $f(x) = x^3 - 1$

84. $f(x) = x^3 - 2$

85. $f(x) = x^3 - x$

86. $f(x) = x^3 - 2x$

87. *Data Analysis*   The average monthly basic rates R for cable television in the United States for the years 1988 through 1997 are given in the table, where t represents the time (in years), with $t = 0$ corresponding to 1990. (Source: Paul Kagan Associates, Inc.)

t	-2	-1	0	1	2
R	13.86	15.21	16.78	18.10	19.08

t	3	4	5	6	7
R	19.39	21.62	23.07	24.41	26.48

(a) Use a graphing utility to sketch a scatter plot of the data.

(b) Use the regression capabilities of a graphing utility to find a cubic model for the data. Then graph the model in the same viewing window as the scatter plot. Compare the model with the data.

(c) Use a graphing utility and the model to create a table of estimated values of R. Compare the estimated values with the actual data.

(d) Use the Remainder Theorem to evaluate the model for the year 2002. Even though the model is relatively accurate for estimating the given data, do you think it is accurate to predict future cable rates? Explain.

88. *Data Analysis*   The number of United States military personnel M (in thousands) on active duty for the years 1989 through 1996 is shown in the table, where t represents the time (in years), with $t = 0$ corresponding to 1990. (Source: U.S. Department of Defense)

t	-1	0	1	2
M	2130	2044	1986	1807

t	3	4	5	6
M	1705	1611	1518	1472

(a) Use a graphing utility to sketch a scatter plot of the data.

(b) Use the regression capabilities of a graphing utility to find a cubic model for the data. Then graph the model in the same viewing window as the scatter plot. Compare the model with the data.

(c) Use a graphing utility and the model to create a table of estimated values of M. Compare the estimated values with the actual data.

(d) Use the Remainder Theorem to evaluate the model for the year 2001. Even though the model is relatively accurate for estimating the given data, would you use this model to predict the number of military personnel in the future? Explain.

89. *Geometry*   An open box is to be made from a rectangular piece of material 15 centimeters by 9 centimeters by cutting equal squares from the corners and turning up the sides.

(a) Let x represent the length of the sides of the squares. Draw a diagram showing the squares removed from the original piece of material and the resulting dimensions of the open box.

(b) Use the diagram in part (a) to write the volume V of the box as a function of x. Determine the domain of the function.

(c) Use a graphing utility to graph the function and approximate the dimensions of the box that yield maximum volume.

(d) Find values of x such that $V = 56$. Which of these values is a physical impossibility in the construction of the box? Explain.

90. *Geometry*   A rectangular package sent by a delivery service can have a maximum combined length and girth (perimeter of a cross section) of 120 inches.

(a) Show that the volume of the package is

$$V(x) = 4x^2(30 - x).$$

(b) Use a graphing utility to graph the function and approximate the dimensions of the package that yield a maximum volume.

(c) Find values of x such that $V = 13,500$. Which of these values is a physical impossibility in the construction of the package? Explain.

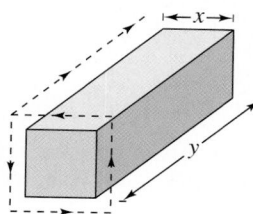

91. *Automobile Emissions*   The number of parts per million of nitric oxide emissions y from a certain car engine is approximated by the model

$$y = -5.05x^3 + 3857x - 38,411.25, \quad 13 \le x \le 18$$

where x is the air-fuel ratio.

(a) Use a graphing utility to graph the emissions function.

(b) It is observed from the graph that two air-fuel ratios produce 2400 parts per million of nitric oxide, with one being 15. Use the graph to approximate the second air-fuel ratio.

(c) Algebraically approximate the second air-fuel ratio that produces 2400 parts per million of nitric oxide. (*Hint:* Because you know that an air-fuel ratio of 15 produces the specified nitric oxide emission, you can use synthetic division.)

92. *Advertising Costs*   A company that manufactures bicycles estimates that the profit for selling a particular model is

$$P = -45x^3 + 2500x^2 - 275,000, \quad 0 \le x \le 50$$

where P is the profit (in dollars) and x is the advertising expense (in tens of thousands of dollars). According to this model, find the smaller of two advertising amounts that yield a profit of $800,000.

Synthesis

True or False?   **In Exercises 93–95, determine whether the statement is true or false. Justify your answer.**

93. If $(7x + 4)$ is a factor of some polynomial function f, then $\frac{4}{7}$ is a root of f.

94. The rational expression $\dfrac{x^3 + 2x^2 - 13x + 10}{x^2 - 4x - 12}$ is improper.

95. $(2x - 1)$ is a factor of the function

$$f(x) = 6x^6 + x^5 - 92x^4 + 45x^3 + 184x^2$$
$$+ \, 4x - 48.$$

Think About It   **In Exercises 96 and 97, perform the division by assuming that n is a positive integer.**

96. $\dfrac{x^{3n} + 9x^{2n} + 27x^n + 27}{x^n + 3}$

97. $\dfrac{x^{3n} - 3x^{2n} + 5x^n - 6}{x^n - 2}$

98. *Think About It*   What does it mean for a divisor to divide evenly into a dividend?

99. *Writing*   Write a short paragraph explaining how you can check polynomial division. Give an example.

Review

In Exercises 100–103, perform the operations and write the result in standard form.

100. $12 - (-7 + 5i) + (-2 + 3i)$

101. $-8i - i(2 + 3i)$

102. $(-3 - 8i)^2$ **103.** $\dfrac{6 - i}{1 - 4i}$

In Exercises 104–107, find a polynomial function that has the given zeros.

104. $0, -12$ **105.** $1, -3, 8$

106. $0, -1, 2, 5$ **107.** $2 + \sqrt{3}, 2 - \sqrt{3}$

3.4   The Fundamental Theorem of Algebra

The Fundamental Theorem of Algebra

You have been using the fact that an *n*th-degree polynomial can have at most *n* real zeros. In the complex number system, this statement can be improved. That is, in the complex number system, every *n*th-degree polynomial function has *precisely n* zeros. This important result is derived from the **Fundamental Theorem of Algebra,** first proved by the famous German mathematician Carl Friedrich Gauss (1777–1855).

The Fundamental Theorem of Algebra

If $f(x)$ is a polynomial of degree n, where $n > 0$, f has at least one zero in the complex number system.

Using the Fundamental Theorem of Algebra and the equivalence of zeros and factors, you obtain the **Linear Factorization Theorem**.

Linear Factorization Theorem

If $f(x)$ is a polynomial of degree n where $n > 0$, f has precisely n linear factors

$$f(x) = a_n(x - c_1)(x - c_2) \cdots (x - c_n)$$

where $c_1, c_2, \ldots, c_n$ are complex numbers.

(A proof of the Linear Factorization Theorem is found in Appendix A.)

Note that neither the Fundamental Theorem of Algebra nor the Linear Factorization Theorem tells you *how* to find the zeros or factors of a polynomial. Such theorems are called *existence theorems*. To find the zeros of a polynomial function, you still must rely on other techniques.

Remember that the *n* zeros of a polynomial function can be real or complex, and they may be repeated. Examples 1 and 2 illustrate several cases.

What You Should Learn:

- How to use the Fundamental Theorem of Algebra to determine the number of zeros of polynomial functions
- How to find all zeros of polynomial functions, including complex zeros
- How to find conjugate pairs of complex zeros
- How to find zeros of polynomials by factoring

Why You Should Learn It:

Being able to find zeros of polynomial functions is an important part of modeling real-life problems. For instance, Exercise 65 on page 270 shows how to determine whether a ball thrown with a given velocity can reach a certain height.

Jed Jacobsohn/Allsport

EXAMPLE 1   Real Zeros of Polynomial Functions

a. The first-degree polynomial $f(x) = x - 2$ has exactly *one* zero: $x = 2$.

b. Counting multiplicity, the second-degree polynomial function

$$f(x) = x^2 - 6x + 9 = (x - 3)(x - 3)$$

has exactly *two* zeros: $x = 3$ and $x = 3$.

Note in Example 1 that you can use a graphing utility to verify graphically the zeros of the polynomial functions.

EXAMPLE 2   Real and Complex Zeros of Polynomial Functions

a. The third-degree polynomial function

$$f(x) = x^3 + 4x = x(x^2 + 4) = x(x - 2i)(x + 2i)$$

has exactly *three* zeros: $x = 0$, $x = 2i$, and $x = -2i$. In the graph in Figure 3.27(a), only the *real* zero $x = 0$ appears as an intercept.

b. The fourth-degree polynomial function

$$f(x) = x^4 - 1 = (x - 1)(x + 1)(x - i)(x + i)$$

has exactly *four* zeros: $x = 1$, $x = -1$, $x = i$, and $x = -i$. In the graph in Figure 3.27(b), only the *real* zeros $x = -1$ and $x = 1$ appear as x-intercepts.

Example 3 shows how to use the methods described in Sections 3.2 and 3.3 (the Rational Zero Test, synthetic division, and factoring) to find all the zeros of a polynomial function, including complex zeros.

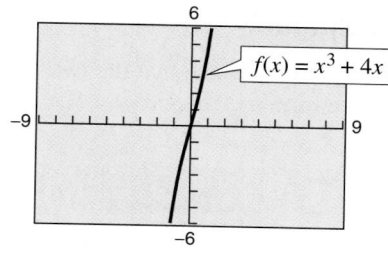

(a)

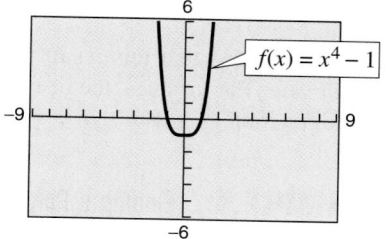

(b)
Figure 3.27

EXAMPLE 3   Finding the Zeros of a Polynomial Function

Write

$$f(x) = x^5 + x^3 + 2x^2 - 12x + 8$$

as the product of linear factors, and list all of its zeros.

Solution

The possible rational zeros are ± 1, ± 2, ± 4, and ± 8. The graph shown in Figure 3.28 indicates that 1 and -2 are good guesses, and that 1 is possibly a repeated zero because it touches the x-axis.

Using synthetic division, you can determine that -2 is a zero and 1 is a repeated zero of f. So, you have

$$f(x) = x^5 + x^3 + 2x^2 - 12x + 8$$
$$= (x - 1)(x - 1)(x + 2)(x^2 + 4).$$

By factoring $x^2 + 4$ as

$$x^2 - (-4) = \left(x - \sqrt{-4}\right)\left(x + \sqrt{-4}\right) = (x - 2i)(x + 2i)$$

you obtain

$$f(x) = (x - 1)(x - 1)(x + 2)(x - 2i)(x + 2i)$$

which gives the following five zeros of f.

$$1, \quad 1, \quad -2, \quad 2i, \quad \text{and} \quad -2i$$

Note from the graph of f shown in Figure 3.28 that the *real* zeros are the only ones that appear as x-intercepts.

You may want to remind students that a graphing calculator is helpful for determining real zeros, which in turn are useful in finding the complex zeros.

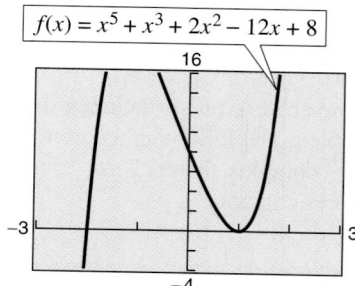

Figure 3.28

Conjugate Pairs

In Example 3, note that the two complex zeros are **conjugates.** That is, they are of the form $a + bi$ and $a - bi$.

Complex Zeros Occur in Conjugate Pairs

Let $f(x)$ be a polynomial function that has *real coefficients*. If $a + bi$, where $b \neq 0$, is a zero of the function, the conjugate $a - bi$ is also a zero of the function.

Be sure you see that this result is true only if the polynomial function has *real coefficients*. For instance, the result applies to the function $f(x) = x^2 + 1$, but not to the function $g(x) = x - i$.

Jean Le Rond d'Alembert (1717–1783) worked independently of Carl Gauss trying to prove the Fundamental Theorem of Algebra. His efforts were such that in France, the Fundamental Theorem of Algebra is frequently known as the Theorem of d'Alembert.

EXAMPLE 4   Finding a Polynomial with Given Zeros

Find a *fourth-degree* polynomial function, with real coefficients, that has -1, -1, and $3i$ as zeros.

Solution

Because $3i$ is a zero *and* the polynomial is stated to have real coefficients, you know that the conjugate $-3i$ must also be a zero. So, from the Linear Factorization Theorem, $f(x)$ can be written as

$$f(x) = a(x + 1)(x + 1)(x - 3i)(x + 3i).$$

For simplicity, let $a = 1$, to obtain

$$f(x) = (x^2 + 2x + 1)(x^2 + 9)$$
$$= x^4 + 2x^3 + 10x^2 + 18x + 9.$$

Factoring a Polynomial

The Linear Factorization Theorem shows that you can write any nth-degree polynomial as the product of n linear factors.

$$f(x) = a(x - c_1)(x - c_2)(x - c_3) \cdots (x - c_n)$$

However, this result includes the possibility that some of the values of c_i are complex. The following theorem says that even if you do not want to get involved with "complex factors," you can still write $f(x)$ as the product of linear and/or quadratic factors.

STUDY T!P

Some graphing utilities can find both real and complex zeros of a function. For instance, to find all the zeros of

$$f(x) = x^4 - 3x^3 + 6x^2 + 2x - 60$$

use the graphing utility's *solve* feature. If your graphing utility can find complex zeros, you will obtain the following solutions.

$$x = 1 + 3i, \quad x = 1 - 3i,$$
$$x = 3, \quad x = -2$$

Factors of a Polynomial

Every polynomial of degree $n > 0$ with real coefficients can be written as the product of linear and quadratic factors with real coefficients, where the quadratic factors have no real zeros.

(For a proof of this theorem, see Appendix A.)

A quadratic factor with no real zeros is said to be **irreducible over the reals.** Be sure you see that this is not the same as being *irreducible over the rationals.* For example, the quadratic

$$x^2 + 1 = (x - i)(x + i)$$

is irreducible over the reals (and therefore over the rationals). On the other hand, the quadratic

$$x^2 - 2 = (x - \sqrt{2})(x + \sqrt{2})$$

is irreducible over the rationals, but *reducible* over the reals.

EXAMPLE 5   Factoring a Polynomial

Write the polynomial

$$f(x) = x^4 - x^2 - 20$$

a. as the product of factors that are irreducible over the *rationals,*

b. as the product of linear factors and quadratic factors that are irreducible over the *reals,* and

c. in completely factored form.

Solution

a. Begin by factoring the polynomial into the product of two quadratic polynomials.

$$x^4 - x^2 - 20 = (x^2 - 5)(x^2 + 4)$$

Both of these factors are irreducible over the rationals.

b. By factoring over the reals, you have

$$x^4 - x^2 - 20 = (x + \sqrt{5})(x - \sqrt{5})(x^2 + 4)$$

where the quadratic factor is irreducible over the reals.

c. In completely factored form, you have

$$x^4 - x^2 - 20 = (x + \sqrt{5})(x - \sqrt{5})(x - 2i)(x + 2i).$$

In Example 5, notice from the completely factored form that the fourth-degree polynomial has four zeros.

Throughout this chapter, the results and theorems have basically been stated in terms of zeros of polynomial functions. Be sure you see that the same results could have been stated in terms of solutions of polynomial equations. This is true because the zeros of the polynomial function

$$f(x) = a_n x^n + a_{n-1} x^{n-1} + \cdots + a_2 x^2 + a_1 x + a_0$$

are precisely the solutions of the polynomial equation

$$a_n x^n + a_{n-1} x^{n-1} + \cdots + a_2 x^2 + a_1 x + a_0 = 0.$$

EXAMPLE 6   Finding the Zeros of a Polynomial Function

Find all the zeros of

$$f(x) = x^4 - 3x^3 + 6x^2 + 2x - 60$$

given that $1 + 3i$ is a zero of f.

Algebraic Solution

Because complex zeros occur in conjugate pairs, you know that $1 - 3i$ is also a zero of f. This means that both

$$x - (1 + 3i) \quad \text{and} \quad x - (1 - 3i)$$

are factors of $f(x)$. Multiplying these two factors produces

$$[x - (1 + 3i)][x - (1 - 3i)] = [(x - 1) - 3i][(x - 1) + 3i]$$
$$= (x - 1)^2 - 9i^2$$
$$= x^2 - 2x + 10.$$

Using long division, you can divide $x^2 - 2x + 10$ into $f(x)$ to obtain the following.

$$
\begin{array}{r}
x^2 - x - 6 \\
x^2 - 2x + 10 \overline{\smash{)}\, x^4 - 3x^3 + 6x^2 + 2x - 60} \\
\underline{x^4 - 2x^3 + 10x^2} \\
-x^3 - 4x^2 + 2x \\
\underline{-x^3 + 2x^2 - 10x} \\
-6x^2 + 12x - 60 \\
\underline{-6x^2 + 12x - 60} \\
0
\end{array}
$$

Therefore, you have

$$f(x) = (x^2 - 2x + 10)(x^2 - x - 6)$$
$$= (x^2 - 2x + 10)(x - 3)(x + 2)$$

and you can conclude that the zeros of f are $1 + 3i$, $1 - 3i$, 3, and -2.

Graphical Solution

Because complex zeros always occur in conjugate pairs, you know that $1 - 3i$ is also a zero of f. Because the polynomial is a fourth-degree polynomial, you know that there are at most two other zeros of the function. Use a graphing utility to graph

$$y = x^4 - 3x^3 + 6x^2 + 2x - 60$$

as shown in Figure 3.29.

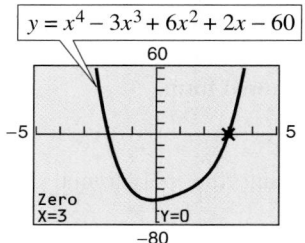

Figure 3.29

You can see that -2 and 3 appear to be x-intercepts of the graph of the function. Use the *zero* or *root* feature or the *zoom* and *trace* features of the graphing utility to confirm that $x = -2$ and $x = 3$ are x-intercepts of the graph. So, you can conclude that the zeros of f are

$$1 + 3i, \quad 1 - 3i, \quad 3, \quad \text{and} \quad -2.$$

In Example 6, if you had not been told that $1 + 3i$ is a zero of f, you could still find all zeros of the function. You could use synthetic division to find the real zeros -2 and 3. Then, you could factor the polynomial as $(x + 2)(x - 3)(x^2 - 2x + 10)$. Finally, by using the Quadratic Formula, you could determine that the zeros are $1 + 3i$, $1 - 3i$, 3, and -2.

W r i t i n g   A b o u t   M a t h   *Factoring a Polynomial*

Compile a list of all the various techniques for factoring a polynomial that have been covered so far in the text. Give an example illustrating each technique, and write a paragraph discussing when the use of each technique is appropriate.

Activities

1. Write as a product of linear factors:
   $f(x) = x^4 - 16$.
   Answer:
   $(x - 2)(x + 2)(x - 2i)(x + 2i)$

2. Find a third-degree polynomial with integer coefficients that has 2, $3 + i$, and $3 - i$ as zeros.
   Answer: $x^3 - 8x^2 + 22x - 20$

3. Use the zero $x = 2i$ to find the zeros of $f(x) = x^4 - x^3 - 2x^2 - 4x - 24$.
   Answer: $-2, 3, 2i, -2i$

3.4   Exercises

In Exercises 1–8, find all the zeros of the function.

1. $f(x) = x(x - 6)^2$

2. $f(x) = x^2(x + 3)(x^2 - 1)$

3. $g(x) = (x - 2)(x + 4)^3$ **4.** $f(x) = (x + 5)(x - 8)^2$

5. $f(x) = (x + 6)(x + i)(x - i)$

6. $h(t) = (t - 3)(t - 2)(t - 3i)(t + 3i)$

7. $f(x) = (x - 2)(x + 3 - 5i)(x + 3 + 5i)$

8. $h(m) = (m - 4)^2(m - 2 + 4i)(m - 2 - 4i)$

Graphical and Analytical Analysis   In Exercises 9–12, find all the zeros of the function. Is there a relationship between the number of real zeros and the number of x-intercepts of the graph? Explain.

9. $f(x) = x^3 - 4x^2$
$\quad + x - 4$

10. $f(x) = x^3 - 4x^2$
$\quad - 4x + 16$

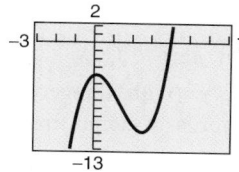

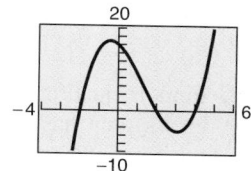

11. $f(x) = x^4 + 4x^2 + 4$ **12.** $f(x) = x^4 - 3x^2 - 4$

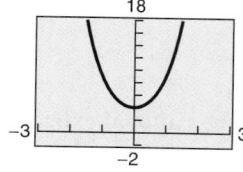

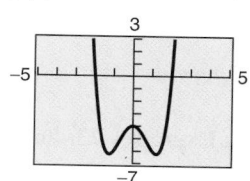

In Exercises 13–32, find all the zeros of the function and write the polynomial as a product of linear factors. Use a graphing utility to graph the function to verify your results graphically. (If your graphing utility can find complex zeros, use it to verify the complex zeros.)

13. $h(x) = x^2 - 4x + 1$ **14.** $g(x) = x^2 + 10x + 23$

15. $f(x) = x^2 - 12x + 26$ **16.** $f(x) = x^2 + 6x - 2$

17. $f(x) = x^2 + 25$ **18.** $f(x) = x^2 - x + 56$

19. $f(x) = x^4 - 81$ **20.** $f(y) = y^4 - 625$

21. $f(z) = z^2 - 2z + 2$

22. $h(x) = x^3 - 3x^2 + 4x - 2$

23. $f(t) = t^3 - 3t^2 - 15t + 125$

24. $f(x) = x^3 + 11x^2 + 39x + 29$

25. $f(x) = 16x^3 - 20x^2 - 4x + 15$

26. $f(s) = 2s^3 - 5s^2 + 12s - 5$

27. $f(x) = x^4 + 10x^2 + 9$

28. $f(x) = x^4 + 29x^2 + 100$

29. $g(x) = x^4 - 4x^3 + 8x^2 - 16x + 16$

30. $h(x) = x^4 + 6x^3 + 10x^2 + 6x + 9$

31. $f(x) = 2x^4 + 5x^3 + 4x^2 + 5x + 2$

32. $g(x) = x^5 - 8x^4 + 28x^3 - 56x^2 + 64x - 32$

In Exercises 33–40, (a) find all zeros of the function, (b) write the polynomial as a product of linear factors, (c) use your factorization to determine the x-intercepts of the graph of the function, and (d) use a graphing utility to verify that the real zeros are the only x-intercepts.

33. $f(x) = x^2 - 14x + 46$ **34.** $f(x) = x^2 - 12x + 34$

35. $f(x) = x^2 + 14x + 44$ **36.** $f(x) = x^2 - 16x + 62$

37. $f(x) = x^3 - 11x + 150$

38. $f(x) = x^3 + 10x^2 + 33x + 34$

39. $f(x) = x^4 + 25x^2 + 144$

40. $f(x) = x^4 - 8x^3 + 17x^2 - 8x + 16$

In Exercises 41–48, find a polynomial function with integer coefficients that has the given zeros. (There are many correct answers.)

41. $1, 5i, -5i$

42. $4, 3i, -3i$

43. $2, 4 + i, 4 - i$

44. $6, -5 + 2i, -5 - 2i$

45. $i, -i, 6i, -6i$

46. $2, 2, 2, 4i, -4i$

47. $-5, -5, 1 + \sqrt{3}i$

48. $0, 0, 4, 1 + \sqrt{2}i$

In Exercises 49–52, write the polynomial (a) as the product of factors that are irreducible over the *rationals*, (b) as the product of linear and quadratic factors that are irreducible over the *reals*, and (c) in completely factored form.

49. $f(x) = x^4 - 6x^2 - 7$ **50.** $f(x) = x^4 + 6x^2 - 27$

51. $f(x) = x^4 - 2x^3 - 3x^2 + 12x - 18$
   (*Hint:* One factor is $x^2 - 6$.)

52. $f(x) = x^4 - 3x^3 - x^2 - 12x - 20$
   (*Hint:* One factor is $x^2 + 4$.)

In Exercises 53–60, use the given zero to find all the zeros of the function.

	Function	*Zero*
53.	$f(x) = 2x^3 + 3x^2 + 50x + 75$	$5i$
54.	$f(x) = 2x^4 - x^3 + 7x^2 - 4x - 4$	$2i$
55.	$g(x) = x^3 - 7x^2 - x + 87$	$5 + 2i$
56.	$g(x) = 4x^3 + 23x^2 + 34x - 10$	$-3 + i$
57.	$h(x) = 3x^3 - 4x^2 + 8x + 8$	$1 - \sqrt{3}i$
58.	$f(x) = x^3 + 4x^2 + 14x + 20$	$-1 - 3i$
59.	$h(x) = 8x^3 - 14x^2 + 18x - 9$	$\frac{1}{2}(1 - \sqrt{5}i)$
60.	$f(x) = 25x^3 - 55x^2 - 54x - 18$	$\frac{1}{5}(-2 + \sqrt{2}i)$

Graphical Analysis **In Exercises 61–64, (a) use the *zero* or *root* feature of a graphing utility to approximate the zeros of the function accurate to three decimal places, (b) determine one of the exact zeros and use synthetic division to verify your result, and (c) find the exact values of the remaining zeros.**

61. $f(x) = x^4 + 3x^3 - 5x^2 - 21x + 22$

62. $f(x) = x^3 + 4x^2 + 14x + 20$

63. $h(x) = 8x^3 - 14x^2 + 18x - 9$

64. $f(x) = 25x^3 - 55x^2 - 54x - 18$

65. *Maximum Height* A baseball is thrown upward from ground level with an initial velocity of 48 feet per second, and its height h (in feet) is

$$h = -16t^2 + 48t, \quad 0 \le t \le 3$$

where t is the time (in seconds). Suppose you are told that the ball reaches a height of 64 feet. Is this possible? Explain.

66. *Profit* The demand equation for a microwave is

$$p = 140 - 0.0001x$$

where p is the unit price (in dollars) of the microwave and x is the number of units produced and sold. The cost equation for the microwave is

$$C = 80x + 150,000$$

where C is the total cost (in dollars) and x is the number of units produced. The total profit obtained by producing and selling x units is

$$P = R - C = xp - C.$$

Suppose you are working in the marketing department that produces this microwave, and you are asked to determine a price p that would yield a profit of 9 million dollars. Is this possible? Explain.

Synthesis

True or False? **In Exercises 67 and 68, decide whether the statement is true or false. Justify your answer.**

67. It is possible for a third-degree polynomial function with integer coefficients to have no real zeros.

68. If $x = 4 + 3i$ is a zero of the function $f(x) = x^4 - 7x^3 - 13x^2 + 265x - 750$, then $x = -3i + 4$ must also be a zero of f.

69. *Exploration* Use a graphing utility to graph the function $f(x) = x^4 - 4x^2 + k$ for different values of k. Find values of k such that the zeros of f satisfy the specified characteristics. (Some parts have many correct answers.)

(a) Four real zeros

(b) Two real zeros each of multiplicity 2

(c) Two real zeros and two complex zeros

(d) Four complex zeros

70. *Think About It* Will the answers to Exercise 69 change for the function g?

(a) $g(x) = f(x - 2)$ (b) $g(x) = f(2x)$

71. Find a quadratic function f (with integer coefficients) that has $\pm\sqrt{b}i$ as zeros. Assume that b is a positive integer.

72. Find a quadratic function f (with integer coefficients) that has $a \pm bi$ as zeros. Assume that b is a positive integer.

Review

In Exercises 73–76, simplify the rational expression.

73. $\dfrac{x^2 - 8x + 15}{x^2 - 9}$ **74.** $\dfrac{x^2 - 4x - 12}{x^2 - 36}$

75. $\dfrac{x^3 - 9x^2 + 20x}{x^2 - 4x}$ **76.** $\dfrac{x^3 - 6x^2 - 5x + 30}{x^3 - 3x^2 - 18x}$

In Exercises 77–80, sketch the graph of the function. Identify the vertex and any intercepts. Use a graphing utility to verify your results.

77. $f(x) = x^2 - 7x - 8$

78. $f(x) = -x^2 + x + 6$

79. $f(x) = 6x^2 + 5x - 6$

80. $f(x) = 4x^2 + 2x - 12$

3.5 Rational Functions and Asymptotes

Introduction to Rational Functions

A **rational function** can be written in the form

$$f(x) = \frac{N(x)}{D(x)}$$

where $N(x)$ and $D(x)$ are polynomials and $D(x)$ is not the zero polynomial. In this section it is assumed that $N(x)$ and $D(x)$ have no common factors.

In general, the *domain* of a rational function of x includes all real numbers except x-values that make the denominator zero. Much of the discussion of rational functions will focus on their graphical behavior near these x-values.

What You Should Learn:

- How to find domains of rational functions
- How to find horizontal and vertical asymptotes of graphs of rational functions
- How to use rational functions to model and solve real-life problems

Why You Should Learn It:

Rational functions are convenient in modeling a wide variety of real-life problems, such as environmental scenarios. For instance, Exercise 31 on page 278 shows how to determine the cost of removing pollutants from a river.

David Woodfull/Tony Stone Images

EXAMPLE 1 Finding the Domain of a Rational Function

Find the domain of $f(x) = 1/x$ and discuss the behavior of f near any excluded x-values.

Solution

Because the denominator is zero when $x = 0$, the domain of f is all real numbers except $x = 0$. To determine the behavior of f near this excluded value, evaluate $f(x)$ to the left and right of $x = 0$, as indicated in the following tables.

x	-1	-0.5	-0.1	-0.01	-0.001	$\rightarrow 0$
$f(x)$	-1	-2	-10	-100	-1000	$\rightarrow -\infty$

x	$0 \leftarrow$	0.001	0.01	0.1	0.5	1
$f(x)$	$\infty \leftarrow$	1000	100	10	2	1

Note that as x approaches 0 *from the left*, $f(x)$ decreases without bound. In contrast, as x approaches 0 *from the right*, $f(x)$ increases without bound. The graph of f is shown in Figure 3.30.

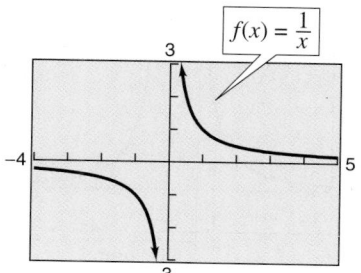

Figure 3.30

Horizontal and Vertical Asymptotes

In Example 1, the behavior of $f(x) = 1/x$ near $x = 0$ is denoted as follows.

$$f(x) \to -\infty \text{ as } x \to 0^-$$

$f(x)$ decreases without bound as x approaches 0 from the left.

$$f(x) \to \infty \text{ as } x \to 0^+$$

$f(x)$ increases without bound as x approaches 0 from the right.

The line $x = 0$ is a **vertical asymptote** of the graph of f, as shown in Figure 3.31. The graph of f also has a **horizontal asymptote**—the line $y = 0$. This means the values of $f(x) = 1/x$ approach zero as x increases or decreases without bound.

$$f(x) \to 0 \text{ as } x \to -\infty$$

$f(x)$ approaches 0 as x decreases without bound.

$$f(x) \to 0 \text{ as } x \to \infty$$

$f(x)$ approaches 0 as x increases without bound.

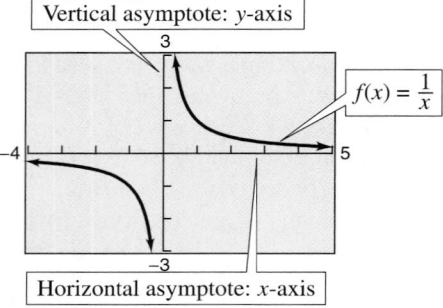

Vertical asymptote: y-axis

$f(x) = \dfrac{1}{x}$

Horizontal asymptote: x-axis

Figure 3.31

Definition of Vertical and Horizontal Asymptotes

1. The line $x = a$ is a **vertical asymptote** of the graph of f if $f(x) \to \infty$ or $f(x) \to -\infty$ as $x \to a$, either from the right or from the left.
2. The line $y = b$ is a **horizontal asymptote** of the graph of f if $f(x) \to b$ as $x \to \infty$ or $x \to -\infty$.

Eventually (as $x \to \infty$ or $x \to -\infty$), the distance between the horizontal asymptote and the points on the graph must approach zero. Figure 3.32 shows the horizontal and vertical asymptotes of the graphs of three rational functions.

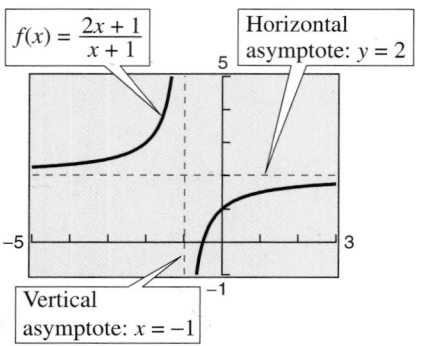

$f(x) = \dfrac{2x + 1}{x + 1}$

Horizontal asymptote: $y = 2$

Vertical asymptote: $x = -1$

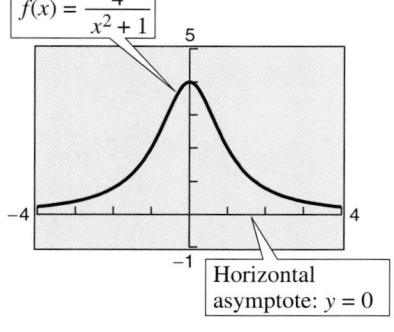

$f(x) = \dfrac{4}{x^2 + 1}$

Horizontal asymptote: $y = 0$

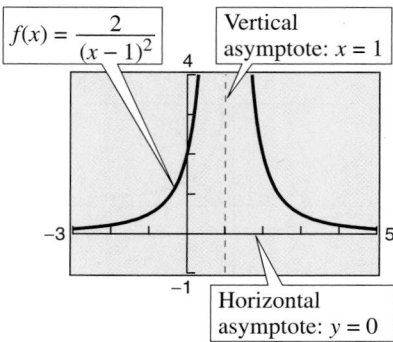

$f(x) = \dfrac{2}{(x - 1)^2}$

Vertical asymptote: $x = 1$

Horizontal asymptote: $y = 0$

Figure 3.32

Library of Functions

A rational function $f(x)$ is the quotient of two polynomials, $f(x) = N(x)/D(x)$. A rational function is not defined at points x for which $D(x) = 0$. Near these points, the graph of the rational function may increase or decrease without bound.

Consult the Library of Functions Summary inside the front cover for a description of the rational functions.

Exploration

Use a graphing utility to graph $g(x) = (3x^2)/(x^2 + 2)$ in a standard viewing window. Graph $g(x)$ again, using a viewing window in which $-100 \le x \le 100$. Graph $g(x)$ a third time, using a viewing window in which $-1000 \le x \le 1000$. Describe the left and right behavior of the graphs. Complete the table.

x	10	100	1000
$g(x)$			

x	-10	-100	-1000
$g(x)$			

As the x-values become very large or very small, what do the values of $g(x)$ approach? What is the horizontal asymptote of the graph of g?

Asymptotes of a Rational Function

Let f be the rational function

$$f(x) = \frac{N(x)}{D(x)}$$

$$= \frac{a_n x^n + a_{n-1} x^{n-1} + \cdots + a_1 x + a_0}{b_m x^m + b_{m-1} x^{m-1} + \cdots + b_1 x + b_0}$$

where $N(x)$ and $D(x)$ have no common factors.

1. The graph of f has vertical asymptotes at the zeros of $D(x)$.
2. The graph of f has at most one horizontal asymptote determined by comparing the degrees of $N(x)$ and $D(x)$.
   a. If $n < m$, the line $y = 0$ (the x-axis) is a horizontal asymptote.
   b. If $n = m$, the line $y = a_n/b_m$ is a horizontal asymptote.
   c. If $n > m$, the graph of f has no horizontal asymptote.

Exploration

Use a graphing utility to compare the graphs of y_1 and y_2.

$$y_1 = \frac{3x^3 - 5x^2 + 4x - 5}{2x^2 - 6x + 7}$$

$$y_2 = \frac{3x^3}{2x^2}$$

Start with a viewing window in which $-5 \leq x \leq 5$ and $-10 \leq y \leq 10$, then zoom out. Write a convincing argument that the shape of the graph of a rational function eventually behaves like the graph of $y = a_n x^n / b_m x^m$, where $a_n x^n$ is the leading term of the numerator and $b_m x^m$ is the leading term of the denominator.

EXAMPLE 2   Finding Horizontal Asymptotes

a. The graph of

$$f(x) = \frac{2x}{3x^2 + 1}$$

has the line $y = 0$ (the x-axis) as a horizontal asymptote, as shown in Figure 3.33(a). Note that the degree of the numerator is *less than* the degree of the denominator.

b. The graph of

$$g(x) = \frac{2x^2}{3x^2 + 1}$$

has the line $y = \frac{2}{3}$ as a horizontal asymptote, as shown in Figure 3.33(b). Note that the degree of the numerator is *equal to* the degree of the denominator, and the horizontal asymptote is given by the ratio of the leading coefficients of the numerator and denominator.

c. The graph of

$$h(x) = \frac{2x^3}{3x^2 + 1}$$

has no horizontal asymptote because the degree of the numerator is *greater than* the degree of the denominator. See Figure 3.33(c).

Although the graph of the function in part (c) does not have a horizontal asymptote, it does have a *slant asymptote*—the line $y = \frac{2}{3}x$. You will study slant asymptotes in the next section.

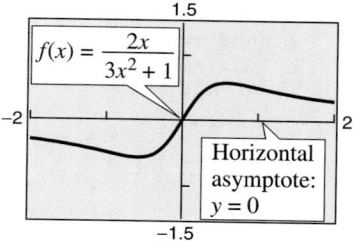

(a)

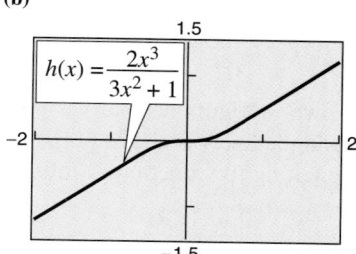

(b)

(c)

Figure 3.33

EXAMPLE 3   Finding a Function's Domain and Asymptotes

For the function f, find (a) the domain of f, (b) the vertical asymptote of f, and (c) the horizontal asymptote of f.

$$f(x) = \frac{3x^3 + 7x^2 + 2}{-4x^3 + 5}$$

Algebraic Solution

a. Because the denominator is zero when $-4x^3 + 5 = 0$, solve this equation to determine that the domain of f is all real numbers except $x = \sqrt[3]{\frac{5}{4}}$.

b. Because the denominator of f has a zero at $x = \sqrt[3]{\frac{5}{4}}$, and $\sqrt[3]{\frac{5}{4}}$ is not a zero of the numerator, the graph of f has the vertical asymptote $x = \sqrt[3]{\frac{5}{4}} \approx 1.08$, as shown in Figure 3.34.

c. Because the degree of the numerator and denominator are the same, the horizontal asymptote is given by the ratio of the leading coefficients.

$$y = \frac{\text{leading coefficient of numerator}}{\text{leading coefficient of denominator}} = -\frac{3}{4}$$

The horizontal asymptote of f, $y = -\frac{3}{4}$, is shown in Figure 3.34.

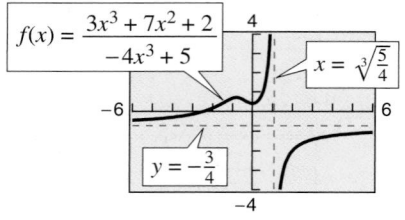

Numerical Solution

a. Because the denominator is zero when $-4x^3 + 5 = 0$, solve this equation to determine that the domain of f is all real numbers except $x = \sqrt[3]{\frac{5}{4}}$.

b. Because the denominator of f has a zero at $x = \sqrt[3]{\frac{5}{4}}$, the graph of f has the vertical asymptote $x = \sqrt[3]{\frac{5}{4}} \approx 1.08$, as shown in Figure 3.34.

c. You can create tables like those shown in Figure 3.35 to estimate that the graph of f has a horizontal asymptote at $y = -\frac{3}{4}$ because the values of $f(x)$ become closer and closer to $-\frac{3}{4}$ as x becomes increasingly large or small.

X	Y1	
1	12	
10	-0.9267	
100	-0.7675	
1000	-0.7518	
10000	-0.7502	
X=		

x Increases Without Bound

X	Y1	
-1	0.66667	
-10	-0.5738	
-100	-0.7325	
-1000	-0.7482	
-10000	-0.7498	
X=		

x Decreases Without Bound

Figure 3.35

EXAMPLE 4   A Graph with Two Horizontal Asymptotes

A function that is not rational can have two horizontal asymptotes—one to the left and one to the right. For instance, the graph of

$$f(x) = \frac{x + 10}{|x| + 2}$$

is shown in Figure 3.36. It has the line $y = -1$ as a horizontal asymptote to the left and the line $y = 1$ as a horizontal asymptote to the right. You can confirm this by rewriting the function as follows.

$$f(x) = \begin{cases} \dfrac{x + 10}{-x + 2}, & x < 0 \qquad |x| = -x \text{ for } x < 0 \\[2ex] \dfrac{x + 10}{x + 2}, & x \geq 0 \qquad |x| = x \text{ for } x \geq 0 \end{cases}$$

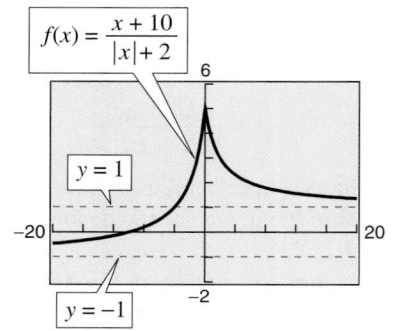

Figure 3.36

Applications

There are many examples of asymptotic behavior in real life. For instance, Example 5 shows how a vertical asymptote can be used to analyze the cost of removing pollutants from smokestack emissions.

EXAMPLE 5   Cost-Benefit Model

A utility company burns coal to generate electricity. The cost of removing a certain *percent* of the pollutants from the smokestack emissions is typically not a linear function. That is, if it costs C dollars to remove 25% of the pollutants, it would cost more than $2C$ dollars to remove 50% of the pollutants. As the percent of removed pollutants approaches 100%, the cost tends to become prohibitive. Suppose that the cost C (in dollars) of removing $p\%$ of the smokestack pollutants is

$$C = \frac{80,000p}{100 - p}, \quad 0 \le p < 100.$$

Sketch the graph of this function. Suppose you are a member of a state legislature that is considering a law that would require utility companies to remove 90% of the pollutants from their smokestack emissions. If the current law requires 85% removal, how much additional cost would there be to the utility company because of the new law?

Solution

The graph of this function is shown in Figure 3.37. Note that the graph has a vertical asymptote at $p = 100$. Because the current law requires 85% removal, the current cost to the utility company is

$$C = \frac{80,000(85)}{100 - 85} \qquad \text{Substitute 85 for } p.$$

$$\approx \$453,333.$$

If the new law increased the percent removal to 90%, the cost to the utility company would be

$$C = \frac{80,000(90)}{100 - 90} \qquad \text{Substitute 90 for } p.$$

$$= \$720,000.$$

So, the new law would require the utility company to spend an additional

$$720,000 - 453,333 = \$266,667.$$

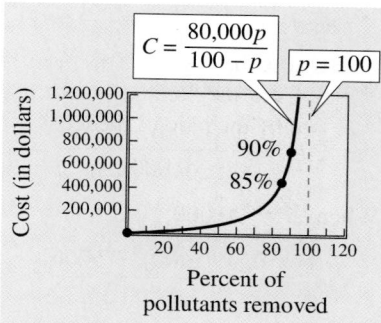

Figure 3.37

Activities

1. Which of the following functions have $x = 0$ as a vertical asymptote? Discuss your answers.

   a. $f(x) = \dfrac{3 + x}{x}$ b. $f(x) = \dfrac{x}{4 - x^2}$

   c. $f(x) = \dfrac{3x^2 - x}{x^3 - x}$

   d. $f(x) = \dfrac{x^3 - x^2 + 1}{x}$

   Answer: (a) and (d). In (a) and (d), $x = 0$ is the zero of the denominator. In (c), the function is not reduced. The numerator and denominator have the common factor of x. So, $x = 0$ is not a vertical asymptote.

2. Identify any horizontal or vertical asymptotes.

   $$f(x) = \frac{3x + 2}{5 - 2x}$$

   Answer: Vertical asymptote: $x = \frac{5}{2}$
   Horizontal asymptote: $y = -\frac{3}{2}$

EXAMPLE 6   Average Cost of Producing a Product

A business has a cost function of $C = 0.5x + 5000$, where C is measured in dollars and x is the number of units produced. The *average cost per unit* is

$$\overline{C} = \frac{C}{x} = \frac{0.5x + 5000}{x}.$$

Find the average cost per unit when $x = 1000, 5000, 10,000$, and $100,000$. What is the horizontal asymptote for this function, and what does it represent?

Point out to students that the result of Example 6 shows one of the major problems of a small business. That is, it is difficult to have competitively low prices when the production level is low.

Algebraic Solution

When $x = 1000$,

$$\overline{C} = \frac{0.5(1000) + 5000}{1000} = \$5.50.$$

When $x = 5000$,

$$\overline{C} = \frac{0.5(5000) + 5000}{5000} = \$1.50.$$

When $x = 10,000$,

$$\overline{C} = \frac{0.5(10,000) + 5000}{10,000} = \$1.00.$$

When $x = 90,000$,

$$\overline{C} = \frac{0.5(90,000) + 5000}{90,000} \approx \$0.56.$$

Because the degree of the numerator and denominator are the same for

$$\overline{C} = \frac{0.5x + 5000}{x}$$

the horizontal asymptote is given by the ratio of the leading coefficients of the numerator and denominator. So, the graph has the line $\overline{C} = \$0.50$ as a horizontal asymptote. This line represents the least possible unit cost for the product.

Graphical Solution

Using a graphing utility to graph the function

$$y = \frac{0.5x + 5000}{x}$$

using a viewing window similar to the graph shown in Figure 3.38. Then use the *trace* or *value* feature to approximate the following.

When $x = 1000$, $y_1 = \$5.50$.   When $x = 5000$, $y_1 = \$1.50$.

When $x = 10,000$, $y_1 = \$1.00$. When $x = 90,000$, $y_1 = \$0.56$.

Continue to use the *trace* or *value* feature to approximate values of $f(x)$ for larger and larger values of x. From this, you can estimate the horizontal asymptote to be $y = \$0.50$. This line represents the least possible cost for the product.

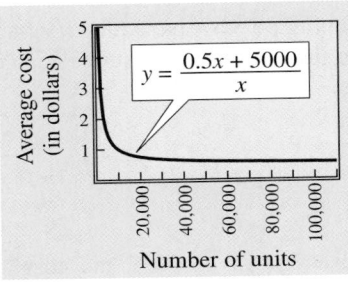

Figure 3.38

Writing About Math   *Common Factors in the Numerator and Denominator*

Consider the function $f(x) = \dfrac{x(x - 1)}{x}$ which has a common factor of x in the numerator and denominator. Use a graphing utility to graph this function. Use the *zoom* and *trace* features to decide whether the function has a vertical asymptote at $x = 0$. Then write a short paragraph explaining why you should check for common factors in the numerator and denominator when graphing a rational function.

3.5 Exercises

In Exercises 1–6, (a) complete each table, (b) determine the vertical and horizontal asymptotes of the function, and (c) find the domain of the function.

x	f(x)
0.5	
0.9	
0.99	
0.999	

x	f(x)
1.5	
1.1	
1.01	
1.001	

x	f(x)
5	
10	
100	
1000	

x	f(x)
−5	
−10	
−100	
−1000	

1. $f(x) = \dfrac{1}{x - 1}$

2. $f(x) = \dfrac{5x}{x - 1}$

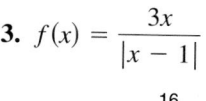

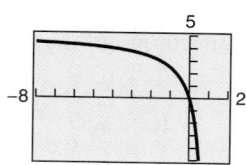

3. $f(x) = \dfrac{3x}{|x - 1|}$

4. $f(x) = \dfrac{3}{|x - 1|}$

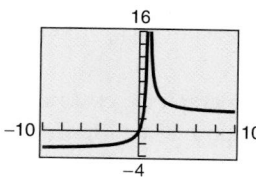

5. $f(x) = \dfrac{3x^2}{x^2 - 1}$

6. $f(x) = \dfrac{4x}{x^2 - 1}$

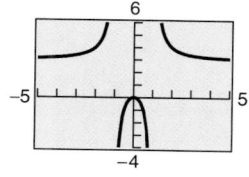

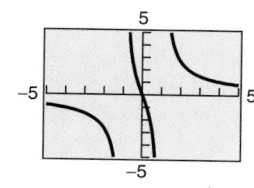

In Exercises 7–12, match the function with its graph. [The graphs are labeled (a), (b), (c), (d), (e), and (f).]

(a)

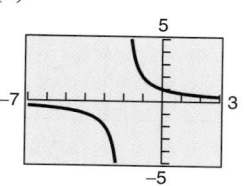

(b)

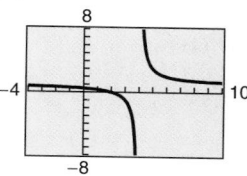

(c)

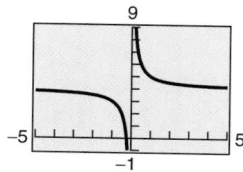

(d)

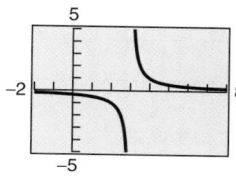

(e)

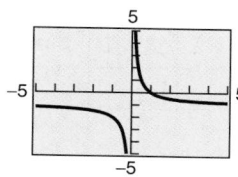

(f)

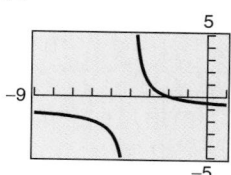

7. $f(x) = \dfrac{2}{x + 2}$

8. $f(x) = \dfrac{1}{x - 3}$

9. $f(x) = \dfrac{4x + 1}{x}$

10. $f(x) = \dfrac{1 - x}{x}$

11. $f(x) = \dfrac{x - 2}{x - 4}$

12. $f(x) = -\dfrac{x + 2}{x + 4}$

In Exercises 13–18, (a) find the domain of the function, (b) identify any horizontal and vertical asymptotes, and (c) verify your answer to part (a) both graphically by using a graphing utility and numerically by creating a table of values.

13. $f(x) = \dfrac{1}{x^2}$

14. $f(x) = \dfrac{3}{(x - 2)^3}$

15. $f(x) = \dfrac{3 + x}{3 - x}$

16. $f(x) = \dfrac{2 - 5x}{2 + 2x}$

17. $f(x) = \dfrac{2x^3}{x^2 - 1}$

18. $f(x) = \dfrac{3x^2 + 1}{x^2 + x + 9}$

Analytical and Numerical Explanation **In Exercises 19–22, (a) determine the domain of *f* and *g*, (b) find any vertical asymptotes of *f*, (c) complete the table, and (d) explain what your results suggest.**

19. $f(x) = \dfrac{x^2 - 4}{x + 2}$, $g(x) = x - 2$

x	-4	-3	-2.5	-2	-1.5	-1	0
$f(x)$							
$g(x)$							

20. $f(x) = \dfrac{x^2(x - 3)}{x^2 - 3x}$, $g(x) = x$

x	-1	0	1	2	3	3.5	4
$f(x)$							
$g(x)$							

21. $f(x) = \dfrac{x - 3}{x^2 - 3x}$, $g(x) = \dfrac{1}{x}$

x	-1	-0.5	0	0.5	2	3	4
$f(x)$							
$g(x)$							

22. $f(x) = \dfrac{2x - 8}{x^2 - 9x + 20}$, $g(x) = \dfrac{2}{x - 5}$

x	0	1	2	3	4	5	6
$f(x)$							
$g(x)$							

Exploration **In Exercises 23–26, determine the value the function *f* approaches as the magnitude of *x* increases. Is *f(x)* greater than or less than this functional value when *x* is positive and large in magnitude? What about when *x* is negative and large in magnitude?**

23. $f(x) = 4 - \dfrac{1}{x}$

24. $f(x) = 2 + \dfrac{1}{x - 3}$

25. $f(x) = \dfrac{2x - 1}{x - 3}$

26. $f(x) = \dfrac{2x - 1}{x^2 + 1}$

In Exercises 27–30, find the zeros (if any) of the rational function. Use a graphing utility to verify your answer.

27. $g(x) = \dfrac{x^2 - 9}{x + 1}$

28. $g(x) = \dfrac{x^3 - 8}{x^2 + 4}$

29. $f(x) = 1 - \dfrac{2}{x - 5}$

30. $h(x) = 6 + \dfrac{4}{x^2 + 2}$

31. *Pollution*   The cost (in millions of dollars) for removing $p\%$ of the industrial and municipal pollutants discharged into a river is

$$C = \frac{255p}{100 - p}, \quad 0 \le p < 100.$$

(a) Find the cost of removing 10% of the pollutants.

(b) Find the cost of removing 40% of the pollutants.

(c) Find the cost of removing 75% of the pollutants.

(d) Use a graphing utility to graph the cost function. Be sure to choose an appropriate viewing window. Explain why you chose the values that you used in your viewing window.

(e) According to this model, would it be possible to remove 100% of the pollutants? Explain.

32. *Recycling*   In a pilot project, a rural township was given recycling bins for separating and storing recyclable products. The cost (in dollars) for supplying bins to $p\%$ of the population is

$$C = \frac{25,000p}{100 - p}, \quad 0 \le p < 100.$$

(a) Find the cost of giving bins to 15% of the population.

(b) Find the cost of giving bins to 50% of the population.

(c) Find the cost of giving bins to 90% of the population.

(d) Use a graphing utility to graph the cost function. Be sure to choose an appropriate viewing window. Explain why you chose the values that you used in your viewing window.

(e) According to this model, would it be possible to supply bins to 100% of the residents? Explain.

33. *Data Analysis* Consider a physics laboratory experiment designed to determine an unknown mass. A flexible metal meter stick is clamped to a table with 50 centimeters overhanging the edge. Known masses M ranging from 200 grams to 2000 grams are attached to the end of the meter stick. For each mass, the meter stick is displaced vertically and then allowed to oscillate. The average time t in seconds of one oscillation for each mass is recorded in the table.

M	200	400	600	800	1000
t	0.450	0.597	0.721	0.831	0.906

M	1200	1400	1600	1800	2000
t	1.003	1.088	1.168	1.218	1.338

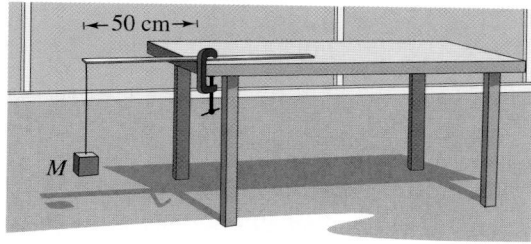

A model for the data is

$$t = \frac{38M + 16{,}965}{10(M + 5000)}.$$

(a) Use a graphing utility to create a table showing the estimated time based on the model for each of the masses shown in the table. What can you conclude?

(b) Use the model to approximate the mass of an object if the average for one oscillation is 1.056 seconds.

34. *Data Analysis* The endpoints of the interval over which distinct vision is possible are called the *near point* and *far point* of the eye. With increasing age these points normally change. The table gives the approximate near points y in centimeters for various ages x.

x	10	20	30	40	50
y	7	10	14	22	40

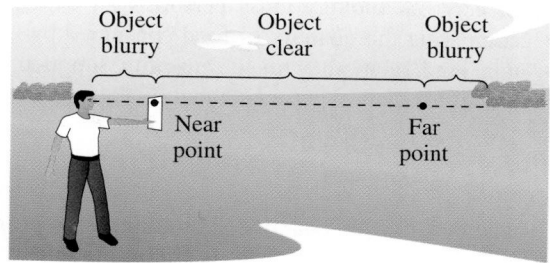

(a) Fit a rational model to the data. Take the reciprocals of the near points to generate the points $(x, 1/y)$. Use the regression capabilities of a graphing utility to fit a line to this data. The resulting line has the form

$$\frac{1}{y} = ax + b.$$

Solve for y.

(b) Use a graphing utility to create a table giving the predicted near point based on the model for each of the ages in the given table.

(c) Do you think the model can be used to predict the near point for a person who is 60 years old? Explain.

35. *Deer Population* The game commission introduces 100 deer into newly acquired state game lands. The population of the herd is

$$N = \frac{20(5 + 3t)}{1 + 0.04t}, \quad t \geq 0$$

where t is the time (in years).

(a) Find the population when t is 5, 10, and 25.

(b) What is the limiting size of the herd as time increases? Explain your reasoning.

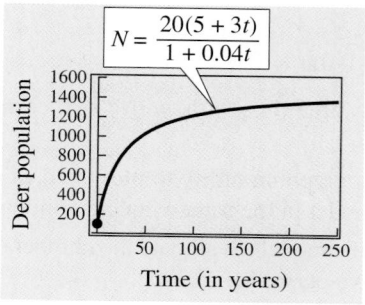

36. *Insects*   A biology class performs an experiment comparing the quantity of food consumed by a certain kind of moth with the quantity supplied. The model for their experimental data is

$$y = \frac{1.568x - 0.001}{6.360x + 1}, \quad x > 0$$

where x is the quantity (in milligrams) of food supplied and y is the quantity (in milligrams) eaten. At what level of consumption will the moth become satiated?

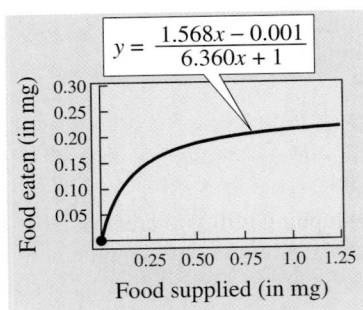

37. *Military*   The number of United States military reserve personnel M (in thousands) for the years 1990 through 1997 is shown in the table.   (Source: U.S. Department of Defense)

Year	1990	1991	1992	1993
M	1671	1786	1883	1867

Year	1994	1995	1996	1997
M	1805	1659	1550	1461

A model for the data is

$$y = \frac{1671.92 + 130.23t}{1 - 0.02t + 0.02t^2}$$

where t is time (in years), with $t = 0$ corresponding to 1990.

(a) Use a graphing utility to plot the data and graph the model in the same viewing window.

(b) Use the model to estimate the number of military reserve personnel in 2002.

(c) Would this model be useful for estimating the number of military reserve personnel for future years? Explain.

Synthesis

True or False?   **In Exercises 38 and 39, determine whether the statement is true or false. Justify your answer.**

38. A rational function can have infinitely many vertical asymptotes.

39. $f(x) = x^3 - 2x^2 - 5x + 6$ is a rational function.

Think About It   **In Exercises 40–43, write a rational function f having the specified characteristics. (There are many correct answers.)**

40. Vertical asymptotes: $x = -2, x = 1$

41. Vertical asymptote: None
Horizontal asymptote: $y = 0$

42. Vertical asymptote: None
Horizontal asymptote: $y = 2$

43. Vertical asymptotes: $x = 0, x = \frac{5}{2}$
Horizontal asymptote: $y = -3$

Review

In Exercises 44–49, find all solutions of the equation.

44. $225x - 50x^3 = 0$

45. $x(10 - x) = 25$

46. $2z^2 - 3z - 35 = 0$

47. $t^3 - 50t = 0$

48. $27x^3 - 147x = 0$

49. $x^4 - 225 = 0$

In Exercises 50–53, divide using synthetic division.

50. $(x^2 + 5x + 6) \div (x - 4)$

51. $(x^2 - 10x + 15) \div (x - 3)$

52. $(2x^2 + x - 11) \div (x + 5)$

53. $(4x^2 + 3x - 10) \div (x + 6)$

In Exercises 54–57, find a polynomial with integer coefficients that has the given zeros. (There are many correct answers.)

54. $8, 5i, -5i$

55. $-2, 6i, -6i$

56. $6, 3 + i, 3 - i$

57. $1, -3 + 2i, -3 - 2i$

3.6 Graphs of Rational Functions

The Graph of a Rational Function

To sketch the graph of a rational function, use the following guidelines.

Guidelines for Graphing Rational Functions

Let $f(x) = N(x)/D(x)$, where $N(x)$ and $D(x)$ are polynomials with no common factors.

1. Find and plot the y-intercept (if any) by evaluating $f(0)$.

2. Set the numerator equal to zero and solve the equation $N(x) = 0$. The real solutions represent the x-intercepts of the graph. Plot these intercepts.

3. Set the denominator equal to zero and solve the equation $D(x) = 0$. The real solutions represent the vertical asymptotes. Sketch these asymptotes using dashed vertical lines.

4. Find and sketch the horizontal asymptote of the graph using a dashed horizontal line.

5. Plot at least one point between and one point beyond each x-intercept and vertical asymptote.

6. Use smooth curves to complete the graph between and beyond the vertical asymptotes.

Testing for symmetry can be useful, especially for simple rational functions. For example, the graph of $f(x) = 1/x$ is symmetrical with respect to the origin, and the graph of $g(x) = 1/x^2$ is symmetrical with respect to the y-axis.

Graphing utilities have difficulty sketching graphs of rational functions that have vertical asymptotes. Often, the utility will connect parts of the graph that are not supposed to be connected. For instance, Figure 3.39(a) shows the graph of

$$f(x) = \frac{1}{x - 2}.$$

Notice that the graph should consist of two *unconnected* portions—one to the left of $x = 2$ and the other to the right of $x = 2$. To eliminate this problem, you can try changing the *mode* of the graphing utility to *dot mode*. The problem with this is that the graph is then represented as a collection of dots rather than as a smooth curve, as shown in Figure 3.39(b).

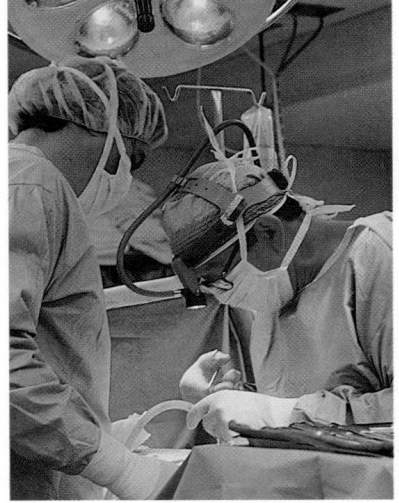

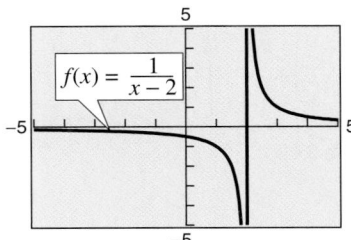

(a) Connected mode

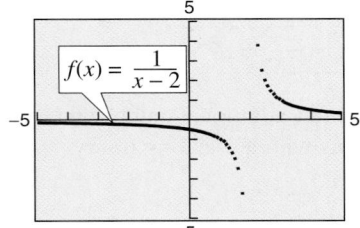

(b) Dot mode

Figure 3.39

EXAMPLE 1   Sketching the Graph of a Rational Function

Sketch the graph of $g(x) = \dfrac{3}{x - 2}$ by hand.

Solution

y-Intercept:	$\left(0, -\frac{3}{2}\right)$, because $g(0) = -\frac{3}{2}$.
x-Intercept:	None, because $3 \neq 0$.
Vertical Asymptote:	$x = 2$, zero of denominator
Horizontal Asymptote:	$y = 0$, degree of $N(x) <$ degree of $D(x)$

Additional Points:

x	-4	1	3	5
$g(x)$	-0.5	-3	3	1

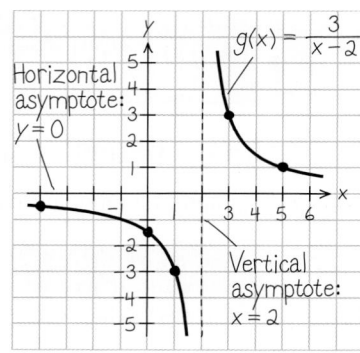

Figure 3.40

By plotting the intercepts, asymptotes, and a few additional points, you can obtain the graph shown in Figure 3.40. Confirm this with a graphing utility.

Note that the graph of g in Example 1 is a vertical stretch and a right shift of the graph of

$$f(x) = \frac{1}{x}$$

because

$$g(x) = \frac{3}{x - 2} = 3\left(\frac{1}{x - 2}\right) = 3f(x - 2).$$

EXAMPLE 2   Sketching the Graph of a Rational Function

Sketch the graph of $f(x) = \dfrac{2x - 1}{x}$ by hand.

Solution

y-Intercept:	None, because $x = 0$ is not in the domain.
x-Intercept:	$\left(\frac{1}{2}, 0\right)$, because $2x - 1 = 0$, or $x = \frac{1}{2}$.
Vertical Asymptote:	$x = 0$, zero of denominator
Horizontal Asymptote:	$y = 2$, degree of $N(x) =$ degree of $D(x)$

Additional Points:

x	-4	-1	$\frac{1}{4}$	4
$f(x)$	2.25	3	-2	1.75

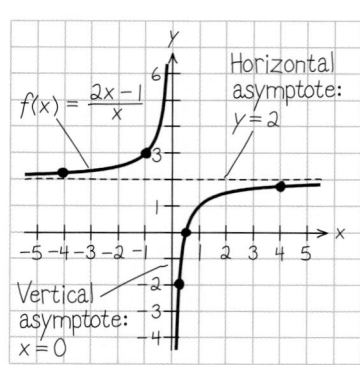

Figure 3.41

By plotting the intercepts, asymptotes, and a few additional points, you can obtain the graph shown in Figure 3.41. Confirm this with a graphing utility.

EXAMPLE 3   Sketching the Graph of a Rational Function

Sketch the graph of $f(x) = \dfrac{x}{x^2 - x - 2}$.

Solution

By factoring the denominator, you have

$$f(x) = \frac{x}{x^2 - x - 2}$$

$$= \frac{x}{(x + 1)(x - 2)}.$$

y-Intercept:	$(0, 0)$, because $f(0) = 0$.
x-Intercept:	$(0, 0)$
Vertical Asymptotes:	$x = -1$, $x = 2$, zeros of denominator
Horizontal Asymptote:	$y = 0$, degree of $N(x) <$ degree of $D(x)$
Additional Points:	

x	-3	-0.5	1	3
$f(x)$	-0.3	0.4	-0.5	0.75

The graph is shown in Figure 3.42.

EXAMPLE 4   Sketching the Graph of a Rational Function

Sketch the graph of $f(x) = \dfrac{2(x^2 - 9)}{x^2 - 4}$.

Solution

By factoring the numerator and denominator, you have

$$f(x) = \frac{2(x^2 - 9)}{x^2 - 4}$$

$$= \frac{2(x - 3)(x + 3)}{(x - 2)(x + 2)}.$$

y-Intercept:	$\left(0, \frac{9}{2}\right)$, because $f(0) = \frac{9}{2}$.
x-Intercepts:	$(-3, 0)$, $(3, 0)$
Vertical Asymptotes:	$x = -2$, $x = 2$, zeros of denominator
Horizontal Asymptote:	$y = 2$, degree of $N(x) =$ degree of $D(x)$
Symmetry:	With respect to y-axis, because $f(-x) = f(x)$.
Additional Points:	

x	0.5	2.5	6
$f(x)$	4.67	-2.44	1.69

The graph is shown in Figure 3.43.

A computer animation of this example appears in the *Interactive* CD-ROM and *Internet* versions of this text.

Use a graphing utility to graph

$$f(x) = 1 + \frac{1}{x - \dfrac{1}{x}}.$$

Set the graphing utility to *dot* mode and use a decimal viewing window. Use the *trace* feature to find three "holes" or "breaks" in the graph. Do all three holes represent zeros of the denominator

$$x - \frac{1}{x}?$$

Explain.

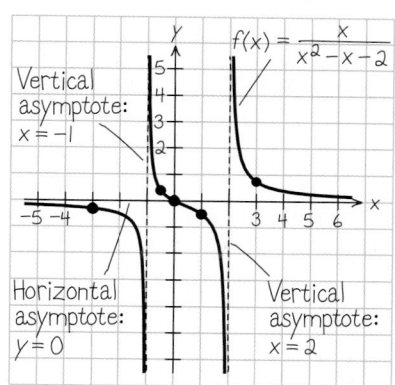

Figure 3.42

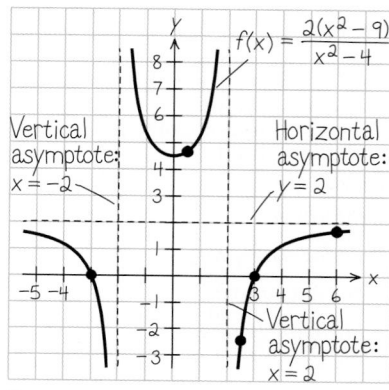

Figure 3.43

Slant Asymptotes

If the degree of the numerator of a rational function is exactly *one more* than the degree of its denominator, the graph of the function has a **slant** (or **oblique**) **asymptote.** For example, the graph of

$$f(x) = \frac{x^2 - x}{x + 1}$$

has a slant asymptote, as shown in Figure 3.44. To find the equation of a slant asymptote, use long division. For instance, by dividing $x + 1$ into $x^2 - x$, you have

$$f(x) = \frac{x^2 - x}{x + 1}$$

$$= \underbrace{x - 2}_{\text{Slant asymptote} \atop (y = x - 2)} + \frac{2}{x + 1}. \qquad \frac{2}{x + 1} \to 0 \text{ as } x \to \pm\infty$$

In Figure 3.44, notice that the graph of f approaches the line $y = x - 2$ as x moves to the right or left.

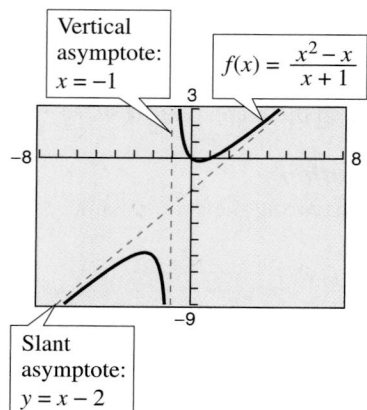

Vertical asymptote: $x = -1$

$f(x) = \dfrac{x^2 - x}{x + 1}$

Slant asymptote: $y = x - 2$

Figure 3.44

EXAMPLE 5 A Rational Function with a Slant Asymptote

Graph the function $f(x) = \dfrac{x^2 - x - 2}{x - 1}$.

Solution

First write $f(x)$ in two different ways. Factoring the numerator

$$f(x) = \frac{x^2 - x - 2}{x - 1} = \frac{(x - 2)(x + 1)}{x - 1}$$

allows you to recognize the x-intercepts, and long division

$$f(x) = \frac{x^2 - x - 2}{x - 1}$$

$$= x - \frac{2}{x - 1} \qquad \frac{2}{x - 1} \to 0 \text{ as } x \to \pm\infty$$

allows you to recognize that the line $y = x$ is a slant asymptote of the graph.

y-Intercept: $(0, 2)$, because $f(0) = 2$.

x-Intercepts: $(-1, 0), (2, 0)$

Vertical Asymptote: $x = 1$, zero of denominator

Slant Asymptote: $y = x$

Additional Points:

x	-2	0.5	1.5	3
$f(x)$	-1.33	4.5	-2.5	2

The graph is shown in Figure 3.45.

> ## Exploration
>
> Do you think it is possible for the graph of a rational function to cross its horizontal asymptote or its slant asymptote? Use the graphs of the following functions to investigate this question. Write a summary of your conclusion. Explain your reasoning.
>
> $$f(x) = \frac{x}{x^2 + 1}$$
>
> $$g(x) = \frac{2x}{3x^2 - 2x + 1}$$
>
> $$h(x) = \frac{x^3}{x^2 + 1}$$

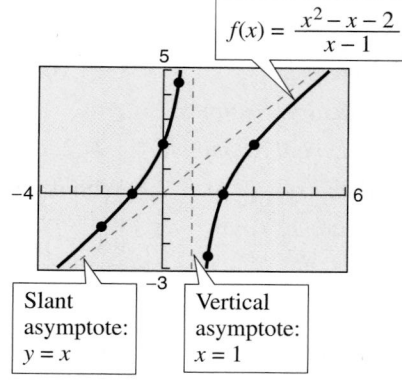

$f(x) = \dfrac{x^2 - x - 2}{x - 1}$

Slant asymptote: $y = x$

Vertical asymptote: $x = 1$

Figure 3.45

Application

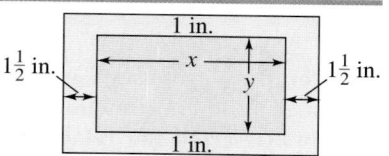

EXAMPLE 6 Finding a Minimum Area

A rectangular page is designed to contain 48 square inches of print. The margins on each side of the page are each $1\frac{1}{2}$ inches. The margins at the top and bottom are each 1 inch. What should the dimensions of the page be so that the minimum amount of paper is used?

Figure 3.46

Graphical Solution

Let A be the area to be minimized. From Figure 3.46, you can write

$$A = (x + 3)(y + 2).$$

The printed area inside the margins is modeled by $48 = xy$ or $y = 48/x$. To find the minimum area, rewrite the equation for A in terms of just one variable by substituting $48/x$ for y.

$$A = (x + 3)\left(\frac{48}{x} + 2\right)$$

$$= \frac{(x + 3)(48 + 2x)}{x}, \quad x > 0$$

The graph of this rational function is shown in Figure 3.47. Because x represents the width of the printed area, you need consider only the portion of the graph for which x is positive. Using a graphing utility, you can approximate the minimum value of A to occur when $x \approx 8.5$ inches. The corresponding value of y is $48/8.5 \approx 5.6$ inches. So, the dimensions should be

$x + 3 \approx 11.5$ inches by $y + 2 \approx 7.6$ inches.

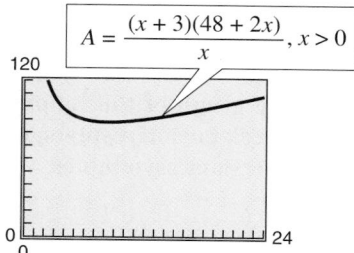

Figure 3.47

Numerical Solution

Let A be the area to be minimized. From Figure 3.46, you can write

$$A = (x + 3)(y + 2).$$

The printed area inside the margins is modeled by $48 = xy$ or $y = 48/x$. To find the minimum area, rewrite the equation for A in terms of just one variable by substituting $48/x$ for y.

$$A = (x + 3)\left(\frac{48}{x} + 2\right) = \frac{(x + 3)(48 + 2x)}{x}, \quad x > 0$$

Use the *table* feature of a graphing utility to create a table of values for the function $y_1 = \dfrac{(x + 3)(48 + 2x)}{x}$ beginning at $x = 1$, as shown in Figure 3.48.

X	Y1
6	90
7	88.571
8	88
9	88
10	88.4
11	89.091
12	90

Y1=88

Figure 3.48

From the table, you can see that the minimum value of y_1 occurs when x is somewhere between 8 and 9. To approximate the minimum value of y_1 to one decimal place, change the table to begin at 8 with an increment of 0.1. The minimum value of y_1 occurs when $x \approx 8.5$, as shown in Figure 3.49. The corresponding value of y is $48/8.5 \approx 5.6$ inches. So, the dimensions should be $x + 3 \approx 11.5$ inches by $y + 2 \approx 7.6$ inches.

X	Y1
8.2	87.961
8.3	87.949
8.4	87.943
8.5	87.941
8.6	87.944
8.7	87.952
8.8	87.964

Y1=87.9411764706

Figure 3.49

If you go on to take a course in calculus, you will learn an analytic technique for finding the exact value of x that produces a minimum area in Example 6. In this case, that value is $x = 6\sqrt{2} \approx 8.485$.

3.6   E x e r c i s e s

In Exercises 1–4, use a graphing utility to graph $f(x) = 2/x$ and the function g in the same viewing window. Describe the relationship between the two graphs.

1. $g(x) = f(x) + 1$ **2.** $g(x) = f(x - 1)$
3. $g(x) = -f(x)$ **4.** $g(x) = \frac{1}{2}f(x + 2)$

In Exercises 5–8, use a graphing utility to graph $f(x) = 2/x^2$ and the function g in the same viewing window. Describe the relationship between the two graphs.

5. $g(x) = f(x) - 2$ **6.** $g(x) = -f(x)$
7. $g(x) = f(x - 2)$ **8.** $g(x) = \frac{1}{4}f(x)$

In Exercises 9–12, use a graphing utility to graph $f(x) = 4/x^3$ and the function g in the same viewing window. Describe the relationship between the two graphs.

9. $g(x) = f(x + 2)$ **10.** $g(x) = f(x) + 1$
11. $g(x) = -f(x)$ **12.** $g(x) = \frac{1}{4}f(x)$

In Exercises 13–30, sketch the graph of the rational function by hand. As sketching aids, check for intercepts, symmetry, vertical asymptotes, and horizontal asymptotes. Use a graphing utility to verify your graph.

13. $f(x) = \dfrac{1}{x + 2}$ **14.** $f(x) = \dfrac{1}{x - 5}$

15. $C(x) = \dfrac{5 + 2x}{1 + x}$ **16.** $P(x) = \dfrac{1 - 3x}{1 - x}$

17. $g(x) = \dfrac{1}{x + 2} + 2$ **18.** $f(t) = \dfrac{1 - 2t}{t}$

19. $f(x) = 2 - \dfrac{3}{x^2}$ **20.** $h(x) = \dfrac{x^2}{x^2 - 9}$

21. $f(x) = \dfrac{x^2}{x^2 - 4}$ **22.** $g(x) = \dfrac{x}{x^2 - 9}$

23. $f(x) = \dfrac{x}{x^2 - 4}$ **24.** $f(x) = -\dfrac{1}{(x - 2)^2}$

25. $g(x) = \dfrac{4(x + 1)}{x(x - 4)}$ **26.** $h(x) = \dfrac{2}{x^2(x - 2)}$

27. $f(x) = \dfrac{3x}{x^2 - x - 2}$ **28.** $f(x) = \dfrac{2x}{x^2 + x - 2}$

29. $f(x) = -\dfrac{4}{\dfrac{5}{x} - 5}$ **30.** $f(x) = 2 + \dfrac{8}{3x - \dfrac{3}{x}}$

In Exercises 31–40, use a graphing utility to obtain the graph of the function. Give its domain and identify any vertical or horizontal asymptotes.

31. $f(x) = \dfrac{2 + x}{1 - x}$ **32.** $f(x) = \dfrac{3 - x}{2 - x}$

33. $f(t) = \dfrac{3t + 1}{t}$ **34.** $h(x) = \dfrac{x - 2}{x - 3}$

35. $h(t) = \dfrac{4}{t^2 + 1}$ **36.** $g(x) = -\dfrac{x}{(x - 2)^2}$

37. $f(x) = \dfrac{x + 1}{x^2 - x - 6}$ **38.** $f(x) = \dfrac{x + 4}{x^2 + x - 6}$

39. $f(x) = \dfrac{20x}{x^2 + 1} - \dfrac{1}{x}$

40. $f(x) = 5\left(\dfrac{1}{x - 4} - \dfrac{1}{x + 2}\right)$

Exploration   In Exercises 41–46, use a graphing utility to obtain the graph of the function. What do you observe about its asymptotes?

41. $h(x) = \dfrac{6x}{\sqrt{x^2 + 1}}$ **42.** $f(x) = -\dfrac{x}{\sqrt{9 + x^2}}$

43. $g(x) = \dfrac{4|x - 2|}{x + 1}$ **44.** $f(x) = -\dfrac{8|3 + x|}{x - 2}$

45. $f(x) = \dfrac{4(x - 1)^2}{x^2 - 4x + 5}$ **46.** $g(x) = \dfrac{3x^4 - 5x + 3}{x^4 + 1}$

In Exercises 47–54, sketch the graph of the rational function. As sketching aids, check for intercepts, symmetry, vertical asymptotes, and slant asymptotes.

47. $f(x) = \dfrac{2x^2 + 1}{x}$ **48.** $g(x) = \dfrac{x^2 + 1}{x}$

49. $h(x) = \dfrac{x^2}{x - 1}$ **50.** $f(x) = \dfrac{x^3}{x^2 - 1}$

51. $g(x) = \dfrac{x^3}{2x^2 - 8}$ **52.** $f(x) = \dfrac{x^2 - 1}{x^2 + 4}$

53. $f(x) = \dfrac{x^3 + 2x^2 + 4}{2x^2 + 1}$ **54.** $f(x) = \dfrac{2x^2 - 5x + 5}{x - 2}$

Graphical Reasoning   In Exercises 55–58, (a) use the graph to estimate any *x*-intercepts of the rational function and (b) set *y* = 0 and solve the resulting equation to confirm your result in part (a).

55. $y = \dfrac{x + 1}{x - 3}$

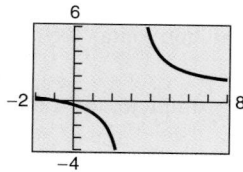

56. $y = \dfrac{2x}{x - 3}$

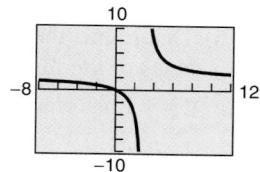

57. $y = \dfrac{1}{x} - x$

58. $y = x - 3 + \dfrac{2}{x}$

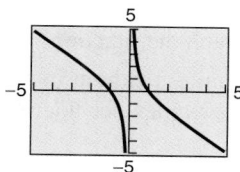
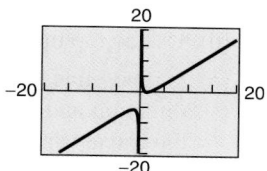

In Exercises 59–62, use a graphing utility to graph the rational function. Give the domain of the function and identify any asymptotes. Then zoom out far enough so that the graph appears as a line. Identify the line.

59. $y = \dfrac{2x^2 + x}{x + 1}$

60. $y = \dfrac{x^2 + 5x + 8}{x + 3}$

61. $y = \dfrac{1 + 3x^2 - x^3}{x^2}$

62. $y = \dfrac{12 - 2x - x^2}{2(4 + x)}$

Graphical Reasoning   In Exercises 63–66, (a) use a graphing utility to graph the function and determine any *x*-intercepts, and (b) set *y* = 0 and solve the resulting equation to confirm your result in part (a).

63. $y = \dfrac{1}{x + 5} + \dfrac{4}{x}$

64. $y = 20\left(\dfrac{2}{x + 1} - \dfrac{3}{x}\right)$

65. $y = x - \dfrac{6}{x - 1}$

66. $y = x - \dfrac{9}{x}$

67. *Concentration of a Mixture*   A 1000-liter tank contains 10 liters of a 25% brine solution. You add *x* liters of a 75% brine solution to the tank.

(a) Show that the concentration *C* of the final mixture is

$$C = \dfrac{3x + 10}{4(x + 10)}.$$

(b) Determine the domain of the function on the basis of the physical constraints of the problem.

(c) Use a graphing utility to graph the function. As the tank is filled, what happens to the rate at which the concentration of brine increases? How close to the horizontal asymptote is the graph of *C* when the tank is full?

68. *Geometry*   A rectangular region of length *x* and width *y* has an area of 500 square meters.

(a) Express the width *y* as a function of *x*.

(b) Determine the domain of the function on the basis of the physical constraints of the problem.

(c) Sketch a graph of the function and determine the width of the rectangle if *x* = 30 meters.

69. *Page Design*   A page that is *x* inches wide and *y* inches high contains 30 square inches of print. The margins at the top and bottom are 2 inches and the margins on each side are 1 inch.

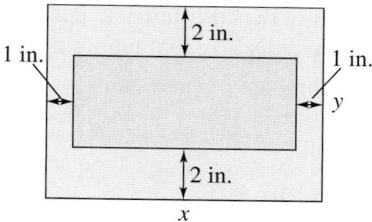

(a) Show that the total area *A* of the page is

$$A = \dfrac{2x(2x + 11)}{x - 2}.$$

(b) Determine the domain of the function on the basis of the physical constraints of the problem.

(c) Use a graphing utility to graph the area function and approximate the page size such that the minimum amount of paper will be used. Verify your answer numerically using the *table* feature of a graphing utility.

70. *Minimum Area*   A right triangle is formed in the first quadrant by the *x*-axis, the *y*-axis, and a line segment through the point (3, 2).

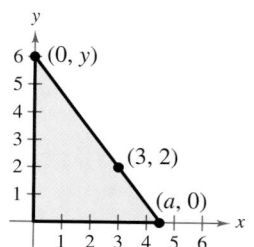

(a) Show that an equation of the line segment is

$$y = \frac{2(a - x)}{a - 3}, \quad 0 \le x \le a.$$

(b) Show that the area of the triangle is $A = \dfrac{a^2}{a - 3}$.

(c) Use a graphing utility to graph the area function and estimate the value of a that yields a minimum area. Estimate the minimum area. Verify your answer numerically using the *table* feature of a graphing utility.

71. Ordering and Transportation Cost   The ordering and transportation cost C for the components used in manufacturing a certain product is

$$C = 100\left(\frac{200}{x^2} + \frac{x}{x + 30}\right), \quad x \ge 1$$

where C is measured in thousands of dollars and x is the order size (in hundreds). Use a graphing utility to obtain the graph of the cost function and, from the graph, estimate the order size that minimizes cost.

72. Average Cost   The cost of producing x units of a product is $C = 0.2x^2 + 10x + 5$, and therefore the average cost per unit is

$$\overline{C} = \frac{C}{x} = \frac{0.2x^2 + 10x + 5}{x}, \quad x > 0.$$

Sketch the graph of the average cost function, and estimate the number of units that should be produced to minimize the average cost per unit.

73. Medicine   The concentration of a certain chemical in the bloodstream t hours after injection into muscle tissue is

$$C = \frac{3t^2 + t}{t^3 + 50}, \quad t \ge 0.$$

(a) Determine the horizontal asymptote of the function and interpret its meaning in the context of the problem.

(b) Use a graphing utility to graph the function and approximate the time when the bloodstream concentration is greatest.

(c) Use a graphing utility to determine when the concentration is less than 0.345.

74. Numerical and Graphical Analysis   A driver averaged 50 miles per hour on the round trip between home and a city 100 miles away. The average speeds for going and returning were x and y miles per hour, respectively.

(a) Show that $y = \dfrac{25x}{x - 25}$.

(b) Determine the vertical and horizontal asymptotes of the function.

(c) Use a graphing utility to complete the table. What do you observe?

x	30	35	40	45	50	55	60
y							

(d) Use a graphing utility to graph the function.

(e) Is it possible to average 20 miles per hour in one direction and still average 50 miles per hour on the round trip? Explain.

75. Comparing Models   The number of kidney transplants K in the United States from 1987 through 1996 is shown in the table.   (Sources: U.S. Department of Health and Human Services; United Network for Organ Sharing)

Year	1987	1988	1989	1990	1991
K	8967	9123	8890	9877	10,122

Year	1992	1993	1994	1995	1996
K	10,231	11,020	11,392	11,891	12,080

For each of the following, let t be the time (in years), with $t = 7$ corresponding to 1987.

(a) A model for the data is

$$K = \frac{8116.17 - 280t}{1 - 0.0447t}.$$

Use a graphing utility to plot the data points and graph the model in the same viewing window.

(b) Use the regression capabilities of a graphing utility to fit a line to the data.

(c) Use the regression capabilities of a graphing utility to fit a parabola to the data.

(d) Which of the three models would you recommend as an estimator of the number of kidney transplants for the years following 1996? Explain your reasoning.

76. *Comparing Models* The number N (in thousands) of insured commercial banks in the United States for the years 1988 through 1997 is shown in the table. (Source: U.S. Federal Deposit Insurance Corporation)

Year	1988	1989	1990	1991	1992
N	13.1	12.7	12.3	11.9	11.5

Year	1993	1994	1995	1996	1997
N	11.0	10.5	9.9	9.5	9.1

For each of the following, let t be the time (in years), with $t = 8$ corresponding to 1988.

(a) Use the regression capabilities of a graphing utility to fit a line to the data. Use a graphing utility to plot the data points and graph the model in the same viewing window.

(b) Fit a rational model to the data. Take the reciprocal of N to generate the points $(t, 1/N)$. Use the regression capabilities of a graphing utility to fit a line to this data. The resulting line has the form

$$\frac{1}{N} = at + b.$$

Solve for N. Use a graphing utility to plot the data points and graph the rational model in the same viewing window.

(c) Use a graphing utility to create a table showing the predicted number of banks based on each model for each of the years in the given table. Which model do you prefer? Why?

Synthesis

True or False? In Exercises 77 and 78, determine whether the statement is true or false. Justify your answer.

77. If the graph of a rational function f has a vertical asymptote at $x = 5$, it is possible to sketch the graph without lifting your pencil from the paper.

78. A rational function can never cross one of its asymptotes.

Think About It In Exercises 79 and 80, use a graphing utility to obtain the graph of the function. Explain why there is no vertical asymptote when a superficial

examination of the function may indicate that there should be one.

79. $h(x) = \dfrac{6 - 2x}{3 - x}$ **80.** $g(x) = \dfrac{x^2 + x - 2}{x - 1}$

81. *Writing* Write a paragraph discussing whether every rational function has a vertical asymptote.

Think About It In Exercises 82–85, write a rational function satisfying the following criteria.

82. Vertical asymptote: $x = 2$
   Slant asymptote: $y = x + 1$
   Zero of the function: $x = -2$

83. Vertical asymptote: $x = -4$
   Slant asymptote: $y = x - 2$
   Zero of the function: $x = 3$

84. Vertical asymptote: $x = -1$
   Horizontal asymptote: $y = 2$
   Zero of the function: $x = 3$

85. Vertical asymptote: $x = 3$
   Horizontal asymptote: $y = -2$
   Zero of the function: $x = -6$

Review

In Exercises 86–91, simplify the expression.

86. $\left(\dfrac{x}{8}\right)^{-3}$ **87.** $(4x^2)^{-2}$

88. $\dfrac{3x^3y^2}{15xy^4}$ **89.** $\dfrac{(4x^2)^{3/2}}{8x^5}$

90. $\dfrac{3^{7/6}}{3^{1/6}}$ **91.** $\dfrac{x^{-2} \cdot x^{1/2}}{x^{-1} \cdot x^{5/2}}$

In Exercises 92–97, sketch a graph of the equation by hand. Use a graphing utility to verify your graph.

92. $-y + 3x + 8 = 0$ **93.** $4x + 5y - 2 = 0$

94. $7x + 3 = 0$ **95.** $4y - 10 = 0$

96. $x - y - 1 = 0$ **97.** $-7 + 8x - 2y = 0$

In Exercises 98–101, use a graphing utility to graph the function and find its domain and range.

98. $f(x) = \sqrt{6 + x^2}$ **99.** $f(x) = \sqrt{121 - x^2}$

100. $f(x) = -|x + 9|$ **101.** $f(x) = -x^2 + 9$

3 Chapter Summary

What did you learn?

3 Review Exercises

3.1 *Graphical Reasoning*   In Exercises 1 and 2, use a graphing utility to graph each equation in the same viewing window. Describe how each graph differs from the graph of $y = x^2$.

1. (a) $y = 2x^2$ (b) $y = -2x^2$
     (c) $y = x^2 + 2$ (d) $y = (x + 2)^2$

2. (a) $y = x^2 - 4$ (b) $y = 4 - x^2$
     (c) $y = (x - 3)^2$ (d) $y = \frac{1}{2}x^2 - 1$

In Exercises 3–6, sketch the graph of the quadratic function. Identify the vertex and the intercepts.

3. $f(x) = \left(x + \frac{3}{2}\right)^2 + 1$ **4.** $f(x) = (x - 4)^2 - 4$
5. $f(x) = \frac{1}{3}(x^2 + 5x - 4)$
6. $f(x) = 3x^2 - 12x + 11$

In Exercises 7 and 8, find the quadratic function that has the indicated vertex and whose graph passes through the given point.

7. Vertex: $(1, -4)$;   Point: $(2, -3)$
8. Vertex: $(2, 3)$;   Point: $(-1, 6)$

In Exercises 9–16, find the maximum or minimum value of the quadratic function.

9. $g(x) = x^2 - 2x$ **10.** $f(x) = x^2 + 8x + 10$
11. $f(x) = 6x - x^2$ **12.** $h(x) = 3 + 4x - x^2$
13. $f(t) = -2t^2 + 4t + 1$ **14.** $h(x) = 4x^2 + 4x + 13$
15. $h(x) = x^2 + 5x - 4$ **16.** $f(x) = 4x^2 + 4x + 5$

17. *Numerical, Graphical, and Analytical Analysis*   A rectangle is inscribed in the region bounded by the x-axis, the y-axis, and the graph of $x + 2y - 8 = 0$.

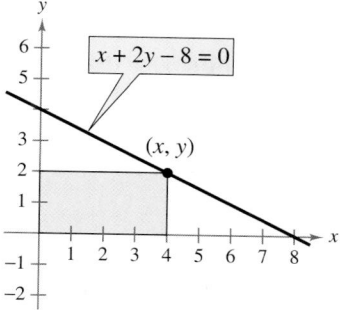

(a) Complete six rows of a table like the one below.

x	y	Area
1	$4 - \frac{1}{2}(1)$	$(1)\left[4 - \frac{1}{2}(1)\right] = \frac{7}{2}$
2	$4 - \frac{1}{2}(2)$	$(2)\left[4 - \frac{1}{2}(2)\right] = 6$

(b) Use a graphing utility to generate additional rows of the table. Use the table to estimate the dimensions that will produce the maximum area.

(c) Write the area A as a function of x. Determine the domain of the function in the context of the problem.

(d) Use a graphing utility to graph the function. Use the graph to approximate the dimensions that will produce the maximum area.

(e) Write the area function in standard form to find algebraically the dimensions that will produce the maximum area.

18. *Maximum Profit*   Let x be the amount (in hundreds of dollars) a company spends on advertising, and let P be the profit, where

$$P = 320 + 15x - \tfrac{1}{2}x^2.$$

(a) Use a graphing utility to graph the function.

(b) Use the *zoom* and *trace* features of a graphing utility to estimate the vertex of the function.

(c) Verify your answer in part (b) both algebraically and numerically by creating a table of values.

(d) Explain what the vertex represents.

3.2   In Exercises 19–22, sketch the graphs of $y = x^n$ and the specified transformations.

19. $y = x^4$
     (a) $f(x) = (x + 5)^4$ (b) $f(x) = x^4 - 4$
     (c) $f(x) = 3 + x^4$ (d) $f(x) = \frac{1}{4}(x - 2)^4$

20. $y = x^5$
     (a) $f(x) = (x + 4)^5$ (b) $f(x) = 6 + x^5$
     (c) $f(x) = 3 - \frac{1}{2}x^5$ (d) $f(x) = 2(x + 3)^5$

21. $y = x^6$
     (a) $f(x) = x^6 - 2$ (b) $f(x) = -\frac{1}{4}x^6$
     (c) $f(x) = -\frac{1}{2}x^6 - 5$ (d) $f(x) = -(x + 7)^6 - 5$

22. $y = x^7$

   (a) $f(x) = -x^7 + 4$ (b) $f(x) = (x + 2)^7 - 1$

   (c) $f(x) = -\frac{1}{3}x^7 + 1$ (d) $f(x) = -(x + 8)^7$

In Exercises 23–26, determine the right-hand and left-hand behavior of the graph of the polynomial function.

23. $f(x) = -x^2 + 6x + 9$

24. $f(x) = \frac{1}{2}x^3 + 2x$

25. $g(x) = \frac{3}{4}(x^4 + 3x^2 + 2)$

26. $h(x) = -x^5 - 7x^2 + 10x$

Graphical Analysis **In Exercises 27 and 28, use a graphing utility to graph the functions f and g in the same viewing window. Zoom out far enough so that the right-hand and left-hand behavior of f and g appear identical.**

27. $f(x) = \frac{1}{2}x^3 - 2x + 1,$ $g(x) = \frac{1}{2}x^3$

28. $f(x) = -x^4 + 2x^3,$ $g(x) = -x^4$

In Exercises 29–34, (a) find the zeros of the function and (b) sketch its graph.

29. $g(x) = x^4 - x^3 - 2x^2$

30. $h(x) = -2x^3 - x^2 + x$

31. $f(t) = t^3 - 3t$ **32.** $f(x) = -(x + 6)^3 - 8$

33. $f(x) = x(x + 3)^2$ **34.** $f(t) = t^4 - 4t^2$

35. *Volume* A rectangular package can have a maximum combined length and girth (perimeter of a cross section) of 216 centimeters.

   (a) Write the volume V as a function of x.

   (b) Use a graphing utility to graph the volume function, and then use the graph to estimate the dimensions of the package of maximum volume.

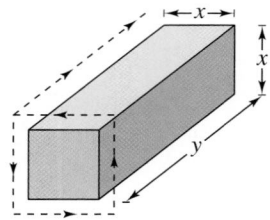

36. *Volume* Rework Exercise 35 for a cylindrical package. (The cross sections are circular.)

In Exercises 37–40, (a) use the Intermediate Value Theorem and a graphing utility to find intervals of length 1 in which the polynomial function is guaranteed to have a zero, and (b) use the *zero* or *root* feature of a graphing utility to approximate the zeros of the function.

37. $f(x) = x^3 + 2x^2 - x - 1$

38. $f(x) = 0.24x^3 - 2.6x - 1.4$

39. $f(x) = x^4 - 6x^2 - 4$

40. $f(x) = 2x^4 + \frac{7}{2}x^3 - 2$

3.3 *Graphical Analysis* **In Exercises 41 and 42, use a graphing utility to graph the two equations in the same viewing window. Use the graphs to verify that the expressions are equivalent. Verify your results algebraically.**

41. $y_1 = \dfrac{x^2}{x - 2},$ $y_2 = x + 2 + \dfrac{4}{x - 2}$

42. $y_1 = \dfrac{x^4 + 1}{x^2 + 2},$ $y_2 = x^2 - 2 + \dfrac{5}{x^2 + 2}$

In Exercises 43–48, divide by long division.

43. $\dfrac{24x^2 - x - 8}{3x - 2}$ **44.** $\dfrac{4x + 7}{3x - 2}$

45. $\dfrac{x^4 - 3x^2 + 2}{x^2 - 1}$ **46.** $\dfrac{3x^4}{x^2 - 1}$

47. $\dfrac{x^4 + x^3 - x^2 + 2x}{x^2 + 2x}$

48. $\dfrac{6x^4 + 10x^3 + 13x^2 - 5x + 2}{2x^2 - 1}$

In Exercises 49–52, divide by synthetic division.

49. $(0.25x^4 - 4x^3) \div (x + 2)$

50. $(0.1x^3 + 0.3x^2 - 0.5) \div (x - 5)$

51. $(6x^4 - 4x^3 - 27x^2 + 18x) \div \left(x - \frac{2}{3}\right)$

52. $(2x^3 + 2x^2 - x + 2) \div \left(x - \frac{1}{2}\right)$

In Exercises 53 and 54, use synthetic division to decide whether the x-values are zeros of the function.

53. $f(x) = 2x^3 + 3x^2 - 20x - 21$

   (a) $x = 4$ (b) $x = -1$

   (c) $x = -\frac{7}{2}$ (d) $x = 0$

54. $f(x) = 20x^4 + 9x^3 - 14x^2 - 3x$

　(a) $x = -1$　　(b) $x = \frac{3}{4}$

　(c) $x = 0$　　(d) $x = 1$

In Exercises 55–58, find a polynomial with integer coefficients that has the given zeros.

55. $-1, -1, \frac{1}{3}, -\frac{1}{2}$

56. $5, 1 - \sqrt{2}, 1 + \sqrt{2}$

57. $\frac{2}{3}, 4, \sqrt{3}i, -\sqrt{3}i$

58. $2, -3, 1 - 2i, 1 + 2i$

In Exercises 59–64, find all the zeros of the function.

59. $f(x) = 4x^3 - 11x^2 + 10x - 3$

60. $f(x) = 10x^3 + 21x^2 - x - 6$

61. $f(x) = 6x^3 - 5x^2 + 24x - 20$

62. $f(x) = x^3 - 1.3x^2 - 1.7x + 0.6$

63. $f(x) = 6x^4 - 25x^3 + 14x^2 + 27x - 18$

64. $f(x) = 5x^4 + 126x^2 + 25$

In Exercises 65 and 66, use synthetic division to verify the upper bound and lower bound of the zeros of f.

65. $f(x) = 4x^3 - 3x^2 + 4x - 3$

　Upper bound: $x = 1$; Lower bound: $x = -\frac{1}{4}$

66. $f(x) = 2x^3 - 5x^2 - 14x + 8$

　Upper bound: $x = 8$; Lower bound: $x = -4$

3.4 In Exercises 67–70, use a graphing utility to (a) graph the function, (b) determine the number of real zeros of the function, and (c) approximate the real zeros of the function to the nearest hundredth.

67. $f(x) = x^4 + 2x + 1$

68. $g(x) = x^3 - 3x^2 + 3x + 2$

69. $h(x) = x^3 - 6x^2 + 12x - 10$

70. $f(x) = x^5 + 2x^3 - 3x - 20$

In Exercises 71–76, find all the zeros of the function and write the polynomial as a product of linear factors. Use a graphing utility to verify your answer.

71. $f(x) = x^3 - 4x^2 + 6x - 4$

72. $f(x) = x^3 - 5x^2 - 7x + 51$

73. $f(x) = x^3 + 6x^2 + 11x + 12$

74. $f(x) = 2x^3 - 9x^2 + 22x - 30$

75. $f(x) = x^4 + 34x^2 + 225$

76. $f(x) = x^4 + 10x^3 + 26x^2 + 10x + 25$

In Exercises 77–82, find a polynomial function with integer coefficients that has the given zeros. (There are many correct answers.)

77. $-2, -2, -5i$

78. $4, 4, 2i$

79. $1, -4, -3 + 5i$

80. $3, 6 + i$

81. $-\frac{2}{3}, -1, 3 + \sqrt{2}i$

82. $-4, -4, 1 + \sqrt{3}i$

In Exercises 83–86, write the polynomial (a) as the product of factors that are irreducible over the rationals, (b) as the product of linear and quadratic factors that are irreducible over the reals, and (c) in completely factored form.

83. $f(x) = x^4 + 2x^2 - 8$

84. $f(x) = x^4 - x^3 - x^2 + 5x - 20$

　(*Hint:* One factor is $x^2 - 5$.)

85. $f(x) = x^4 - 2x^3 + 8x^2 - 18x - 9$

　(*Hint:* One factor is $x^2 + 9$.)

86. $f(x) = x^4 - 4x^3 + 3x^2 + 8x - 16$

　(*Hint:* One factor is $x^2 - x - 4$.)

3.5 In Exercises 87–90, find the domain of the function and identify any horizontal and vertical asymptotes.

87. $f(x) = \dfrac{x - 8}{1 - x}$

88. $f(x) = \dfrac{5x}{x + 12}$

89. $f(x) = \dfrac{2}{x^2 - 3x - 18}$

90. $f(x) = \dfrac{2x^2 + 3}{x^2 + x + 3}$

In Exercises 91–98, determine the horizontal asymptotes of the function.

91. $f(x) = \dfrac{7 + x}{7 - x}$

92. $f(x) = \dfrac{6x}{x^2 - 1}$

93. $f(x) = \dfrac{4x^2}{2x^2 - 3}$

94. $f(x) = \dfrac{3x^2 - 11x - 4}{x^2 + 2}$

95. $f(x) = \dfrac{2x^3}{x^2 + 2x - 8}$

96. $f(x) = \dfrac{3x^2}{2x + 3}$

97. $f(x) = \dfrac{x - 2}{|x| + 2}$

98. $f(x) = \dfrac{2x}{|2x - 1|}$

99. *Average Cost* A business has a cost of $C = 0.5x + 500$ for producing x units. The average cost per unit is

$$\overline{C} = \frac{C}{x} = \frac{0.5x + 500}{x}, \quad x > 0.$$

(a) Use a graphing utility to graph the function.

(b) Find the average cost of producing $x = 50$, 100, 1000, and 10,000 units.

(c) Determine the average cost per unit as x increases without bound. (Find the horizontal asymptote.)

100. *Seizure of Illegal Drugs* The cost in millions of dollars for the U.S. government to seize $p\%$ of a certain illegal drug as it enters the country is

$$C = \frac{528p}{100 - p}, \quad 0 \le p < 100.$$

(a) Find the cost of seizing 25%.

(b) Find the cost of seizing 50%.

(c) Find the cost of seizing 75%.

(d) Use a graphing utility to graph the function.

(e) According to this model, would it be possible to seize 100% of the drug?

3.6 In Exercises 101–110, sketch the graph of the rational function. As a sketching aid, check for intercepts, symmetry, vertical asymptotes, and horizontal asymptotes. Use a graphing utility to verify your graph.

101. $f(x) = \dfrac{2x - 1}{x - 5}$

102. $f(x) = \dfrac{x - 3}{x - 2}$

103. $f(x) = \dfrac{2x}{x^2 + 4}$

104. $f(x) = \dfrac{2x^2}{x^2 - 4}$

105. $f(x) = \dfrac{x^2}{x^2 + 1}$

106. $f(x) = \dfrac{5x}{x^2 + 1}$

107. $f(x) = \dfrac{2}{(x + 1)^2}$

108. $f(x) = \dfrac{4}{(x - 1)^2}$

109. $f(x) = \dfrac{2x}{x^2 + x - 12}$

110. $f(x) = \dfrac{3x - 1}{x^2 + 5x + 4}$

In Exercises 111–116, sketch the graph of the rational function. As a sketching aid, check for intercepts, symmetry, vertical asymptotes, horizontal asymptotes, and slant asymptotes. Use a graphing utility to verify your graph.

111. $f(x) = \dfrac{2x^3}{x^2 + 1}$

112. $f(x) = \dfrac{x^3}{3x^2 - 6}$

113. $f(x) = \dfrac{1}{x + 3} + 2$

114. $f(x) = \dfrac{5x}{x^2 - 4}$

115. $f(x) = \dfrac{x^2 - x + 1}{x - 3}$

116. $f(x) = \dfrac{2x^2 + 7x + 3}{x + 1}$

117. *Population of Fish* The Parks and Wildlife Commission introduces 80,000 fish into a large human-made lake. The population of the fish in thousands is

$$N = \frac{20(4 + 3t)}{1 + 0.05t}, \quad t \ge 0$$

where t is time in years.

(a) Sketch the graph of the function by hand. Use a graphing utility to verify your graph.

(b) Find the populations when t is 5, 10, and 25.

(c) What is the maximum number of fish in the lake as time increases? Explain your reasoning.

118. *Numerical and Graphical Analysis* A right triangle is formed in the first quadrant by the x- and y-axes and a line through the point $(2, 3)$.

(a) Draw a diagram that illustrates the problem. Label the known and unknown quantities.

(b) Verify that the area of the triangle is

$$A = \frac{3x^2}{2(x - 2)}, \quad x > 2.$$

(c) Use a graphing utility to generate a table giving the area for values of x. Start the table with $x = 2.5$ and x-increments of 0.5. Continue until you can approximate the dimensions of the triangle of minimum area.

(d) Use a graphing utility to graph the area function. Use the graph to approximate the dimensions of the triangle of minimum area.

(e) Determine the slant asymptote of the area function. Explain its meaning.

Synthesis

True or False? In Exercises 119 and 120, determine whether the statement is true or false. Justify your answer.

119. The graph of $f(x) = \dfrac{2x^3}{x + 1}$ has a slant asymptote.

120. The graphs of $f(x) = (3x^2 - 10)/x^2$ and $f(x) = (3x^2 - 10)/|x^2|$ are the same, with both having a horizontal asymptote at $x = 3$.

Chapter Project   *Finding Points of Intersection*

You can use the *zoom* feature of a graphing utility to approximate the points of intersection of the graphs of equations.

In this project you will find the points of intersection of the circle and parabola given by

$$x^2 + y^2 - 3x + 5y - 11 = 0 \quad \text{and} \quad y = x^2 - 4x + 5.$$

a. Begin by writing the circle as the union of two functions. Identify the functions that represent the top half and the bottom half of the circle.

b. Use a graphing utility to graph all three functions in the same viewing window, as shown in Figure 3.50. Use the *intersect* feature of the graphing utility to estimate the points of intersection.

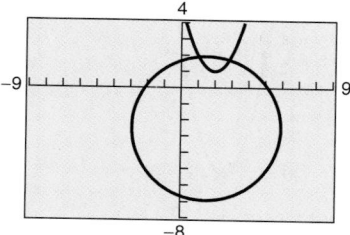

Figure 3.50

Questions for Further Exploration

1. Using a window setting of $1.05 \le x \le 1.06$ and $1.89 \le y \le 1.90$, graph the top half of the circle and the parabola in the example on the same screen. Then use the *trace* or *value* feature to approximate (accurate to three decimal places) the y-coordinate of the point of intersection that is shown on the screen.

2. Another method for finding the points of intersection is to substitute $x^2 - 4x + 5$ for y in the equation of the circle to get a fourth-degree polynomial equation. Graph this polynomial function.

   (a) Find a setting that allows you to approximate the solution $x \approx 1.055$ of the polynomial equation to two more decimal places.

   (b) Find a setting that allows you to approximate the solution $x \approx 2.841$ to two more decimal places.

3. Use a graphing utility to find the points of intersection of the circle and the parabola given by

$$x^2 + y^2 - 5x + 4y - 13 = 0$$
$$y = x^2 - 3x + 2.$$

4. *Market Equilibrium*   The *market equilibrium* of a commodity is the quantity (and corresponding price) at which the supply of the commodity and the demand for the commodity are equal. The supply and demand curves for a business dealing with wheat are

Supply: $p = 1.45 + 0.00014x^2$

Demand: $p = (2.388 - 0.007x)^2$

where p is the price (in dollars) per bushel and x is the quantity (in bushels per day). Use a graphing utility to graph the supply and demand equations and find the market equilibrium. (*Hint:* The *market equilibrium* is the point of intersection of the graphs for $x > 0$.)

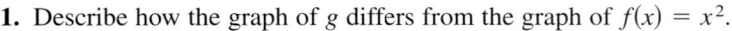

Chapter Test

3

Take this test as you would take a test in class. After you are done, check your work against the answers in the back of the book.

1. Describe how the graph of g differs from the graph of $f(x) = x^2$.

   (a) $g(x) = 2 - x^2$ (b) $g(x) = \left(x - \frac{3}{2}\right)^2$

2. Identify the vertex and intercepts of the graph of $y = x^2 + 4x + 3$.

3. Find an equation of the parabola shown at the right.

4. The path of a ball is given by $y = -\frac{1}{20}x^2 + 3x + 5$, where y is the height in feet and x is the horizontal distance in feet.

   (a) Find the maximum height of the ball.

   (b) Which term determines the height at which the ball was thrown? Does changing this term change the coordinates of the maximum height of the ball? Explain.

5. Divide using long division: $(3x^3 + 4x - 1) \div (x^2 + 1)$.

6. Divide using synthetic division: $(2x^4 - 5x^2 - 3) \div (x - 2)$.

In Exercises 7 and 8, list all the possible rational zeros of the function. Use a graphing utility to graph the function and find all the rational zeros.

7. $g(t) = 2t^4 - 3t^3 + 16t - 24$ 8. $h(x) = 3x^5 + 2x^4 - 3x - 2$

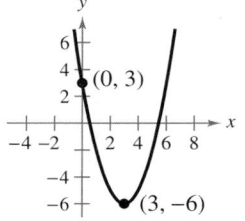

FIGURE FOR 3

In Exercises 9 and 10, use the *zero* or *root* feature of a graphing utility to approximate (accurate to three decimal places) the real zeros of the function.

9. $f(x) = x^4 - x^3 - 1$ 10. $f(x) = 3x^5 + 2x^4 - 12x - 8$

In Exercises 11–13, find a polynomial function with integer coefficients that has the given zeros.

11. $0, 3, 3 + i, 3 - i$ 12. $1 - \sqrt{3}i, 2, 2$ 13. $0, -5, 1 + i$

In Exercises 14–16, sketch the graph of the rational function. As a sketching aid, check for intercepts, symmetry, vertical asymptotes, horizontal asymptotes, and slant asymptotes. Use a graphing utility to verify your graph.

14. $h(x) = \dfrac{4}{x^2} - 1$ 15. $g(x) = \dfrac{x^2 + 2}{x - 1}$ 16. $f(x) = \dfrac{2x^2 + 9}{5x^2 + 2}$

17. Find a rational function with vertical asymptotes at $x = \pm 3$ and a horizontal asymptote at $y = 4$.

18. The average age of the groom in a wedding for a given age of the bride can be approximated by the model

    $$y = -0.00428x^2 + 1.442x - 3.136, \quad 20 \le x \le 55$$

    where y is the age of the groom and x is the age of the bride. For what age of the bride is the average age of the groom 30? (Source: U.S. National Center for Health Statistics)

Exponential and Logarithmic Functions

Louise Gubb/The Image Works

The Big Picture

In this chapter you will learn how to

❑ recognize, evaluate, and graph exponential and logarithmic functions.

❑ rewrite logarithmic functions with different bases.

❑ use properties of logarithms to evaluate, rewrite, expand, or condense logarithmic expressions.

❑ solve exponential and logarithmic equations.

❑ use exponential growth models, exponential decay models, Gaussian models, logistic models, and logarithmic models to solve real-life problems.

❑ fit exponential and logarithmic models to sets of data.

Personal savings as a percent of disposable income was 3.9% in 1997 and disposable per capita income was $21,969. So, the per capita personal savings was $856.79. (Source: U.S. Bureau of Economic Analysis)

Important Vocabulary

As you encounter each new vocabulary term in this chapter, add the term and its definition to your notebook glossary.

- algebraic functions (p. 298)
- transcendental functions (p. 298)
- exponential function with base *a* (p. 298)
- natural base (p. 302)
- natural exponential function (p. 302)
- logarithmic function with base *a* (p. 311)

- common logarithmic function (p. 312)
- natural logarithmic function (p. 315)
- change-of-base formula (p. 322)
- exponential growth model (p. 340)
- exponential decay model (p. 340)
- Gaussian model (p. 340)

- logistic growth model (p. 340)
- logarithmic models (p. 340)
- normally distributed (p. 344)
- bell-shaped curve (p. 344)
- logistic curve (p. 345)
- sigmoidal curve (p. 345)

Additional Resources Text-specific additional resources are available to help you do well in this course. See page xvi for details.

4.1 Exponential Functions and Their Graphs

Exponential Functions

So far, this text has dealt mainly with **algebraic functions,** which include polynomial functions and rational functions. In this chapter you will study two types of nonalgebraic functions—*exponential* functions and *logarithmic* functions. These functions are examples of **transcendental functions.**

Definition of Exponential Function

The **exponential function** f **with base** a is denoted by

$$f(x) = a^x$$

where $a > 0$, $a \neq 1$, and x is any real number.

Note that in the definition of an exponential function, the base $a = 1$ is excluded because it yields $f(x) = 1^x = 1$. This is a constant function, not an exponential function.

You already know how to evaluate a^x for integer and rational values of x. For example, you know that $4^3 = 64$ and $4^{1/2} = 2$. However, to evaluate 4^x for any real number x, you need to interpret forms with *irrational* exponents. For the purposes of this text, it is sufficient to think of

$$a^{\sqrt{2}} \text{ (where } \sqrt{2} \approx 1.41421356)$$

as the number that has the successively closer approximations

$$a^{1.4}, a^{1.41}, a^{1.414}, a^{1.4142}, a^{1.41421}, \ldots$$

Example 1 shows how to use a calculator to evaluate an exponential expression.

EXAMPLE 1 Evaluating Exponential Expressions

Use a calculator to evaluate each expression.

a. $2^{-3.1}$ **b.** $2^{-\pi}$ **c.** $12^{5/7}$ **d.** $(0.6)^{3/2}$

Solution

Number	*Graphing Calculator Keystrokes*	*Display*
a. $2^{-3.1}$	2 [^] [(−)] 3.1 [ENTER]	0.1166291
b. $2^{-\pi}$	2 [^] [(−)] π [ENTER]	0.1133147
c. $12^{5/7}$	12 [^] [(] 5 [÷] 7 [)] [ENTER]	5.8998877
d. $(0.6)^{3/2}$	.6 [^] [(] 3 [÷] 2 [)] [ENTER]	0.4647580

What You Should Learn:

- How to recognize and evaluate exponential functions with base a
- How to graph exponential functions
- How to recognize, evaluate, and graph exponential functions with base e
- How to use exponential functions to model and solve real-life problems

Why You Should Learn It:

Exponential functions are useful in modeling data that increase or decrease quickly. For instance, Exercise 77 on page 309 shows how to use an exponential function to model the amount of defoliation caused by a gypsy moth.

Jenny Hager/The Image Works

Graphs of Exponential Functions

The graphs of all exponential functions have similar characteristics, as shown in Examples 2, 3, and 4.

EXAMPLE 2   Graphs of $y = a^x$

In the same coordinate plane, sketch the graph of each function.

a. $f(x) = 2^x$ **b.** $g(x) = 4^x$

Solution

The table below lists some values for each function, and Figure 4.1 shows the graphs of both functions. Note that both graphs are increasing. Moreover, the graph of $g(x) = 4^x$ is increasing more rapidly than the graph of $f(x) = 2^x$.

x	-2	-1	0	1	2	3
2^x	$\frac{1}{4}$	$\frac{1}{2}$	1	2	4	8
4^x	$\frac{1}{16}$	$\frac{1}{4}$	1	4	16	64

The table in Example 2 was evaluated by hand. You could, of course, use a graphing utility to construct tables with even more values.

EXAMPLE 3   Graphs of $y = a^{-x}$

In the same coordinate plane, sketch the graph of each function.

a. $F(x) = 2^{-x}$ **b.** $G(x) = 4^{-x}$

Solution

The table below lists some values for each function, and Figure 4.2 shows the graphs of both functions. Note that both graphs are decreasing. Moreover, the graph of $G(x) = 4^{-x}$ is decreasing more rapidly than the graph of $F(x) = 2^{-x}$.

x	-3	-2	-1	0	1	2
2^{-x}	8	4	2	1	$\frac{1}{2}$	$\frac{1}{4}$
4^{-x}	64	16	4	1	$\frac{1}{4}$	$\frac{1}{16}$

In Example 3, note that the functions $F(x) = 2^{-x}$ and $G(x) = 4^{-x}$ can be rewritten with positive exponents.

$$F(x) = 2^{-x} = \left(\frac{1}{2}\right)^x \quad \text{and} \quad G(x) = 4^{-x} = \left(\frac{1}{4}\right)^x$$

In general,

$$a^{-x} = \left(\frac{1}{a}\right)^x.$$

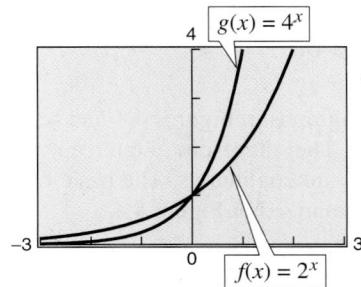

Figure 4.1

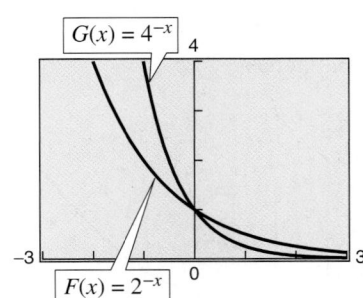

Figure 4.2

Comparing the functions in Examples 2 and 3, observe that

$$F(x) = 2^{-x} = f(-x) \qquad \text{and} \qquad G(x) = 4^{-x} = g(-x).$$

Consequently, the graph of F is a reflection (in the y-axis) of the graph of f, as shown in Figure 4.3(a). The graph of G and g have the same relationship, as shown in Figure 4.3(b).

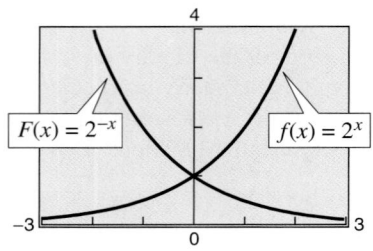

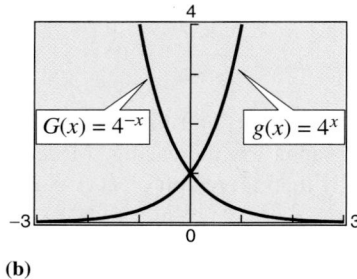

(a)   (b)

Figure 4.3

The graphs in Figures 4.1 and 4.2 are typical of the exponential functions a^x and a^{-x}. They have one y-intercept and one horizontal asymptote (the x-axis), and they are continuous. The basic characteristics of these exponential functions are summarized in Figure 4.4.

Graph of $y = a^x$, $a > 1$

- Domain: $(-\infty, \infty)$
- Range: $(0, \infty)$
- Intercept: $(0, 1)$
- Increasing
- x-axis is a horizontal asymptote
  ($a^x \to 0$ as $x \to -\infty$)
- Continuous

Graph of $y = a^{-x}$, $a > 1$

- Domain: $(-\infty, \infty)$
- Range: $(0, \infty)$
- Intercept: $(0, 1)$
- Decreasing
- x-axis is a horizontal asymptote
  ($a^{-x} \to 0$ as $x \to \infty$)
- Continuous

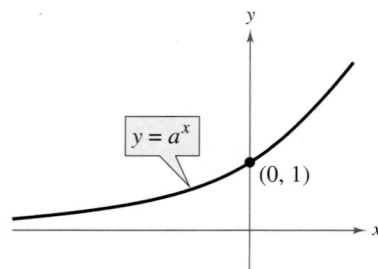

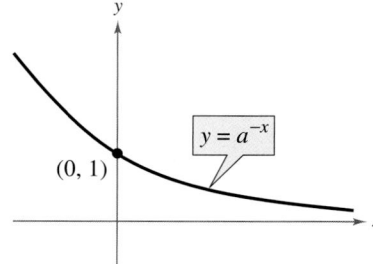

Figure 4.4

In the following example, notice how the graph of $y = a^x$ can be used to sketch the graphs of functions of the form

$$f(x) = b \pm a^{x+c}.$$

A computer animation of this example appears in the *Interactive* CD-ROM and *Internet* versions of this text.

EXAMPLE 4   Transformations of Graphs of Exponential Functions

Each of the following graphs is a transformation of the graph of $f(x) = 3^x$, as shown in Figure 4.5.

a. Because $g(x) = 3^{x+1} = f(x + 1)$, the graph of g can be obtained by shifting the graph of f one unit to the left.

b. Because $h(x) = 3^x - 2 = f(x) - 2$, the graph of h can be obtained by shifting the graph of f down two units.

c. Because $k(x) = -3^x = -f(x)$, the graph of k can be obtained by reflecting the graph of f in the x-axis.

d. Because $j(x) = 3^{-x} = f(-x)$, the graph of j can be obtained by reflecting the graph of f in the y-axis.

STUDY T!P

The following table shows some points of the graphs in Figure 4.5(a). The functions $f(x)$ and $g(x)$ are represented by Y1 and Y2, respectively. Explain how you can use the table to describe the transformation.

X	Y1	Y2
	0.03704	0.1111
-2	0.11111	0.3333
-1	0.33333	1
0	1	3
1	3	9
2	9	27
3	27	81
X=-3		

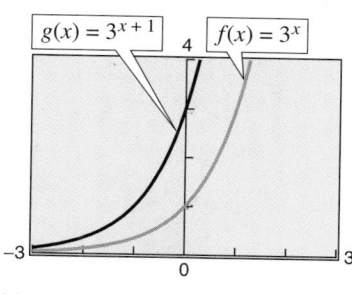

(a)

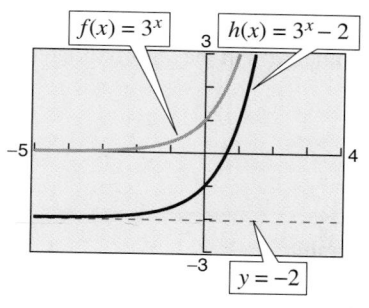

(b)

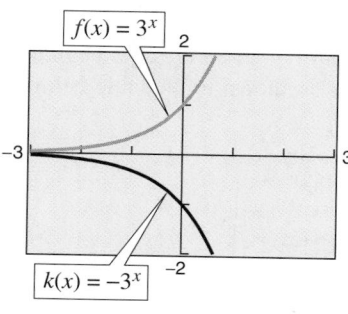

(c)

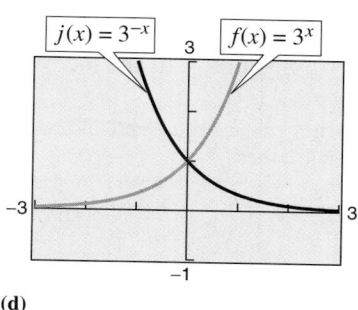

(d)

Figure 4.5

In Figure 4.5, notice that the transformations in parts (a), (c), and (d) keep the x-axis as a horizontal asymptote, but the transformation in part (b) yields a new horizontal asymptote of $y = -2$. Also, be sure to note how the y-intercept is affected by each transformation.

The Natural Base e

For many applications, the convenient choice for a base is the irrational number

$$e \approx 2.71828 \ldots .$$

This number is called the **natural base.** The function $f(x) = e^x$ is the **natural exponential function.** Its graph is shown in Figure 4.6. Be sure you see that for the exponential function $f(x) = e^x$, e is the constant 2.71828 . . . , whereas x is the variable.

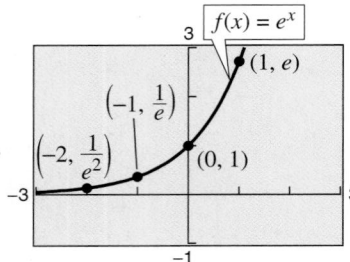

Domain: $(-\infty, \infty)$
Range: $(0, \infty)$
Intercept: $(0, 1)$

Figure 4.6 *The Natural Exponential Function*

In Example 5, you will see that the number e can be approximated by the expression

$$\left(1 + \frac{1}{x}\right)^x \text{ for large values of } x.$$

EXAMPLE 5   Approximation of the Number e

Evaluate the expression $[1 + (1/x)]^x$ for several large values of x to see that the values approach $e \approx 2.71828$ as x increases without bound.

Graphical Solution

Use a graphing utility to graph

$$y_1 = [1 + (1/x)]^x \qquad \text{and} \qquad y_2 = e$$

in the same viewing window, as shown in Figure 4.7. Use the *trace* feature of the graphing utility to verify that as x increases, the graph of y_1 gets closer and closer to the line $y_2 = e$.

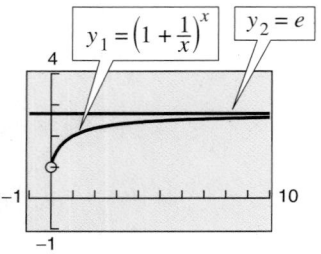

Figure 4.7

Numerical Solution

Create a table of values for the function $y = [1 + (1/x)]^x$, beginning at $x = 10$ and increasing the x-values as shown in the table below.

x	10	100	1000
$\left(1 + \dfrac{1}{x}\right)^x$	2.59374	2.70481	2.71692

x	10,000	100,000	1,000,000
$\left(1 + \dfrac{1}{x}\right)^x$	2.71815	2.71827	2.71828

From the table, it seems reasonable to conclude that

$$\left(1 + \frac{1}{x}\right)^x \to e \text{ as } x \to \infty.$$

EXAMPLE 6   Evaluating the Natural Exponential Function

Use a calculator to evaluate each expression.

a. e^{-2} **b.** e^{-1} **c.** e^1 **d.** e^2

Solution

Number	Graphing Calculator Keystrokes	Display
a. e^{-2}	e^x $(-)$ 2 ENTER	0.1353353
b. e^{-1}	e^x $(-)$ 1 ENTER	0.3678794
c. e^1	e^x 1 ENTER	2.7182818
d. e^2	e^x 2 ENTER	7.3890561

EXAMPLE 7   Graphing Natural Exponential Functions

Sketch the graph of each natural exponential function.

a. $f(x) = 2e^{0.24x}$ **b.** $g(x) = \frac{1}{2}e^{-0.58x}$

Solution

To sketch these two graphs, you can use a calculator to construct a table of values, as shown below.

x	-3	-2	-1	0	1	2	3
$f(x)$	0.974	1.238	1.573	2.000	2.542	3.232	4.109
$g(x)$	2.849	1.595	0.893	0.500	0.280	0.157	0.088

After constructing the table, plot the points and connect them with smooth curves, as shown in Figure 4.8. Note that the graph in part (a) is increasing, whereas the graph in part (b) is decreasing. Use a graphing calculator to verify these graphs.

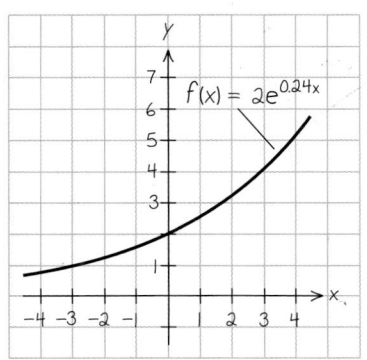

(a)

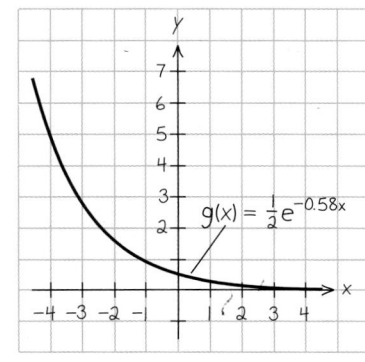

(b)

Figure 4.8

The *Interactive* CD-ROM and *Internet* versions of this text show every example with its solution; clicking on the *Try It!* button brings up similar problems. Guided Examples and Integrated Examples show step-by-step solutions to additional examples. Integrated Examples are related to several concepts in the section.

Compound Interest

One of the most familiar examples of exponential growth is that of an investment earning *continuously compounded interest.* Suppose a principal P is invested at an annual interest rate r, compounded once a year. If the interest is added to the principal at the end of the year, the balance is $P_1 = P + Pr = P(1 + r)$. This pattern of multiplying the previous principal by $1 + r$ is then repeated each successive year, as shown in the table.

Time in Years	Balance After Each Compounding
0	$P = P$
1	$P_1 = P(1 + r)$
2	$P_2 = P_1(1 + r) = P(1 + r)(1 + r) = P(1 + r)^2$
⋮	⋮
n	$P_n = P(1 + r)^n$

Exploration

Use the formula

$$A = P\left(1 + \frac{r}{n}\right)^{nt}$$

to calculate the amount in an account when $P = \$3000$, $r = 6\%$, $t = 10$ years, and the number of compoundings is (1) by the day, (2) by the hour, (3) by the minute, and (4) by the second. Use these results to present an argument that increasing the number of compoundings does not mean unlimited growth of the amount in the account.

To accommodate more frequent (quarterly, monthly, or daily) compounding of interest, let n be the number of compoundings per year and let t be the number of years. (The product nt represents the total number of times the interest will be compounded.) Then the interest rate per compounding period is r/n, and the account balance after t years is

$$A = P\left(1 + \frac{r}{n}\right)^{nt}. \qquad \text{Amount with } n \text{ compoundings per year}$$

If you let the number of compoundings n increase without bound, you approach **continuous compounding.** In the formula for n compoundings per year, let $m = n/r$. This produces

$$A = P\left(1 + \frac{r}{n}\right)^{nt} = P\left(1 + \frac{1}{m}\right)^{mrt} = P\left[\left(1 + \frac{1}{m}\right)^m\right]^{rt}.$$

As m increases without bound, you know from Example 5 that $[1 + (1/m)]^m$ approaches e. So, for continuous compounding, it follows that

$$P\left[\left(1 + \frac{1}{m}\right)^m\right]^{rt} \rightarrow P[e]^{rt}$$

and you can write $A = Pe^{rt}$. This result is part of the reason that e is the "natural" choice for a base of an exponential function.

STUDY T!P

The interest rate r in the formula for compound interest should be written as a decimal. For example, an interest rate of 7% would be written $r = 0.07$.

A computer simulation of this concept appears in the *Interactive* CD-ROM and *Internet* versions of this text.

You may want to point out to your students that the option of continuous compounding is not offered to consumers very often. However, it can be used to figure the maximum earnings (regardless of compounding periods) that a principal may earn at a particular interest rate.

Formulas for Compound Interest

After t years, the balance A in an account with principal P and annual interest rate r (expressed as a decimal) is given by the following formulas.

1. For n compoundings per year: $A = P\left(1 + \frac{r}{n}\right)^{nt}$

2. For continuous compounding: $A = Pe^{rt}$

EXAMPLE 8 Finding the Balance for Compound Interest

A sum of $9000 is invested at an annual interest rate of 8.5%, compounded annually. Find the balance in the account after 3 years.

Algebraic Solution

In this case,

$$P = 9000, r = 8.5\% = 0.085, n = 1, t = 3.$$

Using the formula for compound interest with n compoundings per year, you have

$$A = P\left(1 + \frac{r}{n}\right)^{nt} \qquad \text{Formula for compound interest}$$

$$A = 9000\left(1 + \frac{0.085}{1}\right)^{1(3)} \qquad \begin{array}{l}\text{Substitute values}\\ \text{for } P, r, n, \text{ and } t.\end{array}$$

$$= 9000(1.085)^3 \qquad \text{Simplify.}$$

$$\approx \$11,495.60. \qquad \text{Use a calculator.}$$

So, the balance in the account after 3 years will be about $11,495.60.

Graphical Solution

Substitute values for P, r, and n into the formula for compound interest with n compoundings per year as follows.

$$A = P\left(1 + \frac{r}{n}\right)^{nt} \qquad \text{Formula for compound interest}$$

$$= 9000\left(1 + \frac{0.085}{1}\right)^{(1)t} \qquad \text{Substitute values for } P, r, \text{ and } n.$$

$$= 9000(1 + 0.085)^t \qquad \text{Simplify.}$$

Use a graphing utility to graph $y = 9000(1 + 0.085)^x$, as shown in Figure 4.9. Using the *value* feature or *zoom* and *trace* features, you can approximate the value of y when $x = 3$ to be about 11,495.60. So, the balance in the account after 3 years will be about $11,495.60.

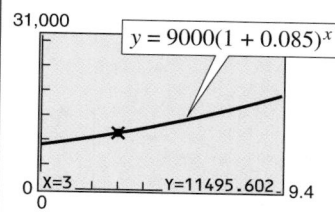

Figure 4.9

EXAMPLE 9 Finding Compound Interest

A total of $12,000 is invested at an annual interest rate of 9%. Find the balance after 5 years if it is compounded

a. quarterly. **b.** monthly. **c.** continuously.

Solution

a. For quarterly compoundings, $n = 4$. So, in 5 years at 9%, the balance is

$$A = P\left(1 + \frac{r}{n}\right)^{nt} = 12,000\left(1 + \frac{0.09}{4}\right)^{4(5)} = \$18,726.11.$$

b. For monthly compoundings, $n = 12$. So, in 5 years at 9%, the balance is

$$A = P\left(1 + \frac{r}{n}\right)^{nt} = 12,000\left(1 + \frac{0.09}{12}\right)^{12(5)} = \$18,788.17.$$

c. For continuous compounding, the balance is

$$A = Pe^{rt} = 12,000e^{0.09(5)} = \$18,819.75.$$

Note that continuous compounding yields more than quarterly or monthly compounding.

Activities

1. Sketch the graph of the functions $f(x) = e^x$ and $g(x) = 1 + e^x$ on the same coordinate system.

2. Determine the balance A at the end of 20 years if $1500 is invested at 6.5% interest and the interest is compounded (a) quarterly and (b) continuously.
   Answer: (a) $5446.73 (b) $5503.95

3. Determine the amount of money that should be invested at 9% interest, compounded monthly, to produce a final balance of $30,000 in 15 years.
   Answer: $7816.48

Other Applications

Exponential functions are used in various other applications.

EXAMPLE 10   Radioactive Decay

Let y represent the mass of a quantity of a radioactive element whose half-life is 25 years. After t years, the mass (in grams) is $y = 10\left(\frac{1}{2}\right)^{t/25}$.

a. What is the initial mass (when $t = 0$)?

b. How much of the initial mass is present after 80 years?

Algebraic Solution

a. $y = 10\left(\frac{1}{2}\right)^{t/25}$ Write original equation.

$= 10\left(\frac{1}{2}\right)^{0/25}$ Substitute 0 for t.

$= 10$ Simplify.

So, the initial mass is 10 grams.

b. $y = 10\left(\frac{1}{2}\right)^{t/25}$ Write original equation.

$= 10\left(\frac{1}{2}\right)^{80/25}$ Substitute 80 for t.

$= 10\left(\frac{1}{2}\right)^{3.2}$ Simplify.

≈ 1.088 Use a calculator.

So, about 1.088 grams is present after 80 years.

Graphical Solution

Use a graphing utility to graph $y = 10\left(\frac{1}{2}\right)^{x/25}$.

a. Use the *value* feature or *zoom* and *trace* features of the graphing utility to determine that the value of y when $x = 0$ is 10, as shown in Figure 4.10. So, the initial mass is 10 grams.

b. Use the *value* feature or *zoom* and *trace* features of the graphing utility to determine that the value of y when $x = 80$ is about 1.088, as shown in Figure 4.11. So, about 1.088 grams is present after 80 years.

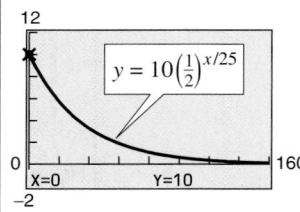

Figure 4.10

Figure 4.11

EXAMPLE 11   Population Growth

The approximate number of fruit flies in an experimental population after t hours is

$$Q(t) = 20e^{0.03t}, \qquad t \geq 0.$$

a. Find the initial number of fruit flies in the population.

b. How large is the population of fruit flies after 72 hours?

c. Sketch the graph of Q.

Solution

a. To find the initial population, evaluate $Q(t)$ at $t = 0$.

$$Q(0) = 20e^{0.03(0)} = 20e^0 = 20(1) = 20 \text{ flies}$$

b. After 72 hours, the population size is

$$Q(72) = 20e^{0.03(72)} = 20e^{2.16} \approx 173 \text{ flies}.$$

c. The graph of Q is shown in Figure 4.12.

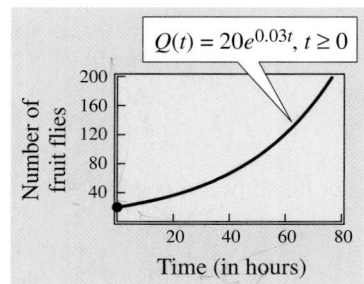

Figure 4.12

4.1   E x e r c i s e s

In Exercises 1–10, use a calculator to evaluate the expression. Round your result to three decimal places.

1. $(3.4)^{6.8}$

2. $5000(2^{-1.5})$

3. $6^{2\pi}$

4. $5^{-\pi}$

5. $\sqrt[3]{7493}$

6. $100^{\sqrt{2}}$

7. $e^{1/2}$

8. $e^{-3/4}$

9. $e^{9.2}$

10. $e^{3.78}$

Think About It   In Exercises 11–14, use properties of exponents to determine which functions (if any) are the same.

11. $f(x) = 3^{x-2}$
$g(x) = 3^x - 9$
$h(x) = \frac{1}{9}(3^x)$

12. $f(x) = 4^x + 12$
$g(x) = 2^{2x+6}$
$h(x) = 64(4^x)$

13. $f(x) = 16(4^{-x})$
$g(x) = \left(\frac{1}{4}\right)^{x-2}$
$h(x) = 16(2^{-2x})$

14. $f(x) = 5^{-x} + 3$
$g(x) = 5^{3-x}$
$h(x) = -5^{x-3}$

In Exercises 15–22, match the exponential function with its graph. [The graphs are labeled (a), (b), (c), (d), (e), (f), (g), and (h).]

(a)
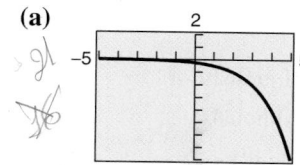

(b)
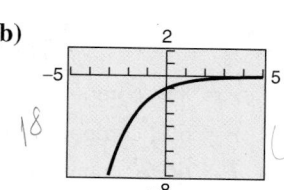

(c)
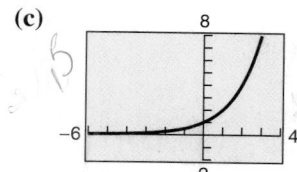

(d)
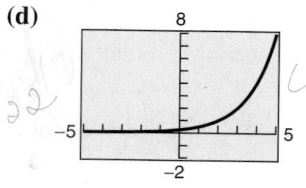

(e)
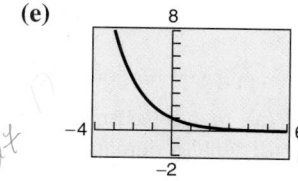

(f)
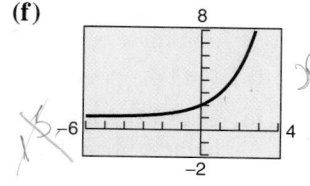

(g)
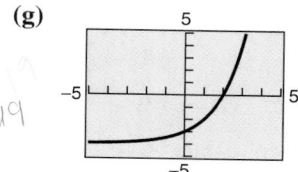

(h)
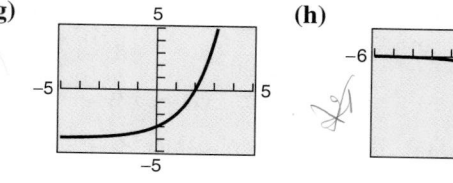

15. $f(x) = 2^x$

16. $f(x) = -2^x$

17. $f(x) = 2^{-x}$

18. $f(x) = -2^{-x}$

19. $f(x) = 2^x - 4$

20. $f(x) = 2^x + 1$

21. $f(x) = -2^{x-2}$

22. $f(x) = 2^{x-2}$

In Exercises 23–26, use the graph of f to describe the transformation that yields the graph of g.

23. $f(x) = 3^x$, $g(x) = 3^{x-5}$

24. $f(x) = -2^x$, $g(x) = 5 - 2^x$

25. $f(x) = \left(\frac{3}{5}\right)^x$, $g(x) = -\left(\frac{3}{5}\right)^{x+4}$

26. $f(x) = 0.3^x$, $g(x) = -0.3^x + 5$

In Exercises 27–34, graph the exponential function *by hand*. Identify the following features of the graph.

(a) Asymptotes

(b) Intercepts

(c) Increasing or decreasing

27. $g(x) = 5^x$

28. $f(x) = \left(\frac{3}{2}\right)^x$

29. $f(x) = \left(\frac{1}{5}\right)^x = 5^{-x}$

30. $h(x) = \left(\frac{3}{2}\right)^{-x}$

31. $h(x) = 5^{x-2}$

32. $g(x) = \left(\frac{3}{2}\right)^{x+2}$

33. $g(x) = 5^{-x} - 3$

34. $f(x) = \left(\frac{3}{2}\right)^{-x} + 2$

In Exercises 35–44, use a graphing utility to construct a table of values for the function. Then sketch the graph of the function.

35. $f(x) = \left(\frac{5}{2}\right)^x$

36. $f(x) = \left(\frac{5}{2}\right)^{-x}$

37. $f(x) = 6^x$

38. $f(x) = 2^{x-1}$

39. $f(x) = 3^{x+2}$

40. $f(x) = e^{-x}$

41. $f(x) = 3e^{x+4}$

42. $f(x) = 2e^{-0.5x}$

43. $f(x) = 2 + e^{x-5}$

44. $f(x) = 4^{x-3} + 3$

The *Interactive* CD-ROM and *Internet* versions of this text contain step-by-step solutions to all odd-numbered Section and Review Exercises. They also provide Tutorial Exercises, which link to Guided Examples for additional help.

In Exercises 45–52, use a graphing utility to graph the exponential function. Identify any asymptotes of the graph.

45. $y = 2^{-x^2}$

46. $y = 3^{-|x|}$

47. $y = 3^{x-2} + 1$

48. $y = 4^{x+1} - 2$

49. $y = 1.08^{-5x}$

50. $s(t) = 2e^{0.12t}$

51. $s(t) = 3e^{-0.2t}$

52. $g(x) = 1 + e^{-x}$

53. *Exploration* Consider the functions $f(x) = 3^x$ and $g(x) = 4^x$.

(a) Use a graphing utility to complete the table, and use the table to estimate the solution of the inequality $4^x < 3^x$.

x	-1	-0.5	0	0.5	1
$f(x)$					
$g(x)$					

(b) Use a graphing utility to graph $f(x)$ and $g(x)$ in the same viewing window. Use the graphs to solve the inequalities.

(i) $4^x < 3^x$ (ii) $4^x > 3^x$

54. *Exploration* Consider the functions $f(x) = \left(\frac{1}{2}\right)^x$ and $g(x) = \left(\frac{1}{4}\right)^x$.

(a) Use a graphing utility to complete the table, and use the table to estimate the solution of the inequality $\left(\frac{1}{4}\right)^x < \left(\frac{1}{2}\right)^x$.

x	-1	-0.5	0	0.5	1
$f(x)$					
$g(x)$					

(b) Use a graphing utility to graph $f(x)$ and $g(x)$ in the same viewing window. Use the graphs to solve the inequalities.

(i) $\left(\frac{1}{4}\right)^x < \left(\frac{1}{2}\right)^x$ (ii) $\left(\frac{1}{4}\right)^x > \left(\frac{1}{2}\right)^x$

In Exercises 55–58, use a graphing utility to (a) graph the function and (b) find any asymptotes numerically by creating a table of values for the function.

55. $f(x) = \dfrac{8}{1 + e^{-0.5x}}$

56. $g(x) = \dfrac{8}{1 + e^{-0.5/x}}$

57. $f(x) = -\dfrac{6}{2 - e^{0.2x}}$

58. $f(x) = \dfrac{6}{2 - e^{0.2/x}}$

In Exercises 59–62, (a) use a graphing utility to graph the function, (b) use the graph to find the open intervals on which the function is increasing and decreasing, and (c) approximate any relative maximum or minimum values.

59. $f(x) = x^2 e^{-x}$

60. $f(x) = 2x^2 e^{x+1}$

61. $f(x) = x(2^{3-x})$

62. $f(x) = -\left(\frac{1}{2}x\right)3^{x+4}$

Compound Interest **In Exercises 63–66, complete the table to determine the balance A for P dollars invested at rate r for t years and compounded n times per year.**

n	1	2	4	12	365	Continuous
A						

63. $P = \$2500$, $r = 8\%$, $t = 10$ years

64. $P = \$1000$, $r = 6\%$, $t = 10$ years

65. $P = \$2500$, $r = 8\%$, $t = 20$ years

66. $P = \$1000$, $r = 6\%$, $t = 40$ years

Compound Interest **In Exercises 67–70, complete the table to determine the balance A for \$12,000 invested at a rate r for t years.**

t	1	10	20	30	40	50
A						

67. $r = 8\%$, compounded continuously

68. $r = 6\%$, compounded continuously

69. $r = 6.5\%$, compounded monthly

70. $r = 7.5\%$, compounded daily

71. *Demand Function* The demand equation for a certain product is

$$p = 5000\left(1 - \frac{4}{4 + e^{-0.002x}}\right)$$

where p is the price and x is the number of units.

(a) Use a graphing utility to graph the demand function for $x > 0$ and $p > 0$.

(b) Find the price p for a demand of $x = 500$ units.

(c) Use the graph in part (a) to approximate the highest price that will still yield a demand of at least 600 units.

(d) Verify your answers to parts (b) and (c) numerically by creating a table of values for the function.

72. *Graphical Reasoning* There are two options for investing $500. The first earns 7% compounded annually, and the second earns 7% simple interest. The figure shows the growth of each investment over a 30-year period.

(a) Identify the two types of investments in the figure. Explain your reasoning.

(b) Verify your answer in part (a) by finding the equations that model the investment growth and using a graphing utility to graph the models.

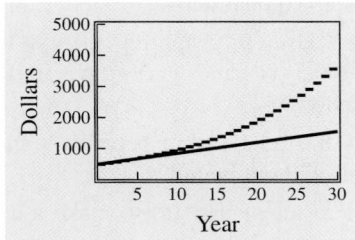

73. *Bacteria Growth* A certain type of bacteria increases according to the model

$$P(t) = 100e^{0.2197t}$$

where t is the time in hours.

(a) Use a graphing utility to graph the model.

(b) Use a graphing utility to approximate $P(0)$, $P(5)$, and $P(10)$.

(c) Verify your answers in part (b) algebraically.

74. *Population Growth* The population of a town increases according to the model

$$P(t) = 2500e^{0.0293t}$$

where t is the time in years, with $t = 0$ corresponding to 1990.

(a) Find the population in 1992, 1995, and 1998.

(b) Use a graphing utility to graph the function for the years 1990 through 2015.

(c) Use a graphing utility to approximate the population in 2005 and 2010.

(d) Verify your answers in part (c) algebraically.

75. *Radioactive Decay* Let Q (in grams) represent the mass of a quantity of radium 226, which has a half-life of 1620 years. The quantity of radium present after t years is

$$Q = 25\left(\tfrac{1}{2}\right)^{t/1620}.$$

(a) Determine the initial quantity (when $t = 0$).

(b) Determine the quantity present after 1000 years.

(c) Use a graphing utility to graph the function over the interval $t = 0$ to $t = 5000$.

(d) When will the quantity of radium be 0 grams? Explain.

76. *Radioactive Decay* Let Q (in grams) represent the mass of a quantity of carbon 14, which has a half-life of 5730 years. The quantity present after t years is $Q = 10\left(\tfrac{1}{2}\right)^{t/5730}$.

(a) Determine the initial quantity (when $t = 0$).

(b) Determine the quantity present after 2000 years.

(c) Sketch the graph of the function over the interval $t = 0$ to $t = 10,000$.

77. *Data Analysis* To estimate the amount of defoliation caused by gypsy moths, a forester counts the number x of egg masses on $\frac{1}{40}$ of an acre (circle of radius 18.6 feet) during the fall. The percent of defoliation y the next spring is shown in the table. (Source: USDA Forest Service)

x	0	25	50	75	100
y	12	44	81	96	99

(a) Use a graphing utility to plot the data points.

(b) A model for the data is $y = \dfrac{300}{3 + 17e^{-0.065x}}$. Use a graphing utility to graph the model in the same viewing window used in part (a). How well does the model fit the data?

(c) Use a graphing utility to create a table comparing the model with the sample data.

(d) Estimate the percent of defoliation if 36 egg masses are counted on $\frac{1}{40}$ acre.

(e) Use the graph to estimate the number of egg masses per $\frac{1}{40}$ acre if approximately $\frac{2}{3}$ of the forest is defoliated the next spring.

78. *Data Analysis* A cup of water at an initial temperature of 78°C is placed in a room at a constant temperature of 21°C. The temperature of the water is measured every 5 minutes for a period of $\frac{1}{2}$ hour. The results are recorded in the table, where t is the time (in minutes) and T is the temperature (in degrees Celsius).

t	0	5	10	15	20	25	30
T	78.0°	66.0°	57.5°	51.2°	46.3°	42.5°	39.6°

(a) Use the regression capabilities of a graphing utility to fit a line to the data. Use the graphing utility to plot the data points and the regression line in the same viewing window. Does the data appear linear? Explain.

(b) Use the regression capabilities of a graphing utility to fit a parabola to the data. Use the graphing utility to plot the data points and the regression parabola in the same viewing window. Does the data appear quadratic? Even though the quadratic model appears to be a "good" fit, explain why it may not be a good model for predicting the temperature of the water when $t = 60$.

(c) The graph of the model should be asymptotic with the temperature of the room. Subtract the room temperature from each of the temperatures in the table. Use a graphing utility to fit an exponential model to the revised data. Add the room temperature to this regression model. Use a graphing utility to plot the original data points and the model in the same viewing window.

(d) Explain why the procedure in part (c) was necessary for finding the exponential model.

79. Inflation   If the annual rate of inflation averages 4% over the next 10 years, the approximate cost C of goods or services during any year in that decade will be $C(t) = P(1.04)^t$, where t is the time (in years) and P is the present cost. Assume the price of an oil change for your car is presently $23.95.

(a) Use a graphing utility to graph the function.

(b) Use the graph in part (a) to approximate the price of an oil change 10 years from now.

(c) Verify your answer in part (b) algebraically.

80. Depreciation   After t years, the value of a car that costs $20,000 is $V(t) = 20,000\left(\frac{3}{4}\right)^t$.

(a) Use a graphing utility to graph the function.

(b) Use a graphing utility to create a table of values that shows the value V for $t = 1$ to 10 years.

Synthesis

True or False?   In Exercises 81 and 82, determine whether the statement is true or false. Justify your answer.

81. The x-axis is an asymptote for the graph of $f(x) = 10^x$.

82. $e = \dfrac{271,801}{99,990}$

83. Exploration   Use a graphing utility to graph $y_1 = e^x$ and each of the functions $y_2 = x^2$, $y_3 = x^3$, $y_4 = \sqrt{x}$, and $y_5 = |x|$.

(a) Which function increases at the fastest rate for "large" values of x?

(b) Use the result of part (a) to make a conjecture about the rates of growth of $y_1 = e^x$ and $y = x^n$ where n is a natural number and x is "large."

(c) Use the results of parts (a) and (b) to describe what is implied when it is stated that a quantity is growing exponentially.

84. Conjecture   Use a graphing utility to graph $f(x) = (1 + 0.5/x)^x$ and $g(x) = e^{0.5}$ in the same viewing window.

(a) What is the relationship between f and g as x increases without bound?

(b) Use the result of part (a) to make a conjecture about the value of $(1 + r/x)^x$ as x increases without bound.

85. Think About It   Without a graphing utility, explain why you know $2^{\sqrt{2}}$ is greater than 2, but less than 4.

86. Think About It   Which functions are exponential? Why?

(a) $3x$ (b) $3x^2$ (c) 3^x (d) 2^{-x}

87. Pattern Recognition   Use a graphing utility to compare the graph of the function $y = e^x$ with the graphs of the following functions.

(a) $y_1 = 1 + \dfrac{x}{1!}$ (b) $y_2 = 1 + \dfrac{x}{1!} + \dfrac{x^2}{2!}$

(c) $y_3 = 1 + \dfrac{x}{1!} + \dfrac{x^2}{2!} + \dfrac{x^3}{3!}$

In your opinion, which function is the best approximation of $y = e^x$?

Review

In Exercises 88–91, determine whether the function has an inverse. If it does, find f^{-1}.

88. $f(x) = 5x - 7$ **89.** $f(x) = -\frac{2}{3}x + \frac{5}{2}$

90. $f(x) = \sqrt[3]{x + 8}$ **91.** $f(x) = \sqrt{x^2 + 6}$

In Exercises 92–95, sketch the graph of the rational function.

92. $f(x) = \dfrac{2x}{x - 7}$ **93.** $f(x) = \dfrac{x^2 + 3}{x + 1}$

94. $f(x) = \dfrac{4x}{x^2 + 11x + 24}$ **95.** $f(x) = \dfrac{2x^3}{(x - 2)^2}$

4.2 Logarithmic Functions and Their Graphs

Logarithmic Functions

In Section 1.7, you studied the concept of the inverse of a function. There, you learned if a function has the property such that no horizontal line intersects its graph more than once, the function must have an inverse. By looking back at the graphs of the exponential functions introduced in Section 4.1, you will see that every function of the form

$$f(x) = a^x, \quad a > 0, a \neq 1$$

passes the Horizontal Line Test and therefore must have an inverse. This inverse function is called the **logarithmic function with base *a*.**

Definition of Logarithmic Function

For $x > 0$ and $0 < a \neq 1$,

$$y = \log_a x \quad \text{if and only if} \quad x = a^y.$$

The function

$$f(x) = \log_a x$$

is called the **logarithmic function with base *a*.**

The equations

$$y = \log_a x \qquad \text{Logarithmic form}$$

and

$$x = a^y \qquad \text{Exponential form}$$

are equivalent. The first equation is in logarithmic form and the second is in exponential form.

When evaluating logarithms, remember that *a logarithm is an exponent.* This means that $\log_a x$ is the exponent to which *a* must be raised to obtain *x*. For instance, $\log_2 8 = 3$ because 2 must be raised to the third power to get 8.

What You Should Learn:

- How to recognize and evaluate logarithmic functions with base *a*
- How to graph logarithmic functions
- How to recognize, evaluate, and graph natural logarithmic functions
- How to use logarithmic functions to model and solve real-life problems

Why You Should Learn It:

Logarithmic functions are useful in modeling data that increase or decrease slowly. For instance, Exercise 81 on page 320 shows how to use a logarithmic function to model the minimum required ventilation rates in public school classrooms.

Mark Richards/PhotoEdit

EXAMPLE 1   Evaluating Logarithms

Evaluate each expression.

a. $\log_2 32$ **b.** $\log_3 27$ **c.** $\log_4 2$
d. $\log_{10} \frac{1}{100}$ **e.** $\log_3 1$ **f.** $\log_2 2$

Solution

a. $\log_2 32 = 5$ because $2^5 = 32.$ **e.** $\log_3 1 = 0$ because $3^0 = 1.$
b. $\log_3 27 = 3$ because $3^3 = 27.$ **f.** $\log_2 2 = 1$ because $2^1 = 2.$
c. $\log_4 2 = \frac{1}{2}$ because $4^{1/2} = \sqrt{4} = 2.$
d. $\log_{10} \frac{1}{100} = -2$ because $10^{-2} = \frac{1}{10^2} = \frac{1}{100}.$

The logarithmic function with base 10 is called the **common logarithmic function.** On most calculators, this function is denoted by $\boxed{\text{LOG}}$. Because $\log_a x$ is the inverse function of a^x, it follows that the domain of $\log_a x$ is the range of a^x, $(0, \infty)$. In other words, $\log_a x$ is defined only if x is positive.

The logarithmic function can be one of the most difficult for students to understand. Remind students that a logarithm is an exponent. Converting back and forth from logarithmic form to exponential form supports this concept.

EXAMPLE 2   Evaluating Logarithms on a Calculator

Use a calculator to evaluate each expression.

a. $\log_{10} 10$ **b.** $2 \log_{10} 2.5$ **c.** $\log_{10}(-2)$

Solution

Number	Graphing Calculator Keystrokes	Display
a. $\log_{10} 10$	$\boxed{\text{LOG}}$ 10 $\boxed{\text{ENTER}}$	1
b. $2\log_{10} 2.5$	2 $\boxed{\text{LOG}}$ 2.5 $\boxed{\text{ENTER}}$	0.7958800
c. $\log_{10}(-2)$	$\boxed{\text{LOG}}$ $\boxed{(-)}$ 2 $\boxed{\text{ENTER}}$	ERROR

Note that the calculator displays an error message when you try to evaluate $\log_{10}(-2)$. The reason for this is that the domain of every logarithmic function is the set of *positive* real numbers. In this case, there is no *real* power to which 10 can be raised to get -2.

The following properties follow directly from the definition of the logarithmic function with base a.

Properties of Logarithms

1. $\log_a 1 = 0$ because $a^0 = 1$.
2. $\log_a a = 1$ because $a^1 = a$.
3. $\log_a a^x = x$ and $a^{\log_a x} = x$.   Inverse Properties
4. If $\log_a x = \log_a y$, then $x = y$.   One-to-One Property

EXAMPLE 3   Using Properties of Logarithms

Solve each equation for x.

a. $\log_2 x = \log_2 3$

b. $\log_4 4 = x$

Solution

a. Using the One-to-One Property (Property 4), you can conclude that $x = 3$.

b. Using Property 2, you can conclude that $x = 1$.

Library of Functions

The logarithmic function is the inverse of the exponential function. Its domain is the set of positive real numbers and its range is the set of all real numbers. Because of the inverse properties of logarithms and exponents, the exponential equation $a^0 = 1$ implies that $\log_a 1 = 0$.

Consult the Library of Functions Summary inside the front cover for a description of the logarithmic function.

Graphs of Logarithmic Functions

To sketch the graph of $y = \log_a x$, you can use the fact that the graphs of inverse functions are reflections of each other in the line $y = x$.

Show graphically and algebraically that the logarithmic function is the inverse of the exponential function.

EXAMPLE 4   Graphs of Exponential and Logarithmic Functions

In the same coordinate plane, sketch the graph of each function.

a. $f(x) = 2^x$ **b.** $g(x) = \log_2 x$

A computer animation of this example appears in the *Interactive* CD-ROM and *Internet* versions of this text.

Solution
a. For $f(x) = 2^x$, construct a table of values.

x	-2	-1	0	1	2	3
2^x	$\frac{1}{4}$	$\frac{1}{2}$	1	2	4	8

By plotting these points and connecting them with a smooth curve, you obtain the graph of $f(x)$ shown in Figure 4.13.

b. Because $g(x) = \log_2 x$ is the inverse of $f(x) = 2^x$, the graph of g is obtained by plotting the points $(2^x, x)$ and connecting them with a smooth curve. The graph of g is a reflection of the graph of f in the line $y = x$, as shown in Figure 4.13.

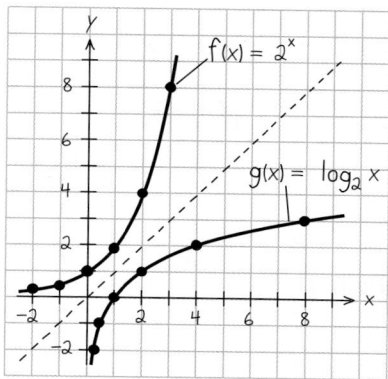

Figure 4.13

Before you can confirm the result of Example 4 using a graphing utility, you need to know how to enter $\log_2 x$. You will learn how to do this using the *change-of-base formula* discussed in Section 4.3.

EXAMPLE 5   Sketching the Graph of a Logarithmic Function

Sketch the graph of the common logarithmic function $f(x) = \log_{10} x$.

Solution
Begin by constructing a table of values. Note that some of the values can be obtained without a calculator using the Inverse Property of logarithms. Others require a calculator. Next, plot the points and connect them with a smooth curve, as shown in Figure 4.14.

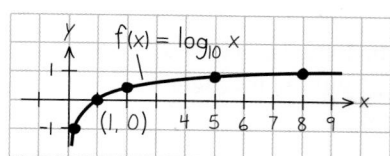

Figure 4.14

x	Without Calculator				With Calculator		
	$\frac{1}{100}$	$\frac{1}{10}$	1	10	2	5	8
$\log_{10} x$	-2	-1	0	1	0.301	0.699	0.903

In Example 5, you can also sketch the graph of $f(x) = \log_{10} x$ as follows. Evaluate the inverse of f, $g(x) = 10^x$ for several values of x. Plot the points, sketch the graph of g, then reflect the graph in the line $y = x$ to obtain the graph of f.

The nature of the graph in Figure 4.14 is typical of functions of the form $f(x) = \log_a x, a > 1$. They have one x-intercept and one vertical asymptote. Notice how slowly the graph rises for $x > 1$. In Figure 4.14, you would need to move out to $x = 100$ before the graph rose to $y = 2$, and $x = 1000$ before the graph rose to $y = 3$. The basic characteristics of logarithmic graphs are summarized in Figure 4.15.

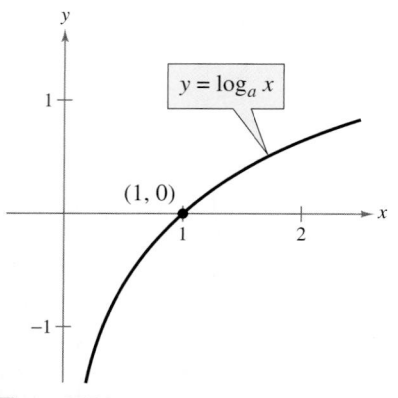

Figure 4.15

Graph of $y = \log_a x, \; a > 1$

- Domain: $(0, \infty)$
- Range: $(-\infty, \infty)$
- Intercept: $(1, 0)$
- Increasing
- y-axis is a vertical asymptote $(\log_a x \to -\infty \text{ as } x \to 0^+)$
- Continuous
- Reflection of graph of $y = a^x$ in the line $y = x$

In Figure 4.15, the vertical asymptote occurs at $x = 0$, where $\log_a x$ is *undefined*.

EXAMPLE 6   Transformations of Graphs of Logarithmic Functions

The graph of each of the following functions is similar to the graph of $f(x) = \log_{10} x$, as shown in Figure 4.16.

a. Because $g(x) = \log_{10}(x - 1) = f(x - 1)$, the graph of g can be obtained by shifting the graph of f one unit to the right.

b. Because $h(x) = 2 + \log_{10} x = 2 + f(x)$, the graph of h can be obtained by shifting the graph of f two units up.

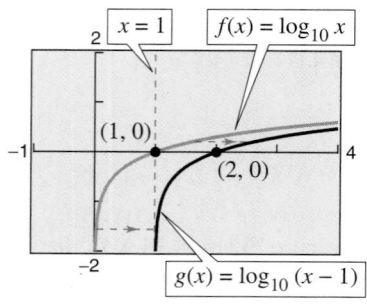

(a)

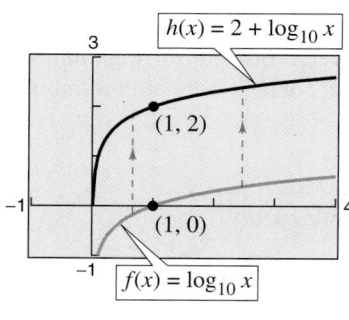

(b)

Figure 4.16

A computer animation of this example appears in the *Interactive* CD-ROM and *Internet* versions of this text.

Point out to your students that they can use their understanding of transformations to identify the vertical asymptote of logarithmic functions. For instance, they know that $f(x - 2)$ shifts the graph of $f(x)$ two units to the right.

In Figure 4.16, notice that the transformation in part (b) keeps the y-axis as a vertical asymptote, but the transformation in part (a) yields the new vertical asymptote $x = 1$.

The Natural Logarithmic Function

The most widely used base for logarithmic functions is the number e, where

$$e \approx 2.718281828 \ldots .$$

The logarithmic function with base e is the **natural logarithmic function** and is denoted by the special symbol $\ln x$, read as "the natural log of x" or "el en of x."

The Natural Logarithmic Function

The function defined by

$$f(x) = \log_e x = \ln x, \qquad x > 0$$

is called the **natural logarithmic function.**

On most calculators, the natural logarithm is denoted by $\boxed{\text{LN}}$, as illustrated in Example 7.

EXAMPLE 7 Evaluating the Natural Logarithmic Function

Use a calculator to evaluate each expression.

a. $\ln 2$ **b.** $\ln 0.3$ **c.** $\ln e^2$ **d.** $\ln(-1)$

Solution

Number	Graphing Calculator Keystrokes	Display
a. $\ln 2$	$\boxed{\text{LN}}$ 2 $\boxed{\text{ENTER}}$	0.6931472
b. $\ln 0.3$	$\boxed{\text{LN}}$ .3 $\boxed{\text{ENTER}}$	-1.2039728
c. $\ln e^2$	$\boxed{\text{LN}}$ $\boxed{e^x}$ 2 $\boxed{\text{ENTER}}$	2
d. $\ln(-1)$	$\boxed{\text{LN}}$ $\boxed{(-)}$ 1 $\boxed{\text{ENTER}}$	ERROR

In Example 7, be sure you see that $\ln(-1)$ gives an error message on most calculators. This occurs because the domain of $\ln x$ is the set of *positive* real numbers. So, $\ln(-1)$ is undefined.

The four properties of logarithms listed on page 312 are also valid for natural logarithms.

Exploration

Because the natural exponential function $y = e^x$ passes the Horizontal Line Test, it has an inverse. Use the *draw inverse* feature of your graphing utility to graph $y = e^x$ and its inverse. Compare this graph with that of the natural logarithmic function. What can you conclude?

Properties of Natural Logarithms

1. $\ln 1 = 0$ because $e^0 = 1$.

2. $\ln e = 1$ because $e^1 = e$.

3. $\ln e^x = x$ and $e^{\ln x} = x$.   Inverse Properties

4. If $\ln x = \ln y$, then $x = y$.   One-to-One Property

EXAMPLE 8   Using Properties of Natural Logarithms

Use the properties of natural logarithms to rewrite each expression.

a. $\ln \dfrac{1}{e}$ **b.** $\ln e^2$ **c.** $\ln e^0$ **d.** $2 \ln e$

Solution

a. $\ln \dfrac{1}{e} = \ln e^{-1} = -1$ Inverse Property

b. $\ln e^2 = 2$ Inverse Property

c. $\ln e^0 = 0$ Property 1

d. $2 \ln e = 2(1) = 2$ Property 2

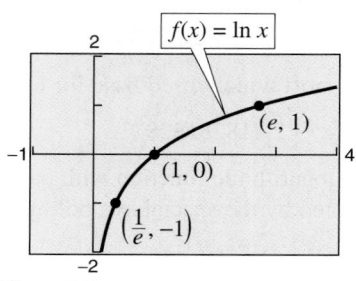

Figure 4.17

The graph of the natural logarithmic function is shown in Figure 4.17. Try using a graphing utility to confirm this graph and to verify that the domain of the natural logarithmic function is $(0, \infty)$.

EXAMPLE 9   Finding the Domains of Logarithmic Functions

Find the domain of each function.

a. $f(x) = \ln(x - 2)$ **b.** $g(x) = \ln(2 - x)$ **c.** $h(x) = \ln x^2$

Algebraic Solution

a. Because $\ln(x - 2)$ is defined only if

$$x - 2 > 0,$$

it follows that the domain of f is $(2, \infty)$.

b. Because $\ln(2 - x)$ is defined only if

$$2 - x > 0,$$

it follows that the domain of g is $(-\infty, 2)$.

c. Because $\ln x^2$ is defined only if

$$x^2 > 0,$$

it follows that the domain of h is all real numbers except $x = 0$.

Graphical Solution

a. Use a graphing utility to graph the equation $y = \ln(x - 2)$ using a decimal setting, as shown in Figure 4.18. Use the *trace* feature to see that the x-coordinates of the points on the graph appear to extend from the right of 2 to $+\infty$. So, you can estimate the domain to be $(2, \infty)$.

b. Use a graphing utility to graph the equation $y = \ln(2 - x)$ using a decimal setting, as shown in Figure 4.19. Use the *trace* feature to see that the x-coordinates of the points on the graph appear to extend from $-\infty$ to the left of 2. So, you can estimate the domain to be $(-\infty, 2)$.

c. Use a graphing utility to graph the equation $y = \ln x^2$ using a decimal setting, as shown in Figure 4.20. Use the *trace* feature to see that the x-coordinates of the points on the graph appear to include all real numbers except $x = 0$. So, you can estimate the domain to be all real numbers except $x = 0$.

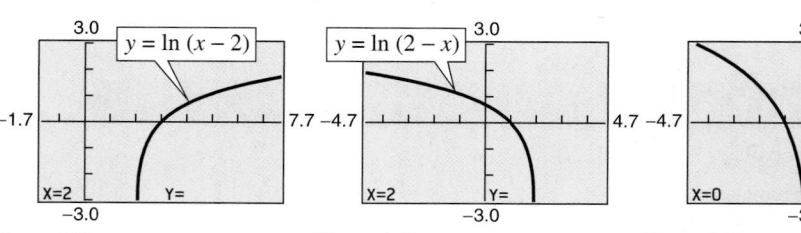

Figure 4.18   **Figure 4.19**   **Figure 4.20**

In Example 9, suppose you had been asked to analyze the function $h(x) = \ln|x - 2|$. How would the domain of this function compare with the domains of the functions given in parts (a) and (b) of the example?

Application

Exponential and logarithmic functions are used to model many situations in real life, as shown in the next example.

EXAMPLE 10   Human Memory Model

Students participating in a psychological experiment attended several lectures on a subject. At the end of the last lecture, and every month for the next year, the students were tested to see how much of the material they remembered. The average scores for the group were given by the *human memory model*

$$f(t) = 75 - 6 \ln(t + 1), \qquad 0 \le t \le 12$$

where *t* is the time in months.

a. What was the average score on the original ($t = 0$) exam?

b. What was the average score at the end of $t = 2$ months?

c. What was the average score at the end of $t = 6$ months?

Algebraic Solution

a. The original average score was

$$f(0) = 75 - 6 \ln 1$$

$$= 75 - 6(0)$$

$$= 75.$$

b. After 2 months, the average score was

$$f(2) = 75 - 6 \ln 3$$

$$\approx 75 - 6(1.0986)$$

$$\approx 68.4.$$

c. After 6 months, the average score was

$$f(6) = 75 - 6 \ln 7$$

$$\approx 75 - 6(1.9459)$$

$$\approx 63.3.$$

Graphical Solution

Use a graphing utility to graph the function $y = 75 - 6 \ln(x + 1)$ as shown in Figure 4.21. Then use the *value* or *trace* feature to approximate the following.

a. When $x = 0$, $y = 75$. So, the original average score was 75.

b. When $x = 2$, $y \approx 68.4$. So, the average score after 2 months was about 68.4.

c. When $x = 6$, $y \approx 63.3$. So, the average score after 6 months was about 63.3.

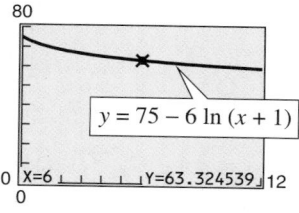

Figure 4.21

Writing About Math   *Analyzing a Human Memory Model*

Use a graphing utility to determine how many months it would take for the average score in Example 10 to decrease to 60. Explain your method of solving the problem. Describe another way that you can use a graphing utility to determine the answer. Also, make a statement about the general shape of the model. Would the students forget more quickly soon after the test or as time passes? Explain your reasoning.

4.2 Exercises

In Exercises 1–8, write the logarithmic equation in exponential form. For example, the exponential form of $\log_5 25 = 2$ is $5^2 = 25$.

1. $\log_4 64 = 3$ **2.** $\log_3 81 = 4$

3. $\log_7 \frac{1}{49} = -2$ **4.** $\log_{10} \frac{1}{1000} = -3$

5. $\log_{32} 4 = \frac{2}{5}$ **6.** $\log_{16} 8 = \frac{3}{4}$

7. $\ln 1 = 0$ **8.** $\ln 4 = 1.386\ldots$

In Exercises 9–18, write the exponential equation in logarithmic form.

9. $5^3 = 125$ **10.** $8^2 = 64$

11. $81^{1/4} = 3$ **12.** $9^{3/2} = 27$

13. $6^{-2} = \frac{1}{36}$ **14.** $10^{-3} = 0.001$

15. $e^3 = 20.0855\ldots$ **16.** $e^x = 4$

17. $e^{2.6} = 13.463\ldots$ **18.** $e^\pi = 23.140\ldots$

In Exercises 19–24, evaluate the expression without using a calculator.

19. $\log_2 16$ **20.** $\log_{27} 9$

21. $\log_{16}\left(\frac{1}{4}\right)$ **22.** $\log_2\left(\frac{1}{8}\right)$

23. $\log_{10} 0.01$ **24.** $\log_{10} 0.1$

In Exercises 25–30, solve the equation for x.

25. $\log_7 x = \log_7 9$ **26.** $\log_5 5 = x$

27. $\ln e^8 = x$ **28.** $\ln 1 = \ln x$

29. $\log_6 6^2 = x$ **30.** $\log_2 2^{-1} = x$

In Exercises 31–42, use a calculator to evaluate the logarithm. Round to three decimal places.

31. $\log_{10} 345$ **32.** $\log_{10} 145$

33. $\log_{10}\left(\frac{4}{5}\right)$ **34.** $\log_{10}\frac{25}{2}$

35. $\ln\left(4 + \sqrt{3}\right)$ **36.** $\ln\left(\sqrt{5} - 2\right)$

37. $\ln\sqrt{42}$ **38.** $\ln\sqrt{752}$

39. $6\log_{10} 14.8$ **40.** $-3\log_{10} 0.09$

41. $12\ln 6.4$ **42.** $-5.5\ln 34$

In Exercises 43–46, describe the relationship between the graphs of f and g. What is the relationship between the functions f and g?

43. $f(x) = 3^x$ **44.** $f(x) = 5^x$
    $g(x) = \log_3 x$ $g(x) = \log_5 x$

45. $f(x) = e^x$ **46.** $f(x) = 10^x$
    $g(x) = \ln x$ $g(x) = \log_{10} x$

In Exercises 47–52, use the graph of $y = \log_3 x$ to match the given function with its graph. [The graphs are labeled (a), (b), (c), (d), (e), and (f).]

(a)  (b)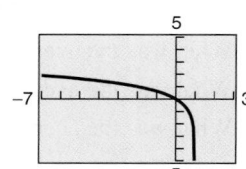

(c) 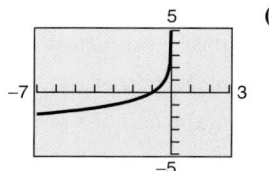 (d)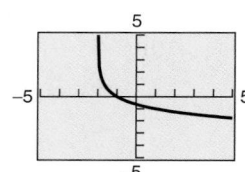

(e) 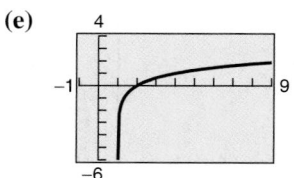 (f)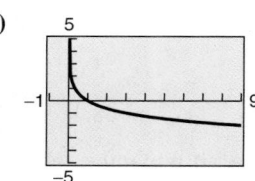

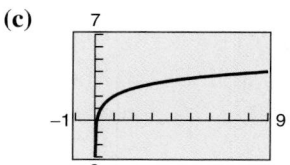

47. $f(x) = \log_3 x + 2$ **48.** $f(x) = -\log_3 x$

49. $f(x) = -\log_3(x + 2)$ **50.** $f(x) = \log_3(x - 1)$

51. $f(x) = \log_3(1 - x)$ **52.** $f(x) = -\log_3(-x)$

In Exercises 53–60, find the domain, vertical asymptote, and x-intercept of the logarithmic function, and sketch its graph by hand. Verify using a graphing utility.

53. $f(x) = \log_4 x$ **54.** $g(x) = \log_6 x$

55. $h(x) = \log_4(x - 3)$ **56.** $f(x) = -\log_6(x + 2)$

57. $y = -\log_3 x + 2$ **58.** $y = \log_5(x - 1) + 4$

59. $f(x) = 6 + \log_6(x - 3)$

60. $f(x) = -\log_3(x + 2) - 4$

In Exercises 61–66, use a graphing utility to graph the logarithmic function. Determine the domain and identify any vertical asymptote and *x*-intercept.

61. $y = \log_{10}\left(\frac{x}{5}\right)$

62. $y = \log_{10}(-x)$

63. $f(x) = \ln(x - 2)$

64. $h(x) = \ln(x + 1)$

65. $g(x) = \ln(-x)$

66. $f(x) = \ln(3 - x)$

In Exercises 67–70, (a) use a graphing utility to graph the function, (b) find the domain, (c) use the graph to determine the intervals in which the function is increasing and decreasing, and (d) approximate any relative maximum or minimum values of the function.

67. $f(x) = \dfrac{x}{2} - \ln\dfrac{x}{4}$

68. $g(x) = \dfrac{12 \ln x}{x}$

69. $h(x) = 4x \ln x$

70. $f(x) = \dfrac{x}{\ln x}$

71. *Population Growth* The population of a town will double in

$$t = \frac{10 \ln 2}{\ln 67 - \ln 50} \text{ years.}$$

Find *t*.

72. *Work* The work (in foot-pounds) done in compressing an initial volume of 9 cubic feet of air at a pressure of 15 pounds per square inch to a volume of 3 cubic feet is $W = 19{,}440(\ln 9 - \ln 3)$. Find *W*.

73. *Human Memory Model* Students in a mathematics class were given an exam and then tested monthly with an equivalent exam. The average score for the class was given by the human memory model

$$f(t) = 80 - 17 \log_{10}(t + 1), \quad 0 \le t \le 12$$

where *t* is the time in months.

(a) What was the average score on the original exam (*t* = 0)?

(b) What was the average score after 4 months?

(c) What was the average score after 10 months?

(d) Verify your answers in parts (a), (b), and (c) using a graphing utility.

74. *Investment Time* A principal *P*, invested at $5\frac{1}{2}\%$ and compounded continuously, increases to an amount *K* times the original principal after *t* years, where $t = (\ln K)/0.055$.

(a) Complete the table and interpret your results.

K	1	2	4	6	8	10	12
t							

(b) Use a graphing utility to graph the function.

75. *Data Analysis* The table shows the temperatures *T* (in °F) at which water boils at selected pressures *p* (in pounds per square inch). (Source: Standard Handbook of Mechanical Engineers)

p	5	10	14.696 (1 atm)
T	162.24°	193.21°	212.00°

p	20	30	40
T	227.96°	250.33°	267.25°

p	60	80	100
T	292.71°	312.03°	327.81°

A model that approximates this data is

$$T = 87.97 + 34.96 \ln p + 7.91\sqrt{p}.$$

(a) Use a graphing utility to plot the data points and graph the model in the same viewing window. How well does the model fit the data?

(b) Use the graph to estimate the pressure required for the boiling point of water to exceed 300°F.

(c) Calculate *T* when the pressure is 74 pounds per square inch. Verify your answer graphically.

76. *Data Analysis* A meteorologist measures the atmospheric pressure *P* (in Pascals) at altitude *h* (in kilometers). The data is shown below.

h	0	5	10	15	20
P	101,293	54,735	23,294	12,157	5069

A model for the data is

$$P = 102{,}303e^{-0.137h}.$$

(a) Use a graphing utility to plot the data points and graph the model in the same viewing window.

(b) Use a graphing utility to plot the points $(h, \ln P)$. Use the regression capabilities of the graphing utility to fit a regression line to the revised data points.

(c) The line in part (b) has the form $\ln P = ah + b$. Write the line in exponential form.

(d) Verify graphically and algebraically that the result of part (c) is equivalent to the given exponential model for the data.

77. World Population Growth The time t in years for the world population to double if it is increasing at a continuous rate of r is

$$t = \frac{\ln 2}{r}.$$

Complete the table. What do your results imply?

r	0.005	0.010	0.015	0.020	0.025	0.030
t						

78. Tractrix A person walking along a dock (the y-axis) drags a boat by a 10-foot rope. The boat travels along a path known as a tractrix. The equation of this path is

$$y = 10 \ln\left(\frac{10 + \sqrt{100 - x^2}}{x}\right) - \sqrt{100 - x^2}.$$

(a) Use a graphing utility to obtain a graph of the function. What is the domain of the function?

(b) Identify any asymptotes of the graph.

(c) Determine the position of the person when the x-coordinate of the position of the boat is $x = 2$.

(d) Let $(0, p)$ be the position of the person. Determine p as a function of x, the x-coordinate of the position of the boat.

(e) Use a graphing utility to graph the function p. When does the position of the person change most for a small change in the position of the boat? Explain.

79. Sound Intensity The relationship between the number of decibels β and the intensity of a sound I in watts per square meter is

$$\beta = 10 \log_{10}\left(\frac{I}{10^{-12}}\right).$$

(a) Determine the number of decibels of a sound with an intensity of 1 watt per square meter.

(b) Determine the number of decibels of a sound with an intensity of 10^{-2} watt per square meter.

(c) The intensity of the sound in part (a) is 100 times as great as that in part (b). Is the number of decibels 100 times as great? Explain.

Ventilation Rates **In Exercises 80 and 81, use the model**

$$y = 80.4 - 11 \ln x, \quad 100 \le x \le 1500$$

which approximates the minimum required ventilation rate in terms of the air space per child in a public school classroom. In the model, x is the air space per child (in cubic feet) and y is the ventilation rate (in cubic feet per minute).

80. Use a graphing utility to graph the function and approximate the required ventilation rate if there is 300 cubic feet of air space per child.

81. A classroom is designed for 30 students. The air-conditioning system in the room has the capacity to move 450 cubic feet of air per minute.

(a) Determine the ventilation rate per child, assuming that the room is filled to capacity.

(b) Use the graph of Exercise 80 to estimate the air space required per child.

(c) Determine the minimum number of square feet of floor space required for the room if the ceiling height is 30 feet.

Monthly Payment **In Exercises 82–85, use the model**

$$t = 16.625 \ln\left(\frac{x}{x - 750}\right), \quad x > 750$$

which approximates the length of a home mortgage of $150,000 at 6% in terms of the monthly payment. In the model, t is the length of the mortgage in years and x is the monthly payment in dollars.

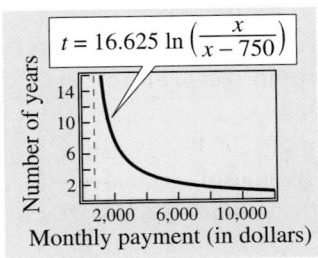

82. Use the model to approximate the length of a $150,000 mortgage (at 6%) if the monthly payment is $897.72.

83. Use the model to approximate the length of a $150,000 mortgage (at 6%) if the monthly payment is $1659.24.

84. Approximate the total amount paid over the term of the mortgage in Exercise 82 with a monthly payment of $897.72. What amount of the total is interest costs?

85. Approximate the total amount paid over the term of the mortgage in Exercise 83 with a monthly payment of $1659.24. What amount of the total is interest costs?

Synthesis

True or False? **In Exercises 86 and 87, determine whether the statement is true or false. Justify your answer.**

86. You can determine the graph of $f(x) = \log_6 x$ by graphing $g(x) = 6^x$ and reflecting it in the x-axis.

87. The graph of $f(x) = \log_3 x$ contains the point $(27, 3)$.

88. *Exploration*   The table of values was obtained by evaluating a function. Determine which of the statements may be true and which must be false.

x	1	2	8
y	0	1	3

(a) y is an exponential function of x.

(b) y is a logarithmic function of x.

(c) x is an exponential function of y.

(d) y is a linear function of x.

89. *Exploration*   Use a graphing utility to compare the graph of the function $y = \ln x$ with the graphs of the following functions.

(a) $y = x - 1$

(b) $y = (x - 1) - \frac{1}{2}(x - 1)^2$

(c) $y = (x - 1) - \frac{1}{2}(x - 1)^2 + \frac{1}{3}(x - 1)^3$

90. *Finding a Pattern*   Identify the pattern of successive polynomials given in Exercise 89. Extend the pattern one more term and compare the graph of the resulting polynomial function with the graph of $y = \ln x$. What do you think the pattern implies?

91. *Numerical and Graphical Analysis*   (a) Use a graphing utility to complete the table for the function

$$f(x) = \frac{\ln x}{x}.$$

x	1	5	10	10^2	10^4	10^6
$f(x)$						

(b) Use the table to determine what $f(x)$ approaches as x increases without bound.

(c) Use a graphing utility to check the result of part (b).

Review

In Exercises 92–95, find the vertical and horizontal asymptotes of the rational function.

92. $f(x) = \dfrac{4}{-8 - x}$

93. $f(x) = \dfrac{2x^3 - 3}{x^2}$

94. $f(x) = \dfrac{x + 5}{2x^2 + x - 15}$

95. $f(x) = \dfrac{2x^2(x - 5)}{x - 7}$

In Exercises 96–99, evaluate the expression. Round your answer to three decimal places.

96. e^{12}

97. $e^{7/2}$

98. e^{-5}

99. $6e^{-8}$

4.3 Properties of Logarithms

Change of Base

Most calculators have only two types of log keys, one for common logarithms (base 10) and one for natural logarithms (base e). Although common logs and natural logs are the most frequently used, you may occasionally need to evaluate logarithms to other bases. To do this, you can use the following **change-of-base formula.**

Change-of-Base Formula

Let a, b, and x be positive real numbers such that $a \neq 1$ and $b \neq 1$. Then $\log_a x$ can be converted to a different base using any of the following formulas.

Base b	*Base 10*	*Base e*
$\log_a x = \dfrac{\log_b x}{\log_b a}$	$\log_a x = \dfrac{\log_{10} x}{\log_{10} a}$	$\log_a x = \dfrac{\ln x}{\ln a}$

One way to look at the change-of-base formula is that logarithms to base a are simply *constant multiples* of logarithms to base b. The constant multiplier is $1/(\log_b a)$.

EXAMPLE 1   Changing Bases Using Common Logarithms

a. $\log_4 30 = \dfrac{\log_{10} 30}{\log_{10} 4}$ $\log_a x = \dfrac{\log_{10} x}{\log_{10} a}$

$\approx \dfrac{1.47712}{0.60206}$ Use a calculator.

≈ 2.4534 Use a calculator.

b. $\log_2 x = \dfrac{\log_{10} x}{\log_{10} 2} \approx \dfrac{\log_{10} x}{0.30103} \approx 3.3219 \log_{10} x$

EXAMPLE 2   Changing Bases Using Natural Logarithms

a. $\log_4 30 = \dfrac{\ln 30}{\ln 4}$ $\log_a x = \dfrac{\ln x}{\ln a}$

$\approx \dfrac{3.40120}{1.38629}$ Use a calculator.

≈ 2.4535 Use a calculator.

b. $\log_2 x = \dfrac{\ln x}{\ln 2} \approx \dfrac{\ln x}{0.693147} \approx 1.4427 \ln x$

In Examples 1 and 2, the result is the same whether common logarithms or natural logarithms are used in the change-of-base formula.

Properties of Logarithms

You know from the previous section that the logarithmic function with base a is the *inverse* of the exponential function with base a. So, it makes sense that the properties of exponents should have corresponding properties involving logarithms. For instance, the exponential property $a^0 = 1$ has the corresponding logarithmic property $\log_a 1 = 0$.

Properties of Logarithms

Let a be a positive number such that $a \neq 1$, and let n be a real number. If u and v are positive real numbers, the following properties are true.

1. $\log_a(uv) = \log_a u + \log_a v$	**1.** $\ln(uv) = \ln u + \ln v$
2. $\log_a \dfrac{u}{v} = \log_a u - \log_a v$	**2.** $\ln \dfrac{u}{v} = \ln u - \ln v$
3. $\log_a u^n = n \log_a u$	**3.** $\ln u^n = n \ln u$

For a proof of Property 1, see Appendix A.

EXAMPLE 3   Using Properties of Logarithms

Write the logarithm in terms of $\ln 2$ and $\ln 3$.

a. $\ln 6$ **b.** $\ln \dfrac{2}{27}$

Solution

a. $\ln 6 = \ln(2 \cdot 3)$ Rewrite 6 as $2 \cdot 3$.

     $= \ln 2 + \ln 3$ Property 1

b. $\ln \dfrac{2}{27} = \ln 2 - \ln 27$ Property 2

     $= \ln 2 - \ln 3^3$ Rewrite 27 as 3^3.

     $= \ln 2 - 3 \ln 3$ Property 3

EXAMPLE 4   Using Properties of Logarithms

Use the properties of logarithms to verify that $-\ln \frac{1}{2} = \ln 2$.

Solution

     $-\ln \frac{1}{2} = -\ln(2^{-1})$ Rewrite $\frac{1}{2}$ as 2^{-1}.

     $= -(-1) \ln 2$ Property 3

     $= \ln 2$ Simplify.

Try checking this result on your calculator.

Rewriting Logarithmic Expressions

The properties of logarithms are useful for rewriting logarithmic expressions in forms that simplify the operations of algebra. This is true because they convert complicated products, quotients, and exponential forms into simpler sums, differences, and products, respectively.

EXAMPLE 5   Expanding the Logarithm of a Product

Use the properties of logarithms to expand $\log_{10} 5x^3 y$.

Solution

$$\log_{10} 5x^3 y = \log_{10} 5 + \log_{10} x^3 y \qquad \text{Property 1}$$

$$= \log_{10} 5 + \log_{10} x^3 + \log_{10} y \qquad \text{Property 1}$$

$$= \log_{10} 5 + 3 \log_{10} x + \log_{10} y \qquad \text{Property 3}$$

EXAMPLE 6   Expanding the Logarithm of a Quotient

Use the properties of logarithms to expand $\ln \dfrac{\sqrt{3x - 5}}{7}$.

Solution

$$\ln \frac{\sqrt{3x - 5}}{7} = \ln \left[\frac{(3x - 5)^{1/2}}{7} \right] \qquad \text{Rewrite rational exponent.}$$

$$= \ln(3x - 5)^{1/2} - \ln 7 \qquad \text{Property 2}$$

$$= \frac{1}{2} \ln(3x - 5) - \ln 7 \qquad \text{Property 3}$$

In Examples 5 and 6, the properties of logarithms were used to *expand* logarithmic expressions. In Example 7, this procedure is reversed and the properties of logarithms are used to *condense* logarithmic expressions.

EXAMPLE 7   Condensing a Logarithmic Expression

Use the properties of logarithms to condense each logarithmic expression.

a. $\frac{1}{2} \log_{10} x + 3 \log_{10}(x + 1)$ **b.** $2 \ln(x + 2) - \ln x$

Solution

a. $\frac{1}{2} \log_{10} x + 3 \log_{10}(x + 1) = \log_{10} x^{1/2} + \log_{10}(x + 1)^3 \qquad \text{Property 3}$

$$= \log_{10} \left[\sqrt{x} \cdot (x + 1)^3 \right] \qquad \text{Property 1}$$

b. $2 \ln(x + 2) - \ln x = \ln(x + 2)^2 - \ln x \qquad \text{Property 3}$

$$= \ln \frac{(x + 2)^2}{x} \qquad \text{Property 2}$$

A common error made in expanding logarithmic expressions is to rewrite $\log ax^n$ as $n \log ax$ instead of $\log a + n \log x$.

Exploration

Use a graphing utility to graph the functions

$$y = \ln x - \ln(x - 3)$$

and

$$y = \ln \frac{x}{x - 3}$$

in the same viewing window. Does the graphing utility show the functions with the same domain? If so, should it? Explain your reasoning.

A common error made in condensing logarithmic expressions is to rewrite $\log x - \log y$ as

$$\frac{\log x}{\log y}$$

instead of

$$\log \frac{x}{y}.$$

Application

EXAMPLE 8   Finding a Mathematical Model

The table shows the mean distance from the sun x and the orbital period y of the six planets that are closest to the sun. In the table, the mean distance is given in terms of astronomical units (where the earth's mean distance is defined as 1.0), and the period is given in terms of years. Find an equation that expresses y as a function of x.

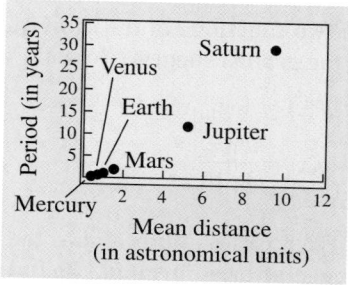

Figure 4.22

Planet	Mercury	Venus	Earth	Mars	Jupiter	Saturn
Mean Distance, x	0.387	0.723	1.0	1.524	5.203	9.539
Period, y	0.241	0.615	1.0	1.881	11.862	29.458

Algebraic Solution

The points in the table are plotted in Figure 4.22. From this figure it is not clear how to find an equation that relates y and x. To solve this problem, take the natural log of each of the x- and y-values shown in the table. This produces the following results.

Planet	Mercury	Venus	Earth
$\ln x = X$	-0.949	-0.324	0.0
$\ln y = Y$	-1.423	-0.486	0.0

Planet	Mars	Jupiter	Saturn
$\ln x = X$	0.421	1.649	2.255
$\ln y = Y$	0.632	2.473	3.383

Now, by plotting the points in the table, you can see that all six of the points appear to lie in a line.

Choose any two points to determine the slope of the line. Using the two points $(0.421, 0.632)$ and $(0, 0)$, you can determine the slope of the line.

$$m = \frac{0.632 - 0}{0.421 - 0} \approx 1.5 = \frac{3}{2}$$

By the point-slope form, the equation of the line is $Y = \frac{3}{2}X$, where $Y = \ln y$ and $X = \ln x$. You can therefore conclude that $\ln y = \frac{3}{2}\ln x$.

Graphical Solution

The points in the table are plotted in Figure 4.22. From this figure it is not clear how to find an equation that relates y and x. To solve this problem, take the natural log of each of the x- and y-values given in the table. This produces the following results.

Planet	Mercury	Venus	Earth	Mars	Jupiter	Saturn
$\ln x = X$	-0.949	-0.324	0.0	0.421	1.649	2.255
$\ln y = Y$	-1.423	-0.486	0.0	0.632	2.473	3.383

Now, by plotting the points in the table, you can see that all six of the points appear to lie in a line, as shown in Figure 4.23.

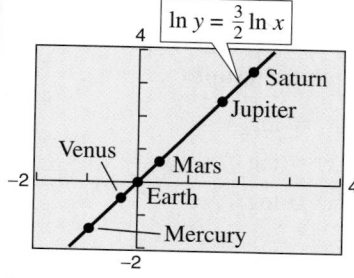

Figure 4.23

Using the regression features of a graphing utility, you can find a linear model for the data $Y = 1.5X = \frac{3}{2}X$, where $Y = \ln y$ and $X = \ln x$. From the model, you can see that the slope of the line is $\frac{3}{2}$. So, you can conclude that $\ln y = \frac{3}{2}\ln x$.

In Example 8, try to convert this to $y = f(x)$ form. You will get a function of the form $y = ax^b$, which is a power model.

4.3 Exercises

In Exercises 1 and 2, use a graphing utility to graph the two functions in the same viewing window. What do the graphs suggest? Explain your reasoning.

1. $f(x) = \log_{10} x$

$g(x) = \dfrac{\ln x}{\ln 10}$

2. $f(x) = \ln x$

$g(x) = \dfrac{\log_{10} x}{\log_{10} e}$

In Exercises 3–10, evaluate the logarithm using the change-of-base formula. Round your result to three decimal places.

3. $\log_3 7$

4. $\log_7 4$

5. $\log_{1/2} 4$

6. $\log_{1/8} 64$

7. $\log_9(0.8)$

8. $\log_{1/3}(0.015)$

9. $\log_{15} 1460$

10. $\log_{20} 135$

In Exercises 11–18, rewrite the logarithm as a multiple of (a) a common logarithm and (b) a natural logarithm.

11. $\log_5 x$

12. $\log_3 x$

13. $\log_{1/5} x$

14. $\log_{1/3} x$

15. $\log_x \frac{3}{10}$

16. $\log_x \frac{3}{4}$

17. $\log_{2.6} x$

18. $\log_{7.1} x$

In Exercises 19–26, use the change-of-base formula to rewrite the logarithm as a multiple of a logarithm. Then use a graphing utility to sketch the graph.

19. $f(x) = \log_2 x$

20. $f(x) = \log_4 x$

21. $f(x) = \log_{1/2} x$

22. $f(x) = \log_{1/4} x$

23. $f(x) = \log_{11.8} x$

24. $f(x) = \log_{12.4} x$

25. $f(x) = \log_3 x^{1/2}$

26. $f(x) = \log_5 \dfrac{x}{3}$

In Exercises 27–46, use the properties of logarithms to write the expression as a sum, difference, and/or constant multiple of logarithms. (Assume all variables are positive.)

27. $\log_{10} 5x$

28. $\log_{10} 10z$

29. $\log_{10} \dfrac{5}{x}$

30. $\log_{10} \dfrac{y}{2}$

31. $\log_8 x^4$

32. $\log_6 z^{-3}$

33. $\ln \sqrt{z}$

34. $\ln \sqrt[3]{t}$

35. $\ln xyz$

36. $\ln \dfrac{xy}{z}$

37. $\ln \sqrt{a-1}, \quad a > 1$

38. $\ln\left(\dfrac{x^2-1}{x^3}\right), \quad x > 1$

39. $\ln z(z-1)^2, \quad z > 1$

40. $\ln \sqrt{\dfrac{x^2}{y^3}}$

41. $\ln \sqrt[3]{\dfrac{x}{y}}$

42. $\ln \dfrac{x}{\sqrt{x^2+1}}$

43. $\ln \dfrac{x^4\sqrt{y}}{z^5}$

44. $\ln \sqrt{x^2(x+2)}$

45. $\log_b \dfrac{x^2}{y^2 z^3}$

46. $\log_b \dfrac{\sqrt{x}y^4}{z^4}$

Graphical Analysis In Exercises 47 and 48, use a graphing utility to graph the two equations in the same viewing window. What do the graphs suggest? Explain your reasoning.

47. $y_1 = \ln[x^3(x+4)], \qquad y_2 = 3 \ln x + \ln(x+4)$

48. $y_1 = \ln\left(\dfrac{\sqrt{x}}{x-2}\right), \qquad y_2 = \frac{1}{2} \ln x - \ln(x-2)$

In Exercises 49–68, write the expression as the logarithm of a single quantity.

49. $\ln x + \ln 4$

50. $\ln y + \ln z$

51. $\log_4 z - \log_4 y$

52. $\log_5 8 - \log_5 t$

53. $2 \log_2(x+3)$

54. $-6 \log_6 2x$

55. $\frac{1}{3} \log_3 7x$

56. $\frac{5}{2} \log_7(z-4)$

57. $\ln x - 3 \ln(x+1)$

58. $2 \ln 8 + 5 \ln z$

59. $\ln(x-2) - \ln(x+2)$

60. $3 \ln x + 2 \ln y - 4 \ln z$

61. $\ln x - 2[\ln(x+2) + \ln(x-2)]$

62. $4[\ln z + \ln(z+5)] - 2 \ln(z-5)$

63. $\frac{1}{3}[2 \ln(x+3) + \ln x - \ln(x^2-1)]$

64. $2[\ln x - \ln(x+1) - \ln(x-1)]$

65. $\frac{1}{3}[\ln y + 2 \ln(y+4)] - \ln(y-1)$

66. $\frac{1}{2}[\ln(x+1) + 2 \ln(x-1)] + 3 \ln x$

67. $2 \ln 3 - \frac{1}{2} \ln(x^2+1)$

68. $\frac{3}{2} \ln 5t^6 - \frac{3}{4} \ln t^4$

Graphical Analysis In Exercises 69 and 70, use a graphing utility to graph the two equations in the same viewing window. What do the graphs suggest? Verify your conclusion algebraically.

69. $y_1 = 2[\ln 8 - \ln(x^2 + 1)]$,　$y_2 = \ln\left[\dfrac{64}{(x^2 + 1)^2}\right]$

70. $y_1 = \ln x + \frac{1}{3}\ln(x + 1)$,　$y_2 = \ln\left(x\sqrt[3]{x + 1}\right)$

Think About It In Exercises 71 and 72, use a graphing utility to graph the two equations in the same viewing window. Are the expressions equivalent? Explain.

71. $y_1 = \ln x^2$,　$y_2 = 2\ln x$

72. $y_1 = \frac{1}{4}\ln[x^4(x^2 + 1)]$,　$y_2 = \ln x + \frac{1}{4}\ln(x^2 + 1)$

In Exercises 73–86, find the exact value of the logarithm without using a calculator. (If this is not possible, state the reason.)

73. $\log_3 9$

74. $\log_6 \sqrt[3]{6}$

75. $\log_4 16^{3.4}$

76. $\log_5\left(\frac{1}{125}\right)$

77. $\log_2(-4)$

78. $\log_4(-16)$

79. $\log_5 75 - \log_5 3$

80. $\log_4 2 + \log_4 32$

81. $\ln e^3 - \ln e^7$

82. $3\ln e^4$

83. $\log_{10} 0$

84. $\ln 1$

85. $\ln e^{8.5}$

86. $\ln \sqrt[5]{e^3}$

In Exercises 87–94, use the properties of logarithms to simplify the logarithmic expression.

87. $\log_4 8$

88. $\log_5\left(\frac{1}{15}\right)$

89. $\log_7 \sqrt{70}$

90. $\log_2(4^2 \cdot 3^4)$

91. $\log_5\left(\frac{1}{250}\right)$

92. $\log_{10}\left(\frac{9}{300}\right)$

93. $\ln(5e^6)$

94. $\ln \dfrac{6}{e^2}$

95. *Sound Intensity* The relationship between the number of decibels β and the intensity of a sound I in watts per square meter is

$$\beta = 10 \log_{10}\left(\frac{I}{10^{-12}}\right).$$

(a) Use the properties of logarithms to write the formula in a simpler form.

(b) Use a graphing utility to complete the table.

I	10^{-4}	10^{-6}	10^{-8}	10^{-10}	10^{-12}	10^{-14}
β						

(c) Verify your answers in part (b) algebraically.

96. *Human Memory Model* Students participating in a psychological experiment attended several lectures. After the last lecture, and every month for the next year, the students were tested to see how much of the material they remembered. The average scores for the group were given by the memory model

$$f(t) = 90 - 15 \log_{10}(t + 1), \quad 0 \le t \le 12$$

where t is the time (in months).

(a) Use a graphing utility to graph the function over the specified domain.

(b) What was the average score on the original exam $(t = 0)$?

(c) What was the average score after 6 months?

(d) What was the average score after 12 months?

(e) When would the average score have decreased to 75?

97. *Comparing Models* A cup of water at an initial temperature of 78°C is placed in a room at a constant temperature of 21°C. The temperature of the water is measured every 5 minutes during a half-hour period. The results are recorded as ordered pairs of the form (t, T), where t is the time (in minutes) and T is the temperature (in degrees Celsius).

(0, 78.0°), (5, 66.0°), (10, 57.5°), (15, 51.2°), (20, 46.3°), (25, 42.5°), (30, 39.6°)

(a) The graph of the model for the data should be asymptotic with the temperature of the room. Subtract the room temperature from each of the temperatures in the ordered pairs. Use a graphing utility to plot the data points (t, T) and $(t, T - 21)$.

(b) Use the regression capabilities of a graphing utility to fit an exponential model to the revised data. This model will be of the form

$$T - 21 = ab^x.$$

Solve for T and graph the model. Compare the result with the plot of the original data.

(c) Take the natural logarithms of the revised temperatures. Use a graphing utility to plot the points $(t, \ln(T - 21))$ and observe that the points appear linear. Use the regression capabilities of a graphing utility to fit a line to this data. The resulting line has the form

$$\ln(T - 21) = at + b.$$

Use the properties of logarithms to solve for T. Verify that the result is equivalent to the model in part (b).

(d) Fit a rational model to the data. Take the reciprocals of the y-coordinates of the revised data to generate the points

$$\left(t, \frac{1}{T - 21}\right).$$

Use a graphing utility to plot these points and observe that they appear linear. Use the regression capabilities of a graphing utility to fit a line to this data. The resulting line has the form

$$\frac{1}{T - 21} = at + b.$$

Solve for T, and use a graphing utility to graph the rational function and the original data points.

98. *Writing*   Write a short paragraph explaining why the transformations of the data in Exercise 97 were necessary to obtain the models. Why did taking the logarithms of the temperatures lead to a linear scatter plot? Why did taking the reciprocals of the temperatures lead to a linear scatter plot?

Synthesis

True or False?   **In Exercises 99–104, determine whether the statement is true or false given that $f(x) = \ln x$. Justify your answer.**

99. $f(0) = 0$

100. $f(ax) = f(a) + f(x), \quad a > 0, x > 0$

101. $f(x - 2) = f(x) - f(2), \quad x > 2$

102. $\sqrt{f(x)} = \frac{1}{2}f(x)$

103. If $f(u) = 2f(v)$, then $v = u^2$.

104. If $f(x) < 0$, then $0 < x < 1$.

105. *Think About It*   Use a graphing utility to graph

$$f(x) = \ln\frac{x}{2}, \quad g(x) = \frac{\ln x}{\ln 2}, \quad h(x) = \ln x - \ln 2$$

in the same viewing window. Which two functions have identical graphs? Explain why.

106. *Exploration*   Approximate the natural logarithms of as many integers as possible between 1 and 20, given that $\ln 2 \approx 0.6931$, $\ln 3 \approx 1.0986$, and $\ln 5 \approx 1.6094$. (Do not use a calculator.)

107. Prove that $\log_b \dfrac{u}{v} = \log_b u - \log_b v$.

108. Prove that $\log_b u^n = n \log_b u$.

Review

In Exercises 109–112, simplify the expression.

109. $\dfrac{24xy^{-2}}{16x^{-3}y}$ **110.** $\left(\dfrac{2x^2}{3y}\right)^{-3}$

111. $(18x^3y^4)^{-3}(18x^3y^4)^3$ **112.** $xy(x^{-1} + y^{-1})^{-1}$

In Exercises 113–118, find all solutions of the equation. Be sure to check all your solutions.

113. $x^2 - 6x + 2 = 0$ **114.** $2x^3 + 20x^2 + 50x = 0$

115. $x^4 - 19x^2 + 48 = 0$ **116.** $9x^4 - 37x^2 + 4 = 0$

117. $x^3 - 6x^2 - 4x + 24 = 0$

118. $9x^4 - 226x^2 + 25 = 0$

In Exercises 119–126, use a calculator to evaluate the expression. Round the result to three decimal places.

119. $1.6^{-2\pi}$ **120.** $\sqrt[5]{8251}$

121. $260^{\sqrt{3}}$ **122.** $170(4^{-1.1})$

123. $\log_{10}(220)$ **124.** $\log_{10}\left(\frac{7}{5}\right)$

125. $\ln 2.008$ **126.** $\ln\left(5 - \sqrt{7}\right)$

4.4 Solving Exponential and Logarithmic Equations

Introduction

So far in this chapter, you have studied the definitions, graphs, and properties of exponential and logarithmic functions. In this section, you will study procedures for *solving equations* involving exponential and logarithmic functions.

There are two basic strategies for solving exponential or logarithmic equations. The first is based on the One-to-One Properties and the second is based on the Inverse Properties. For $a > 0$ and $a \neq 1$, the following properties are true for all x and y for which $\log_a x$ and $\log_a y$ are defined.

One-to-One Properties

$a^x = a^y$ if and only if $x = y$.

$\log_a x = \log_a y$ if and only if $x = y$.

Inverse Properties

$$a^{\log_a x} = x$$

$$\log_a a^x = x$$

What You Should Learn:

- How to solve simple exponential and logarithmic equations
- How to solve more complicated exponential equations
- How to solve more complicated logarithmic equations
- How to use exponential and logarithmic equations to model and solve real-life problems

Why You Should Learn It:

Exponential and logarithmic equations can be used to model and solve real-life problems. For instance, Exercise 126 on page 339 shows how to use a logarithmic function to model crumple zones for automobile crash tests.

Index Stock

EXAMPLE 1 Solving Simple Exponential and Logarithmic Equations

Original Equation	Rewritten Equation	Solution	Property
a. $2^x = 32$	$2^x = 2^5$	$x = 5$	One-to-One
b. $\ln x - \ln 3 = 0$	$\ln x = \ln 3$	$x = 3$	One-to-One
c. $\left(\frac{1}{3}\right)^x = 9$	$3^{-x} = 3^2$	$x = -2$	One-to-One
d. $e^x = 7$	$\ln e^x = \ln 7$	$x = \ln 7$	Inverse
e. $\ln = -3$	$e^{\ln x} = e^{-3}$	$x = e^{-3}$	Inverse
f. $\log x = -1$	$10^{\log x} = 10^{-1}$	$x = 10^{-1} = \frac{1}{10}$	Inverse

The strategies used in Example 1 are summarized as follows.

Strategies for Solving Exponential and Logarithmic Equations

1. Rewrite the given equation in a form to use the One-to-One Properties of exponential or logarithmic functions.

2. Rewrite an *exponential* equation in logarithmic form and apply the Inverse Property of logarithmic functions.

3. Rewrite a *logarithmic* equation in exponential form and apply the Inverse Property of exponential functions.

Before starting this section, have students review the logarithmic properties.

Solving Exponential Equations

EXAMPLE 2   Solving Exponential Equations

Solve each equation.   **a.** $e^x = 72$ **b.** $3(2^x) = 42$

Algebraic Solution

a.
$e^x = 72$	Write original equation.
$\ln e^x = \ln 72$	Take natural log of each side.
$x = \ln 72$	Inverse Property
$x \approx 4.277$	Use a calculator.

The solution is $\ln 72 \approx 4.277$. Check this solution in the original equation.

b.
$3(2^x) = 42$	Write original equation.
$2^x = 14$	Divide each side by 3.
$\log_2 2^x = \log_2 14$	Take log (base 2) of each side.
$x = \log_2 14$	Inverse Property
$x = \dfrac{\ln 14}{\ln 2}$	Change-of-base formula
$x \approx 3.807$	Use a calculator.

The solution is $\log_2 14 \approx 3.807$. Check this solution in the original equation.

Graphical Solution

a. Use a graphing utility to graph the left- and right-hand sides of the equation as $y_1 = e^x$ and $y_2 = 72$ in the same viewing window. Use the *intersect* feature or the *zoom* and *trace* features of the graphing utility to approximate the intersection point, as shown in Figure 4.24. So, the approximate solution is 4.277.

b. Use a graphing utility to graph $y_1 = 3(2^x)$ and $y_2 = 42$ in the same viewing window. Use the *intersect* feature or the *zoom* and *trace* features to approximate the intersection point, as shown in Figure 4.25. So, the approximate solution is 3.807.

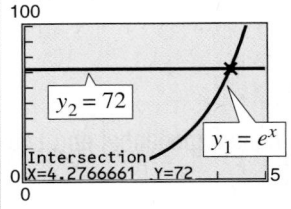

Figure 4.24

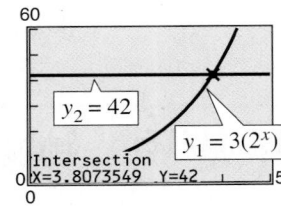

Figure 4.25

EXAMPLE 3   Solving an Exponential Equation

Solve $4e^{2x} = 5$.

Algebraic Solution

$4e^{2x} = 5$	Write original equation.
$e^{2x} = \dfrac{5}{4}$	Divide each side by 4.
$\ln e^{2x} = \ln \dfrac{5}{4}$	Take logarithm of each side.
$2x = \ln \dfrac{5}{4}$	Inverse Property
$x = \dfrac{1}{2} \ln \dfrac{5}{4}$	Solve for x.
$x \approx 0.112$	Use a calculator.

The solution is $\frac{1}{2} \ln \frac{5}{4} \approx 0.112$. Check this solution in the original equation.

Graphical Solution

Rather than graph both sides of the equation you are solving as separate graphs, as you did in Example 2, another way to graphically solve the equation is to first rewrite the equation as $4e^{2x} - 5 = 0$, then use a graphing utility to graph $y = 4e^{2x} - 5$. Use the *zero* or *root* feature or the *zoom* and *trace* features of the graphing utility to approximate the value of x for which $y = 0$. From Figure 4.26, you can see that the zero occurs when $x \approx 0.112$. So, the approximate solution is 0.112.

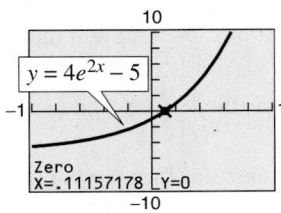

Figure 4.26

EXAMPLE 4   Solving an Exponential Equation

Solve $2(3^{2t-5}) - 4 = 11$.

Solution

$2(3^{2t-5}) - 4 = 11$	Write original equation.
$2(3^{2t-5}) = 15$	Add 4 to each side.
$3^{2t-5} = \frac{15}{2}$	Divide each side by 2.
$\log_3 3^{2t-5} = \log_3 \frac{15}{2}$	Take log (base 3) of each side.
$2t - 5 = \log_3 \frac{15}{2}$	Inverse Property
$2t = 5 + \log_3 7.5$	Add 5 to each side.
$t = \frac{5}{2} + \frac{1}{2}\log_3 7.5$	Divide each side by 2.
$t \approx 3.417$	Use a calculator.

The solution is $\frac{5}{2} + \frac{1}{2}\log_3 7.5 \approx 3.417$. Check this in the original equation.

When an equation involves two or more exponential expressions, you can still use a procedure similar to that demonstrated in the previous three examples. However, the algebra is a bit more complicated.

EXAMPLE 5   Solving an Exponential Equation in Quadratic Form

Solve $e^{2x} - 3e^x + 2 = 0$.

Algebraic Solution

$e^{2x} - 3e^x + 2 = 0$	Write original equation.
$(e^x)^2 - 3e^x + 2 = 0$	Write in quadratic form.
$(e^x - 2)(e^x - 1) = 0$	Factor.
$e^x - 2 = 0$	Set 1st factor equal to 0.
$e^x = 2$	Add 2 to each side.
$x = \ln 2$	Inverse Property
$e^x - 1 = 0$	Set 2nd factor equal to 0.
$e^x = 1$	Add 1 to each side.
$x = \ln 1$	Inverse Property
$x = 0$	Simplify.

The solutions are $\ln 2 \approx 0.693$ and 0. Check these in the original equation.

Graphical Solution

Use a graphing utility to graph $y = e^{2x} - 3e^x + 2$. Use the *zero* or *root* feature or the *zoom* and *trace* features of the graphing utility to approximate the values of x for which $y = 0$. In Figure 4.27, you can see that the zeros occur when $x = 0$ and when $x \approx 0.693$. So, the approximate solutions are 0 and 0.693.

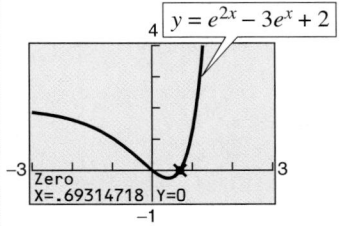

Figure 4.27

Solving Logarithmic Equations

To solve a logarithmic equation, you can write it in exponential form.

$$\ln x = 3 \qquad \text{Logarithmic form}$$

$$e^{\ln x} = e^3 \qquad \text{Exponentiate each side.}$$

$$x = e^3 \qquad \text{Exponential form}$$

This procedure is called *exponentiating* both sides of an equation. It is applied after the logarithmic expression has been isolated.

EXAMPLE 6   Solving Logarithmic Equations

Solve each logarithmic equation.

a. $\ln x = 2$ **b.** $\log_3(5x - 1) = \log_3(x + 7)$

Solution

a. $\ln x = 2$ Write original equation.

$$e^{\ln x} = e^2 \qquad \text{Exponentiate each side.}$$

$$x = e^2 \qquad \text{Inverse Property}$$

$$x \approx 7.389 \qquad \text{Use a calculator.}$$

The solution is $e^2 \approx 7.389$. Check this in the original equation.

b. $\log_3(5x - 1) = \log_3(x + 7)$ Write original equation.

$$5x - 1 = x + 7 \qquad \text{One-to-One Property}$$

$$4x = 8 \qquad \text{Add } -x \text{ and 1 to each side.}$$

$$x = 2 \qquad \text{Divide each side by 4.}$$

The solution is 2. Check this in the original equation.

EXAMPLE 7   Solving a Logarithmic Equation

Solve $5 + 2 \ln x = 4$.

Algebraic Solution

$5 + 2 \ln x = 4$ Write original equation.

$2 \ln x = -1$ Subtract 5 from each side.

$\ln x = -\frac{1}{2}$ Divide each side by 2.

$e^{\ln x} = e^{-1/2}$ Exponentiate each side.

$x = e^{-1/2}$ Inverse property

$x \approx 0.607$ Use a calculator.

The solution is $e^{-1/2} \approx 0.607$. Check this in the original equation.

Graphical Solution

Use a graphing utility to graph $y_1 = 5 + 2 \ln x$ and $y_2 = 4$ in the same viewing window. Use the *intersect* feature or the *zoom* and *trace* features to approximate the intersection point, as shown in Figure 4.28. So, the approximate solution is 0.607.

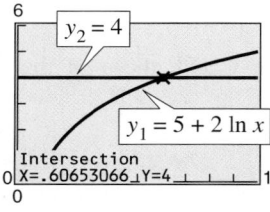

Figure 4.28

EXAMPLE 8   Solving a Logarithmic Equation

Solve $2 \log_5 3x = 4$.

Solution

$2 \log_5 3x = 4$	Write original equation.
$\log_5 3x = 2$	Divide each side by 2.
$5^{\log_5 3x} = 5^2$	Exponentiate each side (base 5).
$3x = 25$	Inverse Property.
$x = \frac{25}{3}$	Divide each side by 3.

The solution is $\frac{25}{3}$. Check this in the original equation. Or, perform a graphical check by graphing

$$y_1 = 2 \log_5 3x = 2\left(\frac{\log_{10} 3x}{\log_{10} 5}\right) \qquad \text{and} \qquad y_2 = 4$$

in the same viewing window. The two graphs should intersect when $x = \frac{25}{3}$ and $y = 4$, as shown in Figure 4.29.

Because the domain of a logarithmic function generally does not include all real numbers, you should be sure to check for extraneous solutions of logarithmic equations, as shown in the next example.

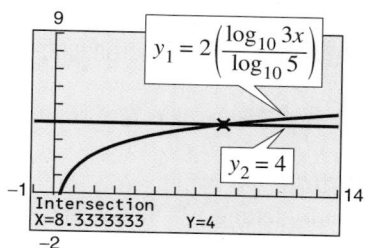

Figure 4.29

EXAMPLE 9   Checking for Extraneous Solutions

Solve for x in the equation $\ln(x - 2) + \ln(2x - 3) = 2 \ln x$.

Algebraic Solution

$\ln(x - 2) + \ln(2x - 3) = 2 \ln x$	Write original equation.
$\ln[(x - 2)(2x - 3)] = \ln x^2$	Use properties of logarithms.
$\ln(2x^2 - 7x + 6) = \ln x^2$	
$2x^2 - 7x + 6 = x^2$	One-to-One Property
$x^2 - 7x + 6 = 0$	Write in general form.
$(x - 6)(x - 1) = 0$	Factor.
$x - 6 = 0 \implies x = 6$	Set 1st factor equal to 0.
$x - 1 = 0 \implies x = 1$	Set 2nd factor equal to 0.

Finally, by checking these two "solutions" in the original equation, you can conclude that $x = 1$ is not valid. This is because when $x = 1$, $\ln(x - 2) + \ln(2x - 3) = \ln(-1) + \ln(-1)$, which is invalid because -1 is not in the domain of the natural log function. So, the only solution is 6.

Graphical Solution

First rewrite the original equation as $\ln(x - 2) + \ln(2x - 3) - 2 \ln x = 0$. Then use a graphing utility to graph $y = \ln(x - 2) + \ln(2x - 3) - 2 \ln x$, as shown in Figure 4.30. Use the *zero* or *root* feature or the *zoom* and *trace* features of the graphing utility to determine that 6 is an approximate solution. You can verify that 6 is an exact solution by substituting $x = 6$ in the original equation.

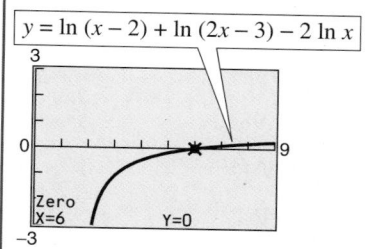

Figure 4.30

EXAMPLE 10   The Change-of-Base Formula

Prove the change-of-base formula: $\log_a x = \dfrac{\log_b x}{\log_b a}$.

Solution

Begin by letting $y = \log_a x$ and writing the equivalent exponential form $a^y = x$. Now, taking the logarithms *with base b* of both sides produces the following.

$$\log_b a^y = \log_b x$$

$$y \log_b a = \log_b x$$

$$y = \frac{\log_b x}{\log_b a}$$

$$\log_a x = \frac{\log_b x}{\log_a a}$$

Approximating Solutions

Equations that involve combinations of algebraic functions, exponential functions, and/or logarithmic functions can be very difficult to solve by algebraic procedures. Here again, you can take advantage of a graphing utility.

EXAMPLE 11   Approximating the Solution of an Equation

Approximate the solution of $\ln x = x^2 - 2$.

Solution

To begin, write the equation so that all terms on one side are equal to 0.

$$\ln x - x^2 + 2 = 0$$

Then use a graphing utility to graph

$$y = -x^2 + 2 + \ln x$$

as shown in Figure 4.31. From this graph, you can see that the equation has two solutions. Next, using the *zero* or *root* feature or the *zoom* and *trace* features, you can approximate the two solutions to be 0.138 and 1.564.

Check

$\ln x = x^2 - 2$	Write original equation.
$\ln(0.138) \overset{?}{\approx} (0.138)^2 - 2$	Substitute 0.138 for x.
$-1.9805 \approx -1.9810$	Solution checks. ✓
$\ln(1.564) \overset{?}{\approx} (1.564)^2 - 2$	Substitute 1.564 for x.
$0.4472 \approx 0.4461$	Solution checks. ✓

So, the two solutions 0.138 and 1.564 seem reasonable.

Activities

1. Solve for x: $7^x = 3$.

   Answer: $x = \log_7 3$
   $$= \frac{\ln 3}{\ln 7}$$
   $$\approx 0.5646$$

2. Solve for x:

   $\log_{10}(x + 4) + \log_{10}(x + 1) = .1$

   Answer: $x = 1$ ($x = -6$ is not in the domain.)

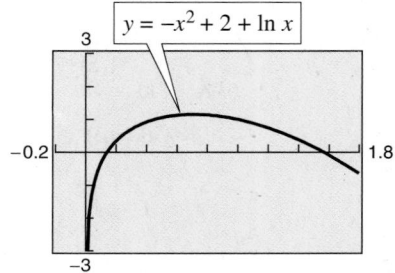

Figure 4.31

Applications

EXAMPLE 12 Doubling an Investment

You have deposited $500 in an account that pays 6.75% interest, compounded continuously. How long will it take your money to double?

Solution

Using the formula for continuous compounding, you can find that the balance in the account is

$$A = Pe^{rt}$$

$$= 500e^{0.0675t}.$$

To find the time required for the balance to double, let $A = 1000$, and solve the resulting equation for t.

$500e^{0.0675t} = 1000$	Substitute 1000 for A.
$e^{0.0675t} = 2$	Divide each side by 500.
$\ln e^{0.0675t} = \ln 2$	Take natural log of each side.
$0.0675t = \ln 2$	Inverse Property
$t = \dfrac{\ln 2}{0.0675}$	Divide each side by 0.0675.
$t \approx 10.27$	Use a calculator.

The balance in the account will double after approximately 10.27 years. This result is demonstrated graphically in Figure 4.32.

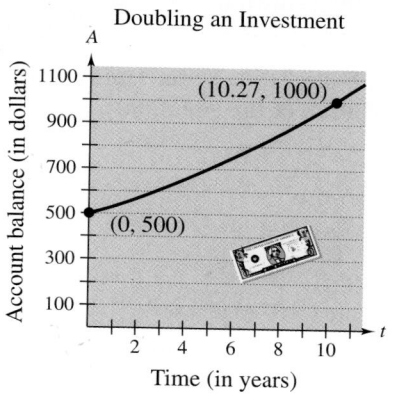

Doubling an Investment

Figure 4.32

EXAMPLE 13 Consumer Price Index for Sugar

From 1970 to 1997, the Consumer Price Index (CPI) value y for a fixed amount of sugar for the year t can be modeled by the equation

$$y = -171.8 + 87.1 \ln t$$

where $t = 10$ represents 1970 (see Figure 4.33). During which year did the price of sugar reach 4.5 times its 1970 price of 28.8 on the CPI?   (Source: U.S. Bureau of Labor Statistics)

Solution

$-171.8 + 87.1 \ln t = y$	Write original equation.
$-171.8 + 87.1 \ln t = 129.6$	Substitute $(4.5)(28.8) = 129.6$ for y.
$87.1 \ln t = 301.4$	Add 171.8 to each side.
$\ln t = 3.460$	Divide each side by 87.1.
$e^{\ln t} = e^{3.460}$	Exponentiate each side.
$t \approx 31.8$	Inverse Property

The solution is 31.8 years. Because $t = 10$ represents 1970, it follows that the price of sugar reached 4.5 times its 1970 price in late 1991.

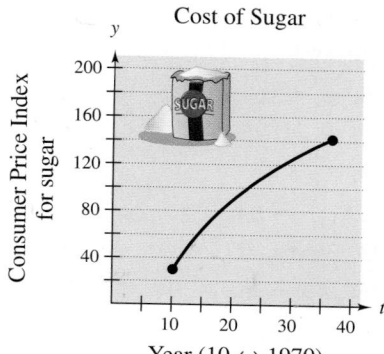

Cost of Sugar

Figure 4.33

4.4 Exercises

In Exercises 1–8, determine whether each x-value is a solution of the equation.

1. $4^{2x-7} = 64$
   (a) $x = 5$
   (b) $x = 2$

2. $2^{3x+1} = 32$
   (a) $x = -1$
   (b) $x = 2$

3. $3e^{x+2} = 75$
   (a) $x = -2 + e^{25}$
   (b) $x = -2 + \ln 25$
   (c) $x \approx 1.2189$

4. $-4e^{x-1} = -60$
   (a) $x = 1 + \ln 15$
   (b) $x \approx 3.7081$
   (c) $x = \ln 16$

5. $\log_4(3x) = 3$
   (a) $x \approx 20.3560$
   (b) $x = -4$
   (c) $x = \frac{64}{3}$

6. $\log_6\left(\frac{5}{3}x\right) = 2$
   (a) $x \approx 20.2882$
   (b) $x = \frac{108}{5}$
   (c) $x = 7.2$

7. $\ln(x - 1) = 3.8$
   (a) $x = 1 + e^{3.8}$
   (b) $x \approx 45.7012$
   (c) $x = 1 + \ln 3.8$

8. $\frac{1}{5}\ln(2 + x) = \frac{1}{2}$
   (a) $x = e^{2.5} - 2$
   (b) $x \approx \frac{4073}{400}$
   (c) $x = \frac{1}{2}$

In Exercises 9–14, use a graphing utility to graph f and g in the same viewing window. Approximate the point of intersection of the graphs of f and g. Then solve the equation $f(x) = g(x)$ algebraically.

9. $f(x) = 2^x$
   $g(x) = 8$

10. $f(x) = 27^x$
   $g(x) = 9$

11. $f(x) = \log_3 x$
   $g(x) = 2$

12. $f(x) = 3\log_5 x$
   $g(x) = 6$

13. $f(x) = \ln(x - 4)$
   $g(x) = 0$

14. $f(x) = \ln e^{x-2}$
   $g(x) = 3x + 2$

In Exercises 15–36, solve for x.

15. $4^x = 16$

16. $3^x = 243$

17. $5^x = 625$

18. $7^x = \frac{1}{49}$

19. $8^x = 4$

20. $\left(\frac{1}{2}\right)^x = 32$

21. $\left(\frac{1}{4}\right)^x = 64$

22. $\left(\frac{3}{4}\right)^x = \frac{27}{64}$

23. $3^{x-1} = 27$

24. $\ln x - \ln 2 = 0$

25. $\ln x - \ln 5 = 0$

26. $e^x = 2$

27. $e^x = 4$

28. $\ln x = -1$

29. $\ln x = -7$

30. $\log_4 x = 3$

31. $\log_x 625 = 4$

32. $\log_{10} x - 2 = 0$

33. $\log_{10} x = -1$

34. $\log_{10} x = -\frac{1}{2}$

35. $\ln(2x - 1) = 0$

36. $\ln(3x + 5) = 8$

In Exercises 37–42, simplify the expression.

37. $\ln e^{x^2}$

38. $\ln e^{2x-1}$

39. $e^{\ln(5x+2)}$

40. $-1 + \ln e^{2x}$

41. $e^{\ln x^2}$

42. $-8 + e^{\ln x^3}$

In Exercises 43–60, solve the exponential equation algebraically. Round your result to three decimal places. Use a graphing utility to verify your answer.

43. $10^x = 570$

44. $6^{5x} = 3000$

45. $e^x = 10$

46. $4e^{2x} = 40$

47. $5^{-t/2} = 0.20$

48. $4^{-3t} = 0.10$

49. $2^{3-x} = 565$

50. $8^{-2-x} = 431$

51. $500e^{-x} = 300$

52. $1000e^{-4x} = 75$

53. $7 - 2e^x = 5$

54. $-14 + 3e^x = 11$

55. $e^{2x} - 4e^x - 5 = 0$

56. $e^{2x} - 5e^x + 6 = 0$

57. $50(120 - e^{x/2}) = 600$

58. $\dfrac{525}{1 + e^{-x}} = 275$

59. $\left(1 + \dfrac{0.10}{12}\right)^{12t} = 2$

60. $\left(16 + \dfrac{0.878}{26}\right)^{3t} = 30$

In Exercises 61–64, let $f(x)$ represent the left side of the equation. Complete the table to obtain a rough estimate of the solution, and then use a graphing utility to graph both sides of the equation to obtain a better estimate of the solution. Round your result to three decimal places.

61. $e^{3x} = 12$

x	0.6	0.7	0.8	0.9	1.0
$f(x)$					

62. $e^{2x} = 50$

x	1.6	1.7	1.8	1.9	2.0
$f(x)$					

63. $20(100 - e^{x/2}) = 500$

x	5	6	7	8	9
$f(x)$					

64. $\dfrac{400}{1 + e^{-x}} = 350$

x	0	1	2	3	4
$f(x)$					

In Exercises 65–74, use the *zero* or *root* feature or the *zoom* and *trace* features of a graphing utility to find an approximate solution of the exponential equation accurate to three decimal places.

65. $2^{3x} = 50$

66. $4^{-x/2} = 0.10$

67. $2^{-3x} = 0.90$

68. $8(10^{3x}) = 12$

69. $5(10^{x-6}) = 7$

70. $8(3^{6-x}) = 40$

71. $\left(1 + \dfrac{0.065}{365}\right)^{365t} = 4$

72. $\left(4 - \dfrac{2.471}{40}\right)^{9t} = 21$

73. $\dfrac{3000}{2 + e^{2x}} = 2$

74. $\dfrac{119}{e^{6x} - 14} = 7$

In Exercises 75–78, use a graphing utility to graph the function and approximate its zero accurate to three decimal places.

75. $g(x) = 6e^{1-x} - 25$

76. $f(x) = 3e^{3x/2} - 962$

77. $g(t) = e^{0.09t} - 3$

78. $h(t) = e^{0.125t} - 8$

In Exercises 79–98, solve the logarithmic equation algebraically. Round the result to three decimal places. Verify your answer using a graphing utility.

79. $\ln x = -3$

80. $\ln x = 2$

81. $\ln 4x = 2.1$

82. $\ln 4x = 1$

83. $2 \ln 3x = 19$

84. $2 \ln x = 7$

85. $\log_{10}(z - 3) = 2$

86. $\log_{10} x^2 = 6$

87. $7 \log_4(0.6x) = 12$

88. $4 \log_{10}(x - 6) = 11$

89. $\ln \sqrt{x + 2} = 1$

90. $\ln \sqrt{x - 8} = 5$

91. $\ln(x + 1)^2 = 2$

92. $\ln(x^2 + 1) = 8$

93. $\log_4 x - \log_4(x - 1) = \frac{1}{2}$

94. $\log_3 x + \log_3(x^2 - 8) = \log_3 8x$

95. $\ln(x + 5) = \ln(x - 1) - \ln(x + 1)$

96. $\ln(x + 1) - \ln(x - 2) = \ln x^2$

97. $\log_{10} 8x - \log_{10}(1 + \sqrt{x}) = 2$

98. $\log_{10} 4x - \log_{10}(12 + \sqrt{x}) = 2$

In Exercises 99–102, let $f(x)$ represent the left side of the equation. Complete the table to obtain a rough estimate of the solution, and then use a graphing utility to graph both sides of the equation to obtain a better estimate of the solution. Round your result to three decimal places.

99. $\ln 2x = 2.4$

x	2	3	4	5	6
$f(x)$					

100. $3 \ln 5x = 10$

x	4	5	6	7	8
$f(x)$					

101. $6 \log_3(0.5x) = 11$

x	12	13	14	15	16
$f(x)$					

102. $5 \log_{10}(x - 2) = 11$

x	150	155	160	165	170
$f(x)$					

In Exercises 103–110, use the *zero* or *root* feature or the *zoom* and *trace* features of a graphing utility to find an approximate solution of the logarithmic equation accurate to three decimal places.

103. $\log_{10}(z - 4) = 1$

104. $\log_{10} x^2 = 4$

105. $3 \ln x = 5$

106. $\ln 4x = 3$

107. $\ln x + \ln(x - 3) = 1$

108. $\log_2 x + \log_2(x + 5) = \log_2(x + 4)$

109. $\ln(x - 5) = \ln(x - 3) - \ln(x + 3)$

110. $\ln x + \ln(x^2 + 4) = 10$

In Exercises 111–116, use a graphing utility to approximate the point of intersection of the graphs. Round your result to three decimal places.

111. $y_1 = 7$
   $y_2 = 2^x$

112. $y_1 = -4$
   $y_2 = -3^{x+1} - 2$

113. $y_1 = 8$

$\quad\;\; y_2 = 4e^{-0.2x}$

114. $y_1 = 500$

$\quad\;\; y_2 = 1500e^{-x/2}$

115. $y_1 = 3$

$\quad\;\; y_2 = \ln x$

116. $y_1 = 10$

$\quad\;\; y_2 = 4\ln(x - 2)$

Compound Interest **In Exercises 117 and 118, find the time required for a $1000 investment to (a) double at interest rate r, compounded continuously, and (b) triple at interest rate r, compounded continuously.**

117. $r = 0.085$

118. $r = 0.12$

119. *Average Heights* The percentages of American males and females between the ages of 18 and 24 who are at least x inches tall are

$$m(x) = \frac{100}{1 + e^{-0.6114(x - 69.71)}} \quad \text{Males}$$

$$f(x) = \frac{100}{1 + e^{-0.66607(x - 64.51)}} \quad \text{Females}$$

where m and f are the percentages and x is the height in inches.   (Source: U.S. National Center for Health Statistics)

(a) Use a graphing utility to graph the two functions in the same viewing window.

(b) Use the graph to determine the horizontal asymptotes of the functions.

(c) What is the median height for each sex?

120. *Human Memory Model* In a group project in learning theory, a mathematical model for the proportion P of correct responses after n trials was found to be

$$P = \frac{0.83}{1 + e^{-0.2n}}.$$

(a) Use a graphing utility to graph the function.

(b) Use the graph to determine the horizontal asymptotes of the function. Interpret the meaning of the upper asymptote in the context of the problem.

(c) After how many trials will 60% of the responses be correct?

121. *Demand Function* The demand equation for a camera is

$$p = 500 - 0.5(e^{0.004x}).$$

Find the demands x for prices of (a) $p = \$350$ and (b) $p = \$300$.

122. *Demand Function* The demand equation for a camcorder is

$$p = 5000\left(1 - \frac{4}{4 + e^{-0.002x}}\right).$$

Find the demands x for prices of (a) $p = \$600$ and (b) $p = \$400$.

123. *Forest Yield* The yield V (in millions of cubic feet per acre) for a forest at age t years is

$$V = 6.7e^{-48.1/t}.$$

(a) Use a graphing utility to graph the function.

(b) Determine the horizontal asymptote of the function. Interpret its meaning in the context of the problem.

(c) Find the time necessary to obtain a yield of 1.3 million cubic feet.

124. *Trees per Acre* The number of trees per acre N of a certain species is approximated by the model

$$N = 68(10^{-0.04x}), \quad 5 \le x \le 40$$

where x is the average diameter of the trees (in inches) three feet above the ground. Use the model to approximate the average diameter of the trees in a test plot when $N = 21$.

125. *Data Analysis* An object at a temperature of 160°C is removed from a furnace and placed in a room at 20°C. The temperature T of the object is measured each hour h and recorded in the table.

h	0	1	2	3	4	5
T	160°	90°	56°	38°	29°	24°

A model for this data is

$$T = 20[1 + 7(2^{-h})].$$

(a) Use a graphing utility to plot the data points and graph the model in the same viewing window.

(b) Use the graph to identify the horizontal asymptote of the model and interpret the asymptote in the context of the problem.

(c) Approximate the time when the temperature of the object is 100°C.

126. *Automobiles* Automobiles are designed with crumple zones that help protect their occupants in crashes. The crumple zones allow the occupants to move short distances when the automobiles come to abrupt stops. The greater the distance moved, the less g's the crash victims experience. (One g is equal to the acceleration due to gravity. For very short periods of time, humans have withstood as much as 40 g's.) In crash tests with vehicles moving at 90 kilometers per hour, analysts measured the number of g's experienced during deceleration y by crash dummies that were permitted to move x meters during impact. The data is shown in the table.

x	0.2	0.4	0.6	0.8	1
y	158	80	53	40	32

(a) Use the regression capabilities of a graphing utility to find a natural logarithmic model for the data. A second model for the data is

$$y = -3.00 + 11.88 \ln x + (36.94/x).$$

Graph both models with the data points in the same viewing window. Which model do you think is a better choice? Comment on accuracy and simplicity.

(b) Use both models to estimate the distance traveled during impact if the passenger deceleration must not exceed 30 g's. Comment on the difference in distances traveled given by the two models and the practical implications of choosing a model when designing the crumple zones.

127. *Comparing Mathematical Models* The table shows the number y (in millions) of single compact discs (CDs) shipped annually by manufacturers from 1993 through 1997, where $x = 3$ represents 1993. (Source: Recording Industry Association of America)

x	3	4	5	6	7
y	7.8	9.3	21.5	43.2	66.7

(a) Create a scatter plot of the data. Find a linear model for the data, and add its graph to your scatter plot. Using this model, approximate the year that corresponds to an annual shipment of single CDs of 100 million.

(b) Create a new table giving values for $\ln x$ and $\ln y$ and create a scatter plot of this transformed data. Use the method illustrated in Example 8 in Section 4.3 to find a model for the transformed data, and add its graph to your scatter plot. According to this model, approximate the year that corresponds to an annual shipment of single CDs of 100 million.

(c) Solve the model in part (b) for y, and add its graph to your scatter plot in part (a). Which model better fits the original data? Which model will better predict future shipping levels? Explain.

Synthesis

True or False? **In Exercises 128 and 129, determine whether the statement is true or false. Justify your answer.**

128. You can approximate the solution to the equation $\frac{2}{3}e^x = 42$ by graphing $y = \frac{2}{3}e^x - 42$ and finding its x-intercept.

129. A logarithmic equation can have, at most, one extraneous solution.

130. *Think About It* Is the time required for an investment to quadruple twice as long as the time for it to double? Give a reason for your answer and give an example to verify your answer algebraically.

131. *Writing* Write a paragraph explaining whether or not the time required for an investment to double is dependent on the size of the investment.

Review

In Exercises 132–135, sketch the graph of the function.

132. $f(x) = 3^{x+3} - 5$

133. $f(x) = -3^{-x-3} + 5$

134. $f(x) = -2^{x+2} - 6$

135. $f(x) = \left(\frac{1}{2}\right)^{-x} + 3$

In Exercises 136–139, evaluate the logarithm using the change-of-base formula. Round your result to three decimal places.

136. $\log_7 11$

137. $\log_3 22$

138. $\log_9 6$

139. $\log_{21} 140$

4.5 Exponential and Logarithmic Models

What You Should Learn:

- How to recognize the five most common types of models involving exponential or logarithmic functions
- How to use exponential growth and decay functions to model and solve real-life problems
- How to use Gaussian functions to model and solve real-life problems
- How to use logistic growth functions to model and solve real-life problems
- How to use logarithmic functions to model and solve real-life problems
- How to fit exponential and logarithmic models to sets of data

Introduction

The five most common types of mathematical models involving exponential functions and logarithmic functions are as follows.

1. **Exponential growth model:** $\quad y = ae^{bx}, \quad\quad b > 0$
2. **Exponential decay model:** $\quad y = ae^{-bx}, \quad\quad b > 0$
3. **Gaussian model:** $\quad\quad\quad\quad\quad y = ae^{-(x-b)^2/c}$
4. **Logistic growth model:** $\quad\quad y = \dfrac{a}{1 + be^{-rx}}$
5. **Logarithmic models:** $\quad\quad y = a + b \ln x, \quad\quad y = a + b \log_{10} x$

The basic shapes of these graphs are shown in Figure 4.34.

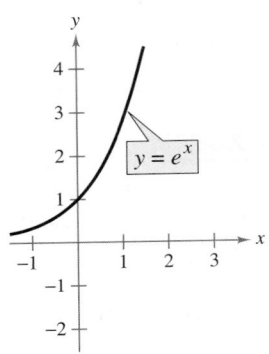

Exponential Growth Model

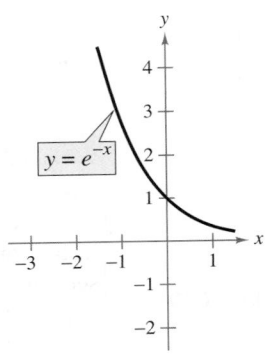

Exponential Decay Model

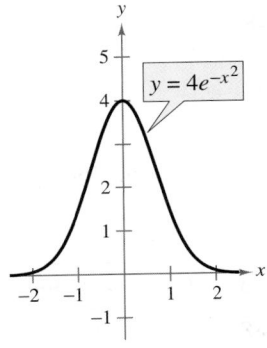

Gaussian Model

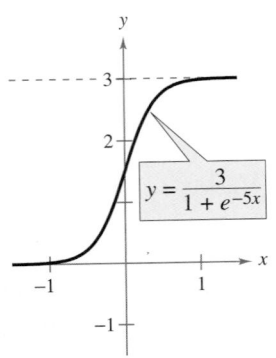

Logistic Growth Model

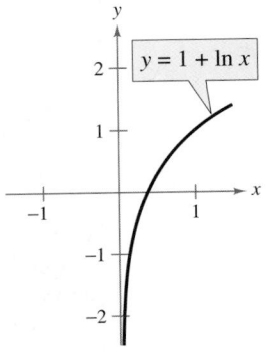

Natural Logarithmic Model

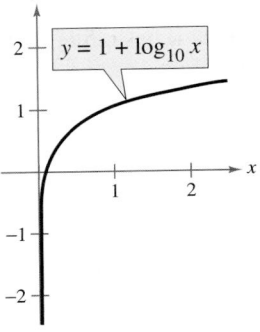

Common Logarithmic Model

Figure 4.34

Why You Should Learn It:

Exponential and logarithmic functions can be used to model and solve a variety of business applications. In Exercise 44 on page 350, you will compare an exponential decay model and a linear model for the depreciation of a computer over three years.

This section shows students real-world applications for logarithmic and exponential functions.

You can often gain quite a bit of insight into a situation modeled by an exponential or logarithmic function by identifying and interpreting the function's asymptotes. Use the graphs in Figure 4.34 to identify the asymptotes of each function.

Exponential Growth and Decay

EXAMPLE 1   Population Growth

Estimates of the world population (in millions) from 1992 through 2000 are shown in the table. The scatter plot of the data is shown in Figure 4.35.   (Source: U.S. Bureau of the Census)

Year	1992	1993	1994	1995	1996	1997	1998	1999	2000
Population	5445	5527	5607	5688	5767	5847	5926	6005	6083

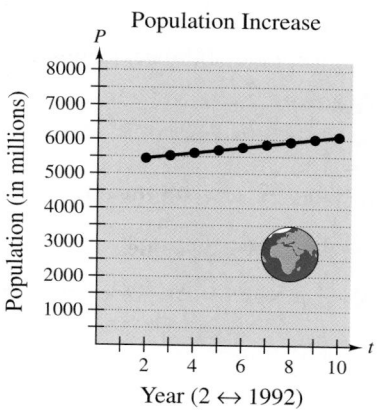

Population Increase

Year (2 ↔ 1992)

Figure 4.35

An exponential growth model that approximates this data is

$$P = 5303e^{0.013838t}, \quad 2 \le t \le 10$$

where P is the population (in millions) and $t = 2$ represents 1992. Compare the values given by the model with the estimates given by the U.S. Bureau of the Census. According to this model, what year corresponds to a world population of 6.5 billion?

Algebraic Solution

The following table compares the two sets of population figures.

Year	1992	1993	1994	1995	1996	1997	1998	1999	2000
Population	5445	5527	5607	5688	5767	5847	5926	6005	6083
Model	5452	5528	5605	5683	5762	5842	5924	6006	6090

To find the year for which the world population is 6.5 billion, let $P = 6500$ in the model and solve for t.

$5303e^{0.013838t} = P$	Write original model.
$5303e^{0.013838t} = 6500$	Substitute 6500 for P.
$e^{0.013838t} \approx 1.2257$	Divide each side by 5303.
$\ln e^{0.013838t} \approx \ln 1.2257$	Take natural log of each side.
$0.013838t \approx 0.2035$	Inverse Property
$t \approx 14.71$	Divide each side by 0.013838.

According to the model, the year 2004 corresponds to a population of 6.5 billion.

Graphical Solution

Use a graphing utility to graph the model $y = 5303e^{0.013838x}$ and the data in the same viewing window. You can see in Figure 4.36 that the model appears to closely fit the data.

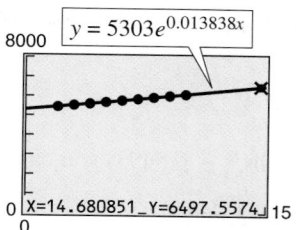

$y = 5303e^{0.013838x}$

Figure 4.36

Use the *zoom* and *trace* features of the graphing utility to find that the approximate value of x for which $y = 6500$ is $x \approx 14.71$. So, according to the model, the year 2004 corresponds to a world population of 6.5 billion.

An exponential model increases (or decreases) by the same percent each year. What is the annual percent increase for the model above?

In Example 1, you were given the exponential growth model. But suppose this model had not been given; how could you have found such a model? One technique for doing this is demonstrated in Example 2.

EXAMPLE 2   Modeling Population Growth

In a research experiment, a population of fruit flies is increasing in accordance with the law of exponential growth. After 2 days there are 100 flies, and after 4 days there are 300 flies. How many flies will there be after 5 days?

Solution

Let y be the number of flies at time t. From the given information, you know that $y = 100$ when $t = 2$ and $y = 300$ when $t = 4$. Substituting this information into the model $y = ae^{bt}$ produces

$$100 = ae^{2b} \quad \text{and} \quad 300 = ae^{4b}.$$

To solve for b, solve for a in the first equation.

$$100 = ae^{2b} \quad \Longrightarrow \quad a = \frac{100}{e^{2b}} \qquad \text{Solve for } a \text{ in the first equation.}$$

Then substitute the result into the second equation.

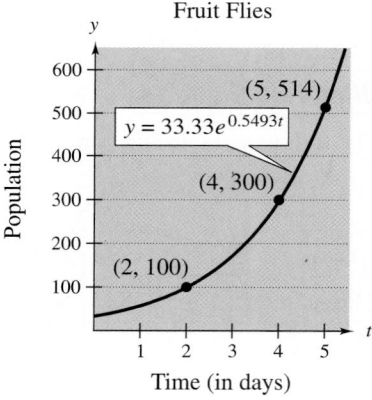
Fruit Flies

$$300 = ae^{4b} \qquad\qquad \text{Write second equation.}$$

$$300 = \left(\frac{100}{e^{2b}}\right)e^{4b} \qquad \text{Substitute } 100/e^{2b} \text{ for } a.$$

$$\frac{300}{100} = e^{2b} \qquad\qquad \text{Divide each side by 100.}$$

$$\ln\frac{300}{100} = \ln e^{2b} \qquad \text{Take natural log of each side.}$$

$$\ln 3 = 2b \qquad\qquad \text{Inverse Property}$$

$$\frac{1}{2}\ln 3 = b \qquad\qquad \text{Solve for } b.$$

Figure 4.37

Using $b = \frac{1}{2}\ln 3 \approx 0.5493$, you can determine that

$$a = \frac{100}{e^{2[(1/2)\ln 3]}} \qquad \text{Substitute } \tfrac{1}{2}\ln 3 \text{ for } b.$$

$$= \frac{100}{e^{\ln 3}} \qquad\qquad \text{Simplify.}$$

$$= \frac{100}{3} \qquad\qquad \text{Inverse Property}$$

$$\approx 33.33 \qquad\qquad \text{Simplify.}$$

So, the exponential growth model is

$$y = 33.33e^{0.5493t},$$

as shown in Figure 4.37. This implies that after 5 days, the population is

$$y = 33.33e^{0.5493(5)} \approx 520 \text{ flies.}$$

In living organic material, the ratio of the content of radioactive carbon (carbon 14) to the content of nonradioactive carbon (carbon 12) is about 1 to 10^{12}. When organic material dies, its carbon 12 content remains fixed, whereas its radioactive carbon 14 begins to decay with a half-life of about 5700 years. To estimate the age of dead organic material, scientists use the following formula, which denotes the ratio of carbon 14 to carbon 12 present at any time t (in years).

$$R = \frac{1}{10^{12}} e^{-t/8223}$$

The graph of R is shown in Figure 4.38. Note that R decreases as t increases.

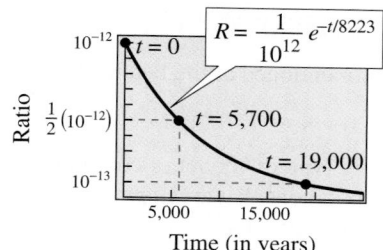

Figure 4.38

EXAMPLE 3 Carbon Dating

The ratio of carbon 14 to carbon 12 in a newly discovered fossil is

$$R = \frac{1}{10^{13}}.$$

Estimate the age of the fossil.

Algebraic Solution

In the carbon dating model, substitute the given value of R to obtain the following.

$\dfrac{1}{10^{12}} e^{-t/8223} = R$	Write original formula.
$\dfrac{e^{-t/8223}}{10^{12}} = \dfrac{1}{10^{13}}$	Substitute $\dfrac{1}{10^{13}}$ for R.
$e^{-t/8223} = \dfrac{1}{10}$	Multiply each side by 10^{12}.
$\ln e^{-t/8223} = \ln \dfrac{1}{10}$	Take natural log of each side.
$-\dfrac{t}{8223} \approx -2.3026$	Inverse Property
$t \approx 18{,}934$	Multiply each side by -8223.

So, to the nearest thousand years, you can estimate the age of the fossil to be 19,000 years.

Graphical Solution

Use a graphing utility to graph the formula for the ratio of carbon 14 to carbon 12 at any time t as

$$y_1 = \frac{1}{10^{12}} e^{-x/8223}.$$

In the same viewing window, graph $y_2 = 1/(10^{13})$. Use the *intersect* feature or the *zoom* and *trace* features of the graphing utility to estimate that $x \approx 18{,}934$ when $y = 1/(10^{13})$, as shown in Figure 4.39.

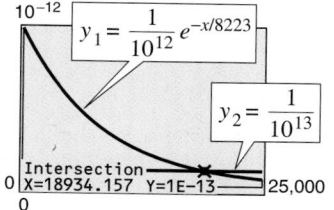

Figure 4.39

So, to the nearest thousand years, you can estimate the age of the fossil to be 19,000 years.

The carbon dating model in Example 3 assumed that the carbon 14 to carbon 12 ratio was 1 part in 10,000,000,000,000. Suppose an error in measurement occurred and the actual ratio was only 1 part in 8,000,000,000,000. The fossil age corresponding to the actual ratio would then be approximately 17,000 years. Try checking this result.

Gaussian Models

As mentioned at the beginning of this section, Gaussian models are of the form

$$y = ae^{-(x-b)^2/c}.$$

This type of model is commonly used in probability and statistics to represent populations that are **normally distributed.** For *standard* normal distributions, the model takes the form

$$y = \frac{1}{\sigma\sqrt{2\pi}}e^{-x^2/2\sigma^2}$$

where σ is the standard deviation (σ is the lowercase Greek letter sigma). The graph of a Gaussian model is called a **bell-shaped curve.** Try assigning a value to σ and sketching a normal distribution curve with a graphing utility. Can you see why it is called a bell-shaped curve?

EXAMPLE 4 SAT Scores

In 1997, the Scholastic Aptitude Test (SAT) math scores for college-bound seniors roughly followed the normal distribution

$$y = 0.0036e^{-(x-511)^2/25{,}088}, \qquad 200 \le x \le 800$$

where x is the SAT score for mathematics. Use a graphing utility to graph this function. From the graph, estimate the average SAT score. (Source: College Board)

Solution

The graph of the function is given in Figure 4.40. On this bell-shaped curve, the maximum value of the curve represents the average score. Using the *maximum* feature or the *zoom* and *trace* features, you can see that the average mathematics score for college-bound seniors in 1997 was 511.

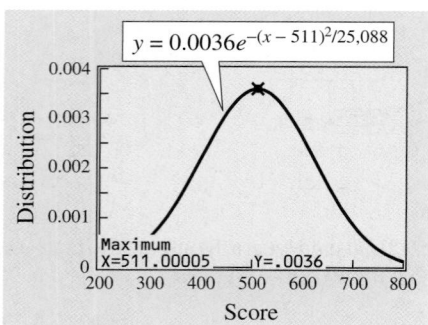

Figure 4.40

In Example 4, note that 50% of the seniors who took the test received a score lower than 511.

Logistic Growth Models

Some populations initially have rapid growth, followed by a declining rate of growth, as indicated by the graph in Figure 4.41. One model for describing this type of growth pattern is the **logistic curve** given by the function

$$y = \frac{a}{1 + be^{-rx}}$$

where y is the population size and x is the time. An example is a bacteria culture allowed to grow initially under ideal conditions and then under less favorable conditions that inhibit growth. A logistic growth curve is also called a **sigmoidal curve**.

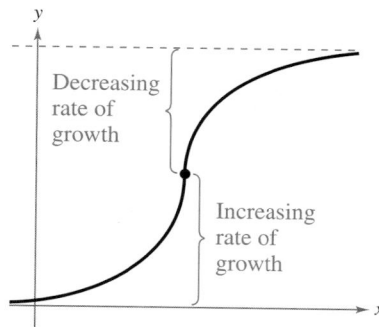

Figure 4.41 *Logistic Curve*

EXAMPLE 5   Spread of a Virus

On a college campus of 5000 students, one student returns from vacation with a contagious flu virus. The spread of the virus is modeled by

$$y = \frac{5000}{1 + 4999e^{-0.8t}}, \qquad t \geq 0$$

where y is the total number infected after t days. The college will cancel classes when 40% or more of the students are ill.

a. How many students are infected after 5 days?

b. After how many days will the college cancel classes?

Some graphing utilities are capable of fitting logistic growth models to data. You might make up a list of data (derived from a logistic model) that your students can graph (to identify the best-fitting form of model) during class and then fit a logistic model to practice interpreting the logistic model.

Algebraic Solution

a. After 5 days, the number infected is

$$y = \frac{5000}{1 + 4999e^{-0.8(5)}} = \frac{5000}{1 + 4999e^{-4}} \approx 54.$$

b. In this case, the number of infected students is $(0.40)(5000) = 2000$. Therefore, you solve for t in the following equation.

$$2000 = \frac{5000}{1 + 4999e^{-0.8t}}$$

$$1 + 4999e^{-0.8t} = 2.5$$

$$e^{-0.8t} \approx \frac{1.5}{4999}$$

$$\ln e^{-0.8t} \approx \ln \frac{1.5}{4999}$$

$$-0.8t \approx \ln \frac{1.5}{4999}$$

$$t = -\frac{1}{0.8} \ln \frac{1.5}{4999}$$

$$t \approx 10.14$$

So, after about 10 days, at least 40% of the students will be infected, and classes will be canceled.

Graphical Solution

a. Use a graphing utility to graph $y = \dfrac{5000}{1 + 4999e^{-0.8x}}$. Use the *value* feature or *zoom* and *trace* features of the graphing utility to estimate that $y = 54$ when $x = 5$. So, after 5 days, about 54 people will be infected.

b. In this case, the number infected must be $(0.40)(5000) = 2000$ to cancel classes. Use a graphing utility to graph

$$y_1 = \frac{5000}{1 + 4999e^{-0.8x}}. \qquad \text{and} \qquad y_2 = 2000$$

in the same viewing window. Use the *intersect* feature or the *zoom* and *trace* features of the graphing utility to find the point of intersection of the graphs. In Figure 4.42, you can see that the point of intersection occurs near $x \approx 10.14$. So, a short time after 10 days, at least 40% of the students will be infected, and the college will cancel classes.

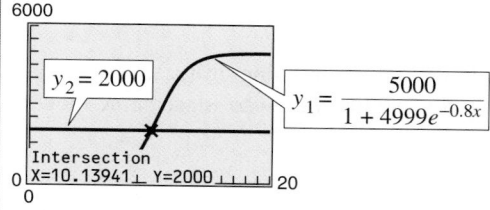

Figure 4.42

Logarithmic Models

EXAMPLE 6   Magnitudes of Earthquakes

On the Richter scale, the magnitude R of an earthquake of intensity I is

$$R = \log_{10} \frac{I}{I_0}$$

where $I_0 = 1$ is the minimum intensity used for comparison. Find the intensities per unit of area for the following earthquakes. (Intensity is a measure of the wave energy of the earthquake.)

More than 15,000 people were killed in the 7.4 magnitude earthquake in Izmit, Turkey, on August 17, 1999.

a. Tokyo and Yokohama, Japan, in 1923; $R = 8.3$

b. Izmit, Turkey, in 1999; $R = 7.4$

Solution
a. Because $I_0 = 1$ and $R = 8.3$, you have

$$8.3 = \log_{10} I$$

$$I = 10^{8.3} \approx 199{,}526{,}000. \qquad \text{Intensity}$$

b. For $R = 7.4$, you have $7.4 = \log_{10} I$, and $I = 10^{7.4} \approx 25{,}119{,}000$.

Note that an increase of 0.9 units on the Richter scale (from 7.4 to 8.3) represents an intensity change by a factor of

$$\frac{199{,}526{,}000}{25{,}119{,}000} \approx 8.$$

In other words, the earthquake in 1923 had a magnitude about 8 times greater than that of the 1999 quake.

Fitting Models to Data

EXAMPLE 7   Fitting a Logarithmic Model

The data in the table gives the yield y (in milligrams) of a chemical reaction after x minutes.

x	1	2	3	4	5	6	7	8
y	1.5	7.4	10.2	13.4	15.8	16.3	18.2	18.3

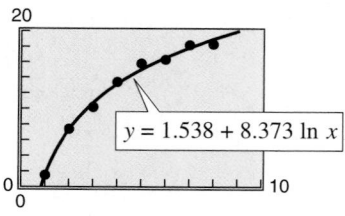

Figure 4.43

Use a graphing utility to fit a logarithmic model to the data.

Solution
Enter the data in the table into a graphing utility. Use the regression capabilities of the graphing utility to find the following logarithmic model.

$$y = 1.538 + 8.373 \ln x$$

When you graph the data and the model in the same viewing window, as shown in Figure 4.43, you can see that the model is a good fit to the data.

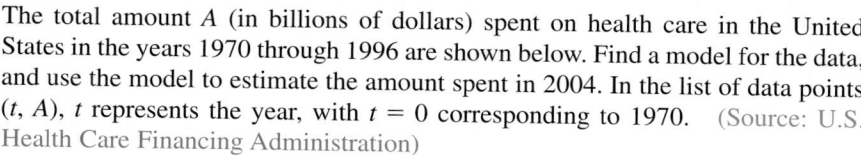

EXAMPLE 8 Fitting an Exponential Model

The total amount A (in billions of dollars) spent on health care in the United States in the years 1970 through 1996 are shown below. Find a model for the data, and use the model to estimate the amount spent in 2004. In the list of data points (t, A), t represents the year, with $t = 0$ corresponding to 1970. (Source: U.S. Health Care Financing Administration)

(0, 74.3), (1, 82.2), (2, 92.3), (3, 102.4), (4, 115.9), (5, 132.6),
(6, 151.9), (7, 172.6), (8, 193.2), (9, 218.3), (10, 247.3), (11, 291.4),
(12, 328.2), (13, 360.8), (14, 396.0), (15, 428.7), (16, 466.0), (17, 506.2),
(18, 562.3), (19, 623.9), (20, 699.5), (21, 766.8), (22, 836.6), (23, 895.1),
(24, 945.7), (25, 991.4), (26, 1035.1)

Solution

Enter the data into a graphing utility. Then graph the data, as shown in Figure 4.44. From the scatter plot, it appears that an exponential model is a good fit. Use the regression capabilities of the graphing utility to find the following exponential model.

$$A = 81.10(1.11)^t \quad \text{or} \quad A = 81.10e^{0.1044t}$$

From the model, you can see that the amount spent on health care from 1970 through 1996 had an average annual increase of 10%. From this model, you can estimate the 2004 amount to be

$$A = 81.10(1.11)^{34} \approx 2818.4 \text{ billion dollars}$$

which is more than twice the amount spent in 1996.

STUDY T!P

You can change an exponential model of the form $y = ab^x$ to one of the form $y = ae^{cx}$ by rewriting b in the form

$$b = e^{\ln b}.$$

For instance, $y = 3(2^x)$ can be written as

$$y = 3(2^x)$$
$$= 3e^{(\ln 2)x}$$
$$\approx 3e^{0.693x}.$$

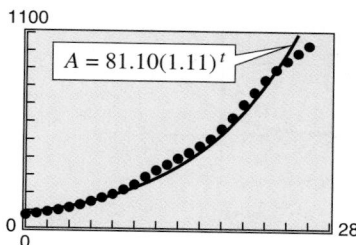

1100

$A = 81.10(1.11)^t$

0

0   28

Figure 4.44

Writing About Math *Fitting a Model to Data*

The numbers y (in millions) of vinyl single records sold in the United States in the years 1984 through 1997 are listed below. The data is given as ordered pairs of the form (t, y), where t is the year, with $t = 4$ representing 1984. Create a scatter plot of the data. Decide which type of model best fits this data. Then find the model. Write a paragraph explaining why you think the model you chose is a good fit to the data.

(4, 131.5), (5, 120.7), (6, 93.9), (7, 82.0),
(8, 65.6), (9, 36.6), (10, 27.6), (11, 22.0),
(12, 19.8), (13, 15.1), (14, 11.7), (15, 10.2),
(16, 10.1), (17, 7.5)

Alternate Writing About Math
Use your school's library or some other reference source to find an application that fits one of the five models discussed in this section. After you have collected data for the model, plot the corresponding points and find an equation that describes the points you have plotted. Write a summary of your findings.

4.5 Exercises

In Exercises 1–6, match the function with its graph.
[The graphs are labeled (a), (b), (c), (d), (e), and (f).]

(a)
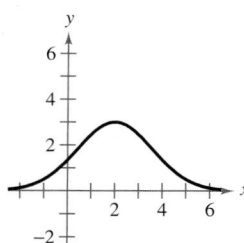

(b)
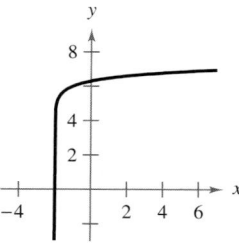

(c)
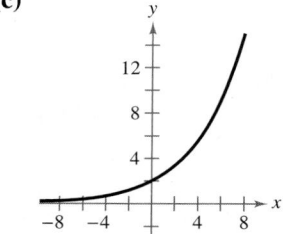

(d)
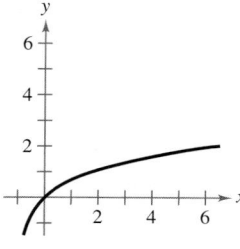

(e)
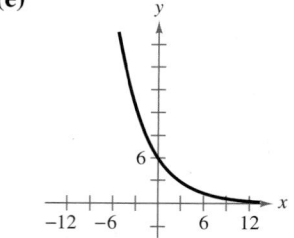

(f)
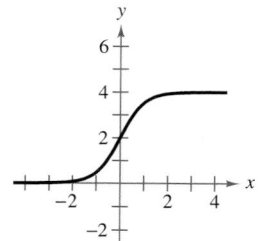

1. $y = 2e^{x/4}$ **2.** $y = 6e^{-x/4}$

3. $y = 6 + \log_{10}(x + 2)$ **4.** $y = 3e^{-(x-2)^2/5}$

5. $y = \ln(x + 1)$ **6.** $y = \dfrac{4}{1 + e^{-2x}}$

In Exercises 7–14, determine whether the scatter plot
could best be modeled by a linear model, a quadratic
model, an exponential model, a logarithmic model, a
Gaussian model, or a logistic model.

7.
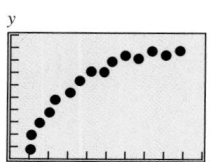

8.
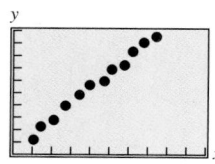

9.
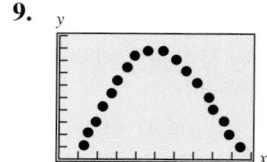

10.
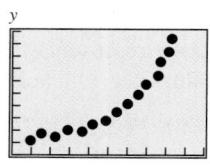

11.
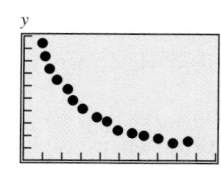

12.
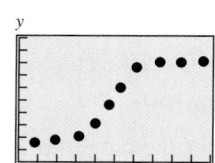

13.
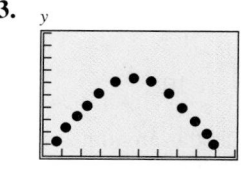

14.
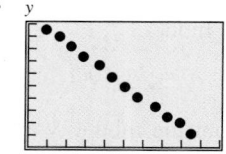

In Exercises 15–18, sketch a scatter plot of the data.
Decide whether the data could best be modeled by a
linear, an exponential, or a logarithmic model.

15. $(1, 2.0)$, $(1.5, 3.5)$, $(2, 4.0)$, $(4, 5.8)$, $(6, 7.0)$, $(8, 7.8)$

16. $(1, 11.0)$, $(1.5, 9.6)$, $(2, 8.2)$, $(4, 4.5)$, $(6, 2.5)$, $(8, 1.4)$

17. $(1, 7.5)$, $(1.5, 7.0)$, $(2, 6.8)$, $(4, 5.0)$, $(6, 3.5)$, $(8, 2.0)$

18. $(1, 5.0)$, $(1.5, 6.0)$, $(2, 6.4)$, $(4, 7.8)$, $(6, 8.6)$, $(8, 9.0)$

Compound Interest In Exercises 19–26, complete the
table for a savings account in which interest is
compounded continuously.

Initial Investment	Annual % Rate	Time to Double	Amount After 10 Years
19. $1000	12%		
20. $20,000	$10\frac{1}{2}$%		
21. $750		$7\frac{3}{4}$ yr	
22. $10,000		12 yr	
23. $500			$1292.85
24. $600			$1505.00
25.	4.5%		$10,000.00
26.	8%		$20,000.00

27. Compound Interest (a) Complete the table for the time t necessary for P dollars to triple if interest is compounded continuously at rate r.

r	2%	4%	6%	8%	10%	12%
t						

(b) Draw a scatter plot of the data in part (a). Use the regression capabilities of a graphing utility to find a model for the data.

28. Compound Interest (a) Complete the table for the time t necessary for P dollars to triple if interest is compounded annually at rate r.

r	2%	4%	6%	8%	10%	12%
t						

(b) Draw a scatter plot of the data in part (a). Use the regression capabilities of a graphing utility to find a model for the data.

29. Comparing Investments If $1 is invested in an account over a 10-year period, the amount in the account, where t represents the time in years, is

$$A = 1 + 0.075[\![t]\!] \quad \text{or} \quad A = e^{0.07t}$$

depending on whether the account pays simple interest at $7\frac{1}{2}\%$ or continuous compound interest at 7%. Use a graphing utility to graph each function in the same viewing window. Which grows at a faster rate?

30. Comparing Investments If $1 is invested in an account over a 10-year period, the amount in the account, where t represents the time in years, is

$$A = 1 + 0.06[\![t]\!] \quad \text{or} \quad A = \left(1 + \frac{0.055}{365}\right)^{[\![365t]\!]}$$

depending on whether the account pays simple interest at 6% or compound interest at $5\frac{1}{2}\%$ compounded daily. Use a graphing utility to graph each function in the same viewing window. Which grows at a faster rate?

In Exercises 31–34, complete the table for the given radioactive isotope.

Isotope	Half-Life (years)	Initial Quantity	Amount After 1000 Years
31. ^{226}Ra	1620	10 g	
32. ^{226}Ra	1620		1.5 g
33. ^{14}C	5730	3 g	
34. ^{230}Pu	24,360		0.4 g

35. Population The population P of a city is

$$P = 105,300e^{0.015t}$$

where $t = 0$ represents 2000. According to this model, when will the population reach 150,000?

36. Population The population P of a city is

$$P = 240,360e^{0.012t}$$

where $t = 0$ represents 2000. According to this model, when will the population reach 275,000?

37. Population The population P of a city is

$$P = 2500e^{kt}$$

where $t = 0$ represents 2000. In 1945, the population was 1350. Find the value of k, and use this value to estimate the population in the year 2010.

38. Population The table shows the population (in millions) of a country in 1997 and the projected population (in millions) for the year 2020. (Source: U.S. Bureau of the Census)

Country	1997	2020
Croatia	5.0	4.8
Mali	9.9	20.4
Singapore	3.5	4.3
Sweden	8.9	9.5

(a) Find the exponential growth model $y = ae^{bt}$ for the population in each country by letting $t = 0$ correspond to 1997. Use the model to estimate the population of each country in 2030.

(b) You can see that the populations of Mali and Sweden are growing at different rates. What constant in the equation $y = ae^{bt}$ is determined by these different growth rates? Discuss the relationship between the different growth rates and the magnitude of the constant.

(c) You can see that the population of Singapore is increasing while the population of Croatia is decreasing. What constant in the equation $y = ae^{bt}$ reflects this difference? Explain.

39. Bacteria Growth The number of bacteria N in a culture is given by the model

$$N = 100e^{kt}$$

where t is the time (in hours). If $N = 300$ when $t = 5$, estimate the time required for the population to double in size. Verify your estimate graphically.

40. Bacteria Growth The number of bacteria N in a culture is given by the model

$$N = 250e^{kt}$$

where t is the time (in hours). If $N = 280$ when $t = 10$, estimate the time required for the population to double in size. Verify your estimate graphically.

41. Radioactive Decay The half-life of radioactive radium (radium 226) is 1620 years. What percent of a present amount of radioactive radium will remain after 100 years?

42. Radioactive Decay Carbon 14 dating assumes that the carbon dioxide on earth today has the same radioactive content as it did centuries ago. If this is true, the amount of carbon 14 absorbed by a tree that grew several centuries ago should be the same as the amount of carbon 14 absorbed by a tree growing today. A piece of ancient charcoal contains only 15% as much radioactive carbon as a piece of modern charcoal. How long ago was the tree burned to make the ancient charcoal if the half-life of carbon 14 is 5730 years?

43. Depreciation A car that cost $22,000 new has a book value of $13,000 after 2 years.

(a) Find the linear model $V = mt + b$.

(b) Find the exponential model $V = ae^{kt}$.

(c) Use a graphing utility to graph the two models in the same viewing window. Which model depreciates faster in the first 2 years?

(d) Use each model to find the book values of the car after 1 year and after 3 years.

(e) Interpret the slope of the linear model.

44. Depreciation A computer that cost $4600 new has a book value of $3000 after 2 years.

(a) Find the linear model $V = mt + b$.

(b) Find the exponential model $V = ae^{kt}$.

(c) Use a graphing utility to graph the two models in the same viewing window. Which model depreciates faster in the first year?

(d) Use each model to find the book values of the computer after 1 year and after 3 years.

(e) Interpret the slope of the linear model.

45. Sales The sales S (in thousands of units) of a new product after it has been on the market t years are

$$S(t) = 100(1 - e^{kt}).$$

Fifteen thousand units of the new product were sold the first year.

(a) Complete the model by solving for k.

(b) Use a graphing utility to graph the model.

(c) Use the graph to estimate the number of units sold after 5 years.

46. Sales and Advertising The sales S (in thousands of units) of a product after x hundred dollars is spent on advertising is

$$S = 10(1 - e^{kx}).$$

When $500 is spent on advertising, 2500 units are sold.

(a) Complete the model by solving for k.

(b) Estimate the number of units that will be sold if advertising expenditures are raised to $700.

47. Learning Curve The management at a factory has found that the maximum number of units a worker can produce in a day is 30. The learning curve for the number of units N produced per day after a new employee has worked t days is

$$N = 30(1 - e^{kt}).$$

After 20 days on the job, a new employee produces 19 units.

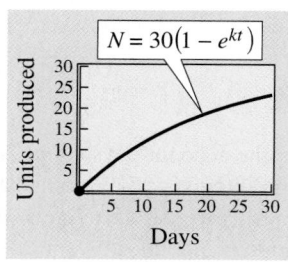

(a) Find the learning curve for this employee (first find the value of k).

(b) How many days should pass before this employee is producing 25 units per day?

(c) Is the employee's production increasing at a linear rate? Explain your reasoning.

48. *Endangered Species* A conservation organization releases 100 animals of an endangered species into a game preserve. The organization believes that the preserve has a carrying capacity of 1000 animals and that the growth of the herd will follow the logistic curve

$$p(t) = \frac{1000}{1 + 9e^{-0.1656t}}$$

where t is measured in months.

(a) Use a graphing utility to graph the function. Use the graph to determine the horizontal asymptotes and interpret the meaning of the larger asymptote in the context of the problem.

(b) Estimate the population after 5 months.

(c) When will the population reach 500?

Earthquake Magnitudes **In Exercises 49 and 50, use the Richter scale (see page 346) for measuring the magnitudes of earthquakes.**

49. Find the magnitude R of an earthquake of intensity I (let $I_0 = 1$).

(a) Taiwan in 1999, $I = 39,811,000$

(b) Hector Mine, California, in 1999, $I = 12,589,000$

50. Find the intensity I of an earthquake measuring R on the Richter scale (let $I_0 = 1$).

(a) Chile in 1906, $R = 8.6$

(b) Los Angeles in 1971, $R = 6.7$

Intensity of Sound **In Exercises 51–54, use the following information. For Exercises 51 and 52, determine the level of sound (in decibels) for the given sound intensity.**

  The level of sound β (in decibels) with an intensity I is $\beta(I) = 10 \log_{10}(I/I_0)$, where I_0 is an intensity of 10^{-12} watt per square meter, corresponding roughly to the faintest sound that can be heard by the human ear.

51. (a) $I = 10^{-10}$ watt per m^2 (faint whisper)

(b) $I = 10^{-5}$ watt per m^2 (busy street corner)

(c) $I = 10^0$ watt per m^2 (threshold of pain)

52. (a) $I = 10^{-3.5}$ watt per m^2 (jet 4 miles from takeoff)

(b) $I = 10^{-3}$ watt per m^2 (diesel truck at 25 feet)

(c) $I = 10^{-1.5}$ watt per m^2 (auto horn at 3 feet)

53. *Noise Level* As a result of the installation of noise suppression materials, the noise level in an audito-

rium was reduced from 93 to 80 decibels. Find the percent decrease in the intensity level of the noise due to the installation of these materials.

54. *Noise Level* As a result of the installation of a muffler, the level of noise emitted by an engine was reduced from 88 to 72 decibels. Find the percent decrease in the intensity level of the noise due to the installation of the muffler.

Acidity **In Exercises 55–58, use the acidity model given by pH $= -\log_{10}[H^+]$, where acidity (pH) is a measure of the hydrogen ion concentration $[H^+]$ (measured in moles of hydrogen per liter) of a solution.**

55. Find the pH if $[H^+] = 2.3 \times 10^{-5}$.

56. Compute $[H^+]$ for a solution in which pH $= 5.8$.

57. A certain fruit has a pH of 2.5, and an antacid tablet has a pH of 9.5. The hydrogen ion concentration of the fruit is how many times that of the tablet?

58. If the pH of a solution is decreased by one unit, the hydrogen ion concentration is increased by what factor?

59. *Finance* A $120,000 home mortgage for 30 years at $7\frac{1}{2}\%$ has a monthly payment of $839.06. Part of the monthly payment goes for the interest charge on the unpaid balance, and the remainder of the payment is used to reduce the principal. The amount that goes for interest is

$$u = M - \left(M - \frac{Pr}{12}\right)\left(1 + \frac{r}{12}\right)^{12t}$$

and the amount that goes toward reduction of the principal is

$$v = \left(M - \frac{Pr}{12}\right)\left(1 + \frac{r}{12}\right)^{12t}.$$

In these formulas, P is the size of the mortgage, r is the interest rate, M is the monthly payment, and t is the time (in years).

(a) Use a graphing utility to graph each function in the same viewing window. (The viewing window should show all 30 years of mortgage payments.)

(b) In the early years of the mortgage, the larger part of the monthly payment goes for what purpose? Approximate the time when the monthly payment is evenly divided between interest and principal reduction.

(c) Repeat (a) and (b) for a repayment period of 20 years ($M = \$966.71$). What can you conclude?

60. Finance   The total interest u paid on a home mortgage of P dollars at interest rate r for t years is

$$u = P\left[\frac{rt}{1 - \left(\dfrac{1}{1 + r/12}\right)^{12t}} - 1\right].$$

Consider a \$120,000 home mortgage at $7\frac{1}{2}\%$.

(a) Use a graphing utility to graph the total interest function.

(b) Approximate the length of the mortgage when the total interest paid is the same as the size of the mortgage. Is it possible that a person could pay twice as much in interest charges as the size of one's mortgage?

In Exercises 61–64, find the exponential model $y = ae^{bx}$ **that fits the points given in the graph or table.**

61.

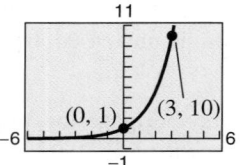

62.

x	y
0	4
5	1

63.

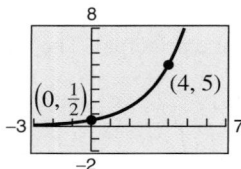

64.

x	y
0	1
3	$\frac{1}{4}$

65. Data Analysis   The time t (in seconds) required to attain a speed of s miles per hour from a standing start for a particular car is given in the table. (Source: *Road & Track*, March 1995)

s	30	40	50	60	70	80	90
t	3.4	5.0	7.0	9.3	12.0	15.8	20.0

Two models for this data are as follows.

$$t_1 = 40.757 + 0.556s - 15.817 \ln s$$

$$t_2 = 1.2259 + 0.0023s^2$$

(a) Use a graphing utility to fit a linear model t_3 and an exponential model t_4 to the data.

(b) Use a graphing utility to graph the data points and each model.

(c) Create a table to compare the data with estimates obtained from each model.

(d) Use the results of part (c) to find the sum of the absolute values of the differences between the data and the estimated values given by each model. Based on the four sums, which model do you think best fits the data? Explain.

66. Comparing Models   Suppose that in 1995 a car had a retail price of \$21,800. A local dealership used the following guide for the approximate value of the car for the years 1995 through 2000.

Year	1995	1996	1997
Value	\$21,800	\$19,530	\$19,210

Year	1998	1999	2000
Value	\$17,945	\$17,120	\$16,080

Let V represent the value of the automobile in the year t, with $t = 0$ corresponding to 1995.

(a) Use the regression capabilities of a graphing utility to find linear and quadratic models for the data. Use the graphing utility to plot the data and graph the models in the same viewing window.

(b) What does the slope represent in the linear model in part (a)?

(c) Do you think the quadratic model is realistic? Explain.

(d) Use the regression capabilities of a graphing utility to fit an exponential model to the data. Use the graphing utility to plot the data and graph the model in the same viewing window. How well does the model fit the data?

(e) Fit a rational model to the data. Take the reciprocal of the depreciated values of the automobile to generate the points $(t, 1/V)$. Use the regression capabilities of a graphing utility to fit a line to this data. The resulting line has the form

$$\frac{1}{V} = at + b.$$

Solve for V and use the graphing utility to graph the rational function and the original data points in the same viewing window. How well does the model fit the data?

(f) Determine the horizontal asymptotes of the exponential and rational models. Interpret their meanings in the context of the problem.

67. Forensics At 8:30 A.M., a coroner was called to the home of a person who had died during the night. In order to estimate the time of death, the coroner took the person's temperature twice. At 9:00 A.M. the temperature was 85.7°F, and at 9:30 A.M. the temperature was 82.8°F. From these two temperatures the coroner was able to determine that the time elapsed since death and the body temperature were related by the formula

$$t = -2.5 \ln \frac{T - 70}{98.6 - 70}$$

where t is the time (in hours elapsed since the person died) and T is the temperature (in degrees Fahrenheit) of the person's body. Assume the person had a normal body temperature of 98.6°F at death, and the room temperature was a constant 70°F. (This formula is derived from a general cooling principle called Newton's Law of Cooling.) Use the formula to estimate the time of death of the person.

68. Foreign Travel The numbers of United States citizens y (in millions) who traveled to foreign countries in the years 1988 through 1996 are shown in the table, where $t = 8$ represents the year 1988. (Source: U.S. Travel and Tourism Administration, U.S. Department of Commerce)

t	8	9	10	11	12
y	40.7	41.1	44.6	41.6	43.9

t	13	14	15	16
y	44.4	46.5	50.8	52.3

(a) Use the regression capabilities of a graphing utility to find a model that best fits the data.

(b) Use the graphing utility to plot the data and graph the model in the same viewing window.

(c) Use the model to estimate the number of foreign travelers in the year 2005.

69. World Population The world population y (in billions) for the years 1987 through 1998 is shown in the table, where $x = 7$ corresponds to 1987. (Source: U.S. Bureau of the Census)

x	7	8	9	10	11	12
y	5.02	5.11	5.19	5.28	5.37	5.45

x	13	14	15	16	17	18
y	5.53	5.61	5.69	5.77	5.85	5.93

(a) Use the regression capabilities of a graphing utility to fit a linear model to the data.

(b) Use the regression capabilities of a graphing utility to fit an exponential model to the data.

(c) Population growth is often exponential. For the 12 years of data in the table, is the exponential model better than the linear model? Explain.

(d) Use each model to estimate the population in the year 2005.

70. Atmospheric Pressure The atmospheric pressure decreases with increasing altitude. At sea level, the average air pressure is 1.033227 kilograms per square centimeter, and this pressure is called one atmosphere. Variations in weather conditions cause changes in the atmospheric pressure of up to ±5 percent. The table shows the pressures p (in atmospheres) at given altitudes h (in kilometers).

h	0	5	10	15	20	25
p	1	0.55	0.25	0.12	0.06	0.02

(a) Use a graphing utility to attempt to find the logarithmic model $p = a + b \ln h$ for the data. Explain why the result is an error message.

(b) Use a graphing utility to find the logarithmic model $h = a + b \ln p$ for the data.

(c) Use a graphing utility to plot the data and graph the logarithmic model.

(d) Use the model to estimate the altitude at which the pressure is 0.75 atmosphere.

(e) Use the graph to estimate the pressure at an altitude of 13 kilometers.

71. National Health Expenditures The table shows the national health expenditures y (in billions of dollars) for the years 1987 through 1996. The years are represented by x, where $x = 7$ corresponds to 1987. (Source: U.S. Health Care Financing Administration)

x	7	8	9	10	11
y	500.1	559.6	622.0	699.5	766.8

x	12	13	14	15	16
y	836.6	895.1	945.7	991.4	1035.1

(a) Use a graphing utility to find an exponential model for the data. Use the graphing utility to plot the data and graph the exponential model in the same viewing window.

(b) Use a graphing utility to find a logarithmic model for the data. Use the graphing utility to plot the data and graph the logarithmic model in the same viewing window.

(c) Use the graphs plotted in parts (a) and (b) to determine which model is better. If the rate of growth of health care costs could be slowed, which model may be better for the future? Explain.

72. Comparing Models The amounts y (in billions of dollars) donated to charity (by individuals, foundations, corporations, and charitable bequests) in the years 1987 through 1996 in the United States are shown in the table, where $x = 7$ corresponds to 1987. (Source: AAFRC Trust for Philanthropy)

x	7	8	9	10	11
y	90.0	98.1	106.7	111.5	117.2

x	12	13	14	15	16
y	121.1	126.5	129.3	140.5	150.7

(a) Use the regression capabilities of a graphing utility to find the following models for the data.

$y_1 = ax + b$

$y_2 = a + b \ln x$

$y_3 = ab^x$

(b) Use the graphing utility to graph the data and each of the models. Use the graphs to select the model that you think best fits the data.

(c) For each of the models y_i ($i = 1, 2,$ and 3), complete the table.

x	y	$y - y_i$	$(y - y_i)^2$
7	90.0		
8	98.1		
9	106.7		
10	111.5		
11	117.2		
12	121.1		
13	126.5		
14	129.3		
15	140.5		
16	150.7		

(d) For each model, find the sum of the entries in the last column of the table in part (c). Use the results to select the best model for the data.

(e) Explain what the sums in part (d) represent.

73. Comparing Models A V-8 car engine is coupled to a dynamometer, and the horsepower y is measured at different engine speeds x (in thousands of revolutions per minute). The results are shown in the table.

x	1	2	3	4	5	6
y	40	85	140	200	225	245

(a) Use the regression capabilities of a graphing utility to find the following models for the data.

$y_1 = ax^3 + bx^2 + cx + d$

$y_2 = a + b \ln x$

$y_3 = ab^x$

(b) Use the graphing utility to graph the data and each of the models. Use the graphs to select the model that you think best fits the data.

(c) For each of the models y_i ($i = 1$, 2, and 3), complete the table.

x	y	$y - y_i$	$(y - y_i)^2$
1	40		
2	85		
3	140		
4	200		
5	225		
6	245		

(d) For each model, find the sum of the entries in the last column of the table in part (c). Use the results to select the best model for the data.

(e) Explain what the sums in part (d) represent.

Synthesis

True or False? **In Exercises 74–78, determine whether the statement is true or false. Justify your answer.**

74. The domain of a logistic growth function cannot be the set of real numbers.

75. The graph of a logistic growth function will always have an x-intercept.

76. The graph of a Gaussian model will never have an x-intercept.

77. The graph of a Gaussian model will always have a maximum point.

78. The graph of

$$f(x) = \frac{4}{1 + 6e^{-2x}} + 5$$

is the graph of

$$f(x) = \frac{4}{1 + 6e^{-2x}}$$

shifted to the right five units.

Review

In Exercises 79–84, match the equation with its graph, and identify any intercepts. [The graphs are labeled (a), (b), (c), (d), (e), and (f).]

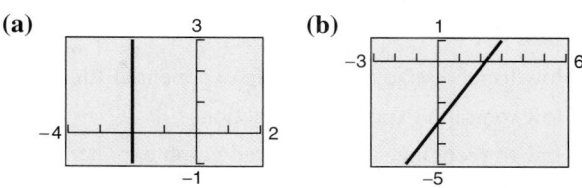

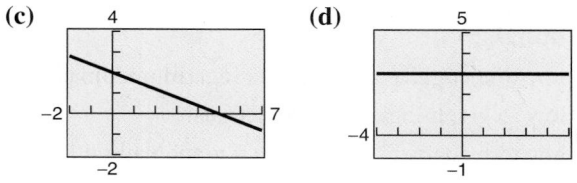

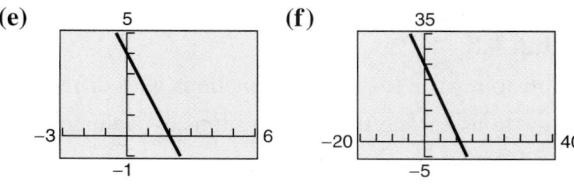

79. $4x - 3y - 9 = 0$

80. $2x + 5y - 10 = 0$

81. $y = 25 - 2.25x$

82. $\frac{x}{2} + \frac{y}{4} = 1$

83. $y - 3 = 0$

84. $x + 2 = 0$

In Exercises 85–88, divide using synthetic division.

85. $\dfrac{4x^3 + 4x^2 - 39x + 36}{x + 4}$

86. $\dfrac{8x^3 - 36x^2 + 54x - 27}{x - \frac{3}{2}}$

87. $(2x^3 - 8x^2 + 3x - 9) \div (x - 4)$

88. $(x^4 - 3x + 1) \div (x + 5)$

In Exercises 89–92, graph the exponential function.

89. $f(x) = 2^{x-1} + 5$

90. $f(x) = -2^{-x-1} - 1$

91. $f(x) = 3^x - 4$

92. $f(x) = -3^x + 4$

4 Chapter Summary

What did you learn?

4 Review Exercises

In Exercises 1–4, use a calculator to evaluate the expression. Round your answer to three decimal places.

1. $(1.45)^{2\pi}$

2. $\sqrt[5]{6240}$

3. $1.59^{-2\sqrt{3}}$

4. $136(5^{-1.1})$

In Exercises 5–10, match the function with its graph. [The graphs are labeled (a), (b), (c), (d), (e), and (f).]

(a)

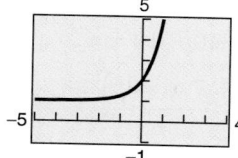

(b)

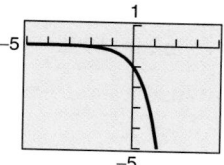

(c)

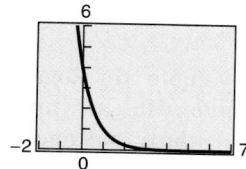

(d)

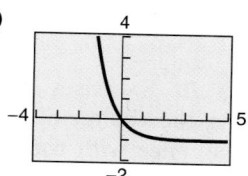

(e)

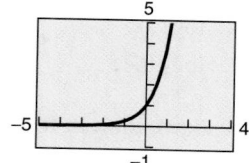

(f)

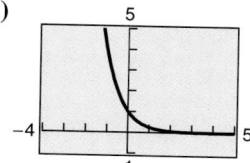

5. $f(x) = 4^x$

6. $f(x) = 4^{-x}$

7. $f(x) = -4^x$

8. $f(x) = 4^x + 1$

9. $f(x) = 4^{-x} - 1$

10. $f(x) = 4^{-x+1}$

In Exercises 11–20, sketch the graph of the function. Use a graphing utility to verify your graph.

11. $f(x) = 6^x$

12. $f(x) = 0.3^x$

13. $g(x) = 6^{-x}$

14. $g(x) = 0.3^{-x}$

15. $h(x) = e^{-x/2}$

16. $f(x) = e^{x+2}$

17. $h(x) = 2 - e^{-x/2}$

18. $f(x) = 3 - e^{-x-2}$

19. $s(t) = 4e^{-2/t}$, $t > 0$

20. $f(x) = 6e^{-3/x}$, $x > 0$

In Exercises 21–26, use a graphing utility to graph the function. Identify any asymptotes.

21. $g(t) = 8 - 0.5e^{-t/4}$

22. $h(x) = 12(1 + e^{-x/2})$

23. $g(x) = 200e^{4/x}$

24. $f(x) = -8e^{-4/x}$

25. $f(x) = \dfrac{10}{1 + 2^{-0.05x}}$

26. $f(x) = -\dfrac{12}{1 + 4^{-x}}$

In Exercises 27–30, use a calculator to evaluate the expression. Round your result to three decimal places.

27. $e^{-8/3}$

28. $e^{\sqrt{5}}$

29. $6e^{4.12}$

30. $-\frac{5}{3}e^{-3/5}$

In Exercises 31 and 32, complete the table to determine the amount of money P that should be invested at rate r to produce a final balance of \$200,000 in t years.

t	1	10	20	30	40	50
P						

31. $r = 8\%$, compounded continuously

32. $r = 10\%$, compounded monthly

33. **Depreciation**   After t years, the value of a car that originally cost \$26,000 is

$$V(t) = 26{,}000\left(\frac{3}{4}\right)^t.$$

(a) Use a graphing utility to graph the function.

(b) Find the value of the car 2 years after it was purchased.

(c) According to the model, when does the car depreciate most rapidly? Is this realistic? Explain.

34. **Fuel Efficiency**   A certain automobile gets 28 miles per gallon of gasoline for speeds up to 50 miles per hour. Over 50 miles per hour, the number of miles per gallon drops at the rate of 12% for each additional 10 miles per hour. If s is the speed and y is the number of miles per gallon, then

$$y = 28e^{0.6 - 0.012s}, \quad s \geq 50.$$

Use the model to complete the table.

s	50	55	60	65	70
y	28				

4.2 **In Exercises 35–38, write the exponential equation in logarithmic form.**

35. $4^3 = 64$

36. $3^5 = 243$

37. $25^{3/2} = 125$

38. $12^{-1} = \frac{1}{12}$

In Exercises 39–44, evaluate the expression without using a graphing utility.

39. $\log_8 8^{-0.34}$

40. $\log_7 1$

41. $\log_6 216$

42. $\log_4 1024$

43. $\log_{36} \frac{1}{6}$

44. $\log_{10} 0.001$

In Exercises 45–52, sketch the graph of the function. Use a graphing utility to verify your graph.

45. $g(x) = -\log_2 x + 5$

46. $g(x) = \log_5(x - 3)$

47. $f(x) = \log_2(x - 1) + 6$

48. $f(x) = \log_5(x + 2) - 3$

49. $f(x) = \ln x + 3$

50. $f(x) = \ln(x - 3)$

51. $h(x) = \frac{1}{2} \ln x$

52. $f(x) = \frac{1}{4} \ln x$

In Exercises 53–56, use a graphing utility to graph the function and determine its domain.

53. $y = \log_{10}(x^2 + 1)$

54. $y = -2 \log_{10}(4 - x^2)$

55. $y = \sqrt{x} \ln(x + 1)$

56. $y = \dfrac{14 \ln x}{x}$

In Exercises 57–60, evaluate the expression without using a graphing utility.

57. $\ln e^7$

58. $\ln 1$

59. $6 \ln e^{-3}$

60. $-\frac{3}{2} \ln e^{-10/11}$

61. *Climb Rate* The time t (in minutes) for a small plane to climb to an altitude of h feet is

$$t = 50 \log_{10} \frac{18,000}{18,000 - h}$$

where 18,000 feet is the plane's absolute ceiling.

(a) Determine the domain of the function appropriate for the context of the problem.

(b) Use a graphing utility to graph the time function and identify any asymptotes.

(c) As the plane approaches its absolute ceiling, what can be said about the time required to further increase its altitude?

(d) Find the time for the plane to climb to an altitude of 4000 feet.

62. *Earthquake Magnitudes* The magnitude M of an earthquake measured on the Richter scale can be found using the model

$$M = \frac{2}{3}(\log_{10} E - 11.4)$$

where E is the energy of the earthquake (in ergs). Use a graphing utility and the table shown below to find the ratio of the magnitudes of the earthquakes.

Earthquake	E (ergs)
San Francisco, 1906	7.079×10^{23}
Japan, 1933	5.623×10^{24}
Armenia, 1988	3.981×10^{21}
Russia, 1995	6.310×10^{22}
Indonesia, 1996	4.467×10^{22}

(a) Japan and San Francisco

(b) Russia and Indonesia

(c) Indonesia and Armenia

4.3 **In Exercises 63–66, evaluate the logarithm using the change-of-base formula. Do each problem twice, once with common logarithms and once with natural logarithms. Round the result to three decimal places.**

63. $\log_4 9$

64. $\log_{1/2} 5$

65. $\log_{12} 200$

66. $\log_3 0.28$

In Exercises 67–70, rewrite the expression in terms of ln 4 and ln 5.

67. $\ln 20$

68. $\ln 45 - 2 \ln 3$

69. $\ln \frac{5}{64}$

70. $\ln \frac{2}{5}$

In Exercises 71–74, approximate the logarithm using the properties of logarithms, given that $\log_b 2 \approx 0.3562$, $\log_b 3 \approx 0.5646$, and $\log_b 5 \approx 0.8271$.

71. $\log_b 25$

72. $\log_b\left(\frac{25}{9}\right)$

73. $\log_b \sqrt{3}$

74. $\log_b 30$

In Exercises 75–80, rewrite the expression as a sum, difference, and/or multiple of logarithms.

75. $\log_5 5x^2$

76. $\log_7 \dfrac{\sqrt{x}}{4}$

77. $\log_{10} \dfrac{5\sqrt{y}}{x^2}$

78. $\ln \left|\dfrac{x - 1}{x + 1}\right|$

79. $\ln[(x^2 + 1)(x - 1)]$

80. $\ln \sqrt[5]{\dfrac{4x^2 - 1}{4x^2 + 1}}$

In Exercises 81–86, write the expression as the logarithm of a single quantity.

81. $\log_2 5 + \log_2 x$

82. $\log_6 y - 2\log_6 z$

83. $\frac{1}{2}\ln|2x - 1| - 2\ln|x + 1|$

84. $5\ln|x - 2| - \ln|x + 2| - 3\ln|x|$

85. $\ln 3 + \frac{1}{3}\ln(4 - x^2) - \ln x$

86. $3[\ln x - 2\ln(x^2 + 1)] + 2\ln 5$

87. *Snow Removal* The number of miles s of roads cleared of snow is approximated by the model

$$s = 25 - \dfrac{13\ln(h/12)}{\ln 3}, \quad 2 \le h \le 15$$

where h is the depth of the snow (in inches).

(a) Use a graphing utility to graph the function.

(b) Complete the table.

h	4	6	8	10	12	14
s						

(c) Using the graph of the function and the table, what conclusion can you make as the depth of the snow increases?

88. *Human Memory Model* Students in a sociology class were given an exam and then were retested monthly with an equivalent exam. The average score for the class was given by the human memory model, $f(t) = 85 - 14\log_{10}(t + 1), \quad 0 \le t \le 4$, where t is the time in months. How did the average score change over the 4-month period?

4.4 **In Exercises 89–94, solve for x.**

89. $8^x = 512$

90. $3^x = 729$

91. $6^x = \frac{1}{216}$

92. $6^{x-2} = 1296$

93. $\log_7 x = 4$

94. $\log_x 243 = 5$

In Exercises 95–104, solve the exponential equation. Round the result to three decimal places.

95. $e^x = 12$

96. $e^{3x} = 25$

97. $3e^{-5x} = 132$

98. $14e^{3x+2} = 560$

99. $e^x + 13 = 35$

100. $e^x - 28 = -8$

101. $-4(5^x) = -68$

102. $2(12^x) = 190$

103. $e^{2x} - 7e^x + 10 = 0$

104. $e^{2x} - 6e^x + 8 = 0$

In Exercises 105–116, solve the logarithmic equation. Round the result to three decimal places.

105. $\ln 3x = 8.2$

106. $\ln 5x = 7.2$

107. $2\ln 4x = 15$

108. $4\ln 3x = 15$

109. $\ln x - \ln 3 = 2$

110. $\ln\sqrt{x + 8} = 3$

111. $\ln\sqrt{x + 1} = 2$

112. $\ln x - \ln 5 = 4$

113. $\log_{10}(x - 1) = \log_{10}(x - 2) - \log_{10}(x + 2)$

114. $\log_{10}(x + 2) - \log_{10} x = \log_{10}(x + 5)$

115. $\log_{10}(1 - x) = -1$

116. $\log_{10}(-x - 4) = 2$

117. *Finance* You deposit $7550 into an account that pays 7.25% interest, compounded continuously. How long will it take the money to triple?

118. *Economics* The demand equation for a certain product is modeled by $p = 500 - 0.5e^{0.004x}$. Find the demand x that corresponds to a price of (a) $p = \$450$ and (b) $p = \$400$.

4.5 **In Exercises 119–124, match the function on page 360 with its graph. [The graphs are labeled (a), (b), (c), (d), (e), and (f).]**

(a)

(b)

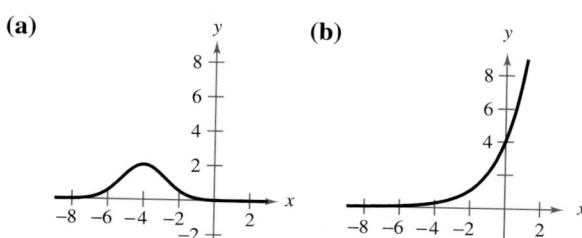

(c)

(d)

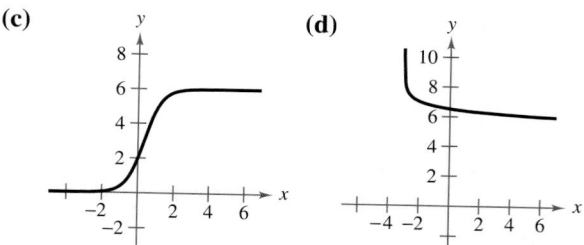

(e)

(f)

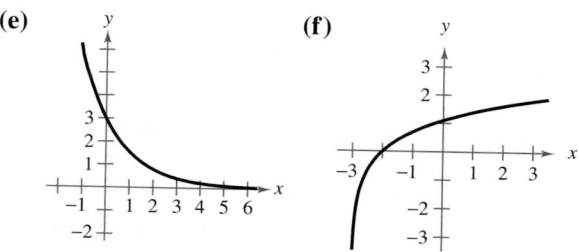

119. $y = 3e^{-2x/3}$

120. $y = 4e^{2x/3}$

121. $y = \ln(x + 3)$

122. $y = 7 - \log_{10}(x + 3)$

123. $y = 2e^{-(x+4)^2/3}$

124. $y = \dfrac{6}{1 + 2e^{-2x}}$

125. Population   The population of a town is modeled by

$$P = 12,620e^{0.0118t}$$

where $t = 0$ represents 2000. According to this model, when will the population reach 17,000?

126. Radioactive Decay   The half-life of radioactive uranium II (^{234}U) is 250,000 years. What percent of the present amount of radioactive uranium II will remain after 5000 years?

127. Compound Interest   A deposit of $10,000 is made in a savings account for which the interest is compounded continuously. The balance will double in 12 years.

(a) What is the annual interest rate for this account?

(b) Find the balance after 1 year.

(c) The *effective yield* of a savings plan is the percent increase in the balance after 1 year. Find the effective yield.

128. Test Scores   The test scores for a biology test follow a normal distribution modeled by

$$y = 0.0499e^{-(x-71)^2/128}.$$

(a) Use a graphing utility to graph the equation.

(b) From the graph, estimate the average test score.

129. Typing Speed   In a typing class, the average number of words per minute N typed after t weeks of lessons was found to be

$$N = \frac{157}{1 + 5.4e^{-0.12t}}.$$

Find the time necessary to type (a) 50 words per minute and (b) 75 words per minute.

130. Earthquake Magnitude   On the Richter scale, the magnitude R of an earthquake I is

$$R = \log_{10}\frac{I}{I_0}$$

where $I_0 = 1$ is the minimum intensity used for comparison. Find the intensity per unit of area for the following values of R.

(a) $R = 8.4$ (b) $R = 6.85$ (c) $R = 9.1$

In Exercises 131–134, find the exponential function $y = Ae^{bx}$ that passes through the two points.

131. $(0, 2), (4, 3)$

132. $(0, 2), (5, 1)$

133. $\left(0, \frac{1}{2}\right), (5, 5)$

134. $(0, 4), \left(5, \frac{1}{2}\right)$

135. Exponential Model   Use a graphing utility to find an exponential model $y = ab^x$ through the points $(0, 250)$, $(4, 135)$, $(6, 92)$, and $(10, 67)$. Graph the data and the exponential model in the same viewing window.

136. Net Profit   The table shows the net profit P (in millions of dollars) of the Bristol-Myers Squibb Company for 1990 through 1998. (Source: Bristol-Myers Squibb Company)

Year	1990	1991	1992	1993	1994
P	1748.0	2056.0	2108.0	2269.0	2330.6

Year	1995	1996	1997	1998
P	2600.0	2850.0	3205.0	3141.0

(a) Make a scatter plot of the data. Let t represent the year, with $t = 0$ corresponding to 1990.

(b) Use a graphing utility to find an exponential model $P = ab^t$ for the data. Let $t = 0$ represent 1990.

Synthesis

True or False? **In Exercises 137–142, determine whether the equation or statement is true or false. Justify your answer.**

137. $\log_b b^{2x} = 2x$

138. $e^{x-1} = \dfrac{e^x}{e}$

139. $\ln(x + y) = \ln x + \ln y$

140. $\ln(x + y) = \ln(xy)$

141. $\log_{10}\left(\dfrac{10}{x}\right) = 1 - \log_{10} x$

142. The domain of the function $f(x) = \ln x$ is the set of all real numbers.

Chapter Project *A Graphical Approach to Compound Interest*

In this project, you will use a graphing utility to compare savings plans. For instance, suppose you are depositing $1000 in a savings account and are given the following options.

- 6.2% annual interest rate, compounded annually
- 6.1% annual interest rate, compounded quarterly
- 6.0% annual interest rate, compounded continuously

a. For each option, write a function that gives the balance as a function of the time t (in years).

b. Graph all three functions in the same viewing window. Can you find a viewing window that distinguishes among the graphs of the three functions? If so, describe the viewing window.

c. Find the balances for the three options after 25, 50, 75, and 100 years. Is the option that yields the greatest balance after 25 years the same option that yields the greatest balances after 50, 75, and 100 years? Explain.

d. The *effective yield* of a savings plan is the percent increase in the balance after 1 year. Find the effective yields for the three options listed above. How can the effective yield be used to decide which option is best?

Questions for Further Exploration

1. You deposit $25,000 in an account to accrue interest for 40 years. The account pays 4% compounded annually. Assume that the income tax on the earned interest is 30%. Which of the following plans produces a larger balance after all income tax is paid?

(a) *Deferred*   The income tax on the interest that is earned is paid in one lump sum at the end of 40 years.

(b) *Not Deferred*   The income tax on the interest that is earned each year is paid at the end of each year.

2. Which of the following would produce a larger balance? Explain.

(a) 4.02% annual interest rate, compounded monthly

(b) 4% annual interest rate, compounded continuously

3. You deposit $1000 in each of two savings accounts. The interest for the accounts is paid according to the two options described in Question 2. How long would it take for the balance in one of the accounts to exceed the balance in the other account by $100? By $100,000?

4. No income tax is due on the interest earned in some types of investments. You deposit $25,000 into an account. Which of the following plans is better? Explain.

(a) *Tax-Free*   The account pays 5%, compounded annually. There is no income tax on the earned interest.

(b) *Tax-Deferred*   The account pays 7%, compounded annually. At maturity, the earned interest is taxable at a rate of 40%.

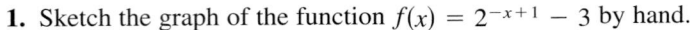

4 Chapter Test

Take this test as you would take a test in class. After you are done, check your work against the answers in the back of the book.

The *Interactive* CD-ROM and *Internet* versions of this text provide answers to the Chapter Tests and Cumulative Tests. They also offer Chapter Pre-Tests (that test key skills and concepts covered in previous chapters) and Chapter Post-Tests, both of which have randomly generated exercises with diagnostic capabilities.

1. Sketch the graph of the function $f(x) = 2^{-x+1} - 3$ by hand.

2. Use a graphing utility to graph f and determine its horizontal asymptotes.

$$f(x) = \frac{1000}{1 + 4e^{-0.2x}}$$

3. Determine the principal that will yield \$200,000 when invested at 8% compounded daily for 20 years.

4. Write the logarithmic equation $\log_4 64 = 3$ in exponential form.

5. Sketch the graph of the function $g(x) = \log_3(x - 2)$ by hand.

6. Use the properties of logarithms to expand $\ln\left(\dfrac{6x^2}{\sqrt{x^2 + 1}}\right)$.

In Exercises 7 and 8, evaluate the expression without using a calculator.

7. $\log_5 25$

8. $-2 \ln e^2 + 1$

In Exercises 9–11, solve the equation. Round to three decimal places.

9. $8 + \frac{1}{4}e^{x/2} = 450$

10. $\left(1 + \dfrac{0.06}{4}\right)^{4t} = 3$

11. $3.6 - 5 \ln(x + 4) = 22$

12. A truck that costs \$28,000 new has a depreciated value of \$20,000 after 1 year. Find the value of the truck when it is 3 years old by using the exponential model $y = ae^{bx}$.

13. The average time between incoming calls at a switchboard is 3 minutes. The probability of waiting less than t minutes for the next incoming call is approximated by the model $F(t) = 1 - e^{-t/3}$. If a call has just come in, find the probability that the next call will come within (a) $\frac{1}{2}$ minute, (b) 2 minutes, and (c) 5 minutes.

14. The population of a certain species t years after it is introduced into a new habitat is $p(t) = \dfrac{1200}{1 + 3e^{-t/5}}$. (a) Determine the initial size of the population. (b) Determine the population after 5 years. (c) After how many years will the population be 800?

15. By observation, identify the equation that corresponds to the graph shown at the right. Explain your reasoning.

    (a) $y = 6e^{-x^2/2}$ (b) $y = \dfrac{6}{1 + e^{-x/2}}$ (c) $y = 6(1 - e^{-x^2/2})$

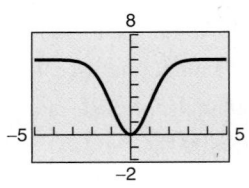

FIGURE FOR 15

16. The numbers of cellular-phone subscribers y (in millions) for the years 1993 through 1997 are (3, 16.0), (4, 24.1), (5, 33.8), (6, 44.0), and (7, 55.3), where x is the time (in years) and $x = 3$ corresponds to 1993. Use a graphing utility to fit an exponential model to the data. Sketch a scatter plot of the data and graph the model in the same viewing window. (Source: Cellular Telecommunications Industry Association)

Systems of Equations and Inequalities

5.1   Solving Systems of Equations

5.2   Systems of Linear Equations in Two Variables

5.3   Multivariable Linear Systems

5.4   Systems of Inequalities

5.5   Linear Programming

Ron Watts/CORBIS

The Big Picture

In this chapter you will learn how to

❑ solve systems of equations by substitution, by elimination, by Gaussian elimination, and graphically.

❑ recognize linear systems in row-echelon form and to use back substitution to solve the system.

❑ solve nonsquare systems of equations.

❑ sketch the graphs of inequalities in two variables and solve systems of inequalities.

❑ solve linear programming problems.

❑ use systems of equations and inequalities to model and solve real-life problems.

In 1996, 57 million newspapers were printed daily in the United States. With a population of over 265 million, there were about 215 newspapers per 1000 people. (Source: U.S. Bureau of the Census and Editor & Publisher, Co.)

Important Vocabulary

As you encounter each new vocabulary term in this chapter, add the term and its definition to your notebook glossary.

- systems of equations (p. 364)
- solution of a system of equations (p. 364)
- method of substitution (p. 364)
- point of intersection (p. 365)
- break-even point (p. 369)
- method of elimination (p. 375)
- equivalent systems (p. 376)
- consistent system (p. 377)
- inconsistent system (p. 377)
- row-echelon form (p. 385)

- ordered triple (p. 385)
- Gaussian elimination (p. 386)
- nonsquare system of equations (p. 389)
- three-dimensional coordinate system (p. 390)
- graph of an equation in three variables (p. 390)
- partial fraction (p. 391)
- partial fraction decomposition (p. 391)
- basic equation (p. 392)

- solution of an inequality (p. 401)
- graph of an inequality (p. 401)
- linear inequalities (p. 402)
- solution of a system of inequalities (p. 403)
- optimization (p. 411)
- linear programming (p. 411)
- objective function (p. 411)
- constraints (p. 411)
- feasible solutions (p. 411)

Additional Resources   Text-specific additional resources are available to help you do well in this course. See page xvi for details.

5.1 Solving Systems of Equations

The Method of Substitution

Up to this point in the text, most problems have involved either a function of one variable or a single equation in two variables. However, many problems in science, business, and engineering involve two or more equations in two or more variables. To solve such problems, you need to find solutions of **systems of equations.** Here is an example of a system of two equations in two unknowns, x and y.

$$\begin{cases} 2x + y = 5 & \text{Equation 1} \\ 3x - 2y = 4 & \text{Equation 2} \end{cases}$$

A **solution** of this system is an ordered pair that satisfies each equation in the system. Finding the set of all such solutions is called **solving the system of equations.** For instance, the ordered pair $(2, 1)$ is a solution of this system. To check this, you can substitute 2 for x and 1 for y in *each* equation.

Check $(2, 1)$ *in Equation 1:*

$$2x + y = 5 \qquad \text{Write Equation 1.}$$
$$2(2) + 1 \overset{?}{=} 5 \qquad \text{Substitute 2 for } x \text{ and 1 for } y.$$
$$4 + 1 = 5 \qquad \text{Solution checks in Equation 1. } \checkmark$$

Check $(2, 1)$ *in Equation 2:*

$$3x - 2y = 4 \qquad \text{Write Equation 2.}$$
$$3(2) - 2(1) \overset{?}{=} 4 \qquad \text{Substitute 2 for } x \text{ and 1 for } y.$$
$$6 - 2 = 4 \qquad \text{Solution checks in Equation 2. } \checkmark$$

In this chapter you will study four ways to solve equations, beginning with the **method of substitution.**

Method	Section	Type of System
1. Substitution	5.1	Linear or nonlinear, 2 variables
2. Graphical	5.1	Linear or nonlinear, 2 variables
3. Elimination	5.2	Linear, 2 variables
4. Gaussian Elimination	5.3	Linear, 3 or more variables

The Method of Substitution

1. Solve one of the equations for one variable in terms of the other.
2. Substitute the expression found in Step 1 into the other equation to obtain an equation in one variable.
3. Solve the equation obtained in Step 2.
4. Back-substitute the solution in Step 3 into the expression obtained in Step 1 to find the value of the other variable.
5. Check that the solution satisfies each of the original equations.

What You Should Learn:

- How to use the method of substitution to solve systems of equations in two variables
- How to solve systems of equations graphically
- How to use systems of equations to model and solve real-life problems

Why You Should Learn It:

You can use systems of equations in situations where the variables must satisfy two or more conditions. For instance, Exercise 73 on page 373 shows how to use a system of equations to compare two models for estimating the number of board feet in a 16-foot log.

Bruce Hands/Tony Stone Images

You may want to compare and contrast solving a problem with a system of two equations versus solving a problem with one equation. Notice that for Example 3 in Section 2.1, the problem can be solved using one equation

$$4w + 2w = 84$$

or it can be solved using a system of two equations

$$\begin{cases} l = 2w \\ 2l + 2w = 84 \end{cases}.$$

In the algebraic solution of Example 1, you use the method of substitution to solve the system of equations. In the graphical solution, note that the solution of the system corresponds to the **point of intersection** of the graphs.

EXAMPLE 1   Solving a System of Equations

Solve the system of equations.

$$\begin{cases} x + y = 4 \quad & \text{Equation 1} \\ x - y = 2 \quad & \text{Equation 2} \end{cases}$$

Algebraic Solution

Begin by solving for y in Equation 1.

$y = 4 - x$ Solve for y in Equation 1.

Next, substitute this expression for y into Equation 2 and solve the resulting single-variable equation for x.

$x - y = 2$	Write Equation 2.
$x - (4 - x) = 2$	Substitute $4 - x$ for y.
$x - 4 + x = 2$	Simplify.
$2x = 6$	Combine like terms.
$x = 3$	Divide each side by 2.

Finally, you can solve for y by *back-substituting* $x = 3$ into the equation $y = 4 - x$, to obtain

$y = 4 - x$	Write Equation 1.
$y = 4 - 3$	Substitute 3 for x.
$y = 1$.	Solve for y.

The solution is the ordered pair $(3, 1)$. Check this as follows.

Check $(3, 1)$ *in Equation 1:*

$x + y = 4$	Write Equation 1.
$3 + 1 \overset{?}{=} 4$	Substitute for x and y.
$4 = 4$	Solution checks in Equation 1. ✓

Check $(3, 1)$ *in Equation 2:*

$x - y = 2$	Write Equation 2.
$3 - 1 \overset{?}{=} 2$	Substitute for x and y.
$2 = 2$	Solution checks in Equation 2. ✓

Graphical Solution

Begin by solving both equations for y. Then use a graphing utility to graph the equations

$$y_1 = 4 - x \quad \text{and} \quad y_2 = x - 2$$

in the same viewing window. Use the *intersect* feature or the *zoom* and *trace* features of the graphing utility to approximate the point of intersection of the graphs. In Figure 5.1, the point of intersection is $(3, 1)$.

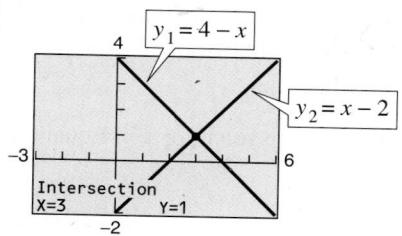

Figure 5.1

Check that $(3, 1)$ is the exact solution as follows.

Check $(3, 1)$ *in Equation 1:*

$x + y = 4$	Write Equation 1.
$3 + 1 \overset{?}{=} 4$	Substitute for x and y.
$4 = 4$	Solution checks in Equation 1. ✓

Check $(3, 1)$ *in Equation 2:*

$x - y = 2$	Write Equation 2.
$3 - 1 \overset{?}{=} 2$	Substitute for x and y.
$2 = 2$	Solution checks in Equation 2. ✓

In the algebraic solution of Example 1, note that the term *back-substitution* implies that you work *backward*. First you solve for one of the variables, and then you substitute that value *back* into one of the equations in the system to find the value of the other variable.

EXAMPLE 2   Solving a System by Substitution

A total of $12,000 is invested in two funds paying 9% and 11% simple interest. The yearly interest is $1180. How much is invested at each rate?

Solution

Verbal Model:

$$\boxed{\begin{array}{c}9\% \\ \text{fund}\end{array}} + \boxed{\begin{array}{c}11\% \\ \text{fund}\end{array}} = \boxed{\begin{array}{c}\text{Total} \\ \text{investment}\end{array}}$$

$$\boxed{\begin{array}{c}9\% \\ \text{interest}\end{array}} + \boxed{\begin{array}{c}11\% \\ \text{interest}\end{array}} = \boxed{\begin{array}{c}\text{Total} \\ \text{interest}\end{array}}$$

Labels:
Amount in 9% fund $= x$ (dollars)
Interest for 9% fund $= 0.09x$ (dollars)
Amount in 11% fund $= y$ (dollars)
Interest for 11% fund $= 0.11y$ (dollars)
Total investment $= \$12{,}000$ (dollars)
Total interest $= \$1180$ (dollars)

System:
$$\begin{cases} x + y = 12{,}000 & \text{Equation 1} \\ 0.09x + 0.11y = 1{,}180 & \text{Equation 2} \end{cases}$$

To begin, it is convenient to multiply both sides of Equation 2 by 100 to obtain $9x + 11y = 118{,}000$. This eliminates the need to work with decimals.

$$9x + 11y = 118{,}000 \qquad \text{Revised Equation 2}$$

To solve this system, you can solve for x in Equation 1.

$$x = 12{,}000 - y \qquad \text{Revised Equation 1}$$

Next, substitute this expression for x into Revised Equation 2 and solve the resulting equation for y.

$$9x + 11y = 118{,}000 \qquad \text{Write Revised Equation 2.}$$
$$9(12{,}000 - y) + 11y = 118{,}000 \qquad \text{Substitute } 12{,}000 - y \text{ for } x.$$
$$108{,}000 - 9y + 11y = 118{,}000 \qquad \text{Distributive Property}$$
$$2y = 10{,}000 \qquad \text{Combine like terms.}$$
$$y = 5000 \qquad \text{Divide each side by 2.}$$

Finally, back-substitute the value $y = 5000$ to solve for x.

$$x = 12{,}000 - y \qquad \text{Write Revised Equation 1.}$$
$$x = 12{,}000 - 5000 \qquad \text{Substitute 5000 for } y.$$
$$x = 7000 \qquad \text{Simplify.}$$

The solution is $(7000, 5000)$. This means that $7000 is invested at 9% and $5000 is invested at 11% to yield yearly interest of $1180. Check this in the original system.

The equations in Examples 1 and 2 are linear. Substitution can also be used to solve systems in which one or both of the equations are nonlinear.

The *Interactive* CD-ROM and *Internet* versions of this text offer a built-in graphing calculator, which can be used with the Examples, Explorations, and Exercises.

STUDY T!P

One way to check the answers you obtain in this section is to use a graphing utility. For instance, enter the two equations in Example 2

$$y_1 = 12{,}000 - x$$
$$y_2 = \frac{1180 - 0.09x}{0.11}$$

and find an appropriate viewing window that shows where the lines intersect. Then use the *intersect* feature or the *zoom* and *trace* features to find their point of intersection.

EXAMPLE 3   Substitution: Two-Solution Case

Solve the system of equations.

$$\begin{cases} x^2 + 4x - y = 7 & \text{Equation 1} \\ 2x - y = -1 & \text{Equation 2} \end{cases}$$

A computer animation of this concept appears in the *Interactive* CD-ROM and *Internet* versions of this text.

Algebraic Solution

Begin by solving for y in Equation 2 to obtain $y = 2x + 1$. Next, substitute this expression for y into Equation 1 and solve for x.

$x^2 + 4x - y = 7$	Write Equation 1.
$x^2 + 4x - (2x + 1) = 7$	Substitute $2x + 1$ for y.
$x^2 + 2x - 8 = 0$	Write in general form.
$(x + 4)(x - 2) = 0$	Factor.
$x + 4 = 0 \Longrightarrow x = -4$	Set 1st factor equal to 0.
$x - 2 = 0 \Longrightarrow x = 2$	Set 2nd factor equal to 0.

Back-substituting these values of x to solve for the corresponding values of y produces the solutions $(-4, -7)$ and $(2, 5)$. Check these in the original system.

Graphical Solution

To graph each equation, first solve both equations for y. Then use a graphing utility to graph the equations in the same viewing window. Use the *intersect* feature or the *zoom* and *trace* features to approximate the points of intersection of the graphs. In Figure 5.2, the points of intersection are $(-4, -7)$ and $(2, 5)$. Check that $(-4, -7)$ and $(2, 5)$ are the exact solutions by substituting *both* ordered pairs into *both* equations.

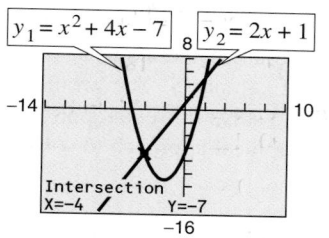

Figure 5.2

EXAMPLE 4   Substitution: No-Solution Case

Solve the system of equations.

$$\begin{cases} -x + y = 4 & \text{Equation 1} \\ x^2 + y = 3 & \text{Equation 2} \end{cases}$$

Solution

Begin by solving for y in Equation 1 to obtain $y = x + 4$. Next, substitute this expression for y into Equation 2 and solve for x.

$x^2 + y = 3$	Write Equation 2.
$x^2 + (x + 4) = 3$	Substitute $x + 4$ for y.
$x^2 + x + 1 = 0$	Simplify.
$x = \dfrac{-1 \pm \sqrt{1 - 4}}{2}$	Quadratic Formula

STUDY T!P

When using substitution, solve for the variable that is not raised to a power in either equation. For instance, in Example 4 it would not be practical to solve for x in Equation 2. Can you see why?

Because this yields two complex values, the equation $x^2 + x + 1 = 0$ has no *real* solution. So, the original system of equations has no *real* solution.

Try graphing the system of equations in Example 4. Do the graphs of the equations intersect? Why or why not?

From Examples 2, 3, and 4, you can see that a system of two equations in two unknowns can have exactly one solution, more than one solution, or no solution. For instance, in Figure 5.3(a), the two equations graph as two lines with a *single point* of intersection. The two equations in Example 3 graph as a parabola and a line with *two points* of intersection, as shown in Figure 5.3(b). The two equations in Example 4 graph as a line and a parabola that happen to have *no points* of intersection, as shown in Figure 5.3(c).

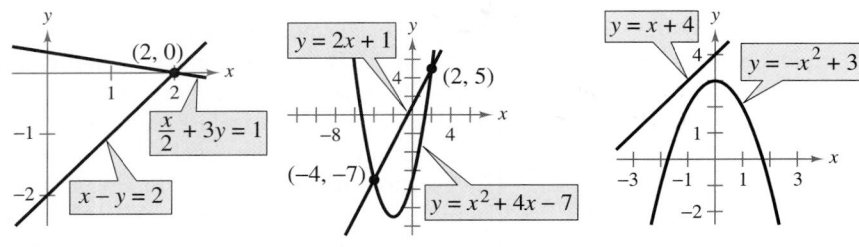

(a) One Intersection Point **(b) Two Intersection Points** **(c) No Intersection Points**
Figure 5.3

Example 5 shows the value of a graphical approach to solving systems of equations in two variables. Notice what would happen if you tried only the substitution method in Example 5. You would obtain the equation $x + \ln x = 1$. It would be difficult to solve this equation for x using standard algebraic techniques. In such cases, a graphical approach to solving a system of equations is more convenient.

EXAMPLE 5   Solving a System of Equations Graphically

Solve the system of equations.

$$\begin{cases} y = \ln x & \text{Equation 1} \\ x + y = 1 & \text{Equation 2} \end{cases}$$

Solution

From the graphs of these equations, shown in Figure 5.4, it is clear that there is only one point of intersection. Use the *intersect* feature or the *zoom* and *trace* features of a graphing utility to approximate the solution point as $(1, 0)$. You can confirm this by substituting in *both* equations.

Check

$$0 = \ln 1 \qquad \text{Equation 1 checks.} \checkmark$$

$$1 + 0 = 1 \qquad \text{Equation 2 checks.} \checkmark$$

So, the solution is $(1, 0)$.

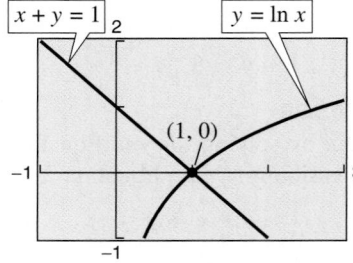

Figure 5.4

Applications

The total cost C of producing x units of a product typically has two components: the initial cost and the cost per unit. When enough units have been sold so that the total revenue R equals the total cost, the sales are said to have reached the **break-even point.** You will find that the break-even point corresponds to the point of intersection of the cost and revenue curves.

EXAMPLE 6   Break-Even Analysis

A small business invests \$10,000 in equipment to produce a product. Each unit of the product costs \$0.65 to produce and is sold for \$1.20. How many items must be sold before the business breaks even?

Solution

The total cost of producing x units is

| Total cost | = | Cost per unit | · | Number of units | + | Initial cost |

$$C = 0.65x + 10,000. \qquad \text{Equation 1}$$

The revenue obtained by selling x units is

| Total revenue | = | Price per unit | · | Number of units |

$$R = 1.2x. \qquad \text{Equation 2}$$

Because the break-even point occurs when $R = C$, you have

$$1.2x = 0.65x + 10,000 \qquad \text{Equate R and C.}$$

$$0.55x = 10,000 \qquad \text{Subtract } 0.65x \text{ from each side.}$$

$$x = \frac{10,000}{0.55} \qquad \text{Divide each side by 0.55.}$$

$$x \approx 18,182 \text{ units.} \qquad \text{Use a calculator.}$$

Note in Figure 5.5 that sales less than the break-even point correspond to an overall loss, whereas sales greater than the break-even point correspond to a profit. Verify the break-even point using the *intersect* feature or the *zoom* and *trace* features of a graphing utility.

Another way to view the solution in Example 6 is to consider the profit function

$$P = R - C.$$

The break-even point occurs when the profit is 0, which is the same as saying that $R = C$.

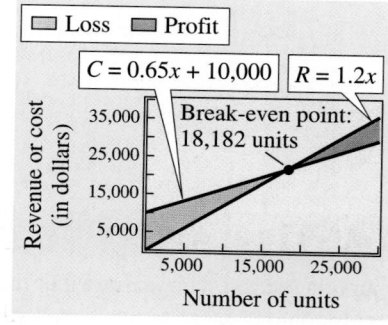

Figure 5.5

EXAMPLE 7 State Populations

From 1990 to 1997, the population of Arizona was increasing at a faster rate than the population of Alabama. Two models that approximate the populations P (in thousands) are

$$\begin{cases} P = 3631.2 + 131.7t & \text{Arizona} \\ P = 4055.6 + 39.9t & \text{Alabama} \end{cases}$$

where $t = 0$ represents 1990. According to these two models, when would you expect the population of Arizona to have exceeded the population of Alabama? (Source: U.S. Bureau of the Census)

Algebraic Solution

Because the first equation has already been solved for P in terms of t, you can substitute this value into the second equation and solve for t, as follows.

$$3631.2 + 131.7t = 4055.6 + 39.9t$$

$$131.7t - 39.9t = 4055.6 - 3631.2$$

$$91.8t = 424.4$$

$$t \approx 4.6$$

So, from the given models, you would expect that the population of Arizona exceeded the population of Alabama sometime during 1994.

Graphical Solution

Use a graphing utility to graph $y_1 = 3631.2 + 131.7x$ and $y_2 = 4055.6 + 39.9x$ in the same viewing window. Use the *intersect* feature or the *zoom* and *trace* features of the graphing utility to approximate the point of intersection of the graphs. In Figure 5.6, the point of intersection occurs when $x \approx 4.6$.

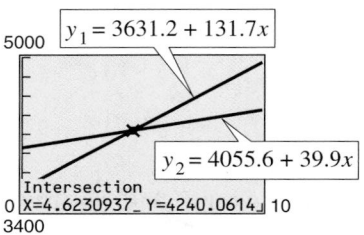

Figure 5.6

So, from the graph, it appears that the population of Arizona exceeded the population of Alabama sometime during 1994.

Writing About Math *Points of Intersection*

In this section, you learned that the graphs of two equations can intersect at zero, one, or more points. Use a graphing utility to graph each of the following systems. Decide whether the system has no solution, one solution, two solutions, or more than two solutions.

a. $\begin{cases} -0.5x^2 + 0.25x + y = -1.5 \\ \qquad\qquad 1.75x + y = -2.625 \end{cases}$

b. $\begin{cases} -0.5x^2 + 0.25x + y = -1.5 \\ \qquad\qquad -1.25x + y = -4.5 \end{cases}$

c. $\begin{cases} -0.5x^2 + 0.25x + y = -1.5 \\ \qquad\qquad 3.5x + y = 2.25 \end{cases}$

Create three other systems of equations, one with no solution, one with one solution, and one with two solutions. Write a short paragraph that explains how you created these systems. Include a description of how you can check that the systems have the appropriate number of solutions.

Suggestion
Ask your students to make up their own problems involving a choice of solution methods. Students can then form groups and trade their problems with other members of their groups. Make sure that students are able to interpret attributes such as slopes and points of intersection.

5.1 Exercises

In Exercises 1–4, decide whether each ordered pair is a solution of the system of equations.

1. $\begin{cases} 4x - y = 1 \\ 6x + y = -6 \end{cases}$ (a) $(0, -3)$ (b) $(-1, -5)$
  (c) $\left(-\frac{3}{2}, 3\right)$ (d) $\left(-\frac{1}{2}, -3\right)$

2. $\begin{cases} 4x^2 + y = 3 \\ -x - y = 11 \end{cases}$ (a) $(2, -13)$ (b) $(-2, -9)$
  (c) $\left(-\frac{3}{2}, 6\right)$ (d) $\left(-\frac{7}{4}, -\frac{37}{4}\right)$

3. $\begin{cases} y = -2e^x \\ 3x - y = 2 \end{cases}$ (a) $(-2, 0)$ (b) $(0, -2)$
  (c) $(0, -3)$ (d) $(-1, -5)$

4. $\begin{cases} -\log_{10} x + 3 = y \\ \frac{1}{9}x + y = \frac{28}{9} \end{cases}$ (a) $(100, 1)$ (b) $(10, 2)$
  (c) $(1, 3)$ (d) $(1, 1)$

In Exercises 5–14, solve the system by the method of substitution. Check your solution graphically.

5. $\begin{cases} 2x + y = 6 \\ -x + y = 0 \end{cases}$ **6.** $\begin{cases} x - y = -4 \\ x + 2y = 5 \end{cases}$

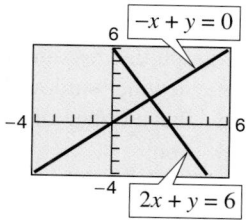 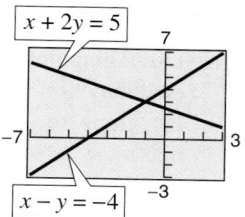

7. $\begin{cases} x - y = -4 \\ x^2 - y = -2 \end{cases}$ **8.** $\begin{cases} -2x + y = -5 \\ x^2 + y^2 = 25 \end{cases}$

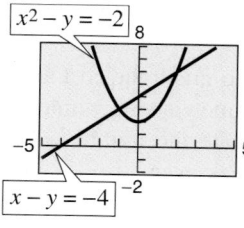 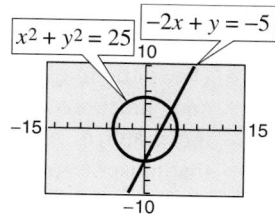

9. $\begin{cases} 3x + y = 2 \\ x^3 - 2 + y = 0 \end{cases}$ **10.** $\begin{cases} x + y = 0 \\ x^3 - 5x - y = 0 \end{cases}$

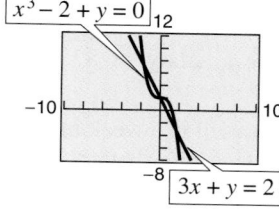 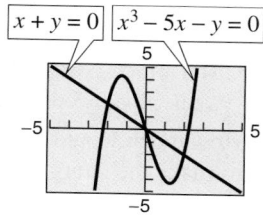

11. $\begin{cases} x^2 + y = 0 \\ x^2 - 4x - y = 0 \end{cases}$ **12.** $\begin{cases} y = -2x^2 + 2 \\ y = 2(x^4 - 2x^2 + 1) \end{cases}$

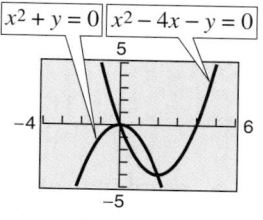 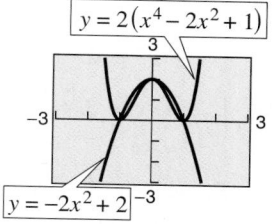

13. $\begin{cases} -\frac{7}{2}x - y = -18 \\ 8x^2 - 2y^3 = 0 \end{cases}$ **14.** $\begin{cases} y = x^3 - 3x^2 + 4 \\ y = -2x + 4 \end{cases}$

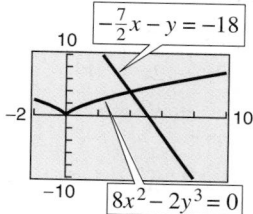 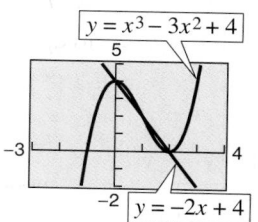

In Exercises 15–28, solve the system by substitution. Use a graphing utility to verify your result.

15. $\begin{cases} x - y = 0 \\ 5x - 3y = 10 \end{cases}$ **16.** $\begin{cases} x + 2y = 1 \\ 5x - 4y = -23 \end{cases}$

17. $\begin{cases} 2x - y + 2 = 0 \\ 4x + y - 5 = 0 \end{cases}$ **18.** $\begin{cases} 6x - 3y - 4 = 0 \\ x + 2y - 4 = 0 \end{cases}$

19. $\begin{cases} 1.5x + 0.8y = 2.3 \\ 0.3x - 0.2y = 0.1 \end{cases}$ **20.** $\begin{cases} 0.5x + 3.2y = 9.0 \\ 0.2x - 1.6y = -3.6 \end{cases}$

21. $\begin{cases} \frac{1}{5}x + \frac{1}{2}y = 8 \\ x + y = 20 \end{cases}$ **22.** $\begin{cases} \frac{1}{2}x + \frac{3}{4}y = 10 \\ \frac{3}{4}x - y = 4 \end{cases}$

23. $\begin{cases} 8x + 4y = 7 \\ 2x + y = 0 \end{cases}$ **24.** $\begin{cases} 2x - y = 4 \\ -4x + 2y = -12 \end{cases}$

25. $\begin{cases} -\frac{5}{3}x + y = 5 \\ -5x + 3y = 6 \end{cases}$ **26.** $\begin{cases} -\frac{2}{3}x + y = -2 \\ 2x - 3y = 6 \end{cases}$

27. $\begin{cases} x - y = 0 \\ 2x + y = 0 \end{cases}$ **28.** $\begin{cases} x - 2y = 0 \\ 3x - y = 0 \end{cases}$

The *Interactive* CD-ROM and *Internet* versions of this text contain step-by-step solutions to all odd-numbered Section and Review Exercises. They also provide Tutorial Exercises, which link to Guided Examples for additional help.

In Exercises 29–36, solve the system of equations graphically. Verify your solutions algebraically.

29. $\begin{cases} -x + 2y = 2 \\ 3x + y = 15 \end{cases}$

30. $\begin{cases} x + y = 0 \\ 3x - 2y = 10 \end{cases}$

31. $\begin{cases} x - 3y = -2 \\ 5x + 3y = 17 \end{cases}$

32. $\begin{cases} -x + 2y = 1 \\ x - y = 2 \end{cases}$

33. $\begin{cases} x + y = 4 \\ x^2 + y^2 - 4x = 0 \end{cases}$

34. $\begin{cases} -x + y = 3 \\ x^2 - 6x - 27 + y^2 = 0 \end{cases}$

35. $\begin{cases} x - y + 3 = 0 \\ x^2 - 4x + 7 = y \end{cases}$

36. $\begin{cases} y^2 - 4x + 11 = 0 \\ -\frac{1}{2}x + y = -\frac{1}{2} \end{cases}$

In Exercises 37–50, use a graphing utility to approximate all points of intersection of the graph of the system of equations. Verify your solutions by checking them in the original system.

37. $\begin{cases} 7x + 8y = 24 \\ x - 8y = 8 \end{cases}$

38. $\begin{cases} x - y = 0 \\ 5x - 2y = 6 \end{cases}$

39. $\begin{cases} 2x - y + 3 = 0 \\ x^2 + y^2 - 4x = 0 \end{cases}$

40. $\begin{cases} 3x - 2y = 0 \\ x^2 + y^2 = 4 \end{cases}$

41. $\begin{cases} x^2 + y^2 = 8 \\ y = x^2 \end{cases}$

42. $\begin{cases} x^2 + y^2 = 25 \\ (x - 8)^2 + y^2 = 41 \end{cases}$

43. $\begin{cases} y = e^x \\ x - y + 1 = 0 \end{cases}$

44. $\begin{cases} y = -4e^{-x} \\ y + 3x + 8 = 0 \end{cases}$

45. $\begin{cases} x + 2y = 8 \\ y = \log_2 x \end{cases}$

46. $\begin{cases} y = -2 + \ln(x - 1) \\ 3y + 2x = 9 \end{cases}$

47. $\begin{cases} y = \sqrt{x} \\ y = x \end{cases}$

48. $\begin{cases} x - y = 3 \\ x - y^2 = 1 \end{cases}$

49. $\begin{cases} x^2 + y^2 = 169 \\ x^2 - 8y = 104 \end{cases}$

50. $\begin{cases} x^2 + y^2 = 4 \\ 2x^2 - y = 2 \end{cases}$

In Exercises 51–62, solve the system graphically or algebraically. Explain your choice of method.

51. $\begin{cases} y = 2x \\ y = x^2 + 1 \end{cases}$

52. $\begin{cases} x + y = 4 \\ x^2 + y = 2 \end{cases}$

53. $\begin{cases} 3x - 7y + 6 = 0 \\ x^2 - y^2 = 4 \end{cases}$

54. $\begin{cases} x^2 + y^2 = 25 \\ 2x + y = 10 \end{cases}$

55. $\begin{cases} x - 2y = 4 \\ x^2 - y = 0 \end{cases}$

56. $\begin{cases} y = (x + 1)^3 \\ y = \sqrt{x - 1} \end{cases}$

57. $\begin{cases} y - e^{-x} = 1 \\ y - \ln x = 3 \end{cases}$

58. $\begin{cases} x^2 + y = 4 \\ e^x - y = 0 \end{cases}$

59. $\begin{cases} y = x^3 - 2x^2 + 1 \\ y = 1 - x^2 \end{cases}$

60. $\begin{cases} y = x^3 - 2x^2 + x - 1 \\ y = -x^2 + 3x - 1 \end{cases}$

61. $\begin{cases} xy - 1 = 0 \\ 2x - 4y + 7 = 0 \end{cases}$

62. $\begin{cases} x - 2y = 1 \\ y = \sqrt{x - 1} \end{cases}$

Break-Even Analysis   In Exercises 63–66, use a graphing utility to graph the cost and revenue functions in the same viewing window. Find the sales x necessary to break even ($R = C$) and the corresponding revenue R obtained by selling x units. (Round to the nearest whole unit.)

Cost	Revenue
63. $C = 8650x + 250,000$	$R = 9950x$
64. $C = 2.65x + 350,000$	$R = 4.15x$
65. $C = 5.5\sqrt{x} + 10,000$	$R = 3.29x$
66. $C = 7.8\sqrt{x} + 18,500$	$R = 12.84x$

67. *Break-Even Point* A small business invests $16,000 to produce an item that will sell for $5.95. Each unit can be produced for $3.45.

(a) Write cost and revenue functions for x units produced and sold.

(b) Use a graphing utility to graph the cost and revenue functions in the same viewing window. Use the graph to approximate the number of units that must be sold to break even.

(c) Verify the result of part (b) algebraically.

68. *Break-Even Point* A small business has an initial investment of $5000. The unit cost of the product is $21.60, and the selling price is $34.10.

(a) Write cost and revenue functions for x units produced and sold.

(b) Use a graphing utility to graph the cost and revenue functions in the same viewing window. Use the graph to approximate the number of units that must be sold to break even.

(c) Verify the result of part (b) algebraically.

69. *Choice of Two Jobs* You are offered two different jobs selling dental supplies.

• One company offers a straight commission of 6% of sales.

• The other company offers a salary of $250 per week plus 3% of sales.

How much would you have to sell in a week in order to make the straight commission offer better?

70. *Choice of Two Jobs*   You are offered two different jobs selling college textbooks.

- One company offers an annual salary of $25,000 plus a year-end bonus of 1% of your total sales.
- The other company offers an annual salary of $20,000 plus a year-end bonus of 2% of your total sales.

Determine the annual sales that make the second offer better.

71. *Finance*   A total of $20,000 is invested in two funds paying 6.5% and 8.5% simple interest. The 6.5% investment has a lower risk. The investor wants a yearly interest check of $1600 from the investment.

(a) Write a system of equations in which one equation represents the total amount invested and the other equation represents the $1600 required in interest. Let x and y represent the amounts invested at 6.5% and 8.5%, respectively.

(b) Use a graphing utility to graph the two equations in the same viewing window. As the amount invested at 6.5% increases, how do the amount invested at 8.5% and the amount of interest each change? Explain.

(c) What is the most that can be invested at 6.5% to meet the requirement of $1600 per year in interest?

72. *Finance*   A total of $25,000 is invested in two funds paying 6% and 8.5% simple interest. The 6% investment has a lower risk. The investor wants a yearly interest income of $2000 from the two investments.

(a) Write a system of equations in which one equation represents the total amount invested and the other equation represents the $2000 required in interest. Let x and y represent the amounts invested at 6% and 8.5%, respectively.

(b) Use a graphing utility to graph the two equations in the same viewing window. As the amount invested at 6% increases, how do the amount invested at 8.5% and the amount of interest each change? Explain.

(c) What is the most that can be invested at 6% to meet the requirement of $2000 per year in interest?

73. *Log Volume*   You are offered two different rules for estimating the number of board feet in a log that is 16 feet long. A board foot is a unit of measure for lumber equal to a board one foot square and one inch thick. One rule is the *Doyle Log Rule* and is modeled by

$$V = (D - 4)^2, \quad 5 \le D \le 40$$

and the other rule is the *Scribner Log Rule* and is modeled by

$$V = 0.79D^2 - 2D - 4, \quad 5 \le D \le 40$$

where D is the diameter of the log and V is its volume in board feet.

(a) Use a graphing utility to graph the log rules in the same viewing window.

(b) For what diameter do the two rules agree?

(c) If you were selling large logs, which rule would you use? Explain your reasoning.

Geometry   **In Exercises 74–77, find the dimensions of the rectangle meeting the specified conditions.**

74. The perimeter is 30 meters and the length is 3 meters greater than the width.

75. The perimeter is 280 centimeters and the width is 20 centimeters less than the length.

76. The perimeter is 42 inches and the width is three-fourths the length.

77. The perimeter is 210 feet and the length is $1\frac{1}{2}$ times the width.

78. *Geometry*   What are the dimensions of a rectangular tract of land if its perimeter is 40 miles and its area is 96 square miles?

79. *Geometry*   What are the dimensions of an isosceles right triangle with a 2-inch hypotenuse and an area of 1 square inch?

80. *Data Analysis*   The table shows the amount y (in millions of short tons) of paperboard produced in the United States in the years 1993 through 1996. (Source: American Forest and Paper Association)

Year	1993	1994	1995	1996
y	43.1	45.7	46.6	47.9

(a) Use the regression capabilities of a graphing utility to find a linear model and a quadratic model that represent the data in the interval from 1993 through 1996. (Let $t = 3$ represent 1993.)

(b) Use the graphing utility to graph the data and the two models in the same viewing window.

(c) Approximate the points of intersection of the graphs of the models.

(d) Use the models to estimate newsprint production in 1998. Which model do you think gives the more accurate estimate? Explain.

81. ***Data Analysis*** The table shows the average hourly earnings E of production workers in manufacturing industries in the United States for the years 1992 to 1997. (Source: U.S. Bureau of Labor Statistics)

Year	1992	1993	1994
E	$11.46	$11.74	$12.06

Year	1995	1996	1997
E	$12.37	$12.78	$13.17

Let t represent the time in years, with $t = 2$ corresponding to 1992.

(a) Use the regression capabilities of a graphing utility to fit a linear model and a quadratic model to the data.

(b) Use the graphing utility to graph the data and the two models in the same viewing window.

(c) Approximate the points of intersections of the graphs of the models.

(d) Use the models to estimate the average hourly earnings in 2000. Which model do you think gives the more accurate estimate? Explain.

Synthesis

True or False? **In Exercises 82 and 83, determine whether the statement is true or false. Justify your answer.**

82. In order to solve a system of equations by substitution, you must always solve for y in one of the two equations and then back-substitute.

83. If a system consists of a parabola and a circle, then it can have at most two solutions.

84. ***Think About It*** When solving a system of equations by substitution, how do you recognize that the system has no solution?

85. ***Writing*** Write a brief paragraph describing any advantages of substitution over the graphical method of solving a system of equations.

86. ***Exploration*** Find an equation of a line whose graph intersects the graph of the parabola $y = x^2$ at the following numbers of points. (There are many correct answers.)

(a) Two points

(b) One point

(c) No points

87. ***Conjecture***

(a) Use a graphing utility to graph the system of equations

$$\begin{cases} y = b^x \\ y = x^b \end{cases}$$

for $b = 2$ and $b = 4$.

(b) For a fixed value of $b > 1$, make a conjecture about the number of points of intersection of the graphs in part (a).

Review

In Exercises 88–93, find the general form of the equation of the line through the two points.

88. $(-2, 7), (5, 5)$ **89.** $(3.5, 4), (10, 6)$

90. $(6, 3), (10, 3)$ **91.** $(4, -2), (4, 5)$

92. $\left(\frac{3}{5}, 0\right), (4, 6)$ **93.** $\left(-\frac{7}{3}, 8\right), \left(\frac{5}{2}, \frac{1}{2}\right)$

In Exercises 94–97, find the domain of the function and identify any horizontal or vertical asymptotes.

94. $f(x) = \dfrac{5}{x - 6}$ **95.** $f(x) = \dfrac{2x - 7}{3x + 2}$

96. $f(x) = \dfrac{x^2 + 2}{x^2 - 16}$ **97.** $f(x) = 3 - \dfrac{2}{x^2}$

In Exercises 98–101, solve the equation. Round your result to three decimal places.

98. $6^{7-x} = 1249$ **99.** $8(10^{2x}) = 28$

100. $e^{2x} - 9e^x + 18 = 0$

101. $\log_{10}(x + 3) - \log_{10} x = \log_{10}(x + 8)$

5.2 Systems of Linear Equations in Two Variables

The Method of Elimination

In Section 5.1, you studied two methods for solving a system of equations: substitution and graphing. Now you will study the **method of elimination.** The key step in this method is to obtain, for one of the variables, coefficients that differ only in sign so that *adding* the equations eliminates the variable.

$$\begin{cases} 3x + 5y = 7 & \text{Equation 1} \\ -3x - 2y = -1 & \text{Equation 2} \end{cases}$$
$$3y = 6 \qquad \text{Add equations.}$$

Note that by adding the two equations, you eliminate the variable x and obtain a single equation in y. Solving this equation for y produces $y = 2$, which you can then back-substitute into one of the original equations to solve for x.

EXAMPLE 1   The Method of Elimination

Solve the system of linear equations.

$$\begin{cases} 3x + 2y = 4 & \text{Equation 1} \\ 5x - 2y = 8 & \text{Equation 2} \end{cases}$$

Solution
You can eliminate y by adding the two equations.

$$3x + 2y = 4 \qquad \text{Write Equation 1.}$$
$$\underline{5x - 2y = 8} \qquad \text{Write Equation 2.}$$
$$8x = 12 \qquad \text{Add equations.}$$

So, $x = \frac{3}{2}$. By back-substituting, you can solve for y.

$$3x + 2y = 4 \qquad \text{Write Equation 1.}$$
$$3\left(\tfrac{3}{2}\right) + 2y = 4 \qquad \text{Substitute } \tfrac{3}{2} \text{ for } x.$$
$$y = -\tfrac{1}{4} \qquad \text{Solve for } y.$$

The solution is $\left(\frac{3}{2}, -\frac{1}{4}\right)$. You can check the solution *algebraically* by substituting into the original system, or graphically as shown in Section 5.1.

Check

$$3\left(\tfrac{3}{2}\right) + 2\left(-\tfrac{1}{4}\right) \stackrel{?}{=} 4 \qquad \text{Substitute into Equation 1.}$$
$$\tfrac{9}{2} - \tfrac{1}{2} = 4 \qquad \text{Equation 1 checks. } \checkmark$$
$$5\left(\tfrac{3}{2}\right) - 2\left(-\tfrac{1}{4}\right) \stackrel{?}{=} 8 \qquad \text{Substitute into Equation 2.}$$
$$\tfrac{15}{2} + \tfrac{1}{2} = 8 \qquad \text{Equation 2 checks. } \checkmark$$

Try using substitution to solve the system given in Example 1. Which method is easier? Many people find that the method of elimination is more efficient.

What You Should Learn:

- How to use the method of elimination to solve systems of linear equations in two variables
- How to graphically interpret the number of solutions of systems of linear equations in two variables
- How to use systems of linear equations in two variables to model and solve real-life problems

Why You Should Learn It:

The method of elimination is one method of solving a system of linear equations. For instance, Exercises 72 on page 383 shows how to use a system of linear equations to recover information about types of shoes that were sold in a shoe store.

Frank Siteman/PhotoEdit

The Method of Elimination

To use the **method of elimination** to solve a system of two linear equations in x and y, perform the following steps.

1. Obtain coefficients for x (or y) that differ only in sign by multiplying all terms of one or both equations by suitably chosen constants.

2. Add the equations to eliminate one variable; solve the resulting equation.

3. Back-substitute the value obtained in Step 2 into either of the original equations and solve for the other variable.

4. Check your solution in both of the original equations.

Consider having your students solve Example 2 by eliminating the x-terms instead of the y-terms to reinforce the fact that either variable may be eliminated first.

Remind your students to multiply the constants as well. A common error is to forget to multiply the constant terms. For instance, in Example 2, students may rewrite Equation 2 as

$$6x - 12y = 14$$

rather than as

$$6x - 12y = 42.$$

EXAMPLE 2   The Method of Elimination

Solve the system of linear equations.

$$\begin{cases} 5x + 3y = 9 & \text{Equation 1} \\ 2x - 4y = 14 & \text{Equation 2} \end{cases}$$

Algebraic Solution

You can obtain coefficients that differ only in sign by multiplying Equation 1 by 4 and multiplying Equation 2 by 3.

$$5x + 3y = 9 \quad\Longrightarrow\quad 20x + 12y = 36 \qquad \text{Multiply Equation 1 by 4.}$$

$$2x - 4y = 14 \quad\Longrightarrow\quad \underline{6x - 12y = 42} \qquad \text{Multiply Equation 2 by 3.}$$

$$26x \qquad\quad = 78 \qquad \text{Add equations.}$$

From this equation, you can see that $x = 3$. By back-substituting this value of x into Equation 2, you can solve for y.

$$2x - 4y = 14 \qquad \text{Write Equation 2.}$$

$$2(3) - 4y = 14 \qquad \text{Substitute 3 for } x.$$

$$-4y = 8 \qquad \text{Combine like terms.}$$

$$y = -2 \qquad \text{Solve for } y.$$

The solution is $(3, -2)$. You can check the solution algebraically by substituting into the original system.

Graphical Solution

Solve each equation for y. Then use a graphing utility to graph $y_1 = 3 - \frac{5}{3}x$ and $y_2 = -\frac{7}{2} + \frac{1}{2}x$ in the same viewing window. Use the *intersect* feature or the *zoom* and *trace* features to approximate the point of intersection of the graphs. From the graphs in Figure 5.7, the point of intersection is $(3, -2)$, so the approximate solution is $(3, -2)$. You can determine that this is the exact solution by checking $(3, -2)$ in both equations.

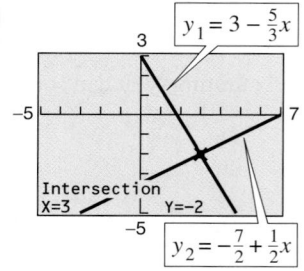

Figure 5.7

In Example 2, the two systems of linear equations

$$\begin{cases} 5x + 3y = 9 \\ 2x - 4y = 14 \end{cases} \quad \text{and} \quad \begin{cases} 20x + 12y = 36 \\ 6x - 12y = 42 \end{cases}$$

are called **equivalent systems** because they have precisely the same solution set. The operations that can be performed on a system of linear equations to produce an equivalent system are (1) interchanging any two equations, (2) multiplying an equation by a nonzero constant, and (3) adding a multiple of one equation to any other equation in the system.

Graphical Interpretation of Two-Variable Systems

It is possible for a *general* system of equations to have exactly one solution, two or more solutions, or no solution. If a system of *linear* equations has two different solutions, it must have an *infinite* number of solutions. To see why this is true, consider the following graphical interpretations of a system of two linear equations in two variables. (Remember that the graph of a linear equation in two variables is a straight line.)

Graphical Interpretation of Solutions

For a system of two linear equations in two variables, the number of solutions is one of the following.

Number of Solutions	*Graphical Interpretation*
1. Exactly one solution	The two lines intersect at one point.
2. Infinitely many solutions	The two lines are identical.
3. No solution	The two lines are parallel.

A system of linear equations is **consistent** if it has at least one solution. It is **inconsistent** if it has no solution.

Exploration

Use a graphing utility to graph each system of equations.

a. $\begin{cases} y = 5x + 1 \\ y - x = -5 \end{cases}$

b. $\begin{cases} 3y = 4x - 1 \\ -8x + 2 = -6y \end{cases}$

c. $\begin{cases} 2y = -x + 3 \\ -4 = y + \frac{1}{2}x \end{cases}$

Determine the number of solutions each system has. Explain your reasoning.

EXAMPLE 3   Recognizing Graphs of Linear Systems

Match each system of linear equations (a, b, c) with its graph (i, ii, iii) in Figure 5.8. Describe the number of solutions. Then state whether the system is consistent or inconsistent.

a. $\begin{cases} 2x - 3y = 3 \\ -4x + 6y = 6 \end{cases}$ **b.** $\begin{cases} 2x - 3y = 3 \\ x + 2y = 5 \end{cases}$ **c.** $\begin{cases} 2x - 3y = 3 \\ -4x + 6y = -6 \end{cases}$

A computer simulation of this example appears in the *Interactive* CD-ROM and *Internet* versions of this text.

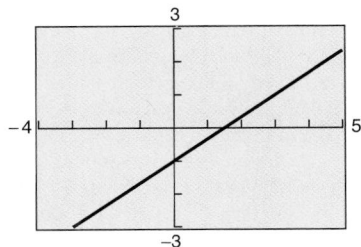

i.

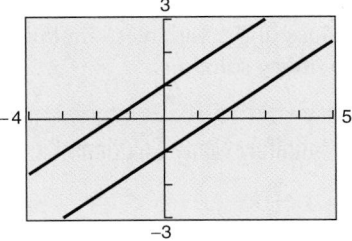

ii.

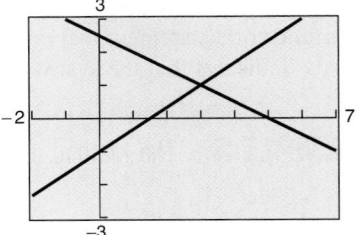

iii.

Figure 5.8

Solution

a. The graph is a pair of parallel lines (ii). The lines have no point of intersection, so the system has no solution. The system is inconsistent.

b. The graph is a pair of intersecting lines (iii). The lines have one point of intersection, so the system has exactly one solution. The system is consistent.

c. The graph is a pair of lines that coincide (i). The lines have infinitely many points of intersection, so the system has infinitely many solutions. The system is consistent.

In Examples 4 and 5, you can use the method of elimination to determine that a system of linear equations has no solution or infinitely many solutions.

EXAMPLE 4   The Method of Elimination: No-Solution Case

Solve the system of linear equations.

$$\begin{cases} x - 2y = 3 & \text{Equation 1} \\ -2x + 4y = 1 & \text{Equation 2} \end{cases}$$

Algebraic Solution

To obtain coefficients that differ only in sign, multiply Equation 1 by 2.

$$\begin{array}{ll} x - 2y = 3 & \Longrightarrow \quad 2x - 4y = 6 \\ -2x + 4y = 1 & \Longrightarrow \quad -2x + 4y = 1 \\ \hline & \qquad\qquad\quad 0 = 7 \end{array}$$

By adding the equations, you obtain $0 = 7$. Because there are no values of x and y for which $0 = 7$, this is a false statement. So, you can conclude that the system is inconsistent and has no solution.

Graphical Solution

Solve each equation for y: $y_1 = -\frac{3}{2} + \frac{1}{2}x$ $y_2 = \frac{1}{4} + \frac{1}{2}x$

Notice that the lines have the same slope, so they are parallel. You can use a graphing utility to verify this by graphing both equations as shown in Figure 5.9. Then try using the *intersect* feature to find a point of intersection. Because the graphing utility cannot find a point of intersection, you will get an error. Use the *zoom* feature and then try using the *intersect* feature again. Because repeated zooming yields the same error message, you can conclude that the lines are parallel, and, therefore, the system has no solution.

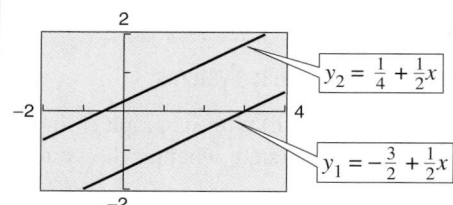

Figure 5.9

In Example 4, note that the occurrence of a false statement, such as $0 = 7$, indicates that the system has no solution. In the next example, note that the occurrence of a statement that is true for all values of the variables—in this case, $0 = 0$—indicates that the system has infinitely many solutions.

In Example 4, remind your students that the solution is "no solution." Students often incorrectly think that it is sufficient to give their answer as "false statement." Similarly, in Example 5, stress that the solution is "infinitely many solutions" and not just "a true statement."

EXAMPLE 5   The Method of Elimination: Infinitely Many Solutions Case

Solve the system of linear equations: $\begin{cases} 2x - y = 1 & \text{Equation 1} \\ 4x - 2y = 2 & \text{Equation 2} \end{cases}$

Solution

To obtain coefficients that differ only in sign, multiply Equation 2 by $-\frac{1}{2}$.

$$\begin{array}{lll} 2x - y = 1 & \Longrightarrow \quad 2x - y = 1 & \text{Write Equation 1.} \\ 4x - 2y = 2 & \Longrightarrow \quad -2x + y = -1 & \text{Multiply Equation 2 by } -\frac{1}{2}. \\ \hline & \qquad\qquad\quad 0 = 0 & \text{Add equations.} \end{array}$$

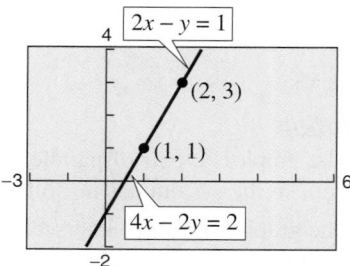

Figure 5.10

Because $0 = 0$ for all values of x and y, the two equations turn out to be equivalent (have the same solution set). You can conclude that the system has infinitely many solutions. The solution set consists of all points (x, y) lying on the line $2x - y = 1$, as shown in Figure 5.10.

Example 6 illustrates a strategy for solving a system of linear equations that has decimal coefficients.

EXAMPLE 6   A Linear System Having Decimal Coefficients

Solve the system of linear equations.

$$\begin{cases} 0.02x - 0.05y = -0.38 \\ 0.03x + 0.04y = 1.04 \end{cases}$$

Equation 1

Equation 2

Solution

Because the coefficients are two-place decimals, begin by multiplying each equation by 100 to produce a system with integer coefficients.

$$\begin{cases} 2x - 5y = -38 \\ 3x + 4y = 104 \end{cases}$$

Revised Equation 1

Revised Equation 2

Now, to obtain coefficients that differ only in sign, multiply Revised Equation 1 by 3 and multiply Revised Equation 2 by -2.

$2x - 5y = -38$ $\Longrightarrow$ $6x - 15y = -114$ Multiply Revised Equation 1 by 3.

$\underline{3x + 4y = 104}$ $\Longrightarrow$ $\underline{-6x - 8y = -208}$ Multiply Revised Equation 2 by -2.

$-23y = -322$ Add equations.

So, you can conclude that

$$y = \frac{-322}{-23} = 14.$$

Back-substituting this value into Revised Equation 2 produces the following.

$3x + 4y = 104$ Write revised Equation 2.

$3x + 4(14) = 104$ Substitute 14 for y.

$3x = 48$ Combine like terms.

$x = 16$ Solve for x.

The solution is $(16, 14)$. Check this in the original system, as follows.

Check

$0.02(16) - 0.05(14) \stackrel{?}{=} -0.38$ Substitute into Equation 1.

$0.32 - 0.70 = -0.38$ Equation 1 checks. ✓

$0.03(16) + 0.04(14) \stackrel{?}{=} 1.04$ Substitute into Equation 2.

$0.48 + 0.56 = 1.04$ Equation 2 checks. ✓

STUDY T!P

The general solution of the linear system

$$\begin{cases} ax + by = c \\ dx + ey = f \end{cases}$$

is $x = (ce - bf)/(ae - db)$ and $y = (af - cd)/(ae - db)$. If $ae - db = 0$, the system does not have a unique solution. A program called SOLVE for solving such a system is given on our website, *college.hmco.com*. Try using this program to check the solution of the system in Example 6.

The *Interactive* CD-ROM and *Internet* versions of this text show every example with its solution; clicking on the *Try It!* button brings up similar problems. Guided Examples and Integrated Examples show step-by-step solutions to additional examples. Integrated Examples are related to several concepts in the section.

Applications

At this point, you may be asking the question "How can I tell which application problems can be solved using a system of linear equations?" The answer comes from the following considerations.

1. Does the problem involve more than one unknown quantity?

2. Are there two (or more) equations or conditions to be satisfied?

If one or both of these conditions occur, the appropriate mathematical model for the problem may be a system of linear equations. Example 7 shows how to construct such a model.

EXAMPLE 7   An Application of a Linear System

An airplane flying into a headwind travels the 2000-mile flying distance between two cities in 4 hours and 24 minutes. On the return flight, the same distance is traveled in 4 hours. Find the airspeed of the plane and the speed of the wind, assuming that both remain constant.

Solution
The two unknown quantities are the speeds of the wind and the plane. If r_1 is the speed of the plane and r_2 is the speed of the wind, then

$r_1 - r_2 =$ speed of the plane *against* the wind

$r_1 + r_2 =$ speed of the plane *with* the wind

as shown in Figure 5.11. Using the formula

Distance $=$ (rate)(time)

for these two speeds, you obtain the following equations.

$$2000 = (r_1 - r_2)\left(4 + \frac{24}{60}\right)$$

$$2000 = (r_1 + r_2)(4)$$

These two equations simplify as follows.

$$\begin{cases} 5000 = 11r_1 - 11r_2 \\ 500 = r_1 + r_2 \end{cases}$$ Equation 1

                                        Equation 2

By elimination, the solution is

$$r_1 = \frac{5250}{11} \approx 477.27 \text{ miles per hour}$$ Speed of plane

$$r_2 = \frac{250}{11} \approx 22.73 \text{ miles per hour.}$$ Speed of wind

Check this solution in the original statement of the problem.

Original flight

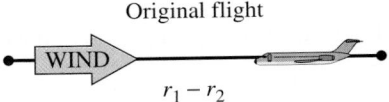

$r_1 - r_2$

Return flight

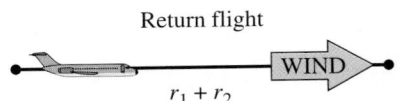

$r_1 + r_2$

Figure 5.11

5.2 Exercises

In Exercises 1–10, solve the system of equations by the method of elimination. Label each graphed line with its equation.

1. $\begin{cases} 2x + y = 5 \\ x - y = 1 \end{cases}$

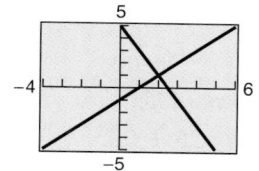

2. $\begin{cases} x + 3y = 1 \\ -x + 2y = 4 \end{cases}$

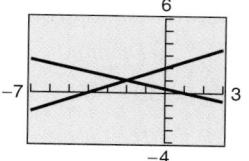

3. $\begin{cases} x + y = 0 \\ 3x + 2y = 1 \end{cases}$

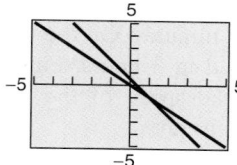

4. $\begin{cases} 2x - y = 3 \\ 4x + 3y = 21 \end{cases}$

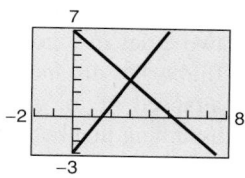

5. $\begin{cases} x - y = 2 \\ -2x + 2y = 5 \end{cases}$

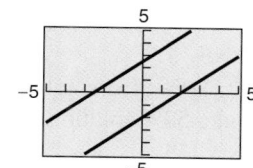

6. $\begin{cases} 3x + 2y = 3 \\ 6x + 4y = 14 \end{cases}$

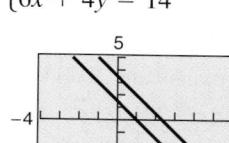

7. $\begin{cases} 3x - 2y = 5 \\ -6x + 4y = -10 \end{cases}$

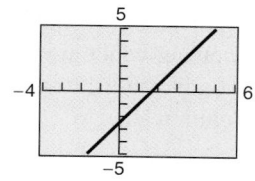

8. $\begin{cases} 9x - 3y = -15 \\ -3x + y = 5 \end{cases}$

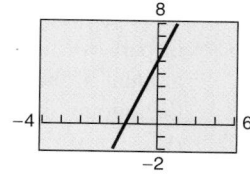

9. $\begin{cases} 9x + 3y = 1 \\ 3x - 6y = 5 \end{cases}$

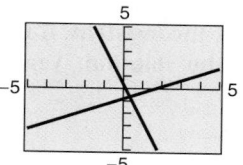

10. $\begin{cases} 5x + 3y = -18 \\ 2x - 6y = 1 \end{cases}$

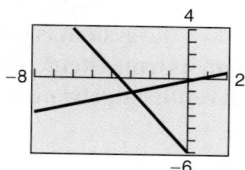

In Exercises 11–20, solve the system by the method of elimination and check any solution algebraically.

11. $\begin{cases} x + 2y = 4 \\ x - 2y = 1 \end{cases}$

12. $\begin{cases} 3x - 5y = 2 \\ 2x + 5y = 13 \end{cases}$

13. $\begin{cases} 2x + 3y = 18 \\ 5x - y = 11 \end{cases}$

14. $\begin{cases} x + 7y = 12 \\ 3x - 5y = 10 \end{cases}$

15. $\begin{cases} 3x + 2y = 10 \\ 2x + 5y = 3 \end{cases}$

16. $\begin{cases} 2r + 4s = 5 \\ 16r + 50s = 55 \end{cases}$

17. $\begin{cases} 5u + 6v = 24 \\ 3u + 5v = 18 \end{cases}$

18. $\begin{cases} 3x + 11y = 4 \\ -2x - 5y = 9 \end{cases}$

19. $\begin{cases} 1.8x + 1.2y = 4 \\ 9x + 6y = 3 \end{cases}$

20. $\begin{cases} 3.1x - 2.9y = -10.2 \\ 31x - 12y = 34 \end{cases}$

In Exercises 21–32, solve the system by the method of elimination and verify any solution using a graphing utility.

21. $\begin{cases} 4b + 3m = 3 \\ 3b + 11m = 13 \end{cases}$

22. $\begin{cases} 2x + 5y = 8 \\ 5x + 8y = 10 \end{cases}$

23. $\begin{cases} \dfrac{x}{4} + \dfrac{y}{6} = 1 \\ \dfrac{1}{2}x - \dfrac{1}{2}y = \dfrac{1}{6} \end{cases}$

24. $\begin{cases} \dfrac{2}{3}x + \dfrac{1}{6}y = \dfrac{2}{3} \\ \dfrac{10}{3}x - \dfrac{5}{6}y = \dfrac{10}{3} \end{cases}$

25. $\begin{cases} \frac{3}{4}x + y = \frac{1}{8} \\ \frac{9}{4}x + 3y = \frac{3}{8} \end{cases}$

26. $\begin{cases} \frac{2}{5}x - \frac{3}{2}y = 4 \\ \frac{1}{5}x - \frac{3}{4}y = -2 \end{cases}$

27. $\begin{cases} \dfrac{x+3}{4} + \dfrac{y-1}{3} = 1 \\ 2x - y = 12 \end{cases}$

28. $\begin{cases} \dfrac{x-1}{2} + \dfrac{y+2}{3} = 4 \\ x - 2y = 5 \end{cases}$

29. $\begin{cases} 2.5x - 3y = 1.5 \\ 2x - 2.4y = 1.2 \end{cases}$

30. $\begin{cases} 0.2x - 0.5y = -27.8 \\ 0.3x + 0.4y = 68.7 \end{cases}$

31. $\begin{cases} 0.02x - 0.05y = -0.19 \\ 0.03x + 0.04y = 0.52 \end{cases}$

32. $\begin{cases} 0.05x - 0.03y = 0.21 \\ 0.07x + 0.02y = 0.16 \end{cases}$

In Exercises 33–40, use a graphing utility to graph the lines in the system. Use the graphs to determine whether the system is consistent or inconsistent. If the system is consistent, determine the solution. Verify your results algebraically.

33. $\begin{cases} 2x - 5y = 0 \\ x - y = 3 \end{cases}$

34. $\begin{cases} 2x + y = 5 \\ x - 2y = -1 \end{cases}$

35. $\begin{cases} \frac{3}{5}x - y = 3 \\ -3x + 5y = 9 \end{cases}$

36. $\begin{cases} 4x - 6y = 9 \\ \frac{16}{3}x - 8y = 12 \end{cases}$

37. $\begin{cases} x + 7y = 2 \\ 4x - y = 9 \end{cases}$

38. $\begin{cases} 8x - 14y = 5 \\ 2x - 3.5y = 1.25 \end{cases}$

39. $\begin{cases} -x + 7y = 3 \\ -\frac{1}{7}x + y = 5 \end{cases}$

40. $\begin{cases} -7x + 6y = -4 \\ y + \frac{7}{6}x = -1 \end{cases}$

In Exercises 41–48, use a graphing utility to graph the two equations. Use the graphs to approximate the solution of the system.

41. $\begin{cases} 8x + 9y = 42 \\ 6x - y = 16 \end{cases}$

42. $\begin{cases} 4y = -8 \\ 7x - 2y = 25 \end{cases}$

43. $\begin{cases} \frac{3}{2}x - \frac{1}{5}y = 8 \\ -2x + 3y = 3 \end{cases}$

44. $\begin{cases} \frac{3}{4}x - \frac{5}{2}y = -9 \\ -x + 6y = 28 \end{cases}$

45. $\begin{cases} 0.5x + 2.2y = 9 \\ 6x + 0.4y = -22 \end{cases}$

46. $\begin{cases} 2.4x + 3.8y = -17.6 \\ 4x - 0.2y = -3.2 \end{cases}$

47. $\begin{cases} 7x - 2y = 24 \\ 5x + 6y = -20 \end{cases}$

48. $\begin{cases} 10x - 13y = -20 \\ 8x + 11y = -16 \end{cases}$

In Exercises 49–56, use any method to solve the system.

49. $\begin{cases} 3x - 5y = 7 \\ 2x + y = 9 \end{cases}$

50. $\begin{cases} -x + 3y = 17 \\ 4x + 3y = 7 \end{cases}$

51. $\begin{cases} y = 2x - 5 \\ y = 5x - 11 \end{cases}$

52. $\begin{cases} 7x + 3y = 16 \\ y = x + 2 \end{cases}$

53. $\begin{cases} x - 5y = 21 \\ 6x + 5y = 21 \end{cases}$

54. $\begin{cases} y = -3x - 8 \\ y = 15 - 2x \end{cases}$

55. $\begin{cases} -2x + 8y = 19 \\ y = x - 3 \end{cases}$

56. $\begin{cases} 4x - 3y = 6 \\ -5x + 7y = -1 \end{cases}$

Exploration In Exercises 57–60, find a system of linear equations that has the given solution. (There are many correct answers.)

57. $(6, 3)$

58. $(8, -2)$

59. $\left(3, \frac{5}{2}\right)$

60. $\left(-\frac{2}{3}, -10\right)$

Supply and Demand In Exercises 61–64, find the *point of equilibrium* of the demand and supply equations. The point of equilibrium is defined by the price *p* and the number of units *x* that satisfy both the demand and supply equations.

	Demand	*Supply*
61.	$p = 50 - 0.5x$	$p = 0.125x$
62.	$p = 100 - 0.05x$	$p = 25 + 0.1x$
63.	$p = 140 - 0.00002x$	$p = 80 + 0.00001x$
64.	$p = 400 - 0.0002x$	$p = 225 + 0.0005x$

65. *Airplane Speed* An airplane flying into a headwind travels the 1800-mile flying distance between two cities in 3 hours and 36 minutes. On the return flight, the distance is traveled in 3 hours. Find the airspeed of the plane and the speed of the wind, assuming that both remain constant.

66. *Airplane Speed* Two planes start from the same airport and fly in opposite directions. The second plane starts $\frac{1}{2}$ hour after the first plane, but its speed is 80 kilometers per hour faster. Find the airspeed of each plane if 2 hours after the first plane departs the planes are 3200 kilometers apart.

67. *Acid Mixture* Ten liters of a 30% acid solution is obtained by mixing a 20% and a 50% solution.

(a) Write a system of equations. One equation represents the amount of final mixture required and the other represents the amount of acid in the final mixture. Let *x* and *y* represent the amounts of 20% and 50% solutions, respectively.

(b) Use a graphing utility to graph the two equations in part (a) in the same viewing window. As the amount of the 20% solution increases, how does the amount of the 50% solution change?

(c) How much of each solution is required to obtain the specified concentration in the final mixture?

68. *Fuel Mixture* Five hundred gallons of 89-octane gasoline is obtained by mixing 87-octane gasoline with 92-octane gasoline.

(a) Write a system of equations. One equation represents the amount of final mixture required and the other represents the amount of 87- and

92-octane gasoline in the final mixture. Let x and y represent the number of 87-octane gallons and 92-octane gallons, respectively.

(b) Use a graphing utility to graph the two equations in part (a). As the amount of 87-octane gasoline increases, how does the amount of 92-octane gasoline change?

(c) How much of each type of gasoline is required to obtain the 500 gallons of 89-octane gasoline?

69. Finance   A total of $12,000 is invested in two corporate bonds that pay 7.5% and 9% simple interest. The investor wants an annual interest income of $990 from the investments. What is the most that can be invested in the 7.5% bond?

70. Finance   A total of $32,000 is invested in two municipal bonds that pay 5.75% and 6.25% simple interest. The investor wants an annual interest income of $1900 from the investments. What is the most that can be invested in the 5.75% bond?

71. Ticket Sales   Five hundred tickets were sold for one performance of a play. The tickets for adults and children sold for $7.50 and $4.00, respectively, and the total receipts for the performance were $3312.50. How many of each kind of ticket were sold?

72. Shoe Sales   On Saturday night, the manager of a shoe store evaluates the receipts of the previous week's sales. Two hundred and forty pairs of two different styles of tennis shoes were sold. One style sold for $66.95 and the other sold for $84.95. The total receipts were $17,652. The cash register that was supposed to record the number of each type of shoe sold malfunctioned. Can you recover the information? If so, how many shoes of each type were sold?

73. Driving Distances   In a trip of 300 kilometers, two people drive. One person drives three times as far as the other. Find the distance that each person drives.

74. Truck Scheduling   A contractor hires two trucking companies to haul 1600 tons of crushed stone for a highway construction project. The contracts state that one company is to haul four times as much as the other. Find the amount hauled by each company.

Fitting a Line to Data   **In Exercises 75–78, find the least squares regression line $y = ax + b$ for the points $(x_1, y_1), (x_2, y_2), \ldots , (x_n, y_n)$ by solving the system for a and b. Then use the regression capabilities of a graphing utility to confirm your result. (For an explanation of how the coefficients of a and b in the system are obtained, see Appendix B.)**

75. $\begin{cases} 5b + 10a = 20.2 \\ 10b + 30a = 50.1 \end{cases}$ **76.** $\begin{cases} 5b + 10a = 11.7 \\ 10b + 30a = 25.6 \end{cases}$

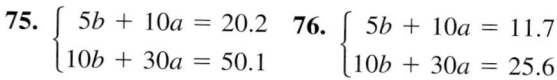

77. $\begin{cases} 7b + 21a = 35.1 \\ 21b + 91a = 114.2 \end{cases}$ **78.** $\begin{cases} 6b + 15a = 23.6 \\ 15b + 55a = 48.8 \end{cases}$

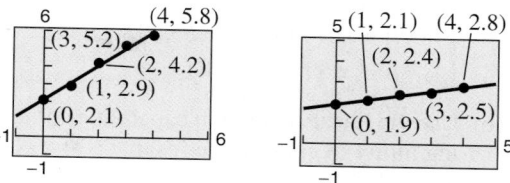

79. Data Analysis   A farmer used four test plots to determine the relationship between wheat yield (in bushels per acre) and the amount of fertilizer (in hundreds of pounds per acre). The results are shown in the table.

Fertilizer, x	1.0	1.5	2.0	2.5
Yield, y	32	41	48	53

(a) Find the least squares regression line $y = ax + b$ for the data by solving the system for a and b.

$$\begin{cases} 4b + 7.0a = 174 \\ 7b + 13.5a = 322 \end{cases}$$

(b) Use the linear regression capabilities of a graphing utility to confirm the result.

(c) Plot the data and the linear regression model.

(d) Use the line to estimate the yield for a fertilizer application of 160 pounds per acre.

80. Data Analysis   A store manager wants to know the demand for a certain product as a function of the price. The daily sales for the different prices of the product are shown in the table.

Price, x	$1.00	$1.25	$1.50
Demand, y	450	375	330

(a) Find the least squares regression line $y = ax + b$ for the data by solving the system for a and b.

$$\begin{cases} 3.00b + 3.7500a = 1155.00 \\ 3.75b + 4.8125a = 1413.75 \end{cases}$$

(b) Use the linear regression capabilities of a graphing utility to confirm the result.

(c) Plot the data and the linear regression model.

(d) Then, use the line to predict the demand when the price is \$1.40.

Synthesis

True or False? **In Exercises 81–83, determine whether the statement is true or false. Justify your answer.**

81. If a system of linear equations has two distinct solutions, then it has an infinite number of solutions.

82. Solving a system of equations graphically will always give an exact solution.

83. If a system of linear equations has no solution, then the lines must be parallel.

Think About It **In Exercises 84 and 85, the graphs of the two equations appear to be parallel. Yet, when the system is solved algebraically, it is found that the system does have a solution. Find the solution and explain why it does not appear on the portion of the graph that is shown.**

84. $\begin{cases} 100y - x = 200 \\ 99y - x = -198 \end{cases}$ **85.** $\begin{cases} 21x - 20y = 0 \\ 13x - 12y = 120 \end{cases}$

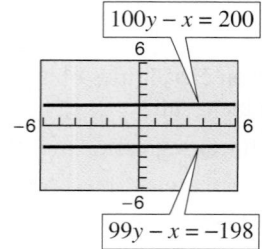

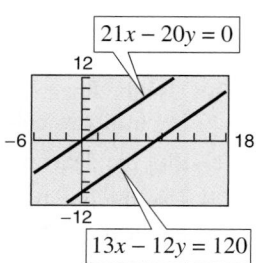

86. *Writing* Briefly explain whether or not it is possible for a consistent system of linear equations to have exactly two solutions.

87. *Think About It* Give examples of (a) a system of linear equations that has no solution and (b) a system that has an infinite number of solutions.

Exploration **In Exercises 88 and 89, find the value of k such that the system of equations is inconsistent.**

88. $\begin{cases} 4x - 8y = -3 \\ 2x + ky = 16 \end{cases}$ **89.** $\begin{cases} 15x + 3y = 6 \\ -10x + ky = 9 \end{cases}$

Advanced Applications **In Exercises 90 and 91, solve the system of equations for u and v. While solving for these variables, consider the transcendental functions as constants. (Systems of this type are found in a course in differential equations.)**

90. $\begin{cases} ue^x + vxe^x = 0 \\ ue^x + v(x + 1)e^x = e^x \ln x \end{cases}$

91. $\begin{cases} ue^{2x} + vxe^{2x} = 0 \\ u(2e^{2x}) + v(2x + 1)e^{2x} = \dfrac{e^{2x}}{x} \end{cases}$

Review

In Exercises 92–95, use a graphing utility to graph the functions. Use the graph to determine the domain and range.

92. $f(x) = x^2 - 2x$ **93.** $g(x) = \sqrt[3]{x - 2}$

94. $h(x) = \sqrt{25 - x^2}$ **95.** $s(t) = 4/(9 - t^2)$

In Exercises 96–103, solve the inequality and graph the solution on a real number line.

96. $-11 - 6x \geq 33$ **97.** $2(x - 3) > -5x + 1$

98. $8x - 15 \leq -4(2x - 1)$

99. $-6 \leq 3x - 10 < 6$

100. $|x - 8| < 10$ **101.** $|x + 10| \geq -3$

102. $2x^2 + 3x - 35 < 0$ **103.** $3x^2 + 12x > 0$

In Exercises 104–107, write the expression as the logarithm of a single quantity.

104. $\ln x + \ln 6$ **105.** $\ln x - 5 \ln(x + 3)$

106. $\log_9 12 - \log_9 x$ **107.** $\frac{1}{4} \log_6 3 + \frac{1}{4} \log_6 x$

In Exercises 108 and 109, solve the system by the method of substitution.

108. $\begin{cases} 4x - y = -16 \\ -5x + 3y = 6 \end{cases}$ **109.** $\begin{cases} -12x + 9y = 51 \\ -x - 7y = -19 \end{cases}$

Row-Echelon Form and Back-Substitution

The method of elimination can be applied to a system of linear equations in more than two variables. When elimination is used to solve a system of linear equations, the goal is to rewrite the system in a form to which back-substitution can be applied. Consider the following two systems of linear equations.

System of 3 Linear Equations in 3 Variables (See Example 2):

$$\begin{cases} x - 2y + 3z = 9 \\ -x + 3y = -4 \\ 2x - 5y + 5z = 17 \end{cases}$$

Equivalent System in Row-Echelon Form (See Example 1):

$$\begin{cases} x - 2y + 3z = 9 \\ y + 3z = 5 \\ z = 2 \end{cases}$$

The second system is said to be in **row-echelon form,** which means that it has a "stair-step" pattern with leading coefficients of 1. After comparing the two systems, it should be clear that it is easier to solve the system in row-echelon form.

EXAMPLE 1 Using Back-Substitution

Solve the system of linear equations.

$$\begin{cases} x - 2y + 3z = 9 & \text{Equation 1} \\ y + 3z = 5 & \text{Equation 2} \\ z = 2 & \text{Equation 3} \end{cases}$$

Solution

From Equation 3, you know the value of z. To solve for y, substitute $z = 2$ into Equation 2 to obtain

$$y + 3(2) = 5 \qquad \text{Substitute 2 for } z.$$
$$y = -1. \qquad \text{Solve for } y.$$

Finally, substitute $y = -1$ and $z = 2$ into Equation 1 to obtain

$$x - 2(-1) + 3(2) = 9 \qquad \text{Substitute } -1 \text{ for } y \text{ and 2 for } z.$$
$$x = 1. \qquad \text{Solve for } x.$$

The solution is $x = 1$, $y = -1$, and $z = 2$, which can be written as the **ordered triple** $(1, -1, 2)$. Check this in the original system of equations as follows.

Check
$$1 - 2(-1) + 3(2) = 9 \checkmark$$
$$-1 + 3(2) = 5 \checkmark$$
$$2 = 2 \checkmark$$

What You Should Learn:

- How to recognize linear systems in row-echelon form and use back-substitution to solve the systems
- How to use Gaussian Elimination to solve systems of linear equations
- How to solve nonsquare systems of linear equations
- How to graphically interpret three-variable systems
- How to use systems of linear equations to write partial fraction decompositions of rational expressions
- How to use systems of linear equations in three or more variables to model and solve real-life problems

Why You Should Learn It:

Systems of linear equations in three or more variables can be used to model and solve real-life problems. For instance, Exercise 109 on page 399 shows how to use a system of linear equations to analyze an automobile's braking system.

Andy Sacks/Tony Stone Images

Gaussian Elimination

Two systems of equations are *equivalent* if they have the same solution set. To solve a system that is not in row-echelon form, first convert it to an *equivalent* system that *is* in row-echelon form by using one or more of the elementary row operations shown below. This process is called **Gaussian elimination,** after the German mathematician Carl Friedrich Gauss (1777–1855).

> ## Elementary Row Operations
>
> 1. Interchange two equations.
> 2. Multiply one of the equations by a nonzero constant.
> 3. Add a multiple of one equation to another equation.

EXAMPLE 2   Using Gaussian Elimination to Solve a System

Solve the system of linear equations.

$$\begin{cases} x - 2y + 3z = 9 & \text{Equation 1} \\ -x + 3y \phantom{{}+3z} = -4 & \text{Equation 2} \\ 2x - 5y + 5z = 17 & \text{Equation 3} \end{cases}$$

Solution

Because the leading coefficient of the first equation is 1, you can begin by saving the x in the upper left position and eliminating the other x's from the first column.

$$\begin{cases} x - 2y + 3z = 9 \\ \phantom{x -{}} y + 3z = 5 \\ 2x - 5y + 5z = 17 \end{cases}$$

> Adding the first equation to the second equation produces a new second equation.

$$\begin{cases} x - 2y + 3z = 9 \\ \phantom{x -{}} y + 3z = 5 \\ \phantom{2x -{}} -y - z = -1 \end{cases}$$

> Adding -2 times the first equation to the third equation produces a new third equation.

Now that all but the first x have been eliminated from the first column, go to work on the second column. (You need to eliminate y from the third equation.)

$$\begin{cases} x - 2y + 3z = 9 \\ \phantom{x -{}} y + 3z = 5 \\ \phantom{x - 2y +{}} 2z = 4 \end{cases}$$

> Adding the second equation to the third equation produces a new third equation.

Finally, you need a coefficient of 1 for z in the third equation.

$$\begin{cases} x - 2y + 3z = 9 \\ \phantom{x -{}} y + 3z = 5 \\ z = 2 \end{cases}$$

> Multiplying the third equation by $\frac{1}{2}$ produces a new third equation.

This is the same system that was solved in Example 1. As in that example, you can conclude that the solution is $x = 1$, $y = -1$, and $z = 2$, written as $(1, -1, 2)$. Check this in the original system of the equations.

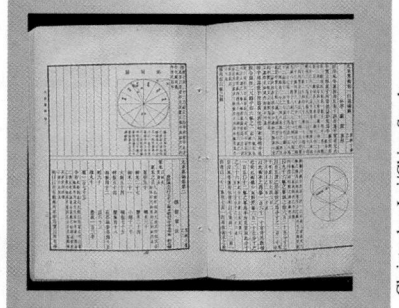

One of the most influential Chinese mathematics books was the *Chui-chang suan-shu* or *Nine Chapters on the Mathematical Art* (written in approximately 250 B.C.). Chapter Eight contained solutions of systems of linear equations using positive and negative numbers. One such system was

$$\begin{cases} 3x + 2y + 3z = 39 \\ 2x + 3y + 3z = 34. \\ 2x + 2y + 3z = 26 \end{cases}$$

This system was solved using column operations on a matrix. Matrices (plural for matrix) will be discussed in the next chapter.

Arithmetic errors are often made when performing elementary row operations. Have students note the operation performed in each step so that they can go back and check their work.

STUDY TIP

The goal of Gaussian elimination is to use elementary row operations on a system in order to isolate one variable. You can then solve for the value of the variable and use back-substitution to find the values of the remaining variables.

The next example involves an inconsistent system—one that has no solution. The key to recognizing an inconsistent system is that at some stage in the elimination process, you obtain a false statement such as $0 = -2$.

EXAMPLE 3   An Inconsistent System

Solve the system of linear equations.

$$\begin{cases} x - 3y + z = 1 & \text{Equation 1} \\ 2x - y - 2z = 2 & \text{Equation 2} \\ x + 2y - 3z = -1 & \text{Equation 3} \end{cases}$$

Solution

$$\begin{cases} x - 3y + z = 1 \\ 5y - 4z = 0 \\ x + 2y - 3z = -1 \end{cases}$$

Adding -2 times the first equation to the second equation produces a new second equation.

$$\begin{cases} x - 3y + z = 1 \\ 5y - 4z = 0 \\ 5y - 4z = -2 \end{cases}$$

Adding -1 times the first equation to the third equation produces a new third equation.

$$\begin{cases} x - 3y + z = 1 \\ 5y - 4z = 0 \\ 0 = -2 \end{cases}$$

Adding -1 times the second equation to the third equation produces a new third equation.

Because $0 = -2$ is a false statement, you can conclude that this system is inconsistent and therefore has no solution. Moreover, because this system is equivalent to the original system, you can conclude that the original system also has no solution.

As with a system of linear equations in two variables, the number of solutions of a system of linear equations in more than two variables must fall into one of three categories.

The Number of Solutions of a Linear System

For a system of linear equations, exactly one of the following is true.

1. There is exactly one solution.
2. There are infinitely many solutions.
3. There is no solution.

A system of linear equations is called *consistent* if it has at least one solution. A consistent system with exactly one solution is **independent**. A consistent system with infinitely many solutions is **dependent**. A system of linear equations is called *inconsistent* if it has no solution.

EXAMPLE 4   A System with Infinitely Many Solutions

Solve the system of linear equations.

$$\begin{cases} x + y - 3z = -1 & \text{Equation 1} \\ \phantom{x + {}} y - z = 0 & \text{Equation 2} \\ -x + 2y \phantom{{}- 3z} = 1 & \text{Equation 3} \end{cases}$$

Look closely at the equations in the first step of the solution to Example 4 and remind students how to recognize equivalent equations (see Section 5.2 for information on equivalent systems). Because original Equations 2 and 3 are equivalent, there are infinitely many solutions.

Solution

$$\begin{cases} x + y - 3z = -1 \\ \phantom{x + {}} y - z = 0 \\ \phantom{x + {}} 3y - 3z = 0 \end{cases}$$

> Adding the first equation to the third equation produces a new third equation.

$$\begin{cases} x + y - 3z = -1 \\ \phantom{x + {}} y - z = 0 \\ 0 = 0 \end{cases}$$

> Adding -3 times the second equation to the third equation produces a new third equation.

This means that Equation 3 depends on Equations 1 and 2 in the sense that it gives us no additional information about the variables. So, the original system is equivalent to the system

$$\begin{cases} x + y - 3z = -1 \\ \phantom{x + {}} y - z = 0 \end{cases}.$$

In the last equation, solve for y in terms of z to obtain $y = z$. Back-substituting for y into the previous equation produces $x = 2z - 1$. Finally, letting $z = a$, where a is a real number, the solutions to the given system are all of the form

$$x = 2a - 1, \qquad y = a, \qquad \text{and} \qquad z = a.$$

So, every ordered triple of the form

$$(2a - 1, a, a), \qquad a \text{ is a real number}$$

is a solution of the system.

In Example 4, there are other ways to write the same infinite set of solutions. For instance, the solutions could have been written as

$$\left(b, \tfrac{1}{2}(b + 1), \tfrac{1}{2}(b + 1)\right), \qquad b \text{ is a real number.}$$

To convince yourself that this description produces the same set of solutions, consider the following.

STUDY T!P

There are an infinite number of solutions to Example 4, but they all are of a specific form. By selecting, for example, a-values of 0, 1, and 3, you can verify that $(-1, 0, 0)$, $(1, 1, 1)$, and $(5, 3, 3)$ are specific solutions. It is incorrect to say simply that the solution to Example 4 is "infinite." You must also specify the form of the solutions.

Substitution	*Solution*	
$a = 0$	$(2(0) - 1, 0, 0) = (-1, 0, 0)$	Same solution
$b = -1$	$\left(-1, \tfrac{1}{2}(-1 + 1), \tfrac{1}{2}(-1 + 1)\right) = (-1, 0, 0)$	
$a = 1$	$(2(1) - 1, 1, 1) = (1, 1, 1)$	Same solution
$b = 1$	$\left(1, \tfrac{1}{2}(1 + 1), \tfrac{1}{2}(1 + 1)\right) = (1, 1, 1)$	
$a = 2$	$(2(2) - 1, 2, 2) = (3, 2, 2)$	Same solution
$b = 3$	$\left(3, \tfrac{1}{2}(3 + 1), \tfrac{1}{2}(3 + 1)\right) = (3, 2, 2)$	

Nonsquare Systems

So far, each system of linear equations has been *square*, which means that the number of equations is equal to the number of variables. In a **nonsquare system of equations,** the number of equations differs from the number of variables. A system of linear equations cannot have a unique solution unless there are at least as many equations as there are variables in the system.

Activities

Solve the systems of equations.

1. $\begin{cases} x - y + z = 4 \\ x + 3y - 2z = -3 \\ 3x + 2y + z = 5 \end{cases}$

   Answer: $(2, -1, 1)$

2. $\begin{cases} x - 2y - z = -5 \\ 2x + y + z = 5 \end{cases}$

   Answer: $(a, 3a, 5 - 5a)$

3. $\begin{cases} x - 2y + z = 4 \\ 3x - 6y + 3z = 7 \\ 2x + y + 4z = 2 \end{cases}$

   Answer: No solution

EXAMPLE 5 A System with Fewer Equations Than Variables

Solve the system of linear equations.

$$\begin{cases} x - 2y + z = 2 & \text{Equation 1} \\ 2x - y - z = 1 & \text{Equation 2} \end{cases}$$

Solution

Begin by rewriting the system in row-echelon form.

$$\begin{cases} x - 2y + z = 2 \\ \phantom{x - {}} 3y - 3z = -3 \end{cases}$$

Adding -2 times the first equation to the second equation produces a new second equation.

$$\begin{cases} x - 2y + z = 2 \\ y - z = -1 \end{cases}$$

Multiplying the second equation by $\frac{1}{3}$ produces a new second equation.

Solving for y in terms of z, you get $y = z - 1$, and back-substitution into Equation 1 yields

$$x - 2(z - 1) + z = 2$$

$$x - 2z + 2 + z = 2$$

$$x = z.$$

Finally, by letting $z = a$ where a is a real number, you have the solution

$$x = a, \qquad y = a - 1, \qquad \text{and} \qquad z = a.$$

So, every ordered triple of the form

$$(a, a - 1, a), \qquad a \text{ is a real number}$$

is a solution of the system.

In Example 5, try choosing some values of a to obtain different solutions of the system, such as $(1, 0, 1)$, $(2, 1, 2)$, and $(3, 2, 3)$. Then check each of the solutions in the original system as follows.

Check: $(1, 0, 1)$

$$1 - 2(0) + 1 = 2$$
$$2 = 2 \checkmark$$
$$2(1) - 0 - 1 = 1$$
$$1 = 1 \checkmark$$

Check: $(2, 1, 2)$

$$2 - 2(1) + 2 = 2$$
$$2 = 2 \checkmark$$
$$2(2) - 1 - 2 = 1$$
$$1 = 1 \checkmark$$

Check: $(3, 2, 3)$

$$3 - 2(2) + 3 = 2$$
$$2 = 2 \checkmark$$
$$2(3) - 2 - 3 = 1$$
$$1 = 1 \checkmark$$

Graphical Interpretation of Three-Variable Systems

Solutions of equations with three variables can be pictured with a **three-dimensional coordinate system.** To construct such a system, begin with the *xy*-coordinate plane in a horizontal position. Then draw the *z*-axis as a vertical line through the origin.

Every ordered triple (x, y, z) corresponds to a point on the three-dimensional coordinate system. For instance, the points corresponding to

$$(-2, 5, 4), \qquad (2, -5, 3), \qquad \text{and} \qquad (3, 3, -2)$$

are shown in Figure 5.12.

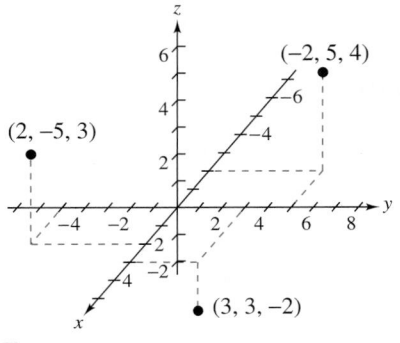

Figure 5.12

The **graph of an equation in three variables** consists of all points (x, y, z) that are solutions of the equation. The graph of a linear equation in three variables is a *plane*. Sketching graphs on a three-dimensional coordinate system is difficult because the sketch itself is only two-dimensional.

One technique for sketching a plane is to find the three points at which the plane intersects the axes. For instance, the plane

$$3x + 2y + 4z = 12$$

intersects the *x*-axis at the point $(4, 0, 0)$, the *y*-axis at the point $(0, 6, 0)$, and the *z*-axis at the point $(0, 0, 3)$.

By plotting these three points, connecting them with line segments, and shading the resulting triangular region, you can sketch a portion of the graph, as shown in Figure 5.13.

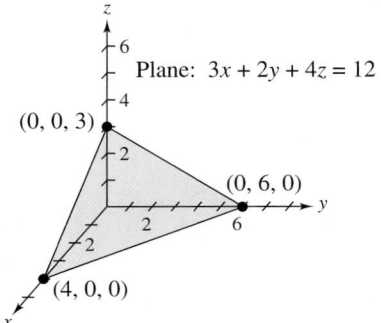

Figure 5.13

The graph of a system of three linear equations in three variables consists of *three* planes. When these planes intersect in a single point, the system has exactly one solution. [See Figure 5.14(a).] When the three planes have no point in common, the system has no solution. [See Figures 5.14(b) and (c).] When the three planes intersect in a line or a plane, the system has infinitely many solutions. [See Figures 5.14(d) and (e).]

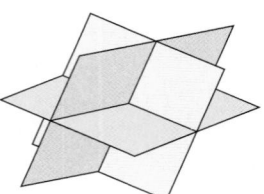  

(a) **Solution: one point**   (b) **Solution: none**   (c) **Solution: none**

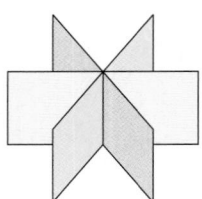

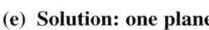

(d) **Solution: one line**   (e) **Solution: one plane**

Figure 5.14

Partial Fraction Decomposition and Other Applications

A rational expression can be often written as the sum of two or more simpler rational expressions. For example, the rational expression

$$\frac{x + 7}{x^2 - x - 6}$$

can be written as the sum of two fractions with linear denominators. That is,

Partial fraction decomposition of
$$\frac{x + 7}{x^2 - x - 6}$$

$$\frac{x + 7}{x^2 - x - 6} = \overbrace{\frac{2}{x - 3}}^{} + \overbrace{\frac{-1}{x + 2}}^{}.$$

$$\underbrace{\phantom{\frac{2}{x-3}}}_{\substack{\text{Partial} \\ \text{fraction}}} \quad \underbrace{\phantom{\frac{-1}{x+2}}}_{\substack{\text{Partial} \\ \text{fraction}}}$$

Each fraction on the right side of the equation is a **partial fraction,** and together they make up the **partial fraction decomposition** of the left side.

The method of partial fractions was introduced by **John Bernoulli (1667–1748),** a Swiss mathematician who was instrumental in the early development of calculus. Bernoulli was a professor at the University of Basel and taught many outstanding students, the most famous of whom was Leonhard Euler.

The Granger Collection

Decomposition of $N(x)/D(x)$ into Partial Fractions

1. *Divide if improper:* If $N(x)/D(x)$ is an improper fraction (degree of $N(x) \geq$ degree of $D(x)$), divide the denominator into the numerator to obtain

$$\frac{N(x)}{D(x)} = (\text{polynomial}) + \frac{N_1(x)}{D(x)}$$

and apply Steps 2, 3, and 4 (below) to the proper rational expression $N_1(x)/D(x)$.

2. *Factor denominator:* Completely factor the denominator into factors of the form

$$(px + q)^m \quad \text{and} \quad (ax^2 + bx + c)^n$$

where $(ax^2 + bx + c)$ is irreducible.

3. *Linear factors:* For *each* factor of the form $(px + q)^m$, the partial fraction decomposition must include the following sum of m fractions.

$$\frac{A_1}{(px + q)} + \frac{A_2}{(px + q)^2} + \cdots + \frac{A_m}{(px + q)^m}$$

4. *Quadratic factors:* For *each* factor of the form $(ax^2 + bx + c)^n$, the partial fraction decomposition must include the following sum of n fractions.

$$\frac{B_1 x + C_1}{ax^2 + bx + c} + \frac{B_2 x + C_2}{(ax^2 + bx + c)^2} + \cdots + \frac{B_n x + C_n}{(ax^2 + bx + c)^n}$$

One of the most important applications of partial fractions is in calculus. If you go on to take a course in calculus, you will learn how partial fractions can be used in a calculus operation called antidifferentiation.

EXAMPLE 6 Partial Fraction Decomposition: Distinct Linear Factors

Write the partial fraction decomposition for

$$\frac{x + 7}{x^2 - x - 6}.$$

Solution

Because $x^2 - x - 6 = (x - 3)(x + 2)$, you should include one partial fraction with a constant numerator for each linear factor of the denominator and write

$$\frac{x + 7}{x^2 - x - 6} = \frac{A}{x - 3} + \frac{B}{x + 2}.$$

Multiplying both sides of this equation by the least common denominator, $(x - 3)(x + 2)$, leads to the **basic equation**

$$
\begin{aligned}
x + 7 &= A(x + 2) + B(x - 3) &\quad& \text{Basic equation} \\
&= Ax + 2A + Bx - 3B \\
&= (A + B)x + 2A - 3B. &\quad& \text{Write in polynomial form.}
\end{aligned}
$$

By equating coefficients of like terms on opposite sides of the equation, you obtain the following system of linear equations.

$$
\begin{cases}
A + B = 1 \\
2A - 3B = 7
\end{cases}
$$

You can solve the system of linear equations as follows.

$$
\begin{array}{lll}
A + B = 1 & \Longrightarrow\quad 3A + 3B = 3 & \text{Multiply Equation 1 by 3.} \\
2A - 3B = 7 & \Longrightarrow\quad \underline{2A - 3B = 7} & \text{Equation 2} \\
& 5A = 10 & \text{Add equations}
\end{array}
$$

From this equation, you can see that $A = 2$. By back-substituting this value of A into Equation 1, you can determine that $B = -1$.

Therefore, the partial fraction decomposition is

$$\frac{x + 7}{x^2 - x - 6} = \frac{2}{x - 3} - \frac{1}{x + 2}.$$

Check this result by combining the two partial fractions on the right side of the equation.

You can graphically check the decomposition found in Example 1. To do this, graph

$$y_1 = \frac{x + 7}{x^2 - x - 6} \quad \text{and} \quad y_2 = \frac{2}{x - 3} - \frac{1}{x + 2}$$

in the same viewing window. Their graphs should be identical, as shown in Figure 5.15.

Activities

1. Write the partial fraction decomposition.

$$\frac{5x - 10}{(x + 2)(2x - 1)}$$

Answer: $\dfrac{4}{x + 2} - \dfrac{3}{2x - 1}$

2. Write the partial fraction decomposition.

$$\frac{4x^3 + 9x^2 - 2x + 6}{x(x + 2)}$$

Answer: $4x + 1 + \dfrac{3}{x} - \dfrac{7}{x + 2}$

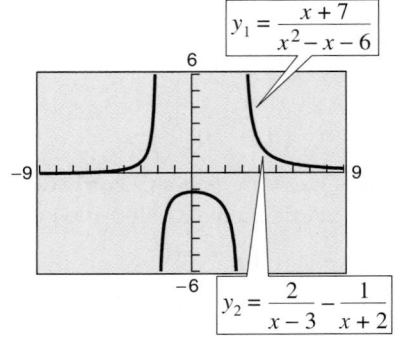

Figure 5.15

The next example shows how to find the partial fraction decomposition for a rational function whose denominator has a repeated linear factor.

EXAMPLE 7   Partial Fraction Decomposition: Repeated Linear Factors

Write the partial fraction decomposition for

$$\frac{5x^2 + 20x + 6}{x^3 + 2x^2 + x}.$$

Solution

Because the denominator factors as

$$x^3 + 2x^2 + x = x(x^2 + 2x + 1)$$

$$= x(x + 1)^2$$

you should include one partial fraction with a constant numerator for each power of x and $(x + 1)$ and write

$$\frac{5x^2 + 20x + 6}{x(x + 1)^2} = \frac{A}{x} + \frac{B}{x + 1} + \frac{C}{(x + 1)^2}.$$

Multiplying by the LCD, $x(x + 1)^2$, leads to the basic equation

$$5x^2 + 20x + 6 = A(x + 1)^2 + Bx(x + 1) + Cx \qquad \text{Basic equation}$$

$$= Ax^2 + 2Ax + A + Bx^2 + Bx + Cx$$

$$= (A + B)x^2 + (2A + B + C)x + A. \qquad \text{Polynomial form}$$

By equating coefficients of like terms on opposite sides of the equation, you obtain the following system of linear equations.

$$\begin{cases} A + B & = 5 \\ 2A + B + C & = 20 \\ A & = 6 \end{cases}$$

Substituting 6 for A in the first equation produces

$$6 + B = 5$$

$$B = -1.$$

Substituting 6 for A and -1 for B in the second equation produces

$$2(6) + (-1) + C = 20$$

$$C = 9.$$

Therefore, the partial fraction decomposition is

$$\frac{5x^2 + 20x + 6}{x(x + 1)^2} = \frac{6}{x} - \frac{1}{x + 1} + \frac{9}{(x + 1)^2}.$$

Exploration

Partial fraction decomposition is practical only for rational functions whose denominators factor "nicely." For example, the factorization of the denominator $x^2 - x - 5$ is

$$\left(x - \frac{1 - \sqrt{21}}{2}\right)\left(x - \frac{1 + \sqrt{21}}{2}\right).$$

Write the basic equation and try to complete the decomposition for

$$\frac{x + 7}{x^2 - x - 5}.$$

What problems do you encounter?

Have students check some of their answers or the answers to some of the examples by combining the partial fractions.

EXAMPLE 8 Vertical Motion

The height at time t of an object that is moving in a (vertical) line with constant acceleration a is given by the *position equation* $s = \frac{1}{2}at^2 + v_0 t + s_0$. The height s is measured in feet, t is measured in seconds, v_0 is the initial velocity (in feet per second) at $t = 0$, and s_0 is the initial height. Find the values of a, v_0, and s_0, if $s = 52$ at $t = 1$, $s = 52$ at $t = 2$, and $s = 20$ at $t = 3$, as shown in Figure 5.16.

Solution

You can obtain three linear equations in a, v_0, and s_0 as follows.

When $t = 1$:　　$\frac{1}{2}a(1)^2 + v_0(1) + s_0 = 52$ ⟹ $a + 2v_0 + 2s_0 = 104$

When $t = 2$:　　$\frac{1}{2}a(2)^2 + v_0(2) + s_0 = 52$ ⟹ $2a + 2v_0 + s_0 = 52$

When $t = 3$:　　$\frac{1}{2}a(3)^2 + v_0(3) + s_0 = 20$ ⟹ $9a + 6v_0 + 2s_0 = 40$

Solving this system yields $a = -32$, $v_0 = 48$, and $s_0 = 20$.

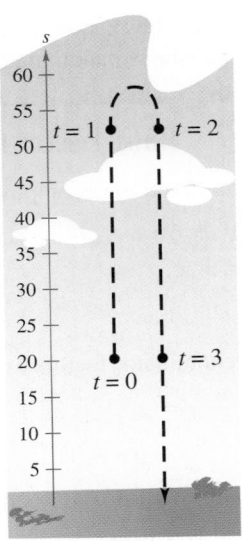

Figure 5.16

EXAMPLE 9 Data Analysis: Curve-Fitting

Find a quadratic equation, $y = ax^2 + bx + c$, whose graph passes through the points $(-1, 3)$, $(1, 1)$, and $(2, 6)$.

Solution

Because the graph of $y = ax^2 + bx + c$ passes through the points $(-1, 3)$, $(1, 1)$, and $(2, 6)$, you can write the following.

　When $x = -1$, $y = 3$:　　$a(-1)^2 + b(-1) + c = 3$

　When $x = 1$, $y = 1$:　　$a(1)^2 + b(1) + c = 1$

　When $x = 2$, $y = 6$:　　$a(2)^2 + b(2) + c = 6$

This produces the following system of linear equations.

$$\begin{cases} a - b + c = 3 & \text{Equation 1} \\ a + b + c = 1 & \text{Equation 2} \\ 4a + 2b + c = 6 & \text{Equation 3} \end{cases}$$

The solution of this system is $a = 2$, $b = -1$, and $c = 0$. So, the equation of the parabola is $y = 2x^2 - x$, as shown in Figure 5.17. From the graph, you can check to see that the parabola passes through the given points $(-1, 3)$, $(1, 1)$, and $(2, 6)$.

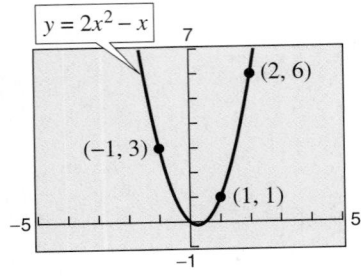

Figure 5.17

> ## STUDY T!P
>
> When you use a system of linear equations to solve an application, it is wise to interpret your solution in the context of the problem to see if it makes sense. For instance, in Example 8 the solution results in a position equation of
>
> $$s = -16t^2 + 48t + 20$$
>
> which implies that the object was thrown upward at a velocity of 48 feet per second from a height of 20 feet. The object undergoes a constant downward acceleration of 32 feet per second squared. (Physics will tell you that this is the value of the acceleration due to gravity.)

5.3   E x e r c i s e s

In Exercises 1–4, decide whether each ordered triple is a solution of the system of equations.

1. $\begin{cases} 3x - y + z = 1 \\ 2x - 3z = -14 \\ 5y + 2z = 8 \end{cases}$

(a) $(2, 5, 0)$ (b) $(-2, 0, 4)$
(c) $(0, -1, 3)$ (d) $(-1, 0, 4)$

2. $\begin{cases} 3x + 4y - z = 17 \\ 5x - y + 2z = -2 \\ 2x - 3y + 7z = -21 \end{cases}$

(a) $(3, 2, 0)$ (b) $(1, 3, -2)$
(c) $(4, 1, -3)$ (d) $(1, 5, -1)$

3. $\begin{cases} 4x + y - z = 0 \\ -8x - 6y + z = -\frac{7}{4} \\ 3x - y = -\frac{9}{4} \end{cases}$

(a) $(0, 1, 1)$ (b) $\left(-\frac{3}{2}, \frac{5}{4}, -\frac{5}{4}\right)$
(c) $\left(-\frac{1}{2}, \frac{3}{4}, -\frac{5}{4}\right)$ (d) $\left(-\frac{1}{2}, 2, 0\right)$

4. $\begin{cases} -4x - y - 8z = -6 \\ y + z = 0 \\ 4x - 7y = 6 \end{cases}$

(a) $(-2, -2, 2)$ (b) $\left(-\frac{33}{2}, -10, 10\right)$
(c) $\left(\frac{1}{8}, -\frac{1}{2}, \frac{1}{2}\right)$ (d) $\left(-\frac{11}{2}, -4, 4\right)$

In Exercises 5–10, use back-substitution to solve the system of linear equations.

5. $\begin{cases} 2x - y + 5z = 24 \\ y + 2z = 4 \\ z = 6 \end{cases}$

6. $\begin{cases} 4x - 3y - 2z = 21 \\ 6y - 5z = -10 \\ z = -4 \end{cases}$

7. $\begin{cases} 2x + y - 3z = 10 \\ y = -2 \\ y - z = 4 \end{cases}$

8. $\begin{cases} x = 8 \\ 2x + 3y = 10 \\ x - y + 2z = 22 \end{cases}$

9. $\begin{cases} 4x - 2y + z = 8 \\ 2z = 4 \\ -y + z = 4 \end{cases}$

10. $\begin{cases} 5x - 8z = 22 \\ 3y - 5z = 10 \\ z = -4 \end{cases}$

In Exercises 11 and 12, perform the row operation and write the equivalent system.

11. Add Equation 1 to Equation 2.

$\begin{cases} x - 2y + 3z = 5 & \text{Equation 1} \\ -x + 3y - 5z = 4 & \text{Equation 2} \\ 2x - 3z = 0 & \text{Equation 3} \end{cases}$

What did this operation accomplish?

12. Add -2 times Equation 1 to Equation 3.

$\begin{cases} x - 2y + 3z = 5 & \text{Equation 1} \\ -x + 3y - 5z = 4 & \text{Equation 2} \\ 2x - 3z = 0 & \text{Equation 3} \end{cases}$

What did this operation accomplish?

In Exercises 13–40, solve the system of linear equations and check any solution algebraically.

13. $\begin{cases} x + y + z = 6 \\ 2x - y + z = -1 \\ 3x - z = -7 \end{cases}$

14. $\begin{cases} x + y + z = 2 \\ -x + 3y + 2z = 8 \\ 4x + y = 4 \end{cases}$

15. $\begin{cases} 2x + 2z = 6 \\ 5x + 3y = 11 \\ 3y - 4z = 1 \end{cases}$

16. $\begin{cases} 4x + y - 3z = 11 \\ 2x - 3y + 2z = 9 \\ x + y + z = -3 \end{cases}$

17. $\begin{cases} 6y + 4z = -18 \\ 3x + 3y = 9 \\ 2x - 3z = 12 \end{cases}$

18. $\begin{cases} 2x + 4y + z = -4 \\ 2x - 4y + 6z = 13 \\ 4x - 2y + z = 6 \end{cases}$

19. $\begin{cases} 3x - 2y + 4z = 1 \\ x + y - 2z = 3 \\ 2x - 3y + 6z = 8 \end{cases}$

20. $\begin{cases} 5x - 3y + 2z = 3 \\ 2x + 4y - z = 7 \\ x - 11y + 4z = 3 \end{cases}$

21. $\begin{cases} 3x + 3y + 5z = 1 \\ 3x + 5y + 9z = 0 \\ 5x + 9y + 17z = 0 \end{cases}$

22. $\begin{cases} 2x + y + 3z = 1 \\ 2x + 6y + 8z = 3 \\ 6x + 8y + 18z = 5 \end{cases}$

23. $\begin{cases} x + 2y - 7z = -4 \\ 2x + y + z = 13 \\ 3x + 9y - 36z = -33 \end{cases}$

24. $\begin{cases} 2x + y - 3z = 4 \\ 4x + 2z = 10 \\ -2x + 3y - 13z = -8 \end{cases}$

25. $\begin{cases} 3x - 3y + 6z = 6 \\ x + 2y - z = 5 \\ 5x - 8y + 13z = 7 \end{cases}$ **26.** $\begin{cases} x + 4z = 13 \\ 4x - 2y + z = 7 \\ 2x - 2y - 7z = -19 \end{cases}$

27. $\begin{cases} x - 2y + 3z = 4 \\ 3x - y + 2z = 0 \\ x + 3y - 4z = -2 \end{cases}$

28. $\begin{cases} -x + 3y + z = 4 \\ 4x - 2y - 5z = -7 \\ 2x + 4y - 3z = 12 \end{cases}$ **29.** $\begin{cases} x + 4z = 1 \\ x + y + 10z = 10 \\ 2x - y + 2z = -5 \end{cases}$

30. $\begin{cases} 3x - 2y - 6z = -4 \\ -3x + 2y + 6z = 1 \\ x - y - 5z = -3 \end{cases}$

31. $\begin{cases} 2x + 3y = 0 \\ 4x + 3y - z = 0 \\ 8x + 3y + 3z = 0 \end{cases}$ **32.** $\begin{cases} 4x + 3y + 17z = 0 \\ 5x + 4y + 22z = 0 \\ 4x + 2y + 19z = 0 \end{cases}$

33. $\begin{cases} x - 2y + 5z = 2 \\ 4x - z = 0 \end{cases}$

34. $\begin{cases} x - 3y + 2z = 18 \\ 5x - 13y + 12z = 80 \end{cases}$

35. $\begin{cases} 2x - 3y + z = -2 \\ -4x + 9y = 7 \end{cases}$

36. $\begin{cases} 2x + 3y + 3z = 7 \\ 4x + 18y + 15z = 44 \end{cases}$

37. $\begin{cases} 12x + 5y + z = 0 \\ 23x + 4y - z = 0 \end{cases}$ **38.** $\begin{cases} 10x - 3y + 2z = 0 \\ 19x - 5y - z = 0 \end{cases}$

39. $\begin{cases} x + 3w = 4 \\ 2y - z - w = 0 \\ 3y - 2w = 1 \\ 2x - y + 4z = 5 \end{cases}$

40. $\begin{cases} x + y + z + w = 6 \\ 2x + 3y - w = 0 \\ -3x + 4y + z + 2w = 4 \\ x + 2y - z + w = 0 \end{cases}$

Exploration **In Exercises 41–44, find a system of linear equations that has the given solution. (There are many correct answers.)**

41. $(4, -1, 2)$ **42.** $(-5, -2, 1)$

43. $\left(3, -\frac{1}{2}, \frac{7}{4}\right)$ **44.** $\left(-\frac{3}{2}, 4, -7\right)$

Three-Dimensional Graphics **In Exercises 45–48, sketch the plane represented by the linear equation. Then list four points that lie in the plane.**

45. $2x + 3y + 4z = 12$ **46.** $x + y + z = 6$

47. $2x + y + z = 4$ **48.** $x + 2y + 2z = 6$

In Exercises 49–54, write the form of the partial fraction decomposition of the rational expression. Do not solve for the constants.

49. $\dfrac{7}{x^2 - 14x}$ **50.** $\dfrac{x - 2}{x^2 + 4x + 3}$

51. $\dfrac{12}{x^3 - 10x^2}$ **52.** $\dfrac{x^2 - 3x + 2}{4x^3 + 11x^2}$

53. $\dfrac{4x^2 + 3}{(x - 5)^3}$ **54.** $\dfrac{6x + 5}{(x + 2)^4}$

In Exercises 55–72, write the partial fraction decomposition for the rational expression. Check your result algebraically by combining the fractions.

55. $\dfrac{1}{x^2 - 1}$ **56.** $\dfrac{1}{4x^2 - 9}$

57. $\dfrac{1}{x^2 + x}$ **58.** $\dfrac{3}{x^2 - 3x}$

59. $\dfrac{1}{2x^2 + x}$ **60.** $\dfrac{5}{x^2 + x - 6}$

61. $\dfrac{3}{x^2 + x - 2}$ **62.** $\dfrac{x + 1}{x^2 + 4x + 3}$

63. $\dfrac{x^2 + 12x + 12}{x^3 - 4x}$ **64.** $\dfrac{x + 2}{x(x - 4)}$

65. $\dfrac{4x^2 + 2x - 1}{x^2(x + 1)}$ **66.** $\dfrac{2x - 3}{(x - 1)^2}$

67. $\dfrac{3x}{(x - 3)^2}$ **68.** $\dfrac{6x^2 + 1}{x^2(x - 1)^3}$

69. $\dfrac{2x^3 - x^2 + x + 5}{x^2 + 3x + 2}$ **70.** $\dfrac{x^3 + 2x^2 - x + 1}{x^2 + 3x - 4}$

71. $\dfrac{x^4}{(x - 1)^3}$ **72.** $\dfrac{4x^4}{(2x - 1)^3}$

In Exercises 73–78, write the partial fraction decomposition for the rational expression. Use a graphing utility to check your result graphically.

73. $\dfrac{5 - x}{2x^2 + x - 1}$

74. $\dfrac{3x^2 - 7x - 2}{x^3 - x}$

75. $\dfrac{x - 1}{x^3 + x^2}$

76. $\dfrac{4x^2 - 1}{2x(x + 1)^2}$

77. $\dfrac{2x^3 - 4x^2 - 15x + 5}{x^2 - 2x - 8}$

78. $\dfrac{x^3 - x + 3}{x^2 + x - 2}$

Graphical Analysis In Exercises 79 and 80, write the partial fraction decomposition for the rational function. Identify the graph of the rational function and the graphs of each term of its decomposition. State any relationship between the vertical asymptotes of the rational function and the vertical asymptotes of the terms of the decomposition.

79. $y = \dfrac{x - 12}{x(x - 4)}$

80. $y = \dfrac{2(4x - 3)}{x^2 - 9}$

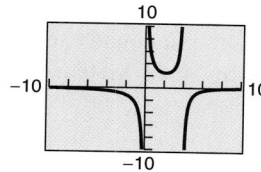
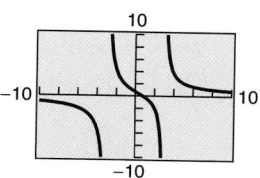

Vertical Motion In Exercises 81–84, find the position equation $s = \frac{1}{2}at^2 + v_0 t + s_0$ for an object at the given heights moving vertically at the specified times.

81. At $t = 1$ second, $s = 128$ feet
At $t = 2$ seconds, $s = 80$ feet
At $t = 3$ seconds, $s = 0$ feet

82. At $t = 1$ second, $s = 48$ feet
At $t = 2$ seconds, $s = 64$ feet
At $t = 3$ seconds, $s = 48$ feet

83. At $t = 1$ second, $s = 452$ feet
At $t = 2$ seconds, $s = 260$ feet
At $t = 3$ seconds, $s = 116$ feet

84. At $t = 1$ second, $s = 132$ feet
At $t = 2$ seconds, $s = 100$ feet
At $t = 3$ seconds, $s = 36$ feet

In Exercises 85–88, find the equation of the parabola

$$y = ax^2 + bx + c$$

that passes through the given points. To verify your result, use a graphing utility to plot the points and graph the parabola.

85. $(0, 0), (2, -2), (4, 0)$

86. $(0, 3), (1, 4), (2, 3)$

87. $(2, 0), (3, -1), (4, 0)$

88. $(1, 3), (2, 2), (3, -3)$

In Exercises 89–92, find the equation of the circle

$$x^2 + y^2 + Dx + Ey + F = 0$$

that passes through the given points. To verify your result, use a graphing utility to plot the points and graph the circle.

89. $(0, 0), (2, 2), (4, 0)$

90. $(0, 0), (0, 6), (3, 3)$

91. $(-3, -1), (2, 4), (-6, 8)$

92. $(-6, -1), (-4, 3), (2, -5)$

93. *Investments* An inheritance of \$16,000 was divided among three investments yielding a total of \$990 in interest per year. The interest rates were 5%, 6%, and 7%. Find the amount in each investment if the 5% and 6% investments were \$3000 and \$2000 less than the 7% investment.

94. *Investments* A total of \$1520 a year is received in interest from three investments. The interest rates for the three investments are 5%, 7%, and 8%. The 5% investment is half of the 7% investment, and the 7% investment is \$1500 less than the 8% investment. Find the amount in each investment.

95. *Borrowing* A small corporation borrowed \$775,000 to expand its product line. Some of the money was borrowed at 8%, some at 9%, and some at 10%. How much was borrowed at each rate if the annual interest was \$67,000 and the amount borrowed at 8% was four times the amount borrowed at 10%?

96. *Borrowing* A small corporation borrowed \$800,000 to expand its product line. Some of the money was borrowed at 8%, some at 9%, and some at 10%. How much was borrowed at each rate if the annual interest was \$67,000 and the amount borrowed at 8% was five times the amount borrowed at 10%?

Investment Portfolio   **In Exercises 97 and 98, consider an investor with a portfolio totaling $500,000 that is invested in certificates of deposit, municipal bonds, blue-chip stocks, and growth or speculative stocks. How much is put in each type of investment?**

97. The certificates of deposit pay 10% annually, and the municipal bonds pay 8% annually. Over a 5-year period, the investor expects the blue-chip stocks to return 12% annually and the growth stocks to return 13% annually. The investor wants a combined annual return of 10% as well as only one-fourth of the portfolio invested in stocks.

98. The certificates of deposit pay 9% annually, and the municipal bonds pay 5% annually. Over a 5-year period, the investor expects the blue-chip stocks to return 12% annually and the growth stocks to return 14% annually. The investor wants a combined annual return of 10% and also wants to have only one-fourth of the portfolio invested in stocks.

99. *Crop Spraying*   A mixture of 12 liters of chemical A, 16 liters of chemical B, and 26 liters of chemical C is required to kill a certain destructive crop insect. Commercial spray X contains 1, 2, and 2 parts, respectively, of these chemicals. Commercial spray Y contains only chemical C. Commercial spray Z contains only chemicals A and B in equal amounts. How much of each type of commercial spray is needed to get the desired mixture?

100. *Chemistry*   A chemist needs 10 liters of a 25% acid solution. The solution is to be mixed from three solutions whose concentrations are 10%, 20%, and 50%. How many liters of each solution should the chemist use to satisfy the following?

    (a) Use as little as possible of the 50% solution.

    (b) Use as much as possible of the 50% solution.

    (c) Use 2 liters of the 50% solution.

101. *Truck Scheduling*   A small company that manufactures products A and B has an order for 15 units of product A and 16 units of product B. The company has trucks of three different sizes that can haul the products A and B in the amounts shown in the table. How many trucks of each size are needed to deliver the order? Give *two* possible solutions.

Truck	Large	Medium	Small
Product A	6	4	0
Product B	3	4	3

102. *Electrical Networks*   When Kirchhoff's Laws are applied to the electrical network in the figure, the currents I_1, I_2, and I_3 are the solution of the system

$$\begin{cases} I_1 - I_2 + I_3 = 0 \\ 3I_1 + 2I_2 \quad\quad = 7. \\ \quad\quad 2I_2 + 4I_3 = 8 \end{cases}$$

Find the currents.

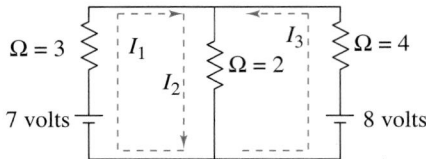

103. *Pulley System*   A system of pulleys is loaded with 128-pound and 32-pound weights. The tensions t_1 and t_2 in the ropes and the acceleration a of the 32-pound weight are found by solving the system

$$\begin{cases} t_1 - 2t_2 \quad\quad = 0 \\ t_1 \quad\quad - 2a = 128 \\ \quad t_2 + a = 32 \end{cases}$$

where t_1 and t_2 are measured in pounds and a is in feet per second squared. Solve the system.

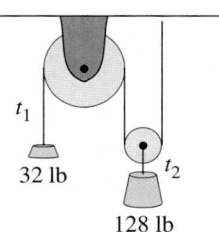

104. *Pulley System*   If the 32-pound weight is replaced with a 64-pound weight in the pulley system described in Exercise 103, the new pulley system is modeled by the following system of equations.

$$\begin{cases} t_1 - 2t_2 \quad\quad = 0 \\ t_1 \quad\quad - 2a = 128 \\ \quad t_2 + 2a = 64 \end{cases}$$

Solve the system, and use your answer for the acceleration to describe what (if anything) is happening in the system.

Fitting a Parabola   **In Exercises 105–108, find the least squares regression parabola $y = ax^2 + bx + c$ for the points $(x_1, y_1), (x_2, y_2), \ldots , (x_n, y_n)$ by solv-**

ing the following system of linear equations for a, b, and c. Then use the regression capabilities of a graphing utility to confirm the result. (For an explanation of how the coefficients of a, b, and c in the system are obtained, see Appendix B.)

105.

$$\begin{cases} 4c & + & 40a & = & 19 \\ & 40b & & = & -12 \\ 40c & + & 544a & = & 160 \end{cases}$$

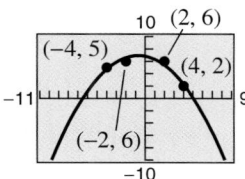

106.

$$\begin{cases} 5c & + & 10a & = & 8 \\ & 10b & & = & 12 \\ 10c & + & 34a & = & 22 \end{cases}$$

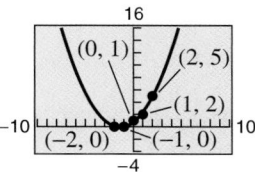

107.

$$\begin{cases} 4c + 9b + 29a = 20 \\ 9c + 29b + 99a = 70 \\ 29c + 99b + 353a = 254 \end{cases}$$

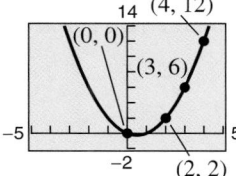

108.

$$\begin{cases} 4c + 6b + 14a = 25 \\ 6c + 14b + 36a = 21 \\ 14c + 36b + 98a = 33 \end{cases}$$

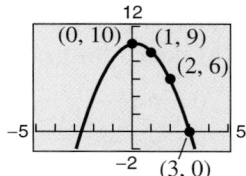

109. *Analyzing Data*   During the testing of a new braking system on an automobile, the speeds (in miles per hour) and the stopping distances (in feet) were recorded as follows.

Speed, x	20	30	40	50	60
Stopping Distance, y	25	55	105	188	300

(a) Find the least squares regression parabola for the data. Use a graphing utility to graph the parabola and the data in the same viewing window.

(b) Use the model to estimate the stopping distance for a speed of 70 miles per hour.

110. *Analyzing Data*   A wildlife management team studied the reproduction rates of deer in five 5-acre tracts of a wildlife preserve. For each tract, the number of females and the percent of females that had offspring the following year were recorded. The results are shown in the table.

Number, x	80	100	120	140	160
Percent, y	80	75	68	55	30

(a) Find the least squares regression parabola for the data.

(b) Use a graphing utility to graph the parabola and the data in the same viewing window.

(c) Use the model to predict the percent of females that would have offspring if $x = 170$.

111. *Exhaust Temperatures*   The magnitude of the range of exhaust temperatures (in degrees Fahrenheit) in an experimental diesel engine is approximated by

$$R = \frac{2000(4 - 3x)}{(11 - 7x)(7 - 4x)}, \quad 0 \le x \le 1$$

where x is the relative load.

(a) Write the partial fraction decomposition for the rational function.

(b) The decomposition in part (a) is the difference of two fractions. The absolute values of the terms give the expected maximum and minimum temperatures of the exhaust gases. Use a graphing utility to graph each term.

112. *Cellular Phone Revenues*   The amount of service revenue R (in billions of dollars) for cellular phones in the United States for the years 1991 through 1997 can be approximated by the model

$$R = \frac{-2617 + 4423t}{t(411 - 38t)}, \quad 1 \le t \le 7$$

where t represents the year with $t = 1$ corresponding to 1991. Write the partial fraction decomposition for the rational function. (Source: Cellular Telecommunications Industry Association)

Synthesis

True or False?   In Exercises 113–115, determine whether the statement is true or false. Justify your answer.

113. The system $\begin{cases} x + 4y - 5z = 8 \\ \quad\quad 2y + \quad z = 5 \\ \quad\quad\quad\quad\quad z = 1 \end{cases}$ is in row-echelon form.

114. If a system of three linear equations is inconsistent, then its graph has no common point.

115. For the rational expression

$$\frac{x}{(x + 10)(x - 10)^2}$$

the partial fraction decomposition is of the form

$$\frac{A}{x + 10} + \frac{B}{(x - 10)^2}.$$

116. *Error Analysis* Suppose you are tutoring a student in algebra. In trying to find a partial fraction decomposition, your student writes the following.

$$\frac{x^2 + 1}{x(x - 1)} = \frac{A}{x} + \frac{B}{x - 1}$$

$$x^2 + 1 = A(x - 1) + Bx \qquad \text{Basic equation}$$

$$x^2 + 1 = (A + B)x - A$$

Your student then forms the following system of linear equations.

$$\begin{cases} A + B = 0 \\ -A \quad\ = 1 \end{cases}$$

Solve the system and check the partial fraction decomposition it yields. Has your student worked the problem correctly? If not, what went wrong?

In Exercises 117–120, write the partial fraction decomposition for the rational expression. Check your result algebraically. Then assign a value to the constant a and check the result graphically.

117. $\dfrac{1}{a^2 - x^2}$

118. $\dfrac{1}{(x + 1)(a - x)}$

119. $\dfrac{1}{y(a - y)}$

120. $\dfrac{1}{x(x + a)}$

121. *Think About It* Are the two systems of equations equivalent? Give reasons for your answer.

$$\begin{cases} x + 3y - z = 6 \\ 2x - y + 2z = 1 \\ 3x + 2y - z = 2 \end{cases} \qquad \begin{cases} x + 3y - z = 6 \\ \quad -7y + 4z = 1 \\ \quad -7y - 4z = -16 \end{cases}$$

122. *Think About It* When using Gaussian elimination to solve a system of linear equations, how can you recognize that it has no solution? Give an example that illustrates your answer.

Advanced Applications **In Exercises 123–126, find values of $x, y,$ and λ that satisfy the system. These systems arise in certain optimization problems in calculus; λ is called a Lagrange multiplier.**

123. $\begin{cases} y + \lambda = 0 \\ x + \lambda = 0 \\ x + y - 10 = 0 \end{cases}$

124. $\begin{cases} 2x + \lambda = 0 \\ 2y + \lambda = 0 \\ x + y - 4 = 0 \end{cases}$

125. $\begin{cases} 2x - 2x\lambda = 0 \\ -2y + \lambda = 0 \\ y - x^2 = 0 \end{cases}$

126. $\begin{cases} 2 + 2x + 2\lambda = 0 \\ 2x + 1 + \lambda = 0 \\ 2x + y - 100 = 0 \end{cases}$

Review

In Exercises 127–134, sketch the graph of the function.

127. $f(x) = -3x + 7$

128. $f(x) = 6 - x$

129. $f(x) = -2x^2$

130. $f(x) = \frac{1}{4}x^2 + 1$

131. $f(x) = x^2 - 9x + 18$

132. $f(x) = 2x^2 - 9x - 5$

133. $f(x) = -x^2(x - 3)$

134. $f(x) = \frac{1}{2}x^3 - 1$

In Exercises 135–138, (a) determine the real zeros of f and (b) sketch the graph of f.

135. $f(x) = x^3 + x^2 - 12x$

136. $f(x) = -8x^4 + 32x^2$

137. $f(x) = 2x^3 + 5x^2 - 21x - 36$

138. $f(x) = 6x^3 - 29x^2 - 6x + 5$

In Exercises 139–142, use a graphing utility to create a table of values. Then sketch the graph of the equation by hand.

139. $y = 4^{-x-4} - 5$

140. $y = \left(\frac{5}{2}\right)^{x-1} - 4$

141. $y = 2.9^{0.8x} - 3$

142. $y = -3.5^{x+2} - 6$

In Exercises 143–146, solve the system by elimination.

143. $\begin{cases} 3x + 3y = 7 \\ 3x + 5y = 3 \end{cases}$

144. $\begin{cases} 6x - 5y = 3 \\ 10x - 12y = 5 \end{cases}$

145. $\begin{cases} 2x + y = 120 \\ x + 2y = 120 \end{cases}$

146. $\begin{cases} 12x + 42y = -17 \\ 30x - 18y = 19 \end{cases}$

5.4 Systems of Inequalities

The Graph of an Inequality

The statements $3x - 2y < 6$ and $2x^2 + 3y^2 \geq 6$ are inequalities in two variables. An ordered pair (a, b) is a **solution of an inequality** in x and y if the inequality is true when a and b are substituted for x and y, respectively. The **graph of an inequality** is the collection of all solutions of the inequality. To sketch the graph of an inequality, begin by sketching the graph of the *corresponding equation*. The graph of the equation will normally separate the plane into two or more regions. In each such region, one of the following must be true.

1. *All* points in the region are solutions of the inequality.
2. *No* point in the region is a solution of the inequality.

So, you can determine whether the points in an entire region satisfy the inequality by simply testing *one* point in the region.

> ### Sketching the Graph of an Inequality in Two Variables
>
> 1. Replace the inequality sign with an equal sign, and sketch the graph of the corresponding equation. (Use a dashed line for < or > and a solid line for ≤ or ≥.)
> 2. Test one point in each of the regions formed by the graph in Step 1. If the point satisfies the inequality, shade the entire region to denote that every point in the region satisfies the inequality.

EXAMPLE 1   Sketching the Graph of an Inequality

To sketch the graph of $y \geq x^2 - 1$, begin by graphing the corresponding *equation* $y = x^2 - 1$, which is a parabola, as shown in Figure 5.18. By testing the point $(0, 0)$ *above* the parabola and the point $(0, -2)$ *below* the parabola, you can see that $(0, 0)$ satisfies the inequality because $0 \geq 0^2 - 1$ and that $(0, -2)$ does not satisfy the inequality because $-2 \ngeq 0^2 - 1$. So, the points that satisfy the inequality are those lying above (or on) the parabola.

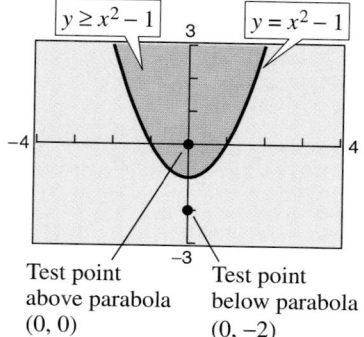

Test point
above parabola
$(0, 0)$

Test point
below parabola
$(0, -2)$

Figure 5.18

What You Should Learn:

- How to sketch graphs of inequalities in two variables
- How to solve systems of inequalities
- How to use systems of inequalities in two variables to model and solve real-life problems

Why You Should Learn It:

Systems of inequalities in two variables can be used to model and solve real-life problems. For instance, Exercise 69 on page 409 shows how to use a system of inequalities to analyze the compositions of dietary supplements.

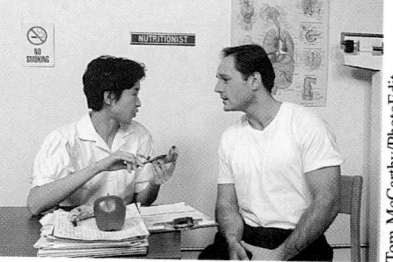

Tom McCarthy/PhotoEdit

The inequality given in Example 1 is a nonlinear inequality in two variables. Most of the following examples involve **linear inequalities** such as $ax + by < c$. The graph of a linear inequality is a half-plane lying on one side of the line $ax + by = c$.

EXAMPLE 2   Sketching the Graphs of Linear Inequalities

Sketch the graph of each linear inequality.

a. $x > -2$ **b.** $y \le 3$

Solution

a. The graph of the corresponding equation $x = -2$ is a vertical line. The points that satisfy the inequality $x > -2$ are those lying to the right of (but not on) this line, as shown in Figure 5.19.

b. The graph of the corresponding equation $y = 3$ is a horizontal line. The points that satisfy the inequality $y \le 3$ are those lying below (or on) this line, as shown in Figure 5.20.

> **STUDY TIP**
>
> A graphing utility can be used to graph an inequality. For instance, to graph $y \ge x - 2$, enter $y = x - 2$ and use the *shade* feature of the graphing utility to shade the correct part of the graph. Consult your user's manual for instructions.

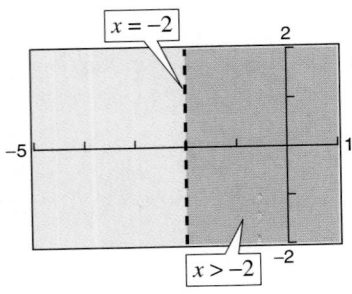

Figure 5.19

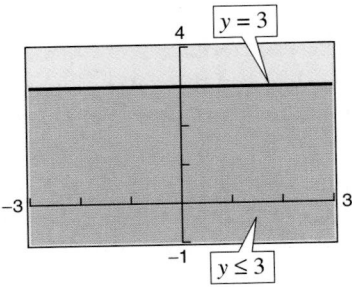

Figure 5.20

EXAMPLE 3   Sketching the Graph of a Linear Inequality

Sketch the graph of $x - y < 2$.

Solution

The graph of the corresponding equation $x - y = 2$ is a line, as shown in Figure 5.21. Because the origin $(0, 0)$ satisfies the inequality, the graph consists of the half-plane lying above the line. (Try checking a point below the line. Regardless of which point below the line you choose, you will see that it does not satisfy the inequality.)

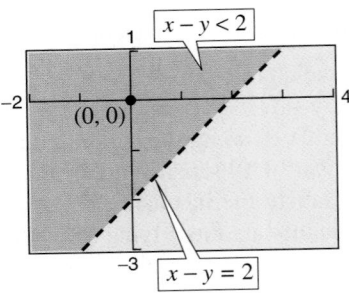

Figure 5.21

To graph a linear inequality, it can help to write the inequality in slope-intercept form. For instance, by writing $x - y < 2$ in Example 3 in the form

$$y > x - 2$$

you can see that the solution points lie *above* the line $y = x - 2$ (or $x - y = 2$), as shown in Figure 5.21.

Systems of Inequalities

Many practical problems in business, science, and engineering involve systems of linear inequalities. A **solution of a system of inequalities** in x and y is a point (x, y) that satisfies each inequality in the system.

To sketch the graph of a system of inequalities in two variables, first sketch the graph of each individual inequality (on the same coordinate system) and then find the region that is *common* to every graph in the system. For systems of *linear* inequalities, it is helpful to find the vertices of the solution region.

EXAMPLE 4   Solving a System of Inequalities

Sketch the graph (and label the vertices) of the solution set of the system.

$$\begin{cases} x - y < 2 & \text{Inequality 1} \\ x > -2 & \text{Inequality 2} \\ y \le 3 & \text{Inequality 3} \end{cases}$$

A computer animation of this example appears in the *Interactive* CD-ROM and *Internet* versions of this text.

Solution

The graphs of these inequalities are shown in Figures 5.19 through 5.21. The triangular region common to all three graphs can be found by superimposing the graphs on the same coordinate system, as shown in Figure 5.22. To find the vertices of the region, solve the three systems of corresponding equations obtained by taking pairs of equations representing the boundaries of the individual regions and solving these pairs of equations.

Vertex A: $(-2, -4)$ $\qquad$ *Vertex B:* $(5, 3)$ $\qquad$ *Vertex C:* $(-2, 3)$

$$\begin{cases} x - y = 2 \\ x = -2 \end{cases} \qquad \begin{cases} x - y = 2 \\ y = 3 \end{cases} \qquad \begin{cases} x = -2 \\ y = 3 \end{cases}$$

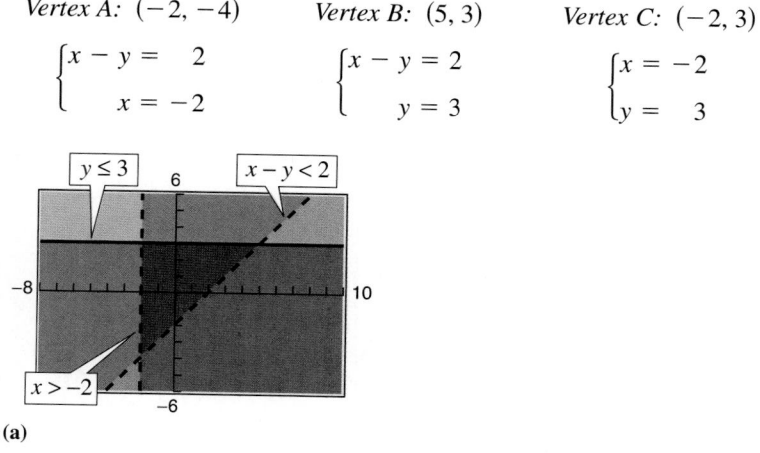

(a)

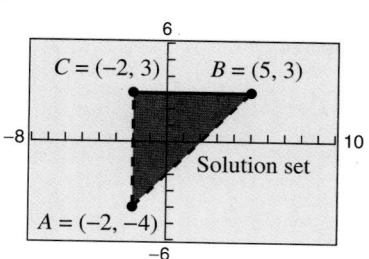

(b)

Figure 5.22

For the triangular region shown in Figure 5.22, each point of intersection of a pair of boundary lines corresponds to a vertex. With more complicated regions, two border lines can sometimes intersect at a point that is not a vertex of the region, as shown in Figure 5.23. To keep track of which points of intersection are actually vertices of the region, you should sketch the region and refer to your sketch as you find each point of intersection.

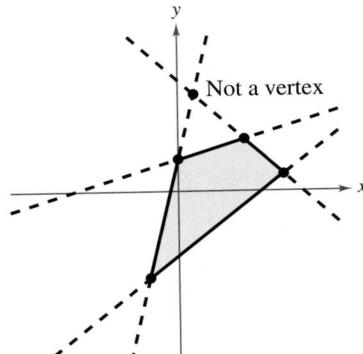

Figure 5.23

EXAMPLE 5   Solving a System of Inequalities

Sketch the region containing all points that satisfy the system.

$$\begin{cases} x^2 - y \le 1 & \text{Inequality 1} \\ -x + y \le 1 & \text{Inequality 2} \end{cases}$$

Solution

As shown in Figure 5.24, the points that satisfy the inequality $x^2 - y \le 1$ are the points lying above (or on) the parabola

$$y = x^2 - 1. \qquad \text{Parabola}$$

The points that satisfy the inequality $-x + y \le 1$ are the points lying below (or on) the line

$$y = x + 1. \qquad \text{Line}$$

To find the points of intersection of the parabola and the line, solve the system of corresponding equations.

$$\begin{cases} x^2 - y = 1 \\ -x + y = 1 \end{cases}$$

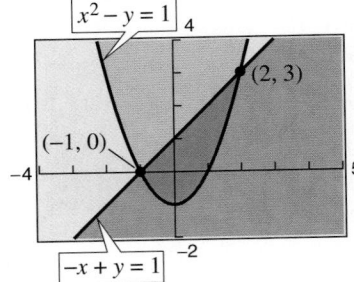

Figure 5.24

Using the method of substitution, you can find the solutions to be $(-1, 0)$ and $(2, 3)$. So, the region containing all points that satisfy the system are indicated by the purple shaded region in Figure 5.24.

When solving a system of inequalities, you should be aware that the system might have no solution, or it might be represented by an unbounded region in the plane. These two possibilities are shown in Examples 6 and 7.

EXAMPLE 6   A System with No Solution

Sketch the solution set of the system.

$$\begin{cases} x + y > 3 & \text{Inequality 1} \\ x + y < -1 & \text{Inequality 2} \end{cases}$$

Solution

From the way the system is written, it is clear that the system has no solutions, because the quantity $(x + y)$ cannot be both less than -1 and greater than 3. Graphically, the inequality $x + y > 3$ is represented by the half-plane lying above the line $x + y = 3$, and the inequality $x + y < -1$ is represented by the half-plane lying below the line $x + y = -1$, as shown in Figure 5.25. These two half-planes have no points in common. So the system of inequalities has no solution.

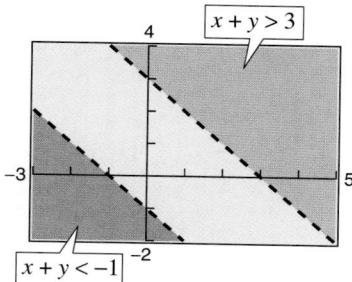

Figure 5.25   *No Solution*

EXAMPLE 7   An Unbounded Solution Set

Sketch the solution set of the system.

$$\begin{cases} x + y < 3 & \text{Inequality 1} \\ x + 2y > 3 & \text{Inequality 2} \end{cases}$$

Solution

The graph of the inequality $x + y < 3$ is the half-plane that lies below the line $x + y = 3$, as shown in Figure 5.26. The graph of the inequality $x + 2y > 3$ is the half-plane that lies above the line $x + 2y = 3$. The intersection of these two half-planes is an *infinite wedge* that has a vertex at $(3, 0)$. This unbounded region representing the solution set has an infinite number of points.

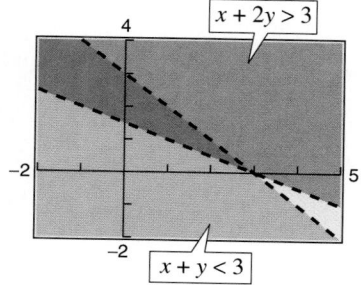

Figure 5.26   *Unbounded Region*

Applications

The next example discusses two concepts that economists call *consumer surplus* and *producer surplus*. As shown in Figure 5.27, the *point of equilibrium* is defined by the price *p* and the number of units *x* that satisfy both the demand and supply equations. Consumer surplus is defined as the area of the region that lies *below* the demand curve, *above* the horizontal line passing through the equilibrium point, and to the right of the *p*-axis. Similarly, the producer surplus is defined as the area of the region that lies *above* the supply curve, *below* the horizontal line passing through the equilibrium point, and to the right of the *p*-axis. The consumer surplus is a measure of the amount that consumers would have been willing to pay *above what they actually paid*, whereas the producer surplus is a measure of the amount that producers would have been willing to receive *below what they actually received*.

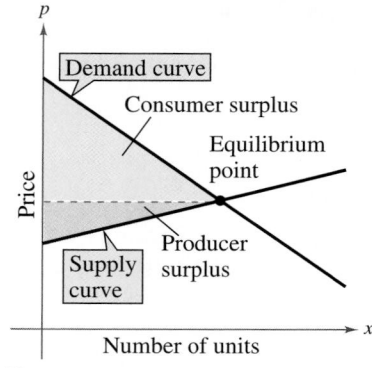

Figure 5.27

EXAMPLE 8   Consumer Surplus and Producer Surplus

The demand and supply functions for a certain type of calculator are

$$\begin{cases} p = 150 - 0.00001x & \text{Demand equation} \\ p = 60 + 0.00002x & \text{Supply equation} \end{cases}$$

where *p* is the price (in dollars) and *x* represents the number of units. Find the consumer surplus and producer surplus for these two equations.

Solution

Begin by finding the point of equilibrium by solving the equation

$$60 + 0.00002x = 150 - 0.00001x.$$

In Example 8 in Section 5.2, you saw that the solution is $x = 3{,}000{,}000$, which corresponds to an equilibrium price of $p = \$120$. So, the consumer surplus and producer surplus are the areas of the following triangular regions.

Consumer Surplus	Producer Surplus
$\begin{cases} p \le 150 - 0.00001x \\ p \ge 120 \\ x \ge 0 \end{cases}$	$\begin{cases} p \ge 60 + 0.00002x \\ p \le 120 \\ x \ge 0 \end{cases}$

In Figure 5.28, you can see that these regions are triangles. So, the consumer and producer surpluses are

Consumer surplus $= \tfrac{1}{2}$ (base)(height)

$\qquad = \tfrac{1}{2}(3{,}000{,}000)(30)$

$\qquad = \$45{,}000{,}000$

Producer surplus $= \tfrac{1}{2}$ (base)(height)

$\qquad = \tfrac{1}{2}(3{,}000{,}000)(60)$

$\qquad = \$90{,}000{,}000$

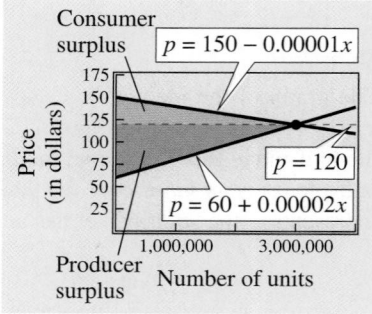

Figure 5.28

EXAMPLE 9　Nutrition

The liquid portion of a diet is to provide at least 300 calories, 36 units of vitamin A, and 90 units of vitamin C daily. A cup of dietary drink X provides 60 calories, 12 units of vitamin A, and 10 units of vitamin C. A cup of dietary drink Y provides 60 calories, 6 units of vitamin A, and 30 units of vitamin C. Set up a system of linear inequalities that must be satisfied in order to meet the minimum daily requirements for calories and vitamins.

Solution

Begin by letting x and y represent the following.

x = number of cups of dietary drink X

y = number of cups of dietary drink Y

To meet the minimum daily requirements, the following inequalities must be satisfied.

$$\begin{cases} 60x + 60y \geq 300 & \text{Calories} \\ 12x + 6y \geq 36 & \text{Vitamin A} \\ 10x + 30y \geq 90 & \text{Vitamin C} \\ x \geq 0 \\ y \geq 0 \end{cases}$$

The last two inequalities are included because x and y cannot be negative. The graph of this system of inequalities is shown in Figure 5.29. (More is said about this application in Example 6 in Section 5.5.)

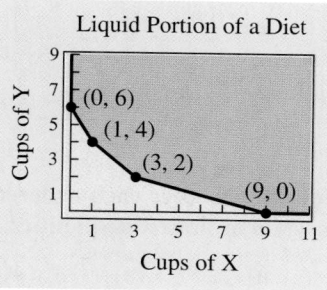

Liquid Portion of a Diet

Figure 5.29

In the following Group Activity, consider grouping students with the same model of graphing calculator together so that they can help one another.

Group Activity

Consult the user's guide for your graphing utility to find how to graph a system of inequalities. Then use the graphing utility to graph the following systems.

$$\begin{cases} y \leq 4 - x^2 \\ y \geq 2x - 3 \end{cases} \qquad \begin{cases} y \leq 4 - x^2 \\ y \geq x^2 - 4 \end{cases}$$

Writing About Math　*Creating a System of Inequalities*

Plot the points $(0, 0)$, $(4, 0)$, $(3, 2)$, and $(0, 2)$ in a coordinate plane. Draw the quadrilateral that has these four points as its vertices. Write a system of linear inequalities that has the quadrilateral as its solution. Explain how you found the system of inequalities.

5.4 Exercises

In Exercises 1–8, match the inequality with its graph. [The graphs are labeled (a), (b), (c), (d), (e), (f), (g), and (h).]

(a)

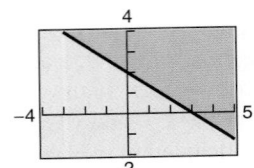

(b)

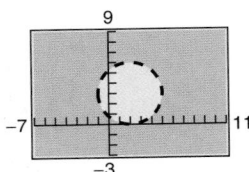

(c)

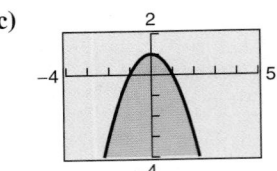

(d)

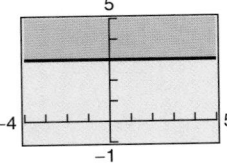

(e)

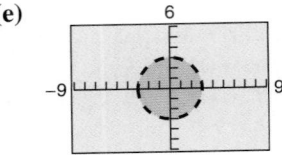

(f)

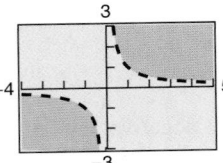

(g)

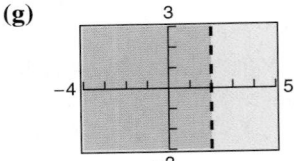

(h)

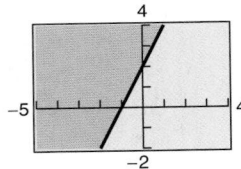

1. $x < 2$

2. $y \geq 3$

3. $2x + 3y \geq 6$

4. $2x - y \leq -2$

5. $x^2 + y^2 < 9$

6. $(x - 2)^2 + (y - 3)^2 > 9$

7. $xy > 1$

8. $y \leq 1 - x^2$

In Exercises 9–20, sketch the graph of the inequality.

9. $x \geq 2$

10. $x \leq -5$

11. $y \geq -1$

12. $y \leq 3$

13. $y < 2 - x$

14. $y > 2x - 4$

15. $2y - x \geq 4$

16. $5x + 3y \geq -15$

17. $y^2 - x < 0$

18. $4x + y^2 > 1$

19. $(x + 1)^2 + y^2 < 9$

20. $(x - 1)^2 + (y - 4)^2 > 9$

In Exercises 21–32, use a graphing utility to graph the inequality. Be sure to shade the region representing the solution.

21. $y \geq \frac{2}{3}x - 1$

22. $y \leq 6 - \frac{3}{2}x$

23. $y < -3.8x + 1.1$

24. $y \geq -20.74 + 2.66x$

25. $x^2 + 5y - 10 \leq 0$

26. $2x^2 - y - 3 > 0$

27. $y \leq \dfrac{1}{1 + x^2}$

28. $y > \dfrac{-10}{x^2 + x + 4}$

29. $y < \ln x$

30. $y \geq 4 - \ln(x + 5)$

31. $y > 3^{-x-4}$

32. $y \leq 2^{2x-1} - 3$

In Exercises 33–36, write an inequality for the shaded region shown in the graph.

33.

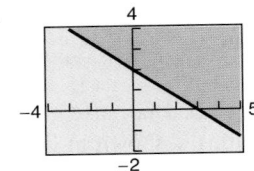

34.

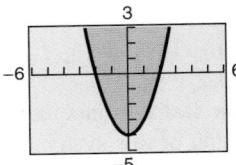

35.

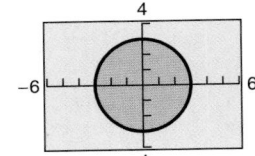

36.

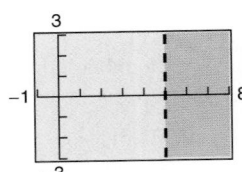

In Exercises 37 and 38, decide whether each ordered pair is a solution of the system of linear inequalities.

37. $\begin{cases} -2x + 5y \geq 3 \\ \qquad\quad y < 4 \\ -4x + 2y < 7 \end{cases}$ (a) $(0, 2)$ (b) $(-6, 4)$ (c) $(-8, -2)$ (d) $(-3, 2)$

38. $\begin{cases} 3x + y > 1 \\ -y - \frac{1}{2}x^2 \leq -4 \\ -15x + 4y > 0 \end{cases}$ (a) $(0, 10)$ (b) $(0, -1)$ (c) $(2, 9)$ (d) $(-1, 6)$

In Exercises 39–50, sketch the graph of the solution of the system of inequalities. Verify your sketch by using a graphing utility to graph the system, shading the region that represents the solution of the system.

39. $\begin{cases} x + y \le 1 \\ -x + y \le 1 \\ y \ge 0 \end{cases}$ **40.** $\begin{cases} 3x + 2y < 6 \\ x > 0 \\ y > 0 \end{cases}$

41. $\begin{cases} -3x + 2y < 6 \\ x - 4y > -2 \\ 2x + y < 3 \end{cases}$ **42.** $\begin{cases} x - 7y > -36 \\ 5x + 2y > 5 \\ 6x - 5y > 6 \end{cases}$

43. $\begin{cases} 2x + y > 2 \\ 6x + 3y < 2 \end{cases}$ **44.** $\begin{cases} x - 2y < -6 \\ 5x - 3y > -9 \end{cases}$

45. $\begin{cases} -x^2 + y \ge 5 \\ \frac{1}{4}x + y < 3 \end{cases}$ **46.** $\begin{cases} y^2 - 3x \ge 9 \\ x + y \ge -3 \end{cases}$

47. $\begin{cases} x > y^2 \\ x < y + 2 \end{cases}$ **48.** $\begin{cases} x - y^2 > 0 \\ x - y < 2 \end{cases}$

49. $\begin{cases} x^2 + y^2 \le 9 \\ x^2 + y^2 \ge 1 \end{cases}$ **50.** $\begin{cases} x < 2y - y^2 \\ 0 < x + y \end{cases}$

In Exercises 51–56, use a graphing utility to graph the inequalities. Be sure to shade the region representing the solution of the system.

51. $\begin{cases} y \le \sqrt{3x} + 1 \\ y \ge x^2 + 1 \end{cases}$ **52.** $\begin{cases} y < -x^2 + 2x + 3 \\ y > x^2 - 4x + 3 \end{cases}$

53. $\begin{cases} y < x^3 - 2x + 1 \\ y > -2x \\ x \le 1 \end{cases}$ **54.** $\begin{cases} y \ge x^4 - 2x^2 + 1 \\ y \le 1 - x^2 \end{cases}$

55. $\begin{cases} x^2 y \ge 1 \\ 0 < x \le 4 \\ \phantom{0<} y \le 4 \end{cases}$ **56.** $\begin{cases} y \le e^{-x^2/2} \\ y \ge 0 \\ -2 \le x \le 2 \end{cases}$

In Exercises 57–64, find a set of inequalities to describe the region.

57. 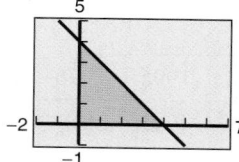   **58.**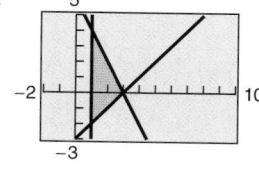

59. 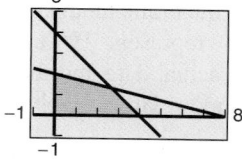   **60.**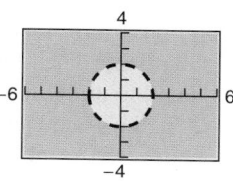

61. Rectangular region with vertices at $(2, 1)$, $(5, 1)$, $(5, 7)$, and $(2, 7)$

62. Parallelogrammatic region with vertices at $(0, 0)$, $(4, 0)$, $(1, 4)$, and $(5, 4)$

63. Triangular region with vertices at $(0, 0)$, $(5, 0)$, and $(2, 3)$

64. Triangular region with vertices at $(-1, 0)$, $(1, 0)$, and $(0, 1)$

In Exercises 65–69, (a) find a system of inequalities that models the problem and (b) use a graphing utility to graph the systems, shading the region that represents the solution of the system.

65. *Investment*   A person plans to invest some or all of $20,000 in two different interest-bearing accounts. Each account is to contain at least $5000, and one account should have at least twice the amount that is in the other account.

66. *Concert Ticket Sales*   One type of concert ticket costs $15 and another costs $25. The promoter of the concert must sell at least 15,000 tickets, including at least 8000 of the $15 tickets and at least 4000 of the $25 tickets, and the gross receipts must total at least $275,000 in order for the concert to be held.

67. *Furniture Production*   A furniture company can sell all the tables and chairs it produces. Each table requires 1 hour of assembly and $1\frac{1}{3}$ hours of finishing. Each chair requires $1\frac{1}{2}$ hours of assembly and $1\frac{1}{2}$ hours of finishing. The company's assembly center is available 12 hours per day, and its finishing center is available 15 hours per day.

68. *Computer Inventory*   A store sells two models of a certain brand of computer. Because of the demand, it is necessary to stock at least twice as many units of model A as units of model B. The costs to the store for the two models are $800 and $1200, respectively. The management does not want more than $20,000 in computer inventory at any one time, and it wants at least four model A computers and two model B computers in inventory at all times.

69. *Diet Supplement*   A dietitian is asked to design a special diet using two different foods. The minimum daily requirements in the new diet are 280 units of calcium, 160 units of iron, and 180 units of vitamin B. Each ounce of food X contains 20 units of calcium, 15 units of iron, and 10 units of vitamin B. Each ounce of food Y contains 10 units of calcium, 10 units of iron, and 20 units of vitamin B.

70. Physical Fitness Facility You plan an exercise facility that has an indoor running track with an exercise floor inside the track. The track must be at least 125 meters long, and the exercise floor must have an area of at least 500 square meters.

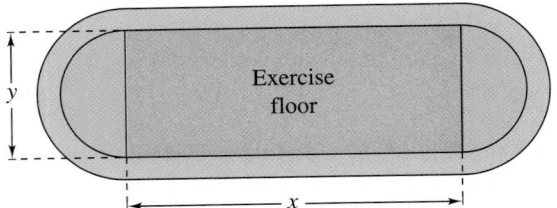

(a) Find a system of inequalities describing the requirements of the exercise facility.

(b) Sketch the graph of the system in part (a).

71. Graphical Reasoning Two concentric circles have radii of x and y meters, where $y > x$. The area between the boundaries of the circles must be at least 10 square meters.

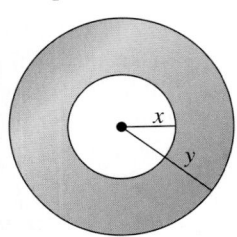

(a) Find an inequality describing the constraints on the circles.

(b) Use a graphing utility to graph the inequality in part (a). Graph the line $y = x$ in the same viewing window.

(c) Identify the graph of the line in relation to the boundary of the inequality. Explain its meaning in the context of the problem.

Consumer and Producer Surpluses In Exercises 72–75, use a graphing utility to graph the system representing the consumer surplus and producer surplus for the supply and demand equations. Be sure to shade the region representing the solution of the system. Find the consumer surplus and the producer surplus.

	Demand	Supply
72.	$p = 50 - 0.5x$	$p = 0.125x$
73.	$p = 60 - x$	$p = 10 + \frac{7}{3}x$
74.	$p = 300 - x$	$p = 100 + x$
75.	$p = 140 - 0.00002x$	$p = 80 + 0.00001x$

Synthesis

True or False? **In Exercises 76 and 77, determine whether the statement is true or false. Justify your answer.**

76. The area of the figure defined by the system below is 99 square units.

$$\begin{cases} x \geq -3 \\ x \leq 6 \\ y \leq 5 \\ y \geq -6 \end{cases}$$

77. The graph below shows the solution of the system

$$\begin{cases} y \leq 6 \\ -4x - 9y > 6. \\ 3x + y^2 \geq 2 \end{cases}$$

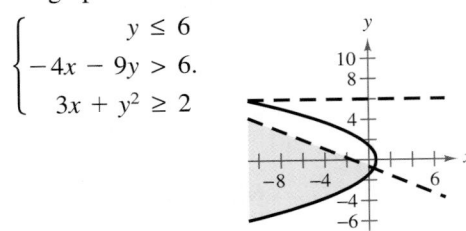

78. Think About It After graphing the boundary of an inequality in x and y, how do you decide on which side of the boundary the solution set of the inequality lies?

79. Writing Describe the difference between the solution set of a system of equations and the solution set of a system of inequalities.

Review

In Exercises 80–83, find the equation of the line passing through the two points.

80. $(-2, 6), (4, -4)$ **81.** $(-8, 0), (3, -1)$

82. $\left(\frac{3}{4}, -2\right), \left(-\frac{7}{2}, 5\right)$ **83.** $(3.4, -5.2), (-2.6, 0.8)$

84. Mortgage Loans The table shows the number of outstanding mortgage loans M (in millions) in the United States for the years 1992 to 1997. (Source: Mortgage Bankers Association of America)

Year	1992	1993	1994	1995	1996	1997
M	42.6	45.3	47.6	49.2	50.1	51.2

Use the regression capabilities of a graphing utility to find a linear model and a quadratic model that represent the data. Let $t = 0$ represent 1990. Use a graphing utility to plot the actual data and the models in the same viewing window. How closely do the models represent the data?

5.5 Linear Programming

Linear Programming: A Graphical Approach

Many applications in business and economics involve a process called **optimization,** in which you are asked to find the minimum or maximum value of a quantity. In this section you will study an optimization strategy called **linear programming.**

A two-dimensional linear programming problem consists of a linear **objective function** and a system of linear inequalities called **constraints.** The objective function gives the quantity that is to be maximized (or minimized), and the constraints determine the set of **feasible solutions.** For example, suppose you are asked to maximize the value of

$$z = ax + by \qquad \text{Objective function}$$

subject to a set of constraints that determines the region in Figure 5.30. Because every point in the region satisfies each constraint, it is not clear how you should go about finding the point that yields a maximum value of z. Fortunately, it can be shown that if there is an optimal solution, it must occur at one of the vertices. So, *you can find the maximum value by testing z at each of the vertices.*

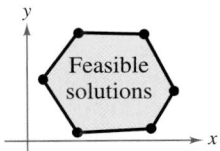

Figure 5.30

What You Should Learn:

- How to solve linear programming problems
- How to use linear programming to model and solve real-life problems

Why You Should Learn It:

Linear programming is a powerful tool used in business and industry to effectively manage resources in order to maximize profits or minimize costs. For instance, Exercise 41 on page 419 shows how to use linear programming to analyze the profitability of two models of compact disc players.

Jeff Greenberg/Unicorn Stock Photos

Optimal Solution of a Linear Programming Problem

If a linear programming problem has a solution, it must occur at a vertex of the set of feasible solutions. If there is more than one solution, at least one of them must occur at such a vertex. In either case, the value of the objective function is unique.

Here are some guidelines for solving a linear programming problem in two variables in which an objective function is to be maximized *or* minimized.

Solving a Linear Programming Problem

1. Sketch the region corresponding to the system of constraints. (The points inside or on the boundary of the region are *feasible solutions.*)
2. Find the vertices of the region.
3. Test the objective function at each of the vertices and select the values of the variables that optimize the objective function. For a bounded region, both a minimum and a maximum value will exist. (For an unbounded region, *if* an optimal solution exists, it will occur at a vertex.)

It is important that students immediately become familiar with the terminology of this section. Emphasize the fact that linear programming is powerful in that it quickly identifies those few points out of many that can be easily tested to find the point that gives the maximum or minimum value.

EXAMPLE 1   Solving a Linear Programming Problem

Find the maximum value of

$$z = 3x + 2y \qquad \text{Objective function}$$

subject to the following constraints.

$$
\left.
\begin{array}{r}
x \geq 0 \\
y \geq 0 \\
x + 2y \leq 4 \\
x - y \leq 1
\end{array}
\right\} \qquad \text{Constraints}
$$

Solution

The constraints form the region shown in Figure 5.31. At the four vertices of this region, the objective function has the following values.

At $(0, 0)$: $z = 3(0) + 2(0) = 0$

At $(1, 0)$: $z = 3(1) + 2(0) = 3$

At $(2, 1)$: $z = 3(2) + 2(1) = 8$ Maximum value of z

At $(0, 2)$: $z = 3(0) + 2(2) = 4$

So, the maximum value of z is 8, and this occurs when $x = 2$ and $y = 1$.

In Example 1, try testing some of the *interior* points in the region. You will see that the corresponding values of z are less than 8. Here are some examples.

At $(1, 1)$: $z = 3(1) + 2(1) = 5$

At $\left(1, \frac{1}{2}\right)$: $z = 3(1) + 2\left(\frac{1}{2}\right) = 4$

At $\left(\frac{1}{2}, \frac{3}{2}\right)$: $z = 3\left(\frac{1}{2}\right) + 2\left(\frac{3}{2}\right) = \frac{9}{2}$

To see why the maximum value of the objective function in Example 1 must occur at a vertex, consider writing the objective function in the form

$$y = -\frac{3}{2}x + \frac{z}{2} \qquad \text{Family of lines}$$

where $z/2$ is the y-intercept of the objective function. This equation represents a family of lines, each of slope $-\frac{3}{2}$. Of these infinitely many lines, you want the one that has the largest z-value while still intersecting the region determined by the constraints. In other words, of all the lines with a slope of $-\frac{3}{2}$, you want the one that has the largest y-intercept *and* intersects the given region, as shown in Figure 5.32. It should be clear that such a line will pass through one (or more) of the vertices of the region.

A computer animation of this example appears in the *Interactive* CD-ROM and *Internet* versions of this text.

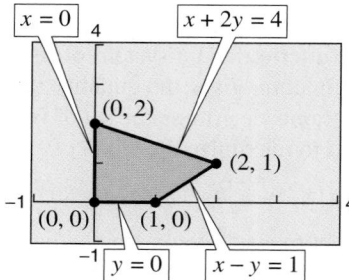

Figure 5.31

STUDY T!P

Remember that a vertex of a region can be found using a system of linear equations. The system will consist of the equations of the lines passing through the vertex.

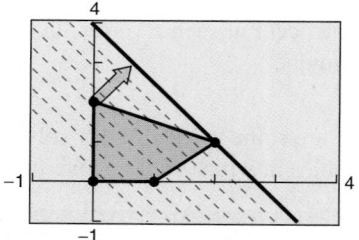

Figure 5.32

The next example shows that the same basic procedure can be used to solve a problem in which the objective function is to be *minimized*.

EXAMPLE 2 Minimizing an Objective Function

Find the minimum value of

$$z = 5x + 7y \qquad \text{Objective function}$$

where $x \geq 0$ and $y \geq 0$, subject to the following constraints.

$$\left.\begin{array}{rcl} 2x + 3y &\geq& 6 \\ 3x - y &\leq& 15 \\ -x + y &\leq& 4 \\ 2x + 5y &\leq& 27 \end{array}\right\} \qquad \text{Constraints}$$

Solution

The region bounded by the constraints is shown in Figure 5.33. By testing the objective function at each vertex, you obtain the following.

At $(0, 2)$: $z = 5(0) + 7(2) = 14$ Minimum value of z

At $(0, 4)$: $z = 5(0) + 7(4) = 28$

At $(1, 5)$: $z = 5(1) + 7(5) = 40$

At $(6, 3)$: $z = 5(6) + 7(3) = 51$

At $(5, 0)$: $z = 5(5) + 7(0) = 25$

At $(3, 0)$: $z = 5(3) + 7(0) = 15$

So, the minimum value of z is 14, and this occurs when $x = 0$ and $y = 2$.

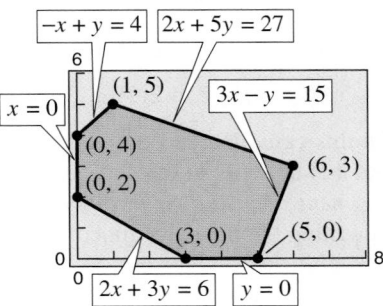

Figure 5.33

EXAMPLE 3 Maximizing an Objective Function

Find the maximum value of

$$z = 5x + 7y \qquad \text{Objective function}$$

where $x \geq 0$ and $y \geq 0$, subject to the following constraints.

$$\left.\begin{array}{rcl} 2x + 3y &\geq& 6 \\ 3x - y &\leq& 15 \\ -x + y &\leq& 4 \\ 2x + 5y &\leq& 27 \end{array}\right\} \qquad \text{Constraints}$$

Solution

This linear programming problem is identical to that given in Example 2 above, except that the objective function is *maximized* instead of minimized. Using the values of z at the vertices shown above, you can conclude that the maximum value of z is 51, and that this value occurs when $x = 6$ and $y = 3$.

It is possible for the maximum (or minimum) value in a linear programming problem to occur at *two* different vertices. For instance, at the vertices of the region shown in Figure 5.34, the objective function

$$z = 2x + 2y \qquad \text{Objective function}$$

has the following values.

At $(0, 0)$: $\quad z = 2(0) + 2(0) = \quad 0$

At $(0, 4)$: $\quad z = 2(0) + 2(4) = \quad 8$

At $(2, 4)$: $\quad z = 2(2) + 2(4) = 12 \qquad$ Maximum value of z

At $(5, 1)$: $\quad z = 2(5) + 2(1) = 12 \qquad$ Maximum value of z

At $(5, 0)$: $\quad z = 2(5) + 2(0) = 10$

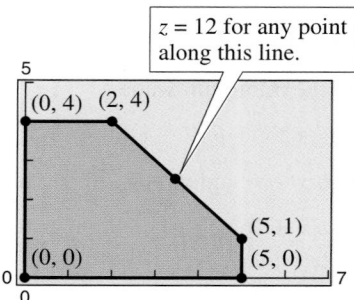

Figure 5.34

In this case, you can conclude that the objective function has a maximum value (of 12) not only at the vertices $(2, 4)$ and $(5, 1)$, but also at *any point on the line segment connecting these two vertices*, as shown in Figure 5.34. Note that by rewriting the objective function as

$$y = -x + \frac{1}{2}z$$

you can see that it has the same slope as the line through the vertices $(2, 4)$ and $(5, 1)$.

Some linear programming problems have no optimal solution. This can occur if the region determined by the constraints is *unbounded*.

EXAMPLE 4   An Unbounded Region

Find the maximum value of

$$z = 4x + 2y \qquad \text{Objective function}$$

where $x \geq 0$ and $y \geq 0$, subject to the following constraints.

$$\left. \begin{array}{r} x + 2y \geq 4 \\ 3x + y \geq 7 \\ -x + 2y \leq 7 \end{array} \right\} \qquad \text{Constraints}$$

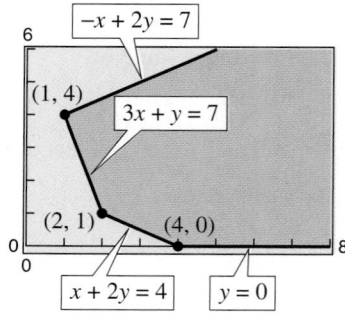

Figure 5.35

Solution

The region determined by the constraints is shown in Figure 5.35. For this unbounded region, there is no maximum value of z. To see this, note that the point $(x, 0)$ lies in the region for all values of $x \geq 4$. By choosing large values of x, you can obtain values of $z = 4(x) + 2(0) = 4x$ that are as large as you want. So, there is no maximum value of z. For the vertices of the region, the objective function has the following values. So, there *is* a minimum value of $z = 10$, which occurs at the vertex $(2, 1)$.

At $(1, 4)$: $\quad z = 4(1) + 2(4) = 12$

At $(2, 1)$: $\quad z = 4(2) + 2(1) = 10 \qquad$ Minimum value of z

At $(4, 0)$: $\quad z = 4(4) + 2(0) = 16$

Applications

Example 5 shows how linear programming can be used to find the maximum profit in a business application.

EXAMPLE 5   Maximum Profit

A manufacturer wants to maximize the profit for two products. Product I yields a profit of $1.50 per unit, and product II yields a profit of $2.00 per unit. Market tests and available resources have indicated the following constraints.

1. The combined production level should not exceed 1200 units per month.

2. The demand for product II is no more than half the demand for product I.

3. The production level of product I is less than or equal to 600 units plus three times the production level of product II.

Solution

If you let x be the number of units of product I and y be the number of units of product II, the objective function (for the combined profit) is

$$P = 1.5x + 2y. \qquad \text{Objective function}$$

The three constraints translate into the following linear inequalities.

1. $x + y \le 1200$ ➡️ $x + y \le 1200$

2. $y \le \frac{1}{2}x$ ➡️ $-x + 2y \le 0$

3. $x \le 3y + 600$ ➡️ $x - 3y \le 600$

Because neither x nor y can be negative, you also have the two additional constraints of $x \ge 0$ and $y \ge 0$. Figure 5.36 shows the region determined by the constraints. To find the maximum profit, test the value of P at the vertices of the region.

At $(0, 0)$: $\quad P = 1.5(0) + 2(0)$

$\qquad\qquad\quad\ = 0$

At $(800, 400)$: $\quad P = 1.5(800) + 2(400)$

$\qquad\qquad\quad\ = 2000 \qquad$ Maximum profit

At $(1050, 150)$: $\ P = 1.5(1050) + 2(150)$

$\qquad\qquad\quad\ = 1875$

At $(600, 0)$: $\quad P = 1.5(600) + 2(0)$

$\qquad\qquad\quad\ = 900$

So, the maximum profit is $2000, and it occurs when the monthly production consists of 800 units of product I and 400 units of product II.

In Example 5, suppose the manufacturer improved the production of product I so that it yielded a profit of $2.50 per unit. This would change the vertex at which the maximum profit would occur. In this case, a maximum profit of $2925 would result from producing 1050 units of product I and 150 units of product II.

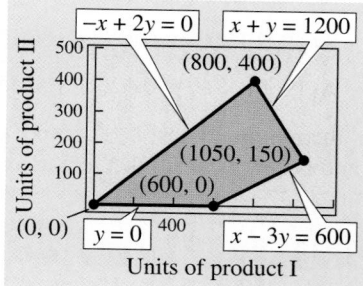

Figure 5.36

EXAMPLE 6 Minimum Cost

The liquid portion of a diet is to provide at least 300 calories, 36 units of vitamin A, and 90 units of vitamin C daily. A cup of dietary drink X costs $0.12 and provides 60 calories, 12 units of vitamin A, and 10 units of vitamin C. A cup of dietary drink Y costs $0.15 and provides 60 calories, 6 units of vitamin A, and 30 units of vitamin C. How many cups of each drink should be consumed each day to minimize the cost and still meet the daily requirements?

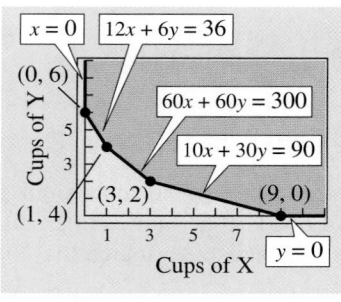

Figure 5.37

Solution

As in Example 9 on page 407, let x be the number of cups of dietary drink X and let y be the number of cups of dietary drink Y.

For Calories:	$60x + 60y \geq 300$	
For Vitamin A:	$12x + 6y \geq 36$	
For Vitamin C:	$10x + 30y \geq 90$	Constraints
	$x \geq 0$	
	$y \geq 0$	

The cost C is given by $C = 0.12x + 0.15y$.   Objective function

The graph of the region determined by the constraints is shown in Figure 5.37. To determine the minimum cost, test C at each vertex of the region.

At $(0, 6)$: $C = 0.12(0) + 0.15(6) = 0.90$

At $(1, 4)$: $C = 0.12(1) + 0.15(4) = 0.72$

At $(3, 2)$: $C = 0.12(3) + 0.15(2) = 0.66$ Minimum value of C

At $(9, 0)$: $C = 0.12(9) + 0.15(0) = 1.08$

So, the minimum cost is $0.66 per day, and this occurs when three cups of drink X and two cups of drink Y are consumed each day.

Writing About Math *Creating a Linear Programming Problem*

Sketch the region determined by the constraints.

$$\left. \begin{array}{r} x \geq 0 \\ y \geq 0 \\ x + 2y \leq 10 \\ x + y \leq 7 \end{array} \right\} \quad \text{Constraints}$$

Find, if possible, an objective function of the form $z = ax + by$ that has a maximum at the indicated vertex of the region.

a. Maximum at $(0, 5)$ 　　　　　**b.** Maximum at $(4, 3)$

c. Maximum at $(7, 0)$ 　　　　　**d.** Maximum at $(0, 0)$

Write a short paragraph explaining how you found each objective function.

5.5 E x e r c i s e s

In Exercises 1–12, find the minimum and maximum values of the objective function and where they occur, subject to the indicated constraints. (For each exercise, the graph of the region determined by the constraints is provided.)

1. Objective function:
$z = 3x + 5y$
Constraints:
$x \geq 0$
$y \geq 0$
$x + y \leq 6$

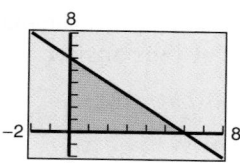

2. Objective function:
$z = 2x + 8y$
Constraints:
$x \geq 0$
$y \geq 0$
$2x + y \leq 4$

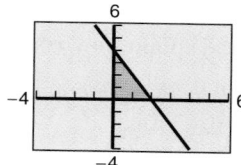

3. Objective function:
$z = 10x + 7y$
Constraints:
(See Exercise 1.)

4. Objective function:
$z = 7x + 3y$
Constraints:
(See Exercise 2.)

5. Objective function:
$z = 5x + 2y$
Constraints:
$x \geq 0$
$y \geq 0$
$x + 3y \leq 15$
$4x + y \leq 16$

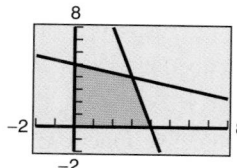

6. Objective function:
$z = 4x + 3y$
Constraints:
$x \geq 0$
$2x + 3y \geq 6$
$3x - 2y \leq 9$
$x + 5y \leq 20$

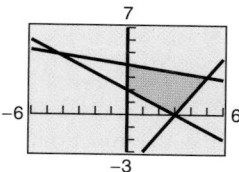

7. Objective function:
$z = 5x + 0.5y$
Constraints:
(See Exercise 5.)

8. Objective function:
$z = x + 6y$
Constraints:
(See Exercise 6.)

9. Objective function:
$z = 10x + 7y$
Constraints:
$0 \leq x \leq 60$
$0 \leq y \leq 45$
$5x + 6y \leq 420$

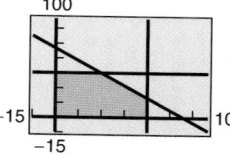

10. Objective function:
$z = 50x + 35y$
Constraints:
$x \geq 0$
$y \geq 0$
$8x + 9y \leq 7200$
$8x + 9y \geq 5400$

11. Objective function:
$z = 25x + 30y$
Constraints:
(See Exercise 9.)

12. Objective function:
$z = 16x + 18y$
Constraints:
(See Exercise 10.)

In Exercises 13–20, sketch the constraint region. Then find the minimum and maximum values of the objective function and where they occur, subject to the constraints.

13. Objective function:
$z = 6x + 10y$
Constraints:
$x \geq 0$
$y \geq 0$
$2x + 5y \leq 10$

14. Objective function:
$z = 4x + 6y$
Constraints:
$-x + y \leq 11$
$x + y \leq 27$
$2x + 5y \leq 90$
$x \geq 0$
$y \geq 0$

15. Objective function:
$z = 9x + 24y$
Constraints:
(See Exercise 13.)

16. Objective function:
$z = 7x + 2y$
Constraints:
(See Exercise 14.)

17. Objective function:
$z = 4x + 3y$
Constraints:
$x \geq 0$
$2x + 3y \geq 6$
$3x - 2y \leq 9$
$x + 5y \leq 20$

18. Objective function:
$z = 4x + 5y$
Constraints:
$x \geq 0$
$y \geq 0$
$2x + 2y \leq 10$
$x + 2y \leq 6$

19. Objective function:

$z = 3x + 7y$

Constraints:

(See Exercise 17.)

20. Objective function:

$z = 2x - y$

Constraints:

(See Exercise 18.)

In Exercises 21–26, use a graphing utility to sketch the region determined by the constraints. Then find the minimum and maximum values of the objective function and where they occur, subject to the constraints.

21. Objective function:

$z = 4x + y$

Constraints:

$$x \geq 0$$
$$y \geq 0$$
$$x + 2y \leq 40$$
$$2x + 3y \geq 72$$

22. Objective function:

$z = x$

Constraints:

$$x \geq 0$$
$$y \geq 0$$
$$2x + 3y \leq 60$$
$$2x + y \leq 28$$
$$4x + y \leq 48$$

23. Objective function:

$z = x + 4y$

Constraints:

(See Exercise 21.)

24. Objective function:

$z = y$

Constraints:

(See Exercise 22.)

25. Objective function:

$z = 2x + 3y$

Constraints:

(See Exercise 21.)

26. Objective function:

$z = 3x + 2y$

Constraints:

(See Exercise 22.)

Exploration In Exercises 27–30, perform the following: (a) use a graphing utility to graph the region bounded by the following constraints.

$$3x + y \leq 15$$
$$4x + 3y \leq 30$$
$$x \geq 0$$
$$y \geq 0$$

(b) Graph the objective function for the given maximum value of z in the same viewing window as the graph of the constraints. (c) Use the graph to determine the feasible point or points that yield the maximum. Explain how you arrived at your answer.

Objective Function	Maximum
27. $z = 2x + y$	$z = 12$
28. $z = 5x + y$	$z = 25$

Objective Function	Maximum
29. $z = x + y$	$z = 10$
30. $z = 3x + y$	$z = 15$

Exploration In Exercises 31–34, perform the following: (a) use a graphing utility to graph the region bounded by the following constraints.

$$x + 4y \leq 20$$
$$x + y \leq 8$$
$$3x + 2y \leq 21$$
$$x \geq 0$$
$$y \geq 0$$

(b) Graph the objective function for the given maximum value of z in the same viewing window as the graph of the constraints. (c) Use the graph to determine the feasible point or points that yield the maximum. Explain how you arrived at your answer.

Objective Function	Maximum
31. $z = x + 5y$	$z = 25$
32. $z = 2x + 4y$	$z = 24$
33. $z = 4x + 5y$	$z = 36$
34. $z = 4x + y$	$z = 28$

In Exercises 35–40, the linear programming problem has an unusual characteristic. Sketch a graph of the solution region for the problem and describe the unusual characteristic. The objective function is to be maximized in each case.

35. Objective function:

$z = 2.5x + y$

Constraints:

$$x \geq 0$$
$$y \geq 0$$
$$3x + 5y \leq 15$$
$$5x + 2y \leq 10$$

36. Objective function:

$z = x + y$

Constraints:

$$x \geq 0$$
$$y \geq 0$$
$$-x + y \leq 1$$
$$-x + 2y \leq 4$$

37. Objective function:

$z = -x + 2y$

Constraints:

$$x \geq 0$$
$$y \geq 0$$
$$x \leq 10$$
$$x + y \leq 7$$

38. Objective function:

$z = x + y$

Constraints:

$$x \geq 0$$
$$y \geq 0$$
$$-x + y \leq 0$$
$$-3x + y \geq 3$$

39. Objective function:

$$z = 3x + 4y$$

Constraints:

$$x \geq 0$$
$$y \geq 0$$
$$x + y \leq 1$$
$$2x + y \leq 4$$

40. Objective function:

$$z = x + 2y$$

Constraints:

$$x \geq 0$$
$$y \geq 0$$
$$x + 2y \leq 4$$
$$2x + y \leq 4$$

41. *Maximum Profit* A merchant plans to sell two models of compact disc players at costs of $250 and $400. The $250 model yields a profit of $45, and the $400 model yields a profit of $50. The merchant estimates that the total monthly demand will not exceed 250 units. The merchant does not want to invest more than $70,000 in inventory for these products. Find the number of units of each model that should be stocked in order to maximize profit. What is the maximum profit?

42. *Maximum Profit* A fruit grower has 150 acres of land available to raise two crops, A and B. It takes 1 day to trim an acre of crop A and 2 days to trim an acre of crop B, and there are 240 days per year available for trimming. It takes 0.3 day to pick an acre of crop A and 0.1 day to pick an acre of crop B, and there are 30 days available for picking. The profits are $140 per acre for crop A and $235 per acre for crop B. Find the number of acres of each fruit that should be planted to maximize profit. What is the maximum profit?

43. *Minimum Cost* Two gasolines, type A ($1.13 per gallon) and type B ($1.28 per gallon), have octane ratings of 80 and 92, respectively. Determine the blend of minimum cost with an octane rating of at least 90. What is the minimum cost? (*Hint:* Let x be the fraction of each gallon that is type A and let y be the fraction that is type B.)

44. *Maximum Revenue* An accounting firm has 900 hours of staff time and 100 hours of reviewing time available each week. The firm charges $2000 for an audit and $300 for a tax return. Each audit requires 100 hours of staff time and 10 hours of review time. Each tax return requires 12.5 hours of staff time and 2.5 hours of review time. What numbers of audits and tax returns will yield the maximum revenue? What is the maximum revenue?

45. *Maximum Revenue* The accounting firm in Exercise 44 lowers its charge for an audit to $1000. What numbers of audits and tax returns will yield the maximum revenue? What is the maximum revenue?

46. *Maximum Profit* A manufacturer produces two models of bicycles. The amounts of time (in hours) required for assembling, painting, and packaging the two models are as follows.

	Model A	Model B
Assembling	2	2.5
Painting	4	1
Packaging	1	0.75

The total amounts of time available for assembling, painting, and packaging are 4000, 4800, and 1500 hours, respectively. The profits per unit are $45 for model A and $50 for model B. How many of each model should be produced to maximize profit? What is the maximum profit?

47. *Maximum Profit* A manufacturer produces two models of snowboards. The amounts of time (in hours) required for assembling, painting, and packaging the two models are as follows.

	Model A	Model B
Assembling	2.5	3
Painting	2	1
Packaging	0.75	1.25

The total amounts of time available for assembling, painting, and packaging are 4000, 2500, and 1500 hours, respectively. The profits per unit are $50 for model A and $52 for model B. How many of each model should be produced to maximize profit? What is the maximum profit?

48. *Minimum Cost* A farming cooperative mixes two brands of cattle feed. Brand X costs $25 per bag and contains 2 units of nutritional element A, 2 units of element B, and 2 units of element C. Brand Y costs $20 per bag and contains 1 unit of nutritional element A, 9 units of element B, and 3 units of element C. The minimum requirements for nutrients A, B, and C are 12 units, 36 units, and 24 units, respectively. Find the number of bags of each brand that should be mixed to produce a mixture having a minimum cost per bag. What is the minimum cost per mixed bag?

Synthesis

True or False? **In Exercises 49 and 50, determine whether the statement is true or false. Justify your answer.**

49. If an objective function has a maximum value at the adjacent vertices $(4, 7)$ and $(8, 3)$, you can conclude that it also has a maximum value at the points $(4.5, 6.5)$ and $(7.8, 3.2)$.

50. When solving a linear programming problem, if the objective function has a maximum value at two adjacent vertices, you can assume that there is an infinite number of points that will produce the maximum value.

Think About It **In Exercises 51–54, find an objective function that has a maximum or minimum value at the indicated vertex of the constraint region shown below. (There are many correct answers.)**

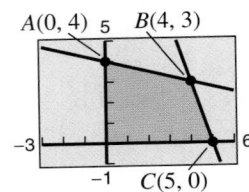

51. The maximum occurs at vertex A.

52. The maximum occurs at vertex B.

53. The maximum occurs at vertex C.

54. The minimum occurs at vertex C.

In Exercises 55 and 56, determine values of t such that the objective function has a maximum value at each indicated vertex.

55. Objective function:

$z = 3x + ty$

Constraints:

$x \geq 0$

$y \geq 0$

$x + 3y \leq 15$

$4x + y \leq 16$

(a) $(0, 5)$

(b) $(3, 4)$

56. Objective function:

$z = 3x + ty$

Constraints:

$x \geq 0$

$y \geq 0$

$x + 2y \leq 4$

$x - y \leq 1$

(a) $(2, 1)$

(b) $(0, 2)$

Review

In Exercises 57–60, simplify the compound fraction.

57. $\dfrac{\left(\dfrac{9}{x}\right)}{\left(\dfrac{6}{x} + 2\right)}$

58. $\dfrac{\left(1 + \dfrac{2}{x}\right)}{\left(x - \dfrac{4}{x}\right)}$

59. $\dfrac{\left(\dfrac{4}{x^2 - 9} + \dfrac{2}{x - 2}\right)}{\left(\dfrac{1}{x + 3} + \dfrac{1}{x - 3}\right)}$

60. $\dfrac{\left(\dfrac{1}{x + 1} + \dfrac{1}{2}\right)}{\left(\dfrac{3}{2x^2 + 4x + 2}\right)}$

In Exercises 61–66, solve the equation algebraically. Round your result to three decimal places.

61. $e^{2x} + 2e^x - 15 = 0$

62. $e^{2x} - 10e^x + 24 = 0$

63. $8(62 - e^{x/4}) = 192$

64. $\dfrac{150}{e^{-x} - 4} = 75$

65. $7 \ln 3x = 12$

66. $\ln(x + 9)^2 = 2$

In Exercises 67–70, use any method to solve the system.

67. $\begin{cases} -3x + 5y = -9 \\ x - 4y = 10 \end{cases}$

68. $\begin{cases} 5x - y = -13 \\ -x + 2y = 17 \end{cases}$

69. $\begin{cases} 4x + 5y = 6 \\ 5x - 11y = -27 \end{cases}$

70. $\begin{cases} -\frac{3}{2}x + 2y = 9 \\ 5x - \frac{1}{2}y = 44 \end{cases}$

In Exercises 71–74, sketch the graph of the solution of the system of inequalities. Use a graphing utility to verify your solution.

71. $\begin{cases} 2x + y \leq 7 \\ y \leq 4 \\ x \geq -1 \\ y \geq 0 \end{cases}$

72. $\begin{cases} x + y \leq 6 \\ y \geq -2 \\ x \geq -5 \end{cases}$

73. $\begin{cases} x^2 + y \leq 1 \\ y - 3x \geq -3 \\ y \geq -3 \end{cases}$

74. $\begin{cases} x^2 + y^2 \leq 9 \\ x + y \leq 3 \\ x \geq 0 \end{cases}$

5 Chapter Summary

What did you learn?

	Review Exercises
Section 5.1	
☐ How to use the method of substitution to solve systems of equations in two variables	1–6
☐ How to solve systems of equations graphically	7–12
☐ How to use systems of equations to model and solve real-life problems	13–16
Section 5.2	
☐ How to use the method of elimination to solve systems of linear equations in two variables	17–24
☐ How to graphically interpret the number of solutions of systems of linear equations in two variables	25–30
☐ How to use systems of linear equations in two variables to model and solve real-life problems	31–34
Section 5.3	
☐ How to recognize linear systems in row-echelon form and use back-substitution to solve the systems	35, 36
☐ How to use Gaussian elimination to solve systems of linear equations	37–42
☐ How to solve nonsquare systems of linear equations	43, 44
☐ How to graphically interpret three-variable systems	45, 46
☐ How to use systems of linear equations to write partial fraction decompositions of rational expressions	47–52
☐ How to use systems of linear equations in three or more variables to model and solve real-life problems	53, 54
Section 5.4	
☐ How to sketch graphs of inequalities in two variables	55–60
☐ How to solve systems of inequalities	61–70
☐ How to use systems of inequalities in two variables to model and solve real-life problems	71–76
Section 5.5	
☐ How to solve linear programming problems	77–80
☐ How to use linear programming to model and solve real-life problems	81, 82

5 Review Exercises

5.1 In Exercises 1–6, solve the system by the method of substitution.

1. $\begin{cases} x + y = 2 \\ x - y = 0 \end{cases}$

2. $\begin{cases} 2x = 3(y - 1) \\ y = x \end{cases}$

3. $\begin{cases} x^2 - y^2 = 9 \\ x - y = 1 \end{cases}$

4. $\begin{cases} x^2 + y^2 = 169 \\ 3x + 2y = 39 \end{cases}$

5. $\begin{cases} y = 2x^2 \\ y = x^4 - 2x^2 \end{cases}$

6. $\begin{cases} x = y + 3 \\ x = y^2 + 1 \end{cases}$

In Exercises 7–12, use a graphing utility to solve the system of equations. If you cannot identify the exact solution, find the solution accurate to two decimal places.

7. $\begin{cases} 5x + 6y = 7 \\ -x - 4y = 0 \end{cases}$

8. $\begin{cases} 8x - 3y = -3 \\ 2x + 5y = 28 \end{cases}$

9. $\begin{cases} y^2 - 2y + x = 0 \\ x + y = 0 \end{cases}$

10. $\begin{cases} y = 2x^2 - 4x + 1 \\ y = x^2 - 4x + 3 \end{cases}$

11. $\begin{cases} y = 2(6 - x) \\ y = 2^{x-2} \end{cases}$

12. $\begin{cases} y = \ln(x - 1) - 3 \\ y = 4 - \frac{1}{2}x \end{cases}$

13. **Break-Even Point** You set up a business and make an initial investment of $10,000. The unit cost of the product is $2.85 and the selling price is $4.95. How many units must you sell to break even?

14. **Choice of Two Jobs** You are offered two sales jobs. One company offers an annual salary of $22,500 plus a year-end bonus of 1.5% of your total sales. The other company offers a salary of $20,000 plus a year-end bonus of 2% of total sales. What amount of sales will make the second offer better? Explain.

15. **Geometry** The perimeter of a rectangle is 480 meters and its length is 1.5 times its width. Find the dimensions of the rectangle.

16. **Geometry** The perimeter of a rectangle is 68 feet and its width is $\frac{8}{9}$ times its length. Find the dimensions of the rectangle.

5.2 In Exercises 17–24, solve by elimination.

17. $\begin{cases} 2x - y = 2 \\ 6x + 8y = 39 \end{cases}$

18. $\begin{cases} 40x + 30y = 24 \\ 20x - 50y = -14 \end{cases}$

19. $\begin{cases} \frac{1}{5}x + \frac{3}{10}y = \frac{7}{50} \\ \frac{2}{5}x + \frac{1}{2}y = \frac{1}{5} \end{cases}$

20. $\begin{cases} \frac{5}{12}x - \frac{3}{4}y = \frac{25}{4} \\ -x + \frac{7}{8}y = -\frac{38}{5} \end{cases}$

21. $\begin{cases} 3x - 2y = 0 \\ 3x + 2(y + 5) = 10 \end{cases}$

22. $\begin{cases} 7x + 12y = 63 \\ 2x + 3y = 15 \end{cases}$

23. $\begin{cases} 1.25x - 2y = 3.5 \\ 5x - 8y = 14 \end{cases}$

24. $\begin{cases} 1.5x + 2.5y = 8.5 \\ 6x + 10y = 24 \end{cases}$

In Exercises 25–30, use a graphing utility to graph the system. Use the graph to determine whether the system is consistent or inconsistent. If the system is consistent, determine the solution. Verify your results algebraically.

25. $\begin{cases} 3x + 2y = 0 \\ x - y = 4 \end{cases}$

26. $\begin{cases} x + y = 6 \\ -2y = -12 + 2x \end{cases}$

27. $\begin{cases} \frac{1}{4}x - \frac{1}{5}y = 2 \\ -5x + 4y = 8 \end{cases}$

28. $\begin{cases} \frac{7}{2}x - 7y = -1 \\ -x + 2y = 4 \end{cases}$

29. $\begin{cases} 8x - 2y = 11 \\ -4x + y = -5.5 \end{cases}$

30. $\begin{cases} -x + 3.2y = 10.4 \\ 3x - 9.6y = 6.4 \end{cases}$

31. **Flying Speeds** Two planes leave Pittsburgh and Philadelphia at the same time, each going to the other city. One plane flies 25 miles per hour faster than the other. Find the air speed of each plane if the cities are 275 miles apart and the planes pass each other after 40 minutes of flying time.

32. **Finance** A total of $46,000 is invested in two corporate bonds that pay 6.75% and 7.25% simple interest. The investor wants an annual interest income of $3245 from the investments. What is the most that can be invested in the 6.75% bond?

Supply and Demand In Exercises 33 and 34, find the point of equilibrium.

Demand Function	Supply Function
33. $p = 37 - 0.0002x$	$p = 22 + 0.00001x$
34. $p = 120 - 0.0001x$	$p = 45 + 0.0002x$

5.3 In Exercises 35 and 36, use back-substitution to solve the system of linear equations.

35. $\begin{cases} x - 4y + 3z = 3 \\ -y + z = -1 \\ z = -5 \end{cases}$

36. $\begin{cases} x - 7y + 8z = 85 \\ y - 9z = -35 \\ z = 3 \end{cases}$

In Exercises 37–40, solve the system of linear equations and check any solution algebraically.

37. $\begin{cases} x + 3y - z = 13 \\ 2x \quad\quad - 5z = 23 \\ 4x - y - 2z = 14 \end{cases}$

38. $\begin{cases} x + 2y + 6z = 4 \\ -3x + 2y - z = -4 \\ 4x + \quad\quad 2z = 16 \end{cases}$

39. $\begin{cases} x - 2y + z = -6 \\ 2x - 3y \quad\quad = -7 \\ -x + 3y - 3z = 11 \end{cases}$

40. $\begin{cases} 2x + \quad\quad 6z = -9 \\ 3x - 2y + 11z = -16 \\ 3x - y + 7z = -11 \end{cases}$

In Exercises 41 and 42, find the equation of the parabola $y = ax^2 + bx + c$ that passes through the given points. Use a graphing utility to verify your result.

41.

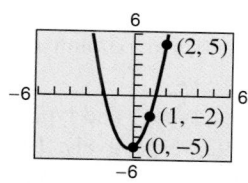

42.

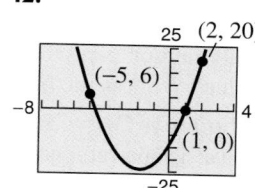

In Exercises 43 and 44, solve the nonsquare system of equations.

43. $\begin{cases} 5x - 12y + 7z = 16 \\ 3x - 7y + 4z = 9 \end{cases}$ **44.** $\begin{cases} 2x + 5y - 19z = 34 \\ 3x + 8y - 31z = 54 \end{cases}$

In Exercises 45 and 46, sketch the plane represented by the linear equation. Then list four points that lie in the plane.

45. $2x - 4y + z = 8$ **46.** $3x + 3y - z = 9$

In Exercises 47–52, write the partial fraction decomposition for the rational expression.

47. $\dfrac{4 - x}{x^2 + 6x + 8}$ **48.** $\dfrac{-x}{x^2 + 3x + 2}$

49. $\dfrac{x^2}{x^2 + 2x - 15}$ **50.** $\dfrac{9}{x^2 - 9}$

51. $\dfrac{x^2 + 2x}{x^3 - x^2 + x - 1}$ **52.** $\dfrac{3x^3 + 4x}{(x^2 + 1)^2}$

53. *Agriculture* A mixture of 6 gallons of chemical A, 8 gallons of chemical B, and 13 gallons of chemical C is required to kill a certain destructive crop insect. Commercial spray X contains 1, 2, and 2 parts, respectively, of these chemicals. Commercial spray Y contains only chemical C. Commercial spray Z contains chemicals A, B, and C in equal amounts. How much of each type of commercial spray is needed to get the desired mixture?

54. *Investments* An inheritance of $20,000 was divided among three investments yielding $1780 in interest per year. The interest rates for the three investments were 7%, 9%, and 11%. Find the amount placed in each investment if the second and third were $3000 and $1000 less than the first, respectively.

5.4 In Exercises 55–60, sketch the graph of the inequality.

55. $x \le 6$ **56.** $y \ge -10$

57. $y \le 5 - \frac{1}{2}x$ **58.** $3y - x \ge 7$

59. $y - 4x^2 > -1$ **60.** $y \ge 2e^x - 6$

In Exercises 61–64, match the system of inequalities with the graph of its solution. [The graphs are labeled (a), (b), (c), and (d).]

(a)

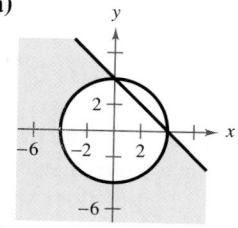

(b)

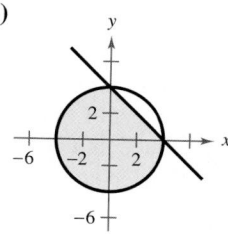

(c)

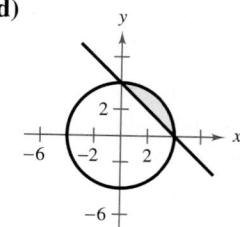

(d)

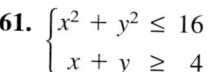

61. $\begin{cases} x^2 + y^2 \le 16 \\ x + y \ge 4 \end{cases}$ **62.** $\begin{cases} x^2 + y^2 \le 16 \\ x + y \le 4 \end{cases}$

63. $\begin{cases} x^2 + y^2 \ge 16 \\ x + y \ge 4 \end{cases}$ **64.** $\begin{cases} x^2 + y^2 \ge 16 \\ x + y \le 4 \end{cases}$

In Exercises 65–70, sketch a graph of the solution set of the system of inequalities. Use a graphing utility to verify your result.

65. $\begin{cases} x + 2y \le 160 \\ 3x + y \le 180 \\ x \ge 0 \\ y \ge 0 \end{cases}$ 66. $\begin{cases} 2x + 3y \le 24 \\ 2x + y \le 16 \\ x \ge 0 \\ y \ge 0 \end{cases}$

67. $\begin{cases} y < x + 1 \\ y > x^2 - 1 \end{cases}$ 68. $\begin{cases} y \le 6 - 2x - x^2 \\ y \ge x + 6 \end{cases}$

69. $\begin{cases} 2x - 3y \ge 0 \\ 2x - y \le 8 \\ y \ge 0 \end{cases}$ 70. $\begin{cases} x^2 + y^2 \le 9 \\ (x - 3)^2 + y^2 \le 9 \end{cases}$

In Exercises 71 and 72, derive a set of inequalities to describe the region.

71. *Parallelogram:* Vertices at $(1, 5), (3, 1), (6, 10), (8, 6)$

72. *Triangle:* Vertices at $(1, 2), (6, 7), (8, 1)$

In Exercises 73 and 74, find a system of inequalities that models the description. Use a graphing utility to graph and shade the solution of the system.

73. *Fruit Distribution*   A Pennsylvania fruit grower has at most 1500 bushels of apples that are to be divided between markets in Harrisburg and philadelphia. These two markets need at least 400 bushels and 600 bushels, respectively.

74. *Inventory Costs*   A warehouse operator has 24,000 square feet of floor space in which to store two products. Each unit of product I requires 20 square feet of floor space and costs $12 per day to store. Each unit of product II requires 30 square feet of floor space and costs $8 per day to store. The total storage cost per day cannot exceed $12,400.

In Exercises 75 and 76, use a graphing utility to shade the regions representing the consumer and producer surpluses for the equations. Find the surpluses.

	Demand	*Supply*
75.	$p = 160 - 0.0001x$	$p = 70 + 0.0002x$
76.	$p = 130 - 0.0002x$	$p = 30 + 0.0003x$

5.5   **In Exercises 77–80, use a graphing utility to graph the region determined by the constraints. Then find the minimum or maximum values of the objective function and where they occur, subject to the constraints.**

77. Maximize:
$$z = 3x + 4y$$
Constraints:
$$x \ge 0$$
$$y \ge 0$$
$$2x + 5y \le 50$$
$$4x + y \le 28$$

78. Minimize:
$$z = 10x + 7y$$
Constraints:
$$x \ge 0$$
$$y \ge 0$$
$$2x + y \ge 100$$
$$x + y \ge 75$$

79. Minimize:
$$z = 1.75x + 2.25y$$
Constraints:
$$x \ge 0$$
$$y \ge 0$$
$$2x + y \ge 25$$
$$3x + 2y \ge 45$$

80. Maximize:
$$z = 50x + 70y$$
Constraints:
$$x \ge 0$$
$$y \ge 0$$
$$x + 2y \le 1500$$
$$5x + 2y \le 3500$$

81. *Maximum Revenue*   A student is working part time as a cosmetologist to pay college expenses. The student may work no more than 24 hours per week. Haircuts cost $17 and require an average of 20 minutes, and permanents cost $60 and require an average of 1 hour and 10 minutes. What combination of haircuts and/or permanent will yield a maximum revenue? What is the maximum revenue?

82. *Minimum Cost*   Two gasolines, type A and type B, have octane ratings of 80 and 92, respectively. Type A costs $1.25 per gallon and type B costs $1.55 per gallon. Determine the blend of minimum cost with an octane rating of at least 88. (*Hint:* Let x be the fraction of each gallon that is type A and let y be the fraction that is type B.) What is the minimum cost?

Synthesis

True or False?   **In Exercises 83 and 84, determine whether the statement is true or false. Justify your answer.**

83. The system $\begin{cases} y \le 5 \\ y \ge -2 \\ y \ge \frac{7}{2}x - 9 \\ y \ge -\frac{7}{2}x + 26 \end{cases}$ represents a region shaped like an isosceles trapezoid.

84. It is possible for an objective function of a linear programming problem to have exactly ten maximum value points.

Chapter Project *Fitting Models to Data*

In this project, you will find and use models relating to newspaper circulation in the United States by using *least squares regression analysis*. This procedure can be performed easily with a computer or graphing utility.

The numbers of morning and evening newspapers published in the United States from 1990 through 1997 are shown in the table.

a. Use the regression capabilities of a graphing utility to find linear models for both sets of data. Then use the models to estimate the numbers of morning and evening newspapers published in 2003. In the table, $t = 0$ represents 1990. (Source: Editor and Publisher Company)

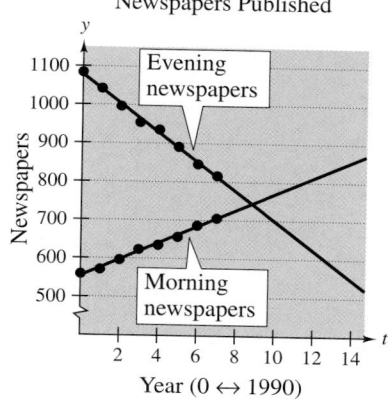

Newspapers Published

Year ($0 \leftrightarrow 1990$)

Year, t	0	1	2	3	4	5	6	7
Morning	559	571	596	623	635	656	686	705
Evening	1084	1042	996	954	935	891	846	816

b. Use the models you found in part (a) to predict the year when the number of morning papers published is equal to the number of evening papers published. Use the graph of the models shown to verify your result.

Questions for Further Exploration

1. The numbers (in millions) of morning newspapers sold each day in the United States from 1990 to 1997 are shown in the table below. In the table $t = 0$ represents 1990. Find a linear model that represents the data. Use your model to estimate the number of morning papers sold each day in 2003.

Year, t	0	1	2	3

Year, t	4	5	6	7

2. From 1990 through 1997, the number of morning newspapers published and sold increased. Did the average circulation per morning paper (number sold ÷ number published) increase or decrease? Explain.

3. If you had the opportunity to invest in a company that published only one type of newspaper (morning or evening), which would you choose? Explain your reasoning.

5 Chapter Test

Take this test as you would take a test in class. After you are done, check your work against the answers in the back of the book.

The *Interactive* CD-ROM and *Internet* versions of this text provide answers to the Chapter Tests and Cumulative Tests. They also offer Chapter Pre-Tests (that test key skills and concepts covered in previous chapters) and Chapter Post-Tests, both of which have randomly generated exercises with diagnostic capabilities.

In Exercises 1–3, solve the system by the method of substitution.

1. $\begin{cases} x - y = 6 \\ 3x + 5y = 2 \end{cases}$
2. $\begin{cases} y = x - 1 \\ y = (x - 1)^3 \end{cases}$
3. $\begin{cases} 4x - y^2 = 7 \\ x - y = 3 \end{cases}$

In Exercises 4–6, solve the system graphically.

4. $\begin{cases} 4x - 3y = -15 \\ 4x + 3y = -9 \end{cases}$
5. $\begin{cases} y = 16 - x^2 \\ y = x + 4 \end{cases}$
6. $\begin{cases} y - \ln x = 8 \\ 3x + y + 10 = 21 \end{cases}$

In Exercises 7–9, solve the linear system by elimination.

7. $\begin{cases} 2x + 5y = -11 \\ 5x - y = 19 \end{cases}$
8. $\begin{cases} x - 2y + 3z = -5 \\ 2x \quad - z = -4 \\ 3y + z = 17 \end{cases}$
9. $\begin{cases} 5x + 5y - z = 0 \\ 10x + 5y + 2z = 0 \\ 5x + 15y - 9z = 0 \end{cases}$

10. Find a system of linear equations that has the solution $\left(\frac{4}{3}, -8\right)$.

11. Find a system of linear equations that has the solution $\left(-\frac{1}{2}, 5, -\frac{9}{4}\right)$.

12. Find the equation of the parabola $y = ax^2 + bx + c$ passing through the points $(0, 6)$, $(-2, 2)$, and $\left(3, \frac{9}{2}\right)$.

13. Write the partial fraction decomposition for the rational expression $\dfrac{5x - 2}{(x - 1)^2}$.

In Exercises 14–16, sketch the graph of the inequality.

14. $x \geq -7$
15. $-4x + 6y < -11$
16. $(x - 4)^2 + y^2 < 16$

In Exercises 17–19, graph the inequalities and shade the region representing the solution.

17. $\begin{cases} 2x + y \leq 6 \\ 2x - y \leq 0 \\ x \geq -5 \end{cases}$
18. $\begin{cases} y < -x^4 + x^2 + 4 \\ y > 4x \end{cases}$
19. $\begin{cases} x^2 + y^2 \leq 16 \\ x \geq 1 \\ y \geq -3 \end{cases}$

20. Derive a set of inequalities to describe the region in the figure at the right.

21. Find the maximum value of the objective function $z = 20x + 12y$ subject to the constraints $x \geq 0$, $y \geq 0$, $x + 4y \leq 32$, and $3x + 2y \leq 36$.

22. A merchant plans to sell two models of compact disc players at costs of $275 and $400. The $275 model yields a profit of $55 and the $400 model yields a profit of $75. The merchant estimates that the total monthly demand will not exceed 300 units. The merchant does not want to invest more than $100,000 in inventory for these products. Find the number of units of each model that should be stocked in order to maximize profit.

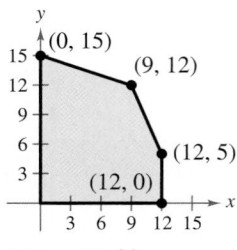

FIGURE FOR 20

3–5   Cumulative Test

Take this test to review the material from earlier chapters. After you are done, check your work against the answers in the back of the book.

In Exercises 1–3, sketch the graph of the function. Use a graphing utility to verify the graph.

1. $f(x) = -\frac{1}{2}(x^2 + 4x)$ **2.** $f(x) = \frac{1}{4}x(x - 2)^2$ **3.** $f(x) = x^3 + 2x^2 - 9x - 18$

4. Find all the zeros of $f(x) = x^3 + 2x^2 + 4x + 8$.

5. Use a graphing utility to approximate any real zeros of $g(x) = x^3 + 4x^2 - 11$ to the nearest hundredth.

6. Divide $(4x^2 + 14x - 9)$ by $(x + 3)$ using long division.

7. Divide $(2x^3 - 5x^2 + 6x - 20)$ by $(x - 6)$ using synthetic division.

8. Find a polynomial function with integer coefficients that has the zeros $0, -3$, and $1 + \sqrt{5}i$.

In Exercises 9–11, sketch the graph of the rational function. Be sure to label all asymptotes. Use a graphing utility to verify the graph.

9. $f(x) = \dfrac{2x}{x - 3}$ **10.** $f(x) = \dfrac{5x}{x^2 + x - 6}$ **11.** $f(x) = \dfrac{x^2 - 3x + 8}{x - 2}$

12. Write a rational function that has no vertical asymptotes and a horizontal asymptote at $y = 4$.

In Exercises 13–16, use a calculator to evaluate the expression. Round your result to three decimal places.

13. $(1.85)^{3.1}$ **14.** $58^{\sqrt{5}}$ **15.** $e^{-20/11}$ **16.** $4e^{2.56}$

In Exercises 17–20, sketch the graph of the function by hand. Use a graphing utility to verify the graph.

17. $f(x) = -3^{x+4} - 5$ **18.** $f(x) = -\left(\frac{1}{2}\right)^{-x} - 3$

19. $f(x) = 4 + \log_{10}(x - 3)$ **20.** $f(x) = \ln(4 - x)$

In Exercises 21–24, evaluate the logarithm using the change-of-base formula. Round your result to three decimal places.

21. $\log_5 21$ **22.** $\log_9 6.8$ **23.** $\log_3 8.61$ **24.** $\log_2\left(\frac{3}{2}\right)$

25. Write $2 \ln x - \frac{1}{2}\ln(x + 5)$ as a logarithm of a single quantity.

In Exercises 26–28, solve the equation algebraically. Round your result to three decimal places and verify your result graphically.

26. $6e^{2x} = 72$ **27.** $4e^{x-3} + 21 = 30$ **28.** $\log_2 x + \log_2 5 = 6$

29. Find the exponential function $y = ae^{bx}$ that passes through the points $\left(0, \frac{5}{2}\right)$ and $(6, 14)$.

In Exercises 30–32, use any method to solve the system of equations.

30. $\begin{cases} 4x - 5y = 29 \\ -x + 9y = 16 \end{cases}$
   31. $\begin{cases} 2x - y^2 = 0 \\ x - y = 4 \end{cases}$
   32. $\begin{cases} y = \log_3 x \\ y = -\frac{1}{3}x + 2 \end{cases}$

33. Find the equation of the circle $x^2 + y^2 + Dx + Ey + F = 0$ that passes through the points $(0, 0)$, $(0, -2)$, and $(3, 0)$.

In Exercises 34–36, sketch the graph of the solution of the system of inequalities. Verify your sketch using a graphing utility.

34. $\begin{cases} -2x + y \le 10 \\ y \le 6 \\ x \le 0 \end{cases}$
   35. $\begin{cases} -x + y^2 \le 4 \\ 2x + 9y \ge -8 \\ x \le 5 \end{cases}$
   36. $\begin{cases} x^2 + y^2 \le 25 \\ x^2 + y^2 \ge 4 \end{cases}$

37. Derive a set of inequalities to describe the trapezoidal region with vertices at $(1, 2)$, $(3, 8)$, $(6, 8)$, and $(8, 2)$.

38. *Finance* You deposit $2500 in an account earning 7.5% interest, compounded continuously. Find the balance after 25 years.

39. *Inflation* If the inflation rate averages 4.5% over the next 10 years, the approximate cost C of goods or services t years from now is $C(t) = P(1.045)^t$, where P is the present cost. If the price of a tire is presently $69.95, estimate the price 10 years from now.

40. *Population* The population P of a city is $P = 135{,}200e^{0.018t}$, where $t = 0$ represents 1990. Use a graphing utility to graph the model and determine when the population reaches 190,000. Verify your answer algebraically.

41. *Break-Even Point* A small business invests $24,000 to produce an item that will sell for $6.95. Each unit can be produced for $2.75.

(a) Write cost and revenue functions for x units produced and sold.

(b) Use a graphing utility to graph the cost and revenue functions in the same viewing window. Use the graph to approximate the number of units that must be sold to break even.

(c) Verify the result to part (b) algebraically.

42. *Geometry* What are the dimensions of a rectangle if its perimeter is 76 meters and its area is 352 square meters?

43. *Airplane Speed* An airplane flying into a headwind travels the 2448-mile flying distance between Anchorage, Alaska, and Colorado Springs, Colorado, in 4 hours and 48 minutes. On the return flight, the distance is traveled in 4 hours and 15 minutes. Find the airspeed of the plane and the speed of the wind, assuming that both remain constant.

44. *Minimum Cost* A pet supply company mixes two brands of dry dog food. Brand X costs $15 per bag and contains eight units of nutritional element A, one unit of element B, and two units of element C. Brand Y cost $30 per bag and contains two units of element A, one unit of element B, and seven units of element C. Each bag of mixed dog food must contain at least 16 units, 5 units, and 20 units of nutritional elements A, B, and C, respectively. Find the numbers of bags of brands X and Y that should be combined to produce a mixture meeting the minimum nutritional requirements and having a minimum cost. What is the minimum cost?

Matrices and Determinants

Superstock

The Big Picture

In this chapter you will learn how to

❏ write matrices, identify their order, and perform elementary row operations.

❏ use Gaussian elimination and Gauss-Jordan elimination with matrices to solve systems of linear equations.

❏ add, subtract, and multiply two matrices, and multiply a matrix by a real number.

❏ verify that two matrices are inverses of each other and find inverses of matrices.

❏ use inverse matrices to solve systems of linear equations.

❏ find the determinants of square matrices.

❏ use Cramer's Rule to solve systems of linear equations.

Heating and shaping iron changes its physical properties. Molten iron in a steelmaking furnace reaches temperatures of 2800°F.

Important Vocabulary

As you encounter each new vocabulary term in this chapter, add the term and its definition to your notebook glossary.

- matrix (p. 430)
- entry of a matrix (p. 430)
- order of a matrix (p. 430)
- square matrix (p. 430)
- main diagonal (p. 430)
- row matrix (p. 430)
- column matrix (p. 430)
- augmented matrix (p. 431)
- coefficient matrix (p. 431)
- elementary row operations (p. 432)
- row-equivalent matrices (p. 432)
- row-echelon form (p. 434)

- reduced row-echelon form (p. 434)
- Gauss-Jordan elimination (p. 437)
- scalar multiple (p. 446)
- zero matrix (p. 449)
- additive identity (p. 449)
- matrix multiplication (p. 450)
- identity matrix of order n (p. 452)
- inverse of a matrix (p. 460)
- invertible or nonsingular matrix (p. 461)
- singular matrix (p. 461)
- determinant (p. 469)

- minors (p. 471)
- cofactors (p. 471)
- expanding by cofactors (p. 472)
- triangular matrix (p. 473)
- upper triangular matrix (p. 473)
- lower triangular matrix (p. 473)
- diagonal matrix (p. 473)
- collinear points (p. 478)
- Cramer's Rule (p. 479)
- uncoded row matrices (p. 482)
- coded row matrices (p. 482)

Additional Resources Text-specific additional resources are available to help you do well in this course. See page xvi for details.

6.1 Matrices and Systems of Equations

Matrices

In this section you will study a streamlined technique for solving systems of linear equations. This technique involves the use of a rectangular array of real numbers called a **matrix.** The plural of matrix is *matrices.*

Definition of Matrix

If m and n are positive integers, an $m \times n$ (read "m by n") matrix is a rectangular array

$$\begin{bmatrix} a_{11} & a_{12} & a_{13} & \cdots & a_{1n} \\ a_{21} & a_{22} & a_{23} & \cdots & a_{2n} \\ a_{31} & a_{32} & a_{33} & \cdots & a_{3n} \\ \vdots & \vdots & \vdots & & \vdots \\ a_{m1} & a_{m2} & a_{m3} & \cdots & a_{mn} \end{bmatrix} \Bigg\} m \text{ rows}$$

$\underbrace{\qquad\qquad\qquad}_{n \text{ columns}}$

in which each **entry** a_{ij} of the matrix is a real number. An $m \times n$ matrix has m rows (horizontal lines) and n columns (vertical lines).

The entry in the ith row and jth column is denoted by the *double subscript* notation a_{ij}. For instance, the entry a_{23} is the entry in the second row and third column. A matrix having m rows and n columns is said to be of **order** $m \times n$. If $m = n$, the matrix is **square** of order n. For a square matrix, the entries $a_{11}, a_{22}, a_{33}, \ldots$ are the **main diagonal** entries.

EXAMPLE 1 Order of Matrices

Determine the order of each matrix.

a. $[2]$ **b.** $\begin{bmatrix} 1 & -3 & 0 & \frac{1}{2} \end{bmatrix}$ **c.** $\begin{bmatrix} 0 & 0 \\ 0 & 0 \end{bmatrix}$ **d.** $\begin{bmatrix} 5 & 0 \\ 2 & -2 \\ -7 & 4 \end{bmatrix}$

Solution

a. *Order:* 1×1

$[2]$ 1 row, 1 column

b. *Order:* 1×4

$\begin{bmatrix} 1 & -3 & 0 & \frac{1}{2} \end{bmatrix}$ 1 row, 4 columns

c. *Order:* 2×2

$\begin{bmatrix} 0 & 0 \\ 0 & 0 \end{bmatrix}$ 2 rows, 2 columns

d. *Order:* 3×2

$\begin{bmatrix} 5 & 0 \\ 2 & -2 \\ -7 & 4 \end{bmatrix}$ 3 rows, 2 columns

A matrix that has only one row [such as the matrix in Example 1(b)] is called a **row matrix,** and a matrix that has only one column is called a **column matrix.**

What You Should Learn:

- How to write matrices and identify their orders
- How to perform elementary row operations on matrices
- How to use matrices and Gaussian elimination to solve systems of linear equations
- How to use matrices and Gauss-Jordan elimination to solve systems of linear equations

Why You Should Learn It:

Matrices can be used to solve systems of linear equations in two or more variables. For instance, Exercise 82 on page 443 shows how a matrix can be used to help find a model for the parabolic path of a baseball.

Amwell/Tony Stone Images

Encourage your students to become familiar with the terms in this chapter.

A matrix derived from a system of linear equations (each written in standard form with the constant term on the right) is the **augmented matrix** of the system. Moreover, the matrix derived from the coefficients of the system (but not including the constant terms) is the **coefficient matrix** of the system.

System
$$\begin{cases} x - 4y + 3z = 5 \\ -x + 3y - z = -3 \\ 2x \quad\quad - 4z = 6 \end{cases}$$

Augmented Matrix
$$\left[\begin{array}{ccc:c} 1 & -4 & 3 & 5 \\ -1 & 3 & -1 & -3 \\ 2 & 0 & -4 & 6 \end{array}\right]$$

Coefficient Matrix
$$\left[\begin{array}{ccc} 1 & -4 & 3 \\ -1 & 3 & -1 \\ 2 & 0 & -4 \end{array}\right]$$

You may want to make sure that the way a linear system matches up with a matrix is clear to your students.

Note the use of 0 for the missing y-variable in the third equation, and also note the fourth column (of constant terms) in the augmented matrix. The optional dotted line in the augmented matrix helps to identify the constant terms.

When forming either the coefficient matrix or the augmented matrix of a system, you should begin by vertically aligning the variables in the equations and using 0's for the missing variables.

EXAMPLE 2   Writing an Augmented Matrix

Write the augmented matrix for the system of linear equations.
$$\begin{cases} x + 3y = 9 \\ -y + 4z = -2 \\ x - 5z = 0 \end{cases}$$
What is the order of the augmented matrix?

Solution
Begin by writing the linear system and aligning the variables.
$$\begin{cases} x + 3y \quad\quad = 9 \\ -y + 4z = -2 \\ x \quad\quad - 5z = 0 \end{cases}$$

Next, use the coefficients and constant terms as the matrix entries. Include zeros for each missing coefficient.
$$\left[\begin{array}{ccc:c} 1 & 3 & 0 & 9 \\ 0 & -1 & 4 & -2 \\ 1 & 0 & -5 & 0 \end{array}\right]$$

The augmented matrix has 3 rows and 4 columns, so it is a 3×4 matrix.

Elementary Row Operations

In Section 5.3, you studied three operations that can be used on a system of linear equations to produce an equivalent system.

1. Interchange two equations.

2. Multiply an equation by a nonzero constant.

3. Add a multiple of an equation to another equation.

In matrix terminology these three operations correspond to **elementary row operations.** An elementary row operation on an augmented matrix corresponds to a new (but equivalent) system of linear equations. Two matrices are **row-equivalent** if one can be obtained from the other by a sequence of elementary row operations.

The *Interactive* CD-ROM and *Internet* versions of this text show every example with its solution; clicking on the *Try It!* button brings up similar problems. Guided Examples and Integrated Examples show step-by-step solutions to additional examples. Integrated Examples are related to several concepts in the section.

Elementary Row Operations

1. Interchange two rows.

2. Multiply a row by a nonzero constant.

3. Add a multiple of a row to another row.

Although elementary row operations are simple to perform, they involve a lot of arithmetic. Because it is easy to make a mistake, you should get in the habit of noting the elementary row operations performed in each step so that you can go back and check your work.

EXAMPLE 3   Elementary Row Operations

a. Interchange the first and second rows.

Original Matrix

$$\begin{bmatrix} 0 & 1 & 3 & 4 \\ -1 & 2 & 0 & 3 \\ 2 & -3 & 4 & 1 \end{bmatrix}$$

New Row-Equivalent Matrix

$$\begin{matrix} R_2 \\ R_1 \end{matrix} \begin{bmatrix} -1 & 2 & 0 & 3 \\ 0 & 1 & 3 & 4 \\ 2 & -3 & 4 & 1 \end{bmatrix}$$

b. Multiply the first row by $\frac{1}{2}$.

Original Matrix

$$\begin{bmatrix} 2 & -4 & 6 & -2 \\ 1 & 3 & -3 & 0 \\ 5 & -2 & 1 & 2 \end{bmatrix}$$

New Row-Equivalent Matrix

$$\frac{1}{2}R_1 \rightarrow \begin{bmatrix} 1 & -2 & 3 & -1 \\ 1 & 3 & -3 & 0 \\ 5 & -2 & 1 & 2 \end{bmatrix}$$

c. Add -2 times the first row to the third row.

Original Matrix

$$\begin{bmatrix} 1 & 2 & -4 & 3 \\ 0 & 3 & -2 & -1 \\ 2 & 1 & 5 & -2 \end{bmatrix}$$

New Row-Equivalent Matrix

$$\begin{bmatrix} 1 & 2 & -4 & 3 \\ 0 & 3 & -2 & -1 \\ -2R_1 + R_3 \rightarrow 0 & -3 & 13 & -8 \end{bmatrix}$$

Note that the elementary row operation is written beside the row that is *changed*.

Gaussian Elimination with Back Substitution

In Example 2 of Section 5.3, you used Gaussian elimination with back-substitution to solve a system of linear equations. The next example demonstrates the matrix version of Gaussian elimination. The two methods are essentially the same. The basic difference is that with matrices you do not need to keep writing the variables.

EXAMPLE 4   Using Elementary Row Operations

Linear System   *Associated Augmented Matrix*

$$\begin{cases} x - 2y + 3z = 9 \\ -x + 3y \quad\;\; = -4 \\ 2x - 5y + 5z = 17 \end{cases}$$

$$\begin{bmatrix} 1 & -2 & 3 & \vdots & 9 \\ -1 & 3 & 0 & \vdots & -4 \\ 2 & -5 & 5 & \vdots & 17 \end{bmatrix}$$

Add the first equation to the second equation.

Add the first row to the second row $(R_1 + R_2)$.

The *Interactive* CD-ROM and *Internet* versions of this text offer a built-in graphing calculator, which can be used with the Examples, Explorations, and Exercises.

$$\begin{cases} x - 2y + 3z = 9 \\ y + 3z = 5 \\ 2x - 5y + 5z = 17 \end{cases}$$

$$R_1 + R_2 \rightarrow \begin{bmatrix} 1 & -2 & 3 & \vdots & 9 \\ 0 & 1 & 3 & \vdots & 5 \\ 2 & -5 & 5 & \vdots & 17 \end{bmatrix}$$

Add -2 times the first equation to the third equation.

Add -2 times the first row to the third row $(-2R_1 + R_3)$.

$$\begin{cases} x - 2y + 3z = 9 \\ y + 3z = 5 \\ -y - z = -1 \end{cases}$$

$$-2R_1 + R_3 \rightarrow \begin{bmatrix} 1 & -2 & 3 & \vdots & 9 \\ 0 & 1 & 3 & \vdots & 5 \\ 0 & -1 & -1 & \vdots & -1 \end{bmatrix}$$

Add the second equation to the third equation.

Add the second row to the third row $(R_2 + R_3)$.

$$\begin{cases} x - 2y + 3z = 9 \\ y + 3z = 5 \\ 2z = 4 \end{cases}$$

$$R_2 + R_3 \rightarrow \begin{bmatrix} 1 & -2 & 3 & \vdots & 9 \\ 0 & 1 & 3 & \vdots & 5 \\ 0 & 0 & 2 & \vdots & 4 \end{bmatrix}$$

Multiply the third equation by $\frac{1}{2}$.

Multiply the third row by $\frac{1}{2}$.

$$\begin{cases} x - 2y + 3z = 9 \\ y + 3z = 5 \\ z = 2 \end{cases}$$

$$\tfrac{1}{2}R_3 \rightarrow \begin{bmatrix} 1 & -2 & 3 & \vdots & 9 \\ 0 & 1 & 3 & \vdots & 5 \\ 0 & 0 & 1 & \vdots & 2 \end{bmatrix}$$

At this point, you can use back-substitution to find that the solution is $x = 1$, $y = -1$, and $z = 2$, as was done in Example 2 of Section 5.3.

Remember that you should check a solution by substituting the values of x, y, and z into each equation in the original system.

The last matrix in Example 4 is said to be in **row-echelon form.** The term *echelon* refers to the stair-step pattern formed by the nonzero elements of the matrix. To be in this form, a matrix must have the properties listed on page 434.

Row-Echelon Form and Reduced Row-Echelon Form

A matrix in **row-echelon form** has the following properties.

1. All rows consisting entirely of zeros occur at the bottom of the matrix.

2. For each row that does not consist entirely of zeros, the first nonzero entry is 1 (called a **leading 1**).

3. For two successive (nonzero) rows, the leading 1 in the higher row is farther to the left than the leading 1 in the lower row.

A matrix in *row-echelon form* is in **reduced row-echelon form** if every column that has a leading 1 has zeros in every position above and below its leading 1.

> **STUDY TIP**
>
> Some graphing utilities can automatically transform a matrix to row-echelon form and reduced row-echelon form. Consult your user's manual to see whether your graphing utility has this capability. If so, use it to verify the results in this section.

It is worth mentioning that the row-echelon form of a matrix is not unique. That is, two different sequences of elementary row operations may yield different row-echelon forms.

EXAMPLE 5   Row-Echelon Form

Decide whether each matrix is in row-echelon form. If it is, decide whether the matrix is in reduced row-echelon form.

a. $\begin{bmatrix} 1 & 2 & -1 & 4 \\ 0 & 1 & 0 & 3 \\ 0 & 0 & 1 & -2 \end{bmatrix}$
  b. $\begin{bmatrix} 1 & 2 & -1 & 2 \\ 0 & 0 & 0 & 0 \\ 0 & 1 & 2 & -4 \end{bmatrix}$

c. $\begin{bmatrix} 1 & -5 & 2 & -1 & 3 \\ 0 & 0 & 1 & 3 & -2 \\ 0 & 0 & 0 & 1 & 4 \\ 0 & 0 & 0 & 0 & 1 \end{bmatrix}$
  d. $\begin{bmatrix} 1 & 0 & 0 & -1 \\ 0 & 1 & 0 & 2 \\ 0 & 0 & 1 & 3 \\ 0 & 0 & 0 & 0 \end{bmatrix}$

e. $\begin{bmatrix} 1 & 2 & -3 & 4 \\ 0 & 2 & 1 & -1 \\ 0 & 0 & 1 & -3 \end{bmatrix}$
  f. $\begin{bmatrix} 0 & 1 & 0 & 5 \\ 0 & 0 & 1 & 3 \\ 0 & 0 & 0 & 0 \end{bmatrix}$

Solution

The matrices in (a), (c), (d), and (f) are in row-echelon form. The matrices in (d) and (f) are in reduced form because every column that has a leading 1 has zeros in every position above and below its leading 1. The matrix in (b) is not in row-echelon form because a row of all zeros does not occur at the bottom of the matrix. The matrix in (e) is not in row-echelon form because the first nonzero entry in row 2 is not a leading 1.

Every matrix has a row-equivalent matrix that is in row-echelon form. For instance, in Example 5, you can change the matrix in part (e) to row-echelon form by multiplying its second row by $\frac{1}{2}$. What elementary row operation could you perform on the matrix in part (b) so that it would be in row-echelon form?

You have seen that the row-echelon form of a given matrix is *not* unique; however, the *reduced* row-echelon form of a given matrix *is* unique.

Gaussian elimination with back-substitution works well for solving systems of linear equations by hand or with a computer. For this algorithm, the order in which the elementary row operations are performed is important. You should operate from *left to right by columns*, using elementary row operations to obtain zeros in all entries directly below the leading 1's.

EXAMPLE 6   Gaussian Elimination with Back-Substitution

Solve the system $\begin{cases} \quad\; y + z - 2w = -3 \\ x + 2y - z \qquad\quad = 2 \\ 2x + 4y + z - 3w = -2 \\ x - 4y - 7z - w = -19 \end{cases}$

A computer animation of this example appears in the *Interactive* CD-ROM and *Internet* versions of this text.

Solution

Interchange rows 1 and 2 in order to have a 1 in the upper left corner.

$$\begin{matrix} {\scriptstyle R_2} \\ {\scriptstyle R_1} \end{matrix} \begin{bmatrix} 1 & 2 & -1 & 0 & \vdots & 2 \\ 0 & 1 & 1 & -2 & \vdots & -3 \\ 2 & 4 & 1 & -3 & \vdots & -2 \\ 1 & -4 & -7 & -1 & \vdots & -19 \end{bmatrix}$$

First column has leading 1 in upper left corner.

$$\begin{matrix} \\ \\ -2R_1 + R_3 \rightarrow \\ -R_1 + R_4 \rightarrow \end{matrix} \begin{bmatrix} 1 & 2 & -1 & 0 & \vdots & 2 \\ 0 & 1 & 1 & -2 & \vdots & -3 \\ 0 & 0 & 3 & -3 & \vdots & -6 \\ 0 & -6 & -6 & -1 & \vdots & -21 \end{bmatrix}$$

First column has zeros below its leading 1.

$$\begin{matrix} \\ \\ \\ 6R_2 + R_4 \rightarrow \end{matrix} \begin{bmatrix} 1 & 2 & -1 & 0 & \vdots & 2 \\ 0 & 1 & 1 & -2 & \vdots & -3 \\ 0 & 0 & 3 & -3 & \vdots & -6 \\ 0 & 0 & 0 & -13 & \vdots & -39 \end{bmatrix}$$

Second column has zeros below its leading 1.

$$\begin{matrix} \\ \\ \tfrac{1}{3}R_3 \rightarrow \\ \\ \end{matrix} \begin{bmatrix} 1 & 2 & -1 & 0 & \vdots & 2 \\ 0 & 1 & 1 & -2 & \vdots & -3 \\ 0 & 0 & 1 & -1 & \vdots & -2 \\ 0 & 0 & 0 & -13 & \vdots & -39 \end{bmatrix}$$

Third column has zeros below its leading 1.

$$\begin{matrix} \\ \\ \\ -\tfrac{1}{13}R_4 \rightarrow \end{matrix} \begin{bmatrix} 1 & 2 & -1 & 0 & \vdots & 2 \\ 0 & 1 & 1 & -2 & \vdots & -3 \\ 0 & 0 & 1 & -1 & \vdots & -2 \\ 0 & 0 & 0 & 1 & \vdots & 3 \end{bmatrix}$$

Fourth column has a leading 1.

The matrix is now in row-echelon form, and the corresponding system is

$$\begin{cases} x + 2y - z \qquad\quad = 2 \\ \quad\; y + z - 2w = -3. \\ \qquad\quad z - w = -2 \\ \qquad\qquad\quad w = 3 \end{cases}$$

Using back-substitution, you can determine that the solution is $x = -1$, $y = 2$, $z = 1$, and $w = 3$. Check this in the original system of equations.

The following steps summarize the procedure used in Example 6.

Gaussian Elimination with Back-Substitution

1. Write the augmented matrix of the system of linear equations.
2. Use elementary row operations to rewrite the augmented matrix in row-echelon form.
3. Write the system of linear equations corresponding to the matrix in row-echelon form and use back-substitution to find the solution.

When solving a system of linear equations, remember that it is possible for the system to have no solution. If, in the elimination process, you obtain a row with zeros except for the last entry, it is unnecessary to continue the elimination process. You can simply conclude that the system is inconsistent.

EXAMPLE 7   A System with No Solution

Solve the system.

$$\begin{cases} x - y + 2z = 4 \\ x + z = 6 \\ 2x - 3y + 5z = 4 \\ 3x + 2y - z = 1 \end{cases}$$

Solution

$$\begin{bmatrix} 1 & -1 & 2 & \vdots & 4 \\ 1 & 0 & 1 & \vdots & 6 \\ 2 & -3 & 5 & \vdots & 4 \\ 3 & 2 & -1 & \vdots & 1 \end{bmatrix} \quad -R_1 + R_2 \rightarrow \begin{bmatrix} 1 & -1 & 2 & \vdots & 4 \\ 0 & 1 & -1 & \vdots & 2 \\ 2 & -3 & 5 & \vdots & 4 \\ 3 & 2 & -1 & \vdots & 1 \end{bmatrix}$$

$$-2R_1 + R_3 \rightarrow \begin{bmatrix} 1 & -1 & 2 & \vdots & 4 \\ 0 & 1 & -1 & \vdots & 2 \\ 0 & -1 & 1 & \vdots & -4 \\ 3 & 2 & -1 & \vdots & 1 \end{bmatrix}$$

$$-3R_1 + R_4 \rightarrow \begin{bmatrix} 1 & -1 & 2 & \vdots & 4 \\ 0 & 1 & -1 & \vdots & 2 \\ 0 & -1 & 1 & \vdots & -4 \\ 0 & 5 & -7 & \vdots & -11 \end{bmatrix}$$

$$R_2 + R_3 \rightarrow \begin{bmatrix} 1 & -1 & 2 & \vdots & 4 \\ 0 & 1 & -1 & \vdots & 2 \\ 0 & 0 & 0 & \vdots & -2 \\ 0 & 5 & -7 & \vdots & -11 \end{bmatrix}$$

Note that the third row of this matrix consists of zeros except for the last entry. Converting this row back to a linear equation yields $0 = -2$, which is a false statement. This means that the original system of linear equations is *inconsistent* and the system has no solution.

Gauss-Jordan Elimination

With Gaussian elimination, elementary row operations are applied to a matrix to obtain a (row-equivalent) row-echelon form. A second method of elimination, called **Gauss-Jordan elimination,** after Carl Friedrich Gauss (1777–1855) and Wilhelm Jordan (1842–1899), continues the reduction process until a reduced row-echelon form is obtained. This procedure is demonstrated in Example 8.

EXAMPLE 8 Gauss-Jordan Elimination

Use Gauss-Jordan elimination to solve the system.

$$\begin{cases} x - 2y + 3z = 9 \\ -x + 3y = -4 \\ 2x - 5y + 5z = 17 \end{cases}$$

Solution

In Example 4, Gaussian elimination was used to obtain the row-echelon form

$$\begin{bmatrix} 1 & -2 & 3 & \vdots & 9 \\ 0 & 1 & 3 & \vdots & 5 \\ 0 & 0 & 1 & \vdots & 2 \end{bmatrix}.$$

Now, rather than using back-substitution, apply additional elementary row operations until you obtain a matrix in *reduced* row-echelon form. To do this, you must produce zeros above each of the leading 1's, as follows.

$$\begin{matrix} 2R_2 + R_1 \rightarrow \\ \\ \\ \end{matrix} \begin{bmatrix} 1 & 0 & 9 & \vdots & 19 \\ 0 & 1 & 3 & \vdots & 5 \\ 0 & 0 & 1 & \vdots & 2 \end{bmatrix}$$

Second column has zeros above its leading 1.

$$\begin{matrix} -9R_3 + R_1 \rightarrow \\ -3R_3 + R_2 \rightarrow \\ \\ \end{matrix} \begin{bmatrix} 1 & 0 & 0 & \vdots & 1 \\ 0 & 1 & 0 & \vdots & -1 \\ 0 & 0 & 1 & \vdots & 2 \end{bmatrix}$$

Third column has zeros above its leading 1.

Now, converting back to a system of linear equations, you have

$$\begin{cases} x = 1 \\ y = -1 \\ z = 2 \end{cases}$$

which is the same solution that was obtained using Gaussian elimination.

The beauty of Gauss-Jordan elimination is that, from the reduced row-echelon form, you can simply read the solution. Which technique do you prefer: Gaussian elimination or Gauss-Jordan elimination?

STUDY T!P

For a demonstration of a graphical approach to Gauss-Jordan elimination on a 2×3 matrix, see the graphing calculator program ROWOPS, available for several models of graphing calculators on our website at *college.hmco.com*.

The elimination procedures described in this section employ an algorithmic approach that is easily adapted to computer use. However, the procedure makes no effort to avoid fractional coefficients. For instance, if the system given in Example 8 had been listed as

$$\begin{cases} 2x - 5y + 5z = 17 \\ x - 2y + 3z = 9 \\ -x + 3y = -4 \end{cases}$$

the procedure would have required multiplication of the first row by $\frac{1}{2}$, which would have introduced fractions in the first row. For hand computations, fractions can sometimes be avoided by judiciously choosing the order in which the elementary row operations are applied.

EXAMPLE 9   A System with an Infinite Number of Solutions

Solve the system.

$$2x + 4y - 2z = 0$$

$$3x + 5y = 1$$

Solution

$$\begin{bmatrix} 2 & 4 & -2 & \vdots & 0 \\ 3 & 5 & 0 & \vdots & 1 \end{bmatrix} \quad \tfrac{1}{2}R_1 \rightarrow \begin{bmatrix} 1 & 2 & -1 & \vdots & 0 \\ 3 & 5 & 0 & \vdots & 1 \end{bmatrix}$$

$$-3R_1 + R_2 \rightarrow \begin{bmatrix} 1 & 2 & -1 & \vdots & 0 \\ 0 & -1 & 3 & \vdots & 1 \end{bmatrix}$$

$$-R_2 \rightarrow \begin{bmatrix} 1 & 2 & -1 & \vdots & 0 \\ 0 & 1 & -3 & \vdots & -1 \end{bmatrix}$$

$$-2R_2 + R_1 \rightarrow \begin{bmatrix} 1 & 0 & 5 & \vdots & 2 \\ 0 & 1 & -3 & \vdots & -1 \end{bmatrix}$$

The corresponding system of equations is

$$\begin{cases} x + 5z = 2 \\ y - 3z = -1 \end{cases}.$$

Solving for x and y in terms of z, you have $x = -5z + 2$ and $y = 3z - 1$. Then, letting $z = a$, where a is a real number, the solution set has the form

$$(-5a + 2, 3a - 1, a).$$

Recall from Section 5.3 that a solution set of this form represents an infinite number of solutions. Try substituting values for a to obtain a few solutions. Then check each solution in the original system of equations.

Activities

1. Write two or three sentences comparing Gaussian elimination with back-substitution and Gauss-Jordan elimination.

2. Set up the augmented matrix needed to solve the system.

$$\begin{cases} 2x + 5y - z + w = 13 \\ x - 4y + 3w = 7 \\ 5x + w = 13 \\ x + 2y + 3z = 1 \end{cases}$$

Answer:

$$\begin{bmatrix} 2 & 5 & -1 & 1 & \vdots & 13 \\ 1 & -4 & 0 & 3 & \vdots & 7 \\ 5 & 0 & 0 & 1 & \vdots & 13 \\ 1 & 2 & 3 & 0 & \vdots & 1 \end{bmatrix}$$

3. Use Gauss-Jordan elimination to solve the system.

$$\begin{cases} x + 2y + z = -4 \\ 2x - y + z = -4 \\ x + 3y - z = -7 \end{cases}$$

Answer: $(-3, -1, 1)$

EXAMPLE 10   Analysis of a Network

Set up a system of linear equations representing the network shown in Figure 6.1.

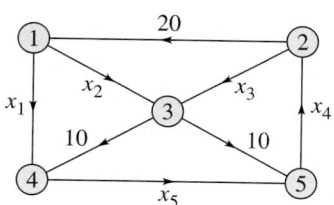

Figure 6.1

Solution

In a network, it is assumed that the total flow into a junction is equal to the total flow out of the junction. For example, because Junction 1 in Figure 6.1 has 20 units flowing into it, there must be 20 units flowing out of it. This is represented by the linear equation $x_1 + x_2 = 20$. A linear equation can be written for each of the network's five junctions, so the network is modeled by the following system.

$$
\begin{cases}
x_1 + x_2 & = 20 & \text{Junction 1} \\
x_3 - x_4 & = -20 & \text{Junction 2} \\
x_2 + x_3 & = 20. & \text{Junction 3} \\
x_1 \qquad\quad - x_5 & = -10 & \text{Junction 4} \\
- x_4 + x_5 & = -10 & \text{Junction 5}
\end{cases}
$$

Using Gauss-Jordan elimination on the augmented matrix produces the matrix in reduced row-echelon form.

Augmented Matrix

$$
\begin{bmatrix}
1 & 1 & 0 & 0 & 0 & \vdots & 20 \\
0 & 0 & 1 & -1 & 0 & \vdots & -20 \\
0 & 1 & 1 & 0 & 0 & \vdots & 20 \\
1 & 0 & 0 & 0 & -1 & \vdots & -10 \\
0 & 0 & 0 & -1 & 1 & \vdots & -10
\end{bmatrix}
$$

Matrix in Reduced Row-Echelon Form

$$
\begin{bmatrix}
1 & 0 & 0 & 0 & -1 & \vdots & -10 \\
0 & 1 & 0 & 0 & 1 & \vdots & 30 \\
0 & 0 & 1 & 0 & -1 & \vdots & -10 \\
0 & 0 & 0 & 1 & -1 & \vdots & 10 \\
0 & 0 & 0 & 0 & 0 & \vdots & 0
\end{bmatrix}
$$

Exercises containing systems with no solutions: 50, 53

Exercises containing systems with infinitely many solutions: 52, 57, 58, 60, 61, 62, 64, 65, 66

Letting $x_5 = t$, where t is a real number, you have $x_1 = t - 10$, $x_2 = -t + 30$, $x_3 = t - 10$, and $x_4 = t + 10$. So, this system has an infinite number of solutions.

Writing About Math   *Error Analysis*

One of your classmates has submitted the following steps for a solution of a system by Gauss-Jordan elimination. Find the error(s) in the solution. Write a short paragraph explaining the error(s) to your classmate.

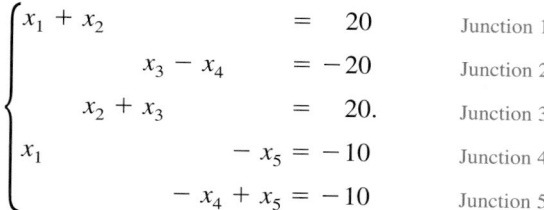

Writing About Math Suggestion
Because it can be difficult for students to find their own errors when applying Gauss-Jordan elimination to matrices, you might consider making up several more examples of common errors for additional practice.

6.1 **Exercises**

In Exercises 1–6, determine the order of the matrix.

1. $\begin{bmatrix} 3 & -2 \\ 7 & 0 \\ 0 & 9 \end{bmatrix}$

2. $\begin{bmatrix} 6 & -3 & 10 & 8 \end{bmatrix}$

3. $\begin{bmatrix} 4 \\ 32 \\ 3 \end{bmatrix}$

4. $\begin{bmatrix} -3 & 7 & 15 & 0 \\ 0 & 0 & 3 & 3 \\ 1 & 1 & 6 & 7 \end{bmatrix}$

5. $\begin{bmatrix} 33 & 45 \\ -9 & 20 \end{bmatrix}$

6. $\begin{bmatrix} 9 \end{bmatrix}$

In Exercises 7–10, write the augmented matrix for the system of linear equations.

7. $\begin{cases} 4x - 5y = 33 \\ -x + 5y = -27 \end{cases}$

8. $\begin{cases} 7x + 4y = 22 \\ 5x - 9y = 15 \end{cases}$

9. $\begin{cases} x + 10y - 2z = 2 \\ 5x - 3y + 4z = 0 \\ 2x + y = 6 \end{cases}$

10. $\begin{cases} -x - 8y + 5z = 17 \\ -6x + 12z = -24 \\ 3x + y - 8z = 11 \end{cases}$

In Exercises 11–14, write the system of linear equations represented by the augmented matrix. (Use variables x, y, z, and w.)

11. $\left[\begin{array}{cc:c} 1 & 2 & 7 \\ 2 & -3 & 4 \end{array}\right]$

12. $\left[\begin{array}{cc:c} 7 & -5 & 0 \\ 8 & 3 & -2 \end{array}\right]$

13. $\left[\begin{array}{cccc:c} 9 & 12 & 3 & 0 & 0 \\ -2 & 18 & 5 & 2 & 10 \\ 1 & 7 & -8 & 0 & -4 \end{array}\right]$

14. $\left[\begin{array}{cccc:c} 6 & 2 & -1 & -5 & -25 \\ -1 & 0 & 7 & 3 & 7 \\ 4 & -1 & -10 & 6 & 23 \\ 0 & 8 & 1 & -11 & -21 \end{array}\right]$

In Exercises 15–18, determine whether the matrix is in row-echelon form. If it is, determine if it is also in reduced row-echelon form.

15. $\begin{bmatrix} 1 & 0 & 0 & 0 \\ 0 & 1 & 1 & 5 \\ 0 & 0 & 0 & 0 \end{bmatrix}$

16. $\begin{bmatrix} 1 & 3 & 0 & 0 \\ 0 & 0 & 1 & 8 \\ 0 & 0 & 0 & 0 \end{bmatrix}$

17. $\begin{bmatrix} 2 & 0 & 4 & 0 \\ 0 & -1 & 3 & 6 \\ 0 & 0 & 1 & 5 \end{bmatrix}$

18. $\begin{bmatrix} 1 & 0 & 2 & 1 \\ 0 & 1 & -3 & 10 \\ 0 & 0 & 1 & 0 \end{bmatrix}$

In Exercises 19–22, fill in the blanks using elementary row operations to form a row-equivalent matrix.

19. $\begin{bmatrix} 1 & 4 & 3 \\ 2 & 10 & 5 \end{bmatrix}$

$\begin{bmatrix} 1 & 4 & 3 \\ 0 & & -1 \end{bmatrix}$

20. $\begin{bmatrix} 3 & 6 & 8 \\ 4 & -3 & 6 \end{bmatrix}$

$\begin{bmatrix} 1 & & \frac{8}{3} \\ 4 & -3 & 6 \end{bmatrix}$

21. $\begin{bmatrix} 1 & 1 & 4 & -1 \\ 3 & 8 & 10 & 3 \\ -2 & 1 & 12 & 6 \end{bmatrix}$

$\begin{bmatrix} 1 & 1 & 4 & -1 \\ 0 & 5 & & \\ 0 & 3 & & \end{bmatrix}$

$\begin{bmatrix} 1 & 1 & 4 & -1 \\ 0 & 1 & -\frac{2}{5} & \frac{6}{5} \\ 0 & 3 & & \end{bmatrix}$

22. $\begin{bmatrix} 2 & 4 & 8 & 3 \\ 1 & -1 & -3 & 2 \\ 2 & 6 & 4 & 9 \end{bmatrix}$

$\begin{bmatrix} 1 & & & \\ 1 & -1 & -3 & 2 \\ 2 & 6 & 4 & 9 \end{bmatrix}$

$\begin{bmatrix} 1 & 2 & 4 & \frac{3}{2} \\ 0 & & -7 & \frac{1}{2} \\ 0 & 2 & & \end{bmatrix}$

In Exercises 23–26, identify the elementary row operation being performed to obtain the new row-equivalent matrix.

23. *Original Matrix*   *New Row-Equivalent Matrix*

$\begin{bmatrix} -2 & 5 & 1 \\ 3 & -1 & -8 \end{bmatrix}$ $\begin{bmatrix} 13 & 0 & -39 \\ 3 & -1 & -8 \end{bmatrix}$

24. *Original Matrix*   *New Row-Equivalent Matrix*

$\begin{bmatrix} 3 & -1 & -4 \\ -4 & 3 & 7 \end{bmatrix}$ $\begin{bmatrix} 3 & -1 & -4 \\ 5 & 0 & -5 \end{bmatrix}$

25. *Original Matrix*   *New Row-Equivalent Matrix*

$\begin{bmatrix} 0 & -1 & -5 & 5 \\ -1 & 3 & -7 & 6 \\ 4 & -5 & 1 & 3 \end{bmatrix}$ $\begin{bmatrix} -1 & 3 & -7 & 6 \\ 0 & -1 & -5 & 5 \\ 4 & -5 & 1 & 3 \end{bmatrix}$

26. *Original Matrix*   *New Row-Equivalent Matrix*

$\begin{bmatrix} -1 & -2 & 3 & -2 \\ 2 & -5 & 1 & -7 \\ 5 & 4 & -7 & 6 \end{bmatrix}$ $\begin{bmatrix} -1 & -2 & 3 & -2 \\ 2 & -5 & 1 & -7 \\ 0 & -6 & 8 & -4 \end{bmatrix}$

The *Interactive* CD-ROM and *Internet* versions of this text contain step-by-step solutions to all odd-numbered Section and Review Exercises. They also provide Tutorial Exercises that link to Guided Examples for addtional help.

27. Perform the sequence of row operations on the matrix. What did the operations accomplish?

$$\begin{bmatrix} 1 & 2 & 3 \\ 2 & -1 & -4 \\ 3 & 1 & -1 \end{bmatrix}$$

(a) Add -2 times Row 1 to Row 2.

(b) Add -3 times Row 1 to Row 3.

(c) Add -1 times Row 2 to Row 3.

(d) Multiply Row 2 by $-\frac{1}{5}$.

(e) Add -2 times Row 2 to Row 1.

28. Perform the sequence of row operations on the matrix. What did the operations accomplish?

$$\begin{bmatrix} 7 & 1 \\ 0 & 2 \\ -3 & 4 \\ 4 & 1 \end{bmatrix}$$

(a) Add Row 3 to Row 4.

(b) Interchange Rows 1 and 4.

(c) Add 3 times Row 1 to Row 3.

(d) Add -7 times Row 1 to Row 4.

(e) Multiply Row 2 by $\frac{1}{2}$.

(f) Add the appropriate multiples of Row 2 to Rows 1, 3, and 4 so that each entry not on the main diagonal is zero.

29. Repeat steps (a) through (e) in Exercise 27 using a graphing utility.

30. Repeat steps (a) through (f) in Exercise 28 using a graphing utility.

In Exercises 31–34, write the matrix in row-echelon form. Remember that the row-echelon form of a matrix is not unique.

31. $\begin{bmatrix} 1 & 1 & 0 & 5 \\ -2 & -1 & 2 & -10 \\ 3 & 6 & 7 & 14 \end{bmatrix}$

32. $\begin{bmatrix} 1 & 2 & -1 & 3 \\ 3 & 7 & -5 & 14 \\ -2 & -1 & -3 & 8 \end{bmatrix}$

33. $\begin{bmatrix} 1 & -1 & -1 & 1 \\ 5 & -4 & 1 & 8 \\ -6 & 8 & 18 & 0 \end{bmatrix}$

34. $\begin{bmatrix} 1 & -3 & 0 & -7 \\ -3 & 10 & 1 & 23 \\ 4 & -10 & 2 & -24 \end{bmatrix}$

In Exercises 35–38, use the matrix capabilities of a graphing utility to write the matrix in reduced row-echelon form.

35. $\begin{bmatrix} 3 & 3 & 3 \\ -1 & 0 & -4 \\ 2 & 4 & -2 \end{bmatrix}$ **36.** $\begin{bmatrix} 1 & 3 & 2 \\ 5 & 15 & 9 \\ 2 & 6 & 10 \end{bmatrix}$

37. $\begin{bmatrix} -3 & 5 & 1 & 12 \\ 1 & -1 & 1 & 4 \end{bmatrix}$

38. $\begin{bmatrix} 5 & 1 & 2 & 4 \\ -1 & 5 & 10 & -32 \end{bmatrix}$

In Exercises 39–42, write the system of linear equations represented by the augmented matrix. Then use back-substitution to find the solution. (Use variables x, y, and z.)

39. $\begin{bmatrix} 1 & -2 & \vdots & 4 \\ 0 & 1 & \vdots & -3 \end{bmatrix}$ **40.** $\begin{bmatrix} 1 & 5 & \vdots & 0 \\ 0 & 1 & \vdots & -1 \end{bmatrix}$

41. $\begin{bmatrix} 1 & -1 & 2 & \vdots & 4 \\ 0 & 1 & -1 & \vdots & 2 \\ 0 & 0 & 1 & \vdots & -2 \end{bmatrix}$

42. $\begin{bmatrix} 1 & 2 & -2 & \vdots & -1 \\ 0 & 1 & 1 & \vdots & 9 \\ 0 & 0 & 1 & \vdots & -3 \end{bmatrix}$

In Exercises 43–46, an augmented matrix that represents a system of linear equations (in variables x, y, and z) has been reduced using Gauss-Jordan elimination. Write the solution represented by the augmented matrix.

43. $\begin{bmatrix} 1 & 0 & \vdots & 7 \\ 0 & 1 & \vdots & -5 \end{bmatrix}$ **44.** $\begin{bmatrix} 1 & 0 & \vdots & -2 \\ 0 & 1 & \vdots & 4 \end{bmatrix}$

45. $\begin{bmatrix} 1 & 0 & 0 & \vdots & -4 \\ 0 & 1 & 0 & \vdots & -8 \\ 0 & 0 & 1 & \vdots & 2 \end{bmatrix}$

46. $\begin{bmatrix} 1 & 0 & 0 & \vdots & 3 \\ 0 & 1 & 0 & \vdots & -1 \\ 0 & 0 & 1 & \vdots & 0 \end{bmatrix}$

In Exercises 47–60, use matrices to solve the system of equations if possible. Use Gaussian elimination with back-substitution or Gauss-Jordan elimination.

47. $\begin{cases} x + 2y = 7 \\ 2x + y = 8 \end{cases}$ **48.** $\begin{cases} 2x + 6y = 14 \\ 2x + 3y = 2 \end{cases}$

49. $\begin{cases} -3x + 5y = -28 \\ 3x + 4y = 10 \\ 4x - 8y = 40 \end{cases}$ **50.** $\begin{cases} x + 2y = 0 \\ x + y = 6 \\ 3x - 2y = 8 \end{cases}$

51. $\begin{cases} 8x - 4y = 13 \\ 5x + 2y = 7 \end{cases}$ **52.** $\begin{cases} x - 3y = 5 \\ -2x + 6y = -10 \end{cases}$

53. $\begin{cases} -x + 2y = 1.5 \\ 2x - 4y = 3 \end{cases}$ **54.** $\begin{cases} 2x - y = -0.1 \\ 3x + 2y = 1.6 \end{cases}$

55. $\begin{cases} x - 3z = -2 \\ 3x + y - 2z = 5 \\ 2x + 2y + z = 4 \end{cases}$ **56.** $\begin{cases} 2x - y + 3z = 26 \\ 2y - z = 12 \\ 7x - 5y = -8 \end{cases}$

57. $\begin{cases} x + y - 5z = 3 \\ x - 2z = 1 \\ 2x - y - z = 0 \end{cases}$ **58.** $\begin{cases} 2x + 3z = 3 \\ 4x - 3y + 7z = 5 \\ 8x - 9y + 15z = 9 \end{cases}$

59. $\begin{cases} x + 2y = 0 \\ -x - y = 0 \end{cases}$ **60.** $\begin{cases} x + 2y = 0 \\ 2x + 4y = 0 \end{cases}$

In Exercises 61–66, use the matrix capabilities of a graphing utility to reduce the augmented matrix and solve the system of equations.

61. $\begin{cases} 3x + 3y + 12z = 6 \\ x + y + 4z = 2 \\ 2x + 5y + 20z = 10 \\ -x + 2y + 8z = 4 \end{cases}$

62. $\begin{cases} 2x + 10y + 2z = 6 \\ x + 5y + 2z = 6 \\ x + 5y + z = 3 \\ -3x - 15y - 3z = -9 \end{cases}$

63. $\begin{cases} 2x + y - z + 2w = -6 \\ 3x + 4y + w = 1 \\ x + 5y + 2z + 6w = -3 \\ 5x + 2y - z - w = 3 \end{cases}$

64. $\begin{cases} x + 2y + 2z + 4w = 11 \\ 3x + 6y + 5z + 12w = 30 \end{cases}$

65. $\begin{cases} x + y + z = 0 \\ 2x + 3y + z = 0 \\ 3x + 5y + z = 0 \end{cases}$ **66.** $\begin{cases} x + 2y + z + 3w = 0 \\ x - y + w = 0 \\ y - z + 2w = 0 \end{cases}$

In Exercises 67–70, determine whether the two systems of linear equations yield the same solutions. If so, find the solutions.

67. (a) $\begin{cases} x - 2y + z = -6 \\ y - 5z = 16 \\ z = -3 \end{cases}$ (b) $\begin{cases} x + y - 2z = 6 \\ y + 3z = -8 \\ z = -3 \end{cases}$

68. (a) $\begin{cases} x - 3y + 4z = -11 \\ y - z = -4 \\ z = 2 \end{cases}$ (b) $\begin{cases} x + 4y = -11 \\ y + 3z = 4 \\ z = 2 \end{cases}$

69. (a) $\begin{cases} x - 4y + 5z = 27 \\ y - 7z = -54 \\ z = 8 \end{cases}$ (b) $\begin{cases} x - 6y + z = 15 \\ y + 5z = 42 \\ z = 8 \end{cases}$

70. (a) $\begin{cases} x + 3y - z = 19 \\ y + 6z = -18 \\ z = -4 \end{cases}$ (b) $\begin{cases} x - y + 3z = -15 \\ y - 2z = 14 \\ z = -4 \end{cases}$

In Exercises 71–76, find the specified equation that passes through the points. Use a graphing utility to verify your result.

71. Parabola:
$y = ax^2 + bx + c$

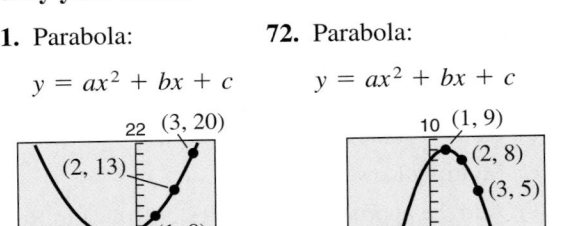

72. Parabola:
$y = ax^2 + bx + c$

73. Cubic:
$y = ax^3 + bx^2 + cx + d$

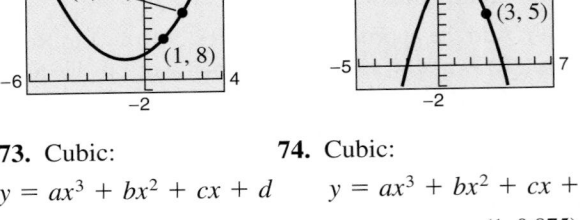

74. Cubic:
$y = ax^3 + bx^2 + cx + d$

75. Quartic:
$y = ax^4 + bx^3 + cx^2 + dx + e$

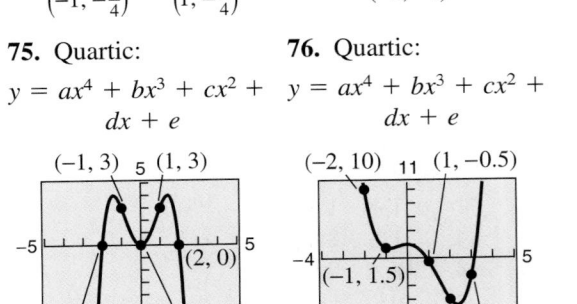

76. Quartic:
$y = ax^4 + bx^3 + cx^2 + dx + e$

77. *Borrowing Money*   A small corporation borrowed $1,500,000 to expand its product line. Some of the money was borrowed at 8%, some at 9%, and some at 12%. How much was borrowed at each rate if the annual interest was $133,000 and the amount borrowed at 8% was 4 times the amount borrowed at 12%?

78. *Borrowing Money*   A small corporation borrowed $500,000 to build a new office building. Some of the money was borrowed at 9%, some at 10%, and some at 12%. How much was borrowed at each rate if the annual interest was $52,000 and the amount borrowed at 10% was $2\frac{1}{2}$ times the amount borrowed at 9%?

79. *Electrical Network*   The currents in an electrical network are given by the solution of the system

$$\begin{cases} I_1 - I_2 + I_3 = 0 \\ 2I_1 + 2I_2 \qquad = 7 \\ \qquad 2I_2 + 4I_3 = 8 \end{cases}$$

where I_1, I_2, and I_3 are measured in amperes. Solve the system of equations.

80. Redo Exercise 79 for the system

$$\begin{cases} 3I_1 - 4I_2 + I_3 = -\frac{9}{8} \\ I_1 + 6I_2 \qquad = 12. \\ \qquad 3I_2 + 2I_3 = 8 \end{cases}$$

81. *Data Analysis*   The bar graph gives the value y (in millions of dollars) for new orders of civil jet transport aircraft built by U.S. companies for the years 1995 through 1997. (Source: Aerospace Industries Association of America)

(a) Find the equation of the parabola that passes through the points. Let $t = 5$ represent 1995.

(b) Use a graphing utility to graph the parabola.

(c) Use the equation in part (a) to estimate y in the year 2000.

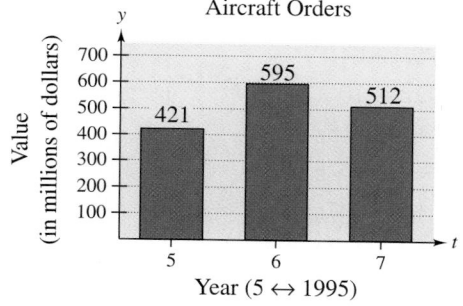

Aircraft Orders
Year (5 ↔ 1995)

82. *Mathematical Modeling*   After the path of a ball thrown by a baseball player is videotaped, it is analyzed on a television set with a grid covering the screen. The tape is paused three times, and the position of the ball is measured each time. The coordinates are approximately (0, 5.0), (15, 9.6), and (30, 12.4). The *x*-coordinate measures the horizontal distance from the player (in feet), and the *y*-coordinate is the height of the ball (in feet).

(a) Find the equation of the parabola $y = ax^2 + bx + c$ that passes through the three points.

(b) Use a graphing utility to graph the parabola. Approximate the maximum height of the ball and the point at which the ball strikes the ground.

(c) Find algebraically the maximum height of the ball and the point at which it strikes the ground.

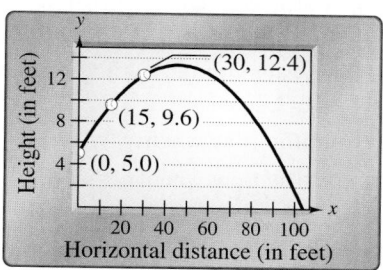

Horizontal distance (in feet)

Network Analysis   **In Exercises 83–85, answer the questions about the specified network.**

83. Water flowing through a network of pipes (in thousands of cubic meters per hour) is shown in the figure.

(a) Solve this system for the water flow represented by x_i, $i = 1, 2, 3, 4, 5, 6$, and 7.

(b) Find the network flow pattern when
$$x_6 = x_7 = 0.$$

(c) Find the network flow pattern when $x_5 = 1000$ and $x_6 = 0$.

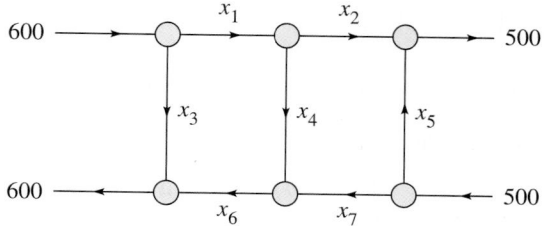

84. The flow of traffic (in vehicles per hour) through a network of streets is shown in the figure.

(a) Solve this system for the traffic flow represented by x_i, $i = 1, 2, 3, 4,$ and 5.

(b) Find the traffic flow when $x_2 = 200$ and $x_3 = 50$.

(c) Find the traffic flow when $x_2 = 150$ and $x_3 = 0$.

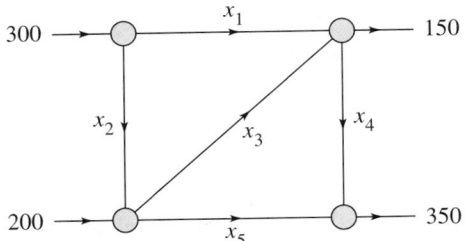

85. The flow of traffic (in vehicles per hour) through a network of streets is shown in the figure.

(a) Solve this system for the traffic flow represented by x_i, $i = 1, 2, 3,$ and 4.

(b) Find the traffic flow when $x_4 = 0$.

(c) Find the traffic flow when $x_4 = 100$.

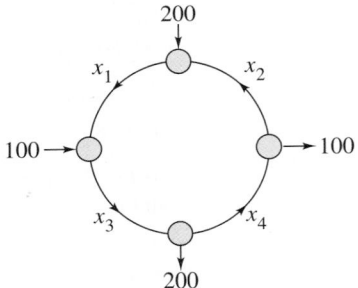

Synthesis

True or False? **In Exercises 86–88, determine whether the statement is true or false. Justify your answer.**

86. $\begin{bmatrix} 6 & 0 & -3 & 10 \\ -2 & 5 & -6 & 2 \end{bmatrix}$ is a 4 × 2 matrix.

87. The matrix $\begin{bmatrix} 0 & 0 & 0 & 0 \\ 0 & 0 & 1 & -4 \\ 0 & 1 & 0 & 2 \\ 1 & 0 & 0 & 5 \end{bmatrix}$ is in reduced row-echelon form.

88. The difference between Gaussian elimination and Gauss-Jordan elimination is that Gaussian elimination reduces a matrix until a reduced row-echelon form is obtained.

89. *Think About It* The augmented matrix represents a system of linear equations (in variables x, y, and z) that has been reduced using Gauss-Jordan elimination. Write a system of equations with *nonzero* coefficients that is represented by the reduced matrix. (There are many correct answers.)

$$\begin{bmatrix} 1 & 0 & 3 & : & -2 \\ 0 & 1 & 4 & : & 1 \\ 0 & 0 & 0 & : & 0 \end{bmatrix}$$

90. Use the system $\begin{cases} x + 3y + z = 3 \\ x + 5y + 5z = 1 \\ 2x + 6y + 3z = 8 \end{cases}$ to write two different row-echelon forms that yield the same solutions.

91. *Think About It*

(a) Describe the row-echelon form of an augmented matrix that corresponds to a system of linear equations that is inconsistent.

(b) Describe the row-echelon form of an augmented matrix that corresponds to a system of linear equations that has an infinite number of solutions.

Review

In Exercises 92–95, sketch the graph of the function. Identify any asymptotes.

92. $f(x) = \dfrac{7}{-x - 1}$

93. $f(x) = \dfrac{4x}{5x^2 + 2}$

94. $f(x) = \dfrac{x^2 - 2x - 3}{x - 4}$

95. $f(x) = \dfrac{x^2 - 36}{x + 1}$

In Exercises 96–99, sketch the graph of the function by hand. Use a graphing utility to verify your sketch.

96. $f(x) = 2^{x-1}$

97. $g(x) = 3^{-x+2}$

98. $h(x) = \ln(x - 1)$

99. $f(x) = 3 + \ln x$

In Exercises 100–103, use any method to solve the system of equations.

100. $\begin{cases} x - 2y = 4 \\ 6x + 2y = 10 \end{cases}$

101. $\begin{cases} 3x - 8y = 47 \\ -5x + 9y = -48 \end{cases}$

102. $\begin{cases} -x + 4y - 5z = 19 \\ 3x - 2y + z = -9 \\ -4x + 3y - 7z = 24 \end{cases}$

103. $\begin{cases} 6x - y + 4z = -11 \\ 5x + 4y - 2z = 0 \\ -8x - y + 5z = 18 \end{cases}$

6.2 Operations with Matrices

Equality of Matrices

In Section 6.1, you used matrices to solve systems of linear equations. Matrices, however, can do much more than this. There is a rich mathematical theory of matrices, and its applications are numerous. This section and the next two introduce some fundamentals of matrix theory. It is standard mathematical convention to represent matrices in any of the following three ways.

Representations of Matrices

1. A matrix can be denoted by an uppercase letter such as A, B, or C.
2. A matrix can be denoted by a representative element enclosed in brackets, such as $[a_{ij}]$, $[b_{ij}]$, or $[c_{ij}]$.
3. A matrix can be denoted by a rectangular array of numbers such as

$$A = [a_{ij}] = \begin{bmatrix} a_{11} & a_{12} & a_{13} & \cdots & a_{1n} \\ a_{21} & a_{22} & a_{23} & \cdots & a_{2n} \\ a_{31} & a_{32} & a_{33} & \cdots & a_{3n} \\ \vdots & \vdots & \vdots & & \vdots \\ a_{m1} & a_{m2} & a_{m3} & \cdots & a_{mn} \end{bmatrix}.$$

Two matrices $A = [a_{ij}]$ and $B = [b_{ij}]$ are **equal** if they have the same order $(m \times n)$ and $a_{ij} = b_{ij}$ for $1 \leq i \leq m$ and $1 \leq j \leq n$. In other words, two matrices are equal if all of their corresponding entries are equal.

Jim Brown/The Stock Market

EXAMPLE 1   Equality of Matrices

Solve for a_{11}, a_{12}, a_{21}, and a_{22} in the following matrix equation.

$$\begin{bmatrix} a_{11} & a_{12} \\ a_{21} & a_{22} \end{bmatrix} = \begin{bmatrix} 2 & -1 \\ -3 & 0 \end{bmatrix}$$

Solution

Because two matrices are equal only if their corresponding entries are equal, you can conclude the following.

$$a_{11} = 2$$
$$a_{12} = -1$$
$$a_{21} = -3$$
$$a_{22} = 0$$

Matrix Addition and Scalar Multiplication

You can add two matrices (of the same order) by adding their corresponding entries.

Definition of Matrix Addition

If $A = [a_{ij}]$ and $B = [b_{ij}]$ are matrices of order $m \times n$, their sum is the $m \times n$ matrix

$$A + B = [a_{ij} + b_{ij}].$$

The sum of two matrices of different orders is undefined.

EXAMPLE 2   Addition of Matrices

a. $\begin{bmatrix} -1 & 2 \\ 0 & 1 \end{bmatrix} + \begin{bmatrix} 1 & 3 \\ -1 & 2 \end{bmatrix} = \begin{bmatrix} -1+1 & 2+3 \\ 0-1 & 1+2 \end{bmatrix} = \begin{bmatrix} 0 & 5 \\ -1 & 3 \end{bmatrix}$

b. $\begin{bmatrix} 0 & 1 & -2 \\ 1 & 2 & 3 \end{bmatrix} + \begin{bmatrix} 0 & 0 & 0 \\ 0 & 0 & 0 \end{bmatrix} = \begin{bmatrix} 0 & 1 & -2 \\ 1 & 2 & 3 \end{bmatrix}$

c. $\begin{bmatrix} 1 \\ -3 \\ -2 \end{bmatrix} + \begin{bmatrix} -1 \\ 3 \\ 2 \end{bmatrix} = \begin{bmatrix} 0 \\ 0 \\ 0 \end{bmatrix}$

d. The sum of

$$A = \begin{bmatrix} 2 & 1 & 0 \\ 4 & 0 & -1 \\ 3 & -2 & 2 \end{bmatrix} \quad \text{and} \quad B = \begin{bmatrix} 0 & 1 \\ -1 & 3 \\ 2 & 4 \end{bmatrix}$$

is undefined because A is of order 3×3 and B is of order 3×2.

Arthur Cayley (1821–1895), a British mathematician, invented matrices around 1858. Cayley was a Cambridge University graduate and a lawyer by profession. His groundbreaking work on matrices was begun as he studied the theory of transformations. Cayley also was instrumental in the development of determinants. Cayley and two American mathematicians, **Benjamin Peirce (1809–1880)** and his son **Charles S. Peirce (1839–1914),** are credited with developing "matrix algebra."

In work with matrices, numbers are usually referred to as **scalars.** In this text, scalars will always be real numbers. You can multiply a matrix A by a scalar c by multiplying each entry in A by c.

Definition of Scalar Multiplication

If $A = [a_{ij}]$ is an $m \times n$ matrix and c is a scalar, the **scalar multiple** of A by c is the $m \times n$ matrix

$$cA = [ca_{ij}].$$

Most graphing utilities can perform matrix addition and scalar multiplication. If you have such a graphing utility, duplicate the matrix operations in Examples 2 and 3. Try adding two matrices of different orders such as

$$A = \begin{bmatrix} 1 & 2 \\ 3 & 4 \end{bmatrix} \quad \text{and} \quad B = \begin{bmatrix} 5 \\ 6 \end{bmatrix}.$$

What error message does your utility display?

The symbol $-A$ represents the scalar product $(-1)A$. Moreover, if A and B are of the same order, $A - B$ represents the sum of A and $(-1)B$. That is,

$$A - B = A + (-1)B.$$ Subtraction of matrices

EXAMPLE 3   Scalar Multiplication and Matrix Subtraction

For the following matrices, find (a) $3A$, (b) $-B$, and (c) $3A - B$.

$$A = \begin{bmatrix} 2 & 2 & 4 \\ -3 & 0 & -1 \\ 2 & 1 & 2 \end{bmatrix} \quad \text{and} \quad B = \begin{bmatrix} 2 & 0 & 0 \\ 1 & -4 & 3 \\ -1 & 3 & 2 \end{bmatrix}$$

Solution

a. $3A = 3\begin{bmatrix} 2 & 2 & 4 \\ -3 & 0 & -1 \\ 2 & 1 & 2 \end{bmatrix}$ Scalar multiplication

$$= \begin{bmatrix} 3(2) & 3(2) & 3(4) \\ 3(-3) & 3(0) & 3(-1) \\ 3(2) & 3(1) & 3(2) \end{bmatrix}$$ Multiply each entry by 3.

$$= \begin{bmatrix} 6 & 6 & 12 \\ -9 & 0 & -3 \\ 6 & 3 & 6 \end{bmatrix}$$ Simplify.

b. $-B = (-1)\begin{bmatrix} 2 & 0 & 0 \\ 1 & -4 & 3 \\ -1 & 3 & 2 \end{bmatrix}$ Definition of negation

$$= \begin{bmatrix} -2 & 0 & 0 \\ -1 & 4 & -3 \\ 1 & -3 & -2 \end{bmatrix}$$ Multiply each entry by -1.

c. $3A - B = \begin{bmatrix} 6 & 6 & 12 \\ -9 & 0 & -3 \\ 6 & 3 & 6 \end{bmatrix} - \begin{bmatrix} 2 & 0 & 0 \\ 1 & -4 & 3 \\ -1 & 3 & 2 \end{bmatrix}$ Matrix subtraction

$$= \begin{bmatrix} 4 & 6 & 12 \\ -10 & 4 & -6 \\ 7 & 0 & 4 \end{bmatrix}$$ Subtract corresponding entries.

It is often convenient to rewrite the scalar multiple cA by factoring c out of every entry in the matrix. For instance, in the following example, the scalar $\frac{1}{2}$ has been factored out of the matrix.

$$\begin{bmatrix} \frac{1}{2} & -\frac{3}{2} \\ \frac{5}{2} & \frac{1}{2} \end{bmatrix} = \begin{bmatrix} \frac{1}{2}(1) & \frac{1}{2}(-3) \\ \frac{1}{2}(5) & \frac{1}{2}(1) \end{bmatrix}$$

$$= \frac{1}{2}\begin{bmatrix} 1 & -3 \\ 5 & 1 \end{bmatrix}$$

The properties of matrix addition and scalar multiplication are similar to those of addition and multiplication of real numbers.

Properties of Matrix Addition and Scalar Multiplication

Let A, B, and C be $m \times n$ matrices and let c and d be scalars.

1. $A + B = B + A$ Commutative Property of Matrix Addition

2. $A + (B + C) = (A + B) + C$ Associative Property of Matrix Addition

3. $(cd)A = c(dA)$ Associative Property of Scalar Multiplication

4. $1A = A$ Scalar Identity

5. $c(A + B) = cA + cB$ Distributive Property

6. $(c + d)A = cA + dA$ Distributive Property

Note that the Associative Property of Matrix Addition allows you to write expressions such as $A + B + C$ without ambiguity because the same sum occurs no matter how the matrices are grouped. In other words, you obtain the same sum whether you group $A + B + C$ as $(A + B) + C$ or as $A + (B + C)$. This same reasoning applies to sums of four or more matrices.

EXAMPLE 4   Addition of More Than Two Matrices

Find the sum.

$$\begin{bmatrix} 1 \\ 2 \\ -3 \end{bmatrix} + \begin{bmatrix} -1 \\ -1 \\ 2 \end{bmatrix} + \begin{bmatrix} 0 \\ 1 \\ 4 \end{bmatrix} + \begin{bmatrix} 2 \\ -3 \\ -2 \end{bmatrix}$$

Solution

By adding corresponding entries, you obtain the following sum of four matrices.

$$\begin{bmatrix} 1 \\ 2 \\ -3 \end{bmatrix} + \begin{bmatrix} -1 \\ -1 \\ 2 \end{bmatrix} + \begin{bmatrix} 0 \\ 1 \\ 4 \end{bmatrix} + \begin{bmatrix} 2 \\ -3 \\ -2 \end{bmatrix} = \begin{bmatrix} 2 \\ -1 \\ 1 \end{bmatrix}$$

EXAMPLE 5   Using the Distributive Property

Evaluate the expression $3\left(\begin{bmatrix} -2 & 0 \\ 4 & 1 \end{bmatrix} + \begin{bmatrix} 4 & -2 \\ 3 & 7 \end{bmatrix} \right)$.

Solution

$$3\left(\begin{bmatrix} -2 & 0 \\ 4 & 1 \end{bmatrix} + \begin{bmatrix} 4 & -2 \\ 3 & 7 \end{bmatrix} \right) = 3\begin{bmatrix} -2 & 0 \\ 4 & 1 \end{bmatrix} + 3\begin{bmatrix} 4 & -2 \\ 3 & 7 \end{bmatrix}$$

$$= \begin{bmatrix} -6 & 0 \\ 12 & 3 \end{bmatrix} + \begin{bmatrix} 12 & -6 \\ 9 & 21 \end{bmatrix}$$

$$= \begin{bmatrix} 6 & -6 \\ 21 & 24 \end{bmatrix}$$

STUDY T!P

In Example 5, you could have added the two matrices first and then multiplied the matrix by 3. The result would have been the same.

One important property of addition of real numbers is that the number 0 is the additive identity. That is, $c + 0 = c$ for any real number c. For matrices, a similar property holds. That is, if A is an $m \times n$ matrix and O is the $m \times n$ **zero matrix** consisting entirely of zeros, then $A + O = A$.

In other words, O is the **additive identity** for the set of all $m \times n$ matrices. For example, the following matrices are the additive identities for the set of all 2×3 and 2×2 matrices.

$$O = \begin{bmatrix} 0 & 0 & 0 \\ 0 & 0 & 0 \end{bmatrix} \quad \text{and} \quad O = \begin{bmatrix} 0 & 0 \\ 0 & 0 \end{bmatrix}$$

$$\underbrace{\phantom{O = \begin{bmatrix} 0 & 0 & 0 \\ 0 & 0 & 0 \end{bmatrix}}}_{\text{Zero } 2 \times 3 \text{ matrix}} \qquad \underbrace{\phantom{O = \begin{bmatrix} 0 & 0 \\ 0 & 0 \end{bmatrix}}}_{\text{Zero } 2 \times 2 \text{ matrix}}$$

The algebra of real numbers and the algebra of matrices have many similarities. For example, compare the following solutions.

Real Numbers	$m \times n$ Matrices
(Solve for x.)	*(Solve for X.)*
$x + a = b$	$X + A = B$
$x + a + (-a) = b + (-a)$	$X + A + (-A) = B + (-A)$
$x + 0 = b - a$	$X + O = B - A$
$x = b - a$	$X = B - A$

The algebra of real numbers and the algebra of matrices also have important differences, which will be discussed later.

EXAMPLE 6   Solving a Matrix Equation

Solve for X in the equation $3X + A = B$, where

$$A = \begin{bmatrix} 1 & -2 \\ 0 & 3 \end{bmatrix} \quad \text{and} \quad B = \begin{bmatrix} -3 & 4 \\ 2 & 1 \end{bmatrix}.$$

Solution

Begin by solving the equation for X to obtain

$$3X = B - A$$
$$X = \tfrac{1}{3}(B - A).$$

Now, using the matrices A and B, you have

$$X = \tfrac{1}{3}\left(\begin{bmatrix} -3 & 4 \\ 2 & 1 \end{bmatrix} - \begin{bmatrix} 1 & -2 \\ 0 & 3 \end{bmatrix} \right)$$

$$= \tfrac{1}{3}\begin{bmatrix} -4 & 6 \\ 2 & -2 \end{bmatrix}$$

$$= \begin{bmatrix} -\tfrac{4}{3} & 2 \\ \tfrac{2}{3} & -\tfrac{2}{3} \end{bmatrix}.$$

Exploration

Use a graphing utility to find the sum of A and B below. Use your result to predict the sum of C and D below. Then check your prediction using a graphing utility.

$$A = \begin{bmatrix} -2 & 1 \\ 0 & 3 \end{bmatrix} \quad B = \begin{bmatrix} 0 & 0 \\ 0 & 0 \end{bmatrix}$$

$$C = \begin{bmatrix} 1 & -1 \\ 2 & -1 \\ 0 & 2 \end{bmatrix} \quad D = \begin{bmatrix} 0 & 0 \\ 0 & 0 \\ 0 & 0 \end{bmatrix}$$

Matrix Multiplication

The third basic matrix operation is **matrix multiplication.** At first glance, the following definition may seem unusual. You will see later, however, that this definition of the product of two matrices has many practical applications.

> ### Definition of Matrix Multiplication
>
> If $A = [a_{ij}]$ is an $m \times n$ matrix and $B = [b_{ij}]$ is an $n \times p$ matrix, the product AB is an $m \times p$ matrix
>
> $$AB = [c_{ij}]$$
>
> where $c_{ij} = a_{i1}b_{1j} + a_{i2}b_{2j} + a_{i3}b_{3j} + \cdots + a_{in}b_{nj}.$

The definition of matrix multiplication indicates a *row-by-column* multiplication, where the entry in the *i*th row and *j*th column of the product AB is obtained by multiplying the entries in the *i*th row of A by the corresponding entries in the *j*th column of B and then adding the results. Example 7 illustrates this process.

EXAMPLE 7   Finding the Product of Two Matrices

Find the product AB where

$$A = \begin{bmatrix} -1 & 3 \\ 4 & -2 \\ 5 & 0 \end{bmatrix} \quad \text{and} \quad B = \begin{bmatrix} -3 & 2 \\ -4 & 1 \end{bmatrix}.$$

Solution

First, note that the product AB is defined because the number of columns of A is equal to the number of rows of B. Moreover, the product AB has order 3×2, and is of the form

$$\begin{bmatrix} -1 & 3 \\ 4 & -2 \\ 5 & 0 \end{bmatrix} \begin{bmatrix} -3 & 2 \\ -4 & 1 \end{bmatrix} = \begin{bmatrix} c_{11} & c_{12} \\ c_{21} & c_{22} \\ c_{31} & c_{32} \end{bmatrix}.$$

To find the entries of the product, multiply each row of A by each column of B, as follows. Use a graphing utility to check this result.

$$AB = \begin{bmatrix} -1 & 3 \\ 4 & -2 \\ 5 & 0 \end{bmatrix} \begin{bmatrix} -3 & 2 \\ -4 & 1 \end{bmatrix}$$

$$= \begin{bmatrix} (-1)(-3) + (3)(-4) & (-1)(2) + (3)(1) \\ (4)(-3) + (-2)(-4) & (4)(2) + (-2)(1) \\ (5)(-3) + (0)(-4) & (5)(2) + (0)(1) \end{bmatrix}$$

$$= \begin{bmatrix} -9 & 1 \\ -4 & 6 \\ -15 & 10 \end{bmatrix}$$

A computer animation of this example appears in the *Interactive* CD-ROM and *Internet* versions of this text.

Be sure you understand that for the product of two matrices to be defined, the number of *columns* of the first matrix must equal the number of *rows* of the second matrix. That is, the middle two indices must be the same and the outside two indices give the order of the product, as shown in the following diagram.

$$A \quad \times \quad B \quad = \quad AB$$

$$m \times n \qquad n \times p \qquad\qquad m \times p$$

equal
order of *AB*

This pattern for the order of the product of matrix multiplication is an effective memory device. You may want to demonstrate this pattern on several multiplication examples.

EXAMPLE 8 Matrix Multiplication

a. $\begin{bmatrix} 1 & 0 & 3 \\ 2 & -1 & -2 \end{bmatrix} \begin{bmatrix} -2 & 4 & 2 \\ 1 & 0 & 0 \\ -1 & 1 & -1 \end{bmatrix} = \begin{bmatrix} -5 & 7 & -1 \\ -3 & 6 & 6 \end{bmatrix}$

      2×3 3×3 2×3

b. $\begin{bmatrix} 3 & 4 \\ -2 & 5 \end{bmatrix} \begin{bmatrix} 1 & 0 \\ 0 & 1 \end{bmatrix} = \begin{bmatrix} 3 & 4 \\ -2 & 5 \end{bmatrix}$

    2×2 2×2 2×2

c. $\begin{bmatrix} 1 & 2 \\ 1 & 1 \end{bmatrix} \begin{bmatrix} -1 & 2 \\ 1 & -1 \end{bmatrix} = \begin{bmatrix} 1 & 0 \\ 0 & 1 \end{bmatrix}$

    2×2 2×2 2×2

d. $\begin{bmatrix} 1 & -2 & -3 \end{bmatrix} \begin{bmatrix} 2 \\ -1 \\ 1 \end{bmatrix} = \begin{bmatrix} 1 \end{bmatrix}$

    1×3 3×1 1×1

e. $\begin{bmatrix} 2 \\ -1 \\ 1 \end{bmatrix} \begin{bmatrix} 1 & -2 & -3 \end{bmatrix} = \begin{bmatrix} 2 & -4 & -6 \\ -1 & 2 & 3 \\ 1 & -2 & -3 \end{bmatrix}$

 3×1 1×3 3×3

f. The product *AB* for the following matrices is not defined.

$$A = \begin{bmatrix} -2 & 1 \\ 1 & -3 \\ 1 & 4 \end{bmatrix} \quad \text{and} \quad B = \begin{bmatrix} -2 & 3 & 1 & 4 \\ 0 & 1 & -1 & 2 \\ 2 & -1 & 0 & 1 \end{bmatrix}$$

          3×2 3×4

In parts (d) and (e) of Example 8, note that the two products are different. Matrix multiplication is not, in general, commutative. That is, for most matrices, $AB \neq BA$. This is one way in which the algebra of real numbers and the algebra of matrices differ.

Exploration

Use a graphing utility to multiply the matrices

$$A = \begin{bmatrix} 1 & 2 \\ 3 & 4 \end{bmatrix} \quad \text{and}$$

$$B = \begin{bmatrix} 0 & 1 \\ 2 & 3 \end{bmatrix}.$$

Do you obtain the same result for the product *AB* as for the product *BA*? What does this tell you about matrix multiplication and commutativity?

In summary, the general pattern for matrix multiplication is as follows. To obtain the entry in the ith row and the jth column of the product AB, use the ith row of A and the jth column of B.

$$\begin{bmatrix} a_{11} & a_{12} & a_{13} & \cdots & a_{1n} \\ a_{21} & a_{22} & a_{23} & \cdots & a_{2n} \\ a_{31} & a_{32} & a_{33} & \cdots & a_{3n} \\ \vdots & \vdots & \vdots & & \vdots \\ a_{i1} & a_{i2} & a_{i3} & \cdots & a_{in} \\ \vdots & \vdots & \vdots & & \vdots \\ a_{m1} & a_{m2} & a_{m3} & \cdots & a_{mn} \end{bmatrix} \begin{bmatrix} b_{11} & b_{12} & \cdots & b_{1j} & \cdots & b_{1p} \\ b_{21} & b_{22} & \cdots & b_{2j} & \cdots & b_{2p} \\ b_{31} & b_{32} & \cdots & b_{3j} & \cdots & b_{3p} \\ \vdots & \vdots & & \vdots & & \vdots \\ b_{n1} & b_{n2} & \cdots & b_{nj} & \cdots & b_{np} \end{bmatrix} = \begin{bmatrix} c_{11} & c_{12} & \cdots & c_{1j} & \cdots & c_{1p} \\ c_{21} & c_{22} & \cdots & c_{2j} & \cdots & c_{2p} \\ \vdots & \vdots & & \vdots & & \vdots \\ c_{i1} & c_{i2} & \cdots & c_{ij} & \cdots & c_{ip} \\ \vdots & \vdots & & \vdots & & \vdots \\ c_{m1} & c_{m2} & \cdots & c_{mj} & \cdots & c_{mp} \end{bmatrix}$$

$$a_{i1}b_{1j} + a_{i2}b_{2j} + a_{i3}b_{3j} + \cdots + a_{in}b_{nj} = c_{ij}$$

Properties of Matrix Multiplication

Let A, B, and C be matrices and let c be a scalar.

1. $A(BC) = (AB)C$ Associative Property of Matrix Multiplication

2. $A(B + C) = AB + AC$ Distributive Property

3. $(A + B)C = AC + BC$ Distributive Property

4. $c(AB) = (cA)B = A(cB)$ Associative Property of Scalar Multiplication

Definition of Identity Multiplication

The $n \times n$ matrix that consists of 1's on its main diagonal and 0's elsewhere is called the **identity matrix of order n** and is denoted by

$$I_n = \begin{bmatrix} 1 & 0 & 0 & \cdots & 0 \\ 0 & 1 & 0 & \cdots & 0 \\ 0 & 0 & 1 & \cdots & 0 \\ \vdots & \vdots & \vdots & & \vdots \\ 0 & 0 & 0 & \cdots & 1 \end{bmatrix}. \quad \text{Identity matrix}$$

Note that an identity matrix must be *square*. When the order is understood to be n, you can denote I_n simply by I.

If A is an $n \times n$ matrix, the identity matrix has the property that $AI_n = A$ and $I_n A = A$. For example,

$$\begin{bmatrix} 3 & -2 & 5 \\ 1 & 0 & 4 \\ -1 & 2 & -3 \end{bmatrix} \begin{bmatrix} 1 & 0 & 0 \\ 0 & 1 & 0 \\ 0 & 0 & 1 \end{bmatrix} = \begin{bmatrix} 3 & -2 & 5 \\ 1 & 0 & 4 \\ -1 & 2 & -3 \end{bmatrix} \quad AI = A$$

and

$$\begin{bmatrix} 1 & 0 & 0 \\ 0 & 1 & 0 \\ 0 & 0 & 1 \end{bmatrix} \begin{bmatrix} 3 & -2 & 5 \\ 1 & 0 & 4 \\ -1 & 2 & -3 \end{bmatrix} = \begin{bmatrix} 3 & -2 & 5 \\ 1 & 0 & 4 \\ -1 & 2 & -3 \end{bmatrix}. \quad IA = A$$

Applications

Matrix multiplication can be used to represent a system of linear equations. Note how the system

$$\begin{cases} a_{11}x_1 + a_{12}x_2 + a_{13}x_3 = b_1 \\ a_{21}x_1 + a_{22}x_2 + a_{23}x_3 = b_2 \\ a_{31}x_1 + a_{32}x_2 + a_{33}x_3 = b_3 \end{cases}$$

can be written as the matrix equation $AX = B$, where A is the *coefficient matrix* of the system, and X and B are column matrices. The column matrix B is also called a *constant* matrix. Its entries are the constant terms in the system of equations.

$$\underbrace{\begin{bmatrix} a_{11} & a_{12} & a_{13} \\ a_{21} & a_{22} & a_{23} \\ a_{31} & a_{32} & a_{33} \end{bmatrix}}_{A} \times \underbrace{\begin{bmatrix} x_1 \\ x_2 \\ x_3 \end{bmatrix}}_{X} = \underbrace{\begin{bmatrix} b_1 \\ b_2 \\ b_3 \end{bmatrix}}_{B}$$

EXAMPLE 9   Solving a System of Linear Equations

Consider the system of linear equations $\begin{cases} x_1 - 2x_2 + x_3 = -4 \\ x_2 + 2x_3 = 4. \\ 2x_1 + 3x_2 - 2x_3 = 2 \end{cases}$

a. Write this system as a matrix equation, $AX = B$.

b. Use Gauss-Jordan elimination on the augmented matrix $[A \vdots B]$ to solve for the matrix X.

A computer animation of this example appears in the *Interactive* CD-ROM and *Internet* versions of this text.

Solution

a. In matrix form $AX = B$, the system can be written as follows.

$$\begin{bmatrix} 1 & -2 & 1 \\ 0 & 1 & 2 \\ 2 & 3 & -2 \end{bmatrix} \begin{bmatrix} x_1 \\ x_2 \\ x_3 \end{bmatrix} = \begin{bmatrix} -4 \\ 4 \\ 2 \end{bmatrix}$$

b. The augmented matrix is

$$[A \vdots B] = \begin{bmatrix} 1 & -2 & 1 & \vdots & -4 \\ 0 & 1 & 2 & \vdots & 4 \\ 2 & 3 & -2 & \vdots & 2 \end{bmatrix}.$$

Using Gauss-Jordan elimination, you can rewrite this equation as

$$[I \vdots X] = \begin{bmatrix} 1 & 0 & 0 & \vdots & -1 \\ 0 & 1 & 0 & \vdots & 2 \\ 0 & 0 & 1 & \vdots & 1 \end{bmatrix}.$$

So, the solution of the system of linear equations is $x_1 = -1$, $x_2 = 2$, and $x_3 = 1$. The solution of the matrix equation is

$$X = \begin{bmatrix} x_1 \\ x_2 \\ x_3 \end{bmatrix} = \begin{bmatrix} -1 \\ 2 \\ 1 \end{bmatrix}.$$

STUDY T!P

You can use some graphing utilities to obtain the reduced row-echelon form of a matrix. Consult your user's manual to determine how to perform this matrix operation. The screen in the figure below shows how one graphing utility displays the reduced row-echelon form of the augmented matrix in Example 9.

```
rref([C])
    [[1 0 0 -1]
     [0 1 0  2]
     [0 0 1  1]]
```

You may also wish to discuss some of the applications problems in the exercise set. See, for example, Exercises 79–86.

EXAMPLE 10   Softball Team Expenses

Two softball teams submit equipment lists to their sponsors.

	Women's Team	Men's Team
Bats	12	15
Balls	45	38
Gloves	15	17

Each bat costs $48, each ball costs $4, and each glove costs $42. Use matrices to find the total cost of equipment for each team.

Solution

The equipment lists and the costs per item can be written in matrix form as

$$E = \begin{bmatrix} 12 & 15 \\ 45 & 38 \\ 15 & 17 \end{bmatrix} \quad \text{and} \quad C = \begin{bmatrix} 48 & 4 & 42 \end{bmatrix}.$$

To find the total cost of the equipment for each team, you need to find the product. Note that you cannot find the total cost using the product EC because EC is not defined. That is, the number of columns of E (2 columns) does not match the number of rows of C (one row). You can find the total cost using the product CE because the number of columns of C (3 columns) matches the number of rows of E (3 rows). Therefore, the total cost of equipment for each team is given by the product

$$CE = \begin{bmatrix} 48 & 4 & 42 \end{bmatrix} \begin{bmatrix} 12 & 15 \\ 45 & 38 \\ 15 & 17 \end{bmatrix}$$

$$= \begin{bmatrix} 1386 & 1586 \end{bmatrix}.$$

So, the total cost of equipment for the women's team is $1386, and the total cost of equipment for the men's team is $1586.

Writing About Math   *Number of Cable Subscribers*

Two competing companies offer cable television to a city with 100,000 households. Company A has 25,000 subscribers, and Company B has 30,000. (The other 45,000 households do not subscribe.) The percent changes in cable subscriptions each year are shown below. Write a short paragraph explaining how matrix multiplication can be used to find the number of subscribers each company will have in one year.

Percent Changes	From Company A	From Company B	From Nonsubscribers
To Company A	0.70	0.15	0.15
To Company B	0.20	0.80	0.15
To Nonsubscriber	0.10	0.05	0.70

Alternate Writing About Math
Determine which of the following matrix multiplications AB is (are) defined. For each case in which AB is defined, what is the order of the resulting matrix?

a. A is of order 1×3
   B is of order 2×1

b. A is of order 2×3
   B is of order 2×3

c. A is of order 3×4
   B is of order 4×2

d. A is of order 3×1
   B is of order 3×3

Write a short paragraph discussing why matrix multiplication is not, in general, commutative. Find an example of two 2×2 matrices such that $AB \neq BA$. Find an example of two 2×2 matrices such that $AB = BA$.

Exercise 62 yields infinitely many solutions. Exercises where it is not possible to perform the given operation: 11a, 11b, 11d, 12a, 12b, 12d, 32c, 33, 40, 44, 45, 69, 70, 71, 74, 75.

6.2 • Operations with Matrices   **455**

6.2   E x e r c i s e s

In Exercises 1–4, find x, y, and z.

1. $\begin{bmatrix} x & -2 \\ 7 & y \end{bmatrix} = \begin{bmatrix} -4 & -2 \\ 7 & 22 \end{bmatrix}$

2. $\begin{bmatrix} -5 & x \\ y & 8 \end{bmatrix} = \begin{bmatrix} -5 & 13 \\ 12 & 8 \end{bmatrix}$

3. $\begin{bmatrix} 16 & 4 & 5 & 4 \\ -3 & 13 & 15 & 12 \\ 0 & 2 & 4 & 0 \end{bmatrix} = \begin{bmatrix} 16 & 4 & 2x+7 & 4 \\ -3 & 13 & & 15 & 3y \\ 0 & 2 & 3z-14 & 0 \end{bmatrix}$

4. $\begin{bmatrix} x+4 & 8 & -3 \\ 1 & 22 & 2y \\ 7 & -2 & z+2 \end{bmatrix} = \begin{bmatrix} 2x+9 & 8 & -3 \\ 1 & 22 & -8 \\ 7 & -2 & 11 \end{bmatrix}$

In Exercises 5–12, if possible, find (a) $A + B$, (b) $A - B$, (c) $3A$, and (d) $3A - 2B$. Use the matrix capabilities of a graphing utility to verify your results.

5. $A = \begin{bmatrix} 1 & -1 \\ 2 & -1 \end{bmatrix}$, $B = \begin{bmatrix} 2 & -1 \\ -1 & 8 \end{bmatrix}$

6. $A = \begin{bmatrix} 1 & 2 \\ 2 & 1 \end{bmatrix}$, $B = \begin{bmatrix} -3 & -2 \\ 4 & 2 \end{bmatrix}$

7. $A = \begin{bmatrix} 8 & -1 \\ 2 & 3 \\ -4 & 5 \end{bmatrix}$, $B = \begin{bmatrix} 1 & 6 \\ -1 & -5 \\ 1 & 10 \end{bmatrix}$

8. $A = \begin{bmatrix} 2 & 1 & 1 \\ -1 & -1 & 5 \end{bmatrix}$, $B = \begin{bmatrix} 6 & -3 & 2 \\ -4 & 1 & -2 \end{bmatrix}$

9. $A = \begin{bmatrix} 2 & 2 & -1 & 0 & 1 \\ 1 & 1 & -2 & 0 & -1 \end{bmatrix}$,

$B = \begin{bmatrix} 1 & 1 & -1 & 1 & 0 \\ -3 & 4 & 9 & -6 & -7 \end{bmatrix}$

10. $A = \begin{bmatrix} -1 & 4 & 0 \\ 3 & -2 & 2 \\ 5 & 4 & -1 \\ 0 & 8 & -6 \\ -4 & -1 & 0 \end{bmatrix}$, $B = \begin{bmatrix} -3 & 5 & 1 \\ 2 & -4 & -7 \\ 10 & -9 & -1 \\ 3 & 2 & -4 \\ 0 & 1 & -2 \end{bmatrix}$

11. $A = \begin{bmatrix} 6 & 0 & 3 \\ -1 & -4 & 0 \end{bmatrix}$, $B = \begin{bmatrix} 8 & -1 \\ 4 & -3 \end{bmatrix}$

12. $A = \begin{bmatrix} 3 \\ 2 \\ -1 \end{bmatrix}$, $B = \begin{bmatrix} -4 & 6 & 2 \end{bmatrix}$

In Exercises 13–18, evaluate the expression.

13. $\begin{bmatrix} -4 & 0 \\ 5 & -6 \end{bmatrix} + \begin{bmatrix} 9 & 1 \\ -2 & -2 \end{bmatrix} + \begin{bmatrix} -12 & -10 \\ 14 & 6 \end{bmatrix}$

14. $\begin{bmatrix} 6 & 9 \\ -1 & 0 \\ 7 & 1 \\ 0 & -10 \end{bmatrix} + \begin{bmatrix} 0 & 5 \\ -2 & -1 \\ 3 & -6 \\ -4 & 2 \end{bmatrix} + \begin{bmatrix} -13 & -7 \\ 4 & -1 \\ -6 & 0 \\ -1 & 25 \end{bmatrix}$

15. $4\left(\begin{bmatrix} -4 & 0 & 1 \\ 0 & 2 & 3 \end{bmatrix} - \begin{bmatrix} 2 & 1 & -2 \\ 3 & -6 & 0 \end{bmatrix} \right)$

16. $\frac{1}{2}([5 \quad -2 \quad 4 \quad 0] + [14 \quad 6 \quad -18 \quad 9])$

17. $-3\left(\begin{bmatrix} 0 & -3 \\ 7 & 2 \end{bmatrix} + \begin{bmatrix} -6 & 3 \\ 8 & 1 \end{bmatrix} \right) - \begin{bmatrix} 4 & -4 \\ 7 & -9 \end{bmatrix}$

18. $-1 \begin{bmatrix} 4 & 11 \\ -2 & -1 \\ 9 & 3 \end{bmatrix} + \frac{1}{6}\left(\begin{bmatrix} -5 & -1 \\ 3 & 4 \\ 0 & 13 \end{bmatrix} + \begin{bmatrix} 7 & 5 \\ -9 & -1 \\ 6 & -1 \end{bmatrix} \right)$

In Exercises 19–22, use the matrix capabilities of a graphing utility to evaluate the expression. Round your results to three decimal places, if necessary.

19. $\frac{3}{7}\begin{bmatrix} 2 & 5 \\ -1 & -4 \end{bmatrix}$

20. $55\left(\begin{bmatrix} 14 & -11 \\ -22 & 19 \end{bmatrix} + \begin{bmatrix} -22 & 20 \\ 13 & 6 \end{bmatrix} \right)$

21. $-\begin{bmatrix} 3.211 & 6.829 \\ -1.004 & 4.914 \\ 0.055 & -3.889 \end{bmatrix} - \begin{bmatrix} -1.630 & -3.090 \\ 5.256 & 8.335 \\ -9.768 & 4.251 \end{bmatrix}$

22. $-12\left(\begin{bmatrix} 6 & 20 \\ 1 & -9 \\ -2 & 5 \end{bmatrix} + \begin{bmatrix} 14 & -15 \\ -8 & -6 \\ 7 & 0 \end{bmatrix} + \begin{bmatrix} -31 & -19 \\ 16 & 10 \\ 24 & 10 \end{bmatrix} \right)$

In Exercises 23–26, solve for X given

$$A = \begin{bmatrix} -2 & -1 \\ 1 & 0 \\ 3 & -4 \end{bmatrix} \quad \text{and} \quad B = \begin{bmatrix} 0 & 3 \\ 2 & 0 \\ -4 & -1 \end{bmatrix}.$$

23. $X = 3A - 2B$
24. $2X = 2A - B$
25. $2X + 3A = B$
26. $2A + 4B = -2X$

In Exercises 27–32, if possible, find (a) AB, (b) BA, and (c) A^2. (*Note:* $A^2 = AA$.) Use the matrix capabilities of a graphing utility to verify your results.

27. $A = \begin{bmatrix} 1 & 2 \\ 5 & 2 \end{bmatrix}$, $B = \begin{bmatrix} 2 & -1 \\ -1 & 8 \end{bmatrix}$

28. $A = \begin{bmatrix} 2 & -1 \\ 1 & -4 \end{bmatrix}$, $B = \begin{bmatrix} -2 & 0 \\ 3 & -3 \end{bmatrix}$

29. $A = \begin{bmatrix} 3 & -1 \\ 1 & 3 \end{bmatrix}$, $B = \begin{bmatrix} 1 & -3 \\ 3 & 1 \end{bmatrix}$

30. $A = \begin{bmatrix} 1 & -1 \\ 1 & 1 \end{bmatrix}$, $B = \begin{bmatrix} 1 & 3 \\ -3 & 1 \end{bmatrix}$

31. $A = \begin{bmatrix} 1 & -1 & 7 \\ 2 & -1 & 8 \\ 3 & 1 & -1 \end{bmatrix}$, $B = \begin{bmatrix} 1 & 1 & 2 \\ 2 & 1 & 1 \\ 1 & -3 & 2 \end{bmatrix}$

32. $A = \begin{bmatrix} 3 & 2 & 1 \end{bmatrix}$, $B = \begin{bmatrix} 2 \\ 3 \\ 0 \end{bmatrix}$

In Exercises 33–40, find AB, if possible.

33. $A = \begin{bmatrix} 2 & 1 \\ -5 & 4 \\ -1 & -6 \end{bmatrix}$, $B = \begin{bmatrix} 0 & -3 & 3 \\ 4 & 0 & 2 \\ 8 & -2 & 7 \end{bmatrix}$

34. $A = \begin{bmatrix} 0 & -1 & 2 \\ 6 & 0 & 3 \\ 7 & -1 & 8 \end{bmatrix}$, $B = \begin{bmatrix} 2 & -1 \\ 4 & -5 \\ 1 & 6 \end{bmatrix}$

35. $A = \begin{bmatrix} -1 & 6 \\ -4 & 5 \\ 0 & 3 \end{bmatrix}$, $B = \begin{bmatrix} 2 & 3 \\ 0 & 9 \end{bmatrix}$

36. $A = \begin{bmatrix} 1 & 0 & 0 \\ 0 & 4 & 0 \\ 0 & 0 & -2 \end{bmatrix}$, $B = \begin{bmatrix} 3 & 0 & 0 \\ 0 & -1 & 0 \\ 0 & 0 & 5 \end{bmatrix}$

37. $A = \begin{bmatrix} 5 & 0 & 0 \\ 0 & -8 & 0 \\ 0 & 0 & 7 \end{bmatrix}$, $B = \begin{bmatrix} \frac{1}{5} & 0 & 0 \\ 0 & -\frac{1}{8} & 0 \\ 0 & 0 & \frac{1}{2} \end{bmatrix}$

38. $A = \begin{bmatrix} 0 & 0 & 5 \\ 0 & 0 & -3 \\ 0 & 0 & 4 \end{bmatrix}$, $B = \begin{bmatrix} 6 & -11 & 4 \\ 8 & 16 & 4 \\ 0 & 0 & 0 \end{bmatrix}$

39. $A = \begin{bmatrix} 10 \\ 11 \end{bmatrix}$, $B = \begin{bmatrix} 4 & -2 & -1 & 8 \end{bmatrix}$

40. $A = \begin{bmatrix} 1 & 0 & 3 & -2 \\ 6 & 13 & 8 & -17 \end{bmatrix}$, $B = \begin{bmatrix} 1 & 6 \\ 4 & 2 \end{bmatrix}$

In Exercises 41–46, use the matrix capabilities of a graphing utility to find AB.

41. $A = \begin{bmatrix} 7 & 5 & -4 \\ -2 & 5 & 1 \\ 10 & -4 & -7 \end{bmatrix}$, $B = \begin{bmatrix} 2 & -2 & 3 \\ 8 & 1 & 4 \\ -4 & 2 & -8 \end{bmatrix}$

42. $A = \begin{bmatrix} 11 & -12 & 4 \\ 14 & 10 & 12 \\ 6 & -2 & 9 \end{bmatrix}$, $B = \begin{bmatrix} 12 & 10 \\ -5 & 12 \\ 15 & 16 \end{bmatrix}$

43. $A = \begin{bmatrix} -3 & 8 & -6 & 8 \\ -12 & 15 & 9 & 6 \\ 5 & -1 & 1 & 5 \end{bmatrix}$,

$B = \begin{bmatrix} 3 & 1 & 6 \\ 24 & 15 & 14 \\ 16 & 10 & 21 \\ 8 & -4 & 10 \end{bmatrix}$

44. $A = \begin{bmatrix} -2 & 6 & 12 \\ 21 & -5 & 6 \\ 13 & -2 & 9 \end{bmatrix}$,

$B = \begin{bmatrix} 3 & 0 \\ -7 & 18 \\ 34 & 14 \\ 0.5 & 1.4 \end{bmatrix}$

45. $A = \begin{bmatrix} 9 & 10 & -38 & 18 \\ 100 & -50 & 250 & 75 \end{bmatrix}$,

$B = \begin{bmatrix} 52 & -85 & 27 & 45 \\ 40 & -35 & 60 & 82 \end{bmatrix}$

46. $A = \begin{bmatrix} 16 & -18 \\ -4 & 13 \\ -9 & 21 \end{bmatrix}$,

$B = \begin{bmatrix} -7 & 20 & -1 \\ 7 & 15 & 26 \end{bmatrix}$

In Exercises 47–50, use the matrix capabilities of a graphing utility to evaluate the expression.

47. $\begin{bmatrix} 3 & 1 \\ 0 & -2 \end{bmatrix} \begin{bmatrix} 1 & 0 \\ -2 & 2 \end{bmatrix} \begin{bmatrix} 1 & 0 \\ 2 & 4 \end{bmatrix}$

48. $-3\left(\begin{bmatrix} 6 & 5 & -1 \\ 1 & -2 & 0 \end{bmatrix} \begin{bmatrix} 0 & 3 \\ -1 & -3 \\ 4 & 1 \end{bmatrix} \right)$

49. $\begin{bmatrix} 0 & 2 & -2 \\ 4 & 1 & 2 \end{bmatrix} \left(\begin{bmatrix} 4 & 0 \\ 0 & -1 \\ -1 & 2 \end{bmatrix} + \begin{bmatrix} -2 & 3 \\ -3 & 5 \\ 0 & -3 \end{bmatrix} \right)$

50. $\begin{bmatrix} 3 \\ -1 \\ 5 \\ 7 \end{bmatrix} \left(\begin{bmatrix} 5 & -6 \end{bmatrix} + \begin{bmatrix} 7 & -1 \end{bmatrix} + \begin{bmatrix} -8 & 9 \end{bmatrix} \right)$

In Exercises 51–56, use matrix multiplication to determine which of the given matrices is a solution of the system of equations. Use a graphing utility to verify your result.

51. $\begin{cases} x + 2y = 4 \\ 3x + 2y = 0 \end{cases}$

(a) $\begin{bmatrix} 2 \\ 1 \end{bmatrix}$ (b) $\begin{bmatrix} -2 \\ 3 \end{bmatrix}$

(c) $\begin{bmatrix} -4 \\ 4 \end{bmatrix}$ (d) $\begin{bmatrix} 2 \\ -3 \end{bmatrix}$

52. $\begin{cases} 6x + 2y = 0 \\ -x + 5y = 16 \end{cases}$

(a) $\begin{bmatrix} -1 \\ 3 \end{bmatrix}$ (b) $\begin{bmatrix} 2 \\ -6 \end{bmatrix}$

(c) $\begin{bmatrix} 3 \\ -9 \end{bmatrix}$ (d) $\begin{bmatrix} -3 \\ 9 \end{bmatrix}$

53. $\begin{cases} -2x - 3y = -6 \\ 4x + 2y = 20 \end{cases}$

(a) $\begin{bmatrix} 3 \\ 0 \end{bmatrix}$ (b) $\begin{bmatrix} 6 \\ -2 \end{bmatrix}$

(c) $\begin{bmatrix} -6 \\ 6 \end{bmatrix}$ (d) $\begin{bmatrix} 4 \\ 2 \end{bmatrix}$

54. $\begin{cases} 5x - 7y = -15 \\ 3x + y = 17 \end{cases}$

(a) $\begin{bmatrix} 4 \\ 5 \end{bmatrix}$ (b) $\begin{bmatrix} 5 \\ 2 \end{bmatrix}$

(c) $\begin{bmatrix} -4 \\ -5 \end{bmatrix}$ (d) $\begin{bmatrix} 2 \\ 11 \end{bmatrix}$

55. $\begin{cases} x - 3y + 4z = 3 \\ 2x - 5y = 19 \\ -2x + 4y - 5z = -6 \end{cases}$

(a) $\begin{bmatrix} 3 \\ 2 \\ -2 \end{bmatrix}$ (b) $\begin{bmatrix} 2 \\ -3 \\ -2 \end{bmatrix}$ (c) $\begin{bmatrix} 1 \\ 3 \\ -2 \end{bmatrix}$ (d) $\begin{bmatrix} 3 \\ -3 \\ 2 \end{bmatrix}$

56. $\begin{cases} -3x + y - 6z = 12 \\ x - 4y + 2z = -26 \\ 4x + y + z = -23 \end{cases}$

(a) $\begin{bmatrix} 6 \\ -8 \\ 3 \end{bmatrix}$ (b) $\begin{bmatrix} 5 \\ 4 \\ -1 \end{bmatrix}$ (c) $\begin{bmatrix} -2 \\ 6 \\ 0 \end{bmatrix}$ (d) $\begin{bmatrix} -8 \\ 6 \\ 3 \end{bmatrix}$

In Exercises 57–64, (a) write each system of equations as a matrix equation $AX = B$ and (b) use Gauss-Jordan elimination on the augmented matrix $[A \,\vdots\, B]$ to solve for the matrix X. Use a graphing utility to check your solution.

57. $\begin{cases} -x_1 + x_2 = 4 \\ -2x_1 + x_2 = 0 \end{cases}$

58. $\begin{cases} 2x_1 + 3x_2 = 5 \\ x_1 + 4x_2 = 10 \end{cases}$

59. $\begin{cases} -2x_1 - 3x_2 = -4 \\ 6x_1 + x_2 = -36 \end{cases}$

60. $\begin{cases} -4x_1 + 9x_2 = -13 \\ x_1 - 3x_2 = 12 \end{cases}$

61. $\begin{cases} x_1 - 2x_2 + 3x_3 = 9 \\ -x_1 + 3x_2 - x_3 = -6 \\ 2x_1 - 5x_2 + 5x_3 = 17 \end{cases}$

62. $\begin{cases} x_1 + x_2 - 3x_3 = -1 \\ -x_1 + 2x_2 = 1 \\ -x_2 + x_3 = 0 \end{cases}$

63. $\begin{cases} x_1 - 5x_2 + 2x_3 = -20 \\ -3x_1 + x_2 - x_3 = 8 \\ -2x_2 + 5x_3 = -16 \end{cases}$

64. $\begin{cases} x_1 - x_2 + 4x_3 = 17 \\ x_1 + 3x_2 = -11 \\ -6x_2 + 5x_3 = 40 \end{cases}$

In Exercises 65–68, use the matrix capabilities of a graphing utility to find

$$f(A) = a_0 I_n + a_1 A + a_2 A^2 + \cdots + a_n A^n.$$

65. $f(x) = x^2 - 5x + 2, \quad A = \begin{bmatrix} 2 & 0 \\ 4 & 5 \end{bmatrix}$

66. $f(x) = x^2 - 7x + 6, \quad A = \begin{bmatrix} 5 & 4 \\ 1 & 2 \end{bmatrix}$

67. $f(x) = x^3 - 10x^2 + 31x - 30, \quad A = \begin{bmatrix} 3 & 1 & 4 \\ 0 & 2 & 6 \\ 0 & 0 & 5 \end{bmatrix}$

68. $f(x) = x^2 - 10x + 24, \quad A = \begin{bmatrix} 8 & -4 \\ 2 & 2 \end{bmatrix}$

Think About It In Exercises 69–78, use matrices A and B each of order 2×3, C of order 3×2, and D of order 2×2. Determine whether the matrices are of proper order to perform the operation(s). If so, give the order of the answer.

69. $A + 2C$

70. $B - 3C$

71. AB

72. BC

73. $BC - D$

74. $CB - D$

75. $(CA)D$

76. $(BC)D$

77. $D(A - 3B)$

78. $(BC - D)A$

79. *Manufacturing* A certain corporation has three factories, each of which manufactures two products. The number of units of product i produced at factory j in one day is represented by a_{ij} in the matrix

$$A = \begin{bmatrix} 60 & 40 & 20 \\ 30 & 90 & 60 \end{bmatrix}.$$

Find the production levels if production is increased by 20%. (*Hint:* Because an increase of 20% corresponds to 100% + 20%, multiply the given matrix by 1.2.)

80. Manufacturing A certain corporation has four factories, each of which manufactures two products. The number of units of product i produced at factory j in one day is represented by a_{ij} in the matrix

$$A = \begin{bmatrix} 100 & 90 & 70 & 30 \\ 40 & 20 & 60 & 60 \end{bmatrix}.$$

Find the production levels if production is increased by 10%.

81. Crop Production A fruit grower raises two crops, which are shipped to three outlets. The number of units of crop i that are shipped to outlet j is represented by a_{ij} in the matrix

$$A = \begin{bmatrix} 100 & 75 & 75 \\ 125 & 150 & 100 \end{bmatrix}.$$

The profit per unit is represented by the matrix

$$B = [\$3.75 \quad \$7.00].$$

Find the product BA and state what each entry of the product represents.

82. Revenue A manufacturer produces three models of a product that are shipped to two warehouses. The number of units of model i that are shipped to warehouse j is represented by a_{ij} in the matrix

$$A = \begin{bmatrix} 5,000 & 4,000 \\ 6,000 & 10,000 \\ 8,000 & 5,000 \end{bmatrix}.$$

The price per unit is represented by the matrix

$$B = [\$20.50 \quad \$26.50 \quad \$29.50].$$

Compute BA and state what each entry of the product represents.

83. Inventory Levels Five models of computers are sold through three retail outlets. The inventories are given by S. The wholesale and retail prices are given by T. Compute ST and interpret the result.

Model

	A	B	C	D	E		
$S =$	3	2	2	3	0	1	
	0	2	3	4	3	2	Outlet
	4	2	1	3	2	3	

Price

	Wholesale	Retail		
	\$840	\$1100	A	
	\$1200	\$1350	B	
$T =$	\$1450	\$1650	C	Model
	\$2650	\$3000	D	
	\$3050	\$3200	E	

84. Labor/Wage Requirements A company that manufactures boats has the following labor-hour and wage requirements. Compute ST and interpret the result.

Labor per Boat

Department

	Cutting	Assembly	Packaging		
	1.0 hr	0.5 hr	0.2 hr	Small	
$S =$	1.6 hr	1.0 hr	0.2 hr	Medium	Boat size
	2.5 hr	2.0 hr	0.4 hr	Large	

Wages per Hour

Plant

	A	B		
	\$12	\$10	Cutting	
$T =$	\$9	\$8	Assembly	Department
	\$6	\$5	Packaging	

85. Voting Preference The matrix

From

	R	D	I	
	0.6	0.1	0.1	R
$P =$	0.2	0.7	0.1	D	To
	0.2	0.2	0.8	I

is called a stochastic matrix. Each entry $p_{ij}(i \neq j)$ represents the proportion of the voting population that changes from party i to party j, and p_{ii} represents the proportion that remains loyal to the party from one election to the next. Compute and interpret P^2.

86. Voting Preference Use a graphing utility to find P^3, P^4, P^5, P^6, P^7, and P^8 for the matrix given in Exercise 85. Can you detect a pattern as P is raised to higher powers?

Synthesis

True or False? In Exercises 87–89, determine whether the statement is true or false. Justify your answer.

87. Two matrices can be added only if they have the same order.

88. $\begin{bmatrix} -6 & -2 \\ 2 & -6 \end{bmatrix}\begin{bmatrix} 4 & 0 \\ 0 & -1 \end{bmatrix} = \begin{bmatrix} 4 & 0 \\ 0 & -1 \end{bmatrix}\begin{bmatrix} -6 & -2 \\ 2 & -6 \end{bmatrix}$

89. $\begin{bmatrix} -2 & 4 \\ -3 & 0 \\ 6 & 1 \end{bmatrix}\begin{bmatrix} 1 & 1 \\ 1 & 1 \end{bmatrix} = \begin{bmatrix} -2 & 4 \\ -3 & 0 \\ 6 & 1 \end{bmatrix}$

90. Think About It If a, b, and c are real numbers such that $c \neq 0$ and $ac = bc$, then $a = b$. However, if A, B, and C are nonzero matrices such that $AC = BC$, then A is *not necessarily* equal to B. Illustrate this using the following matrices.

$$A = \begin{bmatrix} 0 & 1 \\ 0 & 1 \end{bmatrix}, \quad B = \begin{bmatrix} 1 & 0 \\ 1 & 0 \end{bmatrix}, \quad C = \begin{bmatrix} 2 & 3 \\ 2 & 3 \end{bmatrix}$$

91. Think About It If a and b are real numbers such that $ab = 0$, then $a = 0$ or $b = 0$. However, if A and B are matrices such that $AB = 0$, it is *not necessarily* true that $A = 0$ or $B = 0$. Illustrate this using the following matrices.

$$A = \begin{bmatrix} 3 & 3 \\ 4 & 4 \end{bmatrix}, \quad B = \begin{bmatrix} 1 & -1 \\ -1 & 1 \end{bmatrix}$$

Exploration **In Exercises 92 and 93, let $i = \sqrt{-1}$.**

92. Consider the matrix

$$A = \begin{bmatrix} i & 0 \\ 0 & i \end{bmatrix}.$$

Find A^2, A^3, and A^4. Identify any similarities with i^2, i^3, and i^4.

93. Find and identify A^2 for the matrix

$$A = \begin{bmatrix} 0 & -i \\ i & 0 \end{bmatrix}.$$

94. *Exploration* Let A and B be unequal diagonal matrices of the same order. (A *diagonal matrix* is a square matrix in which each entry not on the main diagonal is zero.) Determine the products AB for several pairs of such matrices. Make a conjecture about a quick rule for such products.

95. *Exploration* Consider matrices of the form

$$A = \begin{bmatrix} 0 & a_{12} & a_{13} & a_{14} & \cdots & a_{1n} \\ 0 & 0 & a_{23} & a_{24} & \cdots & a_{2n} \\ 0 & 0 & 0 & a_{34} & \cdots & a_{3n} \\ \vdots & \vdots & \vdots & \vdots & \cdots & \vdots \\ 0 & 0 & 0 & 0 & \cdots & a_{(n-1)n} \\ 0 & 0 & 0 & 0 & \cdots & 0 \end{bmatrix}.$$

(a) Write a 2×2 matrix and a 3×3 matrix in the form of A.

(b) Use a graphing utility to raise each of the matrices to higher powers. Describe the result.

(c) Use the result of part (b) to make a conjecture about powers of A if A is a 4×4 matrix. Use a graphing utility to test your conjecture.

(d) Use the results of parts (b) and (c) to make a conjecture about powers of A if A is an $n \times n$ matrix.

Review

In Exercises 96–101, solve the equation.

96. $3x^2 + 20x - 32 = 0$ **97.** $8x^2 - 10x - 3 = 0$

98. $4x^2 + 10x - 3 = 0$ **99.** $3x^3 + 22x^2 - 45x = 0$

100. $3x^3 - 12x^2 + 5x - 20 = 0$

101. $2x^3 - 5x^2 - 12x + 30 = 0$

In Exercises 102–105, expand the logarithmic expression.

102. $\ln\left(\dfrac{100}{e^2}\right)$ **103.** $\log_2\left(\dfrac{12}{x}\right)$

104. $\ln[x^2(x-2)^3]$ **105.** $\ln\left(\dfrac{x^2-9}{x^4}\right)$

In Exercises 106–109, condense the logarithmic expression.

106. $3 \ln 4 - \frac{1}{3}\ln(x^2 + 3)$

107. $\ln x - 3[\ln(x+6) + \ln(x-6)]$

108. $\frac{1}{2}[2 \ln(x+5) + \ln x - \ln(x-8)]$

109. $\frac{3}{2} \ln 7t^4 - \frac{3}{5} \ln t^5$

In Exercises 110 and 111, solve the system of equations. Check your answer algebraically.

110. $\begin{cases} -x + 4y - 2z = 22 \\ 2x + 5y - 3z = 28 \\ 6x - y - z = -4 \end{cases}$

111. $\begin{cases} 3x - 8y + z = -8 \\ -2x - 4y - 3z = -11 \\ 4x + 9y - 5z = -10 \end{cases}$

6.3 The Inverse of a Square Matrix

The Inverse of a Matrix

This section further develops the algebra of matrices. To begin, consider the real number equation $ax = b$. To solve this equation for x, multiply each side of the equation by a^{-1} (provided that $a \neq 0$).

$$ax = b$$
$$(a^{-1}a)x = a^{-1}b$$
$$(1)x = a^{-1}b$$
$$x = a^{-1}b$$

The number a^{-1} is called the *multiplicative inverse of a* because $a^{-1}a = 1$. The definition of the multiplicative **inverse of a matrix** is similar.

Definition of the Inverse of a Square Matrix

Let A be an $n \times n$ matrix. If there exists a matrix A^{-1} such that

$$AA^{-1} = I_n = A^{-1}A$$

then A^{-1} is called the **inverse** of A. The symbol A^{-1} is read "A inverse."

EXAMPLE 1 The Inverse of a Matrix

Show that B is the inverse of A, where $A = \begin{bmatrix} -1 & 2 \\ -1 & 1 \end{bmatrix}$ and $B = \begin{bmatrix} 1 & -2 \\ 1 & -1 \end{bmatrix}$.

Solution

To show that B is the inverse of A, show that $AB = I = BA$, as follows.

$$AB = \begin{bmatrix} -1 & 2 \\ -1 & 1 \end{bmatrix}\begin{bmatrix} 1 & -2 \\ 1 & -1 \end{bmatrix}$$

$$= \begin{bmatrix} -1 + 2 & 2 - 2 \\ -1 + 1 & 2 - 1 \end{bmatrix}$$

$$= \begin{bmatrix} 1 & 0 \\ 0 & 1 \end{bmatrix}$$

$$BA = \begin{bmatrix} 1 & -2 \\ 1 & -1 \end{bmatrix}\begin{bmatrix} -1 & 2 \\ -1 & 1 \end{bmatrix}$$

$$= \begin{bmatrix} -1 + 2 & 2 - 2 \\ -1 + 1 & 2 - 1 \end{bmatrix}$$

$$= \begin{bmatrix} 1 & 0 \\ 0 & 1 \end{bmatrix}$$

Recall that it is not always true that $AB = BA$, even if both products are defined. However, if A and B are both square matrices and $AB = I_n$, it can be shown that $BA = I_n$. So, in Example 1, you need only to check that $AB = I_2$.

What You Should Learn:

- How to verify that two matrices are inverses of each other
- How to use Gauss-Jordan elimination to find inverses of matrices
- How to use a formula to find inverses of 2×2 matrices
- How to use inverse matrices to solve systems of linear equations

Why You Should Learn It:

Systems of equations can be solved using the inverse of the coefficient matrix, which is particularly useful when the coefficients are the same for several systems, but the constants are different. Exercises 69 and 70 on page 468 show how to use an inverse matrix to find unknown currents in electrical circuits.

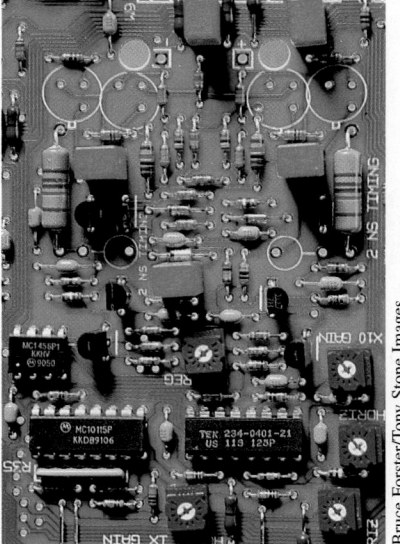

Bruce Forster/Tony Stone Images

If a matrix A has an inverse, A is called **invertible** (or **nonsingular**); otherwise, A is called **singular.** A nonsquare matrix cannot have an inverse. To see this, note that if A is of order $m \times n$ and B is of order $n \times m$ (where $m \neq n$), the products AB and BA are of different orders and so cannot be equal to each other. Not all square matrices possess inverses, as you will see at the bottom of page 463. If, however, a matrix does have an inverse, that inverse is unique. Example 2 shows how to use systems of equations to find the inverse of a matrix.

EXAMPLE 2   Finding the Inverse of a Matrix

Find the inverse of

$$A = \begin{bmatrix} 1 & 4 \\ -1 & -3 \end{bmatrix}.$$

Solution

To find the inverse of A, try to solve the matrix equation $AX = I$ for X.

$$\underset{A}{\begin{bmatrix} 1 & 4 \\ -1 & -3 \end{bmatrix}} \underset{X}{\begin{bmatrix} x_{11} & x_{12} \\ x_{21} & x_{22} \end{bmatrix}} = \underset{I}{\begin{bmatrix} 1 & 0 \\ 0 & 1 \end{bmatrix}}$$

$$\begin{bmatrix} x_{11} + 4x_{21} & x_{12} + 4x_{22} \\ -x_{11} - 3x_{21} & -x_{12} - 3x_{22} \end{bmatrix} = \begin{bmatrix} 1 & 0 \\ 0 & 1 \end{bmatrix}$$

Equating corresponding entries, you obtain the following two systems of linear equations.

$$\begin{cases} x_{11} + 4x_{21} = 1 \\ -x_{11} - 3x_{21} = 0 \end{cases} \qquad \begin{cases} x_{12} + 4x_{22} = 0 \\ -x_{12} - 3x_{22} = 1 \end{cases}$$

Solve the first system using elementary row operations to determine that $x_{11} = -3$ and $x_{21} = 1$. From the second system you can determine that $x_{12} = -4$ and $x_{22} = 1$. Therefore, the inverse of A is

$$X = A^{-1}$$

$$= \begin{bmatrix} -3 & -4 \\ 1 & 1 \end{bmatrix}.$$

You can use matrix multiplication to check this result.

Check

$$AA^{-1} = \begin{bmatrix} 1 & 4 \\ -1 & -3 \end{bmatrix} \begin{bmatrix} -3 & -4 \\ 1 & 1 \end{bmatrix} = \begin{bmatrix} 1 & 0 \\ 0 & 1 \end{bmatrix} \checkmark$$

$$A^{-1}A = \begin{bmatrix} -3 & -4 \\ 1 & 1 \end{bmatrix} \begin{bmatrix} 1 & 4 \\ -1 & -3 \end{bmatrix} = \begin{bmatrix} 1 & 0 \\ 0 & 1 \end{bmatrix} \checkmark$$

Exploration

Most graphing utilities have the capability of finding the inverse of a square matrix. Try using a graphing utility to find the inverse of the matrix

$$A = \begin{bmatrix} 2 & -3 & 1 \\ -1 & 2 & -1 \\ -2 & 0 & 1 \end{bmatrix}.$$

After you find A^{-1}, store it as $[B]$ and use the graphing utility to find $[A] \times [B]$ and $[B] \times [A]$. What can you conclude?

Finding Inverse Matrices

In Example 2, note that the two systems of linear equations have the *same coefficient matrix A*. Rather than solve the two systems represented by

$$\begin{bmatrix} 1 & 4 & \vdots & 1 \\ -1 & -3 & \vdots & 0 \end{bmatrix}$$

and

$$\begin{bmatrix} 1 & 4 & \vdots & 0 \\ -1 & -3 & \vdots & 1 \end{bmatrix}$$

separately, you can solve them *simultaneously* by *adjoining* the identity matrix to the coefficient matrix to obtain

$$\begin{matrix} A & & I \\ \begin{bmatrix} 1 & 4 & \vdots & 1 & 0 \\ -1 & -3 & \vdots & 0 & 1 \end{bmatrix} \end{matrix}.$$

Then, applying Gauss-Jordan elimination to this matrix, you can solve *both* systems with a single elimination process.

$$\begin{bmatrix} 1 & 4 & \vdots & 1 & 0 \\ -1 & -3 & \vdots & 0 & 1 \end{bmatrix}$$

$$R_1 + R_2 \rightarrow \begin{bmatrix} 1 & 4 & \vdots & 1 & 0 \\ 0 & 1 & \vdots & 1 & 1 \end{bmatrix}$$

$$\begin{matrix} -4R_2 + R_1 \rightarrow \\ {} \end{matrix} \begin{bmatrix} 1 & 0 & \vdots & -3 & -4 \\ 0 & 1 & \vdots & 1 & 1 \end{bmatrix}$$

So, from the "doubly augmented" matrix $[A \;\vdots\; I]$, you obtained the matrix $[I \;\vdots\; A^{-1}]$.

$$\begin{matrix} A & \quad & I \\ \begin{bmatrix} 1 & 4 & \vdots & 1 & 0 \\ -1 & -3 & \vdots & 0 & 1 \end{bmatrix} \end{matrix} \implies \begin{matrix} I & \quad & A^{-1} \\ \begin{bmatrix} 1 & 0 & \vdots & -3 & -4 \\ 0 & 1 & \vdots & 1 & 1 \end{bmatrix} \end{matrix}$$

This procedure (or algorithm) works for any square matrix that has an inverse.

Exploration

Select two 2×2 matrices A and B that have inverses. Enter them into your graphing utility and calculate $(AB)^{-1}$. Then calculate $B^{-1}A^{-1}$ and $A^{-1}B^{-1}$. Make a conjecture about the inverse of a product of two invertible matrices.

Finding an Inverse Matrix

Let A be a square matrix of order n.

1. Write the $n \times 2n$ matrix that consists of the given matrix A on the left and the $n \times n$ identity matrix I on the right to obtain $[A \;\vdots\; I]$.

2. If possible, row reduce A to I using elementary row operations on the *entire* matrix $[A \;\vdots\; I]$. The result will be the matrix $[I \;\vdots\; A^{-1}]$. If this is not possible, A is not invertible.

3. Check your work by multiplying to see that $AA^{-1} = I = A^{-1}A$.

EXAMPLE 3   Finding the Inverse of a Matrix

Find the inverse of $A = \begin{bmatrix} 1 & -1 & 0 \\ 1 & 0 & -1 \\ 6 & -2 & -3 \end{bmatrix}$.

A computer animation of this example appears in the *Interactive* CD-ROM and *Internet* versions of this text.

Solution

Begin by adjoining the identity matrix to A to form the matrix

$$[A \ \vdots \ I] = \begin{bmatrix} 1 & -1 & 0 & \vdots & 1 & 0 & 0 \\ 1 & 0 & -1 & \vdots & 0 & 1 & 0 \\ 6 & -2 & -3 & \vdots & 0 & 0 & 1 \end{bmatrix}.$$

Using elementary row operations to obtain the form $[I \ \vdots \ A^{-1}]$ results in

$$\begin{bmatrix} 1 & 0 & 0 & \vdots & -2 & -3 & 1 \\ 0 & 1 & 0 & \vdots & -3 & -3 & 1 \\ 0 & 0 & 1 & \vdots & -2 & -4 & 1 \end{bmatrix}.$$

Therefore, the matrix A is invertible and its inverse is

$$A^{-1} = \begin{bmatrix} -2 & -3 & 1 \\ -3 & -3 & 1 \\ -2 & -4 & 1 \end{bmatrix}.$$

Try using a graphing utility to confirm this result by multiplying A by A^{-1} to obtain I.

The process shown in Example 3 applies to any $n \times n$ matrix A. If A has an inverse, this process will find it. If A does not have an inverse, the process will tell you so. That is, matrix A will not reduce to the identity matrix. For instance, the following matrix has no inverse.

$$A = \begin{bmatrix} 1 & 2 & 0 \\ 3 & -1 & 2 \\ -2 & 3 & -2 \end{bmatrix}$$

To confirm that matrix A above has no inverse, begin by adjoining the identity matrix to A to form

$$[A \ \vdots \ I] = \begin{bmatrix} 1 & 2 & 0 & \vdots & 1 & 0 & 0 \\ 3 & -1 & 2 & \vdots & 0 & 1 & 0 \\ -2 & 3 & -2 & \vdots & 0 & 0 & 1 \end{bmatrix}.$$

Then use elementary row operations to obtain

$$\begin{bmatrix} 1 & 2 & 0 & \vdots & 1 & 0 & 0 \\ 0 & -7 & 2 & \vdots & -3 & 1 & 0 \\ 0 & 0 & 0 & \vdots & -1 & 1 & 1 \end{bmatrix}.$$

At this point in the elimination process you can see that it is impossible to obtain the identity matrix I on the left. Therefore, A is not invertible.

You may want to also demonstrate the singularity of the following matrices.

$$A = \begin{bmatrix} 3 & 6 \\ 1 & 2 \end{bmatrix}$$

$$B = \begin{bmatrix} 3 & 2 & 1 \\ 1 & 0 & -1 \\ 0 & 1 & 2 \end{bmatrix}$$

The Inverse of a 2 × 2 Matrix

Using Gauss-Jordan elimination to find the inverse of a matrix works well (even as a computer technique) for matrices of order 3 × 3 or greater. For 2 × 2 matrices, however, many people prefer to use a formula for the inverse rather than Gauss-Jordan elimination. This simple formula, which works *only* for 2 × 2 matrices, is explained as follows. If A is the 2 × 2 matrix

$$A = \begin{bmatrix} a & b \\ c & d \end{bmatrix}$$

then A is invertible if and only if $ad - bc \neq 0$. If $ad - bc \neq 0$, the inverse is

$$A^{-1} = \frac{1}{ad - bc} \begin{bmatrix} d & -b \\ -c & a \end{bmatrix}.$$

Try verifying this inverse by multiplication. The denominator $ad - bc$ is called the *determinant* of the 2 × 2 matrix A. You will study determinants in the next section.

Exploration

Use a graphing utility with matrix operations to find the inverse of the matrix

$$A = \begin{bmatrix} 1 & -3 \\ -2 & 6 \end{bmatrix}.$$

What message appears on the screen? Why does the graphing utility display this message?

EXAMPLE 4   Finding the Inverse of a 2 × 2 Matrix

If possible, find the inverse of the matrix.

a. $A = \begin{bmatrix} 3 & -1 \\ -2 & 2 \end{bmatrix}$

b. $B = \begin{bmatrix} 3 & -1 \\ -6 & 2 \end{bmatrix}$

Solution

a. For the matrix A, apply the formula for the inverse of a 2 × 2 matrix to obtain

$$ad - bc = (3)(2) - (-1)(-2)$$
$$= 4.$$

Because this quantity is not zero, the inverse is formed by interchanging the entries on the main diagonal, changing the signs of the other two entries, and multiplying by the scalar $\frac{1}{4}$, as follows.

$$A^{-1} = \frac{1}{4} \begin{bmatrix} 2 & 1 \\ 2 & 3 \end{bmatrix}$$

$$= \begin{bmatrix} \frac{1}{2} & \frac{1}{4} \\ \frac{1}{2} & \frac{3}{4} \end{bmatrix}$$

b. For the matrix B, you have

$$ad - bc = (3)(2) - (-1)(-6)$$
$$= 0$$

which means that B is not invertible.

Systems of Linear Equations

You know that a system of linear equations can have exactly one solution, infinitely many solutions, or no solution. If the coefficient matrix A of a *square* system (a system that has the same number of equations as variables) is invertible, the system has a unique solution, which is given as follows.

A System of Equations with a Unique Solution

If A is an invertible matrix, the system of linear equations represented by $AX = B$ has a unique solution

$$X = A^{-1}B.$$

The formula $X = A^{-1}B$ is used on most graphing utilities to solve linear systems that have invertible coefficient matrices. That is, you enter the $n \times n$ coefficient matrix $[A]$ and the $n \times 1$ column matrix $[B]$. The solution X is given by $[A]^{-1}[B]$.

EXAMPLE 5   Solving a System of Equations Using an Inverse

Use an inverse matrix to solve the system.

$$2x + 3y + z = -1$$

$$3x + 3y + z = 1$$

$$2x + 4y + z = -2$$

Solution

Begin by writing the system as $AX = B$.

$$\begin{bmatrix} 2 & 3 & 1 \\ 3 & 3 & 1 \\ 2 & 4 & 1 \end{bmatrix} \begin{bmatrix} x \\ y \\ z \end{bmatrix} = \begin{bmatrix} -1 \\ 1 \\ -2 \end{bmatrix}$$

Then, use Gauss-Jordan elimination to find A^{-1}.

$$A^{-1} = \begin{bmatrix} -1 & 1 & 0 \\ -1 & 0 & 1 \\ 6 & -2 & -3 \end{bmatrix}$$

Finally, multiply B by A^{-1} on the left to obtain the solution.

$$X = A^{-1}B$$

$$= \begin{bmatrix} -1 & 1 & 0 \\ -1 & 0 & 1 \\ 6 & -2 & -3 \end{bmatrix} \begin{bmatrix} -1 \\ 1 \\ -2 \end{bmatrix}$$

$$= \begin{bmatrix} 2 \\ -1 \\ -2 \end{bmatrix}$$

So, the solution is $x = 2$, $y = -1$, and $z = -2$.

Use a graphing utility to verify A^{-1} for the system of equations in Example 5.

Activities

1. Find the inverse of the matrix.

$$A = \begin{bmatrix} 2 & 1 \\ -1 & -1 \end{bmatrix}$$

Answer: $A^{-1} = \begin{bmatrix} 1 & 1 \\ -1 & -2 \end{bmatrix}$

2. Use the inverse matrix

$$A^{-1} = \begin{bmatrix} -3 & -2 \\ -1 & -1 \end{bmatrix}$$

to solve the system of linear equations.

$$-x + 2y = -1$$

$$x - 3y = 6$$

Answer: $x = -9$, $y = -5$

Group Activity Suggestion
Create two linear equations that intersect and carefully graph them on graph paper. Do not write the equations on your graph. Exchange graphs with another student. Use the graph to reconstruct the equations of the two lines. Write the system as the matrix equation $AX = B$. Find A^{-1} and use it to find the point of intersection of the two lines. Does your solution agree with the graph you received? Compare results with the creator of the graph.

STUDY T!P

Remember that matrix multiplication is not commutative. So, you must multiply matrices in the correct order. For instance, in Example 5, you must multiply B by A^{-1} on the left.

In Exercises 18, 19, 20, 24, 32, 35, and 39, the inverse matrix does not exist. In Exercise 59, the system has infinitely many solutions. In Exercise 53, the system has no solution.

6.3 Exercises

In Exercises 1–8, show that B is the inverse of A.

1. $A = \begin{bmatrix} 2 & 1 \\ 5 & 3 \end{bmatrix}$, $B = \begin{bmatrix} 3 & -1 \\ -5 & 2 \end{bmatrix}$

2. $A = \begin{bmatrix} 1 & -1 \\ -1 & 2 \end{bmatrix}$, $B = \begin{bmatrix} 2 & 1 \\ 1 & 1 \end{bmatrix}$

3. $A = \begin{bmatrix} 1 & 2 \\ 3 & 4 \end{bmatrix}$, $B = \begin{bmatrix} -2 & 1 \\ \frac{3}{2} & -\frac{1}{2} \end{bmatrix}$

4. $A = \begin{bmatrix} 1 & -1 \\ 2 & 3 \end{bmatrix}$, $B = \begin{bmatrix} \frac{3}{5} & \frac{1}{5} \\ -\frac{2}{5} & \frac{1}{5} \end{bmatrix}$

5. $A = \begin{bmatrix} 2 & -17 & 11 \\ -1 & 11 & -7 \\ 0 & 3 & -2 \end{bmatrix}$, $B = \begin{bmatrix} 1 & 1 & 2 \\ 2 & 4 & -3 \\ 3 & 6 & -5 \end{bmatrix}$

6. $A = \begin{bmatrix} -4 & 1 & 5 \\ -1 & 2 & 4 \\ 0 & -1 & -1 \end{bmatrix}$, $B = \begin{bmatrix} -\frac{1}{2} & 1 & \frac{3}{2} \\ \frac{1}{4} & -1 & -\frac{11}{4} \\ -\frac{1}{4} & 1 & \frac{7}{4} \end{bmatrix}$

7. $A = \begin{bmatrix} -2 & 2 & 3 \\ 1 & -1 & 0 \\ 0 & 1 & 4 \end{bmatrix}$, $B = \frac{1}{3}\begin{bmatrix} -4 & -5 & 3 \\ -4 & -8 & 3 \\ 1 & 2 & 0 \end{bmatrix}$

8. $A = \begin{bmatrix} -1 & 1 & 0 & -1 \\ 1 & -1 & 1 & 0 \\ -1 & 1 & 2 & 0 \\ 0 & -1 & 1 & 1 \end{bmatrix}$,

$B = \frac{1}{3}\begin{bmatrix} -3 & 1 & 1 & -3 \\ -3 & -1 & 2 & -3 \\ 0 & 1 & 1 & 0 \\ -3 & -2 & 1 & 0 \end{bmatrix}$

In Exercises 9–12, use the matrix capabilities of a graphing utility to show that B is the inverse of A.

9. $A = \begin{bmatrix} -1 & -4 \\ 1 & 2 \end{bmatrix}$, $B = \begin{bmatrix} 1 & 2 \\ -\frac{1}{2} & -\frac{1}{2} \end{bmatrix}$

10. $A = \begin{bmatrix} 11 & -12 \\ 2 & -2 \end{bmatrix}$, $B = \begin{bmatrix} -1 & 6 \\ -1 & \frac{11}{2} \end{bmatrix}$

11. $A = \begin{bmatrix} 1.6 & 2 \\ -3.5 & -4.5 \end{bmatrix}$, $B = \begin{bmatrix} 22.5 & 10 \\ -17.5 & -8 \end{bmatrix}$

12. $A = \begin{bmatrix} 4 & 0 & -2 \\ 1 & 2 & -4 \\ 0 & 3 & 1 \end{bmatrix}$, $B = \begin{bmatrix} 0.28 & -0.12 & 0.08 \\ -0.02 & 0.08 & 0.28 \\ 0.06 & -0.24 & 0.16 \end{bmatrix}$

In Exercises 13–26, find the inverse of the matrix (if it exists).

13. $\begin{bmatrix} 2 & 0 \\ 0 & 3 \end{bmatrix}$

14. $\begin{bmatrix} 1 & 2 \\ 3 & 7 \end{bmatrix}$

15. $\begin{bmatrix} 1 & -2 \\ 2 & -3 \end{bmatrix}$

16. $\begin{bmatrix} -7 & 33 \\ 4 & -19 \end{bmatrix}$

17. $\begin{bmatrix} -1 & 1 \\ -2 & 1 \end{bmatrix}$

18. $\begin{bmatrix} 2 & 4 \\ 4 & 8 \end{bmatrix}$

19. $\begin{bmatrix} 2 & 7 & 1 \\ -3 & -9 & 2 \end{bmatrix}$

20. $\begin{bmatrix} -2 & 5 \\ 6 & -15 \\ 0 & 1 \end{bmatrix}$

21. $\begin{bmatrix} 1 & 1 & 1 \\ 3 & 5 & 4 \\ 3 & 6 & 5 \end{bmatrix}$

22. $\begin{bmatrix} 1 & 2 & 2 \\ 3 & 7 & 9 \\ -1 & -4 & -7 \end{bmatrix}$

23. $\begin{bmatrix} 1 & 0 & 0 \\ 3 & 4 & 0 \\ 2 & 5 & 5 \end{bmatrix}$

24. $\begin{bmatrix} 1 & 0 & 0 \\ 3 & 0 & 0 \\ 2 & 5 & 5 \end{bmatrix}$

25. $\begin{bmatrix} -8 & 0 & 0 & 0 \\ 0 & 1 & 0 & 0 \\ 0 & 0 & 4 & 0 \\ 0 & 0 & 0 & -5 \end{bmatrix}$

26. $\begin{bmatrix} 1 & 3 & -2 & 0 \\ 0 & 2 & 4 & 6 \\ 0 & 0 & -2 & 1 \\ 0 & 0 & 0 & 5 \end{bmatrix}$

In Exercises 27–38, use the matrix capabilities of a graphing utility to find the inverse of the matrix (if it exists).

27. $\begin{bmatrix} 1 & 2 & -1 \\ 3 & 7 & -10 \\ -5 & -7 & -15 \end{bmatrix}$

28. $\begin{bmatrix} 10 & 5 & -7 \\ -5 & 1 & 4 \\ 3 & 2 & -2 \end{bmatrix}$

29. $\begin{bmatrix} 1 & 1 & 2 \\ 3 & 1 & 0 \\ -2 & 0 & 3 \end{bmatrix}$

30. $\begin{bmatrix} 3 & 2 & 2 \\ 2 & 2 & 2 \\ -4 & 4 & 3 \end{bmatrix}$

31. $\begin{bmatrix} -\frac{1}{2} & \frac{3}{4} & \frac{1}{4} \\ 1 & 0 & -\frac{3}{2} \\ 0 & -1 & \frac{1}{2} \end{bmatrix}$

32. $\begin{bmatrix} -\frac{5}{6} & \frac{1}{3} & \frac{11}{6} \\ 0 & \frac{2}{3} & 2 \\ 1 & -\frac{1}{2} & -\frac{5}{2} \end{bmatrix}$

33. $\begin{bmatrix} 0.1 & 0.2 & 0.3 \\ -0.3 & 0.2 & 0.2 \\ 0.5 & 0.4 & 0.4 \end{bmatrix}$

34. $\begin{bmatrix} 0.6 & 0 & -0.3 \\ 0.7 & -1 & 0.2 \\ 1 & 0 & -0.9 \end{bmatrix}$

35. $\begin{bmatrix} 1 & 0 & 3 & 0 \\ 0 & 2 & 0 & 4 \\ 1 & 0 & 3 & 0 \\ 0 & 2 & 0 & 4 \end{bmatrix}$

36. $\begin{bmatrix} 4 & 8 & -7 & 14 \\ 2 & 5 & -4 & 6 \\ 0 & 2 & 1 & -7 \\ 3 & 6 & -5 & 10 \end{bmatrix}$

37. $\begin{bmatrix} -1 & 0 & 1 & 0 \\ 0 & 2 & 0 & -1 \\ 2 & 0 & -1 & 0 \\ 0 & -1 & 0 & 1 \end{bmatrix}$

38. $\begin{bmatrix} 1 & -2 & -1 & -2 \\ 3 & -5 & -2 & -3 \\ 2 & -5 & -2 & -5 \\ -1 & 4 & 4 & 11 \end{bmatrix}$

In Exercises 39–42, use the formula on page 464 to find the inverse of the 2 × 2 matrix.

39. $\begin{bmatrix} -4 & -6 \\ 2 & 3 \end{bmatrix}$　**40.** $\begin{bmatrix} -12 & 3 \\ 5 & -2 \end{bmatrix}$

41. $\begin{bmatrix} \frac{7}{2} & -\frac{3}{4} \\ \frac{1}{5} & \frac{4}{5} \end{bmatrix}$　**42.** $\begin{bmatrix} -\frac{1}{4} & \frac{9}{4} \\ \frac{5}{3} & \frac{8}{9} \end{bmatrix}$

In Exercises 43–46, use an inverse matrix to solve the system of linear equations. (Use the inverse matrix found in Exercise 15.)

43. $\begin{cases} x - 2y = 5 \\ 2x - 3y = 10 \end{cases}$　**44.** $\begin{cases} x - 2y = 0 \\ 2x - 3y = 3 \end{cases}$

45. $\begin{cases} x - 2y = 4 \\ 2x - 3y = 2 \end{cases}$　**46.** $\begin{cases} x - 2y = 1 \\ 2x - 3y = -2 \end{cases}$

In Exercises 47 and 48, use an inverse matrix to solve the system of linear equations. (Use the inverse matrix found in Exercise 21.)

47. $\begin{cases} x + y + z = 0 \\ 3x + 5y + 4z = 5 \\ 3x + 6y + 5z = 2 \end{cases}$　**48.** $\begin{cases} x + y + z = -1 \\ 3x + 5y + 4z = 2 \\ 3x + 6y + 5z = 0 \end{cases}$

In Exercises 49 and 50, use an inverse matrix and the matrix capabilities of a graphing utility to solve the system of linear equations. (Use the inverse matrix found in Exercise 38.)

49. $\begin{cases} x_1 - 2x_2 - x_3 - 2x_4 = 0 \\ 3x_1 - 5x_2 - 2x_3 - 3x_4 = 1 \\ 2x_1 - 5x_2 - 2x_3 - 5x_4 = -1 \\ -x_1 + 4x_2 + 4x_3 + 11x_4 = 2 \end{cases}$

50. $\begin{cases} x_1 - 2x_2 - x_3 - 2x_4 = 1 \\ 3x_1 - 5x_2 - 2x_3 - 3x_4 = -2 \\ 2x_1 - 5x_2 - 2x_3 - 5x_4 = 0 \\ -x_1 + 4x_2 + 4x_3 + 11x_4 = -3 \end{cases}$

In Exercises 51–58, use an inverse matrix (if it exists) to solve the system of linear equations.

51. $\begin{cases} 3x + 4y = -2 \\ 5x + 3y = 4 \end{cases}$　**52.** $\begin{cases} 18x + 12y = 13 \\ 30x + 24y = 23 \end{cases}$

53. $\begin{cases} -0.4x + 0.8y = 1.6 \\ 2x - 4y = 5 \end{cases}$　**54.** $\begin{cases} 0.2x - 0.6y = 2.4 \\ -x + 1.4y = -8.8 \end{cases}$

55. $\begin{cases} -\frac{1}{4}x + \frac{3}{8}y = -2 \\ \frac{3}{2}x + \frac{3}{4}y = -12 \end{cases}$　**56.** $\begin{cases} \frac{5}{6}x - y = -20 \\ \frac{4}{3}x - \frac{7}{2}y = -51 \end{cases}$

57. $\begin{cases} 4x - y + z = -5 \\ 2x + 2y + 3z = 10 \\ 5x - 2y + 6z = 1 \end{cases}$　**58.** $\begin{cases} 4x - 2y + 3z = -2 \\ 2x + 2y + 5z = 16 \\ 8x - 5y - 2z = 4 \end{cases}$

In Exercises 59–64, use the matrix capabilities of a graphing utility to solve (if possible) the system of linear equations.

59. $\begin{cases} 5x - 3y + 2z = 2 \\ 2x + 2y - 3z = 3 \\ -x + 7y - 8z = 4 \end{cases}$　**60.** $\begin{cases} 2x + 3y + 5z = 4 \\ 3x + 5y - 9z = 7 \\ 5x + 9y + 17z = 13 \end{cases}$

61. $\begin{cases} 3x - 2y + z = -29 \\ -4x + y - 3z = 37 \\ x - 5y + z = -24 \end{cases}$

62. $\begin{cases} -8x + 7y - 10z = -151 \\ 12x + 3y - 5z = 86 \\ 15x - 9y + 2z = 187 \end{cases}$

63. $\begin{cases} 7x - 3y + 2w = 41 \\ -2x + y - w = -13 \\ 4x + z - 2w = 12 \\ -x + y - w = -8 \end{cases}$

64. $\begin{cases} 2x + 5y + w = 11 \\ x + 4y + 2z - 2w = -7 \\ 2x - 2y + 5z + w = 3 \\ x - 3w = -1 \end{cases}$

Bond Investments In Exercises 65–68, consider a person who invests in AAA-rated bonds, A-rated bonds, and B-rated bonds. The average yields are 6.5% on AAA-bonds, 7% on A-bonds, and 9% on B-bonds. The person invests twice as much in B-bonds as in A-bonds. Let x, y, and z represent the amounts invested in AAA-, A-, and B-bonds, respectively.

$$x + y + z = \text{(total investment)}$$
$$0.065x + 0.07y + 0.09z = \text{(annual return)}$$
$$2y - z = 0$$

Use the inverse of the coefficient matrix of this system to find the amount invested in each type of bond.

65. Total investment = $25,000
Annual return = $1900

66. Total investment = $45,000
Annual return = $3750

67. Total investment = $12,000
Annual return = $835

68. Total investment = $500,000
Annual return = $38,000

Circuit Analysis **In Exercises 69 and 70, consider the circuit in the figure below. The currents I_1, I_2, and I_3, in amperes, are given by the solution of the system of linear equations**

$$2I_1 \qquad + 4I_3 = E_1$$
$$I_2 + 4I_3 = E_2$$
$$I_1 + I_2 - I_3 = 0$$

where E_1 and E_2 are voltages. Use the inverse of the coefficient matrix of this system to find the unknown currents for the given voltages.

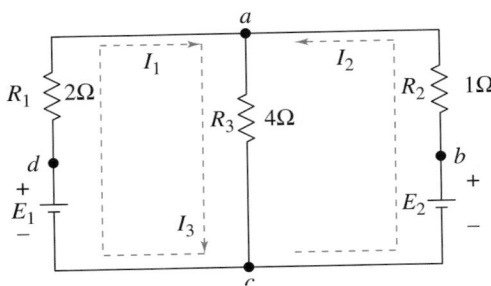

69. $E_1 = 14$ V, $E_2 = 28$ V
70. $E_1 = 10$ V, $E_2 = 10$ V

Synthesis

True or False? **In Exercises 71–73, determine whether the statement is true or false. Justify your answer.**

71. Multiplication of an invertible matrix and its inverse is commutative.

72. If you multiply two matrices and obtain an identity matrix, you can assume the matrices are inverses of each other.

73. No nonsquare matrices have inverses.

74. *Writing* Write a brief paragraph explaining the advantage of using an inverse matrix to solve the systems of linear equations in Exercises 43–50.

75. If A is a 2 × 2 matrix given by $A = \begin{bmatrix} a & b \\ c & d \end{bmatrix}$, then A is invertible if and only if $ad - bc \neq 0$. If $ad - bc \neq 0$, verify that the inverse is

$$A^{-1} = \frac{1}{ad - bc} \begin{bmatrix} d & -b \\ -c & a \end{bmatrix}.$$

Then use the result to find the inverse of each matrix.

(a) $\begin{bmatrix} 5 & -2 \\ 2 & 3 \end{bmatrix}$ (b) $\begin{bmatrix} 7 & 12 \\ -8 & -5 \end{bmatrix}$

76. *Exploration* Consider the matrices of the form

$$A = \begin{bmatrix} a_{11} & 0 & 0 & 0 & \cdots & 0 \\ 0 & a_{22} & 0 & 0 & \cdots & 0 \\ 0 & 0 & a_{33} & 0 & \cdots & 0 \\ \vdots & \vdots & \vdots & \vdots & \cdots & \vdots \\ 0 & 0 & 0 & 0 & \cdots & a_{nn} \end{bmatrix}.$$

(a) Write a 2 × 2 matrix and a 3 × 3 matrix in the form of A. Find the inverse of each.

(b) Use the result of part (a) to make a conjecture about the inverse of a matrix of the form of A.

Review

In Exercises 77–80, find all the real solutions of the polynomial equation.

77. $x^3 + 5x^2 - 6x - 30 = 0$

78. $x^3 - 9x^2 + 14x + 24 = 0$

79. $x^4 - x^3 - 10x^2 - 2x - 24 = 0$

80. $x^4 + 2x^3 - 11x^2 - 12x = 0$

In Exercises 81–84, use a graphing utility to create a table of values for the function. Then sketch its graph by hand.

81. $f(x) = -3^{x-5} + 3$ **82.** $f(x) = 4^{-x-1} + 8$
83. $f(x) = 4 + e^{x-4}$ **84.** $f(x) = -2e^{0.6x} + 4$

In Exercises 85–90, perform the matrix operation.

85. $-3 \begin{bmatrix} -4 & 6 \\ 2 & -8 \\ 1 & 12 \end{bmatrix}$ **86.** $-\frac{1}{12} \begin{bmatrix} -6 & 2 & 0 \\ -4 & -24 & 18 \end{bmatrix}$

87. $\begin{bmatrix} 2 & -7 \\ -3 & -1 \end{bmatrix} - 5 \begin{bmatrix} -1 & 4 \\ 8 & -5 \end{bmatrix}$

88. $10 \begin{bmatrix} 2 & -3 \\ 1 & 0 \end{bmatrix} + \begin{bmatrix} 16 & 17 \\ -7 & 8 \end{bmatrix}$

89. $\begin{bmatrix} -2 & 0 \\ -1 & 4 \end{bmatrix} \begin{bmatrix} -3 & 1 \\ 3 & 2 \end{bmatrix}$

90. $\begin{bmatrix} 6 & -8 \\ 5 & 2 \\ -1 & 0 \end{bmatrix} \begin{bmatrix} 0 & -1 & 2 \\ 4 & -5 & -3 \end{bmatrix}$

6.4 **The Determinant of a Square Matrix**

The Determinant of a Matrix

Every *square* matrix can be associated with a real number called its **determinant.** Determinants have many uses, and several will be discussed in this and the next section. Historically, the use of determinants arose from special number patterns that occur when systems of linear equations are solved. For instance, the system

$$\begin{cases} a_1x + b_1y = c_1 \\ a_2x + b_2y = c_2 \end{cases}$$

has a solution

$$x = \frac{c_1b_2 - c_2b_1}{a_1b_2 - a_2b_1}$$

and

$$y = \frac{a_1c_2 - a_2c_1}{a_1b_2 - a_2b_1}$$

provided that $a_1b_2 - a_2b_1 \neq 0$. Note that the denominator of each fraction is the same. This denominator is called the *determinant* of the coefficient matrix of the system.

Coefficient Matrix	*Determinant*
$A = \begin{bmatrix} a_1 & b_1 \\ a_2 & b_2 \end{bmatrix}$	$\det(A) = a_1b_2 - a_2b_1$

The determinant of the matrix A can also be denoted by vertical bars on both sides of the matrix, as indicated in the following definition.

Definition of the Determinant of a 2 × 2 Matrix

The **determinant** of the matrix

$$A = \begin{bmatrix} a_1 & b_1 \\ a_2 & b_2 \end{bmatrix}$$

is

$$\det(A) = |A| = \begin{vmatrix} a_1 & b_1 \\ a_2 & b_2 \end{vmatrix} = a_1b_2 - a_2b_1.$$

In this text, $\det(A)$ and $|A|$ are used interchangeably to represent the determinant of A. Although vertical bars are also used to denote the absolute value of a real number, the context will show which use is intended.

What You Should Learn:

- How to find determinants of 2×2 matrices
- How to find minors and cofactors of square matrices
- How to find determinants of square matrices
- How to find determinants of triangular matrices

Why You Should Learn It:
Determinants are often used in other branches of mathematics. For instance, Exercises 53–58 on page 475 show some types of determinants that are useful in calculus.

A convenient method for remembering the formula for the determinant of a 2 × 2 matrix is shown in the diagram.

$$\det(A) = \begin{vmatrix} a_1 & b_1 \\ a_2 & b_2 \end{vmatrix} = a_1 b_2 - a_2 b_1$$

Point out to your students that a matrix is an array of numbers, but a determinant is a single numerical value.

Note that the determinant is the difference of the products of the two diagonals of the matrix.

EXAMPLE 1   The Determinant of a 2 × 2 Matrix

Find the determinant of each matrix.

a. $A = \begin{bmatrix} 2 & -3 \\ 1 & 2 \end{bmatrix}$ **b.** $B = \begin{bmatrix} 2 & 1 \\ 4 & 2 \end{bmatrix}$ **c.** $C = \begin{bmatrix} 0 & \frac{3}{2} \\ 2 & 4 \end{bmatrix}$

Solution

a. $\det(A) = \begin{vmatrix} 2 & -3 \\ 1 & 2 \end{vmatrix} = 2(2) - 1(-3)$

$$= 4 + 3$$
$$= 7$$

b. $\det(B) = \begin{vmatrix} 2 & 1 \\ 4 & 2 \end{vmatrix} = 2(2) - 4(1)$

$$= 4 - 4$$
$$= 0$$

c. $\det(C) = \begin{vmatrix} 0 & \frac{3}{2} \\ 2 & 4 \end{vmatrix} = 0(4) - 2\left(\frac{3}{2}\right)$

$$= 0 - 3$$
$$= -3$$

Notice in Example 1 that the determinant of a matrix can be positive, zero, or negative.

The determinant of a matrix of order 1×1 is defined simply as the entry of the matrix. For instance, if $A = [-2]$, $\det(A) = -2$.

Most graphing utilities can evaluate the determinant of a matrix. Consult your user's guide to find how to evaluate a determinant. For instance, you can evaluate the determinant of

$$A = \begin{bmatrix} 2 & -3 \\ 1 & 2 \end{bmatrix}$$

by entering the matrix as $[A]$ and then choosing the determinant feature. The result should be 7, as in Example 1(a). Try evaluating the determinant of

$$B = \begin{bmatrix} 3 & -1 & 1 \\ 0 & 2 & 1 \end{bmatrix}.$$

What happens when you try to evaluate the determinant of a nonsquare matrix?

Minors and Cofactors

To define the determinant of a square matrix of order 3×3 or higher, it is helpful to introduce the concepts of **minors** and **cofactors**.

Minors and Cofactors of a Square Matrix

If A is a square matrix, the **minor** M_{ij} of the entry a_{ij} is the determinant of the matrix obtained by deleting the ith row and jth column of A. The **cofactor** C_{ij} of the entry a_{ij} is

$$C_{ij} = (-1)^{i+j}M_{ij}.$$

EXAMPLE 2   Finding the Minors and Cofactors of a Matrix

Find all the minors and cofactors of

$$A = \begin{bmatrix} 0 & 2 & 1 \\ 3 & -1 & 2 \\ 4 & 0 & 1 \end{bmatrix}.$$

Solution

To find the minor M_{11}, delete the first row and first column of A and evaluate the determinant of the resulting matrix.

$$\begin{bmatrix} 0 & 2 & 1 \\ 3 & -1 & 2 \\ 4 & 0 & 1 \end{bmatrix}$$

$$M_{11} = \begin{vmatrix} -1 & 2 \\ 0 & 1 \end{vmatrix} = -1(1) - 0(2) = -1$$

Similarly, to find M_{12}, delete the first row and second column.

$$\begin{bmatrix} 0 & 2 & 1 \\ 3 & -1 & 2 \\ 4 & 0 & 1 \end{bmatrix}$$

$$M_{12} = \begin{vmatrix} 3 & 2 \\ 4 & 1 \end{vmatrix} = 3(1) - 4(2) = -5$$

Continuing this pattern, you obtain the minors.

$$M_{11} = -1 \qquad M_{12} = -5 \qquad M_{13} = 4$$
$$M_{21} = 2 \qquad M_{22} = -4 \qquad M_{23} = -8$$
$$M_{31} = 5 \qquad M_{32} = -3 \qquad M_{33} = -6$$

Now, to find the cofactors, combine these minors with the checkerboard pattern of signs for a 3×3 matrix shown at the upper right.

$$C_{11} = -1 \qquad C_{12} = 5 \qquad C_{13} = 4$$
$$C_{21} = -2 \qquad C_{22} = -4 \qquad C_{23} = 8$$
$$C_{31} = 5 \qquad C_{32} = 3 \qquad C_{33} = -6$$

Sign Pattern for Cofactors

$$\begin{bmatrix} + & - & + \\ - & + & - \\ + & - & + \end{bmatrix}$$

3×3 matrix

$$\begin{bmatrix} + & - & + & - \\ - & + & - & + \\ + & - & + & - \\ - & + & - & + \end{bmatrix}$$

4×4 matrix

$$\begin{bmatrix} + & - & + & - & + & \cdots \\ - & + & - & + & - & \cdots \\ + & - & + & - & + & \cdots \\ - & + & - & + & - & \cdots \\ + & - & + & - & + & \cdots \\ \vdots & \vdots & \vdots & \vdots & \vdots & \end{bmatrix}$$

$n \times n$ matrix

STUDY T!P

In the sign pattern for cofactors above, notice that *odd* positions (where $i + j$ is odd) have negative signs and *even* positions (where $i + j$ is even) have positive signs.

The Determinant of a Square Matrix

The following definition is called *inductive* because it uses determinants of matrices of order $n - 1$ to define the determinant of a matrix of order n.

> ## Determinant of a Square Matrix
>
> If A is a square matrix (of order 2×2 or greater), the determinant of A is the sum of the entries in any row (or column) of A multiplied by their respective cofactors. For instance, expanding along the first row yields
>
> $$|A| = a_{11}C_{11} + a_{12}C_{12} + \cdots + a_{1n}C_{1n}.$$
>
> Applying this definition to find a determinant is called **expanding by cofactors.**

Try checking that for a 2×2 matrix this definition yields

$$|A| = a_{11}a_{22} - a_{21}a_{12}$$

as previously defined.

You may need to remind your students to use the appropriate signs when expanding a determinant by cofactors. (Refer them back to the Sign Pattern for Cofactors chart on the previous page.)

EXAMPLE 3   The Determinant of a Matrix of Order 3×3

Find the determinant of $A = \begin{bmatrix} 0 & 2 & 1 \\ 3 & -1 & 2 \\ 4 & 0 & 1 \end{bmatrix}$.

Solution

Note that this is the same matrix that was in Example 2. There you found the cofactors of the entries in the first row to be

$$C_{11} = -1, \qquad C_{12} = 5, \qquad \text{and} \qquad C_{13} = 4.$$

So, by the definition of the determinant of a square matrix, you have

$$|A| = a_{11}C_{11} + a_{12}C_{12} + a_{13}C_{13} \qquad \text{First-row expansion}$$

$$= 0(-1) + 2(5) + 1(4)$$

$$= 14.$$

In Example 3, the determinant was found by expanding by the cofactors in the first row. You could have used any row or column. For instance, you could have expanded along the second row to obtain

$$|A| = a_{21}C_{21} + a_{22}C_{22} + a_{23}C_{23} \qquad \text{Second-row expansion}$$

$$= 3(-2) + (-1)(-4) + 2(8)$$

$$= 14.$$

When expanding by cofactors, you do not need to find cofactors of zero entries, because zero times its cofactor is zero.

$$a_{ij}C_{ij} = (0)C_{ij} = 0$$

So, the row (or column) containing the most zeros is usually the best choice for expansion by cofactors.

You might want to consider showing students the following alternative method that can be used to evaluate the determinant of a 3×3 matrix A. (Note that this method works only for 3×3 matrices.) Copy the first and second columns of A to form fourth and fifth columns. The determinant of A is obtained by adding products of the three "downward diagonals" and subtracting the products of the three "upward diagonals" as shown below.

Subtract these products.

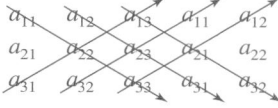

Add these products.

That is,

$$|A| = a_{11}a_{22}a_{33} + a_{12}a_{23}a_{31} +$$

$$a_{13}a_{21}a_{32} - a_{31}a_{22}a_{13} -$$

$$a_{32}a_{23}a_{11} - a_{33}a_{21}a_{12}.$$

Try using this method to find $|A|$ in Example 3.

Triangular Matrices

Evaluating determinants of matrices of order 4 or higher can be tedious. There is, however, an important exception: the determinant of a **triangular** matrix. A triangular matrix is a square matrix with all zero entries either below or above its main diagonal. A square matrix is **upper triangular** if it has all zero entries below its main diagonal and **lower triangular** if it has all zero entries above its main diagonal. A matrix that is both upper and lower triangular is called **diagonal.** That is, a diagonal matrix is a square matrix in which all entries above and below the main diagonal are zero.

Upper Triangular Matrix

$$\begin{bmatrix} a_{11} & a_{12} & a_{13} & \cdots & a_{1n} \\ 0 & a_{22} & a_{23} & \cdots & a_{2n} \\ 0 & 0 & a_{33} & \cdots & a_{3n} \\ \vdots & \vdots & \vdots & & \vdots \\ 0 & 0 & 0 & \cdots & a_{nn} \end{bmatrix}$$

Lower Triangular Matrix

$$\begin{bmatrix} a_{11} & 0 & 0 & \cdots & 0 \\ a_{21} & a_{22} & 0 & \cdots & 0 \\ a_{31} & a_{32} & a_{33} & \cdots & 0 \\ \vdots & \vdots & \vdots & & \vdots \\ a_{n1} & a_{n2} & a_{n3} & \cdots & a_{nn} \end{bmatrix}$$

Diagonal Matrix

$$\begin{bmatrix} a_{11} & 0 & 0 & \cdots & 0 \\ 0 & a_{22} & 0 & \cdots & 0 \\ 0 & 0 & a_{33} & \cdots & 0 \\ \vdots & \vdots & \vdots & & \vdots \\ 0 & 0 & 0 & \cdots & a_{nn} \end{bmatrix}$$

Students may have difficulty choosing the best row or column with which to expand a determinant using cofactors. You might consider using the following matrices as exercises to give students practice in choosing the row or column that yields the most efficient expansion.

$$A = \begin{bmatrix} 0 & -1 & 3 \\ 4 & 0 & 3 \\ 2 & 0 & -3 \end{bmatrix}$$

$$B = \begin{bmatrix} -1 & 3 & 0 & 1 \\ 2 & 0 & 4 & -3 \\ -2 & 1 & 7 & 0 \\ 3 & 2 & 0 & 5 \end{bmatrix}$$

$$C = \begin{bmatrix} -6 & 0 & 1 & 3 & -2 \\ 2 & -1 & 4 & 0 & -3 \\ 7 & 0 & -1 & 0 & 0 \\ 1 & -3 & 0 & 2 & 2 \\ 0 & 4 & 1 & 3 & 2 \end{bmatrix}$$

To find the determinant of a triangular matrix of any order, simply form the product of the entries on the main diagonal.

EXAMPLE 4   The Determinant of a Triangular Matrix

a.
$$\begin{vmatrix} 2 & 0 & 0 & 0 \\ 4 & -2 & 0 & 0 \\ -5 & 6 & 1 & 0 \\ 1 & 5 & 3 & 3 \end{vmatrix} = (2)(-2)(1)(3) = -12$$

b.
$$\begin{vmatrix} -1 & 0 & 0 & 0 & 0 \\ 0 & 3 & 0 & 0 & 0 \\ 0 & 0 & 2 & 0 & 0 \\ 0 & 0 & 0 & 4 & 0 \\ 0 & 0 & 0 & 0 & -2 \end{vmatrix} = (-1)(3)(2)(4)(-2) = 48$$

Writing About Math   *The Determinant of a Triangular Matrix*

Write an argument that explains why the determinant of a 3×3 triangular matrix is the product of its main-diagonal entries.

$$\begin{bmatrix} a_{11} & a_{12} & a_{13} \\ 0 & a_{22} & a_{23} \\ 0 & 0 & a_{33} \end{bmatrix} = a_{11}a_{22}a_{33}$$

6.4 Exercises

In Exercises 1–12, find the determinant of the matrix.

1. $[7]$

2. $[-3]$

3. $\begin{bmatrix} 1 & 4 \\ 7 & 3 \end{bmatrix}$

4. $\begin{bmatrix} -3 & 1 \\ 5 & 2 \end{bmatrix}$

5. $\begin{bmatrix} 6 & 2 \\ -5 & 3 \end{bmatrix}$

6. $\begin{bmatrix} 3 & -3 \\ 4 & -8 \end{bmatrix}$

7. $\begin{bmatrix} -7 & 6 \\ \frac{1}{2} & 3 \end{bmatrix}$

8. $\begin{bmatrix} 4 & -3 \\ 0 & 0 \end{bmatrix}$

9. $\begin{bmatrix} 2 & -1 & 0 \\ 4 & 2 & 1 \\ 4 & 2 & 1 \end{bmatrix}$

10. $\begin{bmatrix} -2 & 2 & 3 \\ 1 & -1 & 0 \\ 0 & 1 & 4 \end{bmatrix}$

11. $\begin{bmatrix} -1 & 2 & -5 \\ 0 & 3 & 4 \\ 0 & 0 & 3 \end{bmatrix}$

12. $\begin{bmatrix} 1 & 0 & 0 \\ -4 & -1 & 0 \\ 5 & 1 & 5 \end{bmatrix}$

In Exercises 13 and 14, use the matrix capabilities of a graphing utility to find the determinant of the matrix.

13. $\begin{bmatrix} 0.3 & 0.2 & 0.2 \\ 0.2 & 0.2 & 0.2 \\ -0.4 & 0.4 & 0.3 \end{bmatrix}$

14. $\begin{bmatrix} 0.1 & 0.2 & 0.3 \\ -0.3 & 0.2 & 0.2 \\ 0.5 & 0.4 & 0.4 \end{bmatrix}$

In Exercises 15–18, find (a) all minors and (b) all cofactors of the matrix.

15. $\begin{bmatrix} 3 & 4 \\ 2 & -5 \end{bmatrix}$

16. $\begin{bmatrix} 11 & 0 \\ -3 & 2 \end{bmatrix}$

17. $\begin{bmatrix} 3 & -2 & 8 \\ 3 & 2 & -6 \\ -1 & 3 & 6 \end{bmatrix}$

18. $\begin{bmatrix} -2 & 9 & 4 \\ 7 & -6 & 0 \\ 6 & 7 & -6 \end{bmatrix}$

In Exercises 19–22, find the determinant of the matrix by the method of expansion by cofactors. Expand using the indicated row or column.

19. $\begin{bmatrix} -3 & 2 & 1 \\ 4 & 5 & 6 \\ 2 & -3 & 1 \end{bmatrix}$
(a) Row 1
(b) Column 2

20. $\begin{bmatrix} -3 & 4 & 2 \\ 6 & 3 & 1 \\ 4 & -7 & -8 \end{bmatrix}$
(a) Row 2
(b) Column 3

21. $\begin{bmatrix} 6 & 0 & -3 & 5 \\ 4 & 13 & 6 & -8 \\ -1 & 0 & 7 & 4 \\ 8 & 6 & 0 & 2 \end{bmatrix}$
(a) Row 2
(b) Column 2

22. $\begin{bmatrix} 10 & 8 & 3 & -7 \\ 4 & 0 & 5 & -6 \\ 0 & 3 & 2 & 7 \\ 1 & 0 & -3 & 2 \end{bmatrix}$
(a) Row 3
(b) Column 1

In Exercises 23–30, find the determinant of the matrix. Expand by cofactors on the row or column that appears to make the computations easiest.

23. $\begin{bmatrix} 1 & 4 & -2 \\ 3 & 2 & 0 \\ -1 & 4 & 3 \end{bmatrix}$

24. $\begin{bmatrix} 2 & -1 & 3 \\ 1 & 4 & 4 \\ 1 & 0 & 2 \end{bmatrix}$

25. $\begin{bmatrix} 2 & 4 & 6 \\ 0 & 3 & 1 \\ 0 & 0 & -5 \end{bmatrix}$

26. $\begin{bmatrix} -3 & 0 & 0 \\ 7 & 11 & 0 \\ 1 & 2 & 2 \end{bmatrix}$

27. $\begin{bmatrix} 2 & 6 & 6 & 2 \\ 2 & 7 & 3 & 6 \\ 1 & 5 & 0 & 1 \\ 3 & 7 & 0 & 7 \end{bmatrix}$

28. $\begin{bmatrix} 3 & 6 & -5 & 4 \\ -2 & 0 & 6 & 0 \\ 1 & 1 & 2 & 2 \\ 0 & 3 & -1 & -1 \end{bmatrix}$

29. $\begin{bmatrix} 3 & 2 & 4 & -1 & 5 \\ -2 & 0 & 1 & 3 & 2 \\ 1 & 0 & 0 & 4 & 0 \\ 6 & 0 & 2 & -1 & 0 \\ 3 & 0 & 5 & 1 & 0 \end{bmatrix}$

30. $\begin{bmatrix} 5 & 2 & 0 & 0 & -2 \\ 0 & 1 & 4 & 3 & 2 \\ 0 & 0 & 2 & 6 & 3 \\ 0 & 0 & 3 & 4 & 1 \\ 0 & 0 & 0 & 0 & 2 \end{bmatrix}$

In Exercises 31–34, evaluate the determinant. Do not use a graphing utility.

31. $\begin{vmatrix} 4 & 0 & 0 & 0 \\ 6 & -5 & 0 & 0 \\ 1 & 3 & 1 & 0 \\ 1 & -2 & 7 & 3 \end{vmatrix}$

32. $\begin{vmatrix} -1 & 3 & 5 & 0 \\ 0 & -10 & 9 & -6 \\ 0 & 0 & 7 & -1 \\ 0 & 0 & 0 & -2 \end{vmatrix}$

33. $\begin{vmatrix} 8 & 0 & 4 & 12 & -1 \\ 0 & -3 & -6 & -10 & 2 \\ 0 & 0 & -1 & 5 & -3 \\ 0 & 0 & 0 & 9 & 7 \\ 0 & 0 & 0 & 0 & 1 \end{vmatrix}$

34.
$$\begin{vmatrix} -2 & 0 & 0 & 0 & 0 \\ -1 & 4 & 0 & 0 & 0 \\ 3 & 5 & 1 & 0 & 0 \\ 6 & -11 & 8 & 10 & 0 \\ 0 & 13 & -9 & 0 & -3 \end{vmatrix}$$

In Exercises 35–38, use the matrix capabilities of a graphing utility to evaluate the determinant.

35.
$$\begin{vmatrix} 1 & -1 & 8 & 4 \\ 2 & 6 & 0 & -4 \\ 2 & 0 & 2 & 6 \\ 0 & 2 & 8 & 0 \end{vmatrix}$$
36.
$$\begin{vmatrix} 0 & -3 & 8 & 2 \\ 8 & 1 & -1 & 6 \\ -4 & 6 & 0 & 9 \\ -7 & 0 & 0 & 14 \end{vmatrix}$$

37.
$$\begin{vmatrix} 3 & -2 & 4 & 3 & 1 \\ -1 & 0 & 2 & 1 & 0 \\ 5 & -1 & 0 & 3 & 2 \\ 4 & 7 & -8 & 0 & 0 \\ 1 & 2 & 3 & 0 & 2 \end{vmatrix}$$

38.
$$\begin{vmatrix} -2 & 0 & 0 & 0 & 0 \\ 0 & 3 & 0 & 0 & 0 \\ 0 & 0 & -1 & 0 & 0 \\ 0 & 0 & 0 & 2 & 0 \\ 0 & 0 & 0 & 0 & -4 \end{vmatrix}$$

In Exercises 39–42, find (a)$|A|$, (b)$|B|$, (c) AB, and (d)$|AB|$.

39. $A = \begin{bmatrix} -1 & 0 \\ 0 & 3 \end{bmatrix}$, $B = \begin{bmatrix} 2 & 0 \\ 0 & -1 \end{bmatrix}$

40. $A = \begin{bmatrix} -2 & 1 \\ 4 & -2 \end{bmatrix}$, $B = \begin{bmatrix} 1 & 2 \\ 0 & -1 \end{bmatrix}$

41. $A = \begin{bmatrix} -1 & 2 & 1 \\ 1 & 0 & 1 \\ 0 & 1 & 0 \end{bmatrix}$, $B = \begin{bmatrix} -1 & 0 & 0 \\ 0 & 2 & 0 \\ 0 & 0 & 3 \end{bmatrix}$

42. $A = \begin{bmatrix} 2 & 0 & 1 \\ 1 & -1 & 2 \\ 3 & 1 & 0 \end{bmatrix}$, $B = \begin{bmatrix} 2 & -1 & 4 \\ 0 & 1 & 3 \\ 3 & -2 & 1 \end{bmatrix}$

In Exercises 43 and 44, use the matrix capabilities of a graphing utility to find (a)$|A|$, (b)$|B|$, (c) AB, and (d)$|AB|$.

43. $A = \begin{bmatrix} 6 & 4 & 0 & 1 \\ 2 & -3 & -2 & -4 \\ 0 & 1 & 5 & 0 \\ -1 & 0 & -1 & 1 \end{bmatrix}$

$B = \begin{bmatrix} 0 & -5 & 0 & -2 \\ -2 & 4 & -1 & -4 \\ 3 & 0 & 1 & 0 \\ 1 & -2 & 3 & 0 \end{bmatrix}$

44. $A = \begin{bmatrix} -1 & 5 & 2 & 0 \\ 0 & 0 & 1 & 1 \\ 3 & -3 & -1 & 0 \\ 4 & 2 & 4 & -1 \end{bmatrix}$, $B = \begin{bmatrix} 1 & 5 & 0 & 0 \\ 10 & -1 & 2 & 4 \\ 2 & 0 & 0 & 1 \\ -3 & 2 & 5 & 0 \end{bmatrix}$

In Exercises 45–48, evaluate the determinants to verify the equation.

45. $\begin{vmatrix} w & x \\ y & z \end{vmatrix} = - \begin{vmatrix} y & z \\ w & x \end{vmatrix}$

46. $\begin{vmatrix} w & cx \\ y & cz \end{vmatrix} = c \begin{vmatrix} w & x \\ y & z \end{vmatrix}$

47. $\begin{vmatrix} w & x \\ y & z \end{vmatrix} = \begin{vmatrix} w & x + cw \\ y & z + cy \end{vmatrix}$

48. $\begin{vmatrix} w & x \\ cw & cx \end{vmatrix} = 0$

In Exercises 49 and 50, evaluate the determinant to verify the equation.

49. $\begin{vmatrix} 1 & x & x^2 \\ 1 & y & y^2 \\ 1 & z & z^2 \end{vmatrix} = (y - x)(z - x)(z - y)$

50. $\begin{vmatrix} a + b & a & a \\ a & a + b & a \\ a & a & a + b \end{vmatrix} = b^2(3a + b)$

In Exercises 51 and 52, solve for x.

51. $\begin{vmatrix} x - 1 & 2 \\ 3 & x - 2 \end{vmatrix} = 0$ **52.** $\begin{vmatrix} x - 2 & -1 \\ -3 & x \end{vmatrix} = 0$

In Exercises 53–58, evaluate the determinant, where the entries are functions. Determinants of this type occur in calculus.

53. $\begin{vmatrix} 4u & -1 \\ -1 & 2v \end{vmatrix}$ **54.** $\begin{vmatrix} 3x^2 & -3y^2 \\ 1 & 1 \end{vmatrix}$

55. $\begin{vmatrix} e^{2x} & e^{3x} \\ 2e^{2x} & 3e^{3x} \end{vmatrix}$ **56.** $\begin{vmatrix} e^{-x} & xe^{-x} \\ -e^{-x} & (1 - x)e^{-x} \end{vmatrix}$

57. $\begin{vmatrix} x & \ln x \\ 1 & 1/x \end{vmatrix}$ **58.** $\begin{vmatrix} x & x \ln x \\ 1 & 1 + \ln x \end{vmatrix}$

Synthesis

True or False? **In Exercises 59 and 60, determine whether the statement is true or false. Justify your answer.**

59. If a square matrix has an entire row of zeros, the determinant will always be zero.

60. If two columns of a square matrix are the same, then the determinant of the matrix will be zero.

61. *Exploration* Find square matrices A and B to demonstrate that

$$|A + B| \neq |A| + |B|.$$

62. *Exploration* Consider square matrices in which the entries are consecutive integers. An example of such a matrix is

$$\begin{bmatrix} 4 & 5 & 6 \\ 7 & 8 & 9 \\ 10 & 11 & 12 \end{bmatrix}.$$

Use a graphing utility to evaluate four determinants of this type. Make a conjecture based on the results. Then verify your conjecture.

63. *Writing* Write a brief paragraph explaining the difference between a square matrix and its determinant.

64. *Think About It* If A is a matrix of order 3×3 such that $|A| = 5$, is it possible to find $|2A|$? Explain.

Properties of Determinants **In Exercises 65–67, a property of determinants is given. State how the property has been applied to the given determinants and use a graphing utility to verify the results.**

65. If A and B are square matrices and B is obtained from A by interchanging two rows of A or interchanging two columns of A, then $|B| = -|A|$.

(a) $\begin{vmatrix} 1 & 3 & 4 \\ -7 & 2 & -5 \\ 6 & 1 & 2 \end{vmatrix} = - \begin{vmatrix} 1 & 4 & 3 \\ -7 & -5 & 2 \\ 6 & 2 & 1 \end{vmatrix}$

(b) $\begin{vmatrix} 1 & 3 & 4 \\ -2 & 2 & 0 \\ 1 & 6 & 2 \end{vmatrix} = - \begin{vmatrix} 1 & 6 & 2 \\ -2 & 2 & 0 \\ 1 & 3 & 4 \end{vmatrix}$

66. If A and B are square matrices and B is obtained from A by adding a multiple of a row of A to another row of A or by adding a multiple of a column of A to another column of A, then $|B| = |A|$.

(a) $\begin{vmatrix} 1 & -3 \\ 5 & 2 \end{vmatrix} = \begin{vmatrix} 1 & -3 \\ 0 & 17 \end{vmatrix}$

(b) $\begin{vmatrix} 5 & 4 & 2 \\ 2 & -3 & 4 \\ 7 & 6 & 3 \end{vmatrix} = \begin{vmatrix} 1 & 10 & -6 \\ 2 & -3 & 4 \\ 7 & 6 & 3 \end{vmatrix}$

67. If A and B are square matrices and B is obtained from A by multiplying a row of A by a nonzero constant c or multiplying a column of A by a nonzero constant c, then $|B| = c|A|$.

(a) $\begin{vmatrix} 5 & 10 & 15 \\ 2 & -3 & 4 \\ 2 & -7 & 1 \end{vmatrix} = 5 \begin{vmatrix} 1 & 2 & 3 \\ 2 & -3 & 4 \\ 2 & -7 & 1 \end{vmatrix}$

(b) $\begin{vmatrix} 1 & 8 & -3 \\ 3 & -12 & 6 \\ 7 & 4 & 9 \end{vmatrix} = 12 \begin{vmatrix} 1 & 2 & -1 \\ 3 & -3 & 2 \\ 7 & 1 & 3 \end{vmatrix}$

Review

In Exercises 68–71, solve the system of equations using substitution or elimination. Verify graphically.

68. $\begin{cases} 3x - 10y = 46 \\ x + y = -2 \end{cases}$

69. $\begin{cases} 5x + 7y = 23 \\ -4x - 2y = -4 \end{cases}$

70. $\begin{cases} -x + 9y = 11 \\ 6x - 3y = -47 \end{cases}$

71. $\begin{cases} 12x - 15y = 3 \\ -13x + 5y = -1 \end{cases}$

In Exercises 72 and 73, sketch the graph of the system of inequalities.

72. $\begin{cases} x + y \leq 8 \\ x \geq -3 \\ 2x - y \leq 4 \end{cases}$

73. $\begin{cases} -x - y \geq -4 \\ y \leq 1 \\ x + y \geq -4 \end{cases}$

In Exercises 74–77, use a graphing utility to find the inverse of the matrix (if it exists).

74. $\begin{bmatrix} -4 & 1 \\ 8 & -1 \end{bmatrix}$

75. $\begin{bmatrix} -5 & -8 \\ 3 & 6 \end{bmatrix}$

76. $\begin{bmatrix} -7 & 2 & 9 \\ 2 & -4 & -6 \\ 3 & 5 & 2 \end{bmatrix}$

77. $\begin{bmatrix} -6 & 2 & 0 \\ 1 & 3 & -2 \\ -2 & 0 & 1 \end{bmatrix}$

6.5　Applications of Matrices and Determinants

Area of a Triangle

In this section, you will study some additional applications of matrices and determinants. The first involves a formula for finding the area of a triangle whose vertices are given by three points on a rectangular coordinate system.

Area of a Triangle

The area of a triangle with vertices (x_1, y_1), (x_2, y_2), and (x_3, y_3) is

$$\text{Area} = \pm \frac{1}{2} \begin{vmatrix} x_1 & y_1 & 1 \\ x_2 & y_2 & 1 \\ x_3 & y_3 & 1 \end{vmatrix}$$

where the symbol $(\pm)$ indicates that the appropriate sign should be chosen to yield a positive area.

EXAMPLE 1　Finding the Area of a Triangle

Find the area of a triangle whose vertices are $(1, 0)$, $(2, 2)$, and $(4, 3)$, as shown in Figure 6.2.

Solution
Let $(x_1, y_1) = (1, 0)$, $(x_2, y_2) = (2, 2)$, and $(x_3, y_3) = (4, 3)$. Then, to find the area of a triangle, evaluate the determinant

$$\begin{vmatrix} x_1 & y_1 & 1 \\ x_2 & y_2 & 1 \\ x_3 & y_3 & 1 \end{vmatrix} = \begin{vmatrix} 1 & 0 & 1 \\ 2 & 2 & 1 \\ 4 & 3 & 1 \end{vmatrix}$$

$$= 1(-1)^2 \begin{vmatrix} 2 & 1 \\ 3 & 1 \end{vmatrix} + 0(-1)^3 \begin{vmatrix} 2 & 1 \\ 4 & 1 \end{vmatrix} + 1(-1)^4 \begin{vmatrix} 2 & 2 \\ 4 & 3 \end{vmatrix}$$

$$= 1(-1) + 0 + 1(-2)$$

$$= -3.$$

Using this value, you can conclude that the area of the triangle is

$$\text{Area} = -\frac{1}{2} \begin{vmatrix} 1 & 0 & 1 \\ 2 & 2 & 1 \\ 4 & 3 & 1 \end{vmatrix}$$

$$= -\frac{1}{2}(-3)$$

$$= \frac{3}{2} \text{ square units.}$$

What You Should Learn:

- How to use determinants to find areas of triangles
- How to use determinants to decide whether points are collinear
- How to use Cramer's Rule to solve systems of linear equations
- How to use matrices to encode and decode messages

Why You Should Learn It:

A determinant can be used to find the area of a region of forest infected with gypsy moths, as shown in Exercise 27 on page 485.

Layne Kennedy/CORBIS

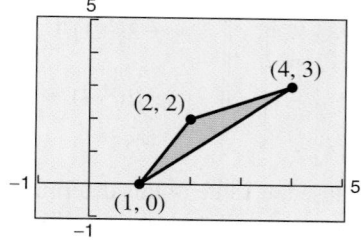

Figure 6.2

Collinear Points

What if the three points in Example 1 had been on the same line? What would have happened had the area formula been applied to three such points? The answer is that the determinant would have been zero. Consider, for instance, the three collinear points $(0, 1)$, $(2, 2)$, and $(4, 3)$, as shown in Figure 6.3. The area of the "triangle" that has these three points as vertices is

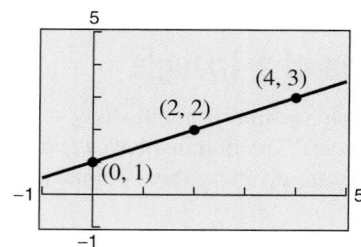

$$\frac{1}{2}\begin{vmatrix} 0 & 1 & 1 \\ 2 & 2 & 1 \\ 4 & 3 & 1 \end{vmatrix} = \frac{1}{2}\left[0(-1)^2\begin{vmatrix} 2 & 1 \\ 3 & 1 \end{vmatrix} + 1(-1)^3\begin{vmatrix} 2 & 1 \\ 4 & 1 \end{vmatrix} + 1(-1)^4\begin{vmatrix} 2 & 2 \\ 4 & 3 \end{vmatrix} \right]$$

$$= \frac{1}{2}[0 + 1(2) + 1(-2)]$$

$$= 0$$

Figure 6.3

This result is generalized as follows.

Three points (x_1, y_1), (x_2, y_2), and (x_3, y_3) are **collinear** (lie on the same line) if and only if

$$\begin{vmatrix} x_1 & y_1 & 1 \\ x_2 & y_2 & 1 \\ x_3 & y_3 & 1 \end{vmatrix} = 0.$$

EXAMPLE 2 Testing for Collinear Points

Determine whether the points $(-2, -2)$, $(1, 1)$, and $(7, 5)$ lie on the same line. (See Figure 6.4.)

Solution

Letting $(x_1, y_1) = (-2, -2)$, $(x_2, y_2) = (1, 1)$, and $(x_3, y_3) = (7, 5)$, you have

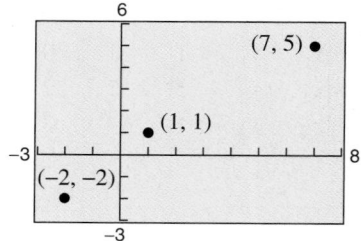

Figure 6.4

$$\begin{vmatrix} x_1 & y_1 & 1 \\ x_2 & y_2 & 1 \\ x_3 & y_3 & 1 \end{vmatrix} = \begin{vmatrix} -2 & -2 & 1 \\ 1 & 1 & 1 \\ 7 & 5 & 1 \end{vmatrix}$$

$$= -2(-1)^2\begin{vmatrix} 1 & 1 \\ 5 & 1 \end{vmatrix} + (-2)(-1)^3\begin{vmatrix} 1 & 1 \\ 7 & 1 \end{vmatrix} + 1(-1)^4\begin{vmatrix} 1 & 1 \\ 7 & 5 \end{vmatrix}$$

$$= -2(-4) + (-2)(6) + 1(-2)$$

$$= -6.$$

Because the value of this determinant is not zero, you can conclude that the three points do not lie on the same line.

Cramer's Rule

So far, you have studied three methods for solving a system of linear equations: substitution, elimination (with equations), and elimination (with matrices). You will now study one more method, **Cramer's Rule,** named after Gabriel Cramer (1704–1752). This rule uses determinants to write the solution of a system of linear equations. To see how Cramer's Rule works, take another look at the solution described at the beginning of Section 6.4. There, it was pointed out that the system

Your students should now be able to solve systems of linear equations by substitution (Section 5.1), elimination (Section 5.2), Gaussian elimination with back-substitution (Section 6.1), Gauss-Jordan elimination (Section 6.1), inverse matrix method (Section 6.3), and now, after this section, Cramer's Rule.

$$a_1 x + b_1 y = c_1$$

$$a_2 x + b_2 y = c_2$$

has a solution

$$x = \frac{c_1 b_2 - c_2 b_1}{a_1 b_2 - a_2 b_1}$$

and

$$y = \frac{a_1 c_2 - a_2 c_1}{a_1 b_2 - a_2 b_1}$$

provided that $a_1 b_2 - a_2 b_1 \neq 0$. Each numerator and denominator in this solution can be expressed as a determinant, as follows.

$$x = \frac{c_1 b_2 - c_2 b_1}{a_1 b_2 - a_2 b_1} = \frac{\begin{vmatrix} c_1 & b_1 \\ c_2 & b_2 \end{vmatrix}}{\begin{vmatrix} a_1 & b_1 \\ a_2 & b_2 \end{vmatrix}}$$

$$y = \frac{a_1 c_2 - a_2 c_1}{a_1 b_2 - a_2 b_1} = \frac{\begin{vmatrix} a_1 & c_1 \\ a_2 & c_2 \end{vmatrix}}{\begin{vmatrix} a_1 & b_1 \\ a_2 & b_2 \end{vmatrix}}$$

Relative to the original system, the denominator for x and y is simply the determinant of the *coefficient* matrix of the system. This determinant is denoted by D. The numerators for x and y are denoted by D_x and D_y, respectively. They are formed by using the column of constants as replacements for the coefficients of x and y, as follows.

Coefficient Matrix	D	D_x	D_y
$\begin{bmatrix} a_1 & b_1 \\ a_2 & b_2 \end{bmatrix}$	$\begin{vmatrix} a_1 & b_1 \\ a_2 & b_2 \end{vmatrix}$	$\begin{vmatrix} c_1 & b_1 \\ c_2 & b_2 \end{vmatrix}$	$\begin{vmatrix} a_1 & c_1 \\ a_2 & c_2 \end{vmatrix}$

EXAMPLE 3   Using Cramer's Rule for a 2 × 2 System

Use Cramer's Rule to solve $\begin{cases} 4x - 2y = 10 \\ 3x - 5y = 11 \end{cases}$.

Solution

To begin, find the determinant of the coefficient matrix.

$$D = \begin{vmatrix} 4 & -2 \\ 3 & -5 \end{vmatrix} = -20 - (-6) = -14$$

Because this determinant is not zero, apply Cramer's Rule.

$$x = \frac{D_x}{D} = \frac{\begin{vmatrix} 10 & -2 \\ 11 & -5 \end{vmatrix}}{-14} = \frac{(-50) - (-22)}{-14} = \frac{-28}{-14} = 2$$

$$y = \frac{D_y}{D} = \frac{\begin{vmatrix} 4 & 10 \\ 3 & 11 \end{vmatrix}}{-14} = \frac{44 - 30}{-14} = \frac{14}{-14} = -1$$

Therefore, the solution is $x = 2$ and $y = -1$. Check this in the original system.

Cramer's Rule generalizes easily to systems of n equations in n variables. The value of each variable is given as the quotient of two determinants. The denominator is the determinant of the coefficient matrix, and the numerator is the determinant of the matrix formed by replacing the column corresponding to the variable (being solved for) with the column representing the constants. For instance, the solution for x_3 in the following system is shown.

$$a_{11}x_1 + a_{12}x_2 + a_{13}x_3 = b_1$$
$$a_{21}x_1 + a_{22}x_2 + a_{23}x_3 = b_2$$
$$a_{31}x_1 + a_{32}x_2 + a_{33}x_3 = b_3$$

$$x_3 = \frac{|A_3|}{|A|} = \frac{\begin{vmatrix} a_{11} & a_{12} & b_1 \\ a_{21} & a_{22} & b_2 \\ a_{31} & a_{32} & b_3 \end{vmatrix}}{\begin{vmatrix} a_{11} & a_{12} & a_{13} \\ a_{21} & a_{22} & a_{23} \\ a_{31} & a_{32} & a_{33} \end{vmatrix}}$$

Cramer's Rule

If a system of n linear equations in n variables has a coefficient matrix A with a *nonzero* determinant $|A|$, the solution is

$$x_1 = \frac{|A_1|}{|A|}, \quad x_2 = \frac{|A_2|}{|A|}, \quad \ldots, \quad x_n = \frac{|A_n|}{|A|}$$

where the ith column of A_i is the column of constants in the system of equations. If the determinant of the coefficient matrix is zero, the system has either no solution or infinitely many solutions.

EXAMPLE 4   Using Cramer's Rule for a 3 × 3 System

Use Cramer's Rule, if possible, to solve the following system of linear equations.

$$\begin{cases} -x & + z = 4 \\ 2x - y + z = -3 \\ y - 3z = 1 \end{cases}$$

Solution

Using the matrix capabilities of a graphing utility to evaluate the determinant of the coefficient matrix A, you find that Cramer's Rule cannot be applied because $|A| = 0$.

EXAMPLE 5   Using Cramer's Rule for a 3 × 3 System

Use Cramer's Rule, if possible, to solve the system of linear equations.

$$\begin{cases} -x + 2y - 3z = 1 \\ 2x \quad + z = 0 \\ 3x - 4y + 4z = 2 \end{cases}$$

A computer animation of this example appears in the *Interactive* CD-ROM and *Internet* versions of this text.

Solution

The coefficient matrix

$$\begin{vmatrix} -1 & 2 & -3 \\ 2 & 0 & 1 \\ 3 & -4 & 4 \end{vmatrix}$$

can be expanded along the second row, as follows.

$$D = 2(-1)^3 \begin{vmatrix} 2 & -3 \\ -4 & 4 \end{vmatrix} + 0(-1)^4 \begin{vmatrix} -1 & -3 \\ 3 & 4 \end{vmatrix} + 1(-1)^5 \begin{vmatrix} -1 & 2 \\ 3 & -4 \end{vmatrix}$$

$$= \; = 2(4) + 0 + (1)(2) = 10$$

Because this determinant is not zero, you can apply Cramer's Rule.

$$x = \frac{D_x}{D} = \frac{\begin{vmatrix} 1 & 2 & -3 \\ 0 & 0 & 1 \\ 2 & -4 & 4 \end{vmatrix}}{10} = \frac{8}{10} = \frac{4}{5}$$

$$y = \frac{D_y}{D} = \frac{\begin{vmatrix} -1 & 1 & -3 \\ 2 & 0 & 1 \\ 3 & 2 & 4 \end{vmatrix}}{10} = \frac{-15}{10} = -\frac{3}{2}$$

$$z = \frac{D_z}{D} = \frac{\begin{vmatrix} -1 & 2 & 1 \\ 2 & 0 & 0 \\ 3 & -4 & 2 \end{vmatrix}}{10} = \frac{-16}{10} = -\frac{8}{5}$$

The solution is $\left(\frac{4}{5}, -\frac{3}{2}, -\frac{8}{5}\right)$. Check this in the original system.

Activities

1. Solve for z using Cramer's Rule.

$$\begin{cases} x - 2y - z = 4 \\ 4x + y + z = 7 \\ x + 3y - 4z = -1 \end{cases}$$

   Answer: $z = 0$

2. Use a determinant to find the area of the triangle with vertices $(1, -3)$, $(2, 3)$, and $(3, 1)$.

   Answer: 4 square units

Cryptography

A **cryptogram** is a message written according to a secret code. (The Greek word *kryptos* means "hidden.") Matrix multiplication can be used to encode and decode messages. To begin, you need to assign a number to each letter in the alphabet (with 0 assigned to a blank space), as follows.

0 = _	9 = I	18 = R
1 = A	10 = J	19 = S
2 = B	11 = K	20 = T
3 = C	12 = L	21 = U
4 = D	13 = M	22 = V
5 = E	14 = N	23 = W
6 = F	15 = O	24 = X
7 = G	16 = P	25 = Y
8 = H	17 = Q	26 = Z

Then the message is converted to numbers and partitioned into **uncoded row matrices**, each having n entries, as demonstrated in Example 6.

EXAMPLE 6   Forming Uncoded Row Matrices

Write the uncoded row matrices of order 1×3 for the message
    MEET ME MONDAY.

Solution

Partitioning the message (including blank spaces, but ignoring punctuation) into groups of three produces the following uncoded row matrices.

$$\begin{bmatrix} 13 & 5 & 5 \end{bmatrix} \quad \begin{bmatrix} 20 & 0 & 13 \end{bmatrix} \quad \begin{bmatrix} 5 & 0 & 13 \end{bmatrix} \quad \begin{bmatrix} 15 & 14 & 4 \end{bmatrix} \quad \begin{bmatrix} 1 & 25 & 0 \end{bmatrix}$$
$$\text{M} \quad \text{E} \quad \text{E} \quad \text{T} \qquad \text{M} \quad \text{E} \qquad \text{M} \quad \text{O} \quad \text{N} \quad \text{D} \quad \text{A} \quad \text{Y}$$

Note that a blank space is used to fill out the last uncoded row matrix.

To encode a message, choose an $n \times n$ invertible matrix A and multiply the uncoded row matrices by A (on the right) to obtain **coded row matrices**. Here is an example.

   Uncoded Matrix   Encoding Matrix A   Coded Matrix

$$\begin{bmatrix} 13 & 5 & 5 \end{bmatrix} \begin{bmatrix} 1 & -2 & 2 \\ -1 & 1 & 3 \\ 1 & -1 & -4 \end{bmatrix} = \begin{bmatrix} 13 & -26 & 21 \end{bmatrix}$$

This technique is further illustrated in Example 7.

EXAMPLE 7 Encoding a Message

Use the following matrix to encode the message MEET ME MONDAY.

$$A = \begin{bmatrix} 1 & -2 & 2 \\ -1 & 1 & 3 \\ 1 & -1 & -4 \end{bmatrix}$$

Solution

The coded row matrices are obtained by multiplying each of the uncoded row matrices found in Example 6 by the matrix A, as follows.

Uncoded Matrix   Encoding Matrix A   Coded Matrix

$$\begin{bmatrix} 13 & 5 & 5 \end{bmatrix} \begin{bmatrix} 1 & -2 & 2 \\ -1 & 1 & 3 \\ 1 & -1 & -4 \end{bmatrix} = \begin{bmatrix} 13 & -26 & 21 \end{bmatrix}$$

$$\begin{bmatrix} 20 & 0 & 13 \end{bmatrix} \begin{bmatrix} 1 & -2 & 2 \\ -1 & 1 & 3 \\ 1 & -1 & -4 \end{bmatrix} = \begin{bmatrix} 33 & -53 & -12 \end{bmatrix}$$

$$\begin{bmatrix} 5 & 0 & 13 \end{bmatrix} \begin{bmatrix} 1 & -2 & 2 \\ -1 & 1 & 3 \\ 1 & -1 & -4 \end{bmatrix} = \begin{bmatrix} 18 & -23 & -42 \end{bmatrix}$$

$$\begin{bmatrix} 15 & 14 & 4 \end{bmatrix} \begin{bmatrix} 1 & -2 & 2 \\ -1 & 1 & 3 \\ 1 & -1 & -4 \end{bmatrix} = \begin{bmatrix} 5 & -20 & 56 \end{bmatrix}$$

$$\begin{bmatrix} 1 & 25 & 0 \end{bmatrix} \begin{bmatrix} 1 & -2 & 2 \\ -1 & 1 & 3 \\ 1 & -1 & -4 \end{bmatrix} = \begin{bmatrix} -24 & 23 & 77 \end{bmatrix}$$

So, the sequence of coded row matrices is

$$\begin{bmatrix} 13 & -26 & 21 \end{bmatrix} \begin{bmatrix} 33 & -53 & -12 \end{bmatrix} \begin{bmatrix} 18 & -23 & -42 \end{bmatrix} \begin{bmatrix} 5 & -20 & 56 \end{bmatrix} \begin{bmatrix} -24 & 23 & 77 \end{bmatrix}.$$

Finally, removing the matrix notation produces the following cryptogram.

$$13 \ -26 \ 21 \ 33 \ -53 \ -12 \ 18 \ -23 \ -42 \ 5 \ -20 \ 56 \ -24 \ 23 \ 77$$

For those who do not know the matrix A, decoding the cryptogram found in Example 7 is difficult. But for an authorized receiver who knows the matrix A, decoding is simple. The receiver need only multiply the coded row matrices by A^{-1} (on the right) to retrieve the uncoded row matrices. Here is an example.

$$\underbrace{\begin{bmatrix} 13 & -26 & 21 \end{bmatrix}}_{\text{Coded}} \underbrace{\begin{bmatrix} -1 & -10 & -8 \\ -1 & -6 & -5 \\ 0 & -1 & -1 \end{bmatrix}}_{A^{-1}} = \underbrace{\begin{bmatrix} 13 & 5 & 5 \end{bmatrix}}_{\text{Uncoded}}$$

STUDY TIP

An efficient method for encoding the message at the left with your graphing utility is to enter A as a 3×3 matrix. Let B be the 5×3 matrix whose rows are the uncoded row matrices

$$B = \begin{bmatrix} 13 & 5 & 5 \\ 20 & 0 & 13 \\ 5 & 0 & 13 \\ 15 & 14 & 4 \\ 1 & 25 & 0 \end{bmatrix}.$$

The product BA gives the coded row matrices.

EXAMPLE 8   Decoding a Message

Use the inverse of the matrix

$$A = \begin{bmatrix} 1 & -2 & 2 \\ -1 & 1 & 3 \\ 1 & -1 & -4 \end{bmatrix}$$

to decode the cryptogram

$$13 \; -26 \; \; 21 \; \; 33 \; -53 \; -12 \; \; 18 \; -23 \; -42 \; \; 5 \; -20 \; \; 56 \; -24 \; \; 23 \; \; 77.$$

Solution
Partition the message into groups of three to form the coded row matrices. Then multiply each coded row matrix by A^{-1} (on the right).

Coded Matrix   Decoding Matrix A^{-1} Decoded Matrix

$$[13 \; -26 \; \; 21] \begin{bmatrix} -1 & -10 & -8 \\ -1 & -6 & -5 \\ 0 & -1 & -1 \end{bmatrix} = [13 \quad 5 \quad 5]$$

$$[33 \; -53 \; -12] \begin{bmatrix} -1 & -10 & -8 \\ -1 & -6 & -5 \\ 0 & -1 & -1 \end{bmatrix} = [20 \quad 0 \quad 13]$$

$$[18 \; -23 \; -42] \begin{bmatrix} -1 & -10 & -8 \\ -1 & -6 & -5 \\ 0 & -1 & -1 \end{bmatrix} = [5 \quad 0 \quad 13]$$

$$[5 \; -20 \quad 56] \begin{bmatrix} -1 & -10 & -8 \\ -1 & -6 & -5 \\ 0 & -1 & -1 \end{bmatrix} = [15 \quad 14 \quad 4]$$

$$[-24 \quad 23 \quad 77] \begin{bmatrix} -1 & -10 & -8 \\ -1 & -6 & -5 \\ 0 & -1 & -1 \end{bmatrix} = [1 \quad 25 \quad 0]$$

So, the message is as follows.

$$[13 \; \; 5 \; \; 5] \quad [20 \; \; 0 \; \; 13] \quad [5 \; \; 0 \; \; 13] \quad [15 \; 14 \; \; 4] \quad [1 \; \; 25 \; \; 0]$$

$$\text{M} \quad \text{E} \quad \text{E} \quad \text{T} \qquad \text{M} \quad \text{E} \qquad \text{M} \quad \text{O} \quad \text{N} \quad \text{D} \quad \text{A} \quad \text{Y}$$

Writing About Math   *Cryptography*

Use your school's library, the Internet, or some other reference source to research a few current real-life uses of cryptography. Write a short summary of these uses. Include a description of how messages are encoded and decoded in each case.

Group Activity Suggestion
Ask each group to work together to decide on their code's number scheme for assigning numbers to letters, to select a message to encode (some of the group members could work on the number scheme while the others are deciding on a message), and to find their invertible encoding matrix *A*. (A few group members could be asked to make up a matrix and the rest of the group could determine if it is invertible. You might also use this as an opportunity to discuss the creation of invertible matrices; suggest starting with the identity matrix and applying a series of elementary row operations.) Students can work together to partition their message into uncoded row matrices; each student can then be responsible for encoding several of the row matrices, and then the group can reassemble the coded message from each member's work. To decode the message they receive, the group can partition the message into coded row matrices, with each member being responsible for decoding several of these matrices, and then reassemble the message from each member's work. Alternatively, to save time, you might supply the entire class with a given number-to-letter code and an invertible matrix *A*. The groups must then only select a message to encode, divide up the message to encode with *A*, trade messages with another group, find A^{-1}, and decode the message they received.

In Exercise 26, Cramer's Rule does not apply.
In Exercises 12, 13, and 14, the points are not collinear.

6.5 • Applications of Matrices and Determinants   **485**

6.5   E x e r c i s e s

In Exercises 1–8, use a determinant to find the area of the triangle with the given vertices.

1.

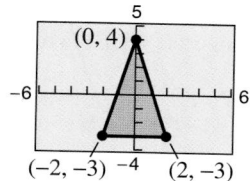

2.

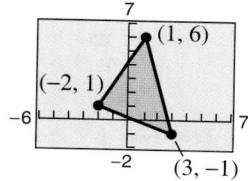

3. $(0, 0), (1, 5), (3, 1)$
4. $(0, 0), (4, 5), (5, -2)$
5. $\left(0, \frac{1}{2}\right), \left(\frac{5}{2}, 0\right), (4, 3)$
6. $\left(\frac{9}{2}, 0\right), (2, 6), \left(0, -\frac{3}{2}\right)$
7. $(4, 5), (6, 1), (7, 9)$
8. $(0, -2), (-1, 4), (3, 5)$

In Exercises 9 and 10, find x such that the triangle has an area of 4.

9. $(-5, 1), (0, 2), (-2, x)$
10. $(-4, 2), (-3, 5), (-1, x)$

In Exercises 11–14, determine whether the points are collinear.

11. $(3, -1), (0, -3), (12, 5)$
12. $(-3, -5), (6, 1), (10, 2)$
13. $\left(2, -\frac{1}{2}\right), (-4, 4), (6, -3)$
14. $\left(0, \frac{1}{2}\right), (2, -1), \left(-4, \frac{7}{2}\right)$

In Exercises 15 and 16, find x such that the points are collinear.

15. $(2, -5), (4, x), (5, -2)$
16. $(-6, 2), (-5, x), (-3, 5)$

In Exercises 17–24, use Cramer's Rule to solve (if possible) the system of equations.

17. $\begin{cases} 3x + 4y = -2 \\ 5x + 3y = 4 \end{cases}$

18. $\begin{cases} 4x - 3y = -10 \\ 6x + 9y = 12 \end{cases}$

19. $\begin{cases} -7x + 11y = -1 \\ 3x - 9y = 9 \end{cases}$

20. $\begin{cases} 6x - 5y = 17 \\ -13x + 3y = -76 \end{cases}$

21. $\begin{cases} -0.4x + 0.8y = 1.6 \\ 0.2x + 0.3y = 2.2 \end{cases}$

22. $\begin{cases} 2.4x - 1.3y = 14.63 \\ -4.6x + 0.5y = -11.51 \end{cases}$

23. $\begin{cases} 4x - y + z = -5 \\ 2x + 2y + 3z = 10 \\ 5x - 2y + 6z = 1 \end{cases}$

24. $\begin{cases} 4x - 2y + 3z = -2 \\ 2x + 2y + 5z = 16 \\ 8x - 5y - 2z = 4 \end{cases}$

In Exercises 25 and 26, use a graphing utility and Cramer's Rule to solve (if possible) the system of equations.

25. $\begin{cases} 3x + 3y + 5z = 1 \\ 3x + 5y + 9z = 2 \\ 5x + 9y + 17z = 4 \end{cases}$

26. $\begin{cases} 2x + 3y + 5z = 4 \\ 3x + 5y + 9z = 7 \\ 5x + 9y + 17z = 13 \end{cases}$

27. *Area of a Region*   A large region of forest has been infected with gypsy moths. The region is roughly triangular, as shown below. From the northernmost vertex A of the region, the distances to the other vertices are 25 miles south and 10 miles east (for vertex B), and 20 miles south and 28 miles east (for vertex C). Use a graphing utility to approximate the number of square miles in this region.

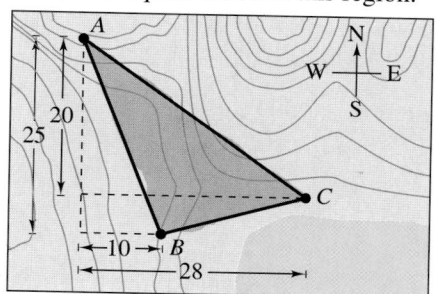

28. *Area of a Region*   You own a triangular tract of land, as shown below. To estimate the number of square feet in the tract, you start at one vertex, walk 65 feet east and 50 feet north to the second vertex, and then walk 85 feet west and 30 feet north to the third vertex. Use a graphing utility to determine how many square feet there are in the tract of land.

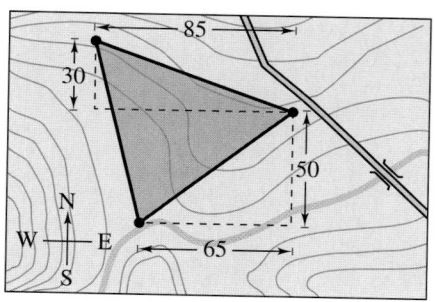

In Exercises 29 and 30, find the uncoded 1×3 row matrices for the message. Then encode the message using the matrix.

Message · *Matrix*

29. TROUBLE IN RIVER CITY $\begin{bmatrix} 1 & -1 & 0 \\ 1 & 0 & -1 \\ -6 & 2 & 3 \end{bmatrix}$

30. PLEASE SEND MONEY $\begin{bmatrix} 4 & 2 & 1 \\ -3 & -3 & -1 \\ 3 & 2 & 1 \end{bmatrix}$

In Exercises 31–34, write a cryptogram for the message using the matrix

$$A = \begin{bmatrix} 1 & 2 & 2 \\ 3 & 7 & 9 \\ -1 & -4 & -7 \end{bmatrix}.$$

31. SHOW ME THE MONEY

32. ICEBERG DEAD AHEAD

33. HAPPY BIRTHDAY

34. OPERATION OVERLORD

In Exercises 35 and 36, use A^{-1} to decode the cryptogram.

35. $A = \begin{bmatrix} 1 & 2 \\ 3 & 5 \end{bmatrix}$ 11 21 64 112 25 50 29 53
23 46 40 75 55 92

36. $A = \begin{bmatrix} -5 & 2 \\ -7 & 3 \end{bmatrix}$ -136 58 -173 72 -120 51
-95 38 -178 73 -70 28
-242 101 -115 47 -90 36
-115 49 -199 82

In Exercises 37 and 38, decode the cryptogram by using the inverse of the matrix

$$A = \begin{bmatrix} 1 & 2 & 2 \\ 3 & 7 & 9 \\ -1 & -4 & -7 \end{bmatrix}.$$

37. 20 17 -15 -12 -56 -104 1 -25 -65 62
143 181

38. 13 -9 -59 61 112 106 -17 -73 -131 11
24 29 65 144 172

39. The following cryptogram was encoded with a 2×2 matrix.

8 21 -15 -10 -13 -13 5 10 5 25 5 19 -1
6 20 40 -18 -18 1 16

The last word of the message is _RON. What is the message?

40. The following cryptogram was encoded with a 2×2 matrix.

5 2 25 11 -2 -7 -15 -15 32 14 -8 -13
38 19 -19 -19 37 16

The last word of the message is _SUE. What is the message?

Synthesis

True or False? **In Exercises 41 and 42, determine whether the statement is true or false. Justify your answer.**

41. Cramer's Rule cannot be used to solve a system of linear equations if the determinant of the coefficient matrix is zero.

42. In a system of linear equations, if the determinant of the coefficient matrix is zero, the system has no solution.

43. *Writing* At this point in the book, you have learned several methods for solving a system of linear equations. Briefly describe which method(s) you find easiest to use and which method(s) you find most difficult to use.

Review

In Exercises 44–47, find the equation of the line that passes through the two given points.

44. $(-1, 5), (7, 3)$ 45. $(0, -6), (-2, 10)$

46. $(3, -3), (10, -1)$ 47. $(-4, 12), (4, 2)$

In Exercises 48 and 49, sketch the graph of the rational function.

48. $f(x) = \dfrac{2x^2}{x^2 + 4}$ 49. $f(x) = \dfrac{2x}{x^2 + 3x - 18}$

In Exercises 50 and 51, use any method to solve the system of equations.

50. $\begin{cases} -x - 3y + 5z = -14 \\ 4x + 2y - z = -1 \\ 5x - 3y + 2z = -11 \end{cases}$

51. $\begin{cases} 5x - y - z = 7 \\ -2x + 3y + z = -5 \\ 4x + 10y - 5z = -37 \end{cases}$

6 Chapter Summary

What did you learn?

Section 6.1

Review Exercises

- [ ] How to write matrices and identify their orders — 1–12
- [ ] How to perform elementary row operations on matrices — 13–18
- [ ] How to use matrices and Gaussian elimination to solve systems of linear equations — 19–26
- [ ] How to use matrices and Gauss-Jordan elimination to solve systems of linear equations — 27–36

Section 6.2

- [ ] How to decide whether two matrices are equal — 37–40
- [ ] How to add and subtract matrices and multiply matrices by a real number — 41–48
- [ ] How to solve matrix equations — 49–52
- [ ] How to multiply two matrices — 53–62
- [ ] How to use matrix operations to model and solve real-life problems — 63, 64

Section 6.3

- [ ] How to verify that two matrices are inverses of each other — 65–68
- [ ] How to use Gauss-Jordan elimination to find inverses of matrices — 69–76
- [ ] How to use a formula to find inverses of 2×2 matrices — 77–82
- [ ] How to use inverse matrices to solve systems of linear equations — 83–96

Section 6.4

- [ ] How to find determinants of 2×2 matrices — 97–100
- [ ] How to find minors and cofactors of square matrices — 101–104
- [ ] How to find determinants of square matrices — 105–114
- [ ] How to find determinants of triangular matrices — 115, 116

Section 6.5

- [ ] How to use determinants to find areas of triangles — 117–120
- [ ] How to use determinants to decide whether points are collinear — 121–124
- [ ] How to use Cramer's Rule to solve systems of linear equations — 125–140
- [ ] How to use matrices to encode and decode messages — 141–144

In Exercises 24, 26, and 36, the system has no solution. In Exercise 25, the system has infinitely many solutions. In Exercises 42 and 54, the operation is not possible. In Exercises 76, 80, 81, 95, and 96, the inverse does not exist. In Exercise 123, the points are not collinear. In Exercise 133, Cramer's Rule does not apply.

6 Review Exercises

6.1 In Exercises 1–6, determine the order of the matrix.

1. $\begin{bmatrix} -3 \\ 1 \\ 10 \end{bmatrix}$

2. $\begin{bmatrix} 3 & -1 & 0 & 6 \\ -2 & 7 & 1 & 4 \end{bmatrix}$

3. $\begin{bmatrix} 14 \end{bmatrix}$

4. $\begin{bmatrix} 6 & 7 & -5 & 0 & -8 \end{bmatrix}$

5. $\begin{bmatrix} 8 & 4 \\ -1 & 6 \\ 0 & 11 \\ 12 & 9 \end{bmatrix}$

6. $\begin{bmatrix} -1 & 0 & 5 \\ 2 & 3 & 20 \end{bmatrix}$

In Exercises 7–10, form the augmented matrix for the system of linear equations.

7. $\begin{cases} 3x - 10y = 15 \\ 5x + 4y = 22 \end{cases}$

8. $\begin{cases} -x + y = 12 \\ 10x - 4y = -90 \end{cases}$

9. $\begin{cases} 8x - 7y + 4z = 12 \\ 3x - 5y + 2z = 20 \\ 5x + 3y - 3z = 26 \end{cases}$

10. $\begin{cases} 3x - 5y + z = 25 \\ -4x \qquad - 2z = -14 \\ 6x + y \qquad = 15 \end{cases}$

In Exercises 11 and 12, write the system of linear equations represented by the augmented matrix. (Use variables $x, y, z,$ and w.)

11. $\begin{bmatrix} 5 & 1 & 7 & \vdots & -9 \\ 4 & 2 & 0 & \vdots & 10 \\ 9 & 4 & 2 & \vdots & 3 \end{bmatrix}$

12. $\begin{bmatrix} 13 & 16 & 7 & 3 & \vdots & 2 \\ 1 & 21 & 8 & 5 & \vdots & 12 \\ 4 & 10 & -4 & 3 & \vdots & -1 \end{bmatrix}$

In Exercises 13 and 14, write the matrix in reduced row-echelon form.

13. $\begin{bmatrix} 0 & 1 & 1 \\ 1 & 2 & 3 \\ 2 & 2 & 2 \end{bmatrix}$

14. $\begin{bmatrix} 1 & 1 & 1 & 0 \\ 1 & 1 & 0 & 1 \\ 1 & 0 & 1 & 1 \\ 0 & 1 & 1 & 1 \end{bmatrix}$

In Exercises 15–18, use the matrix capabilities of a graphing utility to write the matrix in reduced row-echelon form.

15. $\begin{bmatrix} 3 & -2 & 1 & 0 \\ 4 & -3 & 0 & 1 \end{bmatrix}$

16. $\begin{bmatrix} 1 & 1 & 2 & 1 & 0 & 0 \\ -1 & 0 & 3 & 0 & 1 & 0 \\ 1 & 2 & 8 & 0 & 0 & 1 \end{bmatrix}$

17. $\begin{bmatrix} 1 & 3 & 4 \\ 0 & 1 & 1 \\ 2 & 4 & 6 \end{bmatrix}$

18. $\begin{bmatrix} 4 & 8 & 16 \\ 3 & -1 & 2 \\ -2 & 10 & 12 \end{bmatrix}$

In Exercises 19–26, use Gaussian elimination with back-substitution to solve the system of equations.

19. $\begin{cases} 5x + 4y = 2 \\ -x + y = -22 \end{cases}$

20. $\begin{cases} 2x - 5y = 2 \\ 3x - 7y = 1 \end{cases}$

21. $\begin{cases} 2x + y = 0.3 \\ 3x - y = -1.3 \end{cases}$

22. $\begin{cases} 0.2x - 0.1y = 0.07 \\ 0.4x - 0.5y = -0.01 \end{cases}$

23. $\begin{cases} 2x + 3y + 3z = 3 \\ 6x + 6y + 12z = 13 \\ 12x + 9y - z = 2 \end{cases}$

24. $\begin{cases} x + 2y + 6z = 1 \\ 2x + 5y + 15z = 4 \\ 3x + y + 3z = -6 \end{cases}$

25. $\begin{cases} 3x + 21y - 29z = -1 \\ 2x + 15y - 21z = 0 \end{cases}$

26. $\begin{cases} x + 2y + w = 3 \\ -3y + 3z = 0 \\ 4x + 4y + z + 2w = 0 \\ 2x + z = 3 \end{cases}$

In Exercises 27–30, use Gauss-Jordan elimination to solve the system of equations.

27. $\begin{cases} -x + y + 2z = 1 \\ 2x + 3y + z = -2 \\ 5x + 4y + 2z = 4 \end{cases}$

28. $\begin{cases} 4x + 4y + 4z = 5 \\ 4x - 2y - 8z = 1 \\ 5x + 3y + 8z = 6 \end{cases}$

29. $\begin{cases} 2x - y + 9z = -8 \\ -x - 3y + 4z = -15 \\ 5x + 2y - z = 17 \end{cases}$

30. $\begin{cases} -3x + y + 7z = -20 \\ 5x - 2y - z = 34 \\ -x + y + 4z = -8 \end{cases}$

In Exercises 31–36, use the matrix capabilities of a graphing utility to reduce the augmented matrix and solve the system of equations.

31. $\begin{cases} x - 3y = -2 \\ x + y = 2 \end{cases}$

32. $\begin{cases} -x + 3y = 5 \\ 4x - y = 2 \end{cases}$

33. $\begin{cases} x + 2y - z = 7 \\ - y - z = 4 \\ 4x - z = 16 \end{cases}$

34. $\begin{cases} 3x + 6z = 0 \\ -2x + y = 5 \\ y + 2z = 3 \end{cases}$

35. $\begin{cases} 3x - y + 5z - 2w = -44 \\ x + 6y + 4z - w = 1 \\ 5x - y + z + 3w = -15 \\ 4y - z - 8w = 58 \end{cases}$

36. $\begin{cases} 4x + 12y + 2z = 20 \\ x + 6y + 4z = 12 \\ x + 6y + z = 8 \\ -2x - 10y - 2z = -10 \end{cases}$

6.2 **In Exercises 37–40, find x and y.**

37. $\begin{bmatrix} -1 & x \\ y & 9 \end{bmatrix} = \begin{bmatrix} -1 & 12 \\ -7 & 9 \end{bmatrix}$

38. $\begin{bmatrix} -1 & 0 \\ x & 5 \\ -4 & y \end{bmatrix} = \begin{bmatrix} -1 & 0 \\ 8 & 5 \\ -4 & 0 \end{bmatrix}$

39. $\begin{bmatrix} x + 3 & 4 & -4y \\ 0 & -3 & 2 \\ -2 & y + 5 & 6x \end{bmatrix} = \begin{bmatrix} 5x - 1 & 4 & -44 \\ 0 & -3 & 2 \\ -2 & 16 & 6 \end{bmatrix}$

40. $\begin{bmatrix} -9 & 4 & 2 & -5 \\ 0 & -3 & 7 & -4 \\ 6 & -1 & 1 & 0 \end{bmatrix} = \begin{bmatrix} -9 & 4 & x - 10 & -5 \\ 0 & -3 & 7 & 2y \\ \frac{1}{2}x & -1 & 1 & 0 \end{bmatrix}$

In Exercises 41–46, perform the matrix operations. If it is not possible, explain why.

41. $\begin{bmatrix} 7 & 3 \\ -1 & 5 \end{bmatrix} + \begin{bmatrix} 10 & -20 \\ 14 & -3 \end{bmatrix}$

42. $\begin{bmatrix} -11 & 16 & 19 \\ -7 & -2 & 1 \end{bmatrix} - \begin{bmatrix} 6 & 0 \\ 8 & -4 \\ -2 & 10 \end{bmatrix}$

43. $\begin{bmatrix} 2 & 1 & 0 \\ 0 & 5 & -4 \end{bmatrix} - 3\begin{bmatrix} 5 & 3 & -6 \\ 0 & -2 & 5 \end{bmatrix}$

44. $-2\begin{bmatrix} 1 & 2 \\ 5 & -4 \\ 6 & 0 \end{bmatrix} + 8\begin{bmatrix} 7 & 1 \\ 1 & 2 \\ 1 & 4 \end{bmatrix}$

45. $-\begin{bmatrix} 8 & -1 & 8 \\ -2 & 4 & 12 \\ 0 & -6 & 0 \end{bmatrix} - 5\begin{bmatrix} -2 & 0 & -4 \\ 3 & -1 & 1 \\ 6 & 12 & -8 \end{bmatrix}$

46. $6\begin{bmatrix} -4 & -1 & -3 & 4 \\ 2 & -5 & 7 & -10 \end{bmatrix} + 2\begin{bmatrix} -1 & 1 & 13 & -7 \\ 14 & -3 & 8 & -1 \end{bmatrix}$

In Exercises 47 and 48, use a graphing utility to perform the matrix operations.

47. $3\begin{bmatrix} 8 & -2 & 5 \\ 1 & 3 & -1 \end{bmatrix} + 6\begin{bmatrix} 4 & -2 & -3 \\ 2 & 7 & 6 \end{bmatrix}$

48. $-5\begin{bmatrix} 2 & 0 \\ 7 & -2 \\ 8 & 2 \end{bmatrix} + 4\begin{bmatrix} 4 & -2 \\ 6 & 11 \\ -1 & 3 \end{bmatrix}$

In Exercises 49–52, solve for X given

$$A = \begin{bmatrix} -4 & 0 \\ 1 & -5 \\ -3 & 2 \end{bmatrix} \quad \text{and} \quad B = \begin{bmatrix} 1 & 2 \\ -2 & 1 \\ 4 & 4 \end{bmatrix}.$$

49. $X = 3A - 2B$

50. $6X = 4A + 3B$

51. $3X + 2A = B$

52. $2A - 5B = 3X$

In Exercises 53–58, multiply the matrices. If it is not possible, explain why.

53. $\begin{bmatrix} 1 & 2 \\ 5 & -4 \\ 6 & 0 \end{bmatrix}\begin{bmatrix} 6 & -2 & 8 \\ 4 & 0 & 0 \end{bmatrix}$

54. $\begin{bmatrix} 1 & 5 & 6 \\ 2 & -4 & 0 \end{bmatrix}\begin{bmatrix} 6 & -2 & 8 \\ 4 & 0 & 0 \end{bmatrix}$

55. $\begin{bmatrix} 1 & 5 & 6 \\ 2 & -4 & 0 \end{bmatrix}\begin{bmatrix} 6 & 4 \\ -2 & 0 \\ 8 & 0 \end{bmatrix}$

56. $\begin{bmatrix} 1 & 3 & 2 \\ 0 & 2 & -4 \\ 0 & 0 & 3 \end{bmatrix}\begin{bmatrix} 4 & -3 & 2 \\ 0 & 3 & -1 \\ 0 & 0 & 2 \end{bmatrix}$

57. $\begin{bmatrix} 2 & 1 \\ 6 & 0 \end{bmatrix}\left(\begin{bmatrix} 4 & 2 \\ -3 & 1 \end{bmatrix} + \begin{bmatrix} -2 & 4 \\ 0 & 4 \end{bmatrix}\right)$

58. $\begin{bmatrix} 1 & -1 \\ 4 & 2 \end{bmatrix}\left(\begin{bmatrix} 0 & 3 \\ 1 & 2 \end{bmatrix}\begin{bmatrix} 1 & 0 \\ 5 & -3 \end{bmatrix}\right)$

In Exercises 59 and 60, use a graphing utility to multiply the matrices.

59. $\begin{bmatrix} 4 & 1 \\ 11 & -7 \\ 12 & 3 \end{bmatrix} \begin{bmatrix} 3 & -5 & 6 \\ 2 & -2 & -2 \end{bmatrix}$

60. $\begin{bmatrix} -2 & 3 & 10 \\ 4 & -2 & 2 \end{bmatrix} \begin{bmatrix} 1 & 1 \\ -5 & 2 \\ 3 & 2 \end{bmatrix}$

61. Write the system of linear equations represented by the matrix equation

$$\begin{bmatrix} 5 & 4 \\ -1 & 1 \end{bmatrix} \begin{bmatrix} x \\ y \end{bmatrix} = \begin{bmatrix} 2 \\ -22 \end{bmatrix}.$$

62. Write the matrix equation $AX = B$ for the following system of linear equations.

$$\begin{cases} 2x + 3y + z = 10 \\ 2x - 3y - 3z = 22 \\ 4x - 2y + 3z = -2 \end{cases}$$

63. *Manufacturing* A manufacturing company produces three models of a product that are shipped to two warehouses. The number of units of model i that are shipped to warehouse j is represented by a_{ij} in the matrix

$$A = \begin{bmatrix} 8200 & 7400 \\ 6500 & 9800 \\ 5400 & 4800 \end{bmatrix}.$$

The price per unit is represented by the matrix $B = [\$10.25 \quad \$14.50 \quad \$17.75]$.

Use a graphing utility to compute BA and interpret the result.

64. Suppose in Exercise 63 that the number of units of each model shipped to the warehouse is increased by 25% for the following shipment. Use your graphing utility to find a new matrix A_n representing the number of units being shipped to the warehouses. Then calculate BA_n.

6.3 **In Exercises 65–68, show that B is the inverse of A.**

65. $A = \begin{bmatrix} -4 & -1 \\ 7 & 2 \end{bmatrix}$, $B = \begin{bmatrix} -2 & -1 \\ 7 & 4 \end{bmatrix}$

66. $A = \begin{bmatrix} 5 & -1 \\ 11 & -2 \end{bmatrix}$, $B = \begin{bmatrix} -2 & 1 \\ -11 & 5 \end{bmatrix}$

67. $A = \begin{bmatrix} 1 & 1 & 0 \\ 1 & 0 & 1 \\ 6 & 2 & 3 \end{bmatrix}$, $B = \begin{bmatrix} -2 & -3 & 1 \\ 3 & 3 & -1 \\ 2 & 4 & -1 \end{bmatrix}$

68. $A = \begin{bmatrix} 1 & -1 & 0 \\ -1 & 0 & -1 \\ 8 & -4 & 2 \end{bmatrix}$, $B = \begin{bmatrix} -2 & 1 & \frac{1}{2} \\ -3 & 1 & \frac{1}{2} \\ 2 & -2 & -\frac{1}{2} \end{bmatrix}$

In Exercises 69–72, use Gauss-Jordan elimination to find the inverse of the matrix (if it exists).

69. $\begin{bmatrix} -6 & 5 \\ -5 & 4 \end{bmatrix}$

70. $\begin{bmatrix} -3 & -5 \\ 2 & 3 \end{bmatrix}$

71. $\begin{bmatrix} -1 & -2 & -2 \\ 3 & 7 & 9 \\ 1 & 4 & 7 \end{bmatrix}$

72. $\begin{bmatrix} 0 & -2 & 1 \\ -5 & -2 & -3 \\ 7 & 3 & 4 \end{bmatrix}$

In Exercises 73–76, use a graphing utility to find the inverse of the matrix (if it exists).

73. $\begin{bmatrix} 2 & 6 \\ 3 & -6 \end{bmatrix}$

74. $\begin{bmatrix} 3 & -10 \\ 4 & 2 \end{bmatrix}$

75. $\begin{bmatrix} 2 & 0 & 3 \\ -1 & 1 & 1 \\ 2 & -2 & 1 \end{bmatrix}$

76. $\begin{bmatrix} 1 & 4 & 6 \\ 2 & -3 & 1 \\ -1 & 18 & 16 \end{bmatrix}$

In Exercises 77–82, use the formula on page 464 to find the inverse of the matrix (if it exists).

77. $\begin{bmatrix} -7 & 2 \\ -8 & 2 \end{bmatrix}$

78. $\begin{bmatrix} 10 & 4 \\ 7 & 3 \end{bmatrix}$

79. $\begin{bmatrix} -6 & -5 \\ 3 & 3 \end{bmatrix}$

80. $\begin{bmatrix} 10 & 45 \\ 2 & 9 \end{bmatrix}$

81. $\begin{bmatrix} -1 & 20 \\ \frac{3}{10} & -6 \end{bmatrix}$

82. $\begin{bmatrix} -\frac{3}{4} & \frac{5}{2} \\ -\frac{4}{5} & -\frac{8}{3} \end{bmatrix}$

In Exercises 83–90, use an inverse matrix (if it exists) to solve the system of linear equations.

83. $\begin{cases} -x + 4y = 8 \\ 2x - 7y = -5 \end{cases}$

84. $\begin{cases} 5x - y = 13 \\ -9x + 2y = -24 \end{cases}$

85. $\begin{cases} -3x + 10y = 8 \\ 5x - 17y = -13 \end{cases}$

86. $\begin{cases} 4x - 2y = -10 \\ -19x + 9y = 47 \end{cases}$

87. $\begin{cases} 3x + 2y - z = 6 \\ x - y + 2z = -1 \\ 5x + y + z = 7 \end{cases}$

88. $\begin{cases} -x + 4y - 2z = 12 \\ 2x - 9y + 5z = -25 \\ -x + 5y - 4z = 10 \end{cases}$

89. $\begin{cases} -2x + y + 2z = -13 \\ -x - 4y + z = -11 \\ -y - z = 0 \end{cases}$

90. $\begin{cases} 3x - y + 5z = -14 \\ -x + y + 6z = 8 \\ -8x + 4y - z = 44 \end{cases}$

In Exercises 91–96, use a graphing utility to solve the system of linear equations using the inverse of the coefficient matrix (if it exists).

91. $\begin{cases} x + 2y = -1 \\ 3x + 4y = -5 \end{cases}$

92. $\begin{cases} x + 3y = 23 \\ -6x + 2y = -18 \end{cases}$

93. $\begin{cases} -3x - 3y - 4z = 2 \\ y + z = -1 \\ 4x + 3y + 4z = -1 \end{cases}$

94. $\begin{cases} x + 3y + 2z = 2 \\ -2x - 5y - z = 10 \\ 2x + 4y = -12 \end{cases}$

95. $\begin{cases} -x + y + z = 6 \\ 4x - 3y + z = 20 \\ 2x - y + 3z = 8 \end{cases}$

96. $\begin{cases} 2x + 3y - 4z = 1 \\ x - y + 2z = -4 \\ 3x + 7y - 10z = 0 \end{cases}$

6.4 In Exercises 97–100, find the determinant of the matrix.

97. $\begin{bmatrix} 8 & 5 \\ 2 & -4 \end{bmatrix}$

98. $\begin{bmatrix} -9 & 11 \\ 7 & -4 \end{bmatrix}$

99. $\begin{bmatrix} 50 & -30 \\ 10 & 5 \end{bmatrix}$

100. $\begin{bmatrix} 14 & -24 \\ 12 & -15 \end{bmatrix}$

In Exercises 101–104, find all (a) minors and (b) cofactors of the matrix.

101. $\begin{bmatrix} 2 & -1 \\ 7 & 4 \end{bmatrix}$

102. $\begin{bmatrix} 3 & 6 \\ 5 & -4 \end{bmatrix}$

103. $\begin{bmatrix} 3 & 2 & -1 \\ -2 & 5 & 0 \\ 1 & 8 & 6 \end{bmatrix}$

104. $\begin{bmatrix} 8 & 3 & 4 \\ 6 & 5 & -9 \\ -4 & 1 & 2 \end{bmatrix}$

In Exercises 105 and 106, find the determinant of the matrix by the method of expansion by cofactors. Expand using the indicated row or column.

105. $\begin{bmatrix} 5 & 0 & -3 \\ 0 & 12 & 4 \\ 1 & 6 & 3 \end{bmatrix}$ (a) Row 2 (b) Column 2

106. $\begin{bmatrix} 10 & -5 & 5 \\ 30 & 0 & 10 \\ 0 & 10 & 1 \end{bmatrix}$ (a) Row 3 (b) Column 1

In Exercises 107–114, evaluate the determinant. Expand by cofactors on the row or column that appears to make the computations easiest.

107. $\begin{vmatrix} -2 & 4 & 1 \\ -6 & 0 & 2 \\ 5 & 3 & 4 \end{vmatrix}$

108. $\begin{vmatrix} 4 & 7 & -1 \\ 2 & -3 & 4 \\ -5 & 1 & -1 \end{vmatrix}$

109. $\begin{vmatrix} 1 & 0 & -2 \\ 0 & 1 & 0 \\ -2 & 0 & 1 \end{vmatrix}$

110. $\begin{vmatrix} 0 & 3 & 1 \\ 5 & -2 & 1 \\ 1 & 6 & 1 \end{vmatrix}$

111. $\begin{vmatrix} 3 & 0 & -4 & 0 \\ 0 & 8 & 1 & 2 \\ 6 & 1 & 8 & 2 \\ 0 & 3 & -4 & 1 \end{vmatrix}$

112. $\begin{vmatrix} -5 & 6 & 0 & 0 \\ 0 & 1 & -1 & 2 \\ -3 & 4 & -5 & 1 \\ 1 & 6 & 0 & 3 \end{vmatrix}$

113. $\begin{vmatrix} 5 & 3 & 0 & 6 \\ 4 & 6 & 4 & 12 \\ 0 & 2 & -3 & 4 \\ 0 & 1 & -2 & 2 \end{vmatrix}$

114. $\begin{vmatrix} 1 & 4 & 3 & 2 \\ -5 & 6 & 2 & 1 \\ 0 & 0 & 0 & 0 \\ 3 & -2 & 1 & 5 \end{vmatrix}$

In Exercises 115 and 116, evaluate the determinant.

115. $\begin{vmatrix} 8 & 6 & 0 & 2 \\ 0 & -1 & 1 & -4 \\ 0 & 0 & 4 & 5 \\ 0 & 0 & 0 & 3 \end{vmatrix}$

116. $\begin{vmatrix} -5 & 0 & 0 & 0 \\ 7 & -2 & 0 & 0 \\ 11 & 21 & 2 & 0 \\ -6 & 9 & 12 & 14 \end{vmatrix}$

6.5 In Exercises 117–120, use a determinant to find the area of the triangle with the given vertices.

117. $(1, 0), (5, 0), (5, 8)$

118. $(-4, 0), (4, 0), (0, 6)$

119. $\left(\frac{1}{2}, 1\right), \left(2, -\frac{5}{2}\right), \left(\frac{3}{2}, 1\right)$

120. $\left(\frac{3}{2}, 1\right), \left(4, -\frac{1}{2}\right), (4, 2)$

In Exercises 121–124, use a determinant to decide whether the points are collinear.

121. $(-1, 7), (3, -9), (-3, 15)$

122. $(0, -5), (-2, -6), (8, -1)$

123. $(9, -10), (4, -1), (1, 5)$

124. $(-2, -8), (3, 7), (7, 19)$

In Exercises 125–130, use Cramer's Rule to solve (if possible) the system of equations.

125. $\begin{cases} x + 2y = 5 \\ -x + y = 1 \end{cases}$

126. $\begin{cases} 2x - y = -10 \\ 3x + 2y = -1 \end{cases}$

127. $\begin{cases} 5x - 2y = 6 \\ -11x + 3y = -23 \end{cases}$

128. $\begin{cases} 3x + 8y = -7 \\ 9x - 5y = 37 \end{cases}$

129. $\begin{cases} -2x + 3y - 5z = -11 \\ 4x - y + z = -3 \\ -x - 4y + 6z = 15 \end{cases}$

130. $\begin{cases} 5x - 2y + z = 15 \\ 3x - 3y - z = -7 \\ 2x - y - 7z = -3 \end{cases}$

In Exercises 131–134, use a graphing utility and Cramer's Rule (if possible) to solve the system of equations.

131. $\begin{cases} 3x + 6y = 5 \\ 6x + 14y = 11 \end{cases}$

132. $\begin{cases} -0.4x + 0.8y = 1.6 \\ 0.2x + 0.3y = 2.2 \end{cases}$

133. $\begin{cases} 5x - 3y + 2z = 2 \\ 2x + 2y - 3z = 3 \\ x - 7y + 8z = -4 \end{cases}$

134. $\begin{cases} 14x - 21y - 7z = 10 \\ -4x + 2y - 2z = 4 \\ 56x - 21y + 7z = 5 \end{cases}$

In Exercises 135–140, use Cramer's Rule to solve.

135. *Mixture Problem* A florist wants to arrange a dozen flowers consisting of two varieties: carnations and roses. Carnations cost $0.75 each and roses cost $1.50 each. How many of each should the florist use so that the arrangement will cost $12.00?

136. *Mixture Problem* One hundred liters of a 60% acid solution is obtained by mixing a 75% solution with a 50% solution. How many liters of each must be used to obtain the desired mixture?

137. *Fitting a Parabola to Three Points* Find an equation of the parabola $y = ax^2 + bx + c$ that passes through the points $(-1, 2)$, $(0, 3)$, and $(1, 6)$.

138. *Fitting a Parabola to Three Points* Find an equation of the parabola $y = ax^2 + bx + c$ that passes through the points $(0, 1)$, $(2, -11)$, and $(-3, 4)$.

139. *Break-Even Point* A business invests $25,000 in equipment to produce a product. Each unit of the product costs $3.75 to produce and is sold for $5.25. How many items must be sold before the business breaks even?

140. *Break-Even Point* A business invests $48,000 in equipment to produce a product. Each unit of the product costs $2.50 to produce and is sold for $8.75. How many items must be sold before the business breaks even?

In Exercises 141 and 142, find the uncoded 1×3 row matrices for the message. Then encode the message using the matrix.

Message	Matrix

141. LOOK OUT BELOW $\quad \begin{bmatrix} 2 & -2 & 0 \\ 3 & 0 & -3 \\ -6 & 2 & 3 \end{bmatrix}$

142. RETURN TO BASE $\quad \begin{bmatrix} 2 & 1 & 0 \\ -6 & -6 & -2 \\ 3 & 2 & 1 \end{bmatrix}$

In Exercises 143 and 144, decode the cryptogram by using the inverse of the matrix.

$$A = \begin{bmatrix} -5 & 4 & -3 \\ 10 & -7 & 6 \\ 8 & -6 & 5 \end{bmatrix}.$$

143. -5 11 -2 370 -265 225 -57 48 -33 32 -15 20 245 -171 147

144. 145 -105 92 264 -188 160 23 -16 15 129 -84 78 -9 8 -5 159 -118 100 219 -152 133 370 -265 225 -105 84 -63

Synthesis

True or False? In Exercises 145 and 146, determine whether the statement is true or false. Justify your answer.

145. It is possible to find the determinant of a 4×5 matrix.

146. $\begin{vmatrix} a_{11} & a_{12} & a_{13} \\ a_{21} & a_{22} & a_{23} \\ a_{31} + c_1 & a_{32} + c_2 & a_{33} + c_3 \end{vmatrix} =$

$\begin{vmatrix} a_{11} & a_{12} & a_{13} \\ a_{21} & a_{22} & a_{23} \\ a_{31} & a_{32} & a_{33} \end{vmatrix} + \begin{vmatrix} a_{11} & a_{12} & a_{13} \\ a_{21} & a_{22} & a_{23} \\ c_1 & c_2 & c_3 \end{vmatrix}$

147. What is the relationship between the three elementary row operations on an augmented matrix and the operations that lead to equivalent systems of equations?

Chapter Project *Solving Systems of Equations*

Matrices have always been a powerful mathematical tool—especially for dealing with problems that involve a lot of data. With technology available to perform the calculations, matrices have also become a practical mathematical tool. In this project, you will use matrices to represent linear systems that model real-life data.

Three iron alloys contain different percents of carbon, chromium, and iron, shown in the matrix at the right. Alloy X is a type of wrought iron, alloy Y is a type of stainless steel, and alloy Z is a type of cast iron. How much of each of the three alloys can you make with 15 tons of carbon, 39 tons of chromium, and 546 tons of iron?

	Alloy X	Alloy Y	Alloy Z
Carbon	1%	1%	4%
Chromium	0%	15%	3%
Iron	99%	84%	93%

a. Let x, y, and z represent the amounts of the three iron alloys. Write a linear system to model the situation.

b. Write the matrix equation $AX = B$ that represents this system.

c. With a graphing utility or computer, solve the equation in part (b) for X by finding $X = A^{-1}B$.

Chapter Project Investigations

1. Three different gold alloys contain the percents of gold, copper, and silver shown in the following matrix. You have 20,144 grams of gold, 766 grams of copper, and 1990 grams of silver. How much of each alloy can you make?

Percent by Weight

	Alloy X	Alloy Y	Alloy Z
Gold	94%	92%	80%
Copper	4%	2%	4%
Silver	2%	6%	16%

2. The percent (by age group) of the total amounts spent on three types of shoes in 1996 is shown in the following matrix. The total amounts (in millions) spent by each age group on the three types of shoes were \$518.97 (14–17 age group), \$336.16 (18–24 age group), and \$753.37 (25–34 age group). How many dollars worth of gym shoes, jogging shoes, and walking shoes were sold in 1996? (Source: National Sporting Goods Association)

		Gym shoes	Jogging shoes	Walking shoes
Age Group	14–17	0.14	0.13	0.03
	18–24	0.05	0.10	0.04
	25–34	0.10	0.19	0.11

3. The percent (by household size) of the total number of households owning dogs, cats, and birds in 1996 is shown in the following matrix. The total number (in millions) owned by each household size was 923.86 (1-person households), 1975.74 (2-person households), and 3380.4 (3-or-more-person households). How many households owned dogs, cats, and birds in 1996?

		Dogs	Cats	Birds
Family size	1 person	13.2	16.8	12.7
	2 persons	31.0	32.6	27.9
	3 or more persons	55.8	50.6	59.4

6 Chapter Test

Take this test as you would take a test in class. After you are done, check your work against the answers given in the back of the book.

The *Interactive* CD-ROM and *Internet* versions of this text provide answers to the Chapter Tests and Cumulative Tests. They also offer Chapter Pre-Tests (that test key skills and concepts covered in previous chapters) and Chapter Post-Tests, both of which have randomly generated exercises with diagnostic capabilities.

In Exercises 1 and 2, write the matrix in reduced row-echelon form. Use a graphing utility to verify your result.

1. $\begin{bmatrix} 1 & -1 & 5 \\ 6 & 2 & 3 \\ 5 & 3 & -3 \end{bmatrix}$

2. $\begin{bmatrix} 1 & 0 & -1 & 2 \\ -1 & 1 & 1 & -3 \\ 1 & 1 & -1 & 1 \\ 3 & 2 & -3 & 4 \end{bmatrix}$

In Exercises 3 and 4, use matrices and elementary row operations to solve (if possible) the system of equations.

3. $\begin{cases} 2x + y + 2z = 4 \\ 2x + 2y \quad\;\; = 5 \\ 2x - y + 6z = 2 \end{cases}$

4. $\begin{cases} 2x + 3y + z = 10 \\ 2x - 3y - 3z = 22 \\ 4x - 2y + 3z = -2 \end{cases}$

5. Find (a) $A - B$, (b) $3A$, and (c) $3A - 2B$.

$A = \begin{bmatrix} 5 & 4 & 4 \\ -4 & -4 & 0 \end{bmatrix}, \quad B = \begin{bmatrix} 4 & -1 & 6 \\ -4 & 0 & -3 \end{bmatrix}$

6. Find AB, if possible, when $A = \begin{bmatrix} 2 & -2 & 6 \\ 3 & -1 & 7 \\ 2 & 0 & -2 \end{bmatrix}$ and $B = \begin{bmatrix} 4 & 4 \\ 3 & 2 \\ 1 & -2 \end{bmatrix}$.

7. Find A^{-1} for $A = \begin{bmatrix} -6 & 4 \\ 10 & -5 \end{bmatrix}$ and use A^{-1} to solve the system

$\begin{cases} -6x + 4y = 10 \\ 10x - 5y = 20 \end{cases}$.

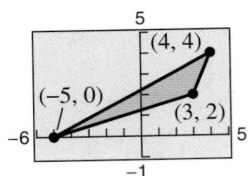

FIGURE FOR 11

In Exercises 8–10, evaluate the determinant.

8. $\begin{vmatrix} -25 & 18 \\ 6 & -7 \end{vmatrix}$

9. $\begin{vmatrix} 4 & 0 & 3 \\ 1 & -8 & 2 \\ 3 & 2 & 2 \end{vmatrix}$

10. $\begin{vmatrix} -10 & 4 & 12 & 21 \\ 0 & 2 & -16 & 0 \\ 0 & 0 & 5 & -9 \\ 0 & 0 & 0 & -3 \end{vmatrix}$

11. Use a determinant to find the area of the triangle in the figure at the right.

In Exercises 12 and 13, use Cramer's Rule to solve (if possible) the system of equations.

12. $\begin{cases} 20x + 8y = 11 \\ 12x - 24y = 21 \end{cases}$

13. $\begin{cases} 13x - 6y = 17 \\ 26x - 12y = 8 \end{cases}$

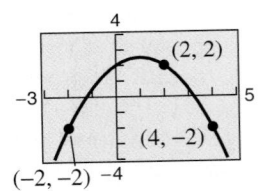

FIGURE FOR 14

14. Find the equation of the parabola $y = ax^2 + bx + c$ that passes through the points in the graph at the right. Use a graphing utility to verify your result.

15. The flow of traffic (in vehicles per hour) through a network of streets is shown in the figure at the right. Solve the system for the traffic flow represented by x_i, $i = 1, 2, 3, 4,$ and 5.

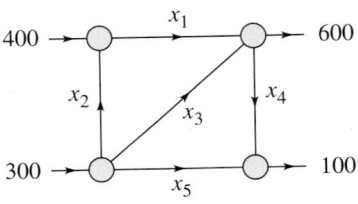

FIGURE FOR 15

Sequences, Series, and Probability

7.1 Sequences and Series
7.2 Arithmetic Sequences and Partial Sums
7.3 Geometric Sequences and Series
7.4 Mathematical Induction

7.5 The Binomial Theorem
7.6 Counting Principles
7.7 Probability

The Big Picture

In this chapter you will learn how to

❑ use sequence, factorial, and summation notation to write the terms and sums of sequences.
❑ recognize, write, and use arithmetic sequences and geometric sequences.
❑ use mathematical induction to prove statements involving a positive integer n.
❑ use the Binomial Theorem and Pascal's Triangle to calculate binomial coefficients and write binomial expansions.
❑ solve counting problems using the Fundamental Counting Principle, permutations, and combinations.
❑ find the probability of events and their complements.

In 1998, the U.S. Postal Service handled 41 percent of the world's mail volume, approximately 630 million pieces every day. (Source: U.S. Postal Service)

Important Vocabulary

As you encounter each new vocabulary term in this chapter, add the term and its definition to your notebook glossary.

- infinite sequence (p. 496)
- finite sequence (p. 496)
- recursive (p. 498)
- factorial (p. 498)
- summation or sigma notation (p. 500)
- infinite series (p. 501)
- finite series or nth partial sum (p. 501)
- arithmetic sequence (p. 507)
- geometric sequence (p. 516)

- infinite geometric series (p. 520)
- mathematical induction (p. 526)
- binomial coefficients (p. 534)
- Binomial Theorem (p. 534)
- Pascal's Triangle (p. 536)
- expanding a binomial (p. 537)
- Fundamental Counting Principle (p. 543)
- permutation (p. 544)

- permutation of n elements taken r at a time (p. 545)
- distinguishable permutation (p. 546)
- combination of n elements taken r at a time (p. 547)
- probability (p. 553)
- independent events (p. 558)
- complement of an event (p. 559)

Additional Resources   Text-specific additional resources are available to help you do well in this course. See page xvi for details.

495

7.1 Sequences and Series

What You Should Learn:

- How to use sequence notation to write the terms of sequences
- How to use factorial notation
- How to use summation notation to write sums
- How to find sums of infinite series
- How to use sequences and series to model and solve real-life problems

Sequences

In mathematics, the word *sequence* is used in much the same way as in ordinary English. Saying that a collection is listed in *sequence* means that it is ordered so that it has a first member, a second member, a third member, and so on.

Mathematically, you can think of a sequence as a *function* whose domain is the set of positive integers. Instead of using function notation, sequences are usually written using subscript notation, as shown in the following definition.

Why You Should Learn It:

Sequences and series are useful in modeling sets of values in order to identify a pattern. For instance, Exercise 115 on page 505 shows how a sequence can be used to model the average daily cost to community hospitals per patient from 1989 to 1996.

Definition of Sequence

.An **infinite sequence** is a function whose domain is the set of positive integers. The function values

$$a_1, a_2, a_3, a_4, \ldots, a_n, \ldots$$

are the **terms** of the sequence. If the domain of the function consists of the first n positive integers only, the sequence is a **finite sequence.**

On occasion, it is convenient to begin subscripting a sequence with 0 instead of 1 so that the terms of the sequence become $a_0, a_1, a_2, a_3, \ldots$.

EXAMPLE 1   Finding the Terms of a Sequence

Find the first four terms of the sequences given by

a. $a_n = 3n - 2$ **b.** $a_n = 3 + (-1)^n$.

Solution

a. The first four terms of the sequence given by $a_n = 3n - 2$ are

$$a_1 = 3(1) - 2 = 1 \qquad \text{1st term}$$
$$a_2 = 3(2) - 2 = 4 \qquad \text{2nd term}$$
$$a_3 = 3(3) - 2 = 7 \qquad \text{3rd term}$$
$$a_4 = 3(4) - 2 = 10. \qquad \text{4th term}$$

b. The first four terms of the sequence given by $a_n = 3 + (-1)^n$ are

$$a_1 = 3 + (-1)^1 = 3 - 1 = 2 \qquad \text{1st term}$$
$$a_2 = 3 + (-1)^2 = 3 + 1 = 4 \qquad \text{2nd term}$$
$$a_3 = 3 + (-1)^3 = 3 - 1 = 2 \qquad \text{3rd term}$$
$$a_4 = 3 + (-1)^4 = 3 + 1 = 4. \qquad \text{4th term}$$

To graph a sequence using a graphing utility, set the mode to *dot* and *sequence* and enter the sequence. Consult your user's manual for instructions. Try graphing the sequences in Example 1 and using the *value* or *trace* feature to identify the terms.

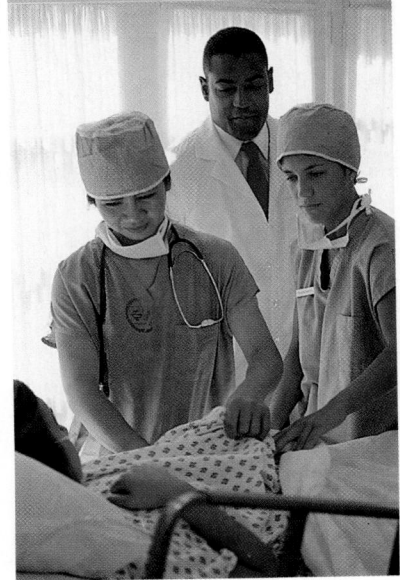
Superstock

EXAMPLE 2   Finding the Terms of a Sequence

Find the first five terms of the sequence given by $a_n = \dfrac{(-1)^n}{2n-1}$.

Algebraic Solution

The first five terms of the sequence given by

$a_n = \dfrac{(-1)^n}{2n-1}$ are as follows.

$a_1 = \dfrac{(-1)^1}{2(1)-1} = \dfrac{-1}{2-1} = -1$ 1st term

$a_2 = \dfrac{(-1)^2}{2(2)-1} = \dfrac{1}{4-1} = \dfrac{1}{3}$ 2nd term

$a_3 = \dfrac{(-1)^3}{2(3)-1} = \dfrac{-1}{6-1} = -\dfrac{1}{5}$ 3rd term

$a_4 = \dfrac{(-1)^4}{2(4)-1} = \dfrac{1}{8-1} = \dfrac{1}{7}$ 4th term

$a_5 = \dfrac{(-1)^5}{2(5)-1} = \dfrac{-1}{10-1} = -\dfrac{1}{9}$ 5th term

Numerical Solution

Use the *table* feature of a graphing utility to create a table showing the terms of the sequence $u_n = (-1)^n/(2n-1)$ for $n = 1, 2, 3, 4,$ and 5. From the table in Figure 7.1, you can estimate the first five terms of the sequence as follows.

$u_1 = -1,$ $u_2 = 0.33333 \approx \dfrac{1}{3},$ $u_3 = -0.2 = -\dfrac{1}{5},$

$u_4 = 0.14286 \approx \dfrac{1}{7}$ and $u_5 = -0.1111 \approx -\dfrac{1}{9}$

n	u(n)
1	-1
2	.33333
3	-.2
4	.14286
5	-.1111

n=1

Figure 7.1

Simply listing the first few terms is not sufficient to define a unique sequence—the *n*th term *must be given*. To see this, consider the following sequences, both of which have the same first three terms.

$\dfrac{1}{2}, \dfrac{1}{4}, \dfrac{1}{8}, \dfrac{1}{16}, \cdots , \dfrac{1}{2^n}, \cdots$

$\dfrac{1}{2}, \dfrac{1}{4}, \dfrac{1}{8}, \dfrac{1}{15}, \cdots , \dfrac{6}{(n+1)(n^2-n+6)}, \cdots$

Remind your students that when they are given the first few terms of a sequence, the best they can do is write an apparent *n*th term for the sequence. There are probably other possible *n*th terms.

EXAMPLE 3   Finding the *n*th Term of a Sequence

Write an expression for the apparent *n*th term (a_n) of each sequence.

a. $1, 3, 5, 7, \ldots$ **b.** $2, 5, 10, 17, \ldots$

Solution

a.   *n*: 1 2 3 4 . . . *n*

Terms: 1 3 5 7 . . . a_n

Apparent Pattern: Each term is 1 less than twice *n*, which implies that

$a_n = 2n - 1.$

b.   *n*: 1 2 3 4 . . . *n*

Terms: 2 5 10 17 . . . a_n

Apparent Pattern: Each term is 1 more than the square of *n*, which implies that

$a_n = n^2 + 1.$

Additional Example
Write an expression for the apparent *n*th term a_n of the sequence

$\dfrac{2}{1}, \dfrac{3}{2}, \dfrac{4}{3}, \dfrac{5}{4}, \cdots$

n: 1 2 3 4 . . . *n*

Terms: $\dfrac{2}{1}, \dfrac{3}{2}, \dfrac{4}{3}, \dfrac{5}{4} \cdots a_n$

Apparent pattern: Each term has a numerator that is 1 greater than its denominator, which implies that

$a_n = \dfrac{n+1}{n}.$

Some sequences are defined **recursively.** To define a sequence recursively, you need to be given one or more of the first few terms. All other terms of the sequence are then defined using previous terms. A well-known example is the Fibonacci sequence shown in Example 4.

EXAMPLE 4   The Fibonacci Sequence: A Recursive Sequence

The Fibonacci sequence is defined recursively as follows.

$$a_0 = 1, \ a_1 = 1, \ a_k = a_{k-2} + a_{k-1}, \qquad \text{where } k \geq 2$$

Write the first six terms of this sequence.

Solution

$a_0 = 1$	0th term is given.
$a_1 = 1$	1st term is given.
$a_2 = a_0 + a_1 = 1 + 1 = 2$	Use recursive formula.
$a_3 = a_1 + a_2 = 1 + 2 = 3$	Use recursive formula.
$a_4 = a_2 + a_3 = 2 + 3 = 5$	Use recursive formula.
$a_5 = a_3 + a_4 = 3 + 5 = 8$	Use recursive formula.

The *Interactive* CD-ROM and *Internet* versions if this text show every example with its solution; clicking on the *Try It!* button brings up similar problems. Guided Examples and Integrated Examples show step-by-step solutions to additional examples. Integrated Examples are related to several concepts in the section.

Point out to your students that the subscripts of a sequence make up the domain of the sequence and that they serve to identify the location of a term within the sequence. For instance, a_4 is the fourth term of the sequence, and a_n is the nth term of the sequence. Sometimes your students may see an entire sequence denoted by the short form $\{a_n\}$.

Factorial Notation

Some very important sequences in mathematics involve terms that are defined with special types of products called **factorials.**

Definition of Factorial

If n is a positive integer, *n* **factorial** is defined by

$$n! = 1 \cdot 2 \cdot 3 \cdot 4 \ \cdots \ (n-1) \cdot n.$$

As a special case, zero factorial is defined as $0! = 1$.

Here are some values of $n!$ for the first several nonnegative integers. Notice that $0! = 1$ by definition.

$$0! = 1$$

$$1! = 1$$

$$2! = 1 \cdot 2 = 2$$

$$3! = 1 \cdot 2 \cdot 3 = 6$$

$$4! = 1 \cdot 2 \cdot 3 \cdot 4 = 24$$

$$5! = 1 \cdot 2 \cdot 3 \cdot 4 \cdot 5 = 120$$

The value of n does not have to be very large before the value of $n!$ becomes huge. For instance, $10! = 3,628,800$.

Factorials follow the same conventions for order of operations as do exponents. For instance,

$$2n! = 2(n!) = 2(1 \cdot 2 \cdot 3 \cdot 4 \cdots n)$$

whereas $(2n)! = 1 \cdot 2 \cdot 3 \cdot 4 \cdots 2n$.

EXAMPLE 5 Finding the Terms of a Sequence Involving Factorials

List the first five terms of the sequence given by $a_n = \dfrac{2^n}{n!}$. Begin with $n = 0$.

Algebraic Solution

$$a_0 = \frac{2^0}{0!} = \frac{1}{1} = 1 \qquad \text{0th term}$$

$$a_1 = \frac{2^1}{1!} = \frac{2}{1} = 2 \qquad \text{1st term}$$

$$a_2 = \frac{2^2}{2!} = \frac{4}{2} = 2 \qquad \text{2nd term}$$

$$a_3 = \frac{2^3}{3!} = \frac{8}{6} = \frac{4}{3} \qquad \text{3rd term}$$

$$a_4 = \frac{2^4}{4!} = \frac{16}{24} = \frac{2}{3} \qquad \text{4th term}$$

Graphical Solution

Using a graphing utility set to *dot* and *sequence* modes, enter the sequence $u_n = 2^n/n!$.

Set the viewing window to $0 \le n \le 4$, $0 \le x \le 6$, and $0 \le y \le 4$. Then graph the sequence as shown in Figure 7.2. Use the *value* or *trace* feature to approximate the first five terms as follows.

$$u_0 = 1, \qquad u_1 = 2, \qquad u_2 = 2, \qquad u_3 \approx 1.333 = \frac{4}{3}, \qquad u_4 \approx 0.666 = \frac{2}{3}$$

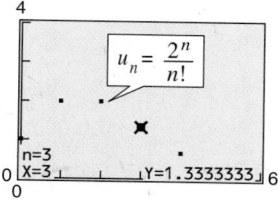

Figure 7.2

When working with fractions involving factorials, you will often find that the fractions can be reduced to simplify the computations.

EXAMPLE 6 Evaluating Factorial Expressions

Evaluate each factorial expression.

a. $\dfrac{8!}{2! \cdot 6!}$ **b.** $\dfrac{2! \cdot 6!}{3! \cdot 5!}$ **c.** $\dfrac{n!}{(n-1)!}$

Solution

a. $\dfrac{8!}{2! \cdot 6!} = \dfrac{1 \cdot 2 \cdot 3 \cdot 4 \cdot 5 \cdot 6 \cdot 7 \cdot 8}{1 \cdot 2 \cdot 1 \cdot 2 \cdot 3 \cdot 4 \cdot 5 \cdot 6} = \dfrac{7 \cdot 8}{2} = 28$

b. $\dfrac{2! \cdot 6!}{3! \cdot 5!} = \dfrac{1 \cdot 2 \cdot 1 \cdot 2 \cdot 3 \cdot 4 \cdot 5 \cdot 6}{1 \cdot 2 \cdot 3 \cdot 1 \cdot 2 \cdot 3 \cdot 4 \cdot 5} = \dfrac{6}{3} = 2$

c. $\dfrac{n!}{(n-1)!} = \dfrac{1 \cdot 2 \cdot 3 \cdots (n-1) \cdot n}{1 \cdot 2 \cdot 3 \cdots (n-1)} = n$

Note in Example 6(a) that you can simplify the computation as follows.

$$\frac{8!}{2!\,6!} = \frac{8 \cdot 7 \cdot 6!}{2!\,6!} = \frac{8 \cdot 7}{2 \cdot 1} = 28$$

Summation Notation

There is a convenient notation for the sum of the terms of a finite sequence. It is called **summation notation** or **sigma notation** because it involves the use of the uppercase Greek letter sigma, written as Σ.

Definition of Summation Notation

The sum of the first n terms of a sequence is represented by

$$\sum_{i=1}^{n} a_i = a_1 + a_2 + a_3 + a_4 + \cdots + a_n$$

where i is called the **index of summation,** n is the **upper limit of summation,** and 1 is the **lower limit of summation.**

EXAMPLE 7 Sigma Notation for Sums

a. $\displaystyle\sum_{i=1}^{5} 3i = 3(1) + 3(2) + 3(3) + 3(4) + 3(5)$

$\qquad\qquad = 3(1 + 2 + 3 + 4 + 5)$

$\qquad\qquad = 3(15) = 45$

b. $\displaystyle\sum_{k=3}^{6} (1 + k^2) = (1 + 3^2) + (1 + 4^2) + (1 + 5^2) + (1 + 6^2)$

$\qquad\qquad\qquad = 10 + 17 + 26 + 37 = 90$

c. $\displaystyle\sum_{n=0}^{8} \frac{1}{n!} = \frac{1}{0!} + \frac{1}{1!} + \frac{1}{2!} + \frac{1}{3!} + \frac{1}{4!} + \frac{1}{5!} + \frac{1}{6!} + \frac{1}{7!} + \frac{1}{8!}$

$\qquad\qquad = 1 + 1 + \frac{1}{2} + \frac{1}{6} + \frac{1}{24} + \frac{1}{120} + \frac{1}{720} + \frac{1}{5040} + \frac{1}{40,320}$

$\qquad\qquad \approx 2.71828$

For this summation, note that the sum is very close to the irrational number $e \approx 2.718281828$. It can be shown that as more terms of the sequence whose nth term is $1/n!$ are added, the sum becomes closer and closer to e.

In Example 7, note that the lower limit of a summation does not have to be 1. Also note that the index of summation does not have to be the letter i. For instance, in part (b) the letter k is the index of summation.

Most graphing utilities are able to sum the first n terms of a sequence. Check your user's manual for a *sum sequence* feature or a *series* feature. Figure 7.3 is an example of how one graphing utility displays the sum of the terms of the sequence

$$a_n = \frac{1}{n!} \quad \text{from} \quad n = 0 \quad \text{to} \quad n = 8.$$

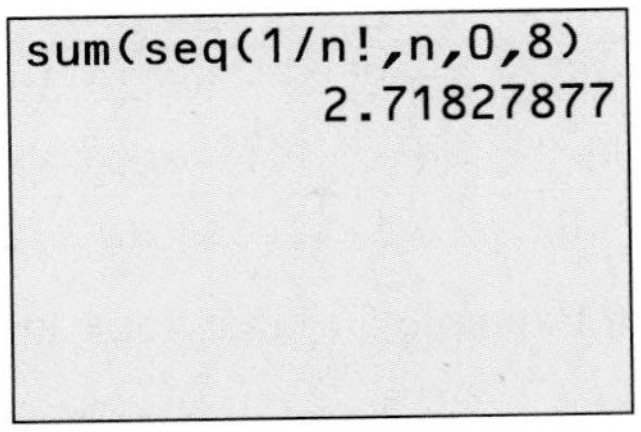

In Example 7(a), note that $\displaystyle\sum_{i=1}^{5} 3i = 3(1 + 2 + 3 + 4 + 5) = 3\sum_{i=1}^{5} i$.

This is an example of one of the *properties of sums* listed on page 501.

Reading and writing the upper and lower limits of summation correctly will help students with problems involving upper and lower limits in calculus.

```
sum(seq(1/n!,n,0,8)
             2.71827877
```

Figure 7.3

Properties of Sums

1. $\sum_{i=1}^{n} ca_i = c \sum_{i=1}^{n} a_i,$ c is any constant.

2. $\sum_{i=1}^{n} (a_i + b_i) = \sum_{i=1}^{n} a_i + \sum_{i=1}^{n} b_i$

3. $\sum_{i=1}^{n} (a_i - b_i) = \sum_{i=1}^{n} a_i - \sum_{i=1}^{n} b_i$

A proof of Property 1 is given in Appendix A.

Series

Many applications involve the sum of the terms of an infinite sequence. Such a sum is called an **infinite series** or simply a **series.**

Definition of a Series

Consider the infinite sequence $a_1, a_2, a_3, \ldots, a_i, \ldots$

1. The sum of all terms of the infinite sequence is called an **infinite series** and is denoted by

$$a_1 + a_2 + a_3 + \cdots + a_i + \cdots = \sum_{i=1}^{\infty} a_i.$$

2. The sum of the first n terms of the sequence is called a **finite series** or the **nth partial sum** of the sequence and is denoted by

$$a_1 + a_2 + a_3 + \cdots + a_n = \sum_{i=1}^{n} a_i.$$

EXAMPLE 8   Finding the Sum of a Series

For the series $\sum_{i=1}^{\infty} \dfrac{3}{10^i}$, find (a) the 3rd partial sum and (b) the sum.

Solution

a. The 3rd partial sum is

$$\sum_{i=1}^{3} \frac{3}{10^i} = \frac{3}{10^1} + \frac{3}{10^2} + \frac{3}{10^3} = 0.3 + 0.03 + 0.003 = 0.333.$$

b. The sum of the series is

$$\sum_{i=1}^{\infty} \frac{3}{10^i} = \frac{3}{10^1} + \frac{3}{10^2} + \frac{3}{10^3} + \frac{3}{10^4} + \frac{3}{10^5} + \cdots$$

$$= 0.3 + 0.03 + 0.003 + 0.0003 + 0.00003 + \cdots$$

$$= 0.33333\ldots \approx \frac{1}{3}.$$

Notice in Example 8(b) that the sum of an infinite series can be a finite number.

Activities

1. Write the first five terms of the sequence. (Assume that n begins with 1.)

   $$a_n = \frac{2n - 1}{2n}$$

   Answer: $\frac{1}{2}, \frac{3}{4}, \frac{5}{6}, \frac{7}{8}, \frac{9}{10}$

2. Write an expression for the apparent nth term of the sequence

   $$0, \frac{1}{2}, \frac{2}{6}, \frac{3}{24}, \frac{4}{120}.$$

   Answer: $\dfrac{n - 1}{n!}$

3. Find the sum.

   $$\sum_{k=1}^{4} (-1)^k 2k$$

   Answer: 4

Application

Sequences have many applications in situations that involve a recognizable pattern. One is illustrated in Example 9.

EXAMPLE 9   Population of the United States

From 1960 to 1997, the resident population of the United States can be approximated by the model

$$a_n = \sqrt{33{,}282 + 801.3n + 6.12n^2}, \qquad n = 0, 1, \ldots, 37$$

where a_n is the population in millions and n represents the calendar year, with $n = 0$ corresponding to 1960. Find the last five terms of this finite sequence. (Source: U.S. Bureau of the Census)

Algebraic Solution

The last five terms of this finite sequence are as follows.

$$a_{33} = \sqrt{33{,}282 + 801.3(33) + 6.12(33)^2}$$
$$\approx 257.7 \qquad \text{1993 population}$$

$$a_{34} = \sqrt{33{,}282 + 801.3(34) + 6.12(34)^2}$$
$$\approx 260.0 \qquad \text{1994 population}$$

$$a_{35} = \sqrt{33{,}282 + 801.3(35) + 6.12(35)^2}$$
$$\approx 262.3 \qquad \text{1995 population}$$

$$a_{36} = \sqrt{33{,}282 + 801.3(36) + 6.12(36)^2}$$
$$\approx 264.7 \qquad \text{1996 population}$$

$$a_{37} = \sqrt{33{,}282 + 801.3(37) + 6.12(37)^2}$$
$$\approx 267.0 \qquad \text{1997 population}$$

Graphical Solution

Using a graphing utility set to *dot* and *sequence* modes, enter the sequence

$$u_n = \sqrt{33{,}282 + 801.3n + 6.12n^2}.$$

Set the viewing window to $0 \le n \le 40$, $0 \le x \le 40$, and $140 \le y \le 280$. Then graph the sequence, as shown in Figure 7.4. Use the *value* or *trace* feature to approximate the last five terms.

$$u_{33} \approx 257.7 \qquad u_{34} \approx 260.0 \qquad u_{35} \approx 262.3$$
$$u_{36} \approx 264.7 \qquad u_{37} \approx 267.0$$

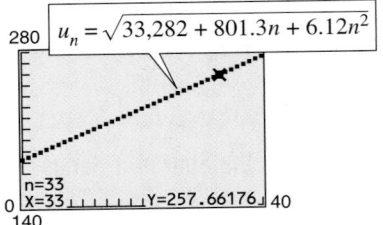

Figure 7.4

Writing About Math

The stars in the figure at the right are formed by placing n equally spaced points on a circle and connecting each point with the third point from it. For these stars, the measure of the angle (in degrees) of each point is

$$d_n = \frac{180(n - 6)}{n}, \qquad n \ge 7.$$

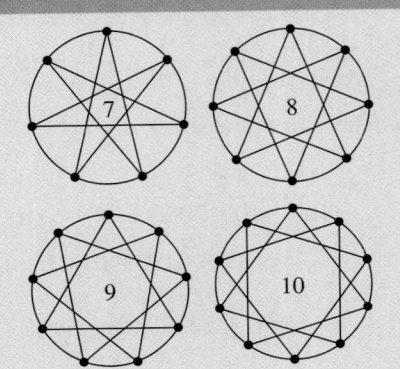

a. Write the first four terms of the sequence.
b. If you form the stars by connecting each point with the fourth point from it, you obtain stars with the following number of points and angle measures: 9 points (20°), 10 points (36°), 11 points $\left(49\frac{1}{11}°\right)$, 12 points (60°). Find a formula for the measure of the angle (in degrees) of each point of an n-pointed star. Explain how you found the formula.

7.1 Exercises

In Exercises 1–22, write the first five terms of the sequence. (Assume n begins with 1.) Use the *table* feature of a graphing utility to verify your results.

1. $a_n = 2n + 5$

2. $a_n = 4n - 7$

3. $a_n = 2^n$

4. $a_n = \left(\frac{1}{2}\right)^n$

5. $a_n = (-2)^n$

6. $a_n = \left(-\frac{1}{2}\right)^n$

7. $a_n = \dfrac{n + 1}{n}$

8. $a_n = \dfrac{n}{n + 1}$

9. $a_n = \dfrac{6n}{3n^2 - 1}$

10. $a_n = \dfrac{3n^2 - n + 4}{2n^2 + 1}$

11. $a_n = \dfrac{1 + (-1)^n}{n}$

12. $a_n = \dfrac{1 + (-1)^n}{2n}$

13. $a_n = 3 - \dfrac{1}{2^n}$

14. $a_n = \dfrac{3^n}{4^n}$

15. $a_n = \dfrac{1}{n^{3/2}}$

16. $a_n = \dfrac{10}{n^{2/3}}$

17. $a_n = \dfrac{3^n}{n!}$

18. $a_n = \dfrac{n!}{2^n}$

19. $a_n = \dfrac{(-1)^n}{n^2}$

20. $a_n = (-1)^n \left(\dfrac{n}{n + 1}\right)$

21. $a_n = (2n - 1)(2n + 1)$ **22.** $a_n = n(n - 1)(n - 2)$

In Exercises 23–28, find the indicated term of the sequence.

23. $a_n = (-1)^n (3n - 2)$

$a_{25} = $ ▢

24. $a_n = (-1)^{n-1}[n(n - 1)]$

$a_{16} = $ ▢

25. $a_n = \dfrac{2^n}{n!}$

26. $a_n = \dfrac{n!}{2n}$

$a_{10} = $ ▢

$a_8 = $ ▢

27. $a_n = \dfrac{4n}{2n^2 - 3}$

28. $a_n = \dfrac{4n^2 - n + 3}{n(n - 1)(n + 2)}$

$a_{12} = $ ▢

$a_{15} = $ ▢

In Exercises 29–34, write the first five terms of the sequence defined recursively.

29. $a_1 = 28, \quad a_{k+1} = a_k - 4$

30. $a_1 = 15, \quad a_{k+1} = a_k + 3$

31. $a_1 = 3, \quad a_{k+1} = 2(a_k - 1)$

32. $a_1 = 32, \quad a_{k+1} = \frac{1}{2}a_k$

33. $a_1 = 2, a_2 = 6, \quad a_{k+2} = a_{k+1} + 2a_k$

34. $a_1 = 52, a_2 = 40, \quad a_{k+2} = \frac{1}{2}a_{k+1} - a_k$

In Exercises 35–40, use a graphing utility to graph the first ten terms of the sequence. (Assume n begins with 1.)

35. $a_n = \dfrac{2}{3}n$

36. $a_n = 2 - \dfrac{4}{n}$

37. $a_n = 16(-0.5)^{n-1}$

38. $a_n = 8(0.75)^{n-1}$

39. $a_n = \dfrac{2n}{n + 1}$

40. $a_n = \dfrac{3n^2}{n^2 + 1}$

In Exercises 41–46, use the *table* feature of a graphing utility to find the first ten terms of the sequence. (Assume n begins with 1.)

41. $a_n = 2(3n - 1) + 5$

42. $a_n = 2n(n + 1)(n + 2)$

43. $a_n = \dfrac{6^n}{n!}$

44. $a_n = \dfrac{n!}{(n^2 - 10)}$

45. $a_n = 1 + \dfrac{n + 1}{n}$

46. $a_n = \dfrac{4n^2}{n + 2}$

In Exercises 47–50, match the sequence with its graph. [The graphs are labeled (a), (b), (c), and (d).]

(a)
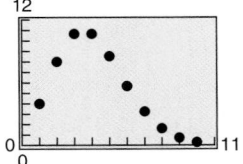

(b)
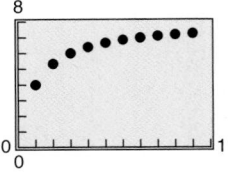

(c)
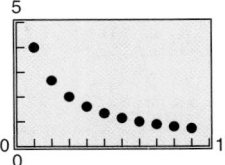

(d)
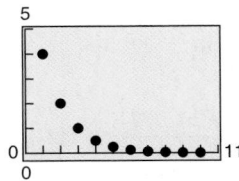

The *Interactive* CD-ROM and *Internet* versions of this text contain step-by-step solutions to all odd-numbered Section and Review Exercises. They also provide Tutorial Exercises, which link to Guided Examples for additional help.

47. $a_n = \dfrac{8}{n+1}$ **48.** $a_n = \dfrac{8n}{n+1}$

49. $a_n = 4(0.5)^{n-1}$ **50.** $a_n = \dfrac{4^n}{n!}$

In Exercises 51–64, write an expression for the apparent *n*th term of the sequence. (Assume *n* begins with 1.)

51. 1, 4, 7, 10, 13, . . .   **52.** 3, 7, 11, 15, 19, . . .

53. 0, 3, 8, 15, 24, . . .   **54.** $1, \frac{1}{4}, \frac{1}{9}, \frac{1}{16}, \frac{1}{25}, \ldots$

55. $\frac{2}{3}, \frac{3}{4}, \frac{4}{5}, \frac{5}{6}, \frac{6}{7}, \ldots$ **56.** $\frac{2}{1}, \frac{3}{3}, \frac{4}{5}, \frac{5}{7}, \frac{6}{9}, \ldots$

57. $\frac{1}{2}, \frac{-1}{4}, \frac{1}{8}, \frac{-1}{16}, \ldots$ **58.** $\frac{1}{3}, -\frac{2}{9}, \frac{4}{27}, -\frac{8}{81}, \ldots$

59. $1 + \frac{1}{1}, 1 + \frac{1}{2}, 1 + \frac{1}{3}, 1 + \frac{1}{4}, 1 + \frac{1}{5}, \ldots$

60. $1 + \frac{1}{2}, 1 + \frac{3}{4}, 1 + \frac{7}{8}, 1 + \frac{15}{16}, 1 + \frac{31}{32}, \ldots$

61. $1, \frac{1}{2}, \frac{1}{6}, \frac{1}{24}, \frac{1}{120}, \ldots$

62. $1, 2, \dfrac{2^2}{2}, \dfrac{2^3}{6}, \dfrac{2^4}{24}, \dfrac{2^5}{120}, \ldots$

63. 1, 3, 1, 3, 1, . . .

64. 1, −1, 1, −1, 1, . . .

In Exercises 65–68, write the first five terms of the sequence defined recursively. Use the pattern to write the *n*th term of the sequence as a function of *n*. (Assume *n* begins with 1.)

65. $a_1 = 6, \quad a_{k+1} = a_k + 2$

66. $a_1 = 25, \quad a_{k+1} = a_k - 5$

67. $a_1 = 81, \quad a_{k+1} = \frac{1}{3}a_k$

68. $a_1 = 14, \quad a_{k+1} = -2a_k$

In Exercises 69–78, simplify the ratio of factorials.

69. $\dfrac{3!}{6!}$ **70.** $\dfrac{4!}{7!}$

71. $\dfrac{10!}{8!}$ **72.** $\dfrac{25!}{23!}$

73. $\dfrac{12!}{4! \cdot 8!}$ **74.** $\dfrac{10! \cdot 3!}{4! \cdot 6!}$

75. $\dfrac{(n+1)!}{n!}$ **76.** $\dfrac{(n+2)!}{n!}$

77. $\dfrac{(2n-1)!}{(2n+1)!}$ **78.** $\dfrac{(2n+2)!}{(2n)!}$

In Exercises 79–90, find the sum.

79. $\displaystyle\sum_{i=1}^{5} (2i + 1)$ **80.** $\displaystyle\sum_{i=1}^{6} (3i - 1)$

81. $\displaystyle\sum_{k=1}^{4} 10$ **82.** $\displaystyle\sum_{k=1}^{5} 6$

83. $\displaystyle\sum_{i=0}^{4} i^2$ **84.** $\displaystyle\sum_{i=0}^{5} 3i^2$

85. $\displaystyle\sum_{k=0}^{3} \dfrac{1}{k^2 + 1}$ **86.** $\displaystyle\sum_{j=3}^{5} \dfrac{1}{j}$

87. $\displaystyle\sum_{i=1}^{4} [(i - 1)^2 + (i + 1)^3]$ **88.** $\displaystyle\sum_{k=2}^{5} (k + 1)(k - 3)$

89. $\displaystyle\sum_{i=1}^{4} 2^i$ **90.** $\displaystyle\sum_{j=0}^{4} (-2)^j$

In Exercises 91–94, use a graphing utility to find the sum.

91. $\displaystyle\sum_{j=1}^{6} (24 - 3j)$ **92.** $\displaystyle\sum_{j=1}^{10} \dfrac{3}{j + 1}$

93. $\displaystyle\sum_{k=0}^{4} \dfrac{(-1)^k}{k + 1}$ **94.** $\displaystyle\sum_{k=0}^{4} \dfrac{(-1)^k}{k!}$

In Exercises 95–104, use sigma notation to write the sum. Then use a graphing utility to find the sum.

95. $\dfrac{1}{3(1)} + \dfrac{1}{3(2)} + \dfrac{1}{3(3)} + \cdots + \dfrac{1}{3(9)}$

96. $\dfrac{5}{1+1} + \dfrac{5}{1+2} + \dfrac{5}{1+3} + \cdots + \dfrac{5}{1+15}$

97. $\left[2\left(\frac{1}{8}\right) + 3\right] + \left[2\left(\frac{2}{8}\right) + 3\right] + \cdots + \left[2\left(\frac{8}{8}\right) + 3\right]$

98. $\left[1 - \left(\frac{1}{6}\right)^2\right] + \left[1 - \left(\frac{2}{6}\right)^2\right] + \cdots + \left[1 - \left(\frac{6}{6}\right)^2\right]$

99. $3 - 9 + 27 - 81 + 243 - 729$

100. $1 - \dfrac{1}{2} + \dfrac{1}{4} - \dfrac{1}{8} + \cdots - \dfrac{1}{128}$

101. $\dfrac{1}{1^2} - \dfrac{1}{2^2} + \dfrac{1}{3^2} - \dfrac{1}{4^2} + \cdots - \dfrac{1}{20^2}$

102. $\dfrac{1}{1 \cdot 3} + \dfrac{1}{2 \cdot 4} + \dfrac{1}{3 \cdot 5} + \cdots + \dfrac{1}{10 \cdot 12}$

103. $\dfrac{1}{4} + \dfrac{3}{8} + \dfrac{7}{16} + \dfrac{15}{32} + \dfrac{31}{64}$

104. $\dfrac{1}{2} + \dfrac{2}{4} + \dfrac{6}{8} + \dfrac{24}{16} + \dfrac{120}{32} + \dfrac{720}{64}$

In Exercises 105–108, find the indicated partial sum of the series.

105. $\sum_{i=1}^{\infty} 5\left(\dfrac{1}{2}\right)^i$,

4th partial sum

106. $\sum_{i=1}^{\infty} 2\left(\dfrac{1}{3}\right)^i$,

5th partial sum

107. $\sum_{n=1}^{\infty} 4\left(-\dfrac{1}{2}\right)^n$,

3rd partial sum

108. $\sum_{n=1}^{\infty} 8\left(-\dfrac{1}{4}\right)^n$,

4th partial sum

In Exercises 109–112, find the sum of the infinite series.

109. $\sum_{i=1}^{\infty} 6\left(\dfrac{1}{10}\right)^i$

110. $\sum_{k=1}^{\infty} 4\left(\dfrac{1}{10}\right)^k$

111. $\sum_{k=1}^{\infty} \left(\dfrac{1}{10}\right)^k$

112. $\sum_{i=1}^{\infty} 2\left(\dfrac{1}{10}\right)^i$

113. ***Compound Interest*** A deposit of $5000 is made in an account that earns 8% interest compounded quarterly. The balance in the account after n quarters is

$$A_n = 5000\left(1 + \dfrac{0.08}{4}\right)^n, \quad n = 1, 2, 3, \ldots.$$

(a) Compute the first eight terms of this sequence.

(b) Find the balance in this account after 10 years by computing the 40th term of the sequence.

114. ***Compound Interest*** A deposit of $100 is made *each month* in an account that earns 12% interest compounded monthly. The balance in the account after n months is

$$A_n = 100(101)\left[(1.01)^n - 1\right], \quad n = 1, 2, 3, \ldots.$$

(a) Compute the first six terms of this sequence.

(b) Find the balance in this account after 5 years by computing the 60th term of the sequence.

(c) Find the balance in this account after 20 years by computing the 240th term of the sequence.

115. ***Per Capita Hospital Care*** The average cost to community hospitals per patient per day from 1989 to 1996 can be approximated by the model
$a_n = 696.39 + 66.44n - 2.37n^2$, $n = -1, \ldots, 6$
where a_n is the cost (in dollars) and n is the year, with $n = 0$ corresponding to 1990. Find the terms of this finite sequence and use a graphing utility to construct a bar graph that represents the sequence.

What does the pattern of the bar graph say about the future of hospital costs? (Source: American Hospital Association)

116. ***Federal Debt*** From 1987 to 1998, the federal debt rose from just over $2 trillion dollars to over $5 trillion dollars. The federal debt from 1987 to 1998 is approximated by the model

$a_n = \sqrt{11.7 + 2.4n}$, $n = -3, \ldots, 8$

where a_n is the debt (in trillions of dollars) and n is the year, with $n = 0$ corresponding to 1990. Find the terms of this finite sequence and use a graphing utility to construct a bar graph that represents the sequence. What does the pattern in the bar graph say about the future of the federal debt? (Source: Bureau of the Public Debt)

117. ***Corporate Income*** The net income a_n (in millions of dollars) of Wal-Mart for the years 1990 through 1998 are shown in the graph. The income can be approximated by the model

$a_n = 1215.16 + 608.19n - 114.83n^2 + 11n^3$,
$n = 0, \ldots, 8$

where $n = 0$ represents 1990. Use this model to approximate the total net income from 1990 through 1998. Compare this sum with the result of adding the incomes shown in the graph. (Source: Wal-Mart Stores, Inc.)

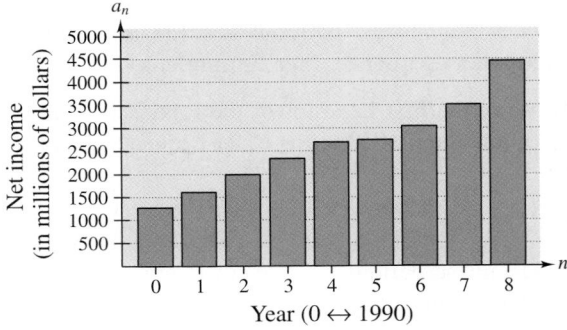

118. ***Corporate Dividends*** The dividends a_n (in dollars) declared per share of common stock of Procter & Gamble Company for the years 1990 through 1998 are shown in the graph. These dividends can be approximated by the model

$a_n = 4.27 + 0.29n - 2.93 \ln n$,
$n = 10, \ldots, 18$

where $n = 10$ represents 1990. Use this model to approximate the total dividends per share of common stock from 1990 through 1998. Compare this sum with the result of adding the dividends shown in the graph. (Source: Procter & Gamble Company)

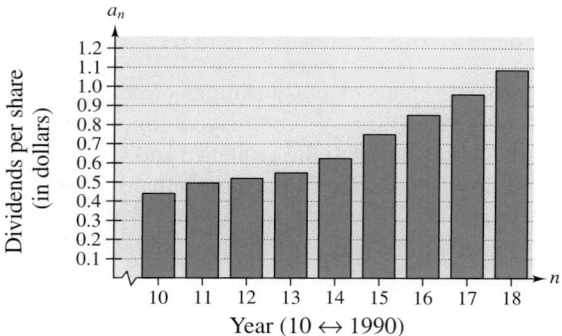

Year (10 ↔ 1990)

Synthesis

True or False? **In Exercises 119 and 120, determine whether the statement is true or false. Justify your answer.**

119. $\displaystyle\sum_{i=1}^{4}(i^2 + 2i) = \sum_{i=1}^{4}i^2 + 2\sum_{i=1}^{4}i$

120. $\displaystyle\sum_{j=1}^{4} 2^j = \sum_{j=3}^{6} 2^{j-2}$

Fibonacci Sequence **In Exercises 121 and 122, use the Fibonacci sequence. (See Example 4.)**

121. Write the first 12 terms of the Fibonacci sequence a_n and the first 10 terms of the sequence given by

$$b_n = \frac{a_{n+1}}{a_n}, \quad n > 1.$$

122. Using the definition for b_n in Exercise 121, show that b_n can be defined recursively by

$$b_n = 1 + \frac{1}{b_{n-1}}.$$

123. Find the first few terms of $a_n = n^2 - n + 11$. Describe any pattern or make an observation about the terms of the sequence.

In Exercises 124–127, find the first five terms of the sequence.

124. $a_n = \dfrac{x^n}{n!}$

125. $a_n = \dfrac{(-1)^n x^{2n+1}}{2n+1}$

126. $a_n = \dfrac{(-1)^n x^{2n}}{(2n)!}$

127. $a_n = \dfrac{(-1)^n x^{2n+1}}{(2n+1)!}$

Review

In Exercises 128 and 129, write the augmented matrix for the system of linear equations.

128. $\begin{cases} -4x + y = -7 \\ 6x - 9y = 3 \end{cases}$

129. $\begin{cases} 2x + y + 3z = -3 \\ -x + 5y = 14 \\ -3x - 6y - 7z = -7 \end{cases}$

In Exercises 130–133, find (a) $A - B$, (b) $2B - 3A$, (c) AB, (d) BA.

130. $A = \begin{bmatrix} 6 & 5 \\ 3 & 4 \end{bmatrix}$, $B = \begin{bmatrix} -2 & 4 \\ 6 & -3 \end{bmatrix}$

131. $A = \begin{bmatrix} 10 & 7 \\ -4 & 6 \end{bmatrix}$, $B = \begin{bmatrix} 0 & -12 \\ 8 & 11 \end{bmatrix}$

132. $A = \begin{bmatrix} -2 & -3 & 6 \\ 4 & 5 & 7 \\ 1 & 7 & 4 \end{bmatrix}$, $B = \begin{bmatrix} 1 & 4 & 2 \\ 0 & 1 & 6 \\ 0 & 3 & 1 \end{bmatrix}$

133. $A = \begin{bmatrix} -1 & 4 & 0 \\ 5 & 1 & 2 \\ 0 & -1 & 3 \end{bmatrix}$, $B = \begin{bmatrix} 0 & 4 & 0 \\ 3 & 1 & -2 \\ -1 & 0 & 2 \end{bmatrix}$

In Exercises 134–137, find the determinant of the matrix.

134. $A = \begin{bmatrix} 3 & 7 \\ -2 & 9 \end{bmatrix}$

135. $A = \begin{bmatrix} -4 & 11 \\ 13 & 20 \end{bmatrix}$

136. $A = \begin{bmatrix} 4 & 0 & 5 \\ 0 & -7 & 2 \\ 9 & 1 & -1 \end{bmatrix}$

137. $A = \begin{bmatrix} 10 & 9 & 12 & 2 \\ -2 & 5 & 8 & 7 \\ -2 & -1 & 0 & 3 \\ -4 & 6 & 2 & 1 \end{bmatrix}$

7.2 Arithmetic Sequences and Partial Sums

Arithmetic Sequences

A sequence whose consecutive terms have a common difference is called an **arithmetic sequence.**

Definition of Arithmetic Sequence

A sequence is **arithmetic** if the differences between consecutive terms are the same. So, the sequence

$$a_1, a_2, a_3, a_4, \ldots, a_n, \ldots$$

is arithmetic if there is a number d such that

$$a_2 - a_1 = a_3 - a_2 = a_4 - a_3 = \cdots = d.$$

The number d is the **common difference** of the arithmetic sequence.

EXAMPLE 1 Examples of Arithmetic Sequences

a. The sequence whose nth term is $4n + 3$ is arithmetic. For this sequence, the common difference between consecutive terms is 4.

$$7, 11, 15, 19, \ldots, 4n + 3, \ldots$$
$$11 - 7 = 4$$

b. The sequence whose nth term is $7 - 5n$ is arithmetic. For this sequence, the common difference between consecutive terms is -5.

$$2, -3, -8, -13, \ldots, 7 - 5n, \ldots$$
$$-3 - 2 = -5$$

c. The sequence whose nth term is $\frac{1}{4}(n + 3)$ is arithmetic. For this sequence, the common difference between consecutive terms is $\frac{1}{4}$.

$$1, \frac{5}{4}, \frac{3}{2}, \frac{7}{4}, \ldots, \frac{n + 3}{4}, \ldots$$
$$\frac{5}{4} - 1 = \frac{1}{4}$$

d. The sequence $1, 4, 9, 16, \ldots$, whose nth term is n^2 is *not* arithmetic. The difference between the first two terms is

$$a_2 - a_1 = 4 - 1 = 3$$

but the difference between the second and third terms is

$$a_3 - a_2 = 9 - 4 = 5.$$

Index Stock

In Example 1, notice that each of the arithmetic sequences in parts (a), (b), and (c) has an nth term that is of the form $dn + c$, where the common difference of the sequence is d. This result is summarized as follows.

The nth Term of an Arithmetic Sequence

The nth term of an arithmetic sequence has the form

$$a_n = dn + c$$

where d is the common difference between consecutive terms of the sequence and $c = a_1 - d$.

An arithmetic sequence $a_n = dn + c$ can be thought of as "counting by d's" after a shift of c units from d. For instance, the sequence

$$2, 6, 10, 14, 18, \ldots$$

has a common difference of 4, so you are counting by 4's after a shift of 2 units below 4 (beginning with $a_1 = 2$). So, the nth term is $4n - 2$. Similarly, the nth term of the sequence

$$6, 11, 16, 21, \ldots$$

is $5n + 1$ because you are counting by 5's after a shift of 1 unit above 5 (beginning with $a_1 = 6$).

EXAMPLE 2   Finding the nth Term of an Arithmetic Sequence

Find a formula for the nth term of the arithmetic sequence whose common difference is 3 and whose first term is 2.

Solution

Because the sequence is arithmetic, you know that the formula for the nth term is of the form $a_n = dn + c$. Moreover, because the common difference is $d = 3$, the formula must have the form $a_n = 3n + c$. Because $a_1 = 2$, it follows that

$$c = a_1 - d = 2 - 3 = -1.$$

So, the formula for the nth term is $a_n = 3n - 1$. The sequence therefore has the following form.

$$2, 5, 8, 11, 14, \ldots, 3n - 1, \ldots$$

A graph of the first 15 terms of the sequence is shown in Figure 7.5. Notice that the points lie on a line. This makes sense because a_n is a linear function of n. In other words, the terms "arithmetic" and "linear" are closely connected.

Another way to find a formula for the nth term of the sequence in Example 2 is to begin by writing the terms of the sequence.

a_1	a_2	a_3	a_4	a_5	a_6	a_7	
2	$2 + 3$	$5 + 3$	$8 + 3$	$11 + 3$	$14 + 3$	$17 + 3$	$\ldots$
2	5	8	11	14	17	20	$\ldots$

From these terms, you can reason that the nth term is of the form

$$a_n = dn + c = 3n - 1.$$

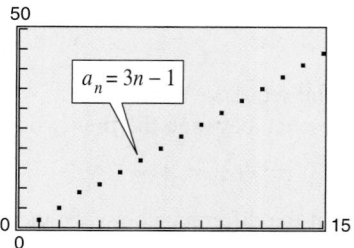

Figure 7.5

EXAMPLE 3   Writing the Terms of an Arithmetic Sequence

The fourth term of an arithmetic sequence is 20, and the 13th term is 65. Write the first several terms of this sequence.

Solution

The fourth and 13th terms of the sequence are related by

$$a_{13} = a_4 + 9d.$$

Using $a_4 = 20$ and $a_{13} = 65$, you can conclude that $d = 5$, which implies that the sequence is as follows.

a_1 a_2 a_3 a_4 a_5 a_6 a_7 a_8 a_9 a_{10} a_{11} a_{12} a_{13} . . .

5,   10, 15, 20, 25, 30, 35, 40, 45, 50,   55,   60,   65,   . . .

If you know the nth term of an arithmetic sequence *and* you know the common difference of the sequence, you can find the $(n + 1)$th term by using the *recursive formula*

$$a_{n+1} = a_n + d. \qquad \text{Recursive formula}$$

With this formula, you can find any term of an arithmetic sequence, *provided* that you know the previous term. For instance, if you know the first term, you can find the second term. Then, knowing the second term, you can find the third term, and so on.

If you substitute $a_1 - d$ for c in the formula $a_n = dn + c$, the nth term of an arithmetic sequence has the alternative recursive formula

$$a_n = a_1 + (n - 1)d. \qquad \text{Alternative recursive formula}$$

Use this formula to solve Example 4. You should get the same answer.

As an aid to learning the formula for the nth term of an arithmetic sequence, consider having your students intuitively find the nth term of each of the following sequences.

1. $a, a + 2, a + 4, a + 6, \ldots$
   Answer: $2n + a - 2$

2. $11, 15, 19, 23, 27, \ldots$
   Answer: $4n + 7$

EXAMPLE 4   Using a Recursive Formula

Find the seventh term of the arithmetic sequence whose first two terms are 2 and 9.

Algebraic Solution

To find the seventh term, first find a formula for the nth term. Because the first term is 2, it follows that

$$c = a_1 - d = 2 - 7 = -5.$$

Therefore, a formula for the nth term is

$$a_n = dn + c$$
$$= 7n - 5$$

which implies that the seventh term is

$$a_7 = 7(7) - 5$$
$$= 44.$$

Numerical Solution

For this sequence, the common difference is $d = 9 - 2 = 7$. Use the *table* feature of a graphing utility to create a table that begins at 2 and increases by 7 in each row, as shown in Figure 7.6. The number in the seventh row of the table is 44, so 44 is the seventh term of the arithmetic sequence.

L1	L2	L3
1	2	- - - - -
2	9	
3	16	
4	23	
5	30	
6	37	
7	44	

L2(7)=44

Figure 7.6

The Sum of a Finite Arithmetic Sequence

There is a simple formula for the *sum* of a finite arithmetic sequence. A proof of the formula is given in Appendix A.

The Sum of a Finite Arithmetic Sequence

The sum of a finite arithmetic sequence with n terms is

$$S_n = \frac{n}{2}(a_1 + a_n).$$

Be sure you see that this formula works only for *arithmetic* sequences. Using this formula reduces the amount of time it takes to find the sum of an arithmetic sequence, as you will see in the following example.

EXAMPLE 5 Finding the Sum of a Finite Arithmetic Sequence

Find the sum: $1 + 3 + 5 + 7 + 9 + 11 + 13 + 15 + 17 + 19$.

Solution

To begin, notice that the sequence is arithmetic (with a common difference of 2). Moreover, the sequence has 10 terms. So, the sum of the sequence is

$$S_n = 1 + 3 + 5 + 7 + 9 + 11 + 13 + 15 + 17 + 19$$

$$= \frac{n}{2}(a_1 + a_n)$$

$$= \frac{10}{2}(1 + 19) \qquad n = 10,\, a_1 = 1,\, a_{10} = 19$$

$$= 5(20)$$

$$= 100.$$

When **Carl Friedrich Gauss (1777–1855)** was ten years old, his teacher asked him to add all the integers from 1 to 100. When Gauss returned with the correct answer after only a few moments the teacher could only look at him in astounded silence. This is what Gauss did:

$$1 + \quad 2 + \quad 3 + \cdots + 100$$
$$100 + \quad 99 + \quad 98 + \cdots + \quad 1$$
$$101 + 101 + 101 + \cdots + 101$$
$$\frac{100 \times 101}{2} = 5050$$

EXAMPLE 6 Finding the Sum of a Finite Arithmetic Sequence

Find the sum of the integers from 1 to 100.

Solution

The integers from 1 to 100 form an arithmetic sequence that has 100 terms. So, you can use the formula for the sum of an arithmetic sequence, as follows.

$$S_n = 1 + 2 + 3 + 4 + 5 + 6 + \cdots + 99 + 100$$

$$= \frac{n}{2}(a_1 + a_n)$$

$$= \frac{100}{2}(1 + 100) \qquad n = 100,\, a_1 = 1,\, a_{100} = 100$$

$$= 50(101)$$

$$= 5050$$

The sum of the first n terms of an infinite sequence is called the **nth partial sum.**

EXAMPLE 7   Finding a Partial Sum of an Arithmetic Sequence

Find the 150th partial sum of the arithmetic sequence

$$5, 16, 27, 38, 49, \ldots.$$

Solution

For this arithmetic sequence, you have $a_1 = 5$ and $d = 16 - 5 = 11$. So,

$$c = a_1 - d = 5 - 11 = -6$$

and the nth term is

$$a_n = 11n - 6.$$

Therefore, $a_{150} = 11(150) - 6 = 1644$, and the sum of the first 150 terms is

$$S_n = \frac{n}{2}(a_1 + a_n)$$

$$= \frac{150}{2}(5 + 1644) \qquad n = 150, a_1 = 5, a_{150} = 1644$$

$$= 75(1649)$$

$$= 123,675.$$

Applications

EXAMPLE 8   Seating Capacity

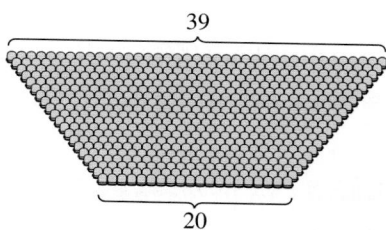

An auditorium has 20 rows of seats. There are 20 seats in the first row, 21 seats in the second row, 22 seats in the third row, and so on. (See Figure 7.7.) How many seats are there in all 20 rows?

Solution

The numbers of seats in the 20 rows form an arithmetic sequence in which the common difference is $d = 1$. Because

$$c = a_1 - d = 20 - 1 = 19$$

you can determine that the formula for the nth term of the sequence is $a_n = n + 19$. So, the 20th term in the sequence is $a_{20} = 20 + 19 = 39$, and the total number of seats is

$$S_n = 20 + 21 + 22 + \cdots + 39$$

$$= \frac{n}{2}(a_1 + a_{20})$$

$$= \frac{20}{2}(20 + 39) \qquad n = 20, a_1 = 20, a_{20} = 39$$

$$= 10(59)$$

$$= 590.$$

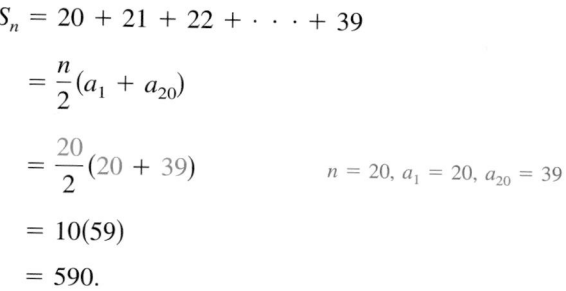

Figure 7.7

EXAMPLE 9 Total Sales

A small business sells \$10,000 worth of products during its first year. The owner of the business has set a goal of increasing annual sales by \$7500 each year for 19 years. Assuming that this goal is met, find the total sales during the first 20 years this business is in operation.

Algebraic Solution

The annual sales form an arithmetic sequence in which $a_1 = 10{,}000$ and $d = 7500$. So,

$$\begin{aligned} c &= a_1 - d \\ &= 10{,}000 - 7500 \\ &= 2500 \end{aligned}$$

and the nth term of the sequence is

$$a_n = 7500n + 2500.$$

This implies that the 20th term of the sequence is

$$\begin{aligned} a_{20} &= 7500(20) + 2500 \\ &= 152{,}500. \end{aligned}$$

The sum of the first 20 terms of the sequence is

$$S_n = \frac{n}{2}(a_1 + a_{20})$$

$$S_{20} = \frac{20}{2}(10{,}000 + 152{,}500) \qquad n = 20,\ a_1 = 10{,}000,\ a_{20} = 152{,}500$$

$$\begin{aligned} &= 10(162{,}500) \\ &= 1{,}625{,}000. \end{aligned}$$

So, the total sales for the first 20 years is \$1,625,500.

Numerical Solution

The annual sales form an arithmetic sequence in which $a_1 = 10{,}000$ and $d = 7500$. So, $c = a_1 - d = 10{,}000 - 7500 = 2500$. Use a graphing utility to create a table that shows the sales $u_n = 7500n + 2500$ for each of the 20 years, as shown in Figure 7.8. Then use the graphing utility to find that the sum of the data in the table is 1,625,000. So, the total sales for the first 20 years is \$1,625,000.

n	u(n)
14	107500
15	115000
16	122500
17	130000
18	137500
19	145000
20	152500
n=20	

Figure 7.8

Writing About Math *Numerical Relationships*

Decide whether it is possible to fill in the blanks in each of the sequences such that the resulting sequence is arithmetic. If so, find a recursive formula for the sequence. Write a short paragraph explaining how you made your decisions.

a. -7, ___, ___, ___, ___, ___, 11

b. 17, ___, ___, ___, ___, ___, ___, ___, ___, 71

c. 2, 6, ___, ___, 162

d. 4, 7.5, ___, ___, ___, ___, ___, ___, ___, ___, 39

e. 8, 12, ___, ___, ___, 60.75

7.2 EXERCISES

In Exercises 1–8, determine whether the sequence is arithmetic. If it is, find the common difference.

1. $10, 8, 6, 4, 2, \ldots$

2. $4, 9, 14, 19, 24, \ldots$

3. $3, \frac{5}{2}, 2, \frac{3}{2}, 1, \ldots$

4. $\frac{1}{3}, \frac{2}{3}, \frac{4}{3}, \frac{8}{3}, \frac{16}{3}, \ldots$

5. $-24, -16, -8, 0, 8, \ldots$

6. $\ln 1, \ln 2, \ln 3, \ln 4, \ln 5, \ldots$

7. $3.7, 4.3, 4.9, 5.5, 6.1, \ldots$

8. $1^2, 2^2, 3^2, 4^2, 5^2, \ldots$

In Exercises 9–16, write the first five terms of the sequence. Determine whether the sequence is arithmetic. If it is, find the common difference.

9. $a_n = 8 + 13n$

10. $a_n = (2^n)n$

11. $a_n = \dfrac{1}{n+1}$

12. $a_n = 1 + (n-1)4$

13. $a_n = 150 - 7n$

14. $a_n = 2^{n-1}$

15. $a_n = 3 + \dfrac{(-1)^n 2}{n}$

16. $a_n = (-1)^n$

In Exercises 17–20, write the first five terms of the arithmetic sequence. Find the common difference and write the nth term of the sequence as a function of n.

17. $a_1 = 15, \quad a_{k+1} = a_k + 9$

18. $a_1 = 200, \quad a_{k+1} = a_k - 20$

19. $a_1 = \frac{7}{2}, \quad a_{k+1} = a_k - \frac{1}{4}$

20. $a_1 = 0.375, \quad a_{k+1} = a_k + 0.25$

In Exercises 21–28, write the first five terms of the arithmetic sequence. Use a graphing utility to verify your results numerically.

21. $a_1 = 5, d = 6$

22. $a_1 = 5, d = -\frac{3}{4}$

23. $a_1 = -2.6, d = -0.4$

24. $a_4 = 16, a_{10} = 46$

25. $a_8 = 26, a_{12} = 42$

26. $a_6 = -38, a_{11} = -73$

27. $a_3 = 19, a_{15} = -1.7$

28. $a_5 = 16, a_{14} = 38.5$

In Exercises 29–34, the first two terms of the arithmetic sequences are given. Find the missing term. Use a graphing utility to verify the result numerically.

29. $a_1 = 5, \quad a_2 = 11, \quad a_{10} = $

30. $a_1 = 3, \quad a_2 = 13, \quad a_9 = $

31. $a_1 = 2, \quad a_2 = -2, \quad a_{14} = $

32. $a_1 = -1, \quad a_2 = -10, \quad a_{25} = $

33. $a_1 = 4.2, \quad a_2 = 6.6, \quad a_7 = $

34. $a_1 = -0.7, \quad a_2 = -13.8, \quad a_8 = $

In Exercises 35–44, find a formula for a_n for the arithmetic sequence.

35. $a_1 = 1, d = 3$

36. $a_1 = 15, d = 4$

37. $a_1 = 100, d = -8$

38. $a_1 = 0, d = -\frac{2}{3}$

39. $4, \frac{3}{2}, -1, -\frac{7}{2}, \ldots$

40. $10, 5, 0, -5, -10, \ldots$

41. $a_1 = 5, a_4 = 15$

42. $a_1 = -4, a_5 = 16$

43. $a_3 = 94, a_6 = 85$

44. $a_5 = 190, a_{10} = 115$

In Exercises 45–48, match the sequence with its graph. [The graphs are labeled (a), (b), (c), and (d).]

(a)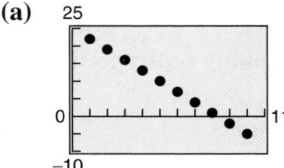

(b)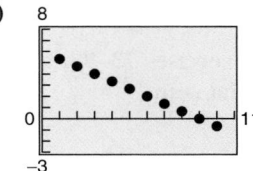

(c)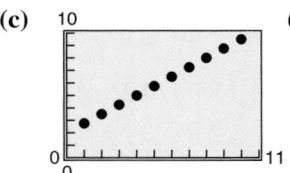

(d)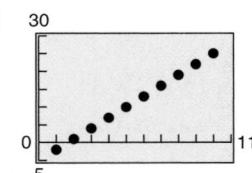

45. $a_n = -\frac{2}{3}n + 6$

46. $a_n = 3n - 5$

47. $a_n = 2 + \frac{3}{4}n$

48. $a_n = 25 - 3n$

In Exercises 49–52, use a graphing utility in *dot* mode to graph the first ten terms of the sequence.

49. $a_n = 15 - \frac{3}{2}n$

50. $a_n = -5 + 2n$

51. $a_n = 0.2n + 3$

52. $a_n = -0.3n + 8$

In Exercises 53–58, use the *table* feature of a graphing utility to find the first ten terms of the sequence.

53. $a_n = 4n - 5$

54. $a_n = 17 + 3n$

55. $a_n = 20 - \frac{3}{4}n$

56. $a_n = \frac{4}{5}n + 12$

57. $a_n = 1.5 + 0.005n$

58. $a_n = -12.4n + 9$

In Exercises 59–64, find the indicated *n*th partial sum of the arithmetic sequence.

59. $8, 26, 44, 62, \ldots, \quad n = 10$

60. $-6, -2, 2, 6, \ldots, \quad n = 50$

61. $0.5, 1.3, 2.1, 2.9, \ldots, \quad n = 10$

62. $40, 29, 18, 7, \ldots, \quad n = 10$

63. $a_1 = 100, \ a_{25} = 220, \quad n = 25$

64. $a_1 = 15, \ a_{100} = 307, \quad n = 100$

In Exercises 65–72, find the partial sum without using a graphing utility.

65. $\displaystyle\sum_{n=1}^{50} n$

66. $\displaystyle\sum_{n=1}^{100} 2n$

67. $\displaystyle\sum_{n=1}^{100} 5n$

68. $\displaystyle\sum_{n=51}^{100} 7n$

69. $\displaystyle\sum_{n=11}^{30} n - \sum_{n=1}^{10} n$

70. $\displaystyle\sum_{n=51}^{100} n - \sum_{n=1}^{50} n$

71. $\displaystyle\sum_{n=1}^{500} (n + 3)$

72. $\displaystyle\sum_{n=1}^{250} (1000 - n)$

In Exercises 73–78, use a graphing utility to find the partial sum.

73. $\displaystyle\sum_{n=1}^{20} (2n + 5)$

74. $\displaystyle\sum_{n=1}^{100} \frac{n + 4}{2}$

75. $\displaystyle\sum_{n=0}^{50} (1000 - 5n)$

76. $\displaystyle\sum_{n=0}^{100} \frac{8 - 3n}{16}$

77. $\displaystyle\sum_{i=1}^{60} \left(250 - \tfrac{8}{3}i\right)$

78. $\displaystyle\sum_{j=1}^{200} (4.5 + 0.025j)$

79. Find the sum of the first 100 positive odd integers.

80. Find the sum of the integers from -10 to 50.

Job Offer **In Exercises 81 and 82, consider a job offer with the given starting salary and guaranteed salary increase for the first 5 years of employment.**

(a) **Determine the person's salary during the sixth year of employment.**

(b) **Determine the person's total compensation from the company through 6 full years of employment.**

(c) **Verify your results in parts (a) and (b) numerically.**

	Starting Salary	*Annual Raise*
81.	$32,500	$1500
82.	$36,800	$1750

83. *Seating Capacity*   Determine the seating capacity of an auditorium with 30 rows of seats if there are 20 seats in the first row, 24 seats in the second row, 28 seats in the third row, and so on.

84. *Seating Capacity*   Determine the seating capacity of an auditorium with 36 rows of seats if there are 15 seats in the first row, 18 seats in the second row, 21 seats in the third row, and so on.

85. *Brick Pattern*   A brick patio has the approximate shape of a trapezoid, as shown in the figure. The patio has 18 rows of bricks. The first row has 14 bricks and the 18th row has 31 bricks. How many bricks are in the patio?

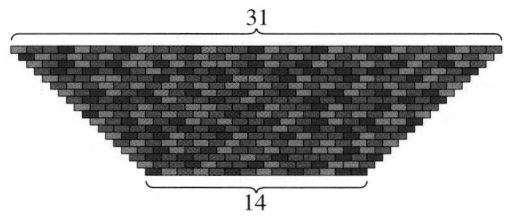

86. *Number of Logs*   Logs are stacked in a pile, as shown in the figure. The top row has 15 logs and the bottom row has 24 logs. How many logs are in the stack?

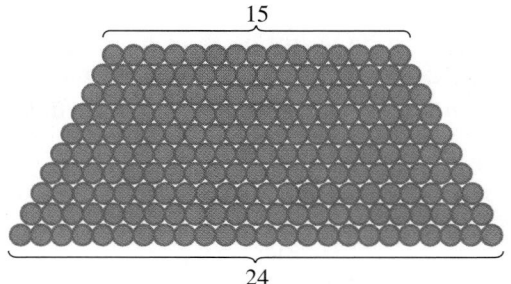

87. *Auditorium Seating*   Each row in a small auditorium has two more seats than the preceding row, as shown in the figure. Find the seating capacity of the auditorium if the front row seats 25 people and there are 15 rows of seats.

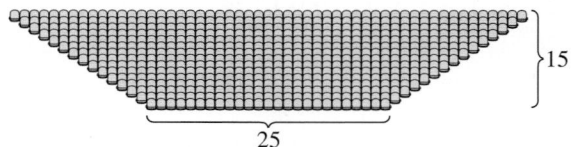

88. *Baling Hay*   In the first two trips around a field baling hay, a farmer makes 93 bales and 89 bales, respectively, as shown in the figure. Because each trip is shorter than the preceding trip, the farmer estimates that the same pattern will continue. Estimate the total number of bales made if there are another six trips around the field.

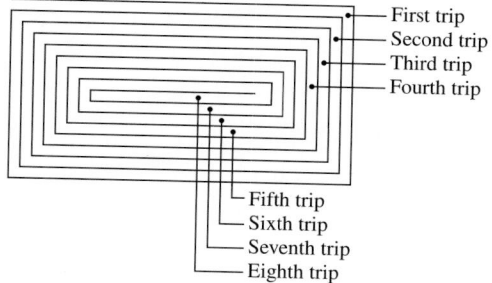

— First trip
— Second trip
— Third trip
— Fourth trip
— Fifth trip
— Sixth trip
— Seventh trip
— Eighth trip

89. *Grandfather Clock*   Each hour, a grandfather clock strikes the number of times corresponding to the hour of the day. How many times does the clock strike in a day?

90. *Falling Object*   An object (with negligible air resistance) is dropped from an airplane. During the first second of fall, the object falls 4.9 meters; during the second second of fall, it falls 14.7 meters; during the third second, it falls 24.5 meters; and during the fourth second, it falls 34.3 meters. If this arithmetic pattern continues, how many meters will the object have fallen after 10 seconds?

Synthesis

True or False?   **In Exercises 91 and 92, determine whether the statement is true or false. Justify your answer.**

91. Given an arithmetic sequence for which only the first and second terms are known, it is possible to find the nth term.

92. If the only known information about a finite arithmetic sequence is its first term and its last term, then it is possible to find the sum of the sequence.

In Exercises 93 and 94, find the first ten terms of the sequence.

93. $a_1 = x, d = 2x$ **94.** $a_1 = -y, d = 5y$

95. *Pattern Recognition*

(a) Compute the following five sums of positive odd integers.

$1 + 3 = \quad$

$1 + 3 + 5 = \quad$

$1 + 3 + 5 + 7 = \quad$

$1 + 3 + 5 + 7 + 9 = \quad$

$1 + 3 + 5 + 7 + 9 + 11 = \quad$

(b) Use the sums in part (a) to make a conjecture about the sums of positive odd integers. Check your conjecture for the sum

$1 + 3 + 5 + 7 + 9 + 11 + 13 = \quad .$

(c) Verify your conjecture algebraically.

96. *Think About It*   The sum of the first 20 terms of an arithmetic sequence with a common difference of 3 is 650. Find the first term.

97. *Think About It*   The sum of the first n terms of an arithmetic sequence with first term a_1 and common difference d is S_n. Determine the sum if the first term is increased by 5. Explain.

Review

In Exercises 98 and 99, use Gauss-Jordan elimination to solve the system of equations.

98. $\begin{cases} 2x - y + 7z = -10 \\ 3x + 2y - 4z = 17 \\ 6x - 5y + z = -20 \end{cases}$

99. $\begin{cases} -x + 4y + 10z = 4 \\ 5x - 3y + z = 31 \\ 8x + 2y - 3z = -5 \end{cases}$

In Exercises 100 and 101, use a determinant to find the area of the triangle with the given vertices.

100. $(0, 0), (4, -3), (2, 6)$ **101.** $(-1, 2), (5, 1), (3, 8)$

In Exercises 102 and 103, simplify the ratio of factorials.

102. $\dfrac{6!}{5! \cdot 2!}$

103. $\dfrac{6! \cdot 8!}{14!}$

7.3 Geometric Sequences and Series

Geometric Sequences

In Section 7.2, you learned that a sequence whose consecutive terms have a common *difference* is an arithmetic sequence. In this section, you will study another important type of sequence called a **geometric sequence.** Consecutive terms of a geometric sequence have a common *ratio.*

Definition of Geometric Sequence

A sequence is a **geometric sequence** if the ratios of consecutive terms are the same.

$$\frac{a_2}{a_1} = \frac{a_3}{a_2} = \frac{a_4}{a_3} = \cdots = r, \qquad r \neq 0$$

The number r is the **common ratio** of the sequence.

EXAMPLE 1   Examples of Geometric Sequences

a. The sequence whose nth term is 2^n is geometric. For this sequence, the common ratio between consecutive terms is 2.

$$\underbrace{2, 4, 8, 16, \ldots, 2^n, \ldots}$$
$$\tfrac{4}{2} = 2$$

b. The sequence whose nth term is $4(3^n)$ is geometric. For this sequence, the common ratio between consecutive terms is 3.

$$\underbrace{12, 36, 108, 324, \ldots, 4(3^n), \ldots}$$
$$\tfrac{36}{12} = 3$$

c. The sequence whose nth term is $\left(-\frac{1}{3}\right)^n$ is geometric. For this sequence, the common ratio between consecutive terms is $-\frac{1}{3}$.

$$\underbrace{-\frac{1}{3}, \frac{1}{9}, -\frac{1}{27}, \frac{1}{81}, \ldots, \left(-\frac{1}{3}\right)^n, \ldots}$$
$$\frac{\frac{1}{9}}{-\frac{1}{3}} = -\frac{1}{3}$$

d. The sequence 1, 4, 9, 16, . . . , whose nth term is n^2 is *not* geometric. The ratio of the second term to first term is

$$\frac{a_2}{a_1} = \frac{4}{1} = 4$$

but the ratio of the third term to the second term is

$$\frac{a_3}{a_2} = \frac{9}{4}.$$

What You Should Learn:

- How to recognize, write, and find the nth terms of geometric sequences
- How to find nth partial sums of geometric sequences
- How to find sums of infinite geometric series
- How to use geometric sequences to model and solve real-life problems

Why You Should Learn It:

Geometric sequences can reduce the amount of time it takes to find the sum of a sequence of numbers with a common ratio. For instance, Exercise 92 on page 523 shows how to use a geometric sequence to estimate the population growth of a city.

Jeff Greenberg/PhotoEdit

In Example 1, each of the geometric sequences in parts (a), (b), and (c) has an nth term in the form ar^n, where the common ratio of the sequence is r.

The *n*th Term of a Geometric Sequence

The nth term of a geometric sequence has the form

$$a_n = a_1 r^{n-1}$$

where r is the common ratio of consecutive terms of the sequence. So, every geometric sequence can be written in the following form.

$$a_1, \quad a_2, \quad a_3, \quad a_4, \quad a_5, \quad \ldots, \quad a_n, \quad \ldots$$

$$a_1, a_1 r, a_1 r^2, a_1 r^3, a_1 r^4, \ldots, a_1 r^{n-1}, \ldots$$

If you know the nth term of a geometric sequence, you can find the $(n+1)$th term by multiplying by r. That is, $a_{n+1} = r a_n$.

EXAMPLE 2   Finding the Terms of a Geometric Sequence

Write the first five terms of the geometric sequence whose first term is $a_1 = 3$ and whose common ratio is $r = 2$.

Solution
Starting with 3, repeatedly multiply by 2 to obtain the following.

$a_1 = 3$ 1st term

$a_2 = 3(2^1) = 6$ 2nd term

$a_3 = 3(2^2) = 12$ 3rd term

$a_4 = 3(2^3) = 24$ 4th term

$a_5 = 3(2^4) = 48$ 5th term

STUDY T!P

You can use a graphing utility to generate the geometric sequence in Example 2 using the following steps.

     3 (enter key)
     2 ⊠ (previous answer key)

Now press the enter key repeatedly to generate the terms of the sequence.

     Most graphing utilities have a built-in function that will display the terms of a geometric sequence. Consult your user's manual for instructions.

EXAMPLE 3   Finding a Term of a Geometric Sequence

Find the 15th term of the geometric sequence whose first term is 20 and whose common ratio is 1.05.

Algebraic Solution

$a_n = a_1 r^{n-1}$ Formula for a geometric sequence

$a_{15} = 20(1.05)^{15-1}$ Substitute for a_1, r, and n.

≈ 39.599 Use a calculator.

Numerical Solution

For this sequence, $r = 1.05$ and $a_1 = 20$. Use the *table* feature of a graphing utility to create a table that shows the value of $u_n = 20(1.05)^{n-1}$ for $n = 1$ through $n = 15$. From Figure 7.9, the number in the fifteenth row is approximately 39.599, so the 15th term of the geometric sequence is about 39.599.

n	u(n)
9	29.549
10	31.027
11	32.578
12	34.207
13	35.917
14	37.713
15	39.599

u(n)=39.59863199

Figure 7.9

EXAMPLE 4 Finding a Term of a Geometric Sequence

Find a formula for the nth term of the following geometric sequence. What is the 9th term of the sequence?

$$5, 15, 45, \ldots$$

Solution

The common ratio of this sequence is

$$r = \frac{15}{5} = 3.$$

Because the first term is $a_1 = 5$, the formula must have the form

$$a_n = a_1 r^{n-1} = 5(3)^{n-1}.$$

You can determine the 9th term ($n = 9$) to be

$$a_9 = 5(3)^{9-1} \qquad \text{Substitute 9 for } n.$$
$$= 5(6561) \qquad \text{Use a calculator.}$$
$$= 32{,}805. \qquad \text{Simplify.}$$

A graph of the first 9 terms of the sequence is shown in Figure 7.10. Notice that the points lie on an exponential curve. This makes sense because a_n is an exponential function of n.

If you know *any* two terms of a geometric sequence, you can use that information to find a formula for the nth term of the sequence.

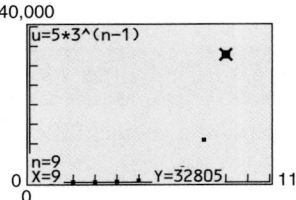

Figure 7.10

EXAMPLE 5 Finding a Term of a Geometric Sequence

The fourth term of a geometric sequence is 125, and the 10th term is 125/64. Find the 14th term. (Assume that the terms of the sequence are positive.)

Solution

The 10th term is related to the fourth term by the equation

$$a_{10} = a_4 r^6. \quad \text{Multiply 4th term by } r^{10-4}.$$

Because $a_{10} = 125/64$ and $a_4 = 125$, you can solve for r as follows.

$$\frac{125}{64} = 125r^6$$

$$\frac{1}{64} = r^6 \quad \Longrightarrow \quad \frac{1}{2} = r$$

You can obtain the 14th term by multiplying the 10th term by r^4.

$$a_{14} = a_{10}r^4$$

$$= \frac{125}{64}\left(\frac{1}{2}\right)^4 = \frac{125}{1024}$$

STUDY TIP

Remember that r is the common ratio of consecutive terms of a geometric sequence. So, in Example 5,

$$a_{10} = a_1 r^9$$

$$= a_1 \cdot r \cdot r \cdot r \cdot r^6$$

$$= a_1 \cdot \frac{a_2}{a_1} \cdot \frac{a_3}{a_2} \cdot \frac{a_4}{a_3} \cdot r^6$$

$$= a_4 r^6.$$

The Sum of a Finite Geometric Sequence

The formula for the sum of a *finite* geometric sequence is as follows. A proof of the formula is given in Appendix A.

The Sum of a Finite Geometric Sequence

The sum of the geometric sequence

$$a_1, \ a_1 r, \ a_1 r^2, \ a_1 r^3, \ a_1 r^4, \ \ldots, \ a_1 r^{n-1}$$

with common ratio $r \neq 1$ is

$$S_n = a_1 \left(\frac{1 - r^n}{1 - r} \right).$$

EXAMPLE 6   Finding the Sum of a Finite Geometric Sequence

Find the sum $\displaystyle \sum_{n=1}^{12} 4(0.3)^n$.

Solution

By writing out a few terms, you have

$$\sum_{n=1}^{12} 4(0.3)^n = 4(0.3) + 4(0.3)^2 + 4(0.3)^3 + \cdots + 4(0.3)^{12}.$$

Now, because $a_1 = 4(0.3)$, $r = 0.3$, and $n = 12$, you can apply the formula for the sum of a finite geometric sequence to obtain

$$\sum_{n=1}^{12} 4(0.3)^n = a_1 \left(\frac{1 - r^n}{1 - r} \right) \qquad \text{Formula for sum of a finite geometric sequence}$$

$$= 4(0.3) \left[\frac{1 - (0.3)^{12}}{1 - 0.3} \right] \qquad \text{Substitute for } a_1, r, \text{ and } n.$$

$$\approx 1.714.$$

When using the formula for the sum of a geometric sequence, be careful to check that the index begins at $i = 1$. If the index begins at $i = 0$, you must adjust the formula for the nth partial sum. For instance, if the index in Example 6 had begun with $n = 0$, the sum would have been

$$\sum_{n=0}^{12} 4(0.3)^n = 4 + \sum_{n=1}^{12} 4(0.3)^n$$

$$\approx 4 + 1.714$$

$$= 5.714.$$

> **STUDY T!P**
>
> Using a graphing calculator, you can calculate the sum of the sequence in Example 6 to be 1.7142848.
>
> Calculate the sum beginning at $n = 0$. You should obtain a sum of 5.7142848.

Geometric Series

The summation of the terms of an infinite geometric sequence is called an **infinite geometric series** or simply a **geometric series.**

The formula for the sum of a *finite* geometric sequence can, depending on the value of r, be extended to produce a formula for the sum of an *infinite* geometric series. Specifically, if the common ratio r has the property that $|r| < 1$, it can be shown that r^n becomes arbitrarily close to zero as n increases without bound. Consequently,

$$a_1\left(\frac{1 - r^n}{1 - r}\right) \longrightarrow a_1\left(\frac{1 - 0}{1 - r}\right) \quad \text{as} \quad n \longrightarrow \infty.$$

This result is summarized as follows.

The Sum of an Infinite Geometric Series

If $|r| < 1$, then the infinite geometric series

$$a_1, a_1r, a_1r^2, a_1r^3, \ldots, a_1r^{n-1}, \ldots$$

has the sum

$$S = \frac{a_1}{1 - r}.$$

EXAMPLE 7   Finding the Sum of an Infinite Geometric Series

Find each sum.

a. $\displaystyle\sum_{n=1}^{\infty} 4(0.6)^{n-1}$ **b.** $3 + 0.3 + 0.03 + 0.003 + \cdots$

Solution

a. $\displaystyle\sum_{n=1}^{\infty} 4(0.6)^{n-1} = 4(1) + 4(0.6) + 4(0.6)^2 + 4(0.6)^3 + \cdots + 4(0.6)^{n-1} + \cdots$

$$= \frac{4}{1 - (0.6)} \qquad \frac{a_1}{1 - r}$$

$$= 10$$

b. $3 + 0.3 + 0.03 + 0.003 + \cdots = 3 + 3(0.1) + 3(0.1)^2 + 3(0.1)^3 + \cdots$

$$= \frac{3}{1 - (0.1)} \qquad \frac{a_1}{1 - r}$$

$$= \frac{10}{3}$$

$$\approx 3.33$$

Application

EXAMPLE 8   Compound Interest

A deposit of $50 is made on the first day of each month in a savings account that pays 6% compounded monthly. What is the balance of this annuity at the end of 2 years?

Solution

The first deposit will gain interest for 24 months, and its balance will be

$$A_{24} = 50\left(1 + \frac{0.06}{12}\right)^{24} = 50(1.005)^{24}.$$

The second deposit will gain interest for 23 months, and its balance will be

$$A_{23} = 50\left(1 + \frac{0.06}{12}\right)^{23} = 50(1.005)^{23}.$$

The last deposit will gain interest for only 1 month, and its balance will be

$$A_1 = 50\left(1 + \frac{0.06}{12}\right)^{1} = 50(1.005).$$

The total balance in the account will be the sum of the balances of the 24 deposits. Using the formula for the sum of a finite geometric sequence, with $A_1 = 50(1.005)$ and $r = 1.005$, you have

$$S_n = a_1\left(\frac{1 - r^n}{1 - r}\right) \qquad \text{Formula for sum of a finite geometric sequence}$$

$$S_{24} = 50(1.005)\left[\frac{1 - (1.005)^{24}}{1 - 1.005}\right] \qquad \text{Substitute values for } a_1, r, \text{ and } n.$$

$$= \$1277.96. \qquad \text{Simplify.}$$

Activities

1. Determine which of the following are geometric sequences.

   a. $3, 6, 9, 12, 15, \ldots$

   b. $2, 4, 8, 16, 32, \ldots$

   c. $1, -1, 1, -1, 1, \ldots$

   d. $4, 2, 1, \frac{1}{2}, \frac{1}{4}, \ldots$

   e. $2, 4, 16, 64, 256, \ldots$

   Answer: b, c, d

2. Find the sum.

   $$\sum_{n=1}^{10} 16\left(\tfrac{1}{2}\right)^n$$

   Answer: 15.984

3. Find the sum.

   $$\sum_{n=0}^{\infty} 16\left(\tfrac{1}{2}\right)^n$$

   Answer: 32

Writing About Math   *An Experiment*

You will need a piece of string or yarn, a pair of scissors, and a tape measure. Measure out any length of string at least 5 feet long. Double over the string and cut it in half. Take one of the resulting halves, double it over, and cut it in half. Continue this process until you are no longer able to cut a length of string in half. How many cuts were you able to make? Construct a sequence of the resulting string lengths after each cut, starting with the original length of the string. Find a formula for the nth term of this sequence. How many cuts could you theoretically make? Write a short paragraph discussing why you were not able to make that many cuts.

7.3 Exercises

In Exercises 1–10, determine whether the sequence is geometric. If it is, find the common ratio.

1. 5, 15, 45, 135, . . . **2.** 3, 15, 75, 375, . . .

3. 6, 18, 30, 42, . . . **4.** 1, −2, 4, −8, . . .

5. 1, $-\frac{1}{2}$, $\frac{1}{4}$, $-\frac{1}{8}$, . . . **6.** 3, 0.6, 0.12, 0.024, . . .

7. $\frac{1}{2}$, $\frac{2}{3}$, $\frac{3}{4}$, $\frac{4}{5}$, . . . **8.** 9, −6, 4, $-\frac{8}{3}$, . . .

9. 1, $\frac{1}{2}$, $\frac{1}{3}$, $\frac{1}{4}$, . . . **10.** $\frac{1}{5}$, $\frac{2}{7}$, $\frac{3}{9}$, $\frac{4}{11}$, . . .

In Exercises 11–20, write the first five terms of the geometric sequence.

11. $a_1 = 8$, $r = 3$ **12.** $a_1 = 10$, $r = 2$

13. $a_1 = 1$, $r = \frac{1}{2}$ **14.** $a_1 = 2$, $r = \frac{1}{3}$

15. $a_1 = 5$, $r = -\frac{1}{10}$ **16.** $a_1 = 6$, $r = -\frac{1}{4}$

17. $a_1 = 3.5$, $r = 5$ **18.** $a_1 = 0.4$, $r = \frac{5}{2}$

19. $a_1 = 1$, $r = e$ **20.** $a_1 = 4$, $r = \sqrt{3}$

In Exercises 21–26, write the first five terms of the geometric sequence. Determine the common ratio and write the nth term of the sequence as a function of n.

21. $a_1 = 64$, $a_{k+1} = \frac{1}{2}a_k$

22. $a_1 = 81$, $a_{k+1} = \frac{1}{3}a_k$

23. $a_1 = 4$, $a_{k+1} = 3a_k$

24. $a_1 = 5$, $a_{k+1} = -2a_k$

25. $a_1 = 6$, $a_{k+1} = -\frac{3}{2}a_k$

26. $a_1 = 36$, $a_{k+1} = -\frac{2}{3}a_k$

In Exercises 27–36, find the nth term of the geometric sequence. Use a graphing utility to verify your answer numerically.

27. $a_1 = 4$, $r = \frac{1}{2}$, $n = 10$

28. $a_1 = 5$, $r = \frac{3}{2}$, $n = 8$

29. $a_1 = 6$, $r = -\frac{1}{3}$, $n = 12$

30. $a_1 = 8$, $r = \sqrt{5}$, $n = 9$

31. $a_1 = 500$, $r = 1.02$, $n = 14$

32. $a_1 = 1000$, $r = 1.005$, $n = 11$

33. $a_1 = 16$, $a_4 = \frac{27}{4}$, $n = 3$

34. $a_2 = 3$, $a_5 = \frac{3}{64}$, $n = 1$

35. $a_2 = -18$, $a_5 = \frac{2}{3}$, $n = 6$

36. $a_3 = \frac{16}{3}$, $a_5 = \frac{64}{27}$, $n = 7$

In Exercises 37–42, find the indicated nth term of the geometric sequence.

37. 9th term: 7, 21, 63, . . .

38. 7th term: 3, 36, 432, . . .

39. 10th term: 5, 30, 180, . . .

40. 22nd term: 4, 8, 16, . . .

41. 12th term: $\frac{3}{16}$, $\frac{3}{4}$, 3, . . .

42. 8th term: $\frac{1}{2}$, 8, 128, . . .

In Exercises 43–46, match the sequence with its graph. [The graphs are labeled (a), (b), (c), and (d).]

(a)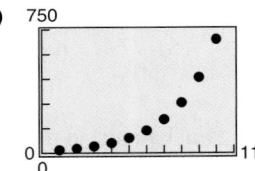

(b)

(c)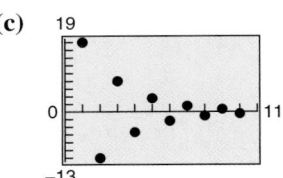

(d)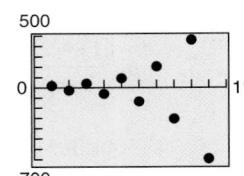

43. $a_n = 18\left(\frac{2}{3}\right)^{n-1}$ **44.** $a_n = 18\left(-\frac{2}{3}\right)^{n-1}$

45. $a_n = 18\left(\frac{3}{2}\right)^{n-1}$ **46.** $a_n = 18\left(-\frac{3}{2}\right)^{n-1}$

In Exercises 47–50, use a graphing utility to graph the first ten terms of the sequence.

47. $a_n = 12(-0.75)^{n-1}$ **48.** $a_n = 12(-0.4)^{n-1}$

49. $a_n = 2(1.3)^{n-1}$ **50.** $a_n = 2(-1.4)^{n-1}$

In Exercises 51 and 52, find the first four terms of the sequence of partial sums of the geometric series. In a sequence of partial sums, the term S_n is the sum of the first n terms of the sequence. For instance, S_2 is the sum of the first two terms.

51. 8, −4, 2, −1, $\frac{1}{2}$, . . . **52.** 8, 12, 18, 27, $\frac{81}{2}$, . . .

In Exercises 53 and 54, use a graphing utility to create a table showing the sequence of partial sums of the first ten terms of the series.

53. $\displaystyle\sum_{n=1}^{\infty} 16\left(\tfrac{1}{2}\right)^{n-1}$

54. $\displaystyle\sum_{n=1}^{\infty} 4(0.2)^{n-1}$

In Exercises 55–64, find the sum. Use a graphing utility to verify your result.

55. $\displaystyle\sum_{n=1}^{9} 2^{n-1}$

56. $\displaystyle\sum_{n=1}^{9} (-2)^{n-1}$

57. $\displaystyle\sum_{i=1}^{7} 64\left(-\tfrac{1}{2}\right)^{i-1}$

58. $\displaystyle\sum_{i=1}^{6} 32\left(\tfrac{1}{4}\right)^{i-1}$

59. $\displaystyle\sum_{n=0}^{20} 3\left(\tfrac{3}{2}\right)^{n}$

60. $\displaystyle\sum_{n=0}^{15} 2\left(\tfrac{4}{3}\right)^{n}$

61. $\displaystyle\sum_{i=1}^{10} 8\left(-\tfrac{1}{4}\right)^{i-1}$

62. $\displaystyle\sum_{i=1}^{10} 5\left(-\tfrac{1}{3}\right)^{i-1}$

63. $\displaystyle\sum_{n=0}^{5} 300(1.06)^{n}$

64. $\displaystyle\sum_{n=0}^{6} 500(1.04)^{n}$

In Exercises 65–68, use summation notation to express the sum.

65. $5 + 15 + 45 + \cdots + 3645$

66. $7 + 14 + 28 + \cdots + 896$

67. $2 - \tfrac{1}{2} + \tfrac{1}{8} - \cdots + \tfrac{1}{2048}$

68. $15 - 3 + \tfrac{3}{5} - \cdots - \tfrac{3}{625}$

In Exercises 69–84, find the sum of the infinite geometric series.

69. $\displaystyle\sum_{n=0}^{\infty} \left(\tfrac{1}{2}\right)^{n}$

70. $\displaystyle\sum_{n=0}^{\infty} 2\left(\tfrac{2}{3}\right)^{n}$

71. $\displaystyle\sum_{n=0}^{\infty} \left(-\tfrac{1}{2}\right)^{n}$

72. $\displaystyle\sum_{n=0}^{\infty} 2\left(-\tfrac{2}{3}\right)^{n}$

73. $\displaystyle\sum_{n=0}^{\infty} 4\left(\tfrac{1}{4}\right)^{n}$

74. $\displaystyle\sum_{n=0}^{\infty} \left(\tfrac{1}{10}\right)^{n}$

75. $\displaystyle\sum_{n=1}^{\infty} 2\left(\tfrac{7}{3}\right)^{n-1}$

76. $\displaystyle\sum_{n=1}^{\infty} \tfrac{1}{2}(2)^{n}$

77. $\displaystyle\sum_{n=0}^{\infty} (0.4)^{n}$

78. $\displaystyle\sum_{n=0}^{\infty} 4(0.2)^{n}$

79. $\displaystyle\sum_{n=0}^{\infty} -3(0.9)^{n}$

80. $\displaystyle\sum_{n=0}^{\infty} -10(0.2)^{n}$

81. $8 + 6 + \tfrac{9}{2} + \tfrac{27}{8} + \cdots$

82. $9 + 6 + 4 + \tfrac{8}{3} + \cdots$

83. $3 - 1 + \tfrac{1}{3} - \tfrac{1}{9} + \cdots$

84. $-6 + 5 - \tfrac{25}{6} + \tfrac{125}{36} - \cdots$

In Exercises 85–88, find the rational number representation of the repeating decimal.

85. $0.\overline{36}$

86. $0.\overline{297}$

87. $0.3\overline{18}$

88. $1.3\overline{8}$

89. *Compound Interest* A principal of $1000 is invested at 8% interest. Find the amount after 10 years if the interest is compounded (a) annually, (b) semiannually, (c) quarterly, (d) monthly, and (e) daily.

90. *Compound Interest* A principal of $2500 is invested at 7% interest. Find the amount after 20 years if the interest is compounded (a) annually, (b) semiannually, (c) quarterly, (d) monthly, and (e) daily.

91. *Depreciation* A company buys a machine for $155,000 and it depreciates at a rate of 30% per year. (In other words, at the end of each year the depreciated value is 70% of what it was at the beginning of the year.) Find the depreciated value of the machine after 5 full years.

92. *Population Growth* A city of 350,000 people is growing at a rate of 1.3% per year. Estimate the population of the city 30 years from now.

93. *Annuities* A deposit of $100 is made at the beginning of each month in an account that pays 6% interest, compounded monthly. The balance A in the account at the end of 5 years is

$$A = 100\left(1 + \frac{0.06}{12}\right)^{1} + \cdots + 100\left(1 + \frac{0.06}{12}\right)^{60}.$$

Find A.

94. *Annuities* A deposit of $50 is made at the beginning of each month in an account that pays 8% interest, compounded monthly. The balance A in the account at the end of 5 years is

$$A = 50\left(1 + \frac{0.08}{12}\right)^{1} + \cdots + 50\left(1 + \frac{0.08}{12}\right)^{60}.$$

Find A.

95. *Annuities* A deposit of P dollars is made at the beginning of each month in an account earning an annual interest rate r, compounded monthly. The balance A after t years is

$$A = P\left(1 + \frac{r}{12}\right) + P\left(1 + \frac{r}{12}\right)^{2} + \cdots + P\left(1 + \frac{r}{12}\right)^{12t}.$$

Show that the balance is

$$A = P\left[\left(1 + \frac{r}{12}\right)^{12t} - 1\right]\left(1 + \frac{12}{r}\right).$$

96. Annuities A deposit of P dollars is made at the beginning of each month in an account earning an annual interest rate r, compounded continuously. The balance A after t years is

$$A = Pe^{r/12} + Pe^{2r/12} + \cdots + Pe^{12tr/12}.$$

Show that the balance is $A = \dfrac{Pe^{r/12}(e^{rt} - 1)}{e^{r/12} - 1}$.

Annuities In Exercises 97–100, consider making monthly deposits of P dollars in a savings account earning an annual interest rate r. Use the results of Exercises 95 and 96 to find the balance A after t years if the interest is compounded (a) monthly and (b) continuously.

97. $P = \$50$, $r = 7\%$, $t = 20$ years

98. $P = \$75$, $r = 9\%$, $t = 25$ years

99. $P = \$100$, $r = 10\%$, $t = 40$ years

100. $P = \$20$, $r = 6\%$, $t = 50$ years

101. Annuities Consider an initial deposit of P dollars in an account earning an annual interest rate r, compounded monthly. At the end of each month, a withdrawal of W dollars will occur and the account will be depleted in t years. The amount of the initial deposit required is

$$P = W\left(1 + \frac{r}{12}\right)^{-1} + W\left(1 + \frac{r}{12}\right)^{-2} + \cdots$$
$$+ W\left(1 + \frac{r}{12}\right)^{-12t}.$$

Show that the initial deposit is

$$P = W\left(\frac{12}{r}\right)\left[1 - \left(1 + \frac{r}{12}\right)^{-12t}\right].$$

102. Annuities Determine the amount required in an individual retirement account for an individual who retires at age 65 and wants an income of $2000 from the account each month for 20 years. Use the result of Exercise 101, and assume that the account earns 9% compounded monthly.

103. Geometry The sides of a square are 16 inches in length. A new square is formed by connecting the midpoints of the sides of the original square, and two of the triangles are shaded. If this process is repeated five more times, determine the total area of the shaded region.

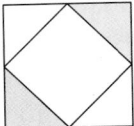 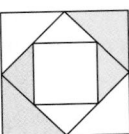 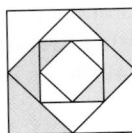 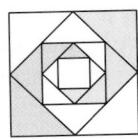

FIGURE FOR 103

104. Geometry The sides of a square are 27 inches in length. New squares are formed by dividing the original square into nine squares. The center square is then shaded. If this process is repeated three more times, determine the total area of the shaded region.

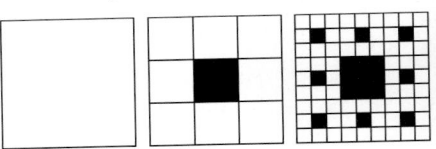

105. Corporate Revenue The annual revenues a_n (in billions of dollars) for the Coca-Cola Company for 1990 through 1996 can be approximated by the model

$$a_n = 3.978e^{0.11n}, \quad n = 0, 1, \ldots, 6$$

where $n = 0$ represents 1990. Use this model and the formula for the sum of a finite geometric sequence to approximate the total revenue earned during this 7-year period. (Source: Coca-Cola Enterprises, Inc.)

106. Distance A ball is dropped from a height of 16 feet. Each time it drops h feet, it rebounds $0.81h$ feet.

(a) Find the total distance traveled by the ball.

(b) The ball takes the following time for each fall.

$$s_1 = -16t^2 + 16, \qquad s_1 = 0 \text{ if } t = 1$$
$$s_2 = -16t^2 + 16(0.81), \qquad s_2 = 0 \text{ if } t = 0.9$$
$$s_3 = -16t^2 + 16(0.81)^2, \qquad s_3 = 0 \text{ if } t = (0.9)^2$$
$$s_4 = -16t^2 + 16(0.81)^3, \qquad s_4 = 0 \text{ if } t = (0.9)^3$$
$$\vdots \qquad\qquad\qquad \vdots$$
$$s_n = -16t^2 + 16(0.81)^{n-1}, \quad s_n = 0 \text{ if } t = (0.9)^{n-1}$$

Beginning with s_2, the ball takes the same amount of time to bounce up as it does to fall, and so the total time elapsed before it comes to rest is

$$t = 1 + 2\sum_{n=1}^{\infty} (0.9)^n.$$

Find this total.

107. *Salary* Suppose you go to work for a company that pays \$0.01 the first day, \$0.02 the second day, \$0.04 the third day, and so on. If the daily wage keeps doubling, what will your total income be for working (a) 29 days? (b) 30 days? (c) 31 days?

108. *Salary* A company is offering a job with a salary of \$30,000 for the first year. Suppose that during the next 39 years, there is a 5% raise each year. Determine the total compensation over the 40-year period.

Synthesis

True or False? **In Exercises 109–111, determine whether the statement is true or false. Justify your answer.**

109. A sequence is geometric if the ratios of consecutive differences of consecutive terms are the same.

110. You can find the nth term of a geometric sequence by multiplying its common ratio by the first term of the sequence raised to the $(n - 1)$ power.

111. A geometric sequence with a common ratio of 1 is also an arithmetic sequence.

In Exercises 112–115, write the first five terms of the geometric sequence.

112. $a_1 = 3, r = \dfrac{x}{2}$ **113.** $a_1 = 8, r = \dfrac{2x}{3}$

114. $a_1 = 5, r = 2x$ **115.** $a_1 = \frac{1}{2}, r = 7x$

In Exercises 116–119, find the nth term of the geometric sequence.

116. $a_1 = 100, r = e^x, n = 9$

117. $a_1 = 6, r = 3e^x, n = 8$

118. $a_1 = 1, r = -\dfrac{x}{3}, n = 7$

119. $a_1 = 4, r = \dfrac{4x}{3}, n = 6$

Graphical Reasoning **In Exercises 120 and 121, use a graphing utility to graph the function. Identify the horizontal asymptote of the graph and determine its relationship to the sum.**

120. $f(x) = 6\left[\dfrac{1 - (0.5)^x}{1 - (0.5)}\right]$, $\displaystyle\sum_{n=0}^{\infty} 6\left(\dfrac{1}{2}\right)^n$

121. $f(x) = 2\left[\dfrac{1 - (0.8)^x}{1 - (0.8)}\right]$, $\displaystyle\sum_{n=0}^{\infty} 2\left(\dfrac{4}{5}\right)^n$

122. *Writing* Write a brief paragraph explaining why the terms of a geometric sequence decrease in magnitude when $-1 < r < 1$.

123. *Writing* Write a brief paragraph explaining how to use the first two terms of a geometric sequence to find the nth term.

Review

124. The ratio of cement to sand in a 90-pound bag of dry mix is 1 to 4. Find the number of pounds of sand in the bag.

125. A truck traveled at an average speed of 50 miles per hour on a 200-mile trip. On the return trip, the average speed was 42 miles per hour. Find the average speed for the round trip.

126. Find two consecutive positive even integers whose product is 624.

127. Suppose your friend can mow a lawn in 4 hours and you can mow it in 6 hours. How long will it take both of you to mow the lawn?

In Exercises 128–131, perform the matrix operation.

128. $\begin{bmatrix} 4 & -1 \\ 6 & 2 \end{bmatrix}\begin{bmatrix} 1 & 3 \\ -2 & 5 \end{bmatrix}$

129. $-4\begin{bmatrix} 7 & 2 \\ -6 & 0 \end{bmatrix} + \begin{bmatrix} -5 & 5 \\ 3 & 1 \end{bmatrix}$

130. $\begin{bmatrix} -1 & 3 & 4 \\ -2 & 8 & 0 \\ 2 & 5 & -1 \end{bmatrix}\begin{bmatrix} -1 & 0 & 4 \\ -4 & 3 & 5 \\ 0 & 2 & -3 \end{bmatrix}$

131. $2\begin{bmatrix} -1 & 3 & 4 \\ -2 & 8 & 0 \\ 2 & 5 & -1 \end{bmatrix} - 4\begin{bmatrix} -1 & 0 & 4 \\ -4 & 3 & 5 \\ 0 & 2 & -3 \end{bmatrix}$

In Exercises 132–135, find the sum.

132. $\displaystyle\sum_{i=1}^{4} (3i + 4)$ **133.** $\displaystyle\sum_{i=0}^{6} 4i^2$

134. $\displaystyle\sum_{k=1}^{5} 12$ **135.** $\displaystyle\sum_{k=0}^{4} \dfrac{2}{k^2 + 2}$

7.4 Mathematical Induction

Introduction

In this section you will study a form of mathematical proof called **mathematical induction.** It is important that you clearly see the logical need for it, so let's take a closer look at a problem discussed in Example 5 on page 510.

$$S_1 = 1 = 1^2$$

$$S_2 = 1 + 3 = 2^2$$

$$S_3 = 1 + 3 + 5 = 3^2$$

$$S_4 = 1 + 3 + 5 + 7 = 4^2$$

$$S_5 = 1 + 3 + 5 + 7 + 9 = 5^2$$

Judging from the pattern formed by these first five sums, it appears that the sum of the first n odd integers is

$$S_n = 1 + 3 + 5 + 7 + 9 + \cdots + (2n - 1) = n^2.$$

Although this particular formula is valid, it is important for you to see that recognizing a pattern and then simply *jumping to the conclusion* that the pattern must be true for all values of n is *not* a logically valid method of proof. There are many examples in which a pattern appears to be developing for small values of n but then fails at some point. One of the most famous cases of this was the conjecture by the French mathematician Pierre de Fermat (1601–1665), who speculated that all numbers of the form

$$F_n = 2^{2^n} + 1, \quad n = 0, 1, 2, \ldots$$

are prime. For $n = 0, 1, 2, 3,$ and 4, the conjecture is true.

$$F_0 = 3$$

$$F_1 = 5$$

$$F_2 = 17$$

$$F_3 = 257$$

$$F_4 = 65,537$$

The size of the next Fermat number ($F_5 = 4,294,967,297$) is so great that it was difficult for Fermat to determine whether or not it was prime. However, another well-known mathematician, Leonhard Euler (1707–1783), later found a factorization

$$F_5 = 4,294,967,297$$

$$= 641(6,700,417)$$

which proved that F_5 is not prime. Therefore Fermat's conjecture was false.

Just because a rule, pattern, or formula seems to work for several values of n, you cannot simply decide that it is valid for *all* values of n without going through a *legitimate proof.*

What You Should Learn:

- How to use mathematical induction to prove statements involving a positive integer n
- How to find sums of powers of integers
- How to find finite differences of sequences

Why You Should Learn It:

Mathematical induction can be used to prove statements involving positive integers. For instance, in Exercises 27–35 on page 532, you are asked to use mathematical induction to prove properties of positive integers.

The Principle of Mathematical Induction

Let P_n be a statement involving the positive integer n. If

1. P_1 is true, and

2. the truth of P_k implies the truth of P_{k+1}, for every positive k,

then P_n must be true for all positive integers n.

To apply the Principle of Mathematical Induction, you need to be able to determine the statement P_{k+1} for a given statement P_k.

EXAMPLE 1   A Preliminary Example

Find P_{k+1} for the following.

a. $P_k : S_k = \dfrac{k^2(k+1)^2}{4}$

b. $P_k : S_k = 1 + 5 + 9 + \cdots + [4(k-1) - 3] + (4k - 3)$

c. $P_k : 3^k \geq 2k + 1$

Solution

a. $P_{k+1} : S_{k+1} = \dfrac{(k+1)^2(k+1+1)^2}{4}$ Substitute $k+1$ for k.

$\qquad\qquad = \dfrac{(k+1)^2(k+2)^2}{4}$ Simplify.

b. $P_{k+1} : S_{k+1} = 1 + 5 + 9 + \cdots + \{4[(k+1) - 1] - 3\} + [4(k+1) - 3]$

$\qquad\qquad = 1 + 5 + 9 + \cdots + (4k - 3) + (4k + 1)$

c. $P_{k+1} : 3^{k+1} \geq 2(k+1) + 1$

$\qquad\qquad 3^{k+1} \geq 2k + 3$

A well-known illustration used to explain why the Principle of Mathematical Induction works is the unending line of dominoes represented by Figure 7.11. If the line actually contains infinitely many dominoes, it is clear that you could not knock down the entire line by knocking down only *one domino* at a time. However, suppose it were true that each domino would knock down the next one as it fell. Then you could knock them all down simply by pushing the first one and starting a chain reaction. Mathematical induction works in the same way. If the truth of P_k implies the truth of P_{k+1} and if P_1 is true, the chain reaction proceeds as follows: P_1 implies P_2, P_2 implies P_3, P_3 implies P_4, and so on.

Figure 7.11

When using mathematical induction to prove a *summation* formula (such as the one in Example 2), it is helpful to think of S_{k+1} as

$$S_{k+1} = S_k + a_{k+1}$$

where a_{k+1} is the $(k + 1)$ term of the original sum.

Your students may benefit from many demonstrations of proof by induction. Consider using proofs of the following.

$3 + 6 + 9 + 12 + \cdots + 3n$

$$= \tfrac{3}{2}n(n + 1)$$

$5 + 7 + 9 + 11 + \cdots + (3 + 2n)$

$$= n(n + 4)$$

EXAMPLE 2   Using Mathematical Induction

Use mathematical induction to prove the following formula.

$$S_n = 1 + 3 + 5 + 7 + \cdots + (2n - 1)$$
$$= n^2$$

Solution

Mathematical induction consists of two distinct parts. First, you must show that the formula is true when $n = 1$.

1. When $n = 1$, the formula is valid, because

$$S_1 = 1 = 1^2.$$

The second part of mathematical induction has two steps. The first step is to assume that the formula is valid for *some* integer k. The second step is to use this assumption to prove that the formula is valid for the next integer, $k + 1$.

2. Assuming that the formula

$$S_k = 1 + 3 + 5 + 7 + \cdots + (2k - 1)$$
$$= k^2$$

is true, you must show that the formula $S_{k+1} = (k + 1)^2$ is true.

$$
\begin{aligned}
S_{k+1} &= 1 + 3 + 5 + 7 + \cdots + (2k - 1) + [2(k + 1) - 1] \\
&= [1 + 3 + 5 + 7 + \cdots + (2k - 1)] + (2k + 2 - 1) \\
&= S_k + (2k + 1) \qquad \text{Group terms to form } S_k. \\
&= k^2 + 2k + 1 \qquad \text{Substitute } k^2 \text{ for } S_k. \\
&= (k + 1)^2
\end{aligned}
$$

Combining the results of parts (1) and (2), you can conclude by mathematical induction that the formula is valid for *all* positive integer values of n.

It occasionally happens that a statement involving natural numbers is not true for the first $k - 1$ positive integers but is true for all values of $n \geq k$. In these instances, you use a slight variation of the Principle of Mathematical Induction in which you verify P_k rather than P_1. This variation is called the *extended principle of mathematical induction*. To see the validity of this, note from Figure 7.11 that all but the first $k - 1$ dominoes can be knocked down by knocking over the kth domino. This suggests that you can prove a statement P_n to be true for $n \geq k$ by showing that P_k is true and that P_k implies P_{k+1}. In Exercises 21–26 in this section, you are asked to apply this extension of mathematical induction.

EXAMPLE 3   Using Mathematical Induction

Use mathematical induction to prove the formula

$$S_n = 1^2 + 2^2 + 3^2 + 4^2 + \cdots + n^2$$

$$= \frac{n(n + 1)(2n + 1)}{6}$$

for all $n \geq 1$.

Solution

1. When $n = 1$, the formula is valid, because

$$S_1 = 1^2 = \frac{1(2)(3)}{6}.$$

2. Assuming that

$$S_k = 1^2 + 2^2 + 3^2 + 4^2 + \cdots + k^2$$

$$= \frac{k(k + 1)(2k + 1)}{6}$$

you must show that

$$S_{k+1} = \frac{(k + 1)(k + 1 + 1)[2(k + 1) + 1]}{6} = \frac{(k + 1)(k + 2)(2k + 3)}{6}.$$

To do this, write the following.

$$S_{k+1} = S_k + a_{k+1}$$

$$= (1^2 + 2^2 + 3^2 + 4^2 + \cdots + k^2) + (k + 1)^2$$

$$= \frac{k(k + 1)(2k + 1)}{6} + (k + 1)^2$$

$$= \frac{k(k + 1)(2k + 1) + 6(k + 1)^2}{6}$$

$$= \frac{(k + 1)[k(2k + 1) + 6(k + 1)]}{6}$$

$$= \frac{(k + 1)(2k^2 + 7k + 6)}{6}$$

$$= \frac{(k + 1)(k + 2)(2k + 3)}{6}$$

Combining the results of parts (1) and (2), you can conclude by mathematical induction that the formula is valid for *all* $n \geq 1$.

When proving a formula with mathematical induction, the only statement that you *need* to verify is P_1. As a check, however, it is a good idea to try verifying some of the other statements. For instance, in Example 3, try verifying P_2 and P_3.

Sums of Powers of Integers

The formula in Example 3 is one of a collection of useful summation formulas. This and other formulas dealing with the sums of various powers of the first n positive integers are summarized as follows.

Sums of Powers of Integers

1. $\displaystyle\sum_{i=1}^{n} i = 1 + 2 + 3 + 4 + \cdots + n = \frac{n(n+1)}{2}$

2. $\displaystyle\sum_{i=1}^{n} i^2 = 1^2 + 2^2 + 3^2 + 4^2 + \cdots + n^2 = \frac{n(n+1)(2n+1)}{6}$

3. $\displaystyle\sum_{i=1}^{n} i^3 = 1^3 + 2^3 + 3^3 + 4^3 + \cdots + n^3 = \frac{n^2(n+1)^2}{4}$

4. $\displaystyle\sum_{i=1}^{n} i^4 = 1^4 + 2^4 + 3^4 + 4^4 + \cdots + n^4 = \frac{n(n+1)(2n+1)(3n^2+3n-1)}{30}$

5. $\displaystyle\sum_{i=1}^{n} i^5 = 1^5 + 2^5 + 3^5 + 4^5 + \cdots + n^5 = \frac{n^2(n+1)^2(2n^2+2n-1)}{12}$

Each of these formulas for sums can be proven by mathematical induction. (See Exercises 13, 14, 17, and 18 in this section.)

EXAMPLE 4   Proving an Inequality by Mathematical Induction

Prove that $n < 2^n$ for all positive integers n.

Solution

1. For $n = 1$ and $n = 2$, the formula is true, because

$$1 < 2^1 \text{ and } 2 < 2^2.$$

2. Assuming that

$$k < 2^k$$

you need to show that $k + 1 < 2^{k+1}$. Note first that

$$2^{k+1} = 2(2^k) > 2(k) = 2k. \qquad \text{By assumption } 2^k > k.$$

Because $2k = k + k > k + 1$ for all $k > 1$, it follows that

$$2^{k+1} > 2k > k + 1$$

or

$$k + 1 < 2^{k+1}.$$

Therefore, $n < 2^n$ for all integers $n \geq 1$.

Finite Differences

The **first differences** of a sequence are found by subtracting consecutive terms. The **second differences** are found by subtracting consecutive first differences. The first and second differences of the sequence 3, 5, 8, 12, 17, 23, . . . are as follows.

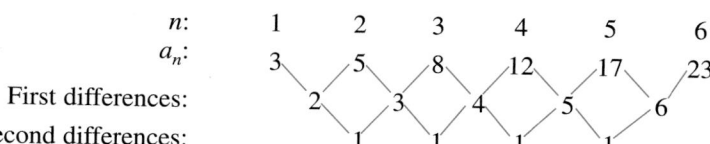

$$n: \quad 1 \quad 2 \quad 3 \quad 4 \quad 5 \quad 6$$
$$a_n: \quad 3 \quad 5 \quad 8 \quad 12 \quad 17 \quad 23$$

First differences: 2   3   4   5   6

Second differences: 1   1   1   1

For this sequence, the second differences are all the same. When this happens, and the second differences are nonzero, the sequence has a perfect quadratic model. If the first differences are all the same nonzero number, the sequence has a linear model—that is, it is arithmetic.

EXAMPLE 5   Finding a Quadratic Model

Find the quadratic model for the sequence 3, 5, 8, 12, 17, 23, ...

Solution

You know from the second differences shown above the model is quadratic and has the form

$$a_n = an^2 + bn + c.$$

By substituting 1, 2, and 3 for n, you can obtain a system of three linear equations in three variables.

$$a_1 = a(1)^2 + b(1) + c = 3 \qquad \text{Substitute 1 for } n.$$

$$a_2 = a(2)^2 + b(2) + c = 5 \qquad \text{Substitute 2 for } n.$$

$$a_3 = a(3)^2 + b(3) + c = 8 \qquad \text{Substitute 3 for } n.$$

You now have a system of three equations in a, b, and c.

$$a + b + c = 3 \qquad \text{Equation 1}$$

$$4a + 2b + c = 5 \qquad \text{Equation 2}$$

$$9a + 3b + c = 8 \qquad \text{Equation 3}$$

Solving this system of equations using techniques discussed in Chapter 5, you can find the solution to be $a = \frac{1}{2}$, $b = \frac{1}{2}$, and $c = 2$. So, the quadratic model is

$$a_n = \frac{1}{2}n^2 + \frac{1}{2}n + 2.$$

Check the values of a_1, a_2, and a_3 as follows.

Check

$$a_1 = \frac{1}{2}(1)^2 + \frac{1}{2}(1) + 2 = 3 \qquad \text{Solution checks. } \checkmark$$

$$a_2 = \frac{1}{2}(2)^2 + \frac{1}{2}(2) + 2 = 5 \qquad \text{Solution checks. } \checkmark$$

$$a_3 = \frac{1}{2}(3)^2 + \frac{1}{2}(3) + 2 = 8 \qquad \text{Solution checks. } \checkmark$$

Group Activity Suggestion

A regular n-sided polygon is a polygon that has n equal sides and n equal angles. For instance, an equilateral triangle is a regular three-sided polygon. Each angle of an equilateral triangle measures 60°, and the sum of all three angles is 180°. Similarly, the sum of the four angles of a four-sided polygon (a square) is 360°.

Polygon	Number of Sides	Sum of Angles
Equilateral triangle	3	180°
Square	4	360°
Regular pentagon	5	540°
Regular hexagon	6	720°

a. The list above gives the sums of angles of four regular polygons. Use this data to write a conjecture about the sum of the angles of any regular n-sided polygon.

b. Discuss how you could *prove* that your formula is valid.

7.4 Exercises

In Exercises 1–6, find P_{k+1} for the given P_k.

1. $P_k = \dfrac{5}{k(k+1)}$

2. $P_k = \dfrac{4}{(k+2)(k+3)}$

3. $P_k = \dfrac{k^2(k+3)^2}{6}$

4. $P_k = \dfrac{k}{2}(5k-3)$

5. $P_k = 1 + 6 + 11 + \cdots + [5(k-1) - 4] + (5k - 4)$

6. $P_k = 7 + 13 + 19 + \cdots + [6(k-1) + 1] + (6k + 1)$

In Exercises 7–20, use mathematical induction to prove the formula for every positive integer n.

7. $2 + 4 + 6 + 8 + \cdots + 2n = n(n+1)$

8. $1 + 5 + 9 + 13 + \cdots + (4n - 3) = n(2n - 1)$

9. $3 + 8 + 13 + 18 + \cdots + (5n - 2) = \dfrac{n}{2}(5n + 1)$

10. $1 + 4 + 7 + 10 + \cdots + (3n - 2) = \dfrac{n}{2}(3n - 1)$

11. $1 + 2 + 2^2 + 2^3 + \cdots + 2^{n-1} = 2^n - 1$

12. $2(1 + 3 + 3^2 + 3^3 + \cdots + 3^{n-1}) = 3^n - 1$

13. $1 + 2 + 3 + 4 + \cdots + n = \dfrac{n(n+1)}{2}$

14. $1^3 + 2^3 + 3^3 + 4^3 + \cdots + n^3 = \dfrac{n^2(n+1)^2}{4}$

15. $1^2 + 3^2 + 5^2 + \cdots + (2n-1)^2 = \dfrac{n(2n-1)(2n+1)}{3}$

16. $\left(1 + \dfrac{1}{1}\right)\left(1 + \dfrac{1}{2}\right)\left(1 + \dfrac{1}{3}\right) \cdots \left(1 + \dfrac{1}{n}\right) = n + 1$

17. $\displaystyle\sum_{i=1}^{n} i^4 = \dfrac{n(n+1)(2n+1)(3n^2 + 3n - 1)}{30}$

18. $\displaystyle\sum_{i=1}^{n} i^5 = \dfrac{n^2(n+1)^2(2n^2 + 2n - 1)}{12}$

19. $\displaystyle\sum_{i=1}^{n} i(i+1) = \dfrac{n(n+1)(n+2)}{3}$

20. $\displaystyle\sum_{i=1}^{n} \dfrac{1}{(2i-1)(2i+1)} = \dfrac{n}{2n+1}$

In Exercises 21–26, prove the inequality for the indicated integer values of n.

21. $n! > 2^n, \quad n \geq 4$

22. $\left(\dfrac{4}{3}\right)^n > n, \quad n \geq 7$

23. $\dfrac{1}{\sqrt{1}} + \dfrac{1}{\sqrt{2}} + \dfrac{1}{\sqrt{3}} + \cdots + \dfrac{1}{\sqrt{n}} > \sqrt{n}, \quad n \geq 2$

24. $\left(\dfrac{x}{y}\right)^{n+1} < \left(\dfrac{x}{y}\right)^{n}, \quad n \geq 1 \text{ and } 0 < x < y$

25. $(1 + a)^n \geq na, \quad n \geq 1, \quad a > 1$

26. $3^n > n\,2^n, \quad n \geq 1$

In Exercises 27–35, use mathematical induction to prove the given property for all positive integers n.

27. $(ab)^n = a^n b^n$

28. $\left(\dfrac{a}{b}\right)^n = \dfrac{a^n}{b^n}$

29. If $x_1 \neq 0$, $x_2 \neq 0$, $\ldots$, $x_n \neq 0$, then
$(x_1 x_2 x_3 \cdots x_n)^{-1} = x_1^{-1} x_2^{-1} x_3^{-1} \cdots x_n^{-1}$.

30. If $x_1 > 0$, $x_2 > 0$, $\ldots$, $x_n > 0$, then
$\ln(x_1 x_2 x_3 \cdots x_n) = \ln x_1 + \ln x_2 + \ln x_3$
$\qquad\qquad\qquad + \cdots + \ln x_n$.

31. Generalized Distributive Law:
$x(y_1 + y_2 + \cdots + y_n) = xy_1 + xy_2 + \cdots + xy_n$

32. $(a + bi)^n$ and $(a - bi)^n$ are complex conjugates for all $n \geq 1$.

33. A factor of $(n^3 + 3n^2 + 2n)$ is 3.

34. A factor of $(2^{2n-1} + 3^{2n-1})$ is 5.

35. A factor of $(9^n - 8n - 1)$ is 64 for all $n \geq 2$.

In Exercises 36–39, write the first five terms of the sequence.

36. $a_0 = 1$
$a_n = a_{n-1} + 2$

37. $a_0 = 10$
$a_n = 4a_{n-1}$

38. $a_0 = 4$
$a_1 = 2$
$a_n = a_{n-1} - a_{n-2}$

39. $a_0 = 0$
$a_1 = 2$
$a_n = a_{n-1} + 2a_{n-2}$

In Exercises 40–49, write the first five terms of the sequence beginning with the given term. Then calculate the first and second differences of the sequence. Does the sequence have a linear model, a quadratic model, or neither?

40. $a_1 = 0$
$a_n = a_{n-1} + 3$

41. $a_1 = 2$
$a_n = n - a_{n-1}$

42. $a_1 = 3$
$a_n = a_{n-1} - n$

43. $a_2 = -3$
$a_n = -2a_{n-1}$

44. $a_0 = 0$
$a_n = a_{n-1} + n$

45. $a_0 = 2$
$a_n = (a_{n-1})^2$

46. $a_1 = 2$
$a_n = a_{n-1} + 2$

47. $a_1 = 0$
$a_n = a_{n-1} + 2n$

48. $a_0 = 1$
$a_n = a_{n-1} + n^2$

49. $a_0 = 0$
$a_n = a_{n-1} - 1$

In Exercises 50–53, find a quadratic model for the sequence with the indicated terms.

50. $a_0 = 3$, $a_1 = 3$, $a_4 = 15$

51. $a_0 = 7$, $a_1 = 6$, $a_3 = 10$

52. $a_0 = -3$, $a_2 = 1$, $a_4 = 9$

53. $a_0 = 3$, $a_2 = 0$, $a_6 = 36$

Synthesis

True or False?   In Exercises 54–56, determine whether the statement is true or false. Justify your answer.

54. If the statement P_k is true and P_k implies P_{k+1}, then P_1 is also true.

55. If a sequence is arithmetic, then the first differences of the sequence are all zero.

56. A sequence with n terms has $n - 1$ second differences.

57. *Writing*   In your own words, explain what is meant by a proof by mathematical induction.

58. *Think About It*   What conclusion can be drawn from the given information about the sequence of statements P_n?

(a) P_3 is true and P_k implies P_{k+1}.

(b) $P_1, P_2, P_3, \ldots, P_{50}$ are all true.

(c) P_1, P_2, and P_3 are all true, but the truth of P_k does not imply that P_{k+1} is true.

(d) P_2 is true and P_{2k} implies P_{2k+2}.

Review

In Exercises 59–62, solve the system of equations.

59. $\begin{cases} x - y = 2 \\ -4x + 5y = -3 \end{cases}$

60. $\begin{cases} x - 3y = 1 \\ 7x - 6y = -38 \end{cases}$

61. $\begin{cases} y = x^2 \\ -3x + 2y = 2 \end{cases}$

62. $\begin{cases} x - y^3 = 0 \\ x - 2y^2 = 0 \end{cases}$

In Exercises 63–66, use Gauss-Jordan elimination to solve the system.

63. $\begin{cases} x - y = -1 \\ x + 2y - 2z = 3 \\ 3x - y + 2z = 3 \end{cases}$

64. $\begin{cases} 2x + y - 2z = 1 \\ x - z = 1 \\ 3x + 3y + z = 12 \end{cases}$

65. $\begin{cases} -3x + y + 5z = 25 \\ x - 2y + 3z = 7 \\ 2x + 3y - z = 0 \end{cases}$

66. $\begin{cases} 2x - y + 4z = 21 \\ -4x + 3y + z = -14 \\ -x - 4y + 7z = 12 \end{cases}$

In Exercises 67 and 68, find the determinant of the matrix.

67. $\begin{bmatrix} 7 & 6 \\ -4 & 2 \end{bmatrix}$

68. $\begin{bmatrix} 2 & 4 & 8 \\ 0 & 6 & -9 \\ 4 & -3 & 8 \end{bmatrix}$

In Exercises 69–72, expand the expression.

69. $(2x^2 - 1)^2$

70. $(2x - y)^2$

71. $(5 - 4x)^3$

72. $(2x - 4y)^3$

7.5   The Binomial Theorem

Binomial Coefficients

Recall that a *binomial* is a polynomial that has two terms. In this section, you will study a formula that provides a quick method of raising a binomial to a power. To begin, look at the expansion of

$$(x + y)^n$$

for several values of n.

$$(x + y)^0 = 1$$

$$(x + y)^1 = x + y$$

$$(x + y)^2 = x^2 + 2xy + y^2$$

$$(x + y)^3 = x^3 + 3x^2y + 3xy^2 + y^3$$

$$(x + y)^4 = x^4 + 4x^3y + 6x^2y^2 + 4xy^3 + y^4$$

$$(x + y)^5 = x^5 + 5x^4y + 10x^3y^2 + 10x^2y^3 + 5xy^4 + y^5$$

There are several observations you can make about these expansions.

1. In each expansion, there are $n + 1$ terms.

2. In each expansion, x and y have symmetric roles. The powers of x decrease by 1 in successive terms, whereas the powers of y increase by 1.

3. The sum of the powers of each term is n. For instance, in the expansion of $(x + y)^5$, the sum of the powers of each term is 5.

$$4 + 1 = 5 \quad 3 + 2 = 5$$

$$(x + y)^5 = x^5 + 5x^4y^1 + 10x^3y^2 + 10x^2y^3 + 5x^1y^4 + y^5$$

4. The coefficients increase and then decrease in a symmetric pattern.

The coefficients of a binomial expansion are called **binomial coefficients.** To find them, you can use the **Binomial Theorem.** A proof of this theorem is given in Appendix A.

What You Should Learn:

- How to use the Binomial Theorem to calculate binomial coefficients
- How to use Pascal's Triangle to calculate binomial coefficients
- How to use binomial coefficients to write binomial expansions

Why You Should Learn It:

You can use binomial coefficients to predict future behavior. For instance, in Exercise 84 on page 540, you are asked to use binomial coefficients to find the probability that a baseball player gets 3 hits during the next 10 times at bat.

Jonathan Daniel/Allsport

The Binomial Theorem

In the expansion of $(x + y)^n$

$$(x + y)^n = x^n + nx^{n-1}y + \cdots +_n C_r\, x^{n-r}y^r + \cdots + nxy^{n-1} + y^n$$

the coefficient of $x^{n-r}y^r$ is

$$_n C_r = \frac{n!}{(n-r)!r!}.$$

The symbol $\binom{n}{r}$ is often used in place of $_n C_r$ to denote binomial coefficients.

EXAMPLE 1   Finding Binomial Coefficients

Find the binomial coefficients.

a. $_8C_2$ **b.** $\binom{10}{3}$ **c.** $_7C_0$ **d.** $\binom{8}{8}$

Solution

a. $_8C_2 = \dfrac{8!}{6! \cdot 2!} = \dfrac{(8 \cdot 7) \cdot 6!}{6! \cdot 2!} = \dfrac{8 \cdot 7}{2 \cdot 1} = 28$

b. $\binom{10}{3} = \dfrac{10!}{7! \cdot 3!} = \dfrac{(10 \cdot 9 \cdot 8) \cdot 7!}{7! \cdot 3!} = \dfrac{10 \cdot 9 \cdot 8}{3 \cdot 2 \cdot 1} = 120$

c. $_7C_0 = \dfrac{7!}{7! \cdot 0!} = 1$

d. $\binom{8}{8} = \dfrac{8!}{0! \cdot 8!} = 1$

When $r \neq 0$ and $r \neq n$, as in parts (a) and (b) above, there is a simple pattern for evaluating binomial coefficients.

$$\underbrace{_8C_2 = \overbrace{\dfrac{8 \cdot 7}{2 \cdot 1}}^{2 \text{ factors}}}_{2 \text{ factorial}} \quad \text{and} \quad \binom{10}{3} = \underbrace{\dfrac{\overbrace{10 \cdot 9 \cdot 8}^{3 \text{ factors}}}{3 \cdot 2 \cdot 1}}_{3 \text{ factorial}}$$

EXAMPLE 2   Finding Binomial Coefficients

Find the binomial coefficients.

a. $_7C_3$ **b.** $_7C_4$ **c.** $_{12}C_1$ **d.** $_{12}C_{11}$

Solution

a. $_7C_3 = \dfrac{7 \cdot 6 \cdot 5}{3 \cdot 2 \cdot 1} = 35$

b. $_7C_4 = \dfrac{7 \cdot 6 \cdot 5 \cdot 4}{4 \cdot 3 \cdot 2 \cdot 1} = 35$

c. $_{12}C_1 = \dfrac{12}{1} = 12$

d. $_{12}C_{11} = \dfrac{12!}{1! \cdot 11!} = \dfrac{(12) \cdot 11!}{1! \cdot 11!} = \dfrac{12}{1} = 12$

It is not a coincidence that the results in parts (a) and (b) of Example 2 are the same and that the results in parts (c) and (d) are the same. In general, it is true that

$$_nC_r = {_nC_{n-r}}.$$

This shows the symmetric property of binomial coefficients that was identified earlier.

STUDY T!P

Most graphing calculators are programmed to evaluate $_nC_r$. Consult your user's manual to evaluate the binomial coefficients in Example 1.

Exploration

Find the following pairs of binomial coefficients.

a. $_7C_0, {_7C_7}$

b. $_8C_0, {_8C_8}$

c. $_{10}C_0, {_{10}C_{10}}$

d. $_7C_1, {_7C_6}$

e. $_8C_1, {_8C_7}$

f. $_{10}C_1, {_{10}C_9}$

What do you observe about the pairs in (a), (b), and (c)? What do you observe about the pairs in (d), (e), and (f)? Write two conjectures from your observations. Develop a convincing argument for your two conjectures.

Pascal's Triangle

There is a convenient way to remember a pattern for binomial coefficients. By arranging the coefficients in a triangular pattern, you obtain the following array, which is called **Pascal's Triangle.** This triangle is named after the famous French mathematician Blaise Pascal (1623–1662).

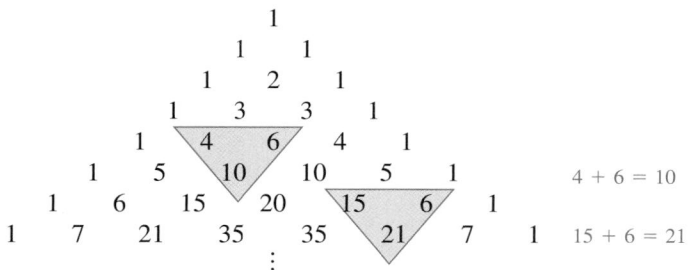

$$4 + 6 = 10$$

$$15 + 6 = 21$$

The first and last number in each row of Pascal's Triangle is 1. Every other number in each row is formed by adding the two numbers immediately above the number. Pascal noticed that numbers in this triangle are precisely the same numbers as the coefficients of binomial expansions.

$$(x + y)^0 = 1$$
$$(x + y)^1 = 1x + 1y$$
$$(x + y)^2 = 1x^2 + 2xy + 1y^2$$
$$(x + y)^3 = 1x^3 + 3x^2y + 3xy^2 + 1y^3$$
$$(x + y)^4 = 1x^4 + 4x^3y + 6x^2y^2 + 4xy^3 + 1y^4$$
$$(x + y)^5 = 1x^5 + 5x^4y + 10x^3y^2 + 10x^2y^3 + 5xy^4 + 1y^5$$
$$(x + y)^6 = 1x^6 + 6x^5y + 15x^4y^2 + 20x^3y^3 + 15x^2y^4 + 6xy^5 + 1y^6$$
$$(x + y)^7 = 1x^7 + 7x^6y + 21x^5y^2 + 35x^4y^3 + 35x^3y^4 + 21x^2y^5 + 7xy^6 + 1y^7$$
$$\vdots$$

The top row in Pascal's Triangle is called the *zero row* because it corresponds to the binomial expansion $(x + y)^0 = 1$.

Similarly, the next row is called the *first row* because it corresponds to the binomial expansion $(x + y)^1 = 1(x) + 1(y)$.

In general, the *nth row* in Pascal's Triangle gives the coefficients of $(x + y)^n$.

Exploration

Complete the following table and describe the result.

n	r	$_nC_r$	$_nC_{n-r}$
9	5		
7	1		
12	4		
6	0		
10	7		

What characteristics of Pascal's Triangle are illustrated by the table?

EXAMPLE 3   Using Pascal's Triangle

Use the seventh row of Pascal's Triangle to find the binomial coefficients.

$$_8C_0, \, _8C_1, \, _8C_2, \, _8C_3, \, _8C_4, \, _8C_5, \, _8C_6, \, _8C_7, \, _8C_8$$

Solution

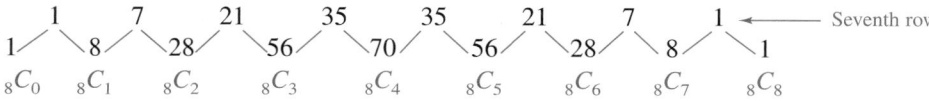

Seventh row

Binomial Expansions

As mentioned at the beginning of this section, when you write out the coefficients for a binomial that is raised to a power, you are **expanding a binomial.** The formulas for binomial coefficients give you an easy way to expand binomials, as demonstrated in the next four examples.

EXAMPLE 4   Expanding a Binomial

Write the expansion for the expression $(x + 1)^3$.

Solution
The binomial coefficients from the third row of Pascal's Triangle are

$$1, 3, 3, 1.$$

Therefore, the expansion is as follows.

$$(x + 1)^3 = (1)x^3 + (3)x^2(1) + (3)x(1^2) + (1)(1^3)$$
$$= x^3 + 3x^2 + 3x + 1$$

To expand binomials representing *differences*, rather than sums, you alternate signs. Here are two examples.

$$(x - 1)^3 = x^3 - 3x^2 + 3x - 1$$
$$(x - 1)^4 = x^4 - 4x^3 + 6x^2 - 4x + 1$$

EXAMPLE 5   Expanding a Binomial

Write the expansion for the expression

$$(2x - 3)^4.$$

Solution
The binomial coefficients from the fourth row of Pascal's Triangle are

$$1, 4, 6, 4, 1.$$

Therefore, the expansion is as follows.

$$(2x - 3)^4 = (1)(2x)^4 - (4)(2x)^3(3) + (6)(2x)^2(3^2) - (4)(2x)(3^3) + (1)(3^4)$$
$$= 16x^4 - 96x^3 + 216x^2 - 216x + 81$$

You can use a graphing utility to check the expansion by graphing the original binomial expression and the expansion in the same viewing window. The graphs should coincide, as shown in Figure 7.12.

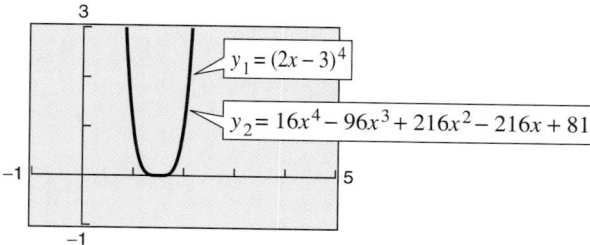

$y_1 = (2x - 3)^4$

$y_2 = 16x^4 - 96x^3 + 216x^2 - 216x + 81$

Figure 7.12

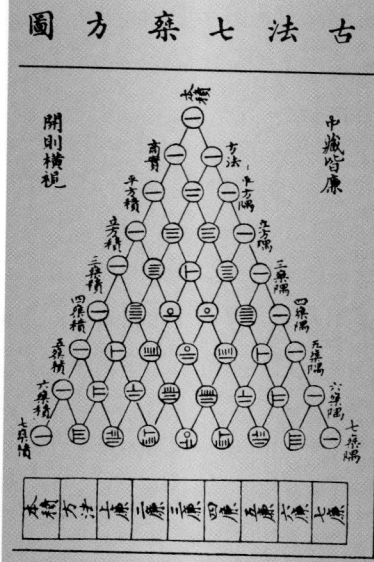

"Pascal's" Triangle and forms of the Binomial Theorem were known in Eastern cultures prior to the Western "discovery" of the theorem. The Chinese text *Precious Mirror* contains a triangle of binomial expansions through the eighth power.

A computer animation of this concept appears in the *Interactive* CD-ROM and *Internet* versions of this text.

Activities

1. Expand and simplify $(x - 3)^4$.

   Answer:
   $x^4 - 12x^3 + 54x^2 - 108x + 81$

2. Find the fifth term in the expansion of $(2x + 1)^9$.

   Answer:
   $$\frac{9 \cdot 8 \cdot 7 \cdot 6 \cdot 5}{5 \cdot 4 \cdot 3 \cdot 2 \cdot 1} (2x)^5(1)^4 = 4032x^5$$

3. Evaluate $_8C_3$.

   Answer: $\dfrac{8 \cdot 7 \cdot 6}{3 \cdot 2 \cdot 1} = 56$

EXAMPLE 6   Expanding a Binomial

Write the expansion for $(x - 2y)^4$.

Solution

Use the fourth row of Pascal's Triangle, as follows.

$$(x - 2y)^4 = (1)x^4 - (4)x^3(2y) + (6)x^2(2y)^2 - (4)x(2y)^3 + (1)(2y)^4$$

$$= x^4 - 8x^3y + 24x^2y^2 - 32xy^3 + 16y^4$$

EXAMPLE 7   Expanding a Binomial

Write the expansion for $(x^2 + 4)^3$.

Solution

Use the third row of Pascal's Triangle, as follows.

$$(x^2 + 4)^3 = (1)(x^2)^3 + (3)(x^2)^2(4) + (3)x^2(4^2) + (1)(4^3)$$

$$= x^6 + 12x^4 + 48x^2 + 64$$

To find a specific term in a binomial expansion, use the fact that from the Binomial Theorem, the $(r + 1)$st term is

$$_nC_r \, x^{n-r}y^r.$$

EXAMPLE 8   Finding a Term in a Binomial Expansion

Find the sixth term of $(a + 2b)^8$.

Solution

For the sixth term in this binomial expansion, use $n = 8$ and $r = 5$ to get

$$_8C_5 \, a^{8-5}(2b)^5 = 56 \cdot a^3 \cdot (2b)^5$$

$$= 56(2^5)a^3b^5$$

$$= 1792a^3b^5.$$

Group Activity
Add the binomial coefficients in each of the first five rows of Pascal's Triangle. What pattern do you see? Work together to use the pattern to find the sum of the terms in the 10th, 15th, and 20th rows of Pascal's Triangle. Check your answer by actually adding the terms of the 10th, 15th, and 20th rows.

Writing About Math   *Error Analysis*

Suppose you are a math instructor and receive the following solutions from one of your students on a quiz. Find the error(s) in each solution and write a short paragraph discussing ways that your student could avoid the error(s) in the future.

a. Find the second term in the expansion of $(2x - 3y)^5$.

$$5(2x)^4(3y)^2 = 720x^4y^2 \quad \times$$

b. Find the fourth term in the expansion of $\left(\frac{1}{2}x + 7y\right)^6$.

$$_6C_4\left(\tfrac{1}{2}x\right)^2(7y)^4 = 9003.75x^2y^4 \quad \times$$

7.5 E x e r c i s e s

In Exercises 1–12, evaluate $_nC_r$.

1. $_7C_5$

2. $_9C_6$

3. $\binom{12}{0}$

4. $\binom{20}{20}$

5. $_{20}C_{15}$

6. $_{12}C_3$

7. $_{14}C_1$

8. $_{18}C_{17}$

9. $\binom{100}{98}$

10. $\binom{10}{7}$

11. $_{100}C_2$

12. $_{13}C_8$

In Exercises 13–18, use a graphing utility to evaluate $_nC_r$.

13. $_{32}C_{28}$

14. $_{17}C_4$

15. $_{22}C_9$

16. $_{52}C_{47}$

17. $_{41}C_{36}$

18. $_{34}C_4$

In Exercises 19–22, evaluate using Pascal's Triangle.

19. $_7C_2$

20. $_6C_4$

21. $_8C_5$

22. $_8C_6$

In Exercises 23–44, use the Binomial Theorem to expand and simplify the expression.

23. $(x + 1)^4$

24. $(x + 1)^6$

25. $(a + 3)^3$

26. $(a + 2)^4$

27. $(y - 2)^4$

28. $(y - 2)^5$

29. $(x + y)^5$

30. $(x + y)^6$

31. $(r + 2s)^6$

32. $(x + 3y)^4$

33. $(x - y)^5$

34. $(2x - y)^5$

35. $(1 - 4x)^3$

36. $(5 - 2y)^3$

37. $(x^2 + 5)^4$

38. $(x^2 + y^2)^6$

39. $\left(\dfrac{1}{x} + y\right)^5$

40. $\left(\dfrac{1}{x} + 2y\right)^6$

41. $2(x - 3)^4 + 5(x - 3)^2$

42. $3(x + 1)^5 - 4(x + 1)^3$

43. $-3(x - 2)^3 - 4(x + 1)^6$

44. $6(x + 2)^5 - 2(x - 1)^2$

In Exercises 45–48, expand the binomial using Pascal's Triangle to determine the coefficients.

45. $(3t - s)^5$

46. $(x + 2y)^5$

47. $(3 - 2z)^4$

48. $(3y + 2)^5$

In Exercises 49–56, find the coefficient a of the given term in the expansion of the binomial.

Binomial	Term
49. $(x + 3)^{12}$	ax^4
50. $(x^2 + 3)^{12}$	ax^{10}
51. $(x - 2y)^{10}$	ax^8y^2
52. $(4x - y)^{10}$	ax^2y^8
53. $(3x - 2y)^9$	ax^6y^3
54. $(2x - 3y)^8$	ax^4y^4
55. $(x^2 + y)^{10}$	ax^8y^6
56. $(z^2 - 1)^{12}$	az^6

In Exercises 57–60, use the Binomial Theorem to expand and simplify the expression.

57. $\left(\sqrt{x} + 5\right)^4$

58. $\left(4\sqrt{t} - 1\right)^3$

59. $(x^{2/3} - y^{1/3})^3$

60. $(u^{3/5} + 2)^5$

In Exercises 61–64, expand the binomial in the difference quotient and simplify.

$$\frac{f(x + h) - f(x)}{h}$$

61. $f(x) = x^3$

62. $f(x) = x^4$

63. $f(x) = \sqrt{x}$

64. $f(x) = \dfrac{1}{x}$

In Exercises 65–70, use the Binomial Theorem to expand the complex number. Simplify your result.

65. $(1 + i)^4$

66. $(4 - i)^5$

67. $(2 - 3i)^6$

68. $\left(5 + \sqrt{-9}\right)^3$

69. $\left(-\dfrac{1}{2} + \dfrac{\sqrt{3}}{2}i\right)^3$

70. $\left(5 - \sqrt{3}i\right)^4$

Approximation   In Exercises 71–74, use the Binomial Theorem to approximate the given quantity accurate to three decimal places. For example, in Exercise 71, use the expansion

$$(1.02)^8 = (1 + 0.02)^8 = 1 + 8(0.02) + 28(0.02)^2 + \cdots.$$

71. $(1.02)^8$

72. $(2.005)^{10}$

73. $(2.99)^{12}$

74. $(1.98)^9$

Graphical Reasoning   In Exercises 75–78, use a graphing utility to obtain the graph of f and g in the same viewing window. What is the relationship between the two graphs? Use the Binomial Theorem to write the polynomial function g in standard form.

75. $f(x) = x^3 - 4x$, $g(x) = f(x + 6)$

76. $f(x) = -x^4 + 4x^2 - 1$, $g(x) = f(x - 4)$

77. $f(x) = -x^2 + 3x + 2$, $g(x) = f(x - 2)$

78. $f(x) = 2x^2 - 4x + 1$, $g(x) = f(x + 3)$

Exploration   In Exercises 79 and 80, use a graphing utility to evaluate and determine which two are equal.

79. (a) $_{12}C_5$

(b) $(_6C_5)^2$

(c) $_{11}C_5 + _{11}C_4$

(d) $_6C_5 + _6C_5$

80. (a) $_{25}C_6$

(b) $2(_{25}C_2 + _{25}C_4)$

(c) $\sum\limits_{k=0}^{5} [(_{10}C_k)(_8C_{5-k})]$

(d) $_{18}C_5$

Graphical Reasoning   In Exercises 81 and 82, use a graphing utility to obtain the graphs of the functions in the given order and in the same viewing window. Compare the graphs. Which two functions have identical graphs and why?

81. (a) $f(x) = (1 - x)^3$

(b) $g(x) = 1 - 3x$

(c) $h(x) = 1 - 3x + 3x^2$

(d) $p(x) = 1 - 3x + 3x^2 - x^3$

82. (a) $f(x) = \left(1 - \frac{1}{2}x\right)^4$

(b) $g(x) = 1 - 2x + \frac{3}{2}x^2$

(c) $h(x) = 1 - 2x + \frac{3}{2}x^2 - \frac{1}{2}x^3$

(d) $p(x) = 1 - 2x + \frac{3}{2}x^2 - \frac{1}{2}x^3 + \frac{1}{16}x^4$

Probability   In Exercises 83–86, consider n independent trials of an experiment where each trial has two possible outcomes, called a **success** and a **failure**, respectively. The probability of a success on each trial is p and the probability of a failure is $q = 1 - p$. In this context, the term $_nC_k \, p^k q^{n-k}$ in the expansion of $(p + q)^n$ gives the probability of k successes in the n trials of the experiment.

83. A fair coin is tossed seven times. To find the probability of obtaining 4 heads, evaluate the term

$$_7C_4\left(\tfrac{1}{2}\right)^4\left(\tfrac{1}{2}\right)^3$$

in the expansion $\left(\tfrac{1}{2} + \tfrac{1}{2}\right)^7$.

84. The probability of a baseball player getting a hit on any given time at bat is $\frac{1}{4}$. To find the probability that the player gets 3 hits during the next 10 times at bat, evaluate the term

$$_{10}C_3\left(\tfrac{1}{4}\right)^3\left(\tfrac{3}{4}\right)^7$$

in the expansion $\left(\tfrac{1}{4} + \tfrac{3}{4}\right)^{10}$.

85. The probability of a sales representative making a sale with any one customer is $\frac{1}{3}$. The sales representative makes 8 contacts a day. To find the probability of making 4 sales, evaluate the term

$$_8C_4\left(\tfrac{1}{3}\right)^4\left(\tfrac{2}{3}\right)^4$$

in the expansion $\left(\tfrac{1}{3} + \tfrac{2}{3}\right)^8$.

86. To find the probability that the sales representative in Exercise 85 makes 4 sales if the probability of a sale with any one customer is $\frac{1}{2}$, evaluate the term

$$_8C_4\left(\tfrac{1}{2}\right)^4\left(\tfrac{1}{2}\right)^4$$

in the expansion $\left(\tfrac{1}{2} + \tfrac{1}{2}\right)^8$.

87. *Life Insurance*   The average amount of life insurance per household f (in thousands of dollars) from 1980 through 1996 can be approximated by

$$f(t) = 0.0348t^2 + 5.1083t + 41.0250, \quad 0 \le t \le 16$$

where $t = 0$ represents 1980. You want to adjust this model so that $t = 0$ corresponds to 1990 rather than 1980. To do this, you shift the graph of f 10 units *to the left* and obtain

$$g(t) = f(t + 10).$$

(Source: American Council of Life Insurance)

(a) Write $g(t)$ in standard form.

(b) Use a graphing utility to graph f and g in the same viewing window.

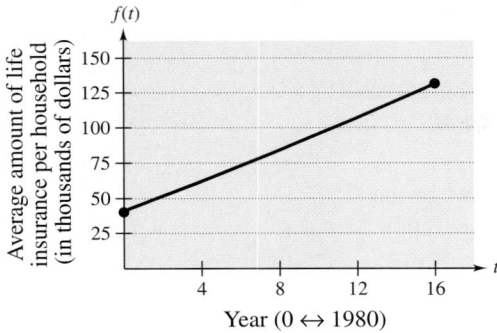

FIGURE FOR 87

88. Health Maintenance Organizations The number of people f (in millions) enrolled in health maintenance organizations in the United States from 1976 through 1997 can be approximated by the model

$$f(t) = 0.0834t^2 + 0.7657t + 5.3680, \quad 0 \le t \le 21$$

where $t = 0$ represents 1976. You want to adjust this model so that $t = 0$ corresponds to 1980 rather than 1976. To do this, you shift the graph of f 4 units *to the left* and obtain $g(t) = f(t + 4)$.   (Source: Group Health Association of America, Interstudy)

(a) Write $g(t)$ in standard form.

(b) Use a graphing utility to graph f and g in the same viewing window.

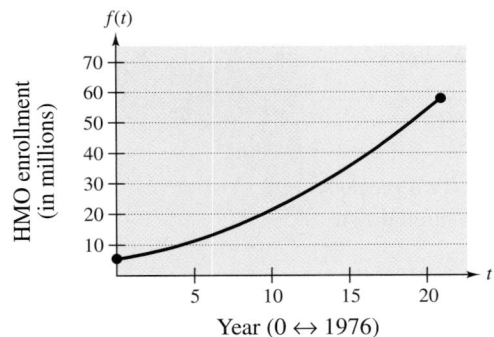

Synthesis

True or False?   In Exercises 89 and 90, determine whether the statement is true or false. Justify your answer.

89. One of the terms in the expansion of $(x - 2y)^{12}$ is $7920x^4y^8$.

90. The x^{10}-term and the x^{14}-term of the expansion of $(x^2 + 3)^{12}$ have identical coefficients.

91. Writing   In your own words, explain how to form the rows of Pascal's Triangle.

92. Form the first nine rows of Pascal's Triangle.

93. Think About It   How many terms are in the expansion of $(x + y)^n$?

94. Think About It   How do the expansions of $(x + y)^n$ and $(x - y)^n$ differ?

In Exercises 95–98, prove the given property for all integers r and n where $0 \le r \le n$.

95. $_nC_r = {_nC_{n-r}}$

96. $_nC_0 - {_nC_1} + {_nC_2} - \cdots \pm {_nC_n} = 0$

97. $_{n+1}C_r = {_nC_r} + {_nC_{r-1}}$

98. The sum of the numbers in the nth row of Pascal's Triangle is 2^n.

Review

In Exercises 99–102, describe the relationship between the graphs of f and g.

99. $g(x) = f(x) + 8$

100. $g(x) = f(x - 3)$

101. $g(x) = f(-x)$

102. $g(x) = -f(x)$

In Exercises 103–108, perform the matrix operation using the given matrices.

$$A = \begin{bmatrix} -2 & 3 & 0 \\ 5 & -1 & 2 \\ 4 & 0 & 1 \end{bmatrix} \quad B = \begin{bmatrix} 0 & -4 & -3 \\ 3 & 1 & 2 \\ -5 & -2 & 6 \end{bmatrix}$$

103. $A + B$

104. $4A - B$

105. $-3A - 5B$

106. $6A + 10B$

107. AB

108. BA

In Exercises 109 and 110, find the inverse of the matrix.

109. $\begin{bmatrix} -6 & 5 \\ -5 & 4 \end{bmatrix}$

110. $\begin{bmatrix} 1.2 & -2.3 \\ -2 & 4 \end{bmatrix}$

7.6 Counting Principles

Simple Counting Problems

The last two sections of this chapter present a brief introduction to some of the basic counting principles and their application to probability. In the next section, you will see that much of probability has to do with counting the number of ways an event can occur.

EXAMPLE 1   Selecting Pairs of Numbers at Random

Eight pieces of paper are numbered from 1 to 8 and placed in a box. One piece of paper is drawn from the box, its number is written down, and the piece of paper is replaced in the box. Then, a piece of paper is again drawn from the box, and its number is written down. Finally, the two numbers are added together. How many different ways can a total of 12 be obtained?

Solution

To solve this problem, count the different ways that a total of 12 can be obtained using two numbers from 1 to 8.

First number	4	5	6	7	8
Second number	8	7	6	5	4

From this list, you can see that a total of 12 can occur in five different ways.

EXAMPLE 2   Selecting Pairs of Numbers at Random

Eight pieces of paper are numbered from 1 to 8 and placed in a box. Two pieces of paper are drawn from the box, and the numbers on the paper are written down and totaled. How many different ways can a total of 12 be obtained?

Solution

To solve this problem, count the different ways that a total of 12 can be obtained using two *different* numbers from 1 to 8.

First number	4	5	7	8
Second number	8	7	5	4

So, a total of 12 can be obtained in four different ways.

The difference between the counting problems in Examples 1 and 2 can be distinguished by saying that the random selection in Example 1 occurs *with replacement,* whereas the random selection in Example 2 occurs *without replacement,* which eliminates the possibility of choosing two 6's.

The Fundamental Counting Principle

Examples 1 and 2 describe simple counting problems in which you can *list* each possible way that an event can occur. When it is possible, this is always the best way to solve a counting problem. However, some events can occur in so many different ways that it is not feasible to write out the entire list. In such cases, you must rely on formulas and counting principles. The most important of these is the **Fundamental Counting Principle.**

Fundamental Counting Principle

Let E_1 and E_2 be two events. The first event E_1 can occur in m_1 different ways. After E_1 has occurred, E_2 can occur in m_2 different ways. The number of ways that the two events can occur is

$$m_1 \cdot m_2.$$

The Fundamental Counting Principle can be extended to three or more events. For instance, the number of ways that three events E_1, E_2, and E_3 can occur is

$$m_1 \cdot m_2 \cdot m_3.$$

You may want to consider opening class by asking students if they can predict which offers more choices for license plates: (a) a plate with three different letters of the alphabet in any order or (b) a plate with four different nonzero digits in any order. You may want to end class by verifying the answer: option (a) offers $26 \cdot 25 \cdot 24 = 15{,}600$ choices and option (b) offers $9 \cdot 8 \cdot 7 \cdot 6 = 3024$ choices.

EXAMPLE 3   Using the Fundamental Counting Principle

How many different pairs of letters from the English alphabet are possible?

Solution

This experiment has two events. The first event is the choice of the first letter, and the second event is the choice of the second letter. Because the English alphabet contains 26 letters, it follows that the number of letter pairs is

$$26 \cdot 26 = 676.$$

EXAMPLE 4   Counting Telephone Numbers

Telephone numbers in the United States have 10 digits. The first three are the *area code* and the next seven are the *local telephone number*. How many different telephone numbers are possible within each area code? (Note that a local telephone number cannot begin with 0 or 1.)

Solution

Because the first digit cannot be 0 or 1, there are only eight choices for the first digit. For each of the other six digits, there are 10 choices.

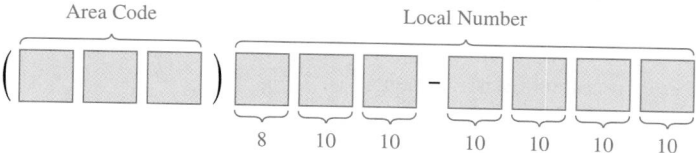

So, the number of local telephone numbers that are possible within each area code is $8 \cdot 10 \cdot 10 \cdot 10 \cdot 10 \cdot 10 \cdot 10 = 8{,}000{,}000.$

Permutations

One important application of the Fundamental Counting Principle is in determining the number of ways that n elements can be arranged (in order). An ordering of n elements is called a **permutation** of the elements.

Definition of Permutation

A **permutation** of n different elements is an ordering of the elements such that one element is first, one is second, one is third, and so on.

EXAMPLE 5   Finding the Number of Permutations of n Elements

How many permutations are possible for the letters A, B, C, D, E, and F?

Solution

Consider the following reasoning.

First position:	Any of the *six* letters
Second position:	Any of the remaining *five* letters
Third position:	Any of the remaining *four* letters
Fourth position:	Any of the remaining *three* letters
Fifth position:	Either of the remaining *two* letters
Sixth position:	The *one* remaining letter

So, the number of choices for the six positions are as follows.

Permutations of six letters

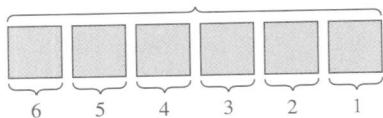

6 5 4 3 2 1

The total number of permutations of the six letters is

$$6! = 6 \cdot 5 \cdot 4 \cdot 3 \cdot 2 \cdot 1$$
$$= 720.$$

Additional Example

a. How many permutations are possible for the numbers 0, 1, 2, 3?

b. Write out the possible permutations of the letters A, B, C.

Solution

a. $4! = 24$

b. ABC, ACB, BAC, BCA, CAB, CBA

Number of Permutations of n Elements

The number of permutations of n elements is

$$n \cdot (n-1) \cdots 4 \cdot 3 \cdot 2 \cdot 1 = n!.$$

In other words, there are $n!$ different ways that n elements can be ordered.

Occasionally, you are interested in ordering a *subset* of a collection of elements rather than the entire collection. For example, you might want to choose (and order) r elements out of a collection of n elements. Such an ordering is called a **permutation of n elements taken r at a time.**

EXAMPLE 6   Counting Horse Race Finishes

Eight horses are running in a race. In how many different ways can these horses come in first, second, and third? (Assume that there are no ties.)

Solution

Here are the different possibilities.

Win (first position):	*Eight* choices
Place (second position):	*Seven* choices
Show (third position):	*Six* choices

The number of choices for the three positions are as follows.

Different orders of horses

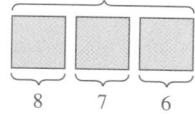

8   7   6

So, there are

$$8 \cdot 7 \cdot 6 = 336$$

different ways the eight horses can come in first, second, and third.

Permutations of *n* Elements Taken *r* at a Time

The number of **permutations of *n* elements taken *r* at a time** is

$$_nP_r = \frac{n!}{(n-r)!}$$

$$= n(n-1)(n-2) \cdots (n-r+1).$$

Using this formula, you can rework Example 6 to find that the number of permutations of eight horses taken three at a time is

$$_8P_3 = \frac{8!}{5!}$$

$$= \frac{8 \cdot 7 \cdot 6 \cdot 5!}{5!}$$

$$= 336$$

which is the same answer.

Most graphing utilities are programmed to evaluate $_nP_r$. Consult your user's manual to learn how to evaluate the permutation $_8P_3$. You should get 336, as shown in Example 6.

Remember that for permutations, order is important. So, if you are looking at the possible permutations of the letters A, B, C, and D taken three at a time, the permutations (A,B,D) and (B,A,D) would be counted as different because the *order* of the elements is different.

Suppose, however, that you are asked to find the possible permutations of the letters A, A, B, and C. The total number of permutations of the four letters would be $_4P_4 = 4!$. However, not all of these arrangements would be *distinguishable* because there are two A's in the list. To find the number of distinguishable permutations, you can use the following formula.

Distinguishable Permutations

Suppose a set of n objects has n_1 of one kind of object, n_2 of a second kind, n_3 of a third kind, and so on, with

$$n = n_1 + n_2 + n_3 + \cdots + n_k.$$

The number of **distinguishable permutations** of the n objects is

$$\frac{n!}{n_1! \cdot n_2! \cdot n_3! \cdots n_k!}.$$

EXAMPLE 7   Distinguishable Permutations

In how many distinguishable ways can the letters in BANANA be written?

Solution

This word has six letters, of which three are A's, two are N's, and one is a B. So, the number of distinguishable ways the letters can be written is

$$\frac{6!}{3! \cdot 2! \cdot 1!} = \frac{6 \cdot 5 \cdot 4 \cdot 3!}{3! \cdot 2!}$$

$$= 60.$$

The 60 different arrangements are as follows.

AAABNN	AAANBN	AAANNB	AABANN
AABNAN	AABNNA	AANABN	AANANB
AANBAN	AANBNA	AANNAB	AANNBA
ABAANN	ABANAN	ABANNA	ABNAAN
ABNANA	ABNNAA	ANAABN	ANAANB
ANABAN	ANABNA	ANANAB	ANANBA
ANBAAN	ANBANA	ANBNAA	ANNAAB
ANNABA	ANNBAA	BAAANN	BAANAN
BAANNA	BANAAN	BANANA	BANNAA
BNAAAN	BNAANA	BNANAA	BNNAAA
NAAABN	NAAANB	NAABAN	NAABNA
NAANAB	NAANBA	NABAAN	NABANA
NABNAA	NANAAB	NANABA	NANBAA
NBAAAN	NBAANA	NBANAA	NBNAAA
NNAAAB	NNAABA	NNABAA	NNBAAA

Additional Example
In how many different ways can the letters in INDIANA be written?

Solution
630

Combinations

When you count the number of possible permutations of a set of elements, order is important. As a final topic in this section, you will look at a method of selecting subsets of a larger set in which order *is not* important. Such subsets are called **combinations of *n* elements taken *r* at a time.** For instance, the combinations

$$\{A, B, C\} \quad \text{and} \quad \{B, A, C\}$$

are equivalent because both sets contain the same three elements, and the order in which the elements are listed is not important. So, you would count only one of the two sets. A common example of how a combination occurs is a card game in which the player is free to reorder the cards after they have been dealt.

Careful attention to detail and numerous examples will help students understand when to count different orders and when not to. You may want to discuss the mis-naming of the "combination lock" according to the definitions presented in this section.

EXAMPLE 8   Combinations of *n* Elements Taken *r* at a Time

In how many different ways can three letters be chosen from the letters A, B, C, D, and E? (The order of the three letters is not important.)

Solution

The following subsets represent the different combinations of three letters that can be chosen from five letters.

$$\{A, B, C\} \quad \{A, B, D\}$$

$$\{A, B, E\} \quad \{A, C, D\}$$

$$\{A, C, E\} \quad \{A, D, E\}$$

$$\{B, C, D\} \quad \{B, C, E\}$$

$$\{B, D, E\} \quad \{C, D, E\}$$

From this list, you can conclude that there are 10 different ways that three letters can be chosen from five letters.

Combinations of *n* Elements Taken *r* at a Time

The number of **combinations of *n* elements taken *r* at a time** is

$$_nC_r = \frac{n!}{(n-r)!r!}.$$

Note that the formula for $_nC_r$ is the same one given for binomial coefficients. To see how this formula is used, solve the counting problem in Example 8. In that problem, you are asked to find the number of combinations of five elements taken three at a time. So, $n = 5$, $r = 3$, and the number of combinations is

$$_5C_3 = \frac{5!}{2!3!} = \frac{5 \cdot 4 \cdot \overset{2}{3!}}{2 \cdot 1 \cdot 3!} = 10$$

which is the same answer obtained in Example 8.

EXAMPLE 9   Counting Card Hands

A standard poker hand consists of five cards dealt from a deck of 52. How many different poker hands are possible?

Solution

Note that after the cards are dealt, the players may reorder them, and therefore order is not important. So, you can find the number of different poker hands by using the formula for the number of combinations of 52 elements taken five at a time, as follows.

$$_{52}C_5 = \frac{52!}{47!5!} = \frac{52 \cdot 51 \cdot 50 \cdot 49 \cdot 48 \cdot 47!}{5 \cdot 4 \cdot 3 \cdot 2 \cdot 1 \cdot 47!} = 2,598,960$$

EXAMPLE 10   The Number of Subsets of a Set

Find the total number of subsets of a set that has 10 elements.

Solution

Begin by considering the number of subsets with 0 elements, the number with 1 element, the number with 2 elements, and so on.

Number of subsets	=	Subsets with 0 elements	+	Subsets with 1 element	+	Subsets with 2 elements	+ · · · +	Subsets with 10 elements

$$= \binom{10}{0} + \binom{10}{1} + \binom{10}{2} + \cdots + \binom{10}{10}$$

Compare this expression to the binomial expansion of $(1 + 1)^{10}$ to see that they are the same.

$$(1 + 1)^{10} = \binom{10}{0}1^{10}1^0 + \binom{10}{1}1^91^1 + \binom{10}{2}1^81^2 + \cdots + \binom{10}{10}1^01^{10}$$

$$= \binom{10}{0} + \binom{10}{1} + \binom{10}{2} + \cdots + \binom{10}{10}$$

This implies that the total number of subsets of a set of 10 elements is

$$(1 + 1)^{10} = 2^{10} = 1024.$$

The result of Example 10 can be generalized to conclude that the total number of subsets of a set of n elements is 2^n.

Writing About Math   *Problem Posing*

According to NASA, each space shuttle astronaut consumes an average of 3000 calories per day. An evening meal normally consists of a main dish, a vegetable dish, and two different desserts. The space shuttle food list contains ten items classified as main dishes, eight vegetable dishes, and 13 desserts. How many different evening meal menus are possible? Write a short paragraph explaining how you determined this number. Create two other problems that could be asked about the evening meal menus and solve them.   (Source: NASA)

Activities

1. Evaluate (a) $_6P_2$ and (b) $_6C_2$.
   Answer: (a) 30 and (b) 15

2. A local building-supply company is hiring extra summer help. They need four additional employees to work outside in the lumberyard and three more to work inside the store. In how many ways can these positions be filled if there are ten applicants for outside work and five for inside work?
   Answer: 2100

3. In how many distinguishable ways can the letters C A L C U L U S be written?
   Answer: 5040 ways

7.6 Exercises

Random Selection **In Exercises 1–8, determine the number of ways a computer can randomly generate one or more such integers from 1 through 12.**

1. An odd integer

2. An even integer

3. A prime integer

4. An integer that is greater than 7

5. An integer that is divisible by 4

6. An integer that is divisible by 3

7. Two integers whose sum is 10

8. Two *distinct* integers whose sum is 10

9. *Entertainment Systems* A customer can choose one of four amplifiers, one of six compact disc players, and one of eight speaker models for an entertainment system. Determine the number of possible system configurations.

10. *Computer Systems* A customer in a computer store can choose one of three monitors, one of two keyboards, and one of seven computers. If all the choices are compatible, determine the number of possible system configurations.

11. *Job Applicants* A college needs two additional faculty members: a chemist and a statistician. In how many ways can these positions be filled if there are three applicants for the chemistry position and six applicants for the statistics position?

12. *Course Schedule* A college student is preparing a course schedule for the next semester. The student must select one of two mathematics courses, one of three science courses, and one of five courses from the social sciences and humanities. How many schedules are possible?

13. *Periodic Table* You are taking a chemistry test and are asked to list the first ten elements *in order* as they appear in the periodic table of elements. Suppose you have no idea of the correct order and simply guess. In how many different orders could you list the elements?

14. *True-False Exam* In how many ways can a ten-question true-false exam be answered? (Assume that no questions are omitted.)

15. *Toboggan Ride* Four people are lining up for a ride on a toboggan, but only two of the four are willing to take the first position. With that constraint, in how many ways can the four people be seated on the toboggan?

16. *Taking a Trip* Four people are taking a long trip in a four-seat car. Three of the people agree to share the driving. In how many different arrangements can the four people sit?

17. *License Plate Numbers* In a certain state the automobile license plates consist of two letters followed by a four-digit number. How many distinct license plate numbers can be formed?

18. *License Plate Numbers* In a certain state the automobile license plates consist of two letters followed by a four-digit number. To avoid confusion between "O" and "zero" and "I" and "one," the letters "O" and "I" are not used. How many distinct license plate numbers can be formed?

19. *Three-Digit Numbers* How many three-digit numbers can be formed under the following conditions?

    (a) The leading digit cannot be zero.

    (b) The leading digit cannot be zero and no repetition of digits is allowed.

    (c) The leading digit cannot be zero and the number must be a multiple of 5.

    (d) The number is at least 400.

20. *Four-Digit Numbers* How many four-digit numbers can be formed under the following conditions?

    (a) The leading digit cannot be zero.

    (b) The leading digit cannot be zero and no repetition of digits is allowed.

    (c) The leading digit cannot be zero and the number must be less than 5000.

    (d) The leading digit cannot be zero and the number must be even.

21. *Combination Lock* A combination lock will open when the right choice of three numbers (from 1 to 40, inclusive) is selected. How many different lock combinations are possible?

22. *Telephone Numbers* In 1997, the Commonwealth of Massachusetts had three area codes: one for the Boston metropolitan area, one for the rest of eastern Massachusetts, and one for western Massachusetts. Using the information about telephone numbers in Example 4, how many telephone numbers could the phone system have accommodated in the state of Massachusetts?

23. *Concert Seats* Three couples have reserved seats in a given row for a concert. In how many different ways can they be seated if
   (a) there are no seating restrictions?
   (b) the two members of each couple wish to sit together?

24. *Single File* In how many orders can five girls and three boys walk through a doorway single file if
   (a) there are no restrictions?
   (b) the girls walk through before the boys?

In Exercises 25–30, evaluate $_nP_r$ using the formula.

25. $_4P_4$

26. $_5P_5$

27. $_8P_3$

28. $_{20}P_2$

29. $_5P_4$

30. $_7P_4$

In Exercises 31 and 32, solve for n.

31. $14 \cdot {_nP_3} = {_{n+2}P_4}$

32. $_nP_5 = 18 \cdot {_{n-2}P_4}$

In Exercises 33–38, evaluate using a graphing utility.

33. $_{20}P_6$

34. $_{100}P_5$

35. $_{120}P_4$

36. $_{10}P_8$

37. $_{20}C_4$

38. $_{10}C_7$

39. *Posing for a Photograph* In how many ways can five children line up in a row?

40. *Riding in a Car* In how many ways can four people sit in a four-passenger car?

41. *Morse Code* In Morse code, all characters are transmitted using a sequence of *dots* and *dashes*.
   (a) How many different characters can be formed with a sequence of four symbols, each of which is a dot or dash?
   (b) How many can be formed with a sequence of one, two, or three symbols?

42. *Assembly Line Production* Four processes are involved in assembling a certain product, and they can be performed in any order. The management

wants to test each order to determine which is the least time consuming. How many different orders will have to be tested?

In Exercises 43–46, find the number of distinguishable permutations of the group of letters.

43. A, A, G, E, E, E, M

44. B, B, B, T, T, T, T, T

45. A, L, G, E, B, R, A

46. M, I, S, S, I, S, S, I, P, P, I

47. Write all permutations of the letters A, B, C, and D.

48. Write all the permutations of the letters A, B, C, and D if the letters B and C must remain between the letters A and D.

49. Write all the possible selections of two letters that can be formed from the letters A, B, C, D, E, and F. (The order of the two letters is not important.)

50. Write all the possible selections of three letters that can be formed from the letters A, B, C, D, E, and F. (The order of the three letters is not important.)

51. *Forming an Experimental Group* In order to conduct a certain experiment, four students are randomly selected from a class of 20. How many different groups of four students are possible?

52. *Test Questions* You can answer any 12 questions from a total of 14 questions on an exam. In how many different ways can you select the questions?

53. *Lottery Choices* There are 40 numbers in a particular state lottery. In how many ways can a player select six of the numbers?

54. *Lottery Choices* There are 50 numbers in a particular state lottery. In how many ways can a player select six of the numbers?

55. *Number of Subsets* How many subsets of five elements can be formed from a set of 100 elements?

56. *Number of Subsets* How many subsets of six elements can be formed from a set of 80 elements?

57. *Geometry* Three points that are not on a line determine three lines. How many lines are determined by nine points, no three of which are on a line?

58. *Defective Units* A shipment of 25 television sets contains three defective units. In how many ways can a vending company purchase four of these units and receive (a) all good units, (b) two good units, and (c) at least two good units?

59. *Job Applicants*   An employer interviews 12 people for four openings in the company. Five of the 12 people are women. If all 12 are qualified, in how many ways can the employer fill the four positions if (a) the selection is random and (b) exactly two women are selected?

60. *Poker Hand*   Five cards are selected from an ordinary deck of 52 playing cards. In how many ways can you get a full house? (A full house consists of three of one kind and two of another. For example, 8-8-8-5-5 and K-K-K-10-10 are full houses.)

61. *Forming a Committee*   Four people are to be selected at random from a group of four couples. In how many ways can this be done, given the following conditions?

(a) There are no restrictions.

(b) The group must have at least one couple.

(c) Each couple must be represented in the group.

62. *Interpersonal Relationships*   The complexity of the interpersonal relationships increases dramatically as the size of a group increases. Determine the number of different two-person relationships in a group of people of size (a) 3, (b) 8, (c) 12, and (d) 20.

In Exercises 63–66, find the number of diagonals of the polygon. (A line segment connecting any two non-adjacent vertices is called a *diagonal* of the polygon.)

63. Pentagon

64. Hexagon

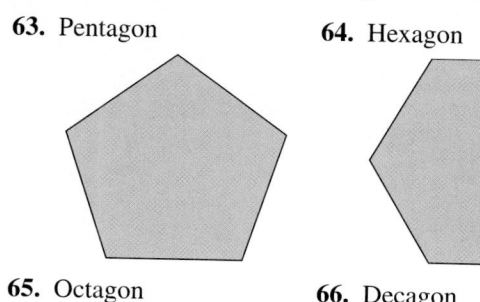
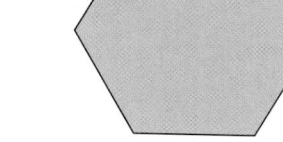

65. Octagon

66. Decagon

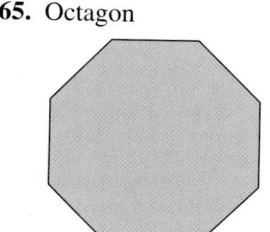
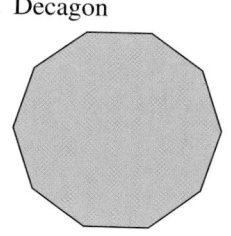

Synthesis

True or False?   **In Exercises 67–69, determine whether the statement is true or false. Justify your answer.**

67. The number of pairs of letters that can be formed from any of the first 13 letters in the alphabet (A–M) is an example of a permutation.

68. The number of permutations of n elements can be derived by using the Fundamental Counting Principle.

69. $_nP_r > {_nC_r}$ always.

70. *Think About It*   Can your calculator evaluate $_{100}P_{80}$? If not, explain why.

71. *Writing*   Explain in words the meaning of $_nP_r$.

72. What is the relationship between $_nC_r$ and $_nC_{n-r}$?

73. Without calculating the numbers, determine which of the following is greater. Explain.

(a) The combinations of 10 elements taken 6 at a time

(b) The permutations of 10 elements taken 6 at a time

In Exercises 74–77, prove the identity.

74. $_nP_{n-1} = {_nP_n}$

75. $_nC_n = {_nC_0}$

76. $_nC_{n-1} = {_nC_1}$

77. $_nC_r = \dfrac{_nP_r}{r!}$

Review

In Exercises 78–81, solve the equation. Round your answer to two decimal places, if necessary.

78. $\sqrt{x-3} = x - 6$

79. $\dfrac{4}{t} + \dfrac{3}{2t} = 1$

80. $\log_2(x-3) = 5$

81. $e^{x/3} = 16$

In Exercises 82–85, use Cramer's Rule to solve the system of equations.

82. $\begin{cases} -5x + 3y = -14 \\ 7x - 2y = 2 \end{cases}$

83. $\begin{cases} 8x + y = 35 \\ 6x + 2y = 10 \end{cases}$

84. $\begin{cases} -3x - 4y = -1 \\ 9x + 5y = -4 \end{cases}$

85. $\begin{cases} 10x - 11y = -74 \\ -8x - 4y = 8 \end{cases}$

In Exercises 86–89, use the Binomial Theorem to expand and simplify the expression.

86. $(x - 4)^3$

87. $(x - 1)^6$

88. $(x^2 + 4)^5$

89. $(3x - y)^4$

7.7 Probability

The Probability of an Event

Any happening whose result is uncertain is called an **experiment.** The possible results of the experiment are **outcomes,** the set of all possible outcomes of the experiment is the **sample space** of the experiment, and any subcollection of a sample space is an **event.**

For instance, when a six-sided die is tossed, the sample space can be represented by the numbers from 1 through 6. For this experiment, each of the outcomes is *equally likely.*

To describe sample spaces in such a way that each outcome is equally likely, you must sometimes distinguish between various outcomes in ways that appear artificial. Example 1 illustrates such a situation.

EXAMPLE 1   Finding the Sample Space

Find the sample space for each of the following.

a. One coin is tossed.

b. Two coins are tossed.

c. Three coins are tossed.

Solution

a. Because the coin will land either heads up (denoted by H) or tails up (denoted by T), the sample space is

$$S = \{H, T\}.$$

b. Because either coin can land heads up or tails up, the possible outcomes are as follows.

HH = heads up on both coins

HT = heads up on first coin and tails up on second coin

TH = tails up on first coin and heads up on second coin

TT = tails up on both coins

So, the sample space is

$$S = \{HH, HT, TH, TT\}.$$

Note that this list distinguishes between the two cases HT and TH, even though these two outcomes appear to be similar.

c. Following the notation of part (b), the sample space is

$$S = \{HHH, HHT, HTH, HTT, THH, THT, TTH, TTT\}.$$

Note that this list distinguishes between the cases HHT, HTH, and THH, and between the cases HTT, THT, and TTH.

What You Should Learn:

- How to find probabilities of events
- How to find probabilities of mutually exclusive events
- How to find probabilities of independent events
- How to find probabilities of complements of events

Why You Should Learn It:

You can use probability to solve a variety of problems that occur in real life. For instance, in Exercise 33 on page 560, you are asked to use probability to help analyze the age distribution of employees who find work through temporary-help agencies.

To calculate the probability of an event, count the number of outcomes in the event and in the sample space. The *number of outcomes* in event E is denoted by $n(E)$ and the number of outcomes in the sample space S is denoted by $n(S)$. The probability that event E will occur is given by $n(E)/n(S)$.

The Probability of an Event

If an event E has $n(E)$ equally likely outcomes and its sample space S has $n(S)$ equally likely outcomes, the **probability** of event E is

$$P(E) = \frac{n(E)}{n(S)}.$$

Because the number of outcomes in an event must be less than or equal to the number of outcomes in the sample space, the probability of an event must be a number from 0 to 1, inclusive. That is,

$$0 \le P(E) \le 1,$$

as indicated in Figure 7.13. If $P(E) = 0$, event E *cannot occur*, and E is called an **impossible event.** If $P(E) = 1$, event E *must occur*, and E is called a **certain event.**

EXAMPLE 2   Finding the Probability of an Event

a. Two coins are tossed. What is the probability that both land heads up?

b. A card is drawn from a standard deck of playing cards. What is the probability that it is an ace?

Solution

a. Following the procedure in Example 1(b), let

$$E = \{HH\}$$

and

$$S = \{HH, HT, TH, TT\}.$$

The probability of getting two heads is

$$P(E) = \frac{n(E)}{n(S)}$$

$$= \frac{1}{4}.$$

b. Because there are 52 cards in a standard deck of playing cards and there are four aces (one in each suit), the probability of drawing an ace is

$$P(E) = \frac{n(E)}{n(S)}$$

$$= \frac{4}{52} = \frac{1}{13}.$$

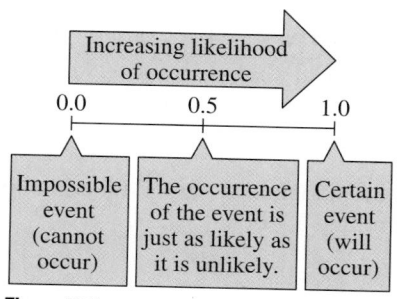

Additional Example

Two coins are tossed. What is the probability that one coin lands heads up and the other coin lands tails up?

Solution

$\frac{1}{2}$

EXAMPLE 3 Finding the Probability of an Event

Two six-sided dice are tossed. What is the probability that the total of the two dice is 7? (See Figure 7.14.)

Solution

Because there are six possible outcomes on each die, you can use the Fundamental Counting Principle to conclude that there are 6 · 6 or 36 different outcomes when two dice are tossed. To find the probability of rolling a total of 7, you must first count the number of ways this can occur.

Figure 7.14

First Die	1	2	3	4	5	6
Second Die	6	5	4	3	2	1

A computer simulation of this example appears in the *Interactive* CD-ROM and *Internet* versions of this text.

So, a total of 7 can be rolled in six ways, which means that the probability of rolling a 7 is

$$P(E) = \frac{n(E)}{n(S)}$$

$$= \frac{6}{36}$$

$$= \frac{1}{6}.$$

You could have written out each sample space in Examples 2 and 3 and simply counted the outcomes in the desired events. For larger sample spaces, however, using the counting principles discussed in Section 7.6 should save you time.

EXAMPLE 4 Finding the Probability of an Event

Twelve-sided dice, as shown in Figure 7.15, can be constructed (in the shape of regular dodecahedrons) so that each of the numbers from 1 to 6 appears twice on each die. Prove that these dice can be used in any game requiring ordinary six-sided dice without changing the probabilities of different outcomes.

Solution

For an ordinary six-sided die, each of the numbers 1, 2, 3, 4, 5, and 6 occurs only once, so the probability of any particular number coming up is

$$P(E) = \frac{n(E)}{n(S)} = \frac{1}{6}.$$

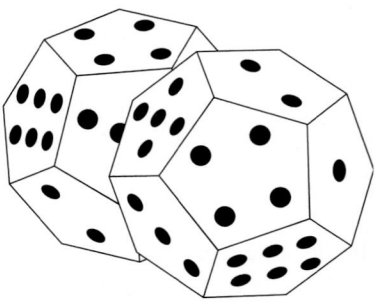

Figure 7.15

For one of the 12-sided dice, each number occurs twice, so the probability of any particular number coming up is

$$P(E) = \frac{n(E)}{n(S)} = \frac{2}{12} = \frac{1}{6}.$$

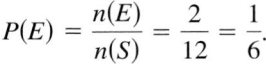

EXAMPLE 5   The Probability of Winning a Lottery

In a state lottery, a player chooses six different numbers from 1 to 40. If these six numbers match the six numbers drawn by the lottery commission, the player wins (or shares) the top prize. What is the probability of winning the top prize?

Solution

To find the number of elements in the sample space, use the formula for the number of combinations of 40 elements taken six at a time.

$$n(S) = {}_{40}C_6$$

$$= \frac{40 \cdot 39 \cdot 38 \cdot 37 \cdot 36 \cdot 35}{6 \cdot 5 \cdot 4 \cdot 3 \cdot 2 \cdot 1}$$

$$= 3{,}838{,}380$$

If a person buys only one ticket, the probability of winning is

$$P(E) = \frac{n(E)}{n(S)}$$

$$= \frac{1}{3{,}838{,}380}.$$

EXAMPLE 6   Random Selection

The numbers of colleges and universities in various regions of the United States in 1996 are shown in Figure 7.16. One institution is selected at random. What is the probability that the institution is in one of the two north central regions?   (Source: U.S. National Center for Education Statistics)

Solution

From the figure, the total number of colleges and universities is 3696. Because there are $397 + 578 = 975$ colleges and universities in the two north central regions, the probability that the institution is in one of these regions is

$$P(E) = \frac{n(E)}{n(S)} = \frac{975}{3696} \approx 0.264.$$

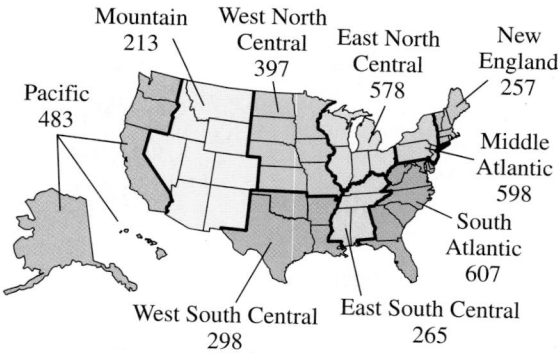

Mountain
213

West North
Central
397

East North
Central
578

New
England
257

Pacific
483

Middle
Atlantic
598

South
Atlantic
607

West South Central
298

East South Central
265

Figure 7.16

Mutually Exclusive Events

Two events A and B (from the same sample space) are **mutually exclusive** if A and B have no outcomes in common. In the terminology of sets, the intersection of A and B is the empty set and

$$P(A \cap B) = 0.$$

For instance, if two dice are tossed, the event A of rolling a total of 6 and the event B of rolling a total of 9 are mutually exclusive. To find the probability that one or the other of two mutually exclusive events will occur, you can *add* their individual probabilities.

Probability of the Union of Two Events

If A and B are events in the same sample space, the probability of A *or* B occurring is

$$P(A \cup B) = P(A) + P(B) - P(A \cap B).$$

If A and B are mutually exclusive, then

$$P(A \cup B) = P(A) + P(B).$$

EXAMPLE 7   The Probability of a Union

One card is selected from a standard deck of 52 playing cards. What is the probability that the card is either a heart or a face card?

Solution

Because the deck has 13 hearts, the probability of selecting a heart (event A) is

$$P(A) = \frac{13}{52}.$$

Similarly, because the deck has 12 face cards, the probability of selecting a face card (event B) is

$$P(B) = \frac{12}{52}.$$

Because three of the cards are hearts and face cards (see Figure 7.17), it follows that

$$P(A \cap B) = \frac{3}{52}.$$

Finally, applying the formula for the probability of the union of two events, you can conclude that the probability of selecting a heart or a face card is

$$P(A \cup B) = P(A) + P(B) - P(A \cap B)$$

$$= \frac{13}{52} + \frac{12}{52} - \frac{3}{52}$$

$$= \frac{22}{52} \approx 0.423.$$

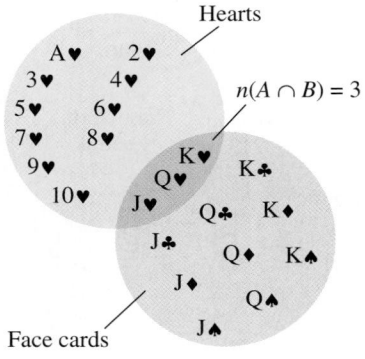

Figure 7.17

EXAMPLE 8   Probability of Mutually Exclusive Events

The personnel department of a company has compiled data on employees' numbers of years of service. The results are shown in the table.

Years of Service	Number of Employees
0–4	157
5–9	89
10–14	74
15–19	63
20–24	42
25–29	38
30–34	37
35–39	21
40–44	8

If an employee is chosen at random, what is the probability that the employee has had nine or fewer years of service?

Solution

To begin, add the number of employees and find that the total is 529. Next, let event A represent choosing an employee with 0 to 4 years of service and let event B represent choosing an employee with 5 to 9 years of service. Then

$$P(A) = \frac{157}{529}$$

and

$$P(B) = \frac{89}{529}.$$

Because A and B have no outcomes in common, you can conclude that these two events are mutually exclusive and that

$$P(A \cup B) = P(A) + P(B)$$

$$= \frac{157}{529} + \frac{89}{529}$$

$$= \frac{246}{529}$$

$$\approx 0.465.$$

So, the probability of choosing an employee who has nine or fewer years of service is about 0.465.

Additional Example
If an employee from Example 8 is chosen at random, what is the probability that the employee has had 30 or more years of service?
Solution
≈ 0.125

Independent Events

Two events are **independent** if the occurrence of one has no effect on the occurrence of the other. To find the probability that two independent events will occur, *multiply* the probabilities of each. For instance, rolling a total of 12 with two six-sided dice has no effect on the outcome of future rolls of the dice.

Probability of Independent Events

If A and B are **independent events,** the probability that both A and B will occur is

$$P(A \text{ and } B) = P(A) \cdot P(B).$$

EXAMPLE 9   Probability of Independent Events

A random number generator on a computer selects three integers from 1 to 20. What is the probability that all three numbers are less than or equal to 5?

Solution
The probability of selecting a number from 1 to 5 is

$$P(A) = \frac{5}{20} = \frac{1}{4}.$$

So, the probability that all three numbers are less than or equal to 5 is

$$P(A) \cdot P(A) \cdot P(A) = \left(\frac{1}{4}\right)\left(\frac{1}{4}\right)\left(\frac{1}{4}\right)$$

$$= \frac{1}{64}.$$

EXAMPLE 10   Probability of Independent Events

In 1997, 58% of the population of the United States were 30 years old or older. Suppose that in a survey, ten people were chosen at random from the population. What is the probability that all ten were 30 years old or older?   (Source: U.S. Bureau of the Census)

Solution
Let A represent choosing a person who was 30 years old or older. Because the probability of choosing a person who was 30 years old or older was 0.58, you can conclude that the probability that all ten people were 30 years old or older is

$$[P(A)]^{10} = (0.58)^{10}$$

$$\approx 0.0043.$$

Activities

1. You have two bags, each of which contains a red marble and a green marble. You select one marble from each bag. Write the sample space.
   Answer: $S = \{RR, RG, GR, GG\}$

2. A person draws two cards from a deck of 52 cards. What is the probability that the two cards drawn will both be face cards if the deck contains 12 face cards?
   Answer: $\frac{11}{221}$

3. A bag contains four red, three yellow, and five green marbles. One marble is selected from the bag. What is the probability that it is a red marble? (Assume that the marbles are of the same size, shape, etc.)
   Answer: $\frac{1}{3}$

4. Use the makeup in your class today.
   a. If two students are chosen at random, what is the probability that both will be female?
   b. If one student is chosen at random, what is the probability that this student was born in a month beginning with the letter J?
   Answers will vary depending on the class.

The Complement of an Event

The **complement of an event** *A* is the collection of all outcomes in the sample space that are *not* in *A*. The complement of event *A* is denoted by *A'*. Because $P(A \text{ or } A') = 1$ and because *A* and *A'* are mutually exclusive, it follows that $P(A) + P(A') = 1$. Therefore, the probability of *A'* is

$$P(A') = 1 - P(A).$$

For instance, if the probability of *winning* a certain game is

$$P(A) = \frac{1}{4}$$

then the probability of *losing* the game is

$$P(A') = 1 - \frac{1}{4}$$

$$= \frac{3}{4}.$$

Exploration

Suppose you are in a class with 22 other people. What is the probability that the birthdays of at least two of the 23 people fall on the same day of the year? What if you know the probability of everyone having the same birthday? Do you think that would help you to find the answer?

Probability of a Complement

Let *A* be an event and let *A'* be its complement. If the probability of *A* is $P(A)$, the probability of the complement is

$$P(A') = 1 - P(A).$$

EXAMPLE 11   Finding the Probability of a Complement

A manufacturer has determined that a certain machine averages one faulty unit for every 1000 it produces. What is the probability that an order of 200 units will have one or more faulty units?

Solution

To solve this problem as stated, you would need to find the probabilities of having exactly one faulty unit, exactly two faulty units, exactly three faulty units, and so on. However, using complements, you can simply find the probability that all units are perfect and then subtract this value from 1. Because the probability that any given unit is perfect is 999/1000, the probability that all 200 units are perfect is

$$P(A) = \left(\frac{999}{1000}\right)^{200}$$

$$\approx 0.8186.$$

Therefore, the probability that at least one unit is faulty is

$$P(A') = 1 - P(A)$$

$$\approx 0.1814.$$

Activity
Consider having students create a book or pamphlet on probability by taking each type of probability situation discussed in this section, defining the terms, giving the formulas needed, and then creating their own examples to illustrate how to calculate probabilities.

7.7 Exercises

In Exercises 1–6, determine the sample space for the given experiment.

1. A coin and a six-sided die are tossed.

2. A six-sided die is tossed twice and the sum of the points is recorded.

3. A taste tester has to rank three varieties of orange juice, A, B, and C, according to preference.

4. Two marbles are selected (without replacement) from a sack containing two red marbles, two blue marbles, and one black marble. The color of each marble is recorded.

5. Two county supervisors are selected from five supervisors, A, B, C, D, and E, to study a recycling plan.

6. A sales representative makes presentations about a product in three homes per day. In each home there may be a sale (denote by S) or there may be no sale (denote by F).

Heads or Tails **In Exercises 7–10, find the probability in the experiment of tossing a coin three times. Use the sample space $S = \{HHH, HHT, HTH, HTT, THH, THT, TTH, TTT\}$.**

7. The probability of getting exactly two tails

8. The probability of getting a head on the first toss

9. The probability of getting at least one head

10. The probability of getting at least two heads

Drawing a Card **In Exercises 11–14, find the probability in the experiment of selecting one card from a standard deck of 52 playing cards.**

11. The card is a face card.

12. The card is not a face card.

13. The card is a black face card.

14. The card is an 8 or lower. (Aces are low.)

Tossing a Die **In Exercises 15–20, find the probability in the experiment of tossing a six-sided die twice.**

15. The sum is 5.

16. The sum is at least 8.

17. The sum is less than 12.

18. The sum is 2, 3, or 12.

19. The sum is odd and no more than 5.

20. The sum is odd or prime.

Drawing Marbles **In Exercises 21–24, find the probability in the experiment of drawing two marbles (without replacement) from a bag containing one green, two yellow, and three red marbles.**

21. Both marbles are red.

22. Both marbles are yellow.

23. Neither marble is yellow.

24. The marbles are of different colors.

In Exercises 25–28, you are given the probability that an event *will* happen. Find the probability that the event *will not* happen.

25. $P(E) = 0.7$

26. $P(E) = 0.36$

27. $P(E) = \frac{1}{3}$

28. $P(E) = \frac{5}{6}$

In Exercises 29–32, you are given the probability that an event *will not* happen. Find the probability that the event *will* happen.

29. $P(E') = 0.15$

30. $P(E') = 0.84$

31. $P(E') = \frac{13}{20}$

32. $P(E') = \frac{59}{100}$

33. *Graphical Reasoning* In 1997 there were approximately 1.3 million temporary help agency workers in the United States. The circle graph shows the age profile of these workers. (Source: U.S. Bureau of Labor Statistics)

   (a) Estimate the number of temporary help agency workers in the age group 16–19.

   (b) What is the probability that a person selected at random from the population of temporary agency workers is in the 25–34 age group?

   (c) What is the probability that a person selected at random from the population of temporary agency workers is in the 35–54 age group?

   (d) What is the probability that a person selected at random from the population of temporary agency workers is 55 or over?

Age of U.S. Workers

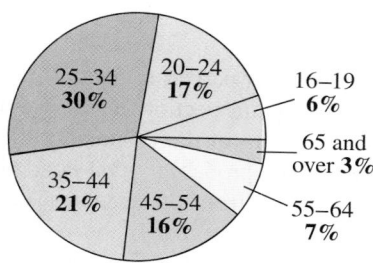

FIGURE FOR 33

34. *Graphical Reasoning*   In 1997 there were approximately 111 million workers in the civilian labor force in the United States. The circle graph shows the educational attainment of these workers.   (Source: U.S. Bureau of Labor Statistics)

(a) Estimate the number of workers whose highest education level was a high school education.

(b) A person is selected at random from the civilian work force. What is the probability that the person's highest education level is 1 to 3 years of college?

(c) A person is selected at random from the civilian work force. What is the probability that the person has had more than a high school education?

Educational Attainment of Workers

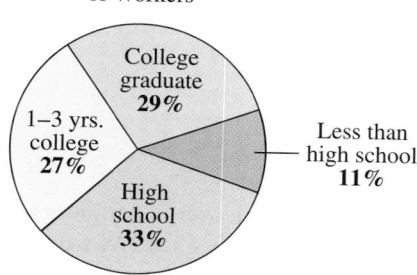

35. *Data Analysis*   A study of the effectiveness of a flu vaccine was conducted with a sample of 500 people. Some in the study were given no vaccine, some were given one injection, and some were given two injections. The results of the study are shown below.

	No Vaccine	One Injection	Two Injections	Total
Flu	7	2	13	22
No flu	149	52	277	478
Total	156	54	290	500

A person is selected at random from the sample. Find the specified probability.

(a) The person had two injections.

(b) The person did not get the flu.

(c) The person got the flu and had one injection.

36. *Data Analysis*   One hundred college students were interviewed to determine their political-party affiliations and whether they favored a balanced-budget amendment to the Constitution. The results of the study are listed in the table.

	Favor	Not favor	Unsure	Total
Democrat	23	25	7	55
Republican	32	9	4	45
Total	55	34	11	100

A person is selected at random from the sample. Find the probability that the described person is selected.

(a) A person who doesn't favor the amendment

(b) A Republican

(c) A Democrat who favors the amendment

37. *Alumni Association*   A college sends a survey to selected members of the class of 2000. Of the 1254 people who graduated that year, 672 are women, of whom 124 went on to graduate school. Of the 582 male graduates, 198 went on to graduate school. If an alumni member is selected at random, what is the probability that the person is (a) female, (b) male, and (c) female and did not attend graduate school?

38. *Post–High School Education*   In a high school graduating class of 128 students, 52 are on the honor roll. Of these, 48 are going on to college; and of the other 76 students, 56 are going on to college. If a student is selected at random from the class, what is the probability that the person chosen is (a) going to college, (b) not going to college, and (c) not going to college and on the honor roll?

39. *Winning an Election*   Taylor, Moore, and Perez are candidates for public office. It is estimated that Moore and Perez have about the same probability of winning, and Taylor is believed to be twice as likely to win as either of the others. Find the probability of each candidate's winning the election.

40. *Payroll Error*   The employees of a company are in six departments: 31 are in sales, 54 are in research, 42 are in marketing, 20 are in engineering, 47 are in finance, and 58 are in production. If one employee's paycheck is lost, what is the probability that the employee is in the research department?

In Exercises 41–52, the sample spaces are large and you should use the counting principles discussed in Section 7.6.

41. *Preparing for a Test*   A class is given a list of 20 study problems from which ten will be part of an upcoming exam. If a given student knows how to solve 15 of the problems, find the probability that the student will be able to answer (a) all ten questions on the exam, (b) exactly eight questions on the exam, and (c) at least nine questions on the exam.

42. *Preparing for a Test*   A class is given a list of eight study problems from which five will be part of an upcoming exam. If a given student knows how to solve six of the problems, find the probability that the student will be able to answer (a) all five questions on the exam, (b) exactly four questions on the exam, and (c) at least four questions on the exam.

43. *Letter Mix-Up*   Four letters and envelopes are addressed to four different people. If the letters are randomly inserted into the envelopes, what is the probability that (a) exactly one is inserted in the correct envelope and (b) at least one is inserted in the correct envelope?

44. *Payroll Mix-Up*   Five paychecks and envelopes are addressed to five different people. If the paychecks are randomly inserted into the envelopes, what is the probability that (a) exactly one is inserted in the correct envelope and (b) at least one is inserted in the correct envelope?

45. *Game Show*   On a game show you are given five digits to arrange in the proper order to form the price of a car. If you are correct, you win the car. What is the probability of winning, given the following conditions?

(a) You guess the position of each digit.

(b) You know the first digit and guess the others.

46. *Card Game*   The deck of a card game is made up of 108 cards. Twenty-five each are red, yellow, blue, and green, and eight are wild cards. Each player is randomly dealt a seven-card hand. (a) What is the probability that a hand will have exactly two wild

cards? (b) What is the probability that a hand will have two wild cards, two red cards, and three blue cards?

47. *Hospital Inspection*   As part of a monthly inspection at a hospital, the inspection team randomly selects reports from eight of the 84 nurses who are on duty. (a) What is the probability that none of the reports selected will be from the ten most experienced nurses on duty? (b) What is the probability that all of the reports selected will be from the 20 least experienced nurses on duty?

48. *Poker Hand*   Five cards are drawn from an ordinary deck of 52 playing cards. What is the probability of getting a full house? (A full house consists of three of one kind and two of another. For example, 3-3-3-7-7 is a full house.)

49. *Defective Units*   A shipment of 12 microwave ovens contains three defective units. A vending company has ordered four of these units, and because all are packaged identically, the selection will be random. What is the probability that

(a) all four units are good?

(b) exactly two units are good?

(c) at least two units are good?

50. *Defective Units*   A shipment of 20 compact disc players contains four defective units. A retail outlet has ordered five of these units, and because all are packaged identically, the selection will be random. What is the probability that

(a) all five units are good?

(b) exactly four units are good?

(c) at least one unit is good?

51. *Random Number Generator*   Two integers (from 1 through 30) are chosen by a random number generator. What is the probability that (a) the numbers are both even, (b) one number is even and one is odd, (c) both numbers are less than 10, and (d) the same number is chosen twice?

52. *Random Number Generator*   Two integers (from 1 through 40) are chosen by a random number generator. What is the probability that (a) the numbers are both even, (b) one number is even and one is odd, (c) both numbers are less than 30, and (d) the same number is chosen twice?

53. *Backup System*   A space vehicle has an independent backup system for one of its communication networks. The probability that either system will function satisfactorily for the duration of a flight is

0.985. What is the probability that during a given flight (a) both systems function satisfactorily, (b) at least one system functions satisfactorily, and (c) both systems fail?

54. Backup Vehicle A fire company keeps two rescue vehicles to serve the community. Because of the demand on the company's time and the chance of mechanical failure, the probability that a specific vehicle is available when needed is 90%. If the availability of one vehicle is *independent* of the other, find the probability that (a) both vehicles are available at a given time, (b) neither vehicle is available at a given time, and (c) at least one vehicle is available at a given time.

55. Making a Sale A sales representative makes sales at approximately one-fifth of all calls. If, on a given day, the representative contacts six potential clients, what is the probability that a sale will be made with (a) all six contacts, (b) none of the contacts, and (c) at least two contacts?

56. A Boy or a Girl? Assume that the probability of the birth of a child of a particular sex is 50%. In a family with four children, what is the probability that (a) all the children are boys, (b) all the children are the same sex, and (c) there is at least one boy?

57. Is That Cash or Charge? Suppose that the methods used by shoppers to pay for merchandise are as shown in the circle graph. If two shoppers are chosen at random, what is the probability that both shoppers paid for their purchases only in cash?

How Shoppers Pay
for Merchandise

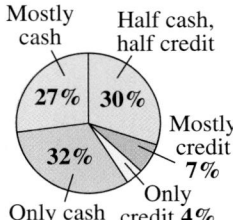

58. Flexible Work Hours In a survey, people were asked if they would prefer to work flexible hours—even if it meant slower career advancement—so they could spend more time with their families. The results of the survey are shown in the circle graph. Suppose that three people from the survey were chosen at random. What is the probability that all three people would prefer flexible work hours?

Flexible Work Hours

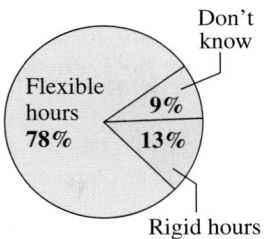

FIGURE FOR 58

59. Geometry You and a friend agree to meet at your favorite fast-food restaurant between 5:00 and 6:00 P.M. The one who arrives first will wait 15 minutes for the other, after which the first person will leave. What is the probability that the two of you will actually meet, assuming that your arrival times are random within the hour?

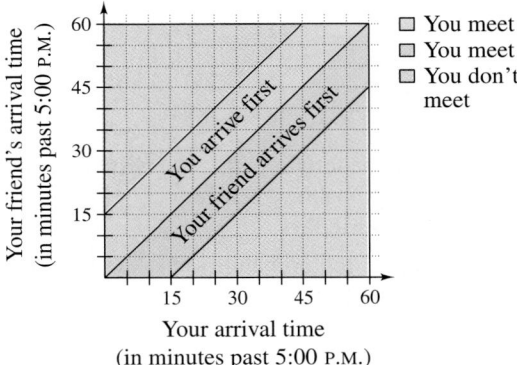

60. Estimating π A coin of diameter d is dropped onto a paper that contains a grid of squares d units on a side.

(a) Find the probability that the coin covers a vertex of one of the squares on the grid.

(b) Perform the experiment 100 times and use the results to approximate π.

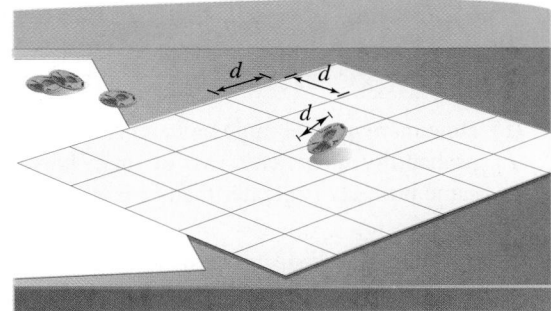

Synthesis

True or False? **In Exercises 61 and 62, determine whether the statement is true or false. Justify your answer.**

61. If the probability of an outcome in a sample space is 1, then the probability of the other outcomes in the sample space is 0.

62. Rolling a number less than 3 on a normal 6-sided die has a probability of $\frac{1}{3}$. The complement of this event is to roll a number greater than 3 and its probability is $\frac{1}{2}$.

63. *Pattern Recognition and Exploration* Consider a group of n people.

(a) Explain why the following gives the probability that the n people have distinct birthdays.

$$n = 2: \quad \frac{365}{365} \cdot \frac{364}{365} = \frac{365 \cdot 364}{365^2}$$

$$n = 3: \quad \frac{365}{365} \cdot \frac{364}{365} \cdot \frac{363}{365} = \frac{365 \cdot 364 \cdot 363}{365^3}$$

(b) Use the pattern in part (a) to write an expression for the probability that four people ($n = 4$) have distinct birthdays.

(c) Let P_n be the probability that the n people have distinct birthdays. Verify that this probability can be obtained recursively by

$$P_1 = 1 \quad \text{and} \quad P_n = \frac{365 - (n - 1)}{365} P_{n-1}.$$

(d) Explain why $Q_n = 1 - P_n$ gives the probability that at least two people in a group of n people have the same birthday.

(e) Use the results of parts (c) and (d) to complete the table.

n	10	15	20	23	30	40	50
P_n							
Q_n							

(f) How many people must be in a group before the probability of at least two of them having the same birthday is greater than $\frac{1}{2}$? Explain.

64. *Think About It* The weather forecast indicates that the probability of rain is 40%. Explain what this means.

Review

In Exercises 65–68, find all real solutions of the rational equation.

65. $\dfrac{2}{x - 5} = 4$

66. $\dfrac{3}{2x + 3} - 4 = \dfrac{-1}{2x + 3}$

67. $\dfrac{3}{x - 2} + \dfrac{x}{x + 2} = 1$

68. $\dfrac{2}{x} - \dfrac{5}{x - 2} = \dfrac{-13}{x^2 - 2x}$

In Exercises 69–72, find all real solutions of the logarithmic equation.

69. $\ln x = 8$

70. $3 - 4 \ln x = 6$

71. $4 \ln 6x = 16$

72. $5 \ln 2x - 4 = 11$

In Exercises 73–76, sketch the graph of the solution of the system of inequalities.

73. $\begin{cases} y \geq -3 \\ x \geq -1 \\ -x - y \geq -8 \end{cases}$

74. $\begin{cases} x \leq 3 \\ y \leq 6 \\ 5x + 2y \geq 10 \end{cases}$

75. $\begin{cases} x^2 + y \geq -2 \\ y \geq x - 4 \end{cases}$

76. $\begin{cases} x^2 + y^2 \leq 4 \\ x + y \geq -2 \end{cases}$

In Exercises 77–80, evaluate $_nC_r$. Verify your result using a graphing utility.

77. $_6C_2$

78. $_9C_5$

79. $_{11}C_8$

80. $_{16}C_{13}$

7   Chapter Summary

What did you learn?

Section 7.1	Review Exercises
☐ How to use sequence notation to write the terms of sequences	1–10
☐ How to use factorial notation	11–14
☐ How to use summation notation to write sums	15–26
☐ How to find sums of infinite series	27–30
☐ How to use sequences and series to model and solve real-life problems	31, 32

Section 7.2	
☐ How to recognize, write, and find the nth terms of arithmetic sequences	33–46
☐ How to find nth partial sums of arithmetic sequences	47–52
☐ How to use arithmetic sequences to model and solve real-life problems	53, 54

Section 7.3	
☐ How to recognize, write, and find the nth terms of geometric sequences	55–66
☐ How to find nth partial sums of geometric sequences	67–76
☐ How to find sums of infinite geometric series	77–80
☐ How to use geometric sequences to model and solve real-life problems	81–84

Section 7.4	
☐ How to use mathematical induction to prove statements involving a positive integer n	85–88
☐ How to find sums of powers of integers	89–92
☐ How to find finite differences of sequences	93–96

Section 7.5	
☐ How to use the Binomial Theorem to calculate binomial coefficients	97–100
☐ How to use Pascal's Triangle to calculate binomial coefficients	101–104
☐ How to use binomial coefficients to write binomial expansions	105–110

Section 7.6	
☐ How to solve simple counting problems	111, 112
☐ How to use the Fundamental Counting Principle to solve more complicated counting problems	113, 114
☐ How to use permutations to solve counting problems	115–117
☐ How to use combinations to solve counting problems	118–120

Section 7.7	
☐ How to find probabilities of events	121–124
☐ How to find probabilities of mutually exclusive events	125
☐ How to find probabilities of independent events	126, 127
☐ How to find probabilities of complements of events	128, 129

7 Review Exercises

7.1 In Exercises 1–6, write the first five terms of the sequence. (Assume n begins with 1.)

1. $a_n = 2 + \dfrac{6}{n}$

2. $a_n = 8 - \dfrac{1}{2^n}$

3. $a_n = \dfrac{5n}{2n - 1}$

4. $a_n = n(n - 1)$

5. $a_n = \dfrac{72}{n!}$

6. $a_n = \dfrac{1}{(n + 1)!}$

In Exercises 7–10, use a graphing utility to graph the first ten terms of the sequence (Assume n begins with 1.)

7. $a_n = \tfrac{3}{2}n$

8. $a_n = \dfrac{3n}{n + 2}$

9. $a_n = 4(0.4)^{n-1}$

10. $a_n = -8(0.5)^{n-1}$

In Exercises 11–14, evaluate the factorial expression.

11. $\dfrac{18!}{20!}$

12. $3! \cdot 2!$

13. $\dfrac{3! \cdot 5!}{6!}$

14. $\dfrac{7! \cdot 6!}{6! \cdot 8!}$

In Exercises 15–22, find the sum. Use a graphing utility to verify your result.

15. $\displaystyle\sum_{i=1}^{6} 5$

16. $\displaystyle\sum_{k=2}^{5} 4k$

17. $\displaystyle\sum_{j=1}^{4} \dfrac{6}{j^2}$

18. $\displaystyle\sum_{i=1}^{8} \dfrac{i}{i + 1}$

19. $\displaystyle\sum_{k=1}^{10} 2k^3$

20. $\displaystyle\sum_{j=0}^{4} (j^2 + 1)$

21. $\displaystyle\sum_{n=0}^{10} (n^2 + 3)$

22. $\displaystyle\sum_{n=1}^{100} \left(\dfrac{1}{n} - \dfrac{1}{n + 1}\right)$

In Exercises 23–26, use sigma notation to write the sum.

23. $\dfrac{1}{2(1)} + \dfrac{1}{2(2)} + \dfrac{1}{2(3)} + \cdots + \dfrac{1}{2(20)}$

24. $2(1^2) + 2(2^2) + 2(3^2) + \cdots + 2(9^2)$

25. $\dfrac{1}{2} + \dfrac{2}{3} + \dfrac{3}{4} + \cdots + \dfrac{9}{10}$

26. $1 - \dfrac{1}{3} + \dfrac{1}{9} - \dfrac{1}{27} + \cdots$

In Exercises 27–30, find (a) the 4th partial sum and (b) the sum of the infinite series.

27. $\displaystyle\sum_{k=1}^{\infty} \dfrac{5}{10^k}$

28. $\displaystyle\sum_{k=1}^{\infty} 8\left(\tfrac{1}{10}\right)^k$

29. $\displaystyle\sum_{k=1}^{\infty} 2\left(\tfrac{1}{100}\right)^k$

30. $\displaystyle\sum_{k=1}^{\infty} 7\left(\tfrac{1}{10}\right)^k$

31. *Compound Interest* A deposit of $2500 is made in an account that earns 8% interest compounded quarterly. The balance in the account after n quarters is

$$a_n = 2500\left(1 + \dfrac{0.08}{4}\right)^n, \qquad n = 1, 2, 3, \ldots$$

(a) Compute the first eight terms of this sequence.

(b) Find the balance in this account after 10 years by computing the 40th term of the sequence.

32. *Corporate Sales* The sales for the Whirlpool Corporation from 1990 to 1998 can be approximated by the model

$$a_n = 29.65n^2 + 186.19n + 6474.70$$

where a_n is the sales (in millions of dollars) and n is the year, with $n = 0$ corresponding to 1990. Find the terms of this finite sequence and use a graphing utility to construct a bar graph that represents the sequence. (Source: Whirlpool Corporation)

7.2 In Exercises 33–36, determine whether the sequence is arithmetic. If it is, find the common difference.

33. $5, -2, -9, -16, -23, \ldots$

34. $0, 1, 3, 6, 10, \ldots$

35. $\tfrac{1}{2}, 1, \tfrac{3}{2}, 2, \tfrac{5}{2}, \ldots$

36. $\tfrac{9}{9}, \tfrac{8}{9}, \tfrac{7}{9}, \tfrac{6}{9}, \tfrac{5}{9}, \ldots$

In Exercises 37–40, write the first five terms of the arithmetic sequence.

37. $a_1 = 3, \ d = 4$

38. $a_1 = 8, \ d = -2$

39. $a_4 = 10, \ a_{10} = 28$

40. $a_2 = 14, \ a_6 = 22$

In Exercises 41–44, write the first five terms of the arithmetic sequence defined recursively. Determine the common difference and write the nth term of the sequence as a function of n.

41. $a_1 = 35, \quad a_{k+1} = a_k - 3$

42. $a_1 = 15, \quad a_{k+1} = a_k + \frac{5}{2}$

43. $a_1 = 9, \quad a_{k+1} = a_k + 7$

44. $a_1 = 100, \quad a_{k+1} = a_k - 5$

In Exercises 45 and 46, write an expression for the nth term of the arithmetic sequence and find the sum of the first 20 terms of the sequence.

45. $a_1 = 100, \quad d = -3$ **46.** $a_1 = 10, \quad a_3 = 28$

In Exercises 47–50, find the sum. Use a graphing utility to verify your result.

47. $\displaystyle\sum_{j=1}^{10} (2j - 3)$ **48.** $\displaystyle\sum_{j=1}^{8} (20 - 3j)$

49. $\displaystyle\sum_{k=1}^{11} \left(\frac{2}{3}k + 4\right)$ **50.** $\displaystyle\sum_{k=1}^{25} \left(\frac{3k + 1}{4}\right)$

51. Find the sum of the first 100 positive multiples of 5.

52. Find the sum of the integers from 20 to 80 (inclusive).

53. *Job Offer* A job has a starting salary of $34,000 and a guaranteed salary increase of $2250 per year for the first 4 years of employment. Determine (a) the salary during the fifth year and (b) the total compensation through 5 full years of employment.

54. *Baling Hay* In his first trip baling hay around a field, a farmer makes 123 bales. In his second trip he makes 11 fewer bales. Because each trip is shorter than the preceding trip, the farmer estimates that the same pattern will continue. Estimate the total number of bales made if there are another six trips around the field.

7.3 In Exercises 55–58, write the first five terms of the geometric sequence.

55. $a_1 = 4, \ r = -\frac{1}{4}$ **56.** $a_1 = 2, \ r = 2$

57. $a_1 = 9, \ a_3 = 4$ **58.** $a_1 = 2, \ a_3 = 12$

In Exercises 59–62, write the first five terms of the geometric sequence defined recursively. Determine the common ratio and write the nth term of the sequence as a function of n.

59. $a_1 = 120, \quad a_{k+1} = \frac{1}{3}a_k$

60. $a_1 = 200, \quad a_{k+1} = 0.1a_k$

61. $a_1 = 25, \quad a_{k+1} = -\frac{3}{5}a_k$

62. $a_1 = 18, \quad a_{k+1} = \frac{5}{3}a_k$

In Exercises 63–66, write an expression for the nth term of the geometric sequence and find the sum of the first 20 terms of the sequence.

63. $a_1 = 16, \quad a_2 = -8$ **64.** $a_3 = 6, \quad a_4 = 1$

65. $a_1 = 100, \quad r = 1.05$ **66.** $a_1 = 5, \quad r = 0.2$

In Exercises 67–72, find the sum.

67. $\displaystyle\sum_{i=1}^{7} 2^{i-1}$ **68.** $\displaystyle\sum_{i=1}^{5} 3^{i-1}$

69. $\displaystyle\sum_{n=1}^{7} (-4)^{n-1}$ **70.** $\displaystyle\sum_{n=1}^{4} 12\left(-\frac{1}{2}\right)^{n-1}$

71. $\displaystyle\sum_{n=0}^{4} 250(1.02)^n$ **72.** $\displaystyle\sum_{n=0}^{5} 400(1.08)^n$

In Exercises 73–76, use a graphing utility to find the sum.

73. $\displaystyle\sum_{i=1}^{10} 10\left(\frac{3}{5}\right)^{i-1}$ **74.** $\displaystyle\sum_{i=1}^{15} 20(0.2)^{i-1}$

75. $\displaystyle\sum_{i=1}^{25} 100(1.06)^{i-1}$ **76.** $\displaystyle\sum_{i=1}^{20} 8\left(\frac{6}{5}\right)^{i-1}$

In Exercises 77–80, find the sum of the infinite series.

77. $\displaystyle\sum_{i=1}^{\infty} \left(\frac{7}{8}\right)^{i-1}$ **78.** $\displaystyle\sum_{i=1}^{\infty} \left(\frac{1}{3}\right)^{i-1}$

79. $\displaystyle\sum_{k=1}^{\infty} 4\left(\frac{2}{3}\right)^{k-1}$ **80.** $\displaystyle\sum_{k=1}^{\infty} 1.3\left(\frac{1}{10}\right)^{k-1}$

81. *Depreciation* A company buys a fleet of six vans for $120,000. During the next 5 years, the fleet will depreciate at a rate of 30% per year. (That is, at the end of each year, the depreciated value is 70% of what it was at the beginning of the year.)

(a) Find the formula for the nth term of a geometric sequence that gives the value of the fleet t full years after it was purchased.

(b) Find the depreciated value of the fleet at the end of 5 full years.

82. **Total Compensation** A job pays a salary of $32,000 the first year. During the next 39 years, there is a 5.5% raise each year. What is the total salary over the 40-year period?

83. **Annuity** A deposit of $75 is made at the beginning of each month in an account that pays 4% interest, compounded monthly. The balance A in the account at the end of 4 years is

$$A = 75\left(1 + \frac{0.04}{12}\right)^1 + \cdots + 75\left(1 + \frac{0.04}{12}\right)^{48}.$$

Find A.

84. **Compound Interest** A deposit of $100 is made at the beginning of each month for 10 years in an account that pays 6.5%, compounded monthly. What is the balance in the account at the end of the 10 years?

7.4 **In Exercises 85–88, use mathematical induction to prove the formula for every positive integer n.**

85. $2 + 7 + \cdots + (5n - 3) = \dfrac{n}{2}(5n - 1)$

86. $1 + \dfrac{3}{2} + 2 + \dfrac{5}{2} + \cdots + \dfrac{1}{2}(n + 1) = \dfrac{n}{4}(n + 3)$

87. $\displaystyle\sum_{i=0}^{n-1} ar^i = \dfrac{a(1 - r^n)}{1 - r}$

88. $\displaystyle\sum_{k=0}^{n-1} (a + kd) = \dfrac{n}{2}[2a + (n - 1)d]$

In Exercises 89–92, find the sum using the formulas for the sums of powers of integers.

89. $\displaystyle\sum_{n=1}^{30} n$

90. $\displaystyle\sum_{n=1}^{10} n^2$

91. $\displaystyle\sum_{n=1}^{7} n^4$

92. $\displaystyle\sum_{n=1}^{6} n^5$

In Exercises 93–96, find the first five terms of the sequence beginning with a_1. Then calculate the first and second differences of the sequence. Does the sequence have a linear model, a quadratic model, or neither?

93. $a_1 = 5$
  $a_n = a_{n-1} + 5$

94. $a_1 = -3$
  $a_n = a_{n-1} - 2n$

95. $a_1 = 16$
  $a_n = a_{n-1} - 1$

96. $a_1 = 1$
  $a_n = n - a_{n-1}$

7.5 **In Exercises 97–100, evaluate $_nC_r$. Use a graphing utility to verify your answer.**

97. $_{10}C_8$

98. $_{12}C_5$

99. $\dbinom{9}{4}$

100. $\dbinom{14}{12}$

In Exercises 101–104, evaluate using Pascal's Triangle.

101. $_6C_3$

102. $_9C_7$

103. $\dbinom{8}{4}$

104. $\dbinom{10}{5}$

In Exercises 105–110, use the Binomial Theorem to expand the binomial. Simplify your answer. (Remember that $i = \sqrt{-1}$.)

105. $(a - 3b)^5$

106. $(3x + y^2)^7$

107. $\left(\dfrac{x}{2} + y\right)^4$

108. $\left(\dfrac{2}{x} - 3x\right)^6$

109. $(5 + 2i)^4$

110. $(4 - 5i)^3$

7.6 **111.** **Numbers in a Hat** If slips of paper numbered 1 through 14 are placed in a hat, in how many ways could two numbers be drawn so that the sum of the numbers was 12? Assume the random selection is without replacement.

112. **Morse Code** In Morse code, each character is transmitted using a sequence of dits and dahs. How many different characters can be formed by a sequence of three dits and dahs? (These can be repeated. For example, dit-dit-dit represents the letter s.)

113. **Course Schedule** A college student is preparing a course schedule for the next semester. The student must select one of four mathematics courses, one of six biology courses, and one of two art courses. How many schedules are possible?

114. **Amateur Radio** A novice amateur radio license consists of two letters, one digit, and then three more letters. How many different licenses can be issued if no restrictions are placed on the letters or digits?

In Exercises 115 and 116, find the number of distinguishable permutations of the group of letters.

115. C, A, L, C, U, L, U, S

116. I, N, V, E, R, T, E, B, R, A, T, E

117. Bike Race There are ten bicyclists entered in a race. In how many different orders could the ten bicyclists finish?

118. Team Captains From a pool of 11 players on a football team, two will be chosen as co-captains. In how many different ways could these positions be filled?

119. Test Questions A student can answer any 15 questions from a total of 20 questions on an exam. In how many different ways could the student select the questions?

120. Magic Act A magician is performing in front of an audience of 68 people. In order to do a demonstration, six people are randomly selected from the audience. How many different groups of six people are possible? Use a graphing utility to find your answer.

7.7 121. Matching Socks A man has five pairs of socks (no two pairs are the same color). If he randomly selects two socks from a drawer, what is the probability that he gets a matched pair?

122. Bookshelf Order A child returns a five-volume set of books to a bookshelf. The child is not able to read and so cannot distinguish one volume from another. What is the probability that the books are shelved in the correct order?

123. Roll of the Dice Are the chances of rolling a 3 with one die the same as rolling a total of 6 with two dice? If not, which has the higher probability?

124. Roll of the Dice A six-sided die is rolled six times. What is the probability that each side appears exactly once?

125. Data Analysis A sample of college students, faculty members, and administrators were asked whether they favored a proposed increase in the annual activity fee to enhance student life on campus. The results of the study are shown in the table.

	Students	Faculty	Admin.	Total
Favor	237	37	18	292
Oppose	163	38	7	208
Total	400	75	25	500

A person is selected at random from the sample. Find the specified probability.

(a) The person is not in favor of the proposal.

(b) The person is a student.

(c) The person is a faculty member and is in favor of the proposal.

126. Card Game Five cards are drawn from an ordinary deck of 52 playing cards. Find the probability of getting two pairs. (For example, the hand could be A-A-5-5-Q or 4-4-7-7-K.)

127. Parental Independence Suppose that in a survey, senior citizens were asked if they would live with their children when they reached the point of not being able to live alone. The results are shown in the figure. If three senior citizens who could not live alone are randomly selected, what is the probability that all three are not living with their children?

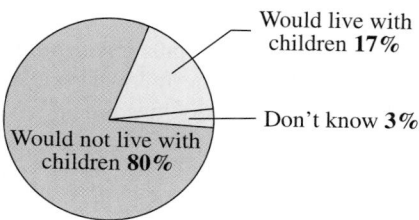

Would live with children **17%**

Don't know **3%**

Would not live with children **80%**

128. Picking a Card You randomly select a card from a 52-card deck. What is the probability that the card is *not* a club?

129. Tossing a Coin Find the probability of obtaining at least one tail when a coin is tossed five times.

Synthesis

True or False? In Exercises 130 and 131, determine whether the statement is true or false. Justify your answer.

130. $\dfrac{(n+2)!}{n!} = (n+2)(n+1)$

131. $\displaystyle\sum_{k=1}^{8} 3k = 3\sum_{k=1}^{8} k$

132. An infinite sequence is a function. What is the domain of the function?

133. How do the two sequences differ?

(a) $a_n = \dfrac{(-1)^n}{n}$ (b) $a_n = \dfrac{(-1)^{n+1}}{n}$

134. In your own words, explain what makes a sequence (a) arithmetic and (b) geometric.

135. The graphs of two sequences are shown below. Identify each sequence as arithmetic or geometric. Explain your reasoning.

(a) (b)

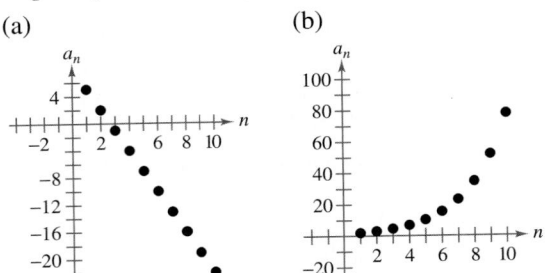

136. *Population Growth*   Consider an idealized population with the characteristic that each member of the population produces one offspring at the end of every time period. If each member has a life span of three time periods and the population begins with ten newborn members, then the following table shows the population during the first five time periods.

Age Bracket	Time Period				
	1	2	3	4	5
0–1	10	10	20	40	70
1–2		10	10	20	40
2–3			10	10	20
Total	10	20	40	70	130

The sequence for the total population has the property that

$$S_n = S_{n-1} + S_{n-2} + S_{n-3}, \quad n > 3.$$

Find the total population during the next five time periods.

137. Explain what a recursive formula is.

138. Explain why the terms of a geometric sequence of positive terms decrease when $0 < r < 1$.

In Exercises 139–142, match the sequence or sum of a sequence with its graph without doing any calculations. Explain your reasoning. [The graphs are labeled (a), (b), (c), and (d).]

(a) (b)

(c) (d)

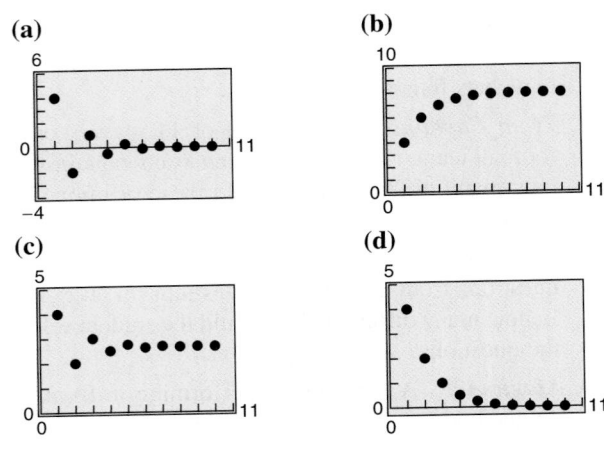

139. $a_n = 4\left(\frac{1}{2}\right)^{n-1}$

140. $a_n = 4\left(-\frac{1}{2}\right)^{n-1}$

141. $a_n = \sum_{k=1}^{n} 4\left(\frac{1}{2}\right)^{k-1}$

142. $a_n = \sum_{k=1}^{n} 4\left(-\frac{1}{2}\right)^{k-1}$

143. *Pattern Recognition*   Use a graphing utility to complete the table. What number is the nth term of the sequence approaching as n gets larger?

$$a_n = \left(1 + \frac{1}{n}\right)^n$$

n	100	500	1000	5000
a_n				

n	10,000	15,000	20,000	25,000
a_n				

144. How do the expansions of $(-x + y)^n$ and $(x - y)^n$ differ?

145. The probability of an event must be a real number in what interval? Is the interval open or closed?

146. The probability of an event is $\frac{2}{3}$. What is the probability that the event does not occur? Explain.

147. The weather forecast indicates that the probability of rain is 60%. Explain what this means.

Chapter Project *Fitting Models to Data*

In this project, you will explore difference quotients and see how they can be used to find average rates.

Suppose you are driving from Atlanta to Miami. The trip is about 700 miles and takes you 12 hours. Your average speed is

$$\text{Average speed} = \frac{\text{distance}}{\text{time}} = \frac{700}{12} \approx 58.3 \text{ miles per hour.}$$

This concept can be generalized as follows. Let f be a function defined on the interval $[a, b]$. The **average rate of change of** f from a to b is

$$\text{Average rate of change} = \frac{f(b) - f(a)}{b - a}.$$

This expression is called a *difference quotient*.

a. Calculate the average rate of change of $f(x) = 3x + 4$ on the interval $[2, 6]$. Select any other interval and show that you obtain the same average rate of change.

b. Calculate the average rates of change of $f(x) = x^2$ on the intervals $[1, 3]$ and $[4, 6]$. Are they equal? Explain.

c. During a one-hour trip, your average speed is 50 miles per hour. Discuss the relationship between this speed and the speeds shown on your speedometer.

Questions for Further Exploration

1. Let $f(x) = x^2 - 2$. Calculate the average rates of change of f on the intervals $[1, 3]$, $[1, 2]$, $[1, 1.5]$, and $[1, 1.1]$.

(a) Find an expression for the average rate of change of f on the interval $[1, 1 + h]$, where h is any real number.

(b) Create a table that shows the average rate of change of f for several values of h. Choose values of h that get closer and closer to 0. What value does the average rate of change of f approach as h approaches 0?

(c) The answer to part (b) is the slope of the tangent line to the graph of f at the point $(1, f(1))$. Graph this line and f in the same viewing window. Describe the behavior of the graphs near the point $(1, f(1))$.

2. The data in the table gives the costs of first-class postage in the United States for selected years from 1971 to 1999, where $t = 0$ corresponds to 1900. (Source: U.S. Postal Service)

t	71	74	75	78	81
Postage	$0.08	$0.10	$0.13	$0.15	$0.20

t	85	88	91	95	99
Postage	$0.22	$0.25	$0.29	$0.32	$0.33

(a) Find the average rate of change of the cost of postage between each two adjacent time intervals.

(b) When was the average rate of change largest? smallest?

(c) Are there intervals over which the average rate of change was zero? What does this mean?

7 Chapter Test

Take this test as you would take a test in class. After you are done, check your work against the answers given in the back of the book.

In Exercises 1 and 2, write the first five terms of the sequence.

1. $a_n = \left(-\frac{2}{3}\right)^{n-1}$. (Begin with $n = 1$.)

2. $a_1 = 12$ and $a_{k+1} = a_k + 4$

3. Simplify $\dfrac{11!\,4!}{4!\,7!}$.

In Exercises 4 and 5, find a formula for the *n*th term of the sequence.

4. Arithmetic: $a_1 = 5000$, $d = -100$

5. Geometric: $a_1 = 4$, $a_{k+1} = \frac{1}{2}a_k$

6. Use sigma notation to write: $\dfrac{2}{3(1)+1} + \dfrac{2}{3(2)+1} + \cdots + \dfrac{2}{3(12)+1}$.

7. Find the sum of the first 50 positive multiples of 3.

In Exercises 8–10, find the sum.

8. $\displaystyle\sum_{n=1}^{7}(8n - 5)$ 9. $\displaystyle\sum_{n=1}^{8}24\left(\frac{1}{6}\right)^{n-1}$ 10. $\displaystyle\sum_{n=1}^{\infty}5\left(\frac{1}{10}\right)^{n-1}$

11. Find the balance in an increasing annuity in which a principal of $50 is deposited at the beginning of each month for 25 years. Assume that the amount in the fund is compounded monthly at 8%.

12. Use mathematical induction to prove the formula

$$3 + 6 + 9 + \cdots + 3n = \frac{3n(n+1)}{2}.$$

In Exercises 13–16, evaluate $_nC_r$.

13. $_9C_3$ 14. $_{20}C_3$ 15. $_{18}C_5$ 16. $_{40}C_{38}$

17. Find the coefficient of the term x^3y^5 in the expansion of $(x + y)^8$.

18. How many distinct license plates can be issued with one letter followed by a three-digit number?

19. Four students are randomly selected from a class of 25 to answer questions from a reading assignment. In how many ways can the four be selected?

20. A card is drawn from a standard deck of 52 playing cards. Find the probability that it is a red face card.

21. Suppose that two spark plugs require replacement in a four-cylinder engine. If the mechanic randomly removes two plugs, find the probability that they are the two defective plugs.

22. Two integers (from 1 to 60) are chosen by a random number generator. What is the probability that (a) both numbers are odd, (b) both numbers are less than 12, and (c) the same number is chosen twice?

Conics and Parametric Equations

8.1 Conics

8.2 Translations of Conics

8.3 Parametric Equations

Mick Rossler/Superstock

The Big Picture

In this chapter you will learn how to

❑ recognize the four basic conics: circles, ellipses, parabolas, and hyperbolas.

❑ recognize, graph, and write equations of conics with vertex or center at the origin.

❑ recognize, graph, and write equations of conics that have been shifted vertically and/or horizontally in the plane.

❑ evaluate sets of parametric equations for given values of the parameter and graph curves that are represented by sets of parametric equations.

❑ rewrite sets of parametric equations as single rectangular equations and find sets of parametric equations for graphs.

Precipitation will fall as snow when the air temperature is below 32°F (or 0°C) from the cloud level down to the earth's surface.

Important Vocabulary

As you encounter each new vocabulary term in this chapter, add the term and its definition to your notebook glossary.

- conic section (p. 574)
- degenerate conic (p. 574)
- parabola (p. 575)
- directrix (p. 575)
- focus of a parabola (p. 575)
- vertex of a parabola (p. 575)
- axis of a parabola (p. 575)
- standard form of the equation of a parabola (p. 575)
- ellipse (p. 577)
- foci of an ellipse (p. 577)

- vertices of an ellipse (p. 577)
- major axis (p. 577)
- center of an ellipse (p. 577)
- minor axis (p. 577)
- standard form of the equation of an ellipse (p. 577)
- hyperbola (p. 579)
- foci of a hyperbola (p. 579)
- branches (p. 579)
- vertices of a hyperbola (p. 579)
- transverse axis (p. 579)

- center of a hyperbola (p. 579)
- standard form of the equation of a hyperbola (p. 579)
- conjugate axis (p. 580)
- asymptotes of a hyperbola (p. 581)
- parameter (p. 597)
- parametric equations (p. 597)
- plane curve (p. 597)
- orientation (p. 598)
- eliminating the parameter (p. 600)

Additional Resources   Text-specific additional resources are available to help you do well in this course. See page xvi for details.

8.1 Conics

Introduction

Conic sections were discovered during the classical Greek period, 600 to 300 B.C. The early Greek studies were largely concerned with the geometrical properties of conics. It was not until the early seventeenth century that the broad applicability of conics became apparent and played a prominent role in the early development of calculus.

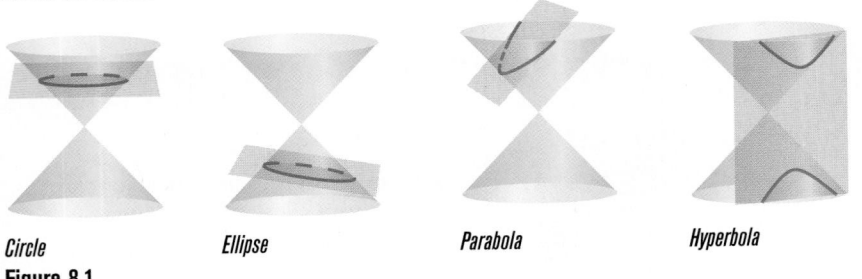

| Circle | Ellipse | Parabola | Hyperbola |

Figure 8.1

A **conic section** (or simply **conic**) is the intersection of a plane and a double-napped cone. Notice in Figure 8.1 that in the formation of the four basic conics, the intersecting plane does not pass through the vertex of the cone. When the plane does pass through the vertex, the resulting figure is a **degenerate conic**, as shown in Figure 8.2.

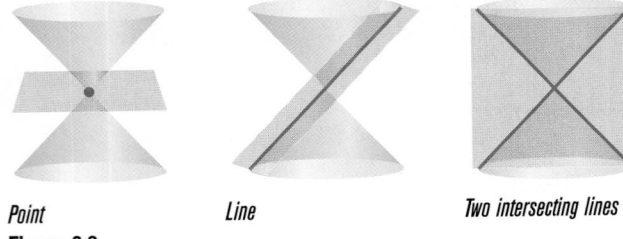

| Point | Line | Two intersecting lines |

Figure 8.2

There are several ways to approach the study of conics. You could begin by defining conics in terms of the intersections of planes and cones, as the Greeks did, or you could define them algebraically, in terms of the general second-degree equation $Ax^2 + Bxy + Cy^2 + Dx + Ey + F = 0$.

However, you will study a third approach, in which each of the conics is defined as a *locus* (collection) of points satisfying a certain geometric property. In Section P.5, you saw how the definition of a circle as *the collection of all points* (x, y) *that are equidistant from a fixed point* (h, k) led easily to the standard equation of a circle

$$(x - h)^2 + (y - k)^2 = r^2. \qquad \text{Equation of circle}$$

For instance, the collection of all points that are 3 units from $(0, 0)$ is a circle of radius 3 centered at the origin, whose equation is

$$x^2 + y^2 = 3^2.$$

What You Should Learn:

- How to recognize the four basic conics: circles, ellipses, parabolas, and hyperbolas
- How to recognize, graph, and write equations of parabolas (vertex at origin)
- How to recognize, graph, and write equations of ellipses (center at origin)
- How to recognize, graph, and write equations of hyperbolas (center at origin)

Why You Should Learn It:

Conics have been used for hundreds of years to model and solve engineering problems. For instance, Exercise 88 on page 585 shows how a parabola can be used to model the cables of a suspension bridge.

Adam Woolfitt/CORBIS

A computer animation of this concept appears in the *Interactive* CD-ROM and *Internet* versions of this text.

Parabolas

In Section 3.1, you learned that the graph of the quadratic function $f(x) = ax^2 + bx + c$ is a parabola that opens upward or downward. The following definition of a parabola is more general in the sense that it is independent of the orientation of the parabola.

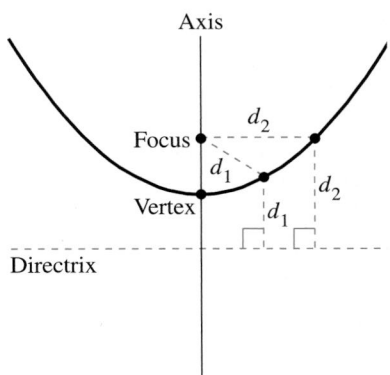

Definition of Parabola

A **parabola** is the set of all points (x, y) in a plane that are equidistant from a fixed line, the **directrix,** and a fixed point, the **focus,** not on the line. (See Figure 8.3.)

Figure 8.3

The midpoint between the focus and the directrix is the **vertex,** and the line passing through the focus and the vertex is the **axis** of the parabola.

A proof of the following standard form of the equation of a parabola is given in Appendix A.

Standard Equation of a Parabola (Vertex at Origin)

The **standard form of the equation of a parabola** with vertex at $(0, 0)$ and directrix $y = -p$ is

$$x^2 = 4py, \qquad p \neq 0. \qquad \text{Vertical axis}$$

For directrix $x = -p$, the equation is

$$y^2 = 4px, \qquad p \neq 0. \qquad \text{Horizontal axis}$$

The focus is on the axis p units (directed distance) from the vertex.

Notice that a parabola can have a vertical or a horizontal axis. Examples of each are shown in Figure 8.4.

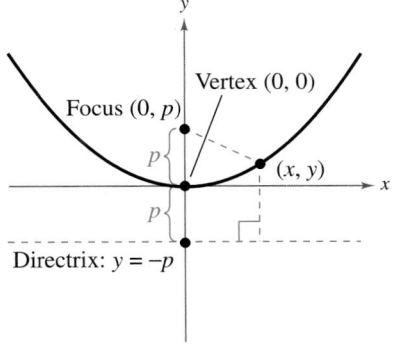

(a) Parabola with vertical axis

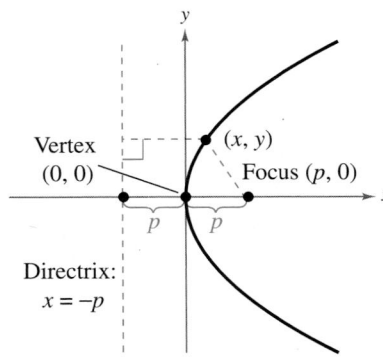

(b) Parabola with horizontal axis

Figure 8.4

EXAMPLE 1   Finding the Focus of a Parabola

Find the focus of the parabola whose equation is $y = -2x^2$.

Solution

Because the squared term in the equation involves x, you know that the axis is vertical, and the equation is of the form $x^2 = 4py$. You can write the given equation in this form as follows.

$$x^2 = -\frac{1}{2}y$$

$$x^2 = 4\left(-\frac{1}{8}\right)y \qquad \text{Write in standard form.}$$

So, $p = -\frac{1}{8}$. Because p is negative, the parabola opens downward (see Figure 8.5), and the focus of the parabola is

$$(0, p) = \left(0, -\frac{1}{8}\right). \qquad \text{Focus}$$

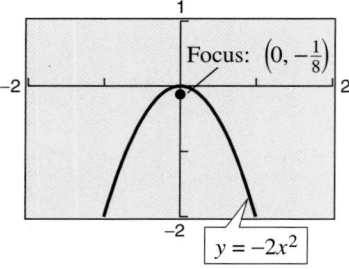

Figure 8.5

EXAMPLE 2   A Parabola with a Horizontal Axis

Write the standard form of the equation of the parabola with vertex at the origin and focus at $(2, 0)$.

Solution

The axis of the parabola is horizontal, passing through $(0, 0)$ and $(2, 0)$, as shown in Figure 8.6. So, the standard form is $y^2 = 4px$. Because the focus is $p = 2$ units from the vertex, the equation is

$$y^2 = 4(2)x$$

$$y^2 = 8x.$$

The equation $y^2 = 8x$ does not define y as a function of x. So, to use a graphing utility to graph $y^2 = 8x$, you need to break the graph into two equations, $y = 2\sqrt{2x}$ and $y = -2\sqrt{2x}$, each of which is a function of x.

Parabolas occur in a wide variety of applications. For instance, a parabolic reflector can be formed by revolving a parabola about its axis. The resulting surface has the property that all incoming rays parallel to the axis are reflected through the focus of the parabola—the principle behind the construction of the parabolic mirrors used in reflecting telescopes. Conversely, the light rays emanating from the focus of a parabolic reflector used in a flashlight are all parallel to one another, as shown in Figure 8.7.

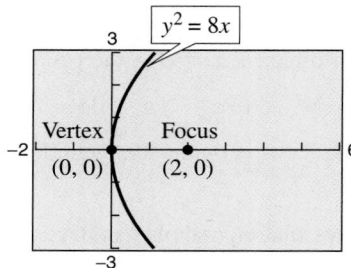

Figure 8.6

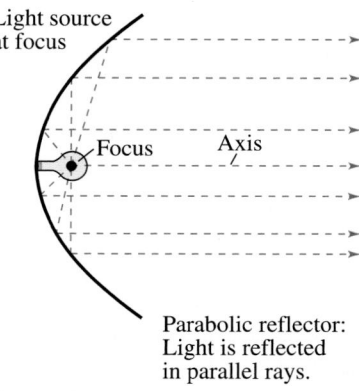

Parabolic reflector: Light is reflected in parallel rays.

Figure 8.7

Ellipses

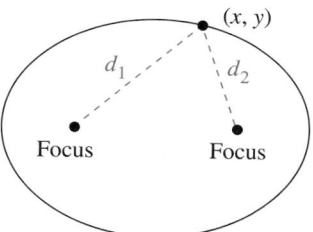

$d_1 + d_2$ is constant.

Definition of Ellipse

An **ellipse** is the set of all points (x, y) in a plane, the sum of whose distances from two distinct fixed points **(foci)** is constant. See Figure 8.8.

The line through the foci intersects the ellipse at two points **(vertices).** The chord joining the vertices is the **major axis,** and its midpoint is the **center** of the ellipse. The chord perpendicular to the major axis at the center is the **minor axis.**

You can visualize the definition of an ellipse by imagining two thumbtacks placed at the foci, as shown in Figure 8.9. If the ends of a fixed length of string are fastened to the thumbtacks and the string is drawn taut with a pencil, the path traced by the pencil will be an ellipse.

The standard form of the equation of an ellipse takes one of two forms, depending on whether the major axis is horizontal or vertical.

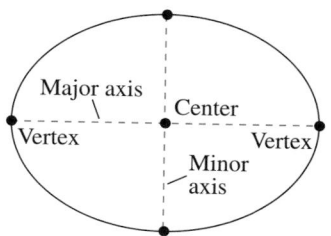

Figure 8.8

A computer animation of this concept appears in the *Interactive* CD-ROM and *Internet* versions of this text.

Standard Equation of an Ellipse (Center at Origin)

The **standard form of the equation of an ellipse** with center at the origin, and major and minor axes of lengths $2a$ and $2b$ (where $0 < b < a$), is

$$\frac{x^2}{a^2} + \frac{y^2}{b^2} = 1 \quad \text{or} \quad \frac{x^2}{b^2} + \frac{y^2}{a^2} = 1.$$

The vertices and foci lie on the major axis, a and c units, respectively, from the center, as shown in Figure 8.10. Moreover, a, b, and c are related by the equation $c^2 = a^2 - b^2$.

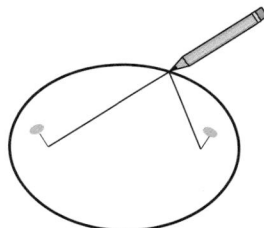

Figure 8.9

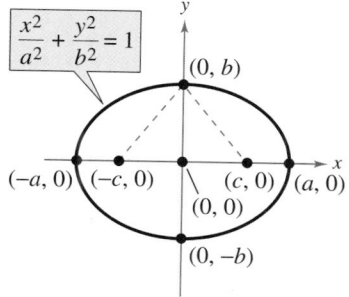

(a) Major axis is horizontal.
Minor axis is vertical.

Figure 8.10

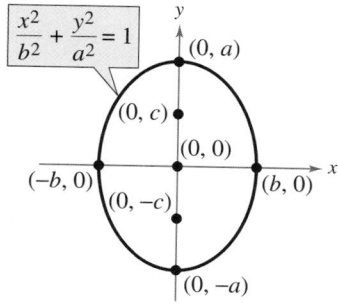

(b) Major axis is vertical.
Minor axis is horizontal.

In Figure 8.10, note that because the sum of the distances from a point on the ellipse to each focus is constant, $c^2 = a^2 - b^2$ as follows.

$$2\sqrt{b^2 + c^2} = (a + c) + (a - c)$$

$$\sqrt{b^2 + c^2} = a$$

$$c^2 = a^2 - b^2$$

Exploration

An ellipse can be drawn using two thumbtacks placed at the foci of the ellipse, a string of fixed length (greater than the distance between the tacks), and a pencil, as shown in Figure 8.9. Try doing this. Vary the distance between the thumbtacks. Explain how to obtain ellipses that are almost circular. Explain how to obtain ellipses that are long and narrow.

EXAMPLE 3   Finding the Standard Equation of an Ellipse

Find the standard form of the equation of the ellipse that has a major axis of length 6 and foci at $(-2, 0)$ and $(2, 0)$, as shown in Figure 8.11.

Solution

Because the foci occur at $(-2, 0)$ and $(2, 0)$, the center of the ellipse is $(0, 0)$ and the major axis is horizontal. So, the ellipse has an equation of the form

$$\frac{x^2}{a^2} + \frac{y^2}{b^2} = 1. \qquad \text{Standard form}$$

Because the length of the major axis is 6, $2a = 6$. This implies that $a = 3$. Moreover, the distance from the center to either focus is $c = 2$. Finally,

$$b^2 = a^2 - c^2 = 3^2 - 2^2 = 9 - 4 = 5.$$

Substituting $a^2 = 9 = 3^2$ and $b^2 = 5 = \left(\sqrt{5}\right)^2$ yields the equation

$$\frac{x^2}{3^2} + \frac{y^2}{\left(\sqrt{5}\right)^2} = 1.$$

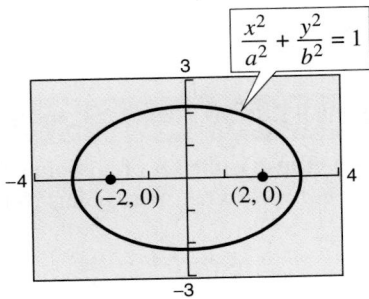

Figure 8.11

The *Interactive* CD-ROM and *Internet* versions of this text show every example with its solution; clicking on the *Try It!* button brings up similar problems. Guided Examples and Integrated Examples show step-by-step solutions to additional examples. Integrated Examples are related to several concepts in the section.

EXAMPLE 4   Sketching an Ellipse

Sketch the ellipse given by $4x^2 + y^2 = 36$, and identify the vertices.

Algebraic Solution

$$4x^2 + y^2 = 36 \qquad \text{Write original equation.}$$

$$\frac{4x^2}{36} + \frac{y^2}{36} = \frac{36}{36} \qquad \text{Divide each side by 36.}$$

$$\frac{x^2}{3^2} + \frac{y^2}{6^2} = 1 \qquad \text{Write in standard form.}$$

Because the denominator of the y^2-term is larger than the denominator of the x^2-term, you can conclude that the major axis is vertical. Moreover, because $a = 6$, the vertices are $(0, -6)$ and $(0, 6)$. Finally, because $b = 3$, the endpoints of the minor axis are $(-3, 0)$ and $(3, 0)$, as shown in Figure 8.12.

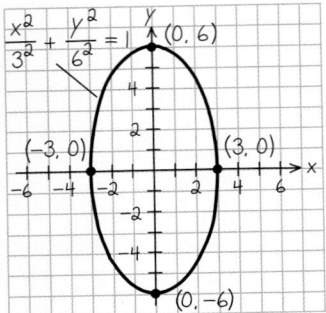

Figure 8.12

Graphical Solution

Solve the equation of the ellipse for y as follows.

$$4x^2 + y^2 = 36$$

$$y^2 = 36 - 4x^2$$

$$y = \pm\sqrt{36 - 4x^2}$$

Then use a graphing utility to graph $y_1 = \sqrt{36 - 4x^2}$ and $y_2 = -\sqrt{36 - 4x^2}$ in the same viewing window. Be sure to use a square setting. From the graph in Figure 8.13, you can see that the major axis is vertical. You can use the *zoom* and *trace* features to approximate the vertices to be $(0, 6)$ and $(0, -6)$.

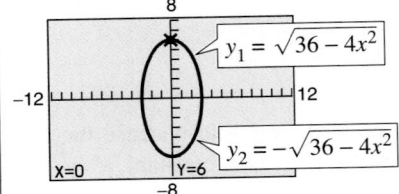

Figure 8.13

Hyperbolas

The definition of a **hyperbola** is similar to that of an ellipse. The difference is that for an ellipse, the *sum* of the distances between the foci and a point on the ellipse is constant, whereas for a hyperbola it is the *difference* of these distances that is constant.

Definition of Hyperbola

A **hyperbola** is the set of all points (x, y) in a plane, the difference of whose distances from two distinct fixed points **(foci)** is a positive constant. (See Figure 8.14.)

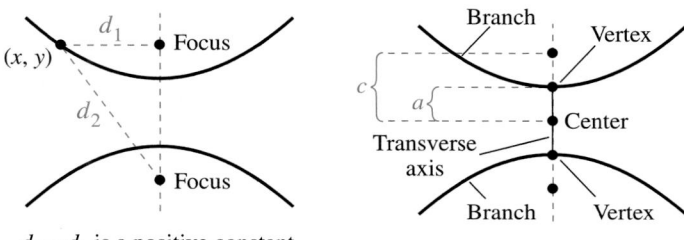

$d_2 - d_1$ is a positive constant.

Figure 8.14

The graph of a hyperbola has two disconnected parts **(branches).** The line through the two foci intersects the hyperbola at two points **(vertices).** The line segment connecting the vertices is the **transverse axis,** and the midpoint of the transverse axis is the **center** of the hyperbola.

Standard Equation of a Hyperbola (Center at Origin)

The **standard form of the equation of a hyperbola** with center at the origin (where $a \neq 0$ and $b \neq 0$) is

$$\frac{x^2}{a^2} - \frac{y^2}{b^2} = 1 \qquad \text{or} \qquad \frac{y^2}{a^2} - \frac{x^2}{b^2} = 1.$$

The vertices and foci are a and c units from the center, respectively. Moreover, a, b, and c are related by the equation $b^2 = c^2 - a^2$. (See Figure 8.15.)

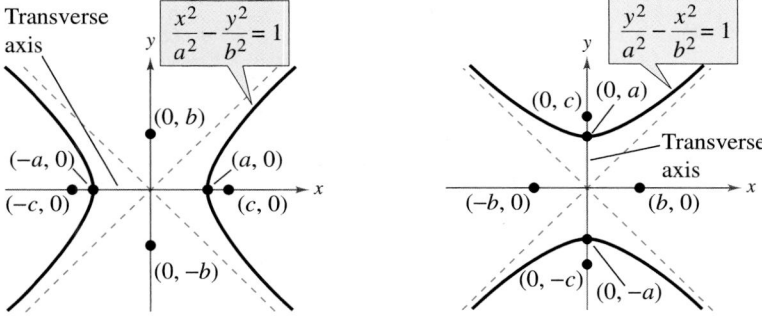

Figure 8.15

EXAMPLE 5   Finding the Standard Equation of a Hyperbola

Find the standard form of the equation of the hyperbola with foci at $(-3, 0)$ and $(3, 0)$ and vertices at $(-2, 0)$ and $(2, 0)$, as shown in Figure 8.16.

Solution

From the graph, you can determine that $c = 3$ because the foci are three units from the center. Moreover, $a = 2$ because the vertices are two units from the center. So, it follows that

$$b^2 = c^2 - a^2$$

$$= 3^2 - 2^2$$

$$= 9 - 4$$

$$= 5.$$

Because the transverse axis is horizontal, the standard form of the equation is

$$\frac{x^2}{a^2} - \frac{y^2}{b^2} = 1.$$

Finally, substitute $a^2 = 4 = 2^2$ and $b^2 = 5 = \left(\sqrt{5}\right)^2$ to obtain

$$\frac{x^2}{2^2} - \frac{y^2}{\left(\sqrt{5}\right)^2} = 1. \qquad \text{Write in standard form.}$$

An important aid in sketching the graph of a hyperbola is the determination of its *asymptotes*, as shown in Figure 8.17. Each hyperbola has two asymptotes that intersect at the center of the hyperbola. Furthermore, the asymptotes pass through the corners of a rectangle of dimensions $2a$ by $2b$. The line segment of length $2b$, joining $(0, b)$ and $(0, -b)$ [or $(-b, 0)$ and $(b, 0)$], is the **conjugate axis** of the hyperbola.

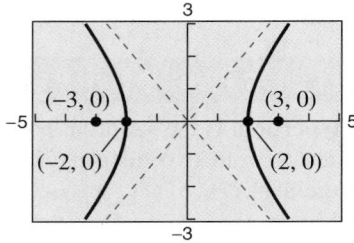

Figure 8.16

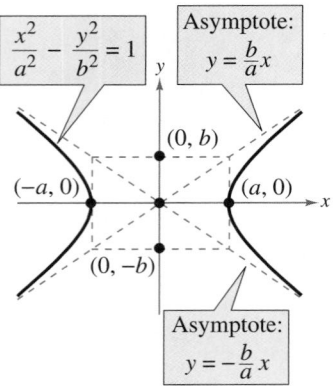

(a) **Transverse axis is horizontal.**
Conjugate axis is vertical.

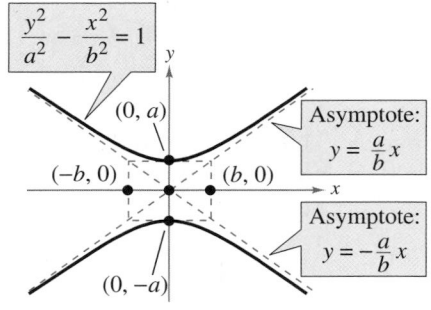

(b) **Transverse axis is vertical.**
Conjugate axis is horizontal.

Figure 8.17

Activities

1. Find an equation of the parabola with vertex at the origin and directrix at $x = 2$.

   Answer: $y^2 = -8x$

2. Find the center and vertices of the ellipse.

   $$\frac{x^2}{16} + \frac{y^2}{9} = 1$$

   Answer: Center $(0, 0)$
   Vertices: $(4, 0)$, $(-4, 0)$

3. Find an equation of the hyperbola with center at the origin, vertices $(0, \pm 2)$, and foci $(0, \pm 3)$.

   Answer: $\dfrac{y^2}{4} - \dfrac{x^2}{5} = 1$

Asymptotes of a Hyperbola (Center at Origin)

The **asymptotes of a hyperbola** with center at $(0, 0)$ are

$$y = \frac{b}{a}x \quad \text{and} \quad y = -\frac{b}{a}x \qquad \text{Transverse axis is horizontal.}$$

or

$$y = \frac{a}{b}x \quad \text{and} \quad y = -\frac{a}{b}x. \qquad \text{Transverse axis is vertical.}$$

EXAMPLE 6   Sketching the Graph of a Hyperbola

Sketch the graph of the hyperbola whose equation is $4x^2 - y^2 = 16$.

Algebraic Solution

$$4x^2 - y^2 = 16 \qquad \text{Write original equation.}$$

$$\frac{4x^2}{16} - \frac{y^2}{16} = \frac{16}{16} \qquad \text{Divide each side by 16.}$$

$$\frac{x^2}{2^2} - \frac{y^2}{4^2} = 1 \qquad \text{Write in standard form.}$$

Because the x^2-term is positive, you can conclude that the transverse axis is horizontal and that the vertices occur at $(-2, 0)$ and $(2, 0)$. Moreover, the endpoints of the conjugate axis occur at $(0, -4)$ and $(0, 4)$, and you can sketch the rectangle shown in Figure 8.18(a). Finally, by drawing the asymptotes through the corners of this rectangle, you can complete the sketch shown in Figure 8.18(b).

Graphical Solution

Solve the equation of the hyperbola for y as follows.

$$4x^2 - y^2 = 16$$

$$4x^2 - 16 = y^2$$

$$\pm\sqrt{4x^2 - 16} = y$$

Then use a graphing utility to graph $y_1 = \sqrt{4x^2 - 16}$ and $y_2 = -\sqrt{4x^2 - 16}$ in the same viewing window. Be sure to use a square setting. From the graph in Figure 8.19, you can see that the transverse axis is horizontal. You can use the *zoom* and *trace* features to approximate the vertices to be $(-2, 0)$ and $(2, 0)$.

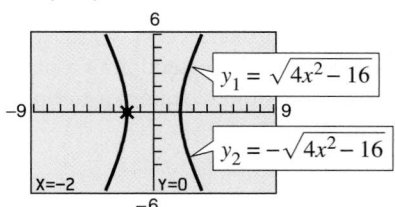

Figure 8.19

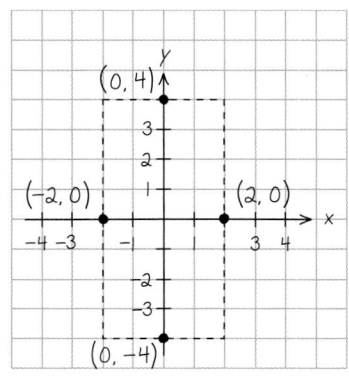

(a)

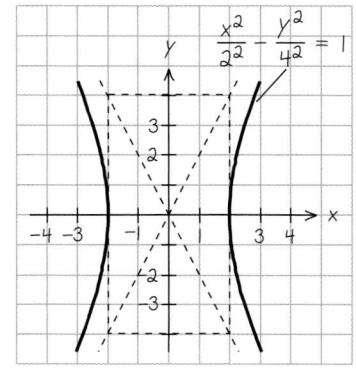

(b)

Figure 8.18

EXAMPLE 7   Finding the Standard Equation of a Hyperbola

Find the standard form of the equation of the hyperbola that has vertices at $(0, -3)$ and $(0, 3)$, and asymptotes $y = -2x$ and $y = 2x$, as shown in Figure 8.20.

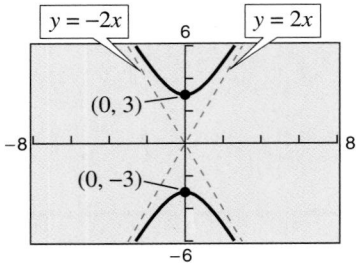

Figure 8.20

Solution

Because the transverse axis is vertical, the asymptotes are of the form

$$y = \frac{a}{b}x \quad \text{and} \quad y = -\frac{a}{b}x.$$

So,

$$\frac{a}{b} = 2$$

and because $a = 3$, you can determine that $b = \frac{3}{2}$. Finally, you can conclude that the hyperbola has the following equation.

$$\frac{y^2}{3^2} - \frac{x^2}{(3/2)^2} = 1 \qquad \text{Write in standard form.}$$

Writing About Math   *Hyperbolas in Applications*

At the beginning of this section, you learned that each type of conic section can be formed by the intersection of a plane and a double-napped cone. The figure below shows three examples of how such intersections can occur in physical situations.

 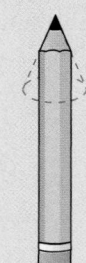 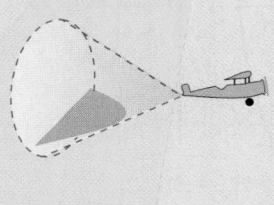

Identify the cone and hyperbola (or portion of a hyperbola) in each of the three situations. Write a short paragraph describing other examples of physical situations in which hyperbolas are formed.

8.1 Exercises

**In Exercises 1–10, match the equation with its graph.
[The graphs are labeled (a), (b), (c), (d), (e), (f), (g),
(h), (i), and (j).]**

(a)
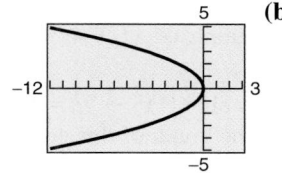

(b)
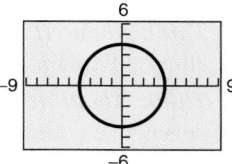

(c)
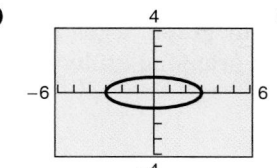

(d)
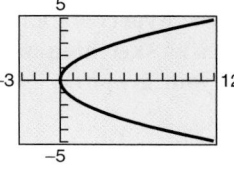

(e)
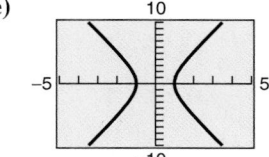

(f)
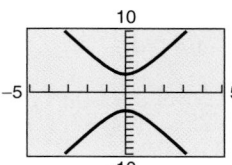

(g)
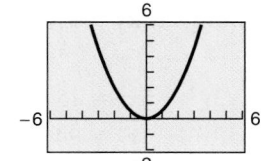

(h)
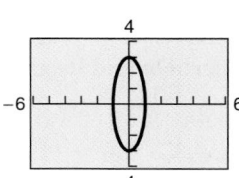

(i)
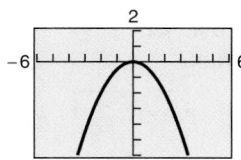

(j)
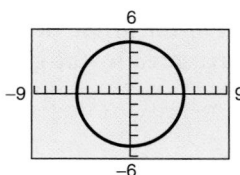

1. $x^2 = 2y$ **2.** $x^2 = -2y$

3. $y^2 = 2x$ **4.** $y^2 = -2x$

5. $9x^2 + y^2 = 9$ **6.** $x^2 + 9y^2 = 9$

7. $9x^2 - y^2 = 9$ **8.** $y^2 - 9x^2 = 9$

9. $x^2 + y^2 = 16$ **10.** $x^2 + y^2 = 25$

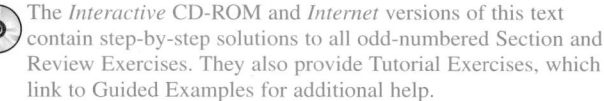

The *Interactive* CD-ROM and *Internet* versions of this text
contain step-by-step solutions to all odd-numbered Section and
Review Exercises. They also provide Tutorial Exercises, which
link to Guided Examples for additional help.

**In Exercises 11–16, find the equation of the circle with
its center at the origin and the given conditions.**

11. Radius: 6

12. Radius: 1

13. Radius: $\frac{9}{4}$

14. Diameter: $\frac{10}{7}$

15. Diameter: $2\sqrt{7}$

16. Diameter: $8\sqrt{13}$

**In Exercises 17–22, find the vertex and focus of the
parabola and sketch its graph. Use a graphing utility
to verify your graph.**

17. $y = \frac{1}{2}x^2$ **18.** $y = 2x^2$

19. $y^2 = -6x$ **20.** $y^2 = 3x$

21. $x^2 + 8y = 0$ **22.** $4x + y^2 = 0$

**In Exercises 23–32, find an equation of the parabola
with vertex at the origin.**

23. Focus: $\left(0, -\frac{3}{2}\right)$ **24.** Focus: $\left(\frac{5}{2}, 0\right)$

25. Focus: $(-2, 0)$ **26.** Focus: $(0, -2)$

27. Directrix: $y = -1$ **28.** Directrix: $y = 2$

29. Directrix: $x = 3$ **30.** Directrix: $x = -2$

31. Horizontal axis and passes through the point $(4, 6)$

32. Vertical axis and passes through the point $(-2, -2)$

**In Exercises 33–36, find an equation of the parabola
and determine the coordinates of the focus.**

33.
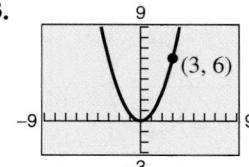

34.
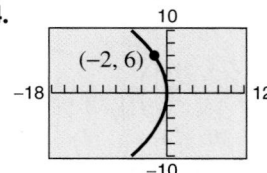

35.
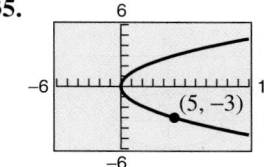

36.
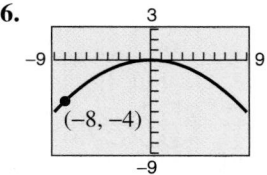

In Exercises 37 and 38, use a graphing utility to graph the parabola and the given line (called one of its *tangent lines*). Identify the point of intersection (called the *point of tangency*).

Parabola	Tangent Line
37. $y^2 - 8x = 0$	$x - y + 2 = 0$
38. $x^2 + 12y = 0$	$x + y - 3 = 0$

In Exercises 39–46, find the center and vertices of the ellipse and sketch its graph. Use a graphing utility to verify your graph.

39. $\dfrac{x^2}{25} + \dfrac{y^2}{16} = 1$ **40.** $\dfrac{x^2}{144} + \dfrac{y^2}{169} = 1$

41. $\dfrac{x^2}{\frac{25}{9}} + \dfrac{y^2}{\frac{16}{9}} = 1$ **42.** $\dfrac{x^2}{4} + \dfrac{y^2}{\frac{1}{4}} = 1$

43. $\dfrac{x^2}{9} + \dfrac{y^2}{5} = 1$ **44.** $\dfrac{x^2}{28} + \dfrac{y^2}{64} = 1$

45. $4x^2 + y^2 = 1$ **46.** $4x^2 + 9y^2 = 36$

In Exercises 47–50, use a graphing utility to graph the ellipse. (*Hint:* Use two equations.)

47. $5x^2 + 3y^2 = 15$ **48.** $x^2 + 4y^2 = 4$

49. $9x^2 + y^2 = 81$ **50.** $4x^2 + 25y^2 = 100$

Think About It In Exercises 51 and 52, which part of the ellipse $4x^2 + 9y^2 = 36$ is represented by the equation?

51. $x = -\dfrac{3}{2}\sqrt{4 - y^2}$ **52.** $y = \dfrac{2}{3}\sqrt{9 - x^2}$

In Exercises 53–62, find an equation of the ellipse with center at the origin.

53.   **54.**

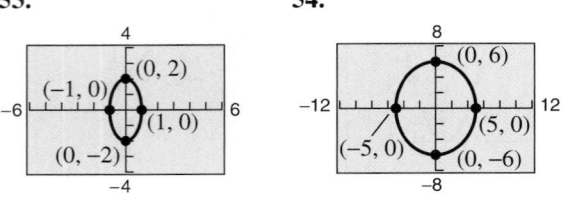

55.   **56.**

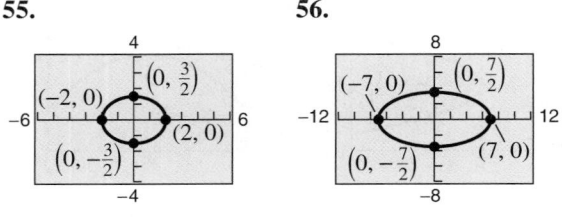

57. Vertices: $(\pm 5, 0)$; Foci: $(\pm 2, 0)$

58. Vertices: $(0, \pm 8)$; Foci: $(0, \pm 4)$

59. Foci: $(\pm 5, 0)$; Major axis of length 12

60. Foci: $(\pm 2, 0)$; Major axis of length 8

61. Vertices: $(0, \pm 5)$; Passes through the point $(4, 2)$

62. Major axis vertical; Passes through the points $(0, 4)$ and $(2, 0)$

63. *Think About It* Is the graph of $x^2 + 4y^4 = 4$ an ellipse? Explain.

64. *Think About It* The graph of $x^2 - y^2 = 0$ is a degenerate conic. Sketch the graph of this equation.

In Exercises 65–72, find the center, vertices, and foci of the hyperbola and sketch its graph, using asymptotes as sketching aids. Use a graphing utility to verify your graph.

65. $x^2 - y^2 = 1$ **66.** $\dfrac{x^2}{9} - \dfrac{y^2}{16} = 1$

67. $\dfrac{y^2}{1} - \dfrac{x^2}{4} = 1$ **68.** $\dfrac{y^2}{9} - \dfrac{x^2}{1} = 1$

69. $\dfrac{y^2}{25} - \dfrac{x^2}{144} = 1$ **70.** $\dfrac{x^2}{36} - \dfrac{y^2}{4} = 1$

71. $4y^2 - x^2 = 1$ **72.** $4y^2 - 9x^2 = 36$

In Exercises 73–76, use a graphing utility to graph the hyperbola and its asymptotes.

73. $2x^2 - 3y^2 = 6$ **74.** $3y^2 - 5x^2 = 15$

75. $4y^2 - 6x^2 = 12$ **76.** $8x^2 - 3y^2 = 24$

Think About It In Exercises 77 and 78, state which part of the graph of the hyperbola $4x^2 - 9y^2 = 36$ is represented by the given equation.

77. $y = -\dfrac{2}{3}\sqrt{x^2 - 9}$ **78.** $x = \dfrac{3}{2}\sqrt{y^2 + 4}$

In Exercises 79–86, find an equation of the specified hyperbola with center at the origin.

79. Vertices: $(0, \pm 2)$; Foci: $(0, \pm 4)$

80. Vertices: $(\pm 3, 0)$; Foci: $(\pm 5, 0)$

81. Vertices: $(\pm 1, 0)$; Asymptotes: $y = \pm 3x$

82. Vertices: $(0, \pm 3)$; Asymptotes: $y = \pm 3x$

83. Foci: $(0, \pm 8)$; Asymptotes: $y = \pm 4x$

84. Foci: $(\pm 10, 0)$; Asymptotes: $y = \pm \dfrac{3}{4}x$

85.

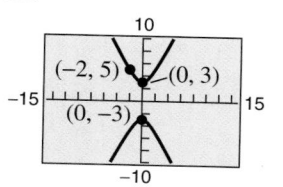

86.

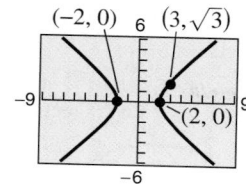

87. *Satellite Antenna* Write an equation for a cross section of the parabolic television dish antenna shown in the figure.

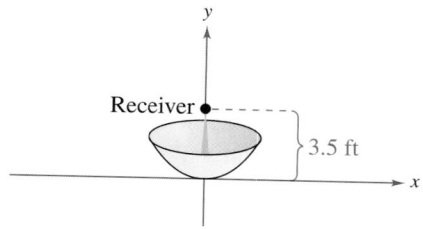

88. *Suspension Bridge* Each cable of a suspension bridge is suspended (in the shape of a parabola) between two towers that are 120 meters apart and rise 20 meters above the roadway. The cables touch the roadway midway between the towers.

(a) Draw a sketch of the bridge. Locate the origin of a rectangular coordinate system at the center of the roadway. Label the coordinates of the known points.

(b) Write an equation that models the cables.

(c) Complete the table by finding the heights of the suspension cables over the roadway at distances of x meters from the center of the bridge.

x	0	20	40	60
y				

89. *Beam Deflection* A simply supported beam is 64 feet long and has a load at the center. The deflection of the beam at its center is 1 inch. The shape of the deflected beam is parabolic.

(a) Find an equation of the parabola. (Assume that the origin is at the center of the beam.)

(b) How far from the center of the beam is the deflection equal to $\frac{1}{2}$ inch?

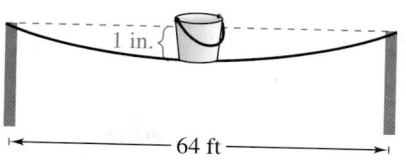

FIGURE FOR 89

90. *Exploration* Consider the equation $x^2 = 4py$.

(a) Use a graphing utility to graph the parabolas for $p = 1$, $p = 2$, $p = 3$, and $p = 4$. Describe the effect on the graph when p increases.

(b) Locate the focus of each parabola in part (a).

(c) For each parabola in part (a), find the length of the chord passing through the focus parallel to the directrix. How can the length of this chord be determined directly from $x^2 = 4py$?

(d) Explain how the result of part (c) can be used as a sketching aid when graphing parabolas.

91. *Fireplace Arch* A fireplace arch is to be built in the shape of a semiellipse. The opening is to have a height of 2 feet at the center and a width of 6 feet along the base. The contractor draws the outline of the ellipse by the method discussed on page 577. Give the required positions of the tacks and the length of the string.

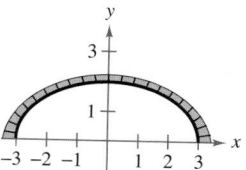

92. *Geometry* Sketch a graph of the ellipse that consists of all points (x, y) such that the sum of the distances between (x, y) and two fixed points is 16 units and the foci are located at the centers of the two sets of concentric circles in the figure.

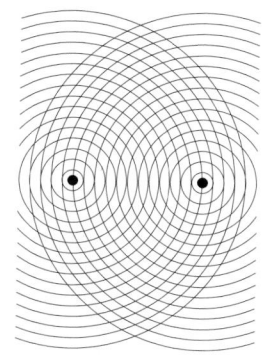

93. *Mountain Tunnel* A semielliptical arch over a tunnel for a road through a mountain has a major axis of 100 feet and a height at the center of 30 feet.

  (a) Draw a diagram to solve the problem. Draw the tunnel on a rectangular coordinate system with the center of the road entering the tunnel at the origin. Identify the coordinates of the known points.

  (b) Find an equation of the semielliptical tunnel.

  (c) Determine the height of the arch 5 feet from the edge of the tunnel.

94. *Exploration* Consider the ellipse

$$\frac{x^2}{a^2} + \frac{y^2}{b^2} = 1, \quad a + b = 20.$$

  (a) The area of the ellipse is given by $A = \pi ab$. Write the area of the ellipse as a function of a.

  (b) Find the equation of an ellipse with an area of 264 square centimeters.

  (c) Complete the table using your equation from part (a) and make a conjecture about the shape of the ellipse with maximum area.

a	8	9	10	11	12	13
A						

  (d) Use a graphing utility to graph the area function to support your conjecture in part (c).

95. *Geometry* The area of the ellipse in the figure is twice the area of the circle. What is the length of the major axis? (The area of an ellipse is $A = \pi ab$.)

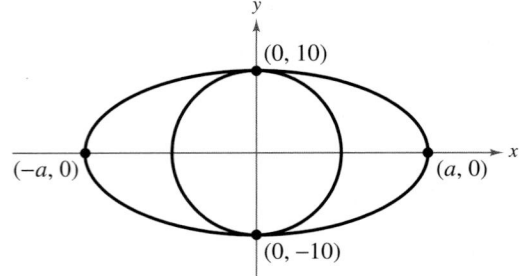

96. *Geometry* A line segment through a focus of an ellipse and with endpoints on the ellipse and perpendicular to the major axis is called a **latus rectum** of the ellipse. Therefore, an ellipse has two latera recta. Knowing the length of the latera recta is helpful in sketching an ellipse because it yields other points on the curve (see figure). Show that the length of each latus rectum is $2b^2/a$.

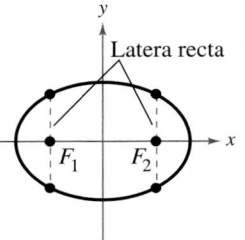

In Exercises 97–100, sketch the graph of the ellipse, making use of the latera recta (see Exercise 96).

97. $\dfrac{x^2}{4} + \dfrac{y^2}{1} = 1$ **98.** $\dfrac{x^2}{9} + \dfrac{y^2}{16} = 1$

99. $9x^2 + 4y^2 = 36$ **100.** $5x^2 + 3y^2 = 15$

101. *Hyperbolic Mirror* A hyperbolic mirror (used in some telescopes) has the property that a light ray directed at the focus will be reflected to the other focus. The focus of a hyperbolic mirror has coordinates $(24, 0)$. Find the vertex of the mirror if its mount has coordinates $(24, 24)$.

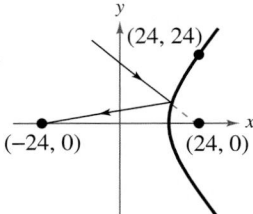

102. *Navigation* Long distance radio navigation for aircraft and ships uses synchronized pulses transmitted by widely separated transmitting stations. These pulses travel at the speed of light (186,000 miles per second). The difference in the times of arrival of these pulses at an aircraft or ship is constant on a hyperbola having the transmitting stations as foci.

Assume that two stations 300 miles apart are positioned on the rectangular coordinate system at points with coordinates $(-150, 0)$ and $(150, 0)$ and that a ship is traveling on a path with coordinates $(x, 75)$. Find the x-coordinate of the position of the ship when the time difference between the pulses from the transmitting stations is 1000 microseconds (0.001 second).

FIGURE FOR 102

Synthesis

True or False In Exercises 103–105, determine whether the statement is true or false. Justify your answer.

103. The equation $9x^2 - 16y^2 = 144$ represents an ellipse.

104. The major axis of the ellipse given by $y^2 + 16x^2 = 64$ is vertical.

105. It is possible for a parabola to intersect its directrix.

106. *Exploration* Let (x_1, y_1) be the coordinates of a point on the parabola $x^2 = 4py$. The equation of the line that just touches the parabola at the point (x_1, y_1), called a *tangent line*, is

$$y - y_1 = \frac{x_1}{2p}(x - x_1).$$

  (a) What is the slope of the tangent line?

  (b) For each parabola in Exercise 90, find the equations of the tangent lines at the endpoints of the chord. Use a graphing utility to graph the parabola and tangent lines.

107. *Think About It* On page 577 (see Figure 8.9) it is noted that an ellipse can be drawn using two thumbtacks, a string of fixed length (greater than the distance between the two tacks), and a pencil.

  (a) What is the length of the string in terms of a?

  (b) Explain why the path is an ellipse.

108. *Writing* Write a paragraph discussing the change in the shape and orientation of the graph of the ellipse

$$\frac{x^2}{a^2} + \frac{y^2}{16} = 1$$

as a increases from 1 to 8.

109. Use the definition of an ellipse to derive the standard form of the equation of an ellipse.

110. Use the definition of a hyperbola to derive the standard form of the equation of a hyperbola.

Review

In Exercises 111–114, factor each expression completely.

111. $12x^2 + 7x - 10$ **112.** $25x^3 - 60x^2 + 36x$

113. $12z^4 + 17z^3 + 5z^2$ **114.** $x^3 + 3x^2 - 4x - 12$

In Exercises 115–118, find a polynomial with integer coefficients that has the given zeros.

115. $0, 3, 4$ **116.** $-6, 1$

117. $-3, 1 + \sqrt{2}, 1 - \sqrt{2}$ **118.** $3, 2 + i, 2 - i$

119. Find all the zeros of $f(x) = 2x^3 - 3x^2 + 50x - 75$

  if one of the zeros is $x = \frac{3}{2}$.

120. List the possible rational zeros of the function

$$g(x) = 6x^4 + 7x^3 - 29x^2 - 28x + 20.$$

121. Use a graphing utility to graph the function

$$h(x) = 2x^4 + x^3 - 19x^2 - 9x + 9.$$

  Use the graph and the Rational Zero Test to find the zeros of h.

In Exercises 122–125, evaluate the determinant. Expand by cofactors on the row or column that appears to make the computations easiest.

122. $\begin{vmatrix} 3 & 8 & -7 \\ 0 & -5 & 4 \\ 8 & 1 & 6 \end{vmatrix}$ **123.** $\begin{vmatrix} 5 & -8 & 0 \\ 9 & 7 & 4 \\ -8 & 7 & 1 \end{vmatrix}$

124. $\begin{vmatrix} 7 & 0 & -14 \\ -2 & 5 & 4 \\ -6 & 2 & 12 \end{vmatrix}$ **125.** $\begin{vmatrix} 3 & 0 & 0 \\ -2 & 5 & 0 \\ 12 & 5 & 7 \end{vmatrix}$

126. *Boarding a Plane* In how many different ways can eleven people board an airplane?

127. *Test Questions* A student can answer any 15 questions from a total of 18 questions on an exam. In how many different ways can the student select the questions?

8.2 Translations of Conics

Vertical and Horizontal Shifts of Conics

In Section 8.1 you looked at conic sections whose graphs were in *standard position* (centered at the origin). In this section you will study the equations of conic sections that have been shifted vertically or horizontally in the plane.

Leo de Wys

Standard Forms of Equations of Conics

Circle: Center $= (h, k)$; Radius $= r$
$$(x - h)^2 + (y - k)^2 = r^2$$

Ellipse: Center $= (h, k)$
    Major axis length $= 2a$
    Minor axis length $= 2b$

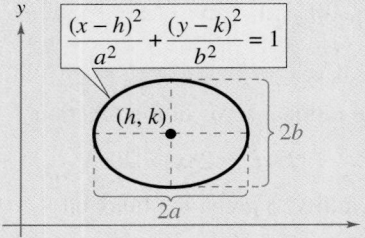

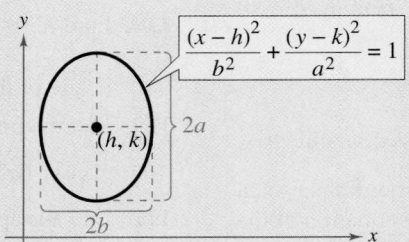

Hyperbola: Center $= (h, k)$
    Transverse axis length $= 2a$
    Conjugate axis length $= 2b$

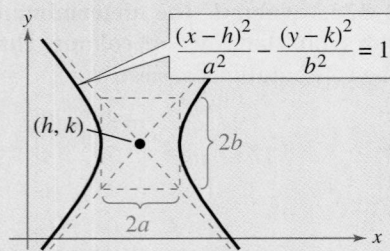

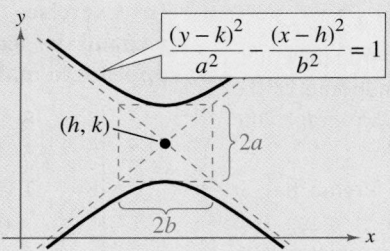

Parabola: Vertex $= (h, k)$
    Directed distance from vertex to focus $= p$

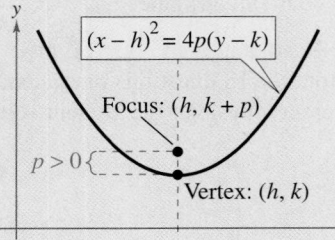

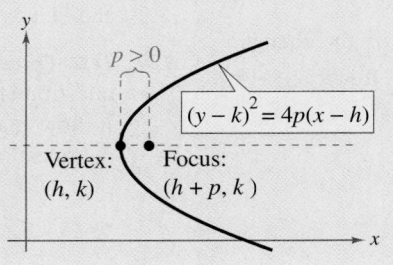

Remind students that these are the standard forms for conics and that conics are in standard position when $h = 0$ and $k = 0$.

EXAMPLE 1   Translations of Conic Sections

Graph each translation.

a. $(x - 1)^2 + (y + 2)^2 = 3^2$

b. $\dfrac{(x - 2)^2}{3^2} + \dfrac{(y - 1)^2}{2^2} = 1$

c. $\dfrac{(x - 3)^2}{1^2} - \dfrac{(y - 2)^2}{3^2} = 1$

d. $(x + 2)^2 = 4(-1)(y - 3)$

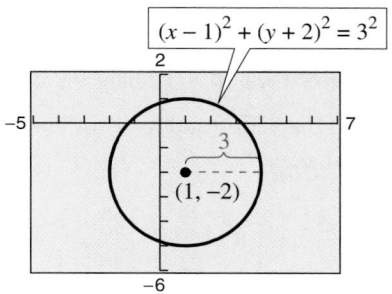

(a)

Solution

a. The graph of

$$(x - 1)^2 + (y + 2)^2 = 3^2$$

is a circle whose center is the point $(1, -2)$ and whose radius is 3, as shown in Figure 8.21(a). Note that the graph of the circle has been shifted 1 unit to the right and 2 units downward from standard position.

b. The graph of

$$\dfrac{(x - 2)^2}{3^2} + \dfrac{(y - 1)^2}{2^2} = 1$$

is an ellipse whose center is the point $(2, 1)$. The major axis of the ellipse is horizontal and of length $2(3) = 6$, and the minor axis of the ellipse is vertical and of length $2(2) = 4$, as shown in Figure 8.21(b). Note that the graph of the ellipse has been shifted 2 units to the right and 1 unit upward from standard position.

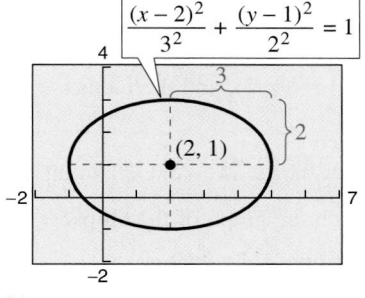

(b)

c. The graph of

$$\dfrac{(x - 3)^2}{1^2} - \dfrac{(y - 2)^2}{3^2} = 1$$

is a hyperbola whose center is the point $(3, 2)$. The transverse axis is horizontal and of length $2(1) = 2$, and the conjugate axis is vertical and of length $2(3) = 6$, as shown in Figure 8.21(c). Note that the graph of the hyperbola has been shifted 3 units to the right and 2 units upward from standard position.

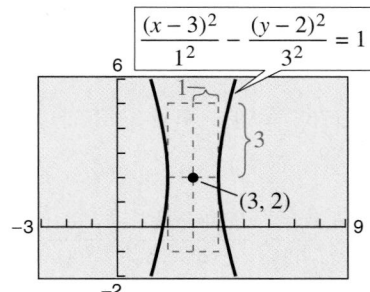

(c)

d. The graph of

$$(x + 2)^2 = 4(-1)(y - 3)$$

is a parabola whose vertex is the point $(-2, 3)$. The axis of the parabola is vertical. The focus is one unit above or below the vertex and, because $p = -1$, it follows that the focus lies *below* the vertex and the parabola opens downward, as shown in Figure 8.21(d). Note that the graph of the parabola has been shifted 2 units to the left and 3 units upward from standard position.

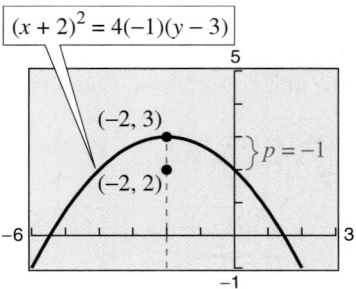

(d)

Figure 8.21

Writing Equations of Conics in Standard Form

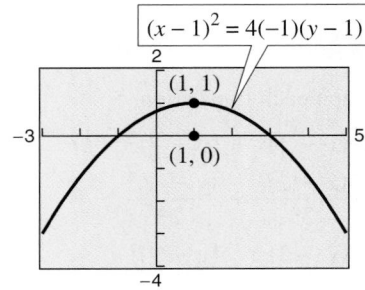

Figure 8.22

EXAMPLE 2   Finding the Standard Form of a Parabola

Find the vertex and focus of the parabola $x^2 - 2x + 4y - 3 = 0$.

Solution

$x^2 - 2x + 4y - 3 = 0$	Write original equation.
$x^2 - 2x + 1 = -4y + 3 + 1$	Group terms and add 1 to each side.
$(x - 1)^2 = -4y + 4$	Write in completed square form.
$(x - 1)^2 = 4(-1)(y - 1)$ $(x - h)^2 = 4p(y - k)$	

From this standard form, it follows that $h = 1$, $k = 1$, and $p = -1$. Because the axis is vertical and p is negative, the parabola opens downward. The vertex is $(h, k) = (1, 1)$, and the focus is $(h, k + p) = (1, 0)$. See Figure 8.22.

> ## STUDY T!P
>
> For a review of completing the square, refer to Section 2.4.
>
> It may be useful to review the process of completing the square in an equation.

EXAMPLE 3   Sketching an Ellipse

Sketch the graph of the ellipse $x^2 + 4y^2 + 6x - 8y + 9 = 0$.

Algebraic Solution

$x^2 + 4y^2 + 6x - 8y + 9 = 0$	Write original equation.
$(x^2 + 6x + \;\;) + (4y^2 - 8y + \;\;) = -9$	Group terms.
$(x^2 + 6x + \;\;) + 4(y^2 - 2y + \;\;) = -9$	Factor 4 out of y-terms.
$(x^2 + 6x + 9) + 4(y^2 - 2y + 1) = -9 + 9 + 4(1)$	Add 9 and $4(1) = 4$ to each side.
$(x + 3)^2 + 4(y - 1)^2 = 4$	Completed square form.
$\dfrac{(x + 3)^2}{4} + \dfrac{(y - 1)^2}{1} = 1$	Standard form

From this standard form, it follows that the center is $(h, k) = (-3, 1)$. Because the denominator of the x-term is $4 = 2^2 = a^2$, the endpoints of the major axis lie two units to the right and left of the center. Similarly, because the denominator of the y-term is $1 = 1^2 = b^2$, the endpoints of the minor axis lie one unit up and down from the center. The ellipse is shown in Figure 8.23.

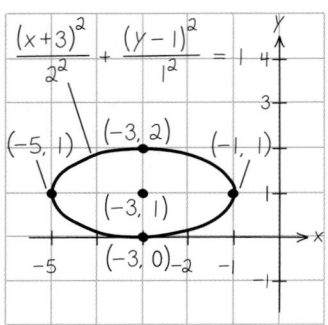

Figure 8.23

Graphical Solution

Write the completed square form of the ellipse as shown in the *Algebraic Solution*. Then solve the equation for y.

$$(y - 1)^2 = 1 - \frac{(x + 3)^2}{4}$$

$$y = 1 \pm \sqrt{1 - \frac{(x + 3)^2}{4}}$$

Then use a graphing utility to graph the two equations for y in the same viewing window, as shown in Figure 8.24. Use the *zoom* and *trace* features to approximate the endpoints of the major and minor axes to be $(-5, 1)$ and $(-1, 1)$, and $(-3, 2)$ and $(-3, 0)$, respectively.

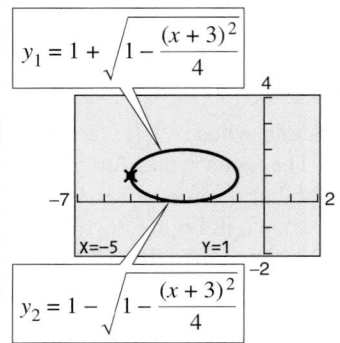

Figure 8.24

EXAMPLE 4   Sketching a Hyperbola

Sketch the graph of the hyperbola given by the equation

$$y^2 - 4x^2 + 4y + 24x - 41 = 0.$$

Solution

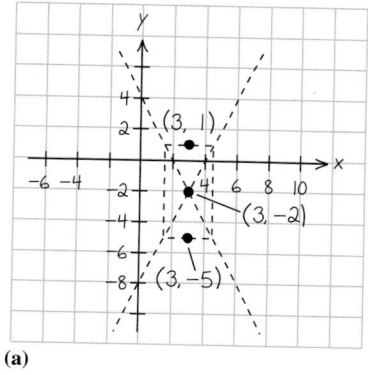

(a)

$$y^2 - 4x^2 + 4y + 24x - 41 = 0 \qquad \text{Write original equation.}$$

$$(y^2 + 4y + \ ) - (4x^2 - 24x + \ ) = 41 \qquad \text{Group terms.}$$

$$(y^2 + 4y + \ ) - 4(x^2 - 6x + \ ) = 41 \qquad \text{Factor 4 out of } x\text{-terms.}$$

$$(y^2 + 4y + 4) - 4(x^2 - 6x + 9) = 41 + 4 - 4(9) \qquad \begin{array}{l}\text{Add 4 and subtract} \\ 4(9) = 36 \text{ from each} \\ \text{side.}\end{array}$$

$$(y + 2)^2 - 4(x - 3)^2 = 9 \qquad \begin{array}{l}\text{Write in completed} \\ \text{square form.}\end{array}$$

$$\frac{(y + 2)^2}{9} - \frac{4(x - 3)^2}{9} = 1 \qquad \text{Divide each side by 9.}$$

$$\frac{(y + 2)^2}{9} - \frac{(x - 3)^2}{\frac{9}{4}} = 1 \qquad \text{Rewrite 4 as } \frac{1}{\frac{1}{4}}.$$

$$\frac{(y + 2)^2}{3^2} - \frac{(x - 3)^2}{\left(\frac{3}{2}\right)^2} = 1 \qquad \frac{(y - k)^2}{a^2} - \frac{(x - h)^2}{b^2} = 1$$

From this standard form, it follows that the transverse axis is vertical and the center lies at $(h, k) = (3, -2)$. Because the denominator of the y-term is $a^2 = 3^2$, you know that the vertices occur three units above and below the center.

$$(3, 1) \qquad \text{and} \qquad (3, -5) \qquad \text{Vertices}$$

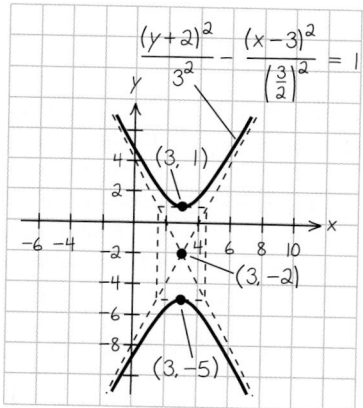

(b)

Figure 8.25

A computer animation of this example appears in the *Interactive* CD-ROM and *Internet* versions of this text.

To sketch the hyperbola, draw a rectangle whose top and bottom pass through the vertices. Because the denominator of the x-term is $b^2 = \left(\frac{3}{2}\right)^2$, locate the sides of the rectangle $\frac{3}{2}$ units to the right and left of the center, as shown in Figure 8.25(a). Finally, sketch the asymptotes by drawing lines through the opposite corners of the rectangle. Using these asymptotes, you can complete the graph of the hyperbola, as shown in Figure 8.25(b).

To find the foci in Example 4, first find c.

$$c^2 = a^2 + b^2 = 9 + \frac{9}{4} = \frac{45}{4} \qquad \Longrightarrow \qquad c = \frac{3\sqrt{5}}{2}$$

Because the transverse axis is vertical, the foci lie c units above and below the center.

$$\left(3, -2 + \tfrac{3}{2}\sqrt{5}\right) \qquad \text{and} \qquad \left(3, -2 - \tfrac{3}{2}\sqrt{5}\right) \qquad \text{Foci}$$

Activities

1. Rewrite in standard form:
   $$4x^2 - 9y^2 - 16x - 18y - 29 = 0.$$
   Answer: $\dfrac{(x - 2)^2}{9} - \dfrac{(y + 1)^2}{4} = 1$

2. Find the vertex, focus, and directrix of the parabola
   $$(x - 1)^2 - 2(y + 6) = 0.$$
   Answer: Vertex: $(1, -6)$
   Focus: $\left(1, -\tfrac{11}{2}\right)$
   Directrix: $y = -\tfrac{13}{2}$

EXAMPLE 5   Writing the Equation of an Ellipse

Write the standard form of the equation of the ellipse whose vertices are $(2, -2)$ and $(2, 4)$. The length of the minor axis of the ellipse is 4, as shown in Figure 8.26.

Solution

The center of the ellipse lies at the midpoint of its vertices. So, the center is

$$(h, k) = (2, 1). \qquad \text{Center}$$

Because the vertices lie on a vertical line and are six units apart, it follows that the major axis is vertical and has a length of $2a = 6$. So, $a = 3$. Moreover, because the minor axis has a length of 4, it follows that $2b = 4$, which implies that $b = 2$. Therefore, the standard form of the ellipse is as follows.

$$\frac{(x - h)^2}{b^2} + \frac{(y - k)^2}{a^2} = 1 \qquad \text{Major axis is vertical.}$$

$$\frac{(x - 2)^2}{2^2} + \frac{(y - 1)^2}{3^2} = 1 \qquad \text{Write in standard form.}$$

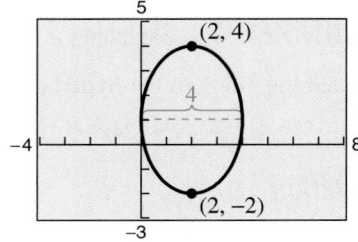

Figure 8.26

An interesting application of conic sections involves the orbits of comets in our solar system. Of the 610 comets identified prior to 1970, 245 have elliptical orbits, 295 have parabolic orbits, and 70 have hyperbolic orbits. For example, Halley's comet has an elliptical orbit, and reappearance of this comet can be predicted every 76 years. The center of the sun is a focus of each of these orbits, and each orbit has a vertex at the point where the comet is closest to the sun, as shown in Figure 8.27.

If p is the distance between the vertex and the focus, and v is the speed of the comet at the vertex, then the orbit is:

an *ellipse* if $v < \sqrt{\dfrac{2GM}{p}}$

a *parabola* if $v = \sqrt{\dfrac{2GM}{p}}$

a *hyperbola* if $v > \sqrt{\dfrac{2GM}{p}}$

where M is the mass of the sun and G is the universal gravitational constant, which is approximately $6.67 \times 10^{-8} \text{cm}^3/(\text{kg} \cdot \text{sec}^2)$.

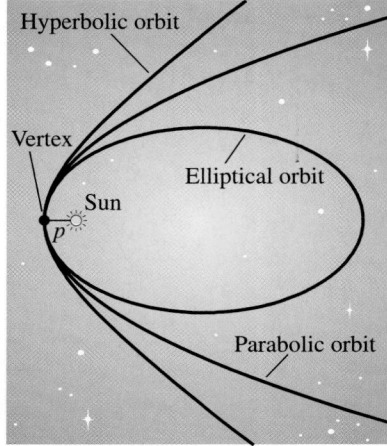

Figure 8.27

Writing About Math   *Identifying Equations of Conics*

Use the Internet to research information about the orbits of comets in our solar system. What can you find about the orbits of comets that have been identified since 1970? Write a summary of your results. Identify your source. Does it seem reliable?

Nicolaus Copernicus (1473–1543) began to study planetary motion when asked to revise the calendar. At that time, the exact length of the year could not be accurately predicted using the theory that the earth was the center of the universe.

8.2 Exercises

In Exercises 1–6, identify the center and radius of each circle.

1. $x^2 + y^2 = 49$ 2. $x^2 + y^2 = 1$

3. $(x + 3)^2 + (y - 8)^2 = 16$

4. $(x + 9)^2 + (y + 1)^2 = 36$

5. $(x - 1)^2 + y^2 = 10$ 6. $x^2 + (y + 12)^2 = 24$

In Exercises 7–10, write the equation of the circle in standard form. Then identify its center and radius.

7. $x^2 + y^2 - 2x + 6y + 9 = 0$

8. $x^2 + y^2 - 10x - 6y + 25 = 0$

9. $4x^2 + 4y^2 + 12x - 24y + 41 = 0$

10. $9x^2 + 9y^2 + 54x - 36y + 17 = 0$

In Exercises 11–18, find the vertex, focus, and directrix of the parabola, and sketch its graph. Use a graphing utility to verify your graph.

11. $(x + 1)^2 + 8(y + 2) = 0$

12. $(x + 3) + (y - 2)^2 = 0$

13. $\left(y - \frac{1}{2}\right)^2 = 2(x - 5)$

14. $\left(x + \frac{1}{2}\right)^2 = 4(y - 3)$

15. $y = \frac{1}{4}(x^2 - 2x + 5)$

16. $4x - y^2 - 2y - 33 = 0$

17. $y^2 + 6y + 8x + 25 = 0$

18. $y^2 - 4y - 4x = 0$

In Exercises 19–22, find the vertex, focus, and directrix of the parabola, and use a graphing utility to sketch its graph.

19. $x^2 + 4x - 2 + 6y = 0$

20. $x^2 - 2x + 8y + 9 = 0$

21. $y^2 + x + y = 0$ 22. $y^2 - 4x - 4 = 0$

In Exercises 23–32, find an equation of the parabola.

23. 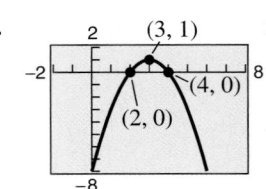   24.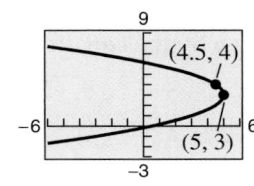

25. 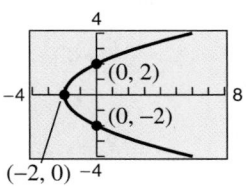   26.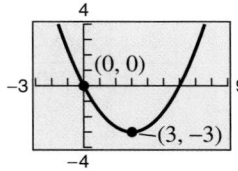

27. Vertex: $(3, 2)$; Focus: $(1, 2)$

28. Vertex: $(-1, 2)$; Focus: $(-1, 0)$

29. Vertex: $(0, 4)$; Directrix: $y = 2$

30. Vertex: $(-2, 1)$; Directrix: $x = 1$

31. Focus: $(2, 2)$; Directrix: $x = -2$

32. Focus: $(0, 0)$; Directrix: $y = 4$

***Think About It*   In Exercises 33 and 34, change the equation so that its graph matches the description.**

33. $(y - 3)^2 = 6(x + 1)$; Upper half of parabola

34. $(y + 1)^2 = 2(x - 2)$; Lower half of parabola

In Exercises 35 and 36, find the center, foci, and vertices of the ellipse, and graph the ellipse using a graphing utility.

35. $12x^2 + 20y^2 - 12x + 40y - 37 = 0$

36. $36x^2 + 9y^2 + 48x - 36y + 43 = 0$

In Exercises 37–44, find the center, foci, and vertices of the ellipse, and sketch its graph. Use a graphing utility to verify your answer.

37. $\dfrac{(x - 1)^2}{9} + \dfrac{(y - 3)^2}{25} = 1$

38. $\dfrac{(x - 6)^2}{16} + \dfrac{(y + 7)^2}{4} = 1$

39. $(x + 2)^2 + \dfrac{(y - 4)^2}{\frac{1}{4}} = 1$

40. $\dfrac{(x - 3)^2}{\frac{25}{9}} + (y - 8)^2 = 1$

41. $9x^2 + 4y^2 + 36x - 24y + 36 = 0$

42. $9x^2 + 4y^2 - 36x + 8y + 31 = 0$

43. $16x^2 + 25y^2 - 32x + 50y + 16 = 0$

44. $9x^2 + 25y^2 - 36x - 50y + 61 = 0$

In Exercises 45–56, find an equation of the ellipse.

45.

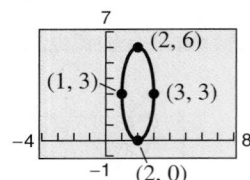

46.

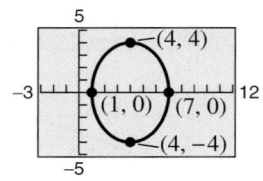

47.

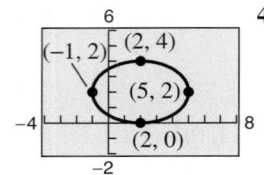

48.

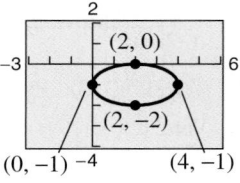

49. Vertices: $(0, 2)$, $(4, 2)$; Minor axis of length 2

50. Foci: $(0, 0)$, $(4, 0)$; Major axis of length 8

51. Foci: $(0, 0)$, $(0, 8)$; Major axis of length 16

52. Center: $(2, -1)$; Vertex: $\left(2, \frac{1}{2}\right)$;
Minor axis of length 2

53. Vertices: $(3, 1)$, $(3, 9)$; Minor axis of length 6

54. Center: $(3, 2)$; $a = 3c$; Foci: $(1, 2)$, $(5, 2)$

55. Center: $(0, 4)$; $a = 2c$; Vertices: $(-4, 4)$, $(4, 4)$

56. Vertices: $(5, 0)$, $(5, 12)$;
Endpoints of the minor axis: $(0, 6)$, $(10, 6)$

Think About It **In Exercises 57 and 58, change the equation so that its graph matches the description.**

57. $\dfrac{(x - 3)^2}{9} + \dfrac{y^2}{4} = 1$; Right half of ellipse

58. $\dfrac{(x + 1)^2}{16} + \dfrac{(y - 2)^2}{25} = 1$; Bottom half of ellipse

In Exercises 59–68, find the center, vertices, and foci of the hyperbola, and sketch its graph. Sketch the asymptotes as an aid in obtaining the graph of the hyperbola. Use a graphing utility to verify your graph.

59. $\dfrac{(x + 1)^2}{4} - \dfrac{(y - 2)^2}{1} = 1$

60. $\dfrac{(x - 1)^2}{144} - \dfrac{(y + 4)^2}{25} = 1$

61. $(y - 6)^2 - (x - 2)^2 = 1$

62. $\dfrac{(y + 1)^2}{\frac{1}{4}} - \dfrac{(x - 3)^2}{\frac{1}{9}} = 1$

63. $9x^2 - y^2 - 36x - 6y + 18 = 0$

64. $x^2 - 9y^2 + 36y - 72 = 0$

65. $x^2 - 9y^2 + 2x - 54y - 80 = 0$

66. $16y^2 - x^2 + 2x + 64y + 63 = 0$

67. $9y^2 - 4x^2 + 8x + 18y + 41 = 0$

68. $9x^2 - 4y^2 + 54x + 8y + 78 = 0$

In Exercises 69 and 70, find the center, vertices, and foci of the hyperbola. Graph the hyperbola and its asymptotes using a graphing utility.

69. $9y^2 - x^2 + 2x + 54y + 62 = 0$

70. $9x^2 - y^2 + 54x + 10y + 55 = 0$

In Exercises 71–80, find an equation of the hyperbola.

71.

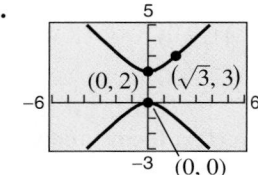

72.

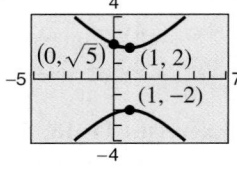

73.

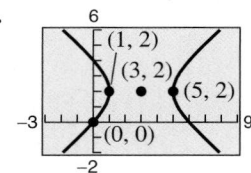

74.

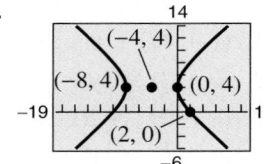

75. Vertices: $(2, 0)$, $(6, 0)$; Foci: $(0, 0)$, $(8, 0)$

76. Vertices: $(2, 3)$, $(2, -3)$; Foci: $(2, 5)$, $(2, -5)$

77. Vertices: $(4, 1)$, $(4, 9)$; Foci: $(4, 0)$, $(4, 10)$

78. Vertices: $(-2, 1)$, $(2, 1)$; Foci: $(-3, 1)$, $(3, 1)$

79. Vertices: $(2, 3)$, $(2, -3)$;
Passes through the point $(0, 5)$

80. Vertices: $(3, 0)$, $(3, 4)$;
Asymptotes: $y = \frac{2}{3}x$, $y = 4 - \frac{2}{3}x$

Think About It **In Exercises 81 and 82, describe the part of the hyperbola**

$$\dfrac{(x - 3)^2}{4} - \dfrac{(y - 1)^2}{9} = 1$$

given by the equation.

81. $x = 3 - \frac{2}{3}\sqrt{9 + (y - 1)^2}$

82. $y = 1 + \frac{3}{2}\sqrt{(x - 3)^2 - 4}$

In Exercises 83–90, classify the graph of the equation as a circle, a parabola, an ellipse, or a hyperbola.

83. $x^2 + y^2 - 6x + 4y + 9 = 0$

84. $x^2 + 4y^2 - 6x + 16y + 21 = 0$

85. $4x^2 - y^2 - 4x - 3 = 0$

86. $y^2 - 4y - 4x = 0$

87. $4x^2 + 3y^2 + 8x - 24y + 51 = 0$

88. $4y^2 - 2x^2 - 4y - 8x - 15 = 0$

89. $25x^2 - 10x - 200y - 119 = 0$

90. $4x^2 + 4y^2 - 16y + 15 = 0$

In Exercises 91 and 92, use a graphing utility to graph the conics in the same viewing window and approximate the coordinates of any points of intersection.

91. $x^2 + 9y^2 = 9$, $y = x^2 - 4$

92. $x^2 + y^2 = 25$, $x^2 - y^2 = 1$

93. *Satellite Orbit*   An earth satellite in a 100-mile-high circular orbit around earth has a velocity of approximately 17,500 miles per hour. If this velocity is multiplied by $\sqrt{2}$, the satellite will have the minimum velocity necessary to escape earth's gravity, and it will follow a parabolic path with the center of earth as the focus.

(a) Find the escape velocity of the satellite.

(b) Find an equation of its path (assume the radius of earth is 4000 miles).

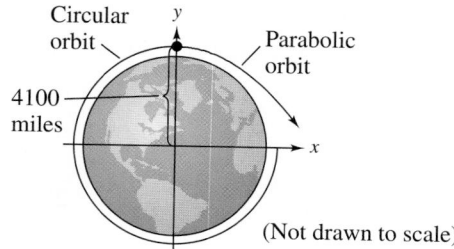

Circular orbit

4100 miles

Parabolic orbit

(Not drawn to scale)

94. *Projectile Motion*   A bomber is flying at an altitude of 30,000 feet and a speed of 540 miles per hour (792 feet per second). How many feet will a bomb dropped from the plane travel horizontally before it hits the target if its path is modeled by

$$y = 30,000 - \frac{x^2}{39,204}?$$

95. *Path of a Projectile*   The path of a softball is given by the equation $y = -0.08x^2 + x + 4$. The coordinates x and y are measured in feet, with $x = 0$ corresponding to the position from which the ball was thrown.

(a) Use a graphing utility to graph the trajectory of the softball.

(b) Move the cursor along the path to approximate the highest point and the distance the ball traveled.

96. *Revenue*   The revenue R generated by the sale of x units is given by $R = 375x - \frac{3}{2}x^2$.

(a) Use a graphing utility to graph the function.

(b) Use the *trace* feature of the graphing utility to approximate *graphically* the sales that will maximize the revenue.

(c) Use the *table* feature of the graphing utility to approximate *numerically* the sales that will maximize the revenue.

(d) Find the coordinates of the vertex to find *algebraically* the sales that will maximize the revenue.

(e) Compare the results of parts (b) (c), and (d). What did you learn as a result of using all three approaches?

In Exercises 97–101, e is called the eccentricity of the ellipse and is defined by $e = c/a$. It measures the flatness of the ellipse.

97. Find an equation of the ellipse with vertices $(\pm 5, 0)$ and eccentricity $e = \frac{3}{5}$.

98. Find an equation of the ellipse with vertices $(0, \pm 8)$ and eccentricity $e = \frac{1}{2}$.

99. *Planetary Motion*   The planet Pluto moves in an elliptical orbit with the sun at one of the foci. The length of half of the major axis is 3.666×10^9 miles and the eccentricity is 0.248. Find the smallest distance (*perihelion*) and the greatest distance (*aphelion*) of Pluto from the sun.

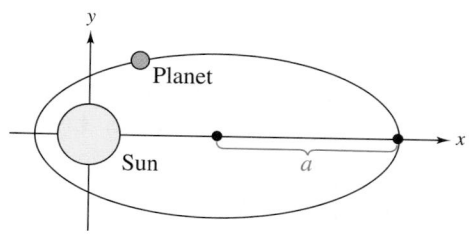

Planet

Sun

a

100. *Satellite Orbit* The first artificial satellite to orbit earth was *Sputnik I* (launched by the former Soviet Union in 1957). Its highest point above earth's surface was 938 kilometers, and its lowest point was 212 kilometers. The center of earth is the focus of the elliptical orbit and the radius of earth is 6378 kilometers. Find the eccentricity of the orbit.

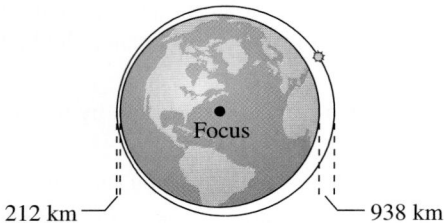

212 km ⎯ 938 km

101. *Orbit of Saturn* Saturn moves in an elliptical orbit with the sun at one of the foci. The smallest distance and the greatest distance of the planet from the sun are 1.3495×10^9 and 1.5045×10^9 kilometers, respectively. Find the eccentricity of the orbit.

102. *Australian Football* In Australia, football by *Australian Rules* (or rugby) is played on elliptical fields. The fields can be a maximum of 170 yards wide and a maximum of 200 yards long. Let the center of a field of maximum size be represented by the point $(0, 85)$. Find an equation of the ellipse that represents this field. (Source: *Oxford Companion to World Sports and Games*)

103. *Astronomy* Halley's comet has an elliptical orbit with the sun at one focus. The eccentricity of the orbit is approximately 0.97. The length of the major axis of the orbit is approximately 36.23 astronomical units. (An astronomical unit is about 93 million miles.) Find an equation of the orbit. Place the center of the orbit at the origin and place the major axis on the *x*-axis.

104. *Astronomy* The comet Encke has an elliptical orbit with the sun at one focus. Encke ranges from 0.34 to 4.08 astronomical units from the sun. Find an equation of the orbit. Place the center of the orbit at the origin and place the major axis on the *x*-axis.

Synthesis

True or False? In Exercises 105 and 106, determine whether the statement is true or false. Justify your answer.

105. The conic represented by the equation $3x^2 + 2y^2 - 18x - 16y + 58 = 0$ is an ellipse.

106. The graphs of $x^2 + 10y - 10x + 5 = 0$ and $x^2 + 16y^2 + 10x - 32y - 23 = 0$ do not intersect.

107. *Exploration* Consider the ellipse $\dfrac{x^2}{a^2} + \dfrac{y^2}{b^2} = 1$.

(a) Show that the equation of the ellipse can be written as

$$\frac{(x - h)^2}{a^2} + \frac{(y - k)^2}{a^2(1 - e^2)} = 1$$

where *e* is the eccentricity.

(b) Use a graphing utility to graph the ellipse

$$\frac{(x - 2)^2}{4} + \frac{(y - 3)^2}{4(1 - e^2)} = 1$$

for $e = 0.95, 0.75, 0.5, 0.25,$ and 0.

(c) Make a conjecture about the change in the shape of the ellipse as *e* approaches 0.

Review

In Exercises 108 and 109, determine whether *f* and *g* are inverse functions. If *g* is not the inverse of *f*, find the correct inverse of *f*.

108. $f(x) = 10 - 7x, \quad g(x) = \dfrac{x - 10}{7}$

109. $f(x) = \sqrt{x + 8}, \quad g(x) = x^2 + 8$

In Exercises 110–113, use sigma notation to write the sum. Then use a graphing utility to find the sum.

110. $\dfrac{1}{6(1)} + \dfrac{1}{6(2)} + \dfrac{1}{6(3)} + \cdots + \dfrac{1}{6(9)}$

111. $\dfrac{7}{2 + 1} + \dfrac{7}{2 + 2} + \dfrac{7}{2 + 3} + \cdots + \dfrac{7}{2 + 12}$

112. $1 - \dfrac{1}{4} + \dfrac{1}{16} - \cdots + \dfrac{1}{65536}$

113. $\dfrac{1}{9} + \dfrac{4}{27} + \dfrac{7}{81} + \dfrac{10}{243}$

In Exercises 114–117, use the Binomial Theorem to expand and simplify the expression.

114. $(x - 4)^4$ **115.** $(x - 3)^6$

116. $(3x + 1)^5$ **117.** $(x^2 - 2)^5$

8.3 Parametric Equations

Plane Curves

Up to this point, you have been representing a graph by a single equation involving *two* variables such as x and y. In this section, you will study situations in which it is useful to introduce a *third* variable to represent a curve in the plane.

To see the usefulness of this procedure, consider the path followed by an object that is propelled into the air at an angle of 45°. If the initial velocity of the object is 48 feet per second, it can be shown that the object follows the parabolic path

$$y = -\frac{x^2}{72} + x \qquad \text{Rectangular equation}$$

as shown in Figure 8.28. However, this equation does not tell the whole story. Although it does tell us *where* the object has been, it doesn't tell us *when* the object was at a given point (x, y) on the path. To determine this time, you can introduce a third variable t, which is called a **parameter.** It is possible to write both x and y as functions of t to obtain the **parametric equations**

$$x = 24\sqrt{2}\,t \qquad \text{Parametric equation for } x$$

$$y = -16t^2 + 24\sqrt{2}\,t. \qquad \text{Parametric equation for } y$$

From this set of equations you can determine that at time $t = 0$, the object is at the point $(0, 0)$. Similarly, at time $t = 1$, the object is at the point $(24\sqrt{2}, 24\sqrt{2} - 16)$, and so on.

Rectangular equation:
$$y = -\frac{x^2}{72} + x$$

Parametric equations:
$$x = 24\sqrt{2}\,t$$
$$y = -16t^2 + 24\sqrt{2}\,t$$

Curvilinear motion: two variables for position, one variable for time
Figure 8.28

For this particular motion problem, x and y are continuous functions of t, and the resulting path is a **plane curve.** (Recall that a *continuous function* is one whose graph can be traced without lifting the pencil from the paper.)

Definition of a Plane Curve

If f and g are continuous functions of t on an interval I, the set of ordered pairs $(f(t), g(t))$ is a **plane curve** C. The equations

$$x = f(t) \qquad \text{and} \qquad y = g(t)$$

are **parametric equations** for C, and t is the **parameter.**

What You Should Learn:

- How to evaluate sets of parametric equations for given values of the parameter
- How to graph curves that are represented by sets of parametric equations
- How to rewrite sets of parametric equations as single rectangular equations by eliminating the parameter
- How to find sets of parametric equations for graphs

Why You Should Learn It:

Parametric equations are useful for modeling the path of an object. For instance, in Exercise 53 on page 604, a set of parametric equations is used to model the path of a baseball.

Superstock

A computer animation of this concept appears in the *Interactive* CD-ROM and *Internet* versions of this text.

Sketching a Plane Curve

One way to sketch a curve represented by a pair of parametric equations is to plot points in the *xy*-plane. Each set of coordinates (x, y) is determined from a value chosen for the parameter *t*. By plotting the resulting points in the order of *increasing* values of *t*, you trace the curve in a specific direction. This is called the **orientation** of the curve.

Library of Functions

Parametric equations consist of a pair of functions $x = f(t)$ and $y = g(t)$, each of which is a function of the parameter *t*. These equations define a plane curve, which might not be the graph of a function, as in Example 1. Most graphing utilities have a *parametric* mode.

EXAMPLE 1   Sketching a Plane Curve

Sketch the curve given by the parametric equations

$$x = t^2 - 4 \quad \text{and} \quad y = \frac{t}{2}, \qquad -2 \le t \le 3.$$

Describe the orientation of the curve.

Solution

Using values of *t* in the given interval, the parametric equations yield the points (x, y) shown in the table.

A computer animation of this example appears in the *Interactive* CD-ROM and *Internet* versions of this text.

t	-2	-1	0	1	2	3
x	0	-3	-4	-3	0	5
y	-1	$-\frac{1}{2}$	0	$\frac{1}{2}$	1	$\frac{3}{2}$

By plotting these points in the order of increasing *t*, you obtain the curve shown in Figure 8.29. The arrows on the curve indicate its orientation as *t* increases from -2 to 3. So, if a particle were moving on this curve, it would start at $(0, -1)$ and then move along the curve to the point $\left(5, \frac{3}{2}\right)$.

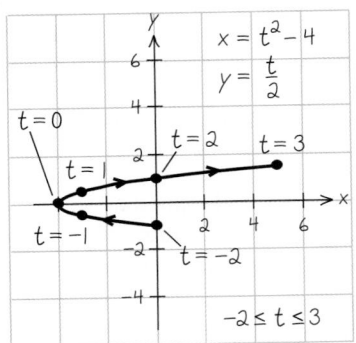

Figure 8.29

The graph shown in Figure 8.29 does not define *y* as a function of *x*. This points out one benefit of parametric equations—they can be used to represent graphs that are more general than graphs of functions.

Two different sets of parametric equations can have the same graph. For example, the set of parametric equations

$$x = 4t^2 - 4 \quad \text{and} \quad y = t, \qquad -1 \le t \le \frac{3}{2}$$

has the same graph as the set given in Example 1. However, by comparing the values of *t* in Figures 8.29 and 8.30, you can see that this second graph is traced out more *rapidly* (considering *t* as time) than the first graph. So, in applications, different parametric representations can be used to represent various *speeds* at which objects travel along a given path.

Another way to display a curve represented by a pair of parametric equations is to use a graphing utility, as shown in Example 2.

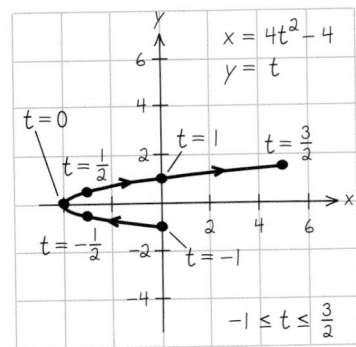

Figure 8.30

Point out to your students the importance of knowing the orientation of the curve, and thus the usefulness of parametric equations.

EXAMPLE 2   Using a Graphing Utility in Parametric Mode

Use a graphing utility to graph the curves represented by the parametric equations. For which curve is y a function of x? (Use $-4 \le t \le 4$.)

a. $x = t^2$ **b.** $x = t$ **c.** $x = t^2$
$\quad y = t^3$ $\quad\;\; y = t^3$ $\quad\;\; y = t$

Solution

Begin by setting the graphing utility to *parametric* mode. When choosing a viewing window, you must set not only minimum and maximum values of x and y but also minimum and maximum values of t.

a. Enter the parametric equations for x and y.

$$X_{1T} = T^2, \qquad Y_{1T} = T^3$$

The curve is shown in Figure 8.31(a). From the graph, you can see that y *is not* a function of x.

b. Enter the parametric equations for x and y.

$$X_{1T} = T, \qquad Y_{1T} = T^3$$

The curve is shown in Figure 8.31(b). From the graph, you can see that y *is a* function of x.

c. Enter the parametric equations for x and y.

$$X_{1T} = T^2, \qquad Y_{1T} = T$$

The curve is shown in Figure 8.31(c). From the graph, you can see that y *is not* a function of x.

The *Interactive* CD-ROM and *Internet* versions of this text offer a built-in graphing calculator, which can be used with the Examples, Explorations, and Exercises.

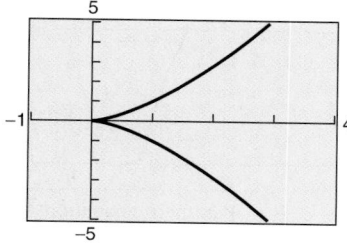

(a)

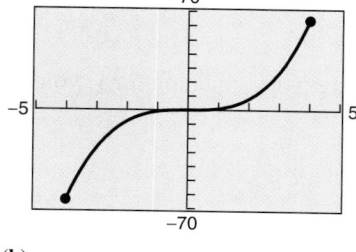

(b)

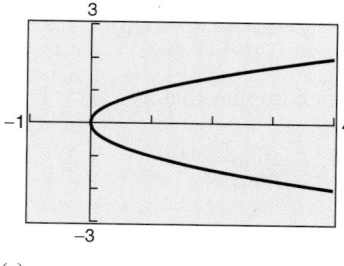

(c)

Figure 8.31

Exploration

Use a graphing utility set in *parametric* mode to graph the curve

$$X_{1T} = T \quad \text{and} \quad Y_{1T} = 1 - T^2.$$

Set the viewing window so that $-4 \le x \le 4$ and $-12 \le y \le 2$. Now, graph the curve with various settings for t. Use the following.

a. $0 \le t \le 3$ **b.** $-3 \le t \le 0$ **c.** $-3 \le t \le 3$

Compare the curves given by the different t settings. Repeat this experiment using $X_{1T} = -T$. How does this change the results?

Eliminating the Parameter

Many curves that are represented by sets of parametric equations have graphs that can also be represented by rectangular equations (in x and y). The process of finding the rectangular equation is called **eliminating the parameter.**

Parametric equations	Solve for t in one equation.	Substitute in second equation.	Rectangular equation

$$x = t^2 - 4 \qquad t = 2y \qquad x = (2y)^2 - 4 \qquad x = 4y^2 - 4$$

$$y = \tfrac{1}{2}t$$

After eliminating the parameter, you can recognize that the curve is a parabola with a horizontal axis and vertex at $(-4, 0)$.

Converting equations from parametric to rectangular form can change the ranges of x and y. In such cases, you should restrict x and y in the rectangular equation so that its graph matches the graph of the parametric equations.

EXAMPLE 3 Eliminating the Parameter

Identify the curve represented by the equations

$$x = \frac{1}{\sqrt{t+1}} \qquad \text{and} \qquad y = \frac{t}{t+1}.$$

Solution

Solving for t in the equation for x produces

$$x^2 = \frac{1}{t+1} \qquad \text{or} \qquad \frac{1}{x^2} = t + 1$$

which implies that $t = (1/x^2) - 1$. Substituting in the equation for y, you obtain

$$
\begin{aligned}
y &= \frac{t}{t+1} \\[4pt]
&= \frac{\left(\dfrac{1}{x^2}\right) - 1}{\left(\dfrac{1}{x^2}\right) - 1 + 1} \\[4pt]
&= \frac{\dfrac{1-x^2}{x^2}}{\left(\dfrac{1}{x^2}\right)} \cdot \frac{x^2}{x^2} \\[4pt]
&= 1 - x^2.
\end{aligned}
$$

From the rectangular equation, you can recognize the curve to be a parabola that opens downward and has its vertex at $(0, 1)$, as shown in Figure 8.32(a). The rectangular equation is defined for all values of x. The parametric equation for x, however, is defined only when $t > -1$. From the graph of the parametric equation, you can see that x is always positive, as shown in Figure 8.32(b). So, you should restrict the domain of x to positive values, as shown in Figure 8.32(c).

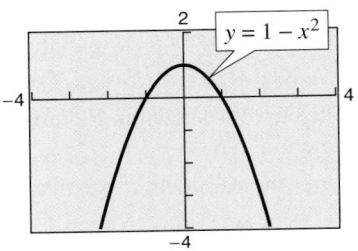

(a)

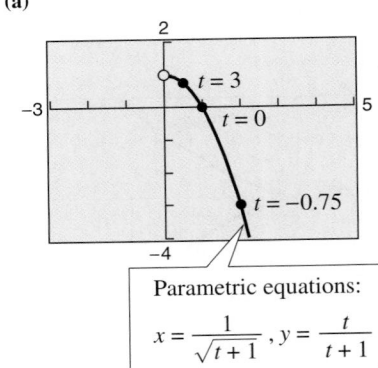

Parametric equations:

$$x = \frac{1}{\sqrt{t+1}}, \; y = \frac{t}{t+1}$$

(b)

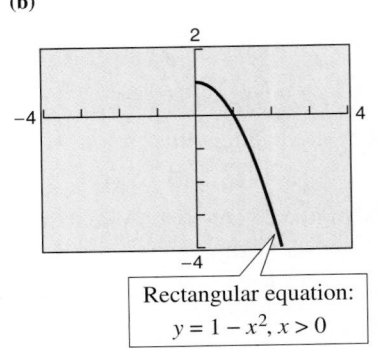

Rectangular equation:

$$y = 1 - x^2, \; x > 0$$

(c)

Figure 8.32

Finding Parametric Equations for a Graph

How can you determine a set of parametric equations for a given graph or a given physical description? From the discussion following Example 1, you know that such a representation is not unique. This is further demonstrated in Example 4.

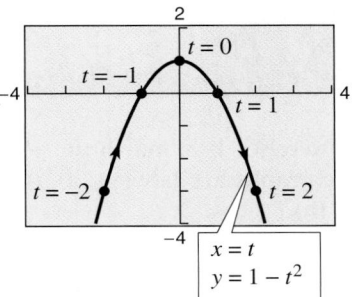

$x = t$
$y = 1 - t^2$

(a)

EXAMPLE 4   Finding Parametric Equations for a Given Graph

Find a set of parametric equations to represent the graph of $y = 1 - x^2$ using the following parameters.

a. $t = x$ **b.** $t = 1 - x$

Solution

a. Letting $t = x$, you obtain the following parametric equations.

$\quad\quad x = t$ Parametric equation for x

$\quad\quad y = 1 - x^2$ Write original rectangular equation.

$\quad\quad\quad = 1 - t^2$ Parametric equation for y

The graph of these equations is shown in Figure 8.33(a).

b. Letting $t = 1 - x$, you obtain the following parametric equations.

$\quad\quad x = 1 - t$ Parametric equation for x

$\quad\quad y = 1 - (1 - t)^2$ Substitute $1 - t$ for x.

$\quad\quad\quad = 2t - t^2$ Parametric equation for y

The graph of these equations is shown in Figure 8.33(b). In this figure, note how the resulting curve is oriented by the increasing values of t. In Figure 8.33(a), the curve has the opposite orientation.

In a parametric mode, the *table* feature of a graphing utility produces a three-column table. The table shown on the right represents the graph in Figure 8.33(b).

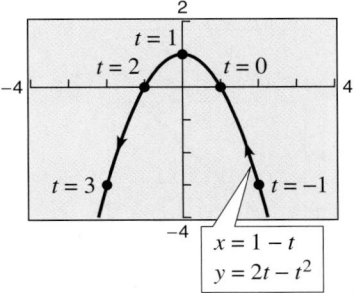

$x = 1 - t$
$y = 2t - t^2$

(b)
Figure 8.33

T	X1T	Y1T
-2	3	-8
-1	2	-3
0	1	0
1	0	1
2	-1	0
3	-2	-3
4	-3	-8
T=-2		

The *folium of Descartes* is a plane curve consisting of single loop, a node, and two branches that are asymptotic to the same line.

Writing About Math   *Changing the Orientation of a Curve*

The orientation of a curve refers to the direction in which the curve is traced as the values of the parameter increase. For instance, as t increases, how is the *folium of Descartes* given by

$$x = \frac{3t}{1 + t^3} \quad \text{and} \quad y = \frac{3t^2}{1 + t^3}, \quad -10 \le t \le 10$$

traced out? Write a short paragraph describing how the curve is traced out. Find a parametric representation for which the curve is traced out in the opposite direction.

8.3   E x e r c i s e s

In Exercises 1–8, match the equation with its graph. [The graphs are labeled (a), (b), (c), (d), (e), (f), (g), and (h).]

(a)
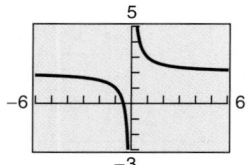

(b)
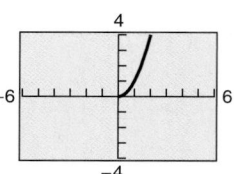

(c)
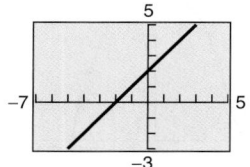

(d)
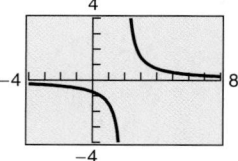

(e)
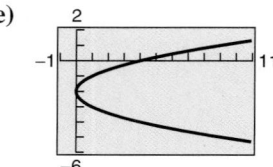

(f)
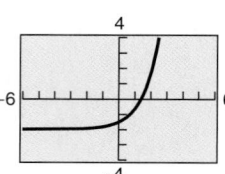

(g)
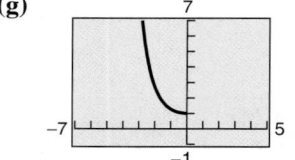

(h)
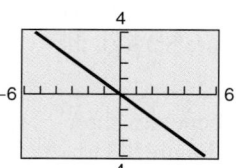

1. $x = t$
  $y = t + 2$

2. $x = t$
  $y = -\frac{3}{4}t$

3. $x = \sqrt{t}$
  $y = t$

4. $x = t^2$
  $y = t - 2$

5. $x = \dfrac{1}{t}$
  $y = t + 2$

6. $x = \dfrac{1}{2}t$
  $y = \dfrac{3}{t - 4}$

7. $x = \ln t$
  $y = \frac{1}{2}t - 2$

8. $x = -2\sqrt{t}$
  $y = e^t$

9. Consider the parametric equations
  $x = \sqrt{t}$ and $y = 2 - t.$

  (a) Complete the table.

t	0	1	2	3	4
x					
y					

  (b) Plot the points (x, y) generated in part (a) and sketch a graph of the parametric equations.

  (c) Use a graphing utility to graph the curve represented by the parametric equations.

  (d) Find the rectangular equation by eliminating the parameter. Sketch its graph. How do the graphs differ from those in parts (b) and (c)?

10. Consider the parametric equations
  $x = 2/t$ and $y = t - 3.$

  (a) Complete the table.

t	-2	-1	1	2	3
x					
y					

  (b) Plot the points (x, y) generated in part (a) and sketch a graph of the parametric equations.

  (c) Use a graphing utility to graph the curve represented by the parametric equations.

  (d) Find the rectangular equation by eliminating the parameter. Sketch its graph. How do the graphs differ from those in parts (b) and (c)?

In Exercises 11–26, sketch the curve represented by the parametric equations (indicate the direction of the curve). Use a graphing utility to confirm your result. Then eliminate the parameter and write the corresponding rectangular equation whose graph represents the curve.

11. $x = t$
  $y = -4t$

12. $x = t$
  $y = \frac{1}{2}t$

13. $x = 3t + 1$
    $y = 2t - 1$

14. $x = 3 - 2t$
    $y = 2 + 3t$

15. $x = \frac{1}{4}t$
    $y = t^2$

16. $x = t$
    $y = t^3$

17. $x = t + 5$
    $y = t^2$

18. $x = \sqrt{t}$
    $y = 1 - t$

19. $x = t^3$
    $y = \frac{5}{2}t^2$

20. $x = t - 1$
    $y = \dfrac{t}{t - 1}$

21. $x = 2t$
    $y = |t - 2|$

22. $x = |t - 1|$
    $y = t + 2$

23. $x = e^{-t}$
    $y = e^{3t}$

24. $x = e^{2t}$
    $y = e^t$

25. $x = t^3$
    $y = 3 \ln t$

26. $x = \ln 2t$
    $y = 2t^2$

In Exercises 27–30, use a graphing utility to graph the curve represented by the parametric equations.

27. $x = 12t$
    $y = -8t^2 + 32t$

28. $x = 3t/(1 + t^3)$
    $y = 3t^2/(1 + t^3)$

29. $x = t/2$
    $y = \ln(t^2 + 1)$

30. $x = 10 - 0.01e^t$
    $y = 0.4t^2$

In Exercises 31–34, determine how the plane curves differ from each other.

31. (a) $x = t$
       $y = 2t + 1$
    (b) $x = 1/t$
        $y = (2/t) + 1$
    (c) $x = e^{-t}$
        $y = 2e^{-t} + 1$
    (d) $x = e^t$
        $y = 2e^t + 1$

32. (a) $x = t$
       $y = t^2 - 1$
    (b) $x = t^2$
        $y = t^4 - 1$
    (c) $x = \dfrac{1}{t}$
        $y = \dfrac{1}{t^2} - 1$
    (d) $x = e^t$
        $y = e^{2t} - 1$

33. (a) $x = 2\sqrt{t}$
       $y = 4 - \sqrt{t}$
    (b) $x = 2\sqrt[3]{t}$
        $y = 4 - \sqrt[3]{t}$
    (c) $x = 2(t + 1)$
        $y = 3 - t$
    (d) $x = -2t^2$
        $y = 4 + t^2$

34. (a) $x = t$
       $y = t$
    (b) $x = t^2$
        $y = t^2$
    (c) $x = -t$
        $y = -t$
    (d) $x = t^3$
        $y = t^3$

35. Graph the parametric equations $x = \sqrt[3]{t}$ and $y = t - 1$. Describe how the graph changes for each of the following.
    (a) $0 \le t \le 1$
    (b) $0 \le t \le 27$
    (c) $-8 \le t \le 27$
    (d) $-27 \le t \le 27$

36. Eliminate the parameter and obtain the standard form of the line through (x_1, y_1) and (x_2, y_2) if
    $$x = x_1 + t(x_2 - x_1)$$
    $$y = y_1 + t(y_2 - y_1).$$

In Exercises 37–40, use the result of Exercise 36 to find a set of parametric equations for the line through the points.

37. $(0, 0), (5, -2)$

38. $(1, 4), (5, -2)$

39. $(-2, 3), (3, 10)$

40. $(-1, -4), (15, 20)$

41. (a) Find a set of parametric equations and the interval for t for the graph of the line from $(3, -1)$ to $(3, 5)$. Use a graphing utility to verify your result.
    (b) Change the parametric equations for the line segment described in part (a) so that the orientation of the graph will be reversed. Use a graphing utility to verify your result.

42. (a) Find a set of parametric equations and the interval for t for the graph of the line from $(-3, 4)$ to $(6, 4)$. Use a graphing utility to verify your result.
    (b) Change the parametric equations for the line segment described in part (a) so that the orientation of the graph will be reversed. Use a graphing utility to verify your result.

In Exercises 43–50, find two different sets of parametric equations for the given rectangular equation.

43. $y = 4x - 3$

44. $y = 5 - 7x$

45. $y = \dfrac{1}{x}$

46. $y = \dfrac{4}{x + 3}$

47. $y = x^2 + 4$

48. $y = 6x^2 - 5$

49. $y = x^3 + 2x$

50. $y = 1 - 8x^3$

Projectile Motion A projectile is launched at a height *h* feet above the ground at an angle of 45° with the horizontal. If the initial velocity is v_0 feet per second, the path of the projectile is modeled by the parametric equations

$$x = \left(\frac{v_0\sqrt{2}}{2}\right)t \quad \text{and} \quad y = h + \left(\frac{v_0\sqrt{2}}{2}\right)t - 16t^2.$$

In Exercises 51 and 52, use a graphing utility to graph the paths of projectiles launched from ground level at the specified values of *h* and v_0. For each case, use the graph to approximate the maximum height and the range of the projectile.

51. (a) $h = 0$, $v_0 = 88$ ft/sec

  (b) $h = 0$, $v_0 = 132$ ft/sec

  (c) $h = 30$, $v_0 = 88$ ft/sec

  (d) $h = 30$, $v_0 = 132$ ft/sec

52. (a) $h = 0$, $v_0 = 60$ ft/sec

  (b) $h = 0$, $v_0 = 100$ ft/sec

  (c) $h = 75$, $v_0 = 60$ ft/sec

  (d) $h = 75°$, $v_0 = 100$ ft/sec

53. *Baseball* The center-field fence in a ballpark is 10 feet high and 400 feet from home plate. The ball is hit at a point 3 feet above the ground and leaves the bat at a speed of 150 feet per second.

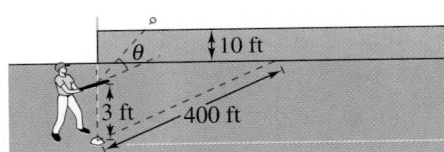

  (a) If the ball leaves the bat at an angle of 15° with the horizontal, the parametric equations for its path are $x = 145t$ and $y = 3 + 39t - 16t^2$. Use a graphing utility to sketch the path of the ball. Is the hit a home run?

  (b) If the ball leaves the bat at an angle of 23° with the horizontal, the parametric equations for its path are $x = 138t$ and $y = 3 + 59t - 16t^2$. Use a graphing utility to sketch the path of the ball. Is the hit a home run?

54. *Football* The quarterback of a football team releases a pass at a height of 7 feet above the playing field, and the football is caught at a height of 4 feet, 30 yards directly downfield. The pass is released at an angle of 35° with the horizontal. The parametric equations for the path of the football are

$$x = 0.82v_0t \quad \text{and} \quad y = 7 + 0.57v_0t - 16t^2$$

where v_0 is the speed of the football (in feet per second) when it is released.

  (a) Find the speed of the football when it is released and write a set of parametric equations for the path of the ball.

  (b) Use a graphing utility to graph the path of the ball and approximate its maximum height.

  (c) Find the time the receiver has to position himself after the quarterback releases the ball.

Synthesis

True or False? In Exercises 55 and 56, determine whether the statement is true or false. Justify your answer.

55. The two sets of parametric equations $x = t$, $y = t^2 + 1$ and $x = 3t$, $y = 9t^2 + 1$ correspond to the same rectangular equation.

56. The graph of the parametric equations $x = t^2$ and $y = t^2$ is the line $y = x$.

57. *Think About It* The graph of the parametric equations $x = t^3$ and $y = t - 1$ is shown below. Would the graph change for the equations $x = (-t)^3$ and $y = -t - 1$? If so, how would it change?

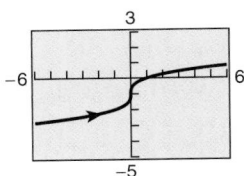

Review

In Exercises 58–61, find all solutions of the equation.

58. $5x^2 + 8 = 0$

59. $x^2 - 6x + 4 = 0$

60. $4x^2 + 4x - 11 = 0$

61. $x^4 - 18x^2 + 18 = 0$

In Exercises 62–67, find the sum. Use a graphing utility to verify your result.

62. $\displaystyle\sum_{n=1}^{50} 8n$

63. $\displaystyle\sum_{n=1}^{200} (n - 8)$

64. $\displaystyle\sum_{n=1}^{40} \left(300 - \frac{1}{2}n\right)$

65. $\displaystyle\sum_{n=1}^{70} \frac{7 - 5n}{12}$

66. $\displaystyle\sum_{n=0}^{18} 8\left(\frac{1}{2}\right)^n$

67. $\displaystyle\sum_{n=0}^{10} 10\left(\frac{2}{3}\right)^n$

8   Chapter Summary

What did you learn?

Section 8.1

	Review Exercises
☐ How to recognize the four basic conics: circles, ellipses, parabolas, and hyperbolas	1–16
☐ How to recognize, graph, and write equations of parabolas (vertex at origin)	17–25
☐ How to recognize, graph, and write equations of ellipses (center at origin)	26–34
☐ How to recognize, graph, and write equations of hyperbolas (center at origin)	35–42

Section 8.2

☐ How to recognize equations of conics that have been shifted vertically and/or horizontally in the plane	43–52
☐ How to write and graph equations of conics that have been shifted vertically and/or horizontally in the plane	53–74

Section 8.3

☐ How to evaluate sets of parametric equations for given values of the parameter	75–78
☐ How to graph curves that are represented by sets of parametric equations	79–88
☐ How to rewrite sets of parametric equations as single rectangular equations by eliminating the parameter	89–100
☐ How to find sets of parametric equations for graphs	101–108

8 Review Exercises

8.1 In Exercises 1–8, match the equation with the correct graph. [The graphs are labeled (a), (b), (c), (d), (e), (f), (g), and (h).]

(a)
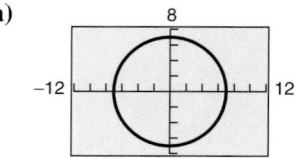

(b)
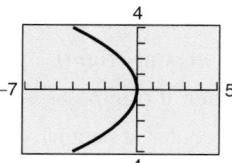

(c)
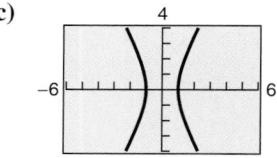

(d)
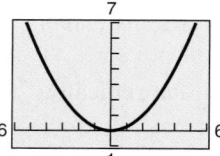

(e)
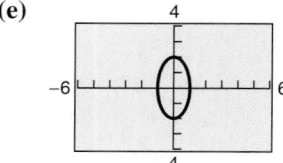

(f)
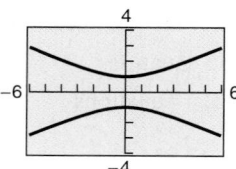

(g)
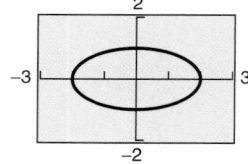

(h)
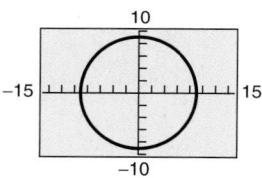

1. $4x^2 + y^2 = 4$

2. $x^2 = 4y$

3. $4x^2 - y^2 = 4$

4. $y^2 = -4x$

5. $x^2 - 5y^2 = -5$

6. $x^2 + y^2 = 49$

7. $x^2 + y^2 = 81$

8. $x^2 + 4y^2 = 4$

In Exercises 9–16, identify the conic.

9. $y^2 = -12x$

10. $16x^2 + y^2 = 16$

11. $\dfrac{x^2}{9} - \dfrac{y^2}{1} = 1$

12. $\dfrac{x^2}{1} + \dfrac{y^2}{9} = 1$

13. $x^2 + 20y = 0$

14. $x^2 + y^2 = 100$

15. $\dfrac{y^2}{49} - \dfrac{x^2}{144} = 1$

16. $\dfrac{x^2}{49} + \dfrac{y^2}{144} = 1$

In Exercises 17–20, find an equation of the specified parabola.

17.
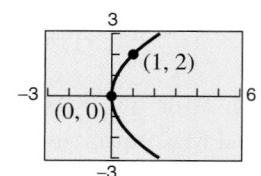

18.
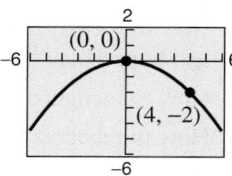

19. Vertex: $(0, 0)$; Focus: $(-6, 0)$

20. Vertex: $(0, 0)$; Focus: $(0, 3)$

In Exercises 21–24, sketch the graph of the parabola. Use a graphing utility to verify your graph.

21. $4x - y^2 = 0$

22. $8y + x^2 = 0$

23. $\frac{1}{2}y^2 + 18x = 0$

24. $\frac{1}{4}y - 8x^2 = 0$

25. *Satellite Antenna* A cross section of a large parabolic antenna is modeled by

$$y = \frac{x^2}{200}, \qquad -100 \le x \le 100.$$

The receiving and transmitting equipment is positioned at the focus. Find the coordinates of the focus.

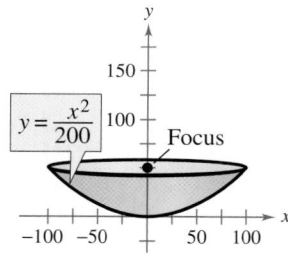

In Exercises 26–29, write the equation of the specified ellipse with center at the origin.

26.
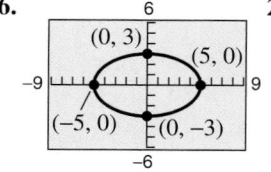

27.
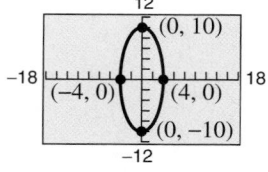

28. Vertices: $(0, \pm6)$; Passes through $(2, 2)$
29. Vertices: $(\pm7, 0)$; Foci: $(\pm6, 0)$

In Exercises 30–33, sketch the graph of the ellipse. Use a graphing utility to verify your graph.

30. $4x^2 + y^2 = 16$ **31.** $2x^2 + 6y^2 = 18$
32. $6x^2 + 4y^2 = 36$ **33.** $3x^2 + 8y^2 = 48$

34. *Semielliptical Archway* A semielliptical archway is to be formed over the entrance to an estate. The arch is to be set on pillars that are 10 feet apart and is to have a height (atop the pillars) of 4 feet. Where should the foci be placed in order to sketch the arch?

In Exercises 35–38, write the equation of the specified hyperbola with center at the origin.

35.
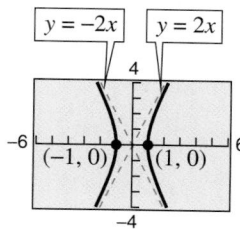

36.
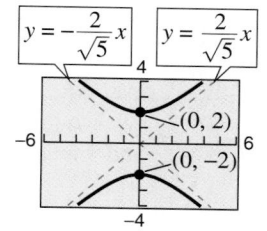

37. Vertices: $(0, \pm1)$; Foci: $(0, \pm3)$
38. Vertices: $(\pm4, 0)$; Foci: $(\pm6, 0)$

In Exercises 39–42, sketch the graph of the hyperbola. Use a graphing utility to verify your graph.

39. $\dfrac{y^2}{9} - \dfrac{x^2}{64} = 1$ **40.** $\dfrac{x^2}{49} - \dfrac{y^2}{36} = 1$
41. $5y^2 - 4x^2 = 20$ **42.** $x^2 - y^2 = \dfrac{9}{4}$

8.2 **In Exercises 43–52, identify the conic.**

43. $x^2 - 6x + 2y + 9 = 0$
44. $y^2 - 12y - 8x + 20 = 0$
45. $x^2 + 9y^2 + 10x - 18y + 25 = 0$
46. $16x^2 + 16y^2 - 16x + 24y - 3 = 0$

47. $4x^2 - 4y^2 - 4x + 8y - 11 = 0$
48. $x^2 - 9y^2 + 10x + 18y + 7 = 0$
49. $x^2 - 10xy + y^2 + 1 = 0$
50. $40x^2 + 36xy + 25y^2 - 52 = 0$
51. $4x^2 + y^2 - 16x + 15 = 0$
52. $9x^2 - y^2 - 72x + 8y + 119 = 0$

In Exercises 53–58, find an equation of the parabola.

53.
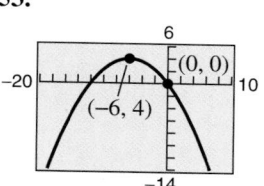

54.
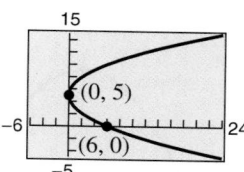

55. Vertex: $(4, 2)$; Focus: $(4, 0)$
56. Vertex: $(2, 0)$; Focus: $(0, 0)$
57. Vertex: $(0, 2)$; Horizontal axis;
  Passes through $(-1, 0)$
58. Vertex: $(2, 2)$; Directrix: $y = 0$

In Exercises 59–64, find an equation of the ellipse.

59.
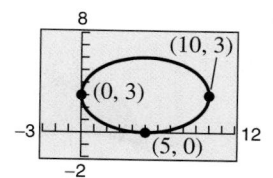

60.
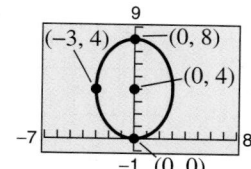

61. Vertices: $(-3, 0)$, $(7, 0)$; Foci: $(0, 0)$, $(4, 0)$
62. Vertices: $(2, 0)$, $(2, 4)$; Foci: $(2, 1)$, $(2, 3)$
63. Vertices: $(0, 1)$, $(4, 1)$;
  Endpoints of the minor axis: $(2, 0)$, $(2, 2)$
64. Vertices: $(-4, -1)$, $(-4, 11)$;
  Endpoints of the minor axis: $(-6, 5)$, $(-2, 5)$

In Exercises 65–70, find an equation of the hyperbola.

65.
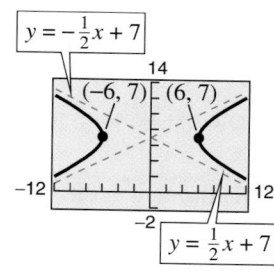

66.
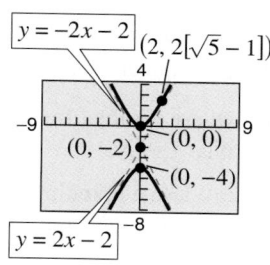

67. Vertices: $(-10, 3)$, $(6, 3)$; Foci: $(-12, 3)$, $(8, 3)$

68. Vertices: $(2, 2)$, $(-2, 2)$; Foci: $(4, 2)$, $(-4, 2)$

69. Foci: $(0, 0)$, $(8, 0)$; Asymptotes: $y = \pm 2(x - 4)$

70. Foci: $(3, \pm 2)$; Asymptotes: $y = \pm 2(x - 3)$

71. *Parabolic Archway*   A parabolic archway is 12 meters high at the vertex. At a height of 10 meters the width of the archway is 8 meters. How wide is the archway at ground level?

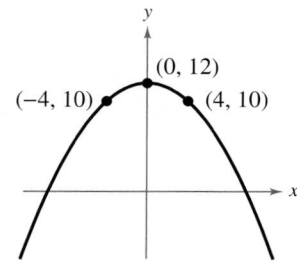

72. *Architecture*   A church window is bounded on top by a parabola and below by the arc of a circle.

   (a) Find equations for the parabola and circle.

   (b) Use a graphing utility to complete the table showing the vertical distance d between the circle and the parabola for the given value of x.

x	0	1	2	3	4
d					

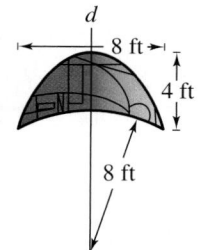

73. *Business*   The sales S (in millions of dollars) for Owens Corning for the years 1994 through 1998 are given in the table.   (Source: Owens Corning)

Year	1994	1995	1996	1997	1998
S	$3351	$3612	$3832	$4373	$5009

A model for this data is

$$S = 76.5t^2 - 510.3t + 4190.2$$

where t is the time (in years), with $t = 4$ corresponding to 1994.

   (a) Use a graphing utility to plot the data in the table and graph the model in the same viewing window.

   (b) Use the model to estimate the earnings for the year 2000.

74. *Heating and Plumbing*   Find the diameter d of the largest water pipe that can be placed behind a ventilation duct of diameter 60 centimeters, as shown in the figure.

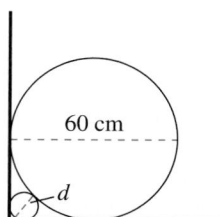

60 cm

d

8.3   In Exercises 75–78, complete the table for each set of parametric equations.

75. $x = 3t - 2$ and $y = 7 - 4t$

t	-2	-1	0	1	2	3
x						
y						

76. $x = \sqrt{t}$ and $y = 8 - t$

t	0	1	2	3	4
x					
y					

77. $x = \dfrac{6}{t}$ and $y = t + 4$

t	-2	-1	1	2	3	4
x						
y						

78. $x = \dfrac{1}{5}t$ and $y = \dfrac{4}{t - 1}$

t	-1	0	2	3	4	5
x						
y						

In Exercises 79–82, match the set of parametric equations with the corresponding graph. In each case the interval for t is $-1 \le t \le 1$. [The graphs are labeled (a), (b), (c), and (d).]

(a)

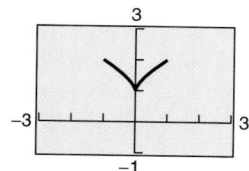

(b)

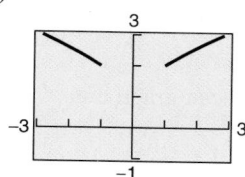

(c)

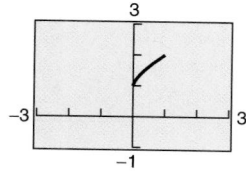

(d)

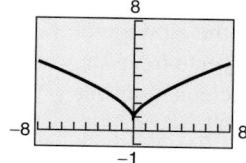

79. $x = t^3$
$\quad y = t^2 + 1$

80. $x = t^6$
$\quad y = t^4 + 1$

81. $x = (2t)^3$
$\quad y = (2t)^2 + 1$

82. $x = 1/t^3$
$\quad y = (1/t^2) + 1$

In Exercises 83–88, sketch the curve represented by the parametric equations.

83. $x = 5t - 1$
$\quad y = 2t + 5$

84. $x = 4t + 1$
$\quad y = 8 - 3t$

85. $x = t^2 + 2$
$\quad y = 4t^2 - 3$

86. $x = \ln 4t$
$\quad y = t^2$

87. $x = t^3$

$\quad y = \frac{1}{2}t^2$

88. $x = \frac{4}{t}$

$\quad y = t^2 - 1$

In Exercises 89–100, sketch the curve represented by the parametric equations and write the corresponding rectangular equation by eliminating the parameter. Verify your result using a graphing utility.

89. $x = \sqrt[3]{t}$
$\quad y = t$

90. $x = t$
$\quad y = \sqrt[3]{t}$

91. $x = \dfrac{1}{t}$

$\quad y = t$

92. $x = t$

$\quad y = \dfrac{1}{t}$

93. $x = 2t$
$\quad y = 4t$

94. $x = t^2$
$\quad y = \sqrt{t}$

95. $x = 1 + 4t$
$\quad y = 2 - 3t$

96. $x = t + 4$
$\quad y = t^2$

97. $x = \dfrac{1}{t}$

$\quad y = t^2$

98. $x = \dfrac{1}{t}$

$\quad y = 2t + 3$

99. $x = 3$
$\quad y = t$

100. $x = t$
$\quad y = 2$

In Exercises 101–104, find two different sets of parametric equations for the given rectangular equation.

101. $y = 6x + 2$

102. $y = 10 - x$

103. $y = x^2 + 2$

104. $y = 2x^3 + 5x$

In Exercises 105–108, find a set of parametric equations for the line through the points.

105. $(3, 5), (8, 5)$

106. $(2, -1), (2, 4)$

107. $(-1, 6), (10, 0)$

108. $(0, 0), \left(\frac{5}{2}, 6\right)$

Synthesis

True or False? In Exercises 109–111, determine whether the statement is true or false. Justify your answer.

109. The graph of $(x^2/4) - y^4 = 1$ is an equation of a hyperbola.

110. The equation

$$Ax^2 + Bxy + Cy^2 + Dx + Ey + F = 0$$

can be a single point.

111. There is only one set of parametric equations that represents the line $y = 3 - 2x$.

112. ***Writing*** In your own words, describe how the graph of each variation differs from the graph of
$\dfrac{x^2}{4} + \dfrac{y^2}{9} = 1.$

(a) $\dfrac{x^2}{9} + \dfrac{y^2}{4} = 1$

(b) $\dfrac{x^2}{4} + \dfrac{y^2}{4} = 1$

(c) $\dfrac{x^2}{4} + \dfrac{y^2}{25} = 1$

(d) $\dfrac{(x - 3)^2}{4} + \dfrac{y^2}{9} = 1$

113. Explain how the central rectangle of a hyperbola can be used to sketch its asymptotes.

Chapter Project *Parametric Equations and Inverse Functions*

In this project, you will use the *parametric* mode of a graphing utility to sketch the inverse of a function.

a. Consider the function given by $f(x) = x^5 + 4x^3 + x - 3$. You can graph this function in *parametric* mode using the following.

$X_{1T} = T$

$Y_{1T} = T \wedge 5 + 4T \wedge 3 + T - 3$

In the graph shown at the right, notice that the function passes the Horizontal Line Test and therefore has an inverse function. To graph the inverse function, you can interchange the roles of x and y in the given parametric equations, as follows.

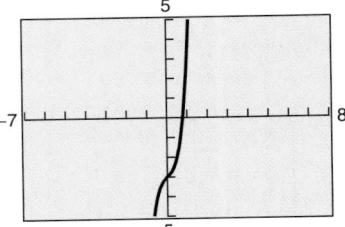

$X_{2T} = T \wedge 5 + 4T \wedge 3 + T - 3$

$Y_{2T} = T$

Sketch the graph of f and f^{-1} in the same viewing window.

b. Compare the graphs of f and f^{-1}.

Questions for Further Exploration

1. Consider the function $f(x) = \sqrt{1 - x}$.

   (a) Use the *parametric* mode of a graphing utility to sketch the graph of f^{-1}.

   (b) Solve for $f^{-1}(x)$ algebraically and compare its graph with the graph found in part (a). Are the graphs the same?

2. Use the *parametric* mode of a graphing utility to sketch the graph of the inverse of $f(x) = e^x$. What is the name of this inverse function?

3. Use the *parametric* mode of a graphing utility to sketch the graph of

$$f(x) = \frac{1}{x^2 - 9}.$$

Why doesn't this function have an inverse? Explain how to restrict the domain of f to define a new function that does have an inverse. Verify your result graphically.

4. In your own words, explain why the graph of an invertible function and its inverse are mirror images of each other about the line $y = x$.

5. The function $F = \frac{9}{5}C + 32$ expresses the relationship between degrees Celsius C and degrees Fahrenheit F.

   (a) Use the *parametric* mode of a graphing utility to graph F and its inverse in the same viewing window.

   (b) Find the point at which the two graphs intersect.

   (c) What is the significance of the point found in part (b)?

6. (a) Do all linear functions have inverses? If not, give an example of one that doesn't.

   (b) Do any quadratic functions have inverses? If so, give an example of one that does.

   (c) Do all cubic functions have inverses? If not, give an example of one that doesn't.

8 Chapter Test

Take this test as you would take a test in class. After you are done, check your work against the answers given in the back of the book.

In Exercises 1–3, graph the conic and identify any vertices and foci.

1. $y^2 - 8x = 0$ **2.** $y^2 - 4x + 4 = 0$ **3.** $x^2 - 4y^2 - 4x = 0$

4. Find an equation of the parabola shown at the right.

5. Find the equation and sketch the graph of a parabola with a focus at $(8, -2)$ and directrix at $x = 4$.

6. Find an equation of the ellipse with vertices $(0, 6)$ and $(10, 6)$, and minor axis of length 4.

7. Find an equation of the ellipse shown at the right.

8. Find an equation of the hyperbola with vertices $(0, \pm 3)$ and asymptotes $y = \pm \frac{3}{2}x$.

9. Use a graphing utility to graph the conic $\dfrac{(y-6)^2}{36} - \dfrac{(x+1)^2}{\frac{1}{16}} = 1$. Describe your viewing window.

10. Use a graphing utility to graph the conics $x^2 + y^2 = 36$ and $x^2 - y^2/4 = 1$ in the same viewing window and approximate the coordinates of any points of intersection.

In Exercises 11–13, sketch the curve represented by the parametric equations. Then eliminate the parameter and write the corresponding rectangular equation whose graph represents the curve.

11. $x = t^2 - 6$ **12.** $x = \sqrt{t^2 + 2}$ **13.** $x = 4t$

     $y = \dfrac{1}{2}t - 1$ $y = \dfrac{t}{4}$ $y = |t - 6|$

In Exercises 14–16, find two different sets of parametric equations for the given rectangular equation.

14. $y = 7x + 6$ **15.** $y = x^2 + 10$ **16.** $y = \frac{1}{4}x - 5$

17. Use a graphing utility to graph the curve represented by the parametric equations $x = 24 - 0.14e^t$ and $y = 0.6t^2$. Describe your viewing window.

18. A parabolic archway is 16 meters high at the vertex. At a height of 14 meters, the width of the archway is 12 meters, as shown in the figure at the right. How wide is the archway at ground level?

19. The moon orbits earth in an elliptical path with the center of earth at one focus, as shown in the figure at the right. The major and minor axes of the orbit have lengths of 768,806 kilometers and 767,746 kilometers, respectively. Find the smallest distance (perigee) and the greatest distance (apogee) from the center of the moon to the center of earth.

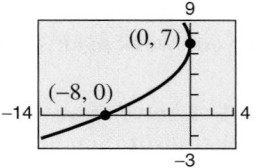

FIGURE FOR 4

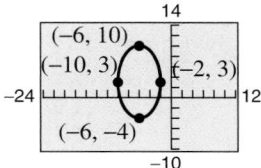

FIGURE FOR 7

The *Interactive* CD-ROM and *Internet* versions of this text provide answers to the Chapter Tests and Cumulative Tests. They also offer Chapter Pre-Tests (which test key skills and concepts covered in previous chapters) and Chapter Post-Tests, both of which have randomly generated exercises with diagnostic capabilities.

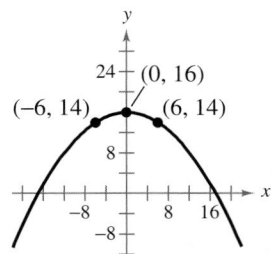

FIGURE FOR 18

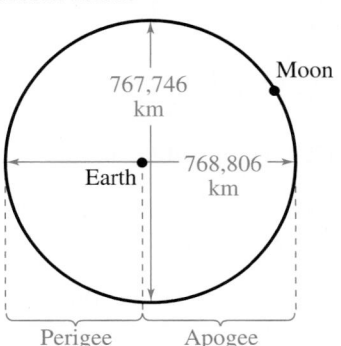

FIGURE FOR 19

6–8 Cumulative Test

Take this test to review the material from earlier chapters. After you are
done, check your work against the answers in the back of the book.

In Exercises 1–4, solve the system of equations. Use either Gaussian elimination with back-substitution or Gauss-Jordan elimination.

1. $\begin{cases} -x - 3y = 5 \\ 4x + 2y = 10 \end{cases}$

2. $\begin{cases} 6x - 10y = -8 \\ 6x + 5y = -23 \end{cases}$

3. $\begin{cases} 2x - 3y + z = 13 \\ -4x + y - 2z = -6 \\ x - 3y + 3z = 12 \end{cases}$

4. $\begin{cases} x - 4y + 3z = 5 \\ 5x + 2y - z = 1 \\ -2x - 8y = 30 \end{cases}$

In Exercises 5–8, perform the matrix operations given

$$A = \begin{bmatrix} -3 & 0 & -4 \\ 2 & 4 & 5 \\ -4 & 8 & 1 \end{bmatrix} \quad \text{and} \quad B = \begin{bmatrix} -1 & 5 & 2 \\ 6 & -3 & 3 \\ 0 & 4 & -2 \end{bmatrix}.$$

5. $3A - 2B$ 6. $5A + 3B$ 7. AB 8. BA

9. Find (a) the inverse of A (if it exists) and (b) the determinant of A.

$$A = \begin{bmatrix} 1 & 2 & -1 \\ 3 & 7 & -10 \\ -5 & -7 & -15 \end{bmatrix}$$

$\begin{cases} x - 3y - 2z = 8 \\ -2x + 7y + 3z = -19 \\ x - y - 3z = 3 \end{cases}$

FOR EXERCISE 10

10. Use an inverse matrix to solve (if possible) the system on the right.

11. Use a determinant to find the area of the triangle with vertices $(0, 0)$, $(6, 2)$,
    and $(8, 10)$.

12. Find the sum of the first 20 terms of the arithmetic sequence 8, 13, 18, 23, ...

13. Simplify: $\dfrac{49!}{46!}$.

In Exercises 14–19, find the sum. Use a graphing utility to verify your result.

14. $\displaystyle\sum_{k=1}^{6} (7k - 2)$

15. $\displaystyle\sum_{k=1}^{5} 8$

16. $\displaystyle\sum_{k=1}^{4} \frac{2}{k^2 + 4}$

17. $\displaystyle\sum_{k=3}^{6} (k - 1)(k + 2)$

18. $\displaystyle\sum_{n=0}^{10} 9\left(\tfrac{3}{4}\right)^n$

19. $\displaystyle\sum_{n=1}^{\infty} 8(0.9)^{n-1}$

20. Find the sum of the integers from 40 to 94 (inclusive).

21. Use mathematical induction to prove the formula
    $$3 + 7 + 11 + 15 + \cdots + (4n - 1) = n(2n + 1).$$

In Exercises 22–25, use the Binomial Theorem to expand and simplify the
expression.

22. $(x + 5)^4$ 23. $(2x + y^2)^5$ 24. $(x - 2y)^6$ 25. $(2x - 1)^8$

In Exercises 26–29, find the number of distinguishable permutations of the group of letters.

26. M, I, A, M, I

27. B, U, B, B, L, E

28. B, A, S, K, E, T, B, A, L, L

29. A, N, T, A, R, C, T, I, C, A

In Exercises 30–33, identify the conic and sketch its graph.

30. $\dfrac{(y + 3)^2}{36} - \dfrac{(x + 5)^2}{121} = 1$

31. $\dfrac{(x - 2)^2}{4} + \dfrac{(y + 1)^2}{9} = 1$

32. $y^2 - x^2 = 16$

33. $x^2 + y^2 - 2x - 4y + 5 = 0$

In Exercises 34–36, find an equation for the graph of the conic.

34.

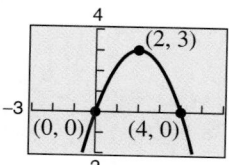

35.

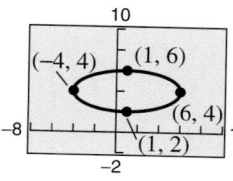

36.

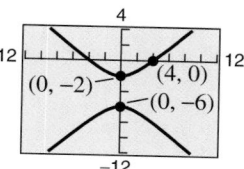

37. Find an equation of the hyperbola with foci $(0, 0)$ and $(0, 4)$, and asymptotes $y = \pm\frac{1}{2}x + 2$.

In Exercises 38–40, (a) sketch the curve represented by the parametric equation, (b) use a graphing utility to verify your graph, and (c) eliminate the parameter and write the corresponding rectangular equation whose graph represents the curve.

38. $x = 2t + 1$
$y = t^2$

39. $x = 8 + 3t$
$y = 4 - t$

40. $x = 4 \ln t$
$y = \frac{1}{2}t^2$

41. From 1992 through 1998, the sales a_n (in millions of dollars) of Bob Evans Farms, Inc., can be approximated by the model

$$a_n = 2.01n^3 - 28.76n^2 + 172.10n + 402.51$$

where $n = 2$ represents 1992. Use the model to approximate the total sales from 1992 through 1998.   (Source: Bob Evans Farms, Inc.)

42. A city of 120,000 people is growing at a rate of 0.9% per year. Estimate the population of the city 40 years from now.

43. The salary for the first year of a job is $28,000. During the next 14 years the salary increases by 5% each year. Determine the total compensation over the 15-year period.

44. On a game show, the digits 3, 4, and 5 must be arranged in the proper order to form the price of an appliance. If they are arranged correctly, the contestant wins the appliance. What is the probability of winning if the contestant knows that the price is at least $400?

45. Statuary Hall is an elliptical room in the United States Capitol in Washington, D.C. The room is 46 feet wide and 96 feet long. Find an equation that models the perimeter of the room.

Appendix A Proofs of Selected Theorems

Section P.5, page 52

The Midpoint Formula

The midpoint of the segment joining the points (x_1, y_1) and (x_2, y_2) is given by the Midpoint Formula

$$\text{Midpoint} = \left(\frac{x_1 + x_2}{2}, \frac{y_1 + y_2}{2} \right).$$

Proof

Using the figure, you must show that

$$d_1 = d_2 \quad \text{and} \quad d_1 + d_2 = d_3.$$

By the Distance Formula, you obtain

$$d_1 = \sqrt{\left(\frac{x_1 + x_2}{2} - x_1 \right)^2 + \left(\frac{y_1 + y_2}{2} - y_1 \right)^2} = \frac{1}{2}\sqrt{(x_2 - x_1)^2 + (y_2 - y_1)^2}$$

$$d_2 = \sqrt{\left(x_2 - \frac{x_1 + x_2}{2} \right)^2 + \left(y_2 - \frac{y_1 + y_2}{2} \right)^2} = \frac{1}{2}\sqrt{(x_2 - x_1)^2 + (y_2 - y_1)^2}$$

$$d_3 = \sqrt{(x_2 - x_1)^2 + (y_2 - y_1)^2}.$$

So, it follows that $d_1 = d_2$ and $d_1 + d_2 = d_3$.

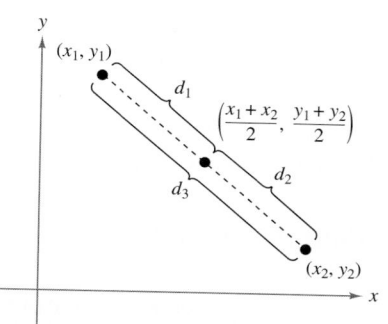

Midpoint Formula

Section 3.3, page 254

The Remainder Theorem

If a polynomial $f(x)$ is divided by $x - k$, the remainder is

$$r = f(k).$$

Proof

From the Division Algorithm, you have

$$f(x) = (x - k)q(x) + r(x)$$

and because either $r(x) = 0$ or the degree of $r(x)$ is less than the degree of $x - k$, you know that $r(x)$ must be a constant. That is, $r(x) = r$. Now, by evaluating $f(x)$ at $x = k$, you have

$$f(k) = (k - k)q(k) + r = (0)q(k) + r = r.$$

Section 3.3, page 254

The Factor Theorem

A polynomial $f(x)$ has a factor $(x - k)$ if and only if $f(k) = 0$.

Proof

Using the Division Algorithm with the factor $(x - k)$, you have

$$f(x) = (x - k)q(x) + r(x).$$

By the Remainder Theorem, $r(x) = r = f(k)$, and you have

$$f(x) = (x - k)q(x) + f(k)$$

where $q(x)$ is a polynomial of lesser degree than $f(x)$. If $f(k) = 0$, then

$$f(x) = (x - k)q(x)$$

and you see that $(x - k)$ is a factor of $f(x)$. Conversely, if $(x - k)$ is a factor of $f(x)$, division of $f(x)$ by $(x - k)$ yields a remainder of 0. So, by the Remainder Theorem, you have $f(k) = 0$.

Section 3.4, page 264

Linear Factorization Theorem

If $f(x)$ is a polynomial of degree n, where $n > 0$, then f has precisely n linear factors

$$f(x) = a_n(x - c_1)(x - c_2) \cdots (x - c_n)$$

where $c_1, c_2, \ldots, c_n$ are complex numbers.

Proof

Using the Fundamental Theorem of Algebra, you know that f must have at least one zero, c_1. Consequently, $(x - c_1)$ is a factor of $f(x)$, and you have

$$f(x) = (x - c_1)f_1(x).$$

If the degree of $f_1(x)$ is greater than zero, you again apply the Fundamental Theorem to conclude that f_1 must have a zero c_2, which implies that

$$f(x) = (x - c_1)(x - c_2)f_2(x).$$

It is clear that the degree of $f_1(x)$ is $n - 1$, that the degree of $f_2(x)$ is $n - 2$, and that you can repeatedly apply the Fundamental Theorem n times until you obtain

$$f(x) = a_n(x - c_1)(x - c_2) \cdots (x - c_n)$$

where a_n is the leading coefficient of the polynomial $f(x)$.

Section 3.4, page 266

Factors of a Polynomial

Every polynomial of degree $n > 0$ with real coefficients can be written as the product of linear and quadratic factors with real coefficients, where the quadratic factors have no real zeros.

Proof

To begin, use the Linear Factorization Theorem to conclude that $f(x)$ can be completely factored in the form

$$f(x) = d(x - c_1)(x - c_2)(x - c_3) \cdots (x - c_n).$$

If each c_i is real, there is nothing more to prove. If any c_i is complex ($c_i = a + bi, b \neq 0$), then, because the coefficients of $f(x)$ are real, you know that the conjugate $c_j = a - bi$ is also a zero. By multiplying the corresponding factors, you obtain

$$(x - c_i)(x - c_j) = [x - (a + bi)][x - (a - bi)]$$
$$= x^2 - 2ax + (a^2 + b^2)$$

where each coefficient is real.

Section 4.3, page 323

Properties of Logarithms

Let a be a positive number such that $a \neq 1$, and let n be a real number. If u and v are positive real numbers, the following properties are true.

1. $\log_a(uv) = \log_a u + \log_a v$ **1.** $\ln(uv) = \ln u + \ln v$

2. $\log_a \dfrac{u}{v} = \log_a u - \log_a v$ **2.** $\ln \dfrac{u}{v} = \ln u - \ln v$

3. $\log_a u^n = n \log_a u$ **3.** $\ln u^n = n \ln u$

Proof

To prove Property 1, let

$$x = \log_a u \quad \text{and} \quad y = \log_a v.$$

The corresponding exponential forms of these two equations are

$$a^x = u \quad \text{and} \quad a^y = v.$$

Multiplying u and v produces $uv = a^x a^y = a^{x+y}$. The corresponding logarithmic form of $uv = a^{x+y}$ is $\log_a(uv) = x + y$. So, $\log_a(uv) = \log_a u + \log_a v$.

Section 7.1, page 501

Properties of Sums

1. $\displaystyle\sum_{i=1}^{n} ca_i = c\sum_{i=1}^{n} a_i,$ c is any constant.

2. $\displaystyle\sum_{i=1}^{n} (a_i + b_i) = \sum_{i=1}^{n} a_i + \sum_{i=1}^{n} b_i$

3. $\displaystyle\sum_{i=1}^{n} (a_i - b_i) = \sum_{i=1}^{n} a_i - \sum_{i=1}^{n} b_i$

Proof

Each of these properties follows directly from the Associative Property of Addition, the Commutative Property of Addition, and the Distributive Property of multiplication over addition. For example, note the use of the Distributive Property in the proof of Property 1.

$$\sum_{i=1}^{n} ca_i = ca_1 + ca_2 + ca_3 + \cdots + ca_n$$

$$= c(a_1 + a_2 + a_3 + \cdots + a_n) = c\sum_{i=1}^{n} a_i$$

Section 7.2, page 510

The Sum of a Finite Arithmetic Sequence

The sum of a finite arithmetic sequence with n terms is

$$S_n = \frac{n}{2}(a_1 + a_n).$$

Proof

Begin by generating the terms of the arithmetic sequence in two ways. In the first way, repeatedly add d to the first term to obtain

$$S_n = a_1 + a_2 + a_3 + \cdots + a_{n-2} + a_{n-1} + a_n$$

$$= a_1 + [a_1 + d] + [a_1 + 2d] + \cdots + [a_1 + (n - 1)d].$$

In the second way, repeatedly subtract d from the nth term to obtain

$$S_n = a_n + a_{n-1} + a_{n-2} + \cdots + a_3 + a_2 + a_1$$

$$= a_n + [a_n - d] + [a_n - 2d] + \cdots + [a_n - (n - 1)d].$$

If you add these two versions of S_n, the multiples of d cancel and you obtain

$$2S_n = \overbrace{(a_1 + a_n) + (a_1 + a_n) + (a_1 + a_n) + \cdots + (a_1 + a_n)}^{n \text{ terms}}$$

$$= n(a_1 + a_n).$$

So, you have $S_n = \dfrac{n}{2}(a_1 + a_n).$

Section 7.3, page 519

The Sum of a Finite Geometric Sequence

The sum of the geometric sequence

$$a_1, \; a_1 r, \; a_1 r^2, \; a_1 r^3, \; a_1 r^4, \; \dots, a_1 r^{n-1}$$

with common ratio $r \neq 1$ is $S_n = a_1 \left(\dfrac{1 - r^n}{1 - r} \right)$.

Proof

Begin by writing out the nth partial sum.

$$S_n = a_1 + a_1 r + a_1 r^2 + \cdots + a_1 r^{n-2} + a_1 r^{n-1}$$

Multiplication by r yields

$$r S_n = a_1 r + a_1 r^2 + a_1 r^3 + \cdots + a_1 r^{n-1} + a_1 r^n.$$

Subtracting the second equation from the first yields

$$S_n - r S_n = a_1 - a_1 r^n.$$

So, $S_n(1 - r) = a_1(1 - r^n)$, and, because $r \neq 1$, you have

$$S_n = a_1 \left(\frac{1 - r^n}{1 - r} \right).$$

Section 7.5, page 534

The Binomial Theorem

In the expansion of $(x + y)^n$

$$(x + y)^n = x^n + nx^{n-1}y + \cdots + {}_nC_r \, x^{n-r}y^r + \cdots + nxy^{n-1} + y^n$$

the coefficient of $x^{n-r}y^r$ is ${}_nC_r = \dfrac{n!}{(n - r)!r!}$.

Proof

The Binomial Theorem can be proved quite nicely using mathematical induction. The steps are straightforward but look a little messy, so only an outline of the proof is presented.

1. If $n = 1$, you have

$$(x + y)^1 = x^1 + y^1 = {}_1C_0 x + {}_1C_1 y$$

   and the formula is valid.

2. Assuming that the formula is true for $n = k$, the coefficient of $x^{k-r}y^r$ is

$$_kC_r = \frac{k!}{(k - r)!r!} = \frac{k(k - 1)(k - 2) \cdots (k - r + 1)}{r!}.$$

To show that the formula is true for $n = k + 1$, look at the coefficient of $x^{k+1-r}y^r$ in the expansion of

$$(x + y)^{k+1} = (x + y)^k(x + y).$$

From the right-hand side, you can determine that the term involving $x^{k+1-r}y^r$ is the sum of two products.

$$({}_kC_r x^{k-r}y^r)(x) + ({}_kC_{r-1}x^{k+1-r}y^{r-1})(y)$$

$$= \left[\frac{k!}{(k-r)!r!} + \frac{k!}{(k-r+1)!(r-1)!}\right]x^{k+1-r}y^r$$

$$= \left[\frac{(k+1-r)k!}{(k+1-r)!r!} + \frac{k!r}{(k+1-r)!r!}\right]x^{k+1-r}y^r$$

$$= \left[\frac{k!(k+1-r+r)}{(k+1-r)!r!}\right]x^{k+1-r}y^r$$

$$= \left[\frac{(k+1)!}{(k+1-r)!r!}\right]x^{k+1-r}y^r$$

$$= {}_{k+1}C_r x^{k+1-r}y^r$$

So, by mathematical induction, the Binomial Theorem is valid for all positive integers n.

Section 8.1, page 575

Standard Equation of a Parabola (Vertex at Origin)

The standard form of the equation of a parabola with vertex at $(0, 0)$ and directrix $y = -p$ is

$$x^2 = 4py, \qquad p \neq 0. \qquad \text{Vertical axis}$$

For directrix $x = -p$, the equation is

$$y^2 = 4px, \qquad p \neq 0. \qquad \text{Horizontal axis}$$

The focus is on the axis p units (directed distance) from the vertex.

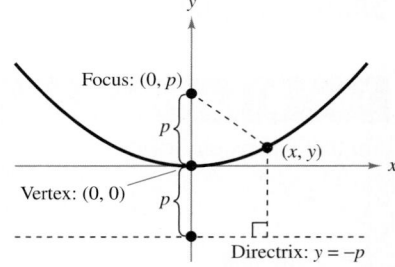

Proof

Because the two cases are similar, a proof will be given for the first case only. Suppose the directrix $(y = -p)$ is parallel to the x-axis. In the figure, you assume that $p > 0$, and because p is the directed distance from the vertex to the focus, the focus must lie above the vertex. Because the point (x, y) is equidistant from $(0, p)$ and $y = -p$, you can apply the Distance Formula to obtain

$$\sqrt{(x - 0)^2 + (y - p)^2} = y + p$$

$$x^2 + (y - p)^2 = (y + p)^2$$

$$x^2 + y^2 - 2py + p^2 = y^2 + 2py + p^2$$

$$x^2 = 4py.$$

Appendix B Concepts in Statistics

Appendix B.1 Representing Data

Line Plots

Statistics is the branch of mathematics that studies techniques for collecting, organizing, and interpreting data. In this section, you will study several ways to organize data. The first is a **line plot,** which uses a portion of a real number line to order numbers. Line plots are especially useful for ordering small sets of numbers (about 50 or less) by hand.

EXAMPLE 1 Constructing a Line Plot

Use a line plot to organize the following test scores. Which number occurs with the greatest frequency?

93, 70, 76, 67, 86, 93, 82, 78, 83, 86, 64, 78, 76, 66, 83,
83, 96, 74, 69, 76, 64, 74, 79, 76, 88, 76, 81, 82, 74, 70

Solution

Begin by scanning the data to find the smallest and largest numbers. For this data, the smallest number is 64 and the largest is 96. Next, draw a portion of a real number line that includes the interval [64, 96]. To create the line plot, start with the first number, 93, and enter an × above 93 on the number line. Continue recording ×'s for each number in the list until you obtain the line plot shown in Figure B.1. From the line plot, you can see that 76 occurs with the greatest frequency.

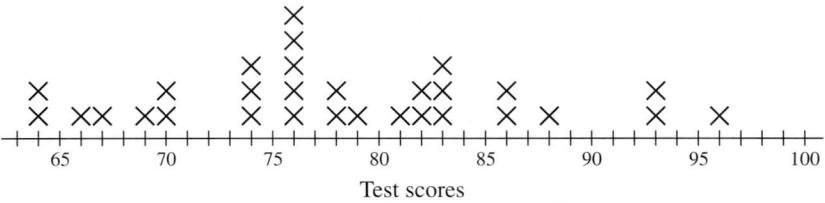

Figure B.1

Test Scores

93, 70, 76, 58, 86, 93, 82, 78,
83, 86, 64, 78, 76, 66, 83, 83,
96, 74, 69, 76, 64, 74, 79, 76,
88, 76, 81, 82, 74, 70

Stems	Leaves
5	8
6	4 4 6 9
7	0 0 4 4 4 6 6 6 6 6 8 8 9
8	1 2 2 3 3 3 6 6 8
9	3 3 6

Stem-and-Leaf Plots

Another type of plot that can be used to organize sets of numbers by hand is a stem-and-leaf plot. A set of test scores and the corresponding stem-and-leaf plot are shown at the right.

Note that the *leaves* represent the units digits of the numbers and the *stems* represent the tens digits. Stem-and-leaf plots can also be used to compare two sets of data, as shown in the following example.

EXAMPLE 2   Comparing Two Sets of Data

Use a stem-and-leaf plot to compare the test scores given on page A7 with the following test scores. Which set of test scores is better?

90, 81, 70, 62, 64, 73, 81, 92, 73, 81, 92, 93, 83, 75, 76,
83, 94, 96, 86, 77, 77, 86, 96, 86, 77, 86, 87, 87, 79, 88

Solution
Begin by ordering the second set of scores.

62, 64, 70, 73, 73, 75, 76, 77, 77, 77, 79, 81, 81, 81, 83,
83, 86, 86, 86, 86, 87, 87, 88, 90, 92, 92, 93, 94, 96, 96

Now that the data has been ordered, you can construct a *double* stem-and-leaf plot by letting the leaves to the right of the stems represent the units digits for the first group of test scores and letting the leaves to the left of the stems represent the units digits for the second group of test scores.

Leaves (2nd Group)	Stems	Leaves (1st Group)
	5	8
4 2	6	4 4 6 9
9 7 7 7 6 5 3 3 0	7	0 0 4 4 4 6 6 6 6 8 8 9
8 7 7 6 6 6 6 3 3 1 1 1	8	1 2 2 3 3 3 6 6 8
6 6 4 3 2 2 0	9	3 3 6

By comparing the two sets of leaves, you can see that the second group of test scores is better than the first group.

AK	5.3	MT	13.2
AL	13.0	NC	12.5
AR	14.3	ND	14.4
AZ	13.2	NE	13.7
CA	11.1	NH	12.1
CO	10.1	NJ	13.7
CT	14.4	NM	11.2
DC	13.9	NV	11.5
DE	12.9	NY	13.4
FL	18.5	OH	13.4
GA	9.9	OK	13.4
HI	13.2	OR	13.3
IA	15.0	PA	15.8
ID	11.3	RI	15.8
IL	12.5	SC	12.1
IN	12.5	SD	14.3
KS	13.5	TN	12.5
KY	12.5	TX	10.1
LA	11.4	UT	8.7
MA	14.1	VA	11.2
MD	11.5	VT	12.3
ME	13.9	WA	11.5
MI	12.4	WI	13.2
MN	12.3	WV	15.1
MO	13.7	WY	11.3
MS	12.2		

EXAMPLE 3   Using a Stem-and-Leaf Plot

The table at the right above shows the percent of the population of each state and the District of Columbia that was at least 65 years old in 1997. Use a stem-and-leaf plot to organize the data.   (Source: U.S. Bureau of the Census)

Solution
Begin by ordering the numbers, as shown below.

5.3, 8.7, 9.9, 10.1, 10.1, 11.1, 11.2, 11.2, 11.3, 11.3, 11.4, 11.5, 11.5, 11.5,
12.1, 12.1, 12.2, 12.3, 12.3, 12.4, 12.5, 12.5, 12.5, 12.5, 12.5, 12.9, 13.0,
13.2, 13.2, 13.2, 13.2, 13.3, 13.4, 13.4, 13.4, 13.5, 13.7, 13.7, 13.7, 13.9,
13.9, 14.1, 14.3, 14.3, 14.4, 14.4, 15.0, 15.1, 15.8, 15.8, 18.5

Next construct the stem-and-leaf plot using the leaves to represent the digits to the right of the decimal points, as shown at the right. From the stem-and-leaf plot, you can see that Alaska has the lowest percent and Florida has the highest percent.

Stems	Leaves
5.	3
6.	
7.	
8.	7
9.	9
10.	1 1
11.	1 2 2 3 3 4 5 5 5
12.	1 1 2 3 3 4 5 5 5 5 5 9
13.	0 2 2 2 2 3 4 4 4 5 7 7 7 9 9
14.	1 3 3 4 4
15.	0 1 8 8
16.	
17.	
18.	5

Histograms and Frequency Distributions

With data such as that given in Example 3, it is useful to group the numbers into intervals and plot the frequency of the data in each interval. For instance, the frequency distribution and the histogram shown in Figure B.2 represent the data given in Example 3.

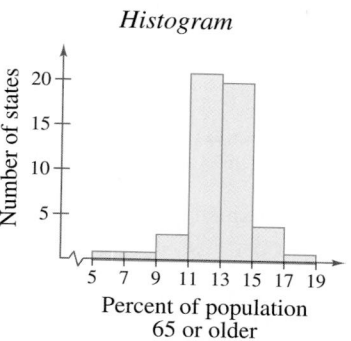

Frequency Distribution

Interval	Tally
[5, 7)	I
[7, 9)	I
[9, 11)	III
[11, 13)	LHT LHT LHT LHT I
[13, 15)	LHT LHT LHT LHT
[15, 17)	IIII
[17, 19)	I

Histogram

Figure B.2

A histogram has a portion of a real number line as its horizontal axis. A histogram is similar to a bar graph, except that the rectangles (bars) in a bar graph can be either horizontal or vertical and the labels of the bars are not necessarily numbers. Another difference between a bar graph and a histogram is that the bars in a bar graph are usually separated by spaces, whereas the bars in a histogram are not.

Interval	Tally
100–109	LHT III
110–119	I
120–129	III
130–139	III
140–149	LHT II
150–159	LHT
160–169	LHT III
170–179	LHT I
180–189	II
190–199	LHT

EXAMPLE 4   Constructing a Histogram

A company has 48 sales representatives who sold the following numbers of units during the first quarter of 2000. Construct a grouped frequency distribution for this data.

107	162	184	170	177	102	145	141
105	193	167	149	195	127	193	191
150	153	164	167	171	163	141	129
109	171	150	138	100	164	147	153
171	163	118	142	107	144	100	132
153	107	124	162	192	134	187	177

Solution

To begin constructing a grouped frequency distribution, you must first decide on the number of groups. There are several ways to group this data. However, because the smallest number is 100 and the largest is 195, it seems that 10 groups of 10 each would be appropriate. The first group would be 100–109, the second group would be 110–119, and so on. By tallying the data into the 10 groups, you obtain the distribution shown at the right above. A histogram for the distribution is shown in Figure B.3.

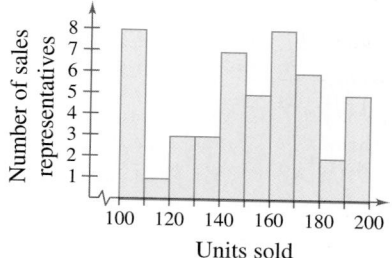

Figure B.3

B.1 Exercises

1. *Gasoline Prices* The line plot shows a sample of prices of unleaded regular gasoline from 25 different cities.

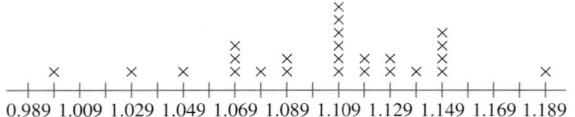

(a) What price occurred with the greatest frequency?

(b) What is the range of prices?

2. *Livestock Weights* The line plot shows the weights (to the nearest hundred pounds) of 30 head of cattle sold by a rancher.

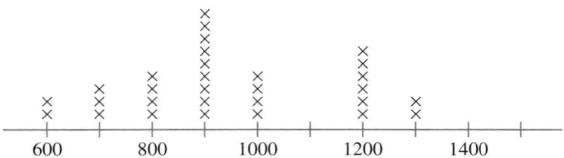

(a) What weight occurred with the greatest frequency?

(b) What is the range of weights?

Quiz and Exam Scores In Exercises 3–6, use the following scores from a math class of 30 students. The scores are for two 25-point quizzes and two 100-point exams.

Quiz #1   20, 15, 14, 20, 16, 19, 10, 21, 24, 15, 15, 14, 15, 21, 19, 15, 20, 18, 18, 22, 18, 16, 18, 19, 21, 19, 16, 20, 14, 12

Quiz #2   22, 22, 23, 22, 21, 24, 22, 19, 21, 23, 23, 25, 24, 22, 22, 23, 23, 23, 23, 22, 24, 23, 22, 24, 21, 24, 16, 21, 16, 14

Exam #1   77, 100, 77, 70, 83, 89, 87, 85, 81, 84, 81, 78, 89, 78, 88, 85, 90, 92, 75, 81, 85, 100, 98, 81, 78, 75, 85, 89, 82, 75

Exam #2   76, 78, 73, 59, 70, 81, 71, 66, 66, 73, 68, 67, 63, 67, 77, 84, 87, 71, 78, 78, 90, 80, 77, 70, 80, 64, 74, 68, 68, 68

3. Construct a line plot for each quiz. For each quiz, which score occurred with the greatest frequency?

4. Construct a line plot for each exam. For each exam, which score occurred with the greatest frequency?

5. Construct a stem-and-leaf plot for Exam #1.

6. Construct a double stem-and-leaf plot to compare the scores for Exam #1 and Exam #2. Which set of scores is higher?

7. *Insurance Coverage* The table shows the total numbers of persons (in thousands) without health insurance coverage in the 50 states and the District of Columbia in 1996. Use a stem-and-leaf plot to organize the data.   (Source: U.S. Bureau of the Census)

AK	89	AL	550	AR	566	AZ	1159	CA	6514
CO	644	CT	368	DC	80	DE	98	FL	2722
GA	1319	HI	101	IA	335	ID	196	IL	1337
IN	600	KS	292	KY	601	LA	890	MA	766
MD	581	ME	146	MI	857	MN	480	MO	700
MS	518	MT	124	NC	1160	ND	62	NE	190
NH	109	NJ	1317	NM	412	NV	255	NY	3132
OH	1292	OK	570	OR	496	PA	1133	RI	93
SC	634	SD	67	TN	841	TX	4680	UT	240
VA	811	VT	65	WA	761	WI	438	WV	261
WY	66								

8. *Snowfall* The data below shows the seasonal snowfall (in inches) at Lincoln, Nebraska for the years 1968 through 1997 (the amounts are listed in order by year). How would you organize this data? Explain your reasoning.   (Source: University of Nebraska–Lincoln)

39.8, 26.2, 49.0, 21.6, 29.2, 33.6, 42.1, 21.1, 21.8, 31.0, 34.4, 23.3, 13.0, 32.3, 38.0, 47.5, 21.5, 18.9, 15.7, 13.0, 19.1, 18.7, 25.8, 23.8, 32.1, 21.3, 21.8, 30.7, 29.0, 44.6

9. *Retirement Contributions* The employees of a company must contribute 7% of their monthly salaries to a company-sponsored retirement plan. The contributed amounts (in dollars) for the company's 35 employees are as follows.

100, 200, 130, 136, 161, 156, 209, 126, 135, 98, 114, 117, 168, 133, 140, 124, 172, 127, 143, 157, 124, 152, 104, 126, 155, 92, 194, 115, 120, 136, 148, 112, 116, 146, 96

(a) Construct a frequency distribution using groups of 20. The first group should be 90–109.

(b) Construct a histogram for this frequency distribution.

Appendix B.2   Measures of Central Tendency and Dispersion

Mean, Median, and Mode

In many real-life situations, it is helpful to describe data by a single number that is most representative of the entire collection of numbers. Such a number is called a **measure of central tendency.** The most commonly used measures are as follows.

1. The **mean,** or **average,** of n numbers is the sum of the numbers divided by n.
2. The **median** of n numbers is the middle number when the numbers are written in order. If n is even, the median is the average of the two middle numbers.
3. The **mode** of n numbers is the number that occurs most frequently. If two numbers tie for most frequent occurrence, the collection has two modes and is called **bimodal.**

EXAMPLE 1   Comparing Measures of Central Tendency

On an interview for a job, the interviewer tells you that the average annual income of the company's 25 employees is $60,849. The actual annual incomes of the 25 employees are shown below. What are the mean, median, and mode of the incomes? Was the person telling you the truth?

$17,305,	$478,320,	$45,678,	$18,980,	$17,408,
$25,676,	$28,906,	$12,500,	$24,540,	$33,450,
$12,500,	$33,855,	$37,450,	$20,432,	$28,956,
$34,983,	$36,540,	$250,921,	$36,853,	$16,430,
$32,654,	$98,213,	$48,980,	$94,024,	$35,671

Solution

The mean of the incomes is

$$\text{Mean} = \frac{17,305 + 478,320 + 45,678 + 18,980 + \cdots + 35,671}{25}$$

$$= \frac{1,521,225}{25} = \$60,849.$$

To find the median, order the incomes as follows.

$12,500,	$12,500,	$16,430,	$17,305,	$17,408,
$18,980,	$20,432,	$24,540,	$25,676,	$28,906,
$28,956,	$32,654,	$33,450,	$33,855,	$34,983,
$35,671,	$36,540,	$36,853,	$37,450,	$45,678,
$48,980,	$94,024,	$98,213,	$250,921,	$478,320

From this list, you can see that the median (the middle number) is $33,450. From the same list, you can see that $12,500 is the only income that occurs more than once. So, the mode is $12,500. Technically, the person was telling the truth because the average is (generally) defined to be the mean. However, of the three measures of central tendency—*Mean:* $60,849 *Median:* $33,450 *Mode:* $12,500—it seems clear that the median is most representative. The mean is inflated by the two highest salaries.

What You Should Learn:

- How to find and interpret the mean, median, and mode of a set of data
- How to determine the measure of central tendency that best represents a set of data
- How to find the standard deviations of a set of data
- How to use box-and-whisker plots

Why You Should Learn It:

Measures of central tendency and dispersion provide a convenient way to describe and compare sets of data. For instance, in Exercise 36 on page A19, the mean and standard deviation are used to analyze the price of gold for the years 1978 through 1997.

Choosing a Measure of Central Tendency

Which of the three measures of central tendency is the most representative? The answer is that it depends on the distribution of the data *and* the way in which you plan to use the data.

For instance, in Example 1, the mean salary of $60,849 does not seem very representative to a potential employee. To a city income tax collector who wants to estimate 1% of the total income of the 25 employees, however, the mean is precisely the right measure.

EXAMPLE 2   Choosing a Measure of Central Tendency

Which measure of central tendency is the most representative of the data given in each of the following frequency distributions?

a. *Number*	*Tally*	b. *Number*	*Tally*	c. *Number*	*Tally*
1	7	1	9	1	6
2	20	2	8	2	1
3	15	3	7	3	2
4	11	4	6	4	3
5	8	5	5	5	5
6	3	6	6	6	5
7	2	7	7	7	4
8	0	8	8	8	3
9	15	9	9	9	0

Solution

a. For this data, the mean is 4.23, the median is 3, and the mode is 2. Of these, the mode is probably the most representative.

b. For this data, the mean and median are each 5 and the modes are 1 and 9 (the distribution is bimodal). Of these, the mean or median is the most representative.

c. For this data, the mean is 4.59, the median is 5, and the mode is 1. Of these, the mean or median is the most representative.

Variance and Standard Deviation

Very different sets of numbers can have the same mean. You will now study two **measures of dispersion,** which give you an idea of how much the numbers in a set differ from the mean of the set. These two measures are called the *variance* of the set and the *standard deviation* of the set.

Definitions of Variance and Standard Deviation

Consider a set of numbers $\{x_1, x_2, \ldots, x_n\}$ with a mean of $\bar{x}$. The **variance** of the set is

$$v = \frac{(x_1 - \bar{x})^2 + (x_2 - \bar{x})^2 + \cdots + (x_n - \bar{x})^2}{n}$$

and the **standard deviation** of the set is $\sigma = \sqrt{v}$ (σ is the lowercase Greek letter *sigma*).

The standard deviation of a set is a measure of how much a typical number in the set differs from the mean. The greater the standard deviation, the more the numbers in the set vary from the mean. For instance, each of the following sets has a mean of 5.

$$\{5, 5, 5, 5\}, \qquad \{4, 4, 6, 6\}, \qquad \text{and} \qquad \{3, 3, 7, 7\}$$

The standard deviations of the sets are 0, 1, and 2.

$$\sigma_1 = \sqrt{\frac{(5 - 5)^2 + (5 - 5)^2 + (5 - 5)^2 + (5 - 5)^2}{4}}$$

$$= 0$$

$$\sigma_2 = \sqrt{\frac{(4 - 5)^2 + (4 - 5)^2 + (6 - 5)^2 + (6 - 5)^2}{4}}$$

$$= 1$$

$$\sigma_3 = \sqrt{\frac{(3 - 5)^2 + (3 - 5)^2 + (7 - 5)^2 + (7 - 5)^2}{4}}$$

$$= 2$$

EXAMPLE 3 Estimations of Standard Deviation

Consider the three sets of data represented by the bar graphs in Figure B.4. Which set has the smallest standard deviation? Which has the largest?

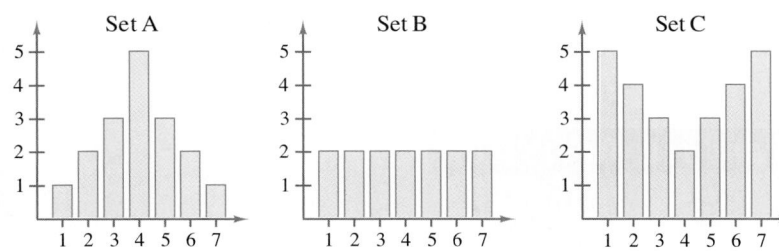

Figure B.4

Solution

Of the three sets, the numbers in set *A* are grouped most closely to the center and the numbers in set *C* are the most dispersed. So, set *A* has the smallest standard deviation and set *C* has the largest standard deviation.

EXAMPLE 4 Find Standard Deviation

Find the standard deviation of each set shown in Example 3.

Solution

Because of the symmetry of each bar graph, you can conclude that each has a mean of $\bar{x} = 4$. The standard deviation of set A is

$$\sigma = \sqrt{\frac{(-3)^2 + 2(-2)^2 + 3(-1)^2 + 5(0)^2 + 3(1)^2 + 2(2)^2 + (3)^2}{17}}$$

$$\approx 1.53.$$

The standard deviation of set B is

$$\sigma = \sqrt{\frac{2(-3)^2 + 2(-2)^2 + 2(-1)^2 + 2(0)^2 + 2(1)^2 + 2(2)^2 + 2(3)^2}{14}}$$

$$= 2.$$

The standard deviation of set C is

$$\sigma = \sqrt{\frac{5(-3)^2 + 4(-2)^2 + 3(-1)^2 + 2(0)^2 + 3(1)^2 + 4(2)^2 + 5(3)^2}{26}}$$

$$\approx 2.22.$$

These values confirm the results of Example 3. That is, set A has the smallest standard deviation and set C has the largest.

The following alternative formula provides a more efficient way to compute the standard deviation.

Alternative Formula for Standard Deviation

The standard deviation of $\{x_1, x_2, \ldots, x_n\}$ is

$$\sigma = \sqrt{\frac{x_1^2 + x_2^2 + \cdots + x_n^2}{n} - \bar{x}^2}.$$

Because of messy computations, this formula is difficult to verify. Conceptually, however, the process is straightforward. It consists of showing that the expressions

$$\sqrt{\frac{(x_1 - \bar{x})^2 + (x_2 - \bar{x})^2 + \cdots + (x_n - \bar{x})^2}{n}}$$

and

$$\sqrt{\frac{x_1^2 + x_2^2 + \cdots + x_n^2}{n} - \bar{x}^2}$$

are equivalent. Try verifying this equivalence for the set $\{x_1, x_2, x_3\}$ with $\bar{x} = (x_1 + x_2 + x_3)/3$.

AK	66	MT	62
AL	40	NC	42
AR	39	ND	47
AZ	51	NE	63
CA	62	NH	59
CO	69	NJ	77
CT	80	NM	45
DC	94	NV	49
DE	44	NY	73
FL	50	OH	55
GA	46	OK	47
HI	80	OR	70
IA	55	PA	61
ID	53	RI	56
IL	61	SC	41
IN	47	SD	49
KS	51	TN	53
KY	53	TX	47
LA	45	UT	66
MA	74	VA	54
MD	68	VT	57
ME	47	WA	68
MI	62	WI	65
MN	67	WV	43
MO	53	WY	52
MS	37		

EXAMPLE 5   Using the Alternative Formula

Use the alternative formula for standard deviation to find the standard deviation of the following set of numbers.

$$5, 6, 6, 7, 7, 8, 8, 8, 9, 10$$

Solution

Begin by finding the mean of the set, which is 7.4. So, the standard deviation is

$$\sigma = \sqrt{\frac{5^2 + 2(6^2) + 2(7^2) + 3(8^2) + 9^2 + 10^2}{10} - (7.4)^2}$$

$$= \sqrt{\frac{568}{10} - 54.76}$$

$$= \sqrt{2.04}$$

$$\approx 1.43.$$

You can use the statistical features of a graphing utility to check this result.

A well-known theorem in statistics, called *Chebychev's Theorem*, states that at least

$$1 - \frac{1}{k^2}$$

of the numbers in a distribution must lie within k standard deviations of the mean. So, 75% of the numbers in a collection must lie within two standard deviations of the mean, and at least 88.9% of the numbers must lie within three standard deviations of the mean. For most distributions, these percentages are low. For instance, in all three distributions shown in Example 3, 100% of the numbers lie within two standard deviations of the mean.

EXAMPLE 6   Describing a Distribution

The table at the right above shows the number of dentists (per 100,000 people) in each state and the District of Columbia. Find the mean and standard deviation of the numbers. What percent of the numbers lie within two standard deviations of the mean?   (Source: American Dental Association)

Solution

Begin by entering the numbers into a graphing utility that has a standard deviation program. After running the program, you should obtain

$$\bar{x} \approx 56.76 \quad \text{and} \quad \sigma = 12.14.$$

The interval that contains all numbers that lie within two standard deviations of the mean is

$$[56.76 - 2(12.14), 56.76 + 2(12.14)] \quad \text{or} \quad [32.48, 81.04].$$

From the histogram in Figure B.5, you can see that all but one of the numbers (98%) lie in this interval—all but the number that corresponds to the number of dentists (per 100,000 people) in Washington, D.C.

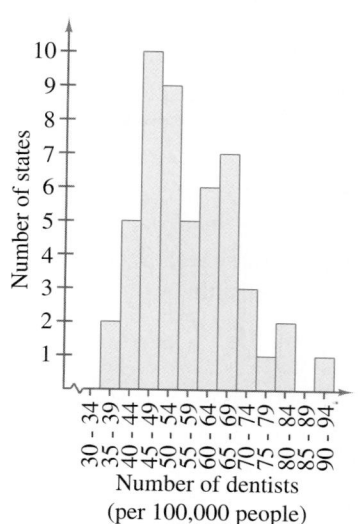

Figure B.5

Box-and-Whisker Plots

Standard deviation is the measure of dispersion that is associated with the mean. Quartiles measure dispersion associated with the median.

Definition of Quartiles

Consider an ordered set of numbers whose median is m. The **lower quartile** is the median of the numbers that occur before m. The upper quartile is the median of the numbers that occur after m.

EXAMPLE 7   Finding Quartiles of a Set

Find the lower and upper quartiles for the following set.

34, 14, 24, 16, 12, 18, 20, 24, 16, 26, 13, 27

Solution

Begin by ordering the set.

12, 13, 14,	16, 16, 18,	20, 24, 24,	26, 27, 34
1st 25%	2nd 25%	3rd 25%	4th 25%

The median of the entire set is 19. The median of the six numbers that are less than 19 is 15. So, the lower quartile is 15. The median of the six numbers that are greater than 19 is 25. So, the upper quartile is 25.

Quartiles are represented graphically by a **box-and-whisker plot,** as shown in Figure B.6. In the plot, notice that five numbers are listed: the smallest number, the lower quartile, the median, the upper quartile, and the largest number. Also notice that the numbers are spaced proportionally, as though they were on a real number line.

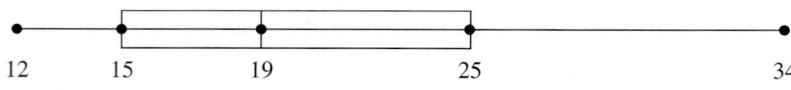

12   15   19   25   34

Figure B.6

The next example shows how to find quartiles when the number of elements in a set is not divisible by 4.

EXAMPLE 8   Sketching Box-and-Whisker Plots

Sketch a box-and-whisker plot for each of the given sets.

a. 27, 28, 30, 42, 45, 50, 50, 61, 62, 64, 66

b. 82, 82, 83, 85, 87, 89, 90, 94, 95, 95, 96, 98, 99

c. 11, 13, 13, 15, 17, 18, 20, 24, 24, 27

Solution

a. This set has 11 numbers. The median is 50 (the sixth number). The lower quartile is 30 (the median of the first five numbers). The upper quartile is 62 (the median of the last five numbers).

b. This set has 13 numbers. The median is 90 (the seventh number). The lower quartile is 84 (the median of the first six numbers). The upper quartile is 95.5 (the median of the last six numbers).

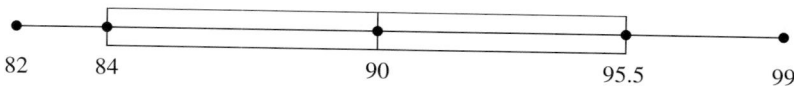

c. This set has 10 numbers. The median is 17.5 (the average of the fifth and sixth numbers). The lower quartile is 13 (the median of the first five numbers). The

B.2   E x e r c i s e s

In Exercises 1–6, find the mean, median, and mode of the set of measurements.

1. 5, 12, 7, 14, 8, 9, 7

2. 30, 37, 32, 39, 33, 34, 32

3. 5, 12, 7, 24, 8, 9, 7

4. 20, 37, 32, 39, 33, 34, 32

5. 5, 12, 7, 14, 9, 7

6. 30, 37, 32, 39, 34, 32

7. *Reasoning*   Compare your answers for Exercises 1 and 3 with those for Exercises 2 and 4. Which of the

measures of central tendency is sensitive to extreme measurements? Explain your reasoning.

8. *Reasoning*

   (a) Add 6 to each measurement in Exercise 1 and calculate the mean, median, and mode of the revised measurements. How are the measures of central tendency changed?

   (b) If a constant k is added to each measurement in a set of data, how will the measures of central tendency change?

9. *Electric Bills* A person had the following monthly bills for electricity. What are the mean and median of the collection of bills?

January	$67.92	February	$59.84
March	$52.00	April	$52.50
May	$57.99	June	$65.35
July	$81.76	August	$74.98
September	$87.82	October	$83.18
November	$65.35	December	$57.00

10. *Car Rental* A car rental company kept the following record of the numbers of miles a rental car was driven. What are the mean, median, and mode of this data?

Monday	410	Tuesday	260
Wednesday	320	Thursday	320
Friday	460	Saturday	150

11. *Six-Child Families* A study was done on families having six children. The table gives the numbers of families in the study with the indicated numbers of girls. Determine the mean, median, and mode of this set of data.

Number of girls	0	1	2	3	4	5	6
Frequency	1	24	45	54	50	19	7

12. *Baseball* A baseball fan examined the records of a favorite baseball player's performance during his last 50 games. The numbers of games in which the player had 0, 1, 2, 3, and 4 hits are recorded in the table.

Number of hits	0	1	2	3	4
Frequency	14	26	7	2	1

(a) Determine the average number of hits per game.

(b) Determine the player's batting average if he had 200 at-bats during the 50-game series.

13. *Think About It* Construct a collection of numbers that has the following properties. If this is not possible, explain why it is not.

Mean = 6, median = 4, mode = 4

14. *Think About It* Construct a collection of numbers that has the following properties. If this is not possible, explain why it is not.

Mean = 6, median = 6, mode = 4

15. *Test Scores* A professor records the following scores for a 100-point exam.

99, 64, 80, 77, 59, 72, 87, 79, 92, 88, 90, 42, 20, 89, 42, 100, 98, 84, 78, 91

Which measure of central tendency best describes these test scores?

16. *Shoe Sales* A salesman sold eight pairs of a certain style of men's shoes. The sizes of the eight pairs were as follows: $10\frac{1}{2}$, 8, 12, $10\frac{1}{2}$, 10, $9\frac{1}{2}$, 11, and $10\frac{1}{2}$. Which measure (or measures) of central tendency best describes the typical shoe size for this data?

In Exercises 17–24, find the mean ($\bar{x}$), variance (v), and standard deviation (σ) of the numbers.

17. 4, 10, 8, 2

18. 3, 15, 6, 9, 2

19. 0, 1, 1, 2, 2, 2, 3, 3, 4

20. 2, 2, 2, 2, 2, 2

21. 1, 2, 3, 4, 5, 6, 7

22. 1, 1, 1, 5, 5, 5

23. 49, 62, 40, 29, 32, 70

24. 1.5, 0.4, 2.1, 0.7, 0.8

In Exercises 25–30, use the alternative formula to find the standard deviation of the numbers.

25. 2, 4, 6, 6, 13, 5

26. 10, 25, 50, 26, 15, 33, 29, 4

27. 246, 336, 473, 167, 219, 359

28. 6.0, 9.1, 4.4, 8.7, 10.4

29. 8.1, 6.9, 3.7, 4.2, 6.1

30. 9.0, 7.5, 3.3, 7.4, 6.0

In Exercises 31 and 32, line plots of sets of data are given. Determine the mean and standard deviation of each set.

31. (a)

(b)

(c)

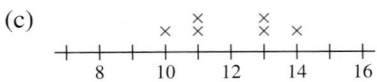

(d)

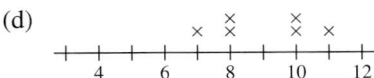

32. (a)

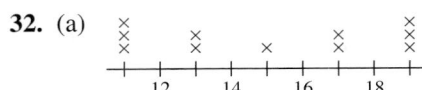

(b)

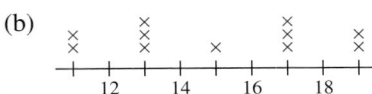

(c)

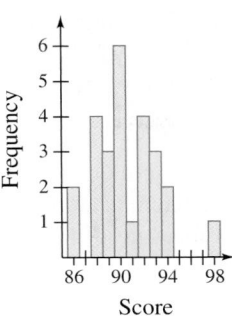

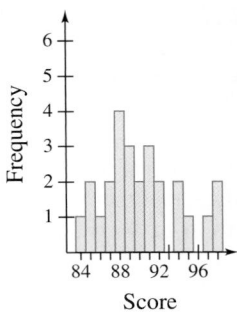

FIGURE FOR 37

In Exercises 38–41, sketch a box-and-whisker plot for the data without the aid of a graphing utility.

38. 23, 15, 14, 23, 13, 14, 13, 20, 12

39. 11, 10, 11, 14, 17, 16, 14, 11, 8, 14, 20

40. 46, 48, 48, 50, 52, 47, 51, 47, 49, 53

41. 25, 20, 22, 28, 24, 28, 25, 19, 27, 29, 28, 21

In Exercises 42–45, use a graphing utility to create a box-and-whisker plot for the data.

42. 19, 12, 14, 9, 14, 15, 17, 13, 19, 11, 10, 19

43. 9, 5, 5, 5, 6, 5, 4, 12, 7, 10, 7, 11, 8, 9, 9

44. 20.1, 43.4, 34.9, 23.9, 33.5, 24.1, 22.5, 42.4, 25.7, 17.4, 23.8, 33.3, 17.3, 36.4, 21.8

45. 78.4, 76.3, 107.5, 78.5, 93.2, 90.3, 77.8, 37.1, 97.1, 75.5, 58.8, 65.6

46. *Product Lifetime* A company has redesigned a product in an attempt to increase the lifetime of the product. The two sets of data list the lifetimes (in months) of 20 units with the original design and 20 units with the new design. Create a box-and-whisker plot for each set of data, and then comment on the differences between the plots.

Original Design

15.1	78.3	56.3	68.9	30.6
27.2	12.5	42.7	72.7	20.2
53.0	13.5	11.0	18.4	85.2
10.8	38.3	85.1	10.0	12.6

New Design

55.8	71.5	25.6	19.0	23.1
37.2	60.0	35.3	18.9	80.5
46.7	31.1	67.9	23.5	99.5
54.0	23.2	45.5	24.8	87.8

33. *Reasoning* Without calculating the standard deviation, explain why the set {4, 4, 20, 20} has a standard deviation of 8.

34. *Reasoning* If the standard deviation of a set of numbers is 0, what does this imply about the set?

35. *Test Scores* An instructor adds five points to each student's exam score. Will this change the mean or standard deviation of the exam scores? Explain.

36. *Price of Gold* The following data represents the average prices of gold (in dollars per fine ounce) for the years 1978 to 1997. Use a computer or calculator to find the mean, variance, and standard deviation of the data. What percent of the data lies within two standard deviations of the mean? (Source: U.S. Bureau of Mines)

194,	308,	613,	460,	376,
424,	361,	318,	368,	448,
438,	383,	385,	363,	345,
361,	385,	386,	389,	333

37. *Think About It* The histograms represent the test scores of two classes of a college course in mathematics. Which histogram has the smaller standard deviation?

Appendix B.3 Least Squares Regression

In many of the examples and exercises in this text, you have been asked to use the regression capabilities of a graphing utility to find mathematical models for sets of data. Another way to find a mathematical model for a set of data is to use the **method of least squares.** As a measure of how well a model fits a set of data points

$$\{(x_1, y_1), (x_2, y_2), (x_3, y_3), \ldots, (x_n, y_n)\}$$

you can add the squares of the differences between the actual y-values and the values given by the model to obtain the **sum of the squared differences.** For instance, the table shows the heights x (in feet) and the diameters y (in inches) of eight trees. The table also shows the values of a linear model $y^* = 0.69x - 40$ for each x-value. The sum of squared differences for the model is 53.3.

x	70	72	75	76	85	78	77	80
y	8.3	10.5	11.0	11.4	12.9	14.0	16.3	18.0
y^*	8.3	9.68	11.75	12.44	18.65	13.82	13.13	15.2

The model that has the least sum of squared differences is the **least squares regression line** for the data. The least squares regression line for the data in the table is $y \approx 0.43x - 20.3$. The sum of squared differences is 43.32.

To find the least squares regression line $y = ax + b$ for the points $\{(x_1, y_1),$ $(x_2, y_2), (x_3, y_3), \ldots, (x_n, y_n)\}$ algebraically, you need to solve the following system for a and b.

$$\begin{cases} nb + \left(\sum_{i=1}^{n} x_i \right) a = \sum_{i=1}^{n} y_i \\ \left(\sum_{i=1}^{n} x_i \right) b + \left(\sum_{i=1}^{n} x_i^2 \right) a = \sum_{i=1}^{n} x_i y_i \end{cases}$$

In the system,

$$\sum_{i=1}^{n} x_i = x_1 + x_2 + \cdots + x_n$$

$$\sum_{i=1}^{n} y_i = y_1 + y_2 + \cdots + y_n$$

$$\sum_{i=1}^{n} x_i^2 = x_1^2 + x_2^2 + \cdots + x_n^2$$

$$\sum_{i=1}^{n} x_i y_i = x_1 y_1 + x_2 y_2 + \cdots + x_n y_n.$$

EXAMPLE 1   Finding a Least Squares Regression Line

Find the least squares regression line for the points $(-3, 0)$, $(-1, 1)$, $(0, 2)$, and $(2, 3)$.

Solution

Begin by constructing a table like that shown below.

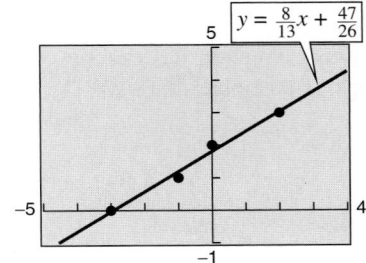

x	y	xy	x^2
-3	0	0	9
-1	1	-1	1
0	2	0	0
2	3	6	4
$\sum_{i=1}^{n} x_i = -2$	$\sum_{i=1}^{n} y_i = 6$	$\sum_{i=1}^{n} x_i y_i = 5$	$\sum_{i=1}^{n} x_i^2 = 14$

Figure B.7

Applying the system for the least squares regression line with $n = 4$ produces

$$\begin{cases} nb + \left(\sum_{i=1}^{n} x_i\right) a = \sum_{i=1}^{n} y_i \\ \left(\sum_{i=1}^{n} x_i\right) b + \left(\sum_{i=1}^{n} x_i^2\right) a = \sum_{i=1}^{n} x_i y_i \end{cases} \implies \begin{cases} 4b - 2a = 6 \\ -2b + 14a = 5 \end{cases}.$$

Solving this system of equations produces $a = \frac{8}{13}$ and $b = \frac{47}{26}$. So, the least squares regression line is $y = \frac{8}{13}x + \frac{47}{26}$, as shown in Figure B.7.

The least squares regression parabola $y = ax^2 + bx + c$ for the points

$$\{(x_1, y_1), (x_2, y_2), (x_3, y_3), \ldots, (x_n, y_n)\}$$

is obtained in a similar manner by solving the following system of three equations in three unknowns for a, b, and c.

$$\begin{cases} nc + \left(\sum_{i=1}^{n} x_i\right) b + \left(\sum_{i=1}^{n} x_i^2\right) a = \sum_{i=1}^{n} y_i \\ \left(\sum_{i=1}^{n} x_i\right) c + \left(\sum_{i=1}^{n} x_i^2\right) b + \left(\sum_{i=1}^{n} x_i^3\right) a = \sum_{i=1}^{n} x_i y_i \\ \left(\sum_{i=1}^{n} x_i^2\right) c + \left(\sum_{i=1}^{n} x_i^3\right) b + \left(\sum_{i=1}^{n} x_i^4\right) a = \sum_{i=1}^{n} x_i^2 y_i \end{cases}$$

Fortunately, graphing utilities have built-in least squares regression capabilities.

Appendix C Solving Linear Equations and Inequalities

Linear Equations

A *linear equation* in one variable x is an equation that can be written in the standard form $ax + b = 0$, where a and b are real numbers with $a \neq 0$.

A linear equation has exactly one solution. To see this, consider the following steps. (Remember that $a \neq 0$.)

$$ax + b = 0 \qquad \text{Original equation}$$

$$ax = -b \qquad \text{Subtract } b \text{ from both sides.}$$

$$x = -\frac{b}{a} \qquad \text{Divide both sides by } a.$$

To solve a linear equation in x, isolate x on one side of the equation by a sequence of *equivalent* (and usually simpler) equations, each having the same solution(s) as the original equation. The operations that yield equivalent equations come from the Substitution Principle and the simplification techniques discussed in Chapter P.

Generating Equivalent Equations

An equation can be transformed into an *equivalent equation* by one or more of the following steps.

	Original Equation	Equivalent Equation
1. Remove symbols of grouping, combine like terms, or reduce fractions on one or both sides of the equation.	$2x - x = 4$	$x = 4$
2. Add (or subtract) the same quantity to (from) *each* side of the equation.	$x + 1 = 6$	$x = 5$
3. Multiply (or divide) *each* side of the equation by the same *nonzero* quantity.	$2x = 6$	$x = 3$
4. Interchange the two sides of the equation.	$2 = x$	$x = 2$

After solving an equation, you should check each solution in the original equation.

EXAMPLE 1   Solving a Linear Equation

a. $3x - 6 = 0$ Original equation

$\qquad 3x = 6$ Add 6 to each side.

$\qquad x = 2$ Divide each side by 3.

b. $4(2x + 3) = 6$ Original equation

$\qquad 8x + 12 = 6$ Distributive Property

$\qquad 8x = -6$ Subtract 12 from each side.

$\qquad x = -\frac{6}{8}$ Divide each side by 8.

$\qquad x = -\frac{3}{4}$ Simplify.

Linear Inequalities

Solving a linear inequality in one variable is much like solving a linear equation in one variable. To solve the inequality, you isolate the variable on one side using transformations that produce *equivalent inequalities*, which have the same solution(s).

Generating Equivalent Inequalities

An inequality can be transformed into an *equivalent inequality* by one or more of the following steps.

	Original Inequality	Equivalent Inequality
1. Remove symbols of grouping, combine like terms, or reduce fractions on one or both sides of the inequality.	$4x + x \geq 2$	$5x \geq 2$
2. Add (or subtract) the same number to (from) *each* side of the inequality.	$x - 3 < 5$	$x < 8$
3. Multiply (or divide) each side of the inequality by the same *positive* number.	$\frac{1}{2}x > 3$	$x > 6$
4. Multiply (or divide) each side of the inequality by the same *negative* number and *reverse* the inequality symbol.	$-2x \leq 6$	$x \geq -3$

EXAMPLE 2   Solving Linear Inequalities

a. $x + 5 \geq 3$ Original inequality

$x + 5 - 5 \geq 3 - 5$ Subtract 5 from each side.

$x \geq -2$ Simplify.

The solution is all real numbers greater than or equal to -2. Check several numbers that are greater than or equal to -2 in the original inequality.

b. $\dfrac{a}{3} \leq 12$ Original inequality

$3 \cdot \dfrac{a}{3} \leq 3 \cdot 12$ Multiply each side by 3.

$a \leq 36$ Simplify.

The solution is all real numbers less than or equal to 36. Check several numbers that are less than or equal to 36 in the original inequality.

c. $-4.2m > 6.3$ Original inequality

$\dfrac{-4.2m}{-4.2} < \dfrac{6.3}{-4.2}$ Divide each side by -4.2 and reverse inequality symbol.

$m < -1.5$ Simplify.

The solution is all real numbers less than -1.5. Check several numbers that are less than -1.5 in the original inequality.

C   E x e r c i s e s

In Exercises 1–18, solve the equation and check your solution.

1. $x + 4 = 7$

2. $x + 6 = 11$

3. $x - 2 = 5$

4. $x - 5 = 1$

5. $3x = 12$

6. $2x = 6$

7. $\dfrac{x}{5} = 4$

8. $\dfrac{x}{4} = 5$

9. $8x + 7 = 39$

10. $12x - 5 = 43$

11. $24 - 7x = 3$

12. $13 + 6x = 61$

13. $15x - 4 = 16$

14. $3x - 8 = 2$

15. $3x - 2(x + 5) = 10$

16. $4x + 2(7 - x) = 5$

17. $2x + 3 = 2x - 2$

18. $8(x - 2) = 4(2x - 4)$

In Exercises 19–36, solve the inequality and check your solution.

19. $x + 5 < 7$

20. $4 + x > -12$

21. $-x - 8 > -17$

22. $-3 + x < 19$

23. $6 + x \leq -8$

24. $x - 10 \geq -6$

25. $\frac{4}{5}x > 8$

26. $\frac{2}{3}x < -4$

27. $-\frac{3}{4}x > -3$

28. $-\frac{1}{6}x < -2$

29. $4x < 12$

30. $2x > -3$

31. $-11x \leq -22$

32. $-7x \geq 21$

33. $x - 3(x + 1) \geq 7$

34. $2(4x - 5) - 3x \leq -15$

35. $7x - 12 < 4x + 6$

36. $11 - 6x \leq 2x + 7$

Looking for solutions to your math problems? These study aids offer more than just the answers!

Two technology options offer complete solutions to every odd-numbered problem, help you practice and assess your skills, and provide problem-solving tools.

Interactive College Algebra: A Graphing Approach 2.0 CD-ROM

- Enhance your understanding with step-by-step solutions to all odd-numbered exercises in the text.
- Assess your skill levels with diagnostic pre- and post-tests for each chapter.
- Strengthen your skills with tutorial exercises accompanied by examples and diagnostics.
- Visualize and graph with a built-in Meridian Graphing Calculator Emulator.
- Enjoy learning with additional interactive features.

Internet College Algebra: A Graphing Approach 1.0

A subscription to this web site offers all of the CD-ROM features listed above, plus:
- Chat rooms for peer support
- Bulletin boards for sharing ideas and insights on each chapter

To purchase Interactive College Algebra: A Graphing Approach 2.0 CD-ROM:

- Visit Houghton Mifflin's College Store at **college.hmco.com** or contact your campus bookstore.

To subscribe online to Internet College Algebra: A Graphing Approach 1.0:

- Visit Houghton Mifflin's College Division web site at **college.hmco.com** and select mathematics.

Use these print supplements for added practice and convenient support.

Study and Solutions Guide to accompany

College Algebra: A Graphing Approach, 3rd Edition

- Work through step-by-step solutions for all odd-numbered exercises in the text.
- Test your skills by taking practice tests with accompanying solutions.
- Find useful study strategies designed to help you succeed.

Student Success Organizer

Ask your instructor about this new study aid.

- Use its practical format to guide you step-by-step through difficult concepts.
- Enhance your organizational skills for approaching problems and assignments.

To purchase these print supplements:

- Visit Houghton Mifflin's College Store at **college.hmco.com** or contact your campus bookstore.

Larson • Hostetler

Answers to Odd-Numbered Exercises and Tests

Chapter P

Section P.1   *(page 9)*

1. (a) 5, 1   (b) $-9, 5, 0, 1, -4, -1$

(c) $-9, -\frac{7}{2}, 5, \frac{2}{3}, 0, 1, -4, -1$ (d) $\sqrt{2}$

3. (a) 1, 20   (b) $-13, 1, -10, 20$

(c) $2.01, 0.666\ldots, -13, 1, -10, 20$

(d) $0.010110111\ldots$

5. (a) $\frac{6}{3}, 3$ (b) $\frac{6}{3}, -2, 3, -3$

(c) $-\frac{1}{3}, \frac{6}{3}, -7.5, -2, 3, -3$ (d) $-\pi, \frac{1}{2}\sqrt{2}$

7. 0.625   **9.** $0.\overline{123}$ **11.** $\frac{23}{5}$ **13.** $\frac{13}{2}$

15. $-\frac{183}{100}$ **17.** $-1 < 2.5$

19. $-4 > -8$ **21.** $\frac{3}{2} < 7$

23. $\frac{5}{6} > \frac{2}{3}$

25. (a) $x \le 5$ is the set of all real numbers less than or equal to 5.

(b)   (c) Unbounded

27. (a) $x < 0$ is the set of all negative real numbers.

(b)   (c) Unbounded

29. (a) $x \ge 4$ is the set of all real numbers greater than or equal to 4.

(b)   (c) Unbounded

31. (a) $-2 < x < 2$ is the set of all real numbers greater than -2 and less than 2.

(b)   (c) Bounded

33. (a) $-1 \le x < 0$ is the set of all negative real numbers greater than or equal to -1.

(b)   (c) Bounded

35. $\frac{127}{90}, \frac{584}{413}, \frac{7071}{5000}, \sqrt{2}, \frac{47}{33}$ **37.** $x < 0; (-\infty, 0)$

39. $y \ge 0; [0, \infty)$ **41.** $12 \le c \le 32; [12, 32]$

43. $W > 45; (45, \infty)$

45. The set of all real numbers greater than -6

47. 10   **49.** $\pi - 3 \approx 0.1416$ **51.** -1 **53.** -9

55. 1 for $x > -2$; undefined for $x = -2$; -1 for $x < -2$

57. $|-3| > -|-3|$ **59.** $-5 = -|5|$

61. $-|-2| = -|2|$ **63.** 4   **65.** 51

67. $\frac{5}{2}$ **69.** $\frac{128}{75}$

71. (a) $-A$ is negative.   (b) $B - A$ is negative.

73. $|x - 5| \le 3$ **75.** $|y - 0| \ge 6$ **77.** 11 miles

79. The temperature dropped 23°.

81. $|\$113{,}356 - \$112{,}700| = \$656 > \$500$

$0.05(\$112{,}700) = \$5635$

Because the actual expenses differ from the budget by more than \$500, there is failure to meet the "budget variance test."

83. $|\$37{,}335 - \$37{,}640| = \$305 < \$500$

$0.05(\$37{,}640) = \$1882$

Because the difference between the actual expenses and the budget is less than \$500 and less than 5% of the budgeted amount, there is compliance with the "budget variance test."

85. $y = \$92.5$ billion, $|y - x| = \$0.3$ billion

There was a surplus of \$0.3 billion.

87. $y = \$517.1$ billion, $|y - x| = \$73.8$ billion

There was a deficit of \$73.8 billion.

89. $y = \$1351.8$ billion, $|y - x| = \$163.9$ billion

There was a deficit of \$163.9 billion.

91. Terms: $7x, 4$; Coefficient: 7

93. Terms: $3x^2, -8x, -11$; Coefficients: $3, -8$

95. Terms: $4x^3, \frac{x}{2}, -5$; Coefficients: $4, \frac{1}{2}$

97. (a) -10 (b) -6 **99.** (a) 14   (b) 2

101. (a) Division by 0 is undefined.   (b) 0

103. Commutative Property of Addition

105. Multiplicative Inverse Property

107. Distributive Property

109. Multiplicative Identity Property

111. Associative and Commutative Properties of Multiplication

113. 0   **115.** Division by 0 is undefined.   **117.** $\frac{1}{2}$

119. $\dfrac{3}{8}$ **121.** $\dfrac{11x}{12}$ **123.** 48   **125.** -2.57

127. 1.56

129. (a)

n	1	0.5	0.01	0.0001	0.000001
$5/n$	5	10	500	50,000	5,000,000

(b) $5/n$ approaches ∞ as n approaches 0.

131. (a) No. If u is negative while v is positive, or vice versa, the expressions will not be equal.

(b) $|u + v| \le |u| + |v|$

133. Answers will vary. Natural numbers are the integers from 1 to infinity. A rational number can be expressed as the ratio of two integers; an irrational number cannot.

135. False. $\dfrac{3 + 5}{4} = 2 = \dfrac{3}{4} + \dfrac{5}{4}$, but $\dfrac{4}{3} + \dfrac{4}{5} = \dfrac{32}{15} \ne \dfrac{4}{3 + 5}$.

Section P. 2   *(page 21)*

1. (a) 48   (b) 81   **3.** (a) 729   (b) -9

5. (a) 243   (b) $-\frac{3}{4}$ **7.** (a) $\frac{5}{6}$ (b) 4   **9.** -1600

11. 2.125   **13.** $\frac{7}{16}$ **15.** -108 **17.** $\frac{3}{2}$

19. (a) $-125z^3$ (b) $5x^6$ **21.** (a) $\dfrac{7}{x}$ (b) $\dfrac{4}{3}(x + y)^2$

23. (a) 1   (b) $\dfrac{1}{4x^4}$ **25.** (a) $\dfrac{x^2}{y^2}$ (b) 1

27. $64^{1/3} = 4$ **29.** $\sqrt{196} = 14$ **31.** $(-216)^{1/3} = -6$

33. $8^{3/4} = 27$ **35.** 3   **37.** 3   **39.** -125 **41.** $\frac{1}{8}$

43. -4 **45.** -7.225 **47.** 21.316   **49.** 14.499

51. (a) $2\sqrt{2}$ (b) $2\sqrt[3]{3}$ **53.** (a) $3y^2\sqrt{6x}$ (b) $\dfrac{4a^2}{|b|}\sqrt{2}$

55. 625   **57.** $\dfrac{2}{x}$ **59.** $\dfrac{1}{x^3}, x > 0$

61. (a) $\dfrac{\sqrt{3}}{3}$ (b) $4\sqrt[3]{4}$

63. (a) $\dfrac{x(5 + \sqrt{3})}{11}$ (b) $3(\sqrt{6} - \sqrt{5})$ **65.** $\dfrac{2}{\sqrt{2}}$

67. $\dfrac{2}{3(\sqrt{5} - \sqrt{3})}$ **69.** (a) $\sqrt{3}$ (b) $\sqrt[3]{(x + 1)^2}$

71. (a) $2\sqrt[4]{2}$ (b) $\sqrt[8]{2x}$ **73.** (a) $34\sqrt{2}$ (b) $22\sqrt{2}$

75. (a) $13\sqrt{x + 1}$ (b) $18\sqrt{5x}$

77. $\sqrt{5} + \sqrt{3} > \sqrt{5 + 3}$ **79.** $5 > \sqrt{3^2 + 2^2}$

81. 5.73×10^7 **83.** 8.99×10^{-5} **85.** 604,800,000

87. 0.0000000000000000001602

89. (a) 954.448   (b) 3.077×10^{10}

91. (a) 67,082.039   (b) 39.791

93. (a) 50,000   (b) 200,000

95. When any positive integer is squared, the units digit is 0, 1, 4, 5, 6, or 9. Therefore, $\sqrt{5233}$ is not an integer.

97. $r = 0.280$ **99.** $t = 13.29$ seconds

101. $8\frac{1}{3}$ minutes   **103.** True. $x^{k+1}/x = x^k x/x = x^k$.

105. $1 = \dfrac{a^n}{a^n} = a^{n-n} = a^0$

Section P.3   *(page 32)*

1. d   **3.** b   **5.** f

7. Answers will vary, but first term is $-2x^3$.

9. Answers will vary, but first term has form $-ax^4, a > 0$.

11. Degree: 2; Leading coefficient: 5

13. Degree: 7; Leading coefficient: 1

15. Degree: 5; Leading coefficient: -2

17. Polynomial: $-2x^3 + 7x + 10$

19. Not a polynomial because of the operation of division.

21. Polynomial: $-x^4 + x^3 + x^2 - x$

23. $-2x - 10$ **25.** $3x^3 - 2x + 2$

27. $8.1x^3 + 29.7x^2 + 11$ **29.** $3x^3 - 6x^2 + 3x$

31. $-15z^2 + 5z$ **33.** $-4x^4 + 4x$ **35.** $7.5x^3 + 15x$

37. $-\frac{1}{4}x^2 - 6x$ **39.** $x^2 + 7x + 12$

41. $6x^2 - 7x - 5$ **43.** $4x^2 - 20xy + 25y^2$

45. $x^2 - 100$ **47.** $x^2 - 4y^2$ **49.** $m^2 - 6m + 9 - n^2$

51. $x^2 + 2xy + y^2 - 6y - 6x + 9$ **53.** $4r^4 - 25$

55. $x^3 + 3x^2 + 3x + 1$ **57.** $8x^3 - 12x^2y + 6xy^2 - y^3$

59. $\frac{1}{4}x^2 - 5x + 25$ **61.** $\frac{1}{16}x^2 - 9$

63. $5.76x^2 + 14.4x + 9$ **65.** $2.25x^2 - 16$

67. $2x^2 + 2x$ **69.** $u^4 - 16$ **71.** $3(x + 2)$

73. $2x(x^2 - 3)$ **75.** $(x - 5)(3x + 8)$

77. $(x - 6)(x + 6)$ **79.** $(4y - 3)(4y + 3)$

81. $\left(2x - \frac{1}{3}\right)\left(2x + \frac{1}{3}\right)$

83. $[(x - 1) - 2][(x - 1) + 2] = (x - 3)(x + 1)$

85. $(x - 2)^2$ **87.** $\left(x + \frac{1}{2}\right)^2$ **89.** $(2t + 1)^2$

91. $\left(3t + \frac{1}{4}\right)^2$ **93.** $(x - 1)(x + 2)$

95. $(s - 2)(s - 3)$ **97.** $-(y - 4)(y + 5)$

99. $(3x - 2)(x - 1)$ **101.** $(2x + 1)(x - 1)$

103. $(5x + 1)(x + 5)$ **105.** $-(5u - 2)(u + 3)$

107. $(x - 2)(x^2 + 2x + 4)$ **109.** $(y + 4)(y^2 - 4y + 16)$

111. $\left(x - \frac{2}{3}\right)\left(x^2 + \frac{2}{3}x + \frac{4}{9}\right)$ **113.** $(2x - 1)(4x^2 + 2x + 1)$

115. $\left(\frac{1}{2}x + 1\right)\left(\frac{1}{4}x^2 - \frac{1}{2}x + 1\right)$ **117.** $(x - 1)(x^2 + 2)$

119. $(2x - 1)(x^2 - 3)$ **121.** $x(x - 3)(x + 3)$

123. $x^2(x - 4)$ **125.** $(x - 1)^2$ **127.** $(2x - 1)^2$

129. $-2x(x - 2)(x + 1)$ **131.** $(9x + 1)(x + 1)$

133. $\frac{1}{96}(3x + 2)(4x - 3)$ **135.** $(3x + 1)(x^2 + 5)$

137. $x(x^2 + 1)(x - 4)$ **139.** $-z(z + 10)$

141. $(x + 1)^2(x - 1)^2$ **143.** $2(t - 2)(t^2 + 2t + 4)$

145. $(2x - 1)(6x - 1)$ **147.** $-(x + 1)(x - 3)(x + 9)$

149. $7(x^2 + 1)(3x^2 - 1)$ **151.** $-2x(x - 5)^3(x + 5)$

153. $-(x^2 + 1)^4\left(\dfrac{x^2}{2} + 1\right)$

155. (a) $500r^2 + 1000r + 500$

(b)

r	$2\frac{1}{2}\%$	3%	4%
$500(1 + r)^2$	525.31	530.45	540.80

r	$4\frac{1}{2}\%$	5%
$500(1 + r)^2$	546.01	551.25

(c) Amount increases with increasing r.

157. $V = x(15 - 2x)\left(\dfrac{45 - 3x}{2}\right)$

$= \dfrac{3}{2}x(x - 15)(2x - 15)$

x (cm)	3	5	7
V (cu cm)	486	375	84

159. (a) $T = 0.14x^2 - 3.33x + 58.40$

(b)

x (mi/hr)	30	40	55
T (ft)	84.50	149.20	298.75

(c) Stopping distance increases at an accelerating rate as speed increases.

161. $(x + 1)(x + 4) = x(x + 4) + 1(x + 4)$

Distributive Property

163. b **165.** a

167.

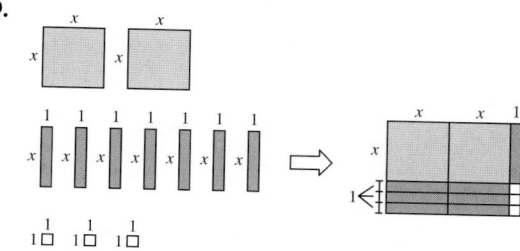

169.

171. $4\pi(r + 1)$ **173.** $4(6 - x)(6 + x)$

175. $-14, 14, -2, 2$ **177.** $-51, 51, -15, 15, -27, 27$

179. $2, -3$ (Answers will vary.)

181. $3, -8$ (Answers will vary.)

183. $9x^2 - 9x - 54 = 9(x^2 - x - 6)$

$= 9(x + 2)(x - 3)$

185. $kx(Q - x)$

187. False. $(x^2 - 1)(x^2 + 1)$ becomes a fourth-degree polynomial.

189. False. Counterexample:

$x^2 + 2^2 \ne (x + 2)^2$ if $x = 3$.

191. n

193. (a) Yes. The sum of two polynomials will have the same degree as the polynomial of greater degree unless the polynomials have equal degree and their leading coefficients are opposites.

(b) No. Same reasoning as in (a).

(c) No. Same reasoning as in (a).

195. A polynomial is in factored form if it is written as a product, not as a sum.

Section P.4 (page 44)

1. All real numbers **3.** All nonnegative real numbers

5. All real numbers x such that $x \ne 2$

7. All real numbers x such that $x \ge -1$

9. $3x, \; x \ne 0$ **11.** $\dfrac{3x}{2}, \; x \ne 0$ **13.** $\dfrac{3y}{y + 1}, \; x \ne 0$

15. $-\dfrac{4y}{5}, \; y \ne \dfrac{1}{2}$ **17.** $-\dfrac{1}{2}, \; x \ne 5$

19. $y - 4, \; y \ne -4$ **21.** $\dfrac{x(x + 3)}{x - 2}, \; x \ne -2$

23. $\dfrac{y - 4}{y + 6}, \; y \ne 3$ **25.** $-(x^2 + 1), \; x \ne 2$ **27.** $z - 2$

29.

x	0	1	2	3	4	5	6
$\dfrac{x^2 - 2x - 3}{x - 3}$	1	2	3	Undef.	5	6	7
$x + 1$	1	2	3	4	5	6	7

The expressions are equivalent except at $x = 3$.

31. Only common factors of the numerator and denominator can be canceled. In this case, factors of terms were incorrectly canceled.

33. $\dfrac{\pi}{4}$ **35.** $\dfrac{1}{5(x - 2)}$, $x \neq 1$ **37.** $\dfrac{r + 1}{r}$, $r \neq 1$

39. $\dfrac{t - 3}{(t + 3)(t - 2)}$, $t \neq -2$ **41.** $\dfrac{3}{2}$, $x \neq -y$

43. $\dfrac{x + 5}{x - 1}$ **45.** $\dfrac{6x + 13}{x + 3}$ **47.** $-\dfrac{2}{x - 2}$

49. $-\dfrac{x^2 + 3}{(x + 1)(x - 2)(x - 3)}$ **51.** $\dfrac{2 - x}{x^2 + 1}$, $x \neq 0$

53. $x^{-2}(x^7 - 2)$ **55.** $x^{-1/2}(3x^2 - 2)$ **57.** $-\dfrac{1}{(x^2 + 1)^5}$

59. $\dfrac{2x^3 - 2x^2 - 5}{(x - 1)^{1/2}}$ **61.** $\dfrac{1}{2}$, $x \neq 2$

63. $x(x + 1)$, $x \neq -1, 0$ **65.** $-\dfrac{2x + h}{x^2(x + h)^2}$, $h \neq 0$

67. $\dfrac{2x - 1}{2x}$, $x > 0$ **69.** $\dfrac{3x - 1}{3}$, $x \neq 0$

71. $\dfrac{1}{\sqrt{x + 2} + \sqrt{x}}$

73. (a) $\dfrac{1}{16}$ minute (b) $\dfrac{x}{16}$ minute(s) (c) $\dfrac{60}{16} = \dfrac{15}{4}$ minutes

75. $\dfrac{11x}{30}$ **77.** $\dfrac{x}{2(2x + 1)}$

79. (a) $r = 9.09\%$ (b) $\dfrac{288(MN - P)}{N(MN + 12P)}$; 9.09%

81. (a)

t	0	2	4	6	8	10
T	75	55.9	48.3	45	43.3	42.3

t	12	14	16	18	20	22
T	41.7	41.3	41.1	40.9	40.7	40.6

(b) 40

83. False. The domain of the left-hand side is $x^n \neq 1$.

85. False. Example: LCD of $1/x$ and $1/x^2$ is x^2, not x^3.

87. No. $\dfrac{ax - b}{b - ax}$ is undefined for values of a, b, and x such that $b = ax$.

Section P.5 (page 54)

1.

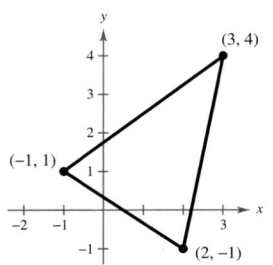

3.

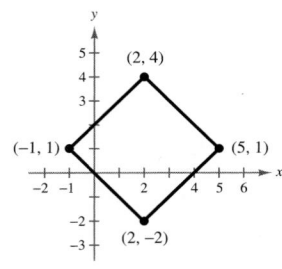

5. A: $(2, 6)$; B: $(-6, -2)$; C: $(4, -4)$; D: $(-3, 2)$

7. A: $(0, 5)$; B: $(-3, -6)$; C: $(1, -4.5)$; D: $(-4, 2)$

9. $(-3, 4)$ **11.** $(-5, -5)$ **13.** Quadrant IV

15. Quadrant II **17.** Quadrant III or IV

19. Quadrant III **21.** Quadrants I and III

23. $(0, 1), (4, 2), (1, 4)$ **25.** 8 **27.** 5 **29.** 13

31. (a)

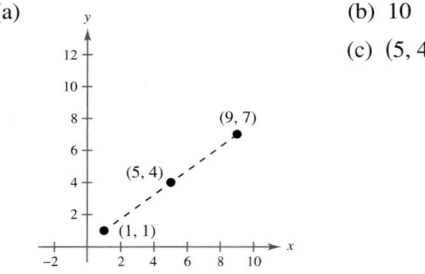

(b) 10

(c) $(5, 4)$

33. (a)

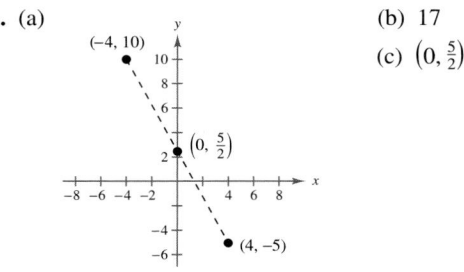

(b) 17

(c) $\left(0, \dfrac{5}{2}\right)$

35. (a)
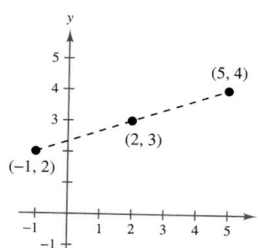
(b) $2\sqrt{10}$
(c) $(2, 3)$

37. (a)
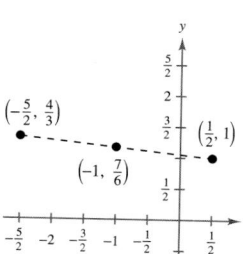
(b) $\dfrac{\sqrt{82}}{3}$
(c) $\left(-1, \dfrac{7}{6}\right)$

39. (a)
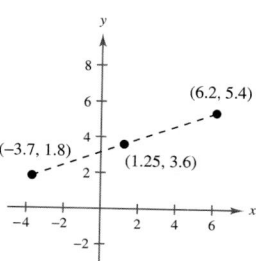
(b) $\sqrt{110.97}$
(c) $(1.25, 3.6)$

41. (a)
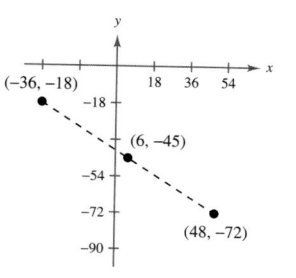
(b) $6\sqrt{277}$
(c) $(6, -45)$

43. (a) $4, 3, 5$ (b) $4^2 + 3^2 = 5^2$

45. (a) $10, 3, \sqrt{109}$ (b) $10^2 + 3^2 = \left(\sqrt{109}\right)^2$

47. \$630,000   **49.** $\left(\sqrt{5}\right)^2 + \left(\sqrt{45}\right)^2 = \left(\sqrt{50}\right)^2$

51. Opposite sides have equal lengths of $2\sqrt{5}$ and $\sqrt{85}$.

53. $(2x_m - x_1, 2y_m - y_1)$;
  (a) $(7, 0)$ (b) $(9, -3)$

55. $x^2 + y^2 = 9$ **57.** $(x - 2)^2 + (y + 1)^2 = 16$

59. $(x + 1)^2 + (y - 2)^2 = 5$

61. $(x - 3)^2 + (y - 4)^2 = 25$

63.
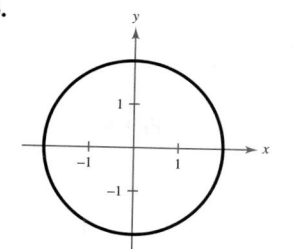
Center: $(0, 0)$
Radius $= 2$

65.
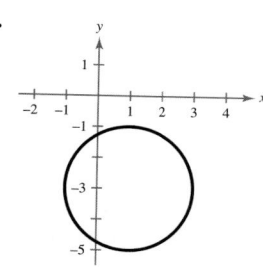
Center: $(1, -3)$
Radius $= 2$

67.
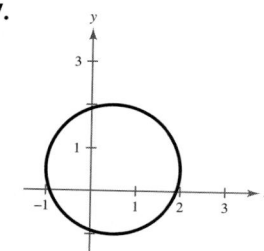
Center: $\left(\dfrac{1}{2}, \dfrac{1}{2}\right)$
Radius $= \dfrac{3}{2}$

69.
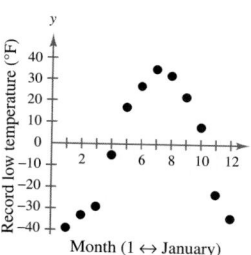

71. \$1.66; 1996   **73.** 167% **75.** 65

77. Answers will vary; for example,
  corn $\approx 14\%$, soybeans $\approx 25\%$, wheat $\approx 29\%$.

79.
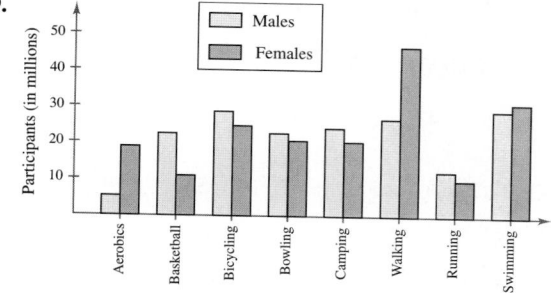

81. (a) $\approx 52\%$

(b) No. The trend limits the amount of funds available for capital improvements in industry. (Answers will vary.)

83. (a) During 1993

(b)

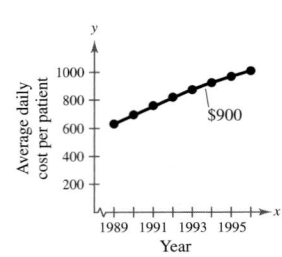

85. ≈ 180.28 kilometers

87. (a) Answers will vary; from 1991 on, the data are nearly in a straight line. Estimate: 7 new members in 2001.

(b) Answers will vary; 1986 and 1987 were the first two years the Hall of Fame was open.

89. $1245.05 million

91. True. The lengths of the sides from $(-8, 4)$ to $(2, 11)$ and from $(2, 11)$ to $(-5, 1)$ are both $\sqrt{149}$.

93. $0; 0$

Review Exercises *(page 60)*

1. (a) 11   (b) $11, -14$

(c) $11, -14, -\frac{8}{9}, \frac{5}{2}, 0.4$ (d) $\sqrt{6}$

3. $0.8\overline{3} < 0.875$

5. The set consists of all real numbers less than or equal to 7.

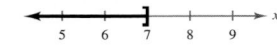

7. 122   **9.** $|x - 7| \geq 4$ **11.** $|y + 30| < 5$

13. (a) -13 (b) 27   **15.** (a) -18 (b) -12

17. Associative Property of Addition

19. Commutative Property of Multiplication   **21.** $\frac{14}{9}$

23. $\frac{1}{24}$ **25.** $\frac{47x}{60}$ **27.** (a) $-8z^3$ (b) $3a^3b^2$

29. (a) $\frac{3u^5}{v^4}$ (b) m^{-2} **31.** 3.3674×10^{10}

33. 483,300,000   **35.** 78   **37.** $2x^2$ **39.** $\frac{3}{4}$

41. $\frac{x}{3}\sqrt[3]{2}$ **43.** $2\sqrt{2}$ **45.** $3\sqrt{3x}$ **47.** $\sqrt{2x}(2x + 1)$

49. $192\sqrt{2}$ in.^{2} **51.** $\frac{\sqrt{x} + 1}{x - 1}$ **53.** $\frac{-3}{\sqrt{2} + \sqrt{11}}$

55. $\sqrt[4]{16}$ **57.** $\frac{1}{16}$ **59.** $(x - 1)^{1/12}$

61. $-2x^4 + x^3 + x^2 - x - 10$ **63.** $-2y^2 + 11y - 8$

65. $-3x^4 - 4x^3 - 9x^2 - x - 13$

67. $2x^5 + 3x^4 - x^3 - 9x^2 - 15x$

69. $x^2 + 2x - 1 - \frac{2}{x}$ **71.** $49x^2 - 16$

73. $8x^3 - 12x^2 + 6x - 1$ **75.** $x^2 - 2xy + y^2 - 36$

77. $\frac{3}{2}x(x - 3)$ **79.** $2(5x - 1)$ **81.** $(x - 3)(x + 4)$

83. $-3x(2x^3 + x^2 - 4)$

85. $R = x(1600 - 0.50x); p = 1600 - 0.50x$

87. $\left(3x - \frac{1}{5}\right)\left(3x + \frac{1}{5}\right)$ **89.** $(4x - 3)(16x^2 + 12x + 9)$

91. $(x - 7)(x - 2)$ **93.** $(3x + 2)(x + 4)$

95. $(x - 6)(x - 1)(x + 1)$ **97.** $(2x + 5)(x^2 - 7)$

99. All positive real numbers

101. All real numbers x such that $x \geq -12, x \neq 0$

103. $\frac{6y}{y + 2}, x \neq 0$ **105.** $\frac{x - 3}{8}, x \neq 6$

107. $\frac{x - 1}{x - 3}, x \neq -1, \frac{1}{2}$ **109.** $\frac{2(x + 3)}{x(x - 1)}, x \neq -3, \frac{3}{2}$

111. $\frac{2x^3 - 4x^2 - 15x + 5}{(x - 4)(x + 2)}$ **113.** $\frac{3x}{(x - 1)(x^2 + x + 1)}$

115. $\frac{y - x}{x + y}, x \neq 0, y \neq 0, x \neq y$

117.   **119.**

Quadrant III   Quadrant III

121. Quadrant I or III

123.

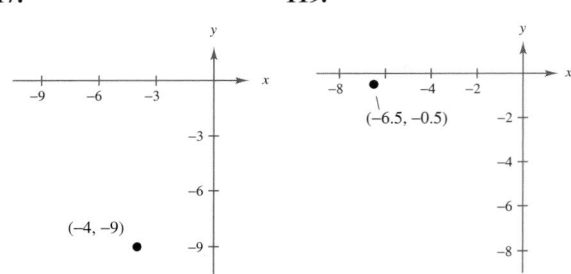

125.

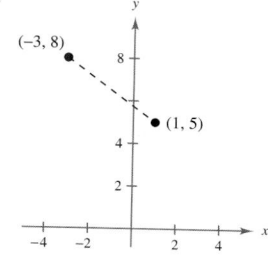

Distance: 5

127.

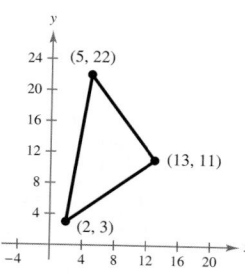

$$2\left(\sqrt{185}\right)^2 = \left(\sqrt{370}\right)^2$$

129.

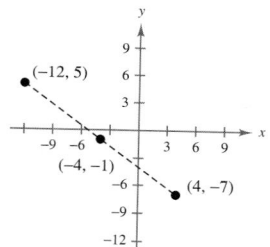

Midpoint: $(-4, -1)$

131. (a) \$352.35 million

(b) The estimate is \$2.95 million over the actual revenue, which is less than a 1% error.

133. $(x - 3)^2 + (y - 2)^2 = 65$

135. False. $(a + b)^2 = a^2 + 2ab + b^2$

137. The numerator and denominator are not equivalent expressions. Factor -1 from numerator: $\dfrac{-1(1 - x)}{(1 - x)} = -1.$

139. You must raise 2 to the fourth power as well. $(2x)^4 = 2^4x^4 = 16x^4$

141. Operations under the radical should be performed first. $\sqrt{3^2 + 4^2} = \sqrt{9 + 16} = \sqrt{25} = 5$

143. The sum of the square roots of two terms is not equivalent to the square root of the sum of the terms.

Chapter Test   *(page 65)*

1. $-\dfrac{10}{3} > -|-4|$ **2.** 56   **3.** (a) -18 (b) $\dfrac{4}{27}$

4. (a) $-\dfrac{27}{125}$ (b) $\dfrac{8}{729}$ **5.** (a) 25   (b) 6

6. (a) 1.8×10^5 (b) 2.7×10^{13}

7. (a) $12z^8$ (b) $(u - 2)^{-7}$ (c) $\dfrac{3x^2}{y^2}$

8. (a) $15z\sqrt{2z}$ (b) $-10\sqrt{y}$ (c) $\dfrac{2}{v}\sqrt[3]{\dfrac{2}{v^2}}$

9. $2x^2 - 3x - 5$ **10.** $x^2 - 5$ **11.** $8,\ x \neq 3$

12. $\dfrac{x - 1}{2x},\ x \neq \pm 1$ **13.** $x^2(2x + 1)(x - 2)$

14. $(x - 2)(x + 2)^2$ **15.** $(2x - 3)(4x^2 + 6x + 9)$

16. (a) $4\sqrt[3]{4}$ (b) $-3\left(1 + \sqrt{3}\right)$ **17.** $\dfrac{5}{6}\sqrt{3}x^2$

18.

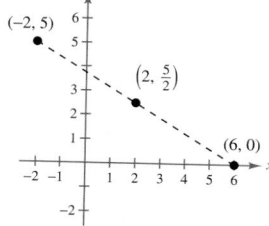

Midpoint: $\left(2, \dfrac{5}{2}\right)$;

Distance: $\sqrt{89}$

19. $l(45 - l)$; Width $= 45 - l$

20.

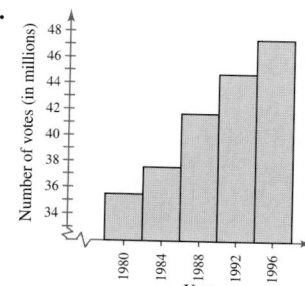

Chapter 1

Section 1.1   *(page 75)*

1. (a) Yes   (b) Yes   **3.** (a) No   (b) Yes

5. (a) No   (b) Yes   **7.** (a) Yes   (b) Yes

9.

x	-1	0	1	$\dfrac{3}{2}$	2
y	5	3	1	0	-1

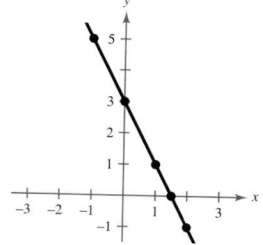

11.

x	-1	0	1	2	3
y	3	0	-1	0	3

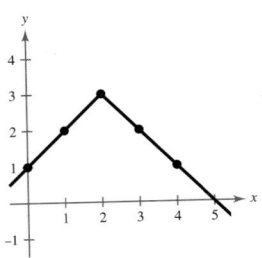

13.

x	0	1	2	3	4
y	1	2	3	2	1

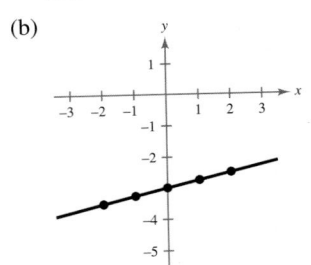

15. (a)

x	-2	-1	0	1	2
y	$-\frac{7}{2}$	$-\frac{13}{4}$	-3	$-\frac{11}{4}$	$-\frac{5}{2}$

(b)

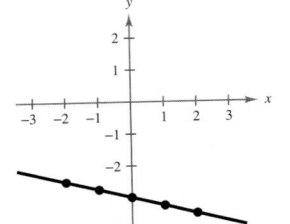

(c)

x	-2	-1	0	1	2
y	$-\frac{5}{2}$	$-\frac{11}{4}$	-3	$-\frac{13}{4}$	$-\frac{7}{2}$

The lines have opposite slopes but the same y-intercept.

17. (d) **19.** (f) **21.** (a)

23.

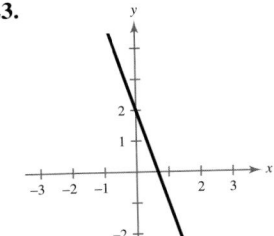

25.

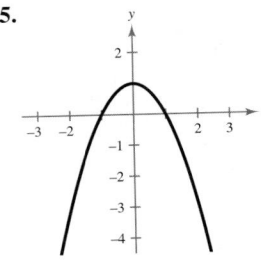

27.

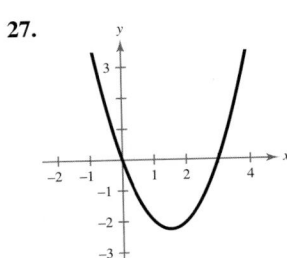

29.

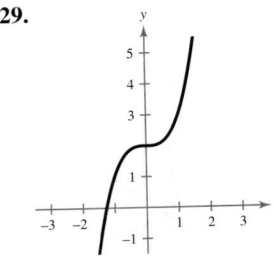

31.

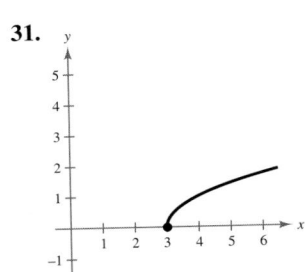

33.

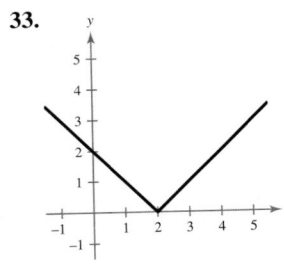

35.

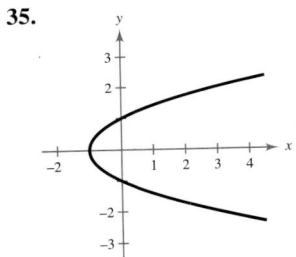

37.

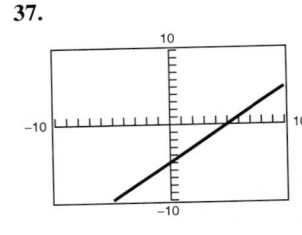

Intercepts: $(5, 0), (0, -5)$

39.

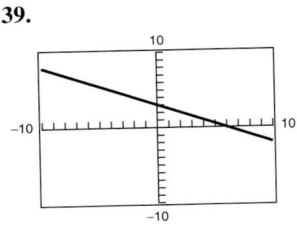

Intercepts: $(6, 0), (0, 3)$

41.

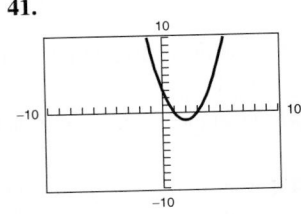

Intercepts: $(3, 0), (1, 0), (0, 3)$

43.

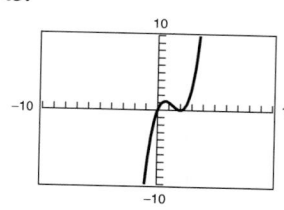

Intercepts: $(0, 0)$, $(2, 0)$

45.

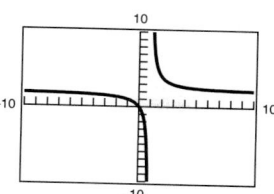

Intercept: $(0, 0)$

47.

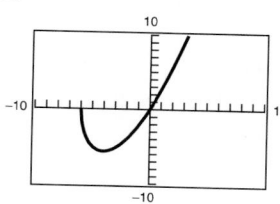

Intercepts: $(-6, 0)$, $(0, 0)$

49.

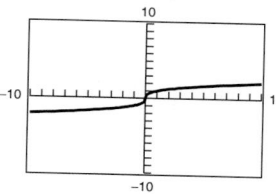

Intercept: $(0, 0)$

51.

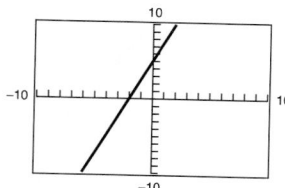 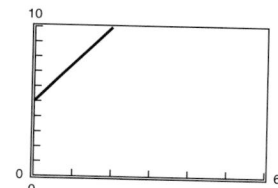

The standard setting gives a more complete graph.

53.

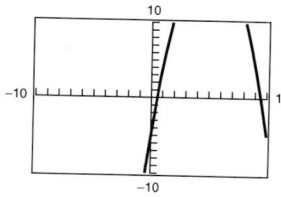 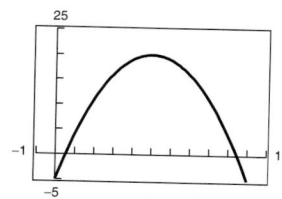

The specified setting gives a more complete graph.

55.

Xmin = -5
Xmax = 5
Xscl = 1
Ymin = -30
Ymax = 10
Yscl = 5

57.

Xmin = -30
Xmax = 30
Xscl = 5
Ymin = -10
Ymax = 50
Yscl = 5

59. $y_1 = \sqrt{64 - x^2}$
$y_2 = -\sqrt{64 - x^2}$

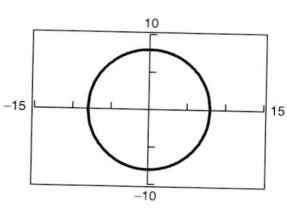

61. $y_1 = \sqrt{49 - x^2}$
$y_2 = -\sqrt{49 - x^2}$

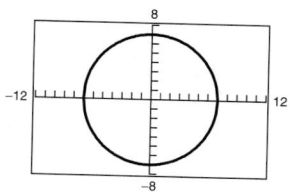

63. The graphs are identical. Distributive Property

65. The graphs are identical. Associative Property of Multiplication

67.

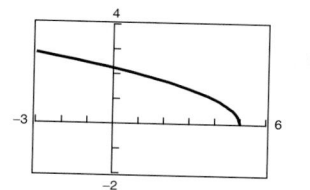

(a) $(2, 1.73)$
(b) $(-4, 3)$

69.

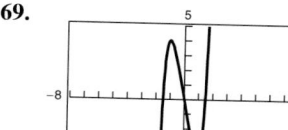

(a) $(-0.5, 2.47)$
(b) $(1, -4)$, $(-1.65, -4)$

71. (a)

Xmin = 0
Xmax = 8
Xscl = 1
Ymin = 60000
Ymax = 230000
Yscl = 10000

(b)

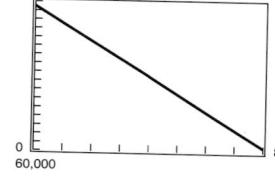

(c) $109,000   (d) $178,000

73. (a)

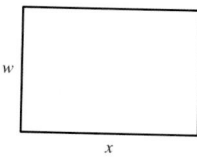

(b) $2w + 2x = 12$
$w + x = 6$
$w = 6 - x$
$A = xw$
$A = x(6 - x)$

(c)

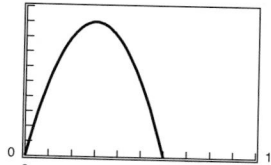

(d) $A \approx 5.4$
(e) $x = 3, w = 3$

75. (a) The life expectancy of a child born in 1950
(b) 1973   (c) ≈ 66.3 years   (d) ≈ 78.7 years

77. (a)

x	10	20	30	40	50
y	107.33	26.56	11.60	6.36	3.94

x	60	70	80	90	100
y	2.62	1.83	1.31	0.96	0.71

(b) $x = 45.64$ (c) $y = 1.103$

(d) They are inversely related.

79. False. $x = 0$ has an infinite number of x-intercepts.

81. Answers will vary. **83.** $-51\sqrt{y}$ **85.** 1000

87. $12x^3 - 4x^2 + 44x$ **89.** $-3x^4 + 8x^2 - 5$

Section 1.2 *(page 87)*

1. (a) L_2 (b) L_3 (c) L_1

3.

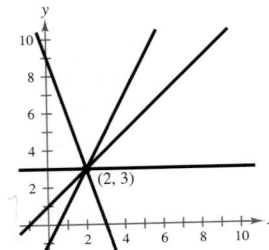

5. $\frac{3}{2}$ **7.** 0 **9.** -4

11. $m = -\frac{5}{2}$ **13.** m is undefined.

15. $(0, 1), (3, 1), (-1, 1)$ **17.** $(-6, 2), (-4, 6), (-3, 8)$

19. $(3, -4), (5, -3), (9, -1)$

21. Perpendicular **23.** Parallel

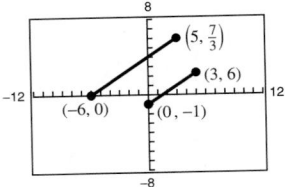

25. (a) $m = 5$;
Intercept: $(0, 3)$
(b)

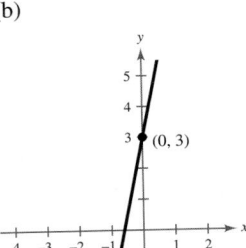

27. (a) m is undefined.
There is no y-intercept.
(b)

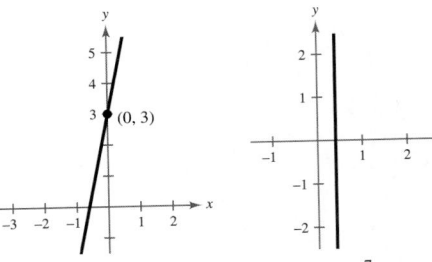

29. (a) $m = 0$;
Intercept: $\left(0, -\frac{5}{3}\right)$
(b)

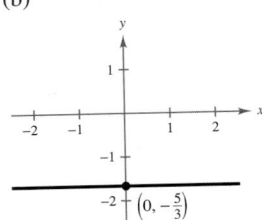

31. (a) $m = -\frac{7}{6}$;
Intercept: $(0, 5)$
(b)

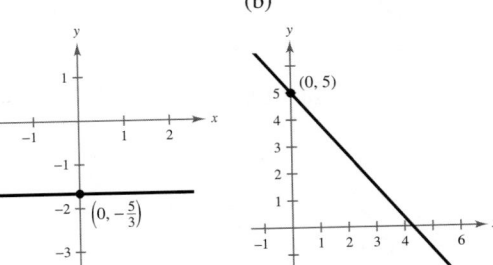

33. $3x - y - 2 = 0$

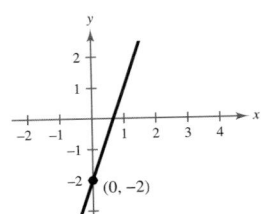

35. $2x + y = 0$

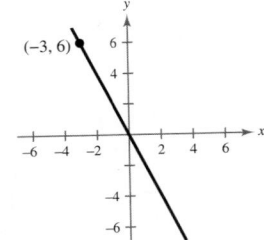

37. $x + 3y - 4 = 0$

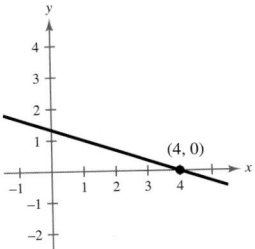

39. $x - 6 = 0$

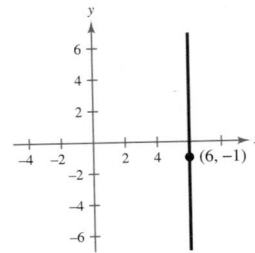

41. $3x + y = 0$

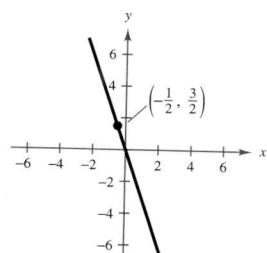

43. $3x + 5y - 10 = 0$

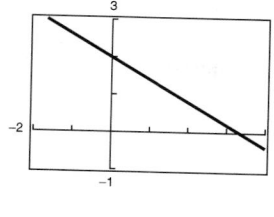

45. $x + 8 = 0$

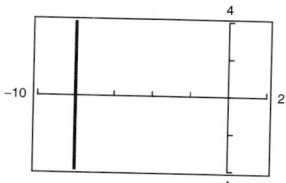

47. $x + 2y - 3 = 0$

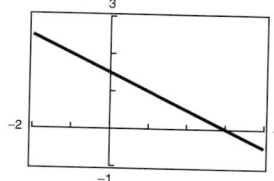

49. $30x + 25y + 18 = 0$

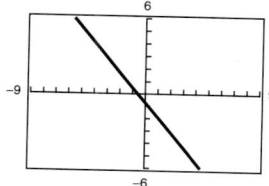

51. $2x - 5y + 1 = 0$

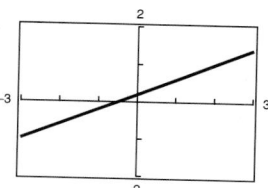

53.

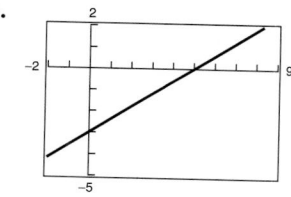

x- and *y*-intercepts

55. $3x + 2y - 6 = 0$ **57.** $12x + 3y + 2 = 0$

59.

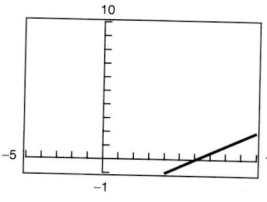 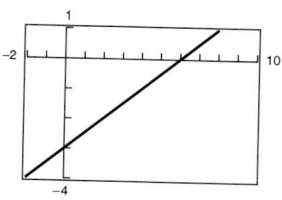

The second setting gives a more complete graph.

61.

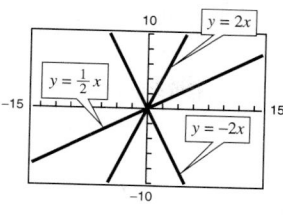

$y = \frac{1}{2}x$ and $y = -2x$
are perpendicular.

63.

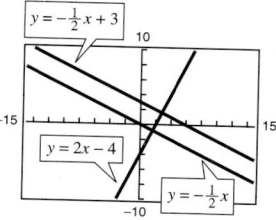

$y = -\frac{1}{2}x$ and $y = -\frac{1}{2}x + 3$
are parallel. Both are perpen-
dicular to $y = 2x - 4$.

65. (a) $2x - y - 3 = 0$ (b) $x + 2y - 4 = 0$

67. (a) $-6x - 8y + 3 = 0$ (b) $96x - 72y + 127 = 0$

69. (a) $10x - 10y + 43 = 0$ (b) $10x + 10y - 93 = 0$

71. $3x - 2y - 1 = 0$

73. (a) Sales increase of $135

(b) No sales increase

(c) Sales decrease of $40

75. (a) Greatest increases per share: 1990 and 1996

Greatest decrease per share: 1997

(b) $37x - 1000y + 943 = 0$

(c) Slope is the average increase per share per year.

(d) $1.46. Answers will vary.

77. 16,667 feet   **79.** $125t - V + 2415 = 0$

81. $2000t + V - 22,400 = 0$

83. (b); slope $= -10$; the amount owed decreases by $10 per
week.

85. (a); slope $= 0.25$; expenses increase by $0.25 per mile.

87. $F = \frac{9}{5}C + 32$ **89.** $39,500

91. (a) $V = -175t + 875$

(b)

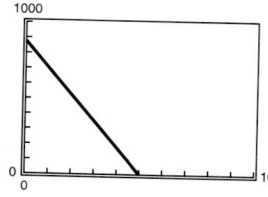

t	0	1	2	3	4	5
V	875	700	525	350	175	0

93. (a) $C = 16.75t + 36,500$ (b) $R = 27t$

(c) $P = 10.25t - 36,500$ (d) $t \approx 3561$ hours

95. (a) Answers will vary. Example: $y = 92.84t + 487.82$

(b) Answers will vary. Example: $1,601,000

(c) Average increase per year

97. False. The line through $(10, -3)$ and $(2, -9)$ is $y = \frac{3}{4}x + \frac{9}{4}$, and $\left(-12, -\frac{37}{2}\right)$ is not on this line.

99. -4

101. No. The slopes of two perpendicular lines have opposite signs (assuming that neither line is vertical or horizontal).

103. Yes. $-10x^2 + 3x + 1$

105. Yes. $-2x^4 - x^3 + 2x^2 + 2$ **107.** No.

109. $(x - 4)(x - 7)$ **111.** $(3x - 1)(x - 5)$

113. $(x + 8)^2 + (y + 5)^2 = \frac{9}{16}$

115. $(x - 2)^2 + (y - 1)^2 = 52$

Section 1.3 *(page 100)*

1. Yes   **3.** No

5. Yes. Each input value is matched with one output value.

7. No. The same input value is matched with two different output values.

9. (a) Function

(b) Not a function because the element 1 in A corresponds to two elements, -2 and 1, in B.

(c) Function   (d) Not a function because the element 2 in A corresponds to no element in B.

11. Each is a function. To each year there corresponds one and only one circulation.

13. Not a function   **15.** Function   **17.** Function

19. Not a function   **21.** Function   **23.** Not a function

25. (a) $\frac{1}{5}$ (b) 1   (c) $\frac{1}{4t + 1}$ (d) $\frac{1}{x + c + 1}$

27. (a) -1 (b) -9 (c) $2x - 5$

29. (a) 0   (b) -0.75 (c) $x^2 + 2x$

31. (a) 1   (b) 2.5   (c) $3 - 2|x|$

33. (a) $-\frac{1}{9}$ (b) Undefined   (c) $\frac{1}{y^2 + 6y}$

35. (a) 1   (b) -1 (c) 1   **37.** (a) -1 (b) 2   (c) 6

39.

x	-2	-1	0	1	2
$f(x)$	1	-2	-3	-2	1

41.

t	-5	-4	-3	-2	-1
$h(t)$	1	$\frac{1}{2}$	0	$\frac{1}{2}$	1

43.

x	-2	-1	0	1	2
$f(x)$	5	$\frac{9}{2}$	4	1	0

45. 5   **47.** $\frac{4}{3}$ **49.** ± 3 **51.** ± 4 **53.** $2, -1$

55. 0, 3   **57.** All real numbers x

59. All real numbers t except $t = 0$

61. All real numbers y such that $y \geq 10$

63. All real numbers x such that $-1 \leq x \leq 1$

65. All real numbers x except $x = 0, -2$

67. All real numbers s such that $s \neq 4$ and $s \geq 1$

69. All real numbers x except $x = 0$

71. $\{(-2, 4), (-1, 1), (0, 0), (1, 1), (2, 4)\}$

73. $\{(-2, 0), (-1, 1), \left(0, \sqrt{2}\right), \left(1, \sqrt{3}\right), (2, 2)\}$

75. $g(x) = -2x^2; c = -2$ **77.** $r(x) = \frac{32}{x}; c = 32$

79. $2, c \neq 0$ **81.** $3 + h, h \neq 0$

83. $3x^2 + 3xc + c^2, c \neq 0$ **85.** $-\frac{1}{t}, t \neq 1$

87. $A = \frac{C^2}{4\pi}$ **89.** $A = \frac{s^2}{2}$

91. (a)

Height, x	Width	Volume, V
1	$24 - 2(1)$	$1[24 - 2(1)]^2 = 484$
2	$24 - 2(2)$	$2[24 - 2(2)]^2 = 800$
3	$24 - 2(3)$	$3[24 - 2(3)]^2 = 972$
4	$24 - 2(4)$	$4[24 - 2(4)]^2 = 1024$
5	$24 - 2(5)$	$5[24 - 2(5)]^2 = 980$
6	$24 - 2(6)$	$6[24 - 2(6)]^2 = 864$

Maximum when $x = 4$

(b) $V = x(24 - 2x)^2, 0 < x < 12$

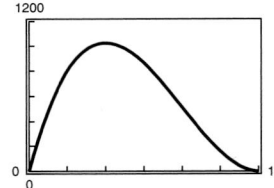

(c) $x = 9, V = 324; x = 10, V = 160$

93. $A = \frac{x^2}{2(x - 2)}, x > 2$

95. (a) $V = x^2 y$
$= x^2(108 - 4x)$
$= 108x^2 - 4x^3$

(b) $0 < x < 27$

(c)

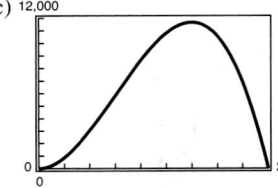

(d) $x = 18$ in., $y = 36$ in.

97. (a) $C = 12.30x + 98,000$ (b) $R = 17.98x$

(c) $P = 5.68x - 98,000$

99. (a) $R = \dfrac{240n - n^2}{20}$

(b)

n	90	100	110	120	130	140	150
$R(n)$	\$675	\$700	\$715	\$720	\$715	\$700	\$675

The revenue is maximum when $n = 120$.

(c)

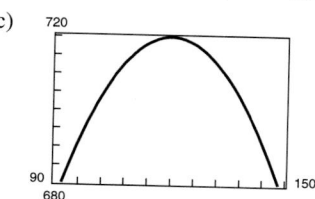

The revenue is maximum when $n = 120$.

101. (a)

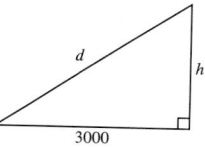

(b) $h = \sqrt{d^2 - 3000^2}$; $d \geq 3000$

(c)

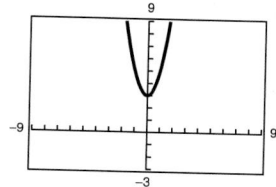

```
Xmin = 3000
Xmax = 20,000
Xscl = 1000
Ymin = 0
Ymax = 20,000
Yscl = 1000
```

(d) ≈ 9539 feet

103. False. Range is $[-1, \infty)$.

105. No. 3 corresponds to both u and v.

107. Function notation is a convenient way of referencing the value of a function for a specific domain value.

109. $\dfrac{x^2 - x - 3}{(x - 4)(x + 5)(x - 1)}$ **111.** $\dfrac{x + 7}{x - 7}$, $x \neq 9$

113.

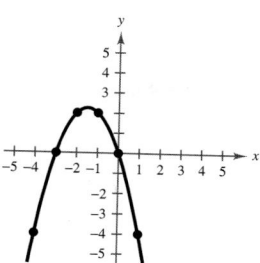

115.

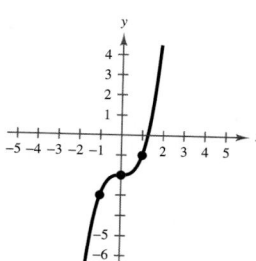

Section 1.4 *(page 114)*

1. Domain: $(-\infty, \infty)$; Range: $(-\infty, 1]$

3. Domain: $(-\infty, -1], [1, \infty)$; Range: $[0, \infty)$

5. Domain: $(-\infty, \infty)$; Range: $[0, \infty)$

7.

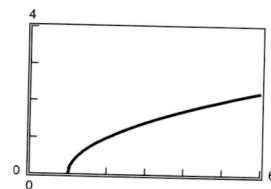

Domain: $(-\infty, \infty)$; Range: $[3, \infty)$

9.

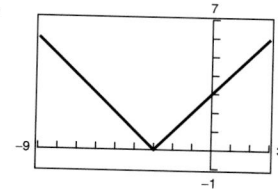

Domain: $[1, \infty)$; Range: $[0, \infty)$

11.

Domain: $(-\infty, \infty)$; Range: $[0, \infty)$

13. Function. Graph the given function over the window shown in the figure.

15. Not a function. Solve for y and graph the resulting two functions.

17. Function. Solve for y and graph the resulting function.

19. (a) Increasing on $(-\infty, \infty)$ (b) Odd function

21. (a) Increasing on $(-\infty, 0)$, $(2, \infty)$

Decreasing on $(0, 2)$

(b) Neither even nor odd

23. (a)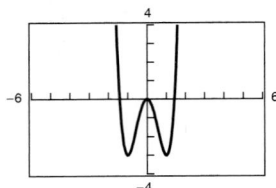

(b) Increasing on $(-1, 0)$, $(1, \infty)$

Decreasing on $(-\infty, -1)$, $(0, 1)$

(c) Even function

25. (a)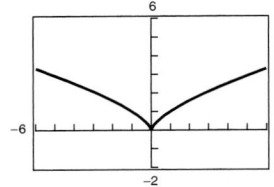

(b) Decreasing on $(-\infty, 0)$; Increasing on $(0, \infty)$

(c) Even function

27. (a)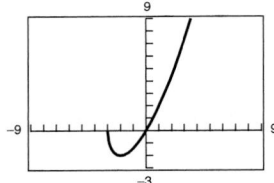

(b) Increasing on $(-2, \infty)$; Decreasing on $(-3, -2)$

(c) Neither even nor odd

29. (a)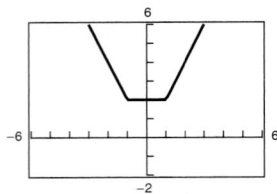

(b) Decreasing on $(-\infty, -1)$; Constant on $(-1, 1)$;

Increasing on $(1, \infty)$

(c) Even function

31.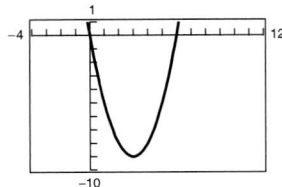

Relative minimum: $(3, -9)$

33.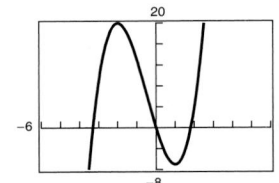

Relative minimum: $(1, -7)$

Relative maximum: $(-2, 20)$

35.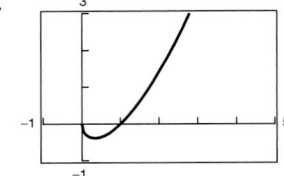

Minimum: $(0.33, -0.38)$

37. (a) Answers will vary.

(b) Relative minimum at $(2, -9)$

(c) Answers will vary.

39. (a) Answers will vary.

(b) Relative minimum at $(1.63, -8.71)$

Relative maximum at $(-1.63, 8.71)$

(c) Answers will vary.

41. (a) Answers will vary.   (b) Relative minimum at $(4, 0)$

(c) Answers will vary.

43.   **45.**

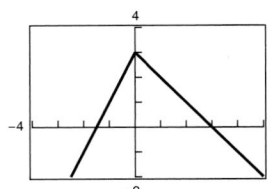   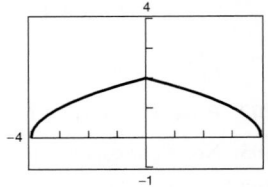

47. Neither even nor odd   **49.** Odd function

51. Odd function   **53.** Even function

55. (a) $\left(\frac{3}{2}, 4\right)$ (b) $\left(\frac{3}{2}, -4\right)$

57. (a) $(-4, 9)$ (b) $(-4, -9)$

59. (a) $(-x, -y)$ (b) $(-x, y)$

61. Even function

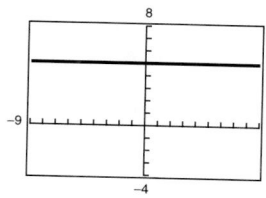

63. Neither even nor odd

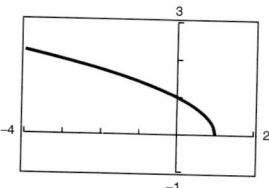

65. Even function

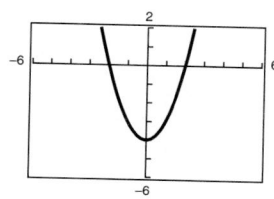

67. Neither even nor odd

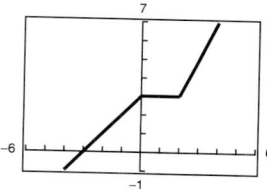

69. Neither even nor odd

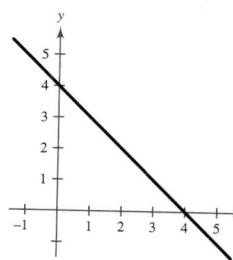

71. Neither even nor odd

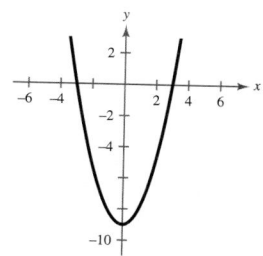

73. $(-\infty, 4]$

75. $(-\infty, -3], [3, \infty)$

77. $[-1, 1]$

79. $[-2, \infty)$

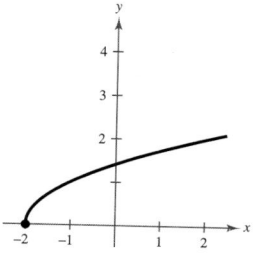

81. $f(x) < 0$ for all x

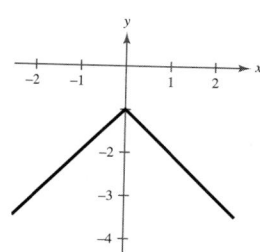

83.

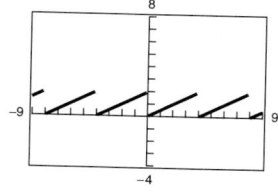

Domain: $(-\infty, \infty)$

Range: $[0, 2)$

Sawtooth pattern

85. (a) Answers will vary.

(b)

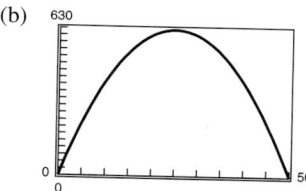

(c) 625 square meters; 25×25 meters

87. (a) C_2 is the appropriate model. The cost of the first minute is \$1.05 and the cost increases \$0.38 when the next minute begins, etc.

(b)

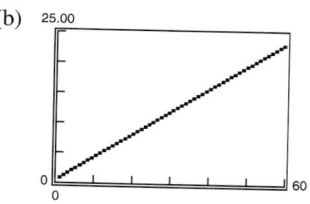

\$7.89

89. $h = -x^2 + 4x - 3, \ 1 \le x \le 3$

91. $h = 2x - x^2, \ 0 \le x \le 2$

93. $L = \frac{1}{2}y^2, \ 0 \le y \le 4$

95. (a) $y = 1.473x^3 - 16.411x^2 + 31.24x - 95.2$

(b) Domain: $[0, 7]$

(c)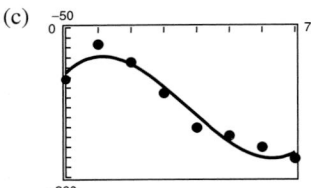

(d) Most accurate: 1992; Least accurate: 1991

(e) Yes. The cubic curve is starting an upswing for future years.

97. False. Counterexample: $f(x) = \sqrt{1 + x^2}$

99. If $y = a_{2n+1}x^{2n+1} + a_{2n-1}x^{2n-1} + \cdots + a_3x^3 + a_1x$, each exponent is odd. Then

$$f(-x) = -a_{2n+1}x^{2n+1} - a_{2n-1}x^{2n-1} - \cdots - a_3x^3 - a_1x,$$

which is equal to $-f(x)$. Therefore, by definition, the original function is odd.

101. (a) Even. g is a reflection in the x-axis.

(b) Even. g is a reflection in the y-axis.

(c) Even. g is a vertical shift downward.

(d) Neither even nor odd. g is shifted to the right and reflected in the x-axis.

103. No. x is not a function of y because horizontal lines can be drawn to intersect the graph twice, so each y-value corresponds to two distinct x-values if $-5 < y < 5$.

105. (a) $d = 10$ (b) Midpoint: $(-1, 3)$

107. (a) $d = \dfrac{\sqrt{733}}{4}$ (b) Midpoint: $\left(-\dfrac{21}{8}, \dfrac{5}{12}\right)$

109. (a) -17 (b) 1 (c) $-x^2 + 3x + 1$

111. (a) 6 (b) -55 (c) $\frac{1}{9}$ **113.** $-h - 6, \, h \neq 0$

Section 1.5 *(page 124)*

1.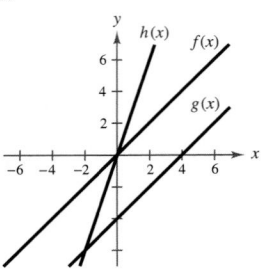

3.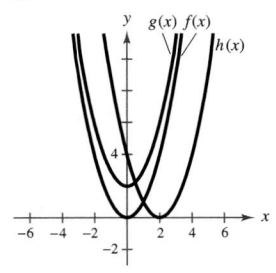

5.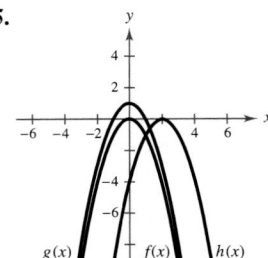

7.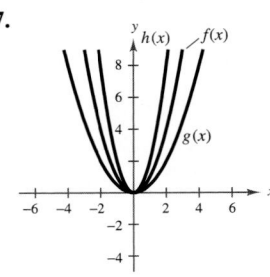

9.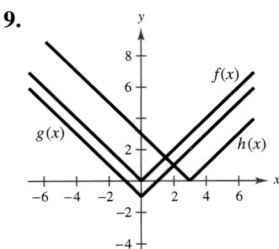

11.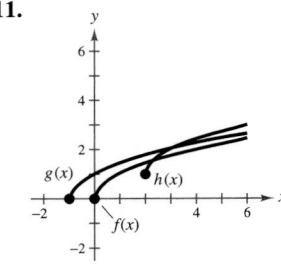

13. (a)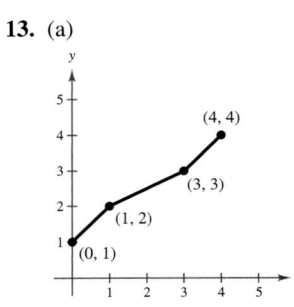

(b)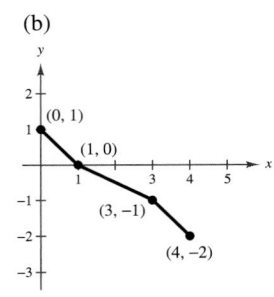

(c)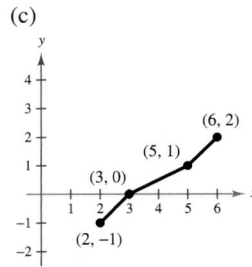

(d)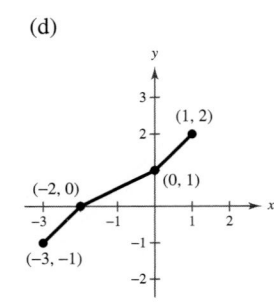

(e)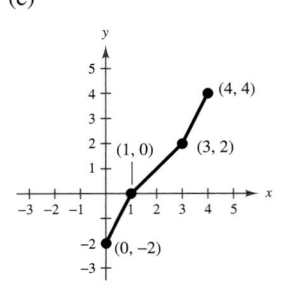

(f)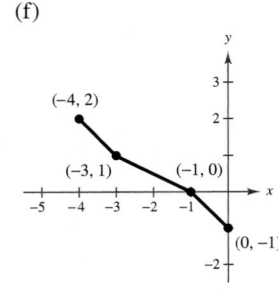

15. Vertical shrink of $y = x$
$y = \frac{1}{2}x$

17. Constant function
$y = 7$

19. Reflection in the x-axis and a vertical shift of $y = \sqrt{x}$
$y = 1 - \sqrt{x}$

21. Horizontal shift of $y = |x|$
$y = |x + 2|$

23. Vertical shift of $y = x^2$
$y = x^2 - 1$

25. Reflection in the x-axis of $y = x^3$ followed by a vertical shift
$y = 1 - x^3$

27. Vertical shift 2 units upward

29. Horizontal shift 2 units to the right

31. Vertical stretch   **33.** Horizontal shift 2 units to the left

35. Reflection in the x-axis   **37.** Vertical shrink

39. Reflection in the x-axis and vertical shift 4 units upward

41. Horizontal shift 2 units to the left and vertical shrink

43. Vertical shrink and vertical shift 2 units upward

45.

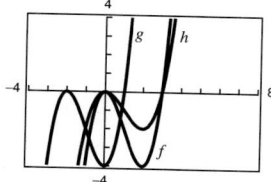

g is a horizontal shift and h is a vertical shrink.

47.

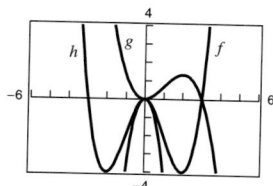

g is a vertical shrink and a reflection in the x-axis and h is a reflection in the y-axis.

49. $g(x) = -(x^3 - 3x^2) + 1$

51. (a) $f(x) = x^2$

(b) Reflection in the x-axis and vertical shift 12 units upward

(c)

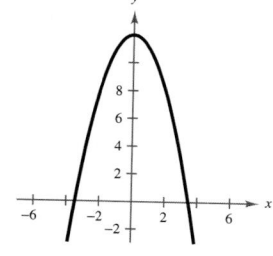

(d) $g(x) = 12 - f(x)$

53. (a) $f(x) = x^2$

(b) Horizontal shift 5 units to the left, reflection in the x-axis, and vertical shift 2 units upward

(c)

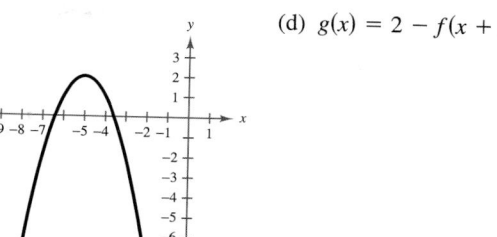

(d) $g(x) = 2 - f(x + 5)$

55. (a) $f(x) = x^2$

(b) Horizontal shift 4 units to the right, vertical stretch, and vertical shift 3 units upward

(c)

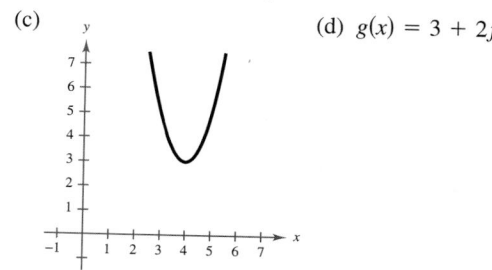

(d) $g(x) = 3 + 2f(x - 4)$

57. (a) $f(x) = x^3$

(b) Vertical shift 7 units upward

(c)

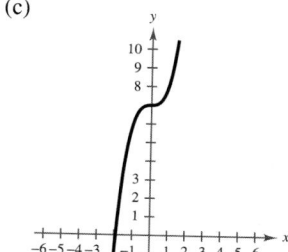

(d) $g(x) = f(x) + 7$

59. (a) $f(x) = x^3$

(b) Horizontal shift 1 unit to the right and vertical shift 2 units upward

(c)

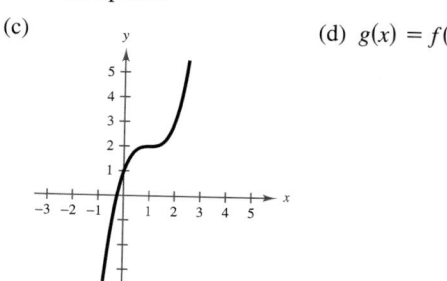

(d) $g(x) = f(x - 1) + 2$

61. (a) $f(x) = x^3$

(b) Horizontal shift 2 units to the right and vertical stretch

(c)

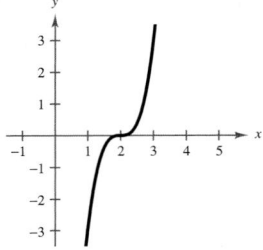

(d) $g(x) = 3f(x - 2)$

63. (a) $f(x) = |x|$

(b) Reflection in the x-axis and vertical shift 2 units downward

(c)

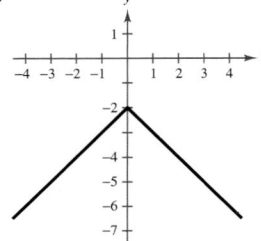

(d) $g(x) = -f(x) - 2$

65. (a) $f(x) = |x|$

(b) Horizontal shift 4 units to the left, reflection in the x-axis, and vertical shift 8 units upward

(c)

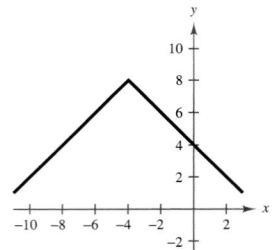

(d) $g(x) = -f(x + 4) + 8$

67. (a) $f(x) = |x|$

(b) Horizontal shift 1 unit to the right, reflection in the x-axis, and vertical stretch

(c)

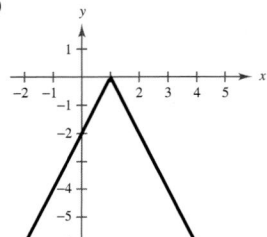

(d) $g(x) = -2f(x - 1)$

69. (a) $f(x) = \sqrt{x}$

(b) Horizontal shift 9 units to the right

(c)

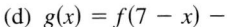

(d) $g(x) = f(x - 9)$

71. (a) $f(x) = \sqrt{x}$

(b) Reflection in the y-axis, horizontal shift 7 units to the right, and vertical shift 2 units downward

(c)

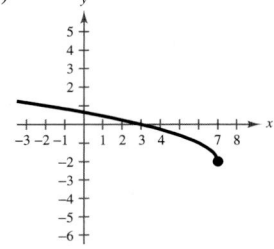

(d) $g(x) = f(7 - x) - 2$

73. (a) $f(x) = \sqrt{x}$

(b) Horizontal shift 1 unit to the right and vertical stretch 4 units

(c)

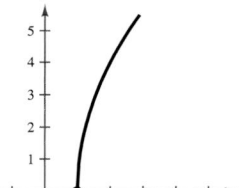

(d) $g(x) = 4f(x - 1)$

75. (a)

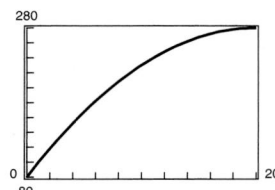

(b) $P(x) = 55 + 20x - 0.5x^2$; vertical shift

(c) $P(x) = 80 + \dfrac{1}{5}x - \dfrac{x^2}{20,000}$; horizontal stretch

77. (a) Vertical shrink and vertical shift

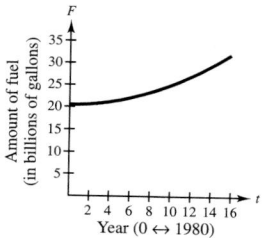

(b) $G(t) = 0.04t^2 + 0.8t + 24.46$; $G(t) = F(t + 10)$

79. (a) To each time t there corresponds one and only one temperature T.

(b) $60°, 72°$

(c) All the temperature changes would be 1 hour later.

(d) The temperature would be decreased by 1 degree.

81. False. The point $(-1, 28)$ does not lie on the graph of $g(x) = -(x - 6)^2 + 3$.

83. $y = x^7$ resembles the cubic graph and $y = x^8$ resembles the quadratic graph. Both are steeper on $(-\infty, -1)$ and $(1, \infty)$ and both are closer to 0 on $-1 < x < 1$.

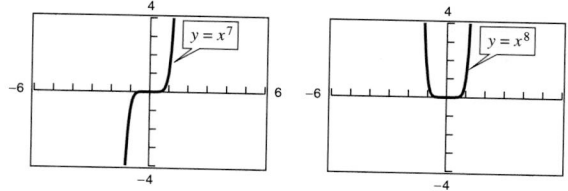

85.

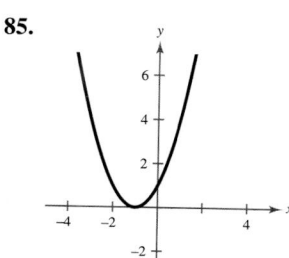

87.   **89.**

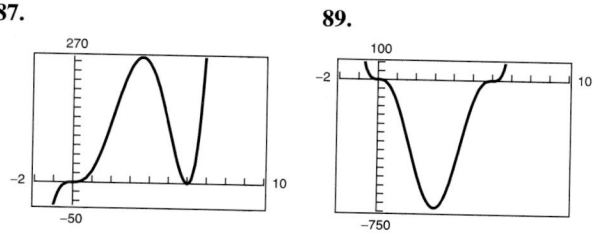

91. All real numbers $x \geq 5$ except $x = 7$

93. All real numbers

95.   **97.**

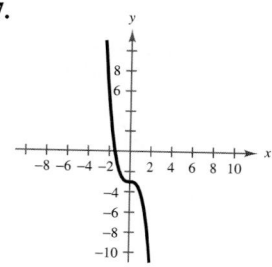

99.

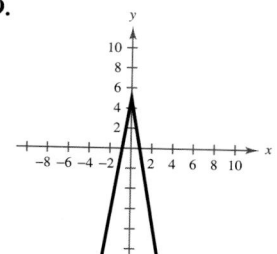

Section 1.6   *(page 134)*

1. (a) $2x$ (b) 2 (c) $x^2 - 1$ (d) $\dfrac{x + 1}{x - 1}, \ x \neq 1$

(e) All $x \neq 1$

3. (a) $x^2 - x + 1$ (b) $x^2 + x - 1$ (c) $x^2 - x^3$

(d) $\dfrac{x^2}{1 - x}, \ x \neq 1$ (e) All $x \neq 1$

5. (a) $x^2 + 5 + \sqrt{1 - x}$ (b) $x^2 + 5 - \sqrt{1 - x}$

(c) $(x^2 + 5)\sqrt{1 - x}$ (d) $\dfrac{x^2 + 5}{\sqrt{1 - x}}, \ x < 1$

(e) $x < 1$

7. (a) $\dfrac{x + 1}{x^2}$ (b) $\dfrac{x - 1}{x^2}$ (c) $\dfrac{1}{x^3}$ (d) $x, \ x \neq 0$

(e) $x \neq 0$

9. 9   **11.** 5   **13.** 0   **15.** 26   **17.** $4t^2 - 2t + 5$

19. $-125t^3 - 100t^2 - 5t - 4$ **21.** $\dfrac{t^2 + 1}{-t - 4}$

23.   **25.**

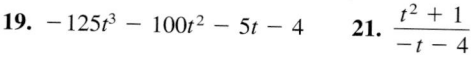

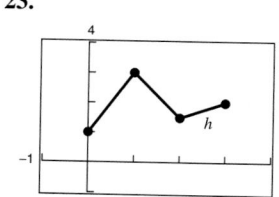

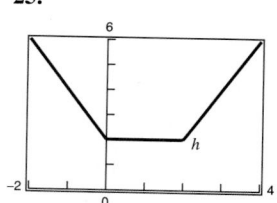

27.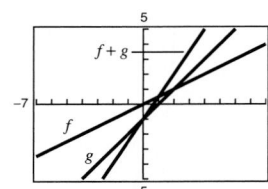

29.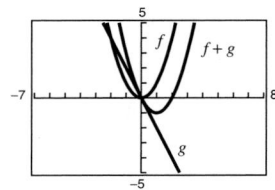

31. 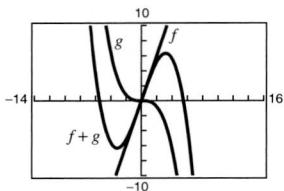 $f(x), 0 \le x \le 2;$
$g(x), x > 6$

33. 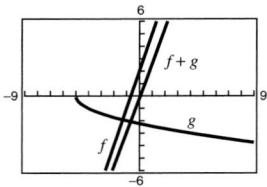 $f(x), 0 \le x \le 2;$
$f(x), x > 6$

35. (a) $(x - 1)^2$ (b) $x^2 - 1$

37. (a) $20 - 3x$ (b) $-3x$

39. (a) $(f \circ g)(x) = \sqrt{x^2 + 4}$
     $(g \circ f)(x) = x + 4, \ x \ge -4$

(b) 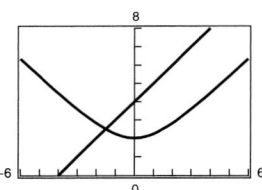   Not equal

41. (a) $(f \circ g)(x) = x - \frac{8}{3}; \ (g \circ f)(x) = x - 8$

(b) 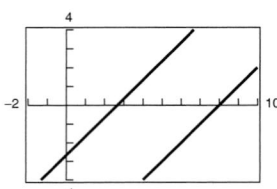   Not equal

43. (a) $(f \circ g)(x) = x^4; \ (g \circ f)(x) = x^4$

(b) 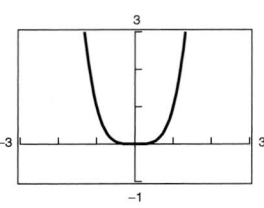   Equal

45. (a) $(f \circ g)(x) = 24 - 5x; \ (g \circ f)(x) = -5x$

(b) $24 - 5x \ne -5x$

(c)

x	0	1	2	3
$g(x)$	4	3	2	1
$(f \circ g)(x)$	24	19	14	9

x	0	1	2	3
$f(x)$	4	9	14	19
$(g \circ f)(x)$	0	-5	-10	-15

47. (a) $(f \circ g)(x) = \sqrt{x^2 + 1}; \ (g \circ f)(x) = x + 1, \ x \ge -6$

(b) $x + 1 \ne \sqrt{x^2 + 1}$

(c)

x	0	1	2	3
$g(x)$	-5	-4	-1	4
$(f \circ g)(x)$	1	$\sqrt{2}$	$\sqrt{5}$	$\sqrt{10}$

x	0	1	2	3
$f(x)$	$\sqrt{6}$	$\sqrt{7}$	$\sqrt{8}$	3
$(g \circ f)(x)$	1	2	3	4

49. (a) $(f \circ g)(x) = |2x + 2|; \ (g \circ f)(x) = 2|x + 3| - 1$

(b) $(f \circ g)(x) = \begin{cases} 2x + 2, & x \ge -1 \\ -2x - 2, & x < -1 \end{cases}$

     $(g \circ f)(x) = \begin{cases} 2x + 5, & x \ge -3 \\ -2x - 7, & x < -3 \end{cases}$

     $(f \circ g)(x) \ne (g \circ f)(x)$

(c)

x	0	-1	-3	-5
$g(x)$	-1	-3	-7	-11
$(f \circ g)(x)$	2	0	4	8

x	0	-1	-3	-5
$f(x)$	3	2	0	2
$(g \circ f)(x)$	5	3	-1	3

51. (a) 3   (b) 0   **53.** (a) 0   (b) 4

55. (a) 0   (b) 4   **57.** $f(x) = x^2, g(x) = 2x + 1$

59. $f(x) = \sqrt[3]{x}, \ g(x) = x^2 - 4$

61. $f(x) = \dfrac{1}{x}, \ g(x) = x + 2$

63. $f(x) = x^2 + 2x, \ g(x) = x + 4$

65. (a) $x \ge 0$ (b) All real numbers   (c) All real numbers

67. (a) All real numbers except $x = 0$ (b) All real numbers

(c) All real numbers except $x = -3$

69. (a) All real numbers except $x = 0$ (b) All real numbers

(c) All real numbers except $x = 1$

71. $3, h \neq 0$ **73.** $-2x - h, h \neq 0$

75. $\dfrac{-4}{x(x + h)}, h \neq 0$

77. $\dfrac{2}{\sqrt{2(x + h) + 1} + \sqrt{2x + 1}}, h \neq 0$

79. (a) $T = \frac{3}{4}x + \frac{1}{15}x^2$

(b)

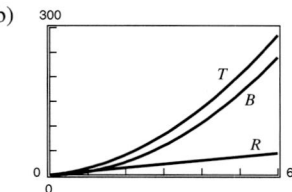

(c) B. For example, $B(60) = 240$ while $R(60)$ is only 45.

81. $y_1 = -0.59x^2 + 7.66x + 144.9$

$y_2 = 16.58x + 245.06$

$y_3 = 1.84x + 21.92$

83. $(A \circ r)(t) = 0.36\pi t^2$

$A \circ r$ represents the area of the circle at time t.

85. (a) $(C \circ x)(t) = 3000t + 750$

$C \circ x$ represents the cost after t production hours.

(b)

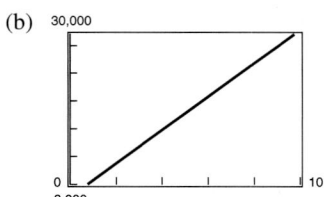

4.75 hours

87. $g(f(x))$ represents 3 percent of an amount over $500,000.

89.

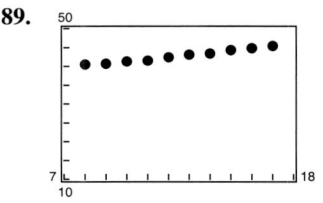 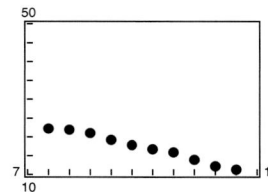

Both data sets appear to be linear.

$y_1 = 0.57x + 35.6$; $y_2 = -1.29x + 33.3$

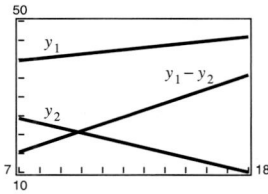

The difference between the morning and evening newspaper circulations is increasing.

91. True   **93.** Odd (Proofs will vary.)

95. $\frac{1}{2}[f(x) + f(-x)] + \frac{1}{2}[f(x) - f(-x)]$

$= \frac{1}{2}[f(x) + f(-x) + f(x) - f(-x)]$

$= \frac{1}{2}[2f(x)]$

$= f(x)$

97. $(0, -5), (1, -5), (2, -7)$ (Answers will vary.)

99. $\left(0, 2\sqrt{6}\right), \left(1, \sqrt{23}\right), \left(2, 2\sqrt{5}\right)$ (Answers will vary.)

101. $10x - y + 38 = 0$ **103.** $30x + 11y - 34 = 0$

105.   **107.**

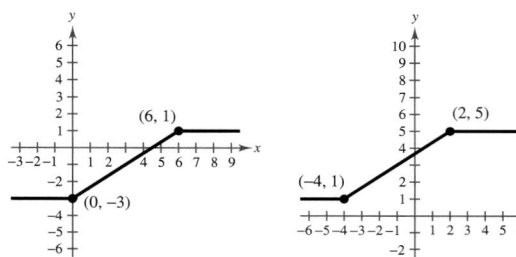

109.

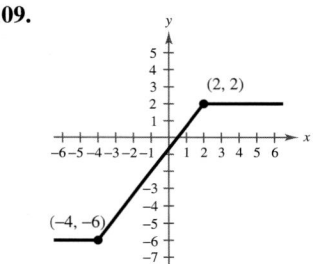

Section 1.7   *(page 145)*

1. (c)   **3.** (a)   **5.** $f^{-1}(x) = \frac{1}{8}x$

7. $f^{-1}(x) = x - 10$ **9.** $f^{-1}(x) = \frac{1}{2}(x - 1)$

11. $f^{-1}(x) = x^3$

13. (a) $f(g(x)) = f\left(\dfrac{x}{2}\right) = 2\left(\dfrac{x}{2}\right) = x$

$g(f(x)) = g(2x) = \dfrac{(2x)}{2} = x$

(b)

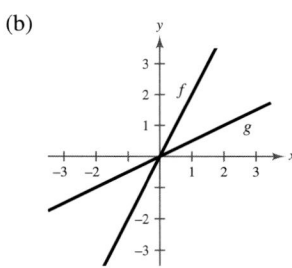

15. (a) $f(g(x)) = f\left(\dfrac{x-1}{5}\right) = 5\left(\dfrac{x-1}{5}\right) + 1 = x$

$g(f(x)) = g(5x+1) = \dfrac{(5x+1)-1}{5} = x$

(b)

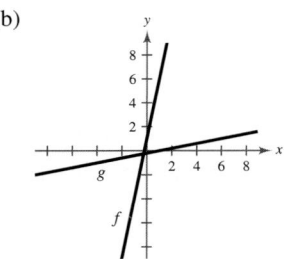

17. $f(g(x)) = f(\sqrt[3]{x}) = (\sqrt[3]{x})^3 = x$

$g(f(x)) = g(x^3) = \sqrt[3]{x^3} = x$

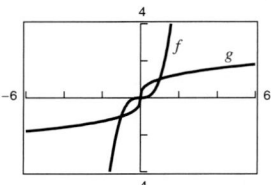

Reflections in the line $y = x$

19. $f(g(x)) = f(x^2 + 4), \quad x \ge 0$

$= \sqrt{(x^2 + 4) - 4} = x$

$g(f(x)) = g(\sqrt{x-4})$

$= (\sqrt{x-4})^2 + 4 = x$

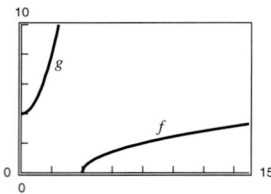

Reflections in the line $y = x$

21. $f(g(x)) = f(\sqrt[3]{1-x}) = 1 - (\sqrt[3]{1-x})^3 = x$

$g(f(x)) = g(1 - x^3) = \sqrt[3]{1 - (1 - x^3)} = x$

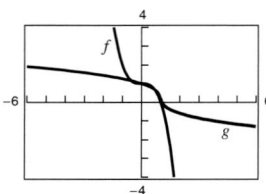

Reflections in the line $y = x$

23. (a) $f(g(x)) = f\left(-\dfrac{2x+6}{7}\right)$

$= -\dfrac{7}{2}\left(-\dfrac{2x+6}{7}\right) - 3 = x$

$g(f(x)) = g\left(-\dfrac{7}{2}x - 3\right)$

$= -\dfrac{2\left(-\frac{7}{2}x - 3\right) + 6}{7} = x$

(b)

x	0	2	-2	6
$f(x)$	-3	-10	4	-24

x	-3	-10	4	-24
$g(x)$	0	2	-2	6

25. (a) $f(g(x)) = f(\sqrt[3]{x-5}) = (\sqrt[3]{x-5})^3 + 5 = x$

$g(f(x)) = g(x^3 + 5) = \sqrt[3]{(x^3 + 5) - 5} = x$

(b)

x	0	1	-1	-2	4
$f(x)$	5	6	4	-3	69

x	5	6	4	-3	69
$g(x)$	0	1	-1	-2	4

27. (a) $f(g(x)) = f(8 + x^2)$

$= -\sqrt{(8 + x^2) - 8}$

$= -\sqrt{x^2} = -(-x) = x, \ x \le 0$

$g(f(x)) = g(-\sqrt{x-8})$

$= 8 + (-\sqrt{x-8})^2$

$= 8 + (x - 8) = x, \ x \ge 8$

(b)

x	8	9	12	15
$f(x)$	0	-1	-2	$-\sqrt{7}$

x	0	-1	-2	$-\sqrt{7}$
$g(x)$	8	9	12	15

29.

One-to-one

31.

Not one-to-one

33.

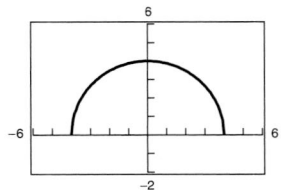

Not one-to-one

35.

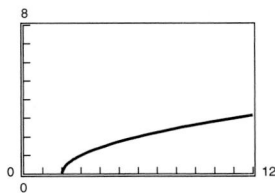

One-to-one

37.

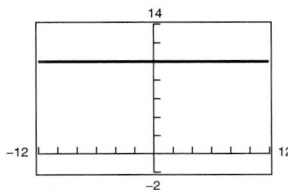

Not one-to-one

39.

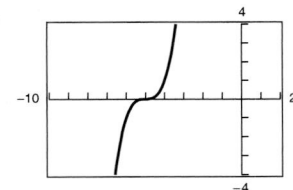

One-to-one

41.

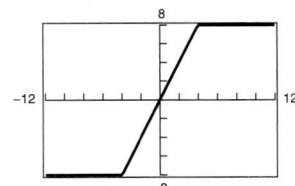

Not one-to-one

43. $f^{-1}(x) = \dfrac{x + 3}{2}$

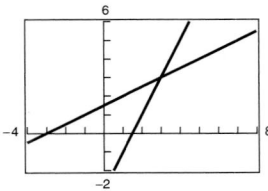

Reflections in the line $y = x$

45. $f^{-1}(x) = \sqrt[5]{x}$

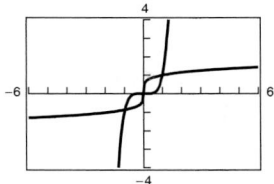

Reflections in the line $y = x$

47. $f^{-1}(x) = x^2, \ x \geq 0$

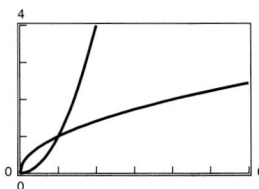

Reflections in the line $y = x$

49. $f^{-1}(x) = \sqrt{4 - x^2}, \ 0 \leq x \leq 2$

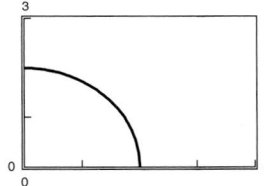

Reflections in the line $y = x$

51. $f^{-1}(x) = x^3 + 1$

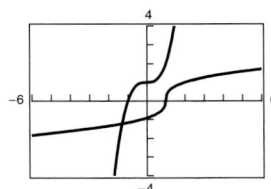

Reflections in the line $y = x$

53. $f^{-1}(x) = \dfrac{4}{x}$

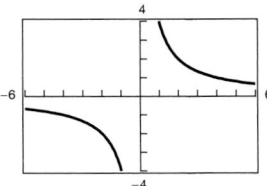

Reflections in the line $y = x$

55. Not one-to-one

57. $f^{-1}(x) = \dfrac{5x - 4}{3}$ **59.** $f^{-1}(x) = \sqrt{x} - 3,\ x \geq 0$

61. Not one-to-one   **63.** $f^{-1}(x) = \dfrac{x^2 - 3}{2},\ x \geq 0$

65. Not one-to-one   **67.** $f^{-1}(x) = \dfrac{x - b}{a}$

69. $y = \sqrt{x} + 2,\ x \geq 0$ **71.** $y = x - 2,\ x \geq 0$

73.

x	-4	-2	2	3
$f^{-1}(x)$	-2	-1	1	3

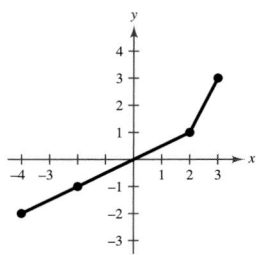

75. (a) and (b)

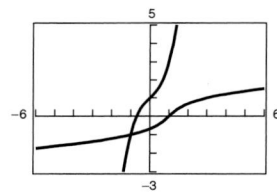

(c) Inverse function because it satisfies the Vertical Line Test

77. (a) and (b)

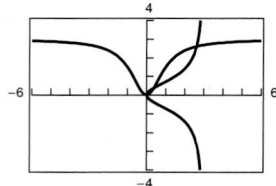

(c) Not an inverse function because it does not satisfy the Vertical Line Test

79. 32   **81.** 600   **83.** $2\sqrt[3]{x + 3}$

85. $\dfrac{x + 1}{2}$ **87.** $\dfrac{x + 1}{2}$

89. (a) $y = \dfrac{x - 8}{0.75}$

   y = number of units produced
   x = hourly wage

(b)

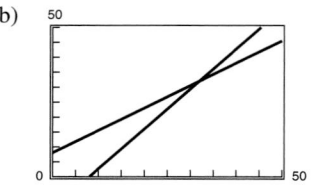

(c) $15.50   (d) 19 units

91. (a) Yes

(b) $f^{-1}(t)$ represents the year new car sales totaled $t billion.

(c) 5, or 1995

(d) No. The inverse is not a function because f is not one-to-one.

93. True   **95.** Answers will vary.   **97.** $9x,\ x \neq 0$

99. $-(x + 6),\ x \neq 6$ **101.** 2   **103.** 0

Review Exercises   *(page 149)*

1.

x	-2	0	2	3	4
y	3	2	1	$\frac{1}{2}$	0

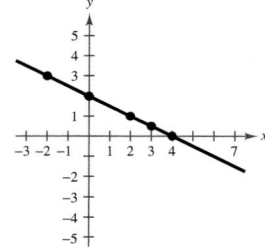

3.

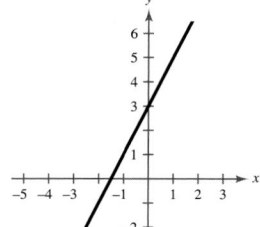

5.

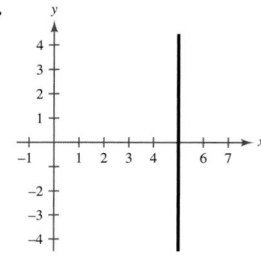

7.

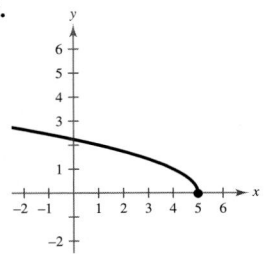

9.

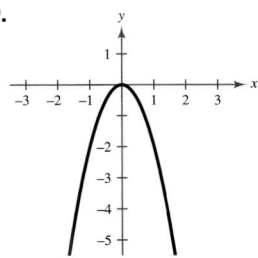

11.

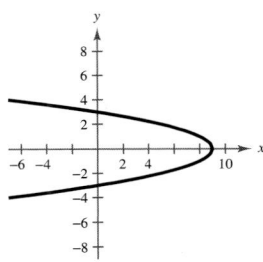

13.

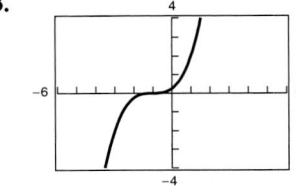

Intercepts: $(-1, 0)$, $\left(0, \frac{1}{4}\right)$

15.

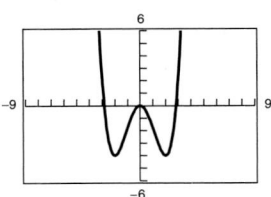

Intercepts: $(0, 0)$, $\left(\pm 2\sqrt{2}, 0\right)$

17.

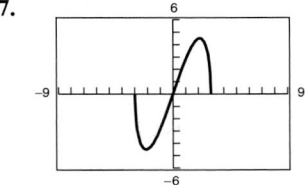

Intercepts: $(0, 0)$, $(\pm 3, 0)$

19.

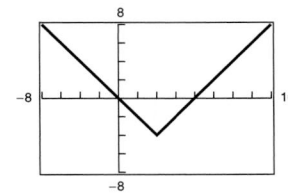

Intercepts: $(0, 0)$, $(8, 0)$

21.

Xmin = -20
Xmax = 50
Xscl = 10
Ymin = -2
Ymax = 1
Yscl = 0.5

23. (a)

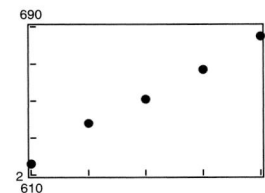

(b) $y = 16.7x + 585$

(c)

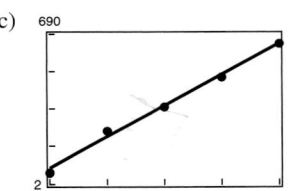

(d) 2000: \$752;
2002: \$785

25.

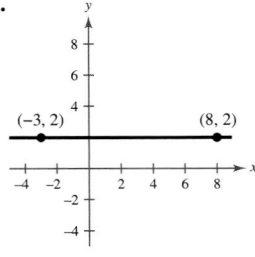

$m = 0$

27.

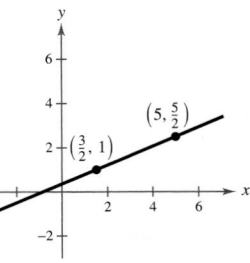

$m = \frac{3}{7}$

29.

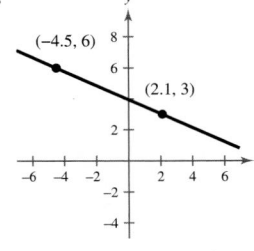

$m = -\frac{5}{11}$

31. $t = \frac{7}{3}$ **33.** $t = 3$

35. (a) $x - 4y - 6 = 0$ (b) $(6, 0), (10, 1), (-2, -2)$

37. (a) $3x - 2y - 10 = 0$ (b) $(4, 1), (2, -2), (-2, 8)$

39. (a) $2x + y + 17 = 0$

(b) $(-5, -7), (-4, -9), (-3, -11)$

41. (a) $5x + 5y + 24 = 0$ (b) $\left(-5, \frac{1}{5}\right), \left(-4, -\frac{4}{5}\right), \left(-6, \frac{6}{5}\right)$

43. (a) $y = 6$ (b) $(0, 6), (1, 6), (-1, 6)$

45. (a) $x = 10$ (b) $(10, 1), (10, 3), (10, -2)$

47. (a) $y = -1$

(b)

49. (a) $y = \frac{5}{12}x + \frac{1}{6}$

(b)

51. (a) $y = \frac{2}{7}x + \frac{2}{7}$

(b)

53. $V = 850t + 12,500$ **55.** $x + y - 1 = 0$

57. \$210,000

59. (a) $5x - 4y - 23 = 0$

(b) $4x + 5y - 2 = 0$

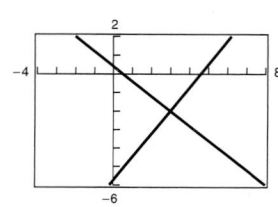

61. (a) $x = -6$

(b) $y = 2$

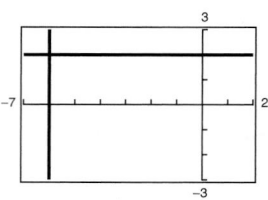

63. (a) Not a function because element 20 in A corresponds to two elements, 4 and 6, in B.

(b) Function

(c) Function

(d) Not a function because 30 in A corresponds to no element in B.

65. Not a function   **67.** Function

69. (a) 5   (b) 17   (c) $t^4 + 1$ (d) $-x^2 - 1$

71. All real numbers   **73.** $[-5, 5]$

75. All real numbers except $s = 3$

77. (a) $C = 5.35x + 16,000$ (b) $P = 2.85x - 16,000$

79. Domain: $(-\infty, \infty)$; Range: $(-\infty, 3]$

81. Domain: $[-6, 6]$; Range: $[0, 6]$

83. (a)

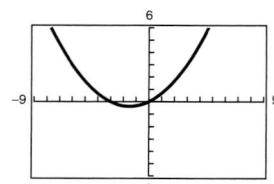

(b) Function

85. (a)

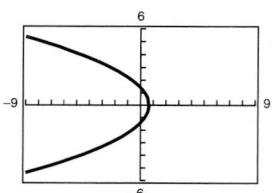

(b) Not a function

87. Increasing on $(-\infty, -1), (1, \infty)$;

Decreasing on $(-1, 1)$

89. Increasing on $(6, \infty)$

91. Relative maximum: $(0, 16)$

Relative minimums: $(-2, 0), (2, 0)$

93. Relative maximum: $(3, 27)$

95.

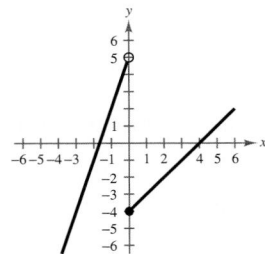

97. Even

99. Constant function $f(x) = C$. $g(x) = -2$

101. Cubic function $f(x) = x^3$. Reflection in x-axis and vertical shift 2 units downward. $g(x) = -x^3 - 2$

103.

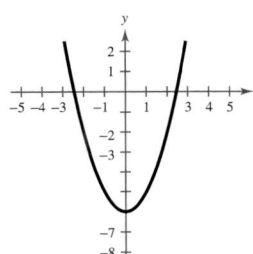

105.

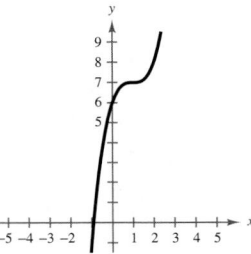

107.

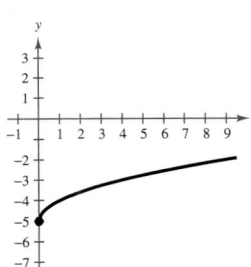

109.

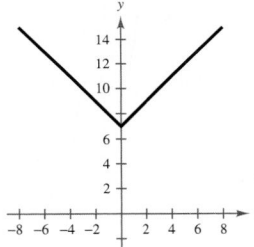

111.

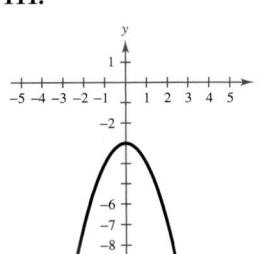

113.

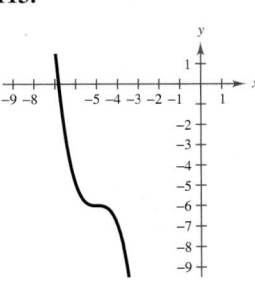

115.

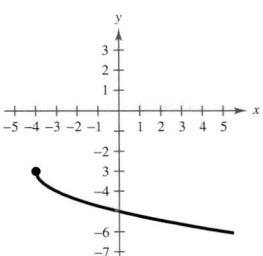

117.

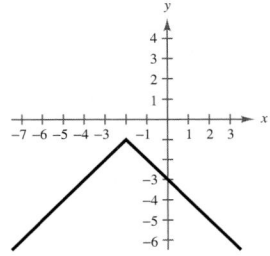

119.

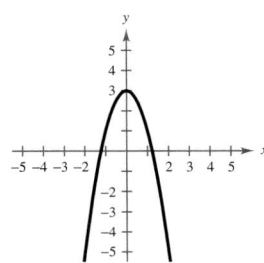

121.

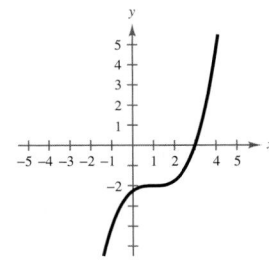

123.

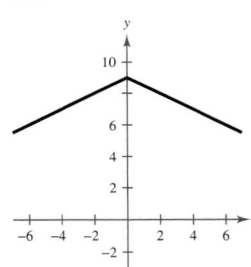

125.

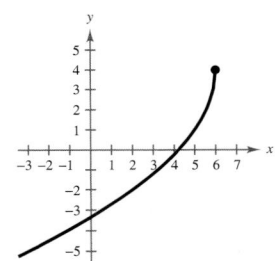

127. -7 **129.** -42 **131.** 5

133. 23   **135.** -97

137. $y_1 = 0.380t^2 + 3.75t + 16.9$

$y_2 = 0.146t^2 + 0.30t + 23.2$

139. $f^{-1}(x) = \dfrac{x}{6}$; $f(f^{-1}(x)) = f\left(\dfrac{x}{6}\right) = 6\left(\dfrac{x}{6}\right) = x$

$f^{-1}(f(x)) = f^{-1}(6x) = \dfrac{6x}{6} = x$

141. $f^{-1}(x) = x + 7$

$f(f^{-1}(x)) = f(x + 7) = (x + 7) - 7 = x$

$f^{-1}(f(x)) = f^{-1}(x - 7) = (x - 7) + 7 = x$

143. (a) $f^{-1}(x) = 2x + 6$

(b)
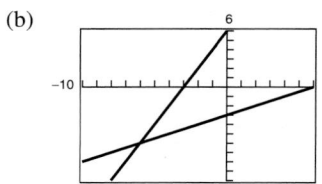

(c) $f^{-1}(f(x)) = f^{-1}\left(\frac{1}{2}x - 3\right)$

$= 2\left(\frac{1}{2}x - 3\right) + 6$

$= x$

$f(f^{-1}(x)) = f(2x + 6)$

$= \frac{1}{2}(2x + 6) - 3$

$= x$

145. (a) $f^{-1}(x) = x^2 - 1, \ x \geq 0$

(b)
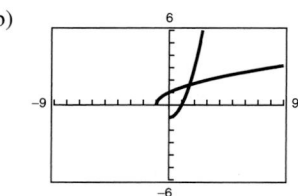

(c) $f^{-1}(f(x)) = f^{-1}\left(\sqrt{x + 1}\right)$

$= (x + 1) - 1$

$= x$

$f(f^{-1}(x)) = f(x^2 - 1), \ x \geq 0$

$= \sqrt{x^2 - 1 + 1}$

$= x$

147. $x \geq 4, \ f^{-1}(x) = \sqrt{\dfrac{x}{2} + 4}$

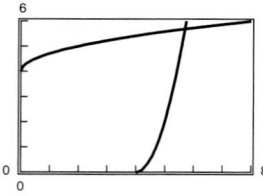

149. $x \geq 2, \ f^{-1}(x) = x + 2, \ x \geq 0$

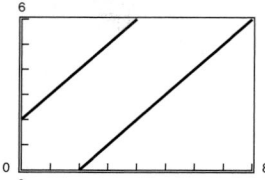

151. $f^{-1}(x) = 12x$ **153.** $f^{-1}(x) = \sqrt[3]{\dfrac{x + 3}{4}}$

155. $f^{-1}(x) = x^2 - 10, \ x \geq 0$

157. False. It is reflected in the x-axis before it is shifted down.

159. False. $f(x) = 4 - x = f^{-1}(x)$

Chapter Test *(page 154)*

1.
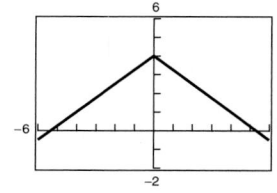

$(0, 4), \left(-\frac{16}{3}, 0\right), \left(\frac{16}{3}, 0\right)$

2.
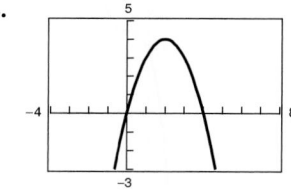

$(0, 0), (4, 0)$

3.
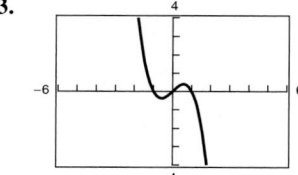

$(0, 0), (1, 0), (-1, 0)$

4.
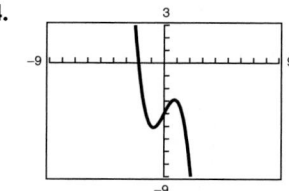

$(-2, 0), (0, -4)$

5.
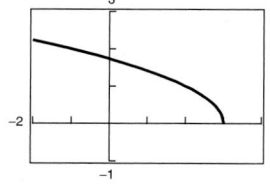

$\left(0, \sqrt{3}\right), (3, 0)$

6.

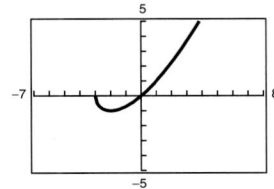

$(-3, 0), (0, 0)$

7. $(1, -4), (5, 2), (7, 5)$

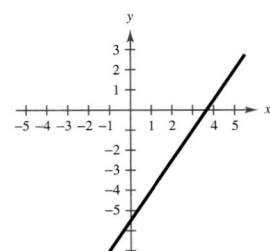

8. $\left(0, -\frac{9}{2}\right), (3, 0)$ **9.** $2x - 5y + 20 = 0$

10. No. To some x there correspond more than one value of y.

11. 7   **12.** $10 - \sqrt{6 - t}$ **13.** $\dfrac{\sqrt{3 - x} - 1}{2 - x}$

14. $(-\infty, 3]$ **15.** $C = 5.60x + 24,000$

$P = 3.60x - 24,000$

16. Increasing: $(-2, 0), (2, \infty)$

Decreasing: $(-\infty, -2), (0, 2)$

17. Increasing: $(-2, 2)$

Constant: $(-\infty, -2), (2, \infty)$

18.

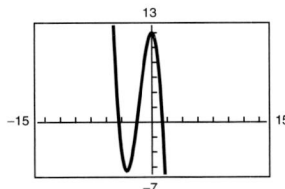

Relative minimum: $(-3.33, -6.52)$

Relative maximum: $(0, 12)$

19.

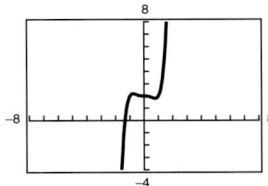

Relative maximum: $(-0.77, 2.19)$

Relative minimum: $(0.77, 1.81)$

20. (a) $f(x) = x^3$

(b) Horizontal shift 5 units to the right, reflection in x-axis, vertical stretch, and then a vertical shift 3 units upward

(c)

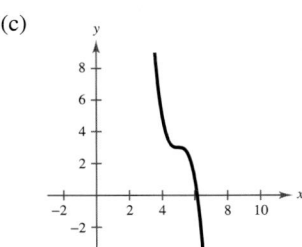

21. (a) $f(x) = \sqrt{x}$

(b) Reflection in y-axis and a horizontal shift 7 units to the left

(c)

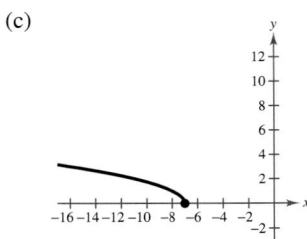

22. (a) $f(x) = |x|$

(b) Reflection in y-axis (no effect), vertical stretch, and vertical shift 7 units downward

(c)

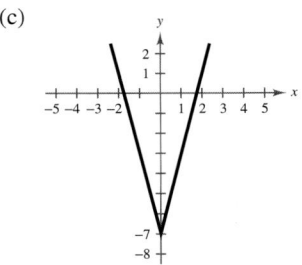

23. (a) $x^2 - \sqrt{2 - x}, \ (-\infty, 2]$ (b) $\dfrac{x^2}{\sqrt{2 - x}}, \ (-\infty, 2)$

(c) $2 - x, \ (-\infty, 2]$ (d) $2 - x^2, \ [0, \infty)$

24. $A = -x^2 + 50x, \ 0 < x < 50$

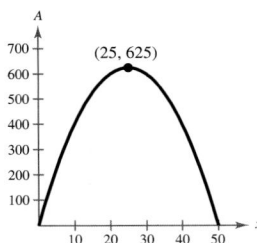

Maximum area $= 625$ square inches

Chapter 2

Section 2.1 *(page 164)*

1. (a) Yes (b) No (c) No (d) No

3. (a) Yes (b) No (c) No (d) No

5. (a) No (b) No (c) No (d) Yes

7. Identity **9.** Identity **11.** Conditional **13.** $-\frac{96}{23}$

15. -4 **17.** $-\frac{6}{5}$ **19.** 10 **21.** 4 **23.** 5

25. $\frac{11}{6}$ **27.** $\frac{5}{3}$ **29.** No solution **31.** $h = \dfrac{2A}{b}$

33. $b = \dfrac{2A - ah}{h}$ **35.** 61.2 inches **37.** 23,437.5 miles

39. (a)
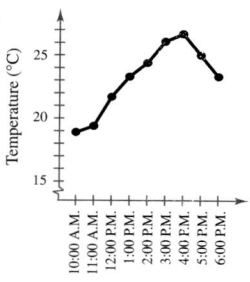
(b) $h = \frac{2}{3}w$; $P = \frac{10}{3}w$
(c) $w = \frac{9}{10}$ meter; $h = \frac{3}{5}$ meter

41. 187 points or 93.5%

43. 3 hours at 58 miles per hour; 2 hours and 45 minutes at 52 miles per hour

45. ≈ 46.3 miles per hour **47.** ≈ 8.33 minutes

49. $21\frac{1}{3}$ meters

51. (a)
(b) 42 feet

53. $16,666.67 **55.** First three quarters: 4.25%
Last quarter: 2.75%

57. 8823 units **59.** $x = 3\frac{2}{3}$ feet

61. (a)
(b) $w = 8$ inches; $h = 12$ inches; $l = 24$ inches

63.

65. (a)
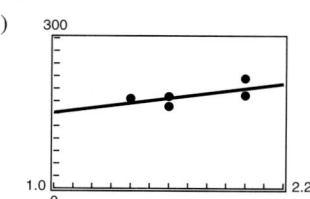
(b) Answers will vary. (c) $y = 4x + 134$
(d) 2000: 214; 2002: 222; 2005: 234

67. (a) $y = 47.77x + 103.8$
(b)
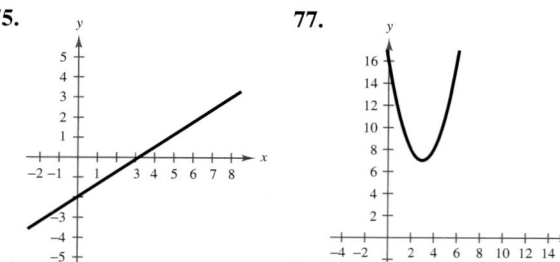
(c) A $1000 advertising increase means a $47.7 thousand = $47,770 sales increase.
(d) $175,300

69. False. $(9.5)^3 < \frac{4}{3}\pi(5.9)^3$.

71. Answers will vary. Example: $9x + 27 = 0$.

73. Equations with the same solution set
$4x + 16 = 0, 2x + 8 = 0$

75.

77.

79.
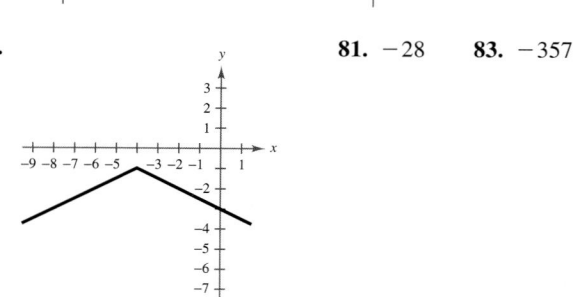

81. -28 **83.** -357

Section 2.2 *(page 176)*

1. $(5, 0), (0, -5)$ **3.** $(-2, 0), (1, 0), (0, -2)$

5. $(-2, 0), (0, 0)$ **7.** No intercepts

9. $(-2, 0), (6, 0), (0, -2)$ **11.** $(1, 0), \left(0, \frac{1}{2}\right)$

13.

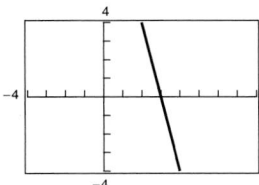

15.

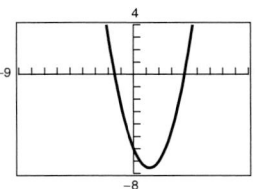

17.

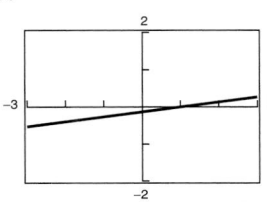

19.

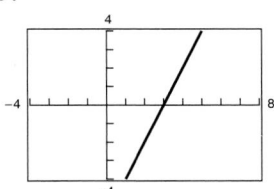

$(3, 0)$

21.

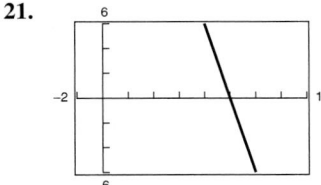

$(10, 0)$

23. $\frac{15}{4}$ **25.** $\frac{89}{13}$

27. 6   **29.** 3, 12   **31.** $1, -1.2$ **33.** $-\frac{5}{8}$

35. 2.172, 7.828   **37.** -1.379 **39.** $0.5, -3, 3$

41. $-0.717, 2.107$ **43.** -1.333 **45.** $-1, 7$

47. (a)

x	-1	0	1	2	3	4
$3.2x - 5.8$	-9	-5.8	-2.6	0.6	3.8	7

(b) $1 < x < 2$

(c)

x	1.5	1.6	1.7	1.8	1.9	2
$3.2x - 5.8$	-1	-0.68	-0.36	-0.04	0.28	0.6

(d) $1.8 < x < 1.9$

To improve accuracy, evaluate the expression in this interval and determine where the sign changes.

(e) $x = 1.8125$

49. $(1, 1)$ **51.** $(2, 2)$ **53.** $(-1, 3), (2, 6)$ **55.** $(4, 1)$

57. $(1.449, 1.899), (-3.449, -7.899)$

59. $(-2, 8), (1.333, 8)$ **61.** $(0, 0), (-2, 8), (2, 8)$

63. (a) 6.46

(b) $\frac{1.73}{0.27} \approx 6.41$. The second method decreases the accuracy.

65. (a) $T(x) = \dfrac{x}{63} + \dfrac{280 - x}{54}$

(b)

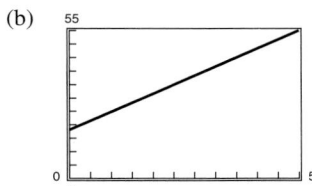

$0 \le x \le 280$

(c) 164.5 miles

67. (a) $C = 0.33(55 - x) + x$

(b)

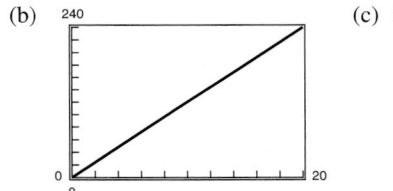

$0 \le x \le 55$

(c) 22.2 gallons

69. (a) $A(x) = 12x$

(b)

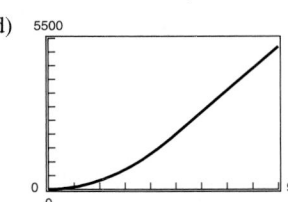

(c) 16.7

71. (a) 5200 cubic feet   (b) $y = \frac{1}{8}x$

(c) Answers will vary.

(d)

5500

0

0   9

(e)

d	3	5	7	9
V	720	2000	3600	5200

(f) 8.5 feet   (g) 38,896 gallons

73. 1994. To answer the question algebraically, solve the equation $0.46t + 30.81 = 33$. To answer the question graphically, graph the model $y = 0.46x + 30.81$ and the horizontal line $y = 33$ and determine where they intersect.

75. (a) The time and quantity when utilization of cucumbers equaled that of nectarines and peaches

    (b) $(3.84, 5.46)$

77. True   **79.** $\dfrac{4\sqrt{3}}{5}$ **81.** $\dfrac{3\left(8 - \sqrt{11}\right)}{53}$

83. $3x^2 + 13x - 30$ **85.** $4x^2 - 81$

87. $6x^4 + 5x^2y - 4y^2$

89. Increasing on $(-\infty, 0)$; Decreasing on $(0, \infty)$

Section 2.3   *(page 186)*

1. $a = -9, b = 4$ **3.** $a = 6, b = 5$ **5.** $4 + 5i$

7. 12 **9.** $-1 - 5i$ **11.** -75 **13.** $0.3i$

15. $11 - i$ **17.** $7 - 3\sqrt{2}\,i$ **19.** $-14 + 20i$

21. $\frac{1}{6} + \frac{7}{6}i$ **23.** $-4.2 + 7.5i$ **25.** $-2\sqrt{3}$

27. -10 **29.** $5 + i$ **31.** $12 + 30i$ **33.** 24

35. $-9 + 40i$ **37.** $\sqrt{-6}\sqrt{-6} = \sqrt{6}\,i\sqrt{6}\,i = 6i^2 = -6$

39. 25 **41.** 41 **43.** 484 **45.** 11 **47.** $-6i$

49. $\frac{16}{41} + \frac{20}{41}i$ **51.** $\frac{3}{5} + \frac{4}{5}i$ **53.** $-7 - 6i$

55. $-\frac{9}{1681} + \frac{40}{1681}i$ **57.** $-\frac{1}{2} - \frac{5}{2}i$ **59.** $-1 + 6i$

61. $-5i$ **63.** $-375\sqrt{3}\,i$ **65.** i **67.** $4 + 3i$

69. $6i$

71.

73.

75. Yes. $0, 0, 0, 0, 0, 0$

77. Yes.

    $0.5i, -0.25 + 0.5i, -0.1875 + 0.25i, -0.0273 + 0.4063i,$

    $-0.1643 + 0.4778i, -0.2013 + 0.3430i$

79. No. $1, 2, 5, 26, 677, 458{,}330$

81. (a) 8 (b) 8 (c) 8

83. (a) $3.12 - 0.97i$ (b) $12.82 + 5.28i$ **85.** True

87. (a) 1 (b) i (c) -1 (d) $-i$

89. Answers will vary.   **91.** $x^3 + x^2 + 2x - 6$

93. $4x^2 - 20x + 25$ **95.** $(-4, 0), (2, 0), (0, -8)$

97. $(-1, 0), (1, 0), (0, -1)$

Section 2.4   *(page 200)*

1. $2x^2 + 5x - 3 = 0$ **3.** $3x^2 - 60x - 10 = 0$

5. $0, -\frac{1}{2}$ **7.** $4, -2$ **9.** $3, -\frac{1}{2}$ **11.** $2, -6$

13. $-a - b, -a + b$ **15.** $\pm\sqrt{7}$; ± 2.65

17. $12 \pm 3\sqrt{2}$; $16.24, 7.76$ **19.** $1 \pm \frac{3}{2}\sqrt{2}$; $-1.62, 2.62$

21. 2 **23.** $-8, 4$ **25.** $-3 \pm \sqrt{7}$ **27.** $1 \pm \dfrac{\sqrt{6}}{3}$

29. $2 \pm 2\sqrt{3}$

31. (a)

    (b) and (c)

    $(-1, 0), (-5, 0)$

33. (a)

    (b) and (c)

    $\left(-\frac{1}{2}, 0\right), \left(\frac{3}{2}, 0\right)$

35. (a)

    (b) and (c)

    $\left(\frac{5}{2}, 0\right)$

37. (a)

    (b) and (c)

    No x-intercepts;

    $2 \pm i$

39. No real solutions   **41.** Two real solutions

43. No real solutions   **45.** $1 \pm \sqrt{3}$ **47.** $-4 \pm 2\sqrt{5}$

49. $\frac{2}{7}$ **51.** $-\frac{3}{2}, -\frac{5}{2}$ **53.** $1 \pm \sqrt{2}$ **55.** $6, -12$

57. $\frac{1}{2} \pm \sqrt{3}$ **59.** $-\frac{1}{2}$ **61.** $0, \pm\frac{3\sqrt{2}}{2}$ **63.** $\pm3, \pm3i$

65. $-3, 0$ **67.** $3, 1, -1$ **69.** $\pm\sqrt{3}, \pm1$

71. $\pm\frac{1}{2}, \pm4$ **73.** $-\frac{1}{5}, -\frac{1}{3}$ **75.** $\frac{1}{4}$

77. (a)

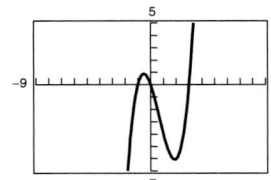

(b) and (c)

$x = 0, 3, -1$

79. (a)

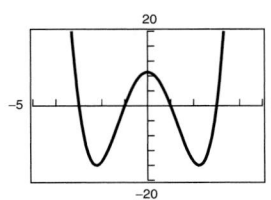

(b) and (c)

$x = \pm3, \pm1$

81. 26   **83.** 0   **85.** 9   **87.** $-59, 69$ **89.** 1

91. (a)

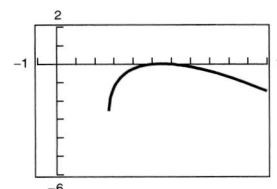

(b) and (c)

$x = 5, 6$

93. (a)

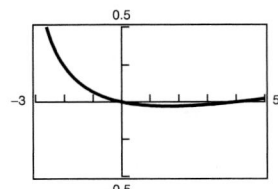

(b) and (c)

$x = 0, 4$

95. $4, -5$ **97.** $\frac{-3 \pm \sqrt{21}}{6}$ **99.** $2, -\frac{3}{2}$

101. $3, -2$ **103.** $\sqrt{3}, -3$

105. (a)

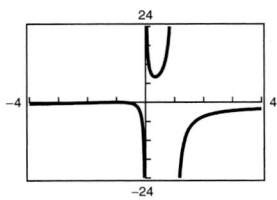

(b) and (c)

$x = -1$

107. (a)

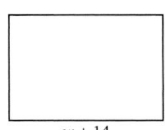

(b) and (c)

$x = 1, -3$

109. $x^2 + x - 30 = 0$ **111.** $21x^2 + 31x - 42 = 0$

113. $x^3 - 4x^2 - 2x + 8 = 0$ **115.** $x^4 - 3x^2 - 4 = 0$

117. $x = 6$ or -4 **119.** $h = \frac{1}{\pi r}\sqrt{S^2 - \pi^2 r^4}$

121. (a)

(b) $1632 = w^2 + 14w$

(c) Width: 34 feet;
length: 48 feet

123. 14 centimeters $\times$ 14 centimeters

125. (a) $s = -16t^2 + 1821$

(b)

t	0	2	4	6	8	10
s	1821	1757	1565	1245	797	221

(c) 10 seconds; ≈ 10.67 seconds

127. (a) $s = -16t^2 + 1368$ (b) 1112 feet

(c) ≈ 9.25 seconds

129. (a) 1995

(b)

t	0	1	2	3	4	5	6
y	6.84	6.91	7.05	7.26	7.54	7.90	8.33

(c)

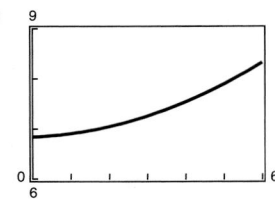

(d) 1991

131. (a)

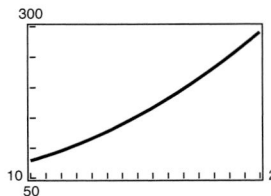

(b) $\approx 16.8°C$ (c) ≈ 2.5 times

133. (a)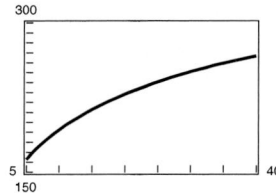

(b) 211.6°F   (c) 24.725 pounds per square inch

135. 50,000 units   **137.** $\dfrac{5\sqrt{2}}{2}$ centimeters

139. Eastbound plane: ≈ 550 miles per hour;

Northbound plane: ≈ 600 miles per hour

141. False. Both solutions are complex.

143. False. For example, $|x| = x^2 + x - 3$ has two extraneous solutions.

145. (a) $0, -\dfrac{b}{a}$ (b) $0, 1$ **147.** $x(x - 7)(x + 2)$

149. $x^{1/3}(9x + 25)$ **151.** Not a function

153. Function   **155.** Not a function

Section 2.5   *(page 214)*

1. (d)   **3.** (c)

5. (a) Yes   (b) No   (c) Yes   (d) No

7. (a) No   (b) Yes   (c) Yes   (d) No

9. $x > -4$

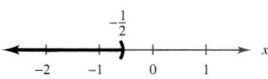

11. $x < -\dfrac{1}{2}$

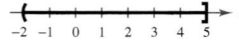

13. $-1 < x < 3$

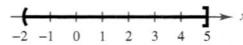

15. $-2 < x \le 5$

17. $-\dfrac{9}{2} < x < \dfrac{15}{2}$

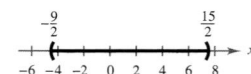

19.

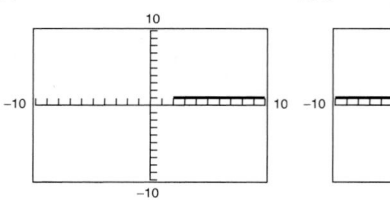

$x > 2$

21.

$x \le 2$

23.

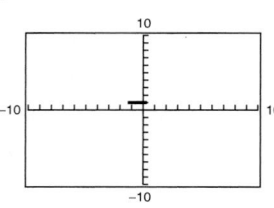

$-\dfrac{4}{3} < x < \dfrac{1}{3}$

25.

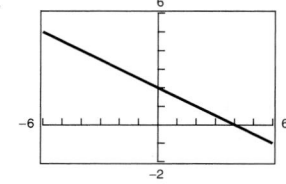

(a) $x \ge 2$ (b) $x \le \dfrac{3}{2}$

27.

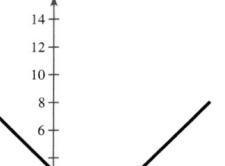

(a) $-2 \le x \le 4$ (b) $x \le 4$

29. $x < -2,\ x > 2$ **31.** $1 < x < 13$

33. $x < -28,\ x > 0$ **35.** $-2 < x < 3$

37.

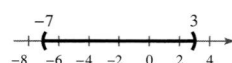

(a) $1 \le x \le 5$

(b) $x \le -1,\ x \ge 7$

39. $|x| \le 3$ **41.** $|x - 7| \ge 3$ **43.** $|x - 12| \le 10$

45. $(-7, 3)$ **47.** $(-\infty, -5],\ [1, \infty)$

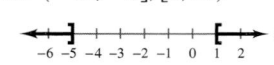

49. $[-2, 0], [2, \infty)$

51.

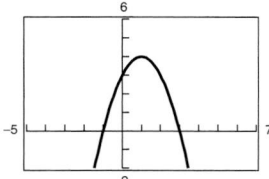

(a) $x \le -1, \ x \ge 3$

(b) $0 \le x \le 2$

53.

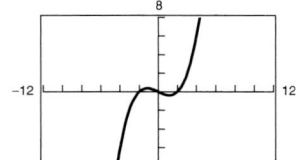

(a) $-2 \le x \le 0,$
$2 \le x < \infty$

(b) $x \le 4$

55. $(-\infty, -1), (0, 1)$ **57.** $(-\infty, -1), (4, \infty)$

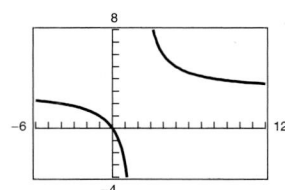

59.

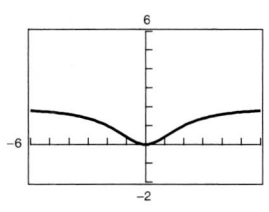

(a) $0 \le x < 2$

(b) $2 < x \le 4$

61.

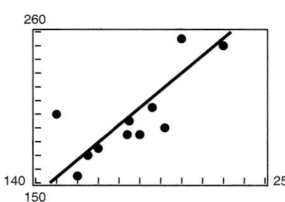

(a) $2 \le |x|$

(b) $-\infty < x < \infty$

63. $[5, \infty)$ **65.** $(-\infty, \infty)$ **67.** $\left[-\frac{5}{2}, \infty\right)$

69. (a) and (b)

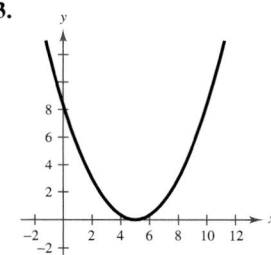

(c) 186.23 pounds

(d) Answers will vary.

71. $[65.8, 71.2]$

73. (a) $333\frac{1}{3}$ vibrations per second (b) 3.6 millimeters

(c) $1.2 < t < 2.4$ (d) $0 < v < 500$

75. False. $10 \ge -x$

77. (a) a, b

(b)

Interval	Expression	Sign
$(-\infty, a)$	$(x - a)$	$-$
	$(x - b)$	$-$
	$(x - a)(x - b)$	$+$
(a, b)	$(x - a)$	$+$
	$(x - b)$	$-$
	$(x - a)(x - b)$	$-$
(b, ∞)	$(x - a)$	$+$
	$(x - b)$	$+$
	$(x - a)(x - b)$	$+$

(c) x-values that are zeros of the function

79. $d = \sqrt{106} \approx 10.296$; Midpoint $= (5.5, 0.5)$

81. $d = \sqrt{180} \approx 13.416$; Midpoint $= (-3, 3)$

83. **85.**

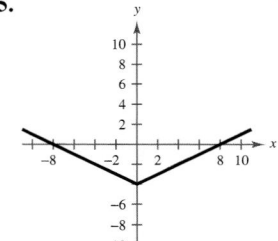

87.

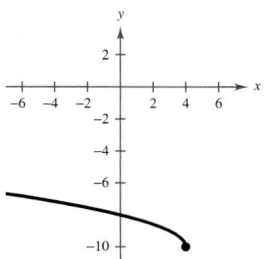

89. $y^{-1} = \dfrac{x - 8}{5}$ **91.** $y^{-1} = x^3 + 7$

Review Exercises *(page 218)*

1. (a) No (b) No (c) No (d) Yes

3. $x = \frac{1}{2}$ **5.** $x = \frac{7}{3}$

7. September: $325,000; October: $364,000

9. $2\frac{6}{7}$ liters **11.** 4 **13.** 56 miles per hour

15. Basketball: ≈ 455.95 cubic inches;

Baseball: ≈ 13.4 cubic inches

17. (a) $y = -1.2x + 64$

(b)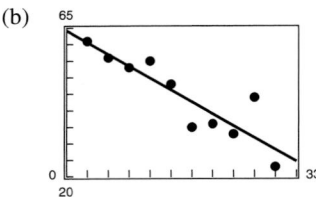

(c) Eliminate the point $(27, 44)$; $y = -1.4x + 66$

19. $(20, 0), (0, -4)$ **21.** $(0, 25), (5, 0), (-5, 0)$

23. 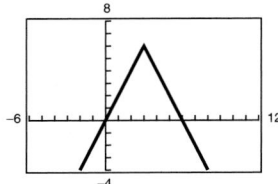 $(0, 0), (6, 0)$

25. $x = 9.4$ **27.** $x = -2.722$ **29.** No solution

31. $(5, 2)$ **33.** $(-1, 8)$ **35.** $3 - 2\sqrt{3}i$ **37.** $1 - 4i$

39. $-\sqrt{2}i$ **41.** $17 + 28i$ **43.** $9 + 20i$ **45.** $-16i$

47. $\frac{17}{26} + \frac{7}{26}i$ **49.** $-\frac{7}{625} - \frac{24}{625}i$

51.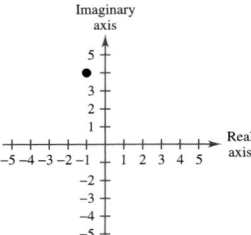

53.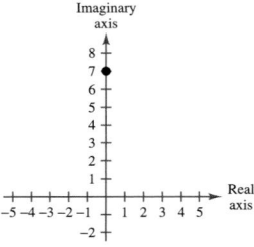

55. $-\frac{5}{2}, 3$ **57.** $\pm\frac{5}{4}$ **59.** $-3 \pm 2\sqrt{3}$

61. $\dfrac{-1 \pm \sqrt{61}}{2}$ **63.** $0, -\dfrac{13}{2}$ **65.** $0, \dfrac{1}{6}$ **67.** $0, \dfrac{3}{2}$

69. 66 **71.** 2 **73.** $\dfrac{38 + 5\sqrt{3}}{24}$ **75.** 79

77. $\pm 2, \pm\frac{2}{3}$ **79.** $\frac{7}{3}$ **81.** $-2, 0$ **83.** $-5, 2$

85. $2, 3$

87. (a) 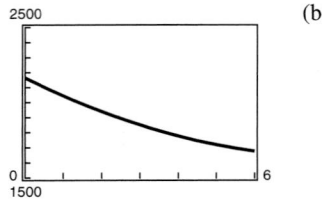 (b) 1991

(c) Eventually the curve begins to rise rapidly. At this point the model is probably not a good predictor.

89. $\left(-\frac{5}{3}, \infty\right)$

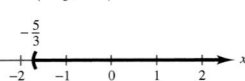

91. $\left(-\frac{1}{2}, \frac{19}{2}\right]$

93. $[-4, 4]$

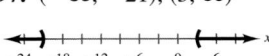

95. $(-\infty, -1), (7, \infty)$

97. $(-\infty, -21), (3, \infty)$

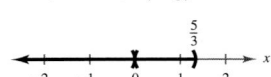

99. $\left[-\frac{1}{4}, 6\right]$

101. $(-\infty, 0), \left(0, \frac{5}{3}\right)$

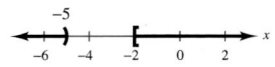

103. $[-5, -1), (1, \infty)$

105. $(-\infty, -5), [-2, \infty)$

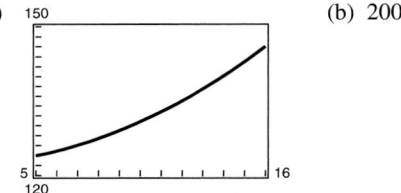

107. (a) 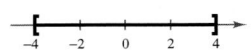 (b) 2001

109. False. $(3 + 2i) + (5 - 2i) = 8$

111. An identity is true for all values of the variable and a conditional equation is true for only some values of the variable.

113. (a) Negative (b) Positive

Chapter Test *(page 222)*

1. $x = 3$ **2.** $x = \frac{2}{15}$ **3.** $-9 - 18i$

4. $6 + \left(2\sqrt{5} + \sqrt{14}\right)i$ **5.** $13 + 4i$ **6.** $-17 + 14i$

7. $\frac{43}{37} + \frac{38}{37}i$ **8.** $\frac{36}{41} + \frac{86}{41}i$

9. 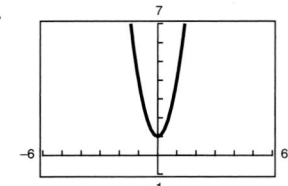 No x-intercepts

No real zeros

10.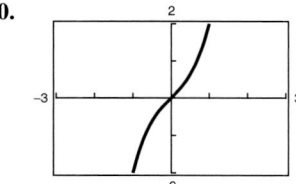
One x-intercept: 0
One real zero: 0

11.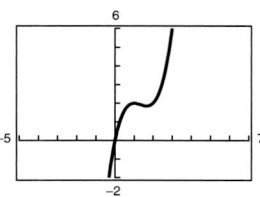
One x-intercept: 0
One real zero: 0

12.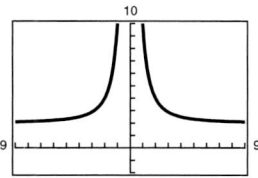
No x-intercepts
No real zeros

13. $x = 1, 9$ **14.** $x = -6 \pm \sqrt{38}$ **15.** $x = \pm\frac{9}{2}$

16. $x = -3, \frac{1}{5}$ **17.** $\pm2, \frac{4}{3}$ **18.** 2   **19.** $\pm\sqrt{58}$

20. $-\frac{5}{2}, \frac{11}{4}$

21. $\left(\frac{7}{6}, \frac{17}{8}\right)$ **22.** (3, 13)

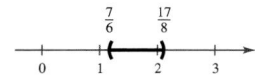   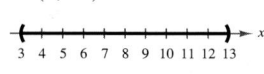

23. $\left(-7, -\frac{2}{3}\right)$

24. $C = 16.4t + 402$; 2002   **25.** \$0.10

Cumulative Test for Chapters P–2
(page 223)

1. $\dfrac{7x^3}{16y^5}$ **2.** $9\sqrt{15}$ **3.** $2x^2y\sqrt{7y}$ **4.** $7x - 10$

5. $x^3 - x^2 - 5x + 6$ **6.** $\dfrac{x - 1}{(x + 1)(x + 3)}$

7. $(3 + x)(7 - x)$ **8.** $x(1 + x)(1 - 6x)$

9. $2(3 - 2x)(9 + 6x + 4x^2)$

10. Midpoint: $(1.5, -2)$; $d = 2\sqrt{61} \approx 15.62$

11. $\left(x + \frac{1}{2}\right)^2 + (y + 8)^2 = \frac{25}{16}$

12. 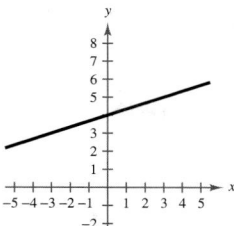   **13.**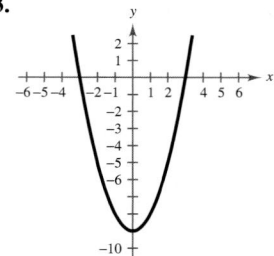

14.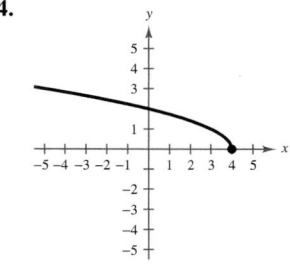

15. (a) $28x + 11y + 52 = 0$
  (b) $\left(0, -\frac{52}{11}\right), \left(-\frac{52}{28}, 0\right), \left(-2, \frac{4}{11}\right)$

16. (a) $2x + y = 0$ (b) $(0, 0), (1, -2), (2, -4)$

17. (a) $x = -\frac{3}{7}$ (b) $\left(-\frac{3}{7}, 0\right), \left(-\frac{3}{7}, 1\right), \left(-\frac{3}{7}, -3\right)$

18. No. It doesn't pass the Vertical Line Test.

19. (a) $\dfrac{3}{2}$ (b) Undefined   (c) $\dfrac{s + 2}{s}$

20. (a) -13 (b) -14 (c) -8

21.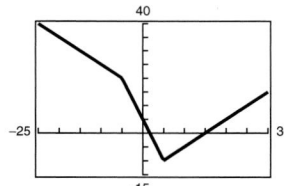
Decreasing on $(-\infty, 5)$
Increasing on $(5, \infty)$

22. (a) 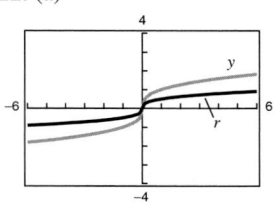   (b)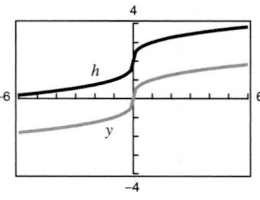

Vertical shrink   Vertical shift
                    Horizontal shift

(c)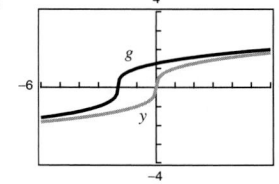

23. -53 **24.** $\frac{197}{16}$ **25.** -79 **26.** 42

27.

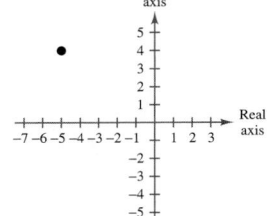

28. $13x^2 - 9x + 6 = 0$

29.

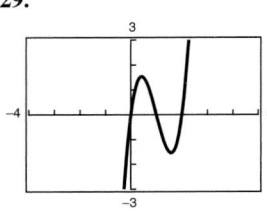

x-intercepts: 0, 1, 2

30.

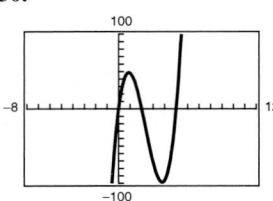

x-intercepts: 0, 2, 5

31.

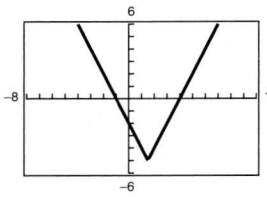

x-intercepts: $-1, 4$

32.

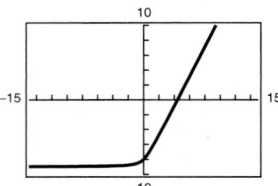

x-intercept: $4.\overline{44}$

33. $X = \pm\sqrt{R^2 - Z^2}$ **34.** $p = \dfrac{k}{3\pi r^2 L}$ **35.** $C = 4$

36. $C = -\frac{4}{5}$ **37.** $(-\infty, 17.143)$

38. $(-\infty, -3], \left[\frac{5}{2}, \infty\right)$ **39.** $(4, \infty)$

40. $S = 119.76t + 914.6$

2000: \$2112.2 million;   2002: \$2351.7 million;
2004: \$2591.2 million

41. $r = 4.297$ inches

42. (a) $A = x(273 - x)$

(b)

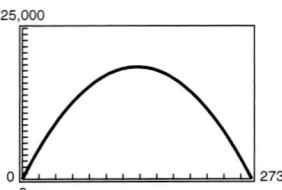

$0 < x < 273$

(c) ≈ 76.2 feet $\times$ 196.8 feet

Chapter 3

Section 3.1   *(page 233)*

1. (g)   **3.** (b)   **5.** (f)   **7.** (e)

9. (a)

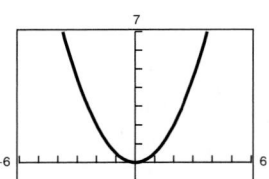

Vertical shrink

(b)

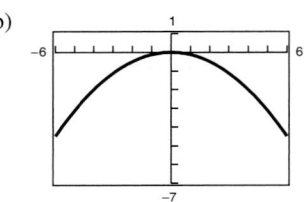

Vertical shrink and reflection in the x-axis

(c)

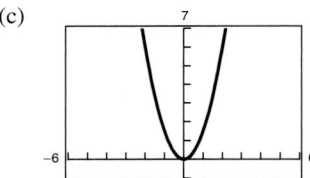

Vertical stretch

(d)

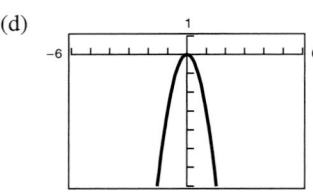

Vertical stretch and reflection in the x-axis

11. (a)

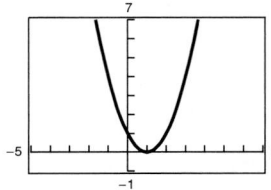

Horizontal shift

(b)

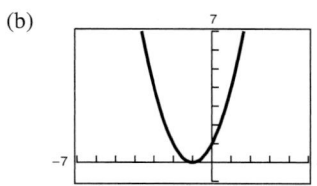

Horizontal shift

(c)

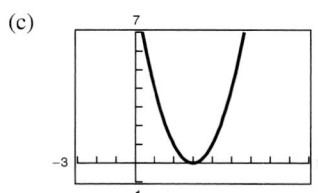

Horizontal shift

(d)

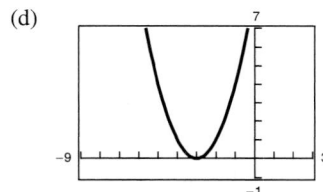

Horizontal shift

13. Vertex: $(0, 25)$

Intercepts:

$(0, 25), (\pm 5, 0)$

15. Vertex: $(0, -4)$

Intercepts:

$(\pm 2\sqrt{2}, 0), (0, -4)$

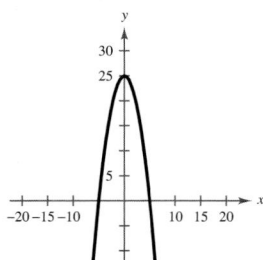

17. Vertex: $(-4, -3)$

Intercepts:

$(\pm\sqrt{3} - 4, 0), (0, 13)$

19. Vertex: $(4, 0)$

Intercepts:

$(4, 0), (0, 16)$

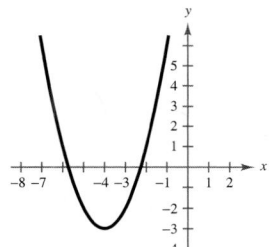

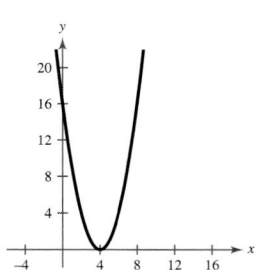

21. Vertex: $\left(\frac{1}{2}, 1\right)$

Intercept: $\left(0, \frac{5}{4}\right)$

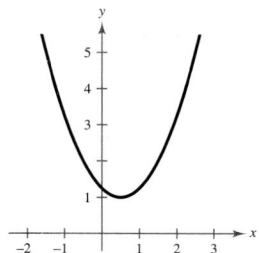

23. Vertex: $(1, 6)$

Intercepts:

$\left(1 \pm \sqrt{6}, 0\right), (0, 5)$

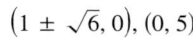
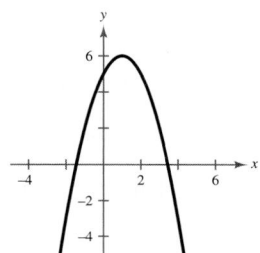

25. Vertex: $\left(\frac{1}{2}, 20\right)$

Intercept: $(0, 21)$

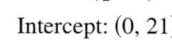
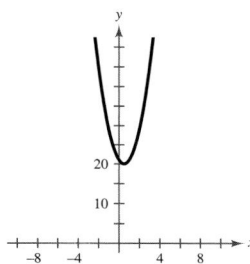

27. Vertex: $(-1, 4)$

Intercepts:

$(1, 0), (-3, 0), (0, 3)$

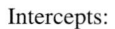
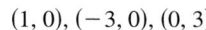
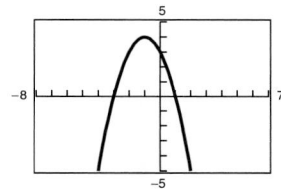

29. Vertex: $(-4, -5)$

Intercepts:

$\left(-4 \pm \sqrt{5}, 0\right), (0, 11)$

31. Vertex: $(4, -1)$

Intercepts:

$\left(4 \pm \frac{1}{2}\sqrt{2}, 0\right), (0, 31)$

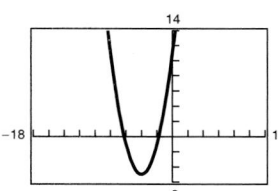

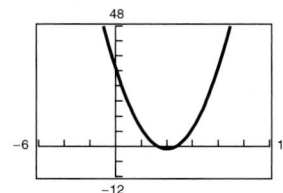

33. Vertex: $(-2, -3)$

Intercepts: $\left(-2 \pm \sqrt{6}, 0\right), (0, -1)$

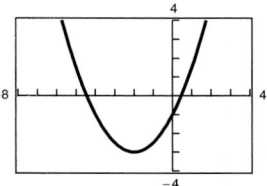

35. $y = (x - 1)^2$ **37.** $y = -(x + 1)^2 + 4$

39. $f(x) = (x + 2)^2 + 5$ **41.** $f(x) = -\frac{1}{2}(x - 3)^2 + 4$

43. $f(x) = 2(x + 2)^2 - 2$ **45.** $f(x) = \frac{19}{81}\left(x - \frac{5}{2}\right)^2 - \frac{3}{4}$

47. $(\pm 4, 0)$; They are the same.

49. $(5, 0), (-1, 0)$; They are the same.

51.

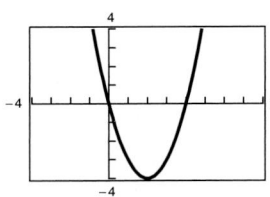

$(0, 0), (4, 0)$; They are the same.

53.

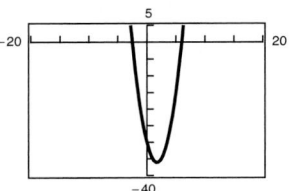

$\left(-\frac{5}{2}, 0\right), (6, 0)$; They are the same.

55.

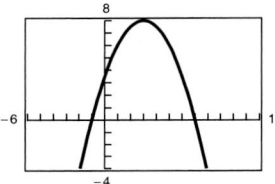

$(7, 0), (-1, 0)$; They are the same.

57. $f(x) = x^2 - 2x - 3$ **59.** $f(x) = 2x^2 + 7x + 3$

     $g(x) = -x^2 + 2x + 3$ $g(x) = -2x^2 - 7x - 3$

61. 55, 55   **63.** 12, 6

65. (a) $A = x(50 - x)$, $0 < x < 50$

    (b)

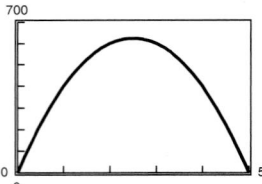

    (c) 25 feet $\times$ 25 feet

67. (a)

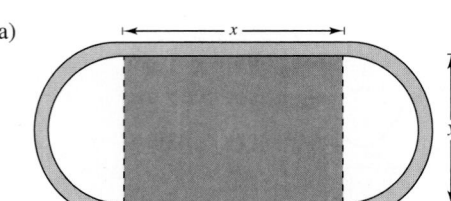

    (b) $r = \frac{1}{2}y$; $d = y\pi$ (c) $y = \dfrac{200 - 2x}{\pi}$

    (d) $A = x\left(\dfrac{200 - 2x}{\pi}\right)$

    (e)

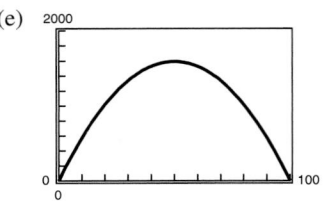

$$x = 50 \text{ meters}, \; y = \frac{100}{\pi} \text{ meters}$$

69. 20   **71.** 350,000 units

73. (a)

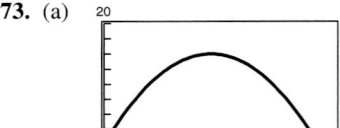
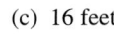

    (b) 4 feet

    (c) 16 feet

    (d) 25.86 feet

75. (a)

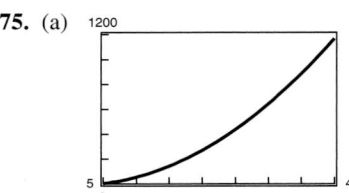

    (b) 166.69 board feet

    (c) 26.59 inches

77. (a)

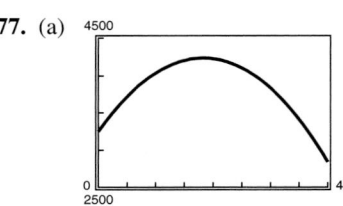

    (b) 4242 cigarettes per person. Answers will vary.

    (c) 9703 cigarettes per smoker per year; 27 cigarettes per smoker per day

79. True   **81.** (a). The profits are positive and rising.

83. $(4, 2)$ **85.** $(2, 11)$ **87.** $20i$ **89.** $52 - 47i$

Section 3.2   *(page 246)*

1. (f)   **3.** (c)   **5.** (e)   **7.** (g)

9. (a)   (b)

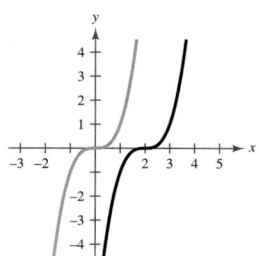   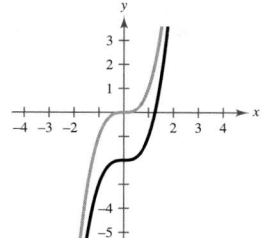

(c)   (d)

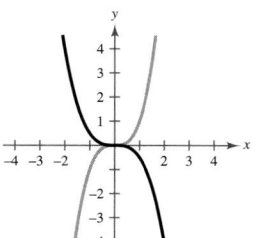   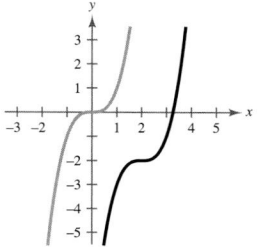

11. (a)   (b)

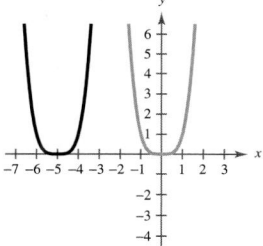   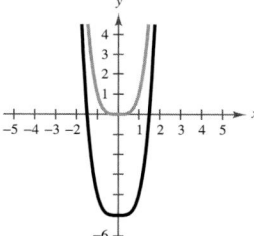

(c)   (d)

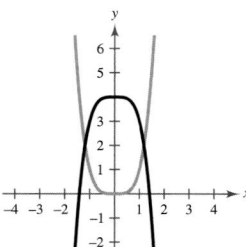   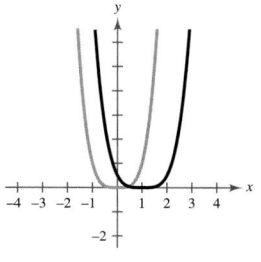

13.   **15.**

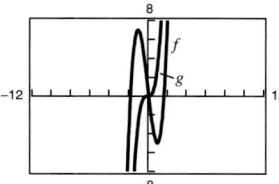   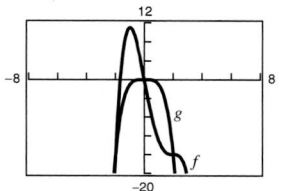

17. Rises to the left.   **19.** Falls to the left.
Rises to the right.   Falls to the right.

21. Rises to the left.   **23.** Rises to the left.
Falls to the right.   Falls to the right.

25. Falls to the left.   **27.** ± 5 **29.** 3
Falls to the right.

31. $1, -2$ **33.** $2, 0$ **35.** $\dfrac{-5 \pm \sqrt{37}}{2}$

37. (a)

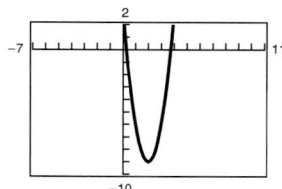

(b) Answers will vary.   (c) $\left(2 - \sqrt{3}, 0\right), \left(2 + \sqrt{3}, 0\right)$

39. (a)

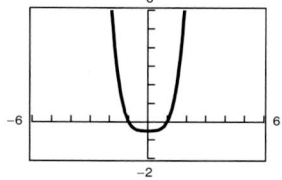

(b) Answers will vary.   (c) $(-1, 0), (1, 0)$

41. (a)

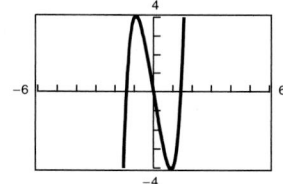

(b) Answers will vary.   (c) $(0, 0), \left(-\sqrt{2}, 0\right), \left(\sqrt{2}, 0\right)$

43. (a)

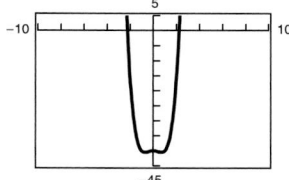

(b) Answers will vary.   (c) $\left(-\sqrt{5}, 0\right), \left(\sqrt{5}, 0\right)$

45. (a)

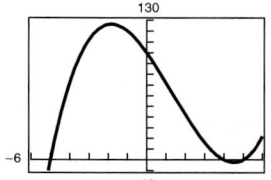

(b) Answers will vary.   (c) $(4, 0), (-5, 0), (5, 0)$

47. (a)

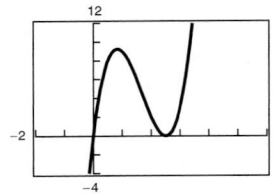

(b) Answers will vary. (c) $(0, 0), \left(\frac{5}{2}, 0\right)$

49.

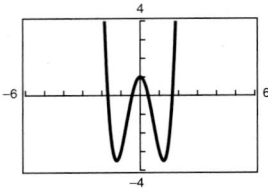

Relative maximum: $(0, 1)$

Relative minimums: $(\pm 1.225, -3.500)$

51.

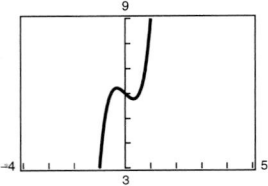

Relative maximum: $(-0.324, 6.218)$

Relative minimum: $(0.324, 5.782)$

53. $f(x) = x^2 - 12x$ **55.** $f(x) = x^2 + 4x - 12$

57. $f(x) = x^3 + 7x^2 + 12x$

59. $f(x) = x^4 - 4x^3 - 9x^2 + 36x$

61. $f(x) = x^2 - 2x - 2$

63. $f(x) = x^3 - 10x^2 + 27x - 22$

65. (a) Falls to the left, rises to the right

(b) $(0, 0), (3, 0), (-3, 0)$

(c)

x	-3.3	-2	-1	1	2	3.3
y	-6.2	10	8	-8	-10	6.2

(d)

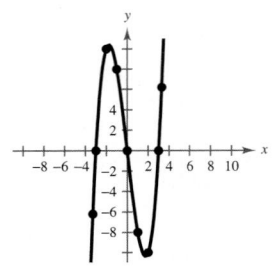

67. (a) Rises to the left and the right

(b) No zeros

(c)

t	-3	-2	-1	0	1	2	3
y	7.5	5.8	4.5	3.8	3.5	3.8	4.5

(d)

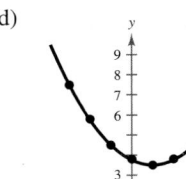

69. (a) Falls to the left, rises to the right

(b) $(0, 0), (3, 0)$

(c)

x	-2.5	-1	1	2	4
y	-34.4	-4	-2	-4	16

(d)

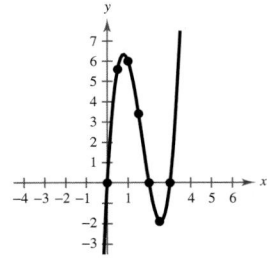

71. (a) Falls to the left, rises to the right

(b) $(0, 0), (2, 0), (3, 0)$

(c)

x	-0.5	0.5	1	1.5	2.5	3.5
y	-13	5.6	6	3.4	-1.9	7.9

(d)

73. (a) Rises to the left, falls to the right

(b) $(0, 0)$, $(-5, 0)$

(c)

x	-6	-4	-3	-2	1	2
y	36	-16	-18	-12	-6	-28

(d)

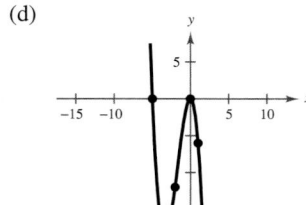

75. (a) Falls to the left, rises to the right

(b) $(0, 0)$, $(4, 0)$

(c)

x	-2	-1	1	2	3	5
y	-24	-5	-3	-8	-9	25

(d)

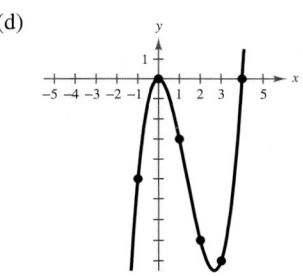

77. (a) Falls to the left and right

(b) $(-2, 0)$, $(2, 0)$

(c)

t	-4	-3	-1	0	1	3
y	-36	-6.3	-2.3	-4	-2.3	-6.3

(d)

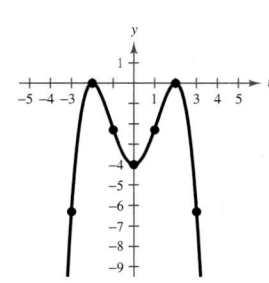

79. (a)

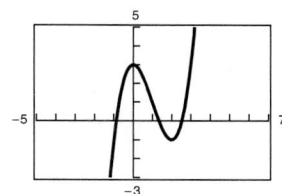

(b) -0.879, 1.347, 2.532

$(-1, 0)$, $(1, 2)$, $(2, 3)$

81. (a)

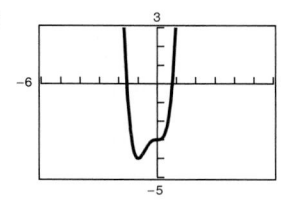

(b) -1.585, 0.779

$(-2, -1)$, $(0, 1)$

83.

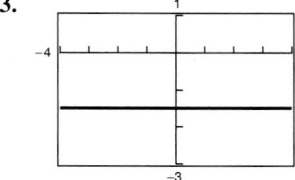

Xmin = -4
Xmax = 4
Xscl = 1
Ymin = -3
Ymax = 1
Yscl = 1

85.

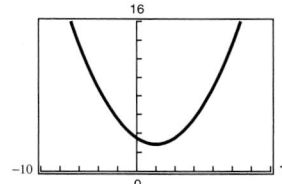

Xmin = -10
Xmax = 14
Xscl = 2
Ymin = 0
Ymax = 16
Yscl = 2

87.

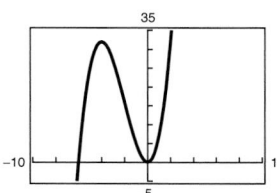

Two x-intercepts

89.

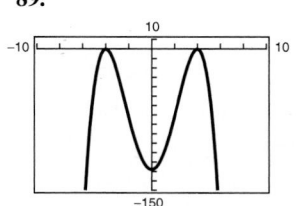

Symmetric to the y-axis
Two x-intercepts

91.

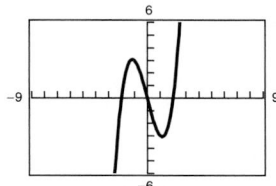

Symmetric to the origin
Three x-intercepts

93.

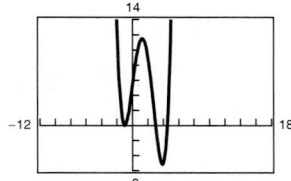

Three x-intercepts

95. (a) and (b)

Height	Width	Volume
1	$36 - 2(1)$	$1[36 - 2(1)]^2 = 1156$
2	$36 - 2(2)$	$2[36 - 2(2)]^2 = 2048$
3	$36 - 2(3)$	$3[36 - 2(3)]^2 = 2700$
4	$36 - 2(4)$	$4[36 - 2(4)]^2 = 3136$
5	$36 - 2(5)$	$5[36 - 2(5)]^2 = 3380$
6	$36 - 2(6)$	$6[36 - 2(6)]^2 = 3456$
7	$36 - 2(7)$	$7[36 - 2(7)]^2 = 3388$

$5 < x < 7$

(c) Answers will vary. Domain: $0 < x < 18$

(d)

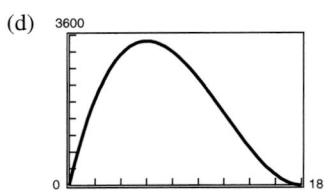

$x = 6$

97. $(200, 160)$

99. (a) $0.002983x^4 - 0.02386x^3 + 0.0194x^2 + 0.113x$

(b)

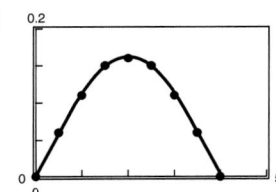

(c) 0. Yes

The model fits well.

101. False. It can have at most three turning points.

103.

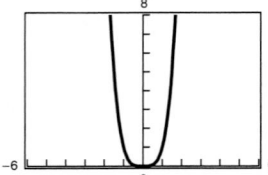

(a) Vertical shift of two units; even

(b) Horizontal shift of two units; neither even nor odd

(c) Reflection in the y-axis; even

(d) Reflection in the x-axis; even

(e) Vertical shrink; even   (f) Vertical shrink; even

(g) $g(x) = x^3$; odd   (h) $g(x) = x^{16}$; even

105. 33   **107.** $-\frac{4}{3} \approx -1.3$ **109.** 72

111. $x \le -\frac{1}{2}, \ x \ge 1$ **113.** $x \le -24, \ x \ge 8$

115. $f(x) = \frac{17}{25}x^2 - 8$ **117.** $f(x) = \frac{1}{5}(x + 5)^2 - 2$

Section 3.3   *(page 260)*

1.

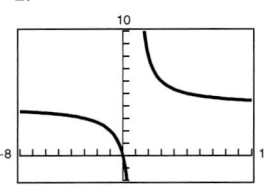

3.

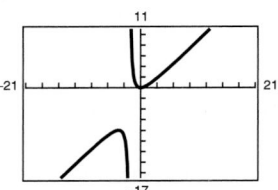

5.

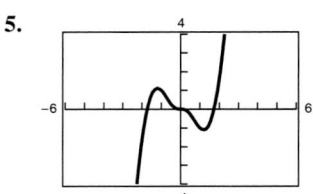

7. $2x + 4$ **9.** $x^2 - 3x + 1$ **11.** $7 - \dfrac{11}{x + 2}$

13. $3x + 5 - \dfrac{2x - 3}{2x^2 + 1}$ **15.** $x^2 + 2x + 4 + \dfrac{2x - 11}{x^2 - 2x + 3}$

17. $2x - \dfrac{17x - 5}{x^2 - 2x + 1}$ **19.** $3x^2 + 2x + 20 + \dfrac{58}{x - 4}$

21. $6x^2 + 25x + 74 + \dfrac{248}{x - 3}$ **23.** $9x^2 - 16$

25. $x^2 - 8x + 64$ **27.** $4x^2 + 14x - 30$

29. $f(x) = (x - 4)(x^2 + 3x - 2) + 3, \ f(4) = 3$

31. $f(x) = \left(x - \sqrt{2}\right)\left[x^2 + \left(3 + \sqrt{2}\right)x + 3\sqrt{2}\right] - 8,$
$f\left(\sqrt{2}\right) = -8$

33. $f(x) = \left(x - 1 + \sqrt{3}\right)\left[4x^2 - \left(2 + 4\sqrt{3}\right)x - \left(2 + 2\sqrt{3}\right)\right],$
$f\left(1 - \sqrt{3}\right) = 0$

35. (a) 1   (b) 4   (c) 4   (d) 1954

37. (a) 97   (b) $-\frac{5}{3}$ (c) 17   (d) -199

39. $(x - 2)(x + 3)(x - 1)$ **41.** $(2x - 1)(x - 5)(x - 2)$
Zeros: $2, -3, 1$ Zeros: $\frac{1}{2}, 5, 2$

43. $\left(x - \sqrt{2}\right)\left(x + \sqrt{2}\right)(x + 2)$
Zeros: $\pm\sqrt{2}, -2$

45. (a) Answers will vary.   (b) $(2x - 1)$
(c) $(x + 2)(x - 1)(2x - 1)$ (d) $-2, 1, \frac{1}{2}$

47. (a) Answers will vary. (b) $(x - 1)$, $(x - 2)$
  (c) $(x - 5)(x + 4)(x - 1)(x - 2)$ (d) $-4, 1, 2, 5$

49. (a) Answers will vary. (b) $(x + 7)$
  (c) $(2x + 1)(3x - 2)(x + 7)$ (d) $-7, -\frac{1}{2}, \frac{2}{3}$

51. $\pm 1, \pm 3$

53. $\pm 1, \pm 3, \pm 5, \pm 9, \pm 15, \pm 45, \pm\frac{1}{2}, \pm\frac{3}{2}, \pm\frac{5}{2}, \pm\frac{9}{2}, \pm\frac{15}{2}, \pm\frac{45}{2}$

55. (a) $\pm 1, \pm 2, \pm 4$
  (b) 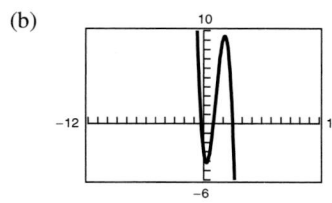 (c) $-2, -1, 2$

57. (a) $\pm 1, \pm 3, \pm\frac{1}{2}, \pm\frac{3}{2}, \pm\frac{1}{4}, \pm\frac{3}{4}$
  (b) 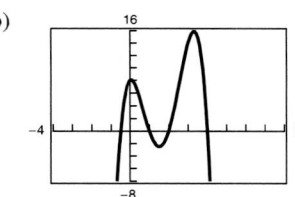 (c) $-\frac{1}{4}, 1, 3$

59. (a) $\pm 1, \pm 2, \pm 4, \pm 8, \pm\frac{1}{2}$
  (b) 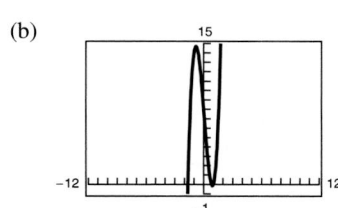 (c) $-\frac{1}{2}, 1, 2, 4$

61. (a) $\pm 1, \pm 2, \pm 4, \pm 8, \pm\frac{1}{2}, \pm\frac{1}{3}, \pm\frac{2}{3}, \pm\frac{4}{3}, \pm\frac{8}{3}, \pm\frac{1}{6}$
  (b) 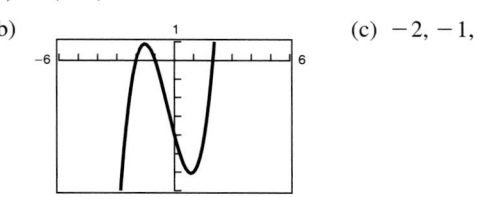 (c) $1, \dfrac{-5 \pm \sqrt{217}}{12}$

63. $-1, 2$ **65.** $0, -1, -3, 4$ **67.** $-2, -\frac{1}{2}, 4$

69. (a) $-2.236, 2, 2.236$ (b) 2
  (c) $f(x) = (x - 2)\left(x - \sqrt{5}\right)\left(x + \sqrt{5}\right)$

71. (a) $-2, 0.268, 3.732$ (b) -2
  (c) $h(t) = (t + 2)\left(t - 2 + \sqrt{3}\right)\left(t - 2 - \sqrt{3}\right)$

73. (a) $0, 3, 4, -1.414, 1.414$ (b) $0, 3, 4$
  (c) $h(x) = x(x - 3)(x - 4)\left(x + \sqrt{2}\right)\left(x - \sqrt{2}\right)$

75.–77. Answers will vary. **79.** $\pm 2, \pm\frac{3}{2}$ **81.** $\pm 1, \frac{1}{4}$

83. (d) **85.** (b)

87. (a) and (b)

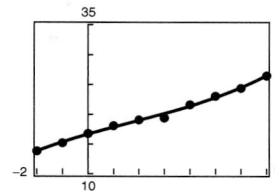

$$R = 0.01326t^3 - 0.0677t^2 + 1.231t + 16.68$$

The model is a good fit.

(c)

t	-2	-1	0	1	2
R	13.84	15.37	16.68	17.86	18.98

t	3	4	5	6	7
R	20.12	21.37	22.8	24.49	26.53

(d) $R(12) = 44.62$. No; the model will turn sharply upward.

89. (a)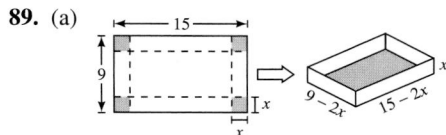

(b) $V = x(9 - 2x)(15 - 2x)$; Domain: $0 < x < \frac{9}{2}$
(c) 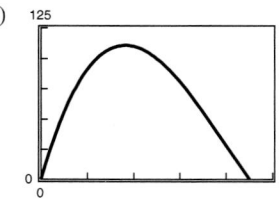 $1.82 \times 5.36 \times 11.36$

(d) $\frac{1}{2}, \frac{7}{2}, 8$; 8 is not in the domain of V.

91. (a) 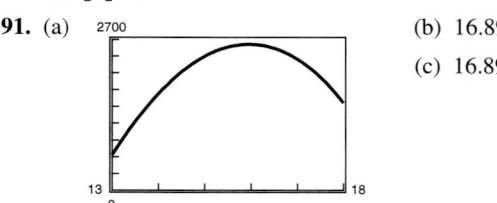 (b) 16.89
  (c) 16.89

93. False. $-\frac{4}{7}$ is the root derived from $(7x + 4)$.

95. True **97.** $x^{2n} - x^n + 3$

99. Multiply the divisor and the quotient to obtain the dividend. Answers will vary.

101. $3 - 10i$ **103.** $\frac{1}{17}(10 + 23i)$

105. $f(x) = x^3 - 6x^2 - 19x + 24$ **107.** $f(x) = x^2 - 4x + 1$

Section 3.4   *(page 269)*

1. $0, 6, 6$ **3.** $2, -4, -4, -4$ **5.** $-6, i, -i$

7. $2, -3 + 5i, -3 - 5i$

9. Zeros: $4, -i, i$. One real zero; same

11. Zeros: $\sqrt{2}i, \sqrt{2}i, -\sqrt{2}i, -\sqrt{2}i$. No real zeros; same

13. $2 \pm \sqrt{3}$

$\left(x - 2 - \sqrt{3}\right)\left(x - 2 + \sqrt{3}\right)$

15. $6 \pm \sqrt{10}$

$\left(x - 6 - \sqrt{10}\right)\left(x - 6 + \sqrt{10}\right)$

17. $\pm 5i$

$(x + 5i)(x - 5i)$

19. $\pm 3, \pm 3i$

$(x + 3)(x - 3)(x + 3i)(x - 3i)$

21. $1 \pm i$

$(z - 1 + i)(z - 1 - i)$

23. $-5, 4 \pm 3i$

$(t + 5)(t - 4 + 3i)(t - 4 - 3i)$

25. $-\frac{3}{4}, 1 \pm \frac{1}{2}i$

$(4x + 3)\left(x - 1 - \frac{1}{2}i\right)\left(x - 1 + \frac{1}{2}i\right)$

27. $\pm i, \pm 3i$

$(x + i)(x - i)(x + 3i)(x - 3i)$

29. $2, 2, \pm 2i$

$(x - 2)^2(x + 2i)(x - 2i)$

31. $-2, -\frac{1}{2}, \pm i$

$(x + 2)(2x + 1)(x - i)(x + i)$

33. (a) $7 \pm \sqrt{3}$ (b) $\left(x - 7 - \sqrt{3}\right)\left(x - 7 + \sqrt{3}\right)$

(c) $\left(7 \pm \sqrt{3}, 0\right)$

35. (a) $-7 \pm \sqrt{5}$ (b) $\left(x + 7 - \sqrt{5}\right)\left(x + 7 + \sqrt{5}\right)$

(c) $\left(-7 \pm \sqrt{5}, 0\right)$

37. (a) $-6, 3 \pm 4i$ (b) $(x + 6)(x - 3 - 4i)(x - 3 + 4i)$

(c) $(-6, 0)$

39. (a) $\pm 4i, \pm 3i$ (b) $(x + 4i)(x - 4i)(x + 3i)(x - 3i)$

(c) None

41. $x^3 - x^2 + 25x - 25$ **43.** $x^3 - 10x^2 + 33x - 34$

45. $x^4 + 37x^2 + 36$ **47.** $x^4 + 8x^3 + 9x^2 - 10x + 100$

49. (a) $(x^2 + 1)(x^2 - 7)$ (b) $(x^2 + 1)\left(x + \sqrt{7}\right)\left(x - \sqrt{7}\right)$

(c) $(x + i)(x - i)\left(x + \sqrt{7}\right)\left(x - \sqrt{7}\right)$

51. (a) $(x^2 - 6)(x^2 - 2x + 3)$

(b) $\left(x + \sqrt{6}\right)\left(x - \sqrt{6}\right)(x^2 - 2x + 3)$

(c) $\left(x + \sqrt{6}\right)\left(x - \sqrt{6}\right)\left(x - 1 - \sqrt{2}i\right)\left(x - 1 + \sqrt{2}i\right)$

53. $-\frac{3}{2}, \pm 5i$ **55.** $-3, 5 \pm 2i$ **57.** $-\frac{2}{3}, 1 \pm \sqrt{3}i$

59. $\frac{3}{4}, \frac{1}{2}\left(1 \pm \sqrt{5}i\right)$

61. (a) $1.000, 2.000$ (b) $1, 2$ (c) $1, 2, -3 \pm \sqrt{2}i$

63. (a) 0.750 (b) $\frac{3}{4}$ (c) $\frac{3}{4}, \frac{1}{2} \pm \frac{\sqrt{5}}{2}i$

65. No. Setting $h = 64$ and solving the resulting equation yields imaginary roots.

67. False. A polynomial can only have an even number of complex zeros, so one of the zeros of a third-degree polynomial must be real.

69. (a) $0 < k < 4$ (b) $k = 4$ (c) $k < 0$ (d) $k > 4$

71. $f(x) = x^2 + b$ **73.** $\dfrac{x - 5}{x + 3}, x \neq 3$

75. $x - 5, x \neq 0, 4$

77. 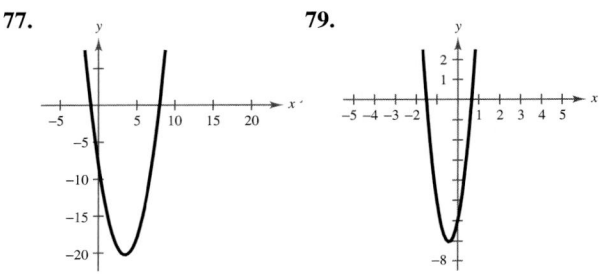   **79.**

Vertex: $(3.5, -20.25)$

Intercepts:

$(-1, 0), (8, 0), (0, -8)$

Vertex: $\left(-\frac{5}{12}, -7\frac{1}{24}\right)$

Intercepts:

$\left(-\frac{3}{2}, 0\right), \left(\frac{2}{3}, 0\right), (0, -6)$

Section 3.5   *(page 277)*

1. (a)

x	$f(x)$	x	$f(x)$
0.5	-2	1.5	2
0.9	-10	1.1	10
0.99	-100	1.01	100
0.999	-1000	1.001	1000

x	$f(x)$	x	$f(x)$
5	0.25	-5	$-0.\overline{16}$
10	$0.\overline{1}$	-10	$-0.\overline{09}$
100	$0.\overline{01}$	-100	$-0.\overline{0099}$
1000	$0.\overline{001}$	-1000	$-0.\overline{000999}$

(b) Vertical asymptote: $x = 1$

Horizontal asymptote: $y = 0$

(c) Domain: all $x \neq 1$

3. (a)

x	$f(x)$	x	$f(x)$
0.5	3	1.5	9
0.9	27	1.1	33
0.99	297	1.01	303
0.999	2997	1.001	3003

x	$f(x)$	x	$f(x)$
5	3.75	-5	-2.5
10	$3.\overline{33}$	-10	-2.727
100	$3.\overline{03}$	-100	-2.97
1000	$3.\overline{003}$	-1000	-2.997

(b) Vertical asymptote: $x = 1$

   Horizontal asymptotes: $y = \pm 3$

(c) Domain: all $x \neq 1$

5. (a)

x	$f(x)$	x	$f(x)$
0.5	-1	1.5	5.4
0.9	-12.79	1.1	17.29
0.99	-147.8	1.01	152.3
0.999	-1498	1.001	1502.3

x	$f(x)$	x	$f(x)$
5	3.125	-5	3.125
10	$3.\overline{03}$	-10	$3.\overline{03}$
100	$3.\overline{0003}$	-100	$3.\overline{0003}$
1000	3	-1000	3.000003

(b) Vertical asymptotes: $x = \pm 1$

   Horizontal asymptote: $y = 3$

(c) Domain: all $x \neq \pm 1$

7. (a)   **9.** (c)   **11.** (b)

13. (a) Domain: all $x \neq 0$

   (b) Vertical asymptote: $x = 0$

   Horizontal asymptote: $y = 0$

15. (a) Domain: all $x \neq 3$

   (b) Vertical asymptote: $x = 3$

   Horizontal asymptote: $y = -1$

17. (a) Domain: all $x \neq \pm 1$

   (b) Vertical asymptotes: $x = \pm 1$

19. (a) Domain of f: all $x \neq -2$

   Domain of g: all real numbers

   (b) Vertical asymptote: None

   (c)

x	-4	-3	-2.5	-2	-1.5	-1	0
$f(x)$	-6	-5	-4.5	Undef.	-3.5	-3	-2
$g(x)$	-6	-5	-4.5	-4	-3.5	-3	-2

   (d) Values differ only where f is undefined.

21. (a) Domain of f: all $x \neq 0, 3$; Domain of g: all $x \neq 0$

   (b) Vertical asymptote: $x = 0$

   (c)

x	-1	-0.5	0	0.5	2	3	4
$f(x)$	-1	-2	Undef.	2	$\frac{1}{2}$	Undef.	$\frac{1}{4}$
$g(x)$	-1	-2	Undef.	2	$\frac{1}{2}$	$\frac{1}{3}$	$\frac{1}{4}$

   (d) Values differ only where f is undefined and g is defined.

23. 4; Less than; Greater than

25. 2; Greater than; Less than

27. ± 3 **29.** 7

31. (a) \$28.33 million   (b) \$170 million

   (c) \$765 million

   (d)

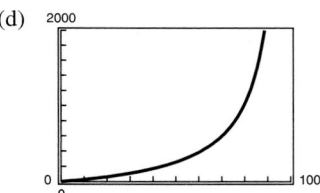

   Answers will vary.

   (e) No. The function is undefined at the 100% level.

33. (a)

M	200	400	600	800	1000
t	0.472	0.596	0.710	0.817	0.916

M	1200	1400	1600	1800	2000
t	1.009	1.096	1.178	1.255	1.328

   The greater the mass, the more time required per oscillation.

   (b) $M \approx 1306$ grams

35. (a) 333 deer, 500 deer, 800 deer

(b) 1500. Because the degrees of the numerator and the denominator are equal, the limiting size is the ratio of the leading coefficients, $60/0.4 = 1500$.

37. (a) 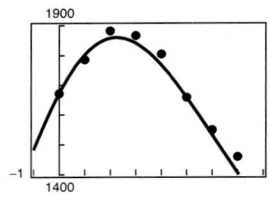 (b) $\approx 889,000$

(c) Not likely. The graph of the model dips quite low in the future.

39. True. Can be written as
$$\frac{N(x)}{D(x)} = \frac{x^3 - 2x^2 - 5x + 6}{1}.$$

41. $f(x) = \dfrac{1}{1 + x^2}$ **43.** $f(x) = \dfrac{-3(x + 1)^2}{x\left(x - \frac{5}{2}\right)}$

45. $x = 5$ **47.** $t = 0, \pm 5\sqrt{2}$

49. $x = \pm\sqrt{15}, \pm\sqrt{15}\,i$ **51.** $x - 7 - \dfrac{6}{x - 3}$

53. $4x - 21 + \dfrac{116}{x + 6}$ **55.** $x^3 + 2x^2 + 36x + 72$

57. $x^3 + 5x^2 + 7x - 13$

Section 3.6   *(page 286)*

1.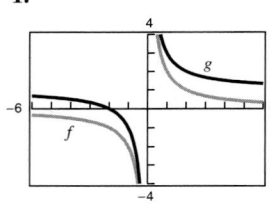

Vertical shift

3.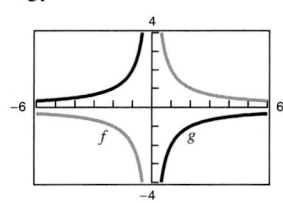

Reflection in the *x*-axis

5.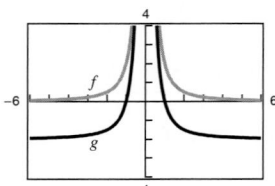

Vertical shift

7.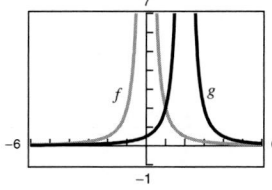

Horizontal shift

9.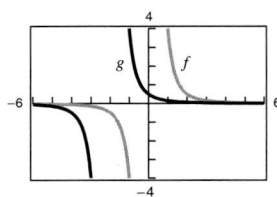

Horizontal shift

11.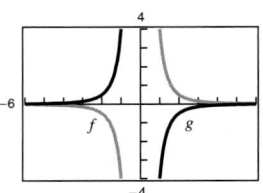

Reflection in the *x*-axis

13.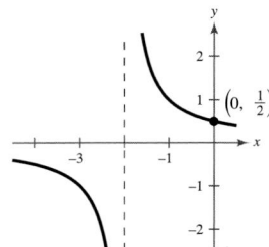

15.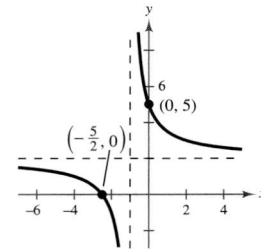

17.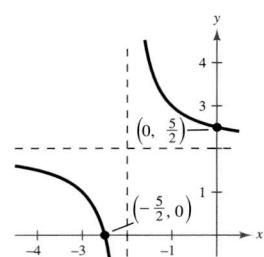

19.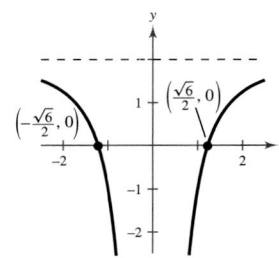

21.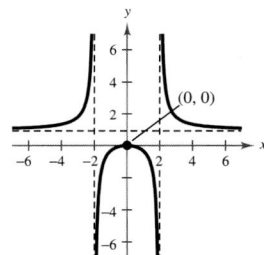

23.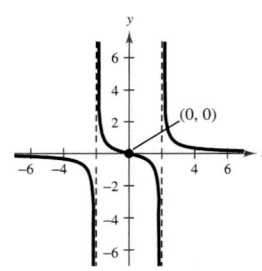

25.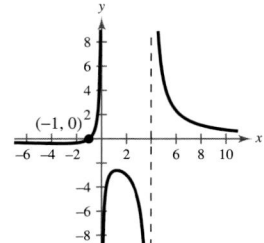

27.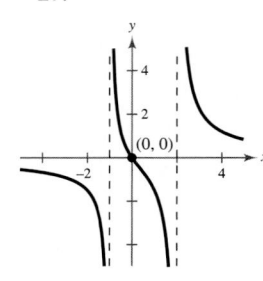

29.

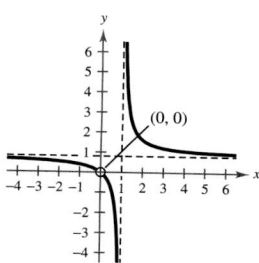

31.

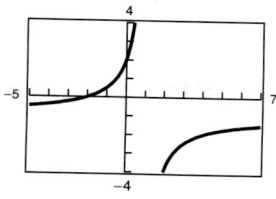

Domain: $(-\infty, 1), (1, \infty)$

$x = 1, y = -1$

43.

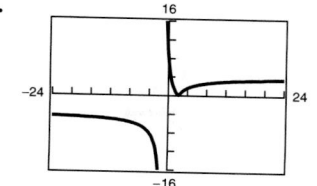

There are two horizontal asymptotes, $y = 4$ and $y = -4$, and one vertical asymptote, $x = -1$.

33.

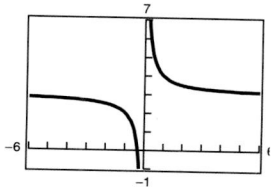

Domain: $(-\infty, 0), (0, \infty)$

$x = 0, y = 3$

35.

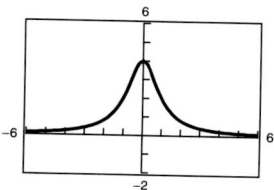

Domain: $(-\infty, \infty)$

$y = 0$

45.

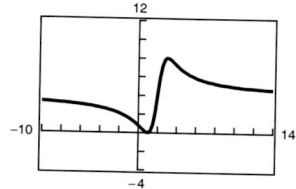

The graph crosses the horizontal asymptote, $y = 4$.

37.

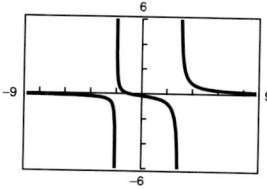

Domain: $(-\infty, -2), (-2, 3), (3, \infty)$

$x = -2, x = 3, y = 0$

47.

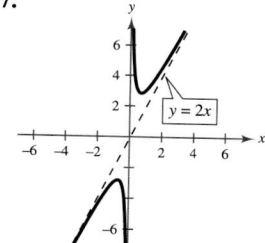

49.

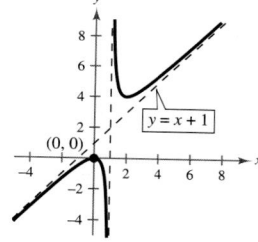

39.

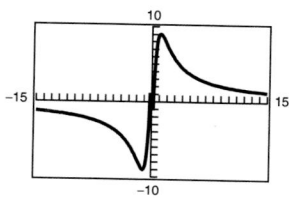

Domain: $(-\infty, 0), (0, \infty)$

$x = 0, y = 0$

51.

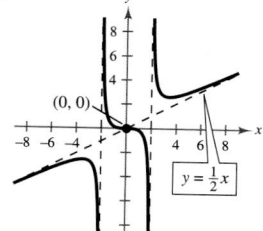

53.

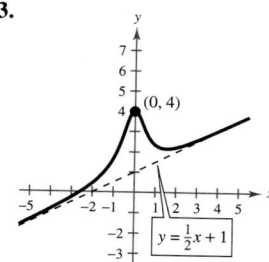

55. $(-1, 0)$ **57.** $(1, 0), (-1, 0)$

59.

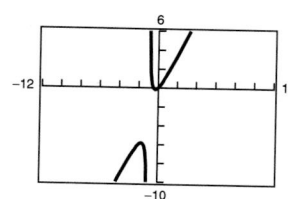

Domain: $(-\infty, -1), (-1, \infty)$

Vertical asymptote: $x = -1$

$y = 2x - 1$

41.

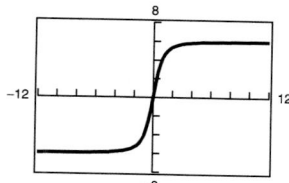

There are two horizontal asymptotes, $y = 6, y = -6$.

61.

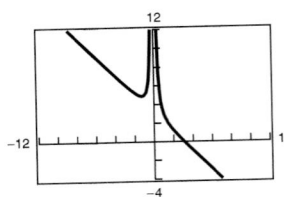

Domain: $(-\infty, 0), (0, \infty)$

Vertical asymptote: $x = 0$

$y = -x + 3$

63.

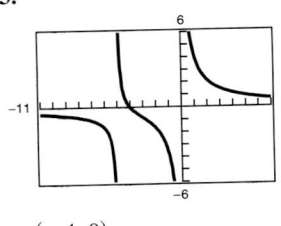

$(-4, 0)$

65.

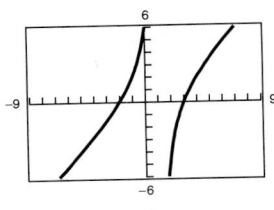

$(3, 0), (-2, 0)$

67. (a) Answers will vary. (b) $[0, 990]$

(c)

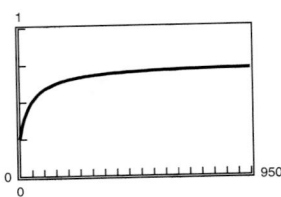

Increases more slowly; the concentration reaches 74.5% when the tank is full.

69. (a) Answers will vary. (b) $(2, \infty)$

(c)

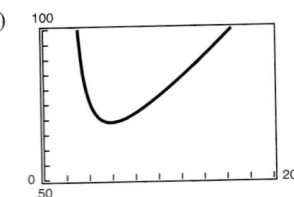

5.9×11.8 inches

71.

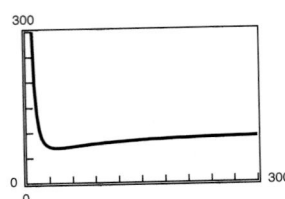

$x \approx 40$

73. (a) $C = 0$. The chemical will eventually dissipate.

(b)

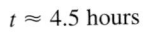
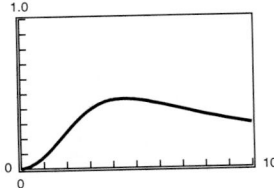

$t \approx 4.5$ hours

(c) Before ≈ 2.6 hours and after ≈ 8.3 hours

75. (a)

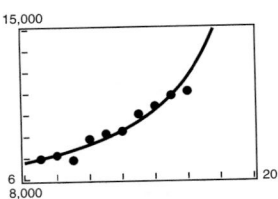

(b) $y = 384.5x + 5938$

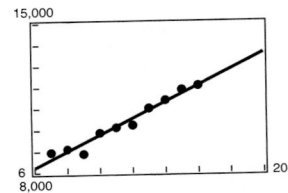

(c) $y = 14.87x^2 + 42.5x + 7781$

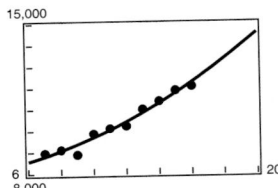

(d) Answers will vary. The rational model seems to start climbing too fast. The quadratic model may fit the data a little better than the linear model, is easy to use, and would be most useful.

77. False. A graph with a vertical asymptote is not continuous.

79.

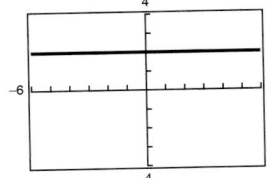

The denominator is a factor of the numerator.

81. No. (Discussions will vary.)

83. $f(x) = \dfrac{x^2 + 2x - 15}{x + 4}$ **85.** $f(x) = \dfrac{-2x - 12}{x - 3}$

87. $\dfrac{1}{16x^4}$ **89.** $\dfrac{1}{x^2}$ **91.** $\dfrac{1}{x^3}$

93.

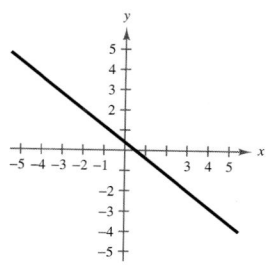

95.

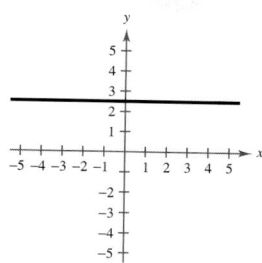

97.

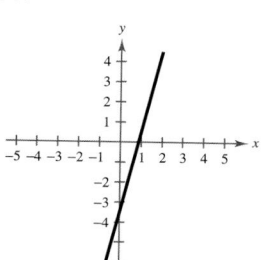

99.

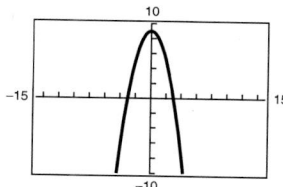

Domain: $-11 \le x \le 11$

Range: $0 \le y \le 11$

101.

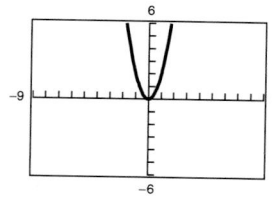

Domain: $(-\infty, \infty)$

Range: $y \le 9$

Review Exercises *(page 291)*

1. (a)

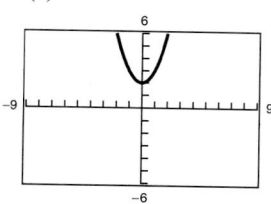

Vertical stretch

(b)

Vertical stretch and reflection in the x-axis

(c)

Vertical shift

(d)

Horizontal shift

3.

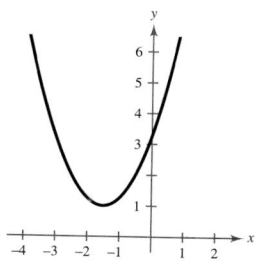

Vertex: $\left(-\dfrac{3}{2}, 1\right)$

Intercept: $\left(0, \dfrac{13}{4}\right)$

5.

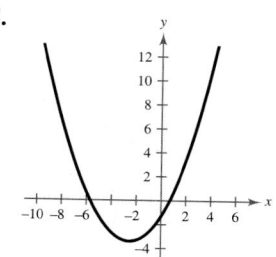

Vertex: $\left(-\dfrac{5}{2}, -\dfrac{41}{12}\right)$

Intercepts:

$\left(0, -\dfrac{4}{3}\right), \left(\dfrac{-5 \pm \sqrt{41}}{2}, 0\right)$

7. $f(x) = (x-1)^2 - 4$ **9.** Minimum: $(1, -1)$

11. Maximum: $(3, 9)$ **13.** Maximum: $(1, 3)$

15. Minimum: $\left(-\dfrac{5}{2}, -\dfrac{41}{4}\right)$

17. (a)

x	y	Area
1	$4 - \frac{1}{2}(1)$	$(1)\left[4 - \frac{1}{2}(1)\right] = \frac{7}{2}$
2	$4 - \frac{1}{2}(2)$	$(2)\left[4 - \frac{1}{2}(2)\right] = 6$
3	$4 - \frac{1}{2}(3)$	$(3)\left[4 - \frac{1}{2}(3)\right] = \frac{15}{2}$
4	$4 - \frac{1}{2}(4)$	$(4)\left[4 - \frac{1}{2}(4)\right] = 8$
5	$4 - \frac{1}{2}(5)$	$(5)\left[4 - \frac{1}{2}(5)\right] = \frac{15}{2}$
6	$4 - \frac{1}{2}(6)$	$(6)\left[4 - \frac{1}{2}(6)\right] = 6$

(b) $x = 4, y = 2$ (c) $A = x\left(\dfrac{8 - x}{2}\right)$, $0 < x < 8$

(d)

$x = 4, y = 2$

(e) $A = -\dfrac{1}{2}(x - 4)^2 + 8$

19. (a)

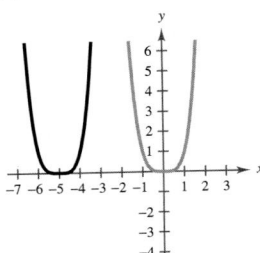

(b)

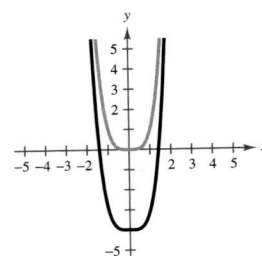

(c)

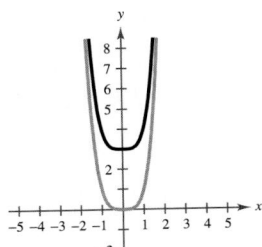

(d)

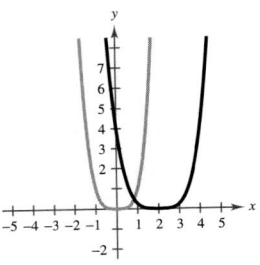

21. (a)

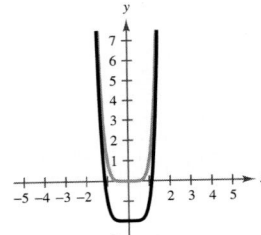

(b)

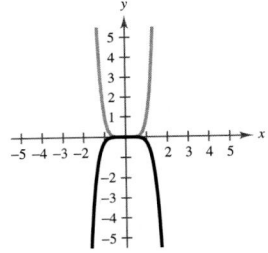

(c)

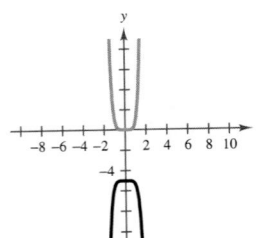

(d)

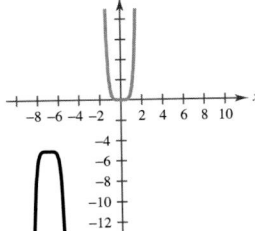

23. Falls to the left.

Falls to the right.

25. Rises to the left.

Rises to the right.

27.

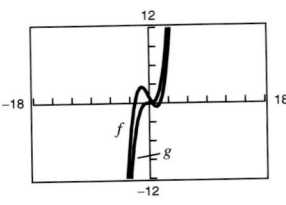

29. (a) $x = -1, 0, 2$

(b)

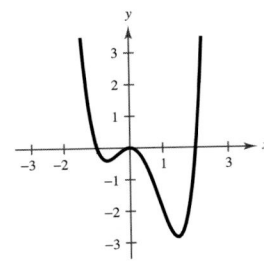

31. (a) $t = 0, \pm\sqrt{3}$

(b)

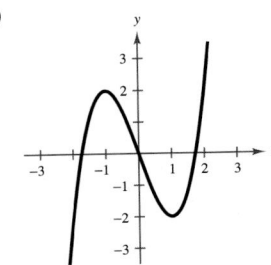

33. (a) $x = -3, 0$

(b)

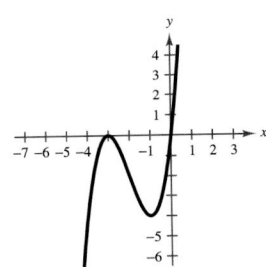

35. (a) $V = x^2(216 - 4x)$

(b)

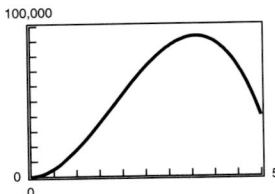

$x = 36$ centimeters, $y = 72$ centimeters

37. (a) $(-3, -2), (-1, 0), (0, 1)$

(b) $(-2.247, 0), (-0.555, 0), (0.802, 0)$

39. (a) $(-3, -2), (2, 3)$ (b) $(-2.570, 0), (2.570, 0)$

41.

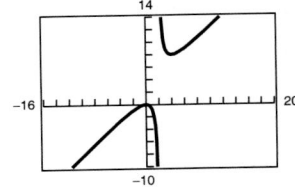

43. $8x + 5 + \dfrac{2}{3x - 2}$

45. $x^2 - 2$, $x \neq \pm 1$ **47.** $x^2 - x + 1$, $x \neq 0, -2$

49. $\dfrac{1}{4}x^3 - \dfrac{9}{2}x^2 + 9x - 18 + \dfrac{36}{x+2}$

51. $6x^3 - 27x$, $x \neq \dfrac{2}{3}$

53. (a) No   (b) Yes   (c) Yes   (d) No

55. $6x^4 + 13x^3 + 7x^2 - x - 1$

57. $3x^4 - 14x^3 + 17x^2 - 42x + 24$ **59.** $\dfrac{3}{4}, 1, 1$

61. $\dfrac{5}{6}, \pm 2i$ **63.** $-1, \dfrac{3}{2}, 3, \dfrac{2}{3}$ **65.** Answers will vary.

67. (a)

(b) Two

(c) $-1, -0.54$

69. (a)

(b) One

(c) 3.26

71. $2, 1 \pm i$

$(x - 2)(x - 1 - i)(x - 1 + i)$

73. $-4, -1 \pm \sqrt{2}\,i$

$(x + 4)\left(x + 1 + \sqrt{2}\,i\right)\left(x + 1 - \sqrt{2}\,i\right)$

75. $\pm 3i, \pm 5i$

$(x - 3i)(x + 3i)(x - 5i)(x + 5i)$

77. $f(x) = x^4 + 4x^3 + 29x^2 + 100x + 100$

79. $f(x) = x^4 + 9x^3 + 48x^2 + 78x - 136$

81. $f(x) = 3x^4 - 13x^3 + 5x^2 + 43x + 22$

83. (a) $(x^2 + 4)(x^2 - 2)$

(b) $(x^2 + 4)\left(x - \sqrt{2}\right)\left(x + \sqrt{2}\right)$

(c) $(x + 2i)(x - 2i)\left(x - \sqrt{2}\right)\left(x + \sqrt{2}\right)$

85. (a) $(x^2 + 9)(x^2 - 2x - 1)$

(b) $(x^2 + 9)\left(x - 1 + \sqrt{2}\right)\left(x - 1 - \sqrt{2}\right)$

(c) $(x + 3i)(x - 3i)\left(x - 1 + \sqrt{2}\right)\left(x - 1 - \sqrt{2}\right)$

87. Domain: all $x \neq 1$

Vertical asymptote: $x = 1$

Horizontal asymptote: $y = -1$

89. Domain: all $x \neq 6, -3$

Vertical asymptotes: $x = 6$, $x = -3$

Horizontal asymptote: $y = 0$

91. $y = -1$ **93.** $y = 2$ **95.** None   **97.** $y = \pm 1$

99. (a)

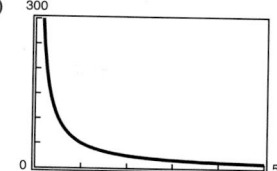

(b) 10.5, 5.5, 1, 0.55

(c) 0.5

101.

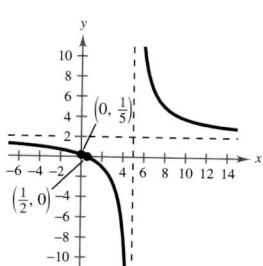

103.

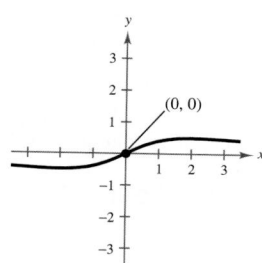

105.

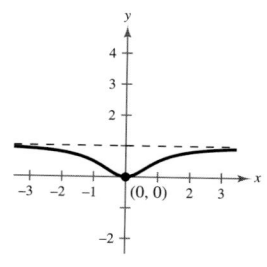

107.

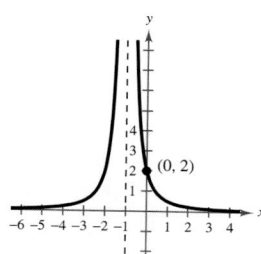

109.

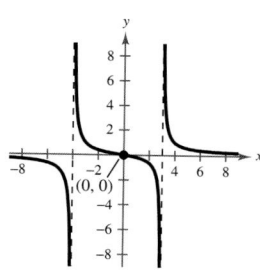

111.

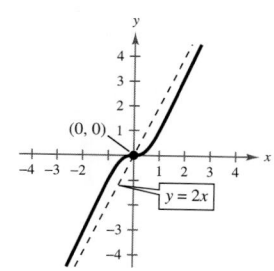

113.

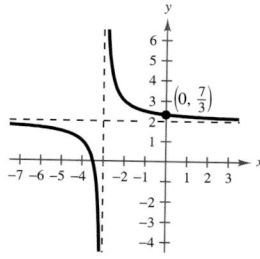

115.

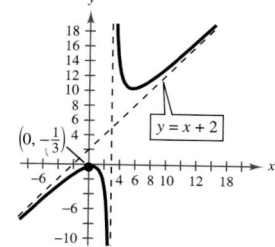

117. (a)

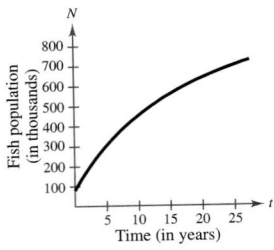

(b) 304,000; 453,333; 702,222

(c) 1,200,000, because N has a horizontal asymptote at $y = 1,200,000$.

119. False. For the graph of a rational function to have a slant asymptote, the degree of its numerator must be exactly one more than the degree of its denominator.

Chapter Test   *(page 296)*

1. (a) Reflection in the x-axis followed by a vertical shift

(b) Horizontal shift

2. Vertex: $(-2, -1)$

Intercepts: $(0, 3), (-3, 0), (-1, 0)$

3. $y = (x - 3)^2 - 6$

4. (a) 50 feet

(b) 5. Changing the constant term results in a vertical shift of the graph and therefore changes the maximum height.

5. $3x + \dfrac{x - 1}{x^2 + 1}$ **6.** $2x^3 + 4x^2 + 3x + 6 + \dfrac{9}{x - 2}$

7. $\pm 1, \pm 2, \pm 3, \pm 4, \pm 6, \pm 8, \pm 12, \pm 24, \pm\frac{1}{2}, \pm\frac{3}{2}$

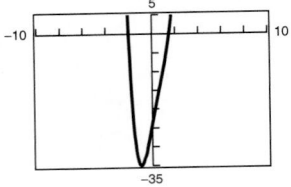

$-2, \frac{3}{2}$

8. $\pm 1, \pm 2, \pm\frac{1}{3}, \pm\frac{2}{3}$

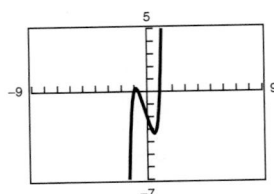

$\pm 1, -\frac{2}{3}$

9. $-0.819, 1.380$ **10.** $-1.414, -0.667, 1.414$

11. $f(x) = x^4 - 9x^3 + 28x^2 - 30x$

12. $f(x) = x^4 - 6x^3 + 16x^2 - 24x + 16$

13. $f(x) = x^4 + 3x^3 - 8x^2 + 10x$

14.

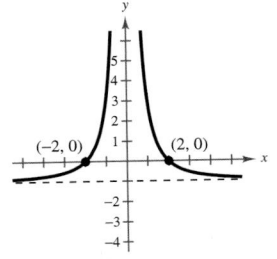

15.

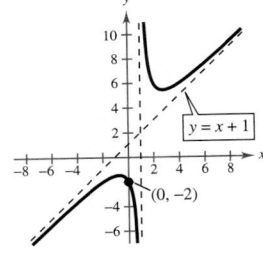

16.

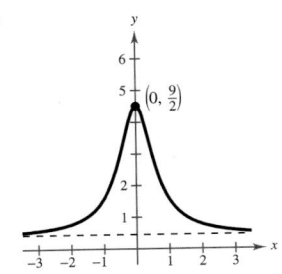

17. $f(x) = \dfrac{4x^2}{x^2 - 9}$ **18.** 24.8 years

Chapter 4

Section 4.1   *(page 307)*

1. 4112.033   **3.** 77,494.076   **5.** 19.568   **7.** 1.649

9. 9897.129   **11.** $f(x) = h(x)$

13. $f(x) = g(x) = h(x)$ **15.** (c)   **17.** (e)   **19.** (g)

21. (a)   **23.** Right shift of 5 units

25. Left shift of 4 units and reflection in x-axis

27.

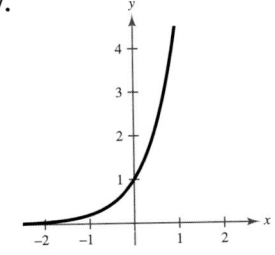

(a) $y = 0$

(b) $(0, 1)$

(c) Increasing

29.

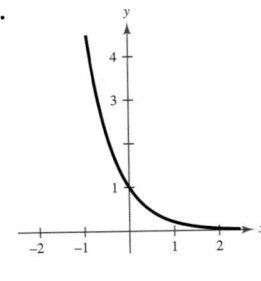

(a) $y = 0$

(b) $(0, 1)$

(c) Decreasing

31.

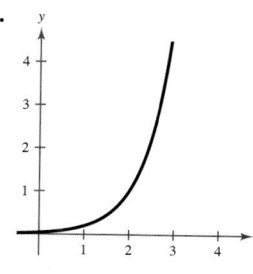

(a) $y = 0$

(b) $\left(0, \frac{1}{25}\right)$

(c) Increasing

33.

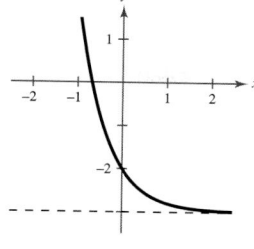

(a) $y = -3$

(b) $(0, -2), (-0.683, 0)$

(c) Decreasing

35.

x	-1	0	1	2	3
$f(x)$	0.4	1	2.5	6.3	15.6

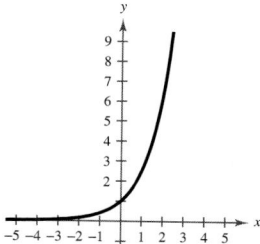

37.

x	-1	0	1	2
$f(x)$	0.2	1	6	36

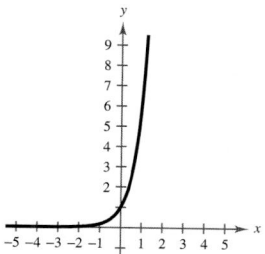

39.

x	-3	-2	0	1
$f(x)$	$\frac{1}{3}$	1	9	27

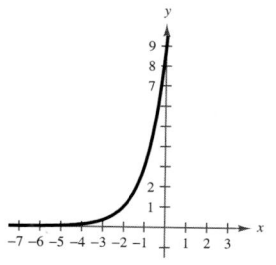

41.

x	-7	-6	-5	-4	-3
$f(x)$	0.1	0.4	1.1	3	8

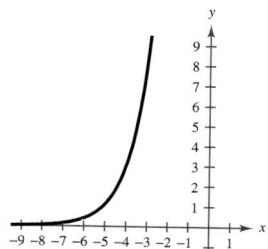

43.

x	2	3	4	5	6	7
$f(x)$	2.0	2.1	2.4	3	4.7	9.3

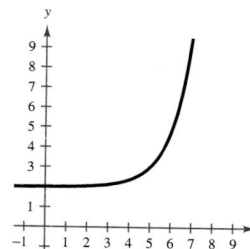

45.

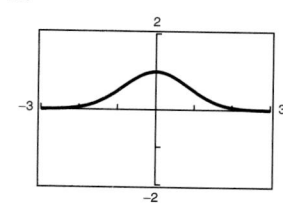

$y = 0$

47.

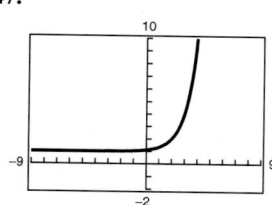

$y = 1$

49.

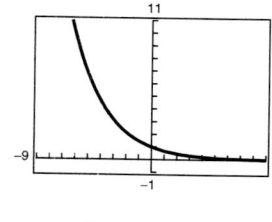

$y = 0$

51.

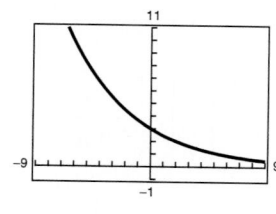

$s(t) = 0$

53. (a)

x	-1	-0.5	0	0.5	1
$f(x)$	0.3333	0.5774	1	1.7321	3
$g(x)$	0.25	0.5	1	2	4

$x < 0$

(b)

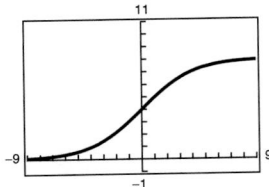

(i) $4^x < 3^x$ when $x < 0$ (ii) $4^x > 3^x$ when $x > 0$

55. (a)

(b)

x	-30	-20	-10	0
$f(x)$	0.0000024	0.00036	0.054	4

x	10	20	30
$f(x)$	7.95	7.9996	7.999998

$y = 0, y = 8$

57. (a)

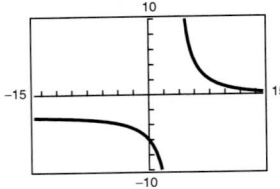

(b)

x	-20	-10	0	3	3.4	3.46
$f(x)$	-3.03	-3.22	-6	-34	-230	-2617

x	3.47	4	5	7	10	15	25
$f(x)$	3516	27	8	2.9	1.1	0.3	0.04

$y = -3, y = 0, x \approx 3.46$

59. (a)

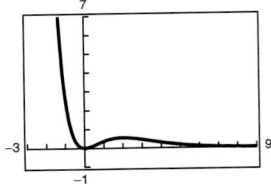

(b) Decreasing on $(-\infty, 0), (2, \infty)$

    Increasing on $(0, 2)$

(c) Relative minimum at $(0, 0)$

    Relative maximum at $(2, 0.541)$

61. (a)

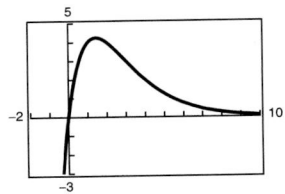

(b) Increasing on $(-\infty, 1.443)$

    Decreasing on $(1.443, \infty)$

(c) Relative maximum at $(1.443, 4.246)$

63.

n	1	2	4	12	365	Continuous
A	5397.3	5477.8	5520.1	5549.1	5563.4	5563.85

65.

n	1	2	4	12	365	Continuous
A	11,652	12,003	12,189	12,317	12,380	12,382.58

67.

t	1	10	20	30	40	50
A	12,999	26,706	59,436	132,278	294,390	655,178

69.

t	1	10	20	30	40	50
A	12,804	22,946	43,877	83,902	160,435	306,782

71. (a)

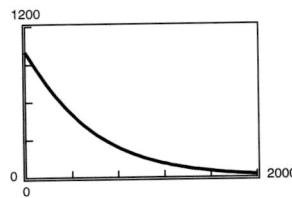

(b) $421.12

(c) $350.13

(d)

x	100	200	300	400
P	849.53	717.64	603.25	504.94

x	500	600	700
P	421.12	350.13	290.35

73. (a)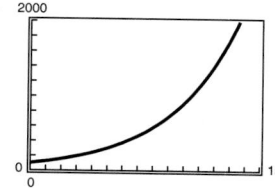

(b) $P(0) = 100$; $P(5) \approx 300$; $P(10) \approx 900$

75. (a) 25 units (b) 16.30 units

(c)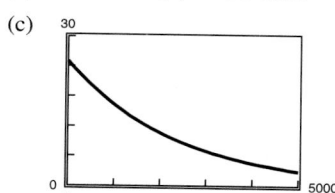

(d) Never. The graph has a horizontal asymptote at $Q = 0$.

77. (a) and (b)

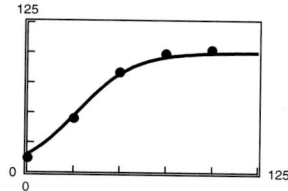

The model fits the data well.

(c)

x	0	25	50	75	100
y	15	47	82	96	99

(d) 64.7% (e) 37.4

79. (a) 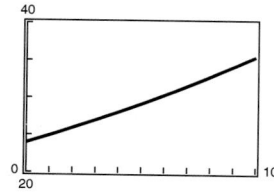 (b) $35.45

81. True

83.

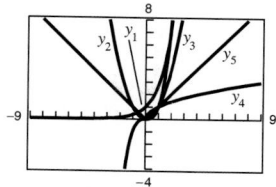

(a) $y = e^x$

(b) The exponential function increases at a faster rate.

(c) It usually implies rapid growth.

85. $1 < \sqrt{2} < 2$, so $2^1 < 2^{\sqrt{2}} < 2^2$

87.

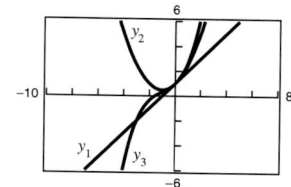

Answers will vary.

89. $f^{-1}(x) = -\frac{3}{2}\left(x - \frac{5}{2}\right)$ **91.** No inverse function

93. 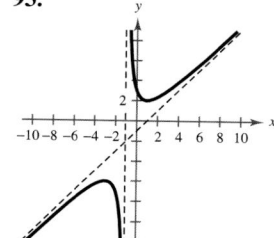 **95.**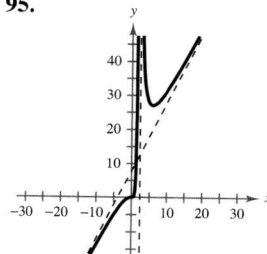

Section 4.2 *(page 318)*

1. $4^3 = 64$ **3.** $7^{-2} = \frac{1}{49}$ **5.** $32^{2/5} = 4$ **7.** $e^0 = 1$

9. $\log_5 125 = 3$ **11.** $\log_{81} 3 = \frac{1}{4}$ **13.** $\log_6 \frac{1}{36} = -2$

15. $\ln 20.0855\ldots = 3$ **17.** $\ln 13.463\ldots = 2.6$

19. 4 **21.** $-\frac{1}{2}$ **23.** -2 **25.** 9 **27.** 8 **29.** 2

31. 2.538 **33.** -0.097 **35.** 1.746 **37.** 1.869

39. 7.022 **41.** 22.276

43. 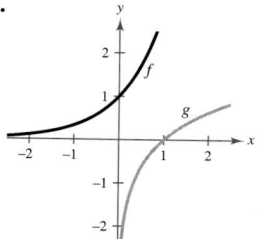 **45.**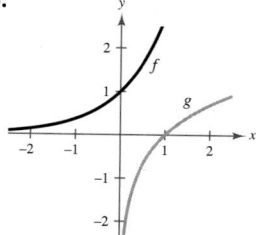

Reflections in the line $y = x$

$g = f^{-1}$

Reflections in the line $y = x$

$g = f^{-1}$

47. (c) **49.** (d) **51.** (b)

53. Domain: $(0, \infty)$

Vertical asymptote: $x = 0$

Intercept: $(1, 0)$

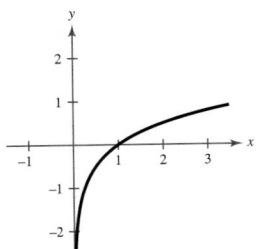

55. Domain: $(3, \infty)$

Vertical asymptote: $x = 3$

Intercept: $(4, 0)$

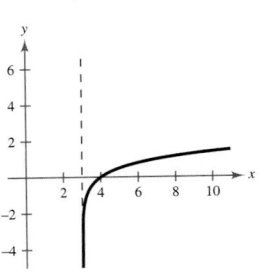

57. Domain: $(0, \infty)$

Vertical asymptote: $x = 0$

Intercept: $(9, 0)$

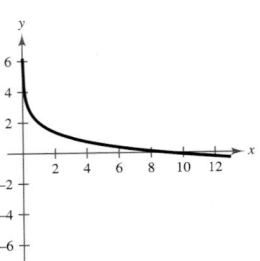

59. Domain: $(3, \infty)$

Vertical asymptote: $x = 3$

Intercept:
$(3 + 6^{-6}, 0) \approx (3, 0)$

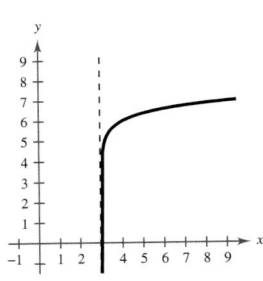

61. Domain: $(0, \infty)$

Vertical asymptote: $x = 0$

Intercept: $(5, 0)$

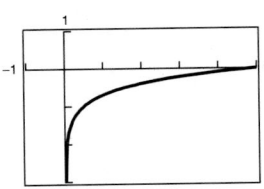

63. Domain: $(2, \infty)$

Vertical asymptote: $x = 2$

Intercept: $(3, 0)$

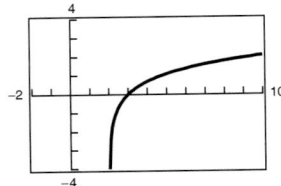

65. Domain: $(-\infty, 0)$

Vertical asymptote: $x = 0$

Intercept: $(-1, 0)$

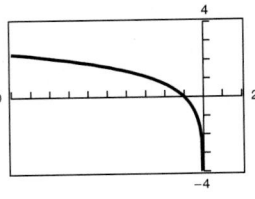

67. (a) 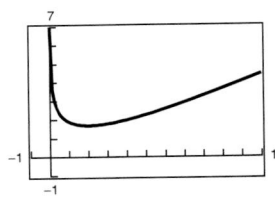 (b) Domain: $(0, \infty)$

(c) Decreasing: $(0, 2)$; Increasing: $(2, \infty)$

(d) Relative minimum: $(2, 1.693)$

69. (a) 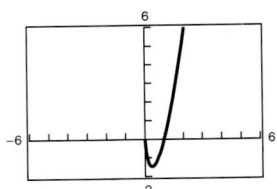 (b) Domain: $(0, \infty)$

(c) Decreasing: $(0, 0.37)$; Increasing: $(0.37, \infty)$

(d) Relative minimum: $(0.37, -1.47)$

71. 23.68 years **73.** (a) 80 (b) 68.1 (c) 62.3

75. (a)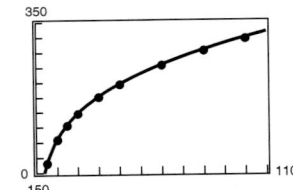

The model fits the data well.

(b) 67.3 pounds per square inch (c) 306.5°F

77.

r	0.005	0.010	0.015
t	138.6	69.3	46.2

r	0.020	0.025	0.030
t	34.7	27.7	23.1

As the growth rate of the population increases, the time for the population to double decreases.

79. (a) 120 decibels (b) 100 decibels (c) No

81. (a) 15 cubic feet per minute (b) 382 cubic feet

(c) 382 square feet

83. 10 years

85. Total amount: $199,108.80; Interest: $49,108.80

87. True   **89.**

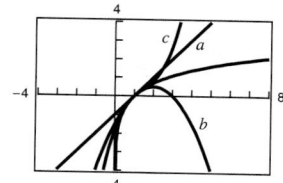

91. (a)

x	1	5	10	10^2	10^4	10^6
$f(x)$	0	0.322	0.230	0.046	0.00092	0.0000138

(b) 0

(c)

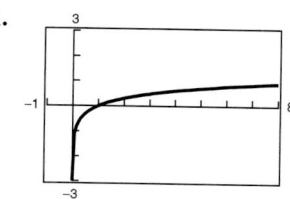

93. Vertical asymptote: $x = 0$

95. Vertical asymptote: $x = 7$ **97.** 33.115   **99.** 0.002

Section 4.3   *(page 326)*

1.

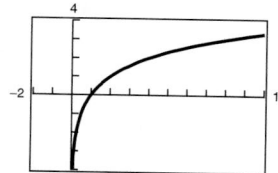

$f = g$

3. 1.771   **5.** -2 **7.** -0.102 **9.** 2.691

11. (a) $\dfrac{\log_{10} x}{\log_{10} 5}$ (b) $\dfrac{\ln x}{\ln 5}$ **13.** (a) $\dfrac{\log_{10} x}{\log_{10} \frac{1}{5}}$ (b) $\dfrac{\ln x}{\ln \frac{1}{5}}$

15. (a) $\dfrac{\log_{10} \frac{3}{10}}{\log_{10} x}$ (b) $\dfrac{\ln \frac{3}{10}}{\ln x}$

17. (a) $\dfrac{\log_{10} x}{\log_{10} 2.6}$ (c) $\dfrac{\ln x}{\ln 2.6}$

19. $\dfrac{\log_{10} x}{\log_{10} 2}$ **21.** $\dfrac{\log_{10} x}{\log_{10} \frac{1}{2}}$

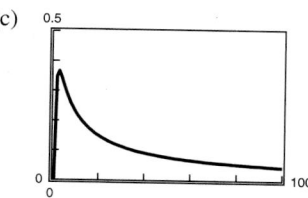

23. $\dfrac{\ln x}{\ln 11.8}$ **25.** $\dfrac{\frac{1}{2}\ln x}{\ln 3}$

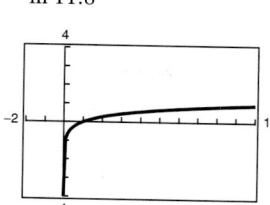   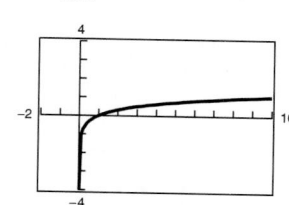

27. $\log_{10} 5 + \log_{10} x$ **29.** $\log_{10} 5 - \log_{10} x$

31. $4 \log_8 x$ **33.** $\frac{1}{2}\ln z$ **35.** $\ln x + \ln y + \ln z$

37. $\frac{1}{2}\ln(a - 1)$ **39.** $\ln z + 2\ln(z - 1)$

41. $\frac{1}{3}\ln x - \frac{1}{3}\ln y$ **43.** $4\ln x + \frac{1}{2}\ln y - 5\ln z$

45. $2\log_b x - 2\log_b y - 3\log_b z$

47.

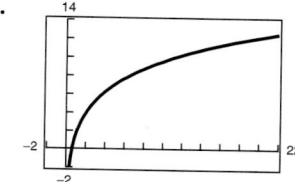

$y_1 = y_2$ for positive values of x.

49. $\ln 4x$ **51.** $\log_4 \dfrac{z}{y}$ **53.** $\log_2(x + 3)^2$

55. $\log_3 \sqrt[3]{7x}$ **57.** $\ln \dfrac{x}{(x + 1)^3}$ **59.** $\ln \dfrac{x - 2}{x + 2}$

61. $\ln \dfrac{x}{(x^2 - 4)^2}$ **63.** $\ln \sqrt[3]{\dfrac{x(x + 3)^2}{x^2 - 1}}$

65. $\ln \dfrac{\sqrt[3]{y(y + 4)^2}}{y - 1}$ **67.** $\ln \dfrac{9}{\sqrt{x^2 + 1}}$

69.   **71.**

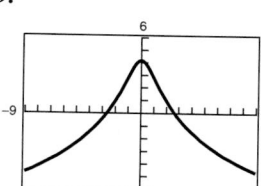

$y_1 = y_2$ No. The domains differ.

73. 2   **75.** 6.8   **77.** -4 is not in the domain of $\log_2 x$.

79. 2   **81.** -4 **83.** 0 is not in the domain of $\log_{10} x$.

85. 8.5   **87.** $\frac{3}{2}$ **89.** $\frac{1}{2}(1 + \log_7 10)$

91. $-3 - \log_5 2$ **93.** $6 + \ln 5$

95. (a) $120 + 10 \log_{10} I$

(b) and (c)

I	10^{-4}	10^{-6}	10^{-8}	10^{-10}	10^{-12}	10^{-14}
B	80	60	40	20	0	-20

97. (a)

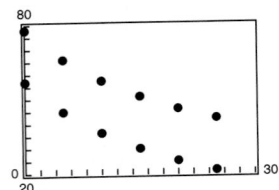

(b) $T = 54.438(0.964)^x + 21$

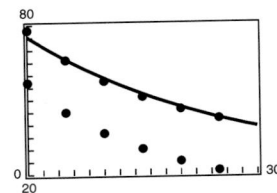

(c) $\ln(T - 21) = -0.037t + 3.997$

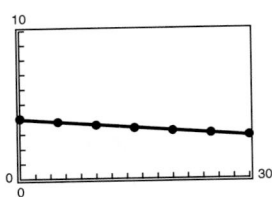

$T = e^{(-0.037t + 3.997)} + 21$

(d)

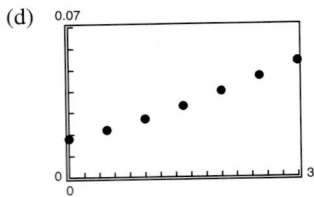

$T = \dfrac{1}{0.0012t + 0.0162} + 21$

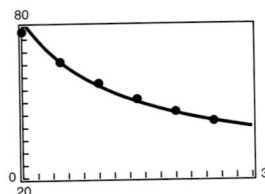

99. False. $\ln 1 = 0$ **101.** False. $f(x) - f(2) = \ln \dfrac{x}{2}$

103. False. $u = v^2$

105.

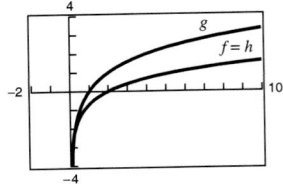

$f(x) = h(x)$

The graphs are identical because for each positive value of x, Property 2 of logarithms holds.

107. Answers will vary.   **109.** $\dfrac{3x^4}{2y^3}$

111. 1, $x \neq 0, y \neq 0$ **113.** $3 \pm \sqrt{7}$ **115.** $\pm 4, \pm \sqrt{3}$

117. $\pm 2, 6$ **119.** 0.052   **121.** 15,235.494

123. 2.342   **125.** 0.697

Section 4.4   *(page 336)*

1. (a) Yes   (b) No   **3.** (a) No   (b) Yes   (c) Yes

5. (a) No   (b) No   (c) Yes

7. (a) Yes   (b) Yes   (c) No

9.   **11.**

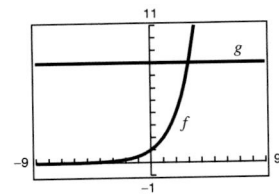   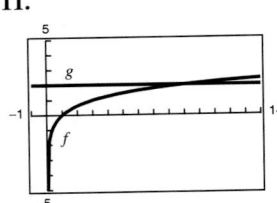

(3, 8)   (9, 2)

13.

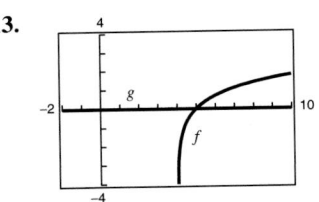

(5, 0)

15. 2   **17.** 4   **19.** $\frac{2}{3}$ **21.** -3 **23.** 4   **25.** 5

27. $\ln 4 \approx 1.386$ **29.** $e^{-7} \approx 0.00091$ **31.** 5

33. 0.1   **35.** 1   **37.** x^2 **39.** $5x + 2$ **41.** x^2

43. 2.756   **45.** $\ln 10 \approx 2.303$ **47.** 2   **49.** -6.142

51. 0.511   **53.** 0   **55.** $\ln 5 \approx 1.609$

57. $2 \ln 108 \approx 9.364$ **59.** 6.960

61.

x	0.6	0.7	0.8	0.9	1.0
$f(x)$	6.05	8.17	11.02	14.88	20.09

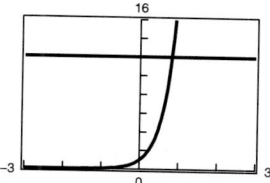

0.828

63.

x	5	6	7	8	9
$f(x)$	1756	1598	1338	908	200

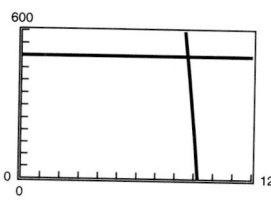

8.635

65. 1.881 **67.** 0.051 **69.** 6.146 **71.** 21.330
73. 3.656

75.

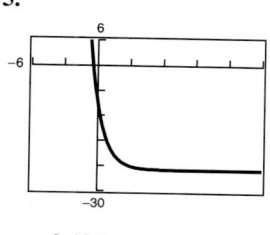

−0.427

77.

12.207

79. 0.050 **81.** 2.042 **83.** 4453.242 **85.** 103
87. 17.945 **89.** 5.389 **91.** 1.718, −3.718 **93.** 2
95. No real solution **97.** 180.384

99.

x	2	3	4	5	6
$f(x)$	1.39	1.79	2.08	2.30	2.48

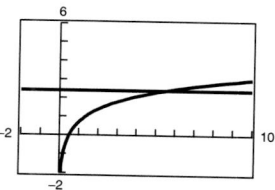

5.512

101.

x	12	13	14	15	16
$f(x)$	9.79	10.22	10.63	11.00	11.36

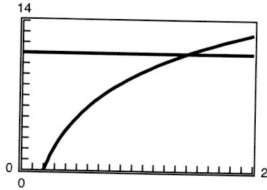

14.988

103. 14 **105.** 5.294 **107.** 3.729 **109.** 5.275
111.

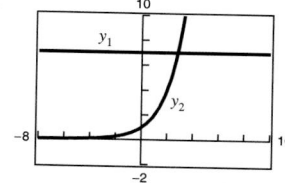

(2.807, 7)

113.

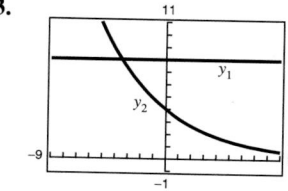

(−3.466, 8)

115.

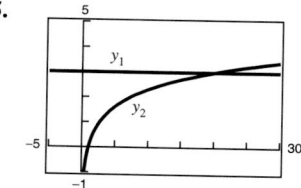

(20.086, 3)

117. (a) 8.2 years (b) 12.9 years
119. (a)

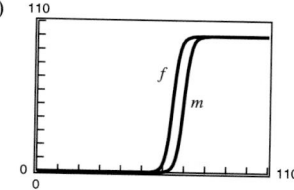

(b) $y = 100$ and $y = 0$
(c) Males: 69.71 inches; Females: 64.51 inches
121. (a) 1426 units (b) 1498 units

123. (a)

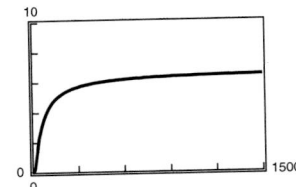

(b) $y = 6.7$. Yield will approach 6.7 million cubic feet per acre.

(c) 29.3 years

125. (a)

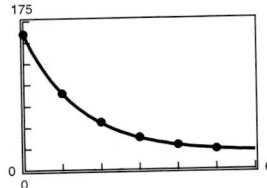

(b) $y = 20$. Room temperature   (c) 0.81 hour

127. (a) $y = 15.17x - 46.15$

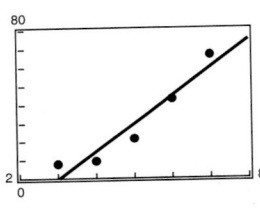

1999

(b) $\ln y = 2.706 \ln x - 1.175$

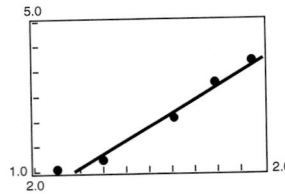

1998

(c) $y = e^{2.706 \ln x - 1.175}$

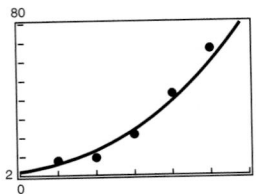

This model better fits the original data and will better predict future shipping levels.

129. False.
For example, $\ln(2x - 1) + \ln(x + 2) = \ln(x^2 - x + 1)$ has 2 extraneous solutions, $x = -1$ and $x = -3$.

131. No. It is dependent on the interest rate.

133.

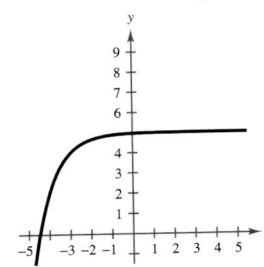

135.

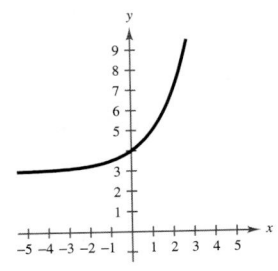

137. 2.814   **139.** 1.623

Section 4.5   *(page 348)*

1. (c)   **3.** (b)   **5.** (d)   **7.** Logarithmic model

9. Gaussian model   **11.** Exponential model

13. Gaussian model

15.

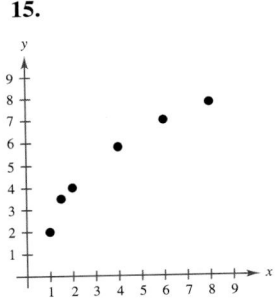

Logarithmic model

17.

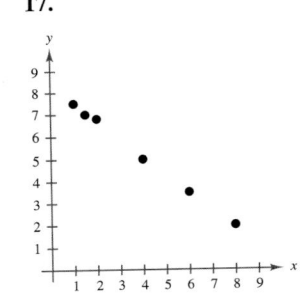

Linear model

	Initial Investment	Annual % Rate	Time to Double	Amount After 10 Years
19.	$1000	12%	5.78 yr	$3320.12
21.	$750	8.94%	7.75 yr	$1833.67
23.	$500	9.5%	7.30 yr	$1292.85
25.	$6376.28	4.5%	15.4 yr	$10,000.00

27. (a)

r	2%	4%	6%	8%	10%	12%
t	54.93	27.47	18.31	13.73	10.99	9.16

(b)

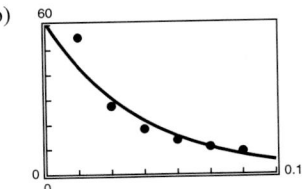

$t = 60.89(3.613 \times 10^{-8})^r$

29.

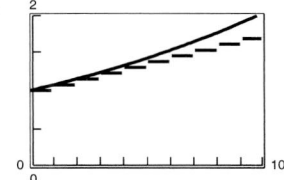

Continuous compounding

Isotope	Half-Life (years)	Initial Quantity	Amount After 1000 Years
31. ^{226}Ra	1620	10 g	6.52 g
33. ^{14}C	5730	3 g	2.66 g

35. 2023 **37.** $k = 0.0112$; 2796 **39.** 3.15 hours

41. 95.8%

43. (a) $V = -4500t + 22{,}000$ (b) $V = 22{,}000e^{-0.263t}$

(c)

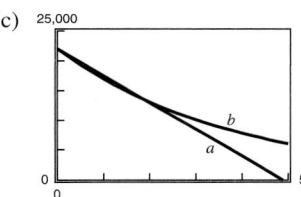

Exponential

(d) 1 year. Straight-line: $17,500; Exponential: $16,912
   3 years. Straight-line: $8500; Exponential: $9995

(e) Value decreases $4500 per year.

45. (a) $S(t) = 100(1 - e^{-0.1625t})$

(b)

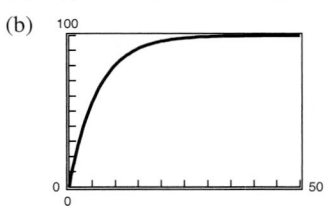

(c) 55,625

47. (a) $N = 30(1 - e^{-0.050t})$ (b) 36 days

(c) No. It is not a linear function.

49. (a) 7.6 (b) 7.1

51. (a) 20 decibels (b) 70 decibels (c) 120 decibels

53. 95% **55.** 4.64 **57.** 10,000,000 times

59. (a)

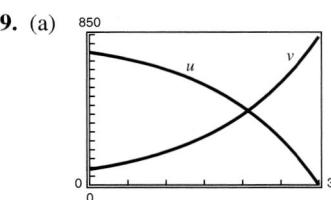

(b) Interest. $t \approx 20.7$ years

(c)

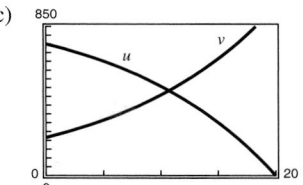

Interest. $t \approx 10.7$ years
Less interest is paid over the life of the loan.

61. $y = e^{0.768x}$ **63.** $y = \frac{1}{2}e^{0.576x}$

65. (a) $t_3 = 0.2729s - 6.0143$; $t_4 = 1.5385e^{0.0291s}$

(b)

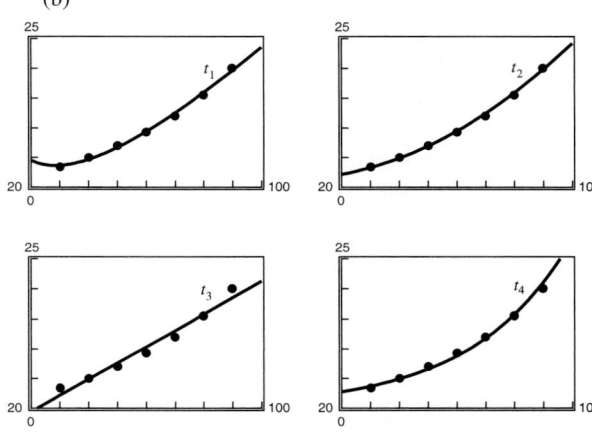

(c)

s	30	40	50	60	70	80	90
t_1	3.6	4.7	6.7	9.4	12.5	15.9	19.6
t_2	3.3	4.9	7.0	9.5	12.5	15.9	19.9
t_3	2.2	4.9	7.6	10.4	13.1	15.8	18.5
t_4	3.7	4.9	6.6	8.8	11.8	15.8	21.1

(d) Model: t_1; Sum ≈ 1.9
   Model: t_2; Sum ≈ 1.1
   Model: t_3; Sum ≈ 5.6
   Model: t_4; Sum ≈ 2.6
   Quadratic model fits best.

67. 7:30 A.M.

69. (a) $y = 0.082x + 4.45$

(b) $y = 4.536(1.015)^x$

(c) The linear model fits the data better; Answers will vary.

(d) Linear: 6.50 billion; Exponential: 6.58 billion

71. (a) $y = 298.794(1.085)^x$

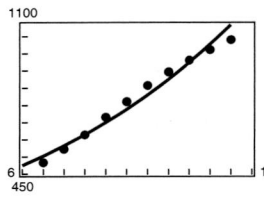

(b) $y = -837.7 + 673.619 \ln x$

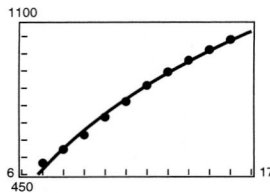

(c) The logarithmic model is better. It will continue to be better if growth of healthcare costs is slowed.

73. (a) $y_1 = -1.81x^3 + 14.58x^2 + 16.39x + 10.00$

$y_2 = 23.07 + 121.08 \ln x$

$y_3 = 38.38(1.4227)^x$

(b)

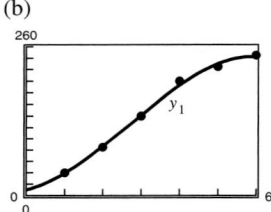 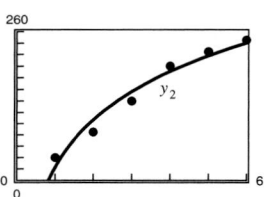

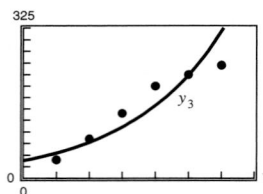

Cubic model

(c)

x	y	$y - y_1$	$(y - y_1)^2$	$y - y_2$	$(y - y_2)^2$
1	40	0.84	0.71	16.93	286.62
2	85	-1.62	2.62	-22.00	483.84
3	140	-1.52	2.31	-16.09	258.89
4	200	7.00	49.00	9.08	82.40
5	225	-5.20	27.04	7.06	49.83
6	245	2.74	7.51	4.98	24.84

x	$y - y_3$	$(y - y_3)^2$
1	-14.60	213.25
2	7.32	53.52
3	29.48	869.01
4	42.76	1828.56
5	1.30	1.68
6	-73.26	5367.34

(d) y_1: 89.19; y_2: 1186.42; y_3: 8333.36

Cubic model

(e) Sum of the squares of the errors

75. False. For example, $y = \dfrac{3}{1 + 2e^{-0.5x}}$ does not have an x-intercept.

77. True   **79.** (b); $(0, -3), \left(\frac{9}{4}, 0\right)$ **81.** (f); $(0, 25), \left(\frac{100}{9}, 0\right)$

83. (d); $(0, 3)$ **85.** $4x^2 - 12x + 9, x \neq -4$

87. $2x^2 + 3 + \dfrac{3}{x - 4}$

89.   **91.**

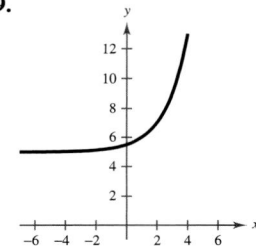 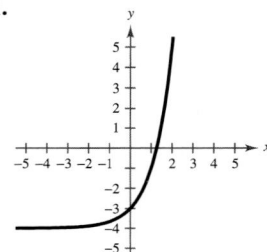

Review Exercises   *(page 357)*

1. 10.325   **3.** 0.201   **5.** (e)   **7.** (b)   **9.** (d)

11.   **13.**

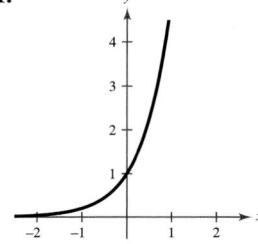 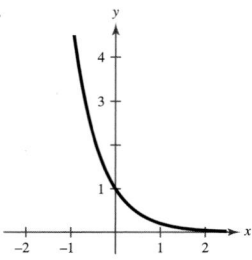

15.
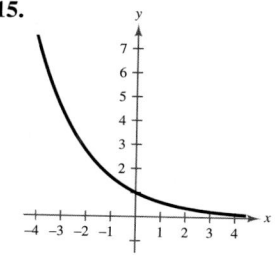

17.
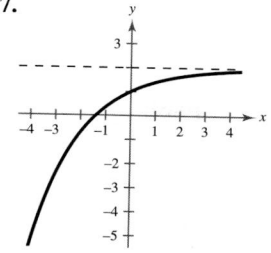

19.
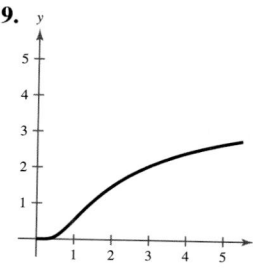

21.
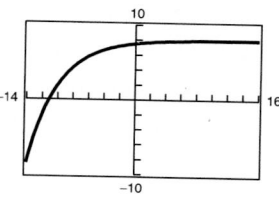

$y = 8$

23.
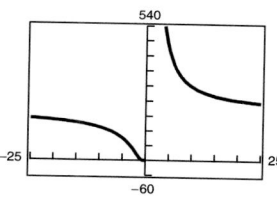

$y = 200, x = 0$

25.
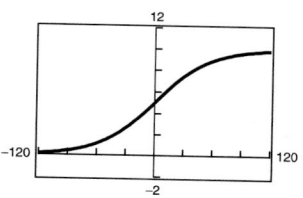

$y = 0, y = 10$

27. 0.069   **29.** 369.355

31.

t	1	10	20
P	\$184,623.27	\$89,865.79	\$40,379.30

t	30	40	50
P	\$18,143.59	\$8152.44	\$3663.13

33. (a)
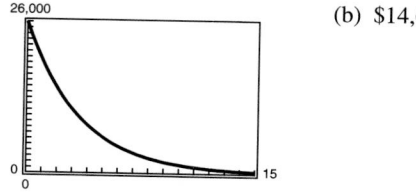

(b) \$14,625

(c) When it is first sold; Yes; Answers will vary.

35. $\log_4 64 = 3$ **37.** $\log_{25} 125 = \frac{3}{2}$ **39.** -0.34

41. 3   **43.** $-\frac{1}{2}$

45.
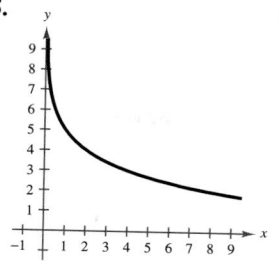

47.
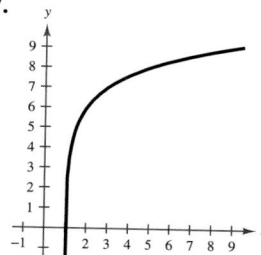

49.
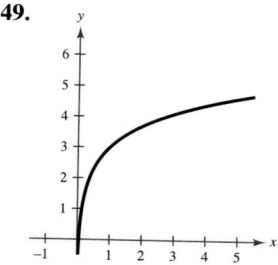

51.
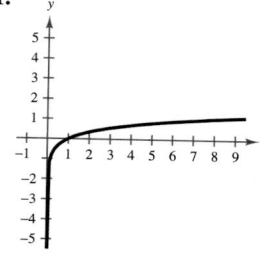

53.
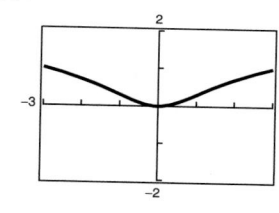

$-\infty < x < \infty$

55.
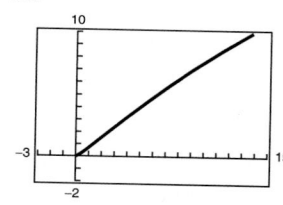

$x \geq 0$

57. 7   **59.** -18

61. (a) $0 \leq h < 18{,}000$

(b)
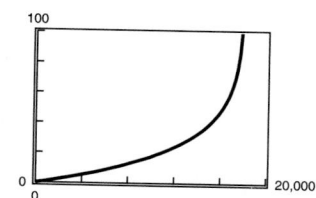

$h = 18{,}000$

(c) The time required to further increase its altitude increases.

(d) 5.46 minutes

63. 1.585   **65.** 2.132   **67.** $\ln 4 + \ln 5$

69. $\ln 5 - 3 \ln 4$ **71.** 1.6542   **73.** 0.2823

75. $1 + 2 \log_5 x$ **77.** $\log_{10} 5 + \frac{1}{2} \log_{10} y - 2 \log_{10} x$

79. $\ln(x^2 + 1) + \ln(x - 1)$ **81.** $\log_2 5x$

83. $\ln \dfrac{\sqrt{|2x - 1|}}{(x + 1)^2}$ **85.** $\ln \dfrac{3\sqrt[3]{4 - x^2}}{x}$

87. (a)

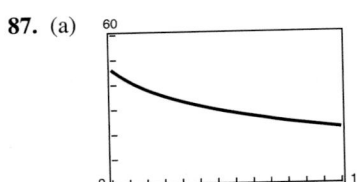

(b)

h	4	6	8	10	12	14
s	38	33	30	27	25	23

(c) The decrease in productivity starts to level off.

89. 3   **91.** −3   **93.** 2401   **95.** $\ln 12 \approx 2.485$

97. $-\dfrac{\ln 44}{5} \approx -0.757$ **99.** $\ln 22 \approx 3.091$

101. $\log_5 17 \approx 1.760$ **103.** $\ln 5 \approx 1.609, \ln 2 \approx 0.693$

105. $\frac{1}{3}e^{8.2} \approx 1213.650$ **107.** $\frac{1}{4}e^{15/2} \approx 452.011$

109. $3e^2 \approx 22.167$ **111.** $e^4 - 1 \approx 53.598$

113. No solution   **115.** $\frac{9}{10}$ **117.** ≈ 15.2 years

119. (e)   **121.** (f)   **123.** (a)   **125.** 2025

127. (a) 5.78%   (b) $10,595.03   (c) 5.95%

129. (a) 7.7 weeks   (b) 13.3 weeks

131. $y = 2e^{0.1014x}$ **133.** $y = \frac{1}{2}e^{0.4605x}$

135. $y = 234.684(0.8746)^x$

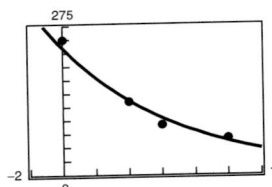

137. True   **139.** False. $\ln(xy) = \ln x + \ln y$ **141.** True

Chapter Test   *(page 362)*

1.

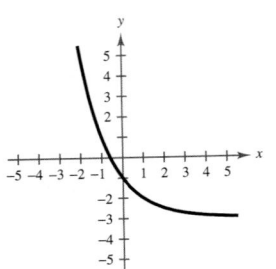

2.

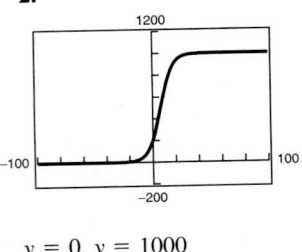

$y = 0, y = 1000$

3. $40,386.38   **4.** $4^3 = 64$

5.

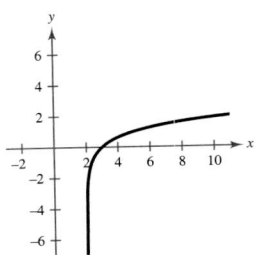

6. $\ln 6 + 2 \ln x - \frac{1}{2}\ln(x^2 + 1)$ **7.** 2   **8.** −3

9. 14.955   **10.** 18.447   **11.** −3.975

12. $10,204   **13.** (a) 0.154   (b) 0.487   (c) 0.811

14. (a) 300   (b) 570   (c) At the end of the 8th year

15. (c); it passes through the point (0, 0). Symmetric to the y-axis, and $y = 6$ is a horizontal asymptote.

16. $y = 6.775(1.361)^x$

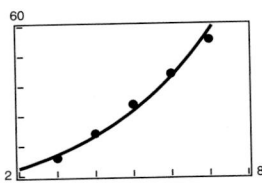

Chapter 5
Section 5.1   *(page 371)*

1. (a) No   (b) No   (c) No   (d) Yes

3. (a) No   (b) Yes   (c) No   (d) No

5. (2, 2)   **7.** $(2, 6), (-1, 3)$

9. $(0, 2), \left(\sqrt{3}, 2 - 3\sqrt{3}\right), \left(-\sqrt{3}, 2 + 3\sqrt{3}\right)$

11. $(0, 0), (2, -4)$ **13.** (4, 4)   **15.** (5, 5)

17. $\left(\frac{1}{2}, 3\right)$ **19.** (1, 1)   **21.** $\left(\frac{20}{3}, \frac{40}{3}\right)$ **23.** No solution

25. No solution   **27.** (0, 0)   **29.** (4, 3)   **31.** $\left(\frac{5}{2}, \frac{3}{2}\right)$

33. $(2, 2), (4, 0)$ **35.** $(1, 4), (4, 7)$

37.

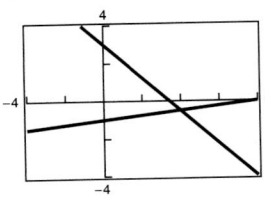

$(4, -0.5)$

39.

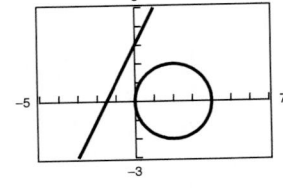

No points of intersection

41.

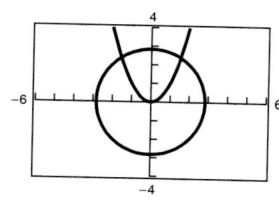

43.

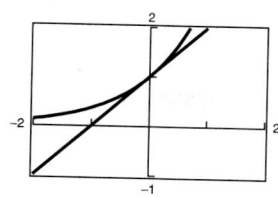

$(\pm 1.540, 2.372)$ $(0, 1)$

45.

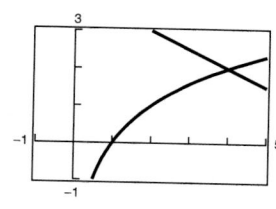

47.

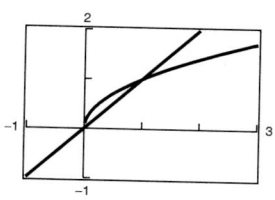

$(4, 2)$ $(0, 0), (1, 1)$

49.

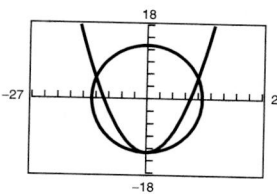

                                  51. $(1, 2)$

$(0, -13), (\pm 12, 5)$

53. $(-2, 0), \left(\frac{29}{10}, \frac{21}{10}\right)$ **55.** No solution   **57.** $(0.287, 1.75)$

59. $(0, 1), (1, 0)$ **61.** $\left(-4, -\frac{1}{4}\right), \left(\frac{1}{2}, 2\right)$

63.

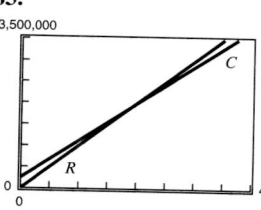

65.

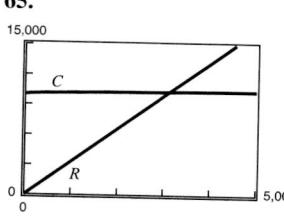

192 units; \$1,910,400   3133 units; \$10,308

67. (a) $C = 3.45x + 16,000; R = 5.95x$

(b)

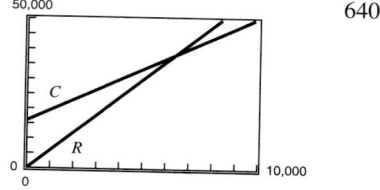

6400 units

69. \$8333.33

71. (a) $\begin{cases} x + y = 20,000 \\ 0.065x + 0.085y = 1600 \end{cases}$

(b)

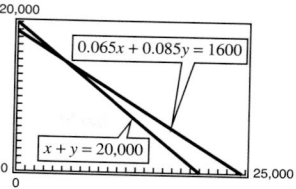

More invested at 6.5% means less invested at 8.5% and less interest.

(c) \$5000

73. (a)

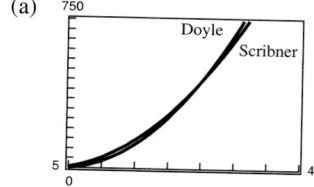

(b) 24.7 inches

(c) Doyle Log Rule; for logs of large diameter, V is larger using the Doyle Log Rule.

75. 60×80 centimeters   **77.** 42×63 feet

79. $2 \times \sqrt{2} \times \sqrt{2}$ inches

81. (a) $E = 0.342t + 10.72$

$E = 0.0163t^2 + 0.196t + 11.00$

(b)

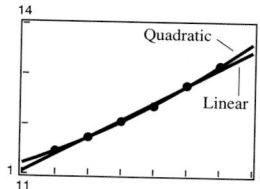

(c) $(6.18, 12.83), (2.78, 11.67)$

(d) Linear: \$14.14; Quadratic: \$14.59. Answers will vary.

83. False. Example: a parabola and a circle can have 4 intersection points.

85. Graphical solutions may be approximate.

87. (a)

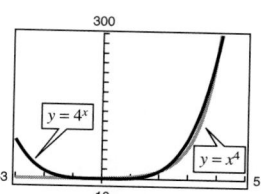

(b) Three points of intersection when b is even

89. $20x - 65y + 190 = 0$ **91.** $x = 4$

93. $45x + 29y - 127 = 0$

95. Domain: $-\infty < x < -\frac{2}{3}, -\frac{2}{3} < x < \infty$

Asymptotes: $x = -\frac{2}{3}, y = \frac{2}{3}$

97. Domain: $-\infty < x < 0, 0 < x < \infty$

Asymptotes: $x = 0, y = 3$

99. 0.272 **101.** 0.405

Section 5.2 *(page 381)*

1. $(2, 1)$ **3.** $(1, -1)$ **5.** Inconsistent

7. All points on $3x - 2y - 5 = 0$ **9.** $\left(\frac{1}{3}, -\frac{2}{3}\right)$

11. $\left(\frac{5}{2}, \frac{3}{4}\right)$ **13.** $(3, 4)$ **15.** $(4, -1)$ **17.** $\left(\frac{12}{7}, \frac{18}{7}\right)$

19. Inconsistent **21.** $\left(-\frac{6}{35}, \frac{43}{35}\right)$ **23.** $\left(\frac{38}{15}, \frac{11}{5}\right)$

25. All points on $6x + 8y - 1 = 0$ **27.** $(5, -2)$

29. All points on $5x - 6y - 3 = 0$ **31.** $(8, 7)$

33.

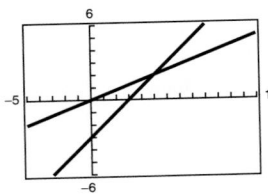

Consistent, $(5, 2)$

35.

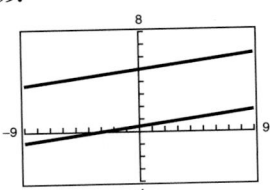

Inconsistent

37.

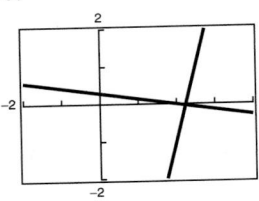

Consistent, $\left(\frac{65}{29}, -\frac{1}{29}\right)$

39.

Inconsistent

41.

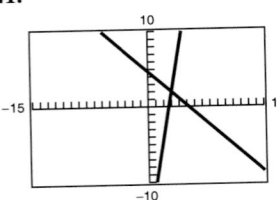

$(3, 2)$

43.

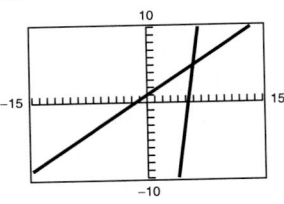

$(6, 5)$

45.

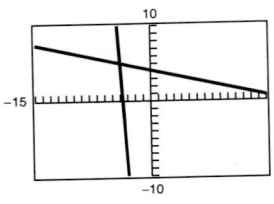

$(-4, 5)$

47.

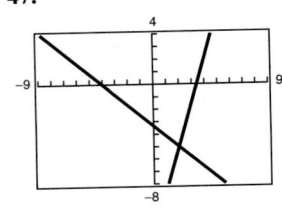

$(2, -5)$

49. $(4, 1)$ **51.** $(2, -1)$ **53.** $(6, -3)$ **55.** $\left(\frac{43}{6}, \frac{25}{6}\right)$

57. $\begin{cases} x - 2y = 0 \\ x - y - 3 = 0 \end{cases}$ **59.** $\begin{cases} 2x + 2y = 11 \\ x - 4y = -7 \end{cases}$

Answer is not unique. Answer is not unique.

61. $(80, 10)$ **63.** $(2,000,000, 100)$

65. Plane: 550 miles per hour; Wind: 50 miles per hour

67. (a) $\begin{cases} x + y = 10 \\ 0.2x + 0.5y = 3 \end{cases}$

(b)

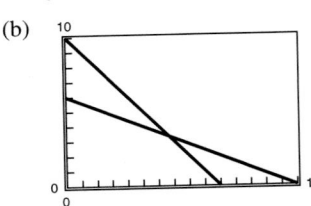

Decreases

(c) 20% solution: $6\frac{2}{3}$ liters; 50% solution: $3\frac{1}{3}$ liters

69. \$6000 **71.** 375 adults, 125 children

73. 225 kilometers and 75 kilometers

75. $y = 0.97x + 2.10$ **77.** $y = 0.318x + 4.061$

79. (a) and (b) $y = 14x + 19$

(c)

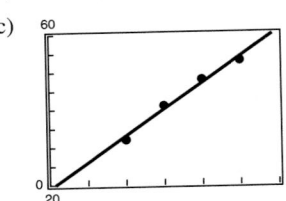

(d) 41.4 bushels

81. True **83.** True

85. $(300, 315)$. It is necessary to change the scale on the axes to see the point of intersection.

87. (a) $\begin{cases} x + y = 10 \\ x + y = 20 \end{cases}$ (b) $\begin{cases} x + y = 4 \\ 3x + 3y = 12 \end{cases}$

89. $k = -2$ **91.** $u = -1, v = \frac{1}{x}$

93.

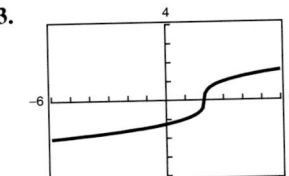

Domain: All real numbers

Range: All real numbers

95.

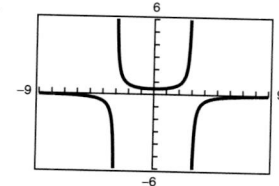

Domain: $-\infty < x < -3,\ -3 < x < 3,\ 3 < x < \infty$
Range: $-\infty < y < 0,\ 0 < y < \infty$

97. $x > 1$

99. $\frac{4}{3} \le x < \frac{16}{3}$

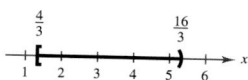

101. $-\infty < x < \infty$

103. $x < -4,\ x > 0$

105. $\ln \dfrac{x}{(x+3)^5}$ **107.** $\log_6 \sqrt[4]{3x}$ **109.** $(-2, 3)$

Section 5.3 *(page 395)*

1. (a) No   (b) No   (c) No   (d) Yes

3. (a) No   (b) No   (c) Yes   (d) No

5. $(-7, -8, 6)$ **7.** $(-3, -2, -6)$ **9.** $\left(\frac{1}{2}, -2, 2\right)$

11.
$$\begin{cases} x - 2y + 3z = 5 \\ \qquad y - 2z = 9 \\ 2x \qquad - 3z = 0 \end{cases}$$

First step in putting the system in row-echelon form

13. $(-1, 3, 4)$ **15.** $(-2, 7, 5)$ **17.** $(6, -3, 0)$

19. Inconsistent   **21.** $\left(1, -\frac{3}{2}, \frac{1}{2}\right)$

23. $(-3a + 10, 5a - 7, a)$ **25.** $(-a + 3, a + 1, a)$

27. Inconsistent   **29.** Inconsistent   **31.** $(0, 0, 0)$

33. $(2a, 21a - 1, 8a)$ **35.** $\left(\frac{1}{2} - \frac{3}{2}a, 1 - \frac{2}{3}a, a\right)$

37. $(9a, -35a, 67a)$ **39.** $(1, 1, 1, 1)$

41.
$$\begin{cases} 3x + \ y - \ z = 9 \\ x + 2y - \ z = 0 \\ -x + \ y + 3z = 1 \end{cases}$$
Answer is not unique.

43.
$$\begin{cases} x + 6y + 4z = 7 \\ 2x - 2y - 4z = 0 \\ -x + \ y + \ z = -\frac{7}{4} \end{cases}$$
Answer is not unique.

45.

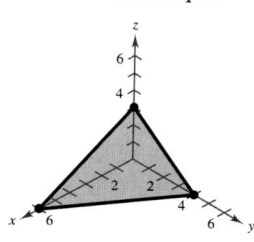

$(6, 0, 0),\ (0, 4, 0),\ (0, 0, 3),\ (4, 0, 1)$

47.

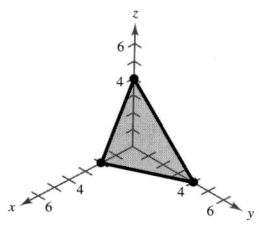

$(2, 0, 0),\ (0, 4, 0),\ (0, 0, 4),\ (0, 2, 2)$

49. $\dfrac{A}{x} + \dfrac{B}{x - 14}$ **51.** $\dfrac{A}{x} + \dfrac{B}{x^2} + \dfrac{C}{x - 10}$

53. $\dfrac{A}{x - 5} + \dfrac{B}{(x - 5)^2} + \dfrac{C}{(x - 5)^3}$

55. $\dfrac{1}{2}\left(\dfrac{1}{x - 1} - \dfrac{1}{x + 1}\right)$ **57.** $\dfrac{1}{x} - \dfrac{1}{x + 1}$

59. $\dfrac{1}{x} - \dfrac{2}{2x + 1}$ **61.** $\dfrac{1}{x - 1} - \dfrac{1}{x + 2}$

63. $-\dfrac{3}{x} - \dfrac{1}{x + 2} + \dfrac{5}{x - 2}$ **65.** $\dfrac{3}{x} - \dfrac{1}{x^2} + \dfrac{1}{x + 1}$

67. $\dfrac{3}{x - 3} + \dfrac{9}{(x - 3)^2}$ **69.** $2x - 7 + \dfrac{17}{x + 2} + \dfrac{1}{x + 1}$

71. $x + 3 + \dfrac{6}{x - 1} + \dfrac{4}{(x - 1)^2} + \dfrac{1}{(x - 1)^3}$

73. $\dfrac{3}{2x - 1} - \dfrac{2}{x + 1}$ **75.** $\dfrac{2}{x} - \dfrac{1}{x^2} - \dfrac{2}{x + 1}$

77. $2x + \dfrac{1}{2}\left(\dfrac{3}{x - 4} - \dfrac{1}{x + 2}\right)$

79. $\dfrac{3}{x} - \dfrac{2}{x - 4}$

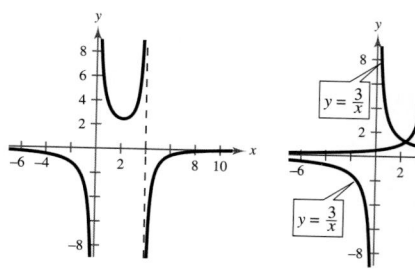

Vertical asymptotes are the same.

81. $s = -16t^2 + 144$ **83.** $s = 24t^2 - 264t + 692$

85. $y = \frac{1}{2}x^2 - 2x$ **87.** $y = x^2 - 6x + 8$

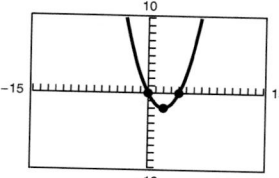

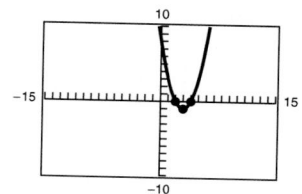

89. $x^2 + y^2 - 4x = 0$

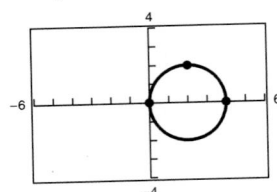

91. $x^2 + y^2 + 6x - 8y = 0$

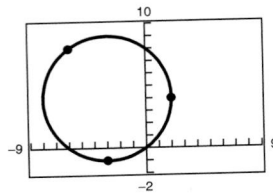

93. $4000 at 5%, $5000 at 6%, $7000 at 7%

95. $366,666.67 at 8%, $316,666.67 at 9%, $91,666.67 at 10%

97. $250,000 - \frac{1}{2}s$ in certificates of deposit

$125,000 + \frac{1}{2}s$ in municipal bonds

$125,000 - s$ in blue-chip stocks

s in growth stocks

99. 20 liters of spray X, 18 liters of spray Y, 16 liters of spray Z

101. Use four medium trucks or two large trucks, one medium truck, and two small trucks. (Other answers possible.)

103. $t_1 = 96$ pounds

$t_2 = 48$ pounds

$a = -16$ feet per second squared

105. $y = -\frac{5}{24}x^2 - \frac{3}{10}x + \frac{41}{6}$ **107.** $y = x^2 - x$

109. (a) $y = 0.14x^2 - 4.4x + 58$ (b) 436 feet

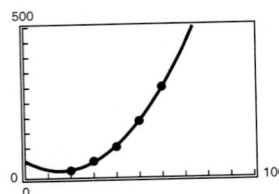

111. (a) $\dfrac{2000}{7 - 4x} - \dfrac{2000}{11 - 7x}$, $0 \le x \le 1$

(b)

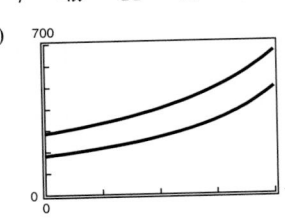

113. False. Leading coefficients are not all 1.

115. False. $\dfrac{A}{x + 10} + \dfrac{B}{x - 10} + \dfrac{C}{(x - 10)^2}$

117. $\dfrac{1}{2a}\left(\dfrac{1}{a + x} + \dfrac{1}{a - x}\right)$ **119.** $\dfrac{1}{a}\left(\dfrac{1}{y} + \dfrac{1}{a - y}\right)$

Answers will vary.   Answers will vary.

121. No. There are two arithmetic errors. They are the constant in the second equation and the coefficient of z in the third equation.

123. $x = 5, y = 5, \lambda = -5$

125. $x = \dfrac{\sqrt{2}}{2}, y = \dfrac{1}{2}, \lambda = 1$

$x = -\dfrac{\sqrt{2}}{2}, y = \dfrac{1}{2}, \lambda = 1$

$x = 0, y = 0, \lambda = 0$

127.

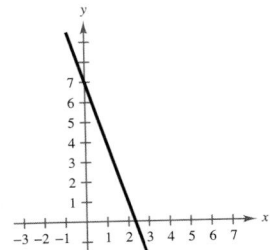

129.

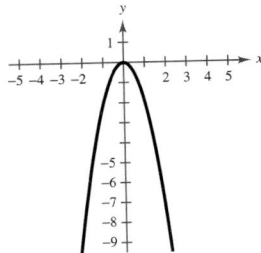

131.

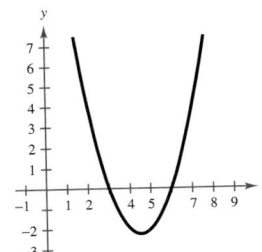

133.

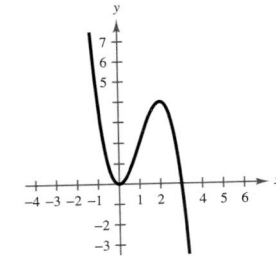

135. (a) $-4, 0, 3$

(b)

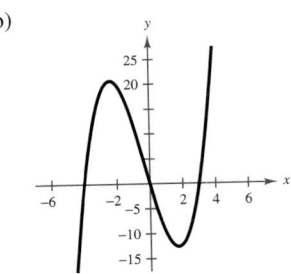

137. (a) $-4, -\frac{3}{2}, 3$

(b)

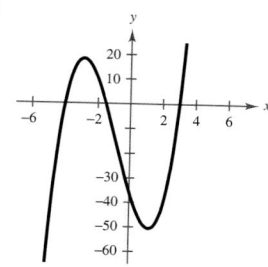

139.

x	-6	-5	-4	-3	0
y	11	-1	-4	-4.75	-4.996

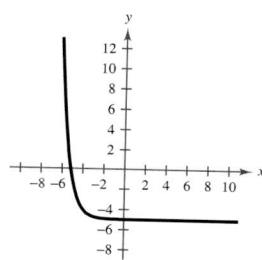

141.

x	-3	-1	0	1	2	3
y	-2.9	-2.6	-2	-0.7	2.5	9.9

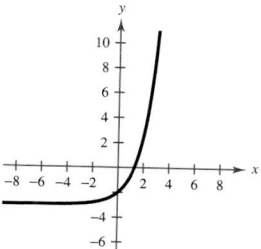

143. $\left(4\frac{1}{3}, -2\right)$ **145.** $(40, 40)$

Section 5.4   *(page 408)*

1. (g)   **3.** (a)   **5.** (e)   **7.** (f)

9.

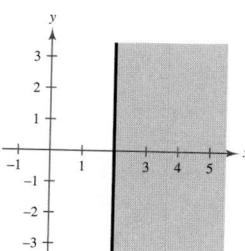

11.

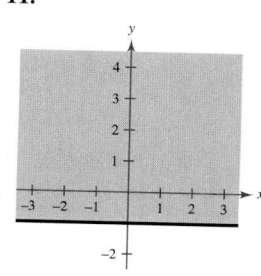

13.

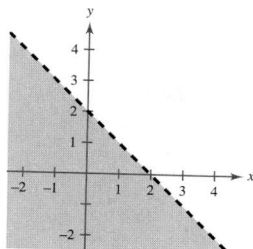

15.

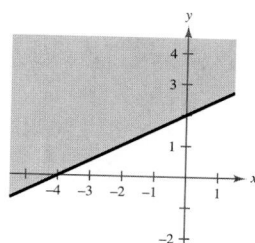

17.

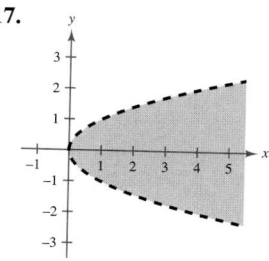

19.

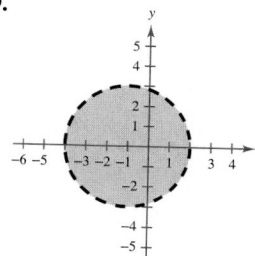

21.

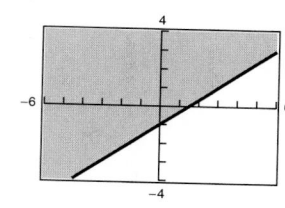

23.

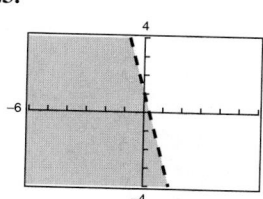

25.

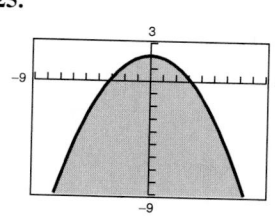

27.

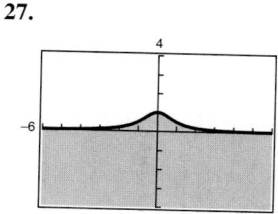

29.

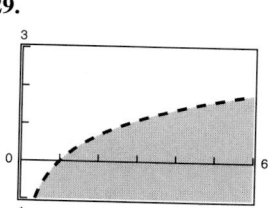

31.

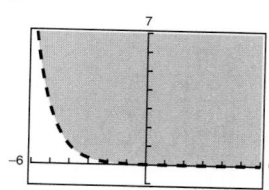

33. $\dfrac{x}{3} + \dfrac{y}{2} \geq 1$ **35.** $x^2 + y^2 \leq 9$

37. (a) Yes   (b) No   (c) No   (d) No

39.

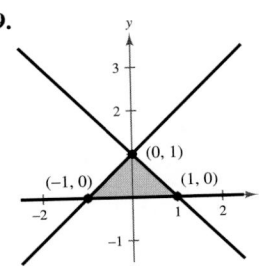

41.

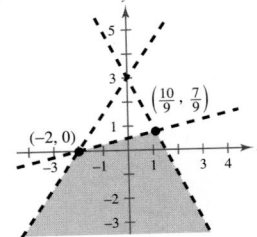

43.

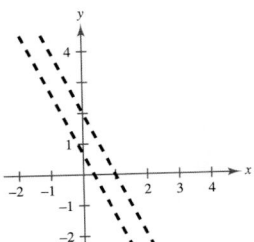

45.

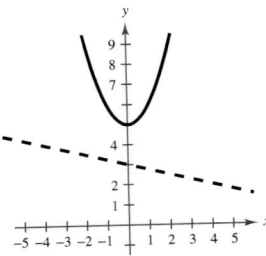

Solution set is empty.

47.

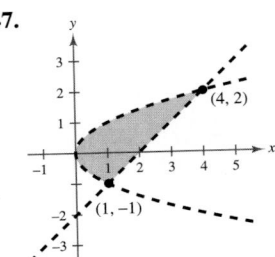

49.

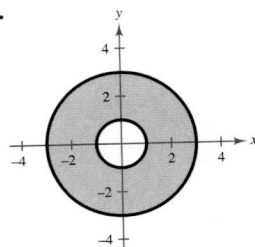

51.

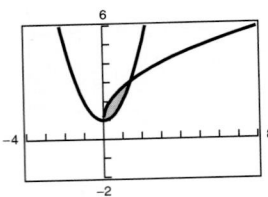

53.

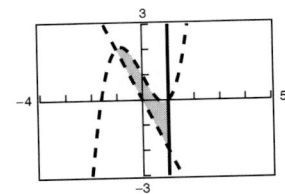

55.

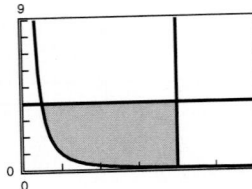

57. $\begin{cases} \frac{1}{4}x + \frac{1}{4}y \le 1 \\ x \ge 0 \\ y \ge 0 \end{cases}$

59. $\begin{cases} y \le 4 - x \\ y \le 2 - \frac{1}{4}x \\ x \ge 0 \\ y \ge 0 \end{cases}$

61. $\begin{cases} 2 \le x \le 5 \\ 1 \le y \le 7 \end{cases}$

63. $\begin{cases} y \le \frac{3}{2}x \\ y \le -x + 5 \\ y \ge 0 \end{cases}$

65. (a) $\begin{cases} x + y \le 20{,}000 \\ y \ge 2x \\ x \ge 5000 \\ y \ge 5000 \end{cases}$

(b)

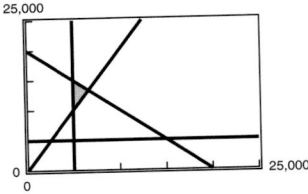

67. (a) $\begin{cases} x + \frac{3}{2}y \le 12 \\ \frac{4}{3}x + \frac{3}{2}y \le 15 \\ x \ge 0 \\ y \ge 0 \end{cases}$

(b)

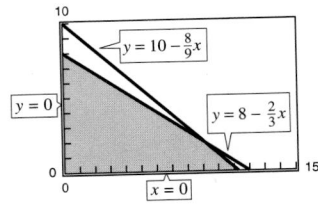

69. (a) $\begin{cases} 20x + 10y \ge 280 \\ 15x + 10y \ge 160 \\ 10x + 20y \ge 180 \\ x \ge 0 \\ y \ge 0 \end{cases}$

(b)

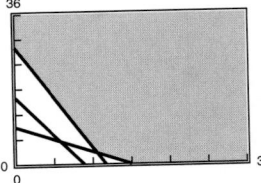

71. (a) $\begin{cases} \pi y^2 - \pi x^2 \ge 10 \\ x > 0 \\ y > x \end{cases}$

(b)

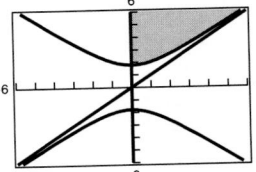

(c) The line is an asymptote to the boundary. The larger the circles, the closer the radii can be and the constraint still be satisfied.

73.

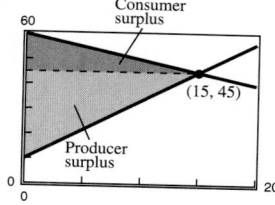

Consumer surplus: 112.5
Producer surplus: 262.5

75.

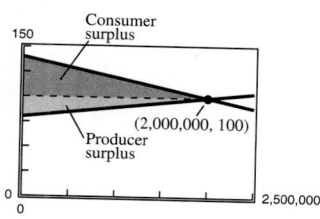

Consumer surplus: 40,000,000
Producer surplus: 20,000,000

77. False. $3x + y^2 \geq 2$ is outside the parabola.

79. Answers will vary.　　**81.** $x + 11y + 8 = 0$

83. $x + y + 1.8 = 0$

Section 5.5 　*(page 417)*

1. Minimum at $(0, 0)$: 0

　　Maximum at $(0, 6)$: 30

3. Minimum at $(0, 0)$: 0

　　Maximum at $(6, 0)$: 60

5. Minimum at $(0, 0)$: 0

　　Maximum at $(3, 4)$: 23

7. Minimum at $(0, 0)$: 0

　　Maximum at $(4, 0)$: 20

9. Minimum at $(0, 0)$: 0

　　Maximum at $(60, 20)$: 740

11. Minimum at $(0, 0)$: 0

　　Maximum at any point on the line segment connecting $(60, 20)$ and $(30, 45)$: 2100

13.

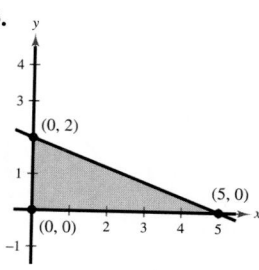

Minimum at $(0, 0)$: 0

Maximum at $(5, 0)$: 30

15.

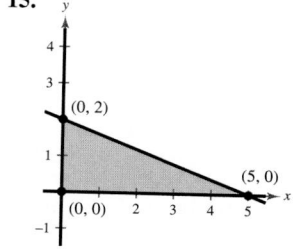

Minimum at $(0, 0)$: 0

Maximum at $(0, 2)$: 48

17.

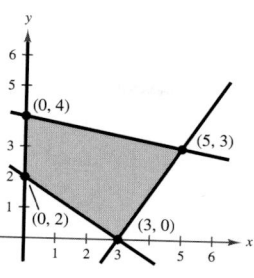

Minimum at $(0, 2)$: 6

Maximum at $(5, 3)$: 29

19.

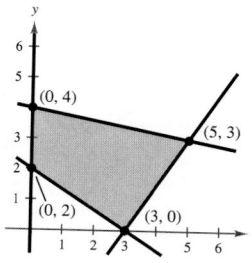

Minimum at $(3, 0)$: 9

Maximum at $(5, 3)$: 36

21.

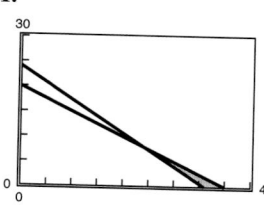

Minimum at $(24, 8)$: 104

Maximum at $(40, 0)$: 160

23.

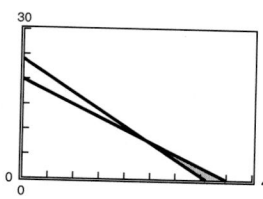

Minimum at $(36, 0)$: 36

Maximum at $(24, 8)$: 56

25.

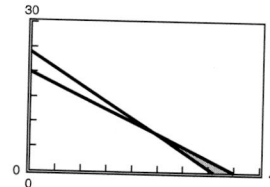

Minimum at any point on the line segment connecting $(24, 8)$ and $(36, 0)$: 72

Maximum at $(40, 0)$: 80

27. (a) and (b)　　　　　　　　(c) $(3, 6)$

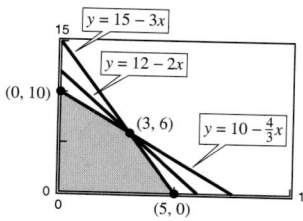

29. (a) and (b)　　　　　　　　(c) $(0, 10)$

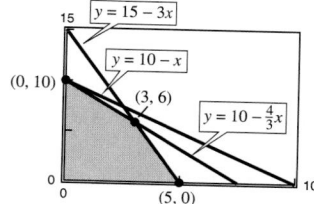

31. (a) and (b)   (c) (0, 5)

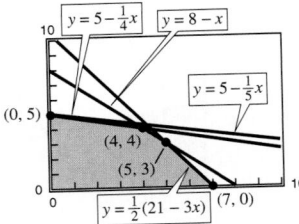

33. (a) and (b)   (c) (4, 4)

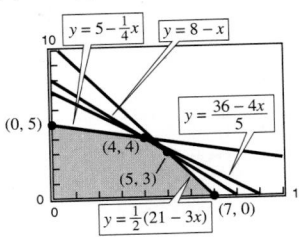

35.

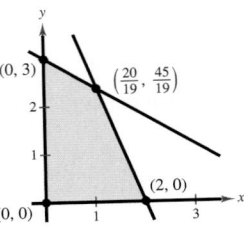

z is maximum at any point on the line segment connecting $(2, 0)$ and $\left(\frac{20}{19}, \frac{45}{19}\right)$.

37.

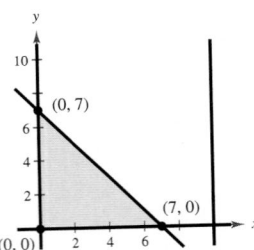

The constraint $x \le 10$ is extraneous.

Maximum at $(0, 7)$: 14

39.

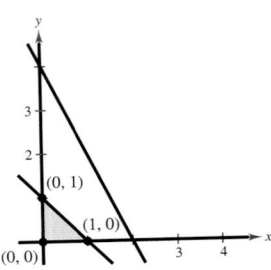

The constraint $2x + y \le 4$ is extraneous.

Maximum at $(0, 1)$: 4

41. 200 units of the $250 model; 50 units of the $400 model

Maximum profit: $11,500

43. Type A: $\frac{1}{6}$ gallon; Type B: $\frac{5}{6}$ gallon

Minimum cost: $1.255 per gallon

45. No audits; 40 tax returns

Maximum revenue: $12,000

47. 1000 units of Model A; 500 units of Model B

Maximum profit: $76,000

49. True   **51.** $z = x + 5y$ (Answer is not unique.)

53. $z = 4x + y$ (Answer is not unique.)

55. (a) $t > 9$ (b) $\frac{3}{4} < t < 9$ **57.** $\dfrac{9}{2(x + 3)}$, $x \ne 0$

59. $\dfrac{x^2 + 2x - 13}{x(x - 2)}$, $x \ne \pm 3$ **61.** 1.099   **63.** 14.550

65. 1.851   **67.** $(-2, -3)$ **69.** $(-1, 2)$

71.   **73.**

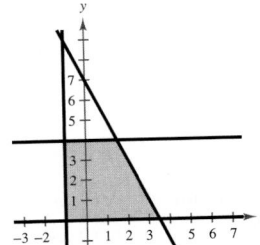   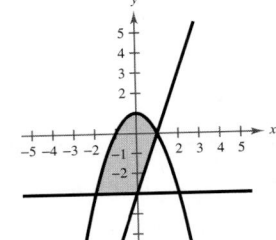

Review Exercises   *(page 422)*

1. $(1, 1)$ **3.** $(5, 4)$ **5.** $(0, 0), (2, 8), (-2, 8)$

7. $\left(2, -\frac{1}{2}\right)$ **9.** $(0, 0), (-3, 3)$ **11.** $(4, 4)$

13. 4762 units   **15.** 96×144 meters   **17.** $\left(\frac{5}{2}, 3\right)$

19. $(-0.5, 0.8)$ **21.** $(0, 0)$ **23.** $\left(\frac{14}{5} + \frac{8}{5}a, a\right)$

25.   **27.**

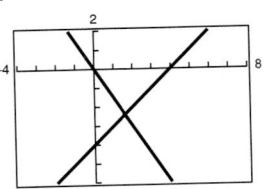   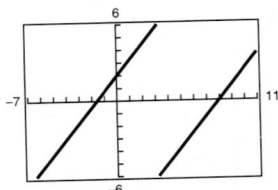

Consistent: $(1.6, -2.4)$ Inconsistent

29.

Consistent: All points on the line $y = 4x - 5.5$

31. 218.75 miles per hour; 193.75 miles per hour

33. $\left(\dfrac{500,000}{7}, \dfrac{159}{7}\right)$ **35.** $(2, -4, -5)$

37. $\left(\dfrac{38}{17}, \dfrac{40}{17}, -\dfrac{63}{17}\right)$ **39.** $(3a + 4, 2a + 5, a)$

41. $y = 2x^2 + x - 5$ **43.** $(a - 4, a - 3, a)$

45.

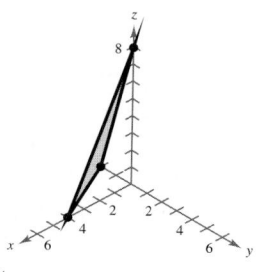

$(0, 0, 8), (0, -2, 0), (4, 0, 0), (1, -1, 2)$

47. $\dfrac{3}{x + 2} - \dfrac{4}{x + 4}$ **49.** $1 + \dfrac{1}{8}\left(\dfrac{9}{x - 3} - \dfrac{25}{x + 5}\right)$

51. $\dfrac{1}{2}\left(\dfrac{3}{x - 1} - \dfrac{x - 3}{x^2 + 1}\right)$

53. Spray X: 10 gallons; Spray Y: 5 gallons; Spray Z: 12 gallons

55.

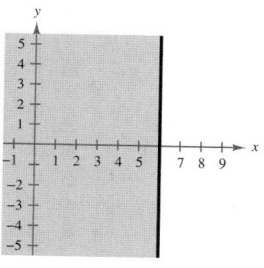

57.

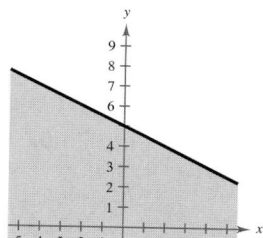

59.

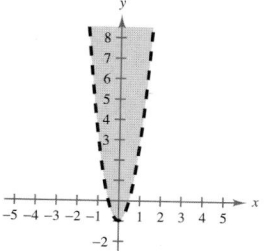

61. (d) **63.** (c)

65.

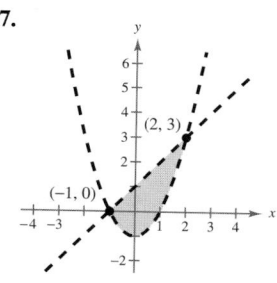

67.

69.

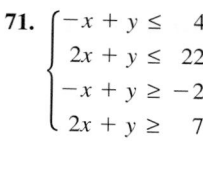

71. $\begin{cases} -x + y \le 4 \\ 2x + y \le 22 \\ -x + y \ge -2 \\ 2x + y \ge 7 \end{cases}$

73. $\begin{cases} x + y \le 1500 \\ x \ge 400 \\ y \ge 600 \end{cases}$

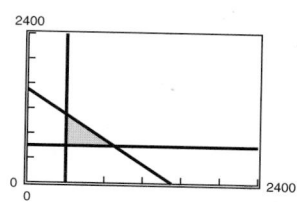

75.

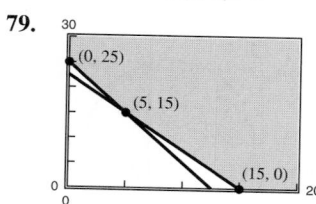

Consumer surplus: 4,500,000

Producer surplus: 9,000,000

77.

Maximum at $(5, 8)$: 47

79.

Minimum at $(15, 0)$: 26.25

81. 20 perms, 2 haircuts

83. False. There is no solution for the system.

Chapter Test *(page 426)*

1. $(4, -2)$ **2.** $(0, -1), (1, 0), (2, 1)$

3. $(8, 5), (2, -1)$ **4.** $(-3, 1)$ **5.** $(3, 7), (-4, 0)$

6. $(1, 8)$ **7.** $\left(\frac{28}{9}, -\frac{31}{9}\right)$ **8.** $(-1, 5, 2)$

9. $\left(-\frac{3}{5}a, \frac{4}{5}a, a\right)$ **10.** $\begin{cases} 9x + 2y = -4 \\ 3x + y = -4 \end{cases}$

11. $\begin{cases} 6x + 2y + 4z = -2 \\ -2x + y + 8z = -12 \\ 2x + y + 4z = -5 \end{cases}$

12. $y = -\frac{1}{2}x^2 + x + 6$ **13.** $\dfrac{5}{x - 1} + \dfrac{3}{(x - 1)^2}$

14.

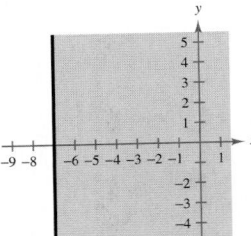

15.

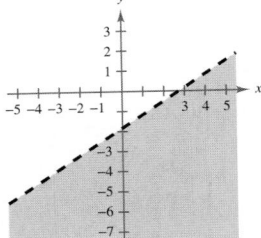

16.

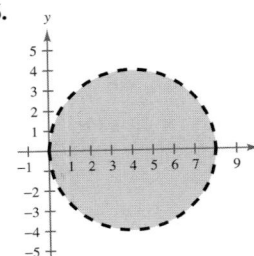

17.

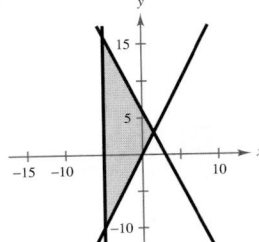

18.

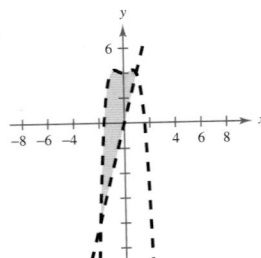

19.

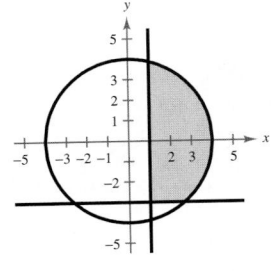

20. $\begin{cases} y \le -\frac{1}{3}x + 15 \\ y \le -\frac{7}{3}x + 99 \\ x \le 12 \\ x \ge 0 \\ y \ge 0 \end{cases}$ **21.** Maximum at $(12, 0)$: 240

22. Stock 160 units of the $275 model and 140 units of the $400 model.

Cumulative Test for Chapters 3–5 *(page 427)*

1.

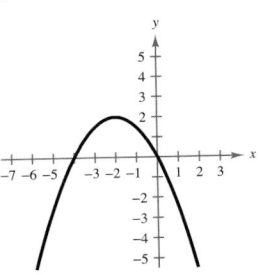

2.

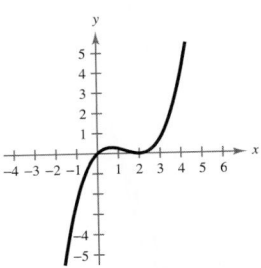

3.

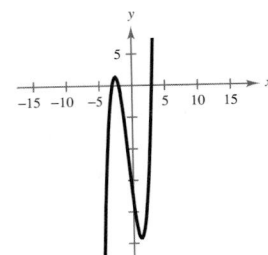

4. $-2, \pm 2i$ **5.** 1.42

6. $4x + 2 - \dfrac{15}{x + 3}$ **7.** $2x^2 + 7x + 48 + \dfrac{268}{x - 6}$

8. $x^4 + x^3 + 18x$

9.

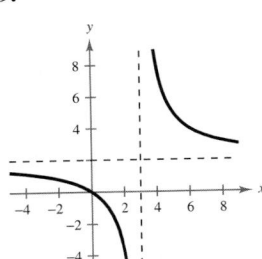

Asymptotes: $x = 3, y = 2$

10.

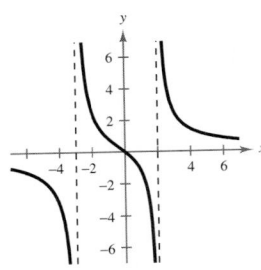

Asymptotes: $x = -3, x = 2, y = 0$

11.

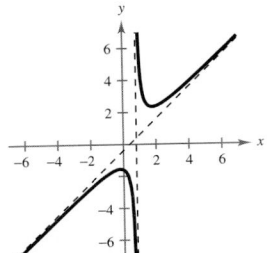

Asymptotes: $x = 2, y = x - 1$

12. $f(x) = \dfrac{4x^2}{x^2 + 1}$ **13.** 6.733   **14.** 8772.934

15. 0.162   **16.** 51.743

17.

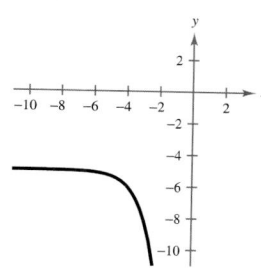

18.

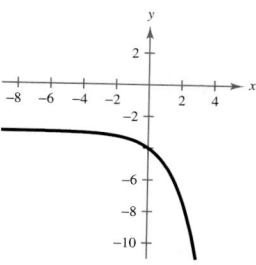

19.

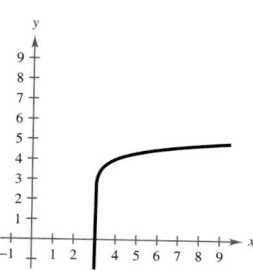

20.

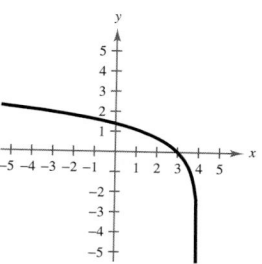

21. 1.892 **22.** 0.872 **23.** 1.960 **24.** 0.585

25. $\ln \dfrac{x^2}{\sqrt{x+5}}$ **26.** $\dfrac{1}{2}\ln 12 \approx 1.242$

27. $\ln\left(\dfrac{9}{4}\right) + 3 \approx 3.811$ **28.** $\dfrac{64}{5} = 12.8$

29. $y = 2.5e^{0.2871x}$ **30.** $(11, 3)$ **31.** $(8, 4), (2, -2)$

32. $(3, 1)$ **33.** $x^2 + y^2 - 3x + 2y = 0$

34.

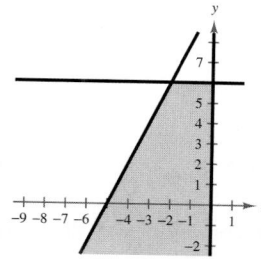

35.

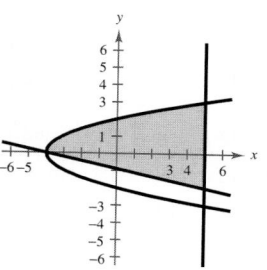

36.

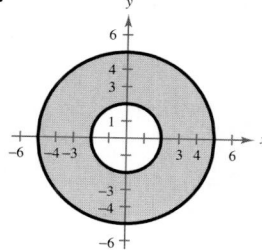

37. $\begin{cases} y \le 3x - 1 \\ y \le -3x + 26 \\ y \le 8 \\ y \ge 2 \end{cases}$

38. $\$16,302.05$ **39.** $\$108.63$

40.

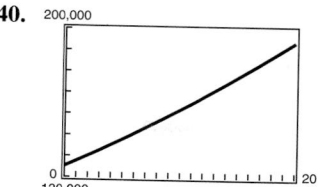

2008

41. (a) $C = 2.75x + 24,000$

$R = 6.95x$

(b)

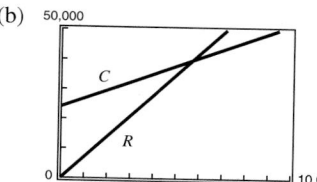

5715 units

(c) Answers will vary.

42. 16×22 meters

43. Airplane: 543 miles per hour

Head wind: 33 miles per hour

44. Three bags of brand X and two bags of brand Y.

Cost: $\$105$

Chapter 6

Section 6.1   *(page 440)*

1. 3×2 **3.** 3×1 **5.** 2×2

7. $\left[\begin{array}{rr:r} 4 & -5 & 33 \\ -1 & 5 & -27 \end{array}\right]$

9. $\left[\begin{array}{rrr:r} 1 & 10 & -2 & 2 \\ 5 & -3 & 4 & 0 \\ 2 & 1 & 0 & 6 \end{array}\right]$

11. $\begin{cases} x + 2y = 7 \\ 2x - 3y = 4 \end{cases}$ **13.** $\begin{cases} 9x + 12y + 3z = 0 \\ -2x + 18y + 5z + 2w = 10 \\ x + 7y - 8z = -4 \end{cases}$

15. Reduced row-echelon form

17. Not in row-echelon form   **19.** $\left[\begin{array}{rrr} 1 & 4 & 3 \\ 0 & 2 & -1 \end{array}\right]$

21. $\left[\begin{array}{rrrr} 1 & 1 & 4 & -1 \\ 0 & 5 & -2 & 6 \\ 0 & 3 & 20 & 4 \end{array}\right], \left[\begin{array}{rrrr} 1 & 1 & 4 & -1 \\ 0 & 1 & -\frac{2}{5} & \frac{6}{5} \\ 0 & 3 & 20 & 4 \end{array}\right]$

23. Add 5 times R_2 to R_1.   **25.** Interchange R_1 and R_2.

27. (a) $\begin{bmatrix} 1 & 2 & 3 \\ 0 & -5 & -10 \\ 3 & 1 & -1 \end{bmatrix}$ (b) $\begin{bmatrix} 1 & 2 & 3 \\ 0 & -5 & -10 \\ 0 & -5 & -10 \end{bmatrix}$

(c) $\begin{bmatrix} 1 & 2 & 3 \\ 0 & -5 & -10 \\ 0 & 0 & 0 \end{bmatrix}$ (d) $\begin{bmatrix} 1 & 2 & 3 \\ 0 & 1 & 2 \\ 0 & 0 & 0 \end{bmatrix}$

(e) $\begin{bmatrix} 1 & 0 & -1 \\ 0 & 1 & 2 \\ 0 & 0 & 0 \end{bmatrix}$

The matrix is in reduced row-echelon form.

29. (a)
```
*row+(-2,[A],1,2)
     [[1   2    3]
      [0  -5  -10]
      [3   1   -1]]
```

(b)
```
*row+(-3,[B],1,3)
     [[1   2    3]
      [0  -5  -10]
      [0  -5  -10]]
```

(c)
```
*row+(-1,[C],2,3)
     [[1   2    3]
      [0  -5  -10]
      [0   0    0]]
```

(d)
```
*row(-1/5,[D],2)
     [[1 2 3]
      [0 1 2]
      [0 0 0]]
```

(e)
```
*row+(-2,[E],2,1)
     [[1 0 -1]
      [0 1  2]
      [0 0  0]]
```

31. $\begin{bmatrix} 1 & 1 & 0 & 5 \\ 0 & 1 & 2 & 0 \\ 0 & 0 & 1 & -1 \end{bmatrix}$ 33. $\begin{bmatrix} 1 & -1 & -1 & 1 \\ 0 & 1 & 6 & 3 \\ 0 & 0 & 0 & 0 \end{bmatrix}$

35. $\begin{bmatrix} 1 & 0 & 0 \\ 0 & 1 & 0 \\ 0 & 0 & 1 \end{bmatrix}$ 37. $\begin{bmatrix} 1 & 0 & 3 & 16 \\ 0 & 1 & 2 & 12 \end{bmatrix}$

39. $\begin{cases} x - 2y = 4 \\ y = -3 \end{cases}$ 41. $\begin{cases} x - y + 2z = 4 \\ y - z = 2 \\ z = -2 \end{cases}$

$(-2, -3)$

$(8, 0, -2)$

43. $(7, -5)$ 45. $(-4, -8, 2)$ 47. $(3, 2)$

49. $(6, -2)$ 51. $\left(\frac{3}{2}, -\frac{1}{4}\right)$ 53. Inconsistent

55. $(4, -3, 2)$ 57. $(2a + 1, 3a + 2, a)$ 59. $(0, 0)$

61. $(0, 2 - 4a, a)$ 63. $(1, 0, 4, -2)$ 65. $(-2a, a, a)$

67. Yes; $(-1, 1, -3)$ 69. No   71. $y = x^2 + 2x + 5$

73. $\frac{1}{4}x^3 + x^2 - x - 2$ 75. $y = -x^4 + 4x^2$

77. $800,000 at 8%, $500,000 at 9%, $200,000 at 12%

79. $I_1 = \frac{13}{10}, I_2 = \frac{11}{5}, I_3 = \frac{9}{10}$

81. (a) $y = -128.5t^2 + 1587.5t - 4304$

(b)
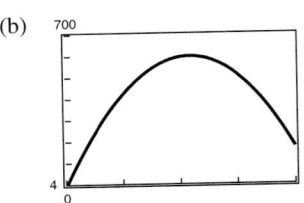

(c) $172 million

83. (a) $x_1 = s, x_2 = t, x_3 = 600 - s,$
$x_4 = s - t, x_5 = 500 - t, x_6 = s, x_7 = t$

(b) $x_1 = 0, x_2 = 0, x_3 = 600, x_4 = 0, x_5 = 500,$
$x_6 = 0, x_7 = 0$

(c) $x_1 = 0, x_2 = -500, x_3 = 600, x_4 = 500,$
$x_5 = 1000, x_6 = 0, x_7 = -500$

85. (a) $x_1 = 100 + t, x_2 = -100 + t, x_3 = 200 + t, x_4 = t$

(b) $x_1 = 100, x_2 = -100, x_3 = 200, x_4 = 0$

(c) $x_1 = 200, x_2 = 0, x_3 = 300, x_4 = 100$

87. False. Rows are not arranged.

89. $\begin{cases} x + y + 7z = -1 \\ x + 2y + 11z = 0 \\ 2x + y + 10z = -3 \end{cases}$

(Answer is not unique.)

91. (a) There exists a row with all zeros except for the entry in the last column.

(b) There are fewer rows with nonzero entries than variables.

93.
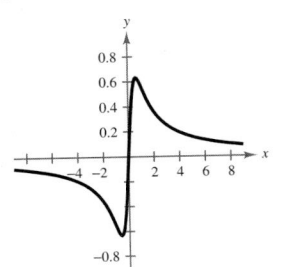

Asymptote: $y = 0$

95.
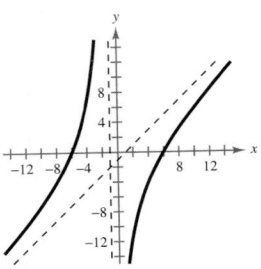

Asymptotes:
$x = -1, y = x - 1$

97.

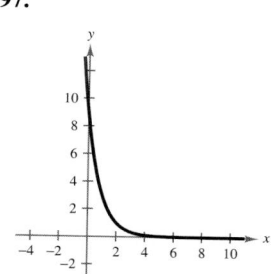

99.

101. $(-3, -7)$ **103.** $(-2, 3, 1)$

Section 6.2   *(page 455)*

1. $x = -4,\ y = 22$ **3.** $x = -1,\ y = 4,\ z = 6$

5. (a) $\begin{bmatrix} 3 & -2 \\ 1 & 7 \end{bmatrix}$ (b) $\begin{bmatrix} -1 & 0 \\ 3 & -9 \end{bmatrix}$

(c) $\begin{bmatrix} 3 & -3 \\ 6 & -3 \end{bmatrix}$ (d) $\begin{bmatrix} -1 & -1 \\ 8 & -19 \end{bmatrix}$

7. (a) $\begin{bmatrix} 9 & 5 \\ 1 & -2 \\ -3 & 15 \end{bmatrix}$ (b) $\begin{bmatrix} 7 & -7 \\ 3 & 8 \\ -5 & -5 \end{bmatrix}$

(c) $\begin{bmatrix} 24 & -3 \\ 6 & 9 \\ -12 & 15 \end{bmatrix}$ (d) $\begin{bmatrix} 22 & -15 \\ 8 & 19 \\ -14 & -5 \end{bmatrix}$

9. (a) $\begin{bmatrix} 3 & 3 & -2 & 1 & 1 \\ -2 & 5 & 7 & -6 & -8 \end{bmatrix}$

(b) $\begin{bmatrix} 1 & 1 & 0 & -1 & 1 \\ 4 & -3 & -11 & 6 & 6 \end{bmatrix}$

(c) $\begin{bmatrix} 6 & 6 & -3 & 0 & 3 \\ 3 & 3 & -6 & 0 & -3 \end{bmatrix}$

(d) $\begin{bmatrix} 4 & 4 & -1 & -2 & 3 \\ 9 & -5 & -24 & 12 & 11 \end{bmatrix}$

11. (a) Not possible   (b) Not possible

(c) $\begin{bmatrix} 18 & 0 & 9 \\ -3 & -12 & 0 \end{bmatrix}$ (d) Not possible

13. $\begin{bmatrix} -7 & -9 \\ 17 & -2 \end{bmatrix}$ **15.** $\begin{bmatrix} -24 & -4 & 12 \\ -12 & 32 & 12 \end{bmatrix}$

17. $\begin{bmatrix} 14 & 4 \\ -52 & 0 \end{bmatrix}$ **19.** $\begin{bmatrix} 0.857 & 2.143 \\ -0.429 & -1.714 \end{bmatrix}$

21. $\begin{bmatrix} -1.581 & -3.739 \\ -4.252 & -13.249 \\ 9.713 & -0.362 \end{bmatrix}$ **23.** $\begin{bmatrix} -6 & -9 \\ -1 & 0 \\ 17 & -10 \end{bmatrix}$

25. $\begin{bmatrix} 3 & 3 \\ -0.5 & 0 \\ -6.5 & 5.5 \end{bmatrix}$

27. (a) $\begin{bmatrix} 0 & 15 \\ 8 & 11 \end{bmatrix}$ (b) $\begin{bmatrix} -3 & 2 \\ 39 & 14 \end{bmatrix}$ (c) $\begin{bmatrix} 11 & 6 \\ 15 & 14 \end{bmatrix}$

29. (a) $\begin{bmatrix} 0 & -10 \\ 10 & 0 \end{bmatrix}$ (b) $\begin{bmatrix} 0 & -10 \\ 10 & 0 \end{bmatrix}$ (c) $\begin{bmatrix} 8 & -6 \\ 6 & 8 \end{bmatrix}$

31. (a) $\begin{bmatrix} 6 & -21 & 15 \\ 8 & -23 & 19 \\ 4 & 7 & 5 \end{bmatrix}$ (b) $\begin{bmatrix} 9 & 0 & 13 \\ 7 & -2 & 21 \\ 1 & 4 & -19 \end{bmatrix}$

(c) $\begin{bmatrix} 20 & 7 & -8 \\ 24 & 7 & -2 \\ 2 & -5 & 30 \end{bmatrix}$

33. Not possible   **35.** $\begin{bmatrix} -2 & 51 \\ -8 & 33 \\ 0 & 27 \end{bmatrix}$ **37.** $\begin{bmatrix} 1 & 0 & 0 \\ 0 & 1 & 0 \\ 0 & 0 & \frac{7}{2} \end{bmatrix}$

39. $\begin{bmatrix} 40 & -20 & -10 & 80 \\ 44 & -22 & -11 & 88 \end{bmatrix}$ **41.** $\begin{bmatrix} 70 & -17 & 73 \\ 32 & 11 & 6 \\ 16 & -38 & 70 \end{bmatrix}$

43. $\begin{bmatrix} 151 & 25 & 48 \\ 516 & 279 & 387 \\ 47 & -20 & 87 \end{bmatrix}$ **45.** Not possible

47. $\begin{bmatrix} 5 & 8 \\ -4 & -16 \end{bmatrix}$ **49.** $\begin{bmatrix} -4 & 10 \\ 3 & 14 \end{bmatrix}$

51. (b)   **53.** (b)   **55.** (b)

57. (a) $\begin{bmatrix} -1 & 1 \\ -2 & 1 \end{bmatrix}\begin{bmatrix} x_1 \\ x_2 \end{bmatrix} = \begin{bmatrix} 4 \\ 0 \end{bmatrix}$ (b) $\begin{bmatrix} 4 \\ 8 \end{bmatrix}$

59. (a) $\begin{bmatrix} -2 & -3 \\ 6 & 1 \end{bmatrix}\begin{bmatrix} x_1 \\ x_2 \end{bmatrix} = \begin{bmatrix} -4 \\ -36 \end{bmatrix}$ (b) $\begin{bmatrix} -7 \\ 6 \end{bmatrix}$

61. (a) $\begin{bmatrix} 1 & -2 & 3 \\ -1 & 3 & -1 \\ 2 & -5 & 5 \end{bmatrix}\begin{bmatrix} x_1 \\ x_2 \\ x_3 \end{bmatrix} = \begin{bmatrix} 9 \\ -6 \\ 17 \end{bmatrix}$ (b) $\begin{bmatrix} 1 \\ -1 \\ 2 \end{bmatrix}$

63. (a) $\begin{bmatrix} 1 & -5 & 2 \\ -3 & 1 & -1 \\ 0 & -2 & 5 \end{bmatrix}\begin{bmatrix} x_1 \\ x_2 \\ x_3 \end{bmatrix} = \begin{bmatrix} -20 \\ 8 \\ -16 \end{bmatrix}$ (b) $\begin{bmatrix} -1 \\ 3 \\ -2 \end{bmatrix}$

65. $\begin{bmatrix} -4 & 0 \\ 8 & 2 \end{bmatrix}$ **67.** $\begin{bmatrix} 0 & 0 & 0 \\ 0 & 0 & 0 \\ 0 & 0 & 0 \end{bmatrix}$

69. Not possible   **71.** Not possible   **73.** 2×2

75. Not possible   **77.** 2×3 **79.** $\begin{bmatrix} 72 & 48 & 24 \\ 36 & 108 & 72 \end{bmatrix}$

81. $BA = [\$1250 \quad \$1331.25 \quad \$981.25]$

Each entry represents the total profit from the two products at one of the three outlets.

83. $\begin{bmatrix} \$15,770 & \$18,300 \\ \$26,500 & \$29,250 \\ \$21,260 & \$24,150 \end{bmatrix}$

The entries are the total wholesale and retail prices of the inventory at each outlet.

85. $\begin{bmatrix} 0.40 & 0.15 & 0.15 \\ 0.28 & 0.53 & 0.17 \\ 0.32 & 0.32 & 0.68 \end{bmatrix}$

P^2 represents the changes in party affiliations after two elections.

87. True. To add two matrices, you add corresponding entries.

89. False. The product is $\begin{bmatrix} 2 & 2 \\ -3 & -3 \\ 7 & 3 \end{bmatrix}$.

91. $AB = 0$, but $A \neq 0$ and $B \neq 0$.   **93.** $A^2 = \begin{bmatrix} 1 & 0 \\ 0 & 1 \end{bmatrix}$

95. (a) $A = \begin{bmatrix} 0 & 2 \\ 0 & 0 \end{bmatrix}$, $B = \begin{bmatrix} 0 & 2 & 3 \\ 0 & 0 & 4 \\ 0 & 0 & 0 \end{bmatrix}$

(Answers will vary.)

(b) A^2 and B^3 are zero matrices.

(c) $A = \begin{bmatrix} 0 & 2 & 3 & 4 \\ 0 & 0 & 5 & 6 \\ 0 & 0 & 0 & 7 \\ 0 & 0 & 0 & 0 \end{bmatrix}$

A^4 is the zero matrix.

(d) A^n is the zero matrix.

97. $\frac{3}{2}, -\frac{1}{4}$ **99.** $-9, 0, \frac{5}{3}$ **101.** $\frac{5}{2}, \pm\sqrt{6}$

103. $2 + \log_2 3 - \log_2 x$

105. $\ln(x + 3) + \ln(x - 3) - 4\ln x$ **107.** $\ln \dfrac{x}{(x^2 - 36)^3}$

109. $\ln(7^{3/2}t^3)$ **111.** $(-1, 1, 3)$

Section 6.3   *(page 466)*

1.–11. Answers will vary.

13. $\begin{bmatrix} \frac{1}{2} & 0 \\ 0 & \frac{1}{3} \end{bmatrix}$ **15.** $\begin{bmatrix} -3 & 2 \\ -2 & 1 \end{bmatrix}$ **17.** $\begin{bmatrix} 1 & -1 \\ 2 & -1 \end{bmatrix}$

19. Does not exist   **21.** $\begin{bmatrix} 1 & 1 & -1 \\ -3 & 2 & -1 \\ 3 & -3 & 2 \end{bmatrix}$

23. $\begin{bmatrix} 1 & 0 & 0 \\ -0.75 & 0.25 & 0 \\ 0.35 & -0.25 & 0.2 \end{bmatrix}$ **25.** $\begin{bmatrix} -\frac{1}{8} & 0 & 0 & 0 \\ 0 & 1 & 0 & 0 \\ 0 & 0 & \frac{1}{4} & 0 \\ 0 & 0 & 0 & -\frac{1}{5} \end{bmatrix}$

27. $\begin{bmatrix} -175 & 37 & -13 \\ 95 & -20 & 7 \\ 14 & -3 & 1 \end{bmatrix}$ **29.** $\frac{1}{2}\begin{bmatrix} -3 & 3 & 2 \\ 9 & -7 & -6 \\ -2 & 2 & 2 \end{bmatrix}$

31. $\begin{bmatrix} -12 & -5 & -9 \\ -4 & -2 & -4 \\ -8 & -4 & -6 \end{bmatrix}$ **33.** $\frac{5}{11}\begin{bmatrix} 0 & -4 & 2 \\ -22 & 11 & 11 \\ 22 & -6 & -8 \end{bmatrix}$

35. Does not exist   **37.** $\begin{bmatrix} 1 & 0 & 1 & 0 \\ 0 & 1 & 0 & 1 \\ 2 & 0 & 1 & 0 \\ 0 & 1 & 0 & 2 \end{bmatrix}$

39. Does not exist   **41.** $\frac{1}{59}\begin{bmatrix} 16 & 15 \\ -4 & 70 \end{bmatrix}$

43. $(5, 0)$ **45.** $(-8, -6)$ **47.** $(3, 8, -11)$

49. $(2, 1, 0, 0)$ **51.** $(2, -2)$ **53.** No solution

55. $(-4, -8)$ **57.** $(-1, 3, 2)$

59. $(0.3125s + 0.8125, 1.1875s + 0.6875, s)$

61. $(-7, 3, -2)$ **63.** $(5, 0, -2, 3)$

65. \$10,000 in AAA-rated bonds, \$5000 in A-rated bonds, \$10,000 in B-rated bonds

67. \$9000 in AAA-rated bonds, \$1000 in A-rated bonds, \$2000 in B-rated bonds

69. $I_1 = -3$ amperes, $I_2 = 8$ amperes, $I_3 = 5$ amperes

71. True   **73.** True

75. Answers will vary.

(a) $\frac{1}{19}\begin{bmatrix} 3 & 2 \\ -2 & 5 \end{bmatrix}$ (b) $\frac{1}{61}\begin{bmatrix} -5 & -12 \\ 8 & 7 \end{bmatrix}$

77. $-5, \pm\sqrt{6}$ **79.** $-3, 4$

81.

x	1	2	3	5	6	7	8
$f(x)$	2.99	2.96	2.89	2.0	0	-6	-24

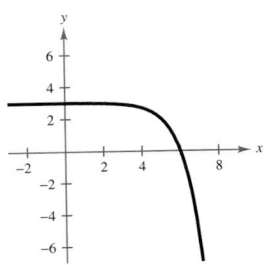

83.

x	0	2	3	5	6	7
$f(x)$	4.02	4.14	4.37	6.7	11.3	24

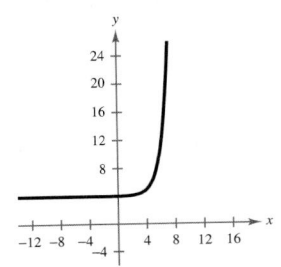

85. $\begin{bmatrix} 12 & -18 \\ -6 & 24 \\ -3 & -36 \end{bmatrix}$ **87.** $\begin{bmatrix} 7 & -27 \\ -43 & 24 \end{bmatrix}$ **89.** $\begin{bmatrix} 6 & -2 \\ 15 & 7 \end{bmatrix}$

Section 6.4 *(page 474)*

1. 7 **3.** −25 **5.** 28 **7.** −24 **9.** 0

11. −9 **13.** −0.002

15. (a) $M_{11} = -5, M_{12} = 2, M_{21} = 4, M_{22} = 3$

(b) $C_{11} = -5, C_{12} = -2, C_{21} = -4, C_{22} = 3$

17. (a) $M_{11} = 30, M_{12} = 12, M_{13} = 11, M_{21} = -36,$

$M_{22} = 26, M_{23} = 7, M_{31} = -4, M_{32} = -42,$

$M_{33} = 12$

(b) $C_{11} = 30, C_{12} = -12, C_{13} = 11, C_{21} = 36, C_{22} = 26,$

$C_{23} = -7, C_{31} = -4, C_{32} = 42, C_{33} = 12$

19. (a) −75 (b) −75 **21.** (a) 170 (b) 170

23. −58 **25.** −30 **27.** −168 **29.** 412

31. −60 **33.** 216 **35.** −336 **37.** 410

39. (a) −3 (b) −2 (c) $\begin{bmatrix} -2 & 0 \\ 0 & -3 \end{bmatrix}$ (d) 6

41. (a) 2 (b) −6 (c) $\begin{bmatrix} 1 & 4 & 3 \\ -1 & 0 & 3 \\ 0 & 2 & 0 \end{bmatrix}$ (d) −12

43. (a) −25 (b) −220

(c) $\begin{bmatrix} -7 & -16 & -1 & -28 \\ -4 & -14 & -11 & 8 \\ 13 & 4 & 4 & -4 \\ -2 & 3 & 2 & 2 \end{bmatrix}$ (d) 5500

45.–49. Answers will vary. **51.** −1, 4 **53.** $8uv - 1$

55. e^{5x} **57.** $1 - \ln x$ **59.** True

61. $A = \begin{bmatrix} 1 & 3 \\ -2 & 4 \end{bmatrix}, B = \begin{bmatrix} -4 & 0 \\ 3 & 5 \end{bmatrix}$

$|A + B| = -30, |A| + |B| = -10$

(Answers will vary.)

63. A square matrix is a square array of numbers. A determinant of a square matrix is a real number.

65. (a) Columns 2 and 3 are interchanged.

(b) Rows 1 and 3 are interchanged.

67. (a) 5 is factored from the first row of the matrix.

(b) 4 and 3 are factored from the second and third columns.

69. (−1, 4) **71.** (0, −0.2)

73.

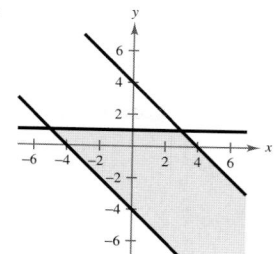

75. $\begin{bmatrix} -1 & -1.33 \\ 0.5 & 0.83 \end{bmatrix}$ **77.** $\begin{bmatrix} -0.25 & 0.17 & 0.33 \\ -0.25 & 0.5 & 1 \\ -0.5 & 0.33 & 1.67 \end{bmatrix}$

Section 6.5 *(page 485)*

1. 14 **3.** 7 **5.** $\frac{33}{8}$ **7.** 10 **9.** $x = \frac{16}{5}, 0$

11. Collinear **13.** Not collinear **15.** $x = -3$

17. (2, −2) **19.** (−3, −2) **21.** $\left(\frac{32}{7}, \frac{30}{7} \right)$

23. (−1, 3, 2) **25.** $\left(0, -\frac{1}{2}, \frac{1}{2} \right)$ **27.** 250 square miles

29. Uncoded: [20 18 15], [21 2 12], [5 0 9], [14 0 18],

[9 22 5], [18 0 3], [9 20 25]

Encoded: −52 10 27 −49 3 34 −49 13 27 −94 22

54 1 1 −7 0 −12 9 −121 41 55

31. 38 74 75 10 −6 −45 −15 −70 −130 23 51 61 44

75 63 80 185 235

33. −5 −41 −87 91 207 257 11 −5 −41 40 80 84 76

177 227

35. HAPPY NEW YEAR **37.** SEND PLANES

39. MEET ME TONIGHT RON **41.** True

43. Answers will vary. **45.** $8x + y + 6 = 0$

47. $5x + 4y - 28 = 0$

49.

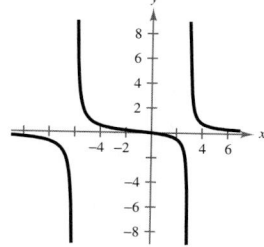

51. (2, −2, 5)

Review Exercises *(page 488)*

1. 3 × 1 **3.** 1 × 1 **5.** 4 × 2

7. $\begin{bmatrix} 3 & -10 & \vdots & 15 \\ 5 & 4 & \vdots & 22 \end{bmatrix}$ **9.** $\begin{bmatrix} 8 & -7 & 4 & \vdots & 12 \\ 3 & -5 & 2 & \vdots & 20 \\ 5 & 3 & -3 & \vdots & 26 \end{bmatrix}$

11. $\begin{cases} 5x + y + 7z = -9 \\ 4x + 2y = 10 \\ 9x + 4y + 2z = 3 \end{cases}$

13. $\begin{bmatrix} 1 & 0 & 0 \\ 0 & 1 & 0 \\ 0 & 0 & 1 \end{bmatrix}$ **15.** $\begin{bmatrix} 1 & 0 & 3 & -2 \\ 0 & 1 & 4 & -3 \end{bmatrix}$

17. $\begin{bmatrix} 1 & 0 & 1 \\ 0 & 1 & 1 \\ 0 & 0 & 0 \end{bmatrix}$ **19.** $(10, -12)$ **21.** $(-0.2, 0.7)$

23. $\left(\frac{1}{2}, -\frac{1}{3}, 1\right)$ **25.** $\left(-2a - 5, \frac{5}{3}a + \frac{2}{3}, a\right)$

27. $(2, -3, 3)$ **29.** $(2, 3, -1)$ **31.** $(1, 1)$

33. $(3, 0, -4)$ **35.** $(2, 6, -10, -3)$

37. $x = 12, y = -7$ **39.** $x = 1, y = 11$

41. $\begin{bmatrix} 17 & -17 \\ 13 & 2 \end{bmatrix}$ **43.** $\begin{bmatrix} -13 & -8 & 18 \\ 0 & 11 & -19 \end{bmatrix}$

45. $\begin{bmatrix} 2 & 1 & 12 \\ -13 & 1 & -17 \\ -30 & -54 & 40 \end{bmatrix}$ **47.** $\begin{bmatrix} 48 & -18 & -3 \\ 15 & 51 & 33 \end{bmatrix}$

49. $\begin{bmatrix} -14 & -4 \\ 7 & -17 \\ -17 & -2 \end{bmatrix}$ **51.** $\frac{1}{3}\begin{bmatrix} 9 & 2 \\ -4 & 11 \\ 10 & 0 \end{bmatrix}$

53. $\begin{bmatrix} 14 & -2 & 8 \\ 14 & -10 & 40 \\ 36 & -12 & 48 \end{bmatrix}$ **55.** $\begin{bmatrix} 44 & 4 \\ 20 & 8 \end{bmatrix}$

57. $\begin{bmatrix} 1 & 17 \\ 12 & 36 \end{bmatrix}$ **59.** $\begin{bmatrix} 14 & -22 & 22 \\ 19 & -41 & 80 \\ 42 & -66 & 66 \end{bmatrix}$

61. $\begin{cases} 5x + 4y = 2 \\ -x + y = -22 \end{cases}$

63. $BA = [\$274,150 \quad \$303,150]$

The entries represent the total value of the units shipped to each warehouse.

65. and 67. Answers will vary.

69. $\begin{bmatrix} 4 & -5 \\ 5 & -6 \end{bmatrix}$ **71.** $\begin{bmatrix} 13 & 6 & -4 \\ -12 & -5 & 3 \\ 5 & 2 & -1 \end{bmatrix}$ **73.** $\begin{bmatrix} \frac{1}{5} & \frac{1}{5} \\ \frac{1}{10} & -\frac{1}{15} \end{bmatrix}$

75. $\begin{bmatrix} \frac{1}{2} & -1 & -\frac{1}{2} \\ \frac{1}{2} & -\frac{2}{3} & -\frac{5}{6} \\ 0 & \frac{2}{3} & \frac{1}{3} \end{bmatrix}$ **77.** $\begin{bmatrix} 1 & -1 \\ 4 & -\frac{7}{2} \end{bmatrix}$ **79.** $\begin{bmatrix} -1 & -\frac{5}{3} \\ 1 & 2 \end{bmatrix}$

81. Does not exist **83.** $(36, 11)$ **85.** $(-6, -1)$

87. $(2, -1, -2)$ **89.** $(6, 1, -1)$ **91.** $(-3, 1)$

93. $(1, 1, -2)$ **95.** No inverse. The system is inconsistent.

97. -42 **99.** 550

101. (a) $M_{11} = 4, M_{12} = 7, M_{21} = -1, M_{22} = 2$

(b) $C_{11} = 4, C_{12} = -7, C_{21} = 1, C_{22} = 2$

103. (a) $M_{11} = 30, M_{12} = -12, M_{13} = -21, M_{21} = 20,$

$M_{22} = 19, M_{23} = 22, M_{31} = 5, M_{32} = -2,$

$M_{33} = 19$

(b) $C_{11} = 30, C_{12} = 12, C_{13} = -21, C_{21} = -20,$

$C_{22} = 19, C_{23} = -22, C_{31} = 5, C_{32} = 2, C_{33} = 19$

105. (a) 96 (b) 96 **107.** 130 **109.** -3

111. 279 **113.** 0 **115.** -96 **117.** 16

119. 1.75 **121.** Collinear **123.** Not collinear

125. $(1, 2)$ **127.** $(4, 7)$ **129.** $(-1, 4, 5)$

131. $\left(\frac{2}{3}, \frac{1}{2}\right)$ **133.** Cramer's rule does not apply.

135. 8 carnations, 4 roses **137.** $y = x^2 + 2x + 3$

139. 16,667 units

141. Uncoded: $[12 \ 15 \ 15], [11 \ 0 \ 15], [21 \ 20 \ 0],$
$[2 \ 5 \ 12], [15 \ 23 \ 0]$

Encoded: $-21 \ 6 \ 0 \ -68 \ 8 \ 45 \ 102 \ -42 \ -60 \ -53$
$20 \ 21 \ 99 \ -30 \ -69$

143. SEE YOU FRIDAY

145. False. Only square matrices have determinants.

147. Elementary row operations correspond to the operations on a system of equations.

Chapter Test (page 494)

1. $\begin{bmatrix} 1 & 0 & 0 \\ 0 & 1 & 0 \\ 0 & 0 & 1 \end{bmatrix}$ **2.** $\begin{bmatrix} 1 & 0 & -1 & 2 \\ 0 & 1 & 0 & -1 \\ 0 & 0 & 0 & 0 \\ 0 & 0 & 0 & 0 \end{bmatrix}$

3. $(-2a + 1.5, 2a + 1, a)$ **4.** $(5, 2, -6)$

5. (a) $\begin{bmatrix} 1 & 5 & -2 \\ 0 & -4 & 3 \end{bmatrix}$ (b) $\begin{bmatrix} 15 & 12 & 12 \\ -12 & -12 & 0 \end{bmatrix}$

(c) $\begin{bmatrix} 7 & 14 & 0 \\ -4 & -12 & 6 \end{bmatrix}$

6. $\begin{bmatrix} 8 & -8 \\ 16 & -4 \\ 6 & 12 \end{bmatrix}$ **7.** $A^{-1} = \begin{bmatrix} \frac{1}{2} & \frac{2}{5} \\ 1 & \frac{3}{5} \end{bmatrix}$; $(13, 22)$

8. 67 **9.** -2 **10.** 300 **11.** 7

12. $\left(\frac{3}{4}, -\frac{1}{2}\right)$

13. Cramer's rule does not apply. System is inconsistent.

14. $y = -\frac{1}{2}x^2 + x + 2$

15. $x_1 = 700 - s - t, x_2 = 300 - s - t, x_3 = s,$

$x_4 = 100 - t, x_5 = t$

Chapter 7

Section 7.1 *(page 503)*

1. 7, 9, 11, 13, 15   **3.** 2, 4, 8, 16, 32

5. $-2, 4, -8, 16, -32$ **7.** $2, \frac{3}{2}, \frac{4}{3}, \frac{5}{4}, \frac{6}{5}$

9. $3, \frac{12}{11}, \frac{9}{13}, \frac{24}{47}, \frac{15}{37}$ **11.** $0, 1, 0, \frac{1}{2}, 0$

13. $\frac{5}{2}, \frac{11}{4}, \frac{23}{8}, \frac{47}{16}, \frac{95}{32}$ **15.** $1, \frac{1}{2^{3/2}}, \frac{1}{3^{3/2}}, \frac{1}{4^{3/2}}, \frac{1}{5^{3/2}}$

17. $3, \frac{9}{2}, \frac{9}{2}, \frac{27}{8}, \frac{81}{40}$ **19.** $-1, \frac{1}{4}, -\frac{1}{9}, \frac{1}{16}, -\frac{1}{25}$

21. 3, 15, 35, 63, 99   **23.** -73 **25.** $\frac{4}{14,175}$

27. $\frac{48}{285} = \frac{16}{95}$ **29.** 28, 24, 20, 16, 12

31. 3, 4, 6, 10, 18   **33.** 2, 6, 10, 22, 42

35.

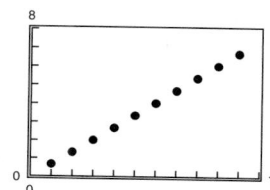

37.

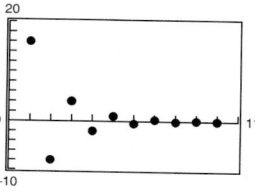

39.

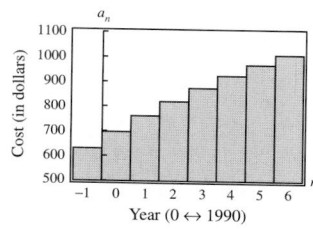

41. 9, 15, 21, 27, 33, 39, 45, 51, 57, 63

43. $6, 18, 36, 54, \frac{324}{5}, \frac{324}{5}, \frac{1944}{35}, \frac{1458}{35}, \frac{972}{35}, \frac{2916}{175}$

45. $3, \frac{5}{2}, \frac{7}{3}, \frac{9}{4}, \frac{11}{5}, \frac{13}{6}, \frac{15}{7}, \frac{17}{8}, \frac{19}{9}, \frac{21}{10}$ **47.** (c)   **49.** (d)

51. $a_n = 3n - 2$ **53.** $a_n = n^2 - 1$ **55.** $a_n = \frac{n+1}{n+2}$

57. $a_n = \frac{(-1)^{n+1}}{2^n}$ **59.** $a_n = 1 + \frac{1}{n}$ **61.** $a_n = \frac{1}{n!}$

63. $(-1)^n + 2(1)^n = (-1)^n + 2$

65. 6, 8, 10, 12, 14; $a_n = 2n + 4$

67. 81, 27, 9, 3, 1; $a_n = \frac{243}{3^n}$ **69.** $\frac{1}{120}$ **71.** 90

73. 495   **75.** $n + 1$ **77.** $\frac{1}{2n(2n+1)}$ **79.** 35

81. 40   **83.** 30   **85.** $\frac{9}{5}$ **87.** 238   **89.** 30

91. 81   **93.** $\frac{47}{60}$ **95.** $\sum_{i=1}^{9} \frac{1}{3i} = 0.94299$

97. $\sum_{i=1}^{8} \left[2\left(\frac{i}{8}\right) + 3 \right] = 33$ **99.** $\sum_{i=1}^{6} (-1)^{i+1} 3i = -546$

101. $\sum_{i=1}^{20} \frac{(-1)^{i+1}}{i^2} = 0.822$ **103.** $\sum_{i=1}^{5} \frac{2^i - 1}{2^{i+1}} = \frac{129}{64}$

105. $\frac{75}{16}$ **107.** $-\frac{3}{2}$ **109.** $\frac{2}{3}$ **111.** $\frac{1}{9}$

113. (a) $A_1 = \$5100.00$, $A_2 = \$5202.00$, $A_3 = \$5306.04$,
$A_4 = \$5412.16$, $A_5 = \$5520.40$, $A_6 = \$5630.81$,
$A_7 = \$5743.43$, $A_8 = \$5858.30$

 (b) $11,040.20

115.

According to the graph, hospital costs are increasing.

117. $23,661.96 million; the sums are approximately the same.

119. True

121. 1, 1, 2, 3, 5, 8, 13, 21, 34, 55, 89, 144;
$1, 2, \frac{3}{2}, \frac{5}{3}, \frac{8}{5}, \frac{13}{8}, \frac{21}{13}, \frac{34}{21}, \frac{55}{34}, \frac{89}{55}$

123. a_n increases by $2(n-1)$. The terms seem to be prime numbers, however, $a_{11} = 121$ is not prime.

125. $-\frac{x^3}{3}, \frac{x^5}{5}, -\frac{x^7}{7}, \frac{x^9}{9}, -\frac{x^{11}}{11}$

127. $-\frac{x^3}{6}, \frac{x^5}{120}, -\frac{x^7}{5040}, \frac{x^9}{362,880}, -\frac{x^{11}}{39,916,800}$

129. $\begin{bmatrix} 2 & 1 & 3 & \vdots & -3 \\ -1 & 5 & 0 & \vdots & 14 \\ -3 & -6 & -7 & \vdots & -7 \end{bmatrix}$

131. (a) $\begin{bmatrix} 10 & 19 \\ -12 & -5 \end{bmatrix}$ (b) $\begin{bmatrix} -30 & -45 \\ 28 & 4 \end{bmatrix}$

 (c) $\begin{bmatrix} 56 & -43 \\ 48 & 114 \end{bmatrix}$ (d) $\begin{bmatrix} 48 & -72 \\ 36 & 122 \end{bmatrix}$

133. (a) $\begin{bmatrix} -1 & 0 & 0 \\ 2 & 0 & 4 \\ 1 & -1 & 1 \end{bmatrix}$ (b) $\begin{bmatrix} 3 & -4 & 0 \\ -9 & -1 & -10 \\ -2 & 3 & -5 \end{bmatrix}$

 (c) $\begin{bmatrix} 12 & 0 & -8 \\ 1 & 21 & 2 \\ -6 & -1 & 8 \end{bmatrix}$ (d) $\begin{bmatrix} 20 & 4 & 8 \\ 2 & 15 & -4 \\ 1 & -6 & 6 \end{bmatrix}$

135. -223 **137.** 664

Section 7.2 *(page 513)*

1. Arithmetic sequence, $d = -2$

3. Arithmetic sequence, $d = -\frac{1}{2}$

5. Arithmetic sequence, $d = 8$

7. Arithmetic sequence, $d = 0.6$

9. 21, 34, 47, 60, 73

Arithmetic sequence, $d = 13$

11. $\frac{1}{2}, \frac{1}{3}, \frac{1}{4}, \frac{1}{5}, \frac{1}{6}$

Not an arithmetic sequence

13. 143, 136, 129, 122, 115

Arithmetic sequence, $d = -7$

15. $1, 4, \frac{7}{3}, \frac{7}{2}, \frac{13}{5}$

Not an arithmetic sequence

17. 15, 24, 33, 42, 51; $d = 9$; $a_n = 9n + 6$

19. $\frac{7}{2}, \frac{13}{4}, 3, \frac{11}{4}, \frac{5}{2}$; $d = -\frac{1}{4}$; $a_n = -\frac{1}{4}n + \frac{15}{4}$

21. 5, 11, 17, 23, 29   **23.** $-2.6, -3, -3.4, -3.8, -4.2$

25. $-2, 2, 6, 10, 14$ **27.** 22.45, 20.725, 19, 17.275, 15.55

29. 59   **31.** -50 **33.** 18.6   **35.** $a_n = -2 + 3n$

37. $a_n = 108 - 8n$ **39.** $a_n = \frac{13}{2} - \frac{5}{2}n$

41. $a_n = \frac{10}{3}n + \frac{5}{3}$ **43.** $a_n = 103 - 3n$

45. (b)   **47.** (c)

49.   **51.**

53. $-1, 3, 7, 11, 15, 19, 23, 27, 31, 35$

55. 19.25, 18.5, 17.75, 17, 16.25, 15.5, 14.75, 14, 13.25, 12.5

57. 1.505, 1.51, 1.515, 1.52, 1.525, 1.53, 1.535, 1.54, 1.545, 1.55

59. 890   **61.** 41   **63.** 4000   **65.** 1275

67. 25,250   **69.** 355   **71.** 126,750   **73.** 520

75. 44,625   **77.** 10,120   **79.** 10,000

81. (a) $40,000   (b) $217,500   **83.** 2340 seats

85. 405 bricks   **87.** 585 seats   **89.** 156 times

91. True   **93.** $x, 3x, 5x, 7x, 9x, 11x, 13x, 15x, 17x, 19x$

95. (a) 4, 9, 16, 25, 36

(b) Sum of first n positive odd integers is n^2; 49

(c) $\frac{n}{2}[1 + (2n - 1)] = n^2$

97. $S_n + 5n$ **99.** $(2, -6, 3)$ **101.** 20 square units

103. $\frac{1}{3003}$

Section 7.3   *(page 522)*

1. Geometric sequence, $r = 3$

3. Not a geometric sequence

5. Geometric sequence, $r = -\frac{1}{2}$

7. Not a geometric sequence

9. Not a geometric sequence   **11.** 8, 24, 72, 216, 648

13. $1, \frac{1}{2}, \frac{1}{4}, \frac{1}{8}, \frac{1}{16}$ **15.** $5, -\frac{1}{2}, \frac{1}{20}, -\frac{1}{200}, \frac{1}{2000}$

17. 3.5, 17.5, 87.5, 437.5, 2187.5   **19.** $1, e, e^2, e^3, e^4$

21. 64, 32, 16, 8, 4; $\frac{1}{2}$ **23.** 4, 12, 36, 108, 324; 3

$a_n = 128\left(\frac{1}{2}\right)^n$ $a_n = \frac{4}{3}(3)^n$

25. $6, -9, \frac{27}{2}, -\frac{81}{4}, \frac{243}{8}$; $-\frac{3}{2}$

$a_n = 6\left(-\frac{3}{2}\right)^{n-1}$

27. $\left(\frac{1}{2}\right)^7$ **29.** $-\dfrac{2}{3^{10}}$ **31.** $500(1.02)^{13}$ **33.** 9

35. $-\frac{2}{9}$ **37.** 45,927   **39.** 50,388,480

41. 786,432   **43.** (a)   **45.** (b)

47.   **49.**

51. 8, 4, 6, 5

55. 511   **57.** 43

53.

n	S_n
1	16
2	24
3	28
4	30
5	31
6	31.5
7	31.75
8	31.875
9	31.9375
10	31.96875

59. 29,921.31   **61.** 6.4   **63.** 2092.60

65. $\displaystyle\sum_{n=1}^{7} 5(3)^{n-1}$ **67.** $\displaystyle\sum_{n=1}^{7} 2\left(-\frac{1}{4}\right)^{n-1}$ **69.** 2   **71.** $\frac{2}{3}$

73. $\frac{16}{3}$ **75.** Series does not have a finite sum.   **77.** $\frac{5}{3}$

79. -30 **81.** 32   **83.** $\frac{9}{4}$ **85.** $\frac{4}{11}$ **87.** $\frac{7}{22}$

89. (a) $2158.92   (b) $2191.12   (c) $2208.04

(d) $2219.64   (e) $2225.35

91. $26,050.85   **93.** $7011.89   **95.** Answers will vary.

97. (a) $26,198.27   (b) $26,263.88

99. (a) $637,678.02   (b) $645,861.43

101. Answers will vary. **103.** 126 square inches

105. \$39.7 billion

107. (a) \$5,368,709.11 (b) \$10,737,418.23

(c) \$21,474,836.47

109. False. Any arithmetic sequence can be used as a counterexample.

111. True. It is an arithmetic sequence with $d = 0$.

113. $8, \dfrac{16x}{3}, \dfrac{32x^2}{9}, \dfrac{64x^3}{27}, \dfrac{128x^4}{81}$

115. $\dfrac{1}{2}, \dfrac{7x}{2}, \dfrac{49x^2}{2}, \dfrac{343x^3}{2}, \dfrac{2401x^4}{2}$

117. $13{,}122e^{7x}$ **119.** $\dfrac{4096x^5}{243}$

121.

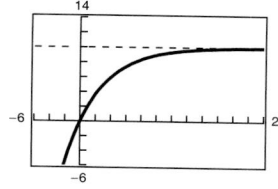

Horizontal asymptote: $y = 10$

Corresponds to the sum of the series

123. Divide the second term by the first to obtain the common ratio. The nth term is the first term times the common ratio raised to the $n - 1$ power.

125. 45.65 miles per hour **127.** 2.4 hours

129. $\begin{bmatrix} -33 & -3 \\ 27 & 1 \end{bmatrix}$ **131.** $\begin{bmatrix} 2 & 6 & -8 \\ 12 & 4 & -20 \\ 4 & 2 & 10 \end{bmatrix}$

133. 364 **135.** $\dfrac{227}{99}$

Section 7.4 (page 532)

1. $\dfrac{5}{(k+1)(k+2)}$ **3.** $\dfrac{(k+1)^2(k+4)^2}{6}$

5. $1 + 6 + 11 + \cdots + (5k - 4) + (5k + 1)$

7.–35. Answers will vary. **37.** 10, 40, 160, 640, 2560

39. 0, 2, 2, 6, 10

41. 2, 0, 3, 1, 4

First differences: $-2, 3, -2, 3$

Second differences: $5, -5, 5$

Neither

43. $-3, 6, -12, 24, -48$

First differences: $9, -18, 36, -72$

Second differences: $-27, 54, -108$

Neither

45. 2, 4, 16, 256, 65,536

First differences: 2, 12, 240, 65,280

Second differences: 10, 288, 65,040

Neither

47. 0, 4, 10, 18, 28

First differences: 4, 6, 8, 10

Second differences: 2, 2, 2

Quadratic

49. $0, -1, -2, -3, -4$

First differences: $-1, -1, -1, -1$

Second differences: 0, 0, 0

Linear

51. $a_n = n^2 - 2n + 7$ **53.** $a_n = \frac{7}{4}n^2 - 5n + 3$

55. False. The first differences are all the same.

57. Answers will vary. **59.** $(7, 5)$ **61.** $\left(-\frac{1}{2}, \frac{1}{4}\right), (2, 4)$

63. $(1, 2, 1)$ **65.** $(-1, 2, 4)$ **67.** 38

69. $4x^4 - 4x^2 + 1$ **71.** $-64x^3 + 240x^2 - 300x + 125$

Section 7.5 (page 539)

1. 21 **3.** 1 **5.** 15,504 **7.** 14 **9.** 4950

11. 4950 **13.** 35,960 **15.** 497,420 **17.** 749,398

19. 21 **21.** 56 **23.** $x^4 + 4x^3 + 6x^2 + 4x + 1$

25. $a^3 + 9a^2 + 27a + 27$

27. $y^4 - 8y^3 + 24y^2 - 32y + 16$

29. $x^5 + 5x^4y + 10x^3y^2 + 10x^2y^3 + 5xy^4 + y^5$

31. $r^6 + 12r^5s + 60r^4s^2 + 160r^3s^3 + 240r^2s^4 + 192rs^5$ $+ 64s^6$

33. $x^5 - 5x^4y + 10x^3y^2 - 10x^2y^3 + 5xy^4 - y^5$

35. $1 - 12x + 48x^2 - 64x^3$

37. $x^8 + 20x^6 + 150x^4 + 500x^2 + 625$

39. $\dfrac{1}{x^5} + \dfrac{5y}{x^4} + \dfrac{10y^2}{x^3} + \dfrac{10y^3}{x^2} + \dfrac{5y^4}{x} + y^5$

41. $2x^4 - 24x^3 + 113x^2 - 246x + 207$

43. $-4x^6 - 24x^5 - 60x^4 - 83x^3 - 42x^2 - 60x + 20$

45. $243t^5 - 405t^4s + 270t^3s^2 - 90t^2s^3 + 15ts^4 - s^5$

47. $81 - 216z + 216z^2 - 96z^3 + 16z^4$ **49.** 3,247,695

51. 180 **53.** $-489{,}888$ **55.** 210

57. $x^2 + 20x^{3/2} + 150x + 500x^{1/2} + 625$

59. $x^2 - 3x^{4/3}y^{1/3} + 3x^{2/3}y^{2/3} - y$

61. $3x^2 + 3xh + h^2, \ h \neq 0$

63. $\dfrac{\sqrt{x+h} - \sqrt{x}}{h} = \dfrac{1}{\sqrt{x+h} + \sqrt{x}}, \ h \neq 0$

65. -4 **67.** $2035 + 828i$ **69.** 1   **71.** 1.172

73. 510,568.785

75.

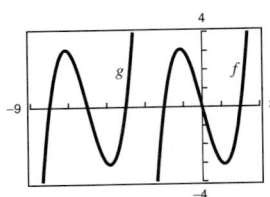

g is shifted 6 units left of f.

$g(x) = x^3 + 18x^2 + 104x + 192$

77.

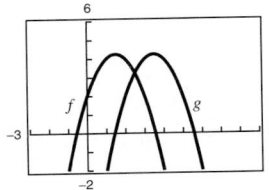

g is shifted 2 units right of f.

$g(x) = -x^2 + 7x - 8$

79. (a) 792   (b) 36   (c) 792   (d) 12

81.

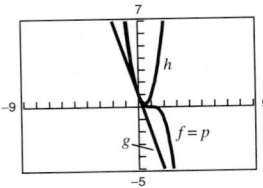

p(x) is the expansion of f(x).

83. 0.273   **85.** 0.171

87. (a) $g(t) = 0.0348t^2 + 5.8043t + 95.588$

(b)

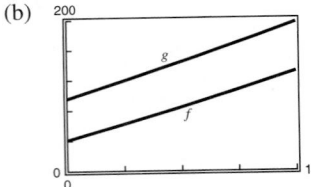

89. False. The correct term is $126,720x^4y^8$.

91. The first and last numbers in each row are 1. Every other number in each row is formed by adding the two numbers immediately above the number.

93. $n + 1$ terms   **95. and 97.** Answers will vary.

99. $g(x)$ is shifted 8 units up from $f(x)$.

101. $g(x)$ is the reflection of $f(x)$ in the y-axis.

103. $\begin{bmatrix} -2 & -1 & -3 \\ 8 & 0 & 4 \\ -1 & -2 & 7 \end{bmatrix}$ **105.** $\begin{bmatrix} 6 & 11 & 15 \\ -30 & -2 & -16 \\ 13 & 10 & -33 \end{bmatrix}$

107. $\begin{bmatrix} 9 & 11 & 12 \\ -13 & -25 & -5 \\ -5 & -18 & -6 \end{bmatrix}$ **109.** $\begin{bmatrix} 4 & -5 \\ 5 & -6 \end{bmatrix}$

Section 7.6   *(page 549)*

1. 6   **3.** 5   **5.** 3   **7.** 9   **9.** 192   **11.** 18

13. 3,628,800   **15.** 12   **17.** 6,760,000

19. (a) 900   (b) 648   (c) 180   (d) 600

21. 64,000   **23.** (a) 720   (b) 48   **25.** 24

27. 336   **29.** 120   **31.** $n = 5$ or $n = 6$

33. 27,907,200   **35.** 197,149,680   **37.** 4845

39. 120   **41.** (a) 16   (b) 14   **43.** 420   **45.** 2520

47. ABCD, ABDC, ACBD, ACDB, ADBC, ADCB, BACD, BADC, CABD, CADB, DABC, DACB, BCAD, BDAC, CBAD, CDAB, DBAC, DCAB, BCDA, BDCA, CBDA, CDBA, DBCA, DCBA

49. AB, AC, AD, AE, AF, BC, BD, BE, BF, CD, CE, CF, DE, DF, EF

51. 4845   **53.** 3,838,380   **55.** 75,287,520   **57.** 36

59. (a) 495   (b) 210   **61.** (a) 70   (b) 54   (c) 16

63. 5   **65.** 20

67. False. Order matters in a permutation.

69. False. $_nP_r = {_nC_r}$ if $r = 1$ or 0.

71. $_nP_r$ represents the number of ways to choose and order r elements out of a collection of n elements.

73. (b). Numerous permutations can be made from each combination.

75. and 77. Answers will vary.   **79.** $\frac{11}{2}$ **81.** 8.32

83. $(6, -13)$ **85.** $(-3, 4)$

87. $x^6 - 6x^5 + 15x^4 - 20x^3 + 15x^2 - 6x + 1$

89. $81x^4 - 108x^3y + 54x^2y^2 - 12xy^3 + y^4$

Section 7.7   *(page 560)*

1. $\{(H, 1), (H, 2), (H, 3), (H, 4), (H, 5), (H, 6),$
$(T, 1), (T, 2), (T, 3), (T, 4), (T, 5), (T, 6)\}$

3. $\{ABC, ACB, BAC, BCA, CAB, CBA\}$

5. $\{(A, B), (A, C), (A, D), (A, E), (B, C), (B, D),$
$(B, E), (C, D), (C, E), (D, E)\}$

7. $\frac{3}{8}$ **9.** $\frac{7}{8}$ **11.** $\frac{3}{13}$ **13.** $\frac{3}{26}$ **15.** $\frac{1}{9}$ **17.** $\frac{35}{36}$

19. $\frac{1}{6}$ **21.** $\frac{1}{5}$ **23.** $\frac{2}{5}$ **25.** 0.3   **27.** $\frac{2}{3}$

29. 0.85   **31.** $\frac{7}{20}$

33. (a) 78,000   (b) 0.3   (c) 0.37   (d) 0.1

35. (a) 0.58   (b) 0.956   (c) 0.004

37. (a) $\frac{672}{1254}$ (b) $\frac{582}{1254}$ (c) $\frac{548}{1254}$

39. $P(\{\text{Taylor wins}\}) = \frac{1}{2}$

$P(\{\text{Moore wins}\}) = P(\{\text{Perez wins}\}) = \frac{1}{4}$

41. (a) $\frac{21}{1292} \approx 0.016$ (b) $\frac{225}{646} \approx 0.348$ (c) $\frac{49}{323} \approx 0.152$

43. (a) $\frac{1}{3}$ (b) $\frac{5}{8}$ **45.** (a) $\frac{1}{120}$ (b) $\frac{1}{24}$

47. (a) 0.346   (b) 0.0000029

49. (a) $\frac{14}{55}$ (b) $\frac{12}{55}$ (c) $\frac{54}{55}$

51. (a) $\frac{1}{4}$ (b) $\frac{1}{2}$ (c) $\frac{9}{100}$ (d) $\frac{1}{30}$

53. (a) 0.9702   (b) 0.9998   (c) 0.0002

55. (a) $\dfrac{1}{15,625}$ (b) $\dfrac{4096}{15,625}$ (c) $\dfrac{11,529}{15,625}$

57. 0.1024   **59.** $\frac{7}{16}$ **61.** True

63. (a) As you consider successive people with distinct birthdays, the probabilities must decrease to take into account the birth dates already used. Because the birth dates of people are independent events, multiply the respective probabilities of distinct birthdays.

(b) $\frac{365}{365} \cdot \frac{364}{365} \cdot \frac{363}{365} \cdot \frac{362}{365}$

(c) Answers will vary.

(d) Q_n is the probability that the birthdays are *not* distinct, which is equivalent to at least two people having the same birthday.

(e)

n	10	15	20	23	30	40	50
P_n	0.88	0.75	0.59	0.49	0.29	0.11	0.03
Q_n	0.12	0.25	0.41	0.51	0.71	0.89	0.97

(f) 23

65. $x = \frac{22}{4} = \frac{11}{2}$ **67.** $x = -10$ **69.** $x = e^8$

71. $x = \frac{1}{6}e^4$

73.

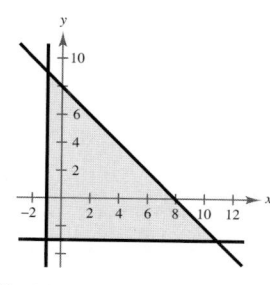

75.

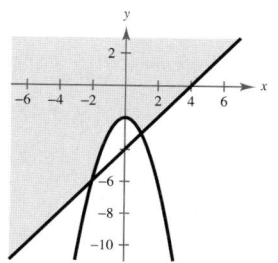

77. 15   **79.** 165

Review Exercises   *(page 566)*

1. $8, 5, 4, \frac{7}{2}, \frac{16}{5}$ **3.** $5, \frac{10}{3}, 3, \frac{20}{7}, \frac{25}{9}$ **5.** $72, 36, 12, 3, \frac{3}{5}$

7. **9.**

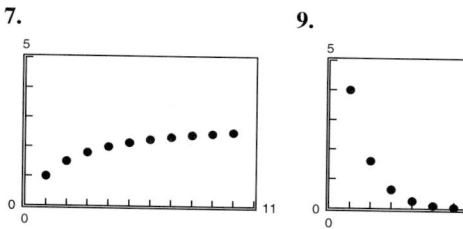

11. $\frac{1}{380}$ **13.** 1   **15.** 30   **17.** $\frac{205}{24}$ **19.** 6050

21. 418   **23.** $\sum_{k=1}^{20} \frac{1}{2k}$ **25.** $\sum_{k=1}^{9} \frac{k}{k+1}$

27. (a) $\frac{1111}{2000}$ (b) $\frac{5}{9}$ **29.** (a) $\frac{2,020,202}{100,000,000}$ (b) $\frac{2}{99}$

31. (a) $a_1 = 2550, a_2 = 2601, a_3 = 2653, a_4 = 2706.10,$

$a_5 = 2760.20, a_6 = 2815.40, a_7 = 2871.70,$

$a_8 = 2929.10$

(b) \$5520.10

33. Arithmetic sequence, $d = -7$

35. Arithmetic sequence, $d = \frac{1}{2}$ **37.** 3, 7, 11, 15, 19

39. 1, 4, 7, 10, 13

41. $35, 32, 29, 26, 23; -3$ **43.** 9, 16, 23, 30, 37; 7

$a_n = 38 - 3n$ $a_n = 2 + 7n$

45. $a_n = 103 - 3n;\ 1430$ **47.** 80   **49.** 88

51. 25,250   **53.** (a) \$43,000   (b) \$192,500

55. $4, -1, \frac{1}{4}, -\frac{1}{16}, \frac{1}{64}$ **57.** $9, 6, 4, \frac{8}{3}, \frac{16}{9}$ or $9, -6, 4, -\frac{8}{3}, \frac{16}{9}$

59. $120, 40, \frac{40}{3}, \frac{40}{9}, \frac{40}{27}; \frac{1}{3}$ **61.** $25, -15, 9, -\frac{27}{5}, \frac{81}{25}; -\frac{3}{5}$

$a_n = 120\left(\frac{1}{3}\right)^{n-1}$ $a_n = 25\left(-\frac{3}{5}\right)^{n-1}$

63. $a_n = 16\left(-\frac{1}{2}\right)^{n-1};\ 10.67$

65. $a_n = 100(1.05)^{n-1};\ 3306.60$ **67.** 127   **69.** 3277

71. 1301.01   **73.** 24.85   **75.** 5486.45   **77.** 8

79. 12   **81.** (a) $a_t = 120,000(0.7)^t$ (b) \$20,168.40

83. \$3909.96   **85. and 87.** Answers will vary.

89. 465   **91.** 4676

93. 5, 10, 15, 20, 25

First differences: 5, 5, 5, 5

Second differences: 0, 0, 0

Linear model

95. 16, 15, 14, 13, 12

First differences: $-1, -1, -1, -1$

Second differences: 0, 0, 0

Linear model

97. 45   **99.** 126   **101.** 20   **103.** 70

105. $a^5 - 15a^4b + 90a^3b^2 - 270a^2b^3 + 405ab^4 - 243b^5$

107. $\dfrac{x^4}{16} + \dfrac{x^3y}{2} + \dfrac{3x^2y^2}{2} + 2xy^3 + y^4$ **109.** $41 + 840i$

111. 10   **113.** 48   **115.** 5040   **117.** 3,628,800

119. 15,504   **121.** $\frac{1}{9}$

123. $P(\{3\}) = \frac{1}{6}$

$P(\{(1, 5), (5, 1), (2, 4), (4, 2), (3, 3)\}) = \frac{5}{36}$

There is a higher probability of rolling a 3 with one die.

125. (a) 0.416   (b) 0.8   (c) 0.074   **127.** 0.512

129. $\frac{31}{32}$ **131.** True

133. (a) Odd-numbered terms are negative.

(b) Even-numbered terms are negative.

135. (a) Arithmetic. There is a constant difference between consecutive terms.

(b) Geometric. Each term is a constant multiple of the preceding term. In this case the common ratio is greater than 1.

137. Each term of the sequence is defined using a previous term or terms.

139. (d)   **141.** (b)

143.

n	100	500	1000	5000
a_n	2.704	2.7156	2.7169	2.7180

n	10,000	15,000	20,000	25,000
a_n	2.71814	2.71819	2.71821	2.71823

a_n approaches e.

145. $0 \le P \le 1$; closed

147. Meteorological records gathered over an extended period of time indicate that under similar weather conditions it will rain 60% of the time.

Chapter Test   *(page 572)*

1. $1, -\frac{2}{3}, \frac{4}{9}, -\frac{8}{27}, \frac{16}{81}$ **2.** 12, 16, 20, 24, 28   **3.** 7920

4. $a_n = 5100 - 100n$ **5.** $a_n = 4\left(\frac{1}{2}\right)^{n-1}$

6. $\displaystyle\sum_{n=1}^{12} \frac{2}{3n + 1}$ **7.** 3825   **8.** 189   **9.** 28.80

10. $\frac{50}{9}$ **11.** \$47,868.33   **12.** Answers will vary.

13. 84   **14.** 1140   **15.** 8568   **16.** 780

17. 56   **18.** 26,000   **19.** 12,650   **20.** $\frac{3}{26}$ **21.** $\frac{1}{6}$

22. (a) $\frac{1}{4}$ (b) $\frac{121}{3600}$ (c) $\frac{1}{60}$

Chapter 8

Section 8.1   *(page 583)*

1. (g)   **3.** (d)   **5.** (h)   **7.** (e)   **9.** (b)

11. $x^2 + y^2 = 36$ **13.** $x^2 + y^2 = \frac{81}{16}$

15. $x^2 + y^2 = 7$

17. Vertex: $(0, 0)$

Focus: $\left(0, \frac{1}{2}\right)$

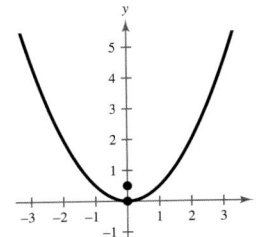

19. Vertex: $(0, 0)$

Focus: $\left(-\frac{3}{2}, 0\right)$

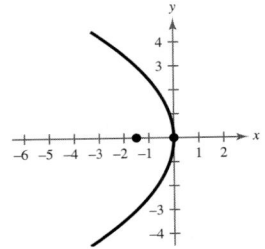

21. Vertex: $(0, 0)$

Focus: $(0, -2)$

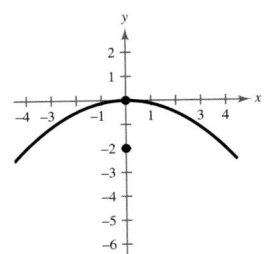

23. $x^2 = -6y$ **25.** $y^2 = -8x$ **27.** $x^2 = 4y$

29. $y^2 = -12x$ **31.** $y^2 = 9x$

33. $y = \frac{2}{3}x^2$; Focus: $\left(0, \frac{3}{8}\right)$ **35.** $x = \frac{5}{9}y^2$; Focus: $\left(\frac{9}{20}, 0\right)$

37.

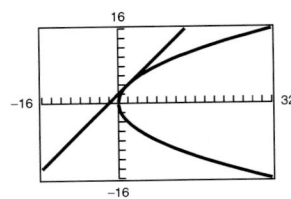

$(2, 4)$

39. Center: $(0, 0)$

Vertices: $(\pm 5, 0)$

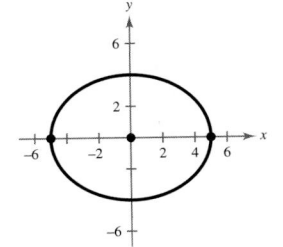

41. Center: $(0, 0)$

Vertices: $\left(\pm \frac{5}{3}, 0\right)$

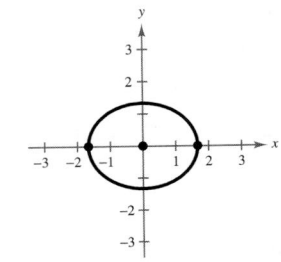

43. Center: $(0, 0)$

Vertices: $(\pm 3, 0)$

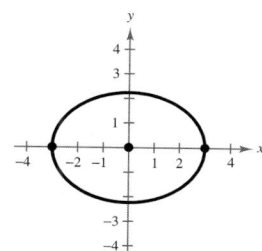

45. Center: $(0, 0)$

Vertices: $(0, \pm 1)$

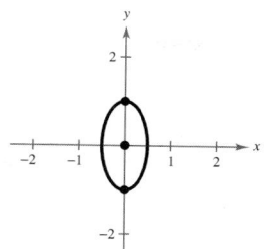

47.

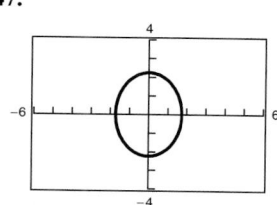

49.

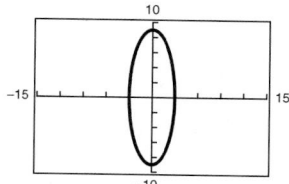

51. Left half

53. $\dfrac{x^2}{1} + \dfrac{y^2}{4} = 1$

55. $\dfrac{x^2}{4} + \dfrac{y^2}{9/4} = 1$

57. $\dfrac{x^2}{25} + \dfrac{y^2}{21} = 1$

59. $\dfrac{x^2}{36} + \dfrac{y^2}{11} = 1$

61. $\dfrac{21x^2}{400} + \dfrac{y^2}{25} = 1$

63. No. Only second-degree equations can be ellipses.

65. Center: $(0, 0)$

Vertices: $(\pm 1, 0)$

Foci: $\left(\pm \sqrt{2}, 0\right)$

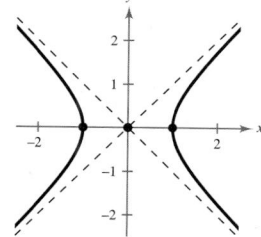

67. Center: $(0, 0)$

Vertices: $(0, \pm 1)$

Foci: $\left(0, \pm \sqrt{5}\right)$

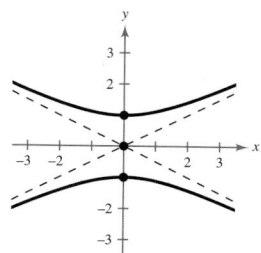

69. Center: $(0, 0)$

Vertices: $(0, \pm 5)$

Foci: $(0, \pm 13)$

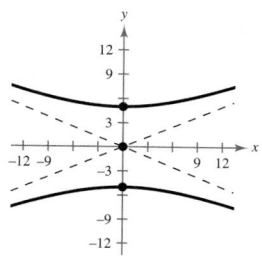

71. Center: $(0, 0)$

Vertices: $\left(0, \pm \dfrac{1}{2}\right)$

Foci: $\left(0, \pm \dfrac{\sqrt{5}}{2}\right)$

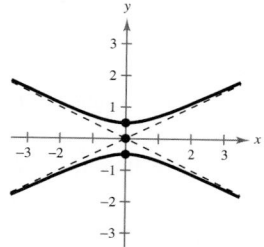

73.

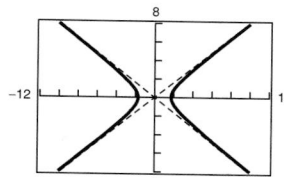

75.

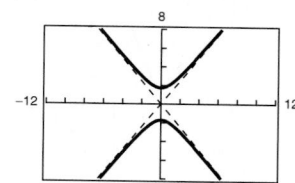

77. Bottom half

79. $\dfrac{y^2}{4} - \dfrac{x^2}{12} = 1$

81. $\dfrac{x^2}{1} - \dfrac{y^2}{9} = 1$

83. $\dfrac{17y^2}{1024} - \dfrac{17x^2}{64} = 1$

85. $\dfrac{y^2}{9} - \dfrac{4x^2}{9} = 1$

87. $y = \dfrac{1}{14}x^2$

89. (a) $y = \dfrac{x^2}{12,288}$ (in feet) (b) 22.6 feet

91. $\left(\pm \sqrt{5}, 0\right)$; 6 feet

93. (a)

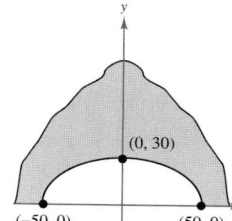

$(0, 30)$

$(-50, 0)$ $(50, 0)$

(b) $\dfrac{x^2}{2500} + \dfrac{y^2}{900} = 1$

(c) 13.08 feet

95. 40

97.

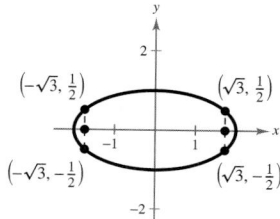

$\left(-\sqrt{3}, \frac{1}{2}\right)$ $\left(\sqrt{3}, \frac{1}{2}\right)$

$\left(-\sqrt{3}, -\frac{1}{2}\right)$ $\left(\sqrt{3}, -\frac{1}{2}\right)$

99.

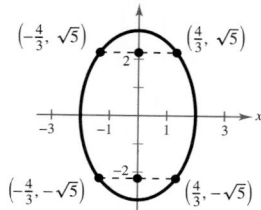

$\left(-\frac{4}{3}, \sqrt{5}\right)$ $\left(\frac{4}{3}, \sqrt{5}\right)$

$\left(-\frac{4}{3}, -\sqrt{5}\right)$ $\left(\frac{4}{3}, -\sqrt{5}\right)$

101. $\left(12\left(\sqrt{5} - 1\right), 0\right) \approx (14.83, 0)$

103. False. Hyperbola

105. False. If the graph intersected the directrix, there would exist points nearer the directrix than the focus.

107. (a) $2a$

(b) The sum of the distances from the two fixed points is constant.

109. Answers will vary. **111.** $(3x - 2)(4x + 5)$

113. $z^2(12z + 5)(z + 1)$ **115.** $f(x) = x^3 - 7x^2 + 12x$

117. $f(x) = x^3 + x^2 - 7x - 3$ **119.** $\frac{3}{2}, \pm 5i$

121.

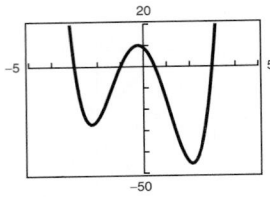

$\pm 3, -1, \frac{1}{2}$

123. 223 **125.** 105 **127.** 816

Section 8.2 *(page 593)*

1. Center: $(0, 0)$
Radius: 7

3. Center: $(-3, 8)$
Radius: 4

5. Center: $(1, 0)$
Radius: $\sqrt{10}$

7. $(x - 1)^2 + (y + 3)^2 = 1$
Center: $(1, -3)$
Radius: 1

9. $\left(x + \frac{3}{2}\right)^2 + (y - 3)^2 = 1$
Center: $\left(-\frac{3}{2}, 3\right)$
Radius: 1

11. Vertex: $(-1, -2)$
Focus: $(-1, -4)$
Directrix: $y = 0$

13. Vertex: $\left(5, \frac{1}{2}\right)$
Focus: $\left(\frac{11}{2}, \frac{1}{2}\right)$
Directrix: $x = \frac{9}{2}$

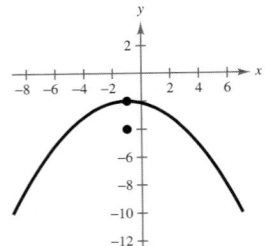

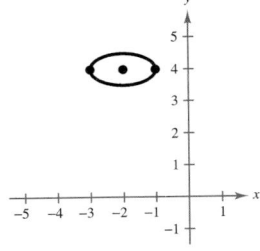

15. Vertex: $(1, 1)$
Focus: $(1, 2)$
Directrix: $y = 0$

17. Vertex: $(-2, -3)$
Focus: $(-4, -3)$
Directrix: $x = 0$

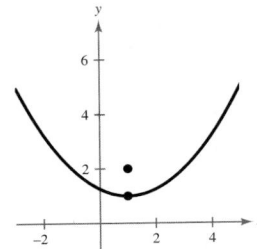

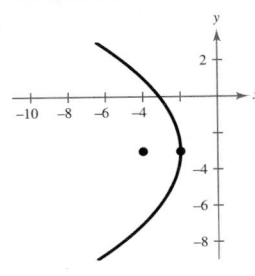

19. Vertex: $(-2, 1)$
Focus: $\left(-2, -\frac{1}{2}\right)$
Directrix: $y = \frac{5}{2}$

21. Vertex: $\left(\frac{1}{4}, -\frac{1}{2}\right)$
Focus: $\left(0, -\frac{1}{2}\right)$
Directrix: $x = \frac{1}{2}$

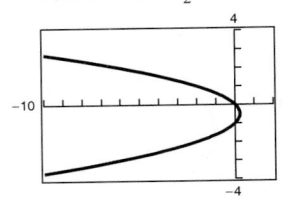

23. $(x - 3)^2 = -(y - 1)$ **25.** $y^2 = 2(x + 2)$

27. $(y - 2)^2 = -8(x - 3)$ **29.** $x^2 = 8(y - 4)$

31. $(y - 2)^2 = 8x$ **33.** $y = \sqrt{6(x + 1)} + 3$

35. Center: $\left(\frac{1}{2}, -1\right)$
Vertices: $\left(\frac{1}{2} \pm \sqrt{5}, -1\right)$
Foci: $\left(\frac{1}{2} \pm \sqrt{2}, -1\right)$

37. Center: $(1, 3)$
Vertices: $(1, -2), (1, 8)$
Foci: $(1, -1), (1, 7)$

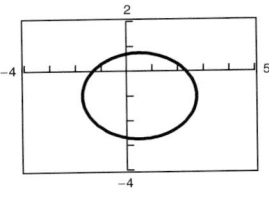

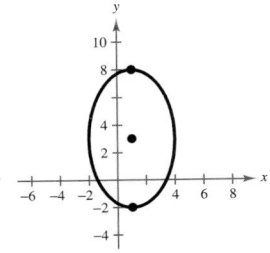

39. Center: $(-2, 4)$
Vertices: $(-1, 4), (-3, 4)$
Foci: $\left(-2 \pm \frac{\sqrt{3}}{2}, 4\right)$

41. Center: $(-2, 3)$
Vertices: $(-2, 6), (-2, 0)$
Foci: $\left(-2, 3 \pm \sqrt{5}\right)$

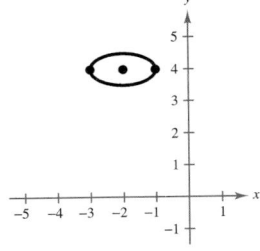

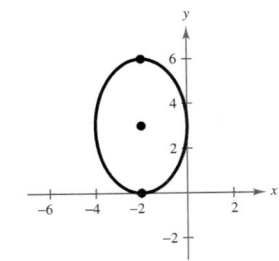

43. Center: $(1, -1)$
Vertices: $\left(\frac{9}{4}, -1\right), \left(-\frac{1}{4}, -1\right)$
Foci: $\left(\frac{7}{4}, -1\right), \left(\frac{1}{4}, -1\right)$

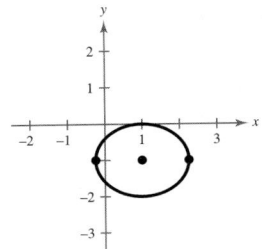

45. $\dfrac{(x-2)^2}{1} + \dfrac{(y-3)^2}{9} = 1$

47. $\dfrac{(x-2)^2}{9} + \dfrac{(y-2)^2}{4} = 1$

49. $\dfrac{(x-2)^2}{4} + \dfrac{(y-2)^2}{1} = 1$ **51.** $\dfrac{x^2}{48} + \dfrac{(y-4)^2}{64} = 1$

53. $\dfrac{(x-3)^2}{9} + \dfrac{(y-5)^2}{16} = 1$ **55.** $\dfrac{x^2}{16} + \dfrac{(y-4)^2}{12} = 1$

57. $x = \frac{3}{2}\left(2 + \sqrt{4 - y^2}\right)$

59. Center: $(-1, 2)$

    Vertices: $(-3, 2), (1, 2)$

    Foci: $\left(-1 \pm \sqrt{5}, 2\right)$

61. Center: $(2, 6)$

    Vertices: $(2, 5), (2, 7)$

    Foci: $\left(2, 6 \pm \sqrt{2}\right)$

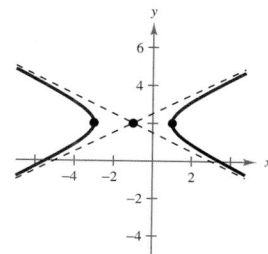
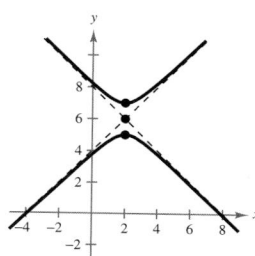

63. Center: $(2, -3)$

    Vertices: $(3, -3), (1, -3)$

    Foci: $\left(2 \pm \sqrt{10}, -3\right)$

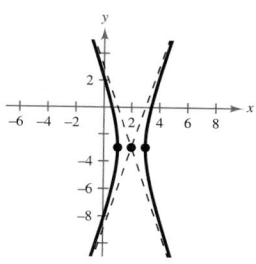

65. The graph of this equation is two lines intersecting at $(-1, -3)$.

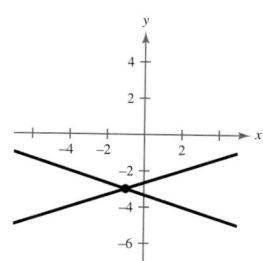

67. Center: $(1, -1)$

    Vertices: $(-2, -1), (4, -1)$

    Foci: $\left(1 \pm \sqrt{13}, -1\right)$

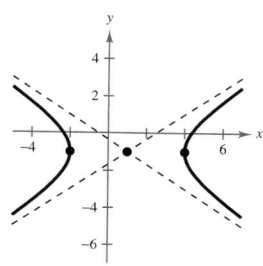

69. Center: $(1, -3)$

    Vertices: $\left(1, -3 \pm \sqrt{2}\right)$

    Foci: $\left(1, -3 \pm 2\sqrt{5}\right)$

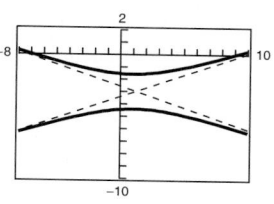

71. $(y-1)^2 - x^2 = 1$ **73.** $\dfrac{(x-3)^2}{4} - \dfrac{(y-2)^2}{16/5} = 1$

75. $\dfrac{(x-4)^2}{4} - \dfrac{y^2}{12} = 1$ **77.** $\dfrac{(y-5)^2}{16} - \dfrac{(x-4)^2}{9} = 1$

79. $\dfrac{y^2}{9} - \dfrac{4(x-2)^2}{9} = 1$ **81.** Left half   **83.** Circle

85. Hyperbola   **87.** Ellipse   **89.** Parabola

91.

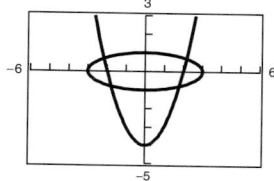

    $(\pm 2.166, 0.692), (\pm 1.788, -0.803)$

93. (a) $17,500\sqrt{2} \approx 24,749$ miles per hour

    (b) $x^2 = -16,400(y - 4100)$

95. (a)

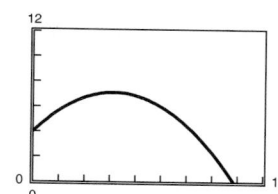

    (b) Highest point: $(6.25, 7.125)$

        Distance: 15.69 feet

97. $\dfrac{x^2}{25} + \dfrac{y^2}{16} = 1$

99. $2,756,832,000$ miles; $4,575,168,000$ miles

101. 0.0543 **103.** $\dfrac{x^2}{328.15} + \dfrac{y^2}{19.39} = 1$ **105.** True

107. (a) Answers will vary.

    (b)

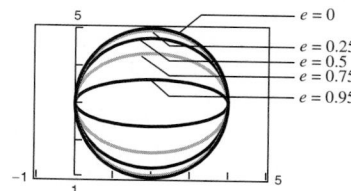

(c) Ellipse becomes more circular.

109. Not inverse functions. $f^{-1}(x) = x^2 - 8, \; x \geq 0$

111. $\displaystyle\sum_{n=1}^{12} \frac{7}{2+n} \approx 12.261$ **113.** $\displaystyle\sum_{n=1}^{4} \frac{-2+3n}{3^{n+1}} \approx 0.387$

115. $x^6 - 18x^5 + 135x^4 - 540x^3 + 1215x^2 - 1458x + 729$

117. $x^{10} - 10x^8 + 40x^6 - 80x^4 + 80x^2 - 32$

Section 8.3   *(page 602)*

1. (c)   **3.** (b)   **5.** (a)   **7.** (f)

9. (a)

t	0	1	2	3	4
x	0	1	$\sqrt{2}$	$\sqrt{3}$	2
y	2	1	0	-1	-2

(b)
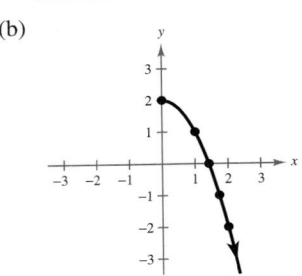

(c)
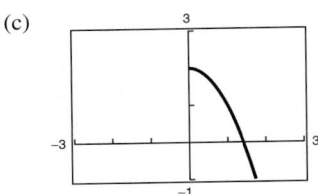

(d) $y = 2 - x^2$

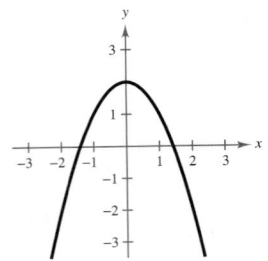

The graph is the entire parabola rather than just the right half.

11.
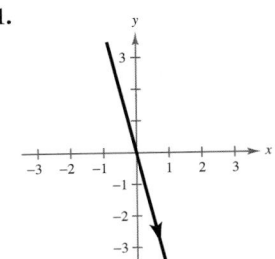

$4x + y = 0$

13.
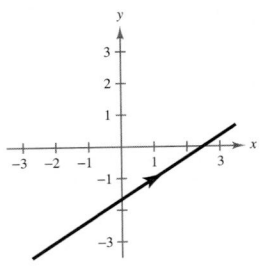

$2x - 3y - 5 = 0$

15.
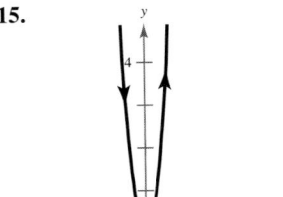

$y = 16x^2$

17.
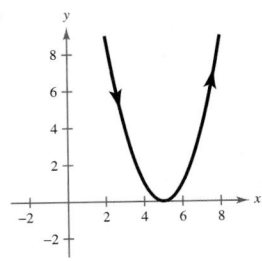

$y = (x - 5)^2$

19.
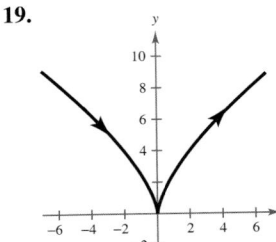

$y = \frac{5}{2}x^{2/3}$

21.
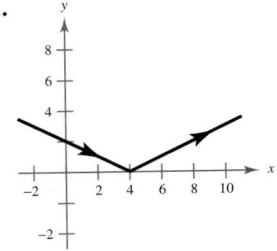

$y = \frac{1}{2}|x - 4|$

23.
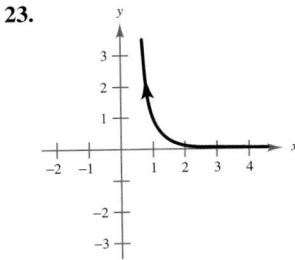

$y = \dfrac{1}{x^3}, \; x > 0$

25.
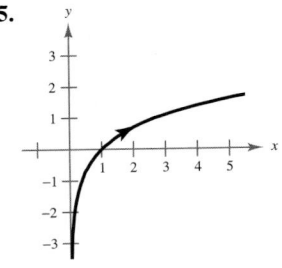

$y = \ln x$

27.
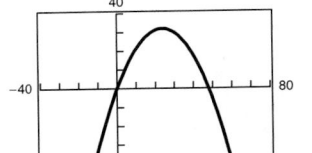

29.
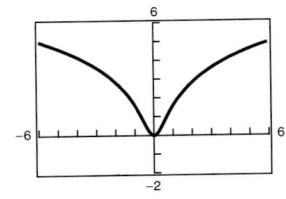

31. Each curve represents a portion of the line $y = 2x + 1$.

Domain	*Orientation*
(a) $(-\infty, \infty)$	Left to right
(b) $(-\infty, 0), (0, \infty)$	Right to left
(c) $(0, \infty)$	Right to left
(d) $(0, \infty)$	Left to right

33. Each curve represents a portion of the line $y = 4 - \frac{1}{2}x$.

Domain	*Orientation*
(a) $[0, \infty)$	Left to right
(b) $(-\infty, \infty)$	Left to right
(c) $(-\infty, \infty)$	Left to right
(d) $(-\infty, 0]$	Right to left for $t \geq 0$

35. Each curve represents a portion of the curve $y = x^3 - 1$.

(a) $0 \leq x \leq 1$ (b) $0 \leq x \leq 3$

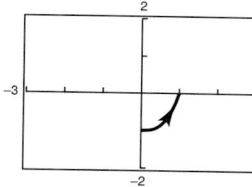 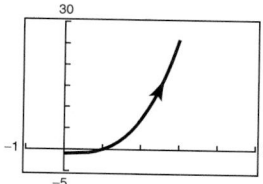

(c) $-2 \leq x \leq 3$ (d) $-3 \leq x \leq 3$

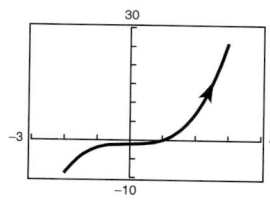 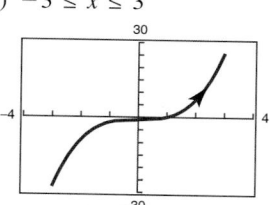

37. $x = 5t$
$y = -2t$

39. $x = 5t - 2$
$y = 7t + 3$

41. (a) Solution is not unique.
$x = 3$
$y = t$
$-1 \leq t \leq 5$

(b) $x = 3$
$y = -t$
$-5 \leq t \leq 1$

43. Answers will vary.
Example:

$x = t, \quad y = 4t - 3$

$x = 2t, y = 8t - 3$

45. Answers will vary.
Example:

$x = t, \quad y = \dfrac{1}{t}$

$x = \dfrac{1}{t}, y = t$

47. Answers will vary.
Example:

$x = t, \quad y = t^2 + 4$

$x = \frac{1}{2}t, y = \frac{1}{4}t^2 + 4$

49. Answers will vary.
Example:

$x = t, \quad y = t^3 + 2t$

$x = \sqrt[3]{t}, y = t + 2\sqrt[3]{t}$

51. (a)   (b)

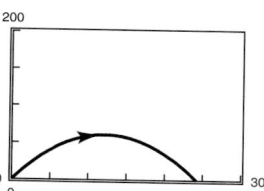 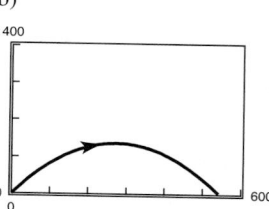

Maximum height: 60.5 feet   Maximum height: 136.1 feet
Range: 242.0 feet   Range: 544.5 feet

(c)   (d)

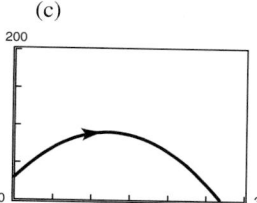 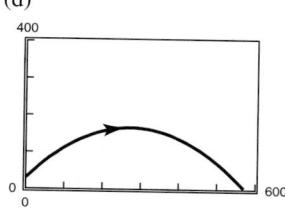

Maximum height: 90.5 feet   Maximum height: 166.1 feet
Range: 269.0 feet   Range: 573.0 feet

53. (a)   (b)

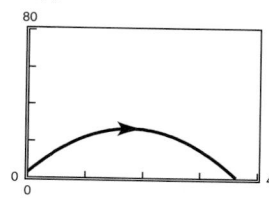 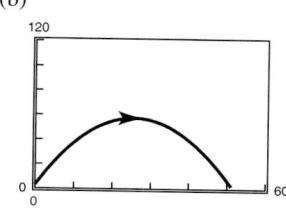

   No   Yes

55. True   **57.** The orientation would be reversed.

59. $x = 3 + \sqrt{5}, x = 3 - \sqrt{5}$

61. $x = \sqrt{9 + 3\sqrt{7}} \approx 4.115$,
$x = -\sqrt{9 + 3\sqrt{7}} \approx -4.115$,
$x = \sqrt{9 - 3\sqrt{7}} \approx 1.031$,
$x = -\sqrt{9 - 3\sqrt{7}} \approx -1.031$

63. 18,500   **65.** $-\frac{11,935}{12}$ **67.** 29.653

Review Exercises   *(page 606)*

1. (e)   **3.** (c)   **5.** (f)   **7.** (h)   **9.** Parabola

11. Hyperbola   **13.** Parabola   **15.** Hyperbola

17. $y^2 = 4x$ **19.** $y^2 = -24x$

21.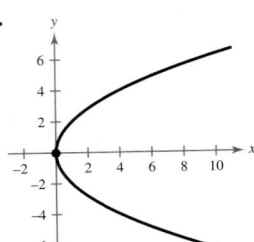

23.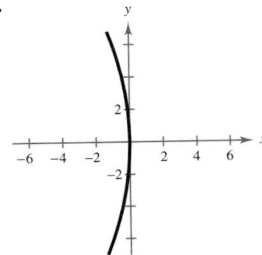

25. (0, 50)

$$\frac{x^2}{16} + \frac{y^2}{100} = 1$$

29. $\frac{x^2}{49} + \frac{y^2}{13} = 1$

27.

31.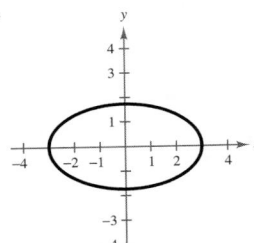

33.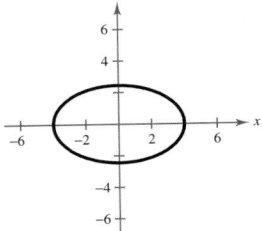

35. $x^2 - \frac{y^2}{4} = 1$ **37.** $y^2 - \frac{x^2}{8} = 1$

39.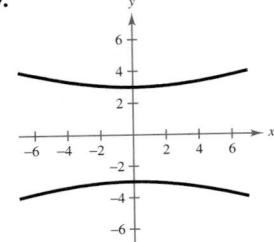

41.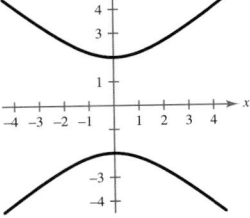

43. Parabola   **45.** Ellipse   **47.** Hyperbola

49. Hyperbola   **51.** Ellipse

53. $(x + 6)^2 = -9(y - 4)$ **55.** $(x - 4)^2 = -8(y - 2)$

57. $(y - 2)^2 = -4x$ **59.** $\frac{(x - 5)^2}{25} + \frac{(y - 3)^2}{9} = 1$

61. $\frac{(x - 2)^2}{25} + \frac{y^2}{21} = 1$ **63.** $\frac{(x - 2)^2}{4} + (y - 1)^2 = 1$

65. $\frac{x^2}{36} - \frac{(y - 7)^2}{9} = 1$ **67.** $\frac{(x + 2)^2}{64} - \frac{(y - 3)^2}{36} = 1$

69. $\frac{5(x - 4)^2}{16} - \frac{5y^2}{64} = 1$ **71.** $8\sqrt{6}$ meters

73. (a) 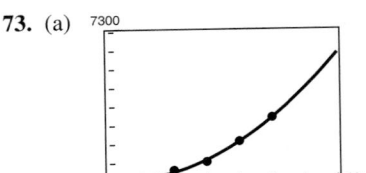   (b) $6737.2 million

75.

t	-2	-1	0	1	2	3
x	-8	-5	-2	1	4	7
y	15	11	7	3	-1	-5

77.

t	-2	-1	1	2	3	4
x	-3	-6	6	3	2	$\frac{3}{2}$
y	2	3	5	6	7	8

79. (a)   **81.** (d)

83.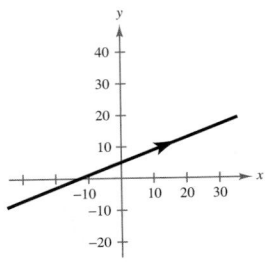

85.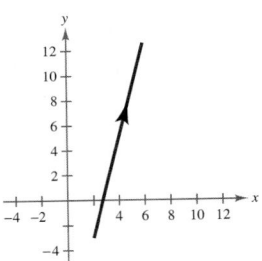

87.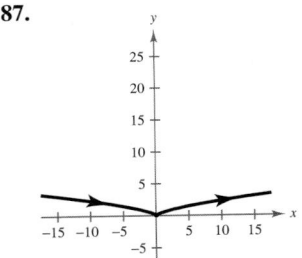

89.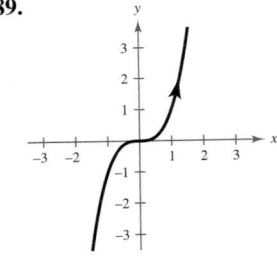

$y = x^3$

91.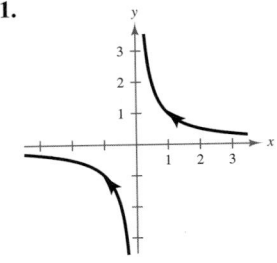

$y = \frac{1}{x}$

93.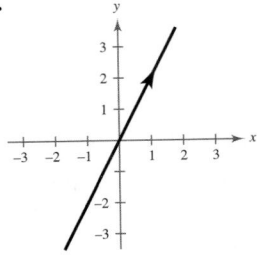

$y = 2x$

95.

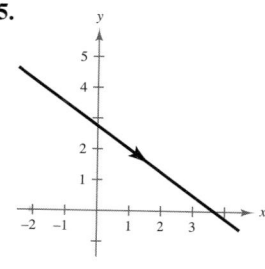

$$3x + 4y - 11 = 0$$

97.

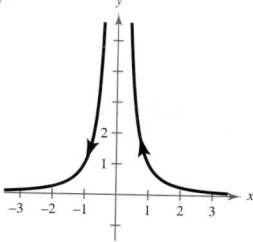

$$y = \frac{1}{x^2}$$

99.

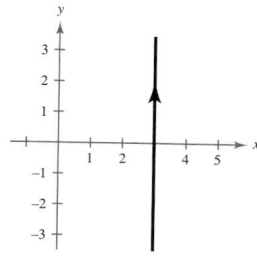

$$x = 3$$

101. Answers will vary. Example:

$$x = t, \quad y = 6t + 2$$
$$x = 2t, \quad y = 12t + 2$$

103. Answers will vary. Example:

$$x = t, \quad y = t^2 + 2$$
$$x = \tfrac{1}{2}t, \quad y = \tfrac{1}{4}t^2 + 2$$

105. Answers will vary. Example:

$$x = t, \quad y = 5$$

107. Answers will vary. Example:

$$x = -1 + 11t, \quad y = 6 - 6t$$

109. False. The equation of a hyperbola is a second-degree equation.

111. False. The following are two sets of parametric equations for the line.

$$x = t, \quad y = 3 - 2t$$
$$x = 3t, \quad y = 3 - 6t$$

113. The extended diagonals of the central rectangle are asymptotes of the hyperbola.

Chapter Test *(page 611)*

1.

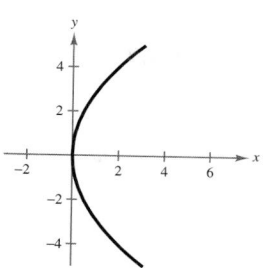

Vertex: $(0, 0)$
Focus: $(2, 0)$

2.

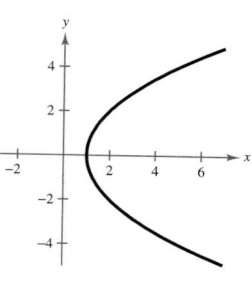

Vertex: $(1, 0)$
Focus: $(2, 0)$

3.

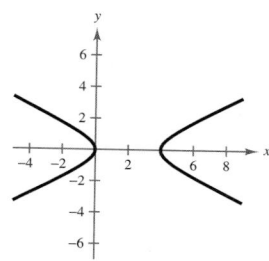

Vertices: $(0, 0), (4, 0)$
Foci: $\left(2 \pm \sqrt{5}, 0\right)$

4. $(y - 7)^2 = -\dfrac{49x}{8}$

5. $(y + 2)^2 = 8(x - 6)$

6. $\dfrac{(x - 5)^2}{25} + \dfrac{(y - 6)^2}{4} = 1$

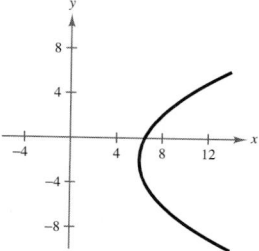

7. $\dfrac{(x + 6)^2}{16} + \dfrac{(y - 3)^2}{49} = 1$

8. $\dfrac{y^2}{9} - \dfrac{x^2}{4} = 1$

9.

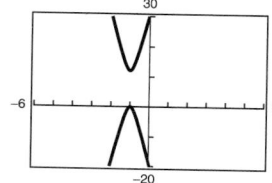

x-axis: tick marks at each unit on the interval $-6 \le x \le 6$

y-axis: tick marks every 10 units on the interval
$-20 \le y \le 30$

10.

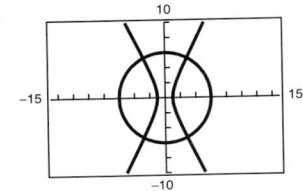

$\left(\sqrt{5}, \pm\sqrt{28}\right), \left(-\sqrt{5}, \pm\sqrt{28}\right) \approx$

$(2.828, \pm5.292), (-2.828, \pm5.292)$

11.

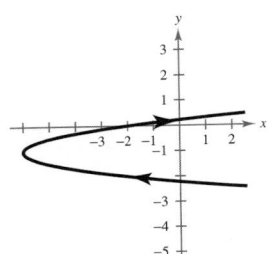

$y = \pm\frac{1}{2}\sqrt{x + 6} - 1$

12.

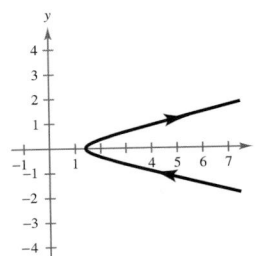

$y = \pm\frac{\sqrt{x^2 - 2}}{4}, \ x \geq \sqrt{2}$

13.

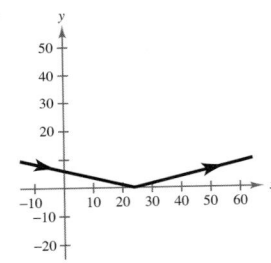

$y = \left|\frac{x}{4} - 6\right|$

14. $x = t, \qquad y = 7t + 6$

$x = t - 1, \ y = 7t - 1$

(Solutions are not unique.)

15. $x = t, \quad y = t^2 + 10$

$x = 2t, \ y = 4t^2 + 10$

(Solutions are not unique.)

16. $x = t + 4, \ y = \dfrac{t}{4} - 4$

$x = 2t, \qquad y = \dfrac{1}{2}t - 5$

(Solutions are not unique.)

17.

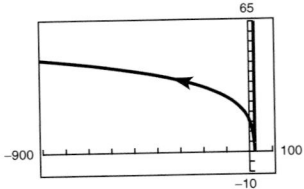

x-axis: tick marks every 100 units on the interval $-900 \leq x \leq 100$

y-axis: tick marks every 5 units on the interval $-10 \leq y \leq 65$

$-10 \leq t \leq 20$

18. ≈ 33.9 meters

19. Perigee: $\approx 364{,}224$ kilometers

Apogee: $\approx 404{,}582$ kilometers

Cumulative Test for Chapters 6–8
(page 612)

1. $(4, -3)$ **2.** $(-3, -1)$ **3.** $(0.6, -4, -0.2)$

4. $(1, -4, -4)$

5. $\begin{bmatrix} -7 & -10 & -16 \\ -6 & 18 & 9 \\ -12 & 16 & 7 \end{bmatrix}$ **6.** $\begin{bmatrix} -18 & 15 & -14 \\ 28 & 11 & 34 \\ -20 & 52 & -1 \end{bmatrix}$

7. $\begin{bmatrix} 3 & -31 & 2 \\ 22 & 18 & 6 \\ 52 & -40 & 14 \end{bmatrix}$ **8.** $\begin{bmatrix} 5 & 36 & 31 \\ -36 & 12 & -36 \\ 16 & 0 & 18 \end{bmatrix}$

9. (a) $\begin{bmatrix} -175 & 37 & -13 \\ 95 & -20 & 7 \\ 14 & -3 & 1 \end{bmatrix}$ (b) 1

10. $(4, -2, 1)$ **11.** 22 square units   **12.** 1110

13. 110,544   **14.** 135   **15.** 40   **16.** ≈ 0.904

17. 96   **18.** ≈ 34.480 **19.** 80   **20.** 3685

21. Answers will vary.

22. $x^4 + 20x^3 + 150x^2 + 500x + 625$

23. $32x^5 + 80x^4y^2 + 80x^3y^4 + 40x^2y^6 + 10xy^8 + y^{10}$

24. $x^6 - 12x^5y + 60x^4y^2 - 160x^3y^3 + 240x^2y^4 - 192xy^5 + 64y^6$

25. $256x^8 - 1024x^7 + 1792x^6 - 1792x^5 + 1120x^4 - 448x^3 + 112x^2 - 16x + 1$

26. 30   **27.** 120   **28.** 453,600   **29.** 151,200

30. Hyperbola

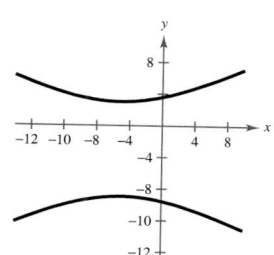

31. Ellipse

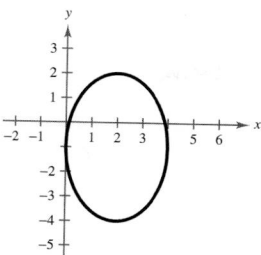

40. (a) and (b)

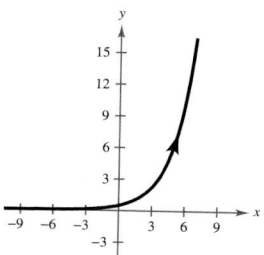

(c) $y = \frac{1}{2}e^{x/2}$

32. Hyperbola

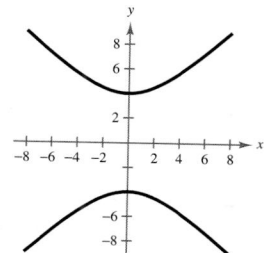

33. Degenerate conic

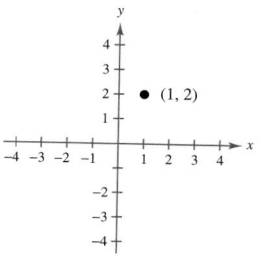

41. $5605.74 million   **42.** 171,723 people

43. $604,199.78   **44.** $\frac{1}{4}$ **45.** $\dfrac{x^2}{23^2} + \dfrac{y^2}{48^2} = 1$

Appendix B

Section B.1   *(page A10)*

1. (a) $1.109   (b) [$0.999, $1.189]

3. Quiz 1:

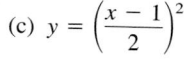

Quiz 2:

22 and 23

34. $(x - 2)^2 = -\frac{4}{3}(y - 3)$

35. $\dfrac{(x - 1)^2}{25} + \dfrac{(y - 4)^2}{4} = 1$ **36.** $\dfrac{(y + 4)^2}{4} - \dfrac{3x^2}{16} = 1$

37. $\dfrac{5(y - 2)^2}{4} - \dfrac{5x^2}{16} = 1$

5.

Stems	Leaves
7	0 5 5 5 7 7 8 8 8
8	1 1 1 1 2 3 4 5 5 5 5 7 8 9 9 9
9	0 2 8
10	0 0

38. (a) and (b)

(c) $y = \left(\dfrac{x - 1}{2}\right)^2$

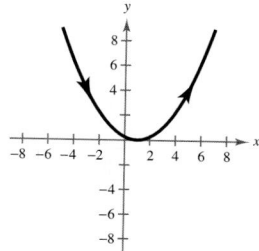

39. (a) and (b)

(c) $y = 4 - \dfrac{x - 8}{3}$

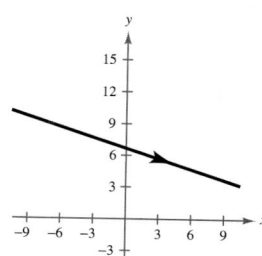

7.

Stems	Leaves
0	89 66 67 65 80 98 62 93
1	09 01 46 24 96 90
2	92 55 40 61
3	68 35
4	12 96 80 38
5	81 18 50 70 66
6	44 00 34 01
7	61 66 00
8	11 57 41 90
9	
10	
11	60 59 33
12	92
13	19 17 37
27	22
31	32
46	80
65	14

9. (a)

Interval	Tally
90–109	ⅢⅢ
110–129	ⅢⅢ ⅢⅢ Ⅰ
130–149	ⅢⅢ ⅢⅢ
150–169	ⅢⅢ Ⅰ
170–189	Ⅰ
190–209	Ⅲ

(b)

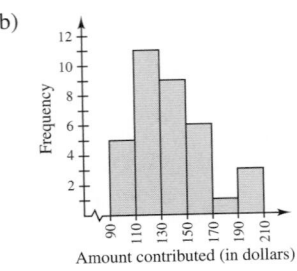

Amount contributed (in dollars)

Section B.2 *(page A17)*

1. Mean: 8.86; median: 8; mode: 7

3. Mean: 10.29; median: 8; mode: 7

5. Mean: 9; median: 8; mode: 7

7. The mean is sensitive to extreme values.

9. Mean: $67.14; median: $65.35

11. Mean: 3.07; median: 3; mode: 3

13. One possibility: $\{4, 4, 10\}$

15. The median gives the most representative description.

17. $\bar{x} = 6$, $v = 10$, $\sigma = 3.16$

19. $\bar{x} = 2$, $v = \frac{4}{3}$, $\sigma = 1.15$ **21.** $\bar{x} = 4$, $v = 4$, $\sigma = 2$

23. $\bar{x} = 47$, $v = 226$, $\sigma = 15.03$ **25.** 3.42

27. 101.55   **29.** 1.65

31. (a) $\bar{x} = 12$; $\sigma = 2.83$ (b) $\bar{x} = 20$; $\sigma = 2.83$

(c) $\bar{x} = 12$; $\sigma = 1.41$ (d) $\bar{x} = 9$; $\sigma = 1.41$

33. $\bar{x} = 12$ and $|x_i - 12| = 8$ for all x_i

35. It will increase the mean by 5, but the standard deviation will not change.

37. First histogram

39.

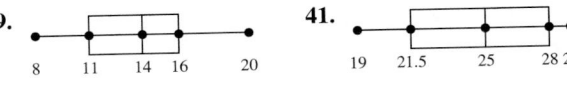

8   11   14 16   20

41.

19   21.5   25   28 29

43.

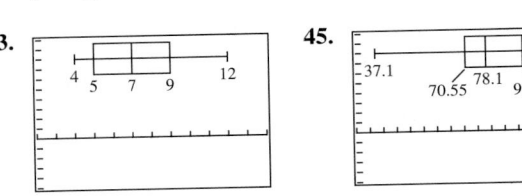

4   5   7   9   12

45.

37.1   70.55   78.1   91.75   107.5

Appendix C *(page A24)*

1. 3   **3.** 7   **5.** 4   **7.** 20   **9.** 4   **11.** 3

13. $\frac{4}{3}$ **15.** 20   **17.** No solution   **19.** $x < 2$

21. $x < 9$ **23.** $x \le -14$ **25.** $x > 10$

27. $x < 4$ **29.** $x < 3$ **31.** $x \ge 2$ **33.** $x \le -5$

35. $x < 6$

Instructor's Answers

Chapter P

Section P.1 *(page 9)*

2. (a) 3 (b) $-7, 0, -2, -8, 3$

(c) $-7, -\frac{7}{3}, 0, 3.12, \frac{5}{4}, -2, -8, 3$ (d) $\sqrt{5}$

4. (a) None (b) $-2, -10$

(c) $0.7575, -4.63, -2, 0.03, -10$

(d) $2.3030030003\ldots, \sqrt{10}$

6. (a) $25, \sqrt{9}, 6, 18$ (b) $25, -17, \sqrt{9}, 6, -4, 18$

(c) $25, -17, -\frac{12}{5}, \sqrt{9}, 3.12, 6, -4, 18$ (d) $\frac{1}{2}\pi$

8. $0.\overline{3}$ **10.** $0.\overline{54}$ **12.** $\frac{123}{10}$ **14.** $\frac{381}{100}$ **16.** $-\frac{249}{100}$

18. $-6 < -2.5$

20. $-3.5 < 1$ **22.** $1 < \frac{16}{3}$

24. $-\frac{8}{7} < -\frac{3}{7}$

26. (a) $x \geq -2$ is the set of all real numbers greater than or equal to -2.

(b) (c) Unbounded

28. (a) $x > 3$ is the set of all real numbers greater than 3.

(b) (c) Unbounded

30. (a) $x < 2$ is the set of all real numbers less than 2.

(b) (c) Unbounded

32. (a) $0 \leq x \leq 5$ is the set of all real numbers greater than or equal to zero and less than or equal to 5.

(b) (c) Bounded

34. (a) $0 < x \leq 6$ is the set of positive real numbers less than or equal to 6.

(b) (c) Bounded

36. $\frac{381}{220}, 1.732, \sqrt{3}, \frac{2103}{1214}, \frac{26}{15}$ **38.** $z \geq 10; [10, \infty)$

40. $y \leq 25; (-\infty, 25]$ **42.** $-1 \leq p < 8; [-1, 8)$

44. $2.5\% \leq r \leq 5\%; [0.025, 0.05]$

46. The set of all real numbers less than or equal to 4

48. 0 **50.** $4 - \pi \approx 0.8584$ **52.** -6 **54.** -1

56. 1 for $x > 1$; undefined for $x = 1$; -1 for $x < 1$

58. $|-4| = |4|$ **60.** $-|-6| < |-6|$

62. $-(-2) > -2$ **64.** $\frac{5}{2}$ **66.** 51

68. $\frac{5}{2}$ **70.** 14.99

72. (a) $-C$ is positive. (b) $A - C$ is positive.

74. $|x + 10| \geq 6$ **76.** $|y - a| \leq 2$ **78.** 17 miles

80. The temperature increased 40°.

82. $|\$9772 - \$9400| = \$372 < \$500$

$0.05(\$9400) = \$470$

Because the difference between the actual expenses and the budget is less than $500 and less than 5% of the budgeted amount, there is compliance with the "budget variance test."

84. $|\$2613 - \$2575| = \$38 < \$500$

$0.05(\$2575) = \$128.75$

Because the difference between the actual expenses and the budget is less than $500 and less than 5% of the budgeted amount, there is compliance with the "budget variance test."

86. $y = \$192.8$ billion, $|y - x| = \$2.8$ billion

There was a deficit of $2.8 billion.

88. $y = \$1032$ billion, $|y - x| = \$221.2$ billion

There was a deficit of $221.2 billion.

90. $y = \$1657.9$ billion, $|y - x| = \$9.9$ billion

There was a deficit of $9.9 billion.

92. Terms: $2x, -9$; Coefficient: 2

94. Terms: $7\sqrt{5}x^2, 3$; Coefficient: $7\sqrt{5}$

96. Terms: $3x^4, 3x^3$; Coefficients: 3, 3

98. (a) 30 (b) -12 **100.** (a) -10 (b) 0

102. (a) $\frac{1}{2}$ (b) Division by 0 is undefined.

104. Multiplicative Inverse Property

106. Additive Inverse Property

108. Additive Identity Property

110. Associative Property of Addition

112. $\frac{1}{7}(7 \cdot 12) = \left(\frac{1}{7} \cdot 7\right)12$ Associative Property of Multiplication

$= 1 \cdot 12$ Multiplicative Inverse Property

$= 12$ Multiplicative Identity Property

114. 0   **116.** 15   **118.** $\frac{2}{7}$ **120.** $\frac{59}{66}$ **122.** $\frac{44}{3x}$

124. $-\frac{14}{5}$ **126.** -0.13 **128.** 10.20

130. (a)

n	1	10	100	10,000	100,000
$5/n$	5	0.5	0.05	0.0005	0.00005

(b) As n approaches infinity, $5/n$ approaches 0.

132. Yes. A nonnegative real number can be 0. A positive real number cannot.

134. False. A contradiction can be shown using numbers such as $a = 2$ and $b = 1$. $2 > 1$, but $\frac{1}{2} \ngtr \frac{1}{1}$.

Section P.2   *(page 21)*

2. (a) 125   (b) $\frac{1}{9}$ **4.** (a) 5184   (b) $-\frac{3}{5}$

6. (a) $\frac{16}{3}$ (b) 1   **8.** (a) $\frac{7}{12}$ (b) $\frac{1}{81}$ **10.** 0.244

12. 5184   **14.** 5   **16.** -80 **18.** $-\frac{4}{27}$

20. (a) $9x^2$ (b) $16x^6$ **22.** (a) $\frac{1}{r^2}$ (b) $\frac{5184}{y^7}$

24. (a) 1   (b) $\frac{1}{(z+2)^4}$ **26.** (a) 3^{3n} (b) $\frac{b^5}{a^5}$

28. $-\sqrt{144} = -12$ **30.** $(614.125)^{1/3} = 8.5$

32. $\sqrt[5]{-243} = -3$ **34.** $\sqrt[4]{16^5} = 32$ **36.** 7

38. 1   **40.** 562   **42.** $\frac{2}{3}$ **44.** -625 **46.** 12.651

48. 0.005   **50.** 0.149   **52.** (a) $\frac{2\sqrt[3]{2}}{3}$ (b) $\frac{5\sqrt{3}}{2}$

54. (a) $3x^2$ (b) $2x\sqrt[5]{3}$ **56.** 64   **58.** $xy^{1/3}$

60. $\frac{x}{5}$ **62.** (a) $\frac{\sqrt{10}}{2}$ (b) $\frac{\sqrt[3]{5x}}{x}$

64. (a) $\frac{\sqrt{14}+2}{2}$ (b) $\frac{2\sqrt{10}+5}{3}$ **66.** $\frac{2}{3\sqrt{2}}$

68. $\frac{1}{2(\sqrt{3}+\sqrt{2})}$ **70.** (a) $\sqrt{x}$ (b) $3x^2$

72. (a) $3\sqrt[4]{3(x+1)}$ (b) $a\sqrt[6]{10ab}$

74. (a) $2\sqrt{x}$ (b) $4\sqrt{y}$

76. (a) $2\sqrt{10}|x|$ (b) $22\sqrt[3]{x}$ **78.** $\sqrt{\frac{3}{11}} = \frac{\sqrt{3}}{\sqrt{11}}$

80. $5 = \sqrt{3^2 + 4^2}$ **82.** 9.46×10^{15}

84. 3.937×10^{-5} **86.** 15,000,000   **88.** 0.00009

90. (a) 4.907×10^{17} (b) 1.479

92. (a) 0.064   (b) 0.030

94. (a) 6.0×10^4 (b) 2.0×10^{11}

96. No. Rationalizing the denominator produces a number equivalent to the original fraction; squaring does not.

98. $T = \frac{\pi}{2} \approx 1.57$ seconds   **100.** 0.026 inches

102. Paper: 7.99×10^7 tons, Metals: 1.61×10^7 tons, Glass: 1.24×10^7 tons, Plastics: 1.97×10^7 tons, Yard waste: 2.81×10^7 tons, Other: 5.35×10^7 tons

104. False. $(a^n)^k = a^{nk}$. In general, $nk \neq n^k$.

106. No. Correct scientific notation would be 5.27×10^6.

Section P.3   *(page 32)*

2. e   **4.** a   **6.** c

8. Answers will vary, but first term is $8x^5$.

10. Answers will vary. Example: $8x^3 + 3x + 14$

12. Degree: 4; Leading coefficient: -3

14. Degree: 1; Leading coefficient: 9

16. Degree: 1; Leading coefficient: 3

18. Not a polynomial   **20.** Polynomial: $\frac{1}{6}x^2 + \frac{1}{3}x - \frac{1}{2}$

22. Not a polynomial   **24.** $x^2 + 2x$ **26.** $-2x^2 - 4$

28. $1.7x^4 - 8.8x - 34.4$ **30.** $4y^4 + 2y^3 - 3y^2$

32. $15x^2 - 6x$ **34.** $4x^4 - 12x$ **36.** $-14y^4 + 8y^3$

38. $-\frac{9}{4}y^2 + 24y$ **40.** $x^2 + 5x - 50$

42. $28x^2 - 29x + 6$ **44.** $64x^2 - 80x + 25$

46. $4x^2 - 9$ **48.** $4x^2 - 9y^2$ **50.** $x^2 + 2xy + y^2 - 1$

52. $x^2 + y^2 - 2xy + 2x - 2y + 1$ **54.** $9a^6 - 16b^4$

56. $x^3 - 6x^2 + 12x - 8$

58. $27x^3 + 54x^2y + 36xy^2 + 8y^3$ **60.** $\frac{9}{25}t^2 + \frac{24}{5}t + 16$

62. $4x^2 - \frac{1}{36}$ **64.** $3.24y^2 - 18y + 25$

66. $10.89y^2 - 1$ **68.** $2x^2 + 8x + 6$ **70.** $x^4 - y^4$

72. $5(y - 6)$ **74.** $2x(2x^2 - 3x + 6)$

76. $(3x - 1)(3x)$ **78.** $\left(x - \frac{1}{2}\right)\left(x + \frac{1}{2}\right)$

80. $(7 - 3y)(7 + 3y)$ **82.** $\left(\frac{5}{6}y - 7\right)\left(\frac{5}{6}y + 7\right)$

84. $-z(z + 10)$ **86.** $(x + 5)^2$ **88.** $\left(x - \frac{2}{3}\right)^2$

90. $(3x - 2)^2$ **92.** $\left(2t + \frac{2}{5}\right)^2$ **94.** $(x + 3)(x + 2)$

96. $(t - 3)(t + 2)$ **98.** $(8 - z)(3 + z)$

100. $(3x - 2)(x + 5)$ **102.** $(2x - 7)(x + 3)$

104. $(8x + 3)(x - 6)$ **106.** $(-6x - 1)(x - 4)$

108. $(x - 3)(x^2 + 3x + 9)$ **110.** $(z + 5)(z^2 - 5z + 25)$

112. $\left(x + \frac{2}{5}\right)\left(x^2 - \frac{2}{5}x + \frac{4}{25}\right)$

114. $(3x + 2)(9x^2 - 6x + 4)$

116. $\left(\frac{3}{4}x - 1\right)\left(\frac{9}{16}x^2 + \frac{3}{4}x + 1\right)$ **118.** $(x^2 - 5)(x + 5)$

120. $(5x^2 + 3)(x - 2)$ **122.** $12(x + 2)(x - 2)$

124. $6(x - 3)(x + 3)$ **126.** $(8 - x)(2 + x)$

128. $(-3x + 1)(3x - 1)$ **130.** $y(2y + 3)(y - 5)$

132. $(5x + 3)(x + 2)$ **134.** $\left(\frac{1}{9}x - 2\right)\left(\frac{1}{9}x + 4\right)$

136. $(5 - x)(1 + x^2)$ **138.** $(u + 2)(3 - u^2)$

140. $(t + 6)(t - 8)$ **142.** $(x + 2)(x + 4)(x - 2)(x - 4)$

144. $5(x + 2)(x^2 - 2x + 4)$ **146.** $(3 - 4x)(23 - 60x)$

148. $5(1 - x)^2(3x + 2)(4x + 3)$

150. $(x - 2)^2(x + 1)^3(7x - 5)$

152. $3(x^2 + 1)^4(x^4 - x^2 + 1)^4(3x + 2)^2(33x^6 + 20x^5 + 3)$

154. $3w^2[15w(9w + 1)^4 + (2w + 1)^5]$

156. (a) $1200r^3 + 3600r^2 + 3600r + 1200$

(b)

r	2%	3%	$3\frac{1}{2}\%$
$1200(1 + r)^3$	\$1273.45	\$1311.27	\$1330.46

r	4%	$4\frac{1}{2}\%$
$1200(1 + r)^3$	\$1349.84	\$1369.40

(c) Amount increases with increasing r.

158. $V = x(26 - 2x)(18 - 2x)$

$\quad = 4x(x - 13)(x - 9)$

x (cm)	1	2	3
V (cu cm)	384	616	720

160. (a) ≈ 233.6 pounds

(b) The difference decreases in magnitude.

162. $(x + a)(x + a) = x(x + a) + a(x + a)$

Distributive Property

164. c **166.** d

168.

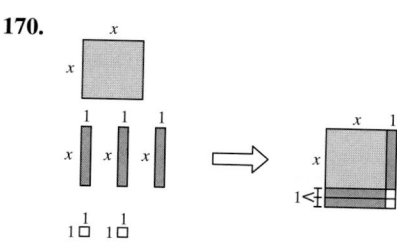

170.

172. $r^2(4 - \pi)$ **174.** $\frac{5}{8}(x + 7)(x - 1)$

176. $1, -1, 4, -4, 11, -11$

178. $25, -25, 14, -14, 11, -11, 10, -10$

180. $-2, -10$ (Answers will vary.)

182. $9, -26$ (Answers will vary.)

184. No. $(3x - 6)$ factors as $3(x - 2)$.

186. (a) $V = \pi h(R - r)(R + r)$

(b) $V = 2\pi\left[\left(\frac{R + r}{2}\right)(R - r)\right]h$

188. True. For example, $x^2 - y^2 = (x - y)(x + y)$.

190. Degree: $m + n$

192. Missing middle term. Square first and last terms and add 2 times the product of these terms:

$x^2 - 2(3x) + 9 = x^2 - 6x + 9$

194. No. $(-3x^2 + 2x + 1) + (3x^2 - x - 2) = x - 1$ is a first-degree polynomial.

Section P.4 *(page 44)*

2. All real numbers **4.** All positive real numbers

6. All real numbers x such that $x \neq -\frac{1}{2}$

8. All real numbers x such that $x \leq 6$

10. $(x + 1), \ x \neq -1$ **12.** $\frac{3}{10y^3}$

14. $\frac{2x^2}{x - 1}, \ y \neq 0$ **16.** $\frac{9x}{2}, \ x \neq -1$

18. $-4, \ x \neq 3$ **20.** $-(x + 5), \ x \neq 5$

22. $\frac{x - 2}{x + 1}, \ x \neq -10$ **24.** $\frac{3 - x}{(x + 10)(x + 1)}$

26. $\frac{1}{x + 1}, \ x \neq \pm 3$ **28.** $\frac{y(y - 3)}{y^2 - y + 1}, \ y \neq -1$

30.

x	0	1	2	3	4	5	6
$\dfrac{x - 3}{x^2 - x - 6}$	$\frac{1}{2}$	$\frac{1}{3}$	$\frac{1}{4}$	Undef.	$\frac{1}{6}$	$\frac{1}{7}$	$\frac{1}{8}$
$\dfrac{1}{x + 2}$	$\frac{1}{2}$	$\frac{1}{3}$	$\frac{1}{4}$	$\frac{1}{5}$	$\frac{1}{6}$	$\frac{1}{7}$	$\frac{1}{8}$

The expressions are equivalent except at $x = 3$.

32. $x^2 + 25$ does not factor to $(x - 5)(x + 5)$.

34. $\frac{x + 5}{4(2x + 3)}$ **36.** $-\frac{x + 13}{5x^2}, \ x \neq 3$

38. $-\frac{8}{5}, \ y \neq -3, 4$ **40.** $\frac{2(y^2 + 2y + 4)}{y^2(y - 3)}, \ y \neq 2$

42. $\dfrac{x+2}{x-2}$, $x \neq 3$ **44.** $\dfrac{x}{x+3}$ **46.** $\dfrac{8-5x}{x-1}$

48. $\dfrac{2x+5}{x-5}$ **50.** $\dfrac{6(2x+3)}{(x-2)(x+1)(x+4)}$

52. $\dfrac{4x+1}{(x-1)(x+1)}$ **54.** $x^{-3}(x^8-5)$

56. $x^{-3/2}(5x^{13/2}-3)$ **58.** $-2x(x-5)^{-4}(x+5)$

60. $2x(8x^4-8x^3+2x^2-1)(2x-1)^{-1/2}$

62. $\dfrac{4x}{x+4}$, $x \neq 0, 4$ **64.** $\dfrac{x+1}{x-1}$, $x \neq 0, 1$

66. $\dfrac{1}{(x+h+1)(x+1)}$, $h \neq 0$ **68.** $-\dfrac{1}{t^2\sqrt{t^2+1}}$

70. $\dfrac{x^2-2}{x^3(1-x^2)^{1/2}}$ **72.** $\dfrac{-1}{\sqrt{z-3}+\sqrt{z}}$ **74.** $\dfrac{8}{15}t$

76. $\dfrac{7x}{16}, \dfrac{13x}{24}, \dfrac{31x}{48}$ **78.** $\dfrac{8(x+2)}{(x+4)^2}$

80. (a) $r = 7.27\%$ (b) $\dfrac{288(NM-P)}{N(12P+NM)}$; 7.27%

82. (a)

Year	1992	1993	1994	1995	1996	1997
Gold	$345	$364	$383	$399	$404	$366
Silver	$4.10	$5.14	$6.17	$5.60	$5.29	$5.13

The models provide a reasonable estimate for the actual prices.

(b) $\dfrac{\text{Price of gold}}{\text{Price of silver}} =$

$$\dfrac{(-38.5t+310.1)(0.09t^2-0.58t+1)}{(0.007t^2-0.176t+1)(0.42t^2-2.56t+4.26)}$$

Year	1992	1993	1994	1995	1996	1997
Ratio	84.10	70.73	62.04	71.19	76.30	71.36

Gold became less expensive compared to silver.

84. False. $\dfrac{x^2-3x+2}{x-1}$ is undefined for $x = 1$.

86. Completely factor the numerator and denominator to determine if they have any common factors.

Section P.5   *(page 54)*

2.
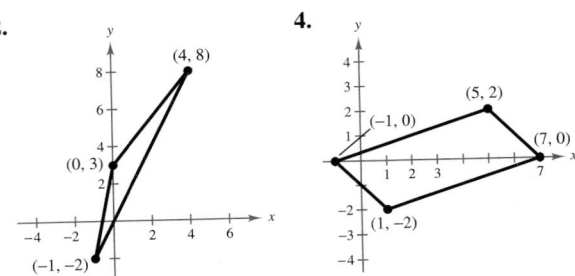

4.

6. A: $(1.5, -4)$; B: $(0, -2)$; C: $(-3, 2.5)$; D: $(-6, 0)$

8. A: $(-4, 0)$; B: $(-5, -5)$; C: $(3.5, -2.5)$; D: $(2, 0)$

10. $(4, -8)$ **12.** $(-12, 0)$ **14.** Quadrant III

16. Quadrant I   **18.** Quadrants I and IV

20. Quadrant III   **22.** Quadrants II and IV

24. $(3, 3)$, $(1, 0)$, $(3, -3)$, $(5, 0)$

26. 7   **28.** 10   **30.** 17

32. (a)
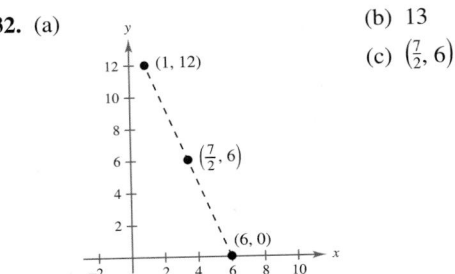
(b) 13
(c) $\left(\dfrac{7}{2}, 6\right)$

34. (a)
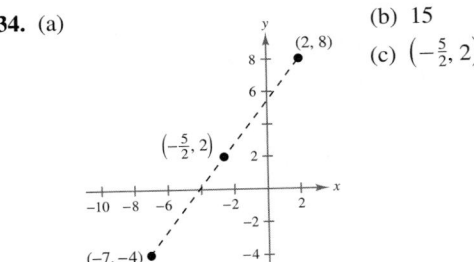
(b) 15
(c) $\left(-\dfrac{5}{2}, 2\right)$

36. (a)
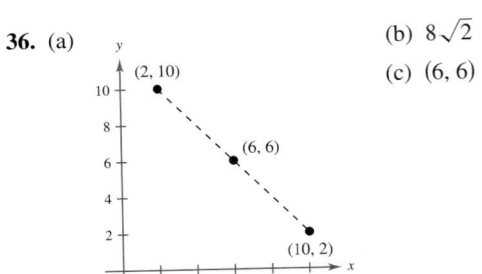
(b) $8\sqrt{2}$
(c) $(6, 6)$

38. (a)

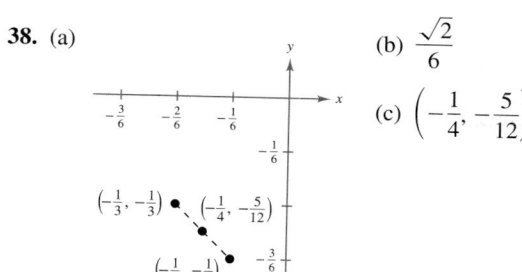

(b) $\dfrac{\sqrt{2}}{6}$

(c) $\left(-\dfrac{1}{4}, -\dfrac{5}{12}\right)$

40. (a)

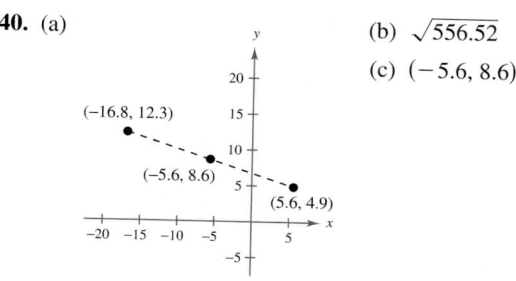

(b) $\sqrt{556.52}$

(c) $(-5.6, 8.6)$

42. (a)

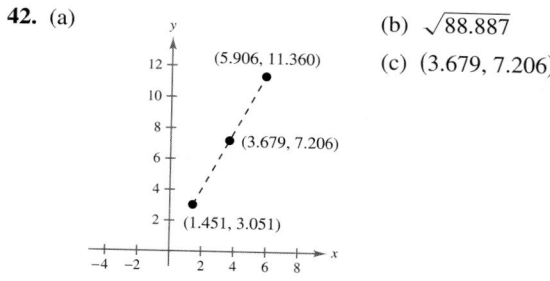

(b) $\sqrt{88.887}$

(c) $(3.679, 7.206)$

44. (a) 5, 12, 13   (b) $5^2 + 12^2 = 13^2$

46. (a) 4, 7, $\sqrt{65}$ (b) $4^2 + 7^2 = \left(\sqrt{65}\right)^2$

48. \$4,925,000   **50.** $\left(\sqrt{29}\right)^2 + \left(\sqrt{29}\right)^2 = \left(\sqrt{58}\right)^2$

52. Opposite sides have equal lengths of $3\sqrt{5}$ and $\sqrt{10}$.

54. $\left(\dfrac{3x_1 + x_2}{4}, \dfrac{3y_1 + y_2}{4}\right), \left(\dfrac{x_1 + x_2}{2}, \dfrac{y_1 + y_2}{2}\right),$

$\left(\dfrac{x_1 + 3x_2}{4}, \dfrac{y_1 + 3y_2}{4}\right)$

(a) $\left(\dfrac{7}{4}, -\dfrac{7}{4}\right), \left(\dfrac{5}{2}, -\dfrac{3}{2}\right), \left(\dfrac{13}{4}, -\dfrac{5}{4}\right)$

(b) $\left(-\dfrac{3}{2}, -\dfrac{9}{4}\right), \left(-1, -\dfrac{3}{2}\right), \left(-\dfrac{1}{2}, -\dfrac{3}{4}\right)$

56. $x^2 + y^2 = 25$ **58.** $x^2 + \left(y - \dfrac{1}{3}\right)^2 = \dfrac{1}{9}$

60. $(x - 3)^2 + (y + 2)^2 = 25$ **62.** $x^2 + y^2 = 17$

64. Center: $(0, 0)$;
Radius = 4

66. Center: $(0, 1)$;
Radius = 2

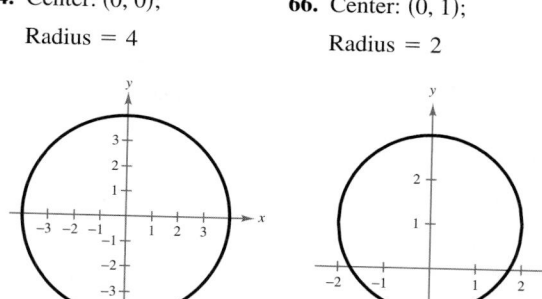

68. Center: $\left(\dfrac{2}{3}, -\dfrac{1}{4}\right)$;
Radius = $\dfrac{5}{3}$

70.

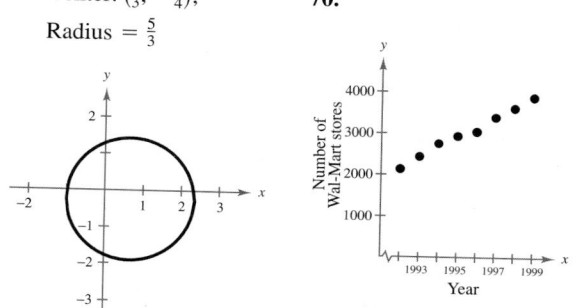

72. \$0.26   **74.** (a) \$250,000   (b) \$750,000

76. No. There are many variables that will affect the final exam score.

78.

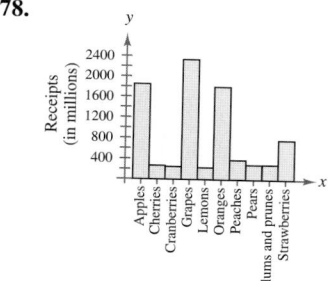

80.

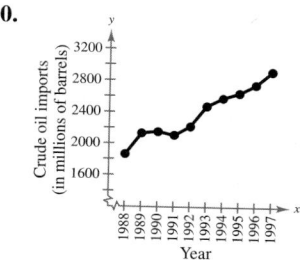

The graph shows crude oil imports on the rise from 1991 to 1997.

82. (a)

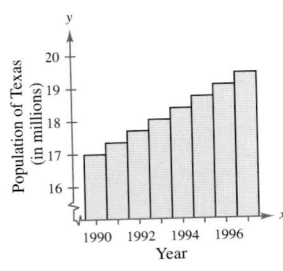

Exceeded 19 million in 1995

(b) $19 = 0.35x + 16.99$, $x \approx 5.74 \Rightarrow 1995$

84. $5\sqrt{74} \approx 43$ yards

86. (a)

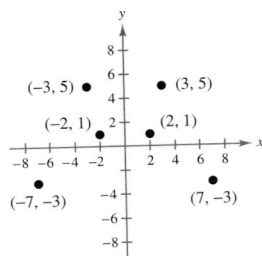

The points are reflected through the y-axis.

(b)

The points are reflected through the x-axis.

(c)

The points are rotated $180°$ about the origin.

88. $1002.6 million   **90.** False; 15 times

92. False; It could be a rhombus.

94. No. Depends on the magnitude of the quantities measured

Review Exercises   *(page 60)*

2. (a) None   (b) $-22, 0$ (c) $-22, -\frac{10}{3}, 0, 5.2, \frac{3}{7}$

(d) $\sqrt{15}$

4. $0.36 < 0.\overline{714285}$

6. The set consists of all real numbers greater than 1.

8. 114   **10.** $|x - 25| \le 10$ **12.** $\left|y - \frac{1}{2}\right| > 2$

14. (a) 50   (b) 6

16. (a) 2   (b) Division by zero is undefined.

18. Multiplicative Inverse Property

20. Additive Identity Property   **22.** $\frac{17}{24}$ **24.** $\frac{5}{12}$

26. $\frac{54}{x}$ **28.** (a) y^{-2} (b) $\frac{8}{15}(b - 3)^3$, $b \ne 3$

30. (a) $\frac{y}{xy + 1}$, $y \ne 0$ (b) x^{-4}, $y \ne 0$

32. 3.048×10^{-1} **34.** 0.00274 **36.** 3

38. $2x\sqrt[5]{2x}$ **40.** $\frac{5}{6}$ **42.** $\frac{5|x|\sqrt{3}}{y^2}$ **44.** $40\sqrt{2}$

46. $-72\sqrt{y}$ **48.** $|x|\sqrt{14}$ **50.** $2 + \sqrt{3}$

52. $\frac{5}{2\sqrt{5}}$ **54.** $16^{1/2}$ **56.** 729   **58.** $6x^{9/10}$

60. $-2x^5 - x^4 + 3x^3 + 15x^2 + 5$

62. $-3x^2 - 7x + 1$ **64.** $2x^3 - x^2 + 3x - 9$

66. $x^5 - 2x^4 + x^3 - x^2 + 2x - 1$

68. $y^6 + y^4 - y^3 - y$ **70.** $9x^2 - 48x + 64$

72. $x^3 - 12x^2 + 48x - 64$ **74.** 41

76. $(x + 3)(x + 5) = 5(x + 3) + x(x + 3)$

Distributive Property

78. $7(x + 5)$ **80.** $x(x^2 - 1) = x(x - 1)(x + 1)$

82. $2x(x^2 + 9x - 2)$

84. (a)

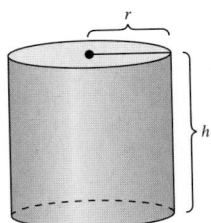

$2\pi r^2 =$ area of top and bottom

$2\pi rh =$ surface area of lateral face

(b) $S = 2\pi r(r + h)$

86. $(x - 13)(x + 13)$ **88.** $(x + 6)(x^2 - 6x + 36)$

90. $(x - 9)(x + 3)$ **92.** $(2x + 1)(x + 10)$

94. $(x - 4)(x^2 - 3)$ **96.** $(4x - 3)(x^2 + 5)$

98. All real numbers   **100.** All real numbers $x \ne \frac{3}{2}$

102. $\dfrac{x}{x^2 + 7}$, $x \neq 0$ **104.** $\dfrac{x-6}{x+5}$, $x \neq -5$

106. $\dfrac{1}{x^2}$, $x \neq \pm 2$ **108.** $\dfrac{1}{5}x(5x-6)$, $x \neq 0, -\dfrac{3}{2}$

110. $\dfrac{x^3 - x + 3}{(x-1)(x+2)}$ **112.** $\dfrac{x+1}{x(x^2+1)}$

114. $-\dfrac{1}{xy(x+y)}$, $x \neq y$

116.

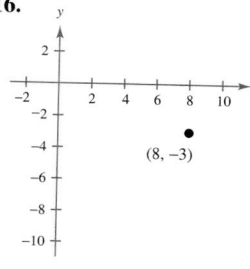

118.

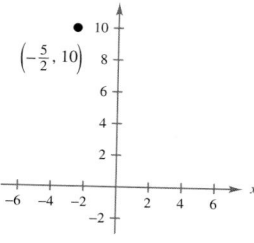

Quadrant IV   Quadrant II

120. Quadrant IV

122. (a)

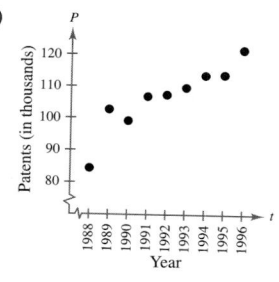

(b) The number of patents issued has increased fairly steadily since 1988.

124.

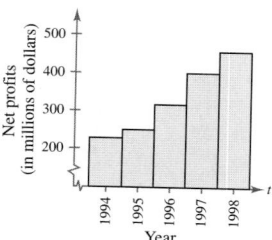

126.

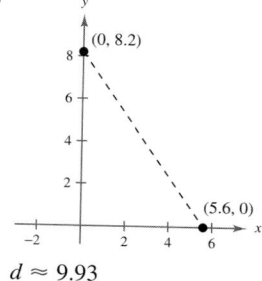

$d \approx 9.93$

128.

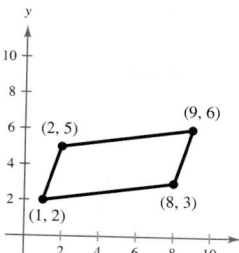

130.

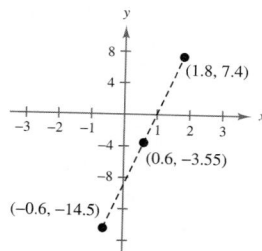

Opposite sides have equal lengths of $\sqrt{10}$ and $5\sqrt{2}$.

Midpoint $= (0.6, -3.55)$

132. $(x-3)^2 + (y+1)^2 = 68$

134. False. $\dfrac{x^3 - 1}{x - 1}$ is undefined at $x = 1$.

136. False. Factors only for even values of n.

138. Didn't distribute $-x^2$ correctly.
$$-x^2(-x^2 + 3) = x^4 - 3x^2$$

140. Answer is not negative. $(-x)^6 = x^6$

142. Can't remove 10 from the radical. $\sqrt{10x} = \sqrt{10}\sqrt{x}$

Chapter 1

Section 1.1   *(page 75)*

2. (a) Yes   (b) No   **4.** (a) No   (b) Yes

6. (a) No   (b) Yes   **8.** (a) Yes   (b) No

10.

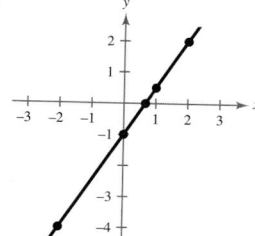

x	y
-2	-4
0	-1
$\frac{2}{3}$	0
1	$\frac{1}{2}$
2	2

12.

x	y
-2	0
-1	3
0	4
1	3
2	0

14.

x	1	2	5	10	17
y	0	1	2	3	4

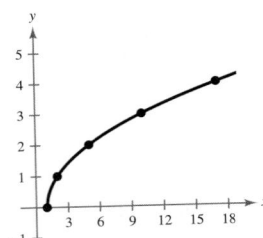

16. (a)

x	-2	-1	0	1	2
y	$-\frac{48}{5}$	-3	Undef.	3	$\frac{48}{5}$

(b)

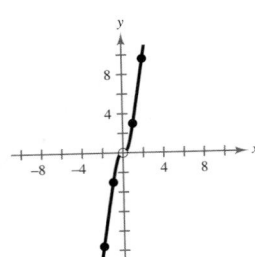

(c)

x	5	10	20	40
y	28.8	59.41	119.7	239.85

y approaches $6x$ as x increases. No. Positive x-values give a positive number divided by a positive number.

18. (c)   **20.** (e)   **22.** (b)

24. 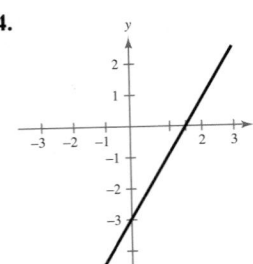   **26.**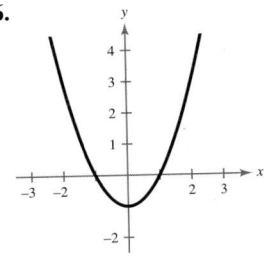

28. 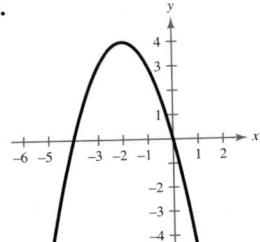   **30.**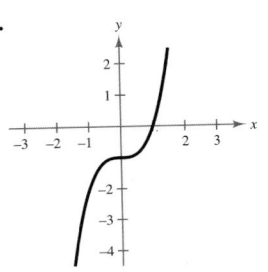

32. 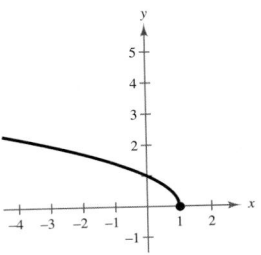   **34.**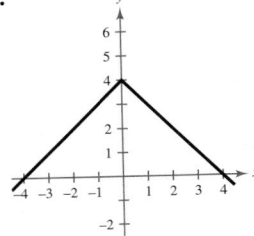

36.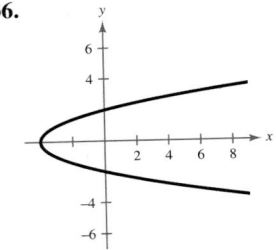

38.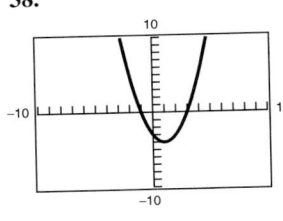

Intercepts:
$(-1, 0), (3, 0), (0, -3)$

40.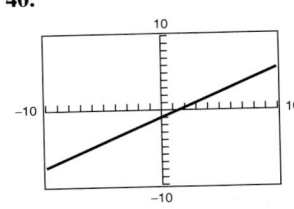

Intercepts: $\left(\frac{3}{2}, 0\right), (0, -1)$

42.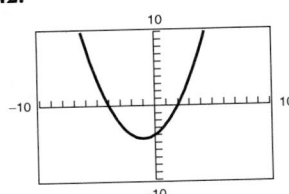

Intercepts:
$(2, 0), (-4, 0), (0, -4)$

44.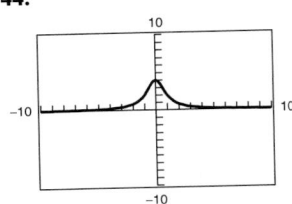

Intercept: $(0, 4)$

46.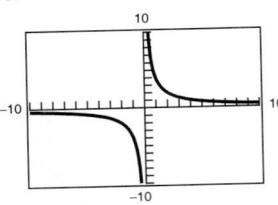

No intercepts

48.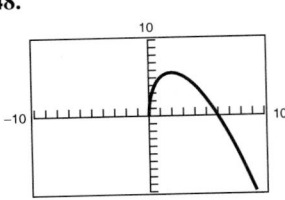

Intercepts: $(0, 0), (6, 0)$

50.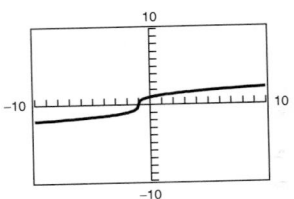

Intercepts: $(-1, 0), (0, 1)$

52.

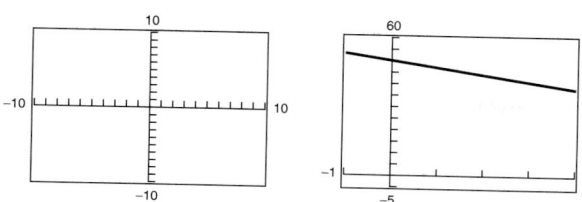

The specified setting gives a more complete graph.

54.

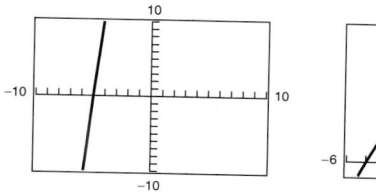 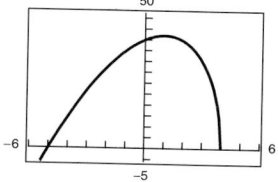

The specified setting gives a more complete graph.

56.

Xmin = -3
Xmax = 5
Xscl = 1
Ymin = -3
Ymax = 5
Yscl = 1

58.

Xmin = -40
Xmax = 40
Xscl = 10
Ymin = -40
Ymax = 40
Yscl = 10

60. $y_1 = 2 + \sqrt{16 - (x - 1)^2}$
$y_2 = 2 - \sqrt{16 - (x - 1)^2}$

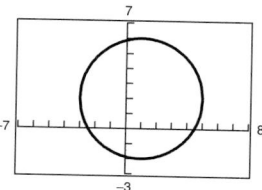

62. $y_1 = 1 + \sqrt{25 - (x - 3)^2}$
$y_2 = 1 - \sqrt{25 - (x - 3)^2}$

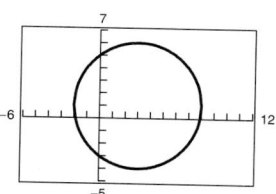

64. The graphs are identical. Associative Property of Addition

66. The graphs appear identical except y_1 has a hole at $x = 3$.
Multiplicative Inverse Property

68.

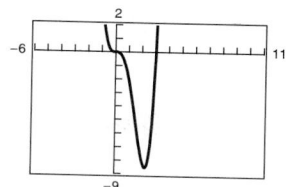

(a) $(2.25, -8.54)$ (b) $(-1.63, 20), (3.48, 20)$

70.

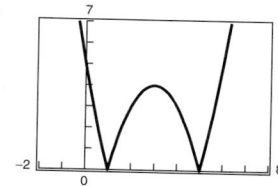

(a) $(2, 3)$

(b) $(0.65, 1.5), (1.42, 1.5), (4.58, 1.5), (5.35, 1.5)$

72. (a)

Xmin = 0
Xmax = 8
Xscl = 1
Ymin = 2400
Ymax = 8200
Yscl = 500

(b)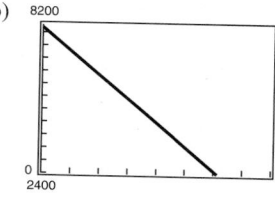

(c) $t = 2.75$ years   (d) $2990.50

74. (a) 1975: $2907; 1992: $13,779   (b) 1988
(c) 2002: $27,142; 2004: $30,589

76. (a)

t	0	1	2	3	4	5	6
y	0.46	0.56	0.65	0.74	0.83	0.92	1.01

1994

(b)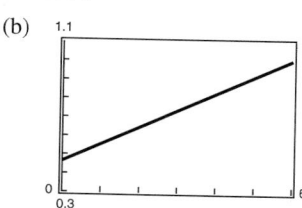

(c) 1994   (d) 0.919   (e) 1.37

78. False. It can also have two intercepts.

80. -2 and 5. a is one and b is the other.   **82.** $27\sqrt{2}$

84. 7^7 **86.** $2x^2 + 8x + 11$ **88.** $2x^2 - 5x - 63$

Section 1.2   *(page 87)*

2. (a) L_2 (b) L_1 (c) L_3

4.

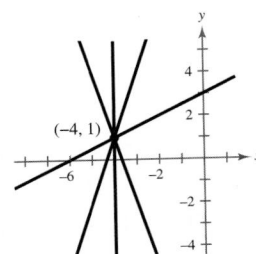

6. $\frac{5}{2}$ **8.** -1 **10.** $\frac{2}{3}$

28. (a) Slope undefined; No intercept

(b)

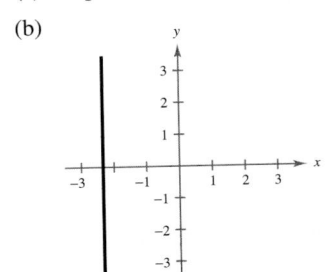

12. $m = -4$

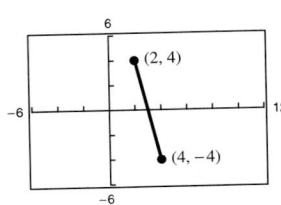

14. $m = 2$

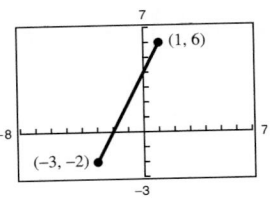

30. (a) $m = 0$; Intercept: $\left(0, -\frac{11}{8}\right)$

(b)

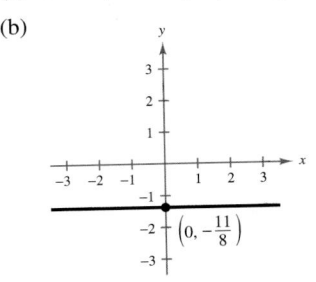

16. $(-4, 0), (-4, 3), (-4, 5)$

18. $(-1, -7), (-2, -5), (-5, 1)$

20. $(-3, -5), (-5, -4), (-7, -3)$

22. Neither parallel nor perpendicular

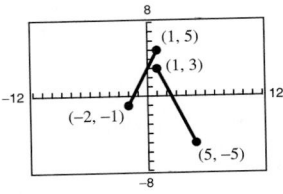

32. (a) $m = 1$; Intercept: $(0, -10)$

(b)

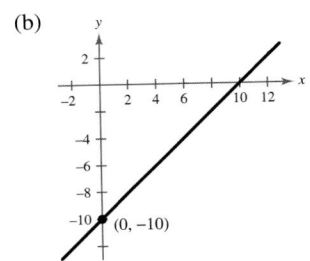

24. Perpendicular

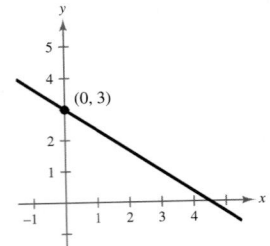

26. (a) $m = -\frac{2}{3}$; Intercept: $(0, 3)$

(b)

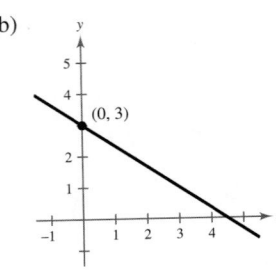

34. $x + y - 10 = 0$

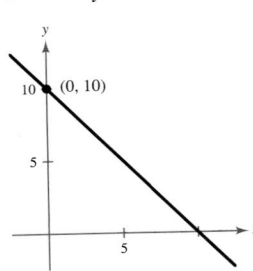

36. $4x - y = 0$

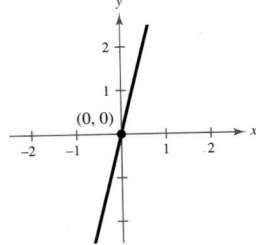

38. $3x - 4y - 14 = 0$

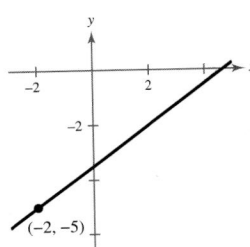

40. $y - 4 = 0$

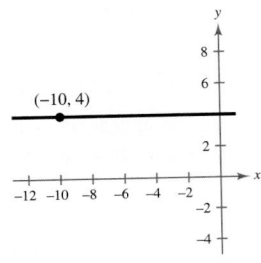

42. $10x + 4y + 11 = 0$

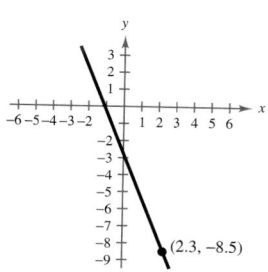

44. $7x - 8y - 4 = 0$

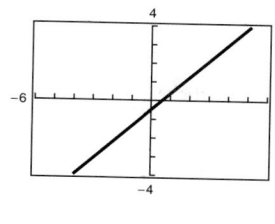

46. $y - 4 = 0$

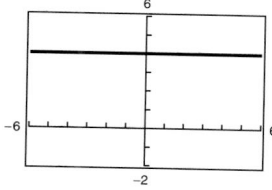

48. $x + 3y - 4 = 0$

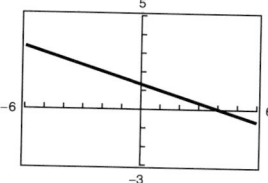

50. $12x + 100y - 159 = 0$

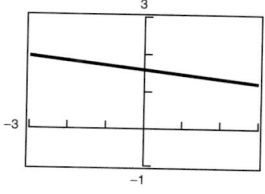

52. $3x + 10y + 18 = 0$

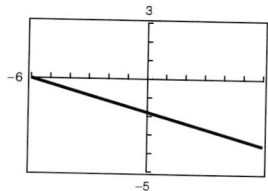

54.

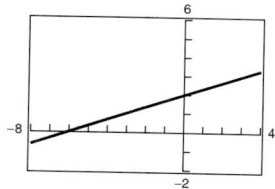

x- and y-intercepts

56. $4x + 5y + 20 = 0$

58. $16x + 15y - 12 = 0$

60.

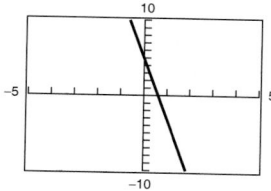 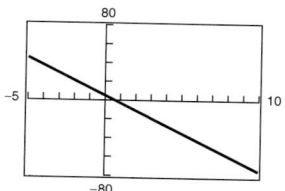

The first setting gives a better view of the intercepts.

62.

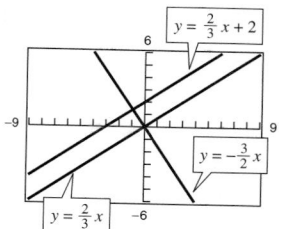

$y = \frac{2}{3}x$ is parallel to $y = \frac{2}{3}x + 2$.

$y = -\frac{3}{2}x$ is perpendicular to $y = \frac{2}{3}x$ and $y = \frac{2}{3}x + 2$.

64.

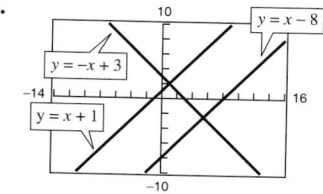

$y = x - 8$ is parallel to $y = x + 1$.

$y = -x + 3$ is perpendicular to $y = x - 8$ and $y = x + 1$.

66. (a) $x + y + 1 = 0$ (b) $x - y + 5 = 0$

68. (a) $40x + 24y - 53 = 0$ (b) $24x - 40y + 9 = 0$

70. (a) $30x + 10y + 131 = 0$ (b) $10x - 30y - 3 = 0$

72. $20x - 6y + 37 = 0$

74. (a) Increase of 400 units   (b) Increase of 100 units

(c) No change

76. (a) Greatest increase: 1996; Smallest increase: 1988

(b) $73x - 1000y + 297 = 0$

(c) Average increase per year from 1988 to 1998

(d) $1.32. Answers will vary.

78. 12 feet   **80.** $4.50t - V + 151.50 = 0$

82. $5600t + V - 250,600 = 0$

84. (c). Slope $= 1.5$. Pay increases by $1.50 per hour for each unit produced.

86. (d). Slope $= -100$. Value decreases by $100 per year.

88.

C	$-17.8°$	$-10°$	$10°$	$20°$	$32.2°$	$177°$
F	$0°$	$14°$	$50°$	$68°$	$90°$	$350.6°$

90. 3014 students

92. (a) $V = 25,000 - 2300t$

(b)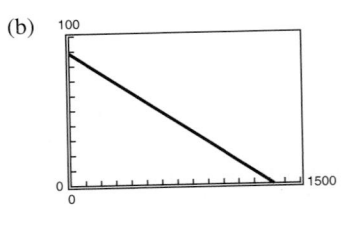

25,000

0

0   10

T	0	1	2	3	4	5
V	25,000	22,700	20,400	18,100	15,800	13,500

T	6	7	8	9	10
V	11,200	8900	6600	4300	2000

94. (a) $x = 50 - \dfrac{p - 580}{15}$

(b)

100

0

0   1500

45

(c) 49

96. False. The slopes $\left(\frac{2}{7} \text{ and } -\frac{11}{7}\right)$ are not equal.

98. Use the slope formula to show that $\overline{AB}$ is perpendicular to $\overline{AC}$.

100. Yes. The rate of change remains the same on a line.

102. Yes. $x + 20$ **104.** No   **106.** No

108. $(x - 9)(x + 3)$ **110.** $(2x - 5)(x + 8)$

112. $x^2 + y^2 = 81$ **114.** $(x - 10)^2 + (y - 1)^2 = 169$

Section 1.3   *(page 100)*

2. No   **4.** Yes   **6.** No. 0 and 1 both have two outputs.

8. Yes. There is one output for each input.

10. (a) Not a function. c matches with both 2 and 3.

(b) Function. Each value from A matches with only one value from B.

(c) Not a function. It is a function from B to A.

(d) Function. Each value from A matches with only one value from B.

12. $f(1994) = 16$ million   **14.** Not a function

16. Not a function   **18.** Function   **20.** Function

22. Not a function   **24.** Function

26. (a) 0

(b) 15

(c) $t^2 - 1$

(d) $x^2 + 2cx + c^2 - 2x - 2c$

28. (a) 7   (b) 0   (c) $1 - 3s$

30. (a) 36π (b) $\dfrac{9\pi}{2}$ (c) $\dfrac{32\pi r^3}{3}$

32. (a) 2   (b) 5   (c) $\sqrt{x} + 2$

34. (a) $\dfrac{11}{4}$ (b) Undefined   (c) $\dfrac{2x^2 + 3}{x^2}$

36. (a) 6   (b) 6   (c) $x^2 + 4$

38. (a) 6   (b) 3   (c) 10

40.

x	3	4	5	6	7
$g(x)$	0	1	$\sqrt{2}$	$\sqrt{3}$	2

42.

x	0	1	$\frac{3}{2}$	$\frac{5}{2}$	4
$f(s)$	-1	-1	-1	1	1

44.

x	1	2	3	4	5
$h(x)$	8	5	0	1	2

46. $-\dfrac{1}{5}$ **48.** $\pm 2\sqrt{3}$ **50.** $0, \pm 1$ **52.** $0, \frac{1}{4}$

54. $-1, 2$ **56.** $0, \pm 2$ **58.** All real numbers x

60. All real numbers $y \neq -5$ **62.** All real numbers t

64. All real numbers x except $-3 < x < 0$

66. All real numbers x except $x = 0, 2$

68. All real numbers x such that $x > -6$

70. All real numbers x except $-3 \leq x \leq 3$

72. $\left\{\left(-2, -\frac{4}{5}\right), (-1, -1), (0, 0), (1, 1), \left(2, \frac{4}{5}\right)\right\}$

74. $\{(-2, 1), (-1, 0), (0, 1), (1, 2), (2, 3)\}$

76. $f(x) = \frac{1}{4}x$; $c = \frac{1}{4}$ **78.** $h(x) = 3\sqrt{|x|}$; $c = 3$

80. $3, h \neq 0$ **82.** $-h - 5, h \neq 0$

84. $3x^2 + 3hx + h^2 + 1, h \neq 0$ **86.** $-\dfrac{1}{2(x + 1)}, x \neq 7$

88. $A = \dfrac{\sqrt{3}}{4}s^2$ **90.** $A = \dfrac{\sqrt{3}}{3}h^2$

92. (a)

Units, x	Price, p	Profit, P
110	$90 - 10(0.15)$	$110[90 - 10(0.15)] - 110(60) = 3135$
120	$90 - 20(0.15)$	$120[90 - 20(0.15)] - 120(60) = 3240$
130	$90 - 30(0.15)$	$130[90 - 30(0.15)] - 130(60) = 3315$
140	$90 - 40(0.15)$	$140[90 - 40(0.15)] - 140(60) = 3360$
150	$90 - 50(0.15)$	$150[90 - 50(0.15)] - 150(60) = 3375$
160	$90 - 60(0.15)$	$160[90 - 60(0.15)] - 160(60) = 3360$

The maximum profit is $3375.

(b) $P = 45x - 0.15x^2$, $x > 100$

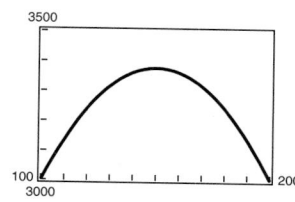

(c) $P(120) = \$3240$, $P(130) = \$3315$, $P(140) = \$3360$

94. $A = 2xy = 2x\sqrt{36 - x^2}$, $0 < x < 6$

96.

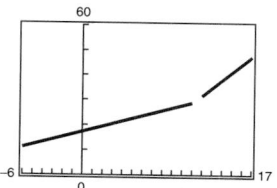

1978: \$15,198, 1988: \$25,558, 1993: \$34,518,
1997: \$47,366

98. (a) $C = 0.95x + 6000$ (b) $\overline{C} = \dfrac{0.95x + 6000}{x}$

100.

y	5	10	20	30	40
$F(y)$	26,474	149,760	847,170	2,334,527	4,792,320

(a) Each time the depth is doubled, the force increases more than 2 times.

(b)

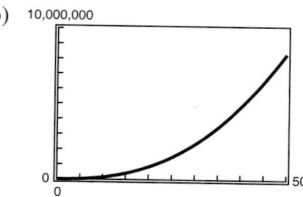

```
Xmin = 0
Xmax = 50
Xscl = 10
Ymin = 0
Ymax = 5,000,000
Yscl = 500,000
```

(c) Depth ≈ 21.37 feet.
Use the *trace* and *zoom* features on a graphing utility.

102. (a) 28

(b) -17. Average decrease per year in the population

(c)

t	1988	1989	1990	1991
N	9.0	19.8	43.9	53.6

t	1992	1993	1994	1995
N	30.9	16.7	10.2	6.9

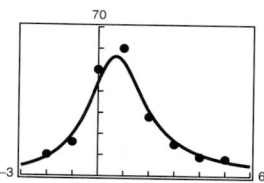

104. True

106. The domain is the set of input values of a function. The range is the set of output values.

108. $\dfrac{12x + 20}{x + 2}$ **110.** $\dfrac{(x + 6)(x + 10)}{5(x + 3)}$, $x \neq 0, \dfrac{1}{2}$

112.   **114.**

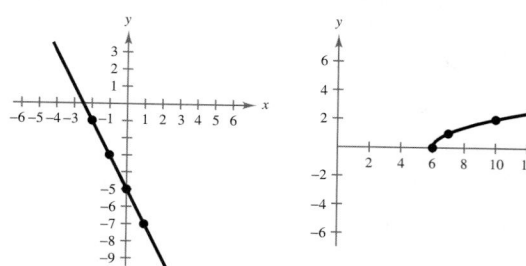

Section 1.4   *(page 114)*

2. Domain: $(-\infty, \infty)$
Range: $(-\infty, \infty)$

4. Domain: $[-4, 4]$
Range: $[0, 4]$

6. Domain: $(-\infty, \infty)$
Range: $(-\infty, 0]$

8.

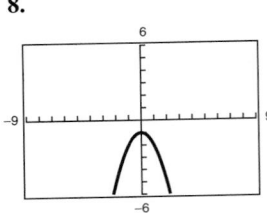

Domain: $(-\infty, \infty)$

Range: $(-\infty, -1]$

10.

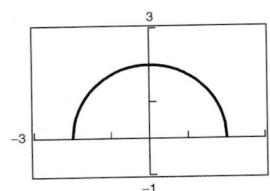

Domain: $[-2, 2]$

Range: $[0, 2]$

Domain: $(-\infty, \infty)$

Range: $(-\infty, 0]$

12.

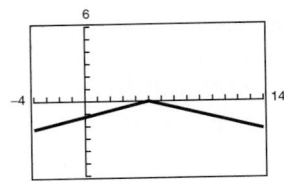

14. Function. Graph the given function over the window shown in the figure.

16. Not a function. Solve for y and graph the resulting two functions.

18. Not a function. Solve for y and graph the resulting two functions.

20. (a) Decreasing on $(-\infty, 2)$; Increasing on $(2, \infty)$

(b) Neither even nor odd

22. (a) Decreasing on $(-\infty, -1)$; Increasing on $(1, \infty)$

(b) Even function

24. (a)

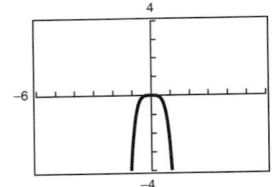

(b) Increasing on $(-\infty, 0)$

Decreasing on $(0, \infty)$

(c) Even function

26. (a)

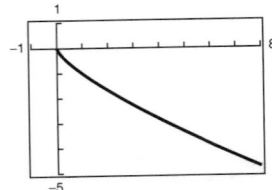

(b) Decreasing on $(0, \infty)$

(c) Neither odd nor even

28. (a)

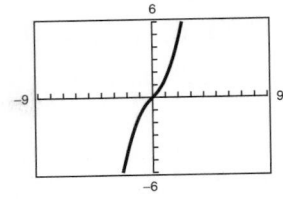

(b) Increasing on $(-\infty, \infty)$

(c) Odd function

30. (a)

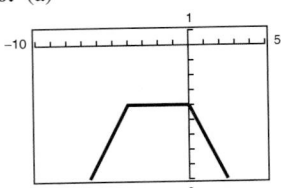

(b) Increasing on $(-\infty, -4)$, constant on $(-4, -1)$, decreasing on $(-1, \infty)$

(c) Neither even nor odd

32.

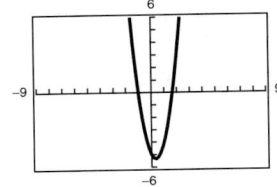

Relative minimum: $(0.33, -5.33)$

34.

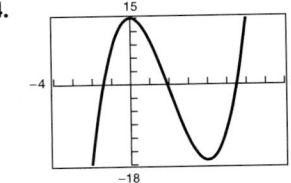

Relative minimum: $(4, -17)$

Relative maximum: $(0, 15)$

36.

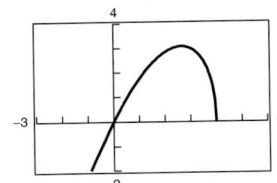

Maximum: $(2.67, 3.08)$

38. (a) Answers will vary.

(b) Relative minimum: $(0, -12)$

(c) Answers will vary.

40. (a) Answers will vary.

(b) Relative minimum: $(-1.53, -7.13)$

Relative maximum: $(1.53, 7.13)$

(c) Answers will vary.

42. (a) Answers will vary. (b) Relative minimum: $(0, 1)$

(c) Answers will vary.

44.

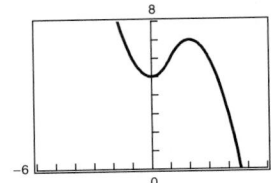

46.

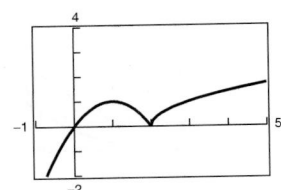

48. Even function   **50.** Neither even nor odd

52. Neither even nor odd   **54.** Neither even nor odd

56. (a) $\left(\frac{5}{3}, -7\right)$ (b) $\left(\frac{5}{3}, 7\right)$

58. (a) $(-5, -1)$ (b) $(-5, 1)$

60. (a) $(-2a, 2c)$ (b) $(-2a, -2c)$

62. Even function   **64.** Neither even nor odd

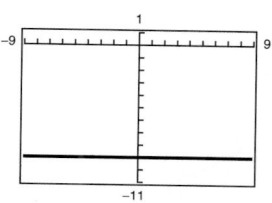   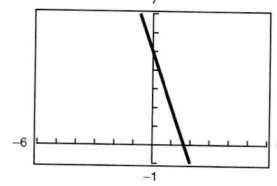

66. Even function   **68.** Neither even nor odd

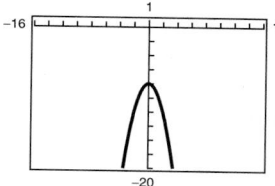   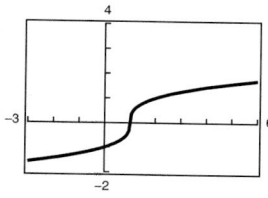

70. Neither even nor odd   **72.** Neither even nor odd

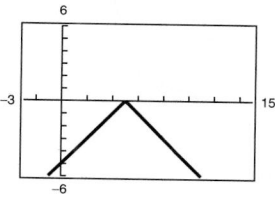   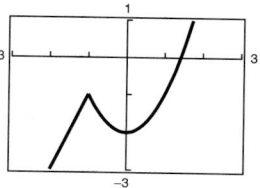

74. $\left[-\frac{1}{2}, \infty\right)$ **76.** $(-\infty, 0], [4, \infty)$

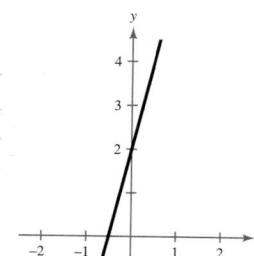   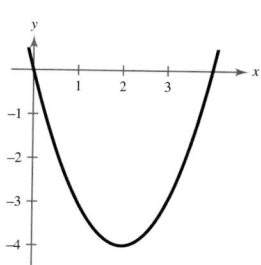

78. $(-\infty, \infty)$ **80.** $x = 3$

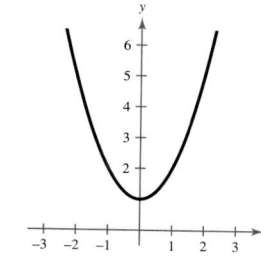   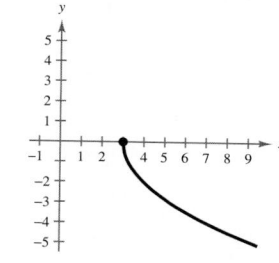

82. $(-\infty, \infty)$ **84.**

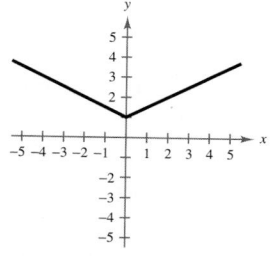   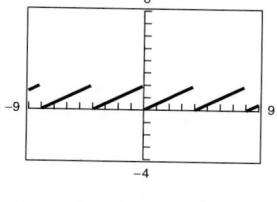

Domain: $(-\infty, \infty)$

Range: $[0, 2)$

Sawtooth pattern

86.

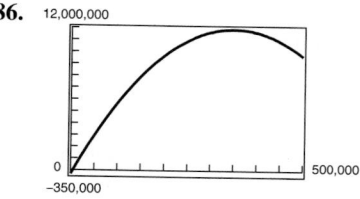

350,000 units

88. $C = 9.80 + 2.50[\![x]\!], \; x > 0$

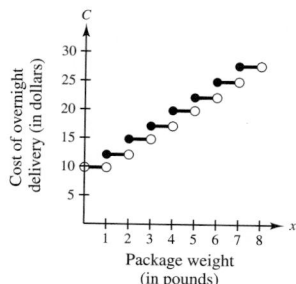

90. $h = 3 - 4x + x^2, \; 0 \le x \le 1$

92. $h = 2 - x^{1/3}, \; 0 \le x \le 8$

94. $L = 2 - \sqrt[3]{2y}, \; 0 \le y \le 4$

96.

Interval	Intake Pipe	Drain Pipe 1	Drain Pipe 2
$[0, 5]$	Open	Closed	Closed
$[5, 10]$	Open	Open	Closed
$[10, 20]$	Closed	Closed	Closed
$[20, 30]$	Closed	Closed	Open
$[30, 40]$	Open	Open	Open
$[40, 45]$	Open	Closed	Open
$[45, 50]$	Open	Open	Open
$[50, 60]$	Open	Open	Closed

98. False. If (x, y) is on the graph of an odd function, then $(-x, -y)$ is also. This is not possible for a domain of $(0, \infty)$.

100. If $y = a_{2n}x^{2n} + a_{2n-2}x^{2n-2} + \cdots + a_2x^2 + a_0$, each exponent is even. Then

$$f(-x) = a_{2n}x^{2n} + a_{2n-2}x^{2n-2} + \cdots + a_2x^2 + a_0$$

which is equal to $f(x)$. Therefore, by definition, the original function is even.

102. Yes. To check whether x is a function of y, determine whether any horizontal line can be drawn to intersect the graph more than once.

104. (a) $d = 4\sqrt{5}$ (b) Midpoint: $(2, 5)$

106. (a) $d = \sqrt{41}$ (b) Midpoint: $\left(\frac{1}{2}, \frac{3}{2}\right)$

108. (a) 29   (b) -6 (c) $5x - 16$

110. (a) 0   (b) 36   (c) $6\sqrt{3}$ **112.** $h + 4, \ h \neq 0$

Section 1.5   *(page 124)*

2.

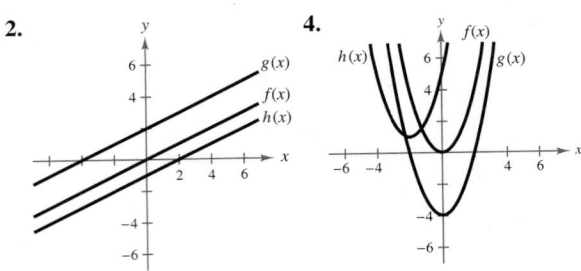

4.

6.

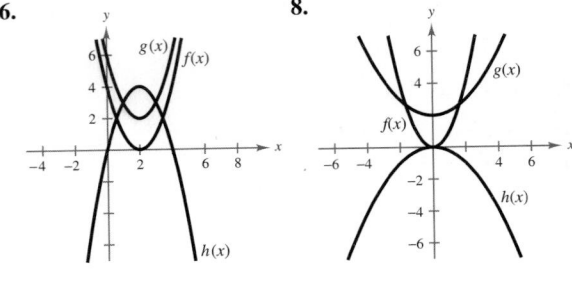

8.

10.

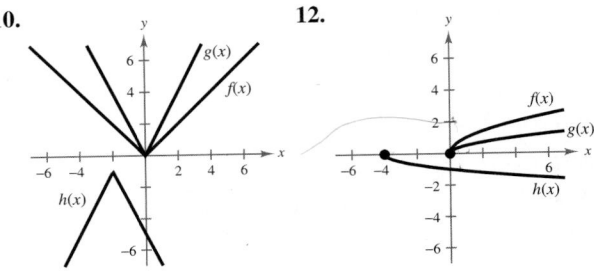

12.

14. (a)

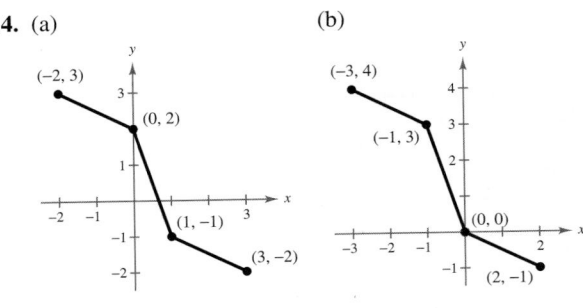

(b)

(c)

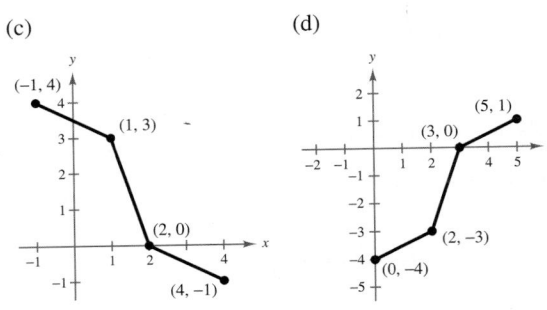

(d)

(e)

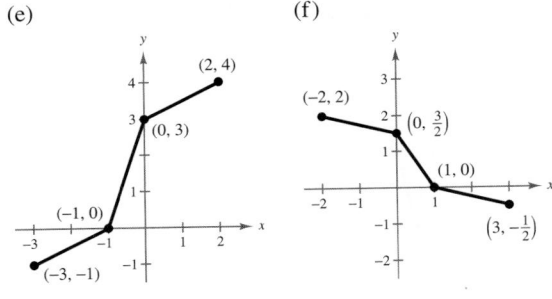

(f)

16. Vertical shift of $y = x$

$$y = x + 3$$

18. Constant function: $y = -8$

20. Horizontal shift of $y = \sqrt{x}$ followed by a reflection in the y-axis

$$y = \sqrt{3 - x}$$

22. Horizontal shift of $y = |x|$, followed by a reflection in the x-axis, followed by a vertical shift

$$y = -|x - 4| - 3$$

24. Horizontal shift of $y = x^2$, followed by a reflection in the x-axis, followed by a vertical shift

$$y = -(x + 1)^2 + 1$$

26. Horizontal and vertical shifts of $y = x^3$

$$y = (x - 1)^3 + 1$$

28. Reflection in x-axis and vertical shift 1 unit downward

30. Horizontal shift 3 units to the left

32. Horizontal shift 3 units to the right followed by a reflection in the y-axis

34. Vertical shift 3 units downward

36. Reflection in y-axis (identical)   **38.** Vertical shrink

40. Horizontal shift 4 units to the right and reflection in x-axis

42. Horizontal shift 1 unit to the right, vertical stretch, reflection in x-axis, and vertical shift 3 units upward

44. Horizontal shift 2 units to the right and vertical stretch

46.

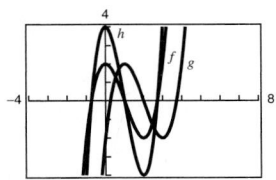

g is a horizontal shift and h is a vertical stretch.

48.

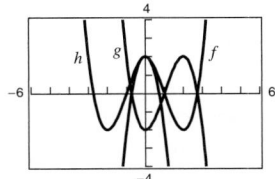

g is a reflection in the x-axis and h is a reflection in the y-axis.

50. $g(x) = (x - 2)^3 - 3(x - 2)^2 + 1$

52. (a) $f(x) = x^2$ (b) Horizontal shift 8 units to the right

(c)

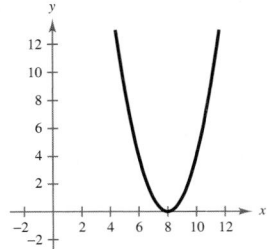

(d) $g(x) = f(x - 8)$

54. (a) $f(x) = x^2$

(b) Horizontal shift 10 units to the left, reflection in the x-axis, and vertical shift 5 units upward

(c)

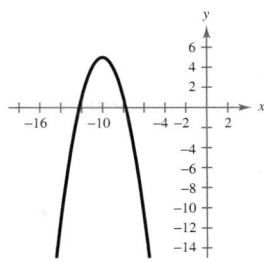

(d) $g(x) = -f(x + 10) + 5$

56. (a) $f(x) = x^2$

(b) Horizontal shift 2 units to the left, vertical shrink, reflection in x-axis, and vertical shift 2 units downward

(c)

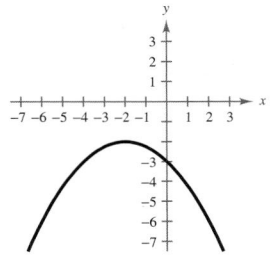

(d) $g(x) = -\frac{1}{4}f(x + 2) - 2$

58. (a) $f(x) = x^3$

(b) Reflection in x-axis and vertical shift 1 unit downward

(c)

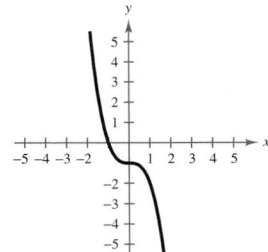

(d) $g(x) = -f(x) - 1$

60. (a) $f(x) = x^3$

(b) Horizontal shift 3 units to the left, reflection in x-axis, and vertical shift 10 units downward

(c)

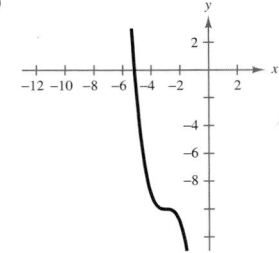

(d) $g(x) = -f(x + 3) - 10$

62. (a) $f(x) = x^3$

(b) Horizontal shift 1 unit to the left, vertical shrink, reflection in x-axis, and vertical shift 5 units downward

(c)

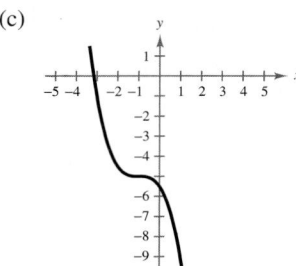

(d) $g(x) = -\frac{1}{2}f(x + 1) - 5$

64. (a) $f(x) = |x|$

(b) Horizontal shift 5 units to the left, reflection in x-axis, and vertical shift 6 units upward

(c)

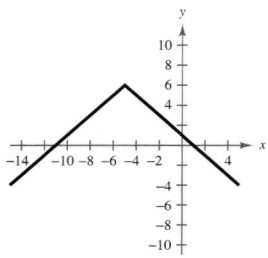

(d) $g(x) = 6 - f(x + 5)$

66. (a) $f(x) = |x|$

(b) Horizontal shift 3 units to the right and vertical shift 9 units upward

(c)

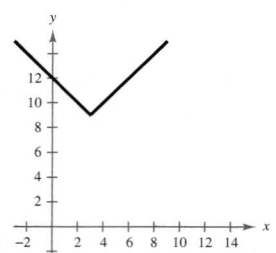

(d) $g(x) = f(x - 3) + 9 = f(-x + 3) + 9$

68. (a) $f(x) = |x|$

(b) Horizontal shift 2 units to the right, vertical shrink, and vertical shift 3 units downward

(c)

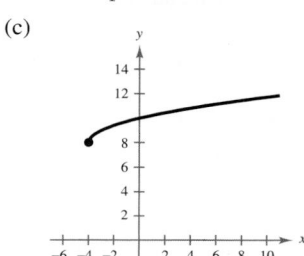

(d) $g(x) = \frac{1}{2}f(x - 2) - 3$

70. (a) $f(x) = \sqrt{x}$

(b) Horizontal shift 4 units to the left and vertical shift 8 units upward

(c)

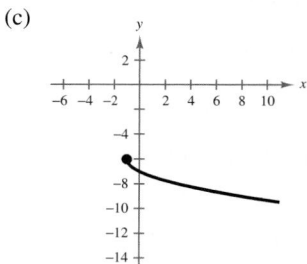

(d) $g(x) = f(x + 4) + 8$

72. (a) $f(x) = \sqrt{x}$

(b) Horizontal shift 1 unit to the left, reflection in x-axis, and vertical shift 6 units downward

(c)

(d) $g(x) = -f(x + 1) - 6$

74. (a) $f(x) = \sqrt{x}$

(b) Horizontal shift 3 units to the left, reflection in x-axis, vertical shrink, and vertical shift 1 unit downward

(c)

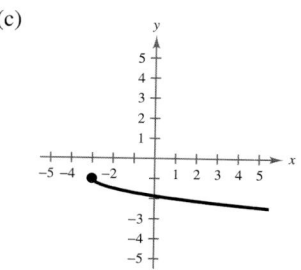

(d) $g(x) = -\frac{1}{2}f(x + 3) - 1$

76. (a)

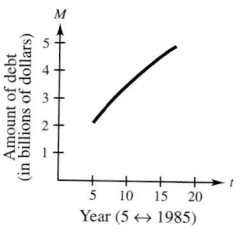

(b) $H(x/1.6) = 0.00078x^2 + 0.0031x - 0.029$

Vertical shrink

78. (a) M is a vertical stretch with a vertical shift 1.25 units downward.

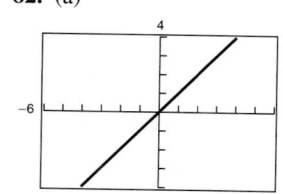

(b) $M(t + 10) = 1.5\sqrt{t + 10} - 1.25$

80. True. The absolute value function is an even function.

82. (a)   (b)

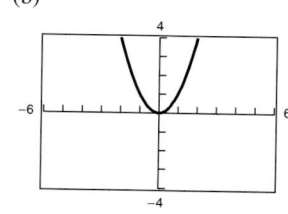

(c)   (d)

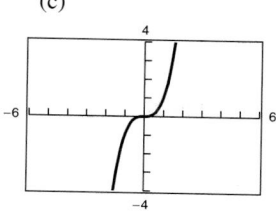
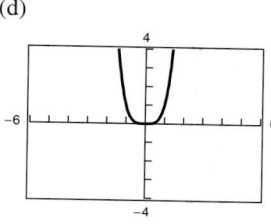

(e)   (f)

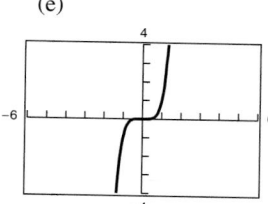
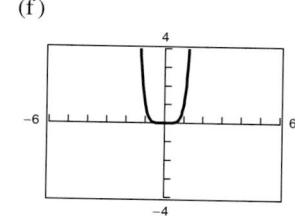

All the graphs pass through the origin. The graphs of the odd powers of x are symmetric with respect to the origin and the graphs of the even powers are symmetric with respect to the y-axis. As the powers increase, the graphs become flatter in the interval $-1 < x < 1$.

84.

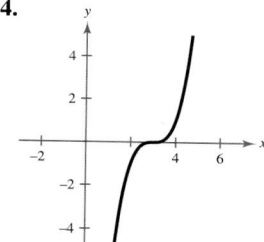

86.   **88.**

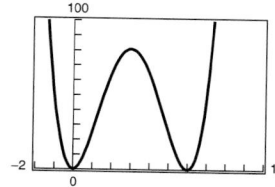
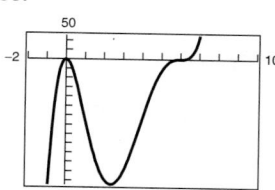

90. All real numbers x except $x = 9$

92. All real numbers x such that $-10 \le x \le 10$

94.

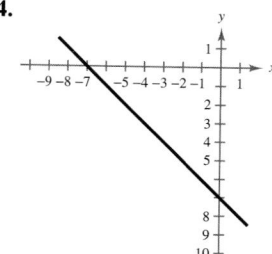

96.

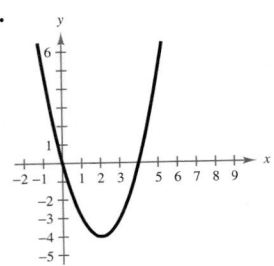

98.

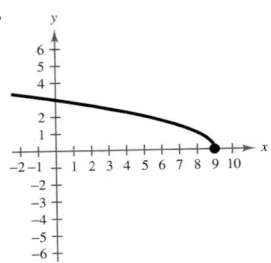

Section 1.6 *(page 134)*

2. (a) $x - 4$

(b) $3x - 6$

(c) $-2x^2 + 7x - 5$

(d) $\dfrac{2x - 5}{1 - x}$, $x \neq 1$

(e) $x \neq 1$

4. (a) $2x$

(b) $2x - 10$

(c) $10x - 25$

(d) $\frac{2}{5}x - 1$

(e) All real numbers x

6. (a) $\sqrt{x^2 - 4} + \dfrac{x^2}{x^2 + 1}$

(b) $\sqrt{x^2 - 4} - \dfrac{x^2}{x^2 + 1}$

(c) $\dfrac{x^2 \sqrt{x^2 - 4}}{x^2 + 1}$

(d) $\dfrac{(x^2 + 1)\sqrt{x^2 - 4}}{x^2}$, $|x| \geq 2$

(e) $|x| \geq 2$

8. (a) $\dfrac{x^4 + x^3 + x}{x + 1}$

(b) $\dfrac{-x^4 - x^3 + x}{x + 1}$

(c) $\dfrac{x^4}{x + 1}$

(d) $\dfrac{1}{x^2(x + 1)}$, $x \neq 0, -1$

(e) $x \neq 0, -1$

10. 11   **12.** -1 **14.** -370 **16.** $-\frac{1}{4}$

18. $t^2 - 7t + 9$ **20.** $27t^6 - 36t^4 + 3t^2 - 4$

22. $\dfrac{t^2 + 4t + 5}{t - 2}$

24.

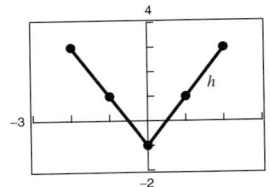

26.

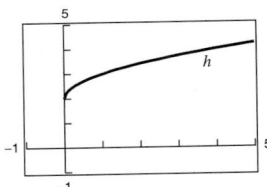

28.

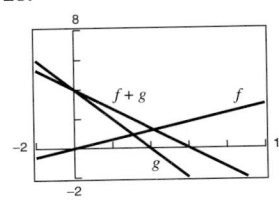

30.

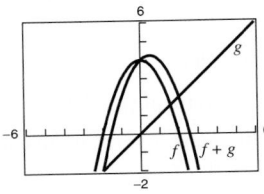

32.

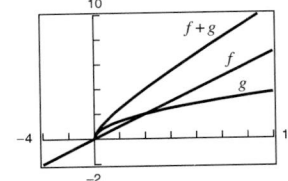

$g(x)$, $0 \leq x \leq 2$; $f(x)$, $x > 6$

34.

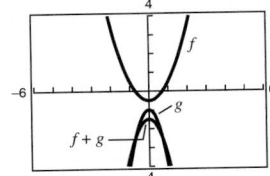

$g(x)$, $0 \leq x \leq 2$; $g(x)$, $x > 6$

36. (a) x (b) x

38. (a) $\dfrac{1}{x^3}$ (b) $\dfrac{1}{x^3}$

40. (a) $(f \circ g)(x) = x$; $(g \circ f)(x) = x$

(b)

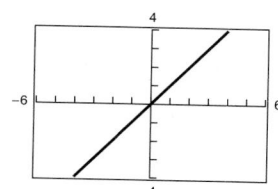

Equal

42. (a) $(f \circ g)(x) = \sqrt[4]{x}$; $(g \circ f)(x) = \sqrt[4]{x}$

(b)

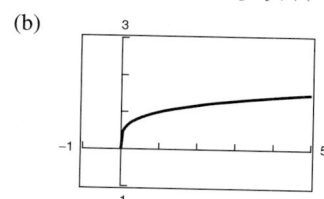

Equal

44. (a) $(f \circ g)(x) = |x + 6|$; $(g \circ f)(x) = |x| + 6$

(b)

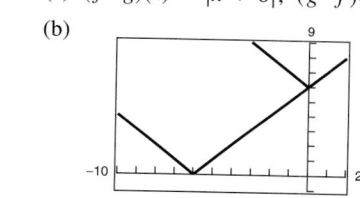

Not equal

46. (a) $(f \circ g)(x) = x$; $(g \circ f)(x) = x$ (b) $x = x$

(c)

x	0	1	2	3
$g(x)$	1	5	9	13
$(f \circ g)(x)$	0	1	2	3

x	0	1	2	3
$f(x)$	$-\frac{1}{4}$	0	$\frac{1}{4}$	$\frac{1}{2}$
$(g \circ f)(x)$	0	1	2	3

48. (a) $(f \circ g)(x) = x + 6$; $(g \circ f)(x) = \sqrt[3]{x^3 + 6}$

(b) $x + 6 \neq \sqrt[3]{x^3 + 6}$

(c)

x	0	1	2	3
$g(x)$	$\sqrt[3]{10}$	$\sqrt[3]{11}$	$\sqrt[3]{12}$	$\sqrt[3]{13}$
$(f \circ g)(x)$	6	7	8	9

x	0	1	2	3
$f(x)$	-4	-3	4	23
$(g \circ f)(x)$	$\sqrt[3]{6}$	$\sqrt[3]{7}$	$\sqrt[3]{14}$	$\sqrt[3]{33}$

50. (a) $(f \circ g)(x) = \dfrac{6}{-3x - 5}$; $(g \circ f)(x) = \dfrac{6}{5 - 3x}$

(b) $\dfrac{6}{-3x - 5} \neq \dfrac{6}{5 - 3x}$

(c)

x	0	1	2	3
$g(x)$	0	-1	-2	-3
$(f \circ g)(x)$	$-\frac{6}{5}$	$-\frac{3}{4}$	$-\frac{6}{11}$	$-\frac{3}{7}$

x	0	1	2	3
$f(x)$	$-\frac{6}{5}$	-3	6	$\frac{3}{2}$
$(g \circ f)(x)$	$\frac{6}{5}$	3	-6	$-\frac{3}{2}$

52. (a) -1 (b) 0   **54.** (a) 2   (b) 2

56. (a) 1   (b) 0   **58.** $f(x) = x^3$, $g(x) = 1 - x$

60. $f(x) = \sqrt{x}$, $g(x) = 9 - x$

62. $f(x) = \dfrac{4}{x^2}$, $g(x) = 5x + 2$

64. $f(x) = x^{3/2}$, $g(x) = x + 3$

66. (a) All real numbers $x \geq -3$ (b) All real numbers

(c) All real numbers $x \geq -6$

68. (a) All real numbers except $x = 0$

(b) All real numbers except $x = 0$

(c) All real numbers except $x = 0$

70. (a) All real numbers except $x = \pm 1$

(b) All real numbers

(c) All real numbers except $x = -2, 0$

72. 5, $h \neq 0$ **74.** $h + 2x$, $h \neq 0$

76. $-\dfrac{4x + 2h}{x^2(x^2 + 2hx + h^2)}$, $h \neq 0$

78. $\dfrac{-2}{\sqrt{x + h} - \sqrt{x}}$, $h \neq 0$

80. (a) $R_3 = 734 - 7.22t - 0.8t^2$

(b)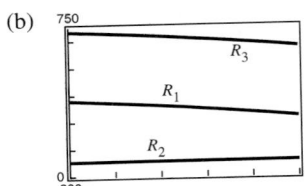

82. 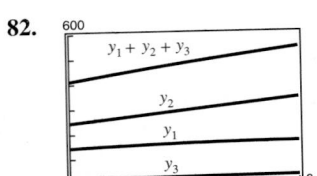 $614 billion

84. (a) $r(x) = \dfrac{x}{2}$ (b) $A(r) = \pi r^2$

(c) $(A \circ r)(x) = \pi \left(\dfrac{x}{2}\right)^2$

$A \circ r$ represents the area of the circular base of the tank with radius $x/2$.

86. $s(t) = \sqrt{(150 - 450t)^2 + (200 - 450t)^2}$

$= 50\sqrt{162t^2 - 126t + 25}$

88. (a) $R = p - 1200$ (b) $S = 0.92p$

(c) $(R \circ S)(p) = 0.92p - 1200$; Cost if discount is taken before rebate

$(S \circ R)(p) = 0.92(p - 1200)$; Cost if rebate is taken before discount

(d) $R \circ S = \$15,728$; $S \circ R = \$15,824$; $R \circ S$ gives a lower cost because if the discount is taken first, its total value is reduced to $0.92(\$1200)$.

90. False. $(f \circ g)(x) = 6x + 1 \neq 6x + 6 = (g \circ f)(x)$

92. To prove that the product of two odd functions f and g is an even function, show that $(fg)(-x) = (fg)(x)$.

$(fg)(-x) = f(-x)g(-x)$

$= [-f(x)][-g(x)] = f(x)g(x) = (fg)(x)$

To prove that the product of two even functions f and g is an even function, show that $(fg)(-x) = (fg)(x)$.

$(fg)(-x) = f(-x)g(-x) = f(x)g(x) = (fg)(x)$

94. Prove $g(-x) = g(x)$.

$g(-x) = \frac{1}{2}[f(-x) + f(x)] = \frac{1}{2}[f(x) + f(-x)] = g(x)$

Prove $h(-x) = -h(x)$.

$h(-x) = \frac{1}{2}[f(-x) - f(x)] = -\frac{1}{2}[f(x) - f(-x)] = -h(x)$

96. (a) $f(x) = (x^2 + 1) + (-2x)$

(b) $f(x) = \dfrac{-1}{(x + 1)(x - 1)} + \dfrac{x}{(x + 1)(x - 1)}$

98. $(0, 1)$, $(5, -74)$, $\left(-1, -\frac{16}{5}\right)$ (Answers will vary.)

100. $(0, 0)$, $\left(1, -\frac{1}{4}\right)$, $(2, -2)$ (Answers will vary.)

102. $x - 3y + 14 = 0$ **104.** $5x + 10y - 11 = 0$

106.   **108.**

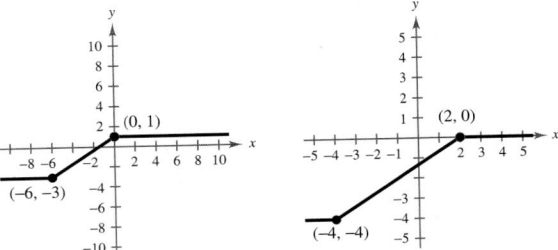

110.

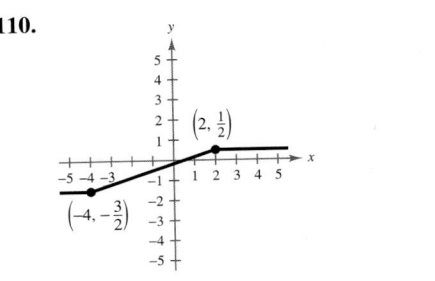

Section 1.7   *(page 145)*

2. (b)

4. (d)

6. $f^{-1}(x) = 5x$

8. $f^{-1}(x) = x + 5$

10. $f^{-1}(x) = 4x + 1$ **12.** $f^{-1}(x) = \sqrt[5]{x}$

14. (a) $f(g(x)) = f(x + 5) = (x + 5) - 5 = x$

$g(f(x)) = g(x - 5) = (x - 5) + 5 = x$

(b)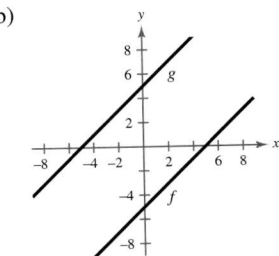

16. (a) $f(g(x)) = f\left(\dfrac{3-x}{4}\right) = 3 - 4\left(\dfrac{3-x}{4}\right) = x$

$g(f(x)) = g(3 - 4x) = \dfrac{3 - (3 - 4x)}{4} = x$

(b)

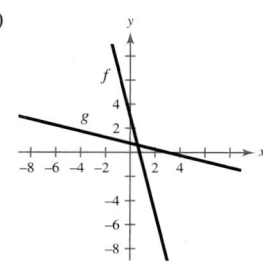

18. $f(g(x)) = f\left(\dfrac{1}{x}\right) = \dfrac{1}{1/x} = x$

$g(f(x)) = g\left(\dfrac{1}{x}\right) = \dfrac{1}{1/x} = x$

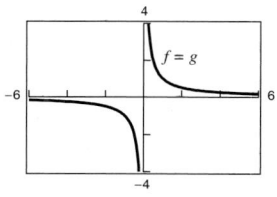

Reflections in the line $y = x$

20. $f(g(x)) = f\left(\sqrt{9-x}\right),\ x \le 9$

$= 9 - \left(\sqrt{9-x}\right)^2 = x$

$g(f(x)) = g(9 - x^2),\ x \ge 0$

$= \sqrt{9 - (9 - x^2)} = x$

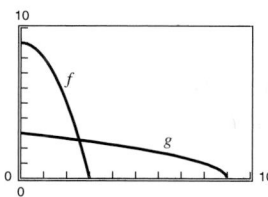

Reflections in the line $y = x$

22. $f(g(x)) = f\left(\dfrac{1-x}{x}\right),\ 0 < x \le 1$

$= \dfrac{1}{1 + (1-x)/x} = \dfrac{x}{x + 1 - x} = x$

$g(f(x)) = g\left(\dfrac{1}{1+x}\right),\ x \ge 0$

$= \dfrac{1 - 1/(1+x)}{1/(1+x)} = \dfrac{1 + x - 1}{1} = x$

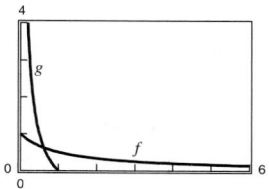

Reflections in the line $y = x$

24. (a) $f(g(x)) = f(3x - 8) = \dfrac{(3x - 8) + 8}{3} = x$

$g(f(x)) = g\left(\dfrac{x+8}{3}\right) = 3\left(\dfrac{x+8}{3}\right) - 8 = x$

(b)

x	-5	-2	0	1	4
$f(x)$	1	2	$\frac{8}{3}$	3	4

x	1	2	$\frac{8}{3}$	3	4
$g(x)$	-5	-2	0	1	4

26. (a) $f(g(x)) = f\left(\sqrt[3]{5x}\right) = \dfrac{\left(\sqrt[3]{5x}\right)^3}{5} = x$

$g(f(x)) = g\left(\dfrac{x^3}{5}\right) = \sqrt[3]{5\left(\dfrac{x^3}{5}\right)} = x$

(b)

x	-2	0	1	5
$f(x)$	$-\frac{8}{5}$	0	$\frac{1}{5}$	25

x	$-\frac{8}{5}$	0	$\frac{1}{5}$	25
$g(x)$	-2	0	1	5

28. (a) $f(g(x)) = f\left(\dfrac{x^3 + 10}{3}\right) = \sqrt[3]{3\left(\dfrac{x^3 + 10}{3}\right) - 10} = x$

$g(f(x)) = g\left(\sqrt[3]{3x - 10}\right)$

$= \dfrac{\left(\sqrt[3]{3x - 10}\right)^3 + 10}{3} = \dfrac{3x - 10 + 10}{3} = x$

(b)

x	-18	0	$\frac{2}{3}$	3	6
$f(x)$	-4	$\sqrt[3]{-10}$	-2	-1	2

x	-4	$\sqrt[3]{-10}$	-2	-1	2
$g(x)$	-18	0	$\frac{2}{3}$	3	6

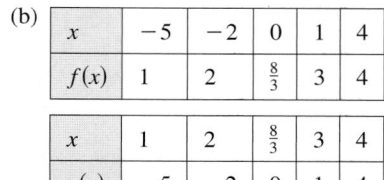

Reflections in the line $y = x$

30.

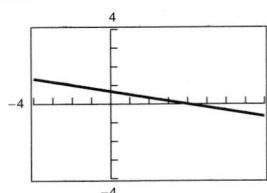

One-to-one

32.

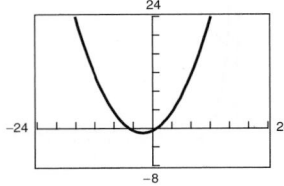

Not one-to-one

34.

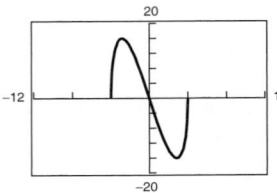

Not one-to-one

36.

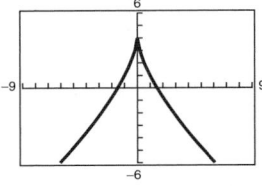

Not one-to-one

38.

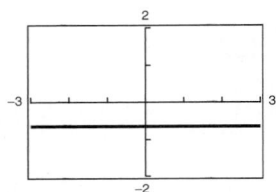

Not one-to-one

40.

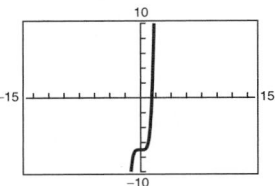

One-to-one

42.

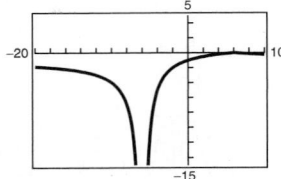

Not one-to-one

44. $f^{-1}(x) = \dfrac{x}{3}$

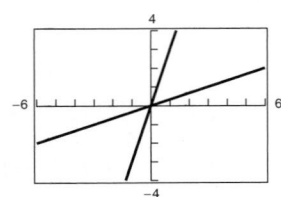

Reflections in the line
$y = x$

46. $f^{-1}(x) = \sqrt[3]{x - 1}$

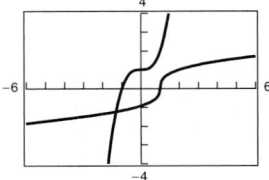

Reflections in the line
$y = x$

48. $f^{-1}(x) = \sqrt{x}$

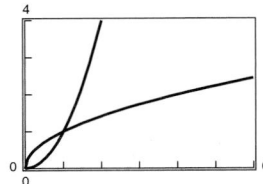

Reflections in the line $y = x$

50. $f^{-1}(x) = -\sqrt{16 - x^2},\ 0 \le x \le 4$

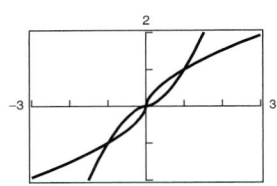

Reflections in the line $y = x$

52. $f^{-1}(x) = x^{5/3}$

54. $f^{-1}(x) = \dfrac{36}{x^2},\ x > 0$

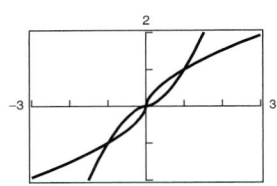

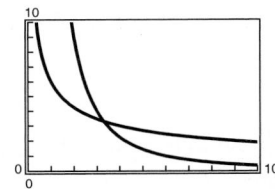

Reflections in the line
$y = x$

Reflections in the line
$y = x$

56. Not one-to-one

58. $f^{-1}(x) = \dfrac{x - 5}{3}$

60. $q^{-1}(x) = -\sqrt{x} + 5$

62. $f^{-1}(x) = 2 - x,\ x \ge 0$

64. $f^{-1}(x) = x^2 + 2,\ x \ge 0$

66. Not one-to-one

68. Not one-to-one

70. $y = \sqrt[4]{1 - x},\ x \le 1$

72. $y = x + 2,\ x \ge 0$

74.

x	-3	-2	0	6
$f^{-1}(x)$	4	3	-1	-2

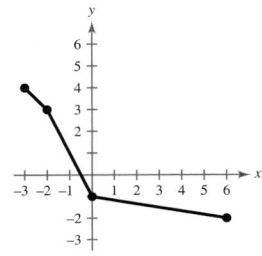

76. (a) and (b)

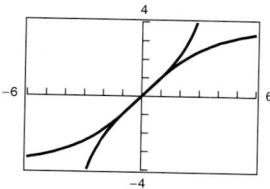

(c) Not an inverse function because it does not satisfy the Vertical Line Test

78. (a) and (b)

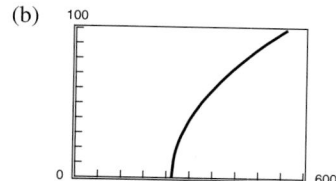

(c) Inverse function because it satisfies the Vertical Line Test

80. 0   **82.** $-\sqrt[9]{4}$ **84.** $2\sqrt[3]{x+3}$

86. $\dfrac{x-3}{2}$ **88.** $\dfrac{x-3}{2}$

90. (a) $y = \sqrt{\dfrac{x-254.50}{0.03}}$

x = degrees Fahrenheit

y = % load

(b)

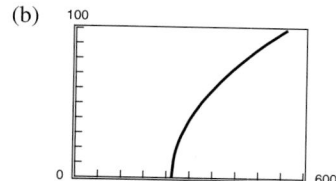

(c) $0 < x < 90.46$

92. False. The inverse of $y = x^2$ is not a function.

94. Answers will vary.   **96.** $k = \dfrac{1}{4}$ **98.** $\dfrac{5xy}{y+5}$, $x \neq 0$

100. $\dfrac{x+8}{x+2}$, $x \neq 5$ **102.** 26   **104.** $\dfrac{1}{3}$

Review Exercises   *(page 149)*

2.

x	-1	0	1	2	3
y	4	0	-2	-2	0

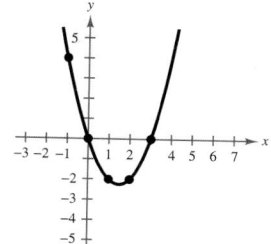

4.

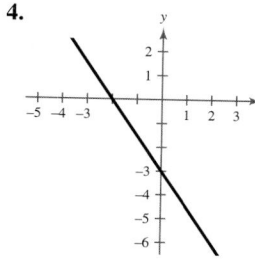

6.

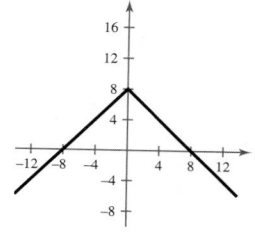

8.

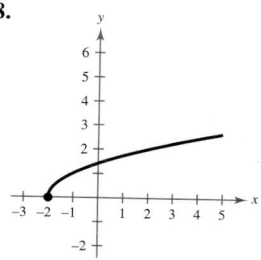

10.

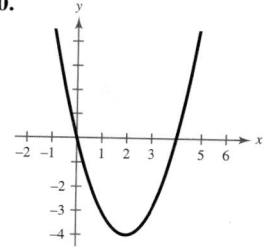

12.

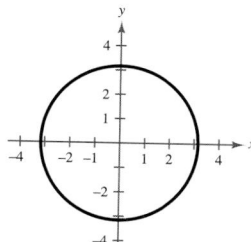

14.

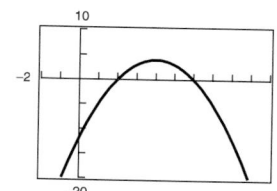

Intercepts:
$(6, 0), (2, 0), (0, -12)$

16.

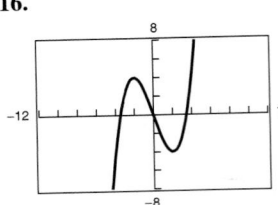

Intercepts: $(0, 0), (\pm 2\sqrt{3}, 0)$

18.

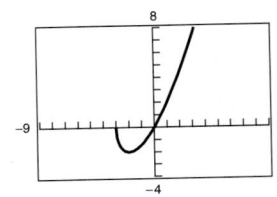

Intercepts: $(0, 0), (-3, 0)$

20.

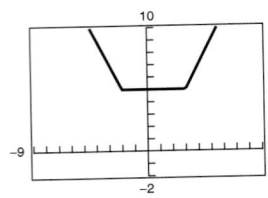

Intercept: $(0, 5)$

22.

Xmin = -2
Xmax = 3
Xscl = 1
Ymin = -20
Ymax = 15
Yscl = 5

24. (a)

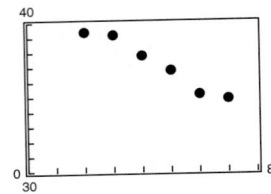

(b) $y = -1.02x + 41.8$

(c)

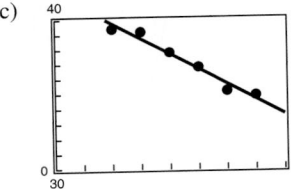

(d) In 2000, $y = 31.6$ thousand personnel on active duty.
In 2002, $y = 29.6$ thousand personnel on active duty.

26.

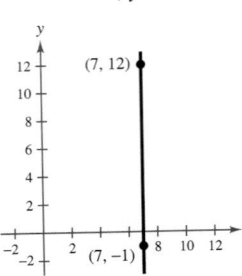

m is undefined.

28.

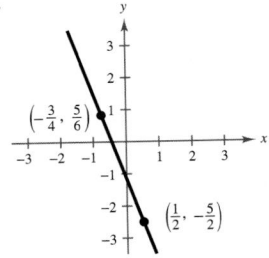

$m = -\frac{8}{3}$

30.

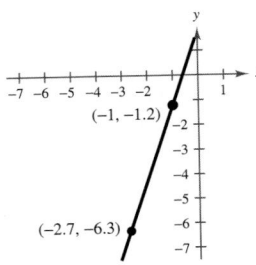

$m = 3$

32. $t = \frac{11}{4}$ **34.** $t = -\frac{53}{3}$

36. (a) $3x + 2y - 1 = 0$ (b) $(-1, 2), (1, -1), (-5, 8)$

38. (a) $2x + 3y - 6 = 0$ (b) $(0, 2), (6, -2), (-3, 4)$

40. (a) $4x - y + 30 = 0$ (b) $(0, 30), (5, 50), (10, 70)$

42. (a) $32x + 40y - 35 = 0$ (b) $\left(3, -\frac{61}{40}\right), \left(\frac{35}{32}, 0\right), \left(-1, \frac{67}{40}\right)$

44. (a) $y = 8$ (b) $(0, 8), (-3, 8), (5, 8)$

46. (a) $x = 5$ (b) $(5, 1), (5, 2), (5, -5)$

48. (a) $x = 0$

(b)

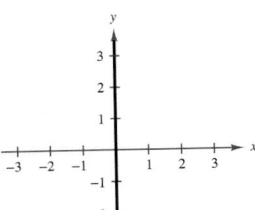

50. (a) $y = -\frac{12}{5}x - \frac{14}{5}$

(b)

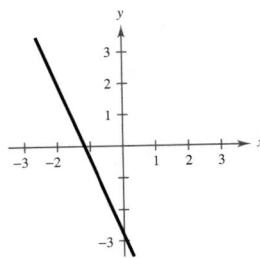

52. (a) $y = -\frac{4}{3}x + \frac{22}{3}$

(b)

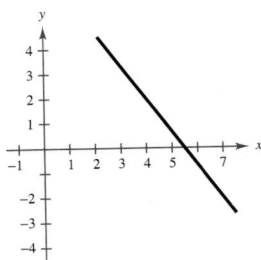

54. $V = 5.15t + 72.95$

56. $32x - 28y - 47 = 0$

58. (a) $V = 3.75t + 85$

(b)

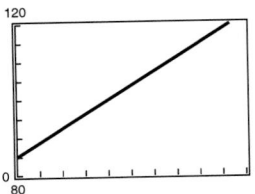

(c) $103.75

60. (a) $2x + 3y + 7 = 0$

(b) $3x - 2y + 30 = 0$

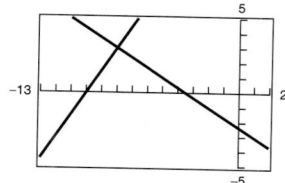

62. (a) $y = -4$

(b) $x = 3$

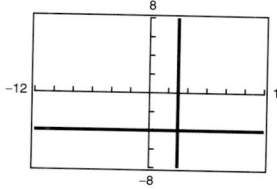

64. (a) Not a function because element u in A corresponds to two elements, 2 and -2, in B.

(b) Function

(c) Function

(d) Not a function because element w in A corresponds to two elements, -2 and 2, in B.

66. Function   **68.** Not a function

70. (a) 16   (b) $(t + 1)^{4/3}$ (c) $\frac{15}{7}$ (d) $x^{4/3}$

72. $(-\infty, \infty)$ **74.** $(-\infty, -8]$ and $[0, \infty)$

76. All real numbers x except $x = -\frac{4}{3}$

78.

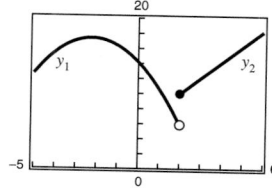

1985: \$12.61 billion

1990: \$14.16 billion

1995: \$16.208 billion

80. Domain: $\left(-\infty, -\frac{\sqrt{2}}{2}\right], \left[\frac{\sqrt{2}}{2}, \infty\right)$; Range: $[0, \infty)$

82. Domain: All real numbers; Range: $[0, \infty)$

84. (a)

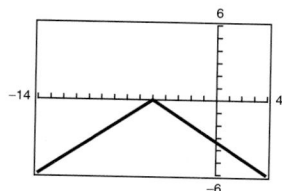

(b) Function

86. (a)

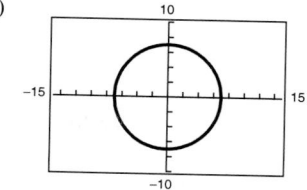

(b) Not a function

88. Increasing on $(3, \infty)$;

Decreasing on $(-\infty, -3)$

90. Increasing on $(-8, \infty)$;

Decreasing on $(-\infty, -8)$

92. Relative minimum: $\left(\frac{1}{2}, -\frac{5}{4}\right)$

94. Relative maximum: $(0, -1)$;

Relative minimum: $(2.67, -10.48)$

96.

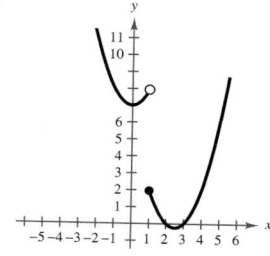

98. Neither even nor odd

100. Absolute value function $f(x) = |x|$

Vertical shift 3 units upward

$g(x) = |x| + 3$

102. Square root function $f(x) = \sqrt{x}$

Horizontal shift 3 units to the right and reflection in x-axis

$g(x) = -\sqrt{x - 3}$

104.   **106.**

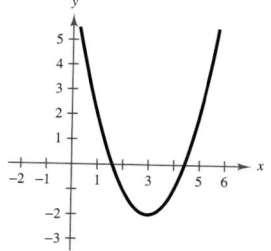   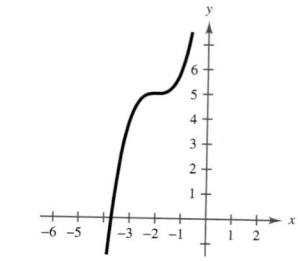

108.

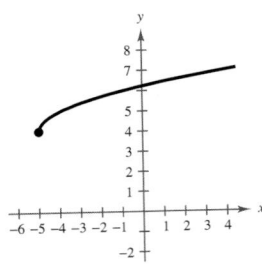

110.

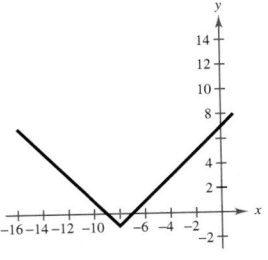

112.

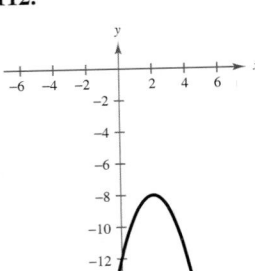

114.

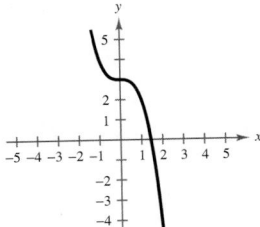

116.

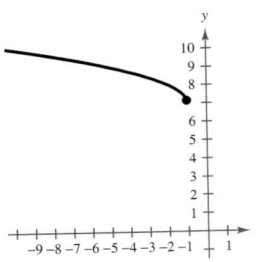

118.

120.

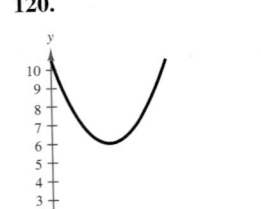

122.

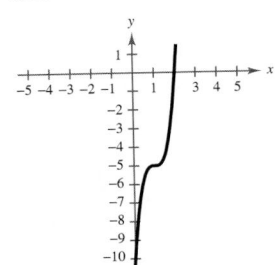

124.

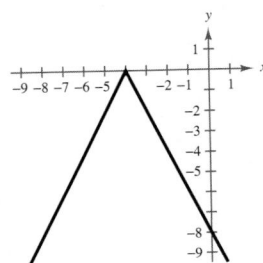

126.

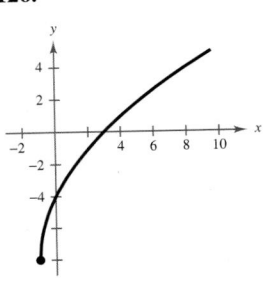

128. 70   **130.** -4 **132.** $\frac{1}{5}$

134. $\sqrt{7}$ **136.** $\sqrt{110}$

138.

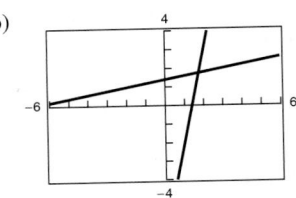

$164.4 billion

140. $f^{-1}(x) = 12x$

$$f(f^{-1}(x)) = f(12x) = \tfrac{1}{12}(12x) = x$$
$$f^{-1}(f(x)) = f^{-1}(\tfrac{1}{12}x) = 12(\tfrac{1}{12}x) = x$$

142. $f^{-1}(x) = x - 5$

$$f(f^{-1}(x)) = f(x - 5) = (x - 5) + 5 = x$$
$$f^{-1}(f(x)) = f^{-1}(x + 5) = (x + 5) - 5 = x$$

144. (a) $f^{-1}(x) = \dfrac{x + 7}{5}$

(b)

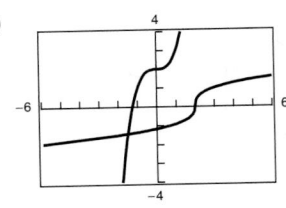

(c) $f^{-1}(f(x)) = f^{-1}(5x - 7) = \dfrac{5x - 7 + 7}{5} = x$

$f(f^{-1}(x)) = f\left(\dfrac{x + 7}{5}\right) = 5\left(\dfrac{x + 7}{5}\right) - 7 = x$

146. (a) $f^{-1}(x) = \sqrt[3]{x - 2}$

(b)

(c) $f^{-1}(f(x)) = f^{-1}(x^3 + 2) = \sqrt[3]{x^3 + 2 - 2} = x$

$f(f^{-1}(x)) = f(\sqrt[3]{x - 2}) = (x - 2) + 2 = x$

148. $x \le 0$; $f^{-1}(x) = -\sqrt{-x + 4},\ x \le 4$

150. $x \geq -4$; $f^{-1}(x) = 2x - 4$, $x \geq 0$

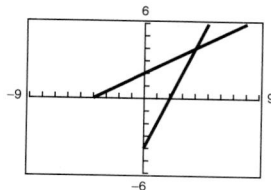

152. $f^{-1}(x) = \dfrac{8x - 3}{7}$ **154.** $f^{-1}(x) = \sqrt[3]{x + 2}$

156. $f^{-1}(x) = -\dfrac{x^2}{16} + 6$, $x \geq 0$

158. True. For odd n, $f(x) = x^n$ is a one-to-one function.

160. Vertical lines of the form $x = c$ are not functions because an infinite number of y-values correspond with the value of $x = c$.

Chapter 2

Section 2.1   *(page 164)*

2. (a) No   (b) Yes   (c) No   (d) No

4. (a) No   (b) No   (c) Yes   (d) No

6. (a) No   (b) Yes   (c) No   (d) No

8. Identity   **10.** Identity   **12.** Conditional

14. $\frac{240}{11}$ **16.** -10 **18.** 6   **20.** $\frac{1}{2}$ **22.** $\frac{9}{7}$

24. $\frac{7}{4}$ **26.** $-\frac{13}{3}$ **28.** No solution   **30.** 0

32. $P = A\left(1 + \dfrac{r}{n}\right)^{-nt}$ **34.** $r = \dfrac{S - a}{S - L}$

36. Yes. The estimated height of a male with a 19-inch thigh bone is 69.4 inches.

38. (a)

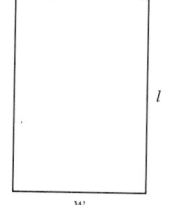

(b) $l = 1.5w$; $P = 5w$

(c) 5 meters $\times$ 7.5 meters

40. (a) Course average $= \dfrac{\text{test 1} + \text{test 2} + \text{test 3} + \text{test 4}}{4}$

(b) 97

42. 3 hours

44. (a) ≈ 3.8 hours; 3.2 hours   (b) 1.1 hours

(c) 25.6 miles

46. $66\frac{2}{3}$ kilometers per hour   **48.** 1.29 seconds

50. (a)

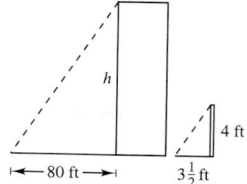

(b) 91.4 feet

52. $4000   **54.** 4.5%   **56.** 50 pounds of each kind

58. $x = 6$ feet   **60.** $h = 27$ feet

62. $r = 22.5$ centimeters

64. (a)

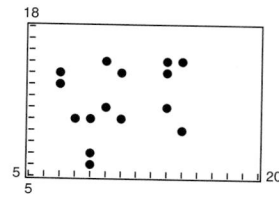

(b) Not linear

66. (a)

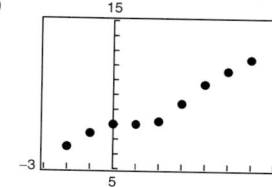

(b) Answers will vary.

(c) $W = 0.72t + 7.7$

(d) 2000: 14.9;
2004: 17.8;
2007: 19.9

68. (a) $P = 21.91t + 447$

(b)

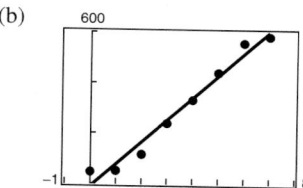

The model fits the data well.

(c)

Year	1990	1991	1992	1993
P (actual)	461.4	462.4	478.6	509.5
P (model)	447	468.9	490.8	512.7

Year	1994	1995	1996	1997
P (actual)	532.9	559.9	589.1	595.6
P (model)	534.6	556.6	578.5	600.4

70. False. Because $|-0.9824|$ is close to 1, the points can be described by a linear model.

72. $2x + \frac{7}{2} = 4$ **74.** Answers will vary.

76.

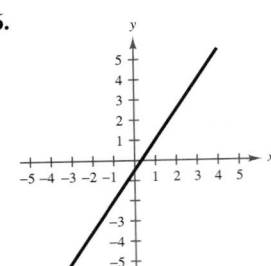

78.

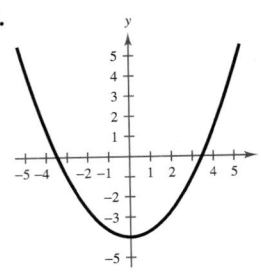

80.

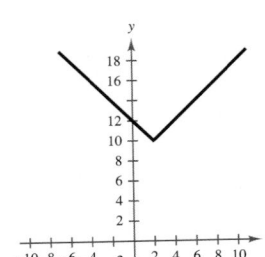

82. -14 **84.** -5

Section 2.2 *(page 176)*

2. $(0, -3), (-4, 0)$ **4.** $(-2, 0), (2, 0), (0, 4)$

6. $(0, 1), (1, 0)$ **8.** $\left(\frac{1}{3}, 0\right)$

10. $(0, 2.5), (5, 0), (-7, 0)$ **12.** $(0, 0)$

14.

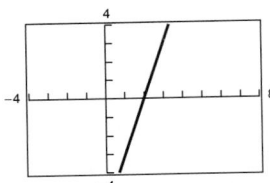

16.

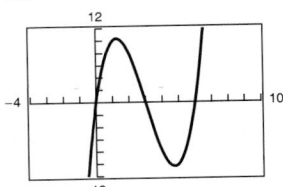

18.

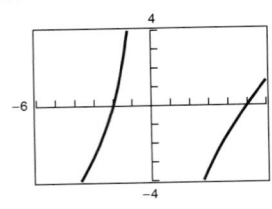

20.

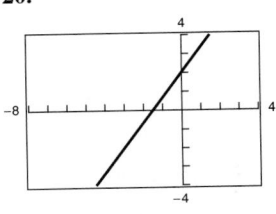

$\left(-\frac{3}{2}, 0\right)$

22.

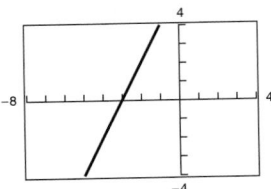

$(-3, 0)$

24. $\frac{8}{3}$ **26.** 950 **28.** 50 **30.** $\frac{89}{13}$ **32.** $-\frac{10}{3}, 3$

34. $\frac{1}{5}$ **36.** 1.268, 4.732 **38.** -2.422

40. $-4.206, -0.735, 1.941$ **42.** 1.638 **44.** ± 3.162

46. 11 **48.** $8.166 < x < 8.167$, so $x \approx 8.17$.

50. $(-1.222, 8.222)$ **52.** $(-1, 3)$

54. $(1, -1), (-2, 8)$ **56.** $(6, 4)$ **58.** $(1.670, 1.660)$

60. $(2.050, 32)$ **62.** $(0, 0), (3, -3)$

64. (a) 13.93. The second method decreases the accuracy.

(b) $\frac{1.87}{0.13} \approx 14.38$

66. (a) $C(x) = 18.65x + 25,000$

(b)

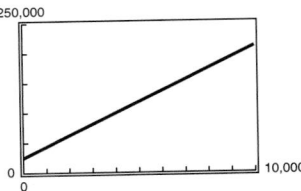

9383 units. Easier to solve algebraically because it is a linear equation.

68. (a)

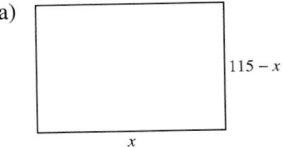

(b) $A(x) = x(115 - x)$

(c)

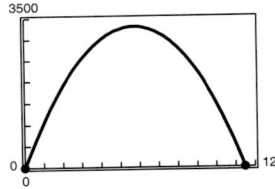

$0 \le x \le 115$

(d) 93.6 meters $\times 21.4$ meters

70. (a) $A(x) = \frac{1}{2}x\left(\frac{2}{3}x + 1\right)$

(b)

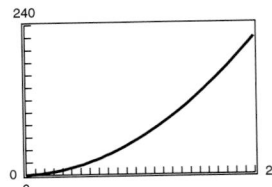

(c) 23.8 units

72. (a) $T = 10,000 + \frac{1}{2}x$ (b) \$6800

(c) \$7600 (d) \$7500

74. 65 inches   **76.** True

78. False. The lines could be identical.

80. $\frac{2}{3}\left(\sqrt{10}+2\right)$ **82.** $\frac{14\left(3\sqrt{10}+1\right)}{89}$

84. $12x^2+31x-91$ **86.** $16x^2+8x+1$

88. $12x^6+17x^3y^2-7y^4$

90. Decreasing on $(-\infty,-0.866)$, $(0,0.866)$

Increasing on $(-0.866,0)$, $(0.866,\infty)$

Section 2.3 *(page 186)*

2. $a=12, b=5$ **4.** $a=0, b=-\frac{5}{2}$ **6.** $3+3i$

8. 42   **10.** $3+i$ **12.** -11 **14.** $0.02i$

16. $8+4i$ **18.** 4   **20.** $17+18i$ **22.** $-\frac{19}{12}-\frac{37}{30}i$

24. $-2.4+17.75i$ **26.** $-5\sqrt{2}$ **28.** -75

30. $6-22i$ **32.** $32-72i$

34. $\left(21+5\sqrt{2}\right)+\left(7\sqrt{5}-3\sqrt{10}\right)i$ **36.** $-8i$

38. $-i\left(\sqrt{-4}-1\right)=-i(2i-1)=2+i$ **40.** 208

42. 11   **44.** 13   **46.** 9   **48.** $5i$ **50.** $\frac{3}{2}+\frac{3}{2}i$

52. $\frac{22}{5}+\frac{9}{5}i$ **54.** $10-4i$ **56.** $\frac{60}{13}-\frac{25}{13}i$

58. $\frac{12}{5}+\frac{9}{5}i$ **60.** $-4+2i$ **62.** i **64.** -8

66. $\frac{1}{8}i$ **68.** $-1-2i$ **70.** $2-6i$

72. 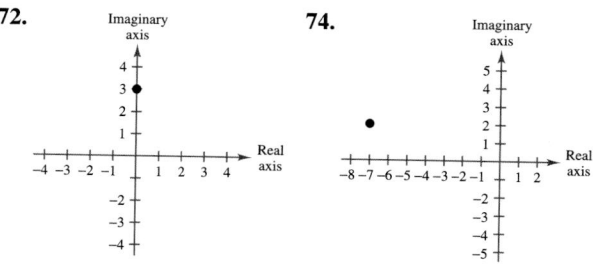   **74.**

76. No. 2, 6, 38, 1446, 2,090,918, 4,371,938,082,726

78. Yes. $-i$, $-1-i$, i, $-1-i$, i, $-1-i$

80. Yes. -1, 0, -1, 0, -1, 0

82. (a) 16   (b) 16   (c) 16   (d) 16

84. False. If the complex number is real, the number equals its conjugate.

86. False. The expression equals 1.   **88.** Answers will vary.

90. $-x^2-3x+12$ **92.** $3x^2+\frac{23}{2}x-2$

94. $\left(-\sqrt{6},0\right),\left(\sqrt{6},0\right),(0,6)$ **96.** $(0,5)$ **98.** 1 liter

Section 2.4   *(page 200)*

2. $x^2-25x=0$ **4.** $2x^2-2x+1=0$ **6.** $-\frac{1}{3},\frac{1}{3}$

8. 9, 1   **10.** $-\frac{3}{2}$, 11   **12.** 2, 6   **14.** $-a$

16. $\pm\frac{5}{3}$; ±1.67 **18.** $5\pm2\sqrt{5}$; 9.47, 0.53

20. $\frac{-7\pm2\sqrt{11}}{4}$; $-3.41, -0.09$ **22.** $-\frac{9}{2}$; -4.50

24. $-1, 3$ **26.** $-4\pm\sqrt{2}$ **28.** $\frac{2}{3}\pm\sqrt{2}$

30. $-\frac{9}{2},\frac{11}{2}$

32. (a)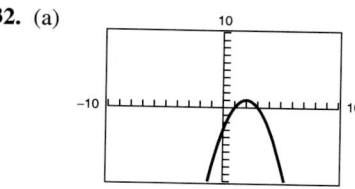

(b) and (c) $(3, 0), (1, 0)$

34. (a)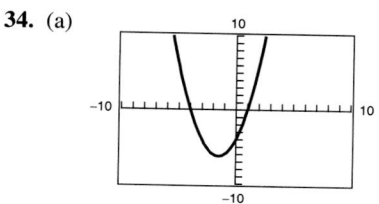

(b) and (c) $(1, 0), (-4, 0)$

36. (a)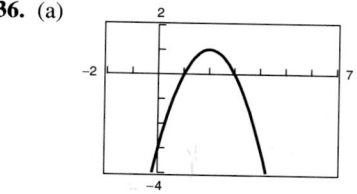

(b) and (c) $(1, 0), (3, 0)$

38. (a)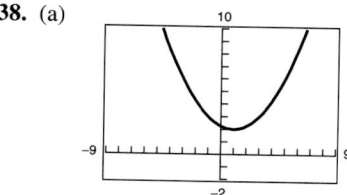

(b) and (c) No x-intercepts; $1\pm2\sqrt{2}i$

40. Two real solutions   **42.** No real solutions

44. Two real solutions   **46.** $5\pm\sqrt{3}$ **48.** $\frac{1}{2}\pm\frac{\sqrt{5}}{2}$

50. $-\frac{4}{3}$ **52.** $-\frac{5}{3},\frac{7}{3}$ **54.** $-3, 0$ **56.** 7

58. $-\frac{3}{2}\pm\sqrt{3}$ **60.** $\pm\frac{b}{a}$ **62.** $0,\pm\frac{5}{2}$

64. $\pm2, 1\pm\sqrt{3}i, -1\pm\sqrt{3}i$ **66.** $0,\frac{4}{3}$

68. $\pm2, -1\pm\sqrt{3}i$ **70.** $\pm2,\pm3i$

72. $\pm\frac{\sqrt{7}}{6},\pm i$ **74.** $2, -\frac{3}{5}$ **76.** $1, -\frac{125}{8}$

CHAPTER 2

78. (a)

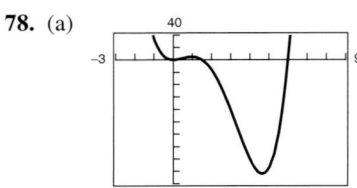

(b) and (c) $(0, 0)$, $\left(\frac{3}{2}, 0\right)$, $(6, 0)$

80. (a)

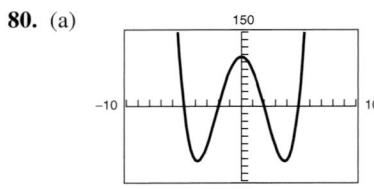

(b) and (c) $(2, 0)$, $(-2, 0)$, $(5, 0)$, $(-5, 0)$

82. -16 **84.** No solution   **86.** 36

88. $-5, 6, \dfrac{1 \pm \sqrt{57}}{2}$ **90.** $0, 1, \dfrac{3}{5}$

92. (a)

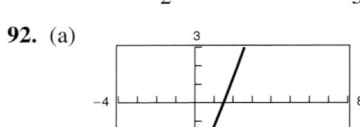

(b) and (c)

$x = \dfrac{3}{2}$

94. (a)

(b) and (c)

$x = 4$

96. $2, -12$ **98.** $\dfrac{1 \pm \sqrt{31}}{3}$ **100.** $\dfrac{3}{4}, -1$

102. $\dfrac{5}{3}, -3$ **104.** $10, -1$

106. (a)

(b) and (c)

$x = 2$

108. (a)

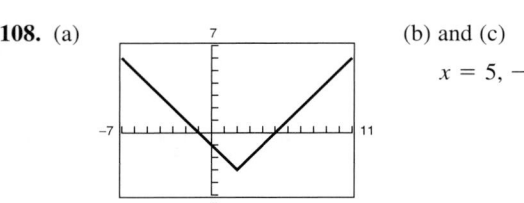

(b) and (c)

$x = 5, -1$

110. $x^3 - 11x^2 + 28x = 0$ **112.** $40x^2 + 37x + 4 = 0$

114. $x^3 - 2x^2 - 5x + 10 = 0$

116. $x^4 - 20x^2 - 576 = 0$ **118.** $x = 4, -20$

120. $Q = \pm\sqrt{LCi^2 + q}$ **122.** 6 inches $\times$ 6 inches

124. (a) $A(x) = \frac{8}{3}x(25 - x)$

(b)

x	y	Area
2	$\frac{92}{3}$	$\frac{368}{3} \approx 123$
4	28	224
6	$\frac{76}{3}$	304
8	$\frac{68}{3}$	$\frac{1088}{3} \approx 363$
10	20	400
12	$\frac{52}{3}$	416
14	$\frac{44}{3}$	$\frac{1232}{3} \approx 411$

Approximate dimensions for maximum area: $24 \times \frac{52}{3}$

(c)

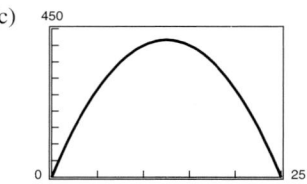

Approximate dimensions for maximum area: $25 \times \frac{50}{3}$

(d) and (e) $15 \times 23\frac{1}{3}$ or 35×10

126. (a) ≈ 22.36 seconds   (b) ≈ 3.73 miles

128. (a) $s = -16t^2 + 45t + 5.5$

(b) 24 feet   (c) ≈ 2.8 seconds

130. (a)

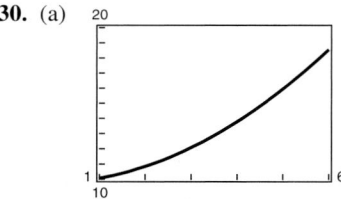

(b) Yes, in late 1997

132. (a)

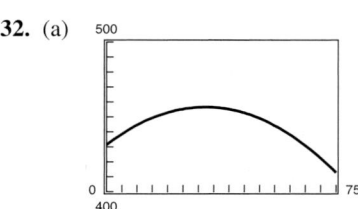

(b) 453 miles; 15 hours

(c) 439 miles; 54.9 miles per hour

134. (a)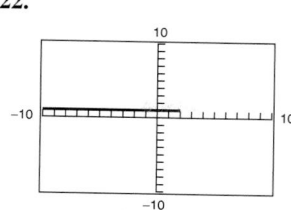

(b) $h \approx 173.21$

h	160	165	170	175	180	185
d	188.7	192.9	197.2	201.6	205.9	210.3

(c) 173.2

(d) Solving graphically or numerically yields an approximate solution. An exact solution is obtained algebraically.

136. 3761 units or 146,239 units

138. $\dfrac{20\sqrt{3}}{3} \approx 11.55$ inches

140. ≈ 541.42 miles and ≈ 258.58 miles

142. False. The product must equal zero to use the Zero-Factor Property.

144. (a) and (b) $x = -5, -\dfrac{10}{3}$ (c) Answers will vary.

146. $x^2(x - 3)(x^2 + 3x + 9)$

148. $(x + 5)(x - \sqrt{2})(x + \sqrt{2})$ **150.** Function

152. Not a function **154.** Function

Section 2.5 *(page 214)*

2. (a) **4.** (b)

6. (a) Yes (b) No (c) No (d) Yes

8. (a) Yes (b) Yes (c) Yes (d) No

10. $x > \dfrac{3}{2}$

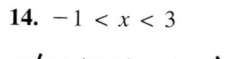

12. $x < -2$

14. $-1 < x < 3$

16. $-4 \leq x < 6$

18. $-3 \leq x < 7$

20.

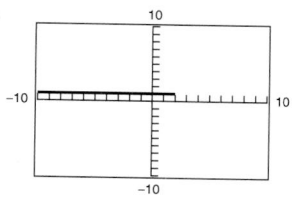

$x \leq 2$

22.

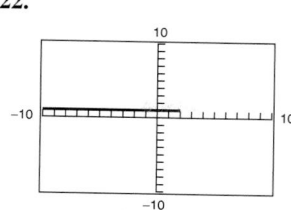

$x < 2$

24.

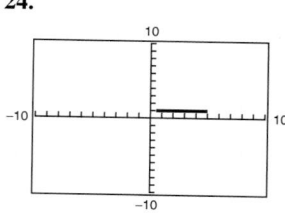

$\dfrac{1}{2} < x \leq 5$

26.

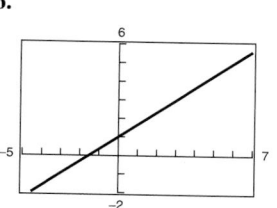

(a) $x \leq 6$ (b) $x \geq -\dfrac{3}{2}$

28.

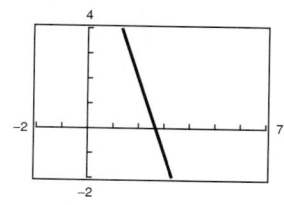

(a) $\dfrac{5}{3} \leq x \leq 3$ (b) $x \geq \dfrac{8}{3}$

30. $16 \leq x \leq 24$

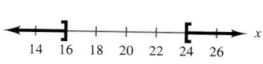

32. $x \leq 16, x \geq 24$

34. $x \leq -7, x \geq 13$

36. $\dfrac{1}{5} \leq x \leq \dfrac{7}{5}$

38.

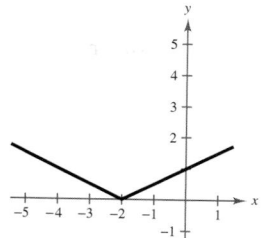

(a) $-10 \leq x \leq 6$

(b) $x \leq -4, x \geq 0$

40. $|x| > 3$ **42.** $|x + 1| \leq 4$ **44.** $|x + 3| > 5$

46. $\left[-6 - 2\sqrt{2}, -6 + 2\sqrt{2}\right]$ **48.** $(-1, 7)$

50. $(-\infty, 3]$

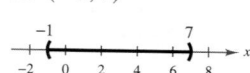

52.

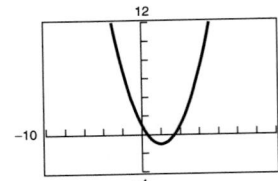

(a) $0 \le x \le 4$

(b) $x \le -2$, $x \ge 6$

54.

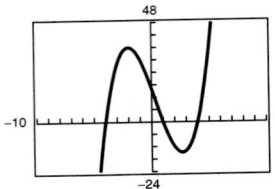

(a) $-\infty < x \le -4$,

$\quad 1 \le x \le 4$

(b) $x = -2$,

$\quad 5 \le x < \infty$

56. $(-\infty, 0)$, $\left(\frac{1}{4}, \infty\right)$

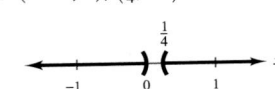

58. $(-2, 3]$

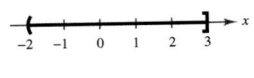

60.

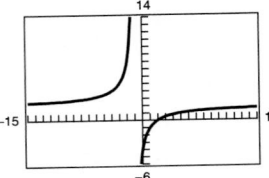

(a) $-1 < x \le 2$

(b) $-2 \le x < -1$

62.

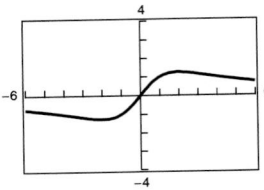

(a) $1 \le x \le 4$

(b) $-\infty < x \le 0$

64. $(-\infty, -2]$, $[2, \infty)$ **66.** $(-\infty, \infty)$ **68.** $[-2, 2]$

70. (a)

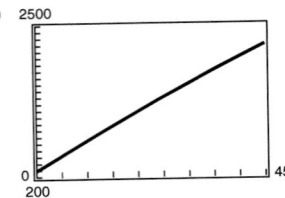

(b) 2002

72. Minimum: 20; Maximum: 80

74. False. Not true if $c < 0$.   **76.** (b)

78. (a) $d = 5\sqrt{5} \approx 11.18$ (b) Midpoint: $(-1.5, 7)$

80. (a) $d = 2\sqrt{65} \approx 16.12$ (b) Midpoint: $(-1, -1)$

82.

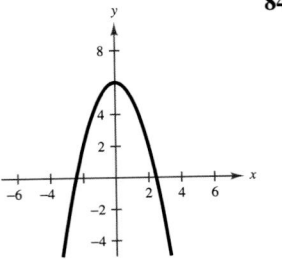

84.

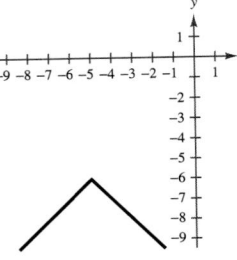

86.

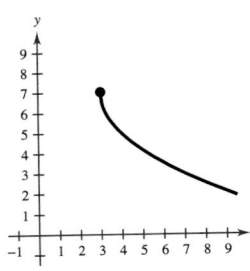

88. $y^{-1} = \dfrac{x}{12}$ **90.** $y^{-1} = \sqrt[3]{x-7}$

Review Exercises   *(page 218)*

2. (a) No   (b) Yes   (c) No   (d) No   **4.** $x = 6$

6. $x = -3$ **8.** 20%   **10.** 2π meters   **12.** 12

14. Base: 20 inches; Height: 8 inches

16. (a) $y = 8.22x + 24.5$

(b)

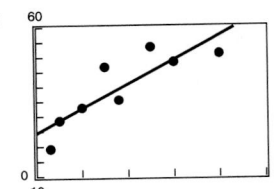

(c) The average increase per year in sales for each additional year of experience

(d) $65,600

18. $(-3, 0)$, $(0, 3)$ **20.** $(1, 0)$, $(8, 0)$, $(0, 8)$

22.

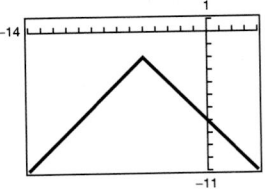

$(0, -7)$

24. $x = 2.2$ **26.** $x = -1.301$ **28.** $x = 0.338, 1.307$

30. $(1, -2)$ **32.** $(4.5, -3.125), (-3, 2.5)$

34. $6 + 5i$ **36.** $2 + 7i$ **38.** $3 + 7i$ **40.** $40 + 65i$

42. $-4 - 46i$ **44.** -80 **46.** $1 - 6i$ **48.** $\frac{4}{3}i$

50.

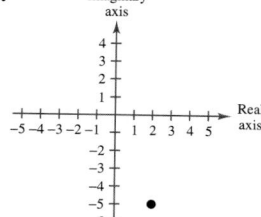

52.

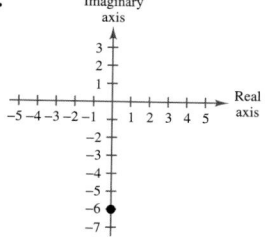

54. $0, 2$ **56.** $-4 \pm 3\sqrt{2}$ **58.** $6 \pm \sqrt{6}$

60. $\frac{1}{2}, -5$ **62.** $2 \pm \sqrt{14}$ **64.** $0, \frac{2}{3}, 8$ **66.** $0, \frac{12}{5}$

68. 5 **70.** $\frac{25}{4}$ **72.** No solution   **74.** $-124, 126$

76. $-2 \pm \dfrac{\sqrt{95}}{5}, -4$ **78.** $\frac{1}{5}$ **80.** $2, 6$ **82.** $-5, 15$

84. $1, 3$

86. (a)

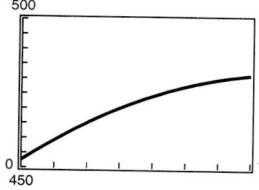

(b) Near the end of 1991

(c) The population will not reach 490,000.

(d) Answers will vary.

(e) According to the model, the population will start to decrease.

88. $(-\infty, 9)$

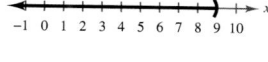

90. $[-3, 9)$

92. $(1, 3)$

94. $(-\infty, 0], [3, \infty)$

96. $\left[-\frac{1}{2}, \frac{7}{2}\right]$

98. $(-\infty, -1], [3, \infty)$

100. $[-4, 0], [4, \infty)$

102. $(-\infty, 3), (5, \infty)$

104. $(-\infty, 3), [20, \infty)$

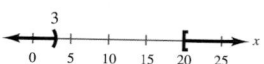

106. $[430.044, 435.244]$

108. False. If a graph has two y-intercepts, one input value ($x = 0$) is matched with two output values, so the graph is not the graph of a function.

110. False. For example, the slope of the regression line for $(1, 4), (2, 3), (3, 2)$, and $(4, 1)$ is -1.

112. The real zeros of a function are the values of x for which the graph of the function crosses the x-axis (the x-intercepts). They are also the values of x which satisfy the equation $f(x) = 0$.

Chapter 3

Section 3.1   *(page 233)*

2. (c)   **4.** (h)   **6.** (a)   **8.** (d)

10. (a)

(b)

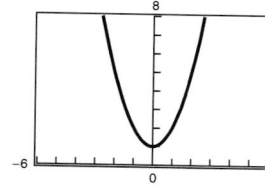

Vertical shift

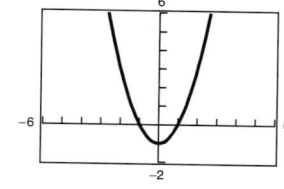

Vertical shift

(c)

(d)

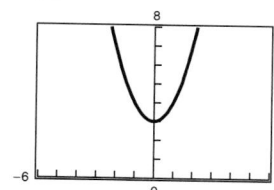

Vertical shift

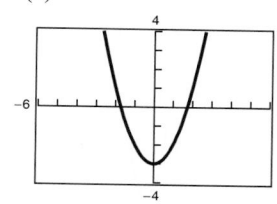

Vertical shift

12. (a)

(b)

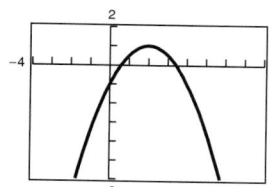

Horizontal shift, vertical shrink, reflection in the x-axis, and vertical shift

Horizontal shift, vertical shrink, and vertical shift

(c)

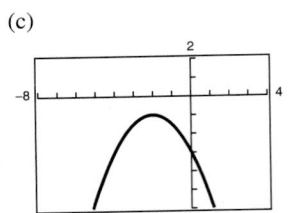

(d)

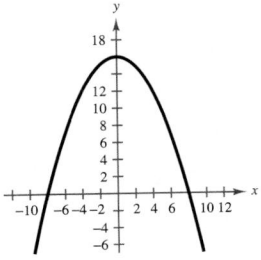

Horizontal shift, vertical shrink, reflection in the x-axis, and vertical shift

Horizontal shift, vertical shrink, and vertical shift

14. Vertex: $(0, -7)$

Intercepts:

$(0, -7), (\pm\sqrt{7}, 0)$

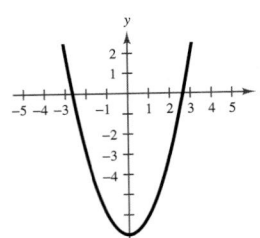

16. Vertex: $(0, 16)$

Intercepts:

$(0, 16), (\pm 8, 0)$

18. Vertex: $(6, 3)$

Intercept: $(0, 39)$

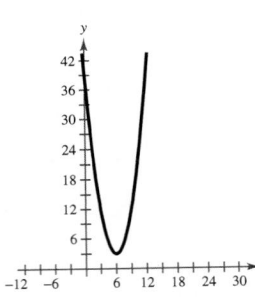

20. Vertex: $(-1, 0)$

Intercepts:

$(-1, 0), (0, 1)$

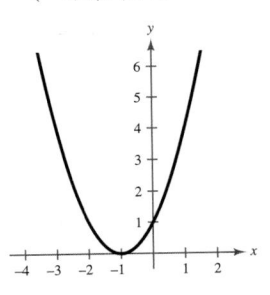

22. Vertex: $\left(-\frac{3}{2}, -2\right)$

Intercepts:

$\left(-\frac{3}{2} \pm \sqrt{2}, 0\right), \left(0, \frac{1}{4}\right)$

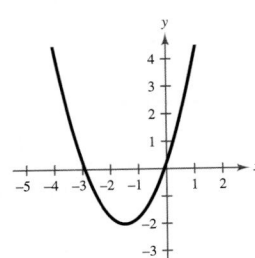

24. Vertex: $(-2, 5)$

Intercepts:

$\left(-2 \pm \sqrt{5}, 0\right), (0, 1)$

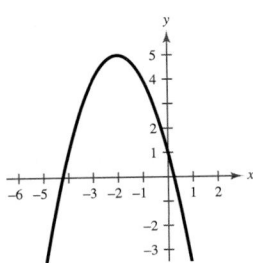

26. Vertex: $\left(\frac{1}{4}, \frac{7}{8}\right)$

Intercept: $(0, 1)$

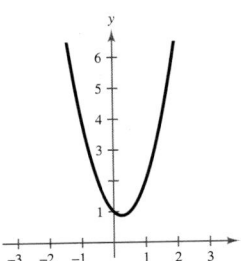

28. Vertex: $\left(-\frac{1}{2}, \frac{121}{4}\right)$

Intercepts:

$(-6, 0), (5, 0), (0, 30)$

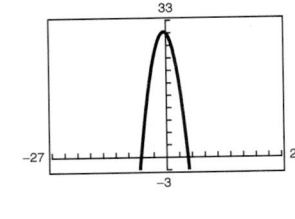

30. Vertex: $(-5, -11)$

Intercepts:

$\left(-5 \pm \sqrt{11}, 0\right), (0, 14)$

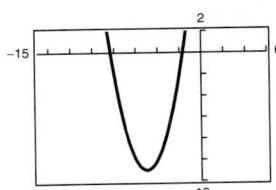

32. Vertex: $(3, -5)$

Intercept: $(0, -41)$

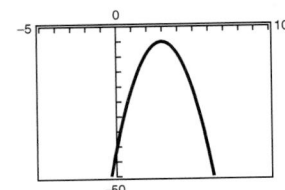

34. Vertex: $\left(-3, -\frac{42}{5}\right)$

Intercepts: $\left(-3 \pm \sqrt{14}, 0\right), (0, -3)$

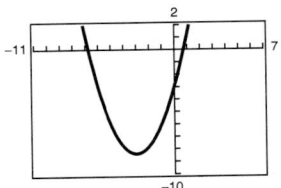

36. $y = -x^2 + 1$

38. $y = (x + 2)^2 - 1$

40. $f(x) = (x - 4)^2 - 1$

42. $f(x) = -\frac{1}{4}(x - 2)^2 + 3$

44. $f(x) = -\frac{24}{49}\left(x + \frac{1}{4}\right)^2 + \frac{3}{2}$

46. $f(x) = -\frac{16}{3}\left(x + \frac{5}{2}\right)^2$

48. $(3, 0)$; They are the same.

50. $(-3, 0), \left(\frac{1}{2}, 0\right)$; They are the same.

52.

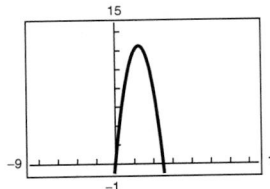

$(0, 0), (5, 0)$; They are the same.

54.

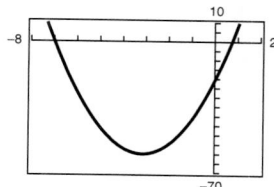

(0.75, 0), (−7, 0); They are the same.

56.

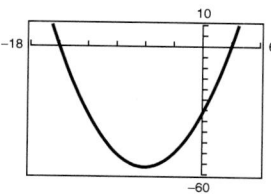

(−15, 0), (3, 0); They are the same.

58. $f(x) = x^2 - 10x$
$g(x) = -x^2 + 10x$

60. $f(x) = 2x^2 + x - 10$
$g(x) = -2x^2 - x + 10$

62. $\dfrac{S}{2}, \dfrac{S}{2}$ **64.** 21, 7

66. (a) $A = x(18 - x)$, $0 < x < 18$

(b)

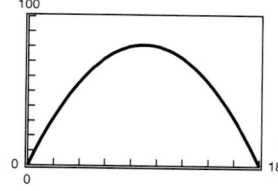

(c) 9 meters × 9 meters

68. (a)

x	y	Area
2	$\frac{1}{3}[200 - 4(2)]$	$(2)(2)(\frac{1}{3})[200 - 4(2)] = 256$
4	$\frac{1}{3}[200 - 4(4)]$	$(2)(4)(\frac{1}{3})[200 - 4(4)] \approx 491$
6	$\frac{1}{3}[200 - 4(6)]$	$(2)(6)(\frac{1}{3})[200 - 4(6)] = 704$
8	$\frac{1}{3}[200 - 4(8)]$	$(2)(8)(\frac{1}{3})[200 - 4(8)] = 896$
10	$\frac{1}{3}[200 - 4(10)]$	$(2)(10)(\frac{1}{3})[200 - 4(10)] \approx 1067$
12	$\frac{1}{3}[200 - 4(12)]$	$(2)(12)(\frac{1}{3})[200 - 4(12)] = 1216$

(b)

x	y	Area
20	$\frac{1}{3}[200 - 4(20)]$	$(2)(20)(\frac{1}{3})[200 - 4(20)] = 1600$
22	$\frac{1}{3}[200 - 4(22)]$	$(2)(22)(\frac{1}{3})[200 - 4(22)] \approx 1643$
24	$\frac{1}{3}[200 - 4(24)]$	$(2)(24)(\frac{1}{3})[200 - 4(24)] = 1664$
26	$\frac{1}{3}[200 - 4(26)]$	$(2)(26)(\frac{1}{3})[200 - 4(26)] = 1664$
28	$\frac{1}{3}[200 - 4(28)]$	$(2)(28)(\frac{1}{3})[200 - 4(28)] \approx 1643$
30	$\frac{1}{3}[200 - 4(30)]$	$(2)(30)(\frac{1}{3})[200 - 4(30)] = 1600$

When x is between 24 and 26 feet, and y is between $34\frac{2}{3}$ and 32 feet

(c) $A = \dfrac{8x(50 - x)}{3}$

(d)

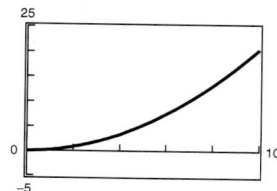

$x = 25$ feet, $y = 33\frac{1}{3}$ feet

(e) $A = -\frac{8}{3}(x - 25)^2 + \frac{5000}{3}$. Maximum area occurs at the vertex, when $x = 25$ feet and $y = 33\frac{1}{3}$ feet.

(f) The results are similar.

70. 122 units   **72.** $2000   **74.** 16 feet

76. (a)

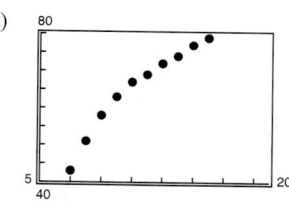

(b) 69.6 miles per hour

78. (a)

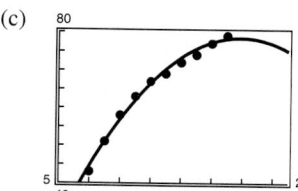

(b) $y = -0.35t^2 + 11.8t - 21$

(c)

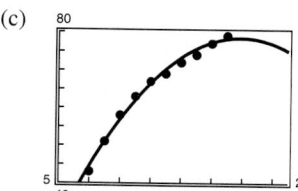

(d) No. The model begins decreasing at a rapid rate.

80. True. The ratio of the x^2-coefficient to the x-coefficient is the same in both.

82. (1.2, 6.8)   **84.** (2, 5), (−3, 0)   **86.** $-5 - 3i$

88. $19 - 25i$

Section 3.2   *(page 246)*

2. (h)   **4.** (a)   **6.** (d)   **8.** (b)

10. (a)   (b)

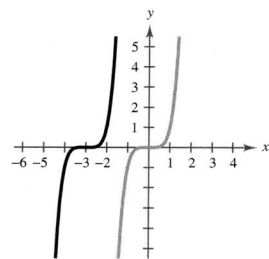

(c)   (d)

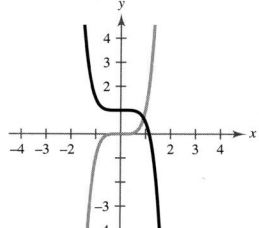

12. (a)   (b)

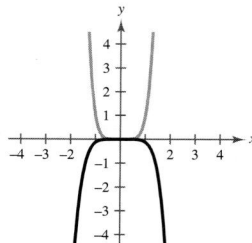

(c)   (d)

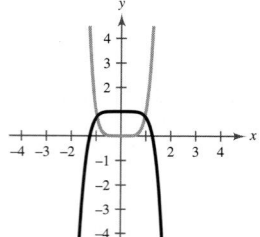

14.   **16.**

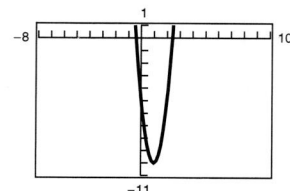

18. Falls to the left   **20.** Falls to the left
    Rises to the right   Falls to the right

22. Falls to the left   **24.** Rises to the left
    Rises to the right   Rises to the right

26. Rises to the left   **28.** ±7
    Falls to the right

30. −5   **32.** 3, 4   **34.** −4, 0, 5   **36.** −2, $\frac{2}{5}$

38. (a)

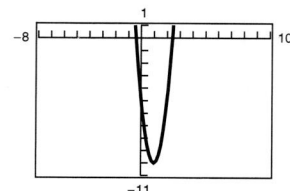

(b) Answers will vary.   (c) $\left(1 \pm \sqrt{2}, 0\right)$

40. (a)

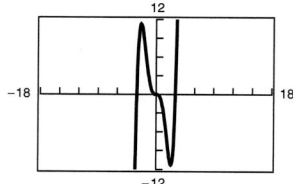

(b) Answers will vary.   (c) $(0, 0), (\pm 3, 0)$

42. (a)

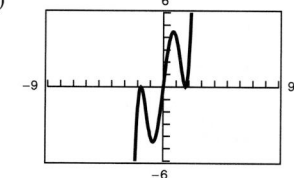

(b) Answers will vary.   (c) $(0, 0), \left(\pm \sqrt{3}, 0\right)$

44. (a)   (b) and (c)
                                        No zeros

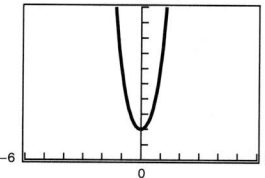

46. (a)

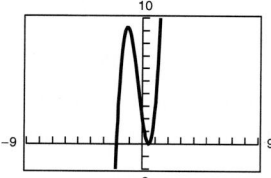

(b) Answers will vary.   (c) $(-2, 0), \left(\frac{1}{2}, 0\right)$

48. (a)

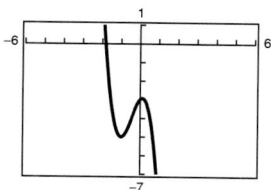

(b) Answers will vary. (c) $(0, 0), (\pm 1, 0), (\pm 2, 0)$

50.

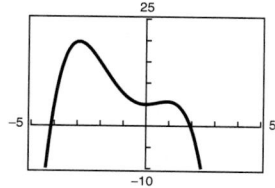

Relative minimum: $(-1, -5)$

Relative maximum: $(0.111, -2.942)$

52.

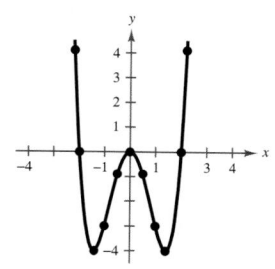

Relative minimum: $(0, 5)$

Relative maximums: $(-2.915, 19.688), (0.915, 5.646)$

54. $f(x) = x^2 + 8x$ **56.** $f(x) = x^2 - x - 20$

58. $f(x) = x^3 - 9x^2 + 14x$ **60.** $f(x) = x^5 - 5x^3 + 4x$

62. $f(x) = x^2 - 12x + 33$

64. $f(x) = x^3 - 8x^2 + 13x + 12$

66. (a) Rises to the left, rises to the right

(b) $(0, 0), (\pm 2, 0)$

(c)

x	-2.2	-1.4	-1	-0.5	0.5	1	1.4	2.2
y	4.1	-4	-3	-0.9	-0.9	-3	-4	4.1

(d)

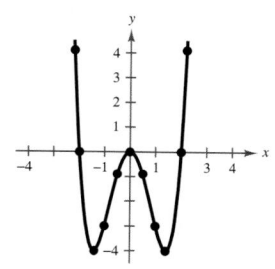

68. (a) Falls to the left, falls to the right

(b) $(2, 0), (8, 0)$

(c)

x	0	1	3	4	5	6	7	9
y	-16	-7	5	8	9	8	5	-7

(d)

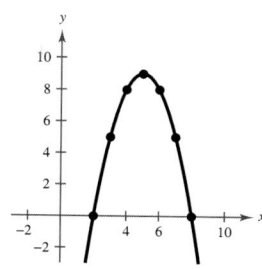

70. (a) Rises to the left, falls to the right

(b) $(1, 0)$

(c)

x	-2	-1	-0.5	0	0.5	2
y	9	2	1.1	1	0.9	-7

(d)

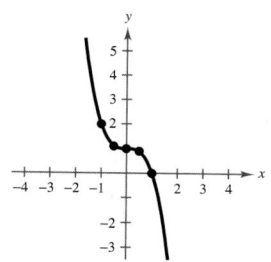

72. (a) Rises to the left, falls to the right

(b) $(-1.5, 0), (0, 0), (2.5, 0)$

(c)

x	-2	-1	-0.8	0.5	1	1.5	2	3
y	18	-7	-7.4	8	15	18	14	-27

(d)

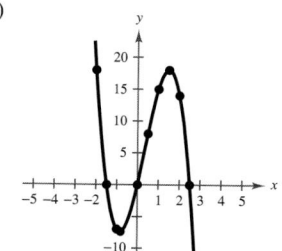

74. (a) Rises to the left, rises to the right

(b) $(0, 0), (\pm 4, 0)$

(c)

x	-5	-3	-2	-1	1	2	3
y	675	-189	-144	-45	-45	-144	-189

(d)

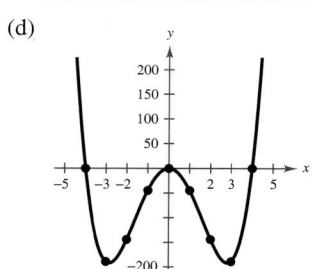

76. (a) Falls to the left, rises to the right

(b) $(0, 0), (4, 0)$

(c)

x	-1	1	2	3	5
y	-8.3	3	10.7	9	41.7

(d)

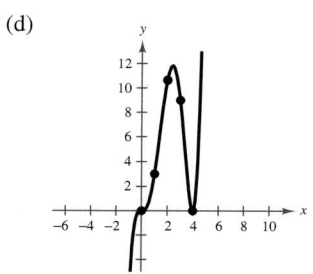

78. (a) Rises to the left, rises to the right

(b) $(-1, 0), (3, 0)$

(c)

x	-2	0	1	2	4
y	2.5	0.9	1.6	0.9	2.5

(d)

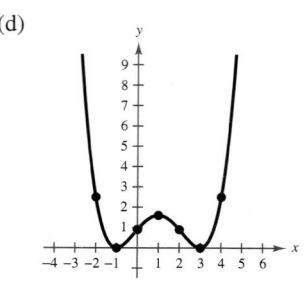

80. (a)

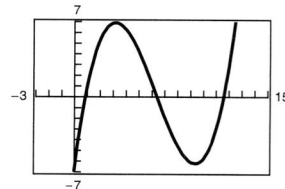

$(0, 1), (6, 7), (11, 12)$

(b) 0.845, 6.385, 11.588

82. (a)

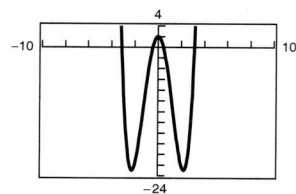

$(0, 1), (-1, 0), (3, 4), (-4, -3)$

(b) $-3.130, -0.452, 0.452, 3.130$

84.

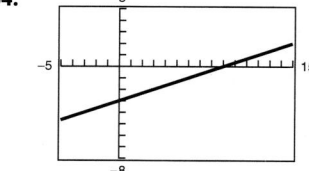

Xmin = -5
Xmax = 15
Xscl = 1
Ymin = -8
Ymax = 5
Yscl = 1

86.

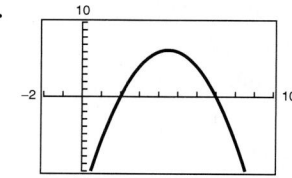

Xmin = -2
Xmax = 10
Xscl = 1
Ymin = -10
Ymax = 10
Yscl = 1

88.

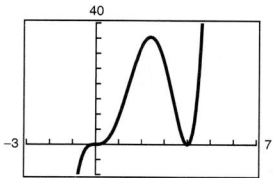

Two x-intercepts

90.

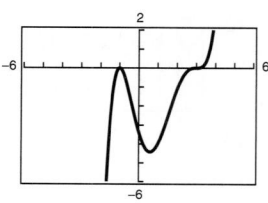

Two x-intercepts

92.

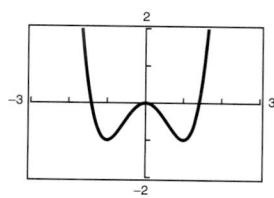

y-axis symmetry

Three x-intercepts

94.

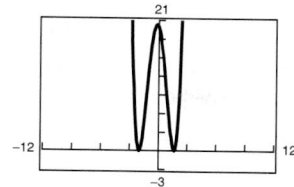

Two x-intercepts

96. (a) Answers will vary.

(b) $0 < x < 6$

(c)

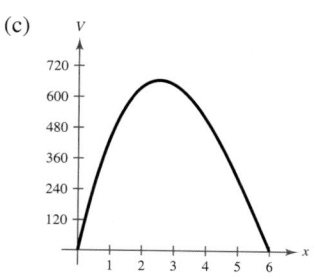

$x \approx 2.54$

98.

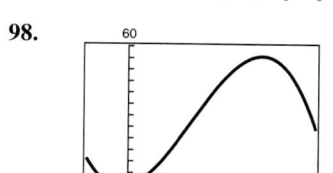

15.22 years

100. (a) $y_1 = 0.0750x^3 - 2.760x^2 + 37.35x - 15.0$

(b) $y_2 = -0.0046x^3 + 0.158x^2 + 2.82x + 59.7$

(c)

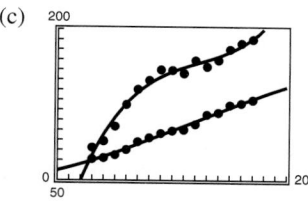

The median price of homes in the South is less than in the Northeast.

102. True   **104.** 69   **106.** $-\frac{1408}{49} \approx -28.73$

108. 109

110. $x > -8$

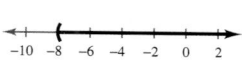

112. $-26 \le x < 7$

114. $f(x) = \frac{1}{2}(x - 3)^2 - 6$ **116.** $f(x) = \frac{14}{9}(x - 4)^2 - 4$

Section 3.3   *(page 260)*

2.

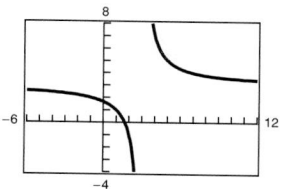

4.

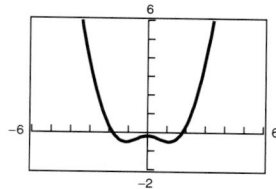

6.

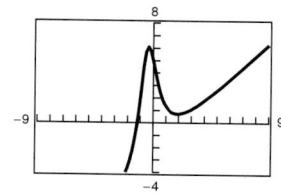

8. $5x + 3$ **10.** $x^3 + 3x^2 - 1$ **12.** $4 - \dfrac{9}{2x + 1}$

14. $x - \dfrac{x + 9}{x^2 + 1}$ **16.** $x^2 + \dfrac{x^2 + 7}{x^3 - 1}$

18. $x + 3 + \dfrac{6x^2 - 8x + 3}{(x - 1)^3}$ **20.** $2x^2 + 8x - 6 + \dfrac{3}{x - 1}$

22. $2x^2 + 2x - 32 + \dfrac{199}{x + 6}$

24. $5x^2 - 10x + 26 - \dfrac{44}{x + 2}$ **26.** $x^2 + 9x + 81$

28. $3x^2 + \dfrac{1}{2}x + \dfrac{3}{4} + \dfrac{49}{8x - 12}$

30. $f(x) = \left(x + \frac{2}{3}\right)(15x^3 - 6x + 4) + \frac{34}{3}, \ f\left(-\frac{2}{3}\right) = \frac{34}{3}$

32. $f(x) = \left(x + \sqrt{5}\right)\left[x^2 + \left(2 - \sqrt{5}\right)x - 2\sqrt{5}\right] + 6,$
$f\left(-\sqrt{5}\right) = 6$

34. $f(x) = \left[x - \left(2 + \sqrt{2}\right)\right]\left[-3x^2 + \left(2 - 3\sqrt{2}\right)x + 8 - 4\sqrt{2}\right],$
$f\left(2 + \sqrt{2}\right) = 0$

36. (a) 14   (b) 3122   (c) 434   (d) 2

38. (a) -2.5 (b) 20   (c) 65.5   (d) 5668

40. $(x + 4)(x + 2)(x - 6)$

Zeros: $-4, -2, 6$

42. $\left(x + \sqrt{3}\right)\left(x - \sqrt{3}\right)(x + 2)$

Zeros: $\pm\sqrt{3}, -2$

44. $\left(x - 2 + \sqrt{5}\right)\left(x - 2 - \sqrt{5}\right)(x + 3)$

Zeros: $2 \pm \sqrt{5}, -3$

CHAPTER 3

46. (a) Answers will vary. (b) $(3x - 1)$
(c) $(x + 3)(x - 2)(3x - 1)$ (d) $-3, 2, \frac{1}{3}$

48. (a) Answers will vary. (b) $(4x + 3), (2x - 1)$
(c) $(4x + 3)(2x - 1)(x - 4)(x + 2)$ (d) $-2, -\frac{3}{4}, \frac{1}{2}, 4$

50. (a) Answers will vary. (b) $x - \sqrt{5}$
(c) $(2x - 1)(x + \sqrt{5})(x - \sqrt{5})$ (d) $\pm\sqrt{5}, \frac{1}{2}$

52. $\pm 1, \pm 2, \pm 4, \pm 8, \pm 16$

54. $\pm 1, \pm 2, \pm\frac{1}{2}, \pm\frac{1}{4}$

56. (a) $\pm\frac{1}{3}, \pm\frac{2}{3}, \pm 1, \pm\frac{4}{3}, \pm 2, \pm\frac{8}{3}, \pm 4, \pm\frac{16}{3}, \pm 8, \pm 16$
(b) 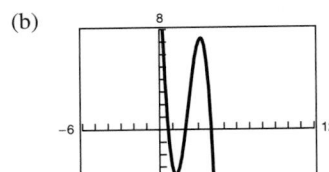 (c) $\frac{2}{3}, 2, 4$

58. (a) $\pm\frac{1}{4}, \pm\frac{1}{2}, \pm\frac{3}{4}, \pm 1, \pm\frac{5}{4}, \pm\frac{3}{2}, \pm\frac{5}{2}, \pm 3, \pm\frac{15}{4}, \pm 5, \pm\frac{15}{2}, \pm 15$
(b) 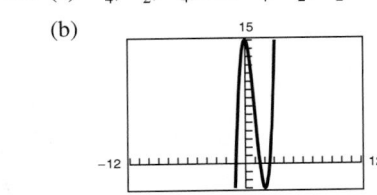 (c) $-1, \frac{3}{2}, \frac{5}{2}$

60. (a) $\pm\frac{1}{4}, \pm\frac{1}{2}, \pm 1, \pm 2, \pm 4$
(b) 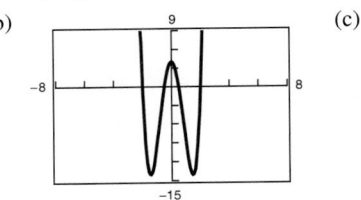 (c) $\pm 2, \pm\frac{1}{2}$

62. (a) $\pm 1, \pm 2, \pm 3, \pm 6, \pm 9, \pm\frac{1}{2}, \pm\frac{3}{2}, \pm\frac{9}{2}, \pm\frac{1}{4}, \pm\frac{3}{4}, \pm\frac{9}{4}, \pm 18$
(b) 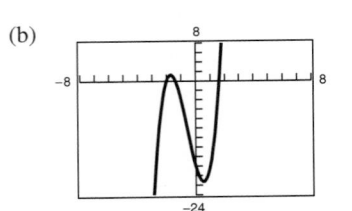 (c) $-2, \frac{1}{8} \pm \frac{\sqrt{145}}{8}$

64. $-5, 6$ **66.** $-6, \frac{1}{2}, 1$ **68.** $-2, 0, 1$

70. (a) $4, \pm 1.414$ (b) 4
(c) $g(x) = (x - 4)(x - \sqrt{2})(x + \sqrt{2})$

72. (a) $0.764, 5.236, 6$ (b) 6
(c) $f(s) = (s - 6)(s - 3 - \sqrt{5})(s - 3 + \sqrt{5})$

74. (a) $x = \pm 3, 1.500, 0.333$ (b) $\pm 3, \frac{3}{2}$
(c) $g(x) = (x + 3)(x - 3)(2x - 3)(3x - 1)$

76.–78. Answers will vary. **80.** $-3, \frac{1}{2}, 4$

82. $-2, -\frac{1}{3}, \frac{1}{2}$ **84.** (a) **86.** (c)

88. (a) and (b)

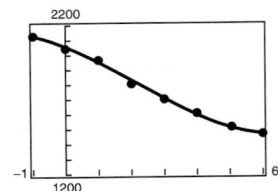

$$M = 2.412t^3 - 15.56t^2 - 90.5t + 2057$$

The model is a good fit.

(c)

t	-1	0	1	2
M	2130	2057	1953	1833

t	3	4	5	6
M	1711	1600	1517	1475

(d) $M(11) \approx 2389$. No. The model turns sharply upward.

90. (a) Answers will vary.

(b) 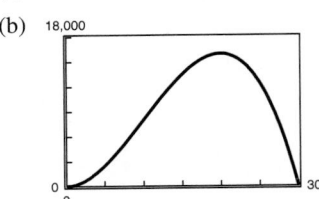 $20 \times 20 \times 40$

(c) $15, \dfrac{15 \pm 15\sqrt{5}}{2}$

$\dfrac{15 - 15\sqrt{5}}{2}$ is negative.

92. $x \approx 31.5$ **94.** True **96.** $x^{2n} + 6x^n + 9$

98. The remainder is 0. **100.** $17 - 2i$

102. $-55 + 48i$ **104.** $f(x) = x^2 + 12x$

106. $f(x) = x^4 - 6x^3 + 3x^2 + 10x$

Section 3.4 *(page 269)*

2. $-3, -1, 0, 0, 1$ **4.** $-5, 8, 8$ **6.** $2, 3, \pm 3i$

8. $4, 4, 2 \pm 4i$

10. Zeros: $-2, 2, 4$. Three real zeros; same

12. Zeros: $\pm 2, \pm i$. Two real zeros; same

14. $-5 \pm \sqrt{2}$

$\left(x + 5 + \sqrt{2}\right)\left(x + 5 - \sqrt{2}\right)$

16. $-3 \pm \sqrt{11}$

$\left(x + 3 + \sqrt{11}\right)\left(x + 3 - \sqrt{11}\right)$

18. $\dfrac{1 \pm \sqrt{223}\,i}{2}$

$\left(x - \dfrac{1 - \sqrt{223}\,i}{2}\right)\left(x - \dfrac{1 + \sqrt{223}\,i}{2}\right)$

20. $\pm 5, \pm 5i$

$(y + 5)(y - 5)(y + 5i)(y - 5i)$

22. $1 \pm i, 1$

$(x - 1)(x - 1 + i)(x - 1 - i)$

24. $-5 \pm 2i, -1$

$(x + 1)(x + 5 + 2i)(x + 5 - 2i)$

26. $1 \pm 2i, \frac{1}{2}$

$(2s - 1)(s - 1 - 2i)(s - 1 + 2i)$

28. $\pm 2i, \pm 5i$

$(x + 2i)(x - 2i)(x + 5i)(x - 5i)$

30. $\pm i, -3, -3$

$(x + 3)^2(x + i)(x - i)$

32. $1 \pm \sqrt{3}\,i, 2, 2, 2$

$(x - 2)^3\left(x - 1 - \sqrt{3}\,i\right)\left(x - 1 + \sqrt{3}\,i\right)$

34. (a) $6 \pm \sqrt{2}$ (b) $\left(x - 6 + \sqrt{2}\right)\left(x - 6 - \sqrt{2}\right)$
(c) $\left(6 \pm \sqrt{2}, 0\right)$

36. (a) $8 \pm \sqrt{2}$ (b) $\left(x - 8 + \sqrt{2}\right)\left(x - 8 - \sqrt{2}\right)$
(c) $\left(8 \pm \sqrt{2}, 0\right)$

38. (a) $-4 \pm i, -2$ (b) $(x + 4 + i)(x + 4 - i)(x + 2)$
(c) $(-2, 0)$

40. (a) $\pm i, 4, 4$ (b) $(x + i)(x - i)(x - 4)^2$ (c) $(4, 0)$

42. $x^3 - 4x^2 + 9x - 36$ **44.** $x^3 + 4x^2 - 31x - 174$

46. $x^5 - 6x^4 + 28x^3 - 104x^2 + 192x - 128$

48. $x^5 - 6x^4 + 11x^3 - 12x^2$

50. (a) $(x^2 + 9)(x^2 - 3)$ (b) $(x^2 + 9)\left(x + \sqrt{3}\right)\left(x - \sqrt{3}\right)$
(c) $(x + 3i)(x - 3i)\left(x + \sqrt{3}\right)\left(x - \sqrt{3}\right)$

52. (a) $(x^2 + 4)(x^2 - 3x - 5)$

(b) $(x^2 + 4)\left(x - \dfrac{3 + \sqrt{29}}{2}\right)\left(x - \dfrac{3 - \sqrt{29}}{2}\right)$

(c) $(x + 2i)(x - 2i)\left(x - \dfrac{3 + \sqrt{29}}{2}\right)\left(x - \dfrac{3 - \sqrt{29}}{2}\right)$

54. $\pm 2i, 1, -\frac{1}{2}$ **56.** $-3 \pm i, \frac{1}{4}$ **58.** $-2, -1 \pm 3i$

60. $3, \frac{1}{5}\left(-2 \pm \sqrt{2}\,i\right)$

62. (a) -2 (b) -2 (c) $-2, -1 \pm 3i$

64. (a) 3 (b) 3 (c) $3, \dfrac{-2 \pm \sqrt{2}\,i}{5}$

66. No. Setting $P = 9{,}000{,}000$ and solving the resulting equation yields imaginary roots.

68. True **70.** (a) No (b) No

72. $f(x) = x^2 - 2ax + a^2 + b^2$ **74.** $\dfrac{x + 2}{x + 6}, x \neq 6$

76. $\dfrac{x^2 - 5}{x(x + 3)}, x \neq 6$

78.

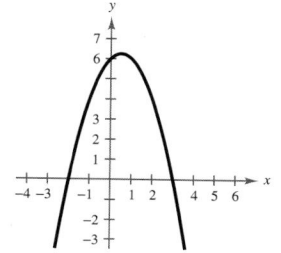

Vertex: $\left(\frac{1}{2}, \frac{25}{4}\right)$

Intercepts:

$(-2, 0), (3, 0), (0, 6)$

80.

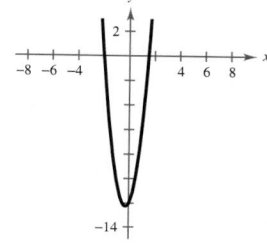

Vertex: $\left(-\frac{1}{4}, -\frac{49}{4}\right)$

Intercepts:

$(-2, 0), (1.5, 0), (0, -12)$

Section 3.5 *(page 277)*

2. (a)

x	$f(x)$	x	$f(x)$
0.5	-5	1.5	15
0.9	-45	1.1	55
0.99	-495	1.01	505
0.999	-4995	1.001	5005

x	$f(x)$	x	$f(x)$
5	6.25	-5	$4.1\overline{6}$
10	$5.\overline{55}$	-10	$4.\overline{54}$
100	$5.\overline{05}$	-100	$4.95\overline{0495}$
1000	$5.\overline{005}$	-1000	4.995

(b) Vertical asymptote: $x = 1$

Horizontal asymptote: $y = 5$

(c) Domain: all $x \neq 1$

4. (a)

x	$f(x)$	x	$f(x)$
0.5	6	1.5	6
0.9	30	1.1	30
0.99	300	1.01	300
0.999	3000	1.001	3000

x	$f(x)$	x	$f(x)$
5	0.75	-5	0.5
10	$0.\overline{33}$	-10	$0.\overline{27}$
100	$0.\overline{03}$	-100	0.0297
1000	$0.\overline{003}$	-1000	0.003

(b) Vertical asymptote: $x = 1$

Horizontal asymptote: $y = 0$

(c) Domain: all $x \neq 1$

6. (a)

x	$f(x)$	x	$f(x)$
0.5	$-2.\overline{66}$	1.5	4.8
0.9	-18.95	1.1	20.95
0.99	-199	1.01	201
0.999	-1999	1.001	2001

x	$f(x)$	x	$f(x)$
5	$0.8\overline{33}$	-5	$-0.8\overline{33}$
10	$0.\overline{40}$	-10	$-0.4\overline{04}$
100	0.04	-100	-0.04
1000	0.004	-1000	-0.004

(b) Vertical asymptotes: $x = \pm 1$

Horizontal asymptote: $y = 0$

(c) Domain: all $x \neq \pm 1$

8. (d)   **10.** (e)   **12.** (f)

14. (a) Domain: all $x \neq 2$

(b) Vertical asymptote: $x = 2$

Horizontal asymptote: $y = 0$

16. (a) Domain: all $x \neq -1$

(b) Vertical asymptote: $x = -1$

Horizontal asymptote: $y = -\frac{5}{2}$

18. (a) Domain: all reals   (b) Horizontal asymptote: $y = 3$

20. (a) Domain of f: all $x \neq 0, 3$

Domain of g: all real numbers

(b) Vertical asymptote: none

(c)

x	-1	0	1	2	3	3.5	4
$f(x)$	-1	Undef.	1	2	Undef.	3.5	4
$g(x)$	-1	0	1	2	3	3.5	4

(d) Values differ only where f is undefined.

22. (a) Domain of f: all $x \neq 4, 5$

Domain of g: all $x \neq 5$

(b) Vertical asymptote: $x = 5$

(c)

x	0	1	2	3	4	5	6
$f(x)$	$-\frac{2}{5}$	$-\frac{1}{2}$	$-\frac{2}{3}$	-1	Undef.	Undef.	2
$g(x)$	$-\frac{2}{5}$	$-\frac{1}{2}$	$-\frac{2}{3}$	-1	-2	Undef.	2

(d) Values differ only where f is undefined and g is defined.

24. 2; Greater than; Less than

26. 0; Greater than; Less than

28. 2   **30.** None

32. (a) \$4411.76   (b) \$25,000   (c) \$225,000

(d)

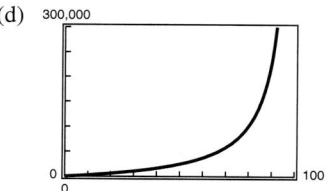

Answers will vary.

(e) No. The function is undefined at the 100% level.

34. (a) $y = \dfrac{1}{-0.0029x + 0.164}$

(b)

x	10	20	30	40	50
y	7.4	9.4	13.0	20.8	52.6

(c) No. The function is negative.

36. ≈ 0.247 milligrams

38. False. The degree of the denominator gives the maximum possible number of vertical asymptotes, and the degree is finite.

40. $f(x) = \dfrac{1}{x^2 + x - 2}$ **42.** $f(x) = \dfrac{2x^2}{1 + x^2}$

44. $0, \pm\dfrac{3\sqrt{2}}{2}$ **46.** $5, -\dfrac{7}{2}$ **48.** $0, \pm\dfrac{7}{3}$

50. $x + 9 + \dfrac{42}{x - 4}$ **52.** $2x - 9 + \dfrac{34}{x + 5}$

54. $x^3 - 8x^2 + 25x - 200$ **56.** $x^3 - 12x^2 + 46x - 60$

Section 3.6   *(page 286)*

2.

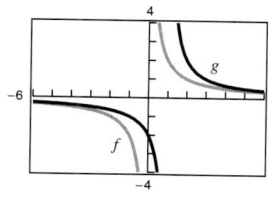

Horizontal shift

4.

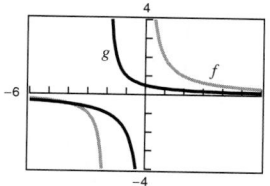

Horizontal shift and
vertical shrink

6.

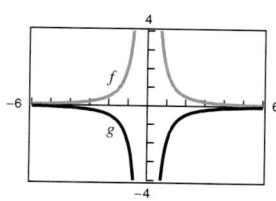

Reflection in the *x*-axis

8.

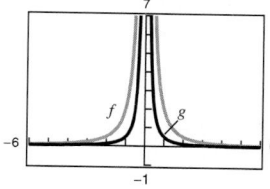

Vertical shrink

10.

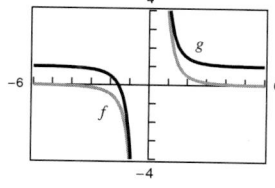

Vertical shift

12.

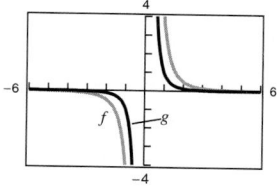

Vertical shrink

14.

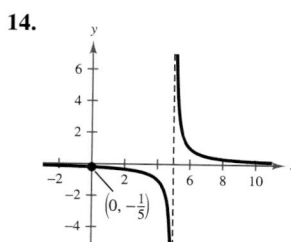

16.

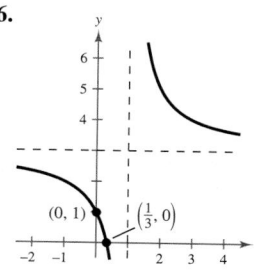

18.

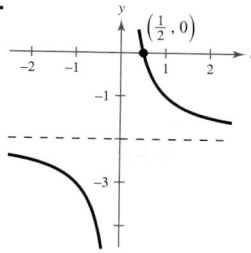

20.

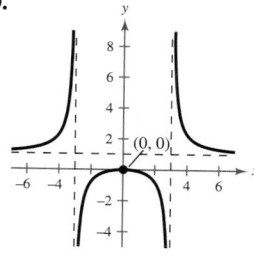

22.

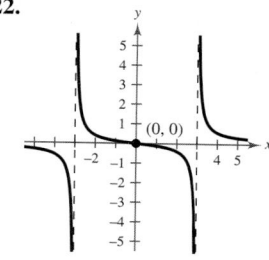

24.

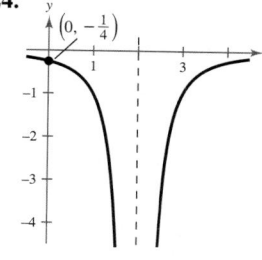

26.

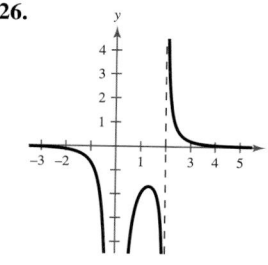

28.

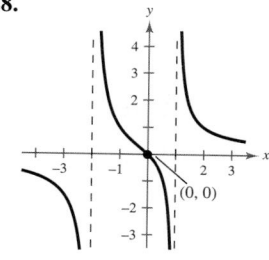

30.

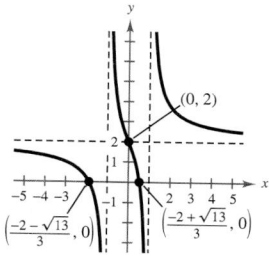

32.

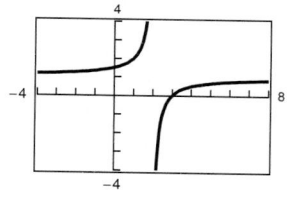

Domain: $(-\infty, 2), (2, \infty)$

$x = 2, y = 1$

34.

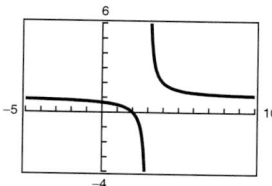

Domain: $(-\infty, 3), (3, \infty)$

$x = 3, y = 1$

36.

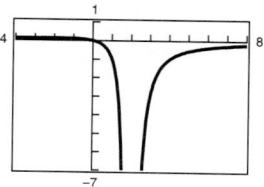

Domain: $(-\infty, 2), (2, \infty)$

$x = 2, y = 0$

CHAPTER 3

38.

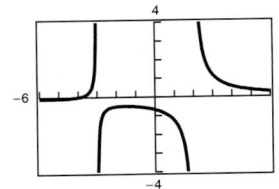

Domain: $(-\infty, -3), (-3, 2), (2, \infty)$

$x = -3, x = 2, y = 0$

40.

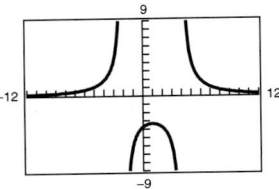

Domain: $(-\infty, -2), (-2, 4), (4, \infty)$

$x = -2, x = 4, y = 0$

42.

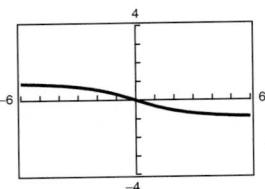

There are two horizontal asymptotes, $y = 1$ and $y = -1$.

44.

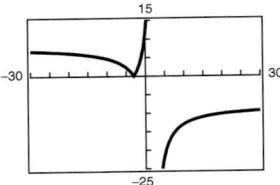

There are two horizontal asymptotes, $y = 8$, $y = -8$, and one vertical asymptote, $x = 2$.

46.

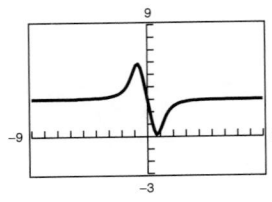

The graph crosses the horizontal asymptote at $y = 3$.

48.

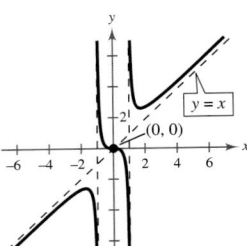

50.

52.

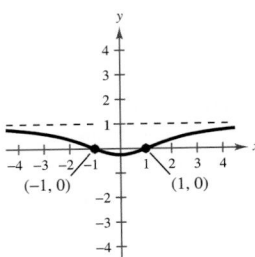

54.

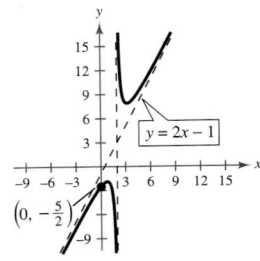

56. $(0, 0)$ **58.** $(1, 0), (2, 0)$

60.

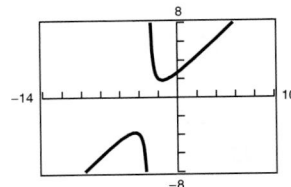

Domain: $(-\infty, -3), (-3, \infty)$

Vertical asymptote: $x = -3$

$y = x + 2$

62.

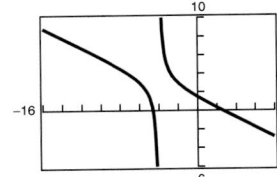

Domain: $(-\infty, -4), (-4, \infty)$

Vertical asymptote: $x = -4$

$y = -\frac{1}{2}x + 1$

64.   **66.**

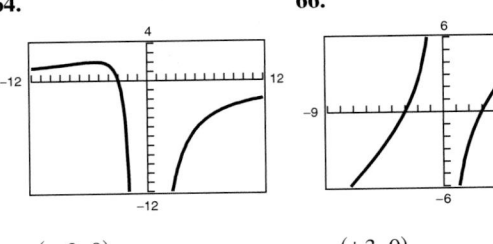

$(-3, 0)$ $(\pm 3, 0)$

68. (a) $y = \dfrac{500}{x}$ (b) $(0, \infty)$

(c)

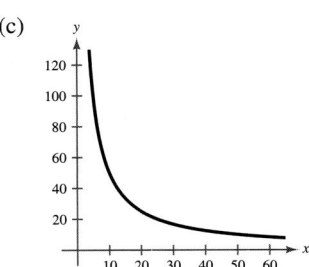

$16\frac{2}{3}$ meters

70. (a) and (b) Answers will vary.

(c)

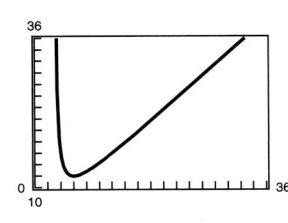

$a = 6, A = 12$

72.

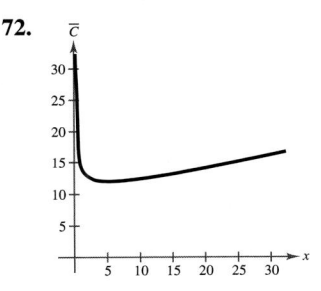

$x \approx 5$

74. (a) Answers will vary.

(b) Vertical asymptote: $x = 25$

Horizontal asymptote: $y = 25$

(c)

x	30	35	40	45	50	55	60
y	150	87.5	66.7	56.3	50	45.8	42.9

(d)

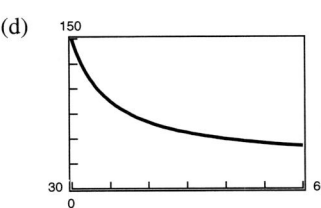

(e) No. At 20 miles per hour you would use more time in one direction than is required for the round trip at an average speed of 50 miles per hour.

76. (a) $N_1 = -0.46t + 16.8$

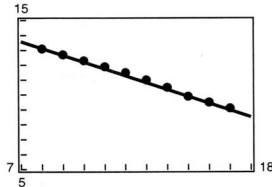

(b) $N_2 = \dfrac{1000}{3.8t + 43.7}$

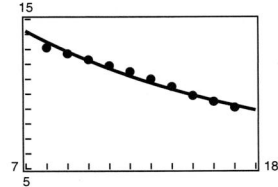

(c)

t	8	9	10	11	12
N_1	13.1	12.7	12.2	11.7	11.3
N_2	13.5	12.8	12.2	11.7	11.2

t	13	14	15	16	17
N_1	10.8	10.4	9.9	9.4	9.0
N_2	10.7	10.3	9.9	9.6	9.2

The linear model seems to follow the data trend a little better.

78. False. It can cross horizontal asymptotes.

80.

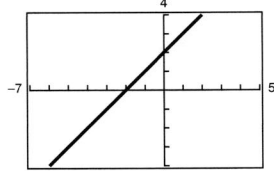

The denominator is a factor of the numerator.

82. $f(x) = \dfrac{x^2 - x - 6}{x - 2}$ **84.** $f(x) = \dfrac{2x - 6}{x + 1}$

86. $\dfrac{512}{x^3}$ **88.** $\dfrac{x^2}{5y^2}, \ x \neq 0$ **90.** 3

CHAPTER 3

92.

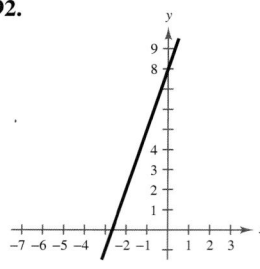

94.

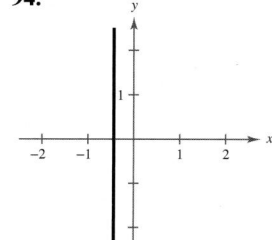

96.

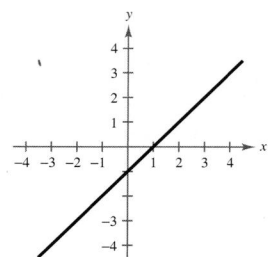

98.

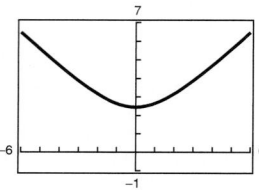

Domain: $(-\infty, \infty)$

Range: $\left[\sqrt{6}, \infty\right)$

100.

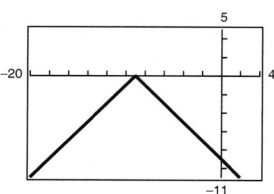

Domain: $(-\infty, \infty)$

Range: $(-\infty, 0]$

Review Exercises *(page 291)*

2. (a)

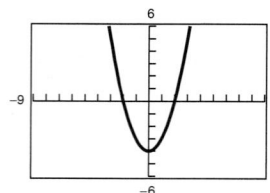

Vertical shift

(b)

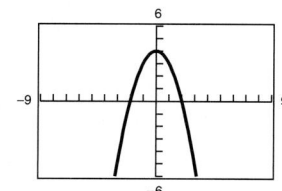

Reflection in the *x*-axis and vertical shift

(c)

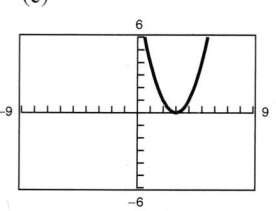

Horizontal shift

(d)

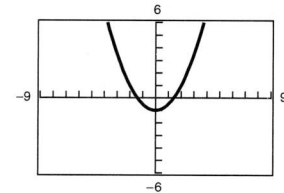

Vertical shrink and vertical shift

4.

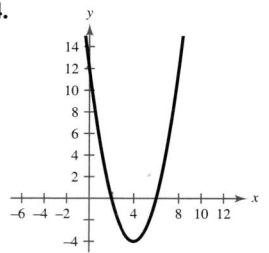

Vertex: $(4, -4)$

Intercepts:

$(0, 12), (2, 0), (6, 0)$

6.

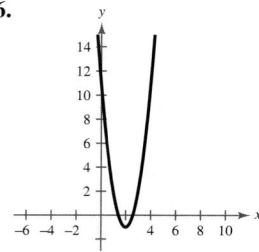

Vertex: $(2, -1)$

Intercepts:

$(0, 11), \left(2 \pm \frac{1}{3}\sqrt{3}, 0\right)$

8. $f(x) = \frac{1}{3}(x - 2)^2 + 3$

10. Minimum: $(-4, -6)$

12. Maximum: $(2, 7)$

14. Minimum: $\left(-\frac{1}{2}, 12\right)$

16. Minimum: $\left(-\frac{1}{2}, 4\right)$

18. (a)

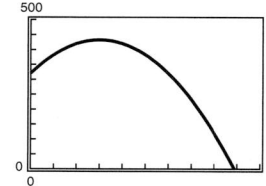

(b) $(15, 432.5)$

(c) Answers will vary.

(d) Maximum profit

20. (a)

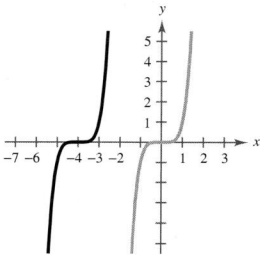

(b)

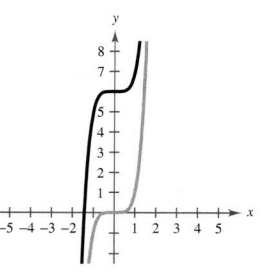

(c)

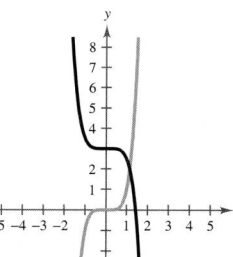

(d)

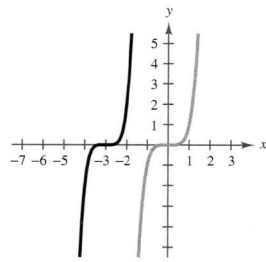

22. (a)   (b)

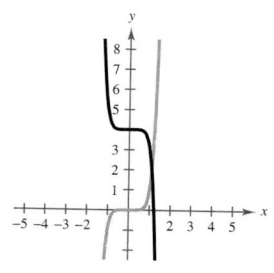   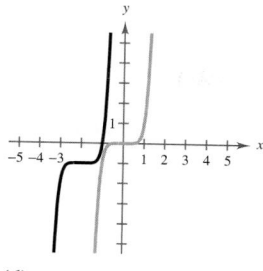

(c)   (d)

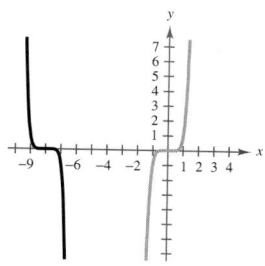

24. Falls to the left   **26.** Rises to the left
Rises to the right   Falls to the right

28.

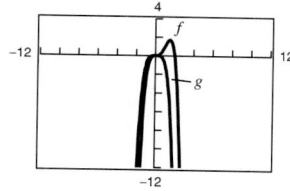

30. (a) $x = 0, \frac{1}{2}, -1$ **32.** (a) $x = -8$
(b)   (b)

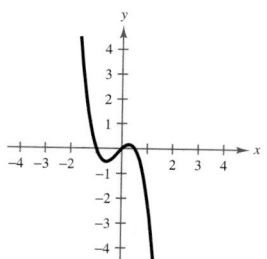   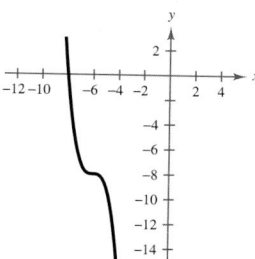

34. (a) $t = 0, 0, -2, 2$
(b)

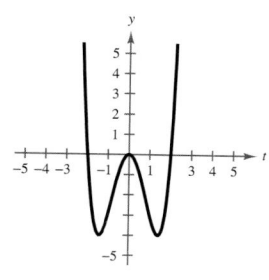

36. (a) $V = \pi r^2(216 - 2\pi r)$

(b) $r = \dfrac{72}{\pi}$, $V = 72$

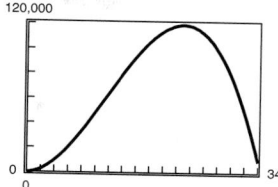

38. (a) $(-3, -2), (-1, 0), (3, 4)$

(b) $-2.979, -0.554, 3.533$

40. (a) $(-2, -1), (0, 1)$ (b) $-1.897, 0.738$

42.

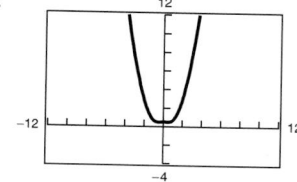

44. $\dfrac{4}{3} + \dfrac{29}{3(3x - 2)}$ **46.** $3x^2 + 3 + \dfrac{3}{x^2 - 1}$

48. $3x^2 + 5x + 8 + \dfrac{10}{2x^2 - 1}$

50. $0.1x^2 + 0.8x + 4 + \dfrac{19.5}{x - 5}$

52. $2x^2 + 3x + \dfrac{1}{2} + \dfrac{9}{2(2x - 1)}$

54. (a) Yes   (b) Yes   (c) Yes   (d) No

56. $x^3 - 7x^2 + 9x + 5$ **58.** $x^4 - x^3 - 3x^2 + 17x - 30$

60. $-2, -\dfrac{3}{5}, \dfrac{1}{2}$ **62.** $-1, 0.3, 2$ **64.** $\pm\dfrac{\sqrt{5}}{5}i, \pm 5i$

66. Answers will vary.

68. (a)

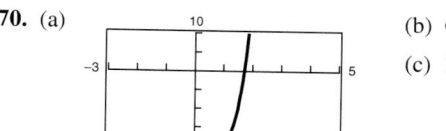

(b) One
(c) -0.44

70. (a)

(b) One
(c) 1.72

72. $-3, 4 \pm i$

$(x + 3)(x - 4 - i)(x - 4 + i)$

74. $2.5, 1 \pm \sqrt{5}i$

$(2x - 5)(x - 1 - \sqrt{5}i)(x - 1 + \sqrt{5}i)$

76. $-5, -5, \pm i$

$(x + 5)(x + 5)(x + i)(x - i)$

78. $f(x) = x^4 - 8x^3 + 20x^2 - 32x + 64$

80. $f(x) = x^3 - 15x^2 + 73x - 111$

82. $f(x) = x^4 + 6x^3 + 4x^2 + 64$

84. (a) $(x^2 - 5)(x^2 - x + 4)$

(b) $(x - \sqrt{5})(x + \sqrt{5})(x^2 - x + 4)$

(c) $(x - \sqrt{5})(x + \sqrt{5})\left(x - \dfrac{1 \pm \sqrt{15}i}{2}\right)\left(x - \dfrac{1 - \sqrt{15}i}{2}\right)$

86. (a) $(x^2 - x - 4)(x^2 - 3x + 4)$

(b) $\left(x - \dfrac{1 + \sqrt{17}}{2}\right)\left(x - \dfrac{1 - \sqrt{17}}{2}\right)(x^2 - 3x + 4)$

(c) $\left(x - \dfrac{1 + \sqrt{17}}{2}\right)\left(x - \dfrac{1 - \sqrt{17}}{2}\right)$

$\left(x - \dfrac{3 + \sqrt{7}i}{2}\right)\left(x - \dfrac{3 - \sqrt{7}i}{2}\right)$

88. Domain: all $x \neq -12$

Vertical asymptote: $x = -12$

Horizontal asymptote: $y = 5$

90. Domain: all real numbers

Horizontal asymptote: $y = 2$

92. $y = 0$ **94.** $y = 3$ **96.** None   **98.** $y = \pm 1$

100. (a) $176 million

(b) $528 million

(c) $1584 million

(d)

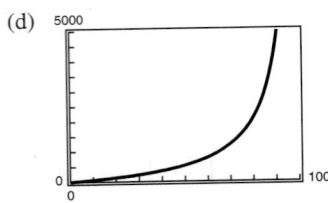

(e) No. As $p \to 100$, the cost approaches ∞.

102.

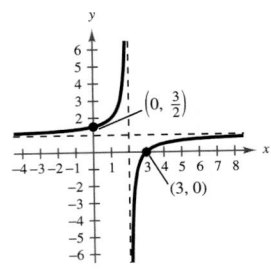

104.

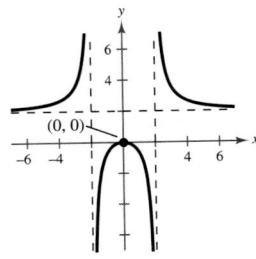

106.

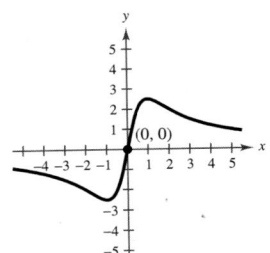

108.

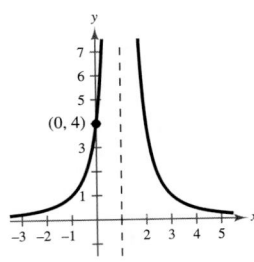

110.

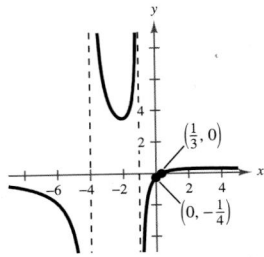

112.

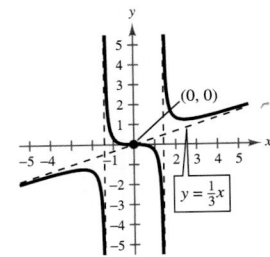

114.

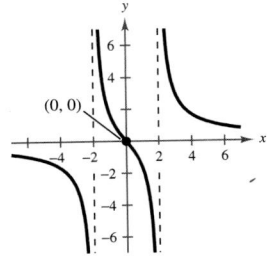

116.

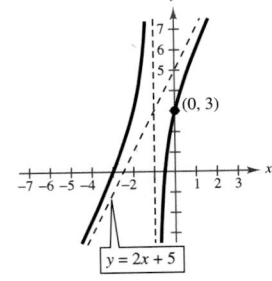

118. (a)

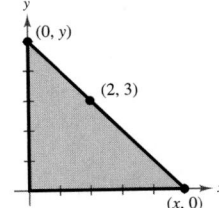

(b) Answers will vary.

(c)

x	2.5	3	3.5	4	4.5
A	18.75	13.50	12.25	12	12.15

$x = 4, y = 6$

(d)

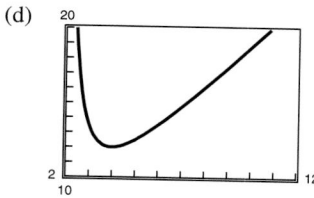

$x = 4, y = 6$

(e) $y = \frac{3}{2}(x + 2)$. The area increases without bound as x increases.

120. False. The horizontal asymptote is $y = 3$.

Chapter 4

Section 4.1   *(page 307)*

2. 1767.767   **4.** 0.006   **6.** 673.639   **8.** 0.472

10. 43.816   **12.** $g(x) = h(x)$ **14.** None are equal.

16. (h)   **18.** (b)   **20.** (f)   **22.** (d)

24. Upward shift of 5 units

26. Reflection in x-axis, then upward shift of 5 units

28.

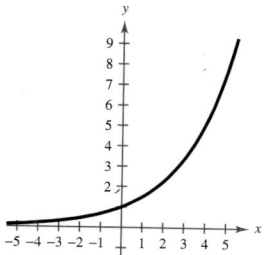

(a) $y = 0$

(b) $(0, 1)$

(c) Increasing

30.

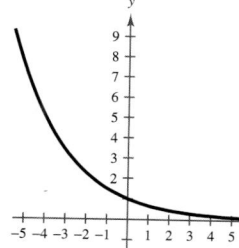

(a) $y = 0$

(b) $(0, 1)$

(c) Decreasing

32.

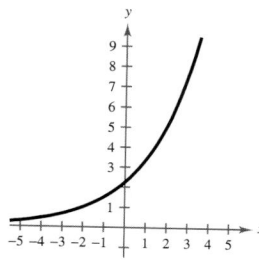

(a) $y = 0$ (b) $(0, 2.25)$

(c) Increasing

34.

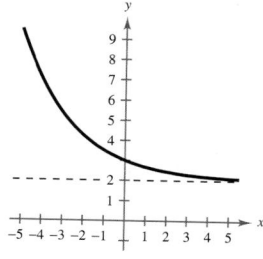

(a) $y = 2$ (b) $(0, 3)$

(c) Decreasing

36.

x	-2	-1	0	1	2
$f(x)$	6.25	2.5	1	0.4	0.16

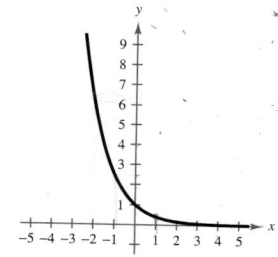

38.

x	-1	0	1	2	3	4
$f(x)$	0.25	0.5	1	2	4	8

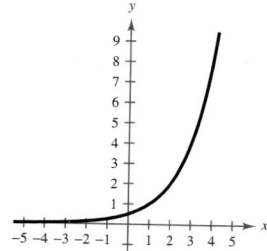

40.

x	-3	-2	-1	0	1
$f(x)$	20	7.4	2.7	1	0.4

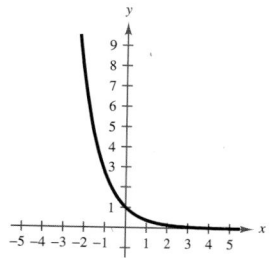

42.

x	-3	-2	-1	0	1	2
$f(x)$	9	5.4	3.3	2	1.2	0.7

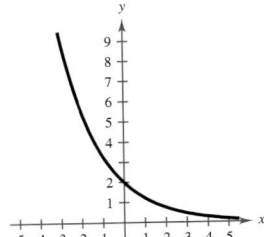

44.

x	-1	0	2	3	4	5
$f(x)$	3.004	3.02	3.25	4	7	19

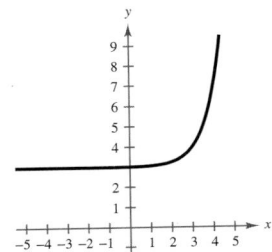

46.

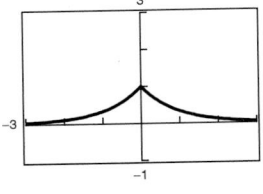

$y = 0$

48.

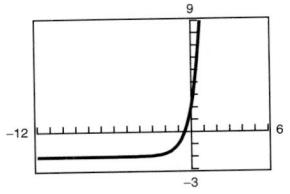

$y = -2$

50.

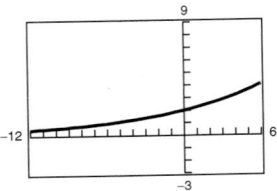

$s(t) = 0$

52.

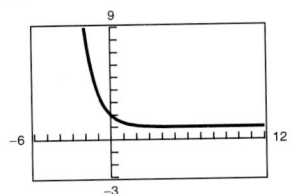

$g(x) = 1$

54. (a)

x	-1	-0.5	0	0.5	1
$f(x)$	2	1.4142	1	0.7071	0.5
$g(x)$	4	2	1	0.5	0.25

$x > 0$

(b)

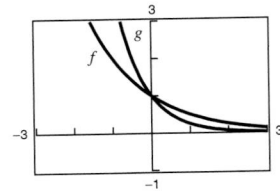

(i) $x > 0$ (ii) $x < 0$

56. (a)

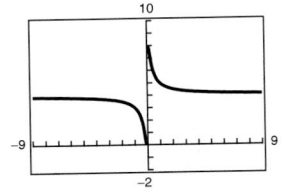

(b)

x	-15	-2	-1	-0.2	-0.1
$f(x)$	3.93	3.5	3.0	0.61	0.05

x	0	0.01	0.2	1	5
$f(x)$	Undef.	8	7.4	4.9	4.2

$y = 4, x = 0$

58. (a)

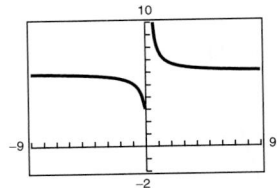

(b)

x	-15	-10	-1	-0.1	-0.001
$f(x)$	5.9	5.9	5.1	3.2	3

x	0	0.01	0.1	0.2	0.288
$f(x)$	Undef.	0	-1.1	-8	-2311

x	$\dfrac{0.2}{\ln 2}$	0.289	1	4	10
$f(x)$	Undef.	2714	7.7	6.3	6.1

$y = 6, x = \dfrac{0.2}{\ln 2}$

60. (a)

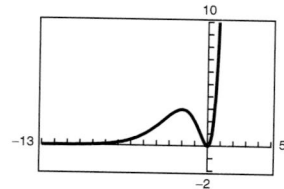

(b) Increasing on $(-\infty, -2), (0, \infty)$

Decreasing on $(-2, 0)$

(c) Relative maximum: $(-2, 2.943)$

Relative minimum: $(0, 0)$

62. (a)

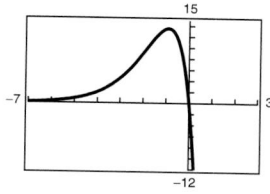

(b) Increasing on $(-\infty, -0.910)$

Decreasing on $(-0.910, \infty)$

(c) Relative maximum: $(-0.910, 13.562)$

64.

n	1	2	4	12	365	Continuous
A	1791	1806	1814	1819	1822	1822

66.

n	1	2	4	12	365	Continuous
A	10,286	10,641	10,828	10,957	11,021	11,023

68.

t	1	10	20	30	40	50
A	12,742	21,865	39,841	72,596	132,278	241,026

70.

t	1	10	20	30	40	50
A	12,935	25,402	53,722	113,827	240,952	510,056

72. (a)

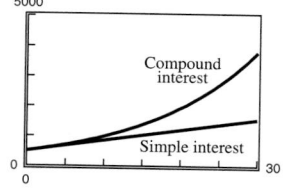

Answers will vary.

(b) $A = 500(1.07)^t$

$A = 500(0.07)t + 500$

74. (a) 1992: 2651; 1995: 2894; 1998: 3160

(b)

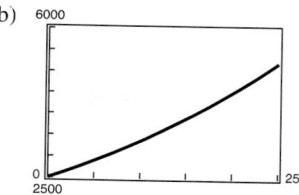

(c) 2005: 3880; 2010: 4492

76. (a) 10 units   (b) 7.85 units

(c)

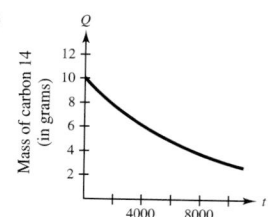

78. (a) $T = -1.24t + 73.0$

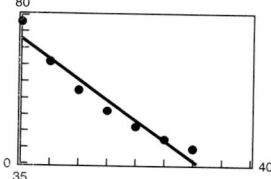

Does not appear linear; the temperature decreases at a slower rate as it approaches the room temperature.

(b) $T = 0.034t^2 - 2.264t + 77.295$

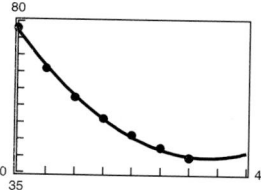

The parabola is a better fit than the line in part (a). It may not be a good model because the parabola is increasing when $t = 60$.

(c) $T = 54.438(0.964)^t + 21$

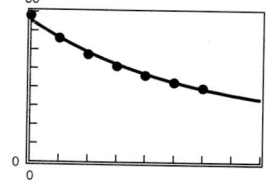

(d) The horizontal asymptote of the exponential model is $T = 0$.

CHAPTER 4

80. (a)

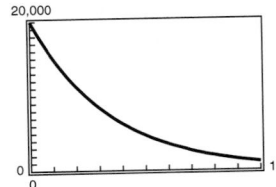

(b)

t	1	2	3	4	5
V	15,000	11,250	8438	6328	4746

t	6	7	8	9	10
V	3560	2670	2002	1502	1126

82. False. e is an irrational number.

84. (a)

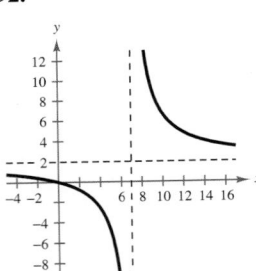

$f(x)$ approaches $g(x) = 1.6487$

(b) e^r

86. (c), (d)   **88.** $f^{-1}(x) = \dfrac{x + 7}{5}$ **90.** $f^{-1}(x) = x^3 - 8$

92.

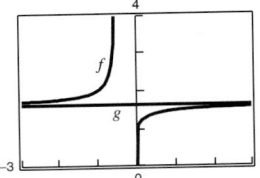

94.

Section 4.2 *(page 318)*

2. $3^4 = 81$ **4.** $10^{-3} = \frac{1}{1000}$ **6.** $16^{3/4} = 8$

8. $e^{1.386\ldots} = 4$ **10.** $\log_8 64 = 2$ **12.** $\log_9 27 = \frac{3}{2}$

14. $\log_{10} 0.001 = -3$ **16.** $\ln 4 = x$

18. $\ln 23.14\ldots = \pi$ **20.** $\frac{2}{3}$ **22.** -3 **24.** -1

26. 1   **28.** 1   **30.** -1 **32.** 2.161   **34.** 1.097

36. -1.444 **38.** 3.311   **40.** 3.137   **42.** -19.395

44.

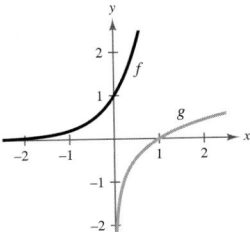

46.

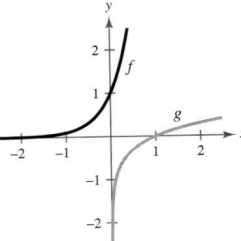

Reflections in the line
$y = x$
$g = f^{-1}$

Reflections in the line
$y = x$
$g = f^{-1}$

48. (f)   **50.** (e)   **52.** (a)

54. Domain: $(0, \infty)$

Vertical asymptote:

$x = 0$

Intercept: $(1, 0)$

56. Domain: $(-2, \infty)$

Vertical asymptote:

$x = -2$

Intercept: $(-1, 0)$

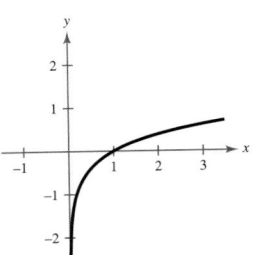

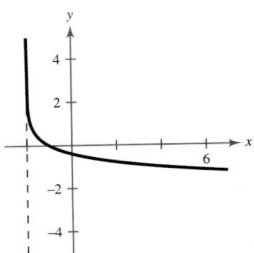

58. Domain: $(1, \infty)$

Vertical asymptote:

$x = 1$

Intercept: $\left(\frac{626}{625}, 0\right)$

60. Domain: $(-2, \infty)$

Vertical asymptote:

$x = -2$

Intercept: $\left(-\frac{161}{81}, 0\right)$

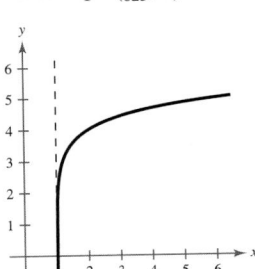

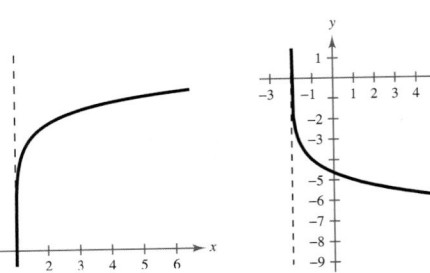

62. Domain: $(-\infty, 0)$

Vertical asymptote: $x = 0$

Intercept: $(-1, 0)$

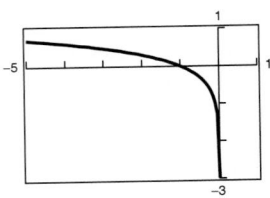

64. Domain: $(-1, \infty)$

Vertical asymptote: $x = -1$

Intercept: $(0, 0)$

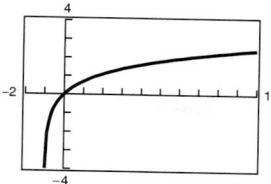

66. Domain: $(-\infty, 3)$

Vertical asymptote: $x = 3$

Intercept: $(2, 0)$

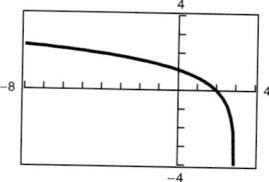

68. (a)

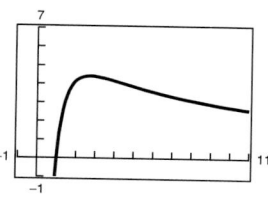

(b) Domain: $(0, \infty)$

(c) Decreasing: $(2.72, \infty)$; Increasing: $(0, 2.72)$

(d) Relative maximum: $(2.72, 4.41)$

70. (a)

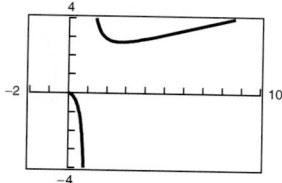

(b) Domain: $(0, 1), (1, \infty)$

(c) Decreasing: $(0, 1), (1, 2.72)$; Increasing: $(2.72, \infty)$

(d) Relative minimum: $(2.72, 2.72)$

72. 21,357 foot-pounds

74. (a)

K	1	2	4	6	8	10	12
t	0	12.6	25.2	32.6	37.8	41.9	45.2

Answers will vary.

(b)

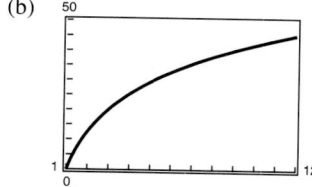

76. (a)

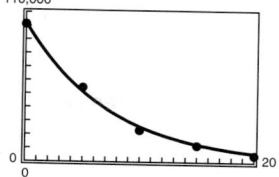

(b) $\ln P = -0.1499h + 11.585$

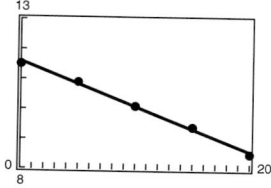

(c) $P = e^{-0.1499h + 11.585}$ or $P = 107,473.5e^{-0.1499h}$

78. (a)

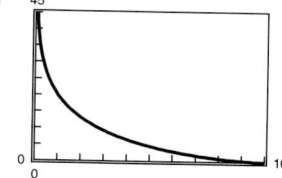

Domain: $0 < x \le 10$

(b) $x = 0$ (c) 22.9   (d) $p = 10 \ln\left(\dfrac{\sqrt{100 - x^2} + 10}{x}\right)$

(e)

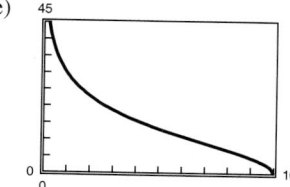

At the beginning of the process

80.

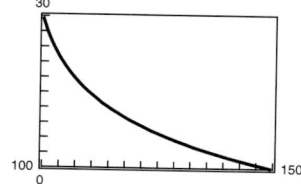

17.66 cubic feet per minute

82. 30 years

84. Total amount: $323,179.20; Interest: $173,179.20

86. False. Reflect $g(x)$ in the line $y = x$.

88. (a) False   (b) True   (c) True   (d) False

90. $y = (x - 1) - \frac{1}{2}(x - 1)^2 + \frac{1}{3}(x - 1)^3 - \frac{1}{4}(x - 1)^4$

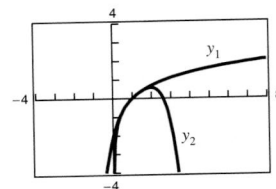

Answers will vary.

92. Vertical asymptote: $x = -8$

Horizontal asymptote: $y = 0$

94. Vertical asymptotes: $x = \frac{5}{2}, x = -3$

Horizontal asymptote: $y = 0$

96. 162,754.791   **98.** 0.007

Section 4.3   *(page 326)*

2.

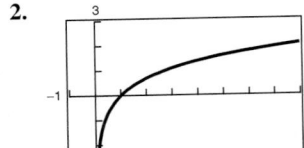

$f = g$

4. 0.712   **6.** -2 **8.** 3.823   **10.** 1.637

12. (a) $\dfrac{\log_{10} x}{\log_{10} 3}$ (b) $\dfrac{\ln x}{\ln 3}$ **14.** (a) $\dfrac{\log_{10} x}{\log_{10} \frac{1}{3}}$ (b) $\dfrac{\ln x}{\ln \frac{1}{3}}$

16. (a) $\dfrac{\log_{10} \frac{3}{4}}{\log_{10} x}$ (b) $\dfrac{\ln \frac{3}{4}}{\ln x}$ **18.** (a) $\dfrac{\log_{10} x}{\log_{10} 7.1}$ (b) $\dfrac{\ln x}{\ln 7.1}$

20. $f(x) = \dfrac{\ln x}{\ln 4}$ **22.** $f(x) = \dfrac{\ln x}{\ln \frac{1}{4}}$

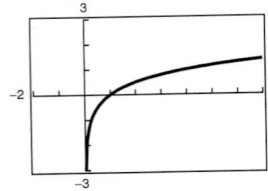

24. $f(x) = \dfrac{\log_{10} x}{\log_{10} 12.4}$ **26.** $f(x) = \dfrac{\log_{10}(x/3)}{\log_{10} 5}$

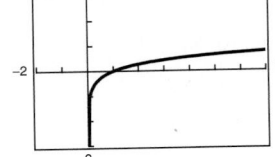 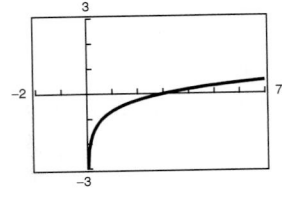

28. $1 + \log_{10} z$ **30.** $\log_{10} y - \log_{10} 2$

32. $-3 \log_6 z$ **34.** $\frac{1}{3} \ln t$ **36.** $\ln x + \ln y - \ln z$

38. $\ln(x + 1) + \ln(x - 1) - 3 \ln x$

40. $\ln x - \frac{3}{2} \ln y$ **42.** $\ln x - \frac{1}{2} \ln(x^2 + 1)$

44. $\ln x + \frac{1}{2} \ln(x + 2)$ **46.** $\frac{1}{2} \log_b x + 4 \log_b y - 4 \log_b z$

48.   **50.** $\ln yz$

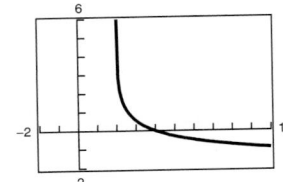

$y_1 = y_2$

52. $\log_5 \dfrac{8}{t}$ **54.** $\log_6(2x)^{-6}$ **56.** $\log_7(z - 4)^{5/2}$

58. $\ln 64z^5$ **60.** $\ln \dfrac{x^3 y^2}{z^4}$ **62.** $\ln \dfrac{z^4(z + 5)^4}{(z - 5)^2}$

64. $\ln\left(\dfrac{x}{x^2 - 1}\right)^2$ **66.** $\ln\left[x^3(x - 1)\sqrt{x - 1}\right]$

68. $\ln 5\sqrt{5}\,t^6$

70.   **72.**

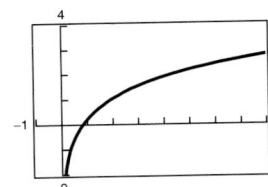 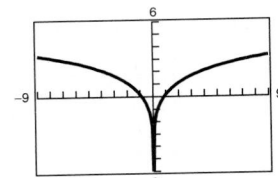

$y_1 = y_2$ for $x > 0$ No. The domains differ.

74. $\frac{1}{3}$ **76.** -3

78. -16 is not in the domain of $\log_4 x$.   **80.** 3   **82.** 12

84. 0   **86.** $\frac{3}{5}$ **88.** $-1 - \log_5 3$ **90.** $4 + 4 \log_2 3$

92. $\log_{10} 3 - 2$ **94.** $\ln 6 - 2$

96. (a)   (b) 90

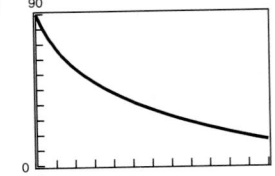

   (c) 77

   (d) 73

   (e) 9 months

98. If $y = ab^x$, you have, by the properties of logarithms, $\ln y = \ln a + (\ln b)x$, which is linear. If $y = 1/(ax + b)$, then $1/y = ax + b$. Answers will vary.

100. True   **102.** False. $f(\sqrt{x}) = \frac{1}{2}f(x)$ **104.** True

106. $\ln 2 \approx 0.6931$ $\ln 10 \approx 2.3025$
  $\ln 3 \approx 1.0986$ $\ln 12 \approx 2.4848$
  $\ln 4 \approx 1.3862$ $\ln 15 \approx 2.7080$
  $\ln 5 \approx 1.6094$ $\ln 16 \approx 2.7724$
  $\ln 6 \approx 1.7917$ $\ln 18 \approx 2.8903$
  $\ln 8 \approx 2.0793$ $\ln 20 \approx 2.9956$
  $\ln 9 \approx 2.1972$

108. Answers will vary.   **110.** $\dfrac{27y^3}{8x^6}$ **112.** $\dfrac{x^2y^2}{x + y}$

114. $0, -5, -5$ **116.** $\pm\frac{1}{3}, \pm 2$ **118.** $\pm\frac{1}{3}, \pm 5$

120. 6.072 **122.** 36.998 **124.** 0.146 **126.** 0.856

Section 4.4   *(page 336)*

2. (a) No   (b) No   **4.** (a) Yes   (b) Yes   (c) No

6. (a) No   (b) Yes   (c) No

8. (a) Yes   (b) Yes   (c) No

10.   **12.**

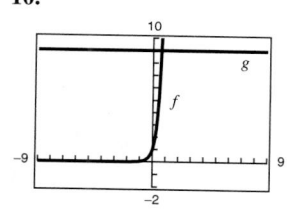   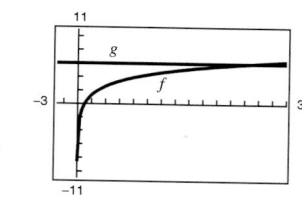

$\left(\frac{2}{3}, 9\right)$ $(25, 6)$

14.   **16.** 5   **18.** -2

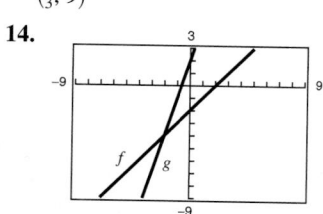

$(-2, -4)$

20. -5 **22.** 3   **24.** 2   **26.** $\ln 2 \approx 0.693$

28. $e^{-1} \approx 0.368$ **30.** 64   **32.** 100

34. $\dfrac{1}{\sqrt{10}} \approx 0.316$ **36.** $\dfrac{1}{3}(e^8 - 5) \approx 991.986$

38. $2x - 1$ **40.** $2x - 1$ **42.** $x^3 - 8$ **44.** 0.894

46. 1.151   **48.** 0.554   **50.** -4.917 **52.** 0.648

54. 2.120   **56.** $\ln 2 \approx 0.693$ and $\ln 3 \approx 1.099$

58. 0.095   **60.** 0.409

62.

x	1.6	1.7	1.8	1.9	2.0
$f(x)$	24.53	29.96	36.60	44.70	54.60

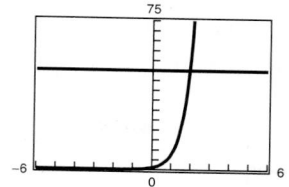

1.956

64.

x	0	1	2	3	4
$f(x)$	200	292	352	381	393

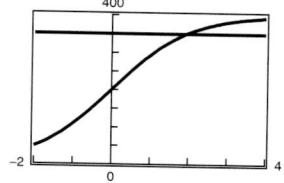

1.946

66. 3.322   **68.** 0.059   **70.** 4.535

72. 0.247   **74.** 0.572

76.   **78.**

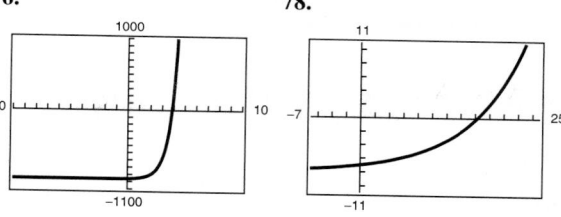

3.847   16.636

80. 7.389   **82.** 0.680   **84.** 33.115   **86.** ± 1000

88. 568.341   **90.** 22,034.466   **92.** ± 54.589

94. 4   **96.** 2.547   **98.** 1146.5

100.

x	4	5	6	7	8
$f(x)$	8.99	9.66	10.20	10.67	11.07

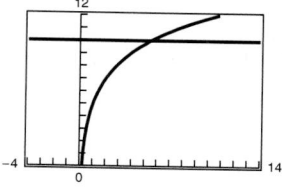

5.606

102.

x	150	155	160	165	170
$f(x)$	10.85	10.92	10.99	11.06	11.13

160.489

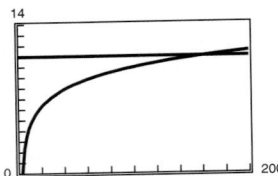

104. ± 100 **106.** 5.021 **108.** 0.828 **110.** 27.984

112.

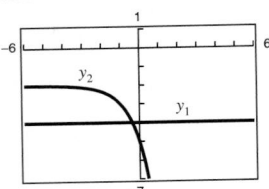

$(-0.369, -4)$

114.

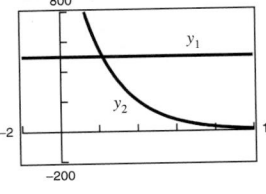

$(2.197, 500)$

116.

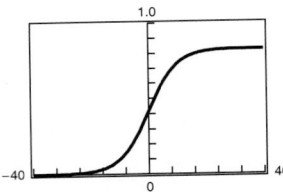

$(14.182, 10)$

118. (a) 5.8 years
(b) 9.2 years

120. (a)

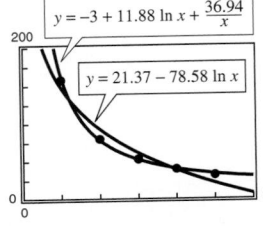

(b) $y = 0$, $y = 0.83$. The proportion of correct responses will approach 0.83 as the number of trials increases.

(c) 5

122. (a) 303 units (b) 528 units **124.** 12.76 inches

126. (a) $y = 21.37 - 78.58 \ln x$

Answers will vary.

$y = -3 + 11.88 \ln x + \frac{36.94}{x}$

$y = 21.37 - 78.58 \ln x$

(b) 1.2 meters, 0.9 meters. Answers will vary.

128. True

130. Yes. Doubling time: $t = \dfrac{\ln 2}{r}$

Quadrupling time: $t = \dfrac{\ln 4}{r} = 2\left(\dfrac{\ln 2}{r}\right)$

132.

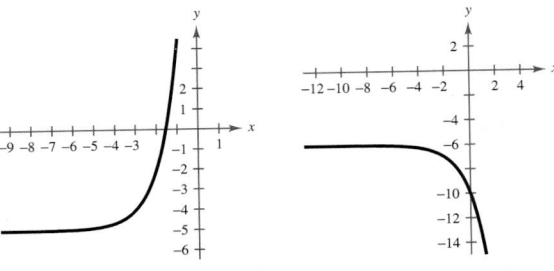

134.

136. 1.232 **138.** 0.815

Section 4.5 *(page 348)*

2. (e) **4.** (a) **6.** (f) **8.** Linear model

10. Exponential model **12.** Logistics model

14. Linear model

16.

18.

Exponential model · Logarithmic model

	Initial Investment	Annual % Rate	Time to Double	Amount After 10 Years
20.	$20,000	10.5%	6.60 yr	$57,153.02
22.	$10,000	5.78%	12 yr	$17,824.70
24.	$600	9.20%	7.53 yr	$1505.00
26.	$8987	8%	8.66 yr	$20,000.00

28. (a)

r	2%	4%	6%	8%	10%	12%
t	55.47	28.01	18.85	14.28	11.53	9.69

(b)

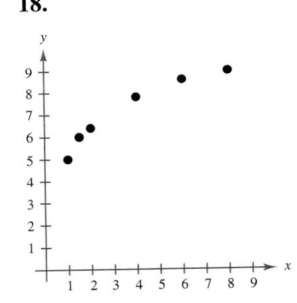

$t = 60.933(5.796 \times 10^{-8})^r$

30.

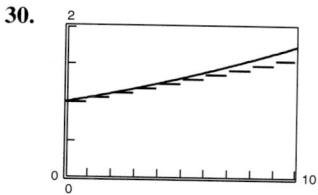

Daily compounding

Isotope	Half-Life (years)	Initial Quantity	Amount After 1000 Years
32. ^{226}Ra	1620	2.30 g	1.5 g
34. ^{230}Pu	24,360	0.41 g	0.4 g

36. 2011

38. (a) Croatia: $y = 5e^{-0.0018t}$; 4.7 million

     Mali: $y = 9.9e^{0.0314t}$; 27.9 million

     Singapore: $y = 3.5e^{0.009t}$; 4.7 million

     Sweden: $y = 8.9e^{0.0028t}$; 9.8 million

   (b) b; Population changes at a faster rate for a greater magnitude of b.

   (c) b; b is positive when the population increases and negative when the population decreases.

40. 61.16 hours   **42.** 15,683 years ago

44. (a) $V = -800t + 4600$ (b) $V = 4600e^{-0.2137t}$

   (c)

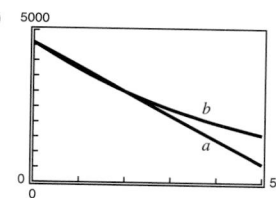

     Exponential model

   (d) 1 year, Linear model: $3800; Exponential model: $3715
3 years, Linear model: $2200; Exponential model: $2423

   (e) The computer's value decreases by $800 per year.

46. (a) $S = 10(1 - e^{-0.0575x})$ (b) 3314 units

48. (a)

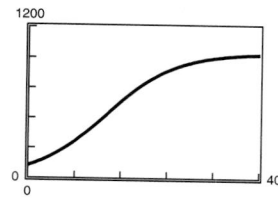

     $y = 0$, $y = 1000$. The population size will approach 1000 as time increases.

   (b) 203   (c) Between 13 and 14 months

50. (a) 398,107,171   (b) 5,011,872

52. (a) 85 decibels   (b) 90 decibels   (c) 105 decibels

54. 97%   **56.** 1.58×10^{-6} moles per liter   **58.** 10

60. (a)

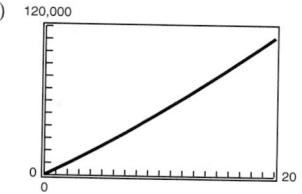

   (b) ≈ 21.2 years. Yes.

62. $y = 4e^{-0.2773x}$ **64.** $y = e^{-0.4621x}$

66. (a) $V = -1059.9x + 21,264$

     $V = 73.75t^2 - 1428.6t + 21,510$

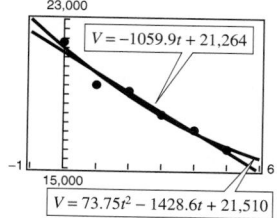

   (b) Average depreciation per year

   (c) No. To the right of the vertex it will increase.

   (d) $V = 21,345.69(0.9449^t)$

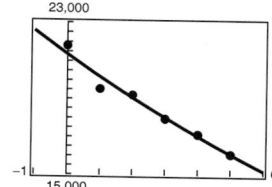

     The model fits the data well.

   (e) $V = \dfrac{1}{3.05 \times 10^{-6}t + 4.66 \times 10^{-5}}$

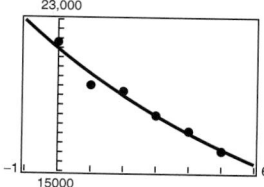

     The rational model fits the data well.

   (f) Both have asymptote $V = 0$. As time goes by, the value of the car approaches 0.

68. (a) $y = 31.432(1.030)^t$

(b)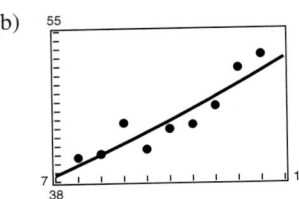

(c) 65.8 million

70. (a) $h = 0$ is not in the domain of the logarithmic function.

(b) $h = 0.863 - 6.447 \ln p$

(c)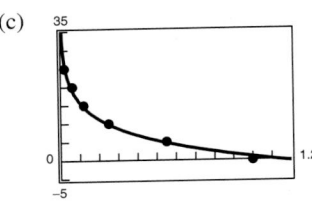

(d) 2.72 kilometers   (e) 0.15 atmosphere

72. (a) $y_1 = 6.09x + 49.1$

$y_2 = -40.7 + 66.366 \ln x$

$y_3 = 65.046(1.053)^x$

(b)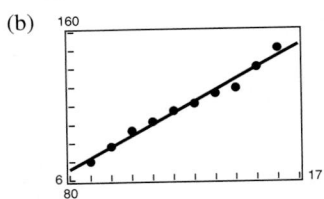

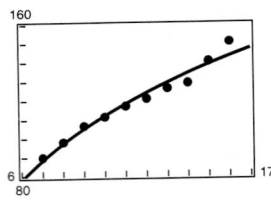

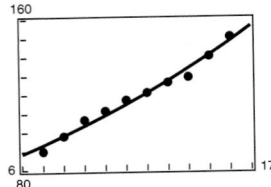

Answers will vary.

(c)

x	y	$y - y_1$	$(y - y_1)^2$	$y - y_2$	$(y - y_2)^2$
7	90.0	-1.73	2.99	1.56	2.43
8	98.1	0.28	0.08	0.80	0.63
9	106.7	2.79	7.78	1.58	2.49
10	111.5	1.5	2.25	-0.61	0.38
11	117.2	1.11	1.23	-1.24	1.53
12	121.1	-1.08	1.17	-3.11	9.69
13	126.5	-1.77	3.13	-3.03	9.15
14	129.3	-5.06	25.60	-5.14	26.46
15	140.5	0.05	0.003	1.48	2.18
16	150.7	4.16	17.31	7.39	54.68

x	$y - y_3$	$(y - y_3)^2$
7	-3.37	11.37
8	-0.22	0.05
9	3.17	10.03
10	2.48	6.15
11	2.40	5.77
12	0.22	0.05
13	-0.79	0.62
14	-4.73	22.42
15	-0.64	0.41
16	2.08	4.33

(d) $\Sigma(y - y_1)^2 = 61.55$ $\Sigma(y - y_2)^2 = 109.63$

$\Sigma(y - y_3)^2 = 61.21$

The exponential model best fits the data.

(e) The sums are the sums of the squares of the errors.

74. False   **76.** True   **78.** False. It is shifted up.

80. (c); $(0, 2), (5, 0)$ **82.** (e); $(0, 4), (2, 0)$

84. (a); $(-2, 0)$ **86.** $8x^2 - 24x + 18,\ x \neq \frac{3}{2}$

88. $x^3 - 5x^2 + 25x - 128 + \dfrac{641}{x + 5}$

90.

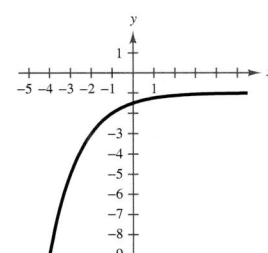

92.

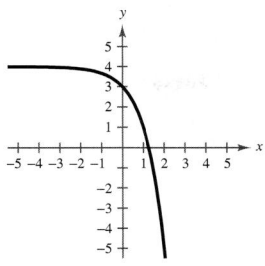

Review Exercises *(page 357)*

2. 5.742   **4.** 23.156   **6.** (f)   **8.** (a)   **10.** (c)

12.

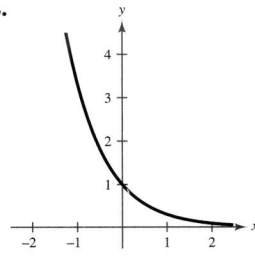

14.

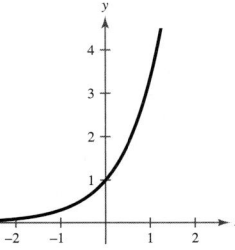

16.

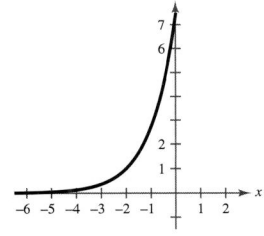

18.

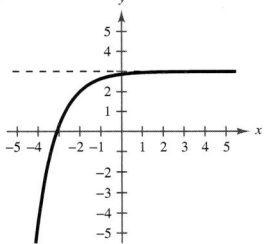

20.

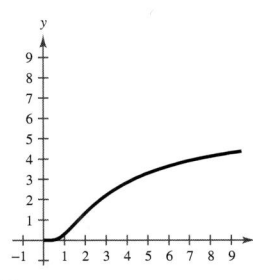

22.

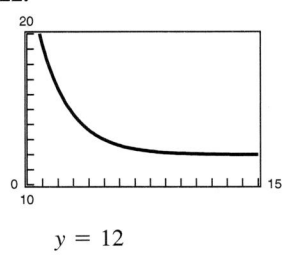

$y = 12$

24.

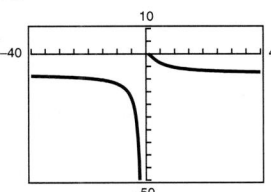

$y = -8, x = 0$

26.

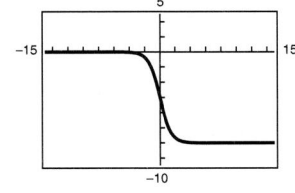

$y = 0, y = -12$

28. 9.356   **30.** −0.915

32.

t	1	10	20
P	\$181,042.49	\$73,881.39	\$27,292.30

t	30	40	50
P	\$10,081.97	\$3724.35	\$1375.80

34.

s	50	55	60	65	70
y	28	26.4	24.8	23.4	22.0

36. $\log_3 243 = 5$ **38.** $\log_{12} \frac{1}{12} = -1$ **40.** 0

42. 5   **44.** −3

46.

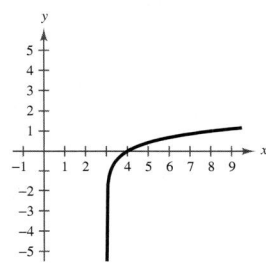

48.

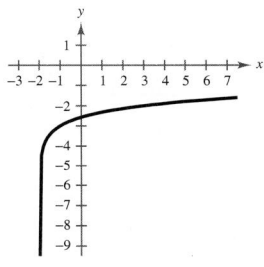

50.

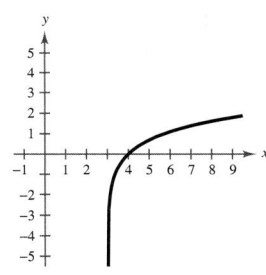

52.

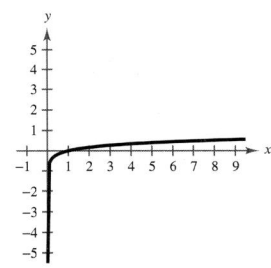

54.

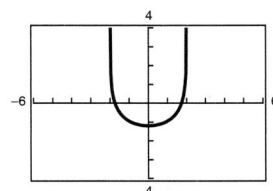

$-2 < x < 2$

56.

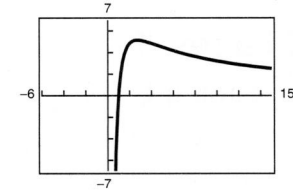

$0 < x < \infty$

58. 0   **60.** $\frac{15}{11}$ **62.** (a) $\frac{8.9}{8.3}$ (b) $\frac{7.6}{7.5}$ (c) $\frac{7.5}{6.8}$

64. −2.322   **66.** −1.159   **68.** ln 5

70. $\frac{1}{2} \ln 4 - \ln 5$ **72.** 0.525   **74.** 1.7479

76. $\frac{1}{2} \log_7 x - \log_7 4$ **78.** $\ln|x - 1| - \ln|x + 1|$

80. $\frac{1}{5}[\ln(2x + 1) + \ln(2x - 1) - \ln(4x^2 + 1)]$

82. $\log_6 \frac{y}{z^2}$ **84.** $\ln \left| \frac{(x - 2)^5}{(x + 2)x^3} \right|$ **86.** $\ln \frac{25x^3}{(x^2 + 1)^6}$

88. The average score dropped about 10 points.

90. 6   **92.** 6   **94.** 3   **96.** $\frac{1}{3}\ln 25 \approx 1.073$

98. $\dfrac{\ln(40) - 2}{3} \approx 0.563$ **100.** $\ln 20 \approx 2.996$

102. $\log_{12} 95 \approx 1.833$ **104.** $\ln 2 \approx 0.693, \ln 4 \approx 1.386$

106. $\frac{1}{5}e^{7.2} \approx 267.886$ **108.** $\frac{1}{3}e^{15/4} \approx 14.174$

110. $e^6 - 8 \approx 395.429$ **112.** $5e^4 \approx 272.991$

114. $-2 + \sqrt{6}$ **116.** -104

118. (a) 1151 units   (b) 1325 units   **120.** (b)

122. (d)   **124.** (c)   **126.** $\approx 98.6\%$

128. (a)   (b) 71

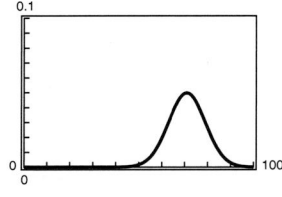

130. (a) 251,188,643   (b) 7,079,458   (c) 1,258,925,412

132. $y = 2e^{-0.1386x}$ **134.** $y = 4e^{-0.4159x}$

136. (a)

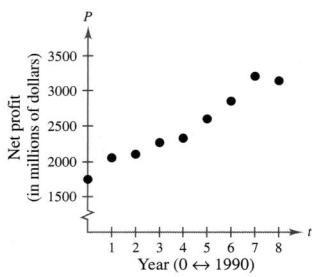

(b) $P = 1812.678(1.0764)^t$

138. True   **140.** False. $\ln(xy) = \ln x + \ln y$

142. False. $0 < x < \infty$

Chapter 5

Section 5.1   *(page 371)*

2. (a) Yes   (b) No   (c) No   (d) Yes

4. (a) No   (b) Yes   (c) Yes   (d) No

6. $(-1, 3)$ **8.** $(0, -5), (4, 3)$

10. $(0, 0), (2, -2), (-2, 2)$ **12.** $(0, 2), (-1, 0), (1, 0)$

14. $(0, 4), (1, 2), (2, 0)$ **16.** $(-3, 2)$ **18.** $\left(\frac{4}{3}, \frac{4}{3}\right)$

20. $(2, 2.5)$ **22.** $\left(\frac{208}{17}, \frac{88}{17}\right)$ **24.** No solution

26. All points on the line $2x - 3y - 6 = 0$ **28.** $(0, 0)$

30. $(2, -2)$ **32.** $(5, 3)$ **34.** $(3, 6), (-3, 0)$

36. $(3, 1), (15, 7)$

38.

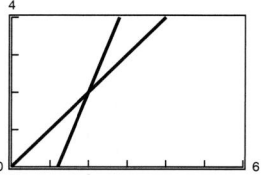

$(2, 2)$

40.

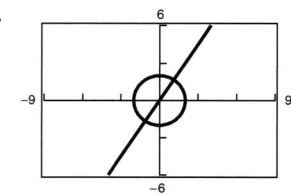

$\left(-\dfrac{4}{\sqrt{13}}, -\dfrac{6}{\sqrt{13}}\right), \left(\dfrac{4}{\sqrt{13}}, \dfrac{6}{\sqrt{13}}\right)$

42.   **44.**

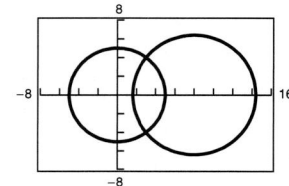   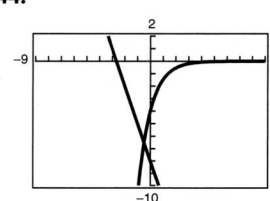

$(3, \pm 4)$ $(-0.490, -6.530)$

46.   **48.**

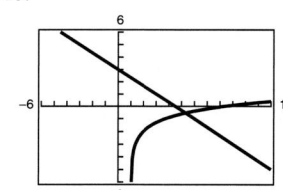   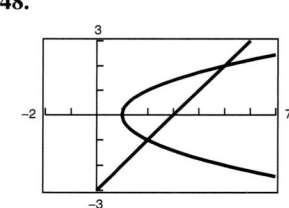

$(5.309, -0.539)$ $(5, 2), (2, -1)$

50.

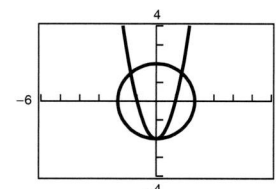

$(0, -2), (\pm 1.323, 1.500)$

52. No solution   **54.** $(3, 4), (5, 0)$ **56.** No solution

58. $(1.058, 2.881), (-1.965, 0.140)$

60. $(0, -1), (2, 1), (-1, -5)$

62. $(5, 2), (1, 0)$

64.

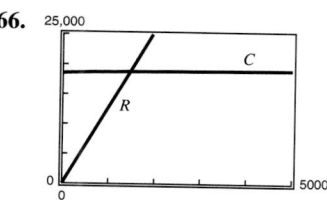

2,500,000

R

C

0

0   500,000

233,333 units; $968,333

66.

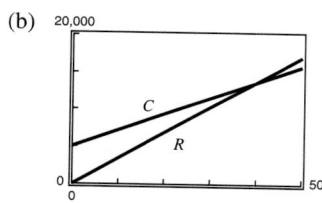

25,000

C

R

0

0   5000

1464 units; $18,798

68. (a) $C = 21.60x + 5000$; $R = 34.10x$

(b)

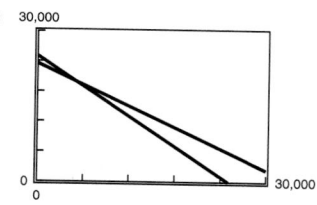

20,000

C

R

0

0   500

400 units

70. Sales greater than $500,000

72. (a) $\begin{cases} x + \quad\quad y = 25,000 \\ 0.06x + 0.085y = \quad\; 2000 \end{cases}$

(b)

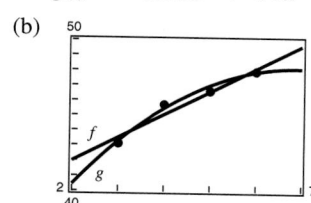

30,000

0

0   30,000

The amount invested at 8.5% and the amount of interest both decrease.

(c) $5000

74. 6×9 meters   **76.** 9×12 inches   **78.** 8×12 miles

80. (a) $f(t) = 1.53t + 38.9$

$g(t) = -0.325t^2 + 4.46t + 32.8$

(b) 50

f

g

2

40   7

(c) $(3.26, 43.89)$, $(5.75, 47.70)$

(d) $f(8) = 51.1$ million

$g(8) = 47.7$ million

Answers will vary.

82. False. You could solve for either variable.

84. For a linear system the result will be a contradictory equation such as $0 = N$, where N is a nonzero real number. For nonlinear systems there may be an equation with imaginary roots.

86. (Answers are not unique.)

   (a) $y = x + 1$ (b) $y = 0$ (c) $y = -2$

88. $2x + 7y - 45 = 0$ **90.** $y = 3$

92. $30x - 17y - 18 = 0$

94. Domain: All real $x \neq 6$

   Asymptotes: $y = 0$, $x = 6$

96. Domain: All real $x \neq \pm 4$

   Asymptotes: $y = 1$, $x = \pm 4$

98. 3.021   **100.** 1.099, 1.792

Section 5.2   *(page 381)*

2. $(-2, 1)$ **4.** $(3, 3)$ **6.** Inconsistent

8. All points on the line $3x - y = -5$ **10.** $\left(-\frac{35}{12}, -\frac{41}{36}\right)$

12. $\left(3, \frac{7}{5}\right)$ **14.** $(5, 1)$ **16.** $\left(\frac{5}{6}, \frac{5}{6}\right)$ **18.** $(-17, 5)$

20. $\left(\frac{130}{31}, 8\right)$ **22.** $\left(-\frac{14}{9}, \frac{20}{9}\right)$ **24.** $(1, 0)$

26. Inconsistent   **28.** $(7, 1)$ **30.** $(101, 96)$

32. $\left(\frac{90}{31}, -\frac{67}{31}\right)$

34.   **36.**

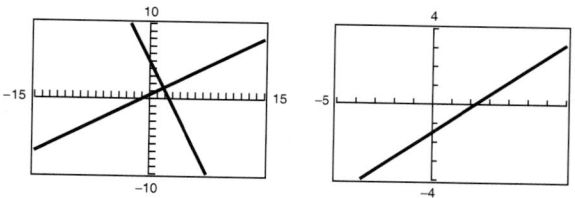

Consistent, $(1.8, 1.4)$ Consistent, all points on the line $4x - 6y - 9 = 0$

38.   **40.**

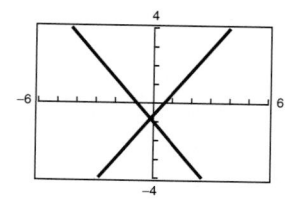

Consistent, all points on the line $8x - 14y = 5$ Consistent, $\left(-\frac{1}{7}, -\frac{5}{6}\right)$

CHAPTER 5

42.

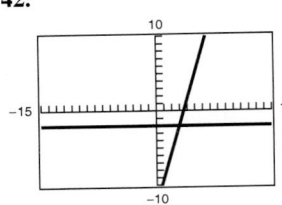

$(3, -2)$

44.

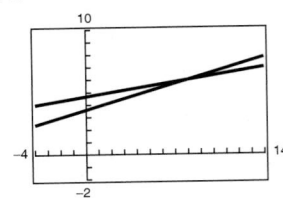

$(8, 6)$

46.

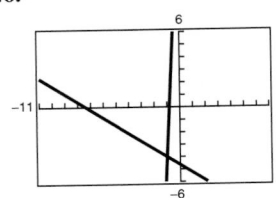

$(-1, -4)$

48.

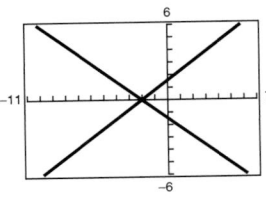

$(-2, 0)$

50. $(-2, 5)$ **52.** $(1, 3)$ **54.** $(-23, 61)$ **56.** $(3, 2)$

58. $\begin{cases} x + y = 6 \\ 2x - y = 18 \end{cases}$ **60.** $\begin{cases} 3x + y = -12 \\ 3x - y = 8 \end{cases}$

Answer is not unique.   Answer is not unique.

62. $(500, 75)$ **64.** $(250{,}000, 350)$

66. First plane: 880 kilometers per hour

Second plane: 960 kilometers per hour

68. (a) $\begin{cases} x + y = 500 \\ 87x + 92y = 44{,}500 \end{cases}$

(b)

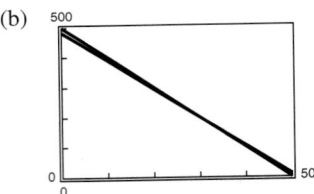

Decreases

(c) 87 octane: 300 gallons; 92 octane: 200 gallons

70. $20,000   **72.** $66.95: 152 pair; $84.95: 88 pair

74. 1280 tons and 320 tons   **76.** $y = 0.22x + 1.9$

78. $y = -0.58x + 5.4$

80. (a) and (b) $y = -240x + 685$

(c)

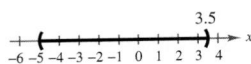

(d) 349 units

82. False. For example, the graphical solution of
$\begin{cases} x + y = 10 \\ 5x - y = 1 \end{cases}$ is an approximate solution.

84. $(39{,}600, 398)$. It is necessary to change the scale on the axes to see the point of intersection.

86. No. Two lines will intersect only once or coincide and the system will have infinitely many solutions.

88. $k = -4$ **90.** $u = -x \ln x; v = \ln x$

92.

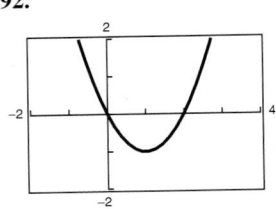

Domain: All real numbers

Range: $-1 \le y < \infty$

94.

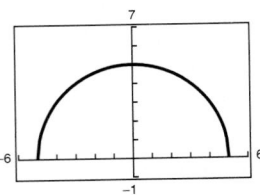

Domain: $-5 \le x \le 5$

Range: $0 \le y \le 5$

96. $x \le -\frac{22}{3}$ **98.** $x \le \frac{19}{16}$

100. $-2 < x < 18$ **102.** $x < 3.5$ and $x > -5$

104. $\ln 6x$ **106.** $\log_9 \dfrac{12}{x}$ **108.** $(-6, -8)$

Section 5.3 *(page 395)*

2. (a) No   (b) Yes   (c) No   (d) No

4. (a) Yes   (b) No   (c) No   (d) Yes

6. $\left(-\frac{1}{2}, -5, -4\right)$ **8.** $(8, -2, 6)$ **10.** $\left(-2, -\frac{10}{3}, -4\right)$

12. $\begin{cases} x - 2y + 3z = 5 \\ -x + 3y - 5z = 4 \\ 4y - 9z = -10 \end{cases}$

Required step in putting the system in row-echelon form

14. $(0, 4, -2)$ **16.** $(2, -3, -2)$ **18.** $\left(\frac{1}{2}, -\frac{3}{2}, 1\right)$

20. Inconsistent   **22.** $\left(\frac{3}{10}, \frac{2}{5}, 0\right)$

24. $\left(-\frac{1}{2}a + \frac{5}{2}, 4a - 1, a\right)$ **26.** $\left(13 - 4a, \frac{45}{2} - \frac{15}{2}a, a\right)$

28. Inconsistent   **30.** Inconsistent   **32.** $(0, 0, 0)$

34. $(-5a + 3, -a - 5, a)$ **36.** $\left(-\frac{3}{8}a - \frac{1}{4}, -\frac{3}{4}a + \frac{5}{2}, a\right)$

38. $\left(\frac{13}{7}a, \frac{48}{7}a, a\right)$ **40.** $(1, 0, 3, 2)$

42. $\begin{cases} x + y + z = -6 \\ -x - y - 7z = 0 \\ 3x - 6y + 3z = 0 \end{cases}$

Answer is not unique.

44. $\begin{cases} 2x + y - z = 8 \\ 4x + 2y + z = -5 \\ -2x + 5y - 3z = 44 \end{cases}$

Answer is not unique.

46.

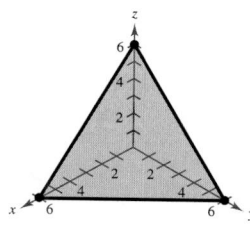

$(6, 0, 0), (0, 6, 0),$
$(0, 0, 6), (2, 3, 1)$

48.

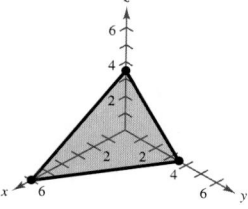

$(6, 0, 0), (0, 3, 0),$
$(0, 0, 3), (2, 1, 1)$

50. $\dfrac{A}{x + 3} + \dfrac{B}{x + 1}$

52. $\dfrac{A}{x} + \dfrac{B}{x^2} + \dfrac{C}{4x + 11}$

54. $\dfrac{A}{x + 2} + \dfrac{B}{(x + 2)^2} + \dfrac{C}{(x + 2)^3} + \dfrac{D}{(x + 2)^4}$

56. $\dfrac{1}{6}\left(\dfrac{1}{2x - 3} - \dfrac{1}{2x + 3}\right)$

58. $\dfrac{1}{x - 3} - \dfrac{1}{x}$

60. $\dfrac{1}{x - 2} - \dfrac{1}{x + 3}$

62. $\dfrac{1}{x + 3}, \; x \neq -1$

64. $\dfrac{1}{2}\left(\dfrac{3}{x - 4} - \dfrac{1}{x}\right)$

66. $\dfrac{2}{x - 1} - \dfrac{1}{(x - 1)^2}$

68. $-\dfrac{3}{x} - \dfrac{1}{x^2} + \dfrac{3}{x - 1} - \dfrac{2}{(x - 1)^2} + \dfrac{7}{(x - 1)^3}$

70. $x - 1 + \dfrac{27}{5(x + 4)} + \dfrac{3}{5(x - 1)}$

72. $\dfrac{1}{2}x + \dfrac{3}{4} + \dfrac{3}{2(2x - 1)} + \dfrac{1}{(2x - 1)^2} + \dfrac{1}{4(2x - 1)^3}$

74. $\dfrac{2}{x} + \dfrac{4}{x + 1} - \dfrac{3}{x - 1}$

76. $\dfrac{1}{2}\left[-\dfrac{1}{x} + \dfrac{5}{x + 1} - \dfrac{3}{(x + 1)^2}\right]$

78. $x - 1 + \dfrac{1}{x + 2} + \dfrac{1}{x - 1}$

80. $\dfrac{3}{x - 3} + \dfrac{5}{x + 3}$

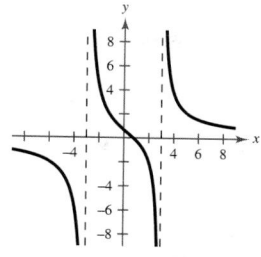

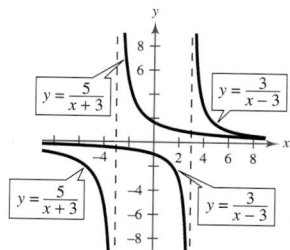

Vertical asymptotes are the same.

82. $s = -16t^2 + 64t$

84. $s = -16t^2 + 16t + 132$

86. $y = -x^2 + 2x + 3$

88. $y = -2x^2 + 5x$

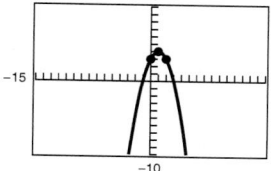

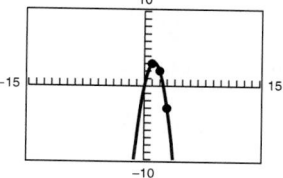

90. $x^2 + y^2 - 6y = 0$

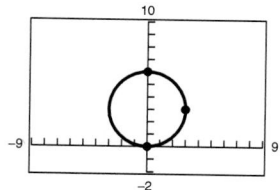

92. $x^2 + y^2 + 2x + 2y - 23 = 0$

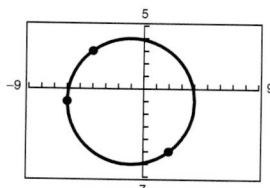

94. $4000 at 5%
$8000 at 7%
$9500 at 8%

96. $625,000 at 8%
$50,000 at 9%
$125,000 at 10%

98. $406{,}250 - \frac{1}{2}s$ in certificates of deposit

$-31{,}250 + \frac{1}{2}s$ in municipal bonds

$125{,}000 - s$ in blue-chip stocks

s in growth stocks

CHAPTER 5

100. (a) No 10% solution, $8\frac{1}{3}$ liters of 20% solution, $1\frac{2}{3}$ liters of 50% solution

(b) No 20% solution, $6\frac{1}{4}$ liters of 10% solution, $3\frac{3}{4}$ liters of 50% solution

(c) 7 liters of 20% solution, 1 liter of 10% solution

102. $I_1 = 1, I_2 = 2, I_3 = 1$

104. $t_1 = 128$ pounds; $t_2 = 64$ pounds; $a = 0$
The system is at rest.

106. $y = \frac{3}{7}x^2 + \frac{6}{5}x + \frac{26}{35}$ **108.** $y = -\frac{5}{4}x^2 + \frac{9}{20}x + \frac{199}{20}$

110. (a) $y = -0.008x^2 + 1.371x + 21.886$

(b)

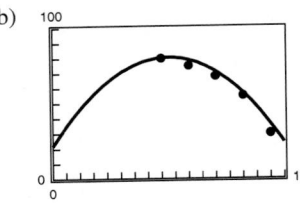

(c) 23.756%

112. $-\dfrac{6.367}{t} + \dfrac{4181.044}{411 - 38t}$ **114.** True

116. The student did not work the problem correctly. Because $\dfrac{x^2 + 1}{x(x - 1)}$ is an improper fraction, the student should begin by dividing to obtain $\dfrac{x^2 + 1}{x(x - 1)} = 1 + \dfrac{x + 1}{x(x - 1)}$, and then decompose $\dfrac{x + 1}{x(x - 1)}$ by the usual methods.

118. $\dfrac{1}{a + 1}\left(\dfrac{1}{x + 1} + \dfrac{1}{a - x}\right)$ **120.** $\dfrac{1}{a}\left(\dfrac{1}{x} - \dfrac{1}{x + a}\right)$

122. There will be a row representing a contradictory equation such as $0 = N$, where N is a nonzero real number.

124. $x = 2, y = 2, \lambda = -4$

126. $x = 0, y = 100, \lambda = -1$

128.

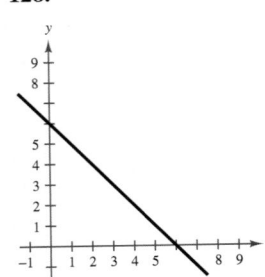

130.

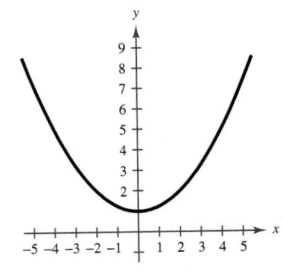

$\left(\frac{1}{3}, -\frac{1}{2}\right)$

132.

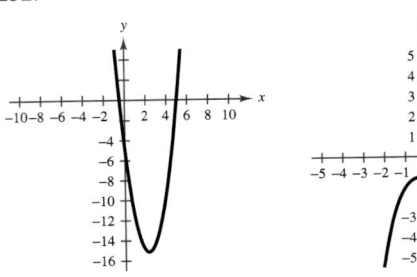

134.

136. (a) $-2, 0, 0, 2$

(b)

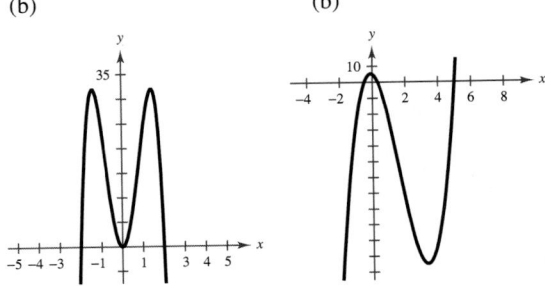

138. (a) $-\frac{1}{2}, \frac{1}{3}, 5$

(b)

140.

x	-5	-1	0	1	2	3	4
y	-3.996	-3.8	-3.6	-3	-1.5	2.25	11.6

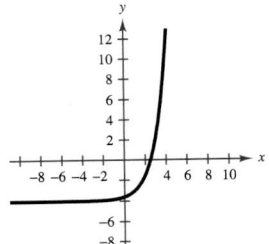

142.

x	-5	-3	-2	-1	0
y	-6.02	-6.3	-7	-9.5	-18.25

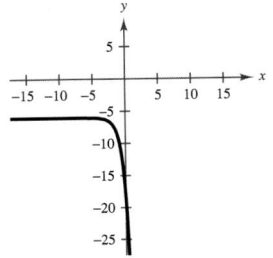

144. $\left(\frac{1}{2}, 0\right)$ **146.**

Section 5.4 *(page 408)*

2. (d)   **4.** (h)   **6.** (b)   **8.** (c)

10.
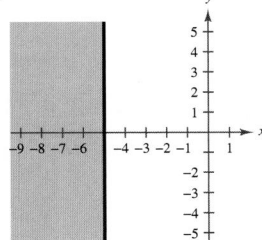

12.
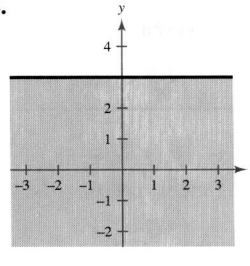

14.
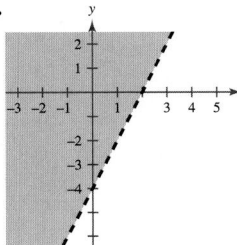

16.
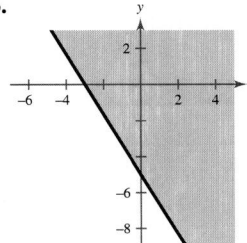

18.
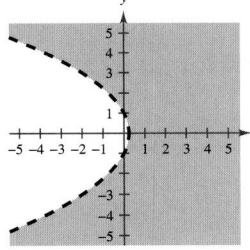

20.
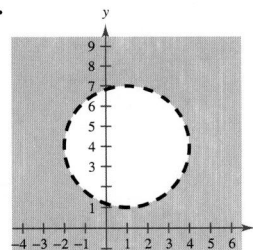

22.
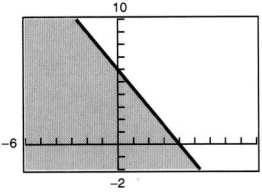

24.
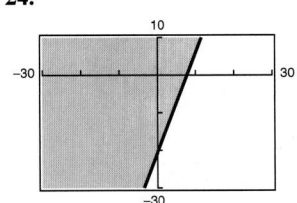

26.
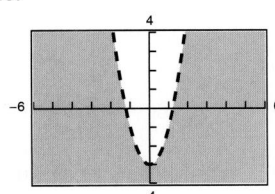

28.
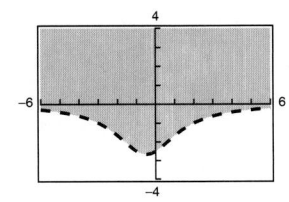

30.
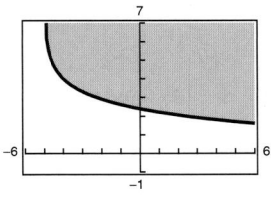

32.
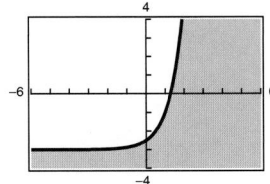

34. $y \geq x^2 - 4$ **36.** $x > 5$

38. (a) Yes   (b) No   (c) Yes   (d) Yes

40.
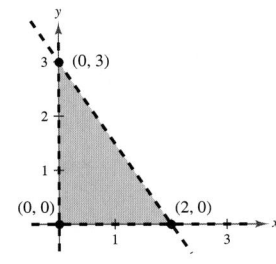

42.
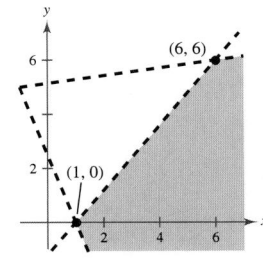

44.
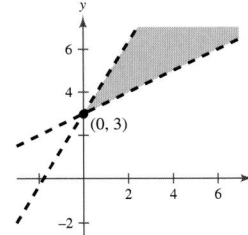

46.
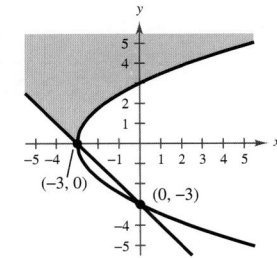

48.
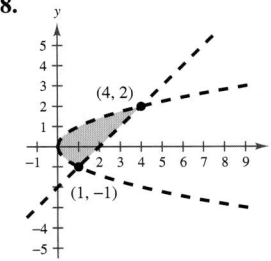

50.
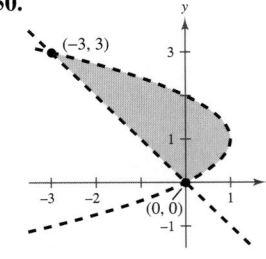

52.
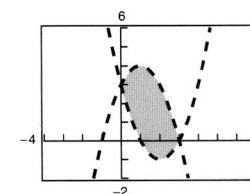

54.
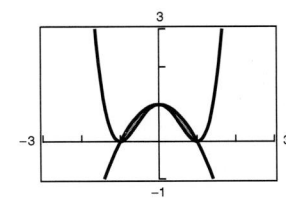

56.

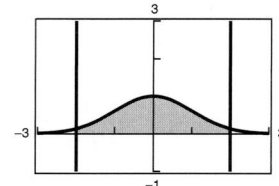

58. $\begin{cases} y \le 6 - 2x \\ y \ge x - 3 \\ x \ge 1 \end{cases}$ **60.** $x^2 + y^2 > 4$

62. $\begin{cases} 4x - y \ge 0 \\ 4x - y \le 16 \\ 0 \le y \le 4 \end{cases}$ **64.** $\begin{cases} y \le x + 1 \\ y \le -x + 1 \\ y \ge 0 \end{cases}$

66. (a) $\begin{cases} x + y \ge 15{,}000 \\ x \ge 8000 \\ y \ge 4000 \\ 15x + 25y \ge 275{,}000 \end{cases}$

(b)

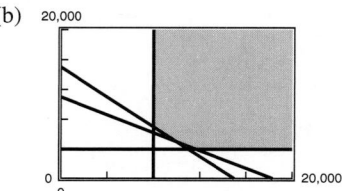

68. (a) $\begin{cases} x \ge 2y \\ 800x + 1200y \le 20{,}000 \\ x \ge 4 \\ y \ge 2 \end{cases}$

(b)

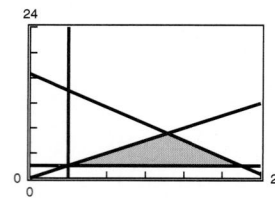

70. (a) $\begin{cases} xy \ge 500 \\ 2x + \pi y \ge 125 \\ x \ge 0 \\ y \ge 0 \end{cases}$ (b)

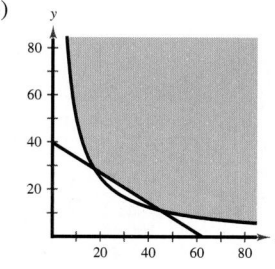

72.

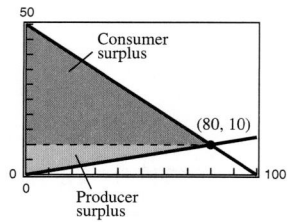

Consumer surplus: 1600
Producer surplus: 400

74.

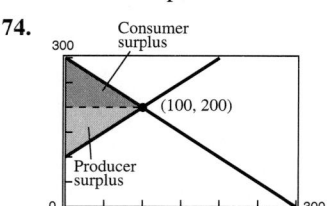

Consumer surplus: 5000
Producer surplus: 5000

76. True **78.** Test a point on either side.

80. $5x + 3y - 8 = 0$ **82.** $28x + 17y + 13 = 0$

84. $y_1 = 1.69x + 40.1$

$y_2 = -0.243x^2 + 3.87x + 35.9$

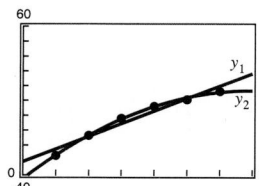

The quadratic model fits the data better.

Section 5.5 *(page 417)*

2. Minimum at $(0, 0)$: 0 **4.** Minimum at $(0, 0)$: 0
Maximum at $(0, 4)$: 32 Maximum at $(2, 0)$: 14

6. Minimum at $(0, 2)$: 6 **8.** Minimum at $(3, 0)$: 3
Maximum at $(5, 3)$: 29 Maximum at $(0, 4)$: 24

10. Minimum at $(0, 600)$: 21,000
Maximum at $(900, 0)$: 45,000

12. Minimum at any point on the line segment connecting $(675, 0)$ and $(0, 600)$: 10,800

Maximum at any point on the line segment connecting $(0, 800)$ and $(900, 0)$: 14,400

14.

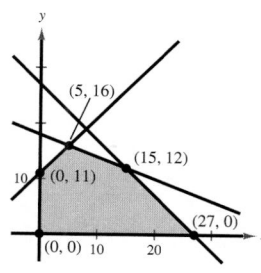

Minimum at $(0, 0)$: 0

Maximum at $(15, 12)$: 132

16.

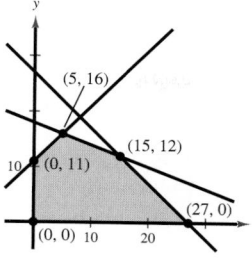

Minimum at $(0, 0)$: 0

Maximum at $(27, 0)$: 189

18.

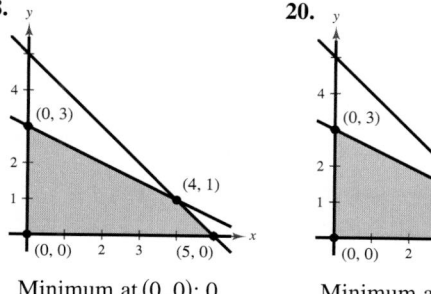

Minimum at $(0, 0)$: 0

Maximum at $(4, 1)$: 21

20.

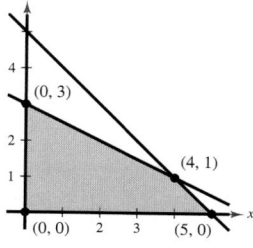

Minimum at $(0, 3)$: -3

Maximum at $(5, 0)$: 10

22.

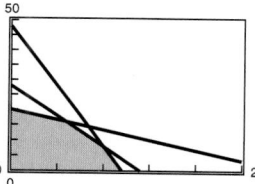

Minimum at any point on the line segment connecting $(0, 0)$ and $(0, 20)$: 0

Maximum at $(12, 0)$: 12

24.

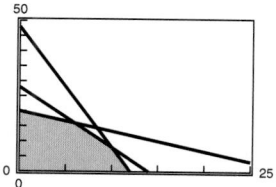

Minimum at any point on the line segment connecting $(0, 0)$ and $(12, 0)$: 0

Maximum at $(0, 20)$: 20

26.

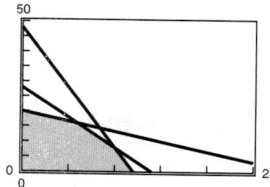

Minimum at $(0, 0)$: 0

Maximum at $(6, 16)$: 50

28. (a) and (b)

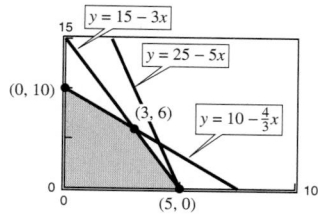

(c) $(5, 0)$

30. (a) and (b)

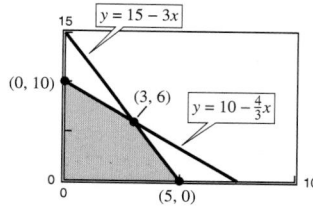

(c) Maximum at any point on the line segment connecting $(3, 6)$ and $(5, 0)$

32. (a) and (b)

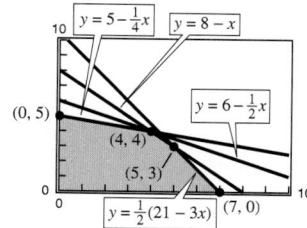

(c) $(4, 4)$

34. (a) and (b)

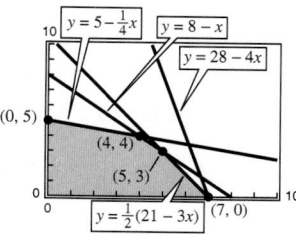

(c) $(7, 0)$

36.

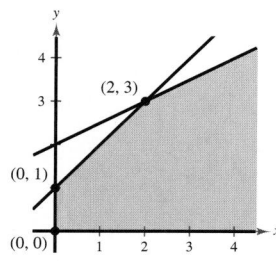

The constraints do not form a closed set of points. Therefore, $z = x + y$ is unbounded.

38.

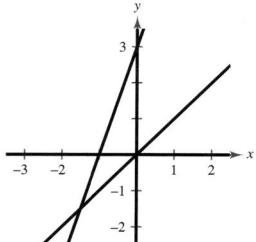

The feasible set is empty.

40.

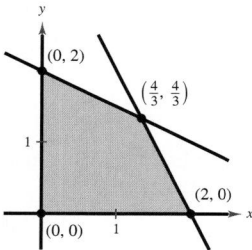

z is maximum at any point on the line segment connecting $(0, 2)$ and $\left(\frac{4}{3}, \frac{4}{3}\right)$.

42. 60 acres of crop A, 90 acres of crop B

Maximum profit: $29,550

44. Eight audits, Eight tax returns

Maximum revenue: $18,400

46. 750 units of Model A, 1000 units of Model B

Maximum profit: $83,750

48. Three bags of Brand X, Six bags of Brand Y

Minimum cost: $21.67 per bag

50. True   **52.** $z = x + y$ (Answer is not unique.)

54. $z = -10x + y$ (Answer is not unique.)

56. (a) $-3 < t < 6$ (b) $t > 6$ **58.** $\dfrac{1}{x - 2}$, $x \neq 0, -2$

60. $\dfrac{(x + 1)(x + 3)}{3}$, $x \neq -1$ **62.** 1.386, 1.792

64. -1.792 **66.** $-6.282, -11.718$

68. $(-1, 8)$ **70.** $(10, 12)$

72.   **74.**

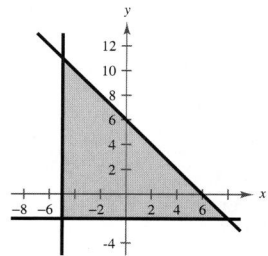   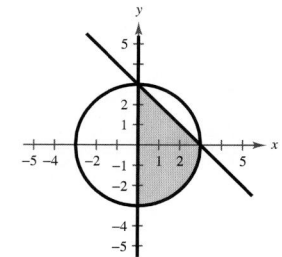

Review Exercises   *(page 422)*

2. $(3, 3)$ **4.** $(13, 0), (5, 12)$ **6.** $(5, 2), (2, -1)$

8. $\left(\frac{3}{2}, 5\right)$ **10.** $(1.41, -0.66), (-1.41, 10.66)$

12. $(9.68, -0.84)$ **14.** More than $500,000

16. 16×18 feet   **18.** $\left(\frac{3}{10}, \frac{2}{5}\right)$ **20.** $\left(\frac{3}{5}, -8\right)$

22. $(-3, 7)$ **24.** No solution

26.

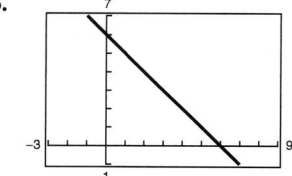

Consistent: All points on the line $y = 6 - x$

28.

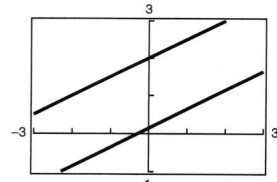

Inconsistent

30.

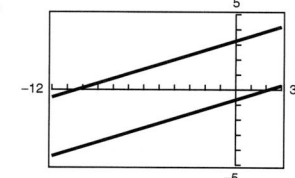

Inconsistent

32. $18,000   **34.** $(250,000, 95)$ **36.** $(5, -8, 3)$

38. $(4.8, 4.4, -1.6)$ **40.** $\left(-\frac{3}{4}, 0, -\frac{5}{4}\right)$

42. $y = 3x^2 + 11x - 4$ **44.** $(2 - 3a, 6 + 5a, a)$

46.

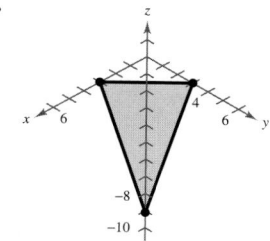

$(0, 0, -9), (0, 3, 0), (3, 0, 0), (1, 1, -3)$

48. $\dfrac{1}{x+1} - \dfrac{2}{x+2}$ **50.** $\dfrac{3}{2}\left(\dfrac{1}{x-3} - \dfrac{1}{x+3}\right)$

52. $\dfrac{3x}{x^2+1} + \dfrac{x}{(x^2+1)^2}$

54. Amount at 7%: $8000, Amount at 9%: $5000,
Amount at 11%: $7000

56.   **58.**

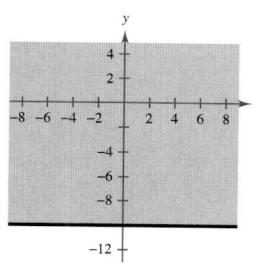 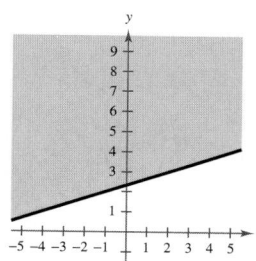

60.

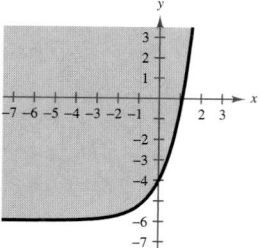

62. (b)   **64.** (a)

66.   **68.**

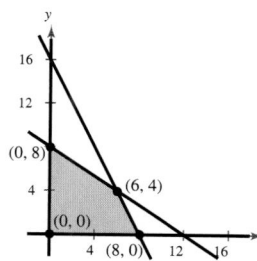 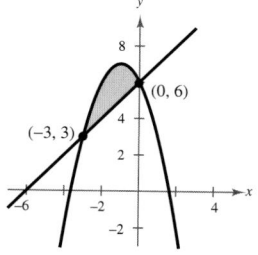

70.

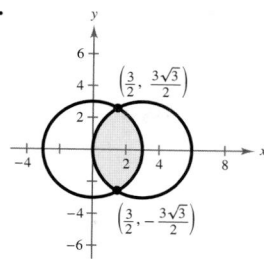

72. $\begin{cases} -x + y \le 1 \\ 3x + y \le 25 \\ x + 7y \ge 15 \end{cases}$

74. $\begin{cases} 20x + 30y \le 24{,}000 \\ 12x + 8y \le 12{,}400 \\ x \ge \phantom{12{,}40}0 \\ y \ge \phantom{12{,}40}0 \end{cases}$

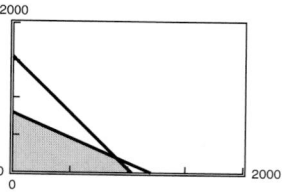

76.

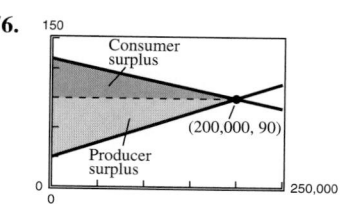

Consumer surplus: 4,000,000
Producer surplus: 6,000,000

78.

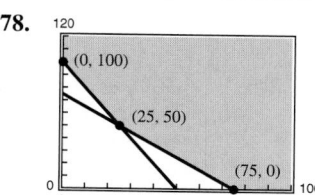

Minimum at $(25, 50)$: 600

80.

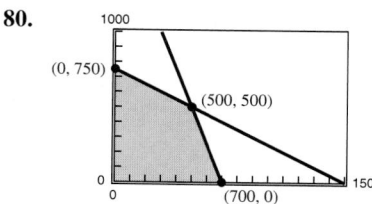

Maximum at $(500, 500)$: 60,000

82. $\frac{1}{3}$ gallon of type A, $\frac{2}{3}$ gallon of type B
Minimum cost: $1.45

84. False. If there is more than one maximum, there are an infinite number of maximum points.

CHAPTER 5

Chapter 6

Section 6.1   *(page 440)*

2. 1×4 **4.** 3×4 **6.** 1×1

8. $\begin{bmatrix} 7 & 4 & \vdots & 22 \\ 5 & -9 & \vdots & 15 \end{bmatrix}$

10. $\begin{bmatrix} -1 & -8 & 5 & \vdots & 17 \\ -6 & 0 & 12 & \vdots & -24 \\ 3 & 1 & -8 & \vdots & 11 \end{bmatrix}$

12. $\begin{cases} 7x - 5y = 0 \\ 8x + 3y = -2 \end{cases}$

14. $\begin{cases} 6x + 2y - z - 5w = -25 \\ -x + 7z + 3w = 7 \\ 4x - y - 10z + 6w = 23 \\ 8y + z - 11w = -21 \end{cases}$

16. Reduced row-echelon form   **18.** Row-echelon form

20. $\begin{bmatrix} 1 & 2 & \frac{8}{3} \\ 4 & -3 & 6 \end{bmatrix}$ **22.** $\begin{bmatrix} 1 & 2 & 4 & \frac{3}{2} \\ 1 & -1 & -3 & 2 \\ 2 & 6 & 4 & 9 \end{bmatrix}$

$\begin{bmatrix} 1 & 2 & 4 & \frac{3}{2} \\ 0 & -3 & -7 & \frac{1}{2} \\ 0 & 2 & -4 & 6 \end{bmatrix}$

24. Add 3 times R_1 to R_2.   **26.** Add 5 times R_1 to R_3.

28. (a) $\begin{bmatrix} 7 & 1 \\ 0 & 2 \\ -3 & 4 \\ 1 & 5 \end{bmatrix}$ (b) $\begin{bmatrix} 1 & 5 \\ 0 & 2 \\ -3 & 4 \\ 7 & 1 \end{bmatrix}$ (c) $\begin{bmatrix} 1 & 5 \\ 0 & 2 \\ 0 & 19 \\ 7 & 1 \end{bmatrix}$

(d) $\begin{bmatrix} 1 & 5 \\ 0 & 2 \\ 0 & 19 \\ 0 & -34 \end{bmatrix}$ (e) $\begin{bmatrix} 1 & 5 \\ 0 & 1 \\ 0 & 19 \\ 0 & -34 \end{bmatrix}$ (f) $\begin{bmatrix} 1 & 0 \\ 0 & 1 \\ 0 & 0 \\ 0 & 0 \end{bmatrix}$

The matrix is in reduced row-echelon form.

30. (a)
```
row+([A],3,4)
            [[ 7  1]
             [ 0  2]
             [-3  4]
             [ 1  5]]
```
(b)
```
rowSwap([B],1,4)
            [[ 1  5]
             [ 0  2]
             [-3  4]
             [ 7  1]]
```
(c)
```
*row+(3,[C],1,3)
            [[ 1  5]
             [ 0  2]
             [ 0 19]
             [ 7  1]]
```
(d)
```
*row+(-7,[D],1,4)
            [[ 1  5]
             [ 0  2]
             [ 0 19]
             [ 0 -34]]
```
(e)
```
*row(.5,[E],2)
            [[ 1  5]
             [ 0  1]
             [ 0 19]
             [ 0 -34]]
```
(f)
```
*row+(-19,[F],2,3)
            [[ 1  5]
             [ 0  1]
             [ 0  0]
             [ 0 -34]]
```
```
*row+(34,[G],2,4)
            [[ 1  5]
             [ 0  1]
             [ 0  0]
             [ 0  0]]
```
```
*row+(-5,[H],2,1)
            [[ 1  0]
             [ 0  1]
             [ 0  0]
             [ 0  0]]
```

32. $\begin{bmatrix} 1 & 2 & -1 & 3 \\ 0 & 1 & -2 & 5 \\ 0 & 0 & 1 & -1 \end{bmatrix}$ **34.** $\begin{bmatrix} 1 & -3 & 0 & -7 \\ 0 & 1 & 1 & 2 \\ 0 & 0 & 0 & 0 \end{bmatrix}$

36. $\begin{bmatrix} 1 & 3 & 0 \\ 0 & 0 & 1 \\ 0 & 0 & 0 \end{bmatrix}$ **38.** $\begin{bmatrix} 1 & 0 & 0 & 2 \\ 0 & 1 & 2 & -6 \end{bmatrix}$

40. $\begin{cases} x + 5y = 0 \\ y = -1 \end{cases}$ **42.** $\begin{cases} x + 2y - 2z = -1 \\ y + z = 9 \\ z = -3 \end{cases}$

$(5, -1)$

$(-31, 12, -3)$

44. $(-2, 4)$ **46.** $(3, -1, 0)$ **48.** $(-5, 4)$

50. Inconsistent   **52.** $(3a + 5, a)$ **54.** $(0.2, 0.5)$

56. $(6, 10, 8)$ **58.** $\left(-\frac{3}{2}a + \frac{3}{2}, \frac{1}{3}a + \frac{1}{3}, a\right)$ **60.** $(-2a, a)$

62. $(-5a, a, 3)$ **64.** $(-2b - 4a + 5, b, 3, a)$

66. $(-2a, -a, a, a)$ **68.** No   **70.** No

72. $y = -x^2 + 2x + 8$ **74.** $y = -\frac{1}{8}x^3 + 2x - 1$

76. $y = \frac{1}{2}x^4 - x^3 - 2x^2 + 2$

78. \$100,000 at 9%, \$250,000 at 10%, \$150,000 at 12%

80. $I_1 = \frac{3}{2}, I_2 = \frac{7}{4}, I_3 = \frac{11}{8}$

82. (a) $y = -0.004x^2 + 0.367x + 5$

(b)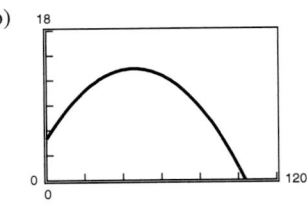

13 feet, 104 feet

(c) 13.418 feet, 103.793 feet

84. (a) $x_1 = 500 - s - t$, $x_2 = -200 + s + t$, $x_3 = s$,
  $x_4 = 350 - t$, $x_5 = t$

(b) $x_1 = 100$, $x_2 = 200$, $x_3 = 50$, $x_4 = 0$, $x_5 = 350$

(c) $x_1 = 150$, $x_2 = 150$, $x_3 = 0$, $x_4 = 0$, $x_5 = 350$

86. False. It is a 2×4 matrix.

88. False. Gauss-Jordan elimination reduces a matrix until a reduced row-echelon form is obtained.

90. $\begin{bmatrix} 1 & 3 & 1 & 3 \\ 0 & 1 & 2 & -1 \\ 0 & 0 & 1 & 2 \end{bmatrix}$, $\begin{bmatrix} 1 & 3 & 1 & 3 \\ 0 & 1 & \frac{7}{4} & -\frac{3}{2} \\ 0 & 0 & 1 & 2 \end{bmatrix}$

(Answers will vary.)

92.

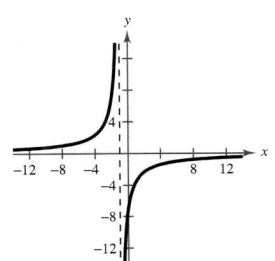

Asymptotes:
  $x = -1, y = 0$

94.

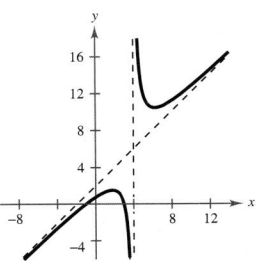

Asymptotes:
  $x = 4, y = x + 2$

96.

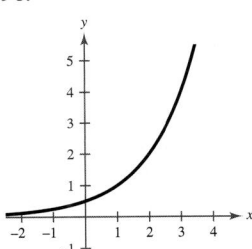

98.

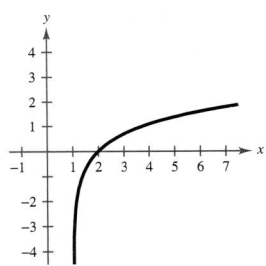

100. $(2, -1)$ **102.** $(-1, 2, -2)$

Section 6.2   *(page 455)*

2. $x = 13, y = 12$ **4.** $x = -5, y = -4, z = 9$

6. (a) $\begin{bmatrix} -2 & 0 \\ 6 & 3 \end{bmatrix}$ (b) $\begin{bmatrix} 4 & 4 \\ -2 & -1 \end{bmatrix}$

(c) $\begin{bmatrix} 3 & 6 \\ 6 & 3 \end{bmatrix}$ (d) $\begin{bmatrix} 9 & 10 \\ -2 & -1 \end{bmatrix}$

8. (a) $\begin{bmatrix} 8 & -2 & 3 \\ -5 & 0 & 3 \end{bmatrix}$ (b) $\begin{bmatrix} -4 & 4 & -1 \\ 3 & -2 & 7 \end{bmatrix}$

(c) $\begin{bmatrix} 6 & 3 & 3 \\ -3 & -3 & 15 \end{bmatrix}$ (d) $\begin{bmatrix} -6 & 9 & -1 \\ 5 & -5 & 19 \end{bmatrix}$

10. (a) $\begin{bmatrix} -4 & 9 & 1 \\ 5 & -6 & -5 \\ 15 & -5 & -2 \\ 3 & 10 & -10 \\ -4 & 0 & -2 \end{bmatrix}$ (b) $\begin{bmatrix} 2 & -1 & -1 \\ 1 & 2 & 9 \\ -5 & 13 & 0 \\ -3 & 6 & -2 \\ -4 & -2 & 2 \end{bmatrix}$

(c) $\begin{bmatrix} -3 & 12 & 0 \\ 9 & -6 & 6 \\ 15 & 12 & -3 \\ 0 & 24 & -18 \\ -12 & -3 & 0 \end{bmatrix}$ (d) $\begin{bmatrix} 3 & 2 & -2 \\ 5 & 2 & 20 \\ -5 & 30 & -1 \\ -6 & 20 & -10 \\ -12 & -5 & 4 \end{bmatrix}$

12. (a) Not possible   (b) Not possible

(c) $\begin{bmatrix} 9 \\ 6 \\ -3 \end{bmatrix}$ (d) Not possible

14. $\begin{bmatrix} -7 & 7 \\ 1 & -2 \\ 4 & -5 \\ -5 & 17 \end{bmatrix}$ **16.** $\begin{bmatrix} 9.5 & 2 & -7 & 4.5 \end{bmatrix}$

18. $\begin{bmatrix} -\frac{11}{3} & -\frac{31}{3} \\ 1 & \frac{3}{2} \\ -8 & -1 \end{bmatrix}$ **20.** $\begin{bmatrix} -440 & 495 \\ -495 & 1375 \end{bmatrix}$

22. $\begin{bmatrix} 132 & 168 \\ -108 & 60 \\ -348 & -180 \end{bmatrix}$ **24.** $\begin{bmatrix} -2 & -2.5 \\ 0 & 0 \\ 5 & -3.5 \end{bmatrix}$

26. $\begin{bmatrix} 2 & -5 \\ -5 & 0 \\ 5 & 6 \end{bmatrix}$

28. (a) $\begin{bmatrix} -7 & 3 \\ -14 & 12 \end{bmatrix}$ (b) $\begin{bmatrix} -4 & 2 \\ 3 & 9 \end{bmatrix}$ (c) $\begin{bmatrix} 3 & 2 \\ -2 & 15 \end{bmatrix}$

30. (a) $\begin{bmatrix} 4 & 2 \\ -2 & 4 \end{bmatrix}$ (b) $\begin{bmatrix} 4 & 2 \\ -2 & 4 \end{bmatrix}$ (c) $\begin{bmatrix} 0 & -2 \\ 2 & 0 \end{bmatrix}$

32. (a) $\begin{bmatrix} 12 \end{bmatrix}$ (b) $\begin{bmatrix} 6 & 4 & 2 \\ 9 & 6 & 3 \\ 0 & 0 & 0 \end{bmatrix}$ (c) Not possible

34. $\begin{bmatrix} -2 & 17 \\ 15 & 12 \\ 18 & 46 \end{bmatrix}$ **36.** $\begin{bmatrix} 3 & 0 & 0 \\ 0 & -4 & 0 \\ 0 & 0 & -10 \end{bmatrix}$

38. $\begin{bmatrix} 0 & 0 & 0 \\ 0 & 0 & 0 \\ 0 & 0 & 0 \end{bmatrix}$ **40.** Not possible

42. $\begin{bmatrix} 252 & 30 \\ 298 & 452 \\ 217 & 180 \end{bmatrix}$ **44.** Not possible

46. $\begin{bmatrix} -238 & 50 & -484 \\ 119 & 115 & 342 \\ 210 & 135 & 555 \end{bmatrix}$ **48.** $\begin{bmatrix} 27 & -6 \\ -6 & -27 \end{bmatrix}$

Approaches the matrix $\begin{bmatrix} 0.2 & 0.2 & 0.2 \\ 0.3 & 0.3 & 0.3 \\ 0.5 & 0.5 & 0.5 \end{bmatrix}$.

88. False. Matrix multiplication is not commutative.

50. $\begin{bmatrix} 12 & 6 \\ -4 & -2 \\ 20 & 10 \\ 28 & 14 \end{bmatrix}$ **52.** (a) **54.** (a) **56.** (d)

90. $AC = BC = \begin{bmatrix} 2 & 3 \\ 2 & 3 \end{bmatrix}$

92. $A^2 = \begin{bmatrix} -1 & 0 \\ 0 & -1 \end{bmatrix}, A^3 = \begin{bmatrix} -i & 0 \\ 0 & -i \end{bmatrix}, A^4 = \begin{bmatrix} 1 & 0 \\ 0 & 1 \end{bmatrix}$

58. (a) $\begin{bmatrix} 2 & 3 \\ 1 & 4 \end{bmatrix}\begin{bmatrix} x_1 \\ x_2 \end{bmatrix} = \begin{bmatrix} 5 \\ 10 \end{bmatrix}$ (b) $\begin{bmatrix} -2 \\ 3 \end{bmatrix}$

94. The product is a diagonal matrix whose entries are the products of the corresponding entries of A and B.

60. (a) $\begin{bmatrix} -4 & 9 \\ 1 & -3 \end{bmatrix}\begin{bmatrix} x_1 \\ x_2 \end{bmatrix} = \begin{bmatrix} -13 \\ 12 \end{bmatrix}$ (b) $\begin{bmatrix} -23 \\ -\frac{35}{3} \end{bmatrix}$

96. $\frac{4}{3}, -8$ **98.** $\dfrac{-5 + \sqrt{37}}{4}, \dfrac{-5 - \sqrt{37}}{4}$

62. (a) $\begin{bmatrix} 1 & 1 & -3 \\ -1 & 2 & 0 \\ 0 & -1 & 1 \end{bmatrix}\begin{bmatrix} x_1 \\ x_2 \\ x_3 \end{bmatrix} = \begin{bmatrix} -1 \\ 1 \\ 0 \end{bmatrix}$ (b) $\begin{bmatrix} 2a - 1 \\ a \\ a \end{bmatrix}$

100. $4, \pm\sqrt{\frac{5}{3}}i$ **102.** $\ln 100 - 2$

104. $2 \ln x + 3 \ln(x - 2)$ **106.** $\ln\left(\dfrac{64}{\sqrt[3]{x^2 + 3}}\right)$

64. (a) $\begin{bmatrix} 1 & -1 & 4 \\ 1 & 3 & 0 \\ 0 & -6 & 5 \end{bmatrix}\begin{bmatrix} x_1 \\ x_2 \\ x_3 \end{bmatrix} = \begin{bmatrix} 17 \\ -11 \\ 40 \end{bmatrix}$ (b) $\begin{bmatrix} 4 \\ -5 \\ 2 \end{bmatrix}$

108. $\ln\left(\dfrac{\sqrt{x}(x + 5)}{\sqrt{x - 8}}\right)$ **110.** $(0, 5, -1)$

Section 6.3 *(page 466)*

66. $\begin{bmatrix} 0 & 0 \\ 0 & 0 \end{bmatrix}$ **68.** $\begin{bmatrix} 0 & 0 \\ 0 & 0 \end{bmatrix}$ **70.** Not possible

2.–12. Answers will vary. **14.** $\begin{bmatrix} 7 & -2 \\ -3 & 1 \end{bmatrix}$

72. 2×2 **74.** Not possible **76.** 2×2 **78.** 2×3

16. $\begin{bmatrix} -19 & -33 \\ -4 & -7 \end{bmatrix}$ **18.** Does not exist

80. $\begin{bmatrix} 110 & 99 & 77 & 33 \\ 44 & 22 & 66 & 66 \end{bmatrix}$ **82.** [\$497,500 \$494,500]

The entries represent the costs of the three models of the product at each of the two warehouses.

20. Does not exist **22.** $\begin{bmatrix} -13 & 6 & 4 \\ 12 & -5 & -3 \\ -5 & 2 & 1 \end{bmatrix}$

84. $\begin{bmatrix} \$17.70 & \$15.00 \\ \$29.40 & \$25.00 \\ \$50.40 & \$43.00 \end{bmatrix}$

The entries are labor costs at each plant for each size of boat.

24. Does not exist **26.** $\frac{1}{10}\begin{bmatrix} 10 & -15 & -40 & 26 \\ 0 & 5 & 10 & -8 \\ 0 & 0 & -5 & 1 \\ 0 & 0 & 0 & 2 \end{bmatrix}$

86. $P^3 = \begin{bmatrix} 0.300 & 0.175 & 0.175 \\ 0.308 & 0.433 & 0.217 \\ 0.392 & 0.392 & 0.608 \end{bmatrix}$

28. $\begin{bmatrix} -10 & -4 & 27 \\ 2 & 1 & -5 \\ -13 & -5 & 35 \end{bmatrix}$ **30.** $\frac{1}{2}\begin{bmatrix} 2 & -2 & 0 \\ 14 & -17 & 2 \\ -16 & 20 & -2 \end{bmatrix}$

$P^4 = \begin{bmatrix} 0.250 & 0.188 & 0.188 \\ 0.315 & 0.377 & 0.248 \\ 0.435 & 0.435 & 0.565 \end{bmatrix}$

32. Does not exist **34.** $\begin{bmatrix} 3.75 & 0 & -1.25 \\ 3.458 & -1 & -1.375 \\ 4.167 & 0 & -2.5 \end{bmatrix}$

$P^5 = \begin{bmatrix} 0.225 & 0.194 & 0.194 \\ 0.314 & 0.345 & 0.267 \\ 0.461 & 0.461 & 0.539 \end{bmatrix}$

36. $\begin{bmatrix} 27 & -10 & 4 & -29 \\ -16 & 5 & -2 & 18 \\ -17 & 4 & -2 & 20 \\ -7 & 2 & -1 & 8 \end{bmatrix}$

$P^6 = \begin{bmatrix} 0.213 & 0.197 & 0.197 \\ 0.311 & 0.326 & 0.280 \\ 0.477 & 0.477 & 0.523 \end{bmatrix}$

38. $\begin{bmatrix} -24 & 7 & 1 & -2 \\ -10 & 3 & 0 & -1 \\ -29 & 7 & 3 & -2 \\ 12 & -3 & -1 & 1 \end{bmatrix}$ **40.** $\frac{1}{9}\begin{bmatrix} -2 & -3 \\ -5 & -12 \end{bmatrix}$

$P^7 = \begin{bmatrix} 0.206 & 0.198 & 0.198 \\ 0.308 & 0.316 & 0.288 \\ 0.486 & 0.486 & 0.514 \end{bmatrix}$

42. $\frac{1}{143}\begin{bmatrix} -32 & 81 \\ 60 & 9 \end{bmatrix}$ **44.** $(6, 3)$ **46.** $(-7, -4)$

$P^8 = \begin{bmatrix} 0.203 & 0.199 & 0.199 \\ 0.305 & 0.309 & 0.292 \\ 0.492 & 0.492 & 0.508 \end{bmatrix}$

48. $(1, 7, -9)$ **50.** $(-32, -13, -37, 15)$

52. $\left(\frac{1}{2}, \frac{1}{3}\right)$ **54.** $(6, -2)$ **56.** $(-12, 10)$

58. $(5, 8, -2)$ **60.** $(-1, 2, 0)$ **62.** $(10, -3, 5)$

64. $(6.21, -0.77, -2.67, 2.40)$

66. \$0 in AAA-rated bonds, \$15,000 in A-rated bonds, \$30,000 in B-rated bonds

68. \$200,000 in AAA-rated bonds, \$100,000 in A-rated bonds, \$200,000 in B-rated bonds

70. $I_1 = \frac{5}{7}$ ampere, $I_2 = \frac{10}{7}$ amperes, $I_3 = \frac{15}{7}$ amperes

72. False. The two matrices may not be square.

74. Answers will vary.

76. (a) Answers will vary.

(b) $A^{-1} = \begin{bmatrix} \frac{1}{a_{11}} & 0 & 0 & 0 & \cdots & 0 \\ 0 & \frac{1}{a_{22}} & 0 & 0 & \cdots & 0 \\ 0 & 0 & \frac{1}{a_{33}} & 0 & \cdots & 0 \\ \vdots & \vdots & \vdots & \vdots & \cdots & \vdots \\ 0 & 0 & 0 & 0 & \cdots & \frac{1}{a_{nn}} \end{bmatrix}$

78. $-1, 4, 6$ **80.** $-4, -1, 0, 3$

82.

x	-3	-2	-1	0	1	2
$f(x)$	24	12	9	8.25	8.06	8.02

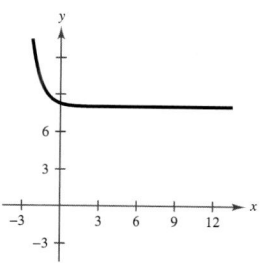

84.

x	-8	-3	-2	-1	0	1	2	3
$f(x)$	3.98	3.7	3.4	2.9	2	0.4	-2.6	-8.1

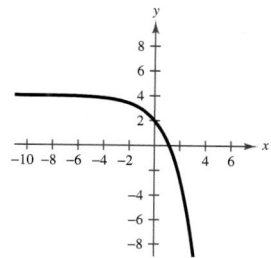

86. $\begin{bmatrix} \frac{1}{2} & -\frac{1}{6} & 0 \\ \frac{1}{3} & 2 & -\frac{3}{2} \end{bmatrix}$ **88.** $\begin{bmatrix} 36 & -13 \\ 3 & 8 \end{bmatrix}$

90. $\begin{bmatrix} -32 & 34 & 36 \\ 8 & -15 & 4 \\ 0 & 1 & -2 \end{bmatrix}$

Section 6.4   *(page 474)*

2. -3 **4.** -11 **6.** -12 **8.** 0   **10.** 3

12. -5 **14.** -0.022

16. (a) $M_{11} = 2, M_{12} = -3, M_{21} = 0, M_{22} = 11$

(b) $C_{11} = 2, C_{12} = 3, C_{21} = 0, C_{22} = 11$

18. (a) $M_{11} = 36, M_{12} = -42, M_{13} = 85, M_{21} = -82,$
$M_{22} = -12, M_{23} = -68, M_{31} = 24, M_{32} = -28,$
$M_{33} = -51$

(b) $C_{11} = 36, C_{12} = 42, C_{13} = 85, C_{21} = 82,$
$C_{22} = -12, C_{23} = 68, C_{31} = 24, C_{32} = 28,$
$C_{33} = -51$

20. 151   **22.** -1167 **24.** 2   **26.** -66

28. -108 **30.** -100 **32.** -140 **34.** 240

36. 7441   **38.** -48

40. (a) 0   (b) -1 (c) $\begin{bmatrix} -2 & -5 \\ 4 & 10 \end{bmatrix}$ (d) 0

42. (a) 0   (b) -7 (c) $\begin{bmatrix} 7 & -4 & 9 \\ 8 & -6 & 3 \\ 6 & -2 & 15 \end{bmatrix}$ (d) 0

44. (a) -46 (b) 89   (c) $\begin{bmatrix} 53 & -10 & 10 & 22 \\ -1 & 2 & 5 & 1 \\ -29 & 18 & -6 & -13 \\ 35 & 16 & -1 & 12 \end{bmatrix}$

(d) -4094

46.–50. Answers will vary.   **52.** $-1, 3$ **54.** $3x^2 + 3y^2$

56. e^{-2x} **58.** x **60.** True

62. 0. Answers will vary.

64. Yes. $|2A| = 8|A| = 8(5) = 40$

66. (a) -5 times Row 1 is added to Row 2.

(b) -2 times Row 2 is added to Row 1.

68. $(2, -4)$ **70.** $\left(-\frac{130}{17}, \frac{19}{51}\right)$

72.

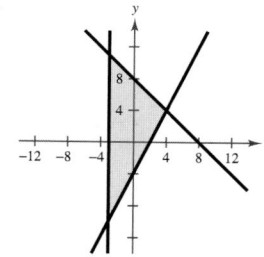

74. $\begin{bmatrix} \frac{1}{4} & \frac{1}{4} \\ 2 & 1 \end{bmatrix}$ **76.** Does not exist

Section 6.5   *(page 485)*

2. $\frac{31}{2}$ **4.** $\frac{33}{2}$ **6.** $\frac{123}{8}$ **8.** $\frac{25}{2}$ **10.** $x = 19, 3$

12. Not collinear   **14.** Collinear   **16.** $x = 3$

18. $(-1, 2)$ **20.** $(7, 5)$ **22.** $\left(\frac{8}{5}, -\frac{83}{10}\right)$

24. $(5, 8, -2)$ **26.** Cramer's Rule does not apply.

28. 3100 square feet

30. Uncoded: $[16, 12, 5], [1, 19, 5], [0, 19, 5], [14, 4, 0],$
$[13, 15, 14], [5, 25, 0]$

Encoded: $43\ 69\ -38\ -45\ -13\ -42\ -47\ -14$
$44\ 16\ 10\ 49\ 9\ 12\ -55\ -65\ -20$

32. $13\ 19\ 10\ -1\ -33\ -77\ 3\ -2\ -14\ 4\ 1\ -9\ -5$
$-25\ -47\ 4\ 1\ -9$

34. $58\ 122\ 139\ 1\ -37\ -95\ 40\ 67\ 55\ 23\ 17\ -19\ 47$
$88\ 88\ 65\ 140\ 164$

36. BRONCOS WIN SUPER BOWL

38. RETURN AT DAWN   **40.** CANCEL ORDERS SUE

42. False. It could have infinitely many solutions.

44. $x + 4y - 19 = 0$ **46.** $2x - 7y - 27 = 0$

48. 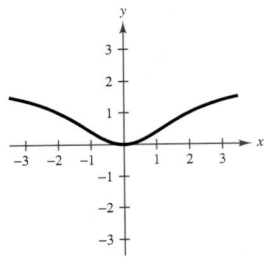   **50.** $(-1, 0, -3)$

Review Exercises   *(page 488)*

2. 2×4 **4.** 1×5 **6.** 2×3

8. $\begin{bmatrix} -1 & 1 & \vdots & 12 \\ 10 & -4 & \vdots & -90 \end{bmatrix}$

10. $\begin{bmatrix} 3 & -5 & 1 & \vdots & 25 \\ -4 & 0 & -2 & \vdots & -14 \\ 6 & 1 & 0 & \vdots & 15 \end{bmatrix}$

12. $\begin{cases} 13x + 16y + 7z + 3w = 2 \\ x + 21y + 8z + 5w = 12 \\ 4x + 10y - 4z + 3w = -1 \end{cases}$

14. $\begin{bmatrix} 1 & 0 & 0 & 0 \\ 0 & 1 & 0 & 0 \\ 0 & 0 & 1 & 0 \\ 0 & 0 & 0 & 1 \end{bmatrix}$

16. $\begin{bmatrix} 1 & 0 & 0 & -6 & -4 & 3 \\ 0 & 1 & 0 & 11 & 6 & -5 \\ 0 & 0 & 1 & -2 & -1 & 1 \end{bmatrix}$ **18.** $\begin{bmatrix} 1 & 0 & \frac{8}{7} \\ 0 & 1 & \frac{10}{7} \\ 0 & 0 & 0 \end{bmatrix}$

20. $(-9, -4)$ **22.** $(0.6, 0.5)$ **24.** Inconsistent

26. Inconsistent   **28.** $\left(\frac{31}{42}, \frac{5}{14}, \frac{13}{84}\right)$ **30.** $(6, -2, 0)$

32. $(1, 2)$ **34.** $(-2, 1, 1)$ **36.** Inconsistent

38. $x = 8, y = 0$ **40.** $x = 12, y = -2$

42. Not possible. The difference of two matrices of different orders is undefined.

44. $\begin{bmatrix} 54 & 4 \\ -2 & 24 \\ -4 & 32 \end{bmatrix}$ **46.** $\begin{bmatrix} -26 & -4 & 8 & 10 \\ 40 & -36 & 58 & -62 \end{bmatrix}$

48. $\begin{bmatrix} 6 & -8 \\ -11 & 54 \\ -44 & 2 \end{bmatrix}$ **50.** $\frac{1}{6}\begin{bmatrix} -13 & 6 \\ -2 & -17 \\ 0 & 20 \end{bmatrix}$

52. $\frac{1}{3}\begin{bmatrix} -13 & -10 \\ 12 & -15 \\ -26 & -16 \end{bmatrix}$ **54.** Not possible

56. $\begin{bmatrix} 4 & 6 & 3 \\ 0 & 6 & -10 \\ 0 & 0 & 6 \end{bmatrix}$ **58.** $\begin{bmatrix} 4 & -3 \\ 82 & -48 \end{bmatrix}$ **60.** $\begin{bmatrix} 13 & 24 \\ 20 & 4 \end{bmatrix}$

62. $\begin{bmatrix} 2 & 3 & 1 \\ 2 & -3 & -3 \\ 4 & -2 & 3 \end{bmatrix}\begin{bmatrix} x \\ y \\ z \end{bmatrix} = \begin{bmatrix} 10 \\ 22 \\ -2 \end{bmatrix}$

64. $A_n = \begin{bmatrix} 10{,}250 & 9250 \\ 8125 & 12{,}250 \\ 6750 & 6000 \end{bmatrix}$;

$BA_n = [\$342{,}687.50 \quad \$378{,}937.50]$

66. and 68. Answers will vary.   **70.** $\begin{bmatrix} 3 & 5 \\ -2 & -3 \end{bmatrix}$

72. $\begin{bmatrix} 1 & 11 & 8 \\ -1 & -7 & -5 \\ -1 & -14 & -10 \end{bmatrix}$ **74.** $\frac{1}{46}\begin{bmatrix} 2 & 10 \\ -4 & 3 \end{bmatrix}$

76. Does not exist   **78.** $\begin{bmatrix} \frac{3}{2} & -2 \\ -\frac{7}{2} & 5 \end{bmatrix}$

80. Does not exist   **82.** $\begin{bmatrix} -\frac{2}{3} & -\frac{5}{8} \\ \frac{1}{5} & -\frac{3}{16} \end{bmatrix}$ **84.** $(2, -3)$

86. $(-2, 1)$ **88.** $(-2, 4, 3)$ **90.** $(-3, 5, 0)$

92. $(5, 6)$ **94.** $(2, -4, 6)$

96. No inverse. System is inconsistent.

98. -41 **100.** 78

102. (a) $M_{11} = -4, M_{12} = 5, M_{21} = 6, M_{22} = 3$
(b) $C_{11} = -4, C_{12} = -5, C_{21} = -6, C_{22} = 3$

104. (a) $M_{11} = 19, M_{12} = -24, M_{13} = 26, M_{21} = 2,$
$M_{22} = 32, M_{23} = 20, M_{31} = -47, M_{32} = -96,$
$M_{33} = 22$

(b) $C_{11} = 19, C_{12} = 24, C_{13} = 26, C_{21} = -2,$
$C_{22} = 32, C_{23} = -20, C_{31} = -47, C_{32} = 96,$
$C_{33} = 22$

106. (a) 650   (b) 650   **108.** -117 **110.** 20

112. -255 **114.** 0   **116.** 280   **118.** 24

120. $\frac{25}{8}$ **122.** Collinear   **124.** Collinear

126. $(-3, 4)$ **128.** $(3, -2)$ **130.** $(6, 8, 1)$

132. $\left(\frac{32}{7}, \frac{30}{7}\right)$ **134.** $\left(\frac{3}{4}, \frac{25}{28}, -\frac{73}{28}\right)$

136. 40 liters of 75% solution, 60 liters of 50% solution

138. $y = -x^2 - 4x + 1$ **140.** 7680 units

142. Uncoded: $\begin{bmatrix} 18 & 5 & 20 \end{bmatrix}, \begin{bmatrix} 21 & 18 & 14 \end{bmatrix}, \begin{bmatrix} 0 & 20 & 15 \end{bmatrix},$
$\begin{bmatrix} 0 & 2 & 1 \end{bmatrix}, \begin{bmatrix} 19 & 5 & 0 \end{bmatrix}$

Encoded: $66\ 28\ 10\ -24\ -59\ -22\ -75\ -90\ -25$
$-9\ -10\ -3\ 8\ -11\ -10$

144. MAY THE FORCE BE WITH YOU   **146.** True

Chapter 7

Section 7.1   *(page 503)*

2. $-3, 1, 5, 9, 13$ **4.** $\frac{1}{2}, \frac{1}{4}, \frac{1}{8}, \frac{1}{16}, \frac{1}{32}$

6. $-\frac{1}{2}, \frac{1}{4}, -\frac{1}{8}, \frac{1}{16}, -\frac{1}{32}$ **8.** $\frac{1}{2}, \frac{2}{3}, \frac{3}{4}, \frac{4}{5}, \frac{5}{6}$

10. $2, \frac{14}{9}, \frac{28}{19}, \frac{16}{11}, \frac{74}{51}$ **12.** $0, \frac{1}{2}, 0, \frac{1}{4}, 0$

14. $\frac{3}{4}, \frac{9}{16}, \frac{27}{64}, \frac{81}{256}, \frac{243}{1024}$ **16.** $10, \frac{10}{\sqrt[3]{4}}, \frac{10}{\sqrt[3]{9}}, \frac{10}{\sqrt[3]{16}}, \frac{10}{\sqrt[3]{25}}$

18. $\frac{1}{2}, \frac{1}{2}, \frac{3}{4}, \frac{3}{2}, \frac{15}{4}$ **20.** $-\frac{1}{2}, \frac{2}{3}, -\frac{3}{4}, \frac{4}{5}, -\frac{5}{6}$

22. $0, 0, 6, 24, 60$ **24.** -240 **26.** 2520   **28.** $\frac{148}{595}$

30. $15, 18, 21, 24, 27$ **32.** $32, 16, 8, 4, 2$

34. $52, 40, -32, -56, 4$

36.

38.

40.

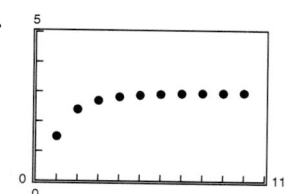

42. 12, 48, 120, 240, 420, 672, 1008, 1440, 1980, 2640

44. $-\frac{1}{9}, -\frac{1}{3}, -6, 4, 8, \frac{360}{13}, \frac{1680}{13}, \frac{2240}{3}, 5111, 40,320$

46. $\frac{4}{3}, 4, \frac{36}{5}, \frac{32}{3}, \frac{100}{7}, 18, \frac{196}{9}, \frac{128}{5}, \frac{324}{11}, \frac{100}{3}$ **48.** (b)   **50.** (a)

52. $a_n = 4n - 1$ **54.** $a_n = \frac{1}{n^2}$ **56.** $a_n = \frac{n+1}{2n-1}$

58. $a_n = \frac{(-2)^{n-1}}{3^n}$ **60.** $a_n = 1 + \frac{2^n - 1}{2^n}$

62. $a_n = \frac{2^{n-1}}{(n-1)!}$ **64.** $a_n = (-1)^{n+1}$

66. 25, 20, 15, 10, 5   **68.** $14, -28, 56, -112, 224$
$a_n = 30 - 5n$ $a_n = 14(-2)^{n-1}$

70. $\frac{1}{210}$ **72.** 600   **74.** 1260   **76.** $(n+2)(n+1)$

78. $(2n+2)(2n+1)$ **80.** 57   **82.** 30   **84.** 165

86. $\frac{47}{60}$ **88.** 14   **90.** 11   **92.** 6.06   **94.** 0.375

96. $\sum_{i=1}^{15} \frac{5}{1+i} = 11.904$ **98.** $\sum_{k=1}^{6} \left[1 - \left(\frac{k}{6}\right)^2\right] = 3.472$

100. $\sum_{n=0}^{7} \left(-\frac{1}{2}\right)^n = 0.664$ **102.** $\sum_{k=1}^{10} \frac{1}{k(k+2)} = 0.663$

104. $\sum_{k=1}^{6} \frac{k!}{2^k} = 18.25$ **106.** $\frac{242}{243}$ **108.** $-\frac{51}{32}$

110. $\frac{4}{9}$ **112.** $\frac{2}{9}$

114. (a) $A_1 = \$101.00, A_2 = \$203.01, A_3 = \$306.04,$
$A_4 = \$410.10, A_5 = \$515.20, A_6 = \$621.35$

(b) $A_{60} = \$8248.64$

(c) $A_{240} = \$99,914.79$

116.

According to the graph, federal debt increases every year.

118. \$5.84; The sums are approximately the same.

120. True   **122.** Answers will vary.

124. $x, \frac{x^2}{2}, \frac{x^3}{6}, \frac{x^4}{24}, \frac{x^5}{120}$

126. $-\frac{x^2}{2}, \frac{x^4}{24}, -\frac{x^6}{720}, \frac{x^8}{40,320}, -\frac{x^{10}}{3,628,800}$

128. $\begin{bmatrix} -4 & 1 & \vdots & -7 \\ 6 & -9 & \vdots & 3 \end{bmatrix}$

130. (a) $\begin{bmatrix} 8 & 1 \\ -3 & 7 \end{bmatrix}$ (b) $\begin{bmatrix} -22 & -7 \\ 3 & -18 \end{bmatrix}$

(c) $\begin{bmatrix} 18 & 9 \\ 18 & 0 \end{bmatrix}$ (d) $\begin{bmatrix} 0 & 6 \\ 27 & 18 \end{bmatrix}$

132. (a) $\begin{bmatrix} -3 & -7 & 4 \\ 4 & 4 & 1 \\ 1 & 4 & 3 \end{bmatrix}$ (b) $\begin{bmatrix} 8 & 17 & -14 \\ -12 & -13 & -9 \\ -3 & -15 & -10 \end{bmatrix}$

(c) $\begin{bmatrix} -2 & 7 & -16 \\ 4 & 42 & 45 \\ 1 & 23 & 48 \end{bmatrix}$ (d) $\begin{bmatrix} 16 & 31 & 42 \\ 10 & 47 & 31 \\ 13 & 22 & 25 \end{bmatrix}$

134. 41   **136.** 335

Section 7.2   *(page 513)*

2. Arithmetic sequence, $d = 5$

4. Not an arithmetic sequence

6. Not an arithmetic sequence

8. Not an arithmetic sequence

10. 2, 8, 24, 64, 160

Not an arithmetic sequence

12. 1, 5, 9, 13, 17

Arithmetic sequence, $d = 4$

14. 1, 2, 4, 8, 16

Not an arithmetic sequence

16. $-1, 1, -1, 1, -1$

Not an arithmetic sequence

18. 200, 180, 160, 140, 120

$d = -20, a_n = 220 - 20n$

20. 0.375, 0.625, 0.875, 1.125, 1.375

$d = 0.25, a_n = 0.25n + 0.125$

22. $5, \frac{17}{4}, \frac{7}{2}, \frac{11}{4}, 2$ **24.** 1, 6, 11, 16, 21

26. $-3, -10, -17, -24, -31$ **28.** 6, 8.5, 11, 13.5, 16

30. 83   **32.** -217 **34.** -92.4 **36.** $a_n = 11 + 4n$

38. $a_n = \frac{2}{3} - \frac{2}{3}n$ **40.** $a_n = 15 - 5n$

42. $a_n = -9 + 5n$ **44.** $a_n = 265 - 15n$

46. (d)   **48.** (a)

50.   **52.**

54. 20, 23, 26, 29, 32, 35, 38, 41, 44, 47

56. $\frac{64}{5}, \frac{68}{5}, \frac{72}{5}, \frac{76}{5}, 16, \frac{84}{5}, \frac{88}{5}, \frac{92}{5}, \frac{96}{5}, 20$

58. $-3.4, -15.8, -28.2, -40.6, -53, -65.4, -77.8,$

$-90.2, -102.6, -115$

60. 4600   **62.** -95 **64.** 16,100   **66.** 10,100

68. 26,425   **70.** 2500   **72.** 218,625   **74.** 2725

76. -896.375 **78.** 1402.5   **80.** 1220

82. (a) \$45,550   (b) \$247,050   **84.** 2430 seats

86. 195 logs   **88.** 632 bales   **90.** 490 meters

92. False. You need to know how many terms are in the sequence.

94. $-y, 4y, 9y, 14y, 19y, 24y, 29y, 34y, 39y, 44y$ **96.** 4

98. $(1, 5, -1)$ **100.** 15   **102.** 3

Section 7.3   *(page 522)*

2. Geometric sequence, $r = 5$

4. Geometric sequence, $r = -2$

6. Geometric sequence, $r = 0.2$

8. Geometric sequence, $r = -\frac{2}{3}$

10. Not a geometric sequence   **12.** 10, 20, 40, 80, 160

14. $2, \frac{2}{3}, \frac{2}{9}, \frac{2}{27}, \frac{2}{81}$ **16.** $6, -\frac{3}{2}, \frac{3}{8}, -\frac{3}{32}, \frac{3}{128}$

18. $0.4, 1, \frac{5}{2}, \frac{25}{4}, \frac{125}{8}$ **20.** $4, 4\sqrt{3}, 12, 12\sqrt{3}, 36$

22. $81, 27, 9, 3, 1; \frac{1}{3}$ **24.** $5, -10, 20, -40, 80; -2$

$a_n = 243\left(\frac{1}{3}\right)^n$ $a_n = 5(-2)^{n-1}$

26. $36, -24, 16, -\frac{32}{3}, \frac{64}{9}; -\frac{2}{3}$

$a_n = 36\left(-\frac{2}{3}\right)^{n-1}$

28. $\frac{10,935}{128}$ **30.** 5000   **32.** $1000(1.005)^{10}$ **34.** 12

36. $\frac{256}{243}$ **38.** 8,957,952   **40.** 8,388,608

42. 134,217,728   **44.** (c)   **46.** (d)

48.   **50.**

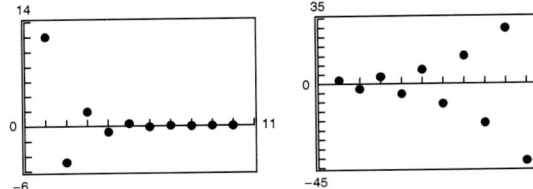

52. 8, 20, 38, 65

54.

n	S_n
1	4
2	4.8
3	4.96
4	4.992
5	4.9984
6	4.99968
7	4.999936
8	4.9999872
9	4.99999744
10	4.999999488

56. 171   **58.** $\frac{1365}{32}$

60. 592.647   **62.** 3.75   **64.** 3949.15

66. $\sum_{n=1}^{8} 7(2)^{n-1}$ **68.** $\sum_{n=1}^{6} 15\left(-\frac{1}{5}\right)^{n-1}$ **70.** 6

72. $\frac{6}{5}$ **74.** $\frac{10}{9}$ **76.** Series does not have a finite sum.

78. 5   **80.** $-\frac{25}{2}$ **82.** 27   **84.** $-\frac{36}{11}$

86. $\frac{11}{37}$ **88.** $\frac{25}{18}$

90. (a) $9674.21   (b) $9898.15   (c) $10,015.98

   (d) $10,096.85   (e) $10,136.64

92. 515,646   **94.** $3698.34   **96.** Answers will vary.

98. (a) $84,714.78   (b) $85,196.05

100. (a) $76,122.54   (b) $76,533.16

102. $222,289.91   **104.** $\frac{2465}{9}$ square inches

106. (a) 152.42 feet   (b) 19 seconds

108. $3,623,993.23

110. False. You can find the nth term by using the formula $a_n = a_1 r^{n-1}$.

112. $3, \dfrac{3x}{2}, \dfrac{3x^2}{4}, \dfrac{3x^3}{8}, \dfrac{3x^4}{16}$ **114.** $5, 10x, 20x^2, 40x^3, 80x^4$

116. $100e^{8x}$ **118.** $\left(-\dfrac{x}{3}\right)^6$

120.

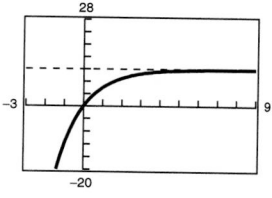

Horizontal asymptote: $y = 12$

Corresponds to the sum of the series

122. Increased powers of real numbers between -1 and 1 approach zero.

124. 72 pounds   **126.** 24 and 26   **128.** $\begin{bmatrix} 6 & 7 \\ 2 & 28 \end{bmatrix}$

130. $\begin{bmatrix} -11 & 17 & -1 \\ -30 & 24 & 32 \\ -22 & 13 & 36 \end{bmatrix}$ **132.** 46   **134.** 60

Section 7.4   *(page 532)*

2. $\dfrac{4}{(k+3)(k+4)}$ **4.** $\dfrac{k+1}{2}(5k+2)$

6. $7 + 13 + 19 + \cdots + (6k+1) + (6k+7)$

8.–34. Answers will vary.

36. 1, 3, 5, 7, 9   **38.** 4, 2, -2, -4, -2

40. 0, 3, 6, 9, 12

   First differences: 3, 3, 3, 3

   Second differences: 0, 0, 0

   Linear

42. 3, 1, -2, -6, -11

   First differences: -2, -3, -4, -5

   Second differences: -1, -1, -1

   Quadratic

44. 0, 1, 3, 6, 10

   First differences: 1, 2, 3, 4

   Second differences: 1, 1, 1

   Quadratic

46. 2, 4, 6, 8, 10

   First differences: 2, 2, 2, 2

   Second differences: 0, 0, 0

   Linear

48. 1, 2, 6, 15, 31

   First differences: 1, 4, 9, 16

   Second differences: 3, 5, 7

   Neither

50. $a_n = n^2 - n + 3$ **52.** $a_n = \frac{1}{2}n^2 + n - 3$

54. False. Not necessarily.

56. False. It has $n - 2$ second differences.

58. (a) P_n is true for all integers $n \geq 3$.

   (b) P_n is true for all integers $1 \leq n \leq 50$.

   (c) P_1, P_2, and P_3 are true.

   (d) P_{2n} is true for any positive integer n.

60. $(-8, -3)$ **62.** $(0, 0), (8, 2)$ **64.** $(4, -1, 3)$

66. $(5, 1, 3)$ **68.** -294 **70.** $4x^2 - 4xy + y^2$

72. $8x^3 - 64y^3 - 48x^2y + 96xy^2$

Section 7.5   *(page 539)*

2. 84   **4.** 1   **6.** 220   **8.** 18   **10.** 120

12. 1287   **14.** 2380   **16.** 2,598,960   **18.** 46,376

20. 15   **22.** 28

24. $x^6 + 6x^5 + 15x^4 + 20x^3 + 15x^2 + 6x + 1$

26. $a^4 + 8a^3 + 24a^2 + 32a + 16$

28. $y^5 - 10y^4 + 40y^3 - 80y^2 + 80y - 32$

30. $x^6 + 6x^5y + 15x^4y^2 + 20x^3y^3 + 15x^2y^4 + 6xy^5 + y^6$

32. $x^4 + 12x^3y + 54x^2y^2 + 108xy^3 + 81y^4$

34. $32x^5 - 80x^4y + 80x^3y^2 - 40x^2y^3 + 10xy^4 - y^5$

36. $125 - 150y + 60y^2 - 8y^3$

38. $x^{12} + 6x^{10}y^2 + 15x^8y^4 + 20x^6y^6 + 15x^4y^8$
$\quad + 6x^2y^{10} + y^{12}$

40. $\dfrac{1}{x^6} + \dfrac{12y}{x^5} + \dfrac{60y^2}{x^4} + \dfrac{160y^3}{x^3} + \dfrac{240y^4}{x^2} + \dfrac{192y^5}{x} + 64y^6$

42. $3x^5 + 15x^4 + 26x^3 + 18x^2 + 3x - 1$

44. $6x^5 + 60x^4 + 240x^3 + 478x^2 + 484x + 190$

46. $x^5 + 10x^4y + 40x^3y^2 + 80x^2y^3 + 80xy^4 + 32y^5$

48. $243y^5 + 810y^4 + 1080y^3 + 720y^2 + 240y + 32$

50. 1,732,104   **52.** 720   **54.** 90,720   **56.** -220

58. $64t^{3/2} - 48t + 12t^{1/2} - 1$

60. $u^3 + 10u^{12/5} + 40u^{9/5} + 80u^{6/5} + 80u^{3/5} + 32$

62. $4x^3 + 6x^2h + 4xh^2 + h^3,\ h \ne 0$

64. $-\dfrac{1}{x(x + h)},\ h \ne 0$ **66.** $404 - 1121i$

68. $-10 + 198i$ **70.** $184 - 440\sqrt{3}\,i$

72. 1049.890   **74.** 467.721

76.

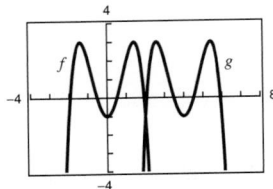

g is shifted 4 units right of f.

$g(x) = -x^4 + 16x^3 - 92x^2 + 224x - 193$

78.

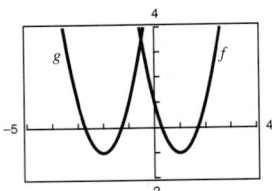

g is shifted 3 units left of f.

$g(x) = 2x^2 + 8x + 7$

80. (a) 177,100   (b) 25,900   (c) 8568   (d) 8568

82.

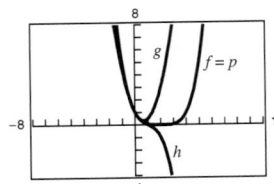

$p(x)$ is the expansion of $f(x)$.

84. 0.2503   **86.** 0.2734

88. (a) $g(t) = 0.0834t^2 + 1.4329t + 9.7652$

(b)

90. False. The x^{10} coefficient is 792×3^7, the x^{14} coefficient is 792×3^5.

92.

$$
\begin{array}{c}
1 \\
1 \quad 1 \\
1 \quad 2 \quad 1 \\
1 \quad 3 \quad 3 \quad 1 \\
1 \quad 4 \quad 6 \quad 4 \quad 1 \\
1 \quad 5 \quad 10 \quad 10 \quad 5 \quad 1 \\
1 \quad 6 \quad 15 \quad 20 \quad 15 \quad 6 \quad 1 \\
1 \quad 7 \quad 21 \quad 35 \quad 35 \quad 21 \quad 7 \quad 1 \\
1 \quad 8 \quad 28 \quad 56 \quad 70 \quad 56 \quad 28 \quad 8 \quad 1
\end{array}
$$

94. Alternating terms of $(x - y)^n$ are negative.

96. and 98. Answers will vary.

100. g is shifted 3 units to the right of f.

102. g is the reflection of f in the x-axis.

104. $\begin{bmatrix} -8 & 16 & 3 \\ 17 & -5 & 6 \\ 21 & 2 & -2 \end{bmatrix}$ **106.** $\begin{bmatrix} -12 & -22 & -30 \\ 60 & 4 & 32 \\ -26 & -20 & 66 \end{bmatrix}$

108. $\begin{bmatrix} -32 & 4 & -11 \\ 7 & 8 & 4 \\ 24 & -13 & 2 \end{bmatrix}$ **110.** $\begin{bmatrix} 20 & 11.5 \\ 10 & 6 \end{bmatrix}$

Section 7.6   *(page 549)*

2. 6   **4.** 5   **6.** 4   **8.** 4   **10.** 42   **12.** 30

14. 1024   **16.** 18   **18.** 5,760,000

20. (a) 9000   (b) 4536   (c) 4000   (d) 4500

22. 24,000,000   **24.** (a) 40,320   (b) 720

26. 120   **28.** 380   **30.** 840   **32.** $n = 9$ or $n = 10$

34. 9,034,502,400   **36.** 1,814,400   **38.** 120

40. 24   **42.** 24   **44.** 56   **46.** 34,650

48. ABCD, ACBD, DBCA, DCBA

50. ABC, ABD, ABE, ABF, ACD, ACE, ACF, ADE, ADF, AEF, BCD, BCE, BCF, BDE, BDF, BEF, CDE, CDF, CEF, DEF

52. 91   **54.** 15,890,700   **56.** 300,500,200

58. (a) 7315   (b) 693   (c) 12,628   **60.** 3744

62. (a) 3   (b) 28   (c) 66   (d) 190   **64.** 9

66. 35   **68.** True

70. For some calculators the answer is too large.

72. They are equal.   **74. and 76.** Answers will vary.

78. 8.30   **80.** 35   **82.** $(-2, -8)$ **84.** $(-1, 1)$
86. $x^3 - 12x^2 + 48x - 64$
88. $x^{10} + 20x^8 + 160x^6 + 640x^4 + 1280x^2 + 1024$

Section 7.7   *(page 560)*

2. $\{2, 3, 4, 5, 6, 7, 8, 9, 10, 11, 12\}$
4. {(red, red), (red, blue), (red, black),
    (blue, blue), (blue, black)}
6. {(SSS), (SSF), (SFS), (SFF), (FSS), (FSF), (FFS), (FFF)}
8. $\frac{1}{2}$ **10.** $\frac{1}{2}$ **12.** $\frac{10}{13}$ **14.** $\frac{8}{13}$ **16.** $\frac{5}{12}$ **18.** $\frac{1}{9}$
20. $\frac{19}{36}$ **22.** $\frac{1}{15}$ **24.** $\frac{11}{15}$ **26.** 0.64   **28.** $\frac{1}{6}$
30. 0.16   **32.** $\frac{41}{100}$
34. (a) 36,630,000   (b) 0.27   (c) 0.56
36. (a) 0.34   (b) 0.45   (c) 0.23
38. (a) $\frac{104}{128} = \frac{13}{16}$ (b) $\frac{24}{128} = \frac{3}{16}$ (c) $\frac{4}{128} = \frac{1}{32}$ **40.** $\frac{3}{14}$
42. (a) $\frac{3}{28}$ (b) $\frac{15}{28}$ (c) $\frac{9}{14}$ **44.** (a) $\frac{3}{8}$ (b) $\frac{19}{30}$
46. (a) 0.076   (b) 0.00069   **48.** $\frac{6}{4165}$
50. (a) $\frac{91}{323} \approx 0.282$ (b) $\frac{455}{969} \approx 0.470$ (c) 1
52. (a) $\frac{1}{4}$ (b) $\frac{1}{2}$ (c) $\frac{841}{1600}$ (d) $\frac{1}{40}$
54. (a) 0.81   (b) 0.01   (c) 0.99
56. (a) $\frac{1}{16}$ (b) $\frac{1}{8}$ (c) $\frac{15}{16}$ **58.** 0.474552
60. (a) $\frac{\pi}{4}$ (b) Answers will vary.
62. False. The complement is to roll a 3 or greater, and its probability is $\frac{2}{3}$.
64. Meteorological records indicate that over an extended period of time with similar weather conditions, it will rain 40% of the time.
66. $x = -1$ **68.** $x = 3$ **70.** $x = e^{-3/4}$
72. $x = \frac{1}{2}e^3$
74.   **76.**

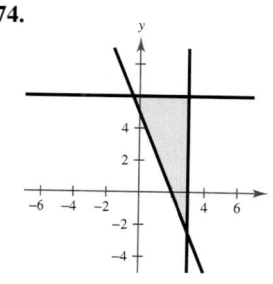

78. 126   **80.** 560

Review Exercises   *(page 566)*

2. $7\frac{1}{2}, 7\frac{3}{4}, 7\frac{7}{8}, 7\frac{15}{16}, 7\frac{31}{32}$ **4.** 0, 2, 6, 12, 20
6. $\frac{1}{2}, \frac{1}{6}, \frac{1}{24}, \frac{1}{120}, \frac{1}{720}$

8.   **10.**

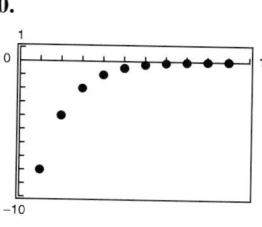

12. 12   **14.** $\frac{1}{8}$ **16.** 56   **18.** 6.17   **20.** 35
22. $\frac{100}{101}$ **24.** $\sum_{k=1}^{9} 2k^2$ **26.** $\sum_{k=0}^{\infty} \left(-\frac{1}{3}\right)^k$
28. (a) 0.8888   (b) $\frac{8}{9}$ **30.** (a) 0.7777   (b) $\frac{7}{9}$
32. 6475, 6691, 6966, 7300, 7694, 8147, 8659, 9231, 9862

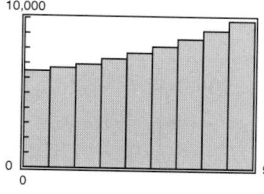

34. Not an arithmetic sequence
36. Arithmetic sequence, $d = -\frac{1}{9}$ **38.** 8, 6, 4, 2, 0
40. 12, 14, 16, 18, 20
42. 15, $17\frac{1}{2}$, 20, $22\frac{1}{2}$, 25; $\frac{5}{2}$ **44.** 100, 95, 90, 85, 80; -5
    $a_n = 12\frac{1}{2} + \frac{5}{2}n$ $a_n = 105 - 5n$
46. $a_n = 1 + 9n$; 1910   **48.** 52   **50.** 250
52. 3050   **54.** 676 bales   **56.** 2, 4, 8, 16, 32
58. $2, 2\sqrt{6}, 12, 12\sqrt{6}, 72$ or $2, -2\sqrt{6}, 12, -12\sqrt{6}, 72$
60. 200, 20, 2, 0.2, 0.02; 0.1; $a_n = 200(0.1)^{n-1}$
62. 18, 30, 50, $\frac{250}{3}, \frac{1250}{9}$; $\frac{5}{3}$; $a_n = 18\left(\frac{5}{3}\right)^{n-1}$
64. $a_n = 216\left(\frac{1}{6}\right)^{n-1}$; 259.2   **66.** $a_n = 5(0.2)^{n-1}$; 6.25
68. 121   **70.** 7.5   **72.** 2934.372   **74.** 25
76. 1493.504   **78.** $\frac{3}{2}$ **80.** $\frac{13}{9}$ **82.** \$4,371,379.65
84. \$16,931.53   **86. and 88.** Answers will vary.
90. 385   **92.** 12,201
94. $-3, -7, -13, -21, -31$
    First differences: $-4, -6, -8, -10$
    Second differences: $-2, -2, -2$
    Quadratic
96. 1, 1, 2, 2, 3
    First differences: 0, 1, 0, 1
    Second differences: 1, -1, 1
    Neither
98. 792   **100.** 91   **102.** 36   **104.** 252

106. $2187x^7 + 5103x^6y^2 + 5103x^5y^4 + 2835x^4y^6 + 945x^3y^8$
$\quad\quad + 189x^2y^{10} + 21xy^{12} + y^{14}$

108. $\dfrac{64}{x^6} - \dfrac{576}{x^4} + \dfrac{2160}{x^2} - 4320 + 4860x^2 - 2916x^4$
$\quad\quad + 729x^6$

110. $-236 - 115i$ **112.** 8 **114.** 118,813,760

116. 19,958,400 **118.** 55 **120.** 109,453,344

122. $\frac{1}{120}$ **124.** $\frac{5}{324}$ **126.** 0.0475 **128.** 0.75

130. True **132.** The set of natural numbers

134. (a) Each term is obtained by adding the same constant (common difference) to the preceding term.
   (b) Each term is obtained by multiplying the same constant (common ratio) by the preceding term.

136. 240, 440, 810, 1490, 2740

138. Increased powers of real numbers between 0 and 1 approach zero.

140. (a) **142.** (c)

144. In $(-x + y)^n$, only terms with odd powers of x are negative. In $(x - y)^n$, only terms with odd powers of y are negative.

146. $\frac{1}{3}$; The sum of possible events must be 1.

Chapter 8

Section 8.1 *(page 583)*

2. (i) **4.** (a) **6.** (c) **8.** (f) **10.** (j)

12. $x^2 + y^2 = 1$ **14.** $x^2 + y^2 = \frac{25}{49}$

16. $x^2 + y^2 = 208$

18. Vertex: $(0, 0)$
  Focus: $\left(0, \frac{1}{8}\right)$

20. Vertex: $(0, 0)$
  Focus: $\left(\frac{3}{4}, 0\right)$

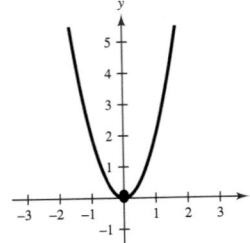
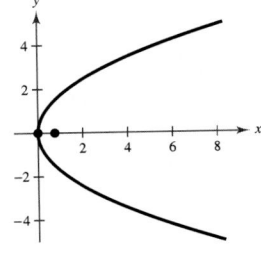

22. Vertex: $(0, 0)$
  Focus: $(-1, 0)$

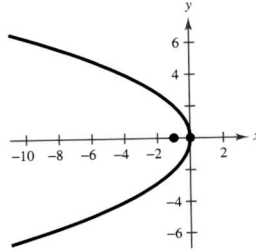

24. $y^2 = 10x$ **26.** $x^2 = -8y$ **28.** $x^2 = -8y$

30. $y^2 = 8x$ **32.** $x^2 = -2y$

34. $y^2 = -18x$; Focus: $\left(-\frac{9}{2}, 0\right)$

36. $x^2 = -16y$; Focus: $(0, -4)$

38.

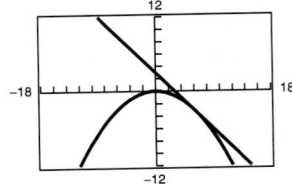

$(6, -3)$

40. Center: $(0, 0)$
  Vertices: $(0, \pm 13)$

42. Center: $(0, 0)$
  Vertices: $(\pm 2, 0)$

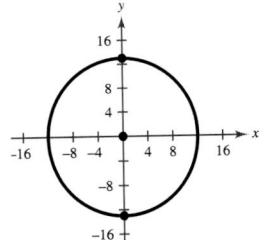
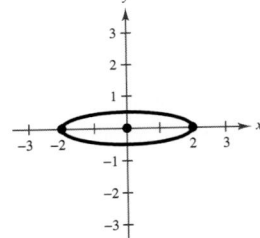

44. Center: $(0, 0)$
  Vertices: $(0, \pm 8)$

46. Center: $(0, 0)$
  Vertices: $(\pm 3, 0)$

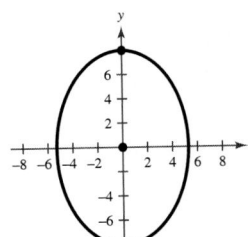
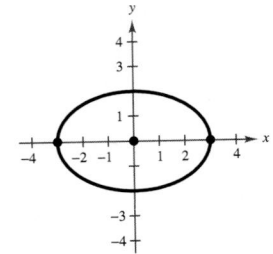

48.

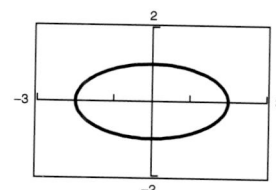

50.

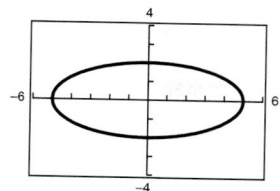

52. Top half   **54.** $\dfrac{x^2}{25} + \dfrac{y^2}{36} = 1$ **56.** $\dfrac{x^2}{49} + \dfrac{4y^2}{49} = 1$

58. $\dfrac{x^2}{48} + \dfrac{y^2}{64} = 1$ **60.** $\dfrac{x^2}{16} + \dfrac{y^2}{12} = 1$

62. $\dfrac{x^2}{4} + \dfrac{y^2}{16} = 1$

64.

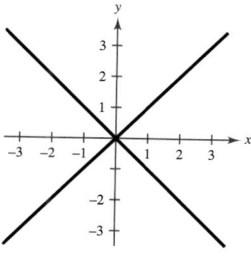

66. Center: $(0, 0)$
Vertices: $(\pm 3, 0)$
Foci: $(\pm 5, 0)$

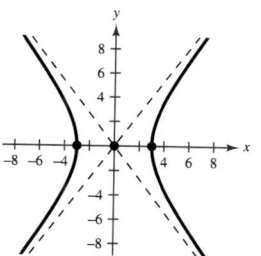

68. Center: $(0, 0)$
Vertices: $(0, \pm 3)$
Foci: $\left(0, \pm \sqrt{10}\right)$

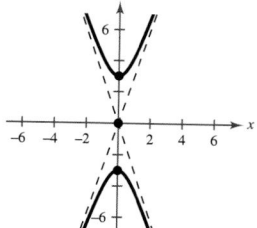

70. Center: $(0, 0)$
Vertices: $(\pm 6, 0)$
Foci: $\left(\pm 2\sqrt{10}, 0\right)$

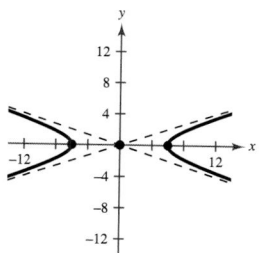

72. Center: $(0, 0)$
Vertices: $(0, \pm 3)$
Foci: $\left(0, \pm \sqrt{13}\right)$

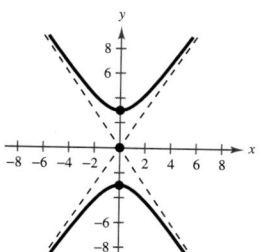

74.

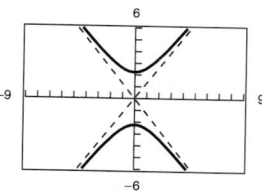

76.

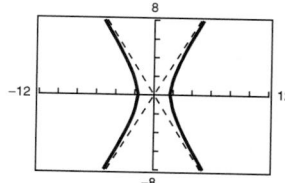

78. Right half   **80.** $\dfrac{x^2}{9} - \dfrac{y^2}{16} = 1$ **82.** $\dfrac{y^2}{9} - x^2 = 1$

84. $\dfrac{x^2}{64} - \dfrac{y^2}{36} = 1$ **86.** $\dfrac{x^2}{4} - \dfrac{5y^2}{12} = 1$

88. (a)

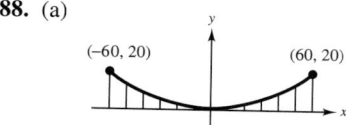

(b) $y = \dfrac{x^2}{180}$

(c)

x	0	20	40	60
y	0	$2\frac{2}{9}$	$8\frac{8}{9}$	20

90. (a)

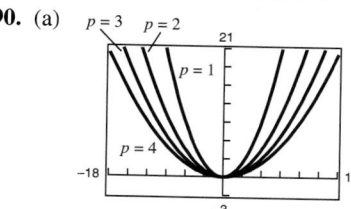

As p increases, the parabola becomes wider.

(b) $(0, 1), (0, 2), (0, 3), (0, 4)$

(c) $4, 8, 12, 16; 4p$

(d) Easy way to determine two additional points on the graph

92.

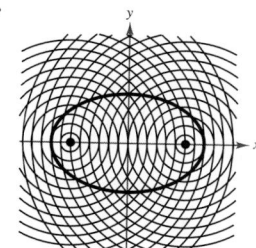

94. (a) $A = \pi a(20 - a)$ (b) $\dfrac{x^2}{196} + \dfrac{y^2}{36} = 1$

(c)

a	8	9	10	11	12	13
A	301.6	311.0	314.2	311.0	301.6	285.9

$a = 10$. Circle

(d)

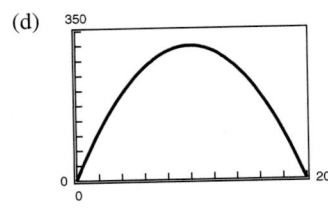

$a = 10$

96. Answers will vary.

98.

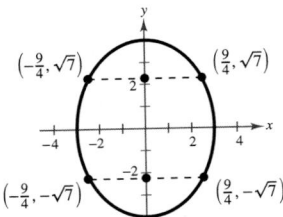

$\left(-\tfrac{9}{4}, \sqrt{7}\right)$ $\left(\tfrac{9}{4}, \sqrt{7}\right)$ $\left(-\tfrac{9}{4}, -\sqrt{7}\right)$ $\left(\tfrac{9}{4}, -\sqrt{7}\right)$

100.

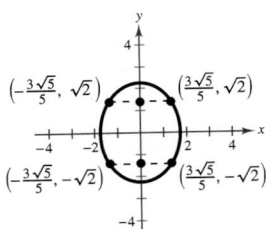

$\left(-\tfrac{3\sqrt{5}}{5}, \sqrt{2}\right)$ $\left(\tfrac{3\sqrt{5}}{5}, \sqrt{2}\right)$ $\left(-\tfrac{3\sqrt{5}}{5}, -\sqrt{2}\right)$ $\left(\tfrac{3\sqrt{5}}{5}, -\sqrt{2}\right)$

102. $x \approx 110.3$ miles   **104.** True

106. (a) $\dfrac{x_1}{2p}$

(b)

$x - y - 1 = 0$ $x - y - 2 = 0$
$x + y + 1 = 0$ $x + y + 2 = 0$

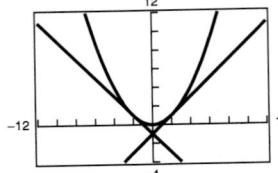   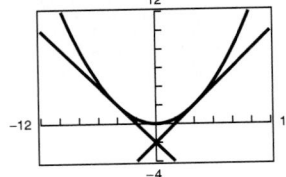

$x - y - 3 = 0$ $x - y - 4 = 0$
$x + y + 3 = 0$ $x + y + 4 = 0$

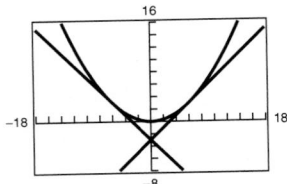   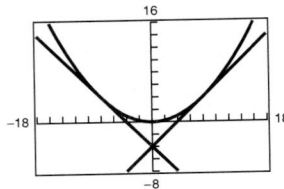

108. The shape continuously changes from an ellipse with a vertical major axis of length 8 and minor axis of length 2 to a circle with a diameter of 8 and then to an ellipse with a horizontal major axis of length 16 and minor axis of length 8.

110. Answers will vary.   **112.** $x(5x - 6)(5x - 6)$

114. $(x + 3)(x + 2)(x - 2)$ **116.** $x^2 + 5x - 6$

118. $x^3 - 7x^2 + 17x - 15$

120. $x = \pm 1, \pm 2, \pm 4, \pm 5, \pm 10, \pm 20, \pm\tfrac{1}{2}, \pm\tfrac{5}{2}, \pm\tfrac{1}{3},$
$\pm\tfrac{2}{3}, \pm\tfrac{4}{3}, \pm\tfrac{5}{3}, \pm\tfrac{10}{3}, \pm\tfrac{20}{3}, \pm\tfrac{1}{6}, \pm\tfrac{5}{6}$

122. -126 **124.** 0   **126.** 39,916,800

Section 8.2   *(page 593)*

2. Center: $(0, 0)$ **4.** Center: $(-9, -1)$
Radius: 1   Radius: 6

6. Center: $(0, -12)$ **8.** $(x - 5)^2 + (y - 3)^2 = 9$
Radius: $2\sqrt{6}$ Center: $(5, 3)$
                    Radius: 3

10. $(x + 3)^2 + (y - 2)^2 = \dfrac{100}{9}$
Center: $(-3, 2)$
Radius: $\dfrac{10}{3}$

12. Vertex: $(-3, 2)$ **14.** Vertex: $\left(-\tfrac{1}{2}, 3\right)$
Focus: $\left(-\tfrac{13}{4}, 2\right)$ Focus: $\left(-\tfrac{1}{2}, 4\right)$
Directrix: $x = -\dfrac{11}{4}$ Directrix: $y = 2$

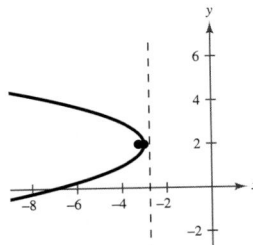   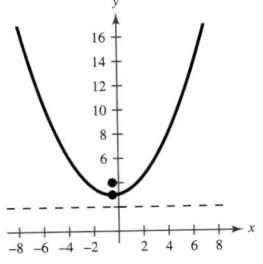

16. Vertex: $(8, -1)$
Focus: $(9, -1)$
Directrix: $x = 7$

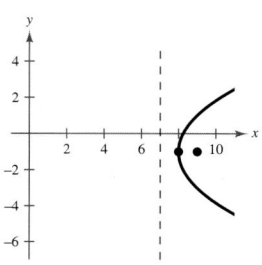

18. Vertex: $(-1, 2)$
Focus: $(0, 2)$
Directrix: $x = -2$

40. Center: $(3, 8)$
Vertices: $\left(\frac{4}{3}, 8\right), \left(\frac{14}{3}, 8\right)$
Foci: $\left(\frac{5}{3}, 8\right), \left(\frac{13}{3}, 8\right)$

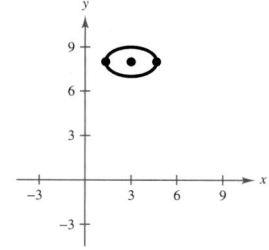

20. Vertex: $(1, -1)$
Focus: $(1, -3)$
Directrix: $y = 1$

22. Vertex: $(-1, 0)$
Focus: $(0, 0)$
Directrix: $x = -2$

42. Center: $(2, -1)$
Vertices: $\left(2, -\frac{5}{2}\right), \left(2, \frac{1}{2}\right)$
Foci: $\left(2, \frac{-2 \pm \sqrt{5}}{2}\right)$

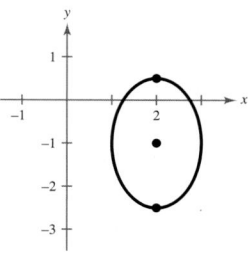

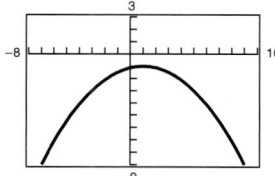

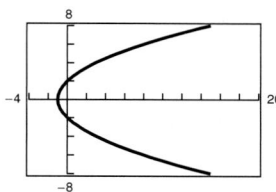

24. $(y - 3)^2 = -2(x - 5)$ **26.** $(x - 3)^2 = 3(y + 3)$
28. $(x + 1)^2 = -8(y - 2)$ **30.** $(y - 1)^2 = -12(x + 2)$
32. $x^2 = -8(y - 2)$ **34.** $y = -\sqrt{2(x - 2)} - 1$

36. Center: $\left(-\frac{2}{3}, 2\right)$

Vertices: $\left(-\frac{2}{3}, 1\right), \left(-\frac{2}{3}, 3\right)$

Foci: $\left(-\frac{2}{3}, \frac{4 \pm \sqrt{3}}{2}\right)$

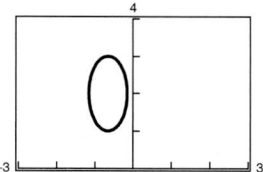

44. Degenerate conic: $(2, 1)$ **46.** $\dfrac{(x - 4)^2}{9} + \dfrac{y^2}{16} = 1$

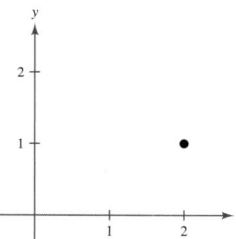

48. $\dfrac{(x - 2)^2}{4} + \dfrac{(y + 1)^2}{1} = 1$ **50.** $\dfrac{(x - 2)^2}{16} + \dfrac{y^2}{12} = 1$

52. $(x - 2)^2 + \dfrac{4(y + 1)^2}{9} = 1$

54. $\dfrac{(x - 3)^2}{36} + \dfrac{(y - 2)^2}{32} = 1$

56. $\dfrac{(x - 5)^2}{25} + \dfrac{(y - 6)^2}{36} = 1$

58. $y = 2 - \frac{5}{4}\sqrt{16 - (x + 1)^2}$

60. Center: $(1, -4)$
Vertices:
$(-11, -4), (13, -4)$
Foci: $(-12, -4), (14, -4)$

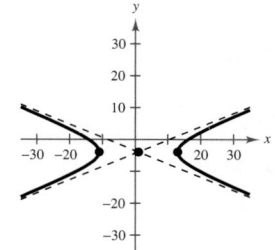

38. Center: $(6, -7)$
Vertices:
$(2, -7), (10, -7)$
Foci: $\left(6 \pm 2\sqrt{3}, -7\right)$

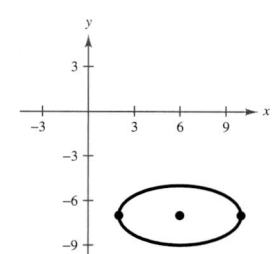

62. Center: $(3, -1)$

Vertices: $\left(3, -\frac{1}{2}\right), \left(3, -\frac{3}{2}\right)$

Foci: $\left(3, -1 \pm \frac{\sqrt{13}}{6}\right)$

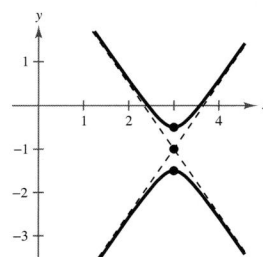

64. Center: $(0, 2)$
Vertices: $(-6, 2), (6, 2)$
Foci: $(\pm 2\sqrt{10}, 2)$

66. The graph of this equation is two lines intersecting at $(1, -2)$.

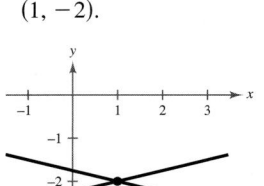

68. Center: $(-3, 1)$

Vertices:

$\left(-3, \frac{1}{2}\right), \left(-3, \frac{3}{2}\right)$

Foci: $\left(-3, 1 \pm \frac{\sqrt{13}}{6}\right)$

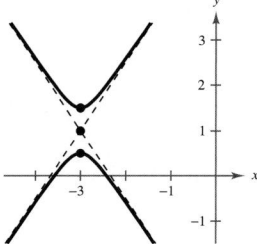

70. Center: $(-3, 5)$

Vertices:

$\left(-\frac{10}{3}, 5\right), \left(-\frac{8}{3}, 5\right)$

Foci: $\left(-3 \pm \frac{\sqrt{10}}{3}, 5\right)$

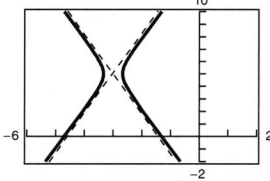

72. $\dfrac{y^2}{4} - \dfrac{(x-1)^2}{4} = 1$ **74.** $\dfrac{(x+4)^2}{16} - \dfrac{(y-4)^2}{64/5} = 1$

76. $\dfrac{y^2}{9} - \dfrac{(x-2)^2}{16} = 1$ **78.** $\dfrac{x^2}{4} - \dfrac{(y-1)^2}{5} = 1$

80. $\dfrac{(y-2)^2}{4} - \dfrac{(x-3)^2}{9} = 1$ **82.** Top half

84. Ellipse   **86.** Parabola   **88.** Hyperbola

90. Circle

92.

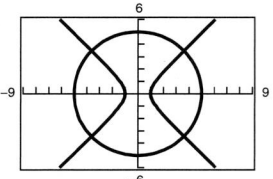

$\left(\sqrt{13}, \pm 2\sqrt{3}\right), \left(-\sqrt{13}, \pm 2\sqrt{3}\right)$

94. 34,295 feet

96. (a)

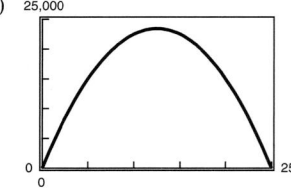

(b) $x = 125$ units

(c) $x = 125$ units

(d) $x = 125$ units

(e) Answers will vary.

98. $\dfrac{y^2}{64} + \dfrac{x^2}{48} = 1$ **100.** $e = \dfrac{c}{a} \approx 0.052$

102. $\dfrac{x^2}{100^2} + \dfrac{(y-85)^2}{85^2} = 1$ **104.** $\dfrac{x^2}{4.88} + \dfrac{y^2}{1.39} = 1$

106. False

108. Not inverse functions. $f^{-1}(x) = \dfrac{10 - x}{7}$

110. $\displaystyle\sum_{n=1}^{9} \dfrac{1}{6n} = 0.4715$ **112.** $\displaystyle\sum_{n=0}^{8} \left(-\dfrac{1}{4}\right)^n = 0.80$

114. $x^4 - 16x^3 + 96x^2 - 256x + 256$

116. $243x^5 + 405x^4 + 270x^3 + 90x^2 + 15x + 1$

Section 8.3   *(page 602)*

2. (h)   **4.** (e)   **6.** (d)   **8.** (g)

10. (a)

t	-2	-1	1	2	3
x	-1	-2	2	1	$\frac{2}{3}$
y	-5	-4	-2	-1	0

(b)

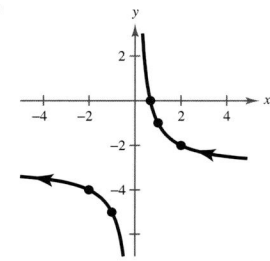

(c)

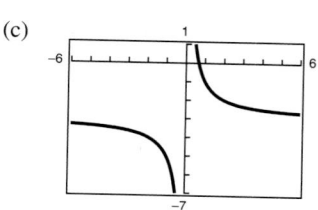

(d) $y = \dfrac{2}{x} - 3$

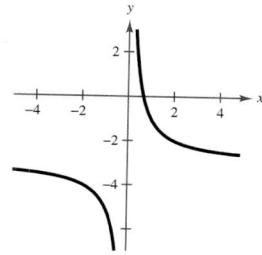

The graphs are the same.

12.

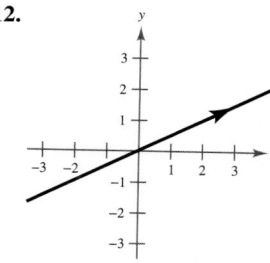

$x - 2y = 0$

14.

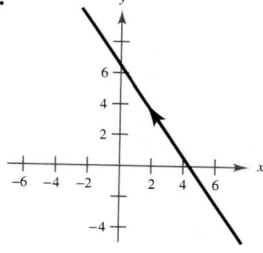

$3x + 2y - 13 = 0$

16.

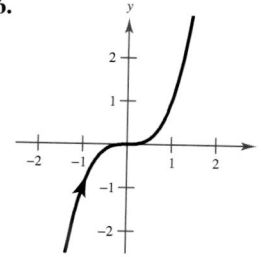

$y = x^3$

18.

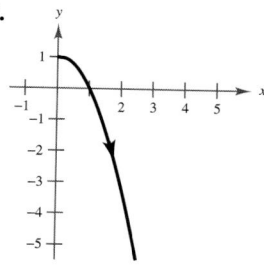

$y = 1 - x^2, \ x \geq 0$

20.

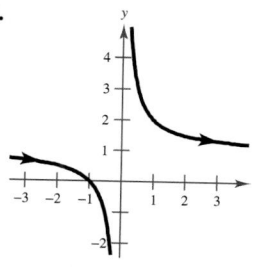

$y = \dfrac{x + 1}{x}$

22.

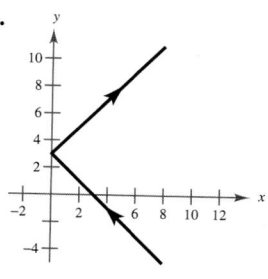

$x = |y - 3|$

24.

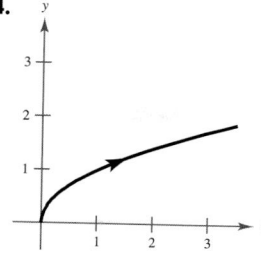

$y = \sqrt{x}, \ x > 0$

26.

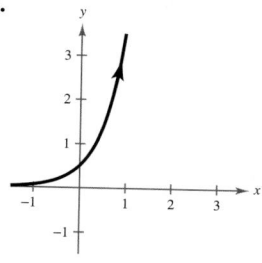

$y = \frac{1}{2}e^{2x}$

28.

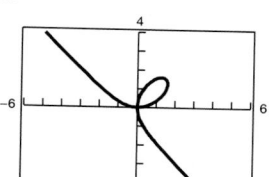

30.

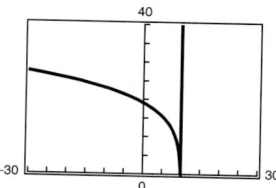

32. Each curve represents a portion of the parabola $y = x^2 - 1$.

	Domain	*Orientation*
(a)	$(-\infty, \infty)$	Left to right
(b)	$(0, \infty)$	Left to right
(c)	$(-\infty, 0), (0, \infty)$	Right to left
(d)	$(0, \infty)$	Left to right

34. Each curve represents a portion of the line $y = x$.

	Domain	*Orientation*
(a)	$(-\infty, \infty)$	Left to right
(b)	$(0, \infty)$	Left to right
(c)	$(-\infty, \infty)$	Right to left
(d)	$(-\infty, \infty)$	Left to right

36. $y = \dfrac{y_2 - y_1}{x_2 - x_1}(x - x_1) + y_1$

38. $x = 1 + 4t$
  $y = 4 - 6t$

40. $x = -1 + 16t$
  $y = -4 + 24t$

42. (a) Solution is not unique.
  $x = t$
  $y = 4$
  $-3 \leq t \leq 6$
  (b) $x = -t$
  $y = 4$
  $-6 \leq t \leq 3$

44. Answers will vary. Example:
  $x = t, \ y = 5 - 7t$
  $x = 2t, \ y = 5 - 14t$

CHAPTER 8

46. Answers will vary. Example:

$$x = t, \quad y = \frac{4}{t + 3}$$

$$x = \frac{4}{t} - 3, \quad y = t$$

48. Answers will vary.
Example:

$x = t, \ y = 6t^2 - 5$

$x = 2t, \ y = 24t^2 - 5$

50. Answers will vary.
Example:

$x = t, \ y = 1 - 8t^3$

$x = \frac{1}{2}t, \ y = 1 - t^3$

52. (a) Maximum height:
28.1 feet

Range: 112.5 feet

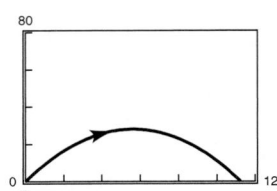

(b) Maximum height:
78.1 feet

Range: 312.5 feet

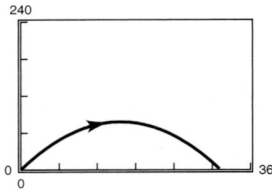

(c) Maximum height:
103.1 feet

Range: 164.0 feet

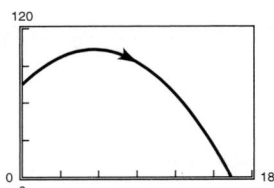

(d) Maximum height:
153.1 feet

Range: 375.0 feet

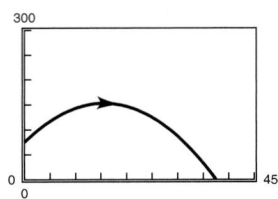

54. (a) $v_0 = 54.22$ feet per second

$x = 44.46t, \ y = 7 + 30.91t - 16t^2$

(b)   21.9 feet

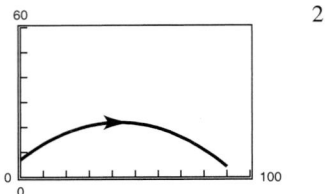

(c) 2.02 seconds

56. False. The graph of the parametric equations does not include negative values of x and y.

58. $x = \sqrt{\frac{8}{5}}i \approx 1.265i, \ x = -\sqrt{\frac{8}{5}}i \approx -1.265i$

60. $x = -\frac{1}{2} + \sqrt{3} \approx 1.232, \ x = -\frac{1}{2} - \sqrt{3} \approx -2.232$

62. 10,200   **64.** 11,590   **66.** 16

Review Exercises *(page 606)*

2. (d)   **4.** (b)   **6.** (a)   **8.** (g)   **10.** Ellipse

12. Ellipse   **14.** Circle   **16.** Ellipse   **18.** $x^2 = -8y$

20. $x^2 = 12y$

22.

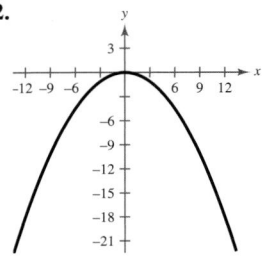

24.

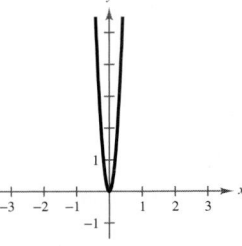

26. $\dfrac{x^2}{25} + \dfrac{y^2}{9} = 1$ **28.** $\dfrac{2x^2}{9} + \dfrac{y^2}{36} = 1$

30.

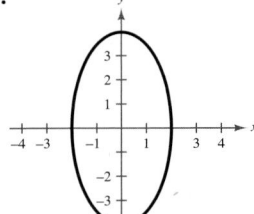

32.

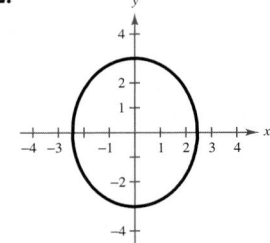

34. The foci should be placed 3 feet on either side of center at the same height as the pillars.

36. $\dfrac{y^2}{4} - \dfrac{x^2}{5} = 1$ **38.** $\dfrac{x^2}{16} - \dfrac{y^2}{20} = 1$

40.

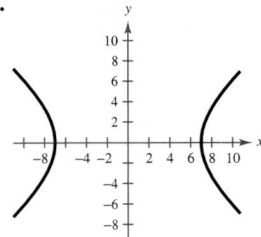

42.

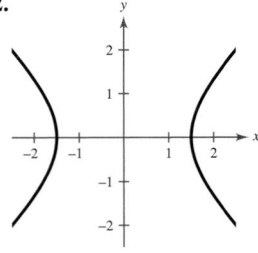

44. Parabola   **46.** Circle   **48.** Hyperbola

50. Ellipse   **52.** Hyperbola   **54.** $(y - 5)^2 = \frac{25}{6}x$

56. $y^2 = -8(x - 2)$ **58.** $(x - 2)^2 = 8(y - 2)$

60. $\dfrac{x^2}{9} + \dfrac{(y-4)^2}{16} = 1$ **62.** $\dfrac{(x-2)^2}{3} + \dfrac{(y-2)^2}{4} = 1$

64. $\dfrac{(x+4)^2}{4} + \dfrac{(y-5)^2}{36} = 1$ **66.** $\dfrac{(y+2)^2}{4} - x^2 = 1$

68. $\dfrac{x^2}{4} - \dfrac{(y-2)^2}{12} = 1$ **70.** $\dfrac{5y^2}{16} - \dfrac{5(x-3)^2}{4} = 1$

72. (a) $y = 4 - \frac{1}{4}x^2$

$x^2 + \left(y + 4\sqrt{3}\right)^2 = 64$

(b)

x	0	1	2	3	4
d	2.928	2.741	2.182	1.262	0

74. Diameter $= \dfrac{60\left(\sqrt{2} - 1\right)}{\sqrt{2} + 1} \approx 10.29$ centimeters

76.

t	0	1	2	3	4
x	0	1	$\sqrt{2}$	$\sqrt{3}$	2
y	8	7	6	5	4

78.

t	-1	0	2	3	4	5
x	$-\frac{1}{5}$	0	$\frac{2}{5}$	$\frac{3}{5}$	$\frac{4}{5}$	1
y	-2	-4	4	2	$\frac{4}{3}$	1

80. (c)   **82.** (b)

84.

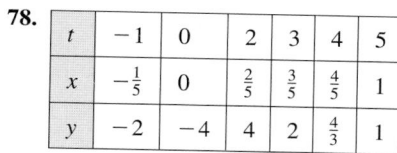

86.

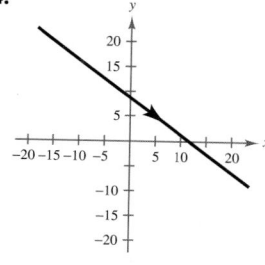

88.

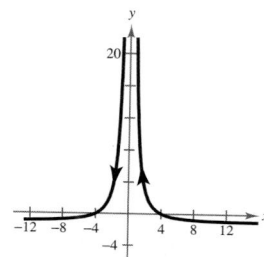

90.

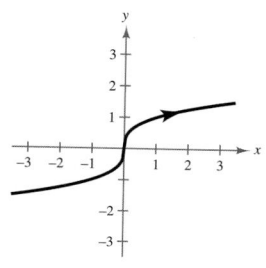

$y = \sqrt[3]{x}$

92.

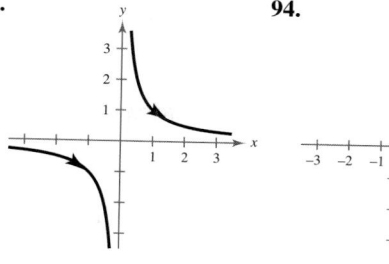

$y = \dfrac{1}{x}$

94.

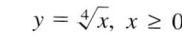

$y = \sqrt[4]{x},\ x \geq 0$

96.

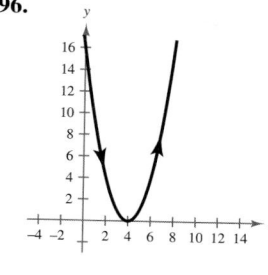

$y = (x - 4)^2$

98.

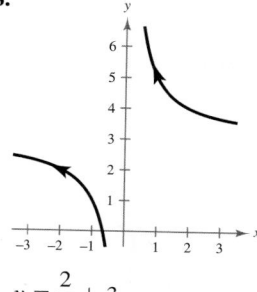

$y = \dfrac{2}{x} + 3$

100.

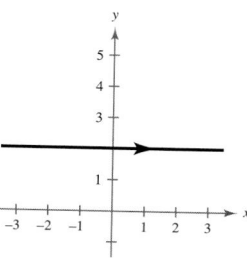

$y = 2$

102. Answers will vary. Example:

$x = t,\ y = 10 - t$

$x = 2t,\ y = 10 - 2t$

104. Answers will vary. Example:

$x = t,\ y = 2t^3 + 5t$

$x = \frac{1}{2}t,\ y = \frac{1}{4}t^3 + \frac{5}{2}t$

106. Answers will vary. Example:

$x = 2,\ y = t$

108. Answers will vary. Example:

$x = 5t,\ y = 12t$

110. True

112. (a) Major axis is horizontal.   (b) Circle

(c) Ellipse is flatter.   (d) Horizontal shift

CHAPTER 8

Explorations

Section P.1 *(page 5)*

a. 6   **b.** 1   **c.** 3   **d.** 3

Absolute value expressions are never negative.

Section P.3 *(page 29)*

$$u^6 - v^6 = (u^3 + v^3)(u^3 - v^3) =$$
$$(u + v)(u - v)(u^2 - uv + v^2)(u^2 + uv + v^2)$$
$$x^6 - 1 = (x + 1)(x - 1)(x^2 - x + 1)(x^2 + x + 1)$$
$$x^6 - 64 = (x + 2)(x - 2)(x^2 - 2x + 4)(x^2 + 2x + 4)$$

Section 1.2 *(page 80)*

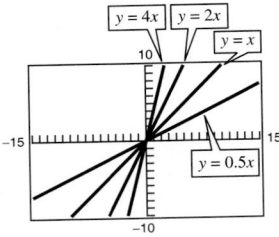

The slopes rise from left to right.

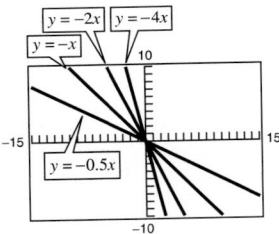

The slopes fall from left to right.

Section 1.2 *(page 84)*

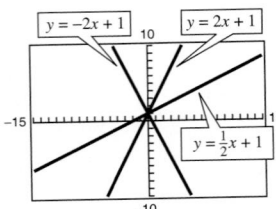

The lines have different slopes and intersect at $(0, 1)$.

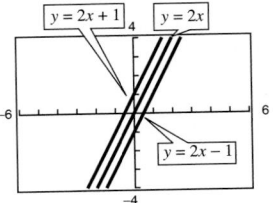

The lines have the same slope and do not intersect.

Section 1.3 *(page 94)*

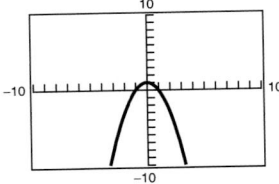

Answers will vary.

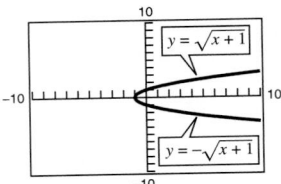

Answers will vary (any value of x greater than -1). y is not a function of x because there are two values of y for each value of x greater than -1.

Section 1.3 *(page 96)*

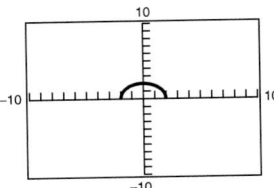

Domain: $[-2, 2]$

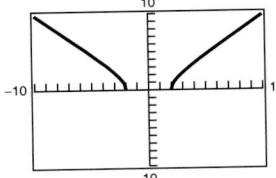

Domain: $(-\infty, -2] \cup [2, \infty]$

Yes, for -2 and 2.

Section 1.5   *(page 119)*

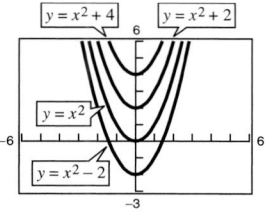

c shifts the graph vertically.

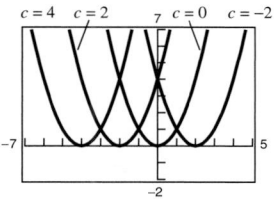

c shifts the graph horizontally.

Section 1.5   *(page 121)*

a.

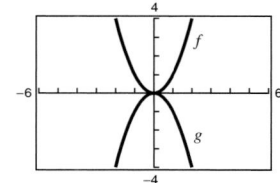

Reflection in the x-axis

b.

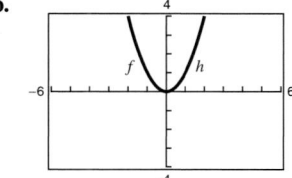

Reflection in the y-axis

Section 1.6   *(page 130)*

No.

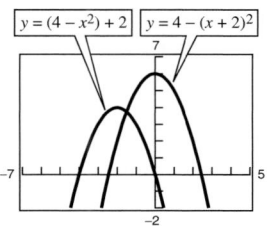

There are two different graphs. Y1 represents $f \circ g$ and Y2 represents $g \circ f$.

Section 1.6   *(page 132)*

a. Yes   **b.** No   **c.** No

Section 1.6   *(page 133)*

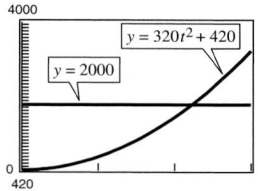

The graphs intersect at the point where the bacteria count reaches 2000. The bacteria count will reach 3200 in about 2.95 hours. Yes. No.

Section 2.2   *(page 171)*

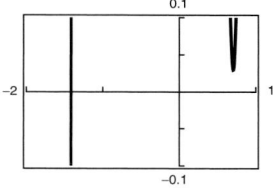

The viewing window for this graph is sufficient to see that there is one real solution.

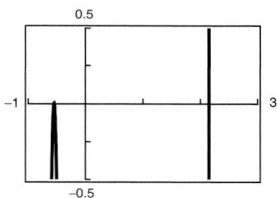

There are three real solutions of
$97x^3 - 102x^2 - 200x - 63 = 0$.

Section 2.3   *(page 182)*

$i, -1, -i, 1, i, -1, -i, 1, i, -1, -i, 1$;   The pattern repeats after every fourth power. Divide the power by 4. If the remainder is 1, the answer is i. If the remainder is 2, the answer is -1. If the remainder is 3, the answer is $-i$. If the remainder is 0, the answer is 1.

Section 2.4 *(page 191)*

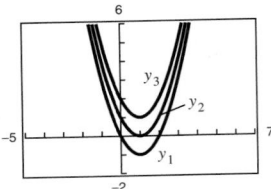

When the discriminant is positive, the number of zeros is 2. When the discriminant is zero, the number of zeros is 1. When the discriminant is negative, the number of zeros is 0.

Section 2.4 *(page 195)*

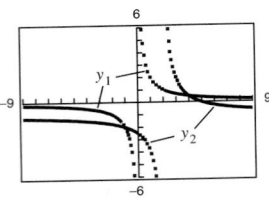

The graphs intersect twice. There are two solutions to Example 12.

Section 2.5 *(page 206)*

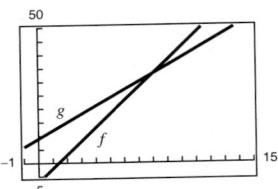

f lies above g for $x > 8$. Where f lies above g, $5x - 7$ is greater than $3x + 9$.

Section 3.1 *(page 227)*

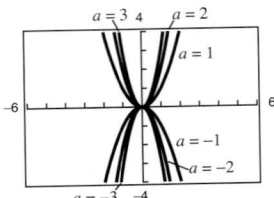

When a is negative the graph opens downward. When a is positive the graph opens upward.

Section 3.1 *(page 229)*

The larger $|a|$ is, the narrower the graph.

A negative h shifts the graph h units to the left. A positive h shifts the graph h units to the right.

A negative k shifts the graph k units downward. A positive k shifts the graph k units upward.

Section 3.2 *(page 238)*

$y = x^8$; $y = x^2$

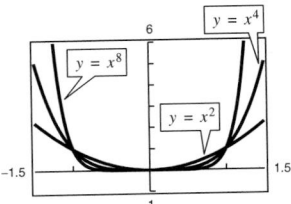

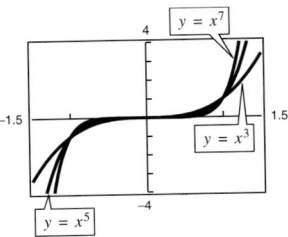

The function on the bottom:

In the intervals $(-\infty, -1)$ and $(0, 1)$, $y = x^7$. In the intervals $(-1, 0)$ and $(1, \infty)$, $y = x^3$.

Section 3.2 *(page 239)*

(a) Degree 3 (odd); $+1$

(b) Degree 5 (odd); $+2$

(c) Degree 5 (odd); -2

(d) Degree 3 (odd); -1

(e) Degree 2 (even); $+2$

(f) Degree 4 (even); $+1$

(g) Degree 2 (even); -1

(h) Degree 6 (even); -1

A function of odd degree falls to the left and rises to the right if the leading coefficient is positive. It rises to the left and falls to the right if the leading coefficient is negative.

A function of even degree rises to the left and to the right if the leading coefficient is positive. It falls to the left and to the right if the leading coefficient is negative.

Section 3.2 *(page 240)*

There is one more zero of a polynomial than there are relative extrema.

Section 3.2 *(page 242)*

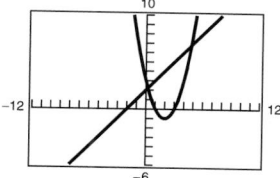

The graph falls to the left and rises to the right. It has three zeros and two relative extrema.

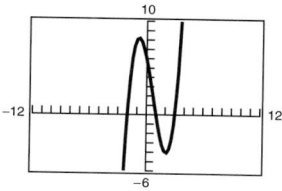

Section 3.3 *(page 259)*

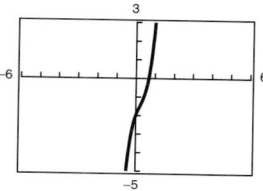

The real zero corresponds to the point where the graph intersects the *x*-axis.

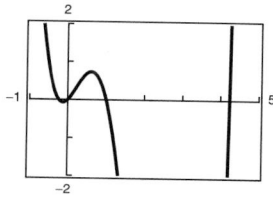

The graph intersects the *x*-axis four times. There are four real zeros.

Section 3.3 *(page 259)*

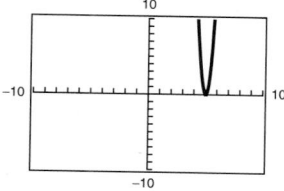

There appears to be one zero at $(5, 0)$. The real zeros are -15, 5.1, and 5.0.

Section 3.5 *(page 272)*

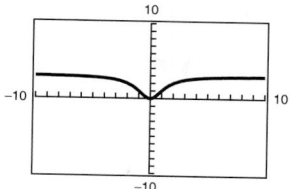

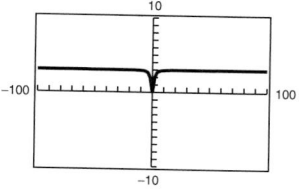

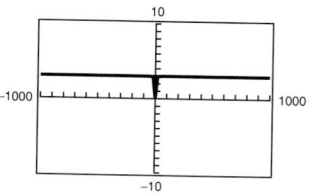

The graph approaches a horizontal line to the right and left.

x	10	100	1000	-10	-100	-1000
$g(x)$	2.941	2.9994	2.999994	2.941	2.9994	2.999994

The values approach 3. The horizontal asymptote is $y = 3$.

Section 3.5 *(page 273)*

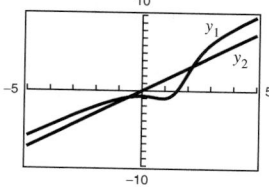
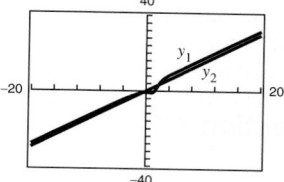

Answers will vary.

Section 3.6 *(page 283)*

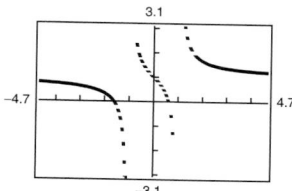

There are holes at $x = 0$, -1, and 1. No. At $x = 0$, the denominator is undefined.

Section 3.6   *(page 284)*

It is possible for the graph of a rational function to cross its horizontal asymptote or its slant asymptote. (Explanations will vary.)

Section 4.1   *(page 300)*

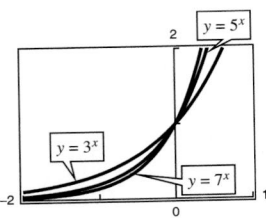

$y = 3^x$ is on top in the interval $(-\infty, 0)$.

$y = 7^x$ is on the bottom in the interval $(-\infty, 0)$.

$y = 7^x$ is on top in the interval $(0, \infty)$.

$y = 3^x$ is on the bottom in the interval $(0, \infty)$.

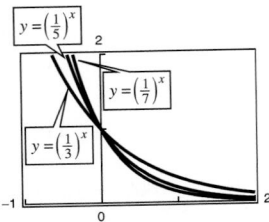

$y = \left(\frac{1}{7}\right)^x$ is on top in the interval $(-\infty, 0)$.

$y = \left(\frac{1}{3}\right)^x$ is on the bottom in the interval $(-\infty, 0)$.

$y = \left(\frac{1}{3}\right)^x$ is on top in the interval $(0, \infty)$.

$y = \left(\frac{1}{7}\right)^x$ is on the bottom in the interval $(0, \infty)$.

For a between 0 and 1 the graph $y = a^x$ rises to the left and falls to the right. For a greater than 1 the graph $y = a^x$ falls to the left and rises to the right.

Section 4.1   *(page 302)*

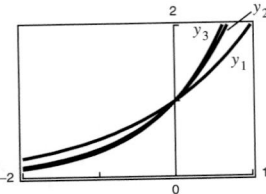

Answers will vary. $e \approx 2.71828$

Section 4.1   *(page 303)*

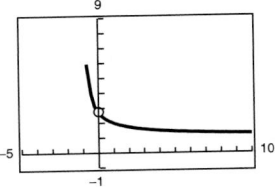

Near $x = 0$ the graph approaches e. There is no y-intercept. In Example 5, as $x \to \infty$ the function approaches e.

x	-0.1	-0.01	-0.001	-0.0001	0
y	2.868	2.732	2.720	2.718	Undef.

x	0.0001	0.001	0.01	0.1
y	2.718	2.717	2.702	2.594

Section 4.1   *(page 304)*

(1) $5466.09   (2) $5466.35

(3) $5466.36   (4) $5466.38

Answers will vary.

Section 4.2   *(page 314)*

The graphs intersect at $x = 100,000,000$. The point of intersection is $(100,000,000, 8)$.

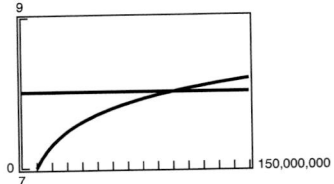

$\log_{10} 100,000,000 = 8$

Section 4.2   *(page 315)*

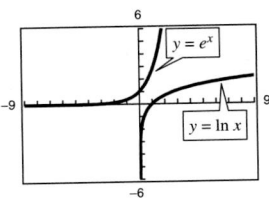

e^x and $\ln x$ are inverse functions.

Section 4.3 *(page 324)*

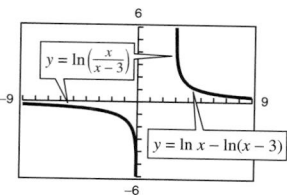

No. Answers will vary.

Section 5.2 *(page 377)*

a.

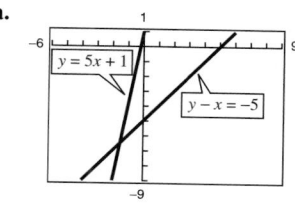

One solution. The lines intersect at one point.

b.

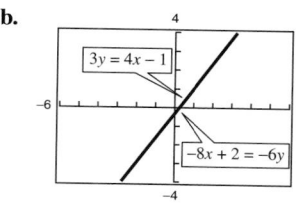

Infinitely many solutions. The lines are identical.

c.

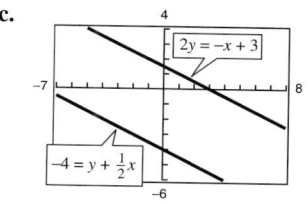

No solution. The lines are parallel.

Section 5.3 *(page 393)*

Answers will vary.

Section 6.2 *(page 447)*

Corresponding entries of A and B are opposites.

$$A + B = \begin{bmatrix} 0 & 0 \\ 0 & 0 \end{bmatrix}$$

Answers will vary.

Section 6.2 *(page 449)*

$$A + B = \begin{bmatrix} -2 & 1 \\ 0 & 3 \end{bmatrix}; \ C + D = \begin{bmatrix} 1 & -1 \\ 2 & -1 \\ 0 & 2 \end{bmatrix}$$

Section 6.2 *(page 451)*

$$AB = \begin{bmatrix} 4 & 7 \\ 8 & 15 \end{bmatrix}; \ BA = \begin{bmatrix} 3 & 4 \\ 11 & 16 \end{bmatrix}$$

No. Matrix multiplication is not commutative.

Section 6.3 *(page 461)*

$$A^{-1} = \begin{bmatrix} -2 & -3 & -1 \\ -3 & -4 & -1 \\ -4 & -6 & -1 \end{bmatrix}; \ AB = BA = \begin{bmatrix} 1 & 0 & 0 \\ 0 & 1 & 0 \\ 0 & 0 & 1 \end{bmatrix}$$

Multiplication of a matrix and its inverse is commutative and gives the identity matrix.

Section 6.3 *(page 462)*

$$(AB)^{-1} = B^{-1}A^{-1}$$

Section 6.3 *(page 464)*

Singular matrix. Row 2 is a multiple of Row 1.

Section 6.4 *(page 473)*

For $n \times n$ triangular matrix A,

$$|cA| = c^n|A|$$

$$|A||B| = |AB|.$$

Section 7.2 *(page 508)*

The differences between consecutive terms are the same in each sequence.

Section 7.3 *(page 520)*

If $|r| = 1$, the geometric series is actually an infinite arithmetic series with a common difference of a_1 or $-a_1$.

Section 7.5 *(page 535)*

a. 1, 1 **b.** 1, 1 **c.** 1, 1 **d.** 7, 7 **e.** 8, 8 **f.** 10, 10

The coefficients of the first and last terms of a binomial expansion are always 1.

The coefficients of the second and next-to-last terms of a binomial expansion to the nth power are always n.

Answers will vary.

Section 7.5 *(page 536)*

126, 126; 7, 7; 495, 495; 1, 1; 120, 120

Symmetry between the right and left sides

Section 7.7 *(page 553)*

Answers will vary. You can expect two heads to occur about 250 times in 1000 coin tosses.

Section 7.7 *(page 559)*

Assuming 365 different birthdays in a year, the probability that at least 2 out of 23 people will have a birthday on the same day of the year is ≈ 0.51. This is the complement of the probability the *nobody* will have the same birthday. Knowing the probability of everybody having the same birthday would not help much.

Section 8.1 *(page 577)*

To obtain ellipses that are almost circular, place the thumbtacks close together. To obtain long and narrow ellipses, move the thumbtacks farther apart.

Section 8.3 *(page 599)*

(a)

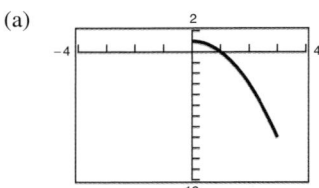

(b)

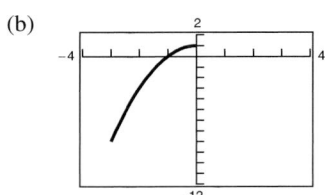

(c)

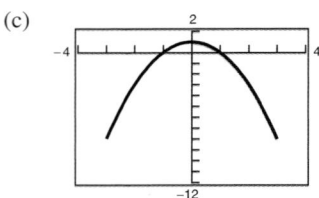

The graphs are portions of a parabola that graph from left to right.

When $X_{1T} = -T$ the graphs are reflections in the x-axis of the previous graphs from right to left.

Writing About Math

Section P. 4 *(page 43)*

x	-3	-2	-1	0	1	2	3
$\dfrac{x^2 - 3x + 2}{x - 2}$	-4	-3	-2	-1	0	Undef.	2
$x - 1$	-4	-3	-2	-1	0	1	2

The expressions are equivalent except at $x = 2$, where the first expression is undefined.

Section 1.1 *(page 74)*

Graph the equations representing each wage scale to determine when they balance. Use this information in your decision. The salaries are the same ($4400 per month) when sales equal $20,000.

Section 1.2 *(page 86)*

a. $\dfrac{7000 - 5500}{10} = 150$ students per year

b. 5950 students in 1993; 6550 in 1997; 6850 in 1999

c. Letting $x = 0$ represent 1990, the equation of the line is $y = 150x + 5500$. The slope of the line is 150, which means that the annual enrollment is increasing by approximately 150 students per year.

d. Answers will vary.

Section 1.3 *(page 99)*

$$f(x) = \begin{cases} 0.51x^2 - 1.47x + 6.31, & 1 \le x \le 6 \\ -1.97x + 26.33, & 6 < x \le 12 \end{cases}$$

You can determine the domain of each part of the graph by inspection of a graph of the data with the two models.

$f(5) = 11.71$; $f(11) = 4.66$. These values represent the revenue for the months of May and November, respectively. These values are quite close to the actual data values.

Section 1.4 *(page 113)*

Examples will vary.

Section 1.7 *(page 144)*

a. Yes, because x and $f(x)$ are one-to-one.

b. No, because x and $f(x)$ are not one-to-one.

Section 2.1 *(page 163)*

Answers will vary.

Section 2.2 *(page 175)*

No. The actual solution is $x = -99$.

Section 2.4 *(page 199)*

The values of A and B are the two x-intercepts. The value of C does not affect the x-intercepts.

$A = -5$, $B = 0$, and C is any negative value.

Section 3.1 *(page 232)*

$y = -x^2 + 5x - 4$

Answers will vary.

Section 3.2 *(page 245)*

1. (b)   **2.** (d)   **3.** (a)   **4.** (c)

No. A polynomial of odd degree will have at least one real zero.

Section 3.3 *(page 259)*

a. $x + 1$

b. $x^2 + x + 1$

c. $x^3 + x^2 + x + 1$

$\dfrac{x^n - 1}{x - 1} = x^{n-1} + x^{n-2} + \cdots + x^2 + x + 1$

Section 3.4 *(page 268)*

Examples will vary.

Section 3.5 *(page 276)*

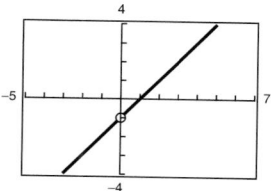

There is no vertical asymptote at $x = 0$. At $x = 0$ there is a point of discontinuity. Explanations will vary.

Section 4.2 *(page 317)*

Eleven months. Students will forget more quickly soon after the test. Explanations will vary.

Section 4.5 *(page 347)*

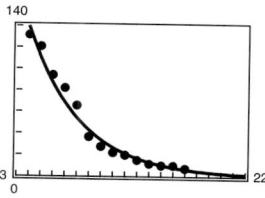

Exponential decay model: $y = 359.057e^{-0.23636x}$

Section 5.1 *(page 370)*

a.

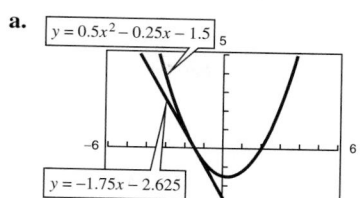

One solution

b.

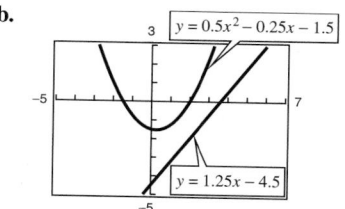

No solution

c.

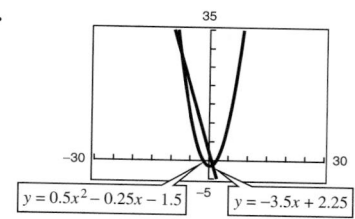

Two solutions

The sets of systems that students create will vary.

Section 5.4 *(page 407)*

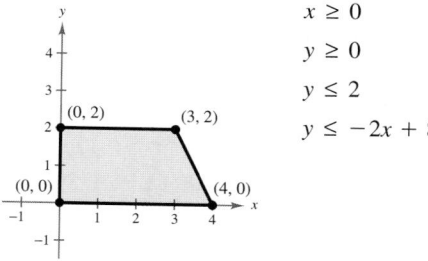

$x \geq 0$

$y \geq 0$

$y \leq 2$

$y \leq -2x + 8$

Answers will vary.

Section 5.5 *(page 416)*

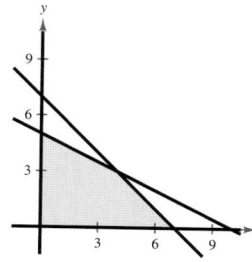

a. $z = -x + y$

b. $z = 3x + 4y$

c. $z = x - y$

d. $z = -x - y$

(Answers are not unique.)

Explanations will vary.

WRITING ABOUT MATH

Section 6.1 *(page 439)*

The student did not apply the row operations to the third column of the matrix containing the constants. The correct solution is:

$$\begin{bmatrix} 1 & 1 & \vdots & 4 \\ 2 & 3 & \vdots & 5 \end{bmatrix} \begin{array}{c} \\ -2R_1 + R_2 \to \end{array} \begin{bmatrix} 1 & 1 & \vdots & 4 \\ 0 & 1 & \vdots & -3 \end{bmatrix}$$

$$-1R_2 + R_1 \to \begin{bmatrix} 1 & 0 & \vdots & 7 \\ 0 & 1 & \vdots & -3 \end{bmatrix}$$

Section 6.2 *(page 454)*

Multiply a 3×1 matrix whose respective row entries are Company A subscribers, Company B subscribers, and nonsubscribers by the 3×3 percent change matrix. (3×3 matrix on the left, and 3×1 matrix on the right)

Section 6.4 *(page 473)*

Arguments will vary.

Section 6.5 *(page 484)*

Uses and descriptions will vary.

Section 7.1 *(page 502)*

$$d_n = \frac{180(n-8)}{n}$$

Explanations will vary.

Section 7.2 *(page 512)*

a. Yes: $-7, -4, -1, 2, 5, 8, 11$;

Recursive formula: $a_{n+1} = a_n + 3$

b. Yes: $17, 23, 29, 35, 41, 47, 53, 59, 65, 71$;

Recursive formula: $a_{n+1} = a_n + 6$

c. No

d. Yes: $4, 7.5, 11, 14.5, 18, 21.5, 25, 28.5, 32, 35.5, 39$;

Recursive formula: $a_{n+1} = a_n + 3.5$

e. No

Explanations will vary.

Section 7.3 *(page 521)*

Sequences will vary. One possibility (when starting with an 8-foot piece of string) is: $96, 48, 24, 12, 6, 3, 1\frac{1}{2}, \frac{3}{4}, \frac{3}{8}, \frac{3}{16}, \frac{3}{32}, \frac{3}{64}$ (and can go no further).

Formula: $a_n = 96\left(\frac{1}{2}\right)^{n-1}$

You could theoretically make an infinite number of cuts.

Section 7.5 *(page 538)*

1. Student incorrectly identified the second term of the binomial $(2x - 3y)$ as $3y$ rather than $-3y$ and raised this term to the incorrect power in the expansion. Correct solution:

$$5(2x)^4(-3y)^1 = -240x^4y$$

2. Student incorrectly identified the fourth term in the expansion of $\left(\frac{1}{2}x + 7y\right)^6$. Correct solution:

$$_6C_3\left(\tfrac{1}{2}x\right)^3(7y)^3 = 20\left(\tfrac{1}{2}x\right)^3(7y)^3$$

$$= 857.5x^3y^3$$

Section 7.6 *(page 548)*

$10 \cdot 8 \cdot {}_{13}C_2 = 6240$ menus

Section 8.1 *(page 582)*

The cone is the light from the lamp. The hyperbola is where the light shines directly on the wall.

The cone is the pencil point. The hyperbola is where the shaved portion of the pencil meets the unshaved portion.

The cone is the plane's exhaust. The hyperbola is the horizontal surface of the earth.

Section 8.2 *(page 592)*

Answers will vary.

Section 8.3 *(page 601)*

The following sequence describes how the folium of Descartes is traced out.

(a)   (b)

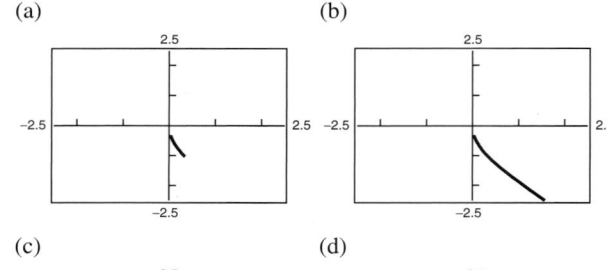

(c)   (d)

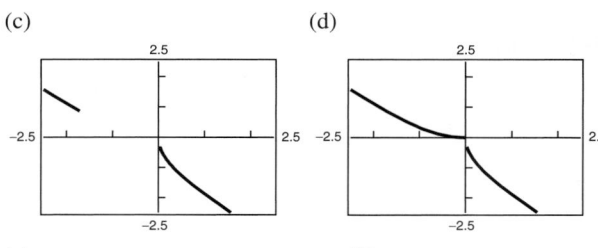

(e)   (f)

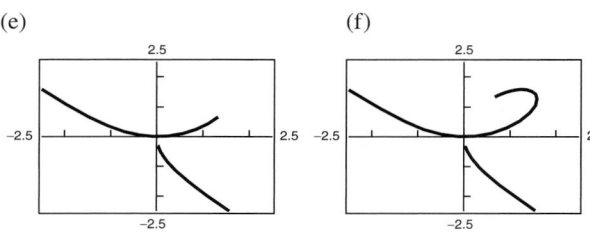

(g)

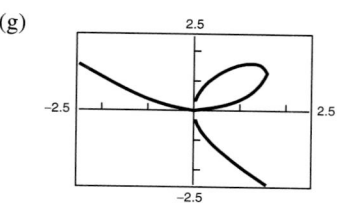

Orientation in opposite direction:

$$x = \frac{-3t}{1 - t^3}, \quad y = \frac{3t^2}{1 - t^3}$$

Chapter Projects

Chapter P *(page 64)*

(a) Base $= x^2$, top $= x^2$, sides $= 4xh$

(b) Surface area $= 2x^2 + 4xh$

(c) $h = \dfrac{108 - x^2}{2x}$ (d) Volume $= 54x - \dfrac{1}{2}x^3$

(e)

Base x	Height	Surface Area	Volume
1.0	53.5	216.0	53.5
1.5	32.3	216.0	79.3
2.0	26.0	216.0	104.0
2.5	20.4	216.0	127.2
3.0	16.5	216.0	148.5
3.5	13.7	216.0	167.6
4.0	11.5	216.0	184.0
4.5	9.8	216.0	197.4
5.0	8.3	216.0	207.5
5.5	7.1	216.0	213.8
6.0	6.0	216.0	216.0
6.5	5.1	216.0	213.7
7.0	4.2	216.0	206.5
7.5	3.5	216.0	194.1
8.0	2.8	216.0	176.0
8.5	2.1	216.0	151.9
9.0	1.5	216.0	121.5
9.5	0.9	216.0	84.3
10.0	0.4	216.0	40.0

The box with the greatest volume is a cube with 6-inch sides.

1. As x gets closer and closer to 0, the height increases without bound. No.

2. $x < \sqrt{108}$; x cannot equal $\sqrt{108}$.

   As x gets closer and closer to $\sqrt{108}$, the height gets closer and closer to (but does not become) 0. No.

3.

Base x	5.9	5.99	5.999
Volume V	215.9105	215.9991005	215.999991

Base x	6.001	6.01	6.1
Volume V	215.999991	215.9990995	215.9095

Yes. x-values closer to 6 yield volumes closer to 216.

4. $x \approx 4.24$, $2x \approx 8.49$, $h \approx 5.66$

   You can use the same method as with a box with square bases.

Chapter 1 *(page 153)*

a. $A = x(50 - x)$

b.

x	0	5	10	15	20	25	30	35	40	45	50
$A(x)$	0	225	400	525	600	625	600	525	400	225	0

25 meters by 25 meters

c.

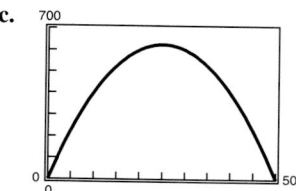

Domain: $0 \le x \le 50$; maximum area when $x = 25$.

d. Complete the square on the right side of the equation $A = 50x - x^2$ to show that the function can be written as $A = 625 - (x - 25)^2$. When $x = 25$ the area is at its maximum.

e. Answers will vary.

1. Yes. A circle with radius ≈ 15.9 meters would have a perimeter of 100 meters and an area ≈ 795.8 square meters.

2. Yes. You quadruple the amount of area.

3. 25 meters by 50 meters

Chapter 2 *(page 221)*

a.

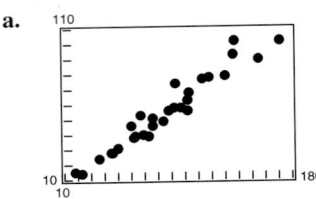

The scatter plot has a positive correlation.

(b) $y = 0.626x + 1.360$; It is a good fit. The r correlation factor is ≈ 0.97. The slope means that for every ≈ 63 measures of exposition, there are ≈ 100 measures of development and recapitulation. The y-intercept has no meaning in this context, because if there were no measures of exposition there could not be any measures of development and recapitulation.

(c)

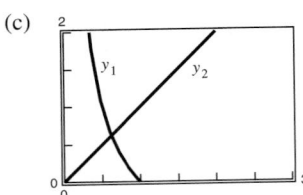

The graphs intersect at $x \approx 0.618$. This value is almost the same as the slope in part (b).

1.

x	y	$x/(x+y)$	x	y	$x/(x+y)$
62	38	0.6200	84	49	0.6316
46	28	0.6216	73	39	0.6518
102	56	0.6456	92	58	0.6133
88	56	0.6111	103	68	0.6023
36	24	0.6000	136	93	0.5939
113	77	0.5947	155	90	0.6327
69	40	0.6330	102	63	0.6182
60	46	0.5660	50	31	0.6173
18	15	0.5455	93	74	0.5569
63	39	0.6176	137	102	0.5732
67	53	0.5583	76	46	0.6230
23	14	0.6216	45	28	0.6164
171	102	0.6264	118	78	0.6020
76	51	0.5984	130	79	0.6220
97	58	0.6258			

These values are close to the golden ratio.

2. (a) Except for the first two terms, each term is the sum of the two preceding terms.

(b) 0.6, 0.625, 0.615, 0.619, 0.618; The ratios appear to be approaching the golden ratio.

3. Answers will vary.

Chapter 3 *(page 295)*

(a) $y = \frac{1}{2}\left(-5 + \sqrt{69 + 12x - 4x^2}\right)$ (top half)

$y = \frac{1}{2}\left(-5 - \sqrt{69 + 12x - 4x^2}\right)$ (bottom half)

(b) $(1.055, 1.893), (2.841, 1.707)$

1.

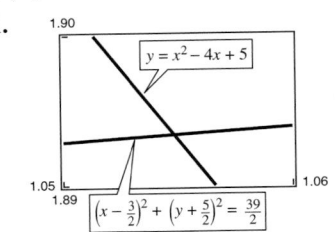

1.893

2.

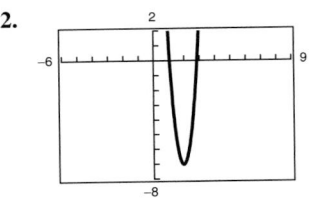

(a) $1.0546518 \le x \le 1.054957$

$-3.5 \times 10^{-5} \le y \le 2.7 \times 10^{-5}$

(b) $2.8408781 \le x \le 2.8411833$

$-1.4 \times 10^{-4} \le y \le 1.7 \times 10^{-4}$

3. $(-0.034, 2.102), (3.236, 2.765)$

4.

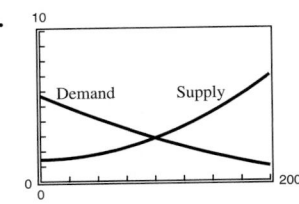

100 bushels

Chapter 4 *(page 361)*

a. $A = 1000(1 + 0.062)^t$, $A = 1000\left(1 + \dfrac{0.061}{4}\right)^{4t}$,

$A = 1000e^{0.06t}$

b.

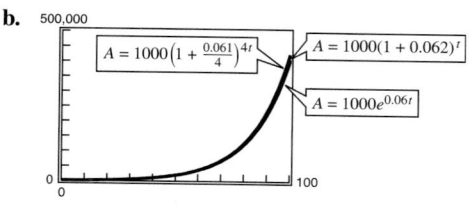

500,000

$A = 1000\left(1 + \frac{0.061}{4}\right)^{4t}$

$A = 1000(1 + 0.062)^t$

$A = 1000e^{0.06t}$

Answers will vary.

c.

	25 yrs	50 yrs	75 yrs	100 yrs
Option 1	$4645.25	$20,240.71	$94,023.15	$409,686.52
Option 2	$4691.21	$20,634.77	$96,802.05	$425,793.73
Option 3	$4627.03	$20,085.54	$92,936.35	$403,428.79

Yes. Compounding quarterly overtakes the slightly higher rate for compounding annually. Compounding continuously does not overtake the higher quarterly rate.

d. Option 1: 6.2%; Option 2: 6.24%; Option 3: 6.18%
The savings plan with the highest effective yield will yield the greatest balance.

1. The tax-deferred plan

2. 4.02% compounded monthly. Continuous compounding will not overtake the higher rate.

3. By $100: 62 years; By $100,000: 204 years

4. The tax-free investment plan is better for the first 16 years. The tax-deferred plan is better for 17 years or more.

Chapter 5 *(page 425)*

a. Morning: $y = 21.3t + 554$

Evening: $y = -38.0t + 1078$

b. 1998

1. $y = 0.61t + 41.1$

49.0 million papers

2. Decreased. The average circulation per morning paper was 73,882 in 1990 and 64,397 in 1997.

3. Answers will vary.

Chapter 6 *(page 493)*

a. $0.01x + 0.01y + 0.04z = 15$
$0.15y + 0.03z = 39$
$0.99x + 0.84y + 0.93z = 546$

b. $\begin{bmatrix} 0.01 & 0.01 & 0.04 \\ 0 & 0.15 & 0.03 \\ 0.99 & 0.84 & 0.93 \end{bmatrix} \begin{bmatrix} x \\ y \\ z \end{bmatrix} = \begin{bmatrix} 15 \\ 39 \\ 546 \end{bmatrix}$

c. $\begin{bmatrix} 100 \\ 200 \\ 300 \end{bmatrix}$

You can make 100 tons of alloy X, 200 tons of alloy Y, and 300 tons of alloy Z.

1. 6600 grams of alloy X, 7500 grams of alloy Y, and 8800 grams of alloy Z

2. $1996 million on gym shoes, $1132 million on jogging shoes, and $3079 million on walking shoes

3. 3120 million had dogs, 2700 million had cats, and 460 million had birds.

Chapter 7 *(page 571)*

a. 3

b. 4; 10; No; x^2 is not a linear function.

c. Answers will vary.

1. 4; 3; 2.5; 2.1

(a) $h + 2$

(b) Tables will vary. f will approach 2 as h approaches 0.

(c)

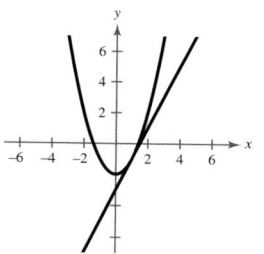

The graphs intersect at one point $(1, -1)$.

2. a. ≈ 0.00667; 0.03; ≈ 0.00667; ≈ 0.01667; 0.005; 0.01; ≈ 0.01333; 0.0075; 0.0025

b. Between 1974 and 1975; Between 1995 and 1999

c. There is no interval in the table that has an average rate of change of zero. For an interval such as 1971 to 1972 the average rate of change is zero. This means that there was no change in that interval.

Chapter 8 *(page 610)*

a.

b. The graphs are inverses of each other.

1. (a)

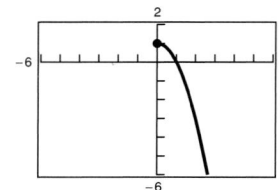

(b) $f^{-1} = 1 - x^2$, $x \geq 0$. Yes.

2.

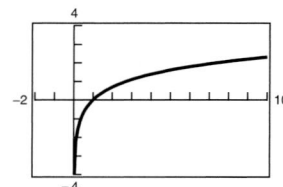

The natural log function

3.

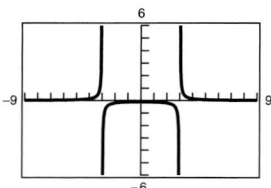

The function does not pass the horizontal line test. You can restrict the domain of the function so that it passes the horizontal line test. An example would be to restrict the domain to $x \geq 0$.

4. Explanations will vary.

5. (a)

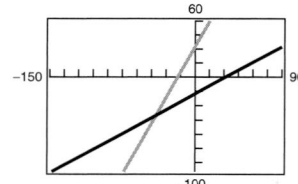

(b) $(-40, -40)$

(c) When the temperature is $-40°$F it is also $-40°$C.

6. (a) No. Examples will vary, but will be horizontal line functions: $f(x) =$ any constant.

(b) For a quadratic function to have an inverse the domain would have to be restricted.

(c) Yes

Appendix B

Section B.1 *(page A10)*

2. (a) 900 pounds   (b) [600, 1300]

4. Exam 1:

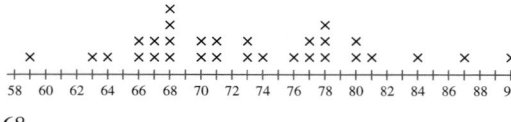

81 and 85

Exam 2:

Leaves (Exam 2)	Stems	Leaves (Exam 1)
9	5	
8 8 8 8 7 7 6 6 4 3	6	
8 8 8 7 7 6 4 3 3 1 1 0 0	7	0 5 5 5 7 7 8 8 8
7 4 1 0 0	8	1 1 1 1 2 3 4 5 5 5 5 7 8 9 9 9
0	9	0 2 8
	10	0 0

Exam 1

8. Organize the data by using a stem-and-leaf plot.

Stem	Leaves
1	3.0 3.0 5.7 8.7 8.9 9.1
2	1.1 1.3 1.5 1.6 1.8 1.8 3.3 3.8 5.8 6.2 9.0 9.2
3	0.7 1.0 2.1 2.3 3.6 4.4 8.0 9.8
4	2.1 4.6 7.5 9.0

Section B.2 *(page A17)*

2. Mean: 33.86; median: 33; mode: 32

4. Mean: 32.43; median: 33; mode: 32

6. Mean: 34; median: 33; mode: 32

8. (a) Mean: 14.86; median: 14; mode: 13

Each is increased by 6.

(b) Each will increase by k.

10. Mean: 320; median: 320; mode: 320

12. (a) Average number of hits = 1

(b) Batting average = 0.250

14. One possibility: $\{4, 4, 6, 7.5, 8.5\}$

16. Median and mode give most representative descriptions.

18. $\bar{x} = 7$, $v = 22$, $\sigma \approx 4.69$ **20.** $\bar{x} = 2$, $v = 0$, $\sigma = 0$

22. $\bar{x} = 3$, $v = 4$, $\sigma = 2$

24. $\bar{x} = 1.1$, $v = 0.38$, $\sigma \approx 0.616$ **26.** 13.53

28. 2.19   **30.** 1.92

32. (a) $\bar{x} = 15$; $\sigma = 3.19$ (b) $\bar{x} = 15$; $\sigma = 2.83$

(c) $\bar{x} = 25$; $\sigma = 2.83$ (d) $\bar{x} = 5$; $\sigma = 3.19$

34. All numbers must be equal.

36. $\bar{x} = 381.9$, $v = 5947.29$, $\sigma = 77.119$
90% lie within two standard deviations.

38.

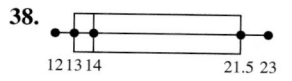

12 13 14   21.5 23

40.

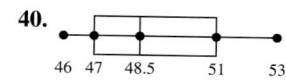

46 47 48.5   51   53

42.

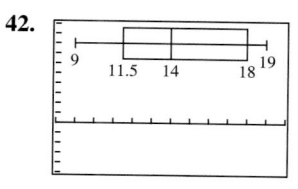

9   11.5   14   18 19

44.

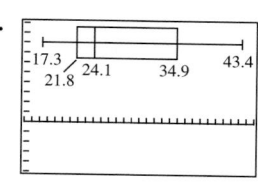

17.3   24.1   34.9   43.4
21.8

46.

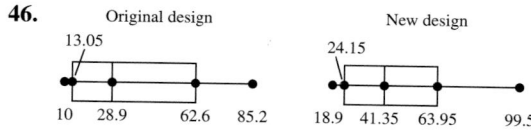

Original design

13.05

10   28.9   62.6   85.2

New design

24.15

18.9   41.35   63.95   99.5

From the plots, you can see that the lifetimes of the units in the sample made by the new design are greater than the lifetimes of the units in the sample made by the original design. (The median increased by more than 12 months.)

Appendix C   *(page A24)*

2. 5   **4.** 6   **6.** 3   **8.** 20   **10.** 4   **12.** 8

14. $\frac{10}{3}$ **16.** $-\frac{9}{2}$ **18.** all real numbers   **20.** $x > -16$

22. $x < 22$ **24.** $x \geq 4$ **26.** $x < -6$ **28.** $x > 12$

30. $x > -\frac{3}{2}$ **32.** $x \leq -3$ **34.** $x \leq -1$ **36.** $x \geq \frac{1}{2}$

Index of Applications

Index

A

Absolute value
  properties of, 5
  of a real number, 5
Absolute value function, 118
Additive identity
  for a complex number, 181
  for a matrix, 449
  for a real number, 7
Additive Identity Property for real
    numbers, 7
Additive inverse, 6
  for a complex number, 181
  for a real number, 6
Additive Inverse Property for real
    numbers, 7
Adjoining matrices, 462
Algebraic expression, 6
  domain of, 37
  evaluating, 6
Algebraic function, 298
Arithmetic combination, 127
Arithmetic sequence, 507
  common difference of, 507
  nth term of, 508
  recursive formula, 509
  sum of a finite, 510
Associative property of addition
  for complex numbers, 182
  for matrices, 448
  for real numbers, 7
Associative property of multiplication
  for complex numbers, 182
  for matrices, 448
  for real numbers, 7
Associative property of scalar multipli-
    cation for matrices, 448
Asymptote
  horizontal, 272
  of a hyperbola, 581
  of a rational function, 273
  slant, 284
  vertical, 272
Augmented matrix, 431
Average of n numbers, A11
Average rate of change, 571
Axis (axes)
  coordinate, 47
  of an ellipse, 577
  imaginary, 184
  of a hyperbola, 579, 580

of a parabola, 227, 575
of symmetry, 227
real, 184

B

Back substitution, 385, 436
Bar graph, 49
Base, 12
  of an exponential function, 298
  of a logarithmic function, 311
Basic rules of algebra, 7
Bell-shaped curve, 344
Bimodal, A11
Binomial, 24, 534
Binomial coefficient, 534
Binomial expansion, 537
Binomial Theorem, 534
Bounded sequence, 184
Break-even point, 369

C

Calculator
  use with exponential expressions,
    298
  use with exponents, 13
  use with logarithmic functions, 312
  use with radicals, 16
  use with scientific notation, 14
Cartesian plane, 47
Center
  of a circle, 53
  of an ellipse, 577
  of a hyperbola, 579
Certain event, 553
Change-of-base formula, 322
Circle, 53
  center of, 53
  radius of, 53
  standard form of equation of, 53,
    574
Closed interval, 3
Coded row matrices, 482
Coefficient matrix, 431
Coefficient of a polynomial, 24
Coefficient of a variable term, 6
Cofactor(s), 471
  expanding by, 472
  of a matrix, 471
Collinear points
  in the plane 478
  tests for, 478

Column matrix, 430
Column of a matrix, 430
Combination of n elements taken r at a
    time, 547
Common logarithmic function, 312
Commutative property of addition
  for complex numbers, 182
  for matrices, 448
  for real numbers, 7
Commutative property of multiplication
  for complex numbers, 182
  for real numbers, 7
Commutative property of scalar multi-
    plication for matrices, 448
Complement of an event, 559
Complete the square, 188
Complex conjugate, 183
Complex fraction, 41
Complex number(s), 180
  addition of, 181
  conjugate of, 183
  dividing, 183
  equality of, 180
  multiplication of, 182
  standard form of, 180
  subtraction of, 181
Composite number, 8
Compound interest, 304
Conditional equation, 156
Conics or conic section, 574
  degenerate, 574
  standard forms of equations of, 588
  translation of, 588
Conjugate, 18
  of a complex number, 183
Conjugate axis of a hyperbola, 580
Conjugate pairs, 266
Consistent system of equations, 377
Constant, 6
Constant term, 6, 24
Constant function, 108, 118, 226
Constraint, 411
Consumer surplus, 406
Continuous compounding, 304
Continuous function, 237
Coordinate, 2
Coordinate axes, 47
  reflections in, 121
Coordinate system
  rectangular, 47
  three-dimensional, 390

FORMULAS FROM GEOMETRY

Triangle

$h = a \sin \theta$

$\text{Area} = \dfrac{1}{2}bh$

Laws of Cosines:

$c^2 = a^2 + b^2 - 2ab \cos \theta$

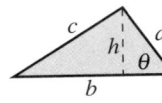

Right Triangle

Pythagorean Theorem:

$c^2 = a^2 + b^2$

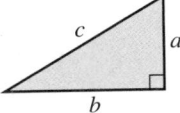

Equilateral Triangle

$h = \dfrac{\sqrt{3}s}{2}$

$\text{Area} = \dfrac{\sqrt{3}s^2}{4}$

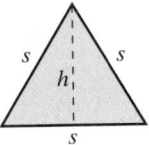

Parallelogram

$\text{Area} = bh$

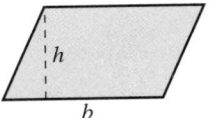

Trapezoid

$\text{Area} = \dfrac{h}{2}(a + b)$

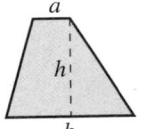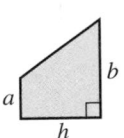

Circle

$\text{Area} = \pi r^2$

$\text{Circumference} = 2\pi r$

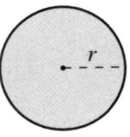

Sector of Circle

$\text{Area} = \dfrac{\theta r^2}{2}$

$s = r\theta$

$(\theta \text{ in radians})$

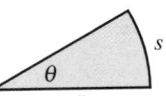

Circular Ring

$\text{Area} = \pi(R^2 - r^2)$

$\qquad = 2\pi pw$

$(p = \text{average radius},$

$\quad w = \text{width of ring})$

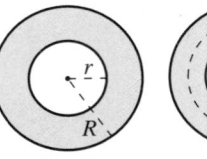

Ellipse

$\text{Area} = \pi ab$

$\text{Circumference} \approx 2\pi \sqrt{\dfrac{a^2 + b^2}{2}}$

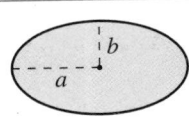

Cone

$(A = \text{area of base})$

$\text{Volume} = \dfrac{Ah}{3}$

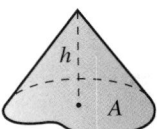

Right Circular Cone

$\text{Volume} = \dfrac{\pi r^2 h}{3}$

$\text{Lateral Surface Area} = \pi r \sqrt{r^2 + h^2}$

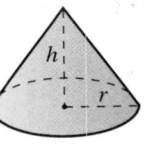

Frustum of Right Circular Cone

$\text{Volume} = \dfrac{\pi(r^2 + rR + R^2)h}{3}$

$\text{Lateral Surface Area} = \pi s(R + r)$

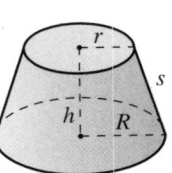

Right Circular Cylinder

$\text{Volume} = \pi r^2 h$

$\text{Lateral Surface Area} = 2\pi rh$

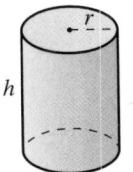

Sphere

$\text{Volume} = \dfrac{4}{3}\pi r^3$

$\text{Surface Area} = 4\pi r^2$

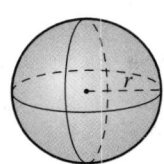